Mid-Atlantic
2003

ExxonMobil Travel Publications

ACKNOWLEDGMENTS

We gratefully acknowledge the help of our representatives for their efficient and perceptive inspection of the lodging and dining establishments listed; the establishments' proprietors for their cooperation in showing their facilities and providing information about them; the many users of previous editions of the Mobil Travel Guides who have taken the time to share their experiences; and for their time and information, the thousands of chambers of commerce, convention and visitors bureaus, city, state, and provincial tourism offices, and government agencies who assisted in our research.

PHOTO CREDITS

C.M. Baker Photography/Kent County Tourism: 9; **Walter Choroszewski Photography:** 92, 95; **Corbis:** Dave Bartruff: 412; Richard T. Nowitz: 469; **Dick Dietrich Photography:** 382; **Folio, Inc.:** Pat Fisher: 41; Everett C. Johnson: 411; Fred J. Maroon: 117; Richard T. Nowitz: 571; Pete Souza: 45 (bottom); **FPG/Getty Images:** Robert Bennett: 26; James Blank: 7; David Doody: 493; Kenneth Garrett: 481; Peter Gridley: 86, 153, 274; **National Park Service, Colonial National Historical Park:** 427; **Photri, Inc.:** D&I MacDonald: 410; James P. Rowan: 441; **Chris Queeney Photography/Greater Wilmington CVB:** 24; **Paul Rezendes Photography:** 143; **W. Lynn Seldon, Jr., Photography:** 152; **Rob & Ann Simpson Photography:** 23; **SuperStock:** 10, 18, 29, 31, 35, 38, 42, 43, 44, 45 (top), 52, 53, 78, 94, 96, 98, 187, 197, 268, 270, 272, 273, 276, 278, 280, 295, 333, 347, 366, 383, 447, 466, 528, 535, 542; **Tom Till Photography:** 547; **Jonathan Wallen Photography:** 209, 560; **Paul Witt/Gettysburg Convention and Visitors Bureau:** 219.

Maps © MapQuest 2002, www.mapquest.com.

Printed by Publications International, Ltd.
7373 North Cicero Avenue
Lincolnwood, Illinois 60712

info@mobiltravelguide.com

ISBN 0-7627-2613-X

Manufactured in China.

10 9 8 7 6 5 4 3 2 1

CONTENTS

Welcome A-21
A Word to Our Readers A-22
How to Use This Book A-25
Making the Most of Your Trip A-33
Important Toll-Free Numbers and On-Line Information A-37
Four- and Five-Star Establishments in the Mid-Atlantic A-39

Mid-Atlantic

US Mileage Chart A-6
Delaware 1
DC .31
Maryland 78
Pennsylvania 163
Virginia 347

West Virginia 521
Appendix A: Attraction List .575
Appendix B: Lodging List . . .608
Appendix C: Restaurant List .627
City Index 639

Maps

Map Legend A-18
Interstate Highway Map of the
    United States A-4
Mid-Atlantic Region A-8
Distance and Driving Time,
    Region A-10
Delaware/Maryland A-12
Pennsylvania A-14
Virginia/West Virginia A-16
Wilmington, DE 23
District of Columbia 36

The Mall, DC 48
Baltimore, MD 93
Inner Harbor, MD 99
Philadelphia, PA 269
Philadelphia, PA 275
Pittsburgh, PA 296
Pittsburgh, PA 300
Richmond, VA 465
Charleston, WV 534

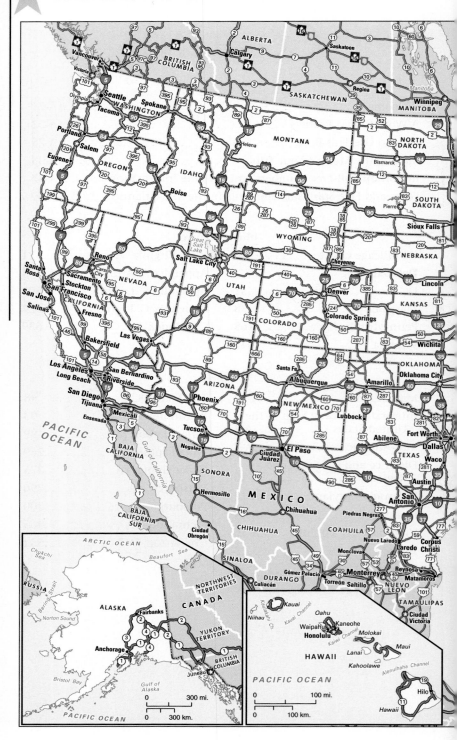

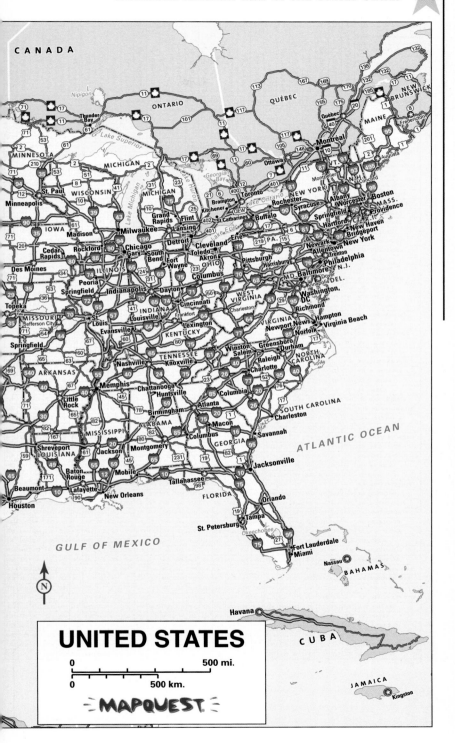

UNITED STATES

0   500 mi.
0   500 km.

MAPQUEST

A-6 Mileage Chart

Distances in chart are in miles. To convert miles to kilometers, multiply the distance in miles by 1.609 Example: New York, NY to Boston, MA = 215 miles or 346 kilometers (215 x 1.609)	ALBUQUERQUE, NM	ATLANTA, GA	BALTIMORE, MD	BILLINGS, MT	BIRMINGHAM, AL	BISMARCK, ND	BOISE, ID	BOSTON, MA	BUFFALO, NY	BURLINGTON, VT	CHARLESTON, SC	CHARLESTON, WV	CHARLOTTE, NC	CHEYENNE, WY	CHICAGO, IL	CINCINNATI, OH	CLEVELAND, OH	DALLAS, TX	DENVER, CO	DES MOINES, IA	DETROIT, MI	EL PASO, TX	HOUSTON, TX	INDIANAPOLIS, IN	JACKSON, MS	KANSAS CITY, MO	LAS VEGAS, NV
ALBUQUERQUE, NM		1490	1902	991	1274	1333	966	2240	1808	2178	1793	1568	1649	538	1352	1409	1619	754	438	1091	1608	263	994	1298	1157	894	578
ATLANTA, GA	1490		679	1889	150	1559	2218	1100	910	1158	317	503	238	1482	717	476	726	792	1403	967	735	1437	800	531	386	801	2067
BALTIMORE, MD	1902	679		1959	795	1551	2401	422	370	481	583	352	441	1665	708	521	377	1399	1690	1031	532	2045	1470	600	1032	1087	2445
BILLINGS, MT	991	1889	1959		1839	413	626	2254	1796	2181	2157	1755	2012	455	1246	1552	1597	1433	554	1007	1534	1255	1673	1432	1836	1088	965
BIRMINGHAM, AL	1274	150	795	1839		1509	2170	1215	909	1241	466	578	389	1434	667	475	725	647	1356	919	734	1292	678	481	241	753	1852
BISMARCK, ND	1333	1559	1551	413	1509		1039	1846	1388	1773	1749	1347	1604	594	838	1144	1189	1342	693	675	1126	1597	1582	1024	1548	801	1378
BOISE, ID	966	2218	2401	626	2170	1039		2697	2239	2624	2520	2182	2375	737	1708	1969	2040	1711	833	1369	1977	1206	1952	1852	2115	1376	760
BOSTON, MA	2240	1100	422	2254	1215	1846	2697		462	214	1003	741	861	1961	1003	862	654	1819	2004	1326	741	2465	1890	940	1453	1427	2757
BUFFALO, NY	1808	910	370	1796	909	1388	2239	462		375	899	431	695	1502	545	442	197	1393	1546	868	277	2039	1513	508	1134	995	2299
BURLINGTON, VT	2178	1158	481	2181	1241	1773	2624	214	375		1061	782	919	1887	930	817	567	1763	1931	1253	652	2409	1916	878	1479	1366	2684
CHARLESTON, SC	1793	317	583	2157	466	1749	2520	1003	899	1061		468	204	1783	907	622	724	1109	1705	1204	879	1754	1110	721	703	1102	2371
CHARLESTON, WV	1568	503	352	1755	578	1347	2182	741	431	782	468		265	1445	506	209	255	1072	1367	802	410	1718	1192	320	816	764	2122
CHARLOTTE, NC	1649	238	441	2012	389	1604	2375	861	695	919	204	265		1637	761	476	520	1031	1559	1057	675	1677	1041	575	625	956	2225
CHEYENNE, WY	538	1482	1665	455	1434	594	737	1961	1502	1887	1783	1445	1637		972	1233	1304	979	100	633	1241	801	1220	1115	1382	640	843
CHICAGO, IL	1352	717	708	1246	667	838	1708	1003	545	930	907	506	761	972		302	346	936	1015	337	283	1543	1108	184	750	532	1768
CINCINNATI, OH	1409	476	521	1552	475	1144	1969	862	442	817	622	209	476	1233	302		253	958	1200	599	261	1605	1079	116	700	597	1955
CLEVELAND, OH	1619	726	377	1597	725	1189	2040	654	197	567	724	255	520	1304	346	253		1208	1347	669	171	1854	1328	319	950	806	2100
DALLAS, TX	754	792	1399	1433	647	1342	1711	1819	1393	1763	1109	1072	1031	979	936	958	1208		887	752	1218	647	241	913	406	554	1331
DENVER, CO	438	1403	1690	554	1356	693	833	2004	1546	1931	1705	1367	1559	100	1015	1200	1347	887		676	1284	701	1127	1088	1290	603	756
DES MOINES, IA	1091	967	1031	1007	919	675	1369	1326	868	1253	1204	802	1057	633	337	599	669	752	676		606	1283	992	481	931	194	1429
DETROIT, MI	1608	735	532	1534	734	1126	1977	741	277	652	879	410	675	1241	283	261	171	1218	1284	606		1799	1338	318	960	795	2037
EL PASO, TX	263	1437	2045	1255	1292	1597	1206	2465	2039	2409	1754	1718	1677	801	1543	1605	1854	647	701	1283	1799		758	1489	1051	1085	717
HOUSTON, TX	994	800	1470	1673	678	1582	1952	1890	1513	1916	1110	1192	1041	1220	1108	1079	1328	241	1127	992	1338	758		1033	445	795	1474
INDIANAPOLIS, IN	1298	531	600	1432	481	1024	1852	940	508	878	721	320	575	1115	184	116	319	913	1088	481	318	1489	1033		675	485	1843
JACKSON, MS	1157	386	1032	1836	241	1548	2115	1453	1134	1479	703	816	625	1382	750	700	950	406	1290	931	960	1051	445	675		747	1735
KANSAS CITY, MO	894	801	1087	1088	753	801	1376	1427	995	1366	1102	764	956	640	532	597	806	554	603	194	795	1085	795	485	747		1358
LAS VEGAS, NV	578	2067	2445	965	1852	1378	760	2757	2299	2684	2371	2122	2225	843	1768	1955	2100	1331	756	1429	2037	717	1474	1843	1735	1358	
LITTLE ROCK, AR	900	528	1072	1530	381	1183	1808	1493	1066	1437	900	745	754	1076	662	632	882	327	984	567	891	974	447	587	269	382	1478
LOS ANGELES, CA	806	2237	2705	1239	2092	1702	1033	3046	2572	2957	2554	2374	2453	1116	2042	2215	2374	1446	1029	1703	2310	801	1558	2104	1851	1632	274
LOUISVILLE, KY	1320	419	602	1547	369	1139	1933	964	545	915	610	251	464	1197	299	106	356	852	1118	595	366	1499	972	112	594	516	1874
MEMPHIS, TN	1033	389	933	1625	241	1337	1954	1353	927	1297	760	606	614	1217	539	493	742	466	1116	720	752	1112	586	464	211	536	1611
MIAMI, FL	2155	661	1109	2554	812	2224	2883	1529	1425	1587	583	994	730	2147	1382	1141	1250	1367	2069	1632	1401	1959	1201	1196	915	1466	2733
MILWAUKEE, WI	1426	813	805	1175	763	767	1748	1100	642	1027	1003	601	857	1012	89	398	443	1010	1055	378	380	1617	1193	279	835	573	1808
MINNEAPOLIS, MN	1339	1129	1121	839	1079	431	1465	1417	958	1343	1319	918	1173	881	409	714	760	999	924	246	697	1530	1240	596	1151	441	1677
MONTRÉAL, QC	2172	1241	564	2093	1289	1685	2535	313	397	92	1145	822	1003	1799	841	815	588	1772	1843	1165	564	2363	1892	872	1514	1359	2596
NASHVILLE, TN	1248	242	716	1648	194	1315	1976	1136	716	1086	543	395	397	1240	474	281	531	681	1162	725	541	1328	801	287	423	559	1826
NEW ORLEANS, LA	1276	473	1142	1955	351	1734	2234	1563	1254	1588	783	926	713	1502	935	820	1070	525	1409	1117	1079	1118	360	826	185	932	1854
NEW YORK, NY	2015	869	192	2049	985	1641	2491	215	400	299	773	515	631	1755	797	636	466	1589	1799	1121	622	2235	1660	715	1223	1202	2552
OKLAHOMA CITY, OK	546	944	1354	1227	729	1136	1506	1694	1262	1632	1248	1022	1102	773	807	863	1073	209	681	546	1062	737	449	752	612	348	1124
OMAHA, NE	973	989	1168	904	941	616	1234	1463	1005	1390	1290	952	1144	497	474	736	806	669	541	136	743	1236	910	618	935	188	1294
ORLANDO, FL	1934	440	904	2333	591	2003	2662	1324	1221	1383	379	790	525	1926	1161	920	1045	1146	1847	1411	1180	1738	980	975	694	1245	2512
PHILADELPHIA, PA	1954	782	104	2019	897	1611	2462	321	414	371	685	454	543	1725	768	576	437	1501	1744	1091	592	2147	1572	655	1135	1141	2500
PHOENIX, AZ	466	1868	2366	1199	1723	1662	993	2706	2274	2644	2184	2035	2107	1004	1819	1876	2085	1077	904	1558	2074	432	1188	1764	1482	1360	285
PITTSBURGH, PA	1670	676	246	1719	763	1311	2161	592	217	587	642	217	438	1425	467	292	136	1246	1460	791	292	1893	1366	370	988	857	2215
PORTLAND, ME	2338	1197	520	2352	1313	1944	2795	107	560	233	1101	839	959	2059	1101	960	751	1917	2102	1424	838	2563	1988	1038	1550	1525	2855
PORTLAND, OR	1395	2647	2830	889	2599	1301	432	3126	2667	3052	2948	2610	2802	1166	2137	2398	2469	2140	1261	1798	2405	1767	2381	2280	2544	1805	1188
RAPID CITY, SD	841	1511	1626	379	1463	320	930	1921	1463	1848	1824	1422	1678	305	913	1219	1264	1077	404	629	1201	1105	1318	1101	1458	710	1035
RENO, NV	1020	2440	2623	960	2392	1372	430	2919	2460	2845	2741	2403	2595	959	1930	2191	2262	1933	1054	1591	2198	1315	2072	2073	2337	1598	442
RICHMOND, VA	1876	527	152	2053	678	1645	2496	572	485	630	428	322	289	1760	802	530	471	1309	1688	1126	627	1955	1330	641	914	1085	2444
ST. LOUIS, MO	1051	549	841	1341	501	1053	1628	1181	749	1119	850	512	704	892	294	350	560	635	855	436	549	1242	863	239	505	252	1610
SALT LAKE CITY, UT	624	1916	2100	548	1868	960	342	2395	1936	2322	2218	1880	2072	436	1406	1667	1738	1410	531	1067	1675	864	1650	1549	1813	1074	417
SAN ANTONIO, TX	818	1000	1671	1500	878	1599	1761	2092	1665	2036	1310	1344	1241	1046	1270	1231	1481	271	946	1009	1490	556	200	1186	644	812	1272
SAN DIEGO, CA	825	2166	2724	1302	2021	1765	1096	3065	2632	3020	2483	2393	2405	1179	2105	2234	2437	1375	1092	1766	2373	730	1487	2122	1780	1695	337
SAN FRANCISCO, CA	1111	2618	2840	1176	2472	1749	646	3135	2677	3062	2934	2620	2759	1176	2146	2407	2478	1827	1271	1807	2415	1181	1938	2290	2232	1814	575
SEATTLE, WA	1463	2705	2775	816	2657	1229	500	3070	2612	2997	2973	2571	2827	1234	2062	2368	2413	2208	1329	1822	2350	1944	2449	2249	2612	1872	1256
TAMPA, FL	1949	455	960	2348	606	2018	2677	1380	1276	1438	434	845	581	1941	1176	935	1101	1161	1862	1426	1194	1753	995	990	709	1259	2526
TORONTO, ON	1841	958	565	1762	958	1354	2204	570	106	419	1006	537	802	1468	510	484	303	1441	1512	834	233	2032	1561	541	1183	1028	2265
VANCOUVER, BC	1597	2838	2908	949	2791	1362	633	3204	2745	3130	3106	2705	2960	1368	2196	2501	2547	2342	1463	1956	2483	2087	2583	2383	2746	2007	1390
WASHINGTON, DC	1896	636	38	1953	758	1545	2395	458	384	517	539	346	397	1659	701	517	370	1362	1686	1025	526	2008	1433	596	996	1083	2441
WICHITA, KS	707	989	1276	1067	838	934	1346	1616	1184	1554	1291	953	1145	613	728	785	995	367	521	390	984	898	608	674	771	192	1276

LITTLE ROCK, AR	LOS ANGELES, CA	LOUISVILLE, KY	MEMPHIS, TN	MIAMI, FL	MILWAUKEE, WI	MINNEAPOLIS, MN	MONTRÉAL, QC	NASHVILLE, TN	NEW ORLEANS, LA	NEW YORK, NY	OKLAHOMA CITY, OK	OMAHA, NE	ORLANDO, FL	PHILADELPHIA, PA	PHOENIX, AZ	PITTSBURGH, PA	PORTLAND, ME	PORTLAND, OR	RAPID CITY, SD	RENO, NV	RICHMOND, VA	SALT LAKE CITY, UT	SAN ANTONIO, TX	SAN DIEGO, CA	SAN FRANCISCO, CA	SEATTLE, WA	ST. LOUIS, MO	TAMPA, FL	TORONTO, ON	VANCOUVER, BC	WASHINGTON, DC	WICHITA, KS
900	806	1320	1033	2155	1426	1339	2172	1248	1276	2015	546	973	1934	1954	466	1670	2338	1395	841	1020	1876	1051	624	818	825	1111	1463	1949	1841	1597	1896	707
528	2237	419	389	661	813	1129	1241	242	473	869	944	989	440	782	1868	676	1197	2647	1511	2440	527	549	1916	1000	2166	2618	2705	455	958	2838	636	989
1072	2705	602	933	1109	805	1121	564	716	1142	192	1354	1168	904	104	2366	246	520	2830	1626	2623	152	841	2100	1671	2724	2840	2775	960	565	2908	38	1276
1530	1239	1547	1625	2554	1175	839	2093	1648	1955	2049	1227	904	2333	2019	1199	1719	2352	889	379	960	2053	1341	548	1500	1302	1176	816	2348	1762	949	1953	1067
381	2092	369	241	812	763	1079	1289	194	351	985	729	941	591	897	1723	763	1313	2599	1463	2392	678	501	1868	878	2021	2472	2657	606	958	2791	758	838
1183	1702	1139	1337	2224	767	431	1685	1315	1734	1641	1136	616	2003	1611	1662	1311	1944	1301	320	1372	1645	1053	960	1599	1765	1749	1229	2018	1354	1362	1545	934
1808	1033	1933	1954	2883	1748	1465	2535	1976	2234	2491	1506	1234	2662	2462	993	2161	2795	432	930	430	2496	1628	342	1761	1096	646	500	2677	2204	633	2395	1346
1493	3046	964	1353	1529	1100	1417	313	1136	1563	215	1694	1463	1324	321	2706	592	107	3126	1921	2919	572	1181	2395	2092	3065	3135	3070	1380	570	3204	458	1616
1066	2572	545	927	1425	642	958	397	716	1254	400	1262	1005	1221	414	2274	217	560	2667	1463	2460	485	749	1936	1665	2632	2677	2612	1276	106	2745	384	1184
1437	2957	915	1297	1587	1027	1343	92	1086	1588	299	1632	1390	1383	371	2644	587	233	3052	1848	2845	630	1119	2322	2036	3020	3062	2997	1438	419	3130	517	1554
900	2554	610	760	583	1003	1319	1145	543	783	773	1248	1290	379	685	2184	642	1101	2948	1824	2741	428	850	2218	1310	2483	2934	2973	434	1006	3106	539	1291
745	2374	251	606	994	601	918	822	395	926	515	1022	952	790	454	2035	217	839	2610	1422	2403	322	512	1880	1344	2393	2620	2571	845	537	2705	346	953
754	2453	464	614	730	857	1173	1003	397	713	631	1102	1144	525	543	2107	438	959	2802	1678	2595	289	704	2072	1241	2405	2759	2827	581	802	2960	397	1145
1076	1116	1197	1217	2147	1012	881	1799	1240	1502	1755	773	497	1926	1725	1004	1425	2059	1166	305	959	1760	892	436	1046	1179	1176	1234	1941	1468	1368	1659	613
662	2042	299	539	1382	89	409	841	474	935	797	807	474	1161	768	1819	467	1101	2137	913	1930	802	294	1406	1270	2105	2146	2062	1176	510	2196	701	728
632	2215	106	493	1141	398	714	815	281	820	636	863	736	920	576	1876	292	960	2398	1219	2191	530	350	1667	1231	2234	2407	2368	935	484	2501	517	785
882	2374	356	742	1250	443	760	588	531	1070	466	1073	806	1045	437	2085	136	751	2469	1264	2262	471	560	1738	1481	2437	2478	2413	1101	303	2547	370	995
327	1446	852	466	1367	1010	999	1772	681	525	1589	209	669	1146	1501	1077	1246	1917	2140	1077	1933	1309	635	1410	271	1375	1827	2208	1161	1441	2342	1362	367
984	1029	1118	1116	2069	1055	924	1843	1162	1409	1799	681	541	1847	1744	904	1460	2102	1261	404	1054	1688	855	531	946	1092	1271	1329	1862	1512	1463	1686	521
567	1703	595	720	1632	378	246	1165	725	1117	1121	546	136	1411	1091	1558	791	1424	1798	629	1591	1126	436	1067	1009	1766	1807	1822	1426	834	1956	1025	390
891	2310	366	752	1401	380	697	564	541	1079	622	1062	743	1180	592	2074	292	838	2405	1201	2198	627	549	1675	1490	2373	2415	2350	1194	233	2483	526	984
974	801	1499	1112	1959	1617	1530	2363	1328	1118	2235	737	1236	1738	2147	432	1893	2563	1767	1105	1315	1955	1242	864	556	730	1181	1944	1753	2032	2087	2008	898
447	1558	972	586	1201	1193	1240	1892	801	360	1660	449	910	980	1572	1188	1366	1988	2381	1318	2072	1330	863	1650	200	1487	1938	2449	995	1561	2583	1433	608
587	2104	112	464	1196	279	596	872	287	826	715	752	618	975	655	1764	370	1038	2280	1101	2073	641	239	1549	1186	2122	2290	2249	990	541	2383	596	674
269	1851	594	211	915	835	1151	1514	423	185	1223	612	935	694	1135	1482	988	1550	2544	1458	2337	914	505	1813	644	1780	2232	2612	709	1183	2746	996	771
382	1632	516	536	1466	573	441	1359	559	932	1202	348	188	1245	1141	1360	857	1525	1805	710	1598	1085	252	1074	812	1695	1814	1872	1259	1028	2007	1083	192
1478	274	1874	1611	2733	1808	1677	2596	1826	1854	2552	1124	1294	2512	2500	285	2215	2855	1188	1035	442	2444	1610	417	1272	337	575	1256	2526	2265	1390	2441	1276
	1706	526	140	1190	747	814	1446	355	455	1262	355	570	969	1175	1367	920	1590	2237	1093	2030	983	416	1507	600	1703	2012	2305	984	1115	2439	1036	464
1706		2126	1839	2759	2082	1951	2869	2054	1917	2820	1352	1567	2538	2760	369	2476	3144	971	1309	519	2682	1856	691	1356	124	385	1148	2553	2538	1291	2702	1513
526	2126		386	1084	394	711	920	175	714	739	774	704	863	678	1786	394	1062	2362	1215	2155	572	264	1631	1125	2144	2372	2364	878	589	2497	596	705
140	1839	386		1051	624	940	1306	215	396	1123	487	724	830	1035	1500	780	1451	2382	1247	2175	843	294	1652	739	1841	2144	2440	845	975	2574	896	597
1190	2759	1084	1051		1478	1794	1671	907	874	1299	1609	1654	232	1211	2390	1167	1627	3312	2176	3105	954	1214	2581	1401	2688	3140	3370	274	1532	3504	1065	1655
747	2082	394	624	1478		337	939	569	1020	894	880	514	1257	865	1892	564	1198	2063	842	1970	899	367	1446	1343	2145	2186	1991	1272	607	2124	799	769
814	1951	711	940	1794	337		1255	886	1337	1211	793	383	1573	1181	1805	881	1515	1727	606	1839	1216	621	1315	1257	2014	2055	1654	1588	924	1788	1115	637
1446	2869	920	1306	1671	939	1255		1094	1632	383	1625	1300	1466	454	2637	607	282	2963	1758	2756	714	1112	2232	2043	2931	2972	2907	1522	330	3041	600	1547
355	2054	175	215	907	569	886	1094		539	906	703	747	686	818	1715	569	1234	2405	1269	2198	626	307	1675	954	2056	2360	2463	701	764	2597	679	748
455	1917	714	396	874	1020	1337	1632	539		1332	731	1121	653	1245	1548	1108	1660	2663	1643	2431	1002	690	1932	560	1846	2298	2731	668	1302	2865	1106	890
1262	2820	739	1123	1299	894	1211	383	906	1332		1469	1258	1094	91	2481	367	313	2920	1716	2713	342	956	2189	1861	2839	2929	2864	1150	507	2998	228	1391
355	1352	774	487	1609	880	793	1625	703	731	1469		463	1388	1408	1012	1124	1792	1934	871	1727	1331	505	1204	466	1370	1657	2002	1403	1295	2136	1350	161
570	1567	704	724	1654	514	383	1300	747	1121	1258	463		1433	1228	1440	928	1561	1662	525	1455	1263	440	932	927	1630	1672	1719	1448	971	1853	1162	307
969	2538	863	830	232	1257	1573	1466	686	653	1094	1388	1433		1006	2169	963	1422	3091	1955	2884	750	993	2360	1180	2467	2918	3149	82	1327	3283	860	1434
1175	2760	678	1035	1211	865	1181	454	818	1245	91	1408	1228	1006		2420	306	419	2890	1686	2683	254	895	2160	1774	2779	2900	2835	1062	522	2968	140	1330
1367	369	1786	1500	2390	1892	1805	2637	1715	1548	2481	1012	1440	2169	2420		2136	2804	1335	1308	883	2343	1517	651	987	358	750	1513	2184	2307	1655	2362	1173
920	2476	394	780	1167	564	881	607	569	1108	367	1124	928	963	306	2136		690	2590	1386	2383	341	611	1859	1519	2494	2599	2534	1019	321	2668	240	1046
1590	3144	1062	1451	1627	1198	1515	282	1234	1660	313	1792	1561	1422	419	2804	690		3223	2019	3016	670	1279	2493	2189	3162	3233	3168	1478	668	3301	556	1714
2237	971	2362	2382	3312	2063	1727	2963	2405	2663	2920	1934	1662	3091	2890	1335	2590	3223		1268	578	2925	2057	771	2322	1093	638	170	3106	2633	313	2824	1775
1093	1309	1215	1247	2176	842	606	1758	1269	1643	1716	871	525	1955	1686	1308	1386	2019	1268		1151	1720	963	628	1335	1372	1368	1195	1970	1429	1328	1620	712
2030	519	2155	2175	3105	1970	1839	2756	2198	2431	2713	1727	1455	2884	2683	883	2383	3016	578	1151		2718	1850	524	1870	642	217	755	2899	2426	898	2617	1568
983	2682	572	843	954	899	1216	714	626	1002	342	1331	1263	750	254	2343	341	670	2925	1720	2718		834	2194	1530	2684	2934	2869	805	660	3003	108	1274
416	1856	264	294	1214	367	621	1112	307	690	956	505	440	993	895	1517	611	1279	2057	963	1850	834		1326	968	1875	2066	2125	1008	782	2259	837	441
1507	691	1631	1652	2581	1446	1315	2232	1675	1932	2189	1204	932	2360	2160	651	1859	2493	771	628	524	2194	1326		1419	754	740	839	2375	1902	973	2094	1044
600	1356	1125	739	1401	1343	1257	2043	954	560	1861	466	927	1180	1774	987	1519	2189	2322	1335	1870	1530	968	1419		1285	1737	2275	1195	1714	2410	1635	624
1703	124	2144	1841	2688	2145	2014	2931	2056	1846	2839	1370	1630	2467	2779	358	2494	3162	1093	1372	642	2684	1875	754	1285		508	1271	2481	2601	1414	2720	1531
2012	385	2372	2144	3140	2186	2055	2972	2360	2298	2929	1657	1672	2918	2900	750	2599	3233	638	1368	217	2934	2066	740	1737	508		816	2933	2643	958	2834	1784
2305	1148	2364	2440	3370	1991	1654	2907	2463	2731	2864	2002	1719	3149	2835	1513	2534	3168	170	1195	755	2869	2125	839	2275	1271	816		3164	2577	140	2769	1843
984	2553	878	845	274	1272	1588	1522	701	668	1150	1403	1448	82	1062	2184	1019	1478	3106	1970	2899	805	1008	2375	1195	2481	2933	3164		1383	3297	916	1448
1115	2538	589	975	1532	607	924	330	764	1302	507	1295	971	1327	522	2307	321	668	2633	1429	2426	660	782	1902	1714	2601	2643	2577	1383		2711	563	1217
2439	1291	2497	2574	3504	2124	1788	3041	2597	2865	2998	2136	1853	3283	2968	1655	2668	3301	313	1328	898	3003	2259	973	2410	1414	958	140	3297	2711		2902	1977
1036	2702	596	896	1065	799	1115	600	679	1106	228	1350	1162	860	140	2362	240	556	2824	1620	2617	108	837	2094	1635	2720	2834	2769	916	563	2902		1272
464	1513	705	597	1655	769	637	1547	748	890	1391	161	307	1434	1330	1173	1046	1714	1775	712	1568	1274	441	1044	624	1531	1784	1843	1448	1217	1977	1272	

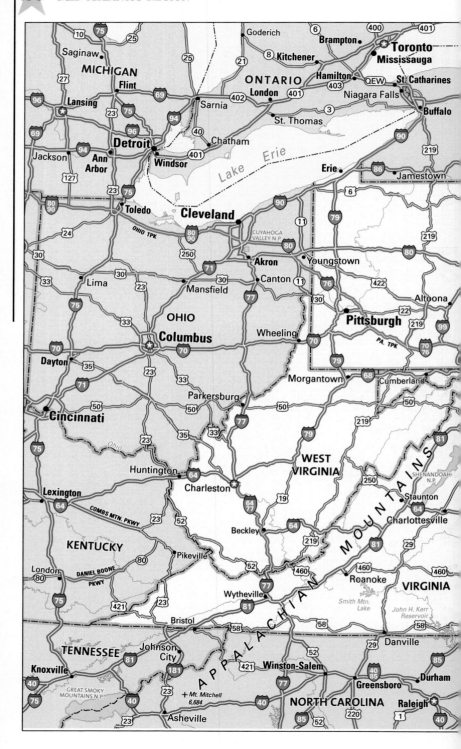

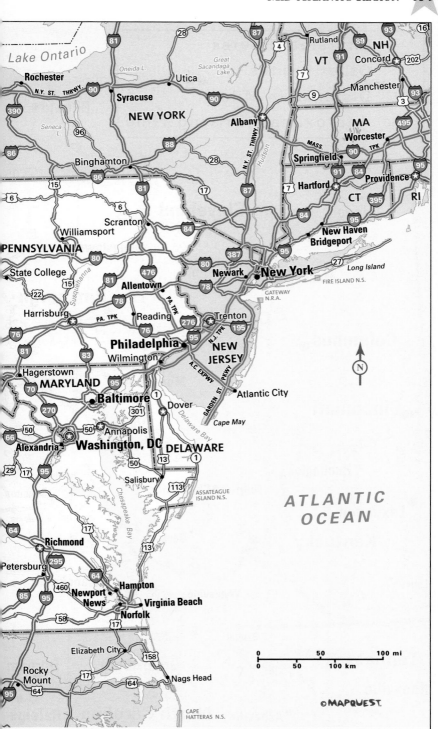

Interstate Routes
Other Routes
277 Distance in Miles
1:50 Approximate Driving Time

Lake

MI

Lake Erie

Buffalo

74
1:30

96
1:35

Erie

186
3:05

106
1:50

Toledo

119
2:00

Cleveland

75
1:15

126
2:05

148
3:05

81
1:20

112
1:50

Youngstown

395
7:10

Mansfield

67
1:05

173
3:30

71
1:10

Pittsburgh

205
3:25

190
3:10

Ohio

78
1:20

173
2:55

Columbus

255
4:15

Morgantown

138
2:20

109
1:50

168
3:40

West
Virginia

Cincinnati

135
2:55

142
2:10

150
3:25

136
2:15

85
1:25

Huntington

52
0:50

Charleston

158
2:30

Staunton

108
1:50

126
2:05

60
0:55

Lexington

316
6:15

Beckley

91
1:30

192
3:50

77
1:15

71
1:10

78
1:20

Roanoke

Kentucky

213
4:10

252
5:00

Wytheville

London

70
1:10

101
2:15

100
1:40

117
1:55

Bristol

APPALACHIAN MOUNTAINS

Greensboro

49
0:50

Durham

Tennessee

83
1:50

176
2:40

23
0:25

Knoxville

109
1:45

Asheville

North Carolina

Raleigh

Ontario

Rochester 88
1:45

New York

152 Syracuse
2:30

146
2:25

Albany

99 2:00
76 1:15

135
2:45

Corning 72
1:35 Binghamton

135
2:15

MA

151 2:30

CT RI

167 3:40

Scranton

61 1:00

176 3:25

Pennsylvania

119 2:00

120 2:20

New York

128 2:10

Harrisburg

165 3:30

New Jersey

91 1:50

109 1:50

75 1:15

83 1:25

Philadelphia

125 2:30

104 1:45

74 1:35

62 1:15

Hagerstown

76 70 1:15

Baltimore

Atlantic City

1:10

38 0:40

94 2:00

Dover

Delaware

157 2:35

Washington, DC
Maryland

Virginia

108 1:50

191 4:10

ATLANTIC
OCEAN

Richmond

152 2:35

91 1:30

Norfolk

127 2:05

82 1:45

Rocky Mount

147 3:15

Nags Head

54 1:10

N

©MAPQUEST.

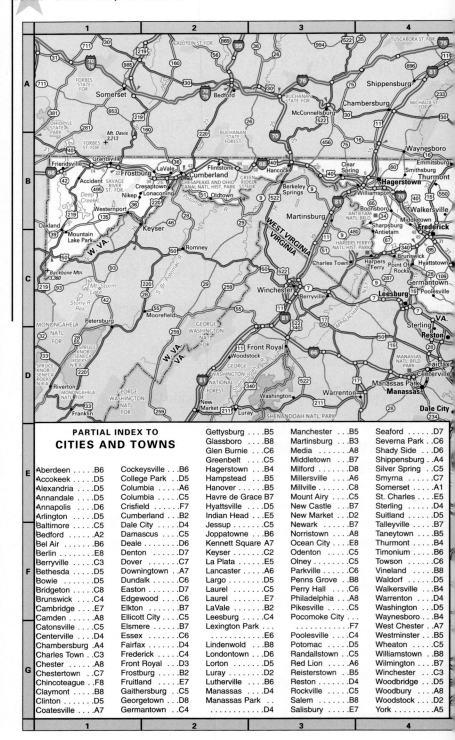

PARTIAL INDEX TO
CITIES AND TOWNS

Aberdeen B6
Accokeek D5
Alexandria D5
Annandale D5
Annapolis D6
Arlington D5
Baltimore C5
Bedford A2
Bel Air B6
Berlin E8
Berryville C3
Bethesda D5
Bowie D5
Bridgeton C8
Brunswick C4
Cambridge E7
Camden A8
Catonsville C5
Centerville D4
Chambersburg .A4
Charles Town . .C3
Chester A8
Chestertown . .C7
Chincoteague . .F8
Claymont B8
Clinton D5
Coatesville A7

Cockeysville . . .B6
College Park . .D5
Columbia A6
Columbia C5
Crisfield F7
Cumberland . . .B2
Dale City D4
Damascus C5
Deale D6
Denton D7
Dover C7
Downingtown . .A7
Dundalk C6
Easton D7
Edgewood C6
Elkton B7
Ellicott City . . .C5
Elsmere B7
Essex C6
Fairfax D4
Frederick C4
Front Royal . . .D3
Frostburg B2
Fruitland E7
Gaithersburg . .C5
Georgetown . . .D8
Germantown . .C4

Gettysburg . . .B5
Glassboro B8
Glen Burnie . . .C6
Greenbelt C5
Hagerstown . . .B4
Hampstead . . .B5
Hanover B5
Havre de Grace B7
Hyattsville D5
Indian Head . . .E5
Jessup C5
Joppatowne . . .B6
Kennett Square A7
Keyser C2
La Plata E5
Lancaster A6
Largo D5
Laurel C5
Laurel E7
LaVale B2
Leesburg C4
Lexington Park . .
. . . . .E6
Lindenwold . . .B8
Londontown . . .D6
Lorton D5
Luray D2
Lutherville B6
Manassas D4
Manassas Park . .
. . . . .D4

Manchester . . .B5
Martinsburg . . .B3
Media A8
Middletown . . .B7
Milford D8
Millersville A6
Millville C8
Mount Airy C5
New Castle . . .B7
New Market . . .D2
Newark B7
Norristown A8
Ocean City . . .E8
Odenton C5
Olney C5
Parkville C6
Penns Grove . .B8
Perry Hall C6
Philadelphia . .A8
Pikesville C5
Pocomoke City . .
. . . . .F7
Poolesville C4
Potomac D5
Randallstown . .C5
Red Lion A6
Reisterstown . .B5
Reston D4
Rockville C5
Salem B8
Salisbury E7

Seaford D7
Severna Park . .C6
Shady Side . . .D6
Shippensburg . .A4
Silver Spring . .C5
Smyrna C7
Somerset A1
St. Charles E5
Sterling D4
Suitland D5
Talleyville B7
Taneytown B5
Thurmont B4
Timonium B6
Towson C6
Vineland B8
Waldorf D5
Walkersville . . .B4
Warrenton D4
Washington . . .D5
Waynesboro . . .B4
West Chester . .A7
Westminster . . .B5
Wheaton C5
Williamstown . .B8
Wilmington B7
Winchester C3
Woodbridge . . .D5
Woodbury A8
Woodstock D2
York A5

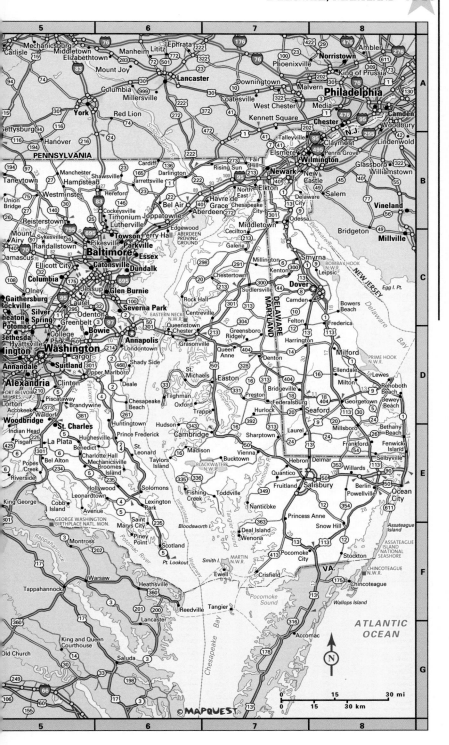

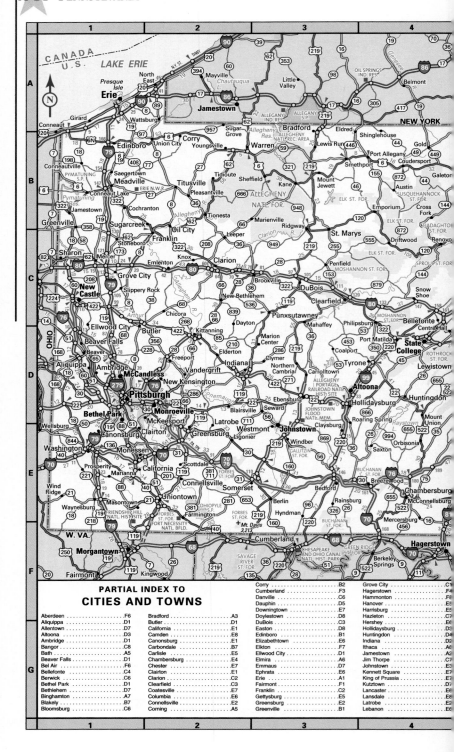

PARTIAL INDEX TO
CITIES AND TOWNS

Aberdeen F6	Bradford A3	Grove City C1
Aliquippa D1	Butler D1	Hagerstown F4
Allentown D7	California E1	Hammonton F8
Altoona D3	Camden E8	Hanover E5
Ambridge D1	Canonsburg E1	Harrisburg E6
Bangor C8	Carbondale B7	Hazleton C7
Bath A5	Carlisle E5	Hershey E6
Beaver Falls D1	Chambersburg E4	Hollidaysburg D3
Bel Air F6	Chester E7	Huntingdon D4
Bellefonte C4	Clairton E1	Indiana D2
Berwick C6	Clarion C2	Ithaca A6
Bethel Park D1	Clearfield C3	Jamestown A2
Bethlehem D7	Coatesville E7	Jim Thorpe C7
Binghamton A7	Columbia E6	Johnstown E3
Blakely B7	Connellsville E2	Kennett Square E7
Bloomsburg C6	Corning A5	King of Prussia D7
	Corry B2	Kutztown D7
	Cumberland F3	Lancaster E6
	Danville C6	Lansdale E8
	Dauphin D5	Latrobe E2
	Downingtown E7	Lebanon E6
	Doylestown D8	
	DuBois C3	
	Easton D8	
	Edinboro B1	
	Elizabethtown E6	
	Elkton F7	
	Ellwood City D1	
	Elmira A6	
	Emmaus D7	
	Ephrata E6	
	Erie A1	
	Fairmont F1	
	Franklin C2	
	Gettysburg E5	
	Greensburg E2	
	Greenville B1	

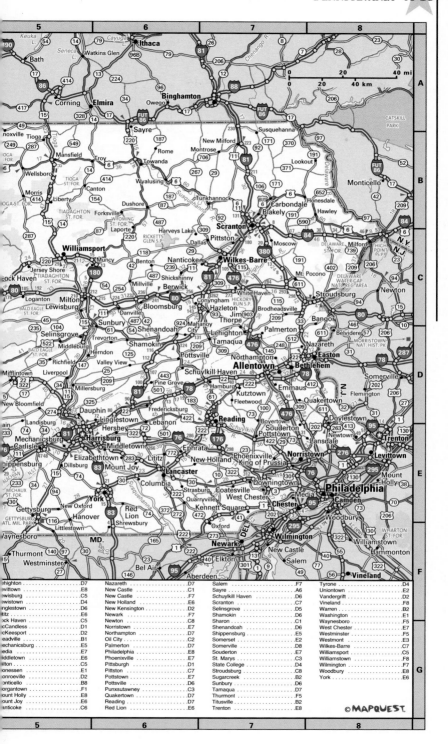

...ehighton ...D7	Nazareth ...D7	Salem ...F7
...ewisburg ...C5	New Castle ...C1	Sayre ...A6
...ewistown ...D4	New Castle ...F7	Schuylkill Haven ...D6
...inglestown ...D6	New Holland ...E6	Scranton ...C7
...ititz ...E6	New Kensington ...D2	Selinsgrove ...D5
...ock Haven ...C5	Newark ...F7	Shamokin ...D6
...cCandless ...D1	Newton ...C8	Sharon ...C1
...cKeesport ...D2	Norristown ...E7	Shenandoah ...D6
...eadville ...B1	Northampton ...D7	Shippensburg ...E5
...echanicsburg ...E5	Oil City ...C2	Somerset ...E2
...edia ...E7	Palmerton ...D7	Somerville ...D8
...iddletown ...E6	Philadelphia ...E8	Souderton ...D7
...ilton ...C5	Phoenixville ...E7	St. Marys ...C3
...onessen ...E1	Pittsburgh ...D1	State College ...D4
...onroeville ...D2	Pittston ...C7	Stroudsburg ...C8
...onticello ...B8	Pottstown ...E7	Sugarcreek ...B2
...organtown ...F1	Pottsville ...D6	Sunbury ...D6
...ount Holly ...E8	Punxsutawney ...C3	Tamaqua ...D7
...ount Joy ...E6	Quakertown ...D7	Thurmont ...F5
...anticoke ...C6	Reading ...D7	Titusville ...B2
	Red Lion ...E6	Trenton ...E8
		Tyrone ...D4
		Uniontown ...E2
		Vandergrift ...D2
		Vineland ...F8
		Warren ...B2
		Washington ...E1
		Waynesboro ...F5
		West Chester ...E7
		Westminster ...F5
		Westmont ...E3
		Wilkes-Barre ...C7
		Williamsport ...C5
		Williamstown ...F8
		Wilmington ...F7
		Woodbury ...E8
		York ...E6

©MAPQUEST.

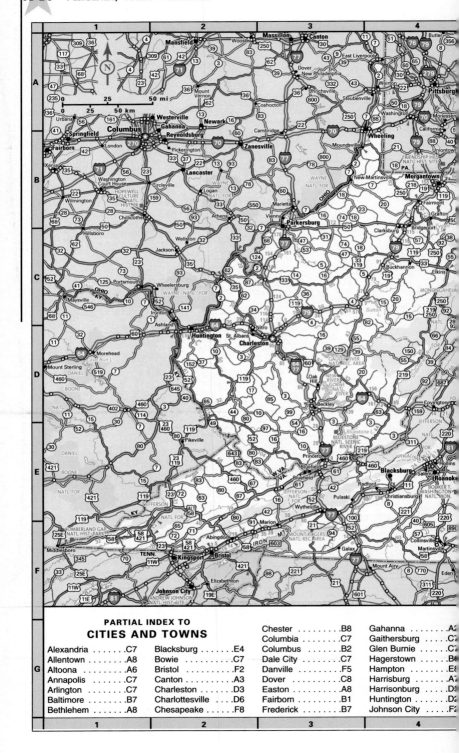

PARTIAL INDEX TO
CITIES AND TOWNS

Alexandria C7
Allentown A8
Altoona A6
Annapolis C7
Arlington C7
Baltimore B7
Bethlehem A8

Blacksburg E4
Bowie C7
Bristol F2
Canton A3
Charleston D3
Charlottesville D6
Chesapeake F8

Chester B8
Columbia C7
Columbus B2
Dale City C7
Danville F5
Dover C8
Easton A8
Fairborn B1
Frederick B7

Gahanna A2
Gaithersburg C7
Glen Burnie C7
Hagerstown B6
Hampton E8
Harrisburg A7
Harrisonburg D5
Huntington D2
Johnson City F2

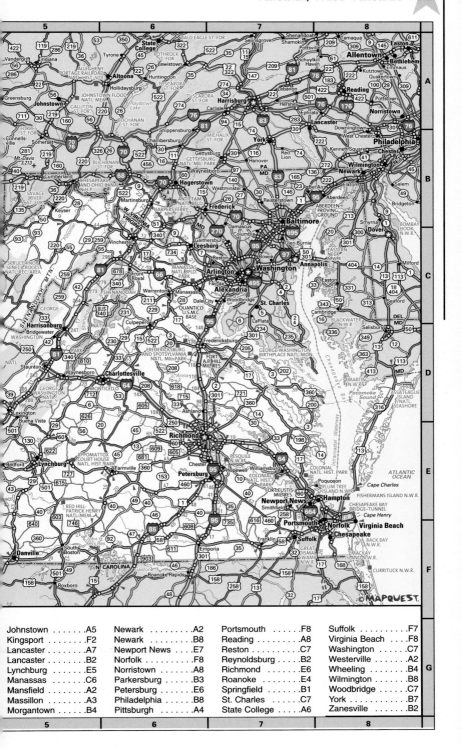

Johnstown	A5	Newark	A2	Portsmouth	F8	Suffolk ... F7
Kingsport	F2	Newark	B8	Reading	A8	Virginia Beach ... F8
Lancaster	A7	Newport News	E7	Reston	C7	Washington ... C7
Lancaster	B2	Norfolk	F8	Reynoldsburg	B2	Westerville ... A2
Lynchburg	E5	Norristown	A8	Richmond	E6	Wheeling ... B4
Manassas	C6	Parkersburg	B3	Roanoke	E4	Wilmington ... B8
Mansfield	A2	Petersburg	E6	Springfield	B1	Woodbridge ... C7
Massillon	A3	Philadelphia	B8	St. Charles	C7	York ... B7
Morgantown	B4	Pittsburgh	A4	State College	A6	Zanesville ... B2

MAP LEGEND

TRANSPORTATION

CONTROLLED ACCESS HIGHWAYS

Free

Toll; Toll Booth

Under Construction

Interchange and Exit Number

Ramp
Downtown maps only

OTHER SYMBOLS

Distances Along Major Highways
Miles in US; kilometers in Canada and Mexico

Tunnel; Pass

One-Way Street

Airport

Railroad
Downtown maps only

Auto Ferry; Passenger Ferry

OTHER HIGHWAYS

Primary Highway

Secondary Highway

Multilane Divided Highway
Primary and secondary highways only

Other Paved Road

Unpaved Road
Check conditions locally

HIGHWAY MARKERS

Interstate Route

US Route

State or Provincial Route

County or Other Route

Business Route

Trans-Canada Highway

Canadian Provincial Autoroute

Mexican Federal Route

RECREATION AND FEATURES OF INTEREST

National Park

National Forest; National Grassland

Other Large Park or Recreation Area

Military Lands

Indian Reservation

Small State Park with and without Camping

Public Campsite

Trail

Point of Interest

Golf Course
Professional tournament location

Hospital
City maps only

Ski Area

CITIES AND TOWNS

National Capital; State or Provincial Capital

County Seat
State maps only

Cities, Towns, and Populated Places
Type size indicates relative importance

Urban Area
State and province maps only

Large Incorporated Cities

OTHER MAP FEATURES

County Boundary and Name

Time Zone Boundary

Mountain Peak; Elevation
Feet in US; meters in Canada and Mexico

+ Mt. Olympus
7,965

Perennial; Intermittent River

Perennial; Intermittent or Dry Water Body

Dam

Swamp

JEFFERSON

It pays for all kinds of fuel.

Speedpass: today's way to pay. Don't go on the road without *Speedpass*. You can pay for gas at the pump or just about anything inside our store. It's fast, free, and links to a check card or major credit card you already have. To join the millions who use *Speedpass*, call **1-87-SPEEDPASS** or visit speedpass.com.

We're drivers too.

With the right gas, a kid could go pretty far.

Next time you stop at an Exxon or Mobil station, consider a new destination: college. ExxonMobil is working with Upromise to help you save for a child's education. How do you start saving? Just join at upromise.com and register your credit cards. It's FREE to join. Then when you buy Exxon or Mobil gas with a credit card registered with Upromise, one cent per gallon will be contributed to your Upromise account*. This account helps you pay for the college education of any child you choose. Contributions from other Upromise participants, like GM, AT&T and Toys"R"Us, are also added to this account.** One more thing: be sure to register the credit card you linked to your *Speedpass*. That way, *Speedpass* gasoline purchases can also contribute to your account. To get your FREE *Speedpass*, go to speedpass.com or call toll free 1-87-SPEEDPASS. Upromise is an easy way to help you save for a child's education. How do we know? We're drivers too.

Join Upromise for FREE at upromise.com
For your FREE *Speedpass*, call 1-87-SPEEDPASS
or visit speedpass.com.
You must have Internet access and a valid email address to join Upromise.
*No contributions are made for diesel fuel purchases.
** Specific terms and conditions apply for each company's contributions.
  Visit upromise.com for details.
Available at Exxon and Mobil stations that accept *Speedpass*.
©2002 Exxon Mobil Corporation. All rights reserved.

EXXON Mobil

We're drivers too.

WELCOME

Dear Traveler,

Since its inception in 1958, Mobil Travel Guide has served as a trusted aid to auto travelers in search of value in lodging, dining, and destinations. Now in its 45th year, Mobil Travel Guide is the hallmark of our ExxonMobil family of travel publications, and we're proud to offer an array of products and services from our Mobil, Exxon, and Esso brands in North America to facilitate life on the road.

Whether business or pleasure venues, our nationwide network of independent, professional evaluators offers their expertise on thousands of travel options, allowing you to plan a quick family getaway, a full-service business meeting, or an unforgettable Five-Star celebration.

Your feedback is important to us as we strive to improve our product offerings and better meet today's travel needs. Whether you travel once a week or once a year, please take the time to complete the customer feedback form at the back of this book. Or, contact us at www.mobiltravelguide.com. We hope to hear from you soon.

Best wishes for safe and enjoyable travels.

Lee R. Raymond
Chairman
Exxon Mobil Corporation

A WORD TO OUR READERS

In this day and age the travel industry is ever-changing, and having accurate, reliable travel information is indispensable. Travelers are back on the roads in enormous numbers. They are going on day trips, long weekends, extended family vacations, and business trips. They are traveling across the country- stopping at National Parks, major cities, small towns, monuments, and landmarks. And for 45 years, the *Mobil Travel Guide* has been providing this invaluable service to the traveling consumer and is committed to continuing this service well into the future.

You, the traveler, deserve the best food and accommodations available in every city, town, or village you visit. But finding suitable accommodations can be problematic. You could try to meet and ask local residents about appropriate places to stay and eat, but that time-consuming option comes with no guarantee of getting the best advice.

The *Mobil Travel Guide* One- to Five-Star rating system is the oldest and most respected lodging and restaurant inspection and rating program in North America. This trusted, well-established tool directs you to satisfying places to eat and stay, as well as to interesting events and attractions in thousands of locations. Mobil Corporation (now known as Exxon Mobil Corporation, following a 1999 merger) began producing the *Mobil Travel Guides* in 1958, following the introduction of the US Highway system in 1956. The first edition covered only 5 southwestern states. Since then, the *Mobil Travel Guide* has become the premier travel guide in North America, covering the 48 contiguous states and major cities in Canadian provinces. Now, ExxonMobil presents the latest edition of our annual Travel Guides series.

For the past 45 years, *Mobil Travel Guide* has been inspecting and rating lodging and restaurants throughout the United States and Canada. Each restaurant, motel, hotel, inn, resort, guest ranch, etc., is inspected and must meet the basic requirements of cleanliness and service to be included in the *Mobil Travel Guide.* Highly trained quality assurance team members travel across the country generating exhaustive inspections reports. *Mobil Travel Guide* management's careful scrutiny of findings detailed in the inspection reports, incognito inspections, where we dine in the restaurant and stay overnight at the lodging to gauge the level of service of the hotel and restaurant, review of our extensive files of reader comments and letters are all used in the final ratings determinations. All of this information is used to arrive at fair, accurate, and useful assessments of lodgings and restaurants. Based upon these elements, *Mobil Travel Guide* determines those establishments eligible for listing. Only facilities meeting *Mobil Travel Guide* standards of cleanliness, maintenance and stable management are listed in the Guide. Deteriorating, poorly managed establishments are deleted. A listing in the *Mobil Travel Guide* constitutes a positive quality recommendation; every rating is an accolade; a recognition of achievement. Once an establishment is chosen for a listing, Mobil's respected and world-famous one- to five-star rating system highlights their distinguishing characteristics.

Although the ten-book set allows us to include many more hotels, restaurants, and attractions than in past years, space limitations still make it impossible for us to include every hotel, motel, and restaurant in America. Instead, our database consists of a generous, representative sampling, with information about places that are above-average in their type. In essence, you can confidently patronize any of the restaurants, places of lodging, and attractions contained in the *Mobil Travel Guide* series.

What do we mean by "representative sampling"? You'll find that the *Mobil Travel Guide* books include information about a great variety of establishments. Perhaps you favor rustic lodgings and restaurants, or perhaps you're most comfortable with elegance and high style. Money may be no object or, like most of us, you may be on a budget. Some travelers place a high premium on 24-hour room service or special menu items. Others look for quiet seclusion. Whatever your travel needs and desires, they will be reflected in the *Mobil Travel Guide* listings.

Allow us to emphasize that we have charged no establishment for inclusion in our guides. We have no relationship with any of the businesses and attractions we list and act only as a consumer advocate. In essence, we do the investigative legwork so you won't have to.

Look over the "How to Use This Book" section that follows. You'll discover just how simple it is to quickly and easily gather all the information you need—before your trip or while on the road. For terrific tips on saving money, travel safety, and other ways to get the most out of your travels, be sure to read our special section, "Making the Most of Your Trip."

Keep in mind that the hospitality business is ever-changing. Restaurants and places of lodging—particularly small chains or stand-alone establishments—can change management or even go out of business with surprising quickness. Although we have made every effort to double-check information during our annual updates, we nevertheless recommend that you call ahead to be sure a place you have selected is open and still offers all the features you want. Phone numbers are provided, and, when available, we also list fax and Web site information.

We hope that all your travel experiences are easy and relaxing. If any aspects of your accommodations or dining motivate you to comment, please drop us a line. We depend a great deal on our readers' remarks, so you can be assured that we will read and assimilate your comments into our research. General comments about our books are also welcome. You can write us at *Mobil Travel Guides*, 1460 Renaissance Drive, Suite 401, Park Ridge, IL, 60068, or send e-mail to info@mobiltravelguide.com.

Take your *Mobil Travel Guide* books along on every trip. You'll be pleased by their convenience, ease of use, and breadth of dependable coverage.

Happy travels in the new millennium!

EDITORIAL CONTRIBUTOR AND CONSULTANT FOR DRIVING TOURS, WALKING TOURS, ATTRACTIONS, EVENTS, AND PHOTOGRAPHY:

Jim Yenckel served as editor and writer for *The Washington Post* for 33 years, including 16 years as a travel writer. He writes a weekly travel column for a chain of newspapers and is a regular contributor to several national magazines including *Budget Travel, Washingtonian,* and *Preservation*.

HOW TO USE
THIS BOOK

The *Mobil Travel Guides* are designed for ease of use. Each state has its own chapter. The chapter begins with a general introduction, which provides both a general geographical and historical orientation to the state; it also covers basic statewide tourist information, from state recreation areas to seatbelt laws. The remainder of each chapter is devoted to the travel destinations within the state—cities and towns, state and national parks, and tourist areas—which, like the states, are arranged alphabetically.

The following is an explanation of the wealth of information you'll find regarding those travel destinations—information on the area, on things to see and do there, and on where to stay and eat.

Maps and Map Coordinates

Next to most destinations is a set of map coordinates. These are referenced to the appropriate state map in the front of this book. In addition, we have provided maps of selected larger cities and of key neighborhoods within the city sections.

Destination Information

Because many travel destinations are close to other cities and towns where visitors might find additional attractions, accommodations, and restaurants, cross-references to those places are included whenever possible. Also listed are addresses and phone numbers for travel information resources—usually the local chamber of commerce or office of tourism—as well as pertinent vital statistics and a brief introduction to the area.

What to See and Do

Almost 20,000 museums, art galleries, amusement parks, universities, historic sites and houses, plantations, churches, state parks, ski areas, and other attractions are described in the *Mobil Travel Guides*. A white star on a red background ⭐ signals that the attraction is one of the best in the state. Because municipal parks, public tennis courts, swimming pools, and small educational institutions are common to most towns, they are generally not represented within the city.

Following the attraction's description, you'll find the months and days it's open, address/location and phone number, and admission costs (see the inside front cover for an explanation of the cost symbols). Note that directions are given from the center of the town under which the attraction is listed, which may not necessarily be the town in which the attraction is located. Zip codes are listed only if they differ from those given for the town.

Driving and Walking Tours

The driving tours are usually day trips—though they can be longer—that make for interesting side trips. This is a way to get off the beaten track and visit an area often overlooked. These trips frequently cover areas of natural beauty or historical significance. The walking tours focus on a particularly interesting area of a city or town. Again, these can be a break from more everyday tourist attractions. The tours often include places to stop for a meal or snack.

Special Events

Special events can either be annual events that last only a short time, such as festivals and fairs, or longer, seasonal events such as horse racing, summer theater and concerts, and professional sports. Special event listings might also include an infrequently occurring occasion that marks a certain date or event, such as a centennial or other commemorative celebration.

Major Cities

Additional information on airports and ground transportation, and suburbs may be included for large cities.

Lodging and Restaurant Listings

ORGANIZATION

For both lodgings and restaurants, when a property is in a town that does not have its own heading, the listing appears under the town nearest its location with the address and town immediately after the establishment name. In large cities, lodgings located within five miles of major commercial airports are listed under a separate "Airport" heading, following the city listings.

LODGING CLASSIFICATIONS

Each property is classified by type according to the characteristics below. Because the following features and services are found at most motels and hotels, they are not shown in those listings:

- Year-round operation with a single rate structure unless otherwise quoted
- European plan (meals not included in room rate)
- Bathroom with tub and/or shower in each room
- Air-conditioned/heated, often with individual room control
- Cots
- Daily maid service
- In-room phones
- Elevators

Motels/Motor Lodges. Accommodations are in low-rise structures with rooms easily accessible to parking (which is usually free). Properties have outdoor room entry and small, functional lobbies. Service is often limited, and dining may not be offered in lower-rated motels and lodges. Shops and businesses are found only in higher-rated properties, as are bellhops, room service, and restaurants serving three meals daily.

Hotels. To be categorized as a hotel, an establishment must have most of the following facilities and services: multiple floors, a restaurant and/or coffee shop, elevators, room service, bellhops, a spacious lobby, and recreational facilities. In addition, the following features and services not shown in listings are also found:

- Valet service (one-day laundry/cleaning service)
- Room service during hours restaurant is open
- Bellhops
- Some oversize beds

Resorts. These specialize in stays of three days or more and usually offer American plan and/or housekeeping accommodations. Their emphasis is on recreational facilities, and a social director is often available. Food services are of primary importance, and guests must be able to eat three meals a day on the premises, either in restaurants or by having access to an on-site grocery store and preparing their own meals.

All Suites. All Suites' guest rooms consist of two rooms, one bedroom and one living room. Higher rated properties offer facilities and services comparable to regular hotels.

B&Bs/Small Inns. Frequently thought of as a small hotel, a bed-and-breakfast or an inn is a place of homelike comfort and warm hospitality. It is often a structure of historic significance, with an equally interesting setting. Meals are a special occasion, and refreshments are frequently served in late afternoon. Rooms are usually individually decorated, often with antiques or furnishings representative of the locale. Phones, bathrooms, or TVs may not be available in every room.

Guest Ranches. Like resorts, guest ranches specialize in stays of three days or more. Guest ranches also offer meal plans and extensive outdoor activities. Horseback riding is usually a feature; there are stables and trails on the ranch property, and trail rides and daily instruction are part of the program. Many guest ranches are working ranches, ranging from casual to rustic, and guests are encouraged to participate in ranch life. Eating is often family style and may also include cookouts. Western saddles are assumed; phone ahead to inquire about English saddle availability.

Extended Stay. These hotels specialize in stays of three days or more and usually offer weekly room rates. Service is often limited and dining might not be offered at lower-rated extended-stay hotels.

Villas/Condos. Similar to Cottage Colonies, these establishments are usually found in recreational areas. They are often separate houses, often luxuriously furnished, and rarely offer restaurants and only a small variety of services on the premises.

Conference Centers. Conference Centers are hotels with extended meeting space facilities designed to house multiday conferences and seminars. Amenities are often geared toward groups staying for longer than one night and often include restaurants and fitness facilities. Larger Conference Center Hotels are often referred to as Convention Center Hotels.

Casinos. Casino Hotels incorporate areas that offer games of chance like Blackjack, Poker, Slot machines, etc. and are only found in states that legalize gambling. Casino Hotels offer a wide range of services and amenities, comparable to regular hotels.

Cottage Colonies. These are housekeeping cottages and cabins that are usually found in recreational areas. Any dining or recreational facilities are noted in our listing.

DINING CLASSIFICATIONS

Restaurants. Most dining establishments fall into this category. All have a full kitchen and offer table service and a complete menu. Parking on or near the premises, in a lot or garage, is assumed. When a property offers valet or other special parking features, or when only street parking is available, it is noted in the listing.

Unrated Dining Spots. These places, listed after Restaurants in many cities, are chosen for their unique atmosphere, specialized menu, or local flavor. They include delis, ice-cream parlors, cafeterias, tearooms, and pizzerias. Because they may not have a full kitchen or table service, they are not given a *Mobil Travel Guides* rating. Often they offer extraordinary value and quick service.

QUALITY RATINGS

The *Mobil Travel Guides* have been rating lodgings and restaurants on a national basis since the first edition was published in 1958. For years the guide was the only source of such ratings, and it remains among the few guidebooks to rate restaurants across the country.

All listed establishments were inspected by experienced field representatives or evaluated by a senior staff member. Ratings are based upon their detailed inspection reports of the individual properties, on written evaluations of staff members who stay and dine anonymously, and on an extensive review of comments from our readers.

You'll find a key to the rating categories, ★ through ★★★★★, on the inside front cover. All establishments in the book are recommended. Even a ★ place is clean, convenient, limited service, usually providing a basic, informal experience. Rating categories reflect both the features the property offers and its quality in relation to similar establishments.

For example, lodging ratings take into account the number and quality of facilities and services, the luxury of appointments, and the attitude and professionalism of staff and management. A ★ establishment provides a comfortable night's lodging. A ★★ property offers more than a facility that rates one star, and the decor is well planned and integrated. Establishments that rate ★★★ are well-appointed, with full services and amenities; the lodging experience is truly excellent, and the range of facilities is extensive. Properties that have been given ★★★★ not only offer many services but also have their own style and personality; they are luxurious, creatively decorated, and superbly maintained. The ★★★★★ properties are among the best in North America, superb in every respect and entirely memorable, year in and year out.

Restaurant evaluations reflect the quality of the food and the ingredients, preparation, presentation, service levels, as well as the property's decor and ambience. A restaurant that has fairly simple goals for menu and decor but that achieves those goals superbly might receive the same number of stars as a restaurant with somewhat loftier ambitions, but the execution of which falls short of the mark. In general, ★ indicates a restaurant that's a good choice in its area, usually fairly simple and perhaps catering to a clientele of locals and families; ★★ denotes restaurants that are more highly recommended in their area; ★★★ restaurants are of national caliber, with professional and attentive service and a skilled chef in the kitchen; ★★★★ reflect superb dining choices, where remarkable food is served in equally remarkable surroundings; and ★★★★★ represent that rare group of the best restaurants in the country, where in addition to near perfection in every detail, there's that special something extra that makes for an unforgettable dining experience.

A list of the four-star and five-star establishments in each region is located just before the state listings.

Each rating is reviewed annually and each establishment must work to maintain its rating (or improve it). Every effort is made to assure that ratings are fair and accurate; the designated ratings are published purely as an aid to travelers. In general, properties that are very new or have recently undergone major management changes are considered difficult to assess fairly and are often listed without ratings.

LODGINGS

Each listing gives the name, address, directions (when there is no street address), neighborhood and/or directions from downtown (in major cities), phone number (local and 800), fax number, number and type of rooms available, room rates, and seasons open (if not year-round). Also included are details on recreational and dining facilities on the property or nearby, the presence of a luxury level, and credit card information. A key to the symbols at the end of each listing is on the inside front cover. (Note that Exxon or Mobil Corporation credit cards cannot be used for payment of meals and room charges.)

All prices quoted in the *Mobil Travel Guide* publications are expected to be in effect at the time of publication and during the entire year; however, prices cannot be guaranteed. In some localities there may be short-term price variations because of special events or holidays. Whenever possible, these price charges are noted. Certain resorts have complicated rate structures that vary with the time of year; always confirm listed rates when you make your plans.

RESTAURANTS

Each listing gives the name, address, directions (when there is no street address), neighborhood and/or directions from downtown (in major cities), phone number, hours and days of operation (if not open daily year-round), reservation policy, cuisine (if other than American), price range for each meal served, children's menu (if offered), specialties, and credit card information. In addition, special features such as chef ownership, ambience, and entertainment are noted. By carefully reading the detailed restaurant information and comparing prices, you can easily determine whether the restaurant is formal and elegant or informal and comfortable for families.

TERMS AND ABBREVIATIONS IN LISTINGS

The following terms and abbreviations are used throughout the listings:

A la carte entrees With a price, refers to the cost of entrees/main dishes that are not accompanied by side dishes.

AP American plan (lodging plus all meals).

Bar Liquor, wine, and beer are served in a bar or cocktail lounge and usually with meals unless otherwise indicated (e.g., "wine, beer").

Business center The property has a designated area accessible to all guests with business services.

Business servs avail The property can perform/arrange at least two of the following services for a guest: audiovisual equipment rental, binding, computer rental, faxing, messenger services, modem availability, notary service, obtaining office supplies, photocopying, shipping, and typing.

Cable Standard cable service; "premium" indicates that HBO, Disney, Showtime, or similar cable services are available.

Ck-in, ck-out Check-in time, check-out time.

Coin lndry Self-service laundry.

Complete meal Soup and/or salad, entree, and dessert, plus nonalcoholic beverage.

Continental bkfst Usually coffee and a roll or doughnut.

Cr cds: A, American Express; C, Carte Blanche; D, Diners Club; DS, Discover; ER, enRoute; JCB, Japanese Credit Bureau; MC, MasterCard; V, Visa.

D Followed by a price, indicates room rate for a "double"—two people in one room in one or two beds (the charge may be higher for two double beds).

Downhill/X-country ski Downhill and/or cross-country skiing within 20 miles of property.

Each addl Extra charge for each additional person beyond the stated number of persons at a reduced price.

Early-bird dinner A meal served at specified hours, typically around 4:30-6:30 pm.

Exc Except.

Exercise equipt Two or more pieces of exercise equipment on the premises.

Exercise rm Both exercise equipment and room, with an instructor on the premises.

Fax Facsimile machines available to all guests.

Golf privileges Privileges at a course within ten miles.

Hols Holidays.

In-rm modem link Every guest room has a connection for a modem that's separate from the phone line.

Kit. or **Kits.** A kitchen or kitchenette that contains stove or microwave, sink, and refrigerator and that is either part of the room or a separate room. If the kitchen is not fully equipped, the listing will indicate "no equipt" or "some equipt."

Luxury level A special section of a lodging, covering at least an entire floor, that offers increased luxury accommodations. Management must provide no less than three of these four services: separate check-in and check-out, concierge, private lounge, and private elevator service (key access). Complimentary breakfast and snacks are commonly offered.

MAP Modified American plan (lodging plus two meals).

Movies Prerecorded videos are available for rental.

No cr cds accepted No credit cards are accepted.

No elvtr In hotels with more than two stories, it's assumed there are elevators; only their absence is noted.

No phones Phones, too, are assumed; only their absence is noted.

Parking There is a parking lot on the premises.

Private club A cocktail lounge or bar available to members and their guests. In motels and hotels where these clubs exist, registered guests can usually use the club as guests of the management; the same is frequently true of restaurants.

Prix fixe A full meal for a stated price; usually one price is quoted.

Res Reservations.

S Followed by a price, indicates room rate for a "single," i.e., one person.

Serv bar A service bar, where drinks are prepared for dining patrons only.

Serv charge Service charge is the amount added to the restaurant check in lieu of a tip.

Table d'hôte A full meal for a stated price, dependent upon entree selection; no a la carte options are available.

Tennis privileges Privileges at tennis courts within five miles.

TV Indicates color television.

Under certain age free Children under that age are not charged if staying in room with a parent.

Valet parking An attendant is available to park and retrieve a car.

VCR VCRs in all guest rooms.

VCR avail VCRs are available for hookup in guest rooms.

Special Information for Travelers with Disabilities

The *Mobil Travel Guides* Ⓓ symbol shown in accommodation and restaurant listings indicates establishments that are at least partially accessible to people with mobility problems.

The *Mobil Travel Guides* criteria for accessibility are unique to our publication. Please do not confuse them with the universal symbol for wheelchair accessibility. When the Ⓓ symbol appears following a listing, the establishment is equipped with facilities to accommodate people using wheelchairs or crutches or otherwise needing easy access to doorways and rest rooms. Travelers with severe mobility problems or with hearing or visual impairments may or may not find facilities they need. Always phone ahead to make sure that an establishment can meet your needs.

All lodgings bearing our Ⓓ symbol have the following facilities:

- ISA-designated parking near access ramps
- Level or ramped entryways to building
- Swinging building entryway doors minimum 39"
- Public rest rooms on main level with space to operate a wheelchair; handrails at commode areas
- Elevators equipped with grab bars and lowered control buttons
- Restaurants with accessible doorways; rest rooms with space to operate wheelchair; handrails at commode areas
- Minimum 39" width entryway to guest rooms
- Low-pile carpet in rooms
- Telephone at bedside and in bathroom
- Bed placed at wheelchair height
- Minimum 39" width doorway to bathroom
- Bath with open sink—no cabinet; room to operate wheelchair
- Handrails at commode areas; tub handrails

- Wheelchair-accessible peephole in room entry door
- Wheelchair-accessible closet rods and shelves

All restaurants bearing our [D] symbol offer the following facilities:

- ISA-designated parking beside access ramps
- Level or ramped front entryways to building
- Tables to accommodate wheelchairs
- Main-floor rest rooms; minimum 39" width entryway
- Rest rooms with space to operate wheelchair; handrails at commode areas

In general, the newest properties are apt to impose the fewest barriers.

To get the kind of service you need and have a right to expect, do not hesitate when making a reservation to question the management in detail about the availability of accessible rooms, parking, entrances, restaurants, lounges, or any other facilities that are important to you, and confirm what is meant by "accessible." Some guests with mobility impairments report that lodging establishments' housekeeping and maintenance departments are most helpful in describing barriers. Also inquire about any special equipment, transportation, or services you may need.

MAKING THE MOST OF YOUR TRIP

A few hardy souls might look with fondness upon the trip where the car broke down and they were stranded for a week. Or maybe even the vacation that cost twice what it was supposed to. For most travelers, though, the best trips are those that are safe, smooth, and within their budget. To help you make your trip the best it can be, we've assembled a few tips and resources.

Saving Money

ON LODGING

After you've seen the published rates, it's time to look for discounts. Many hotels and motels offer them—for senior citizens, business travelers, families, you name it. It never hurts to ask—politely, that is. Sometimes, especially in late afternoon, desk clerks are instructed to fill beds, and you might be offered a lower rate, or a nicer room, to entice you to stay. Look for bargains on stays over multiple nights, in the off-season, and on weekdays or weekends (depending on location). Many hotels in major metropolitan areas, for example, have special weekend package plans that offer considerable savings on rooms; they may include breakfast, cocktails, and meal discounts. Prices can change frequently throughout the year, so phone ahead.

Another way to save money is to choose accommodations that give you more than just a standard room. Rooms with kitchen facilities enable you to cook some meals for yourself, reducing restaurant costs. A suite might save money for two couples traveling together. Even hotel luxury levels can provide good value, as many include breakfast or cocktails in the price of the room.

State and city sales taxes, as well as special room taxes, can increase your room rates as much as 25 percent per day. We are unable to include this specific information in the listings, but we strongly urge that you ask about these taxes when placing reservations to understand the total cost of your lodgings.

Watch out for telephone-usage charges that hotels frequently impose on long-distance calls, credit-card calls, and other phone calls—even those that go unanswered. Before phoning from your room, read the information given to you at check-in, and then be sure to read your bill carefully before checking out. You won't be expected to pay for charges that they did not spell out. (On the other hand, it's not unusual for a hotel to bill you for your calls after you return home.) Consider using your cell phone; or, if public telephones are available in the hotel lobby, your cost savings may outweigh the inconvenience.

ON DINING

There are several ways to get a less expensive meal at a more expensive restaurant. Early-bird dinners are popular in many parts of the country and offer considerable savings. If you're interested in sampling a 4- or 5-star establishment, consider going at lunchtime. While the prices then are probably relatively high, they may be half of those at dinner and come with the same ambience, service, and cuisine.

ON PARK PASSES

Although many national parks, monuments, seashores, historic sites, and recreation areas may be used free of charge, others charge an entrance fee (ranging from $1 to $6 per person to $5 to $15 per carload) and/or a "use fee" for special services and facilities. If you plan to make several visits to federal recreation areas, consider one of the following National Park Service money-saving programs:

Park Pass. This is an annual entrance permit to a specific unit in the National Park Service system that normally charges an entrance fee. The pass admits the permit holder and any accompanying passengers in a private noncommercial vehicle or, in the case of walk-in facilities, the holder's spouse, children, and parents. It is valid for entrance fees only. A Park Pass may be purchased in person or by mail from the National Park Service unit at which the pass will be honored. The cost is $15 to $20, depending upon the area.

Golden Eagle Passport. This pass, available to people who are between 17 and 61, entitles the purchaser and accompanying passengers in a private noncommercial vehicle to enter any outdoor National Park Service unit that charges an entrance fee and admits the purchaser and family to most walk-in fee-charging areas. Like the Park Pass, it is good for one year and does not cover use fees. It may be purchased from the National Park Service, Office of Public Inquiries, Room 1013, US Department of the Interior, 18th and C sts NW, Washington, D.C. 20240, phone 202/208-4747; at any of the ten regional offices throughout the country; and at any National Park Service area that charges a fee. The cost is $50.

Golden Age Passport. Available to citizens and permanent residents of the United States 62 years or older, this is a lifetime entrance permit to fee-charging recreation areas. The fee exemption extends to those accompanying the permit holder in a private noncommercial vehicle or, in the case of walk-in facilities, to the holder's spouse and children. The passport also entitles the holder to a 50 percent discount on use fees charged in park areas but not to fees charged by concessionaires. Golden Age Passports must be obtained in person. The applicant must show proof of age, i.e., a driver's license, birth certificate, or signed affidavit attesting to age (Medicare cards are not acceptable proof). These passports are available at most park service units where they're used, at National Park Service headquarters (see above), at park system regional offices, at National Forest Supervisors' offices, and at most Ranger Station offices. The cost is $10.

Golden Access Passport. Issued to citizens and permanent residents of the United States who are physically disabled or visually impaired, this passport is a free lifetime entrance permit to fee-charging recreation areas. The fee exemption extends to those accompanying the permit holder in a private noncommercial vehicle or, in the case of walk-in facilities, to the holder's spouse and children. The passport also entitles the holder to a 50 percent discount on use fees charged in park areas but not to fees charged by concessionaires. Golden Access Passports must be obtained in person. Proof of eligibility to receive federal benefits is required (under programs such as Disability Retirement, Compensation for Military Service-Connected Disability, Coal Mine

Safety and Health Act, etc.), or an affidavit must be signed attesting to eligibility. These passports are available at the same outlets as Golden Age Passports.

FOR SENIOR CITIZENS

Look for the senior-citizen discount symbol in the lodging and restaurant listings. Always call ahead to confirm that the discount is being offered, and be sure to carry proof of age. At places not listed in the book, it never hurts to ask if a senior-citizen discount is offered. Additional information for mature travelers is available from the American Association of Retired Persons (AARP), 601 E St NW, Washington, D.C. 20049, phone 202/434-2277.

Tipping

Tipping is an expression of appreciation for good service, and often service workers rely on tips as a significant part of their income. However, you never need to tip if service is poor.

IN HOTELS

Door attendants in major city hotels are usually given $1 for getting you a cab. Bellhops expect $1 per bag, usually $2 if you have only one bag. Concierges are tipped according to the service they perform. It's not mandatory to tip when you've asked for suggestions on sightseeing or restaurants or help in making reservations for dining. However, when a concierge books you a table at a restaurant known to be difficult to get into, a gratuity of $5 is appropriate. For obtaining theater or sporting event tickets, $5-$10 is expected. Maids, often overlooked by guests, may be tipped $1-$2 per days of stay.

AT RESTAURANTS

Coffee shop and counter service waitstaff are usually given 8 percent–10 percent of the bill. In full-service restaurants, tip 15 percent of the bill, before sales tax. In fine restaurants, where the staff is large and shares the gratuity, 18 percent–20 percent for the waiter is appropriate. In most cases, tip the maitre d' only if service has been extraordinary and only on the way out; $20 is the minimum in upscale properties in major metropolitan areas. If there is a wine steward, tip him or her at least $6 a bottle, more if the wine was decanted or if the bottle was very expensive. If your bus person has been unusually attentive, $2 pressed into his hand on departure is a nice gesture. An increasing number of restaurants automatically add a service charge to the bill instead of a gratuity. Before tipping, carefully review your check. If you are in doubt, ask your server.

AT AIRPORTS

Curbside luggage handlers expect $1 per bag. Car-rental shuttle drivers who help with your luggage appreciate a $1 or $2 tip.

Staying Safe

The best way to deal with emergencies is to be prepared enough to avoid them. However, unforeseen situations do happen, and you can prepare for them.

IN YOUR CAR

Before your trip, make sure your car has been serviced and is in good working order. Change the oil, check the battery and belts, and make sure tires are inflated properly (this can also improve gas mileage). Other inspections recommended by the car's manufacturer should be made, too.

Next, be sure you have the tools and equipment to deal with a routine breakdown: jack, spare tire, lug wrench, repair kit, emergency tools, jumper cables, spare fan belt, auto fuses, flares and/or reflectors, flashlights, first-aid kit, and, in winter, windshield wiper fluid, a windshield scraper, and snow shovel.

Bring all appropriate and up-to-date documentation—licenses, registration, and insurance cards—and know what's covered by your insurance. Also bring an extra set of keys, just in case.

En route, always buckle up! In most states it is required by law.

If your car does break down, get out of traffic as soon as possible—pull well off the road. Raise the hood and turn on your emergency flashers or tie a white cloth to the roadside door handle or antenna. Stay near your car. Use flares or reflectors to keep your car from being hit.

IN YOUR LODGING

Chances are slim that you will encounter a hotel or motel fire. The ⬛ in a listing indicates that there were smoke detectors and/or sprinkler systems in the rooms we inspected. Once you've checked in, make sure that any smoke detector in your room is working properly. Ascertain the locations of fire extinguishers and at least two fire exits. Never use an elevator in a fire.

For personal security, use the peephole in your room's door.

PROTECTING AGAINST THEFT

To guard against theft wherever you go, don't bring anything of more value than you need. If you do bring valuables, leave them at your hotel rather than in your car, and if you have something very expensive, lock it in a safe. Many hotels have one in each room; others will store your valuables in the hotel's safe. And of course, don't carry more money than you need; use traveler's checks and credit cards, or visit cash machines.

For Travelers with Disabilities

A number of publications can provide assistance. The most complete listing of published material for travelers with disabilities is available from The Disability Bookshop, Twin Peaks Press, Box 129, Vancouver, WA 98666, phone 360/694-2462.

The Reference Section of the National Library Service for the Blind and Physically Handicapped (Library of Congress, Washington, D.C. 20542, phone 202/707-9276 or 202/707-5100) provides information and resources for persons with mobility problems and hearing and vision impairments, as well as information about the NILS talking program (or visit your local library).

IMPORTANT TOLL-FREE NUMBERS AND ONLINE INFORMATION

Hotels and Motels

Adams Mark   800-444-2326
www.adamsmark.com
Amerisuites   800-833-1516
www.amerisuites.com
AMFA Parks & Resorts   800-236-7916
www.amfac.com
Baymont Inns   800-229-6668
www.baymontinns.com
Best Western   800-780-7234
www.bestwestern.com
Budget Host Inn   800-283-4678
www.budgethost.com
Candlewood Suites   888-226-3539
www.candlewoodsuites.com
Clarion Hotels   800-252-7466
www.choicehotels.com
Clubhouse Inns   800-258-2466
www.clubhouseinn.com
Coast Hotels & Resorts   800-663-1144
www.coasthotels.com
Comfort Inns   800-252-7466
www.choicehotels.com
Concorde Hotels   800-888-4747
www.concorde-hotel.com
Country Hearth Inns   800-848-5767
www.countryhearth.com
Country Inns   800-456-4000
www.countryinns.com
Courtyard by Marriott   888-236-2437
www.courtyard.com
Crown Plaza Hotels   800-227-6963
www.crowneplaza.com
Days Inn   800-544-8313
www.daysinn.com
Delta Hotels   800-268-1133
www.deltahotels.com
Destination Hotels & Resorts
  800-434-7347
www.destinationhotels.com
Doubletree   800-222-8733
www.doubletree.com
Drury Inns   800-378-7946
www.druryinn.com
Econolodge   800-553-2666
www.econolodge.com
Embassy Suites   800-362-2779
www.embassysuites.com
Fairfield Inns   800-228-2800
www.fairfieldinn.com
Fairmont Hotels   800-441-1414
www.fairmont.com

Family Inns of America   800-251-9752
www.familyinnsofamerica.com
Forte Hotels   800-300-9147
www.fortehotels.com
Four Points by Sheraton
www.starwood.com   888-625-5144
Four Seasons   800-545-4000
www.fourseasons.com
Hampton Inns   800-426-7866
www.hamptoninn.com
Hilton   800-774-1500
www.hilton.com
Holiday Inn   800-465-4329
www.holiday-inn.com
Homestead Studio Suites
www.stayhsd.com   888-782-9473
Homewood Suites   800-225-5466
www.homewoodsuites.com
Howard Johnson   800-406-1411
www.hojo.com
Hyatt   800-633-7313
www.hyatt.com
Inn Suites Hotels & Suite
www.innsuites.com   800-842-4242
Inter-Continental   888-567-8725
www.interconti.com
Jameson Inns   800-526-3766
www.jamesoninns.com
Kempinski Hotels   800-426-3135
www.kempinski.com
Kimpton Hotels   888-546-7866
www.kimptongroup.com
La Quinta   800-531-5900
www.laquinta.com
Leading Hotels of the World
www.lhw.com   800-223-6800
Loews Hotels   800-235-6397
www.loewshotels.com
Mainstay Suites   800-660-6246
www.choicehotels.com
Mandarin Oriental   800-526-6566
www.mandarin-oriental.com
Marriott   888-236-2427
www.marriott.com
Nikko Hotels   800-645-5687
www.nikkohotels.com
Omni Hotels   800-843-6664
www.omnihotels.com
Preferred Hotels & Resorts Worldwide
www.preferredhotels.com
  800-323-7500
Quality Inn   800-228-5151
www.qualityinn.com

Radisson Hotels	800-333-3333
www.radisson.com	
Ramada	888-298-2054
www.ramada.com	
Red Lion Inns	800-733-5466
www.redlion.com	
Red Roof Inns	800-733-7663
www.redroof.com	
Regal Hotels	800-222-8888
www.regal-hotels.com	
Regent International	800-545-4000
www.regenthotels.com	
Renaissance Hotels	888-236-2427
www.renaissancehotels.com	
Residence Inns	888-236-2427
www.residenceinn.com	
Ritz Carlton	800-241-3333
www.ritzcarlton.com	
Rodeway Inns	800-228-2000
www.rodeway.com	
Rosewood Hotels & Resorts	
	888-767-3966
www.rosewood-hotels.com	
Sheraton	888-625-5144
www.sheraton.com	
Shilo Inns	800-222-2244
www.shiloinns.com	
Shoney's Inns	800-552-4667
www.shoneysinn.com	
Sleep Inns	800-453-3746
www.sleepinn.com	
Small Luxury Hotels	800-525-4800
www.slh.com	
Sofitel	800-763-4835
www.sofitel.com	
Sonesta Hotels & Resorts	
www.sonesta.com	800-766-3782
SRS Worldhotels	800-223-5652
www.srs-worldhotels.com	
Summerfield Suites	800-833-4353
www.summerfieldsuites.com	
Summit International	800-457-4000
www.summithotels.com	
Swissotel	800-637-9477
www.swissotel.com	
The Peninsula Group	
www.peninsula.com	
Travelodge	800-578-7878
www.travelodge.com	
Westin Hotels & Resorts	
www.westin.com	800-937-8461
Wingate Inns	800-228-1000
www.wingateinns.com	
Woodfin Suite Hotels	
www.woodfinsuitehotels.com	
	800-966-3346
Wyndham Hotels & Resorts	
www.wyndham	800-996-3426

Airlines

Air Canada	888-247-2262
www.aircanada.ca	
Alaska	800-252-7522
www.alaska-air.com	
American	800-433-7300
www.aa.com	
America West	800-235-9292
www.americawest.com	
British Airways	800-247-9297
www.british-airways.com	
Continental	800-523-3273
www.flycontinental.com	
Delta	800-221-1212
www.delta-air.com	
Island Air	800-323-3345
www.islandair.com	
Mesa	800-637-2247
www.mesa-air.com	
Northwest	800-225-2525
www.nwa.com	
Southwest	800-435-9792
www.southwest.com	
United	800-241-6522
www.ual.com	
US Air	800-428-4322
www.usair.com	

Car Rentals

Advantage	800-777-5500
www.arac.com	
Alamo	800-327-9633
www.goalamo.com	
Allstate	800-634-6186
www.bnm.com/as.htm	
Avis	800-831-2847
www.avis.com	
Budget	800-527-0700
www.budgetrentacar.com	
Dollar	800-800-4000
www.dollarcar.com	
Enterprise	800-325-8007
www.pickenterprise.com	
Hertz	800-654-3131
www.hertz.com	
National	800-227-7368
www.nationalcar.com	
Payless	800-729-5377
www.800-payless.com	
Rent-A-Wreck.com	800-535-1391
www.rent-a-wreck.com	
Sears	800-527-0770
www.budget.com	
Thrifty	800-847-4389
www.thrifty.com	

Four-Star and Five-Star Establishments in the Mid-Atlantic

Delaware

★★★★ Lodgings
Inn at Montchanin Village, *Wilmington*
The Hotel DuPont, *Wilmington*
★★★★ Restaurant
Krazy Kat's, *Wilmington*

District of Columbia

★★★★ Lodgings
Four Seasons Hotel Washington D.C., *Washington*
The Hay-Adams, *Washington*
Park Hyatt Washington, *Washington*
The Ritz-Carlton,Washington D.C., *Washington*
The St. Regis Washington, *Washington*
The Westin Embassy Row, *Washington*
Willard Inter-Continental Washington, *Washington*
★★★★ Restaurants
Citronelle, *Washington*
Gerard's Place, *Washington*
Kinkead's, *Washington*
Willard Room, *Washington*

Maryland

★★★★ Lodging
The Inn at Perry Cabin, *St. Michael's*
★★★★ Restaurants
Charleston, *Baltimore*
The Dining Room, *St. Michael's*
The Oregon Grille, *Cockeysville*

Pennsylvania

★★★★★ Restaurant
Le Bec-Fin, *Philadelphia*
★★★★ Lodgings
Four Seasons Hotel Philadelphia, *Philadelphia*
The Hotel Hershey, *Hershey*
The Rittenhouse Hotel, *Philadelphia*
The Ritz-Carlton, Philadelphia, *Philadelphia*
★★★★ Restaurants
Brasserie Perrier, *Philadelphia*
Fountain Restaurant, *Philadelphia*
Jake's Restaurant, *Philadelphia*
La Famiglia, *Philadelphia*
Striped Bass, *Philadelphia*

Virginia

★★★★★ Lodgings
The Inn at Little Washington, *Washington*
The Jefferson, *Richmond*
★★★★★ Restaurant
The Inn at Little Washington, *Washington*
★★★★ Lodgings
The Clifton Country Inn, *Charlottesville*
The Homestead, *Hot Springs*
Keswick Hall At Monticello, *Charlottesville*
Morrison House, *Alexandria*
The Ritz-Carlton, Pentagon City, *Arlington County (Ronald Reagan Washington-National Airport Area)*
The Ritz-Carlton, Tyson's Corner, *Tyson's Corner*
Williamsburg Inn, *Williamsburg*

West Virginia

★★★★ Lodging
The Greenbrier, *White Sulphur Springs*
★★★★ Restaurant
The Tavern Room, *White Sulphur Springs*

DELAWARE

D elaware "...is like a diamond, diminutive, but having within it inherent value," wrote John Lofland, the eccentric "Bard of Milford," in 1847. The state is 96 miles long and from 9 to 35 miles wide. With more than half of its 1,982 square miles (excluding marshes) used for farming, Delaware produces a flood of agricultural products. Poultry makes up approximately half of the state's total farm income; soybeans, corn, tomatoes, strawberries, asparagus, fruit, and other crops bring in about $170 million each year. Booming industry in northern and central Delaware balances the agricultural sector of the economy. Consistent state corporate policies have persuaded more than 183,000 corporations to make their headquarters in the "corporate capital of the world." Forty major US banks alone have established lending and credit operations in the state.

Compact but diverse, Delaware has rolling, forested hills in the north, stretches of bare sand dunes in the south, and mile upon mile of lonely marsh along the coast. Visitors can tour a modern agricultural or chemical research center in the morning and search for buried pirate treasure in the afternoon. The *deBraak,* which foundered off Lewes in 1798, was raised in 1986 because of the belief that it may have had a fortune in captured Spanish coin or bullion aboard. The coins that frequently come ashore at Coin Beach below Rehoboth are believed to come from the *Faithful Steward,* a passenger vessel lost in 1785.

Delaware's history started on a grim note. The first colonists, 28 men under Dutch auspices, landed in the spring of 1631 near what is now Lewes. A year later, after an argument with a Lenni-Lenape chief, the bones of all 28 were found mingled with those of their cattle and strewn over their burned fields. In 1638 a group of Swedes established the first permanent settlement, Fort Christina, at a spot now in Wilmington. This was also the first permanent settlement of Swedes in North America. Dutch, English, Scottish, and Irish colonists soon followed, with German, Italian, and Polish groups coming in the late 19th century.

Henry Hudson, in Dutch service, discovered Delaware Bay in 1609. A year later, Thomas Argall reported it to English navigators, naming it for his superior, Lord de la Warr, Governor of Virginia. Ownership changed rapidly from Swedish to Dutch to English hands. Later the area was claimed by both Lord Baltimore and the Penn family. The Maryland-Delaware boundary was set by British court order in 1750 and surveyed as part of the Mason-Dixon Line in 1763-1767. The boundary with New Jersey, also long disputed, was confirmed by the Supreme Court in 1935.

The "First State" (first to adopt the Constitution—December 7, 1787) is proud of its history of sturdy independence, both military and political. During the Revolution, the "Delaware line" was a crack regiment of the Continental Army. After heavy casualties in 1780, the unit was reorganized. The men would "fight

Population: 753,538
Area: 1,982 square miles
Elevation: 0-447 feet
Peak: Ebright Road (New Castle County)
Entered Union: First state to ratify Constitution (December 7, 1787)
Capital: Dover
Motto: Liberty and independence
Nickname: First State, Small Wonder, Diamond State, Blue Hen State
Flower: Peach Blossom
Bird: Blue Hen
Tree: American Holly
Fair: July, 2003, in Harrington (see Dover)
Time Zone: Eastern
Website: www.state.de.us

all day and dance all night," according to a dispatch by General Greene. How well they danced is open to question, but they fought with such gallantry that they were mentioned in nearly all of the General's dispatches.

Delaware statesman John Dickinson, "penman of the Revolution" and one of the state's five delegates to the Constitutional Convention, was instrumental in the decision to write a new document rather than simply patch up the Articles of Confederation. Later he effected the compromise on representation, a problem that had threatened to break up the convention completely.

In addition to Lofland and Dickinson, Delaware has produced many literary figures, including the 19th-century playwright and novelist Robert Montgomery Bird, writer and illustrator Howard Pyle, Henry Seidel Canby (founder of the *Saturday Review*), and novelist John P. Marquand.

A fine highway network tempts motorists to drive through diminutive Delaware without really seeing it. Those who take time to leave the major highways and explore the countryside will find it rewarding.

When to Go/Climate

Delaware's climate is generally mild; long Indian summers are not unusual and there's seldom frost until late autumn. Temperatures at the shore can be 10°F higher in winter or lower in summer than inland temperatures.

AVERAGE HIGH/LOW TEMPERATURES (°F)

WILMINGTON

Jan 39/22	**May** 73/52	**Sept** 78/58
Feb 42/25	**June** 81/62	**Oct** 67/46
Mar 52/33	**July** 86/67	**Nov** 56/37
Apr 63/42	**Aug** 84/66	**Dec** 44/28

Parks and Recreation Finder

Directions to and information about the parks and recreation areas below are given under their respective town/city sections. Please refer to those sections for details.

STATE PARK AND RECREATION AREAS

Key to abbreviations. I.P. = Interstate Park; S.A.P. = State Archaeological Park; S.B. = State Beach; S.C.A. = State Conservation Area; S.C.P. = State Conservation Park; S.Cp. = State Campground; S.F. = State Forest; S.G. = State Garden; S.H.A. = State Historic Area; S.H.P. = State Historic Park; S.H.S. = State Historic Site; S.M.P. = State Marine Park; S.N.A. = State Natural Area; S.P. = State Park; S.P.C. = State Public Campground; S.R. = State Reserve; S.R.A. = State Recreation Area; S.Res. = State Reservoir; S.Res.P. = State Resort Park; S.R.P. = State Rustic Park.

Place Name	Listed Under
Bellevue S.P.	WILMINGTON
Brandywine Creek S.P.	WILMINGTON
Cape Henlopen S.P.	LEWES
Delaware Seashore S.P.	REHOBOTH BEACH
Fenwick Island S.P.	FENWICK ISLAND
Fort Delaware S.P.	same
Holts Landing S.P.	BETHANY BEACH
Killens Pond S.P.	DOVER
Lums Pond S.P.	ODESSA
Trap Pond S.P.	DOVER
White Clay Creek S.P.	NEWARK

CALENDAR HIGHLIGHTS

MAY

Wilmington Garden Day (Wilmington). Tour of famous houses and gardens.

JUNE

Zwaanendael Heritage Garden Tour (Lewes). Tour of the hidden gardens of Lewes. Vendors. Phone 302/645-8073.

JULY

Delaware State Fair (Dover). In Harrington. Arts and crafts, home and trade show, carnival rides, and entertainment; homemaking, agricultural, and livestock exhibits. Phone 302/398-3269.

OCTOBER

Sea Witch Halloween and Fiddlers' Festival (Rehoboth Beach). Phone 800/441-1329, extension 11.

Water-related activities, hiking, riding, various other sports, picnicking, and visitor centers are available in many of these areas. Delaware state parks are open all year, 8 am-sunset, except Fort Delaware (late April-late September). Most areas have fishing, boat ramps, and picnicking. There is a vehicle entrance fee from Memorial Day-Labor Day, daily; May and September-October, weekends and holidays. Camping is available from mid-March-mid-November at Delaware Seashore; April-October at Lums Pond, Trap Pond, and Cape Henlopen; year-round at Killens Pond. There is a two-week maximum stay at campgrounds; reservations encouraged; campsites run from $12-$26/night/site. For further information contact Department of Natural Resources and Environmental Control, Division of Parks and Recreation, 89 Kings Highway, Dover 19901, phone 302/739-4702.

FISHING AND HUNTING

Both fresh and saltwater fishing are excellent. The state owns, leases, or licenses 33,000 acres of game lands and fishing waters. More than 50 well-stocked state and privately owned ponds are scattered throughout the state. Many miles of ocean shoreline between Rehoboth Beach and Indian River Inlet are ideal for surf fishing. Common saltwater fish include trout, bluefish, porgie, sea bass, flounder, and croaker; freshwater fish include bass, bluegill, pickerel, crappie, perch, and trout.

An annual nonresident hunting license is $86; nonresident three-day small game license $35; nonresident trapping license $25; additional single deer permit $10. An annual resident freshwater fishing license is $8.50; nonresident license $15; seven-day nonresident license $5.20. A license is not required for tidal saltwater fishing. For further information on fishing or hunting, contact the Department of Natural Resources and Environmental Control, Division of Fish and Wildlife, 89 Kings Highway, Dover 19901, phone 302/739-4431 or 800/523-3336.

Driving Information

Safety belts are mandatory for all persons in front seat of vehicle. Children under four years and 40 pounds in weight must be in an approved safety seat anywhere in vehicle; children ages 4-15 must use a regulation seat belt anywhere in vehicle. Phone 302/739-5938.

INTERSTATE HIGHWAY SYSTEM

The following alphabetical listing of Delaware towns in *Mobil Travel Guide* shows that these cities are within ten miles of the indicated interstate highway. A highway map, however, should be checked for the nearest exit.

Highway Number   **Cities/Towns within ten miles**

Interstate 95   Newark, New Castle, Wilmington.

Additional Visitor Information

Delaware Tourism Office, 99 Kings Highway, Dover 19901, will provide tourist information. Phone 800/441-8846.

Visitor centers also provide information and brochures on points of interest in the state. Their locations are as follows: Delaware Memorial Bridge Plaza, junction I-295 and the bridge at New Castle; I-95 rest area, Greater Wilmington Convention and Visitors Bureau, Wilmington; Delaware State Information Center, Duke of York and Federal Sts, Dover; Smyrna, 1 mile N on US 13; Bethany-Fenwick Area Chamber of Commerce, DE 1, N of Fenwick Island.

BRANDYWINE VALLEY (APPROX 50 MI)

Cut by slender Brandywine Creek, the Brandywine Valley just north of Wilmington is a serene canvas of rolling hills, broad fields of corn and yellow sunflowers, rambling split-rail fences, horse pastures, ancient stone barns, and narrow country roads lined by towering old trees. Scattered within this scenic realm, one of the Mid-Atlantic's loveliest, is a wonderfully diverse collection of fine arts, history, and house museums, most of which were bequeathed by the du Pont family, the wealthy industrialists whose forebear, Pierre Samuel du Pont, arrived from France in 1800. Pierre's son, Eleuthere Irenee (E. I.) du Pont, established a black powder factory, harnessing the Brandywine for power and creating the du Pont fortune. Brandywine Creek flows southeast from Pennsylvania's Chester County through prosperous Wilmington suburbs to the Delaware River. The wealth here has earned the valley the nickname of "Chateau Country" because of its many grand homes, typically set far back from the road. For more than 30 years, an environmental organization called the Brandywine Conservancy has worked to protect the valley's open pastoral look from the threatening sprawl of both Philadelphia and Wilmington. Begin this one day, 50-mile tour into the scenic and artistic riches of the region in Wilmington. Your first stop is the Delaware Art Museum at 2301 Kentmere Parkway, which features a strong collection of American sculpture and painting, including works by Brandywine resident Andrew Wyeth. To reach the museum from downtown Wilmington, take 12th Street north to State Route 52 north. Take a right on North Bancroft to Kentmere. Founded in 1912, the museum also houses a premier collection of the works of Howard Pyle, a famous Wilmington illustrator of that era. Many of his illustrations depict pirates, witches, and other fanciful characters drawn to accompany adventure stories in magazines and books. More realistic is Pyle's 1911 portrait of General Robert E. Lee surrendering his Confederate army at Appomattox, commissioned to illustrate a piece in Harper's Monthly Magazine. From the museum, return to Route 52 north. Turn right at Route 141 to the Hagley Museum, which sits on the site of the first du Pont powder works, amid 230 acres of gardens and exhibits. The museum recalls industrial life in mid-19th-century America. A bit further upstream along Brandywine Creek is Eleutherian Mills, the lovely Georgian-style house E. I. du Pont built in 1803. Double back on Route 141 to Route 100 north (Montchanin Road) to the village of Montchanin. Here 11 varied structures that served as homes for workers at the du Pont mills have been converted into a luxury retreat, the 37-room Inn at Montchanin Village. Even if you aren't a guest, stroll the block-long cobblestone main street, which is named Privy Lane for the comical row of gray concrete privies standing behind the dwellings in military precision. Today the privies, a reminder of an earlier era, store garden equipment. Consider lunch at the inn's whimsically named restaurant, the Krazy Kat's, one of Brandywine's best. Continue north on Route 100 to Brandywine State Park for a chance to hike along Brandywine Creek. Stay on Route 100 north to Smiths Bridge Road, where you make a left turn. Continue west via Centerville Road to Route 52, and turn south (left). At the sign, turn left into Winterthur, a nine-story museum of American decorative arts set in the midst of 985 acres of gardens. This was the estate of Henry Francis du Pont, who collected antique furniture, porcelain, silver, rugs, and draperies crafted from 1640 to 1860. These items are organized in period rooms, including a 17th-century Lancaster, Pennsylvania, bedroom and an 18th-century Tidewater, Virginia, plantation sitting room. The gardens reflect du Pont's goal of creating a masterpiece of 20th-century American naturalism. Return to Wilmington on Route 52 south.

ATLANTIC BEACHES (APPROX 25 MI)

Graced with a beautiful 25-mile stretch of Atlantic beach, Delaware has done more than many Eastern states to preserve much of the land from excessive development. From north to south, three impressive state parks maintain the coast's natural look, and between these parks, several small resort towns retain an old-fashioned, early-20th-century flavor. The charm quotient is high and honky-tonk lures are minimal. Though most people think of the beach as a summer destination, you will find this one-day, 25-mile drive rewarding any time of the year. Indeed, many visitors, especially bird watchers and shell collectors, enjoy hiking the beaches in spring and fall when the summer sunbathers are absent. Begin in Lewes, a community that dates its founding to a Dutch whaling colony in 1631. Stroll tree-shaded 2nd Street, the main street, to browse the town's shops and view its rich architectural heritage, then drive east about a mile on Savannah Road, following the signs to 3,785-acre Cape Henlopen State Park. On your left, you will pass the dock for the Cape May-Lewes Ferry, which shuttles across Delaware Bay between Delaware and New Jersey, a 70-minute crossing. The park juts between the bay and the ocean, offering hiking and bicycling trails that meander among pine forests, salt marshes, and grass-topped dunes. Just inside the park, the Seaside Nature Center features a small aquarium displaying examples of local sea life, including the region's famed blue crabs. In mid-May, the park is a resting stop for shore birds migrating north from South America to their summer breeding grounds in the Arctic. The park enjoys a long beach of golden sand. From the parking lot, a high boardwalk crosses the dunes, leaving the cars hidden behind. Only a bath house invades the otherwise unblemished seascape. From Lewes, take US 9 west briefly to State Route 1 south, which parallels the coast for the length of this drive. You will detour from it only once—at Rehoboth Beach, the next stop. One of the Mid-Atlantic's most popular beach resorts, Rehoboth hasn't lost its small-town appeal. The beach is long and inviting, and at sunset many people promenade on the boardwalk that links one end of the community to the other. In recent years, Rehoboth has blossomed into a sophisticated destination, evidenced by its numerous fine bed-and-breakfast inns; upscale restaurants; and quality shops selling designer beach attire, expensive antiques, and excellent contemporary crafts and home furnishings. But you can also find more typical beach wear and fare—such as burgers and hot dogs—on the boardwalk. There's even a small amusement arcade called Funland. South of Rehoboth on Route 1 is Dewey Beach, a much smaller resort town with a cluster of lively pubs that have a reputation of attracting a young singles crowd. To the south is 2,656-acre Delaware Seashore State Park, another natural preserve offering such traditional beach activities as swimming, surfing, fishing, picnicking, hiking, and boating on Indian River Bay. Further south is the little resort town of Bethany Beach, favored by families renting a vacation home or condominium, and beyond that is 442-acre Fenwick Island State Park, another natural area. End the tour just across the state line in sprawling Ocean City, Maryland, a bustling beach town that is the antithesis of Delaware's quieter beach experience.

Bethany Beach

(E-8) *See also Fenwick Island, Lewes, Rehoboth Beach*

Founded 1901 **Pop** 903 **Elev** 8 ft
Area code 302 **Zip** 19930
Information Bethany-Fenwick Area Chamber of Commerce, Coastal Hwy/DE 1, PO Box 1450; 302/539-2100 or 800/962-7873
Web www.bethany-fenwick.org

A quiet beach town on the Atlantic Ocean, Bethany Beach was founded as a site for revival camp meetings; hence the biblical name. Surf fishing and swimming are excellent here.

What to See and Do

Holts Landing State Park. A 203-acre park located along the Indian River Bay. Fishing, crabbing, clamming, sailing, boating (launch ramp providing access to bay); picnicking, playground, ball fields. Standard hrs, fees. 8 mi NW via DE 26 and DE 346, N of Millville. Phone 302/539-9060.

Special Event

Boardwalk Arts Festival. The Boardwalk, Garfield Pkwy. Juried, original handmade works; woodcarving, photography, jewelry, batik, watercolor paintings. Early Sept. Phone 302/539-2100.

Motel/Motor Lodge

★ **BETHANY ARMS.** *99 Hollywood St (19930). 302/539-9603. www.beach-net.com/bethanyarms.* 52 units, 2-3 story, 36 kit. units. No elvtr. July-Aug: S, D $105-$160; each addl $10; under 6 free; wkly rates; lower rates mid-Mar-June, Sept-mid-Oct. Closed mid-Oct-mid-Mar. Crib $5. TV; cable. Restaurant adj 7 am-9 pm. Ck-out 11 am. Many refrigerators. Balconies. On ocean; beach. Cr cds: MC, V.

Dover

(C-7) *See also Odessa, Smyrna*

Founded 1717 **Pop** 32,135 **Elev** 36 ft
Area code 302 **Zip** 19901
Information Central Delaware Chamber of Commerce, 9 E Loockerman St, Suite 2-A, PO Box 576, 19903; 302/734-7513
Web www.cdcc.net

State Capitol Building, Dover

The capital of Delaware since 1777, Dover was laid out by William Penn around the city's lovely green. For almost 200 years there were coach houses and inns on King's Road between Philadelphia and Lewes. Circling the green north and south on State Street are fine 18th- and 19th-century houses.

Today, because of Delaware's favorable corporation laws, more than 60,000 US firms pay taxes in Dover. At Dover Air Force Base, south off US 113, the Military Airlift Command operates one of the biggest air cargo terminals in the world, utilizing the giant C5-A Galaxy aircraft. Dover is also the home of Delaware State College, Wesley College, and the Terry campus of Delaware Technical and Community College.

What to See and Do

Delaware Agricultural Museum and Village. Museum of farm life from early settlement to 1960. Main exhibition hall and historic structures representing a late-19th-century farming community; incl gristmill, blacksmith-wheelwright shop, farmhouse, outbuildings, one-rm schoolhouse, store, and train station. Gift shop. (Apr-Dec, Tues-Sun; rest of yr, Mon-Fri) 866 N du Pont Hwy (US 13). Phone 302/734-1618. ¢¢

Delaware Public Archives. Delaware's historical public records.(Mon-Sat; closed hols) 121 Duke of York St. Phone 302/739-5318. **FREE**

Delaware State Museums. Complex of three buildings:

Delaware Archeology Museum. (1790) Housed in an old church, exhibits devoted to archaeology. (Tues-Sat; closed hols) Bank Ln and Governors Ave. Phone 302/739-4266. **FREE**

Johnson Victrola Museum. Tribute to Eldridge Reeves Johnson, founder of the Victor Talking Machine Company. Collection of talking machines, Victrolas, early recordings, and equipt. (Tues-Sat; closed hols) Bank Ln and New St. Phone 302/739-4266. **FREE**

Museum of Small Town Life. Turn-of-the-century drugstore, printing press, pharmacy, carpenter shop, general store, post office, shoemaker's shop, printer's shop; Johnson building. (Tues-Sat; closed hols) 316 S Governors Ave. Phone 302/739-4266. **FREE**

Delaware State Visitor Center. Administered by Delaware State Museums, center offers information on attractions throughout state. Exhibit galleries. (Mon-Sat, Sun afternoons; closed hols) 406 Federal St. Phone 302/739-4266. **FREE**

Dover Heritage Trail. Guided walking tour of historic areas, buildings, and other attractions. (By appt only) Departs from State Visitor Center. Phone 302/739-4266. ¢¢

John Dickinson Plantation. (1740) Restored boyhood residence of Dickinson, the "penman of the Revolution." Reconstructed farm complex. (Tues-Sat; also Sun afternoons Mar-Dec) 6 mi SE, near jct US 113 and DE 9 on Kitts Hummock Rd. Phone 302/739-3277. **FREE**

Killens Pond State Park. A 1,083-acre park with a 66-acre pond. Swimming pool, fishing, boating (rentals); hiking, fitness trails, game fields, picnicking, camping (hookups, dump station). Standard hrs, fees. 13 mi S via US 13. Phone 302/284-4526.

The Old State House. (1792) Delaware's Seat of government since 1777, the State House, restored in 1976, contains a courtroom, ceremonial governor's office, legislative chambers, and county offices, incl Levy Courtroom. A portrait of George Washington in the Senate Chamber was commissioned in 1802 by the legislature as a memorial to the nation's first president. Although Delaware's General Assembly moved to nearby Legislative Hall in 1934, the State House remains the state's symbolic capitol. (Tues-Sun; closed hols) Federal St, The Green. Phone 302/739-4266. **FREE**

Trap Pond State Park. Boating, canoeing, fishing; hiking, biking, camping. Standard fees. Contact RD2 Box 331, Laurel 19956. Phone 302/875-5153.

Special Events

Old Dover Days. Tours of historic houses and gardens not usually open to the public. Crafts exhibits, many other activities. Contact Kent County Tourism, 800/233-KENT. First wkend May.

Dover Downs. 1131 N du Pont Hwy (US 13). Racing events incl NASCAR Winston Cup auto racing (June, Sept); harness racing (mid-Nov-Apr). For fees and schedule, phone 302/674-4600.

Delaware State Fair. 17 mi S on US 13 in Harrington. Arts and crafts, home and trade show, carnival rides,

Celebrating Old Dover Days, Dover

shows; homemaking, agricultural, and livestock exhibits. Phone 302/398-3269. Mid-July.

Harrington Raceway. 17 mi S on US 13, at fairgrounds in Harrington. Harness racing. Betting most nights. Phone 302/398-7223. Sept-Apr.

Motels/Motor Lodges

★ **BUDGET INN.** *1426 N DuPont Hwy (19901). 302/734-4433; fax 302/734-4433.* 68 rms, 2 story. May-Sept: S $42-$50; D $47-$55; each addl $5; lower rates rest of yr. Crib free. TV; cable. Pool; lifeguard. Complimentary coffee in lobby. Restaurant opp 8 am-9 pm. Ck-out 11 am. Coin lndry. Sundries. Cr cds: A, C, D, DS, ER, MC, V.

★ **COMFORT INN.** *222 S DuPont Hwy (19901). 302/674-3300; toll-free 800/228-5150. www.comfortinn.com.* 94 rms, 2 story. May-Sept: S $47-$51; D $51-$55; each addl $5; kit. units $65; family, wkly rates; higher rates NASCAR races; lower rates rest of yr. Crib free. TV; cable. Pool; lifeguard. Complimentary continental bkfst. Restaurant adj 11 am-10 pm. Ck-out noon. Sundries. Some refrigerators. Grill. Cr cds: A, C, D, DS, ER, JCB, MC, V.

Hotel

★★★ **SHERATON INN.** *1570 N DuPont Hwy (19901). 302/678-8500; fax 302/678-9073; toll-free 800/544-5064. www.sheratondover.com.* 152 rms, 7 story. S, D $95; each addl $10; under 18 free. TV; cable. Indoor pool; whirlpool. Restaurant 6:30 am-10 pm. Rm serv to 10:30 pm. Bars 4 pm-1 am; entertainment Mon-Sat. Ck-out noon. Meeting rms. Business servs avail. In-rm modem link. Bellhops. Sundries. Exercise equipt. Cr cds: A, C, D, DS, MC, V.

Restaurants

★★★ **BLUE COAT INN.** *800 N State St (19901). 302/674-1776.* Hrs: 11:30 am-9 pm; Fri to 10 pm; Sat 11:30 am-3 pm, 4:30-10 pm; Sun noon-9 pm. Closed Mon; Dec 25. Res accepted. Bar. Lunch $4.95-$11.95, dinner $8.95-$32.95. Child's menu. Specializes in fresh seafood, steak. Own baking. Entertainment Fri, Sat. Early American decor. Lake setting. Cr cds: A, C, D, DS, MC, V.

★★ **VILLAGE INN.** *DE 9, Little Creek (19901). 302/734-3245.* Hrs: 11 am-2 pm, 4:30-10 pm; Sat 11 am-10 pm; Sun noon-9 pm. Closed Dec 25. Res accepted. Bar. Lunch $4.95-$9.95, dinner $12.95-$19.95. Specialties: stuffed flounder, prime rib. Colonial decor; fireplace, antiques. Cr cds: C, D, DS, ER, MC, V.

Fenwick Island

(E-8) *See also Bethany Beach, Lewes, Rehoboth Beach; also see Ocean City, MD*

Pop 342 **Elev** 4 ft **Area code** 302 **Zip** 19944

Information Bethany-Fenwick Area Chamber of Commerce, Coastal Hwy/DE 1, PO Box 1450, Bethany Beach 19930; 302/539-2100 or 800/962-7873

Web www.bethany-fenwick.org

Fenwick Island, at the southeast corner of Delaware, was named for Thomas Fenwick, a wealthy Virginia landowner who purchased the land in 1686. For a time a dispute raged over whether Fenwick Island was part of Maryland or Pennsylvania. It ended in 1751 when the Transpeninsular Line placed Fenwick Island in Delaware. In 1775 James and Jacob

Brasure, residents of the island, began extracting salt from the ocean and until 1825, "salt making" was big business. In the latter part of the 19th century, Fenwick Island grew as a religious-oriented summer campground. After World War I, Fenwick Island became fashionable as a summer resort.

What to See and Do

DiscoverSea Shipwreck Museum. Contains changing exhibits of shipwreck artifacts recovered on the Delmarva Peninsula. (Memorial Day-Labor Day, daily; rest of yr, Sat, Sun) 708 Ocean Hwy. Phone 302/539-9366 or 888/743-5524. **FREE**

Fenwick Island Lighthouse. Historic 87-ft-tall lighthouse; light was first turned on Aug 1, 1859. (June-Aug, two Wed afternoons per month; also by appt) W of town via DE 54. Phone 410/250-1098.

Fenwick Island State Park. This 208-acre seashore park is located between the Atlantic Ocean and Little Assawoman Bay. Surfing, swimming, bathhouse, surf fishing, sailing (rentals). Standard hrs, fees. 1 mi N on DE 1. Phone 302/539-9060.

Fort Delaware, Fort Delaware State Park

Special Event

Surf Fishing Tournaments. Phone 302/539-2100. Second Sat May and Columbus Day wkend.

Motel/Motor Lodge

★ **ATLANTIC BUDGET INN.** *Ocean Hwy and Rte 54 (19944). 302/539-7673; fax 302/539-7673; toll-free 800/432-8038. www.atlanticbud-getinn.com.* 48 rms, 1-2 story, 3 kit. units. Memorial Day, July 4-Labor Day (3-day min): S, D $90-$105; each addl $8; kit. units $105; lower rates mid-Apr-June, after Labor Day-Oct. Closed rest of yr. Crib $5. TV; cable. Pool; lifeguard. Complimentary coffee in lobby. Restaurant nearby. Ck-out 11 am. Refrigerators, microwaves. Beach 1 blk. Cr cds: A, D, DS, MC, V.

Restaurants

★ ★ **HARPOON HANNA'S.** *DE 54 at the Bay, Fenwick Islands (19944). 302/539-3095.* Hrs: 11-1 am; Sun from 10 am; Sun brunch 10 am-3 pm. Bar. A la carte entrees: lunch $3.95-$7.95, dinner $7.95-$29.95. Sun brunch $3.95-$7.95. Child's menu. Specializes in fresh seafood. Entertainment Fri, Sat. Outdoor dining. Casual, contemporary decor; fireplace. On waterfront. Cr cds: A, C, D, DS, ER, MC, V.

★ ★ **TOM & TERRY'S.** *DE 54 at the Bay (19944). 302/436-4161.* Hrs: 11:30 am-10 pm; early-bird dinner 5-6 pm. Closed Dec 25. Bar. Lunch $6.95-$10.50, dinner $16.95-$22.95. Specializes in fresh local seafood, prime rib. View of Ocean City and bay. Cr cds: DS, MC, V.

Fort Delaware State Park

See also Newark, New Castle, Odessa, Wilmington

(On Pea Patch Island, opposite Delaware City)

This grim gray fort was built as a coastal defense in 1860. The fort was used as a prisoner of war depot for three years, housing up to 12,500 Confederate prisoners at a time. The damp, low-lying terrain and the poor conditions encouraged epidemics, leading to some 2,400 deaths. The fort was modernized in 1896 and remained in commission until 1943.

Restoration of the site is a continuing process. Available are overlook of heronry, picnicking, and living history programs. Museum has scale model of fort, model Civil War relics, orientation video. Special events throughout summer. Boat trip to island from Delaware City (mid-June-Labor Day, Wednesday-Sunday; last weekend April-mid-June and September, Saturday, Sunday, and holidays). No pets. Contact the Park Superintendent, 45 Clinton St, PO Box 170, Delaware City 19706; 302/834-7941. Round trip ¢¢¢

Lewes

(D-8) *See also Bethany Beach, Fenwick Island, Rehoboth Beach*

Settled 1631 **Pop** 2,932 **Elev** 10 ft
Area code 302 **Zip** 19958
Information Chamber of Commerce, Fisher-Martin House, 120 Kings Hwy, PO Box 1; 302/645-8073
Web www.leweschamber.com

Lewes (LOO-is) has been home base to Delaware Bay pilots for 300 years. Weather-beaten, cypress-shingled houses still line the streets where privateers plundered and Captain Kidd bargained away his loot. The treacherous sandbars outside the harbor have claimed their share of ships, and stories of sunken treasure have circulated for centuries. Some buildings show scars from cannonballs that hit their mark when the British bombarded Lewes in the War of 1812. Traces of the original stockade were discovered in 1964.

What to See and Do

Cape Henlopen State Park. More than 3,000 acres at confluence of Delaware Bay and Atlantic Ocean; site of decommissioned Fort Miles, part of coastal defense system during WWII. Supervised swimming, fishing; nature center, programs, trails, picnicking, concession, camping (water hookups, dump station). Standard hrs, fees. 1 mi E of ferry terminal on Cape Henlopen Dr. Phone 302/645-8983.

Lewes-Cape May, NJ, Ferry. Sole connection between US 13 (Ocean Hwy) on the Delmarva Peninsula and southern terminus of Garden State Pkwy (NJ). Trip across Delaware Bay (16 mi) takes 70 min. (Daily; 22 crossings in summer, 10 in winter, 14-18 in spring and fall) Phone 302/645-6313. ¢¢¢¢

Lewes Historical Society Complex. The restored buildings located here were moved here to create a feel for Lewes' early days. (June-Labor Day, Tues-Sat) Tickets at Rabbit's Ferry House. Walking tours and varied events take place during summer season. Shipcarpenter and Third sts. Phone 302/564-7670. Tour ¢¢ Buildings incl

Burton-Ingram House. (ca 1800) Log home made from hand-hewn timbers with cypress shingles. Houses beautiful antiques.

Cannon Ball House & Marine Museum. Built in late 18th century. Originally called the David Rowland Home, it was hit by a cannonball during the War of 1812 and renamed. 118 Front St.

Doctor's Office. (ca 1850) Medical and Dental museum.

DUTCH HERITAGE IN LEWES

As an Atlantic beach destination, historic Lewes (pronounced Loo-is) is an offbeat choice, a place that recommends itself to vacationers for whom sand and sea (about a mile away) are only part of the pleasure. Dating its origins to a Dutch attempt at establishing a whaling station in 1631, it is Delaware's oldest community and enjoys a rich architectural heritage. The neighborhood adjacent to the pleasure boat harbor on the Lewes & Rehoboth Canal is dotted with beautifully restored cottages and mansions from the 18th and 19th centuries, which once housed ship's pilots working Delaware Bay. A one-mile, one-hour stroll through the Historic District is an engaging journey into the past. Begin at the Zwaanendael Museum, a red-brick curiosity with a delightful stair-stepping gable decorated with carved stonework. Built in 1931, it was adapted from the 17th-century town hall of Hoorn in the Netherlands, from which Lewes' first colonists arrived. As the museum, which details the town's history, explains, all 28 (some sources say 32) were killed in a dispute with local Native Americans. In 1682, the area became part of an English grant to William Penn, the founder of Pennsylvania. Behind the museum, the gambrel-roofed Fisher-Martin House (1730) houses the Visitor Information Center. From the museum, head up 2nd Street, Lewes' "main street," in the shade of a canopy of giant, old trees. Take time out to nibble on an ice cream cone while resting on a park bench. At 218 2nd Street, Lewes' oldest home, the little red and yellow shingled Ryves Holt House, is believed to have been built in about 1665. Once a colonial inn, it also housed the Officer of the Port. A few steps to the right at 118 Front Street, which parallels the canal, a cannonball fired by a British vessel in the War of 1812 still juts from the brick foundation of the Cannonball House Marine Museum (1797). Inside are nautical exhibits. Many of the town's Victorian homes are richly adorned with gingerbread trim, and several are brightly painted. One of the prettiest, just off 2nd Street (double back to get here), is the Ann Eliza Baker House, a dazzler in yellow, gold, purple, and orange. This house is a fine example of Lewes' "folk Victorian" style: note the lovely flower gardens and small fountains in this neighborhood. Head north up 3rd Street to Shipcarpenter Street, where the Lewes Historical Society maintains an outdoor museum of early Delaware architecture. Several are "scooter" houses; that is, they are relocated from elsewhere—a local custom. Conclude this tour just up Shipcarpenter to the west at Shipcarpenter Square, an attractive development of restored 18th- and 19th-century scooter homes, all private residences, set around a nicely landscaped mall.

Hiram R. Burton House. (ca 1780) Houses antique furnishings; 18th century kitchen. Also incl a reading rm with materials dedicated to Delaware history. Second and Shipcarpenter sts.

Rabbit's Ferry House. (ca 1789) An 18th century farmhouse with original paneling and period pieces.

Thompson Country Store. (1800) Moved from original location in Tompsonville, DE. Thompson family ran as a store until 1962.

Plank House. Swedish log cabin restored to reflect the home of an early settler.

Restored buildings. Maintained by the Lewes Historical Society. Cannon Ball House and US Lifesaving Station have marine exhibits and lightship *Overfalls*. Other buildings open are Thompson country store, Plank House, Rabbit's Ferry House, Burton-Ingram House, Ellegood House, Hiram R. Burton House, and old doctor's office. (June-Labor Day, Tues-Sat) Tickets at Rabbit's Ferry House. Walking tours and varied events take place during summer season. Phone 302/645-7670.

Zwaanendael Museum. Adaptation of Hoorn, Holland town hall was built in 1931 as memorial to original Dutch founders of Lewes (1631). Highlights the town's maritime heritage with colonial, Native American, and Dutch exhibits. (Tues-Sun; closed hols) Savannah Rd and Kings Hwy. Phone 302/645-1148.

Special Events

Great Delaware Kite Festival. Cape Henlopen State Park (see). Festival heralding the beginning of spring. Fri before Easter. Phone 302/645-8983.

Lewes Garden Tour. Visit hidden gardens of Lewes. Vendors. Phone 302/645-8073. Third Sat June.

Coast Day. University of Delaware Marine Studies Complex. Facilities and research vessel open to public; marine exhibits, research demonstrations, nautical films. Phone 302/645-4346. First Sun Oct.

Motels/Motor Lodges

★ **ANGLER'S MOTEL.** *110 Anglers Rd (19958).* 302/645-2831. 25 rms, 1-2 story, 2 kits. Mid-May-mid-Sept (3-day min wkends, hols): S, D $70-$105; each addl $5; kit. units $85-$105; lower rates rest of yr. Closed Dec-Feb. Crib free. TV; cable. Pool. Restaurant nearby. Ck-out 11 am. Refrigerators. Picnic tables, grills. Sun deck. Overlooks canal, marina opp. Boat docking. Cr cds: A, MC, V.

★ **BEACON.** *514 E Savannah Rd (19958).* 302/645-4888; fax 302/645-8138; toll-free 800/735-4888. www.lewestoday.com/beacon. 66 rms, 3 story. Aug: S, D $105-$155; each addl $5; under 12 free; hol rates; lower rates rest of yr. Closed mid-Nov-Mar. Crib $5. TV; cable (premium), VCR avail (movies). Complimentary coffee in lobby. Restaurant adj 6 am-6 pm. Ck-out 11 am. Meeting rms. Business servs avail. Bellhops. Pool. Refrigerators. Balconies. Cr cds: A, DS, MC, V.

Hotel

★ ★ ★ **ZWAANENDAEL INN.** *142 2nd St (19958).* 302/645-6466; fax 302/645-7196; toll-free 800/824-8754. www.beach-net.com/newdevoninn. 26 rms, 4 story. Mid-June-mid-Oct: S, D $65-$130; suites $110-$170; package plans; lower rates rest of yr. Restaurant 11 am-10 pm. Ck-out 11 am. Business servs avail. Shopping arcade. Built 1926. Cr cds: A, C, D, DS, MC, V.

B&B/Small Inn

★ ★ ★ **INN AT CANAL SQUARE.** *122 Market St (19958).* 302/644-3377; fax 302/644-6565; toll-free 888/644-1911. www.beach-net.com/canalsquare.html. 19 rms, 4 story. Late June-Sept: D $155-$175; each addl $15; 2-bedrm houseboat avail; wkly rates; wkends (2-day min); lower rates rest of yr. Crib $15. TV; cable (premium). Complimentary continental bkfst. Restaurant nearby. Ck-out 11 am. Concierge serv. Meeting rm. Refriger-

ators avail. Balconies. On canal. Cr
cds: A, C, D, DS, MC, V.
🏊 🐾 SC

Restaurants

★ **ASHBY'S OYSTER HOUSE.** *24
Peddlers Village (19958). 302/945-
4070.* Hrs: 11:30-1 am; Sun from 9
am. Closed Thanksgiving, Dec 25.
Bar. Lunch $3.95-$6.95, dinner
$11.95-$19.95. Sun bkfst buffet
$6.95. Child's menu. Specializes in
seafood, raw bar. Casual dining. Cr
cds: A, DS, MC, V.
D SC 🔜

★ ★ ★ **THE BUTTERY.** *102 Second
St (19958). 302/645-7755.
www.butteryrestaurant.com.* French
menu. Hrs: 11 am-2:30 pm, 5-10 pm;
Sun 10:30 am-2:30 pm, 5-10 pm. Res
accepted. Wine, beer. Lunch $16-$20;
dinner $18-$29. Brunch $19. Enter-
tainment. Cr cds: DS, MC, V.
D 🔜

★ ★ **GILLIGAN'S.** *134 Market St
(19958). 302/645-7866.* Hrs: 11 am-
11 pm. Closed Nov-Mar. Bar. A la
carte entrees: lunch $6.50-$10, dinner $13-$20. Wine list. Specializes in
seafood, crab cakes, vegetarian
dishes. Outside dining deck, waterfront bar. Part of exterior resembles
the "good ship Minnow." View of
harbor. Cr cds: A, D, DS, MC, V.
D 🔜

★ **LIGHTHOUSE.** *Savannah Rd at
Anglers Rd (19958). 302/645-6271.
www.lighthouselewes.com.* Hrs: 6 am-
10 pm; Sept-Mar 7 am-9 pm. Closed
Thanksgiving, Dec 24, 25. Bar from
11 am. Bkfst $3.75-$6.95, lunch
$3.25-$12.95, dinner $12.95-$17.95.
Child's menu. Specializes in fresh
seafood. Entertainment wkends. Outdoor dining. Overlooks Lewes Harbor. Cr cds: MC, V.
D 🔜

Newark

(B-7) *See also New Castle, Wilmington*

Settled 1685 **Pop** 28,547 **Elev** 124 ft
Area code 302

Information Greater Wilmington
Convention & Visitors Bureau-
Visitors Center, 100 W 10th St,
Wilmington 19801; 302/737-4059

Newark grew up at the crossroads of
two well-traveled Native American
trails. The site of the only Revolutionary War battle on Delaware soil
is at nearby Cooch's Bridge, southeast of Newark. According to tradition, Betsy Ross's flag was first raised
in battle at Cooch's Bridge on September 3, 1777.

What to See and Do

University of Delaware. (1743)
18,000 students. Founded as a small
private academy; stately elm trees,
fine lawns, and Georgian-style brick
buildings adorn the central campus.
Tours from Visitors Center, 196 S
College Ave (Mon-Fri, Sat). Phone
302/831-8123. On campus is

   **University of Delaware Mineral
Collection.** Also fossil exhibit.
Penny Hall, Academy St. (Mon-Fri,
by appt only; closed hols) Phone
302/831-8242. **FREE**

White Clay Creek State Park. A
1,483-acre day park with farmlands,
forest, and streams. Fishing; nature
and fitness trails, picnicking. Standard hrs, fees. 3 mi NW via DE 896.
Phone 302/368-6900.

Motels/Motor Lodges

★ ★ **BEST WESTERN.** *260 Chapman
Rd (19702). 302/738-3400; fax
302/738-3414; toll-free 800/633-3203.
www.bestwestern.com.* 99 rms, 2 story.
S $55-$65; D $60-$75; each addl $5;
under 18 free; wkend rates. Crib free.
TV; cable. Pool. Restaurant 5-9 pm.
Bar 4 pm-1 am. Ck-out noon. Meeting rms. Business servs avail. Sundries. Cr cds: A, D, DS, MC, V.
D 🏊 🐾 🐾

★ **COMFORT INN.** *1120 S College
Ave (19713). 302/368-8715; fax
302/368-6454; toll-free 800/228-5150.
www.comfortinn.com.* 102 rms, 2
story. S $50-$54; D $56-$60; each
addl $6; under 18 free. Crib free. Pet
accepted. TV; cable, VCR avail
(movies). Pool; lifeguard. Complimentary continental bkfst. Ck-out 11
am. Meeting rm. Business servs avail.

In-rm modem link. Some refrigerators. Cr cds: A, C, D, DS, JCB, MC, V.

★★ **HOLIDAY INN.** *1203 Christiana Rd (19713). 302/737-2700; fax 302/737-3214; toll-free 800/465-4329.* 144 rms, 2 story. S $71-$81; D $77-$87; each addl $6; under 18 free. Crib free. TV; cable. Pool; lifeguard. Restaurant 6:30 am-10 pm. Bar noon-1 am. Ck-out noon. Coin lndry. Meeting rms. Business servs avail. In-rm modem link. Valet serv. Sundries. Cr cds: A, C, D, DS, JCB, MC, V.

★ **HOWARD JOHNSON HOTEL AND SUITES.** *1119 S College Ave (19713). 302/368-8521; fax 302/368-9868; toll-free 800/654-2000. www.hojo.com.* 142 rms, 2 story. S, D $55; each addl $10; under 18 free. Crib free. Pet accepted. TV; cable. Pool. Complimentary continental bkfst. Ck-out noon. Meeting rms. Business servs avail. In-rm modem link. Valet serv. Health club privileges. Private patios, balconies. Cr cds: A, C, D, DS, ER, JCB, MC, V.

★ **MCINTOSH INN.** *100 McIntosh Plaza (19713). 302/453-9100; fax 302/453-9114; toll-free 800/444-2775. www.mcintoshinn.com.* 108 rms. S $41.95; D $46.95; each addl $5. Crib free. TV. Restaurant adj open 24 hrs. Ck-out 11 am. Some refrigerators. Cr cds: A, D, MC, V.

Hotel

★★★ **BRANDYWINE VALLEY COUNTRY ESTATE.** *100 Continental Dr (19713). 302/454-1500; fax 302/454-0233; toll-free 800/348-3133. www.brandywinevalleycountryestate.com.* 266 rms, 4 story. S, D $99-$199; each addl $10; suites $185-$325; family plans; higher rates university graduation. Crib free. TV; cable. Heated pool; whirlpool, poolside serv, lifeguard. Restaurant 6:30 am-10 pm. Bar 11-1 am. Ck-out 11:30 am. Meeting rms. Business center. In-rm modem link. Concierge. RR station transportation. Tennis privileges. Golf privileges. Exercise equipt. Lux-ury level. Cr cds: A, C, D, DS, ER, JCB, MC, V.

Restaurant

★ **KLONDIKE KATE'S.** *158 E Main St (19711). 302/737-6100. www.klondikekates.com.* Hrs: 11-1 am; Sun from 10 am. Closed Thanksgiving, Dec 25. Southwestern menu. Bar. Lunch, dinner $4.95-$12.95. Child's menu. Specializes in fresh seafood, Tex-Mex dishes. Outdoor dining. In former courthouse/jail. Cr cds: A, D, DS, MC, V.

New Castle

(B-7) *See also Newark, Wilmington*

Settled 1651 **Pop** 4,862 **Elev** 19 ft
Area code 302 **Zip** 19720
Information Mayor and Council of New Castle, 220 Delaware St; 302/322-9801
Web www.newcastlecity.net

New Castle—meeting place of the Colonial assemblies, first capital of the state, and an early center of culture and communication—was one of Delaware's first settlements. Its fine harbor made it a busy port in the 18th century until its commerce was taken over by Wilmington, which is closer to Philadelphia. Today, New Castle is a historian's and architect's delight—charming, mellow, and relaxed. Three signers of the Declaration of Independence made their homes here: George Read, Thomas McKean, and George Ross, Jr. (considered a Pennsylvanian by some). New Castle lies at the foot of the Delaware Memorial Bridge, which connects with the southern end of the New Jersey Turnpike.

What to See and Do

Amstel House Museum. (1730) Restored brick mansion of seventh governor of Delaware; an earlier structure was incorporated into the service wing. Houses Colonial furnishings and arts; complete Colonial kitchen. (Mar-Dec, Tues-Sun; rest of yr, Sat and Sun; closed hols) Combination ticket avail with Old Dutch House. 2 E 4th St at Delaware St. Phone 302/322-2794. ¢

George Read II House. (1804) Federal house with elegant interiors: gilded fanlights; silver door hardware; carved woodwork; relief plasterwork. Furnished with period antiques; garden design dates from 1847. (Mar-Dec, Tues-Sun; rest of yr, Sat and Sun) 42 The Strand. Phone 302/322-8411. ¢¢

The Green. Laid out by direction of Peter Stuyvesant, this public square of the old town is surrounded by dozens of historically important buildings. Delaware and 3rd sts.

New Castle Court House Museum. (1732) Original Colonial capitol and oldest surviving courthouse in the state; furnishings and exhibits on display; cupola is the center of a 12-mi circle that delineates Delaware-Pennsylvania border. (Tues-Sun; closed hols) 211 Delaware St, on The Green. Phone 302/323-4453. **FREE**

Old Dutch House. (late 17th century) Thought to be Delaware's oldest dwelling in its original form; Dutch Colonial furnishings; decorative arts. (Mar-Dec, Tues-Sun; rest of yr, Sat and Sun; closed hols) Combination ticket avail with Amstel House Museum. 32 E 3rd St. Phone 302/322-2794. ¢

Old Library Museum. (1892) Unusual semioctagonal Victorian building houses temporary exhibits relating to area. (Sat-Sun) 40 E 3rd St. Phone 302/322-2794. **FREE**

Special Events

Band concerts. Battery Park. Phone 302/328-4188. Wed eves, June-early Aug.

Separation Day. Battery Park. Observance of Delaware's declaration of independence from Great Britain. Regatta, shows, bands, concerts, fireworks. June. Phone 302/322-9802.

Motels/Motor Lodges

★ **RAMADA INN.** *I-295 and US 13 (19720). 302/658-8511; fax 302/658-3071. www.ramada.com.* 131 rms, 2 story. S $75-$81; D $78-$84; each

addl $10; under 18 free. Crib free. TV; cable. Pool; poolside serv, lifeguard. Restaurant 7 am-10 pm. Bar 4:30 pm-midnight. Ck-out noon. Meeting rms. Business servs avail. In-rm modem link. Valet serv. Sundries. RR station, bus depot transportation. Cr cds: A, D, DS, MC, V.
D ⬚ ⬚ ⬚

★ **RODEWAY INN.** *111 S DuPont Hwy (19720). 302/328-6246; fax 302/328-9493; toll-free 800/321-6246. www.rodewayinn.com.* 40 rms. S $49-$59; D $55-$69; each addl $5; under 18 free. Crib $5. Pet accepted. TV; cable. Complimentary continental bkfst. Restaurant adj 11 am-10 pm. Ck-out noon. Business servs avail. Some refrigerators, microwaves. Cr cds: A, C, D, DS, JCB, MC, V.
⬚ ⬚ ⬚ ⬚ ⬚ ⬚

Restaurants

★★ **AIR TRANSPORT COMMAND.** *143 N DuPont Hwy (19720). 302/328-3527.* Hrs: 11 am-4 pm, 5-11 pm; Fri to midnight; Sat 4:30 pm-midnight; Sun 4-10 pm; Sun brunch 10 am-3 pm. Res accepted; required Sat. Bar to 1 am. Lunch $4.50-$8.95, dinner $9.95-$23.95. Sun brunch $14.95. Child's menu. Specialty: prime rib. Outdoor dining. Replica of WWII-era Scottish farmhouse; war memorabilia. Overlooks airfield. Cr cds: A, D, DS, MC, V.
D ⬚

★★ **ARSENAL AT NEW CASTLE.** *30 Market St (19720). 302/328-1290.* Hrs: 11:30 am-2:30 pm, 5-9 pm; Sun 1-8 pm. Closed Mon. Res accepted. Lunch $4.75-$13.95, dinner $11.95-$28.95. Specialties: Delaware crab cakes, crab imperial. Building constructed in 1809 by the Federal government; originally used as arsenal. Colonial decor. Cr cds: A, D, DS, MC, V.
⬚

★★★ **LYNNHAVEN INN.** *154 N DuPont Hwy (19720). 302/328-2041.* Hrs: 11:30 am-9:30 pm; Sat 4-10 pm; Sun 1-9 pm. Closed Dec 24-25. Res accepted. Bar. Lunch $4.95-$11.95, dinner $10.95-$25.95. Child's menu. Specialties: imperial crab, prime rib. Early American decor. Cr cds: A, D, DS, MC, V.
D ⬚

Odessa

(B-7) *See also New Castle, Smyrna, Wilmington*

Settled 1721 **Pop** 286 **Elev** 50 ft
Area code 302 **Zip** 19730

Once a prosperous grain shipping center, Odessa tried to protect its shipping trade by haughtily telling the Delaware Railroad, in 1855, to lay its tracks elsewhere. To glorify itself that same year, the town changed its name from Cantwell's Bridge to that of the Russian grain port on the Black Sea. But the sloops and schooners that transported grain eventually found less short-sighted ports of call. Odessa was an important station on the Underground Railroad for many years before the Civil War. Now it is a crossroads town at the junction of US 13 and DE 299. The town exhibits numerous fine examples of 18th- and 19th-century domestic architecture.

What to See and Do

Fort Delaware State Park. (see) Approx 9 mi NE on Pea Patch Island, opposite Delaware City.

Historic Houses of Odessa. For full tour of houses, arrive by 2 pm. (Tues-Sun; closed hols, Jan-Feb) Individual house tickets avail. Main St. Phone 302/378-4069. ¢¢

Brick Hotel Gallery and Manney Collection of Belter Furniture. Federal, 19th-century building was a hotel and tavern for nearly a century. Gallery houses the largest private collection of Belter furniture in existence. Very high-styled Victorian furniture, Belter parlor and bedrm suites, made in New York in the mid-19th century, were famous for craftsmanship, particularly elaborate carvings. Phone 302/378-4069. ¢¢

Corbit-Sharp House. (1774) Georgian house built by William Corbit, Odessa's leading citizen, was lived in by his family for 150 yrs. Restored and furnished with many family pieces, the interior reflects period from 1774-1818. Maintained by Winterthur Museum,

Garden, and Library (see WIL-MINGTON).

Wilson-Warner House. (1769) Handsome red brick Georgian house, with L-shape plan typical of early Delaware architecture, is accurately furnished to portray life in early 19th century. Maintained by Winterthur Museum, Garden, and Library (see WILMINGTON). Phone 302/378-4069.

Lums Pond State Park. More than 1,800-acre park centered around 200-acre pond. Fishing, boating (rentals); hiking and fitness trails, game courts, picnicking, camping (showers, dump station; Apr-Oct). Standard hrs, fees. Approx 3 mi W on DE 299 to Middletown, then 8 mi N on US 301 and DE 71. Phone 302/368-6989. ¢¢

Rehoboth Beach

(D-8) *See also Bethany Beach, Fenwick Island, Lewes*

Settled 1872 **Pop** 1,495 **Elev** 16 ft
Area code 302 **Zip** 19971
Information Rehoboth Beach-Dewey Beach Chamber of Commerce, 501 Rehoboth Ave, PO Box 216; 302/227-2233 or 800/441-1329
Web www.beach-fun.com

The "nation's summer capital" got its nickname by being a favorite with Washington diplomats and legislators. A 2½-hour drive from Washington, D.C., the largest summer resort in Delaware began as a spot for camp meetings amid sweet-smelling pine groves. In the 1920s, real estate boomed, triggering Rehoboth Beach's rebirth as a resort town with a variety of accommodations, shopping areas, and eateries. Deep sea and freshwater fishing, sailing, swimming, and biking and strolling along cherry tree-lined Rehoboth Avenue have kept it a favorite retreat from Washington's summer heat.

What to See and Do

Delaware Seashore State Park. This seven-mi strip of land separates Rehoboth and Indian River bays from the Atlantic. Bay and ocean swimming, fishing, surfing, boating (marina, launch, rentals); picnicking, concession, primitive and improved campsites (hookups). Standard hrs, fees. 6 mi S on DE 1. Phone 302/227-2800.

Special Events

Bandstand concerts. Bandstand, Rehoboth Ave. Open-air concerts. Phone 302/227-6181. Sat and Sun eves, Memorial Day-Labor Day.

Sea Witch Halloween and Fiddlers' Festival. Phone 800/441-1329, ext 12. Late Oct.

Motels/Motor Lodges

★★ **ADAMS OCEANFRONT VILLAS.** *4 Read St, Dewey Beach (19971). 302/227-3030; fax 302/227-1034; toll-free 800/448-8080. www.adamsoceanfront. com.* 23 rms, 3 story, 12 villas. No elvtr. Late June-Aug: S, D $95-$115; each addl $6; villas (up to 7) $250-$295 (3-day min); lower rates mid-Mar-late June, Sept-Oct. Closed rest of yr. Crib $6. TV; cable (premium). Pool. Complimentary continental bkfst. Ck-out 11 am; villas 10 am. Refrigerators; microwaves avail. Picnic tables, grills; some balconies. On beachfront. Cr cds: MC, V.

★★ **ADMIRAL.** *2 Baltimore Ave (19971). 302/227-2103; fax 302/227-3620; toll-free 888/882-4188. www. admiralrehoboth.com.* 73 rms, 5 story. June-Labor Day: S, D $110-$199; each addl $10; suites $155-$245; wkend rates; 3-day min stay in season; lower rates rest of yr. TV; cable. Indoor pool; whirlpool. Complimentary coffee in lobby. Restaurant adj 7 am-9 pm. Gift shop. Refrigerators; some in-rm whirlpools. Cr cds: A, DS, MC, V.

The boardwalk at Rehoboth Beach

★ **THE ATLANTIC BUDGET INN.** *154 Rehoboth Ave (19971). 302/227-9446; fax 302/227-9446; toll-free 800/245-2112.* 97 rms, 1-4 story, 10 kits. Mid-July-late Aug, hol wkends: D $69-$159; each addl $10; kits. $109-$179; under 11 free; lower rates rest of yr. Crib $6. TV; cable, VCR avail (movies). Pool. Complimentary coffee. Restaurant nearby. Ck-out 11 am. Coin lndry. Some refrigerators, microwaves. Cr cds: A, DS, MC, V.

★ **ATLANTIC VIEW MOTEL.** *2 Clayton St, North Dewey Beach (19971). 302/227-3878; fax 302/227-5372; toll-free 800/777-4162. www.atlanticview. com.* 35 rms, 4 story. No elvtr. Mid-June-Labor Day (2-4-day min): S, D $99-$169; each addl $7; lower rates Apr-mid-June, after Labor Day-mid-Oct. Closed rest of yr. Crib $5. TV; cable (premium). Pool. Complimentary coffee. Restaurant nearby. Ck-out 11 am. Coin lndry. Refrigerators. Balconies. Cr cds: A, DS, MC, V.

★ **BAY RESORT MOTEL.** *126 Belle-vue St, Dewey Beach (19971). 302/227-6400; fax 302/227-5800; toll-free 800/922-9240. www.bayresort.com.* 68 kit. units, 3 story. July-Labor Day: D $119-$199; each addl $10; under 12 free; wkend, wkly rates; lower rates Apr-June and Sept-Oct. Closed rest of yr. Crib $10. TV; cable (premium). Pool. Complimentary continental bkfst. Ck-out 11 am. Coin lndry. Some private patios, balconies. Cr cds: DS, MC, V.

★★ **BEACH VIEW MOTEL.** *6 Wilmington Ave (19971). 302/227-2999; fax 302/226-2640; toll-free 800/288-5962. www.beachviewmotel.com.* 38 rms, 4 story. Mid-June-early Sept: D $80-$155; each addl $7; under 7 free; lower rates Apr-mid-June, early Sept-Nov. Closed rest of yr. Crib $5. TV; cable (premium). Pool. Complimentary continental bkfst. Restaurant adj 8 am-11 pm. Ck-out 11 am. Coin lndry. Refrigerators. Some balconies. Cr cds: A, DS, MC, V.

★★ **BEST WESTERN GOLDEN LEAF.** *1400 Hwy 1 (19971). 302/226-1100; fax 302/226-9785; res 800/422-8566. www.bestwestern.com.* 75 rms, 4 story. Mid-June-Aug: S, D $149-$189; each addl $10; under 12 free; lower rates rest of yr. Crib $10. TV; cable (premium). Pool. Complimentary continental bkfst. Restaurant opp 8 am-9 pm. Ck-out 11 am. Coin lndry. Meeting rms. Business servs avail. Covered parking. Refrigerators, microwaves. Balconies. Ocean ½ blk; swimming beach. Cr cds: A, C, D, DS, ER, JCB, MC, V.

★ **BRIGHTON SUITES HOTELS.** *34 Wilmington Ave (19971). 302/227-5780; fax 302/227-6815; toll-free 800/227-5788. www.brightonsuites. com.* 66 suites, 4 story. July-Aug: suites $189-$239; each addl $10; under 16 free; mid-wk rates; package plans; lower rates rest of yr. Crib $6. TV; cable (premium). Heated pool. Coffee in rms. Restaurant opp 11 am-9 pm. Ck-out 11 am. Meeting rms. Business servs avail. Bellhops in season. Garage parking. Exercise equipt.

Refrigerators, wet bars; microwaves avail. Cr cds: A, C, D, DS, MC, V.

★★ **DINNER BELL INN.** *2 Christian St (19971). 302/227-2561; fax 302/227-0323; toll-free 800/425-2355. www. dinnerbellinn.com.* 28 rms, 2 story, 4 kit. units, 1 cottage. Late June-Aug: D $85-$175; each addl $15; kit. units $150-$210; cottage $250; under 12 free; lower rates Apr-mid-June and late Sept. Closed Jan-Feb. Crib $15. TV; cable (premium). Complimentary continental bkfst. Restaurant 4-10 pm. Bar. Ck-out 11 am. Meeting rm. Business servs avail. Individually decorated rms. Ocean 2 blks. Cr cds: A, MC, V.

★ **ECONO LODGE.** *4361 DE 1 (19971). 302/227-0500; fax 302/227-2170; toll-free 800/645-2690. www. econolodge.com.* 79 rms, 3 story. June-Sept: S, D $85-$135; each addl $10; under 16 free; lower rates rest of yr. Crib free. TV; cable (premium). Pool; lifeguard. Complimentary coffee in lobby. Restaurant nearby. Ck-out 11 am. Coin lndry. Business servs avail. Some refrigerators. Microwaves avail. Lawn games. Balconies. Cr cds: A, C, D, DS, MC, V.

★ **HARBOR VIEW.** *DE 1 (19930). 302/539-0500; fax 302/539-5170.* 60 rms, 2 story, 8 kit. units. July-Aug: S, D $95-$139; each addl $10; kit. units $100-$139; lower rates rest of yr. Crib $10. TV; cable (premium). Pool. Complimentary continental bkfst. Restaurant 5-10 pm; closed Dec-Jan. Ck-out 11 am. Meeting rm. Refrigerators, microwaves. Balconies. Picnic tables, grills. On bay; swimming. Cr cds: A, D, DS, MC, V.

★★ **HENLOPEN HOTEL.** *511 N Boardwalk (19971). 302/227-2551; fax 302/227-8147; toll-free 800/441-8450. www.henlopenhotel.com.* 93 rms, 8 story. July-Aug (2-day min wkends, hols): S, D $179-$279; each addl $10; under 16 free; varied lower rates Apr-May and Sept-Oct. Closed Jan-Mar 15. Crib free. TV; cable. Coffee in rms. Restaurant 8-11 am, 5-10 pm. Ck-out 11 am. Meeting rms. Business servs avail. Some refrigerators. Balconies. On beach; ocean views. Cr cds: A, MC, V.

★★ **OCEANUS MOTEL.** *6 Second St (19971). 302/227-8200; toll-free 800/852-5011. www.oceanusmotel.com.* 38 rms, 3 story. No elvtr. July-Aug: D $129-$169; each addl $10; under 12 free; wkly rates; lower rates Apr-June, Sept-Oct. Closed rest of yr. Crib $7. TV; cable (premium). Pool; lifeguard. Complimentary continental bkfst. Restaurant opp 8-2 am. Ck-out noon. Coin lndry. Refrigerators. Microwaves avail. Cr cds: DS, MC, V.

★★ **SANDCASTLE.** *123 Second St (19971). 302/227-0400; toll-free 800/372-2112. www.thesandcastle motel.com.* 60 rms, 3 story. July-Labor Day: S, D $100-$130; each addl $10; under 12 free; lower rates Mar-July and Labor Day-Dec. Closed rest of yr. Crib $10. TV; cable. Indoor pool. Sauna. Complimentary coffee in lobby. Ck-out 11 am. Refrigerators. Microwaves avail; $5/day. Balconies. Cr cds: A, DS, MC, V.

★ **SEA ESTA MOTEL III.** *1409 DE 1, Dewey Beach (19971). 302/227-4343; fax 302/227-3049; toll-free 800/436-6591. www.seaesta.com.* 33 kit. units, 3 story. July-Aug: S, D $100-$150; each addl $10; under 12 free; lower rates rest of yr. Pet accepted; $5/day. TV; cable (premium). Complimentary coffee in lobby. Restaurant nearby. Ck-out 11 am. Covered parking. Balconies. Ocean 1 blk; swimming beach. Cr cds: A, D, DS, MC, V.

Hotel

★★★ **BOARDWALK PLAZA HOTEL.** *2 Olive Ave (19971). 302/227-7169; fax 302/227-0561; toll-free 800/332-3224. www.boardwalkplaza. com.* 84 units, 4 story. 45 suites, 6 kit. units. Memorial Day-Labor Day: S, D $135-$300; each addl $20; suites $245-$395; kit. units $1,800-$3,000/wk (Memorial Day-Labor Day 1-wk min); under 6 free; lower rates rest of yr. Crib free. TV; cable, VCR avail (movies). Indoor/outdoor pool; poolside serv. Complimentary coffee in rms. Restaurant 7 am-10 pm. Ck-out 11 am. Meeting rms. Business

servs avail. In-rm modem link. Exercise equipt. Minibars; microwaves avail. Some balconies. On beach; ocean swimming. Victorian decor and architectural detail in modern structure; antiques, period furnishings; glass-encased oceanview elvtr; rooftop sun deck. Luxury level. Cr cds: A, D, DS, MC, V.

B&B/Small Inn

★★★ **CHESAPEAKE LANDING.** *101 Chesapeake St (19971). 302/227-2973; fax 302/227-0301. www. chesapeakelanding.com.* 4 rms, 3 with shower only, 3 story. No elvtr. No rm phones. May-Oct: S, D $95-$225; wkends, hols (2-3 day min); lower rates rest of yr. Children over 16 yrs only. TV in common rm; cable, VCR avail (movies). Complimentary full bkfst; afternoon refreshments. Ck-out noon, ck-in 2 pm. In-rm modem link. Luggage handling. Valet serv. Health club privileges. Heated pool. Antiques. Totally nonsmoking. Cr cds: MC, V.

Restaurants

★★ **BLUE MOON.** *35 Baltimore Ave (19971). 302/227-6515.* Hrs: 6-11 pm; Sun brunch noon-3 pm. Closed Jan. Res accepted. Bar 4 pm-1 am. Dinner $9-$26. Sun brunch $6.25-$9.50. Specializes in fresh seafood, vegetarian dishes. Outdoor dining. Cr cds: A, D, DS, MC, V.

★★★ **CHEZ LA MER.** *210 2nd St (19971). 302/227-6494.* Hrs: 5:30-10 pm; Fri, Sat to 10:30 pm. Closed Mon-Wed off season; Thanksgiving; also Dec-Mar. Res accepted. Continental menu. Bar to 1 am. Dinner $16-$23. Child's menu. Specializes in fresh seafood, veal. Outdoor dining. Restored house with French provincial decor. Sun porch. Cr cds: A, D, DS, MC, V.

★ **FULLMOON SALOON.** *15 Wilmington Ave (19971). 302/227-2888.* Hrs: 5 pm-1 am; Sat, Sun from noon. Closed Thanksgiving; also 3 wks Dec. Bar to 1 am. Lunch $4.75-$9.25, dinner $8.75-$19 (cover charge $5 during comedy club). Child's menu.

Specializes in overstuffed sandwiches, steak, seafood. Irish music in
season. Irish pub atmosphere. Cr cds:
MC, V.
[D] [⊣]

★★ **LA LA LAND.** *22 Wilmington
Ave (19971).* 302/227-3887. *www.
lalalandrestaurant.com.* Hrs: 6-11 pm.
Closed Nov-mid-Apr. Res accepted.
Bar 6 pm-1 am. A la carte entrees:
dinner $19-$27. Specialty: rack of
lamb. Outdoor dining. Artistic
atmosphere; hand-painted walls and
chairs; bamboo garden. Cr cds: A, C,
D, DS, MC, V.
[D] [⊣]

★★ **LAMP POST.** *4534 DE 1
(19971).* 302/645-9132. Hrs: 7 am-
9:30 pm; Fri, Sat to 10 pm. Closed
Thanksgiving, Dec 25. Bar. Bkfst
$3.50-$9.50, lunch $3.50-$12, dinner
$8.95-$25. Child's menu. Specializes
in fresh seafood, steak. Parking. Cr
cds: A, DS, MC, V.
[D] [⊣]

★★ **RUSTY RUDDER.** *113 Dickinson
St, Dewey Beach (19971).* 302/227-
3888. *www.dmv.com/rustyrudder.* Hrs:
11:30 am-9 pm, Fri, Sat to 10 pm;
Memorial Day-Labor Day to 11 pm;
Sun to 9 pm; Sun brunch 10 am-2
pm. Bar to 1 am. Lunch $5.95-$8.95,
dinner $14.95-$25.95. Sun brunch
$11.95. Child's menu. Specializes in
prime rib, seafood. Salad bar. Entertainment. Parking. Outdoor dining.
Nautical decor; on bay. Cr cds: A, C,
D, DS, ER, MC, V.
[D] [SC] [⊣]

★★ **SYDNEY'S SIDE STREET.** *25
Christian St (19971).* 302/227-1339.
www.sydneysofrehoboth.com. Hrs: 4
pm-1 am. Closed Thanksgiving, Dec
25; hrs vary Nov-Apr. Res accepted.
Bar. Dinner $9.50-$19.50. Specializes
in New Orleans cuisine. Own
desserts. Blues, jazz eves. Outdoor
dining. Restored old schoolhouse. Cr
cds: A, D, DS, MC, V.
[D] [SC]

★ **TIJUANA TAXI.** *207 Rehoboth Ave
(19971).* 302/227-1986. Hrs: 5-11
pm; Fri, Sat noon-midnight; Sun
noon-11 pm. Closed Super Bowl
Sun, Dec 25. Mexican menu. Bar.
Lunch, dinner $9-$12. Specializes in
chili, nachos, vegetarian dishes.

Street parking. Mexican cantina
atmosphere. Cr cds: MC, V.
[D] [⊣]

Smyrna

(C-7) *See also Dover, Odessa*

Founded 1768 **Pop** 5,679 **Elev** 36 ft
Area code 302 **Zip** 19977
Information Chamber of Commerce,
PO Box 576, Dover 19903; 302/653-
9291; or visit the Smyrna Visitors Cen-
ter, 5500 du Pont Hwy; 302/653-8910

Named in 1806 for the chief seaport
of Turkish Asia Minor, Smyrna in the
1850s was an active shipping center
for produce grown in central
Delaware.

What to See and Do

**Bombay Hook National Wildlife
Refuge.** Annual fall and spring resting and feeding spot for migratory
waterfowl, incl a variety of ducks and
tens of thousands of snow geese and
Canada geese; also home for bald
eagles, shorebirds, deer, fox, and
muskrat. Auto tour route (12 mi),
wildlife foot trails, observation towers; visitor center offering interpretive and environmental education
programs. (Spring and fall, daily,
summer and winter, Mon-Fri)
Golden Eagle, Golden Age, and
Golden Access passports accepted
(see MAKING THE MOST OF YOUR
TRIP). 5 mi E on DE 6, then 3 mi S
on DE 9. Phone 302/653-6872. ¢¢

Smyrna Museum. Furnishings and
memorabilia from early Federal to
late Victorian periods; changing
exhibits. (Sat, limited hrs) 11 S Main
St. Phone 302/653-8844.

Restaurants

★★ **THOMAS ENGLAND HOUSE.**
1165 S DuPont Blvd (US 13) (19977).
302/653-1420. Hrs: 4-10 pm; wkends
to 11 pm; early-bird dinner to 7 pm.
Res accepted; required Sat. Continental menu. Bar. Dinner $9.95-$29.95.
Child's menu. Specializes in fresh
seafood, prime rib. Colonial building;
housed troops during Revolutionary

Bombay Hook National Wildlife Refuge

War; was stop on Underground Railroad. Cr cds: A, D, DS, MC, V.

★ **WAYSIDE INN.** *103 N DuPont Hwy (19977).* 302/653-8047. Hrs: 11 am-9 pm; Sun to 8 pm. Res accepted. Lunch $4.25-$8.50, dinner $10.95-$22.50. Child's menu. Specializes in seafood, prime rib. Cr cds: A, C, D, DS, ER, MC, V.

Wilmington

(B-7) *In PA see also Chester, Kennett Square, Philadelphia*

Settled 1638 **Pop** 72,664 **Elev** 120 ft
Area code 302
Information Greater Wilmington Convention & Visitors Bureau, 100 W 10th St, 19801; 302/652-4088
Web www.wilmcvb.org

Wilmington, the "chemical capital of the world," international hub of industry and shipping, is the largest city in Delaware. The Swedish, Dutch, and British have all left their mark on the city. The first settlement was made by Swedes seeking their fortunes; they founded the colony of New Sweden. In 1655, the little colony was taken without bloodshed by Dutch soldiers under Peter Stuyvesant, governor of New Amsterdam. Nine years later the English became entrenched in the town, which grew, under the influence of wealthy Quakers, as a market and shipping center. Abundant water power in creeks of the Brandywine River Valley plus accessibility to other eastern ports stimulated early industrial growth. When Eleuthère du Pont built his powder mill on Brandywine Creek in 1802, the valley had already known a century of industry. From here come vulcanized fiber, glazed leathers, dyed cotton, rubber hose, autos, and many other products.

What to See and Do

Amtrak Station. Victorian railroad station, which continues to function as such, designed by master architect Frank Furness. Restored. (Daily) Martin Luther King Blvd and French St.

Banning Park. Fishing; tennis; playing fields, picnicking, pavilions. (Daily) 2 mi S on DE 4. Middleboro Rd and Maryland Ave. Phone 302/323-6422. **FREE**

Bellevue State Park. Fishing; nature, fitness, and horseback riding trails, bicycling, tennis, game courts, picnicking (pavilions). Standard hrs, fees. 4 mi NE via I-95, Marsh Rd exit. Phone 302/577-3390.

Brandywine Creek State Park. A 1,000-acre day-use park. Fishing; nature and fitness trails; x-country skiing. Picnicking. Nature center. Standard hrs, fees. 4 mi N on DE 100. Phone 302/577-3534. Per vehicle ¢¢

Brandywine Springs Park. Site of a once-famous resort hotel (1827-1845) for Southern planters and politicos. Here, Lafayette met Washington under the Council Oak before the Battle of Brandywine in 1777. Picnicking, fireplaces, pavilions, baseball fields. Pets on leash only. (Daily) 4 mi W on DE 41, 3300 Faulkland Rd. Phone 302/395-5652. **FREE**

Brandywine Zoo and Park. Designed by Frederick Law Olmsted, the park incl Josephine Garden with fountain and roses; stands of Japanese cherry trees. The zoo, along North Park Dr, features animals from North and South America (daily). Picnicking, playgrounds. On both sides of Brandywine River, from Augustine to Market St bridges. Phone 302/571-7747. ¢¢

Delaware Art Museum. Expanded facility features Howard Pyle Collection of American illustrations with works by Pyle, N. C. Wyeth, and Maxfield Parrish; American painting collection, with works by West, Homer, Church, Glackens, and Hopper; Bancroft Collection of English Pre-Raphaelite art, with works by Rossetti and Burne-Jones; and Phelps Collection of Andrew Wyeth works;

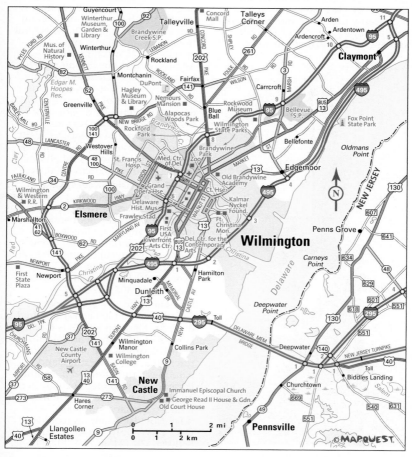

also changing exhibits, children's participatory gallery; store. (Tues-Sun; closed hols) Guided tours by appt. 2301 Kentmere Pkwy. Phone 302/571-9590. ¢¢¢

Delaware History Museum. Changing exhibits on history and decorative arts. (Tues-Sat; closed hols) 504 Market St. Phone 302/656-0637. ¢¢

Delaware Museum of Natural History. Exhibits of shells, birds, mammals; also largest bird egg and a 500-pound clam. (Daily; closed hols) 5 mi NW on DE 52 in Greenville. Phone 302/658-9111. ¢¢

Fort Christina Monument. Monument marks location where Swedes settled in 1638. Presented in 1938 to Wilmington by the people of Sweden, monument consists of black granite plinth surmounted by pioneers' flagship, the *Kalmar Nyckel*, sculpted by Carl Milles. Complex incl nearby log cabin, moved to this location as a reminder of Finnish and Swedish contributions to our nation. Foot of E 7th St. Phone 302/652-5629.

Fort Delaware State Park. (see) Approx 15 mi S on Pea Patch Island, opp Delaware City.

Grand Opera House. (1871) Historic landmark built by Masons, this restored Victorian theater now serves as Delaware's Center for the Performing Arts, home of Opera Delaware (Nov-May) and Delaware Symphony (Sept-May). Facade is fine example of style of the Second Empire interpreted in cast iron. 818 Market St Mall. Phone 302/658-7898.

Hagley Museum. Old riverside stone mill buildings, one-rm schoolhouse, and millwright shop highlight 19th-century explosive manufacturing and community life; 240-acre historic site of E. I. du Pont's original black powder mills, incl exhibit building with working models and dioramas, operating waterwheel, stationary steam engine, and a fully-operable 1875 machine shop. Admission incl bus ride along river for tour of 1803 Eleutherian Mills, residence with antiques reflecting five generations of du Ponts, a 19th-century garden, and a barn with a collection of antique wagons. Museum store. (Mid-Mar-Dec, daily; rest of yr, Sat and Sun, limited hrs Mon-Fri; closed hols) 3 mi NW off DE 141. Phone 302/658-2400. ¢¢¢

Holy Trinity (Old Swedes) Church and Hendrickson House. Founded by Swedish settlers in 1698, the church stands as originally built and still has regular services. The house, a Swedish farmhouse built in 1690, is now a museum containing 17th- and 18th-century artifacts. (Mon-Sat; closed hols) 606 Church St. Donation. Phone 302/652-5629.

Nemours Mansion and Gardens. Country estate (300 acres) of Alfred I. du Pont. Mansion (1910) is modified Louis XVI, by Carrère and Hastings, with 102 rms of rare antique furniture, Asian rugs, tapestries, and paintings dating from 12th century. Formal French gardens extend ⅓ of a mi along main vista from house with terraces, statuary, and pools. Tours (May-Nov, Tues-Sun; res required) Over 16 yrs only. Rockland Rd between DE 141 and US 202. Phone 302/651-6912. ¢¢¢

Kalmar Nyckel at Fort Christina monument, Wilmington

WILMINGTON'S PUBLIC ART

The Brandywine Valley, just outside Wilmington, is noted for its magnificent museums and gardens. What is often overlooked is the wealth of outdoor statuary in public squares and office courtyards in the historic heart of the old city. Much of it is representational, but there are abstract pieces and a whimsical work or two. Indeed, a picture book describing the collection has been published for several years. On a one-hour, one-mile walk through the city's commercial center, you can almost imagine you are in a sculpture garden. Begin at Rodney Square outside the elegant Hotel du Pont at 11th and Market streets. Dominating the view is the famous 1923 statue of Caesar Rodney, which shows him astride his horse galloping toward Philadelphia, about 30 miles north, to cast the deciding vote for the Declaration of Independence in 1776. A city hallmark, the Rodney is one of the world's rare equestrian sculptures of a horse in full gallop, its two front legs in the air and the weight of the statue resting on the two rear hooves. The challenge of balancing the statue was solved in part by weighting the horse's tail. Head north on Market Street to 13th Street and two blocks west (left) to Orange Street to the Brandywine Gateway, where you'll see the intriguing kinetic fountain at the foot of the Hercules Building (facing 13th Street) in Hercules Plaza. Three solid granite balls rest on three marble pillars in the middle of a large pool. The spheres are arranged so that water flowing over them suggests they are rotating. Retrace your path to 8th and Market and then turn east (left) to Spencer and Freedom plazas between French and Market streets. In Spencer Plaza, Father and Son, a larger-than-life bronze statue, touchingly depicts a black man with a child in his arms. It is the work of Charles Parks, a local artist. A plaque notes that this was the one-time site of the Mother African Union Methodist Protestant Church, the first black church in America wholly controlled by descendants of Africans. Just across French Street in Freedom Plaza, in the shadow of a cluster of modern municipal buildings, is an arresting statue, The Holocaust. Both abstract and realistic, it shows the tortured bodies of the victims pressed against three unyielding pillars, a symbol of the force of destruction. On a more positive note, end your tour at the plaque honoring abolitionists Harriet Tubman and Thomas Garrett and the Underground Railway, the road north to freedom for Southern slaves before the Civil War.

Rockwood Museum. A 19th-century Gothic Revival estate with gardens in English Romantic style. On grounds are manor house, conservatory, porter's lodge, and other outbuildings. Museum furnished with English, European, and American decorative arts of the 17th-19th centuries. Guided tours (Mar-Dec, Tues-Sun; Jan and Feb, Tues-Sat). (See SPECIAL EVENTS) 610 Shipley Rd. Phone 302/761-4340. ¢¢

Willingtown Square. Historic square surrounded by four 18th-century houses moved to this location between 1973-1976. Serves as office and conference space. 500 blk Market St Mall. Phone 302/655-7161.

Wilmington & Western Railroad. Round-trip steam-train ride (9 mi) to and from Mt Cuba picnic grove. (May-Oct, Sun; rest of yr, schedule varies) 4 mi SW, near jct DE 2 and DE 41 at Greenbank Station. Phone 302/998-1930. ¢¢

Winterthur Museum, Garden, and Library. Museum houses decorative arts representing period from 1640-1860; collection of over 89,000 objects is displayed in two buildings. First-floor exhibition in the Galleries introduces 200 yrs of American antiques. The Period Rooms (seen on guided tours) were arranged by Henry Francis du Pont in his nine-story country house. Museum is surrounded by 60 acres of naturally landscaped garden, also arranged by du Pont, on a 980-acre estate. The Galleries at Winterthur offer self-guided tours. (Daily; closed hols) Admission varies with tour. 6 mi NW on DE 52. Phone 302/888-4600 or 800/448-3883.

Special Events

**Horse racing.
Delaware Park.**
Thoroughbred racing.
7 mi S on I-95 exit 4B.
Phone 302/994-2521.
Late-Apr-mid-Nov.

**Wilmington Garden
Day.** Tour of famous
gardens and houses.
Phone 302/428-6172.
First Sat May.

**Winterthur Point-to-
Point Races.** Phone
302/888-4600. May.

**Victorian Ice Cream
Festival.** Rockwood
Museum. Victorian
festival featuring high-
wheeled bicycles,
hot-air balloons, mari-
onettes, old-fashioned
medicine show, baby
parade, crafts; home-
made ice cream.
Phone 302/761-4340.
Mid-July.

Winterthur Museum, Wilmington

Harvest Moon Festival.
3 mi NW via US 41, at
Ashland Nature Center in Hockessin.
Cider-pressing demonstrations, hay
rides, nature walks, farm animals, arts
and crafts, musical entertainment,
pony rides, games. Phone 302/239-
2334. First wkend Oct.

Motels/Motor Lodges

★ ★ **BEST WESTERN BRANDY-
WINE VALLEY INN.** *1807 Concord
Pike (19803). 302/656-9436; fax
302/656-8564; toll-free 800/537-7772.
www.bestwestern.com.* 95 rms, 2 story,
12 kit. suites. S $77; D $97; each addl
$5; kit. suites $110; under 18 free.
Crib $5. Pet accepted. TV; cable (pre-
mium), VCR avail. Pool; wading
pool, whirlpool, lifeguard. Complimentary coffee in rms. Restaurant
adj 7 am-11 pm. Ck-out noon. Meeting rms. Business servs avail. In-rm
modem link. Bellhops. Valet serv.
Sundries. Gift shop. Exercise equipt.
Microwaves avail. Cr cds: A, C, D,
DS, MC, V.

★ ★ **COURTYARD BY MARRIOTT.**
*1102 West St (19801). 302/429-7600;
fax 302/429-9167; res 800/321-2211.
www.courtyard.com.* 126 rms, 10 story.
S $139-$170; D $149-$180; each addl

$10; wkend rates. Crib free. Garage
$8.50; free Fri, Sat. TV; cable (pre-
mium). Coffee in rms. Ck-out noon.
Guest lndry. Business servs avail. In-
rm modem link. Airport, RR station,
bus depot transportation. Exercise
equipt. Health club privileges. Refrigerators, wet bar; some in-rm
whirlpools; microwaves avail. Cr cds:
A, C, D, DS, JCB, MC, V.

★ ★ **HOLIDAY INN NORTH.** *4000
Concord Pike (19803). 302/478-2222;
fax 302/479-0850; toll-free 800/465-
4329. www.holiday-inn.com.* 138 rms,
2 story. S, D $99; each addl $6; under
18 free; wkend rates. Crib free. TV;
cable (premium). Pool; lifeguard. Coffee in rms. Restaurant 7 am-10 pm.
Bar 4 pm-midnight. Ck-out noon.
Coin lndry. Meeting rms. Business
servs avail. In-rm modem link. Bellhops. Sundries. Health club privileges. Cr cds: A, C, D, DS, JCB, MC, V.

Hotels

★ ★ **BRANDYWINE SUITES
HOTEL.** *707 N King St (19801).
302/656-9300; fax 302/656-2459; toll-
free 800/756-0070.* 49 suites, 4 story.

S, D $109-$225; under 12 free; wkend rates. Crib free. Parking $7.50. TV; cable (premium), VCR avail (movies). Complimentary continental bkfst, coffee in rms. Restaurant 6:30-8:30 am, 11:30 am-2 pm, 5-10 pm; Sat, Sun 8-10 am, 5-10 pm. Bar 2-10 pm. Ck-out noon. Meeting rms. Business servs avail. In-rm modem link. Free airport, RR station, bus depot transportation. Bathrm phones; microwaves avail. Modern decor with European accents; atrium. Cr cds: A, C, D, MC, V.

★ ★ **DOUBLETREE HOTEL.** *4727 Concord Pike (19803). 302/478-6000; fax 302/477-1492; res 888/478-2923. www.doubletreehotels.com.* 154 rms, 7 story. S, D $129-$189; each addl $10; suites $189-$229; under 18 free. Crib $10. TV; cable (premium), VCR avail (movies). Pool. Restaurant 6:30 am-10 pm. Bar 5-11 pm. Ck-out noon. Meeting rms. Business servs avail. In-rm modem link. Exercise equipt. Health club privileges. Some refrigerators. Cr cds: A, C, D, DS, ER, JCB, MC, V.

★ ★ **HOLIDAY INN SELECT.** *630 Naamans Rd, Claymont (19703). 302/792-2700; fax 302/798-6182. www.holiday-inn.com.* 193 rms, 7 story. S, D $99-$136; each addl $15; suites $150-$275; under 12 free; wkend rates. Pet accepted; $60. TV; cable (premium). Pool. Playground. Coffee in rms. Restaurant 6:30 am-2 pm, 4:30-11 pm. Bar 3:30 pm-1 am. Ck-out noon. Meeting rms. Business servs avail. In-rm modem link. Valet serv. Free airport transportation. Exercise equipt. Some refrigerators; microwaves avail. Cr cds: A, C, D, DS, MC, V.

★ ★ ★ ★ **THE HOTEL DUPONT.** *11th and Market sts (19801). 302/594-3100; fax 302/594-3108; toll-free 800/441-9019. www.dupont.com.* Upon entering this ornate historic property, guests will feel the thrill of a forgotten era. Finished in 1913 by French and Italian craftsmen, the grand lobby boasts 40-foot carved ceilings, gilt detailing, and turn-of-the-century elegance. Rooms are spacious with conservative, tasteful decor and notably large bathrooms, and the staff is helpful and personable. Suites have fireplaces and polished-brass beds. 217 rms, 10 story. S, D $149-$269; suites $395-$495; under 12 free; wkend rates, special packages. Crib free. Valet parking $14, self $10. TV; cable (premium); VCR avail. Restaurants (see BRANDYWINE ROOM and GREEN ROOM). Rm serv 24 hrs. Bar; entertainment. Ck-out noon. Meeting rms. Business center. In-rm modem link. Concierge. Bellhops. Shopping arcade. Barber, beauty shop. Valet serv. Airport transportation. Exercise rm; sauna. Massage. Minibars; refrigerators; microwaves avail. Cr cds: A, C, D, DS, ER, JCB, MC, V.

★ ★ ★ **SHERATON SUITES.** *422 Delaware Ave (19801). 302/654-8300; fax 302/654-6036. www.sheraton.com.* 228 suites, 16 story. S, D $175-$195; each addl $15; under 18 free; wkend rates. Crib free. Garage $9; Fri, Sat free. TV; cable (premium), VCR avail. Indoor pool. Complimentary coffee in rms. Restaurant 6:30-10 am, 11:30 am-10:30 pm; Sun 7 am-10:30 pm. Bar. Ck-out noon. Coin lndry. Meeting rms. Business center. In-rm modem link. Gift shop. Airport transportation. Exercise equipt; sauna. Health club privileges. Refrigerators; microwaves avail. Cr cds: A, C, D, DS, MC, V.

★ ★ ★ **WYNDHAM WILMINGTON.** *700 King St (33140). 302/655-0400. www.wyndham.com.* 219 rms, 9 story. S, D $195-$250; under 17 free. Crib avail. TV; cable (premium). Pool; whirlpool. Restaurant 6:30 am-10 pm. Bar to midnight. Ck-out noon, ck-in 3 pm. Meeting rms. Business center. In-rm modem link. Concierge. Exercise equipt. Minibars; many refrigerators in suites.

B&Bs/Small Inns

★ ★ ★ **THE BOULEVARD BED AND BREAKFAST.** *1909 Baynard Blvd (19802). 302/656-9700; fax 302/656-9701.* 6 rms, 2 share bath, 3 story. S $65-$80; D $70-$85; each addl $10-$15; hol wkends (2-day min). TV; cable (premium), VCR (free movies).

Complimentary full bkfst. Ck-out 11 am, ck-in 2 pm. Business servs avail. In-rm modem link. Brick house built 1913. Antiques. Cr cds: A, MC, V.
⛄ 🐾

★ ★ ★ **DARLEY MANOR INN BED AND BREAKFAST.** *3701 Philadelphia Pike, Claymont (19703). 302/792-2127; fax 302/798-6143; toll-free 800/824-4703. www.dca.net/darley.* 6 rms, 3 story. No elvtr. S, D $95-$109; each addl $10; suites $99-$119. Children over 9 yrs only. TV; cable, VCR. Whirlpool. Complimentary full bkfst. Restaurant nearby. Ck-out noon, ck-in 4 pm. Business servs avail. Exercise equipt. Totally nonsmoking. Cr cds: A, C, D, DS, MC, V.
🛌 ⛄ 🐾

★ ★ ★ ★ **INN AT MONTCHANIN VILLAGE.** *Rte 100 and Kirk Rd, Montchanin (19710). 302/888-2133; fax 302/888-0389; toll-free 800/269-2473. www.montchanin.com.* Nestled in the Brandywine Valley in an old crossroads settlement, this restored 19th-century landmark is on the National Register of Historic Places. Eleven buildings comprise the historic village, housing 27 rooms and suites, many with private, professionally landscaped courtyards and gas fireplaces. Guests will find unique fine dining in a lighthearted atmosphere at Krazy Kat's restaurant. 27 rms, 1-3 story. S, D $150-$180; suites $275-$375; package plans; wkends, hols (2-day min). Crib free. TV; cable, VCR avail. Restaurant (see KRAZY KAT'S). Rm serv Sun-Thurs. Coffee in rms. Ck-out 11 am, ck-in 3 pm. In-rm modem link. Valet serv. Concierge serv. Lighted tennis privileges. Golf privileges, greens fee $65-$99. Health club privileges. Refrigerators, microwaves, wet bars. Some fireplaces, balconies. Totally nonsmoking. Cr cds: A, C, D, MC, V, DS.
🛌 📷 ⛄ 🐾

Restaurants

★ ★ ★ **BACK BURNER.** *425 Hockessin Corner, Hockessin (19707). 302/239-2314. www.backburner.com.* Hrs: 11:15 am-2:15 pm, 5-9 pm; Fri, Sat 11:15 am-2:15 pm, 5:30-9:45 pm. Closed Sun; hols; also wk before Labor Day. Res required. Bar. Wine cellar. Lunch $6-$12, dinner $13-$25. Specialties: black Angus beef,

soft shell crabs, rack of lamb. Elegeant dining in country atmosphere; renovated barn with arched walls, display kitchen. Cr cds: A, C, D, DS, ER, MC, V.
🄳

★ ★ ★ **BISTRO 1717.** *1717 Delaware Ave (19806). 302/777-0464.* Specializes in pan-seared filet mignon, pan-seared scallops with angel hair pasta. Hrs: 11:30 am-10 pm. Closed Sun. Res accepted. Wine list. Lunch, dinner $5.50-$21. Entertainment: guitarist Mon-Thurs. Small French bistro. Cr cds: A, MC, V.
🄳 🄳

★ ★ ★ **BLACK TRUMPET .** *1828 W 11th (19806). 302/777-0454.* Hrs: 11:30 am-2 pm, 5:30-10 pm; Sat from 5:30 pm. Closed Sun; Memorial Day, Dec 25. Res required. French menu. Bar. Wine cellar. A la carte entrees: lunch $6-$12, dinner $15-$24. Specialties: exotic wild mushrooms, grilled chicken breast with potato risotto. Own pastries, ice cream. Intimate atmosphere; original artwork adorns walls. Totally nonsmoking. Cr cds: A, MC, V.

★ ★ **BRANDYWINE ROOM.** *11th and Market sts (19801). 302/594-3156. www.hoteldupont.com.* Hrs: 6-11 pm; Sun 5-10 pm. Closed Fri, Sat. Res accepted. Bar. $18-$32. Specializes in steak, rack of lamb, seafood. Club atmosphere; Wyeth paintings. Cr cds: A, C, D, DS, MC, V, ER, JCB.
🄳

★ ★ ★ **COLUMBUS INN.** *2216 Pennsylvania Ave (19806). 302/571-1492. www.columbusinn.com.* Hrs: 11 am-11 pm; Fri, Sat to midnight. Closed Memorial Day, Labor Day, Dec 25. Res accepted. Continental menu. Bar. Wine cellar. A la carte entrees: lunch $5.95-$11.95, dinner $12-$22. Child's menu. Specializes in fresh seafood, beef. Entertainment Fri, Sat. Valet parking. Early American decor in 200-yr-old house. Fireplaces. Outdoor dining. Family-owned since 1957. Cr cds: A, C, D, DS, ER, MC, V.
🄳 🄳

★ ★ ★ **GREEN ROOM.** *11th and Market sts (19801). 302/594-3154. www.hoteldupont.com.* Hrs: 6:30 am-2 pm; Fri, Sat 7 am-2 pm, 6-10 pm; Sun brunch 10 am-2 pm. Res accepted; required Sun brunch. Continental menu. Bar. Wine list. Bkfst $6.95-$14. A la carte entrees: lunch $10-$20, dinner $25-$35. Sun brunch $32. Child's menu. Specializes in lobster, rack of lamb, filet mignon. Harpist Fri, Sat. Valet parking. Elegant dining rm in historic hotel; gold leaf ceiling, oak paneled. Cr cds: A, D, DS, ER, JCB, MC, V.

D

★ ★ ★ **HARRY'S SAVOY GRILL.** *2020 Naaman's Rd (19810). 302/475-3000. www.harrys-savoy. com.* Hrs: 11 am-10:30 pm; Fri to 11:30 pm; Sat 4:30-11:30 pm; Sun 4-10:30 pm; Sun brunch 10:30 am-3 pm; early-bird dinner Mon-Fri to 6 pm. Closed Dec 25. Res accepted. Bar to 1 am. Wine cellar. A la carte entrees: lunch $6.95-$14.95, dinner $11.95-$20.95. Sun brunch $7.95-$14.95. Child's menu. Specializes in prime rib, fresh seafood. Musicians Fri, Sat; magicians perform at tables Tues eves. Parking. Outdoor dining. Fireplaces. Cr cds: A, D, DS, MC, V.

D

★ **INDIA PALACE.** *101 N Maryland Ave (19804). 302/655-8772.* Hrs: 11:30 am-2:30 pm, 5-10 pm; Fri, Sat to 10:30 pm. Closed Mon. Res accepted. Indian menu. Wine, beer. Lunch $5.95, dinner $6.95-$15.95. Specializes in vegetarian and tandoori meals. Native American art. Cooking observed behind glass wall. Cr cds: A, D, DS, MC, V.

D

★ ★ **J G COOK'S RIVERVIEW INN.** *60 Main St, Pennsville (08070). 856/678-3700. www.riverviewinn.net.* Hrs: 11:30 am-10 pm; Sat to 11 pm. Closed Mon, Sun; also Dec 25. Res accepted. Bar. A la carte entrees: lunch $6.95-$10.95, dinner $14.95-$22.95. Buffet: lunch $8.95. Child's

Hagley Museum on the Brandywine River, Wilmington

menu. Specialties: chicken St. Michael, seafood plank. Parking. Outdoor dining. Cr cds: A, D, DS, MC, V.

★ **KID SHELLEENS.** *1801 W 14th St (19806). 302/658-4600. www.welcome 1492.com.* Hrs: 11 am-midnight; Sun brunch 10 am-2 pm. Closed Thanksgiving, Dec 25. Bar. A la carte entrees: lunch $4.95-$8.95, dinner $7.95-$13.95. Child's menu. Specializes in grilled dishes, fresh seafood. Parking. Outdoor dining. Casual atmosphere. Cr cds: A, DS, MC, V.

D

★ ★ ★ **KRAZY KAT'S.** *Rte 100 and Kirk Rd, Montchanin (19710). 302/888-2133. www.montchanin.com.* Housed in a historically recognized 19th-century blacksmith's shop neighboring the Inn at Montchanin Village, this unique fine dining establishment has a lighthearted atmosphere with a wacky animal-themed decor. However, Executive chef Todd Snyder creates a menu which is far from comic-strip fare. Todd specializes in

French-Asian cuisine. Specialties: wild boar satay, duck breast and crispy leg of confit, seared tuna with daily variety of fresh sushi. Hrs: 7-9 am, 11 am-2 pm, 5:30-10 pm; Sat, Sun 8-11 am, 5:30-10 pm. Res accepted. Wine cellar. Lunch $10-$14, dinner $22-$30. Complete meal: bkfst $3-$15. Totally nonsmoking. Cr cds: A, D, DS, MC, V.
D

★ ★ ★ **PICCOLO MONDO.** *3604 Silverside Rd (19810). 302/478-9028.* Hrs: 11:30 am-2 pm, 5-10 pm; Sat from 5 pm. Closed Sun; hols. Res accepted. Italian menu. Bar. Wine list. A la carte entrees: lunch $6-$9, dinner $10-$18. Specialties: risotto primavera, grilled shrimp on rosemary branch, cannelloni con frutti di mare. Own pastries. Italian decor with open hearth kitchen; wine bottles displayed. Cr cds: A, C, D, DS, ER, MC, V.
D ⊒

★ ★ ★ **POSITANO.** *2401 Pennsylvania Ave (19806). 302/656-6788.* Hrs: 11:30 am-2 pm, 5:30-10 pm. Closed Sun; hols. Res required. Italian, French menu. Wine list. Lunch $8.50-$12.50, dinner $21.75-$32.50. Specializes in veal, fresh seafood. Parking. Elegant and intimate dining. Jacket. Totally nonsmoking. Cr cds: A, D, DS, MC, V.
D

★ ★ ★ **RESTAURANT 821.** *821 Market St (19801). 302/652-8821. www. restaurant821.com.* Specializes in braised short ribs, iron skillet monk fish. Hrs: 11:30 am-10 pm; Fri to 10:30 pm; Sat 5-11 pm. Closed Sun. Res accepted. Wine, beer. Lunch $9-$16; dinner $20-$32. Entertainment. Cr cds: A, C, D, DS, MC, V.
D

★ ★ ★ **SILK PURSE & SOW'S EAR.** *1307 N Scott St (19806). 302/654-7666.* Hrs: 5:30-9:30 pm. Closed Sun, Mon; hols. Res accepted. Eclectic menu. Wine list. A la carte entrees: dinner $13.50-$18.50. Specializes in fresh seasonal ingredients, game, fish. Own baking. In converted town house. Cr cds: A, MC, V.
SC

★ ★ ★ **TAVOLA TOSCANA.** *1412 N DuPont St (19806). 302/654-8001.* Hrs: 11:30 am-2 pm, 5:30-10 pm;

Sun 5:30-9:30 pm. Closed hols. Res accepted; required wkends. Italian menu. Bar. Wine list. A la carte entrees: lunch $10-$15, dinner $18-$24. Specializes in hand-rolled pasta, shared specialty appetizers. Parking. Atmosphere of European bistro. Cr cds: A, D, DS, MC, V.
D ⊒

★ ★ ★ **VINCENTE'S.** *1601 Concord Pike (19803). 302/652-5142.* Hrs: 11 am-10 pm; Sat from 4 pm. Closed Sun; hols. Res accepted. Italian menu. Bar. Extensive wine list. Lunch $6.50-$12.50, dinner $16.95-$28.95. Child's menu. Specializes in veal, steak, seafood. Own pasta, desserts. Contemporary decor; Caesar salad made tableside. Cr cds: A, C, D, DS, ER, MC, V.
D ⊒

★ ★ **WATERWORKS CAFE.** *16th and French Sts (19899). 302/652-6022. www.waterworks-cafe.com.* Hrs: 11:30 am-2:30 pm, 5:30-10 pm; Sat from 5:30 pm. Closed Sun, Mon; hols. Res accepted. Bar to midnight. A la carte entrees: lunch $5.95-$14.95, dinner $13.95-$26.95. Specializes in fresh seafood. Parking. Outdoor dining. Old waterworks on Brandywine River. Cr cds: DS, MC, V.
D ⊒

DISTRICT OF COLUMBIA

Washington

Area code 202

Population: 519,000
Area: 63 square miles
Elevation: 1-410 feet
Peak: Tenleytown
Entered Union: Founded 1790
Flower: American Beauty Rose
Bird: Wood Thrush
Time Zone: Eastern
Website: www.washington.org

Designed by Major Pierre Charles L'Enfant in about 1791, Washington was the first American city ever planned for a specific purpose. It is a beautiful city, with wide, tree-lined streets laid out according to a design that is breathtaking in its scope and imagination. For its purpose the broad plan still works well even though L'Enfant could not have foreseen the automobile or the fact that the United States would come to have a population of more than 250 million people. Nevertheless, L'Enfant's concept was ambitious, allowing for vast growth. Washington, named for the first US president, has been the nation's capital since 1800. The city's business is centered around government and tourism; there is little heavy industry.

Independence Day in Washington D.C.

The District of Columbia and Washington are one and the same. Originally the District was a ten-mile square crossing the Potomac River into Virginia, but the Virginia portion (31 square miles) was turned back to the state in 1846. Residences of workers spill into Virginia and Maryland, as do government offices. In 1800, there were 130 federal employees; at the end of the Civil War there were 7,000; now there are well over 500,000. Although the city was a prime Confederate target in the Civil War, it was barely damaged. The assassination of Abraham Lincoln, however, struck a blow to the nation and drove home to Americans the fact that Washington was not merely a center of government. What happened here affected everyone.

This is a cosmopolitan city. Perhaps no city on earth has a populace with so many different origins. Representatives from all nations and men and women from every state work here—and vote in their home states by absentee ballot. It is a dignified, distinguished capital. Many who visit the city go first to the House of Representatives or Senate office buildings and chat with their representatives, who receive constituent visitors when they can. At these offices visitors obtain tickets to the Senate and House galleries. From the top of the Washington Monument there is a magnificent view of the capital. The Lincoln and Jefferson memorials cannot fail to capture the imagination.

When to Go/Climate

D.C. winters are relatively mild, while summers are hot and humid. The city is alive with color in spring and fall—cherry blossoms bloom in April and May and vibrant fall foliage begins around September.

AVERAGE HIGH/LOW TEMPERATURES (°F)

WASHINGTON NATIONAL AIRPORT

Jan 42/27	**May** 76/57	**Sept** 80/63
Feb 46/29	**June** 85/67	**Oct** 69/50
Mar 57/38	**July** 89/71	**Nov** 58/41
Apr 67/46	**Aug** 87/70	**Dec** 47/32

Visitor Information

Washington D.C. Convention and Visitors Association, 1212 New York Ave NW, Suite 600, Washington, D.C. 20005, has brochures and schedules of events. Phone 202/789-7000 (Monday-Friday, 9 am-5 pm).

The National Park Service maintains information kiosks at several key points in the city as well as a White House Visitor Center at 1450 Pennsylvania Ave NW, which distributes free tickets to tour the White House.

Note: By writing to your representative or senator ahead of time, tickets can be obtained for two Congressional Tours: a guided White House tour that differs slightly from the normal tour and begins at 8:15, 8:30, or 8:45 am (Tuesday-Saturday; specific times are assigned); or passes to the House and Senate visitors' galleries to watch Congressional sessions in progress. Without this ticket, the chambers can only be viewed when Congress is not in session.

Write your senator at the United States Senate, Washington, D.C. 20510. Address your representative at the United States House of Representatives, Washington, D.C. 20515. All tickets are free, but in peak season, which starts in spring, White House tickets may be limited. In the letter include the dates you will be in Washington, first- and second-choice dates for the tours, and the number of people in your party. Also include your home phone number, should your representative's or senator's aide need to contact you. You can also get tickets, if available, directly from the office of your senator or representative after you arrive in Washington.

For additional attractions and accommodations, see ARLINGTON COUNTY (RONALD REAGAN WASHINGTON-NATIONAL AIRPORT AREA) and DULLES

INTERNATIONAL AIRPORT AREA in Virginia. Also see BALTIMORE/WASHINGTON INTERNATIONAL AIRPORT AREA in Maryland.

The following suburbs and towns in the Washington, D.C., area are included in the *Mobil Travel Guide*. For information on any one of them, see the individual alphabetical listing. In Virginia: Alexandria, Arlington County (Ronald Reagan Washington-National Airport Area), Fairfax, Falls Church, McLean, Springfield, Tyson's Corner. In Maryland: Bethesda, Bowie, College Park, Laurel, Rockville, Silver Spring.

Driving in Washington

Since the city is divided into four quarters, or quadrants, emanating from the Capitol, driving may be confusing for the first-time visitor. The quadrants are northeast (NE), northwest (NW), southeast (SE), and southwest (SW). All Washington addresses have these designations listed after the street name. It is advisable to obtain a city map before attempting to drive through the city, especially during rush hours.

Safety belts are mandatory for all persons in front seat of vehicle. All children under 3 yrs must be in an approved safety seat anywhere in vehicle. Children 3-16 yrs must be properly restrained in either a safety belt or child safety seat anywhere in the vehicle. For further information phone 202/939-8018.

What to See and Do

African American Civil War Memorial. Sculpture pays tribute to the more than 200,000 African American soldiers who fought in the Civil War. 1200 U St NW. Phone 202/667-2667. **FREE**

American Red Cross. National headquarters includes three buildings bounded by 17th, 18th, D, and E sts NW. The 17th St building includes marble busts, *Faith, Hope,* and *Charity,* by sculptor Hiram Powers, and three original Tiffany stained-glass windows. (Mon-Fri) 430 17th St NW. Phone 202/737-8300. **FREE**

Anacostia Museum, Smithsonian Institution. An exhibition and research center for black heritage in the historic Anacostia section of southeast Washington. Changing exhibits. (Daily; closed Dec 25) 1901 Fort Place SE. Phone 202/357-2700. **FREE**

Art Museum of the Americas, OAS. Dedicated to Latin American and Caribbean contemporary art; paintings, graphics, sculpture. (Tues-Sun; closed hols) 201 18th St NW. Phone 202/458-6016. **FREE**

Basilica of the National Shrine of the Immaculate Conception. Largest Roman Catholic church in US and one of the largest in the world. Byzantine and Romanesque architecture; extensive and elaborate collection of mosaics and artwork. (Daily) Carillon concerts (Sun afternoons); organ recitals (June-Aug, Sun eves). Guided tours (daily). 400 Michigan Ave, NE. Phone 202/526-8300. **FREE**

Black History Recreation Trail. Trail through Washington neighborhoods highlights important sites in African American history. Phone 202/619-7222.

Blair House. (1824) Guest house for heads of government and state who are visiting the US as guests of the president. Not open to public. 1651 Pennsylvania Ave NW.

B'nai B'rith Klutznick Museum. Permanent exhibition of Jewish ceremonial and folk art. Changing exhibits. (Mon-Fri, Sun; closed hols, Jewish hols) B'nai B'rith International Center, 1640 Rhode Island Ave NW. Phone 202/857-6583. **FREE**

Bureau of Engraving and Printing. Headquarters for making US paper money; guided tours (every ten min). (Mon-Fri; closed hols and Dec 24-Jan 3) 14th and C sts SW, S of Mall; enter on 14th St. Phone 202/874-3019. **FREE**

Capital Children's Museum. Hands-on museum where children of all ages can explore exhibits on computers, human development, and Mexican culture. (Daily; closed hols) 800 3rd St NE. Phone 202/675-4120. ¢¢¢

★ **The Capitol.** The Capitol is the meeting place of Congress—the legislative branch of the government—as well as a symbol of the US government. George Washington laid the cornerstone in 1793, and

The Capitol at night

Chesapeake Canal boat rides

part of the originally planned building opened in 1800. Construction continued on and off over a number of yrs (including rebuilding after the British burned the Capitol in 1814) until the original building, which was crowned with a low copper-covered dome, was completed in 1826. Expansion in the 1850s and 1860s includes the new wings, today's House and Senate chambers, and the cast-iron dome seen today, which was completed during the Civil War. The Rotunda, in the center, is the main ceremonial room of the Capitol where dignitaries have lain in-state. National Statuary Hall, just to the south, houses part of the state statue collection (each state can contribute two), but was originally built for the House as its chamber. (Tour every 30 min, Mon-Sat; closed Jan 1, Thanksgiving, Dec 25) Public dining room on first floor of Senate wing (Mon-Fri). Summer band concerts (see SPECIAL EVENTS). Between Constitution and Independence aves, at Pennsylvania Ave, east end of Mall. Phone 202/225-6827. **FREE**

Congress. Tickets to the House and Senate visitors' galleries can be obtained from the office of your representative or senator. Foreign visitors can obtain passes to the Senate Gallery from the appointment desk, first floor, Senate Wing; and to the House of Representatives Gallery from the check stand, third floor, House wing (identification required).

Old Senate Chamber. Original Senate chamber has been restored to its 1850s appearance. North of rotunda. Phone 202/225-6827.

West Front. Along the Capitol's west front are terraces, gardens, and lawns designed by Frederick Law Olmstead, who also planned New York City's Central Park. Halfway down the hill are the Peace Monument (on the north) and the Garfield Monument (on the south). At the foot of Capitol Hill is Union Sq with a reflecting pool and Grant Monument. Phone 202/225-6827.

Catholic University of America. (1887) 5,510 students. Open to all faiths. Performances at Hartke Theatre (yr-round). 620 Michigan Ave NE. Phone 202/319-5000.

Chesapeake and Ohio Canal Boat Rides. Narrated round-trip canal tours (1 hr) by park rangers in period clothing aboard mule-drawn boats. Ticket office adj. (Apr-Nov, Wed-Sun) Departs 1057 Thomas Jefferson St NW, between 30th and 31st sts. Phone 202/653-5190. ¢¢ (Also see CHESAPEAKE AND OHIO CANAL NATIONAL HISTORIC PARK in Maryland)

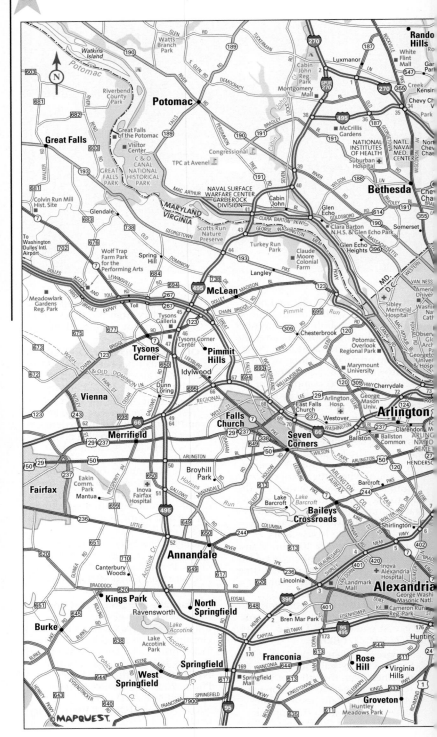

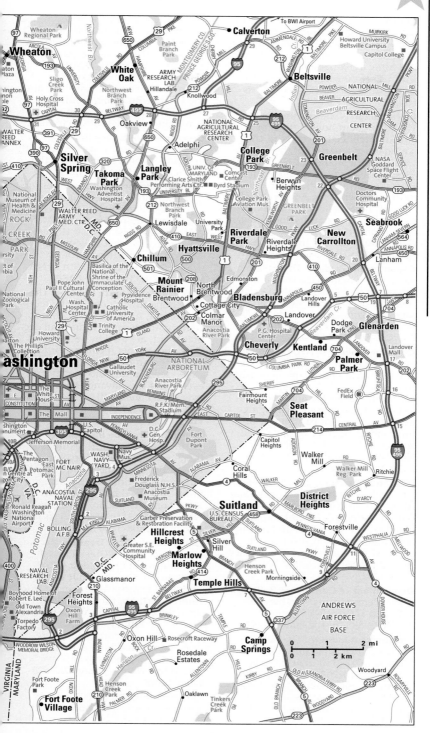

Chinatown. Recognizable by the Chinatown Friendship Archway at 7th and H sts. Archway is decorated in Chinese architectural styles of Qing and Ming dynasties and is topped with nearly 300 painted dragons. G and H sts, between 6th and 8th sts NW.

Clara Barton National Historic Site. Thirty-six-room house (1891) of unusual architecture was both the national headquarters of the Red Cross and the home of Clara Barton for the last 15 yrs of her life. Contents include many items belonging to the founder of the American Red Cross. Period costumes worn during some special programs. Guided tours only. (Daily; closed hols) 5801 Oxford Rd, 8 mi NW in Glen Echo, MD. Phone 301/492-6245. **FREE**

Constitution Gardens. This 50-acre park, with a man-made lake, is also the site of the Signers of the Declaration of Independence Memorial. Along Constitution Ave between 18th and 22nd sts NW. Phone 202/426-6841. **FREE**

Corcoran Gallery of Art. (1869) Oldest and largest private gallery in the city has world's most comprehensive collection of 18th-20th-century American art; Walker and Clark collections of European art; changing exhibitions (fee) of painting, sculpture, and photography. (Mon, Wed-Sun; closed hols) 17th St between New York Ave and E St NW. Phone 202/639-1700. **¢¢**

DAR Headquarters. Includes Memorial Continental Hall (1904) and Constitution Hall (1920); DAR Museum Gallery, located in administration building, has 33 state period rooms; outstanding genealogical research library (fee for nonmembers). Guided tours (Mon-Sat). 1776 D St NW. Phone 202/879-3241. **FREE**

Department of Commerce Building. (1932) Pennsylvania Ave, between 14th and 15th sts NW. Phone 202/482-4883. In the building is the

National Aquarium. The nation's oldest public aquarium was established in 1873. It now exhibits more than 1,700 specimens representing approx 260 species, both freshwater and saltwater. Touch tank; theater. Shark feeding (Mon, Wed, Sat); piranha feeding (Tues, Thurs, Sun). (Daily; closed Dec 25) Phone 202/482-2826. **¢¢**

Department of Energy. Pennsylvania Ave between 12th and 13th sts NW; **Interstate Commerce Commission** (1934), Constitution Ave between 12th and 13th sts NW; **Customs Department**, Constitution Ave between 13th and 14th sts NW; and the **District Building**, Pennsylvania Ave between 13th and 14th sts NW, Washington's ornate 1908 city hall.

Department of Justice Building. (1934) Pennsylvania Ave between 9th and 10th sts NW. (Not open to the public) Across Pennsylvania Ave is

FBI Headquarters. Tours of historical exhibits, includes FBI laboratory; very large firearm collection; demonstration of firearms. (Mon-Fri; closed hols) J. Edgar Hoover Building, 935 Pennsylvania Ave NW, between 9th and 10th sts NW; tour entrance on 9th St NW. Phone 202/324-3447. **FREE**

Department of State Building. The State Department's diplomatic reception rooms, furnished with 18th-century American furniture and decorative art, are used by Secretary of State and cabinet members for formal entertaining. Tours (Mon-Fri; closed federal hols and special events; 3-4 wks advance res; children over 12 yrs preferred). 21st, 22nd, C and D St NW. Phone 202/647-3241. **FREE**

Department of the Interior. (1938) Within is museum with exhibits and dioramas depicting history and activities of the department and its various bureaus. Photo ID required. (Mon-Fri; closed hols) Reference library open to public. 1849 C St NW, between 18th and 19th sts NW. Phone 202/208-3100. **FREE**

Department of the Treasury. According to legend, this Greek Revival building, one of the oldest (1836-1869) in the city, was built in the middle of Pennsylvania Ave because Andrew Jackson, tired of endless wrangling over the location, walked out of the White House, planted his cane in the mud, and said, "Here." The building has been extensively restored. 1500 Pennsylvania Ave NW, E of White House. Phone 202/622-0896. **FREE**

Dumbarton Oaks. (1800) Famous gardens (16 acres) are both formal and romantic in design. Mansion has antiques and European art, including

El Greco's *The Visitation;* galleries of Byzantine art; library of rare books on gardening and horticulture. Museum of pre-Columbian artifacts housed in structure by Philip Johnson. Garden (daily; closed hols); house and museum (Tues-Sun afternoons; closed hols). 1703 32nd St NW; garden entrance 31st and R sts. Phone 202/339-6401. ¢¢

Dupont-Kalorama Museum Walk. A joining of forces of seven museums to create an awareness of the area. Information and brochures are avail at any of the museums concerned. Participating museums are

Anderson House Museum. Museum of the Revolutionary War and national headquarters of the Society of the Cincinnati has portraits by early-American artists; 18th-century paintings; 17th-century tapestries; decorative arts of Europe and Asia; displays of books, medals, swords, silver, glass, and china. (Tues-Sat afternoons; closed hols). 2118 Massachusetts Ave NW. Phone 202/785-2040. **FREE**

Christian Heurich Mansion. (1892) Four-story, 31-room neo-Renaissance/late-Victorian mansion has elaborate furnishings and garden; houses the Historical Society of Washington, D.C., and the society's Library of Washington History; changing exhibits. House tours (Mon-Sat; closed hols). Library (Wed, Fri, Sat; closed hols). 800 Mt Vernon Place NW, City Museum. Phone 202/785-2068. ¢¢

Fondo del Sol. Dedicated to presenting, promoting, and preserving cultures of the Americas, the museum presents exhibitions of contemporary artists and crafters; holds special events; hosts traveling exhibits for museums and other institutions. (Tues-Sat afternoons; closed hols) 2112 R St NW. Phone 202/483-2777. ¢¢

Meridian International Center. Housed in two historic mansions designed by John Russell Pope; hosts international exhibits, concerts, lectures, and symposia promoting international understanding. Period furnishings, Mortlake tapestry; gardens with linden grove. (Wed-Sun

afternoons; closed hols) 1630 Crescent Pl NW. Phone 202/939-5568. **FREE**

Phillips Collection. First museum of modern art in the nation. Founded in 1918, the museum continues to emphasize the work of emerging as well as established international artists. Permanent collection of 19th- and 20th-century Impressionist, Post-Impressionist, and modern painting and sculpture. (Tues-Sun; closed hols) Introductory tours (Wed and Sat). Concerts (Sept-May, Sun). Wkday admission by donation. 1600 21st St NW. Phone 202/387-2151 or 202/387-0961. Wkend admission ¢¢

Emancipation Statue

Textile Museum. Founded in 1925 with the collection of George Hewitt Myers, the museum features changing exhibits of non-Western textiles, Oriental rugs, and other handmade textile art. Guided tours (Sept-May, Wed, Sat, Sun; by appt). (Daily) 2320 S St NW. Phone 202/667-0441. **DONATION**

Woodrow Wilson House. (1915) Red brick Georgian Revival townhouse to which President Wilson retired after leaving office; family furnishings and gifts-of-state. A National Trust for Historic Preser-

Georgetown

vation property. (Tues-Sun; closed Jan 1, Thanksgiving, Dec 25) 2340 S St NW. Phone 202/387-4062. ¢¢

Eastern Market. Meat, fish, and produce sold. Also crafts and farmers market on wkends. (Tues-Sun) 225 7th St SE. Phone 202/546-2698.

Emancipation Statue. Bronze work of Thomas Ball paid for by voluntary subscriptions from emancipated slaves, depicting Lincoln presenting Emancipation Proclamation to black man, was dedicated Apr 14, 1876, the 11th anniversary of Lincoln's assassination, with Fredrick Douglass in attendance. Lincoln Park, E Capitol St NE between 11th and 13th sts NE. Also here is

> **Mary McLeod Bethune Memorial.** Honors the noted educator and advisor to President Lincoln and founder of the National Council of Negro Women.

Embassy Row. This neighborhood, within the city's northwest quadrant, is centered around Sheridan Cir, at the intersection of Massachusetts Ave and 23rd St NW. Dozens of foreign legations can be found in the area and north along Massachusetts Ave.

Explorers Hall. National Geographic Society headquarters. Several traveling exhibits, call for info. (Daily; closed Dec 25) 17th and M sts NW. Phone 202-857-7588 (recording). **FREE**

Federal Reserve Building. (1937) Primarily an office building but noteworthy for its architecture; rotating art exhibits; film (20 min). C St between 20th and 21st sts NW. Phone 202/452-3149. **FREE**

Federal Trade Commission Building. (1938) (Mon-Fri; closed hols) Pennsylvania Ave NW, between 6th and 7th sts. Phone 202/326-2222. **FREE**

Federal Triangle. The Triangle consists of a group of government buildings, of which nine were built for $78 million in the 1930s in modern classic design. The "crown jewel" of the triangle is the Ronald Reagan International Trade Center, located on Pennsylvania Ave at 13th St NW.

⭐ **Ford's Theatre.** Where John Wilkes Booth shot Abraham Lincoln on Apr 14, 1865. Restored as a functioning theater with Broadway and original productions offered throughout the yr. Phone 202/347-4833 for tickets. Tours (daily; closed Dec 25). 511 10th St NW. Phone 202/426-6924. Performance tickets ¢¢¢¢. In basement is

> **Lincoln Museum.** Exhibits and displays focus on Lincoln's life and assassination. (Daily; closed Dec 25) Phone 202/347-4833. **FREE** Across the street is

Petersen House. House where Lincoln died. The house to where President Lincoln was carried after the shooting at Ford's Theatre; he died here the following morning. The house has been restored to its appearance at that time. (Daily; closed Dec 25) 516 10th St NW. **FREE**

Fort Dupont Park. Picnicking, hiking, and bicycling in hilly terrain; cultural arts performances in summer (see SPECIAL EVENTS). Also films, slides, and activities including natural science; environmental education programs; nature discovery room; Junior Ranger program; programs for senior citizens and disabled persons; garden workshops and programmed activities by res. Randle Cir and Minnesota Ave. Phone 202/426-7723 or 202/426-7745. **FREE** Nearby is

> **Fort Dupont Sports Complex.** Skating, ice hockey (fee); tennis courts, basketball courts, ball fields (daily; free), jogging. E on Pennsylvania Ave SE; N on Minnesota Ave; E on Ely Pl. Phone 202-584-5007 (ice rink).

Fort Stevens Park. General Jubal Early and his Confederate troops tried to invade Washington at this point on July 11-12, 1864. President Lincoln risked his life at the fort during the fighting. (Daily) Piney Branch Rd and Quackenbos St NW. Phone 202/895-6000. **FREE**

Fort Washington National Park. Earliest defense of the city (1809), the original fort was destroyed in 1814; reconstructed by 1824. View of Potomac River; picnicking; history exhibits. (Daily) 4 mi S on MD 210, 3½ mi at 13551 Fort Washington Rd in Fort Washington, MD. Phone 301/763-4600. ¢¢

Franciscan Monastery. Within the church and grounds is the "Holy Land of America"; replicas of sacred Holy Land shrines include the Manger at Bethlehem, Garden of Gethsemane, and Holy Sepulchre. Also Grotto at Lourdes and Roman catacombs. Guided tours by the friars (daily). 1400 Quincy St NE. Phone 202/526-6800. **DONATION**

Franklin Delano Roosevelt Memorial. Series of sculptures depicting Franklin and Eleanor Roosevelt. (Daily) West Potomac Park near the Lincoln Memorial. Phone 202/426-6841. **FREE**

Frederick Douglass National Historic Site, "Cedar Hill". This 21-room house on nine acres is where Douglass, a former slave who became Minister to Haiti and a leading black spokesman, lived from 1877 until his death in 1895; visitor center with film, memorabilia. (Daily; closed Jan 1, Thanksgiving, Dec 25) 1411 W St SE. Phone 202/426-5961. **FREE**

General Services Administration Building. (1917) Was originally Department of Interior. 18th, 19th, E, and F sts NW.

Georgetown. Georgetown, a neighborhood within the city's northwest quadrant, is actually older than Washington. In Colonial days it was a busy commercial center along the Potomac. Today Georgetown is an area of fine 18th- and 19th-century residences and fashionable shops and restaurants; the commercial center radiates from the intersection of Pennsylvania Ave and M St, NW of the White House.

Georgetown University. (1789) 12,000 students. Oldest Catholic col-

Georgetown University

lege in US, a Jesuit school. Campus tours (Mon-Sat, by res). Main entrance 37th and O sts NW. Phone 202/687-0100.

George Washington University. (1821) 20,000 students. Theater; art exhibits in Dimock Gallery (Mon-Fri; closed hols) and University Library. 19th to 24th sts NW, F St to Pennsylvania Ave. Phone 202/994-1000.

Government Printing Office. Four buildings with 35 acres of floor space where most of the material issued by US Government, including production and distribution of the Congressional Record, Federal Register, and US passports, is printed. (No public tours; for info on the agency, call 202/512-1991.) Office includes the **Main Government Bookstore,** 710 N Capitol St NW. Nearly 20,000 publications avail (Mon-Fri; closed hols). On N Capitol St, between G and H sts. Phone 202/512-0132.

Great Falls of the Potomac. (See CHESAPEAKE AND OHIO CANAL NATIONAL HISTORICAL PARK in Maryland)

Harness racing. Rosecroft Raceway. (Daily, races Thurs-Sat) 6336 Rosecroft Dr, 8 mi SE in Oxon Hill, MD. Phone 301/567-4000. ¢¢

House Office Buildings. Pedestrian tunnel connects two of the oldest House office buildings with the Capitol. Along Independence Ave, south side of Capitol grounds at Independence and New Jersey aves.

Howard University. (1867) 12,000 students. Main campus has Gallery of Fine Art, with permanent Alain Locke African Collection; changing exhibits (Sept-July, Mon-Fri). Main campus: 2400 6th St NW between W and Harvard sts NW. West Campus: 2900 Van Ness St NW. Three other campuses in area. Phone 202/806-6100.

Islamic Center. Leading mosque in the US has landscaped courtyard, intricate interior mosaics. (Daily; no tours during Fri prayer service) 2551 Massachusetts Ave NW. Phone 202/332-8343.

Iwo Jima Statue

Iwo Jima Statue. (See ARLINGTON COUNTY in Virginia) Across Theodore Roosevelt Bridge on Arlington Blvd.

John F. Kennedy Center for the Performing Arts. Official memorial to President Kennedy. Single structure, designed by Edward Durell Stone, incorporates opera house, concert hall, movie theater, Eisenhower theatre, Terrace theatre, and Theatre lab; two restaurants; library; gift shop. Tours (daily, limited hrs). Some free performances. New Hampshire Ave at F St NW. Phone 202/467-4600.

Judiciary Square. Two square blks of judiciary buildings, includes five federal and district courts, the US District Court (1820), and US Court of Appeals (1910). At D St halfway between 4th and 5th sts is the first completed statue of Abraham Lincoln (1868). D, E, and F sts, between 4th and 5th sts NW.

Kenilworth Aquatic Gardens. Water lilies, lotuses, other water plants bloom from mid-May until frost. Gardens (daily). Guided walks (Memorial Day-Labor Day, Sat, Sun, and hols, also by appt; closed Jan 1, Thanksgiving, Dec 25). Anacostia

Ave and Douglas St NE. Phone 202/426-6905. **FREE**

Korean War Memorial. Massive sculpture honoring Americans who served in the conflict. Adj to the Lincoln Memorial. Phone 202/426-6841. **FREE**

Labor Department. Lobby contains the Labor Hall of Fame, an exhibit depicting labor in US; library on second floor is open to public. (Mon-Fri; closed hols) Francis H. Perkins Building, 200 Constitution Ave NW. **FREE**

Lafayette Square. Statue of Andrew Jackson on horseback in center was first equestrian figure in Washington (1853). One of park benches was known as Bernard Baruch's office in 1930s and is dedicated to him. Phone 202/673-7647. On square is

Decatur House Museum. (1818) Federal townhouse built for naval hero Commodore Stephen Decatur by Benjamin H. Latrobe, second architect of the Capitol. After Decatur's death in 1820, the house was occupied by a succession of American and foreign statespeople and was a center of political and social life in the city. The ground floor family rooms reflect Decatur's Federal-period lifestyle. Operated by National Trust for Historic Preservation. (Tues-Sun; closed Jan 1, Thanksgiving, Dec 25) 748 Jackson Pl NW. Phone 202/842-0920. **FREE**

Library of Congress. (1800) Treasures include a Gutenberg Bible, the first great book printed with movable metal type; the Giant Bible of Mainz, a 500-yr-old illuminated manuscript. Collection includes books, manuscripts, newspapers, maps, recordings, prints, photographs, posters, and more than 30 million books and pamphlets in 60 languages. In the elaborate Jefferson Building is the Great Hall, decorated with murals, mosaics, and marble carvings; exhibition halls. In the Madison Building, a 22-min audiovisual presentation, *America's Library,* provides a good introduction to the library and its facilities. (Mon-Sat; closed federal hols) 10 1st St SE. **FREE** Library complex includes

Folger Shakespeare Library. (1932) Houses the finest collection of Shakespeare materials in the world, including the 1623 First Folio edition and large holdings of rare books and manuscripts of the English and continental Renaissance.

The Lincoln Memorial

Library of Congress

The Great Hall offers yr-round exhibits from the Folger's extensive collection. The Elizabethan Theatre, which was designed to resemble an innyard theater of Shakespeare's day, is the site of the Folger Shakespeare Library's series of museum and performing arts programs, which incl literary readings, drama, lectures, and education and family programs. Self-guided tours. Guided tours (11 am). (Mon-Sat; closed federal hols) 201 E Capitol St SE. Phone 202/544-4600. **FREE**

⭐ **Lincoln Memorial.** Dedicated in 1922, Daniel Chester French's Lincoln looks across a reflecting pool to the Washington Monument and Capitol. Lincoln's Gettysburg Address and Second Inaugural Address are inscribed on the walls of the temple-like structure, which is particularly impressive at night. Tours. (Daily; closed Dec 25) 23rd St NW, at Daniel French and Henry Bacon Dr. Phone 202/426-6841. **FREE**

Martin Luther King Memorial Library. (1972) Main branch of D.C. public library was designed by architect Mies van der Rohe. Martin Luther King mural. Books, periodicals, photographs, films, videocassettes, recordings, microfilms, Washingtoniana, and the *Washington Star* collection. Library for the visually impaired; librarian for the hearing impaired; black studies division;

AP wire service machine; community information service. Underground parking. (Mon-Sat, also Sun afternoons; closed hols) 901 G St NW. **FREE**

MCI Center. Home of the NBA's Washington Wizards, the WNBA's Washington Mystics, and the NHL's Washington Capitals, this 220,000-square-ft venue also has a 19,000-square-ft sports restaurant overlooking the Wizards' practice court. (Daily) 601 F St NW. Phone 202/628-3200.

MCI National Sports Gallery. This 25,000-square-ft museum commemorates and showcases the best of American sports history. Includes sports memorabilia collections; participatory and technology-driving exhibits with basketball, football, hockey, and baseball themes. Rotating exhibits feature special-interest sports. Home of the American Sportscasters Association Hall of Fame and Museum, honoring the memorable voices that brought great sports moments. Phone 202/661-5133. Gallery ¢¢¢

⭐ **Mount Vernon.** (See MOUNT VERNON in Virginia) 18 mi S via George Washington Memorial Pkwy. Phone 703/780-2000.

National Academy of Sciences. (1924) Established in 1863 to stimulate research and communication among scientists and to advise the federal government in science and technology. A famous 21-ft bronze statue of Albert Einstein by Robert Berks is on the front lawn. Art exhibits, concerts. (Schedule varies) 2101 Constitution Ave, between 21st and 22nd sts NW. Phone 202/334-2000. **FREE**

National Archives. (1934) Original copies of the Declaration of Independence, Bill of Rights, Constitution; a 1297 version of the Magna Carta and other historic documents, maps, and photographs. Guided tours by appt only; phone 202/501-5205. Archives also avail to public for genealogical and historical research (Mon-Sat; closed federal hols). (Daily; closed Dec 25) Pennsylvania Ave between 7th and 9th sts NW; exhibition entrance on Constitution Ave. **FREE**

National Building Museum. Deals with architecture, design, engineering, and construction. Permanent exhibits include drawings, blueprints, models, photographs, artifacts; architectural evolution of Washington's buildings and monuments. The museum's enormous Great Hall is supported by eight of the world's largest Corinthian columns. Guided tours (afternoons: wkdays, one tour; wkends, two tours). Museum (Mon-Sat; also Sun afternoons). Housed in Old Pension Building, 401 F St NW. Phone 202/272-2448. **FREE**

National Colonial Farm. Approx 150 acres in Piscataway National Park. A "living history" farm of mid-18th century; crops, herb garden, livestock, methods of the period are used; replicated farm buildings. (Tues-Sun; closed Jan 1, Thanksgiving, Dec 25) I-95 exit 3A, then 10 mi S on MD 210, right on Bryan Point Rd, 3 mi in Accokeek, MD. Phone 301/283-2113. ¢

National Gallery of Art. The West Building (1941), designed by John Russell Pope, contains Western European and American art spanning periods between the 13th and 20th centuries: highlights include the only Leonardo da Vinci painting in the western hemisphere, *Ginevra de' Benci;* a comprehensive collection of Italian paintings and sculpture; major French Impressionists; numerous Rembrandts and examples of the Dutch school; masterpieces from the Mellon, Widener, Kress, Dale, and Rosenwald collections; special exhibitions. The East Building (1978), designed by architect I. M. Pei, houses the gallery's growing collection of 20th-century art, including Picasso's *Family of Saltimbanques* and Jackson Pollock's *Lavender Mist.* (Daily; closed Jan 1, Dec 25) Constitution Ave, between 3rd and 7th sts. Phone 202/737-4215. **FREE**

Declaration of Independence

National Museum of American Art. American paintings, sculpture, prints, and graphic art from the 18th century to the present. (Daily; closed Dec 25) 8th and G sts NW, Gallery Pl. Phone 202/357-2700.

National Museum of Health and Medicine. One of the most important medical collections in America. Interprets the link between history and technology; AIDS education exhibit; an interactive exhibit on human anatomy and lifestyle choices; collection of microscopes, medical teaching aids, tools, and instruments (1862-1965) and famous historical icons exhibits. (Daily; closed Dec 25) Building #54, Walter Reed Army Medical Center. Phone 202/782-2200. **FREE**

National Museum of Women in the Arts. Focus on women's contributions to the arts. More than 1,200 works by women artists from Renaissance to present. Paintings, drawings, sculpture, pottery, prints. Library, research center by appt. Performances. Guided tours (by appt). (Daily; closed Jan 1, Thanksgiving, Dec 25) 1250 New York Ave NW. Phone 202/783-5000. **DONATION**

National Portrait Gallery. Portraits and statues of people who have made significant contributions to the history, development, and culture of the US. (Daily; closed Dec 25) 8th and F sts NW. Phone 202/357-2700.

National Presbyterian Church and Center. Chapel of the President contains memorabilia of past US presidents; faceted glass windows depict history of man and church. Self-guided tours (daily; no tours hols). Guided tours (Sun following service). 4101 Nebraska Ave NW. Phone 202/537-0800.

Navy Yard. Along the Anacostia River at a location chosen by George Washington, the yard was founded in 1799 and was nearly destroyed during the War of 1812. Outside the yard at 636 G St SE is the John Phillip Sousa house, where the "March King" wrote many of his famous compositions; the house is private. M St between 1st and 11th sts SE. Phone 202/433-4882. One blk E is

    Marine Barracks. Parade ground, more than two centuries old, is surrounded by handsome and historic structures including the Commandant's House facing G St, which is said to be the oldest continuously-occupied public building in the city. Spectacular parade is open to public Tues and Fri eves in summer (see SPECIAL EVENTS). Entrance to Navy Yard is at end of 9th St at M St SE. Inside is G St between 8th and 9th sts SE. Phone 202/433-6060.

    Marine Corps Museum. Weapons, uniforms, maps, flags, and other artifacts describe the history of the US Marine Corps. Housed in restored 19th-century structure; also used as marine barracks from 1941-1975. (Mon, Wed-Fri; Sat, Sun by appt only; closed Jan 1, Dec 25) 901 M St. Bldg 58 in Navy Yard. Phone 202/433-3840. **FREE**

Navy Museum. History of US Navy from the Revolutionary War to the space age. Dioramas depict achievements of early naval heroes; displays development of naval weapons; fully rigged foremast fighting top and gun deck from frigate *Constitution* on display; WWII guns that can be trained and elevated; submarine room has operating periscopes. Approx 5,000 objects on display including paintings, ship models, flags, uniforms, naval decorations, and the bathyscaphe *Trieste*. Two-acre outdoor park displays 19th- and 20th-century guns, cannons, other naval artifacts; US Navy destroyer *Barry* located on the waterfront. (Daily; closed hols) Tours (Mon-Fri). Building 76, Washington Navy Yard, 805 Kidder Breese SE. Phone 202/433-4882. **FREE**

New York Avenue Presbyterian Church. The church where Lincoln worshipped; rebuilt 1950-1951, with Lincoln's pew. Dr. Peter Marshall was pastor 1937-1949. Mementos on display include first draft of Emancipation Proclamation. (Daily, services Sun morning; closed hols) 1313 New York Ave, at H St NW. Phone 202/393-3700.

The Octagon. (1799-1801) Federal townhouse built for Colonel John Tayloe III, based on designs by Dr. William Thornton. Served as temporary quarters for President and Mrs. James Madison after White House burned in War of 1812; also site of ratification of the Treaty of Ghent. Restored with period furnishings (1800-1828). Changing exhibits on architecture and allied arts. (Tues-Sun; closed hols) 1799 New York Ave NW, at 18th and E sts NW. Phone 202/638-3221. ¢¢

Old Executive Office Building. (1875) Second Empire/Victorian architecture. Built as War Office; was also home to State Department; now offices for president's staff. Guided tours by appt (Sat morning only). Pennsylvania Ave and 17th St NW. Phone 202/395-5895. **FREE**

Old Stone House. (1765) Believed to be the oldest pre-Revolutionary building in Washington. Constructed on parcel No. 3 of the original tract of land that was then Georgetown, the house was used as both a residence and a place of business; five rooms are furnished with household items that reflect a middle-class residence of the late 18th century. The grounds are lush with fruit trees and seasonal blooms. (Wed-Sun; closed hols) 3051 M St NW. **FREE**

Organization of American States (OAS). Headquarters of OAS, set up to maintain international peace and security and to promote integral development in the Americas. Tropical patio, Hall of Heroes and Flags, Hall of the Americas, Aztec Garden, Council Chamber. (Mon-Fri; closed hols) Constitution Ave and 17th St NW. Phone 202/458-3000. **FREE**

Oxon Hill Farm. Living history farm ca 1898-1914 located on working farm with livestock; participatory activities. Represents life from early 1800s to present. (Daily; closed Jan 1, Thanksgiving, Dec 25) Entrance from Oxon Hill Rd, 300 yds W of jct MD 210 and I-95 in Oxon Hill, MD. Phone 301/839-1177. **FREE**

Pavilion at the Old Post Office. (1899) Romanesque structure which for yrs was headquarters of the US Postal Service has been remodeled into a marketplace with 100 shops and restaurants, and daily entertainment. In the 315-ft tower are replicas of the bells of Westminster Abbey, a Bicentennial gift from Great Britain; the tower, which is the second-highest point in D.C., offers spectacular views from an open-air observation deck (free). Above the Pavilion shops are headquarters for the National Endowment for the Arts. (Daily; closed Jan 1, Thanksgiving, Dec 25) 1100 Pennsylvania Ave NW. Phone 202/289-4224. **FREE**

Potomac Park (East and West). On the banks of the Potomac River, park recreational activities include fishing, pedalboating; golf, tennis, picnicking. Washington's famous cherry trees can be found around the Tidal Basin. Hundreds of **Yoshino and Akebono cherry trees,** a gift from Japan in 1912, come into full bloom in a celebration of spring (see SPECIAL EVENTS), an unforgettable floral display (late-Mar-early-Apr). West Potomac park is the site of the Franklin Delano Roosevelt Memorial. NW and SE of the Jefferson Memorial.

★ **President Kennedy's Gravesite.** (See ARLINGTON COUNTY in Virginia) South Gate, Arlington National Cemetery.

Professional sports.

D.C. United (MLS). RFK Memorial Stadium, 2400 E Capitol St. Phone 202/547-9077.

Washington Capitals (NHL). MCI Center, 601 F St NW. Phone 202/661-5050.

Washington Mystics (WNBA). MCI Center, 601 F St NW. Phone 202/661-5050.

Washington Redskins (NFL). FedEx Field, 1 Redskins Rd. Landover, MD. Phone 301/276-6050.

Washington Wizards (NBA). MCI Center, 601 F St NW. Phone 202/661-5050.

Renwick Gallery. American crafts from 1900-present. A department of the National Museum of American Art. (Daily; closed Dec 25) Pennsylvania Ave NW at 17th St NW. Phone 202/357-2700. **FREE**

Rock Creek Park. More than 1,700 acres with working gristmill; 18-hole golf course, hiking, exercise course, historic sites, tennis courts, picnicking, self-guided nature trails, stables, bridle paths, biking trails, ball fields. Fee for some activities. NW on Beach Dr. Phone 202/895-6000. Also here are

Art Barn. Historic carriage house (1831). Art exhibitions. (Thurs-Sun afternoons). 2401 Tilden St and Beach Dr NW. Phone 202/244-2482. **FREE**

Carter Barron Amphitheater. This 4,200-seat outdoor theater in wooded area is setting for summer performances of symphonic, folk, pop, and jazz music (see SPECIAL EVENTS) and Shakespearean theater. Some fees. 16th St and Colorado Ave NW.

National Zoological Park. A branch of the Smithsonian Institution, the zoo features approx 5,000 animals of 500 species, including two giant pandas; lions, tigers, and cheetahs; great apes; elephants and rhinos; small mammals; reptiles and inver-

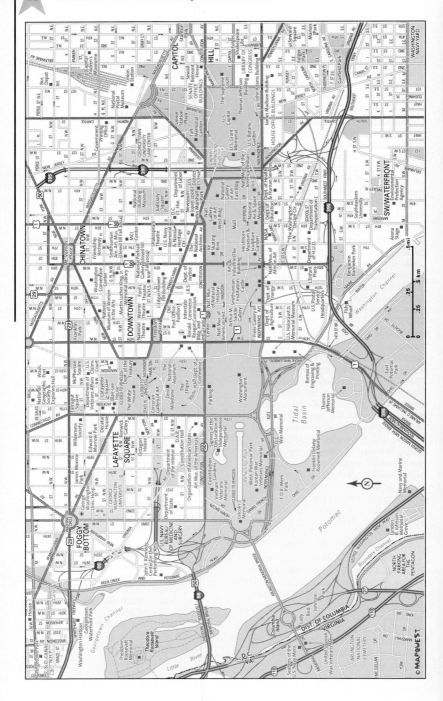

tebrates; birdhouse and wetlands; rain forest exhibit. Picnicking, refreshments. Guided tours (wkends). Metrorail (Red Line) stop. Limited parking (fee). (Daily; closed Dec 25) Main entrance at 3000 blk of Connecticut Ave NW; other entrances at Beach Dr (Rock Creek Pkwy) and jct Adams Mill Rd and Harvard St. Phone 202/673-4800. **FREE**

Nature Center. Planetarium, films, exhibits, nature demonstrations. (Wed-Sun; closed hols) 5200 Glover Rd NW. Phone 202/865-6070. **FREE**

Theodore Roosevelt Memorial. The island is an 88-acre wilderness preserve; the 17-ft statue of Roosevelt was designed by Paul Manship. (Daily; closed Dec 25) N end of Theodore Roosevelt Island, accessible only by footbridge from George Washington Memorial Pkwy, northbound lane, in Arlington, VA. **FREE**

St. John's Church Georgetown Parish. Oldest Episcopal congregation in Georgetown, established 1796; original design of church by William Thornton, architect of the Capitol. Many presidents since Madison have worshiped here. Francis Scott Key was a founding member. Tours (by appt). 3240 O St NW. Phone 202/338-1796.

Senate Office Buildings. Linked by private subway to Capitol. Constitution Ave on both sides of 1st St NE.

Sewall-Belmont House. (1680, 1800) The Sewall-Belmont House is a living monument to Alice Paul, the author of the Equal Rights Amendment. From this house she spearheaded the fight for the passage of the amendment. Now a national landmark, the house contains portraits and sculptures of women from the beginning of the suffrage movement; extensive collection of artifacts of the suffrage and equal rights movements; historic headquarters of the National Woman's Party. (Tues-Fri, also Sat afternoons; closed Jan 1, Thanksgiving, Dec 25) 144 Constitution Ave NE. Phone 202/546-1210. **FREE**

Shops at National Place. Trilevel marketplace—at, above, and below street grade—featuring more than 100 specialty shops and restaurants.

(Daily) 1331 Pennsylvania Ave NW; enter at 13th and F sts. Phone 202/662-1200.

Sightseeing tours.

Gray Line bus tours. Tours of city and area attractions depart from terminal in Union Station. Contact 5500 Tuxedo Rd, Tuxedo, MD 20781. Phone 301/386-8300 or 800/862-1400.

Tourmobile Sightseeing. Narrated shuttle tours to 18 historic sites on the National Mall and in Arlington National Cemetery. Unlimited reboarding throughout day (daily; no tours Dec 25). Additional tours separately or in combinations: Arlington National Cemetery; Mount Vernon (seasonal) and Frederick Douglass Home (seasonal). Phone 202/554-5100. ¢¢¢

Six Flags America. Thrill rides, water attractions, children's rides; wave pool; Wild One Rollercoaster. Entertainment; game gallery. Parking fee. (Mid-May-Labor Day, schedule varies) E via Capital Beltway to exit 15A, then E on Central Ave (MD 214) in Mitchellville, MD, follow signs. Phone 301/249-1500.

★ **Smithsonian Institution.** The majority of Smithsonian museums are located on the National Mall. Smithsonian headquarters is located in the Smithsonian Institution Building, the "Castle" (1855), located at 1000 Jefferson Dr SW, on the Mall. The headquarters contains administrative offices, Smithson's crypt, and the Smithsonian Information Center, which has information on all Smithsonian museums. Many visitors begin their day here. (All buildings open daily; closed Dec 25; Anacostia Museum and National Zoo hrs vary) **FREE** Smithsonian museums on the Mall include

National Museum of Natural History. Gems (including Hope Diamond), minerals; botanical, zoological, and geological materials; live insect "zoo"; Dinosaur Hall, Discovery Room, with hands-on activities for children; living coral reef; cultures of Africa, Asia, the Pacific, and the Americas are explored; Western civilization is traced to its roots. Cafeteria. Special exhibition hall. Constitution Ave, between 9th and 12th sts NW.

Smithsonian Institution

Phone 202/357-2700. **FREE** To the west is

National Museum of American History. Cultural and technological development of the US; Star-Spangled Banner; numismatic exhibit; political history exhibits; gowns of First Ladies; Dorothy's ruby slippers; interactive video stations; ship models; railroad hall. Cafeteria, snack bar, ice cream parlor. Constitution Ave, between 12th and 14th sts NW. Phone 202/357-2700. **FREE** Across the Mall is

Freer Gallery. Asian art with objects dating from Neolithic period to the early 20th century. Also works by late 19th- and early 20th-century American artists, including a major collection of James McNeill Whistler's work, highlighted by the famous Peacock Room. Jefferson Dr at 12th St SW. Next to the Freer is the Smithsonian Institution Building, or "the Castle." Phone 202/357-2700. **FREE** Connected to the Freer is the

Arthur M. Sackler Gallery. Changing exhibitions of Asian art, both Near- and Far-Eastern, from major national and international collections. Permanent collection includes Chinese and South and Southeast Asian art objects presented by Arthur Sackler. Between

the Freer Gallery and the Arts and Industries Building is the **Enid A. Haupt Garden**, four acres that comprise the "roof" of the Sackler Gallery, the International Gallery, an underground Smithsonian research and education complex, and 1050 Independence Ave SW. Phone 202/357-2700. **FREE**

National Museum of African Art. Devoted to collection, study, research, and exhibition of African art. The museum collection, numbering about 6,000 objects, is a primary source for the study of African art and culture; highlighted by traditional arts of sub-Saharan Africa, includes collection of utilitarian ojects. Guided tours by appt. 950 Independence Ave SW. **FREE** To the east is

Arts and Industries Building. The south hall contains the Experimental Gallery, an exhibit space dedicated to innovative and creative exhibits from museums in the Smithsonian and from around the world. Discovery Theater (fee) hosts performances for children. 900 Jefferson Dr SW. **FREE** Directly to the east is

Hirshhorn Museum and Sculpture Garden. Modern, circular museum houses a collection of more than 6,000 works of art donated by Joseph H. Hirshhorn. Emphasis on contemporary art as well as 19th- and 20th-century painting and sculpture. Sculpture garden is on the Mall, between 7th and 9th sts SW. Independence Ave, between 7th and 9th sts SW. **FREE** Directly east is

National Air and Space Museum.
Museum presents exhibits on history of aviation and space age; artifacts include the original *Kitty Hawk Flyer, Spirit of St. Louis,* and *Friendship 7;* also touchable moon rocks. Five-story theater shows IMAX films on air and space travel (fee; for schedule phone 202/357-1686). Museum also encompasses Albert Einstein Planetarium (fee). For a behind-the-scenes look at the restoration of the museums reserve collection of approx 90 aircraft, spacecraft, engines, propellers, and flight-related objects, visit the **Paul E. Garber Facility** in Suitland, MD (15 mi SE via Independence Ave to Pennsylvania Ave to Silver Hill Rd). Guided tours (daily; closed Dec 25; res must be made two wks in advance by contacting Tour Scheduler, Office of Volunteer Services, National Air and Space Museum, Smithsonian Institution, Washington, DC 20560. Phone 202/357-1400). Independence Ave, between 7th and 4th sts SW. Phone 202/357-1387. **FREE**

Supreme Court of the United States.
Designed by Cass Gilbert in Neo-Classical style. Court is in session Oct-Apr (Mon-Wed, at two-wk intervals from first Mon in Oct) and on the first workday of each wk in May and June; court sessions are open to the public (10 am and 1 pm), on a first-come basis; lectures are offered in the courtroom (Mon-Fri exc when court is in session; 20-min lectures hrly on ½-hr); on ground floor are exhibits and film (23 min), cafeteria, snack bar, gift shop (Mon-Fri; closed hols). 1st St NE at Maryland Ave, E of Capitol. Phone 202/479-3211. **FREE**

Theaters. Shakespeare Theatre, Lansburgh Theater, 450 7th St NW, phone 202/547-1122. **The National,** 1321 Pennsylvania Ave NW, phone 202/628-6161. **Arena Stage,** 1101 6th at Maine Ave SW, phone 202/488-3300. **The Warner,** 13th

and E sts NW, phone 202/783-4000. Also see John F. Kennedy Center.

⭐ **Thomas Jefferson Memorial.**
(1943) Memorial honors the third President of the United States and author of both the Declaration of Independence and Bill of Rights. Tours. (Daily; closed Dec 25) S edge of Tidal Basin. **FREE**

Tudor Place. (1805) Twelve-room Federal-style mansion was designed by Dr. William Thornton, architect of Capitol, for Martha Custis Peter, granddaughter of Martha Washington. Peter family lived in house for 180 yrs. All furnishings and objets d'art original. More than five acres of gardens (Mon-Sat). Guided tours (Tues-Sat, by res; closed hols). 1644 31st St NW. Phone 202/965-0400. Garden only ¢ House and garden ¢¢¢

Union Station. Restored Beaux Arts train station designed by Daniel Burnham and completed in 1907 features lavish interior spaces under 96-ft-high, coffered, gold-leafed ceiling. Located within original station and train shed are 130 shops, restaurants, and movie theater complex. Original spaces, such as the presidential suite, have been turned into restaurants without extensive alteration. Also located within the station are the Amtrak depot and Gray Line and Tourmobile Sightseeing operators (see SIGHTSEEING TOURS). (Daily) On Massachusetts Ave between 1st and 2nd sts. Phone 703/371-9441. **FREE**

US Botanic Gardens. The Botanic Garden, one of the oldest in the country, was established by Congress in 1820 for public education and exhibition. It features plants collected by the famous Wilkes Expedition of the South Seas. Conservatory has tropical, subtropical, and desert plants; seasonal displays. Exterior gardens are planted for seasonal blooming; also here is Bartholdi Fountain, designed by sculptor of the Statue of Liberty. (Daily) 100 Maryland Ave, at base of Capitol Hill. Phone 202/225-8333. **FREE**

⭐ **US Holocaust Memorial Museum.**
Interprets the story of the Holocaust through modern exhibition techniques and authentic objects, includ-

Vietnam Veterans Memorial

ing a railroad freight car used to transport Polish Jews from Warsaw, concentration camp uniforms, photographs, diaries. Visitors are taken from Hall of Witness directly to the fourth floor and begin a chronological journey from the roots of the Holocaust to its aftermath. Changing exhibits include "Remember the Children," which interprets Holocaust events from a child's perspective. (Daily; closed Yom Kippur, Dec 25) Permanent exhibits recommended for ages 11 and over only. Entrances at Raoul Wallenberg Pl (15th St SW) and at 14th St SW. Phone 202/488-0400. **FREE**

US National Arboretum. Floral displays spring, summer, fall, and winter on 446 acres; Japanese garden, National Bonsai and Penjing Museum (daily); National Herb Garden, major collections of azaleas (15,000), wildflowers, ferns, magnolias, crabapples, cherries, dogwoods; aquatic plantings; dwarf conifers (world's largest evergreen collection). (Daily; closed Dec 25) Under 16 yrs admitted only with adult. 3501 New York Ave NE. Phone 202/245-2726. **FREE**

US Navy Memorial. Dedicated to those who have served in the Navy in war and in peacetime. A 100-ft diameter granite world map domi-

nates the Plaza, where the *Lone Sailor,* a seven-ft bronze sculpture, stands and the US Navy Band stages performances (Memorial Day-Labor Day, Tues eves). Visitor Center features electronic kiosks with interactive video displays on naval history; also Navy Memorial Log Room and US Presidents Room. (Tues-Sat) Pennsylvania Ave, at 7th and 9th sts NW. Phone 202/737-2300. **FREE** Also here is

At Sea. Underwritten by ExxonMobil, this is an award-winning high-resolution 70mm film that conveys the experience of being at sea aboard a US Navy aircraft carrier. The 241-seat theater employs a two-story, 52-ft-wide screen and six-track digital audio to surround the audience with the sights and sounds of carrier operations. Showings (Mon-Sat, four times daily; Sun, two times). Arleigh and Roberta Burke Theater.

⭐ **Vietnam Veterans Memorial.** Designed by Maya Ying Lyn, the memorial's polished black granite walls are inscribed with the names of the 58,175 US citizens who died in or remain missing from the Vietnam War (a large directory helps visitors locate names). Also Statue of Three Servicemen. Built with private contributions of American citizens. (Daily)

Constitution Ave between Henry Bacon Dr and 21st St NW. Phone 202/634-1568. **FREE**

Voice of America. Live radio broadcasts to foreign countries; 45-min guided tours (Mon-Fri, res required; closed hols). 330 Independence Ave SW between 3rd and 4th sts SW; enter on C St. Phone 202/619-3919. **FREE**

Washington Dolls' House & Toy Museum. Splendid collection of antique doll houses, dolls, toys, and games; museum shop. (Tues-Sun; closed Jan 1, Thanksgiving, Dec 25) 5236 44th St NW. Phone 202/244-0024. ¢¢

Washington Harbour. Dining and shopping complex that features lavish fountains, life-size statuary, and a boardwalk with a view of the Potomac River. 30th and K sts NW.

⭐ **Washington Monument.** Parking lot on north side, off Constitution Ave. The obelisk, tallest masonry structure in the world (555 ft), was dedicated in 1885 to the memory of the first US president. (Daily; extended hrs in summer; closed Dec 25). Elevator to observation room at 500-ft level. To take the 898 steps up or down, arrangements must be made in advance. Mall at 15th St NW. **FREE**

⭐ **Washington National Cathedral.** Cornerstone of the Gothic cathedral was laid in 1907; final stone was set in 1990; structure, built entirely in the manner and materials of medieval cathedrals, took 83 yrs, five architects, and the terms of seven bishops to complete. Details are intentionally irregular to avoid uniform features typical of machine-age building. Tombs of Woodrow Wilson, Helen Keller, and others are within structure. Pilgrim Observation Gallery overlooks Washington from city's highest geographic point. Within the grounds are trees grown from a cutting of England's Glastonbury Thorne, which by legend grew from the staff of Joseph of Arimathea; museum shop; Bishop's Garden, a medieval walled garden; Herb Cottage; greenhouse with potted herbs for sale. Shops (daily). Services (daily). Carillon recitals (Sat). Organ recitals (Sun). Tours (daily). Massachusetts and Wisconsin aves NW. Phone 202/537-6200. **DONATION**

⭐ **The White House.** (1800) Constructed under the supervision of George Washington, the house has been lived in by every president since John Adams. It was burned by the British during the War of 1812 and reconstructed under the guidance of James Monroe (1817-1825). The West Wing, which includes the Oval Office, was built during Theodore Roosevelt's administration (1901-1909); before its construction, executive offices shared the second floor with the president's private quarters. The interior of the White House was gutted and rebuilt, using modern construction techniques, during the Truman administration; President Truman and family resided at Blair House for four yrs during the reconstruction. The Library and the Vermeil Room (on Ground Floor), the East Room, Green, Blue, and Red

Washington Monument amidst Cherry Blossoms

Rooms, and the State Dining Room (on State Floor) are accessible to certain groups for educational tours. Tickets must be obtained through the particular state's Congressman or Senator. (Closed Jan 1, Dec 25, and presidential functions). 1600 Pennsylvania Ave NW. **FREE**

Yellow House. (1733) One of Georgetown's oldest homes, typical of the area's mansions. (Private residence) 1430 33rd St NW.

Special Events

Cherry Blossom Festival. Celebrates the blooming Japanese cherry trees. Also Japanese Lantern Lighting ceremony and marathon run; parade. Late Mar-early Apr. Phone 202/547-1500.

Easter Egg Roll. White House Lawn. First introduced to Washington by Dolley Madison. Mon after Easter. Phone 202/456-2200 (recording).

Georgetown House Tour. Held since 1927, participants view 12 well-known and less well-known houses in Georgetown. St. John's Episcopal Church members serve as hosts and guides, and serve tea in the Parish Hall in the afternoon. Late Apr. Phone 202/338-1796.

Georgetown Garden Tour. Fourteen or more different gardens open to the public. Proceeds go to Georgetown Children's House; includes "Evermay" garden, which features grand expanses, fountains, and sculptures. Self-guided tours. Second Sat in May. Phone 202/333-6896.

Evening Parade. US Marine Barracks, I St between 8th and 9th sts SE. Spectacular parade with Marine Band, US Marine Drum and Bugle Corps, Color Guard, Silent Drill Team, and marching companies. Written request for res suggested at least three wks in advance. Tues and Fri eves, early-May-late Aug. Phone 202/433-6060.

Memorial Day Ceremony. Arlington National Cemetery (See ARLINGTON COUNTY in Virginia). Wreaths placed at Tomb of the Unknown Soldier. The National Symphony Orchestra gives a free concert later in the eve on the lawn of the Capitol. Phone 703/685-2851.

Goodwill Industries Embassy Tour. Six to eight embassies are open to the public; only time embassies are open to public; visitors can view artifacts and design peculiar to each government's legation. Complimentary refreshments and illustrated tour booklet. Walking tour with shuttle bus between embassies. Tickets limited. No children under age ten. Second Sat May. Phone 202/636-4225.

Wolf Trap Farm Park for the Performing Arts. In Vienna, VA, 14 mi NW via Washington Memorial Pkwy, VA 123, US 7, then S on Towlston Rd (Trap Rd), (VA 676), then follow signs. Phone 703/255-1900. (See FAIRFAX in Virginia) Late May-Sept (Filene Center) and mid-Oct-mid-May (The Barns).

Musical programs. In Carter Barron Amphitheater, Rock Creek Park. Mid-June-Aug. Phone 202/619-7222.

Festival of American Folklife. The Mall. Festival of folklife traditions from America and abroad. Sponsored by the Smithsonian Institution and National Park Service. Late June-early July. Phone 202/357-2700.

Fort Dupont Summer Theatre. Fort Dupont Park. Musicals, concerts, plays, dancing. Fri eves, late June-late Aug. Phone 202/426-7723.

July 4 Celebration. Washington Monument and Capitol west steps. Music, celebrations; extensive fireworks. Phone 202/426-6841.

Concerts. Sylvan Theater, Washington Monument grounds, June-Aug, days vary, phone 202/619-7222. US Capitol, west terrace, June-late Aug, Mon-Wed, Fri, Sun, phone 202/619-7222. National Gallery of Art, west garden court, Oct-June, Sun eves; first-come basis, phone 202/842-6941. Phillips Collection, a Dupont-Kalorama museum, Sept-May, Sun, phone 202/387-2151.

Washington National Cathedral Open House. Washington National Cathedral. Special tours, entertainment, food; demonstrations of cathedral arts. Only day of the yr when central tower is open to the public. Sat nearest Sept 29. Phone 202/537-6200.

Taste of D.C. Pennsylvania Ave NW between 9th and 14th sts. Selected D.C. restaurants offer sample-size specialities. Mid-Oct. Phone 202/789-7000.

Pageant of Peace. Ellipse, south of White House. Seasonal music, caroling; giant Christmas tree near the White House is lit by the president. Dec. Phone 202/619-7222.

Motels/Motor Lodges

★ ★ **CHANNEL INN HOTEL.** *650 Water St SW (20024). 202/554-2400; fax 202/863-1164; toll-free 800/368-5668. www.channelinn.com.* 100 rms, 3 story. S, D $115-$145; each addl $10; suites $200; under 13 free; wkend rates. Crib free. TV; cable (premium). Pool; lifeguard. Restaurant 7 am-11 pm; Sun to 9 pm. Bar 11:30-1 am; Fri, Sat to 2 am; Sun to 10 pm; entertainment. Ck-out noon. Meeting rms. In-rm modem link. Bellhops. Garage parking. Health club privileges. Balconies. Near piers. Cr cds: A, C, D, DS, JCB, MC, V.
D ⛝ 🐾 SC

★ **HOTEL ROUGE.** *1315 16th St NW (20036). 202/232-8000; fax 202/667-9827; toll-free 800/368-5689. www.hotelrouge.com.* 137 rms, 10 story. S $170; D $190; each addl $20; under 16 free. Crib free. Garage $20. TV; cable (premium). Restaurant 7 am-2:30 pm, 5-10:30 pm. Bar 5-midnight. Ck-out noon. Coin lndry. Meeting rms. Business center. Exercise equipt. Health club privileges. Microwaves avail. Cr cds: A, C, D, DS, JCB, MC, V.
D 🐾 ⛝ 🐾 SC 🏃

★ **WINDSOR PARK HOTEL.** *2116 Kalorama Rd NW (20008). 202/483-7700; fax 202/332-4547; toll-free 800/247-3064. www.windsorparkhotel.com.* 43 rms, 5 story, 6 suites. S $98-$110; D $108-$122; each addl $10; suites $125-$155; under 16 free; wkend rates (2-day min). TV; cable (premium). Complimentary continental bkfst. Restaurant nearby. Ck-out noon. Business servs avail. Refrigerators. Cr cds: A, C, D, DS, MC, V.
⛝ 🐾 SC

Hotels

★ **CAPITOL HILL SUITES.** *200 C St SE (20003). 202/543-6000; fax 888/627-7811; toll-free 800/424-9165.* 152 kit. rms, 5 story. Feb-June: S $139; D $149; each addl $20; suites $169; under 18 free; lower rates rest

of yr. Crib free. Valet parking $24. TV; cable (premium). Complimentary continental bkfst. Coffee in rms. Restaurant nearby. Ck-out noon. Meeting rms. Business servs avail. Valet serv. Health club privileges. Refrigerators. Cr cds: A, D, DS, MC, V.
⛝ 🐾 SC

★ **CENTER CITY HOTEL.** *1201 13th St NW (20005). 202/682-5300; fax 202/371-9624; toll-free 800/458-2817. www.centercityhotel.com.* 100 rms, 8 story. Apr-Sept: S $85-$115; D $95-$125; each addl $10; under 16 free; wkend rates; lower rates rest of yr. Parking $10 in/out. TV; cable (premium). Complimentary continental bkfst. Coffee in rms. Restaurant. Ck-out 11 am. Coin lndry. Meeting rm. Business servs avail. Cr cds: A, C, D, DS, MC, V.
D ⛝ 🐾 SC

★ ★ ★ **THE CHURCHILL.** *1914 Connecticut Ave NW (20009). 202/797-2000; fax 202/462-0944. www.the churchillhotel.com.* 144 units, 9 story, 36 suites. S, D $229-$329; each addl $30; suites $229-$329; under 12 free; wkend rates. Crib free. Garage parking; valet $21. TV; cable (premium). Restaurant 6:30 am-10:30 pm. Bar noon-11:30 pm; Fri, Sat to 1 am. Meeting rms. Business servs avail. In-rm modem link. Concierge. Exercise equipt. Health club privileges. Bathrm phones; microwaves avail. Refurbished apartment building; built 1904. Cr cds: A, C, D, JCB, MC, V.
⛝ 🐾 SC 🏃

★ ★ **COURTYARD BY MARRIOTT.** *1900 Connecticut Ave NW (20009). 202/332-9300; fax 202/328-7039; res 800/321-2211. www.courtyard.com.* 147 rms, 9 story. S, D $89-$200; each addl $15; under 18 free; wkend rates (2-day min). Crib free. Garage parking, valet $15. TV; cable (premium), VCR avail. Pool; lifeguard. Complimentary coffee in rms. Restaurant 6:30-10:30 am, 5-10 pm. Bar 5-11 pm. Ck-out noon. Coin lndry. Meeting rms. Business servs avail. In-rm modem link. Exercise equipt. Health club privileges. Cr cds: A, C, D, DS, JCB, MC, V.
D ⛝ ⛝ 🐾 🏃

★ ★ **EMBASSY SQUARE SUMMER-FIELD SUITES BY WYNDHAM.** *2000 North St NW (20036). 202/659-9000; fax 202/429-9546; toll-free 800/424-2999. www.staydc.com.* 278 suites, 10 story. Mar-mid-June, mid-Sept-mid-Nov: S $139-$250; D $159-$279; each addl $20; under 18 free; wkly, wkend rates; lower rates rest of yr. Crib free. Garage $15. TV; cable (premium). Pool; lifeguard. Complimentary continental bkfst. Ck-out noon. Coin lndry. Meeting rms. Business servs avail. In-rm modem link. Exercise equipt. Microwaves. Some balconies. Cr cds: A, C, D, DS, MC, V.

⬚ ⬚ ⬚ ⬚ ⬚ ⬚

★ ★ ★ ★ **FOUR SEASONS HOTEL WASHINGTON D.C.** *2800 Pennsylvania Ave NW (20007). 202/342-0444; fax 202/944-2076. www.fshr.com.* Nestled in residential Georgetown along the C&O Canal and Rock Creek Park, this peaceful property has a beautiful garden courtyard entrance and 260 elegant rooms and suites. A relaxing residential feel is evident throughout the design of the lobby and the extensive multilevel health and fitness club offers further pampering with great views, a lap pool, and a full spa. 260 rms, 6 story. S $350-$365; D $350-$395; each addl $30; suites $750-$4,000; under 18 free; wkend rates. Crib free. Pet accepted. Valet parking $25. TV; cable (premium), VCR avail (movies). Indoor pool. Restaurant 7-2 am (see also SEASONS). Rm serv 24 hrs. Afternoon tea. Bar from 11 am. Ck-out noon. Meeting rms. Business center. In-rm modem link. Concierge. Exercise rm; steam rm. Spa. Bathrm phones, minibars; microwaves avail. Some balconies. Cr cds: A, C, D, ER, JCB, MC, V.

⬚ ⬚ ⬚ ⬚ ⬚ ⬚ ⬚

★ ★ **GEORGETOWN INN.** *1310 Wisconsin Ave NW (20007). 202/333-8900; fax 202/333-8308; res 800/528-4261. www.thegeorgetowninn.com.* 96 rms, 6 story, 10 suites. S, D $195-$225; each addl $20; suites $275-$325; under 13 free; wkend, hol rates. Crib free. Valet parking $22. TV; cable (premium), VCR avail. Restaurant 6:30 am-2 pm, 5-11 pm. Bar 11-1 am. Ck-out noon. Meeting rms. Business servs avail. In-rm modem link. Exercise equipt. Refrigerators avail. Cr cds: A, C, D, DS, MC, V.

⬚ ⬚ ⬚ ⬚

★ **GOVERNORS HOUSE HOTEL.** *1615 Rhode Island Ave NW (20036). 202/296-2100; fax 202/463-6614; toll-free 800/821-4367. www.governors housewdc.com.* 149 units, 9 story, 24 kits. Mar-June, Sept-Oct: S $125-$195; D $140-$210; each addl $20; suites $175-$225; kit. units $145-$155; under 16 free; wkend, monthly rates. Crib free. Valet parking $19. TV; cable (premium). Pool; lifeguard. Restaurant 7 am-midnight. Bar from 11:30 am. Ck-out noon. Meeting rms. Business servs avail. In-rm modem link. Exercise rm. Health club privileges. Microwaves avail. On original site of Governor of Pennsylvania's house. Cr cds: A, C, D, DS, JCB, MC, V.

⬚ ⬚ ⬚ ⬚ ⬚

★ ★ ★ **GRAND HYATT WASHINGTON.** *1000 H St NW (20001). 202/582-1234; fax 202/634-4781; res 800/233-1234. www.hyatt.com.* 900 rms, 60 suites, 12 story. S $235-$299; D $250-$299; each addl $25; suites $425-$1,500; under 18 free; wkend rates. Crib free. Garage $20. Valet parking with in/out privileges $26. TV; cable (premium), VCR avail. Restaurant 6:30-1 am. Bar; entertainment. Ck-out noon. Convention facilities. Business center. In-rm modem link. Gift shop. Exercise rm; sauna. Health club privileges. Minibars. 12-story atrium lobby; 3-story cascading waterfall. Luxury level. Cr cds: A, C, D, DS, ER, JCB, MC, V.

⬚ ⬚ ⬚ ⬚ ⬚

★ ★ **THE HAMILTON CROWNE PLAZA.** *1001 14th St NW (20005). 202/682-0111; fax 202/682-9525. www.crownplazawashington.com.* 318 rms, 14 story, 17 suites. S, D $159-$229; suites $400. Crib avail. Valet parking avail. TV; cable. Complimentary coffee in rms. Restaurant 6:30 am-11 pm. Bar. Ck-out noon, ck-in 3 pm. Conference center, meeting rms. Business center. Bellhops. Concierge serv. Dry cleaning. Gift shop. Exercise privileges. Cr cds: A, D, DS, MC, V.

⬚ ⬚ ⬚ ⬚ ⬚ ⬚

★ ★ ★ ★ **THE HAY-ADAMS.** *800 16th St NW (20006). 202/638-6600; fax 202/638-2716; toll-free 800/424-5054. www.hayadams.com.* Situated directly across from the White House, this historic property offers exquisite views of national landmarks and has recently completed a major renovation. Old World charm and modern conveniences are melded to give the guests the best of both worlds. Guest rooms feature lavish tapestries, ornamental fireplaces, high speed internet access, and a refreshment center. 143 rms, 8 story. S, D $275-$500; each addl $30; suites $575-$2,250; under 13 free; wkend rates. Pet accepted, some restrictions. TV; cable (premium). Restaurant (see also LAFAYETTE). Rm serv 24 hrs. Bar 4:30 pm-midnight; Fri, Sat to 1 am. Ck-out noon. Business servs avail. In-rm modem link. Meeting rms. Concierge. Valet parking $28. Health club privileges. Bathrm phones; some refrigerators, minibars, fireplaces. Some balconies. Cr cds: A, C, D, DS, JCB, MC, V.

★ ★ ★ **HENLEY PARK HOTEL.** *926 Massachusetts NW (20001). 202/638-5200; fax 202/414-0513; toll-free 800/222-8474. www.henleypark.com.* 96 rms, 8 story. Mar-May, Oct-Nov: S $165-$235; D $185-$255; each addl $20; suites $295-$375; under 16 free; wkend rates; lower rates rest of yr. Crib free. Valet parking $16. TV; cable (premium). Restaurant 7-10:30 am, 11:30 am-2 pm, 6-10 pm. Rm serv 24 hrs. Bar 11-12:30 am; entertainment. Ck-out noon. Meeting rms. Business servs avail. In-rm modem link. Health club privileges. Bathrm phones, refrigerators, minibars. Wet bar in suites. Tudor detailing; 1918 structure. Cr cds: A, C, D, DS, MC, V.

★ ★ ★ **HILTON AND TOWERS.** *1919 Connecticut Ave NW (20009). 202/483-3000; fax 202/232-0438; toll-free 800/445-8667. www.hilton.com.* 1,118 rms, 10 story. S $169-$355; D $189-$355; each addl $25; suites $444-$500; wkend rates. Crib free. Pet accepted, some restrictions. Garage $15. TV; cable (premium), VCR avail (movies). Heated pool; poolside serv, lifeguard (in season). Supervised children's activities (May-Sept). Restaurants 6:30 am-11:45 pm. Bar 11:30-2 am; entertainment. Ck-out noon. Convention facilities. Business center. In-rm modem link. Gift shop. Lighted tennis, pro. Exer-

cise rm. Minibars. Resort atmosphere; on 7 landscaped acres. Luxury level. Cr cds: A, C, D, DS, JCB, MC, V.

★ ★ ★ **CAPITOL HILTON.** *1001 16th St NW (20036). 202/393-1000; fax 202/639-5784; toll-free 800/445-8667. www.capital.hilton.com.* 544 rms, 12 story. S $195-$325; D $220-$345; each addl $30; suites $495-$1,100; family, wkend rates; package plans. Crib free. TV; cable (premium). Restaurants 6:30 am-midnight (see also FRAN O'BRIEN'S). Rm serv 24 hrs. Bar 11-2 am; entertainment Tues-Fri. Ck-out noon. Convention facilities. Business center. In-rm modem link. Concierge. Shopping arcade. Barber, beauty shop. Full-service spa. Valet parking 24 hrs. Exercise equipt; sauna. Minibars; many wet bars; some refrigerators. Luxury level. Cr cds: A, C, D, DS, JCB, MC, V.

★ ★ ★ **HILTON WASHINGTON EMBASSY ROW.** *2015 Massachusetts Ave NW (20036). 202/265-1600; fax 202/328-7526.* 193 rms, 9 story. S, D $130-$200; each addl $20; under 17 free; family, wkend, wkly, hol rates; higher rates special events. Crib free. Valet parking $15. TV; cable (premium). Complimentary coffee in rms. Restaurant 6:30 am-10 pm. Rm serv 24 hrs. Bar 11:30-1 am; entertainment. Ck-out noon. Meeting rms. Business center. In-rm modem link. Concierge. Free guest lndry. Exercise equipt. Pool; poolside serv, lifeguard. Many bathrm phones; some refrigerators, microwaves, wet bars. Cr cds: A, C, D, DS, MC, V.

★ ★ **HOLIDAY INN CAPITOL.** *550 C St SW (20024). 202/479-4000; fax 202/479-4353; toll-free 800/465-4329. www.holiday-inn.com.* 516 rms, 13 suites, 9 story. S, D $179; suites $219-$299; under 18 free; wkend rates. Crib free. Garage $16. TV; cable (premium). Pool; lifeguard. Coffee in rms. Restaurant 6:30 am-10 pm. Bar 11-1 am. Ck-out noon. Coin lndry. Convention facilities. Business servs avail. In-rm modem link. Exercise equipt. Health club privileges. Microwaves avail. Cr cds: A, C, D, DS, JCB, MC, V.

★ ★ **HOLIDAY INN CAPITOL HILL.**
415 New Jersey Ave NW (20001).
202/638-1616; fax 202/638-0707; toll-free 800/638-1116. www.holiday-inn.com. 343 rms, 10 suites, 10 story.
Feb-May, Sept-Nov: S, D $99-$249;
each addl $10; suites $198-$475;
under 18 free; wknd rates; lower
rates rest of yr. Crib free. TV; cable
(premium). Rooftop pool; poolside
serv, lifeguard. Restaurant 6:30 am-
midnight. Bar 11-2 am. Ck-out noon.
10,000 square-ft of meeting space.
Business servs avail. In-rm modem
link. Sundries. Covered parking.
Exercise equipt. Refrigerators, microwaves avail. Cr cds: A, C, D, DS, JCB,
MC, V.

[D] [≈] [▨] [SC] [≈] [ⅹ]

★ ★ **HOLIDAY INN CENTRAL.**
1501 Rhode Island Ave NW (20005).
202/483-2000; fax 202/797-1078;
toll-free 800/248-0016. www.holiday-inn.com. 212 rms, 16 suites, 10 story.
Apr-May and Oct: S, D $129-$179;
family, wkly, wkend rates; lower
rates rest of yr. Crib free. Covered
parking $16.74. TV; cable (pre-
mium). Pool; lifeguard. Coffee in
lobby. Restaurant 6:30 am-10 pm.
Bar. Ck-out noon. Free guest lndry.
Meeting rms. Business servs avail. In-
rm modem link. Gift shop. Exercise
equipt. Game rm. Some refrigerators.
Balconies. Cr cds: A, C, D, DS, JCB,
MC, V.

[D] [≈] [ⅹ] [▨] [▧] [SC]

★ ★ **HOLIDAY INN GEORGE-
TOWN.** *2101 Wisconsin Ave NW
(20007). 202/338-4600; fax 202/338-
4458; toll-free 800/465-4329.
www.holiday-inn.com.* 296 rms, 4
suites, 7 story. S $110-$140; D $120-
$149; each addl $10; suites $175;
under 18 free. Crib free. Parking
in/out $10. TV; cable (premium).
Pool; lifeguard. Restaurant 6:30 am-2
pm; 5-10 pm. Bar 4-11 pm. Ck-out
noon. Coin lndry. Meeting rms. Business servs avail. In-rm modem link.
Gift shop. Exercise equipt. Refrigerators avail. Cr cds: A, C, D, DS, JCB,
MC, V.

[D] [≈] [ⅹ] [▨] [▧] [SC]

★ ★ ★ **HOTEL GEORGE.** *15 E St
NW (20001). 202/347-4200; fax
202/347-4213; toll-free 800/576-8331.
www.hotelgeorge.com.* 139 rms, 8
story, 5 suites. Feb-June, Sep-Dec: S,
D $295; each addl $25; suites $750-

$875; lower rates rest of yr. Crib
avail, fee. Valet parking $15-$24/day.
TV; cable (premium), VCR avail, CD
avail. Complimentary coffee in rms.
Restaurant 7 am-10:30 pm. Bar. Ck-
out noon. Meeting rms. Business
servs avail. Concierge. Bellhops. Valet
serv. Exercise privileges, sauna, steam
rm. Cr cds: A, D, DS, MC, V.

[D] [ⅹ] [▨] [▧]

★ **HOTEL HARRINGTON.** *436 11th
St NW (20004). 202/628-8140; fax
202/347-3924; res 800/424-8532.
www.hotel-harrington.com.* 260 rms,
11 story, 29 suites. Mar-Oct: S $89; D
$99-$109; each addl $5; suites $115;
under 16 free; package plans; lower
rates rest of yr. Crib avail. Pet
accepted, some restrictions. Garage
$6.50/day. TV; cable (premium).
Restaurants 7 am-midnight. Bar from
11 am. Ck-out noon. Meeting rm.
Gift shop. Coin lndry. Refrigerators
avail. Cr cds: A, D, DS, JCB, MC, V.

[D] [♠] [▨] [▧] [SC]

★ ★ **HOTEL LOMBARDY.** *2019 Pennsylvania Ave NW (20006). 202/828-
2600; fax 202/872-0503; toll-free
800/424-5486. www.hotellombardy.com.*
130 units, 11 story. Mar-May, Sept-
Oct: S $130-$150; D $150-$170; each
addl $20; suites $170-$200; under 16
free; wknd rates; lower rates rest of
yr. Crib free. TV; cable. Restaurant 7
am-2:30 pm, 5:30-9:30 pm; Sat, Sun 7
am-1 pm, 5-9:30 pm. Ck-out noon.
Meeting rms. Business servs avail. In-
rm modem link. Health club privileges. Refrigerators, minibars. Cr cds:
A, C, D, DS, MC, V.

[▨] [▧] [SC]

★ **HOTEL MONTICELLO.** *1075
Thomas Jefferson St NW (20007).
202/337-0900; fax 202/333-6526;
toll-free 800/388-2410. www.hotel
monticello.com.* 47 kit. suites, 7 story.
Feb-mid-June, Sept-mid-Nov: S $135-
$165; D $145-$180; each addl $20;
suites $250-$350; under 16 free;
wkly, monthly rates; higher rates
Cherry Blossom season; lower rates
rest of yr. Crib free. TV; cable (premium). Complimentary continental
bkfst. Ck-out noon. Business servs
avail. In-rm modem link. Limited
free covered parking. Health club
privileges. Bathrm phones. Cr cds: A,
C, D, MC, V.

[▨] [▧] [SC]

★★ **HOTEL WASHINGTON.** *515 15th & Pennsylvania Ave NW (20004). 202/638-5900; fax 202/638-4275; toll-free 800/424-9540. www.hotel washington.com.* 340 rms, 11 story. S $170-$235; D $185-$235; each addl $18; suites $430-$668; under 14 free; wkend rates. Crib free. Pet accepted, some restrictions. TV; cable (premium). Restaurant 7 am-10 pm. Bar 11-1 am. Ck-out noon. Meeting rms. Business center. In-rm modem link. Gift shop. Exercise equipt; sauna. Bathrm phones. Original Jardin d'Armide tapestry (1854). One of the oldest continuously operated hotels in the city. Cr cds: A, C, D, DS, JCB, MC, V.

⬚ ⬚ ⬚ ⬚ ⬚ SC ⬚

★★★ **HYATT REGENCY.** *400 New Jersey Ave NW (20001). 202/737-1234; fax 202/393-7927; toll-free 800/233-1234. www.hyatt.com.* 834 rms, 32 suites, 11 story. S $235; D $260; each addl $25; under 18 free. Crib free. Garage $29. TV; cable (premium). Indoor pool. Restaurants 6:30 am-11 pm. Bar 11-2 am. Coffee shop. Ck-out noon. Meeting rms. Business center. In-rm modem link. Concierge. Gift shop. Barber, beauty shop. Exercise rm; sauna. Health club privileges. Minibars; some refrigerators; microwaves avail. Luxury level. Cr cds: A, C, D, DS, JCB, MC, V.

⬚ ⬚ ⬚ ⬚ ⬚ SC ⬚

★★★ **THE JEFFERSON.** *1200 16th St NW (20036). 202/347-2200; fax 202/331-7982; toll-free 800/235-6397. www.loweshotels.com.* 100 rms, 8 story, 32 suites. Jan-June, Sept-Nov: S $270-$310; D $285-$325; each addl $25; suites $450-$1,200; under 12 free; wkend rates; lower rates rest of yr. Crib free. Garage, valet parking $25. TV; cable (premium). Restaurant 6:30 am-10:30 pm. Rm serv 24 hrs. Afternoon tea 3-5 pm. Bar 11-1 am. Ck-out 1 pm. Business servs avail. In-rm modem link. Concierge. Health club privileges. Microwaves avail. Cr cds: A, C, D, DS, JCB, MC, V.

⬚ ⬚ ⬚

★★★ **JW MARRIOTT HOTEL.** *1331 Pennsylvania Ave NW (20004). 202/393-2000; fax 202/626-6991; toll-free 800/228-9290. www.marriott hotels.com/wasjw.* 772 rms, 42 suites, 12 story. S, D $214-$239; each addl $20; suites $275-$1,550; higher rates Mar-June, Sept-Nov; lower rates rest of yr; family, wkend rates. Crib free. Valet parking $25. TV; cable (premium). Indoor pool; whirlpool. Restaurant 7 am-11 pm. Rm serv 24 hrs. Bars; entertainment. Ck-out noon. Convention facilities. Business center. In-rm modem link. Concierge. Shopping arcade. Exercise rm; sauna. Massage. Game area. Bathrm phones, refrigerator in suites. Private patios on 7th, 12th floors. Luxurious hotel with elegant interior detail; extensive marble, mirrors; large collection of artwork displayed throughout lobby. Luxury level. Cr cds: A, C, D, DS, JCB, MC, V.

⬚ ⬚ ⬚ ⬚ ⬚ SC

★★★ **THE LATHAM HOTEL GEORGETOWN.** *3000 M St NW (20007). 202/726-5000; fax 202/337-4250; toll-free 800/368-5922. www. lathamhotel.com.* 143 rms, 10 story. S, D $179-$245; each addl $20; suites $225-$390; under 17 free; wkend rates. Valet parking $20. TV; cable. Pool. Restaurant (see also CITRONELLE). Bar 11-1 am; Fri, Sat to 2 am. Ck-out noon. Meeting rms. Business servs avail. In-rm modem link. Concierge. Health club privileges. Some minibars. Refrigerators avail. Sun deck. Overlooks historic Chesapeake and Ohio Canal. Cr cds: A, C, D, DS, MC, V.

⬚ ⬚ ⬚ ⬚ SC

★★★ **LOEWS L'ENFANT PLAZA HOTEL.** *480 L'Enfant Plaza SW (20024). 202/484-1000; fax 202/646-4456; res 800/636-5065. www.loews hotels.com.* 370 rms on floors 11-15. S, D $189-$279; each addl $20; suites $370-$1,200; under 18 free; wkend rates. Crib free. Pet accepted. Valet parking $22. TV; cable (premium), VCR (movies avail). Pool; poolside serv, lifeguard. Restaurant 6:30 am-midnight. Bar from 11:30 am. Ck-out 1 pm. Convention facilities. Business center. In-rm modem link. Concierge. Underground shopping arcade with Metro subway stop. Gift shop. Extensive exercise rm. Refrigerators, minibars; microwaves avail.

Many balconies. Cr cds: A, C, D, DS, JCB, MC, V.

⊡ 🦫 ≈ 🛪 ⊠ 🔥 🚶

★ ★ ★ **THE MADISON HOTEL.** *15th and M sts (20005).* 202/862-1708; fax 202/785-1255; toll-free 800/424-8577. *www.themadisonhotel.net.* 353 rms, 14 story. S, D $235-$315; each addl $20; suites $450-$3,000; wkend packages. Crib free. Valet, garage $15. TV; cable (premium). Restaurant 6:30 am-11 pm. Rm serv 24 hrs. Bar 11-2 am. Ck-out 1 pm. Meeting rms. Business center. In-rm modem link. Valet serv. Concierge. Exercise rm. Minibars, bathrm phones, refrigerators, mini-bars. Original paintings, antiques, Oriental rugs. Cr cds: A, C, D, DS, JCB, MC, V.

⊡ 🛪 ⊠ 🔥 🚶

★ ★ ★ **MARRIOTT AT METRO CENTER.** *775 12th St NW (20005).* 202/737-2200; fax 202/347-5886; res 800/228-9290. *www.marriott.com.* 456 rms, 3 suites, 15 story. Late Feb-June, mid-Sept-mid-Nov: S, D $179-$219; wkend rates; higher rates Cherry Blossom festival; lower rates rest of yr. Crib free. Valet parking $22. TV; cable (premium). Indoor pool; whirl-pool. Restaurant 6:30 am-2:30 pm, 5:30-10 pm; Sat, Sun 6:30 am-noon, 5:30-10 pm. Rm serv to midnight. Bar 11 am-midnight. Ck-out noon. Meeting rms. Business center. In-rm modem link. Concierge. Gift shop. Exercise equipt; sauna. Minibars; microwaves avail. Luxury level. Cr cds: A, C, D, DS, JCB, MC, V.

⊡ ≈ 🛪 ⊠ 🔥 🚶

★ ★ ★ **MARRIOTT WARDMAN PARK HOTEL.** *2660 Woodley Rd NW (20008).* 202/328-2000; fax 202/234-0015; res 888/733-3222. *www.marriott. com.* 1,350 rms, 125 suites, 10 story. Mar-June: S, D $149-$209; each addl $30; suites $250-$2,200; under 18 free; lower rates rest of yr. Crib free. Pet accepted. Valet parking $23; garage $19. TV; cable (premium), VCR avail. Heated pool. Complimentary coffee in rms. Restaurants 6:30 am-11 pm. Bar 11-2 am. Ck-out noon. Convention facilities. Business center. Concierge. Gift shop. Exercise equipt; sauna. Some refrigerators. Balconies. Cr cds: A, C, D, DS, MC, V.

⊡ 🦫 ≈ 🛪 ⊠ 🔥 🚶

★ ★ ★ **MARRIOTT WASHINGTON.** *1221 22nd St NW (20037).* 202/872-1500; fax 202/872-1424; toll-free 800/228-9290. *www.marriott.com.* 418 rms, 9 story. S, D $99-$219; suites $250-$500; under 18 free; wkend rates. Crib free. Garage $20. TV; cable (premium). Heated pool; whirlpool, poolside serv, lifeguard. Complimentary coffee in rms. Restaurant 6:30 am-10 pm; Fri, Sat to 11 pm. Bars 11:30 am-midnight. Ck-out noon. Meeting rms. Business center. In-rm modem link. Concierge. Gift shop. Exercise equipt; sauna. Refrigerators avail. Luxury level. Cr cds: A, C, D, DS, MC, V.

⊡ ≈ 🛪 ⊠ 🔥 🚶

★ ★ **MELROSE HOTEL.** *2430 Pennsylvania Ave NW (20037).* 202/955-6400; fax 202/775-8489. *www.melrose hotel.com.* 240 rms, 8 story, 37 suites. S $179-$219; D $199-$229; each addl $20; suites $285-$850; under 17 free; monthly rates; wkend plans. Crib free. Valet garage parking $16. TV; cable, VCR avail. Complimentary coffee in rms. Restaurant 6:30 am-11 pm. Rm serv 24 hrs. Bar 11-1 am. Ck-out noon. Meeting rms. Business servs avail. In-rm modem link. Concierge. Exercise equipt. Bathrm phones; microwaves avail. Classic English furnishings, art. Cr cds: A, C, D, DS, JCB, MC, V.

⊡ 🛪 ⊠ 🔥 SC

★ ★ **NORMANDY INN.** *2118 Wyoming Ave NW (20008).* 202/483-1350; fax 202/387-8241; res 800/423-6953. *www.jurysdoyle.com.* 75 rms, 6 story. S $103-$133; D $113-$143; each addl $10; under 12 free. Crib free. Garage $13-$20. TV; cable (premium). Complimentary coffee in rms. Restaurant nearby. Ck-out noon. Coin lndry. In-rm modem link. Health club privileges. Refrigerators. In residential neighborhood. Cr cds: A, C, D, MC, V.

⊡ ⊠ 🔥

★ ★ ★ **OMNI SHOREHAM HOTEL.** *2500 Calvert St NW (20008).* 202/234-0700; fax 202/265-7972; toll-free 800/843-6664. *www.omnihotels.com.* 836 rms, 34 suites, 8 story. S, D $109-$259; each addl $30; suites $400-$1,600; under 18 free; wkend, hol rates. Crib free. Pet accepted, some restrictions. Valet $26. Self park $22. Garage $14. TV; cable (premium),

2

2

VCR avail. Pool; wading pool, poolside serv, lifeguard. Restaurant 6:30 am-11 pm. Bar 11-2 am; entertainment. Ck-out noon. Meeting rms. Business center. Exercise equipt; sauna. Microwave avail in suites. Cr cds: A, C, D, DS, JCB, MC, V.

★★ **ONE WASHINGTON CIRCLE HOTEL.** 1 Washington Cir NW (20037). 202/872-1680; fax 202/887-4989; toll-free 800/424-9671. www.onewashcirclehotel.com. 151 kit. suites, 9 story. S, D $125-$275; each addl $15; under 18 free; wkend rates. Garage $16. TV; cable (premium), VCR avail. Pool. Coffee in rms. Restaurant 7 am-11:30 pm; Fri, Sat to midnight. Bar; entertainment. Ck-out noon. Meeting rms. Business servs avail. In-rm modem link. Concierge. Exercise equipt. Some bathrm phones; microwaves avail. Balconies. Elegant furnishings; landscaped grounds. Cr cds: A, C, D, MC, V.

★★★★ **PARK HYATT WASHINGTON.** 1201 24th St NW (20037). 202/789-1234; fax 202/419-6795; res 800/233-1234. www.hyatt.com. Just three blocks from Georgetown, this 92-room, 131-suite property is located in the fashionable West End neighborhood just minutes from D.C. monuments. Public spaces and guestrooms have a bright decor of light woods and soothing pastel colors creating an intimate European feel. The Melrose restaurant and bar offer contemporary American cuisine and beautiful outdoor cafe seating. 223 units, 10 story, 131 suites. S, D $350; each addl $25; suites $270-$1,975; under 18 free; wkend rates; lower rates July, Aug. Crib free. TV; cable (premium), VCR avail. Indoor pool; whirlpool, poolside serv. Restaurant (see also MELROSE). Rm serv 24 hrs. Bar 11:30-1 am; Fri, Sat to 2 am; pianist and 4-piece dance band. Ck-out noon. Meeting rms. Underground valet parking. Golf privileges. Exercise rm; steam rm, sauna. Massage. Bathrm phones, refrigerators; microwaves avail. Cr cds: A, C, D, DS, MC, V.

★★ **PHOENIX PARK HOTEL.** 520 N Capitol St NW (20001). 202/638-6900; fax 202/393-3236; toll-free 800/824-5419. www.phoenixparkhotel. com. 148 rms, 9 story. S $179-$219; D $199-$239; each addl $20; suites $350-$750; under 16 free; wkend plans. Crib free. Valet parking $21. TV; cable (premium). Coffee in rms. Restaurant 7-2 am. Bar from 11 am; Fri, Sat to 3 am; entertainment. Ck-out 1 pm. Meeting rms. Business center. In-rm modem link. Exercise equipt. Minibars; some refrigerators. Near Capitol; traditional European decor. Cr cds: A, C, D, DS, MC, V.

★★ **RADISSON BARCELO.** 2121 P St NW (20037). 202/293-3100; fax 202/857-0134; res 800/333-3333. www.radisson.com. 300 rms, 10 story. S, D $160-$180; each addl $20; suites $210-$550; under 17 free; wkend rates. Crib free. Valet parking $18. TV; cable (premium). Pool; lifeguard. Restaurant (see also GABRIEL). Bar 11 am-midnight. Ck-out noon. Meeting rms. Business servs avail. In-rm modem link. Concierge. Gift shop. Exercise equipt; sauna. Bathrm phones, minibars. Cr cds: A, C, D, DS, ER, MC, V.

★★★ **RENAISSANCE MAYFLOWER HOTEL.** 1127 Connecticut Ave NW (20036). 202/347-3000; fax 202/776-9182; toll-free 800/228-7697. www.renaissancehotels. com. 660 rms, 10 story, 186 suites. S, D $124-$289; suites $450-$3,500; under 18 free; wkend rates. Crib free. Valet parking $23. Garage $15-$30. TV; cable (premium). Complimentary coffee. Restaurant 6:30 am-11:30 pm. Rm serv 24 hrs. Bar 11-2 am; entertainment. Ck-out 1 pm. Convention facilities. Business center. In-rm modem link. Concierge. Exercise equipt. Health club privileges. Bathrm phones; refrigerators. Foreign currency exchange. Opened in 1925 for Calvin Coolidge's inauguration; ornate gilded interior, stained-glass skylights. Cr cds: A, C, D, DS, MC, V.

★★★ **RENAISSANCE WASHINGTON D.C. HOTEL.** 999 9th St NW (20001). 202/898-9000; fax 202/289-0947. www.renaissancehotels.com. 791 rms, 10 suites, 16 story. Apr-June, Sept-Nov: S, D $229-$270; each addl

$25; suites $500-$2,000; under 18 free; wkend rates; lower rates rest of yr. Crib free. Pet accepted, some restrictions. Garage $15. TV; cable (premium), VCR avail. Indoor pool; whirlpool. Complimentary coffee in rms. Restaurant 6:30 am-11 pm. Rm serv 24 hrs. Bar 11-1 am. Ck-out 1 pm. Convention facilities. Business center. In-rm modem link. Concierge. Shopping arcade. Exercise rm; sauna. Minibars; some bathrm phones; microwaves avail. Luxury level. Cr cds: A, C, D, DS, ER, MC, V.

★★★★ **THE RITZ-CARLTON, WASHINGTON D.C.** *1150 22nd St NW (20037). 202/835-0500; fax 202/835-1588. www.ritzcarlton.com.* This swank D.C. hotel offers ultimate comfort, with fine bed linens, spacious bathrooms, efficient and attentive service, and an excellent health club. Geared more toward business travelers than families on vacation, it is highly recommended for meetings. The luxurious appointments that the Ritz-Carlton name has come to symbolize are all here. 300 rms, 15 story. S, D $275-$425. Crib avail. TV; cable (premium). Restaurant 6:30 am-11 pm. Bar to midnight. Ck-out noon, ck-in 3 pm. Meeting rms. Business center. In-rm modem link. Concierge. Exercise rm. Minibars; many refrigerators in suites. Cr cds: A, C, D, DS, MC, V.

★★ **RIVER INN.** *924 25th St NW (20037). 202/337-7600; fax 202/337-6520; toll-free 800/424-2741. www.the riverinn.com.* 126 kit. suites. S, D $99-$219; each addl $15; under 18 free; wkend rates; higher rates Apr-May, Sept-Oct. Crib free. Pet accepted, some restrictions; $100. Parking $20. TV; cable (premium). Restaurant 7-10 am, 11:30 am-2 pm, 5-10 pm; Sat 8-10 am, 11 am-2 pm, 5:30-11:30 pm; Sun 8-10 am, 11 am-2 pm, 5-10 pm. Bar. Ck-out noon. Meeting rm. Business servs avail. In-rm modem link. Health club privileges. Microwaves. Cr cds: A, D, MC, V.

★★★★ **THE ST. REGIS WASHINGTON.** *923 16th and K sts NW (20006). 202/638-2626; fax 202/638-4231; toll-free 800/562-5661. www.sheraton.com.* This luxuriously striking property,

built in the style of an Italian Renaissance palace, certainly stands up to its neighbors, which include some of the grandest hotels in the city. The museum-quality lobby, with its gilded ceiling, marble floors, and antique furnishings, creates an elegant and stately feel. Perfect, unpretentious service and sumptuously appointed guestrooms have been luring patrons since 1926. 194 rms, 8 story. S, D $380-$3,800; each addl $25; suites $600-$3,500; under 18 free; wkend rates. Crib free. Pet accepted, some restrictions, fee. Covered valet parking $26. TV; cable (premium), VCR avail. Restaurant 7-10:30 am, noon-2 pm, 6-10 pm; Sat 7-11 am, 6-10 pm; Sun to 11 am. Rm serv 24 hrs. Bar. Ck-out 1 pm. Meeting rms. Business servs avail. In-rm modem link. Concierge. Gift shop. Exercise equipt. Health club privileges. Bathrm phones, refrigerators, minibars; microwaves avail. Italian Renaissance mansion with courtyard terrace. Cr cds: A, C, D, DS, ER, JCB, MC, V.

★★ **TOPAZ HOTEL.** *1733 North St NW (20036). 202/393-3000; fax 202/785-9581; toll-free 800/424-2950. www.topazhotel.com.* 99 kit. units, 10 story. S $140-$195; D $160-$215; each addl $20; under 12 free; wkend plans. Crib free. Garage $13. TV; cable (premium), VCR avail. Complimentary continental bkfst. Complimentary coffee in rms. Restaurant 7 am-2:30 pm, 5-10 pm. wkend hrs vary. Bar 5-10 pm. Ck-out noon. Meeting rms. Business servs avail. In-rm modem link. Health club privileges. Refrigerators, microwaves. On site of "Little White House" where Theodore Roosevelt lived during his vice-presidency and first weeks of his presidency. Cr cds: A, C, D, DS, JCB, MC, V.

★★★ **WASHINGTON COURT HOTEL ON CAPITOL HILL.** *525 New Jersey Ave NW (20001). 202/628-2100; fax 202/879-7918; toll-free 800/321-3010. www.washingtoncourt hotel.com.* 264 rms, 15 story. S, D $195-$275; each addl $25; suites $250-$1,500; under 16 free; wkend rates. Crib free. Pet accepted, some restrictions. Valet parking $24. TV; cable (premium), VCR avail. Restaurant 6:30 am-11 pm. Bar; pianist. Ck-out noon. Meeting rms. Business servs avail. In-rm modem link. Concierge. Exercise equipt. Gift shop. Bathrm phones. Large atrium lobby. Cr cds: A, C, D, DS, MC, V.

D 🔧 🏂 🖼 🐾 **SC**

★ ★ ★ **MONARCH HOTEL.** *2401 M St NW (20037). 202/429-2400; fax 202/457-5010; toll-free 877/222-2266. www.monarchdc.com.* 415 rms, 10 story. S, D $235-$330; each addl $30; suites $1,100-$3,000; under 18 free; wkend, summer rates. Crib free. Covered parking; valet $23. Pet accepted, some restrictions. TV; cable (premium), CD player. Indoor pool; whirlpool. Restaurant 6:30 am-10:30 pm. Rm serv 24 hrs. Bar 4 pm-midnight; entertainment. Ck-out 1 pm. Convention facilities. Business center. In-rm modem link. Concierge. Gift shop. Exercise rm; sauna, steam rm. Squash, racquetball courts. Bathrm phones, refrigerators, minibars. Some balconies. Cr cds: A, C, D, DS, JCB, MC, V.

D 🔧 🏂 🖼 🖼 🐾 **SC** 🏃

★ **WASHINGTON SUITES HOTEL.** *2500 Pennsylvania Ave NW (20037). 202/333-8060; fax 202/338-3818; toll-free 877/736-2500. www.washingtonsuiteshotel.com.* 123 kit. suites, 10 story. S, D $109-$269; each addl $20; under 18 free. Crib free. Pet accepted; $15/day. Garage $23. TV; cable (premium). Coffee in rms. Restaurant adj 11 am-midnight. Ck-out noon. Business servs avail. In-rm modem link. Health club privileges. Microwaves. Cr cds: A, C, D, DS, MC, V.

🔧 🖼 🐾 **SC**

★ ★ ★ **THE WATERGATE.** *2650 Virginia Ave NW (20037). 202/965-2300; fax 202/337-7915; toll-free 800/424-2736. www.swissotel.com.* 232 rms, 13 story. S, D $225-$255; each addl $25; suites $245-$385; under 18 free; wkend, hol rates. Crib free. Pet accepted, some restrictions. Valet parking $25. TV; cable (premium), VCR avail (movies). Indoor pool; whirlpool, lifeguard. Restaurant (see also AQUARELLE). Rm serv 24 hrs. Bar 11:30-1 am; pianist. Ck-out noon. Meeting rms. Business center. In-rm modem link. Concierge. Shopping arcade. Barber, beauty shop.

Exercise rm; sauna, steam rm. Massage. Bathrm phones, minibars; microwaves avail. Many balconies. Kennedy Center adj. Overlooks Potomac River. Cr cds: A, C, D, DS, JCB, MC, V.

D 🔧 🖼 🏂 🖼 🐾 🏃

★ ★ ★ ★ **WESTIN EMBASSY ROW.** *2100 Massachusetts Ave NW (20008). 202/293-2100; fax 202/293-0641; res 800/937-8461. www.westin.com.* Since 1927 this Embassy Row property has welcomed guests with turn-of-the-century style. All 206 rooms and suites are decorated with Federal and Empire furnishings, including rich fabrics and antique reproductions, and boast beautiful views of Washington Cathedral and historic Georgetown. 206 rms, 8 story. S, D $185-$500; suites $400-$3,000; under 18 free; wkend rates. Crib free. Valet parking $23. TV; cable (premium), VCR avail. Restaurant 6:30 am-10:30 pm. Bar 3 pm-1 am; entertainment. Ck-out noon. Meeting rms. Business center. In-rm modem link. Concierge. Tennis privileges. Golf privileges. Exercise equipt; sauna. Massage. Health club privileges. Bathrm phones, minibars. Cr cds: A, C, D, DS, JCB.

D 🏂 🖼 🐾 🖼 🏂 🏃

★ ★ ★ **WESTIN GRAND.** *2350 M St NW (20037). 202/429-0100; fax 202/429-9759; res 800/228-3000. www.westin.com.* 263 rms, 4 story. Sept-June: S $229-$299; D $249-$325; each addl $30; suites $450-$3,000; under 18 free; wkend rates; lower rates rest of yr. Crib free. Covered valet parking $20/day. TV; cable (premium), VCR avail. Heated pool; poolside serv. Restaurant 6:30 am-10:30 pm. Rm serv 24 hrs. Bar. Ck-out noon. Meeting rms. Business center. In-rm modem link. Concierge. Gift shop. Exercise equipt. Minibars. Bathrm phones; some fireplaces; whirlpool in suites. Some balconies. Many rms with view of landscaped interior courtyard. Luxury level. Cr cds: A, C, D, DS, JCB, MC, V.

D 🖼 🏂 🖼 🐾 🏃

★ ★ ★ ★ **WILLARD INTERCONTINENTAL WASHINGTON.** *1401 Pennsylvania Ave NW (20004). 202/637-7440; fax 202/637-7326.*

www.washington.interconti.com. This landmark property is one block from the White House and within walking distance of all major D.C. attractions. The corner building, housing 341 guestrooms and 42 suites, has been a part of Washington society for 150 years, offering a luxurious decor of Federal-, Victorian-, and Edwardian-era style. The Willard Room is a regal destination for regional American and European cuisine. 341 rms, 12 story, 42 suites. S, D $450-$620; each addl $30; suites $850-$4,200; under 14 free; wkend rates. Crib free. Pet accepted, some restrictions. Covered parking, valet $23. TV; cable (premium), VCR avail. 2 restaurants 7:30 am-10 pm (see also WILLARD ROOM). Rm serv 24 hrs. Bar 11-1 am; Sun 11:30 am-midnight. Ck-out noon. Convention facilities. Business center. In-rm modem link. Concierge. Shopping arcade. Exercise equipt. Bathrm phones, minibars; some microwaves avail. Cr cds: A, C, D, DS, MC, V.

[D] [🏃] [🐕] [🛫] [📶] [SC]

★ ★ **WYNDHAM CITY CENTER.**
1143 New Hampshire Ave NW (20037). *202/775-0800; fax 202/331-9491; res* *800/526-7495. www.wyndham.com.* 352 rms, 16 suites, 9 story. Mar-May, Aug-Oct: S $199-$220; D $219-$245; each addl $15; suites $250-$600; under 18 free; lower rates rest of yr. Crib free. Parking $22. TV; cable (premium). Coffee in rms. Restaurant 6 am-10 pm. Bar noon-1 am; entertainment Mon-Fri. Ck-out noon. Meeting rms. Business center. In-rm modem link. Concierge. Gift shop. Exercise equipt. Health club privileges. Some refrigerators. Luxury level. Cr cds: A, C, D, DS, JCB, MC, V.

[D] [🏃] [📶] [🐕] [SC] [🏃]

B&Bs/Small Inns

★ **KALORAMA GUEST HOUSE.**
1854 Mintwood Pl NW (20009). *202/667-6369; fax 202/319-1262.* *www.washingtonpost.com/yp/kgh.* 30 rms, some share bath, 3 story. S $55-$95; D $60-$100; each addl $5; suites $95-$135; wkly rates. TV in common rm. Complimentary continental bkfst; afternoon refreshments. Ck-out 11 am, ck-in noon. Limited parking avail. Business servs avail. Created from four Victorian townhouses

(1890s); rms individually decorated, antiques. Garden. Totally nonsmoking. Cr cds: A, D, DS, MC, V.

[📶] [🐕] [SC]

★ **KALORAMA GUEST HOUSE.**
2700 Cathedral Ave NW (20008). *202/328-0860; fax 202/328-8730.* 19 rms, 7 share baths, 4 story, 2 suites. No rm phones. Mar-mid-June, Sept-Nov: S $45-$95; D $55-$105; each addl $5; wkly rates; lower rates rest of yr. Children over 5 yrs only. TV in sitting rm. Complimentary continental bkfst; afternoon refreshments. Restaurant nearby. Ck-out 11 am, ck-in noon. Free lndry facilities. Limited off-street parking. Sitting rm; antiques. Two early 20th-century townhouses (1910). Cr cds: A, C, D, DS, MC, V.

[📶] [🐕]

★ ★ ★ **MORRISON-CLARK INN.**
1015 L St NW (20001). 202/898-1200; *fax 202/289-8576; toll-free 800/332-7898. www.morrisonclark.com.* 54 units, 4 story, 14 suites. Mar-June, Sept-Nov: S $155-$240; D $175-$260; each addl $20; suites $180-$240; under 12 free; wkend rates; lower rates rest of yr. Crib free. TV; cable (premium), VCR avail. Complimentary continental bkfst. Dining rm (see also MORRISON-CLARK). Ck-out noon, ck-in 3 pm. Luggage handling. Valet serv. Business servs avail. In-rm modem link. Exercise equipt. Health club privileges. Underground parking. Minibars; microwaves avail. Restored Victorian mansion (1864); period furnishings. Cr cds: A, C, D, DS, MC, V.

[🏃] [📶] [🐕] [SC]

★ **TAFT BRIDGE INN.** *2007* *Wyoming Ave NW (20009). 202/387-2007; fax 202/387-5019. www.taft* *bridgeinn.com.* 12 rms, 7 share bath, 3 with shower only, 3 story. Mar-June, Sept-Nov: S $59-$135; D $84-$150; each addl $15; wkly, hol rates; lower rates rest of yr. TV in some rms; cable, VCR avail. Complimentary full bkfst. Restaurant nearby. Ck-out 11 am, ck-in 2 pm. In-rm modem link. Valet serv. Guest lndry. Some balconies. Georgian-style house built in 1905; eclectic antique, art collection. Totally nonsmoking. Cr cds: MC, V.

[📶] [🐕]

★ **WINDSOR INN.** *1842 16th St NW (20009).* 202/667-0300; fax 202/667-4503; toll-free 800/423-9111. 45 rms, 3 story, 9 suites. No elvtr. S $79-$110; D $89-$139; suites $105-$175; under 14 free; wkend rates. Crib free. TV; cable (premium). Complimentary continental bkfst; afternoon refreshments. Restaurant nearby. Ck-out noon, ck-in 2 pm. Business servs avail. Health club privileges. Refrigerator in suites. Originally a boarding house (1922). Cr cds: A, C, D, MC, V.
🖨 🔥 SC

All Suites

★★ **EMBASSY SUITES.** *1250 22nd St NW (20037).* 202/857-3388; fax 202/293-3173; res 800/362-2779. www.embassysuites.com. 318 suites, 9 story. S $159-$369; D $179-$389; each addl $20; 2-bedrm suites $600-$900; under 16 free; wkend rates. Crib free. TV; cable (premium). Indoor pool; whirlpool, lifeguard. Complimentary full bkfst. Complimentary coffee in rms. Restaurant 11 am-11 pm. Bar. Ck-out noon. Meeting rms. Business center. In-rm modem link. Concierge. Exercise equipt; sauna. Game rm. Refrigerators, microwaves, wet bars. Cr cds: A, C, D, DS, JCB, MC, V.
D 🏊 🏃 🖨 🔥 SC 🏃

★★ **EMBASSY SUITES UPTOWN.** *4300 Military Rd NW (20015).* 202/362-9300; fax 202/686-3405; toll-free 800/362-2779. www.embassysuites. com. 198 suites, 8 story. Mar-Oct: S, D $160-$200; each addl $15; wkend rates; lower rates rest of yr. Crib avail. Garage $10. TV; cable (premium). Indoor pool. Complimentary full bkfst. Complimentary coffee in rms. Rm serv 11:30 am-10 pm. Ck-out noon. Coin lndry. Meeting rms. Business servs avail. Exercise rm. Refrigerators, microwaves, wet bars. Atrium. Connected to shopping center. Cr cds: A, C, D, DS, MC, V.
D 🏊 🏃 🖨 🔥 SC

★ **LINCOLN SUITES.** *1823 L St NW (20036).* 202/223-4320; fax 202/223-8546; toll-free 800/424-2970. www.lincolnhotels.com. 99 rms, 10 story, 24 kit. units. S, D, kit. units $175; each addl $15; under 17 free. Crib free. Garage parking $16. TV;

cable (premium). Complimentary coffee in rms. Restaurant 7-10 am, 11:30 am-1:30 pm, 5-10 pm. Bar. Ck-out noon. Meeting rms. Business servs avail. Health club privileges. Refrigerators, microwaves. Cr cds: A, C, D, DS, MC, V.
D 🏊 🔥 SC

★★ **ST. JAMES SUITES.** *950 24th St NW (20037).* 202/457-0500; fax 202/659-4492; toll-free 800/852-8512. www.stjamessuitesdc.com. 195 kit. suites, 12 story. Feb-June, Sept-Oct: suites $139-$169; under 16 free; wkend rates; higher rates: Cherry Blossom Festival; lower rates rest of yr. Crib free. Garage parking $15; valet. TV; cable, VCR avail. Pool; lifeguard. Complimentary continental bkfst. Coffee in rms. Restaurant nearby. Ck-out noon. Coin lndry. Meeting rms. Business servs avail. In-rm modem link. Concierge. Exercise equipt. Cr cds: A, D, DS, MC, V.
D 🏊 🏃 🖨 🔥 SC

Restaurants

★★ **ADITI.** *3299 M St NW (20007).* 202/625-6825. Hrs: 11:30 am-2:30 pm, 5:30-10 pm; Fri, Sat to 10:30 pm. Closed Thanksgiving. Res accepted. Indian menu. Serv bar. Lunch $4.95-$9.95, dinner $4.95-$13.95. Specializes in tandoori char-broiled meats, vegetarian dishes, seafood. Cr cds: A, D, DS, MC, V.
🖨

★★ **ANNA MARIA'S.** *1737 Connecticut Ave NW (20009).* 202/667-1444. Hrs: 11-1 am; Fri to 3 am; Sat 5 pm-3 am; Sun 5 pm-1 am. Closed hols. Res accepted. Italian menu. Bar. Lunch $7.95-$10.95, dinner $12.95-$19.95. Specializes in homemade pasta, veal. Atrium rm; fireplace. Cr cds: A, D, DS, MC, V.
🖨

★★★ **AQUARELLE.** *2650 Virginia Ave NW (20037).* 202/298-4455. Hrs: 7-10:30 am, 11:30 am-2:30 pm, 5-10:30 pm; Sun brunch 11:30 am-2:30 pm; early-bird dinner 5-7:30 pm. Res accepted. Continental menu. Bar 11:30-1 am. Wine cellar. A la carte entrees: bkfst $7-$16, lunch $12-$22, dinner $14-$25. Complete meal: dinner $35-$65. Sun brunch $38. Specialties: quail stuffed with wild game bird mousseline, filet of sea bass in pesto broth, warm plumb tart. Own pasta. Valet parking. Panoramic view of the Potomac River. Cr cds: A, D, DS, MC, V.

⭐ **AUSTIN GRILL.** *2404 Wisconsin Ave NW (20007). 202/337-8080. www.austingrill.com.* Hrs: 11:30 am-11 pm; Mon to 10:30 pm; Fri, Sat to midnight; Sun 11 am-10:30 pm. Closed Thanksgiving, Dec 25. Tex-Mex menu. Bar. Lunch, dinner $4.95-$14.95. Sat, Sun brunch $4.95-$6.95. Specializes in enchiladas, fajitas. Southwestern decor. Cr cds: A, D, DS, MC, V.

⭐⭐ **BACCHUS.** *1827 Jefferson Pl NW (20036). 202/785-0734.* Hrs: noon-2:30 pm, 6-10 pm; Fri to 10:30 pm; Sat 6-10:30 pm. Closed Sun; hols. Res accepted. Lebanese menu. A la carte entrees: lunch $6.50-$10.75, dinner $11.75-$16.25. Specializes in authentic Lebanese cuisine. Valet parking (dinner). Cr cds: A, MC, V.

⭐⭐ **BEDUCI.** *2100 P St NW (20037). 202/223-3824.* Hrs: 11:30 am-2:30 pm, 5:30-10 pm; Fri to 10:30 pm; Sat 5:30-10:30 pm; Sun 5:30-9:30 pm. Closed late Aug; hols. Res accepted. Mediterranean menu. Bar. Lunch $9.50-$23, dinner $10.50-$25. Specializes in game, seafood. Three dining areas. Contemporary decor. Cr cds: A, D, DS, MC, V.

⭐ **BILLY MARTIN'S TAVERN.** *1264 Wisconsin Ave NW (20007). 202/333-7370. www.billymartinstavern.com.* Hrs: 8-1 am; Fri, Sat to 2:30 am; Sat, Sun brunch to 5 pm. Closed Dec 25. Res accepted. Bar. Bkfst $3.95-$7.95, lunch $5.95-$8.95, dinner $6.50-$18.95. Sat, Sun brunch $5.95-$12.95. Specializes in steak, seafood, chops. Parking. Outdoor dining. Established 1933. Family-owned. Cr cds: A, D, DS, MC, V.

⭐⭐⭐ **BISTRO BIS.** *15 E St (20001). 202/661-2700.* Specializes in tuna nicoise, sea scallops, veal chops. Hrs: 7 am-2:30 pm; Sat, Sun 11:30 am-2:30 pm, 5:30-10:30 pm. Closed Dec 25. Res accepted. Wine, beer. Lunch $11-$17; dinner $18.50-$27. Brunch $10.50-$14.95. Child's menu. Entertainment. Cr cds: A, D, DS, MC, V.

⭐⭐ **BISTRO FRANCAIS.** *3128 M St NW (20007). 202/338-3830.* Hrs: 11-3 am; Fri, Sat to 4 am; early-bird dinner 5-7 pm, 10:30 pm-1 am; Sat, Sun brunch 11 am-4 pm. Closed Dec 24, 25. Res accepted. Country French menu. Lunch $6.95-$11.95, dinner $12.95-$19.95. Wkday brunch: $11.95. Sat, Sun brunch $13.95. Specializes in rotisserie chicken, fresh seafood. Cr cds: A, DS, MC, V.

⭐⭐ **BISTROT LEPIC.** *1736 Wisconsin Ave NW (20007). 202/333-0111. www.bistrotlepic.net.* Hrs: 11:30 am-2:30 pm, 5:30-10 pm; Fri, Sat to 10:30 pm; Sun to 9:30 pm. Closed Mon; hols. Res accepted. French menu. Lunch $9.75-$12.95, dinner $13.95-17.95. Specialties: roasted rack of lamb, salmon in braro crust, soft shell crab. Storefront restaurant. Cr cds: A, D, DS, MC, V.

⭐⭐⭐ **BOMBAY CLUB.** *815 Connecticut Ave NW (20006). 202/659-3727.* Hrs: 11:30 am-2:30 pm, 6-10:30 pm; Sat 6-11 pm; Sun 5:30-9 pm; Sun brunch 11:30 am-2:30 pm. Closed hols. Res accepted. Indian menu. Bar 11:30 am-3 pm, 5-11 pm. Lunch, dinner $7-$18.50. Sun brunch $16.50. Specialties: tandoori salmon, lamb Roganjosh, chicken Tikka Makhani. Pianist eves, Sun brunch. Valet parking (dinner). Outdoor dining. Extensive vegetarian menu. Elegant clublike atmosphere reminiscent of British Colonial India. Cr cds: A, DS, MC, V.

⭐⭐ **BOMBAY PALACE.** *2020 K St NW (20006). 202/331-4200. www.bombay-palace.com.* Hrs: 11:30 am-2:30 pm, 5:30-10 pm; Fri, Sat to 10:30 pm. Res accepted. Northern Indian menu. Bar. A la carte entrees: lunch, dinner $8.50-$19.95. Complete meals: lunch, dinner $16.95-$19.95. Specialties: butter chicken, gosht patiala, jumbo prawns tandoori. Indian decor and original art; 350-gallon fish tank. Totally nonsmoking. Cr cds: A, DS, MC, V.

⭐ **BUA.** *1635 P St NW (20036). 202/265-0828. www.buathai.com.* Hrs: 11:30 am-2:30 pm, 5-10:30 pm; Fri, Sat to 11 pm. Closed Thanksgiving,

Dec 25. Res accepted. Thai menu. Bar. A la carte entrees: lunch $5.85-$7.75, dinner $7.50-$12.95. Specializes in seafood. Outdoor dining on 2nd-floor balcony. In townhouse on side street; fireplace. Cr cds: A, C, D, DS, MC, V.
D 🖨

★ **BURMA.** *740 6th St NW (20001). 202/638-1280.* Hrs: 11 am-3 pm, 6-10 pm; Sat, Sun from 6 pm. Closed hols. Res accepted. Burmese menu. Serv bar. Lunch, dinner $5.95-$7.95. Specialties: green tea leaf salad, tamarind fish, mohingar. Burmese decor. Cr cds: A, C, D, DS, MC, V.
🖨

★★ **BUSARA.** *2340 Wisconsin Ave NW (20007). 202/337-2340.* Hrs: 11:30 am-3 pm, 5-11 pm; Fri to midnight; Sat 5 pm-midnight; Sun 5-11 pm. Closed hols. Res required Fri, Sat. Thai menu. Bar. Lunch $5.95-$8.50, dinner $7.25-$15.95. Specialties: panang gai, crispy whole flounder, pad Thai. Outdoor dining in a Japanese garden. New wave decor. Cr cds: A, D, DS, MC, V.
D 🖨

★★ **CAFE ATLANTICO.** *405 8th St NW (20004). 202/393-0812. www.cafeatlanticodc.com.* Hrs: 11:30 am-10 pm; Fri, Sat to 11 pm; Sun 5:30-10 pm. Closed hols. Res accepted. Latin American menu. Bar to midnight. Lunch $7.95-$13.95, dinner $13.95-$19.95. Complete meals (Sun-Wed): dinner $19.95-$21.95. Menu changes bi-weekly. Valet parking. Outdoor dining. Contemporary decor with modern artwork; central circular stairway leads to second dining level. Cr cds: A, DS, MC, V.
D

★★ **CAFE MILANO.** *3251 Prospect St NW (20007). 202/333-6183. www.cafemilanodc.com.* Hrs: 11-1 am; Sun noon-11 pm. Closed Thanksgiving, Dec 25. Res accepted. Italian menu. Bar. Lunch $9-$26, dinner $13-$28. Specialties: strozzapreti moschino, costoletta di vitello. Outdoor dining. Large tie/scarf collection hanging on walls. Cr cds: A, C, D, DS, MC, V.
D 🖨

★ **CAFE MOZART.** *1331 H St NW (20005). 202/347-5732.* Hrs: 7:30 am-

10 pm; Sat from 9 am; Sun from 11 am. Closed Jan 1, Thanksgiving, Dec 25. Res accepted. German, Austrian menu. Bar. Bkfst $3.10-$6.95, lunch $4.85-$21.50, dinner $8.95-$22.50. Child's menu. Specialties: Wiener schnitzel, pork roast, Kasseler rippchen. Entertainment Thurs-Sat. German deli on premises. Cr cds: A, C, D, DS, MC, V.
D 🖨

★★★ **THE CAPITAL GRILLE.** *601 Pennsylvania Ave NW (20004). 202/737-6200. www.thecapitalgrille. com.* Hrs: 11:30 am-3 pm, 5-10 pm; Fri, Sat 5-11 pm; Sun from 2 pm. Closed Thanksgiving, Dec 25. Res accepted. Bar. A la carte entrees: lunch $9.95-$19.95, dinner $15.95-$27.95. Specializes in steak. Free valet parking (dinner). Club atmosphere. Cr cds: A, D, DS, MC, V.
D 🖨

★★ **CASHION'S EAT PLACE.** *1819 Columbia Rd NW (20009). 202/797-1819.* Hrs: 5:30-11 pm; Sun, Tues to 10 pm; Sun brunch 11:30 am-2:30 pm. Closed Mon; hols. Res accepted. Bar. Dinner $10.95-$17.95. Complete meal: dinner $25-$40. Sun brunch $3.95-$8.95. Specializes in lamb, duck, seafood. Own desserts. Valet parking. Outdoor dining. Contemporary decor; skylights. Cr cds: MC, V.
D

★★★ **CATALAN WEST.** *1319 F St NW (20005). 202/628-2299. www. catalanwest.com.* Hrs: 11:30 am-2:30 pm, 5:30-11 pm; Fri, Sat 5:30-midnight. Closed Sun; hols. Res required (lunch). French, Catalonian menu. Bar. A la carte entrees: lunch $13.75-$19.50, dinner $14.74-$25. Specializes in seafood, chicken, lamb. Valet parking. Cr cds: A, DS, MC, V.
D 🖨

★★★ **CHRISTOPHER MARKS.** *1301 Pennsylvania Ave NW (20004). 202/628-5939. www.opentable.com.* Specializes in New England seafood pie, walnut-crusted salmon. Hrs: 11:30 am-11 pm; Sat 4-11 pm; Mon to 10 pm. Closed Sun. Res accepted. Wine, beer. Lunch $7.50-$18; dinner $12-$28. Child's menu. Entertainment. Cr cds: A, C, D, MC, V.
D 🖨

★ ★ ★ ★ **CITRONELLE.** *3000 M St NW (20007). 202/625-2150. www. citronelledc.com.* Chef Michel Richard made his name in the '80s in California, and he opened Citronelle in Georgetown as an outpost to the original Citrus in Santa Barbara. It should come as no surprise that the food is better than ever. Appetizer presentations are stunning, entrees are rich and flavorful, and dessert (Richard was trained as a pastry chef) is not to be missed. Hrs: 6:30-10:30 am, noon-2 pm, 5:30-10 pm; Fri, Sat 5:30-10:30 pm. Res accepted. French menu. Bar. Bkfst $7.50-$12.50, lunch $20-$30, dinner $35-$55. Specialties: foie gras, filet mignon, canard a l'orange. Multilevel dining rm. Contemporary decor with modern art. Cr cds: A, D, DS, MC, V.

★ ★ **CLYDE'S.** *3236 M St NW (20007). 202/333-9180. www.clydes. com.* Hrs: 11:30-2 am; Fri to 3 am; Sat 10-3 am; Sun from 9 am. Closed Dec 25. Res accepted. Bars. Lunch $6.95-$10.95, dinner $9.95-$14.95. Sun brunch $4.25-$9.95. Child's menu. Specializes in seafood, crab cakes, ribs. Garage parking. Atrium dining. Classic saloon decor. Cr cds: A, D, DS, MC, V.
D 🖼

★ ★ **COCO LOCO.** *810 7th St NW (20001). 202/289-2626.* Hrs: 11:30 am-2:30 pm, 5:30-10:30 pm; Sat 5:30-11 pm. Closed Sun. Res accepted. Spanish menu. Bar. A la carte entrees: lunch $4.50-$11, dinner $5-$12. Prix fixe: $29.95. Specialties: stuffed ravioles, grilled chicken, stuffed shrimp. Salad bar. Entertainment. Outdoor dining. Modern tropical decor. Cr cds: A, DS, MC, V.
D 🖼

★ ★ **COPPI'S VIGORELLI.** *3421 Connecticut Ave NW (20008). 202/244-6437.* Hrs: noon-11 pm; Fri to midnight; Sat noon-3 pm, 5 pm-midnight; Sun 5-11 pm. Closed Thanksgiving, Dec 24, 25. Northern Italian menu. Bar. Lunch, dinner $7.95-$15.95. Child's menu. Specialties: wood-oven broiled fish, baked Ligurian risotto. Own pasta. Decor celebrates Italian bicycle racing. Cr cds: A, DS, MC, V.
D 🖼

★ ★ ★ **DC COAST.** *1401 K St NW (20005). 202/216-5988. www.dccoast. com.* Specializes in Chinese-style smoked lobster, mushroom-crusted halibut. Hrs: 11:30 am-2:30 pm, 5:30-10:30 pm; Fri, Sat 5:30-11 pm. Closed Sun; hols. Res accepted. Wine list. Lunch $22; dinner $45. Cr cds: A, C, D, DS, MC, V.
D

★ ★ **DISTRICT CHOPHOUSE.** *509 7th St NW (20004). 202/347-3434. www.districtchophouse.com.* Hrs: 11 am-11 pm; Fri, Sat 11 am-midnight. Sun 2-10 pm. Closed Thanksgiving, Dec 25. Res accepted. Bar. Lunch $8-$24, dinner $19-$27. Child's menu. Specializes in steaks, chops, seafood. Street parking. Brewery. Cr cds: A, DS, MC, V.
D 🖼

★ ★ ★ **FAIRFAX ROOM.** *2100 Massachusetts Ave NW (20008). 202/835-2100. www.westin.com/embassyrow.* Hrs: 6:30-11 am, noon-2:30 pm, 6:30-10:30 pm; Sat, Sun 6-11:30 am, noon-2:30 pm, 6:30-11 pm. Res accepted. American cuisine. Bar. A la carte entrees: bkfst $4.50-$18.50, lunch $12.50-$24.50, dinner $24.50-$34. Specializes in fresh seafood. Own baking. Free valet parking. Tableside cooking. Baby grand piano. Clublike atmosphere in 1928 landmark building. Proper attire required. Cr cds: A, D, DS, MC, V.
D 🖼

★ ★ **FILOMENA.** *1063 Wisconsin Ave NW (20007). 202/338-8800. www. filomena.com.* Hrs: 11:30 am-11 pm; Sat, Sun brunch to 3 pm. Closed Jan 1, Thanksgiving, Dec 25. Res accepted. Italian menu. Bar. A la carte entrees: lunch $5.95-$12.95, dinner $11.95-$29.95. Lunch buffet $8.95. Sat, Sun brunch $11.95. Specializes in pasta, seafood, regional Italian dishes. Own baking, pasta. Italian gardenlike atmosphere; antiques. Overlooks Chesapeake and Ohio Canal. Cr cds: A, D, MC, V.

★ **FRAN O'BRIEN'S STADIUM STEAK HOUSE.** *1001 16th St NW (20036). 202/783-2599. www.fobss. com.* Hrs: 11:30 am-11 pm; Sat, Sun from 5 pm. Closed hols. Res accepted. Bar to midnight. Wine cellar. Lunch $9-$25, dinner $18-$35. Child's menu. Specialties: ribeye steak, filet mignon, Maryland crab cakes with lobster cream sauce. Own desserts. Clublike atmosphere with sport themes; large collection of football memorabilia. Cr cds: A, D, DS, MC, V.

D ⊡

★ **FRATELLI.** *5820 Landover Rd, Cheverly (20784). 301/209-9006.* Hrs: 10 am-10 pm; Fri, Sat 2-10 pm; Sun 2-9 pm. Italian menu. Bar. Lunch $9.95-$13.95, dinner $11.95-$16.95. Specializes in pasta, chicken, seafood. Contemporary decor. Cr cds: A, MC, V.

⊡

★★ **GABRIEL.** *2121 P St NW (20037). 202/956-6690. www. washingtonpost.com/yp/gabriel.* Hrs: 6:30 am-10 pm; Sat 7 am-10:30 pm; Sun to 9 pm; Sun brunch 11 am-3 pm. Closed Dec 25. Res accepted. Spanish/Latin American menu. Bar 11 am-midnight. Bkfst $3.50-$9.50, lunch $7.25-$15, dinner $8-$24. Sun brunch $19.75. Specialties: sauteed scallops, roasted rack of lamb, smoked black bean soup. Mediterranean decor. Cr cds: A, D, DS, MC, V.

D

★★★ **GALILEO.** *1110 21st St NW (20036). 202/293-7191. www.roberto donna.com.* Hrs: 5-10 pm; Fri, Sat 5:30-10:30 pm, Sun 5-10 pm. Closed hols. Res accepted. Northern Italian menu. Bar. Wine cellar. A la carte entrees: lunch $15-$18, dinner $24-$35. Specializes in game, seasonal dishes, pasta, Mediterranean seafood. Free valet parking (dinner) Mon-Sat. Outdoor dining. Mediterranean decor. Cr cds: A, D, DS, MC, V.

D ⊡

★ **GARRETT'S.** *3003 M St NW (20007). 202/333-1033.* Hrs: 11:30 am-10:30 pm; Fri, Sat to 11 pm. Res accepted. Bars 11:30-2 am; Fri, Sat to 3 am. Lunch, dinner $5.50-$14.95. Specializes in steaks, pasta, seafood. 1794 landmark building; originally house of MD governor T.S. Lee. Cr cds: A, D, DS, MC, V.

⊡

★★★ **GEORGIA BROWN'S.** *950 15th St NW (20005). 202/393-4499. www.gbrowns.com.* Hrs: 11:30 am-10:30 pm; Fri to 11:30 pm; Sat 5:30-11:30 pm; Sun 11:30 am-2:30 pm (brunch), 5:30-10:30 pm. Closed Dec 25. Res accepted. South Carolina Low Country menu. Bar. Lunch, dinner $6.95-$22.95. Specialties: head-on Carolina shrimp and grits with spicy sausage, frogmore stew, Southern fried chicken. Jazz, blues Sun afternoons. Valet parking (dinner). View of McPherson Sq. Cr cds: A, D, DS, MC, V.

D

★★★★ **GERARD'S PLACE.** *915 15th St NW (20005). 202/737-4445.* After gaining acclaim in the 1980s for the striking, simple food served at his former Paris restaurant, chef Gerard Pangaud brought his culinary talents to the States at this relaxed and intimate bistro. The frequently changing menu doesn't depend on trendy ingredients and its written descriptions are as poignantly straightforward as the tastes they introduce. French menu. Specializes in contemporary French cooking. Hrs: 11:30 am-2:30 pm, 5:30-10 pm; Fri to 10:30 pm; Sat 5:30-10:30 pm. Closed Sun; hols. Res accepted. Wine list. A la carte entrees: lunch $15.50-$19.50, dinner $16.50-$32.50. Prix fixe: lunch, $29, dinner $78. Outdoor dining. Formal atmosphere. Some modern art. Cr cds: A, D, MC, V.

D ⊡

★ **GRILL FROM IPANEMA.** *1858 Columbia Rd NW (20009). 202/986-0757. www.thegrillfromipanema.com.* Hrs: 5-11 pm; Fri to midnight; Sat noon-midnight; Sun noon-10 pm. Closed Jan 1, Dec 25. Res accepted. Brazilian menu. Bar. Dinner $10-$22.95. Sat, Sun brunch $11.95. Specialties: feijoada, moqueca, caipirinha, bobo de camarao. Cr cds: A, D, DS, MC, V.

D ⊡

★ **GUAPO'S.** *4515 Wisconsin Ave NW (20016). 202/686-3588. www. guaposrestaurant.com.* Hrs: 11:30 am-11:30 pm; Fri, Sat to midnight. Res accepted. Latin American, Mexican menu. Bar. Lunch $6.95-$7.95, dinner $12. Specializes in fajitas. Outdoor dining. Colorful dining rms; Mexican decor. Cr cds: A, D, MC, V.

D ⊡

★ **GUARDS.** *2915 M St NW (20007). 202/965-2350.* Hrs: 11:30-2 am; Fri,

Sat to 3 am; Sun brunch 11:30 am-5 pm. Res accepted. Continental menu. Bar. Lunch $6.95-$12.95, dinner $15.95-$22.95. Sun brunch $5.95-$12.95. Specializes in veal, Angus beef, fresh seafood. Atrium dining rm; English country decor. Cr cds: A, D, DS, MC, V.
⊟

★ **HAAD THAI.** *1100 New York Ave NW (20005). 202/682-1111. www. haadthai.com.* Hrs: 11:30 am-2:30 pm, 5-10:30 pm; Sun from noon. Closed hols. Res accepted. Thai menu. Bar. Lunch $5.95-$8.50, dinner $8.95-$15.95. Specialties: pad Thai, pla yang, surf 'n turf. Tropical atmosphere. Cr cds: A, MC, V.
D

★★ **HOGATE'S.** *800 Water St SW (20024). 202/484-6300. www.hogates. com.* Hrs: 11 am-10 pm; Fri to 11 pm, Sat noon-11 pm; Sun 10:30 am-10 pm; Sun brunch to 2:30 pm. Closed Dec 25. Res accepted. Bar. Lunch $6-$13, dinner $13-$35. Lunch buffet $12.95. Sun brunch $18.95. Child's menu. Specialties: mariner's platter, wood-grilled fish, rum buns. Brunch entertainment. Indoor parking $1.50/hr. Outdoor dining. Overlooks Potomac River. Cr cds: A, D, DS, MC, V.
D ⊟

★★ **HUNAN CHINATOWN.** *624 H St NW (20001). 202/783-5858.* Hrs: 11 am-10 pm; Fri, Sat to 11 pm. Hunan, Szechwan menu. Serv bar. Lunch $6.75-$12, dinner $8.25-$20. Specialties: General Tso's chicken, tea-smoked duck, crispy prawns with walnuts. Parking (dinner). Modern, bilevel dining room. Cr cds: A, D, DS, MC, V.
⊟

★★ **JALEO.** *480 7th St NW (20004). 202/628-7949.* Hrs: 11:30 am-11:30 pm; Sun, Mon to 10 pm; Fri, Sat to midnight. Closed Thanksgiving, Dec 24, 25. Spanish menu. Bar. Lunch $15, dinner $25. Specializes in hot and cold tapas, Spanish-style fish. Sevillanas dancers Wed nights. Valet parking $8. Murals of flamenco dancers. Cr cds: A, D, DS, MC, V.
D

★★★ **THE JEFFERSON.** *16th and M sts (20036). 202/833-6206. www.the*

jefferson.com. Hrs: 6:30-11 am, 11:30 am-2:30 pm, 6-10:30 pm. Sun brunch 10:30 am-2:30 pm. Res accepted. Bar 5 pm-1 am. Wine list. Bkfst $5.50-$15.50, lunch $12-$22, dinner $20-$27. Sun brunch $17.50-$26. Specializes in natural American cuisine. Valet parking. Jeffersonian-era decor. Cr cds: A, D, DS, MC, V.
D ⊟

★ **J. PAUL'S.** *3218 M St NW (20007). 202/333-3450. www.j-pauls.com.* Hrs: 11:30 am-11:30 pm; Fri, Sat 1 am; Sun brunch to 4 pm. Bar to 1:30 am. Lunch, dinner $8.50-$21.95. Sun brunch $7.95-$12.95. Child's menu. Specializes in ribs, crab cakes, burgers. Turn-of-the-century saloon decor; antique bar from Chicago's old Stockyard Inn. Cr cds: A, D, DS, MC, V.
⊟

★★★★ **KINKEAD'S.** *2000 Pennsylvania Ave NW (20006). 202/296-7700. www.kinkead.com.* Chef/proprietor Robert H. Kinkead, Jr. presides over this American seafood restaurant. The spacious facility offers a choice of menus and atmospheres including outdoor seating, a more casual ground-floor bar and cafe with a seafood and raw bar menu, and the second-floor exhibition-kitchen dining room. One popular signature dish is the pepita-crusted salmon with crab, corn, and chiles. Specialties: pepita-crusted salmon, pepper-seared tuna, grilled squid. Hrs: 11:30 am-2:30 pm, 5:30-9:30 pm; Fri, Sat to 10 pm. Closed Jan 1, July 4th, Thanksgiving, Dec 25. Res accepted. Bar to midnight. Lunch $15-$22, dinner $24-$32. Free valet parking (dinner). Jazz pianist. Seafood/raw bar. Cr cds: A, D, DS, MC, V.
D ⊟

★★★ **KOBALT.** *1150 22nd St NW (20037). 202/835-0500. www.ritz carlton.com.* French menu. Specializes in lamb osso bucco with curried risotto, game hen stuffed with foie gras and truffles. Hrs: 6:30-10 am, 11 am-2:30 pm, 6 pm-midnight. Res accepted. Wine list. Bkfst $12.95-$15.95; lunch $15.95-$20.05; dinner $19.95-$32.95. Cr cds: A, C, D, DS, ER, JCB, MC, V.

★★ **KRUPIN'S.** *4620 Wisconsin Ave NW (20016). 202/686-1989.* Hrs: 8 am-10 pm. Closed Dec 25. Bkfst $7, lunch, dinner $8-$12. Child's menu. Specializes in smoked fish, meatloaf, beef stew. Old-fashioned decor. Totally nonsmoking. Cr cds: A, DS, MC, V.

D

★★ **LA CHAUMIERE.** *2813 M St NW (20007). 202/338-1784. www. washingtonpost/yp/lachaumiere.* Hrs: 11:30 am-2:30 pm, 5:30-10:30 pm; Sat from 5:30 pm. Closed Sun; hols. Res accepted. Country French menu. Lunch $13-$18, dinner $14-$28. Specializes in seafood, veal, game. Intimate room with beamed ceiling, open-hearth fireplace. Family-owned. Cr cds: A, MC, V.

D

★★ **LA COLLINE.** *400 N Capitol St NW (20001). 202/737-0400.* Hrs: 7-10 am, 11:30 am-3 pm, 6-10 pm; Sat from 6 pm. Closed Sun; hols. Res accepted. French menu. Bar. Bkfst $3.50-$8.75, lunch $9-$17, dinner $15-$22. Prix fixe: dinner $22-$27. Specializes in seasonal foods, fowl, seafood. Outdoor dining. Across from Union Station. Cr cds: A, D, DS, MC, V.

D

★★★ **LAFAYETTE.** *800 16th St NW (20006). 202/638-2570. www.hay adams.com.* Hrs: 6:30 am-2 pm, 6-10 pm; Sat, Sun from 7 am; Sun brunch 11:30 am-2 pm. Res accepted. Wine list. Bkfst $6-$19, lunch $16.50-$28, dinner $16-$32. Sun brunch $48.50. Specialties: American cuisine with French influence. Pianist. Overlooking Lafayette Park and White House. Cr cds: A, D, DS, MC, V.

★★ **LA FOURCHETTE.** *2429 18th St NW (20009). 202/332-3077.* Hrs: 11:30 am-10:30 pm; Sat 4-11 pm; Sun 4-10 pm. Closed hols. Res accepted. French menu. Lunch, dinner $12.95-$23.95. Specialties: soft-shelled crabs, veal, sweet bread. Outdoor dining. Former townhouse; painted murals on walls. Cr cds: A, D, MC, V.

★★ **LAURIOL PLAZA.** *1835 18th St NW (20009). 202/387-0035. www.lauriolplazarestaurant.com.* Hrs: 11:30 am-11 pm; Fri, Sat to midnight; Sun brunch 11 am-3 pm. Res accepted wkdays. Latin American

menu. Bar. A la carte entrees: lunch, dinner $9-$14. Sun brunch $9-14. Specialties: paella, pollo asado, lomo saltado. Outdoor dining. Oil paintings and exotic flower arrangements. Cr cds: A, DS, MC, V.

D

★★ **LAVANDOU.** *3321 Connecticut Ave NW (20008). 202/966-3002. www.lavandou.net.* Hrs: 11:30 am-10 pm; Fri, Sat to 11 pm. Closed hols. Res accepted, required on wkends. Southern French menu. Serv bar. Lunch $8.95-$14.95, dinner $14.95-$18.95. Complete meals: dinner (to 6:30 pm) $14.95. Specialties: clam a l'ail, grilled fish, truite saumnonee, daube Provençale. French bistro atmosphere features country artifacts. Free parking. Cr cds: A, D, MC, V.

D

★★ **LEBANESE TAVERNA.** *2641 Connecticut Ave NW (20008). 202/265-8681. www.lebanesetaverna. com.* Hrs: 11:30 am-3:00 pm, 5:30-10:30 pm; Fri, Sat to 11 pm; Sun 5-10 pm. Closed hols. Lebanese menu. Bar. Lunch $11-$16, dinner $18-$25. Specializes in falafel, lamb, shish kabob. Contemporary decor. Cr cds: A, D, DS, MC, V.

D

★★ **LEGAL SEAFOODS.** *2020 K St NW (20006). 202/496-1111. www. legalseafoods.com.* Hrs: 11 am-10 pm; Fri to 10:30 pm; Sat 4-10:30 pm. Closed Sun, Thanksgiving, Dec 25. Res accepted. Seafood menu. Bar. Lunch $7-$17, dinner $10-$29. Child's menu. Specializes in fresh fish. Valet parking after 4:30 pm. Family-owned since 1950. Cr cds: A, D, DS, MC, V.

D

★ **LES HALLES.** *1201 Pennsylvania Ave NW (20004). 202/347-6848. www.leshalles.net.* Hrs: 11:30 am-midnight; Sun brunch to 4 pm. Res accepted. French, American menu. Bar. Lunch $25, dinner $35. Sun brunch $14.95. Child's menu. Specialties: onglet, steak, cassoulet. Outdoor dining. Three-level dining area. Cr cds: A, D, DS, MC, V.

D **SC**

★★ **LUIGINO.** *1100 New York Ave NW (20005). 202/371-0595. www.*

luigino.com. Hrs: 11:30 am-2:30 pm, 5:30-10:30 pm; Fri to 11:30 pm; Sat 5:30-11:30 pm; Sun 5-10 pm. Closed hols. Res accepted. Nothern Italian menu. Bar. Lunch $8.25-$15.50, dinner $12.50-$22.50. Child's menu. Specializes in pasta, seafood, game. Outdoor dining. Trattoria with contemporary atmosphere. Cr cds: A, D, DS, MC, V.
[D] [⟶]

★ ★ ★ **MAKOTO RESTAURANT.** *4822 MacArthur Blvd (20007).* *202/298-6866.* Japanese menu. Specializes in sushi, sashimi, steamed salmon with grated turnip and wasabi-spiked broccoli. Hrs: noon-2 pm, 6-10 pm. Closed Mon. Res required. Lunch $20; dinner $50. Cr cds: MC, V.

★ **MARKET INN.** *200 E St SW (20024).* *202/554-2100.* *www.market inndc.com.* Hrs: 11 am-11 pm; Fri to midnight; Sat 4:30 pm-midnight; hols from 5 pm. Closed Thanksgiving, Dec 25. Res accepted. Bar. Lunch $20, dinner $25. Sun brunch $19.95. Child's menu. Specializes in Maine lobster, beef. Entertainment; jazz Sun brunch. Free valet parking. Outdoor dining. English pub ambience. Family-owned. Cr cds: A, D, DS, MC, V.
[D] [⟶]

★ ★ **MCCORMICK AND SCHMICK'S.** *1652 K St NW (20006).* *202/861-2233.* *www.mccormickand schmick.com.* Hrs: 11 am-11 pm; Sat 2 pm-midnight; Sun 4-10 pm. Closed Dec 25. Res accepted. Seafood menu. Bar to midnight; Fri, Sat to 1 am; Sun to 11 pm. Lunch, dinner $9.95-$19.95. Child's menu. Specialties: Alaskan halibut stuffed with Dungeness crab, Bay shrimp and brie; cedar-planked salmon with berry sauce; seared yellowfin tuna with wasabi and soy sauce. Own pastries. Valet parking (dinner). Old-fashioned decor with large, open grill. Cr cds: A, D, DS, MC, V.
[D] [⟶]

★ ★ ★ **MELROSE.** *1201 24th St (20037).* *202/955-3899.* Hrs: 5:30 am-2:30 pm, 5:30-10:30 pm; Fri, Sat to 11 pm; Sun brunch 10:30 am-2:30 pm. Res accepted. Contemporary American menu. Bar 5 pm-1 am; Fri, Sat to 2 am. Wine cellar. Bkfst $8-$15, lunch $15-$20, dinner $22-$32. Sun brunch $50. Child's menu. Specializes in fresh fish, seafood, veal. Own baking. Pianist. Valet parking. Outdoor dining. Dinner dancing Fri and Sat night. Sunlit atrium. Italian fountain. Cr cds: A, D, DS, MC, V.
[D] [⟶]

★ ★ ★ **MENDOCINO GRILL AND WINE BAR.** *2917 M St NW (20007).* *202/333-2912.* Specializes in mustard-spiced yellowfin tuna, grilled loin of Colorado lamb. Hrs: 11:30 am-10 pm; Fri, Sat to 11 pm. Res accepted. Wine list. Lunch $20; dinner $50. Entertainment. Cr cds: A, D, DS, MC, V.
[D]

★ ★ **MESKEREM.** *2434 18th St NW (20009).* *202/462-4100.* *www.meskerem online.com.* Hrs: noon-midnight; Fri, Sat to 1 am. Closed Thanksgiving, Dec 25. Res accepted. Ethiopian menu. Bar. Lunch, dinner $8.50-$11.95. Specializes in lamb, beef, chicken. Own Ethiopian breads. Ethiopian band Fri-Sun. Tri-level dining rm; traditional Ethiopian decor, sunny and bright. Cr cds: A, MC, V.
[D] [⟶]

★ ★ **MONOCLE.** *107 D St NE (20002).* *202/546-4488.* Hrs: 11:30 am-midnight. Closed Sat, Sun; major hols. Res accepted. Bar. A la carte entrees: lunch $13-$17, dinner $16-$25. Child's menu. Specializes in seafood, aged beef. Valet parking. Located in 1865 Jenkens Hill building; fireplace. Close to Capitol; frequented by members of Congress and other politicians. Family-owned. Cr cds: A, D, MC, V.
[⟶]

★ ★ **MORRISON-CLARK.** *1015 L St NW (20001).* *202/289-8580.* *www. morrisonclark.com.* Hrs: Mon-Fri 11:30 am-2 pm, 6-9:30 pm; Sat 6-10 pm; Sun brunch 11 am-2 pm, 6:00 pm-9:00 pm. Closed hols. Res accepted. Bar. Lunch $8-$15, dinner $25-$35. Sun brunch $35. Specialties: lamb, crab cakes. Own desserts. Free valet parking. Outdoor dining. American-style cuisine with Caribbean twist. Elegant Victorian dining rm; antiques; elaborately dressed floor-to-ceiling windows. Cr cds: A, D, DS, MC, V.
[D] [⟶]

★ ★ ★ **MORTON'S OF CHICAGO.**
3251 Prospect St NW (20007).
202/342-6258. www.mortons.com. Hrs:
5:30-11 pm. Closed hols. Res
accepted. Bar. Wine list. A la carte
entrees: dinner $25-$33. Specializes
in steak, lobster, seafood. Valet parking. Collection of Leroy Neiman
paintings. Cr cds: A, D, DS, MC, V.
$\boxed{D}$ $\boxed{=}$

★ **MR. SMITH'S.** *3104 M St NW
(20007). 202/333-3104. www.mrsmiths.
com.* Hrs: 11:30-2 am; Fri, Sat to 3
am; Sat, Sun brunch 11 am-4:30 pm.
Bar. Lunch, dinner $4.95-$14.95. Sat,
Sun brunch $4.50-$8. Specializes in
seafood, pasta, hamburgers. Pianist 9
pm-1 am. Old tavern atmosphere.
Outdoor dining. Family-owned. Cr
cds: A, DS, MC, V.
$\boxed{=}$

★ **MR.YUNG'S.** *740 6th St NW
(20001). 202/628-1098.* Hrs: 11 am-
10:30 pm. Chinese, Cantonese
menu. Serv bar. Lunch $5.95-$7.95,
dinner $9.95-$25.95. Specialties:
sauteed shrimp with snow pea
leaves, steamed lobster in garlic
sauce. Enclosed outdoor dining.
Modern Asian decor. Cr cds: A, D,
MC, V.

★ **MURPHY'S OF D.C.** *2609 24th St
NW (20008). 202/462-7171. www.
murphysofdc.com.* Hrs: 11-2 am. Irish,
American menu. Beer. Lunch, dinner
$5.95-$14.95. Child's menu. Specializes in steak, burgers, seafood. Traditional Irish music. Patio dining.
Wood-burning fireplace. Cr cds: A, D,
MC, V.
$\boxed{=}$

★ ★ **NATHAN'S.** *3150 M St NW
(20007). 202/338-2000.* Hrs: 3-11 pm;
Fri, Sat to 2 am. Res accepted. Northern Italian, American menu. Bar 11-2
am; Fri, Sat to 3 am. Dinner $9-$25.
Sat, Sun brunch $8-$15. Specializes
in steak, seafood. Antiques. Family-
owned. Cr cds: A, D, DS, MC, V.
$\boxed{=}$

★ ★ **NEW HEIGHTS.** *2317 Calvert St
NW (20008). 202/234-4110. www.
newheightsrestaurant.com.* Hrs: 5:30-10
pm; Fri, Sat to 11 pm; Sun brunch 11
am-2:30 pm. Closed hols. Res
accepted. New American cuisine. Bar
from 5 pm. Dinner $17-$28. Sun

brunch $11-$18. Specializes in cala-
mari fritti, grilled salmon, fresh
trout. Menu changes seasonally;
some entrees offered in half-portions.
Outdoor dining. Main dining rm on
2nd floor overlooks Rock Creek Park.
Cr cds: A, D, DS, MC, V.
$\boxed{=}$

★ ★ **OBELISK.** *2029 P St NW
(20036). 202/872-1180.* Hrs: 6-10 pm.
Closed Sun, Mon; hols. Res accepted.
Italian menu. Serv bar. Complete
meals: dinner $58. Specializes in sea-
sonal dishes. Menu changes daily.
Intimate dining rm on 2nd floor of
townhouse. Totally nonsmoking. Cr
cds: D, MC, V.

★ ★ **OCCIDENTAL GRILL.** *1475
Pennsylvania Ave NW (20004).
202/783-1475. www.occidentaldc.com.*
Hrs: 11:30 am-10:30 pm; Fri, Sat to
11 pm. Closed Thanksgiving, Dec 25.
Res accepted. Regional American
menu. Bar. A la carte entrees: lunch
$13-$20, dinner $20-$34. Specializes
in grilled seafood, beef, lamb. Own
desserts. Turn-of-the-century Victorian decor with autographed photos
of celebrities; originally opened
1906. Cr cds: A, D, DS, MC, V.
$\boxed{D}$ $\boxed{=}$

★ ★ **OLD EBBITT GRILL.** *675 15th
St NW (20005). 202/347-4800.
www.clydes.com.* Hrs: 7:30-1 am; Sat
from 8 am; Sun from 9:30 am; Sun
brunch to 4 pm. Res accepted. Bar to
2 am; Fri, Sat to 3 am. Bkfst $7-$10;
lunch, dinner $9-$25. Sun brunch
$7. Specializes in fresh oysters,
seafood, hamburgers. Own pasta.
Valet parking (dinner, Sun brunch).
In old vaudeville theater built in
early 1900s. Victorian decor,
gaslights; atrium dining. Cr cds: A,
D, DS, MC, V.
$\boxed{D}$ $\boxed{=}$

★ ★ **OLD EUROPE.** *2434 Wisconsin
Ave NW (20007). 202/333-7600.
www.old-europe.com.* Hrs: 11:30 am-3
pm, 5-10 pm; Sun 1-9 pm. Closed
July 4, Dec 24, 25. Res accepted. German menu. Serv bar. Lunch $5-$15,
dinner $10-$25. Child's menu. Specialties: schnitzel Old Europe, wiener
schnitzel, sauerbraten. Pianist Wed-
Sun. Cr cds: A, D, MC, V.
$\boxed{D}$ $\boxed{SC}$ $\boxed{=}$

★ ★ **OVAL ROOM.** *800 Connecticut Ave NW (20006). 202/463-8700. www.ovalroom.com.* Hrs: 11:30 am-3:00 pm, 5:30-10 pm; Fri, Sat to 10:30 pm. Closed Sun; July 4th, Dec 25. Res accepted. Bar. A la carte entrees: lunch $11.75-$19.95, dinner $16.95-$27.50. Specializes in New American cuisine. Menu changes seasonally. Valet parking after 5:30 pm. Outdoor dining. "Oval office" theme. Cr cds: A, D, MC, V.
D

★ ★ **PALM.** *1225 19th St NW (20036). 202/293-9091. www.thepalm.com.* Hrs: 11:45 am-10:30 pm; Sat 5:30-10:30 pm; Sun 5:30-9:30 pm. Closed hols. Res accepted. Bar. A la carte entrees: lunch $10, dinner $14.50 and up. Specializes in steak, lobster. Valet parking (dinner). 1920s New York-style steak house. Family-owned. Cr cds: A, D, DS, MC, V.
D

★ ★ **PAOLO'S.** *1303 Wisconsin Ave NW (20007). 202/333-7353. www. paolosristorante.com.* Hrs: 11:30-2 am; Fri, Sat to 3 am; Sun 11-2 am; Sat, Sun brunch to 3 pm. Italian menu. Bar. Lunch $7-$13, dinner $10-$25. Sun brunch $6.95. Specializes in pizza, pasta, seafood. Patio dining; wood-burning pizza oven. Cr cds: A, D, DS, MC, V.
D

★ ★ **PESCE.** *2016 P St NW (20036). 202/466-3474. www.pescebistro.com.* Hrs: 11:30 am-2:30 pm, 5:30-10 pm; Fri, Sat to 10:30 pm; Sun 5-9:30 pm. Closed Jan 1, Labor Day, Dec 25. Lunch $13-$17, dinner $20-$23. Specializes in seafood. Valet parking Mon-Sat. Modern decor. Cr cds: A, D, DS, MC, V.
D

★ **PIZZERIA PARADISO.** *2029 P St NW (20036). 202/223-1245.* Hrs: 11 am-11:30 pm; Fri, Sat to midnight; Sun noon-10 pm. Closed hols. Italian menu. Wine, beer. A la carte entrees: lunch $10-$15, dinner $10-$20. Specializes in pizza, salads, sandwiches. Lively, colorful atmosphere; pizza makers visible from dining area. Totally nonsmoking. Cr cds: D, MC, V.

★ ★ ★ **PRIME RIB.** *2020 K St NW (20006). 202/466-8811. www.theprimerib.com.* Hrs: 11:30 am-3 pm, 5-11 pm; Fri, Sat to 11:30 pm. Closed Sun; hols. Res accepted. Bar. Lunch $18. A la carte entrees: dinner $30. Specializes in roast prime rib, Chesapeake seafood, aged thick-cut steak. Pianist. Free valet parking (dinner). Art Deco decor; 1920s lithographs. 1940s New York supper club atmosphere. Jacket and tie required. Cr cds: A, D, MC, V.
D

★ ★ **PRIMI PIATTI.** *2013 I St NW (20006). 202/223-3600. www.primipiatti.com.* Hrs: 11:30 am-2:30 pm, 5:30-10:30 pm; Fri, Sat 5:30-11:30 pm. Closed Sun; hols. Res accepted. Italian menu. Bar. Lunch $20-$25, dinner $30-$35. Specializes in grilled fish, meat. Own pasta. Outdoor dining. Cr cds: A, D, DS, JCB, MC, V.
D

★ **RAKU.** *1900 Q St NW (20009). 202/265-7258. www.raku/dc.com.* Hrs: 11:30 am-10 pm; Fri, Sat to 11 pm. Closed Thanksgiving, Dec 25. Pan-Asian menu. Bar. Lunch, dinner $7.95-$15.95. Specializes in noodle dishes, dumplings, sushi, satays. Street parking. Outdoor dining. Casual teahouse decor with varied Asian accents. Cr cds: A, MC, V.
D

★ ★ ★ **RED SAGE.** *605 14th St NW (20005). 202/638-4444. www.redsage. com.* Eclectic menu. Specializes in nuevo Latino, modern American and southwestern favorites. Hrs: 11:30 am-2 pm, 5:30-10 pm; Sun from 5 pm. Closed Dec 25. Res accepted. Bar. A la carte entrees: lunch $8.50-$15.50, dinner $18.50-$31. Validated parking. Designed as a contemporary interpretation of the American West; each of dining level's four major areas exhibits a particular style and mood. Cr cds: A, D, DS, MC, V.
D

★ ★ ★ **RESTAURANT NORA.** *2132 Florida Ave NW (20008). 202/462-5143. www.noras.com.* Continental menu. Hrs: 5:30-10 pm; Fri, Sat to 10:30 pm. Closed Sun; hols; last wk Aug, 1st wk Sept. Res accepted. Bar. A la carte: entrees $25-$30. Menu changes daily. Own desserts. Atrium dining. In 1890 building with American folk art, Amish quilts on walls. Totally nonsmoking. Cr cds: A, MC, V.

★ ★ **ROOF TERRACE.** *2700 F St NW (20566). 202/416-8555.* Hrs: 11:30

am-3 pm only on matinee days, 5:30-9 pm on performance eves. Sun brunch 11:30 am-2:30 pm. Res accepted. Lunch $12-$16, dinner $20-$29. Sun brunch $25.95. Child's menu. Specializes in regional American cuisine. Garage parking. Summer outdoor dining. Contemporary decor; floor-to-ceiling windows offer views of Lincoln Memorial, Washington Monument, Potomac River, and Virginia. Totally nonsmoking. Cr cds: A, DS, MC, V.
D

★★ **SAIGON GOURMET.** 2635 Connecticut Ave NW (20008). 202/265-1360. Hrs: 11 am-3 pm, 5-10:30 pm. Closed Thanksgiving. Res accepted. Vietnamese menu. Serv bar. Lunch $5.95-$7.95, dinner $8.95-$13.95. Specialties: Saigon noodles, roasted quail, caramel chicken. Valet parking. Patio dining overlooking upper Connecticut Ave. Cr cds: A, D, DS, MC, V.
D

★ **SAIGONNAIS.** 2307 18th St NW (20009). 202/232-5300. www.dcnet. com/saigonnais. Hrs: 11:30 am-3 pm, 5-11 pm; Sun 5-10:30 pm. Closed Jan 1, Thanksgiving, Dec 25. Res accepted. Serv bar. Vietnamese menu. Lunch $5.95-$12.50, dinner $8.75-$14.50. Specialties: lemongrass beef, shrimp on sugarcane stick. Outdoor dining. Vietnamese artwork. Cr cds: A, MC, V.

★★★ **SAM AND HARRY'S.** 1200 19th St NW (20036). 202/296-4333. www.samandharrys.com. Hrs: 11:30 am-2:30 pm, 5:30-10:30 pm; Sat from 5:30 pm. Closed Sun; hols. Res accepted. Bar. A la carte entrees: lunch $9-$18, dinner $24-$35. Specializes in prime aged beef, Maine lobster, fresh seafood. Valet parking (dinner). Clublike atmosphere with mahogany paneling, paintings of jazz legends. Cr cds: A, D, DS, MC, V.
D

★★ **SEA CATCH.** 1054 31st St NW (20007). 202/337-8855. www.seacatch restaurant.com. Hrs: noon-3 pm, 5:30-10 pm, Fri, Sat to 10:30 pm. Closed Sun. Res accepted. Bar. Lunch $7.25-$18, dinner $15-$32. Specializes in fresh seafood, lobster, crab cakes. Own pastries. Valet parking. Outdoor dining on deck overlooking historic

Chesapeake and Ohio Canal. Cr cds: A, C, D, DS, MC, V.
D

★★★ **SEASONS.** 2800 Pennsylvania Ave NW (20007). 202/342-0444. www.fourseasons.com. Hrs: 6:30-11 am, noon-2:30 pm, 6:30-10:30 pm; Sun brunch 10 am-2:30 pm. Res accepted. Bar 11-2 am. Wine list. Bkfst $9-$21, lunch $14-$23, dinner $25-$40. Child's menu. Specializes in regional and seasonal dishes. Own baking. Pianist. Valet parking. Overlooks Rock Creek Park. Cr cds: A, D, DS, MC, V.
D

★★ **SEQUOIA.** 3000 K St NW (20007). 202/944-4200. www.ark restaurants.com. Hrs: 11:30 am-midnight; Fri, Sat to 1 am; Sat, Sun brunch 10:30 am-4 pm. Res accepted. Bar. Lunch, dinner $5.95-$28.95. Sun brunch $5.95-$20. Specializes in American cuisine. Outdoor dining. Terrace and multistory dining rm windows overlook Kennedy Center, Potomac River, and Roosevelt Island. Cr cds: A, D, DS, MC, V.
D

★★★ **1789.** 1226 36th St NW (20007). 202/965-1789. www.clydes. com. Hrs: 6-10 pm; Fri, Sat to 11 pm. Closed Dec 25. Res accepted. Bar. Wine list. Dinner $18-$32. Prix fixe: pre-theater dinner $25. Specializes in seafood, rack of lamb. Own baking. Valet parking. In restored mansion; 5 dining rms on 3 levels. Federal-period decor. Fireplace. Jacket. Cr cds: A, C, D, DS, MC, V.

★★★ **701 RESTAURANT.** 701 Pennsylvania Ave NW (20004). 202/393-0701. Hrs: 11:30 am-3 pm, 5:30-10:30 pm; Wed, Thurs to 11 pm; Fri to 11:30 pm; Sat 5:30-11:30 pm; Sun 5-9:30 pm. Closed hols. Res accepted. Continental menu. Bar. Wine list. Lunch $8.50-$19.50, dinner $13.50-$23.50. Specializes in seafood, lamb chops, New York strip steak. Pianist Sun-Thurs; Jazz combo Fri, Sat. Free valet parking (dinner). Outdoor dining. Overlooks fountain at Navy Memorial. Cr cds: A, DS, MC, V.
D

★ **SUSHI-KO.** *2309 Wisconsin Ave NW (20007).* *202/333-4187.* *www. heatherfreeman.com.* Hrs: noon-2:30 pm, 6-10:30 pm; Mon from 6 pm; Sat 5-10:30 pm; Sun 5-10 pm. Closed July 4, Thanksgiving, Dec 25. Res accepted. Japanese menu. Lunch $10-$18, dinner $15-$28. Specializes in traditional and modern Japanese dishes. Casual decor. Cr cds: A, MC, V.
D

★★★ **TABERNA DEL ALABARDERO.** *1776 I St NW (20006).* *202/429-2200.* Hrs: 11:30 am-2:30 pm, 6-10:30 pm; Fri to 11 pm; Sat 6-11 pm. Closed Sun; hols. Res accepted. Basque, Spanish menu. Bar. Lunch $14-$20, dinner $16-$28. Complete meals: lunch $17.50, dinner $35. Specializes in beef, fish, paella. Tapas bar. Own baking. Flamenco dancers Mar, Oct. Garage parking (dinner). Outdoor dining. Ornate, 19th-century Spanish decor. Jacket. Cr cds: A, D, DS, MC, V.
D

★★★ **TEATRO GOLDONI.** *1909 K St (20036).* *202/955-9494.* *www.teatro goldoni.com.* Hrs: 11:30 am-3 pm, 5:30-10 pm; Fri 11:30 am-2 pm, 5-10:30 pm; Sat 5-10:30 pm. Closed Sun, hols. Res accepted. Italian menu. Bar. Wine list. Lunch $30, dinner $50. Specialties: grilled wild rockfish with polenta, mushrooms and cherry tomatoes, cappellacci with lobster, foie gras with white truffles. Own pasta, desserts. Valet parking. Gallery setting has look and feel of Italian villa. Cr cds: A, C, D, DS, MC, V.
D 🍸

★ **THAI KINGDOM.** *2021 K St NW (20006).* *202/835-1700.* Hrs: 11:30 am-2:30 pm, 5-10:30 pm; Sat noon-11 pm; Sun noon-10 pm. Closed hols. Res accepted. Thai menu. Bar. A la carte entrees: lunch $6.50-$10, dinner $9.95-$20. Specialties: crispy chili fish, scallops wrapped in minced chicken, Thai Kingdom grilled chicken. Bilevel dining rm with full windows overlooking K St; authentic Thai decor. Cr cds: A, D, DS, MC, V.
D 🍸

★ **TOMBS.** *1226 36th St NW (20007).* *202/337-6668.* *www.clydes.com.* Hrs:

11:30 am-midnight; Sat from 11 am; Sun brunch 9:30 am-3 pm. Closed Thanksgiving, Dec 24, 25. Bar. Brunch, lunch, dinner $5.95-$12.95. Specializes in chicken, pasta, burgers. Vintage crew gear and prints on walls. Cr cds: A, D, DS, MC, V.
🍸

★★ **TONY AND JOE'S SEAFOOD PLACE.** *3000 K St NW (20007).* *202/944-4545.* *www.tonyandjoes.com.* Hrs: 11 am-11 pm; Sun brunch to 3 pm. Closed Dec 25. Res accepted. Bar Fri, Sat to 2 am. Lunch $10-$15, dinner $20-$25. Sun brunch $28-$32. Specializes in seafood. Own desserts. Entertainment Tues-Sat. Outdoor dining. Overlooks Potomac River. Cr cds: A, D, DS, MC, V.
D 🍸

★★ **TONY CHENG'S MONGOLIAN BARBECUE.** *619 H St NW (20001).* *202/842-8669.* Hrs: 11 am-11 pm; Fri, Sat to midnight. Res accepted. Mongolian barbecue menu. Prix fixe: lunch $9.50, dinner $13.95 (serv charge 15%). Food bar encircles Mongolian grill. Diners may select own ingredients to be stir-fried, grilled, or steeped tableside. Asian decor. Cr cds: A, MC, V.
D

★★ **TWO QUAIL.** *320 Massachusetts Ave NW (20002).* *202/543-8030.* Hrs: 11:30 am-2:30 pm, 5-10:30 pm; Sat, Sun from 5 pm. Closed Dec 25. Res accepted. Lunch $7-$14, dinner $11-$19. Specializes in New American cuisine, pork chops, seafood. Country inn atmosphere in Victorian townhouse; eclectic furnishings. Cr cds: A, D, DS, MC, V.

★★★ **VIDALIA.** *1990 M St NW (20036).* *202/659-1990.* *www.vidaliadc. com.* Hrs: 11:30 am-2:30 pm, 5:30-10 pm; Fri to 10:30 pm; Sat 5:30-10:30 pm; Sun 5-9:30 pm. Closed Sun (Jul-Aug); also hols. Res accepted. Bar. Lunch $12.50-$21.50, dinner $20-$30. Specialties: sauteed shrimp with creamed grits, pan-roasted sweetbreads. Country manor house decor. Cr cds: A, D, DS, MC, V.
D

★★★★ **WILLARD ROOM.** *1401 Pennsylvania Ave NW (20004).* *202/637-7440.* *www.washington. interconti.com.* Feel like royalty in this turn-of-the-century dining

room located in the Willard Inter-Continental Hotel. Awe-inspiring with rich oak paneling, creamy brocade fabrics, flowing drapery, and a grand piano. Chef Gerard Madani's menu is an impressive blend of regional American and European cuisine with dishes such as poached turbot with sauteed oyster mushrooms and port wine sauce. Hrs: 11:30 am-2 pm, 6-10 pm; Sat from 6 pm. Res accepted. Wine list. European, regional American menu. A la carte entrees: bkfst $8.50-$15.50; lunch $14.50-$38, dinner $20-$39. Chef tasting menu: 3-course $55; 5-course $85. Specializes in regional seafood, lamb, beef. Seasonal specialties. Own pastries. Pianist. Valet parking (dinner). Cr cds: A, C, D, DS, ER, JCB, MC, V.
D

★ **ZED'S ETHIOPIAN CUISINE.** *1201 28th NW (20007). 202/333-4710. www.zeds.net.* Hrs: 11 am-11 pm. Closed Dec 25. Ethiopian menu. Serv bar. Lunch $6.50-$10, dinner $6.50-$15. Specializes in seafood, beef, vegetarian dishes. No silverware is used at the restaurant; silverware will be provided at customer's request, communal dining from trays. Cr cds: A, D, DS, MC, V.

Unrated Dining Spots

AFTERWORDS. *1517 Connecticut Ave (20036). 202/387-1462. www.kramers. com.* Hrs: 7:30-1 am; Fri, Sat open 24 hrs; Sun brunch 9:30 am-3 pm. Closed Thanksgiving, Dec 25. Bar. Bkfst $5.50-$10, lunch $8-15, dinner $12-$15. Sun brunch $10-$16. Specialties: Thai jambalaya, grilled portobello mushroom sandwich. Entertainment Wed-Sat. Outdoor dining. In two-story greenhouse and terrace behind Kramer Books bookshop. Cr cds: A, D, MC, V.
D ⊟

ARMAND'S CHICAGO PIZZERIA. *4231 Wisconsin Ave NW (20016). 202/686-9450. www.armands.com.* Hrs: 11:30 am-11 pm; Fri, Sat to 11 pm. Closed Thanksgiving, Dec 25. Bar. A la carte entrees: lunch, dinner $7-$12. Buffet: lunch (pizza and salad) $9. Specializes in Chicago-style deep-dish pizza, pasta, sandwiches,

salads. Outdoor dining. Cr cds: A, D, DS, MC, V.
⊟

THE BREAD LINE. *1751 Pennsylvania Ave NW (20006). 202/822-8900.* Hrs: 7 am-3:30 pm. Closed Sat, Sun. Bkfst $1-$2.15, lunch $5.75-$8.25. Specializes in traditional stuffed, grilled and filled breads. Outdoor dining. Food inspired by international street foods. Cr cds: A, MC, V.
D

C.F. FOLKS. *1225 19th St NW (20036). 202/293-0162.* Hrs: 11:45 am-3 pm. Closed Sat, Sun; hols. Lunch $8-$11. Complete meals: lunch $8.50-$12. Specializes in daily and seasonally changing cuisines. Outdoor dining. Old-fashioned lunch counter. Cash only.
D

PHILLIPS' FLAGSHIP. *900 Water St SW (20024). 202/488-8515. www. phillipsfood.com.* Hrs: 11 am-10 pm; Fri to 11 pm; Sat, Sun 11 am-11 pm. Closed Dec 25. Bar. Buffet: lunch $14.95, dinner $24.95; Sun $19.95. A la carte bar menu: $3.50-$9.95. Specializes in seafood. Sushi bar. Garage parking. Outdoor dining. Antiques; Tiffany lamps, stained glass. Cr cds: A, D, DS, V.
D **SC** ⊟

MARYLAND

Maryland prides itself on its varied terrain and diverse economy. Metropolitan life around the great cities of Baltimore and Washington, D.C. (the land was ceded from Maryland in 1791) is balanced by the rural atmosphere in central and southern Maryland and on the Eastern Shore, across the Chesapeake Bay. Green mountains in the western counties contrast with white Atlantic beaches. A flourishing travel industry, agricultural and dairy wealth in central Maryland, the seafood industry of the Bay and its tidal rivers, manufacturing and commerce in the cities, plus federal government and defense contracts combine to make the state prosperous.

Maryland's 3½ centuries of history began in March 1634 when Lord Baltimore's brother, Leonard Calvert, solemnly knelt on tiny St. Clements Island, near the wide mouth of the Potomac, and named his new province in honor of Henrietta Maria, wife of Charles I, King of England. Calvert's awkward little ships, the *Ark* and the *Dove,* then carried the 222 passengers, including religious refugees, to a Native American village a few miles away. They purchased the village and named it Saint Maries Citty (now St. Mary's City). Religious tolerance was practiced from the colony's founding and was assured by law in 1649. The land was cleared, tobacco was planted, and over the years, profits built elegant mansions, many of which still stand.

Population: 5,171,634
Area: 9,838 square miles
Elevation: 0-3,360 feet
Peak: Backbone Mountain (Garrett County)
Entered Union: Seventh of original 13 states (April 28, 1788)
Capital: Annapolis
Motto: Manly deeds, womanly words
Nickname: Old Line State, Free State
Flower: Black-Eyed Susan
Bird: Baltimore Oriole
Tree: White Oak
Fair: August-September 2003, in Timonium (see Towson)
Time Zone: Eastern
Website: www.mdisfun.org

Chesapeake Bay

Maryland was one of the 13 original colonies. Its first capital was St. Mary's City. In 1694 the capital was transferred to Annapolis, where it remains today.

Every war waged on US soil has seen major action by Marylanders. In 1755 British General Edward Braddock, assisted by Lieutenant Colonel George Washington, trained his army at Cumberland for the fight against the French and Indians. In the Revolution, General William Howe invaded Maryland at the head of Chesapeake Bay, and a battle was joined at Brandywine Creek in Pennsylvania before the British moved on to capture Philadelphia. Maryland troops in the Battle of Long Island made a heroic bayonet coverage of the retreat. The courageous action of the "Old Line" gave the state one of its nicknames. The War of 1812 saw Fort McHenry at Baltimore withstand attack by land and sea, with the action immortalized in the national anthem by Francis Scott Key, a Frederick lawyer. In the Civil War, Maryland was a major battleground at Antietam; troops moved back and forth through the state for the four bloody years of destruction.

A border state with commercial characteristics of both North and South, Maryland found its original dependence on tobacco relieved by the emerging Industrial Revolution. Modern factories, mills, and ironworks around Baltimore became important to the state's economy. Educational institutions were established and the port of Baltimore, at the mouth of the Patapsco River, flourished. In the mid-19th century, with the Baltimore & Ohio Railroad and the Chesapeake & Ohio Canal carrying freight to the fast-developing western states, Maryland thrived.

Sports enthusiasts have always thought well of Maryland. The state's thousands of miles of tidal shoreline allow plenty of elbow room for aquatic diversion. Maryland's race tracks include Pimlico (see BALTIMORE), featuring the nationally known Preakness Stakes, and Laurel. The "Maryland Million" is held alternately at Laurel and Pimlico. Deer hunting is allowed in most counties and goose hunting on the Eastern Shore. Historical sites cover the landscape, and more are constantly being opened up to the public by the state and National Park Service. Highways are good; reaching places in the Baltimore-Washington, D.C. area is simplified by direct, high-speed, four-lane highways constructed around, between, and radiating from these cities.

When to Go/Climate

Spring and autumn are popular times to visit Maryland. Winter weather is unpredictable and summers can be hot and humid.

AVERAGE HIGH/LOW TEMPERATURES (°F)

BALTIMORE

Jan 40/23	May 74/53	Sept 79/58
Feb 44/26	June 83/62	Oct 67/46
Mar 54/34	July 87/67	Nov 57/37
Apr 64/43	Aug 85/66	Dec 42/28

Parks and Recreation Finder

Directions to and information about the parks and recreation areas below are given under their respective town/city sections. Please refer to those sections for details.

NATIONAL PARK AND RECREATION AREAS

Key to abbreviations. I.H.S. = International Historic Site; I.P.M. = International Peace Memorial; N.B. = National Battlefield; N.B.P. = National Battlefield Park; N.B.C. = National Battlefield and Cemetery; N.C.A. = National Conservation Area; N.E.M. = National Expansion Memorial; N.F. = National Forest;

CALENDAR HIGHLIGHTS

FEBRUARY

National Outdoor Show (Cambridge). Goose and duck calling, log sawing, crab picking, trap setting contests; entertainment. Phone 800/522-TOUR.

APRIL

Point-to-Point Steeplechase (Cockeysville). Three well-known meets on consecutive weekends—My Lady's Manor, Grand National, and Maryland Hunt Cup. Phone 410/557-9466.

MAY

Maryland Preakness Celebration (Baltimore). Statewide festival; events include hot-air balloon festival, parade, steeplechase, celebrity golf tournament, block parties, and schooner race. Phone 410/837-3030.

Mid-Atlantic Maritime Festival (St. Michael's). Chesapeake Bay Maritime Museum. Nautical celebration with fly-fishing demonstration, skipjack races, boat building contest, boat parade, seafood festival cooking contest. Phone 410/745-2916.

AUGUST

Montgomery County Agricultural Fair (Gaithersburg). One of the East Coast's leading county fairs; emphasis on agriculture, 4-H activities; animal exhibits, home arts, antique farm equipment; tractor pull, horse pull, demolition derby, rodeo; entertainment. Phone 301/926-3100.

State Fair (Towson). Timonium Fairgrounds. Ten-day festival of home arts; entertainment, midway; agricultural demonstrations, thoroughbred horse racing, livestock presentations. Phone 410/252-0200.

SEPTEMBER

New Market Days (Frederick). In New Market. Nostalgic revival of the atmosphere of a 19th-century village; costumed guides, period crafts, and events held in the "Antiques Capital of Maryland." Phone 301/831-6755.

OCTOBER

St. Mary's County Oyster Festival (Leonardtown). County Fairgrounds. National oyster shucking contests; oyster cook-off, seafood and crafts. Phone 301/863-5015.

Autumn Glory Festival (Oakland). Celebrates fall foliage. Features arts and crafts, five-string banjo contest, state fiddle contest, western Maryland tournament of bands, parades, antique show. Phone 301/387-4386.

NOVEMBER

Annapolis by Candlelight (Annapolis). For information, contact Historic Annapolis Foundation. Phone 800/603-4020.

N.G. = National Grassland; N.H.P. = National Historical Park; N.H.C. = National Heritage Corridor; N.H.S. = National Historic Site; N.L. = National Lakeshore; N.M. = National Monument; N.M.P. = National Military Park; N.Mem. = National Memorial; N.P. = National Park; N.Pres. = National Preserve; N.R.A. = National Recreational Area; N.R.R. = National Recreational River; N.Riv. = National River; N.S. = National Seashore; N.S.R. = National Scenic Riverway; N.S.T. = National Scenic Trail; N.Sc. = National Scientific Reserve; N.V.M. = National Volcanic Monument.

Place Name	Listed Under
Antietam N.B.	same
Assateague Island N.S.	OCEAN CITY
Catoctin Mountain N.P.	THURMONT
Chesapeake and Ohio Canal N.H.P.	same
Fort McHenry N.M. and Historic Shrine	BALTIMORE
Hampton N.H.S.	TOWSON
Monocacy N.B.	FREDERICK

STATE PARK AND RECREATION AREAS

Key to abbreviations. I.P. = Interstate Park; S.A.P. = State Archaeological Park; S.B. = State Beach; S.C.A. = State Conservation Area; S.C.P. = State Conservation Park; S.Cp. = State Campground; S.F. = State Forest; S.G. = State Garden; S.H.A. = State Historic Area; S.H.P. = State Historic Park; S.H.S. = State Historic Site; S.M.P. = State Marine Park; S.N.A. = State Natural Area; S.P. = State Park; S.P.C. = State Public Campground; S.R. = State Reserve; S.R.A. = State Recreation Area; S.Res. = State Reservoir; S.Res.P. = State Resort Park; S.R.P. = State Rustic Park.

Place Name	Listed Under
Assateague S.P.	OCEAN CITY
Casselman S.P.	GRANTSVILLE
Cedarville S.F.	WALDORF
Cunningham Falls S.P.	THURMONT
Dans Mountain S.P.	CUMBERLAND
Deep Creek Lake S.P.	OAKLAND
Elk Neck S.F.	ELKTON
Elk Neck S.P.	ELKTON
Fort Frederick S.P.	HAGERSTOWN
Gambrill S.P.	FREDERICK
Garrett S.F.	OAKLAND
Green Ridge S.F.	CUMBERLAND
Greenbrier S.P.	HAGERSTOWN
Gunpowder Falls S.P. (Hammerman Area)	BALTIMORE
Gathland S.P.	BOONSBORO (WASHINGTON COUNTY)
Herrington Manor S.P.	OAKLAND
Janes Island S.P.	CRISFIELD
New Germany S.P.	GRANTSVILLE
Patapsco Valley S.P.	ELLICOTT CITY
Point Lookout S.P.	ST. MARY'S CITY
Potomac S.F.	OAKLAND
Rocky Gap S.P.	CUMBERLAND
Sandy Point S.P.	ANNAPOLIS
Savage River S.F.	GRANTSVILLE
Seneca Creek S.P.	GAITHERSBURG
Smallwood S.P.	LA PLATA
Susquehanna S.P.	HAVRE DE GRACE
Swallow Falls S.P.	OAKLAND
Tuckahoe S.P.	EASTON
Washington Monument S.P.	BOONSBORO (WASHINGTON COUNTY)
Wye Oak S.P.	CHESAPEAKE BAY BRIDGE AREA

Water-related activities, hiking, riding, various other sports, picnicking, and visitor centers, as well as camping, are available in many of these areas. Most state-maintained areas have small charges for parking and special services. Camping: $2-$22/site/night; stays limited to two weeks; most areas are open late March-early December, but season varies from one park to the next; checkout 3 pm; reservations for a stay of one week are available at Assateague—they may be obtained by writing directly to the park (see OCEAN CITY). Pets allowed at the following parks (some special restrictions may apply; phone ahead): Green Ridge Forest, Elk Neck, Patapsco (Hollofield), Point Lookout, Rocky Gap, Savage River Forest, Susquehanna, Swallow Falls, Garrett Forest, Potomac Forest, and Pocomoke River (Milburn Landing). Day use: 8 am-sunset; closed December 25; fee March-October. For complete information, including information on cabins, contact the Maryland Department of Natural Resources, State Forest and Park Service, Tawes State Office Building E-3, 580 Taylor Ave, Annapolis 21401, phone 888/432-2267 or 800/830-3974. It is advisable to call parks before visiting, as some may be closed during the off-season.

FISHING AND HUNTING

Nontidal, nonresident fishing license, $20; five-day, $7; trout stamp, $5. Chesapeake Bay nonresident fishing license, $12; five-day, $4.

Nonresident hunting licenses: consolidated, $86-$135, depending on state of residence; three-day, $35; waterfowl stamp $6; regular deer stamp, $9.50; bow hunting deer stamp, $3.50; black powder deer stamp, $3.50; second deer stamp, $10. For latest information, including *Maryland Sportfishing Guide* or the *Guide to Hunting, Trapping in Maryland,* contact Maryland Department of Natural Resources, Licensing & Registration Service, 580 Taylor Ave B-1, Annapolis 21404-1869, phone 410/260-8200.

Driving Information

Safety belts are mandatory for driver and passengers in front seat of vehicle. Children ten yrs and under must be in an approved passenger restraint anywhere in the vehicle. Children under four years or weighing 40 pounds or less must be in an approved safety seat. Phone 410/486-3101.

INTERSTATE HIGHWAY SYSTEM

The following alphabetical listing of Maryland towns in *Mobil Travel Guide* shows that these cities are within ten miles of the indicated Interstate highways. A highway map should be checked, however, for the nearest exit.

Highway Number	Cities/Towns within ten miles
Interstate 68	Cumberland.
Interstate 70	Baltimore, Columbia, Ellicott City, Frederick, Hagerstown.
Interstate 81	Hagerstown.
Interstate 83	Baltimore, Cockeysville, Towson.
Interstate 95	Aberdeen, Baltimore, College Park, Elkton, Havre de Grace, Laurel, Silver Spring, Towson.

Additional Visitor Information

The Maryland guide to travel, *Destination Maryland,* and a calendar of events can be obtained from the Maryland Office of Tourism Development, 217 E Redwood St, Baltimore 21202, phone 800/543-1036.

There are several visitor information centers in Maryland; visitors who stop by will find information and brochures helpful in planning stops at points of interest. Their locations are as follows: on I-95 (North and South) near Laurel; on I-70 (East and West) between Hagerstown and Frederick; on US 15 S at Emmitsburg; on I-95 S near North East; on US 48 E near Friendsville; on US 13 N near Maryland-Virginia line; in the State House, Annapolis; Crain memorial, on US 301 N, Newburg; and in Bay Country, on US 301 N/S, Centreville. (Daily; closed holidays)

EASTERN SHORE OF THE CHESAPEAKE BAY (APPROX 250 MI)

North America's largest estuary, the Chesapeake Bay commands more than 4,500 miles of shoreline, much of it in Maryland. A vast sea known for its rich history and savory shellfish, it is one of the Mid-Atlantic's most popular destinations. Inviting inns and other lodgings and fine seafood restaurants are plentiful on Maryland's Eastern Shore. A two-day driving tour covering about 250 miles makes a fine introduction to the bay and to the watermen and their families who harvest the seafood that appears on every menu. Begin your drive in Annapolis, Maryland's beautiful old capital, which doubles as the bay's sailing headquarters. In summer, catch the regular Wednesday evening races, when as many as 100 boats may compete. The finish is easily visible from City Dock at the foot of the city's colonial-era streets. From Annapolis, take US 50 east across the soaring Chesapeake Bay Bridge. Just before you reach the bridge, a five-minute detour leads to Sandy Point State Park, the only stop on this drive where you can take a dip in the bay. At the eastern end of the bridge, turn north onto US 301 to State Route 213 north to Chestertown. Founded in 1706, Chestertown is a pretty village with a collection of 18th- and 19th-century homes, several of them situated along the scenic Chester River. After browsing in the shops of High and Cross streets, take Route 20 west to Rock Hall, a sailing and charter fishing port. Retrace your path to Chestertown, and take Route 213 south to US 50 south. In Easton, take Route 33 west to the historic sailing port of St. Michaels, an inviting place to spend the night. One of the Mid-Atlantic's prettiest little towns, its lovely inns, fine restaurants, offbeat shops on Talbot Street, and expansive bay views are irresistible. So, too, are the charming little back streets, lined with lovely homes dating back to the 18th and 19th centuries. Your first stop should be the Chesapeake Bay Maritime Museum, which focuses on the Chesapeake. The museum's 18-acre harbor site features more than a dozen historic structures, including a fully restored 1879 lighthouse complete with flashing light. Stop by Waterman's Wharf, where you can try your skill at crab fishing. The Waterfowling Building displays beautifully carved duck decoys. Boat builders are often at work restoring historic bay work boats for the museum's large collection. The *Patriot*, a cruise ship departing from the museum's dock, takes visitors on a 60-minute tour up the Miles River, a bay tributary. From St. Michaels, follow Route 33 to its end at Tilghman Island, a charter fishing port. Plan on having lunch at one of its waterside seafood houses. On the return trip to St. Michaels, stop about three miles east of the city and take the road south (right) to Bellevue. There you can catch the little Bellevue-Oxford Ferry for a ten-minute ride across the Tred Avon River to Oxford, a sleepy pleasure boat port dating back to 1694. To stretch your legs, take a walk along The Strand, a lovely river promenade, or rent a bicycle and pedal among the quiet streets. From Oxford, return to Annapolis via Route 333 and US 50, stopping briefly in Easton to admire its attractive, colonial-looking town center and to investigate its engaging shops and galleries.

DEEP CREEK LAKE, MARYLAND'S WESTERN PLAYGROUND (APPROX 400 MI)

Out in Western Maryland's Garrett County, the local folks like to call massive Deep Creek Lake the state's "hidden secret." But the secret is getting out, and the massive lake has become the centerpiece for a wealth of vigorous outdoor adventures: water skiing, whitewater rafting, hiking, back-road bicycling, kayaking, fly-fishing, canoeing, sailing, and swimming. On a drive around the lake, you can partake in as many activities as you choose—outfitters are on hand to rent all the necessary equipment—or simply enjoy the sublime mountain views. Maryland's largest fresh water lake, Deep Creek is 12 miles long, but so etched with fingerlike coves that the shoreline stretches for 65 miles. Surrounded by the forested ridges and splashing streams of a mountain wilderness, the lake, at an altitude of 2,300 feet, treats summer visitors to a cooling respite from the city. Begin this two-day, 400-mile drive in Baltimore and head west on I-70 and I-68 to exit 14 at Keysers Ridge. Take US 219 south to the Visitor Center, which is on the right just outside the village of McHenry. Plan to spend the night in one of McHenry's inns, hotels, or motels. The trip from Baltimore to McHenry is about 180 miles, a scenic ride that carries you across a series of green mountain ridges. To break up the trip, pull off I-68 at Cumberland, immediately recognizable by the castlelike spires and turrets of its courthouse and churches. George Washington is said to have assumed his first military command at Fort Cumberland, and his one-room log cabin and remnants of the fort can still be seen here. Cumberland is the terminus of the Chesapeake and Ohio Canal, which originates in Washington D.C., and you can rent a bicycle and ride along the tow path for miles. At Deep Creek Lake, follow the signs to Deep Creek Lake State Park, which maintains a nice 700-foot-long sandy swimming beach, a lovely place to relax after the trip from the city. The Discovery Center, an attractive structure of stone, wood, and soaring windows, features displays about the region's natural history and mining heritage. Ranger talks, walks, and canoe trips are offered. On the second day of your trip, take US 219 south from McHenry to the turn-off to Swallow Falls State Park. For an easy hike, follow the 1½-mile path that scrambles in a loop past four waterfalls. At the trail head, the park has preserved a 37-acre stand of virgin hemlock and white pine estimated to be 300 years old. After ¼ mile, Muddy Creek Falls—the state's highest at 52 feet—cascades down a staircase of rocks into a large pool. You are welcome to splash in the many pools along this trail. Next, follow signs south to the town of Oakland and then begin your scenic return to Baltimore via Route 135 northeast to US 220 north to I-68 east. Just beyond Bloomington on Route 135, make a detour left on Savage River Road. For about 5½ miles along this road, the Savage River splashes. So narrow, mean, and harrowing is the course, say local tourism officials, that it was picked as the site of the 1989 Whitewater World Championships and the 1992 US Canoe & Kayak Team Olympic Trials. A couple of suspension bridges built for these events still leap the river. While here, imagine yourself trying to negotiate a kayak through the frenzied chaos of water and rocks. Retrace your path to Route 135 northeast. About ten miles east of Cumberland, take a break at Rocky Gap State Park, two minutes off the interstate, which tempts with a couple of fine sandy beaches in a forested mountain setting.

Aberdeen (B-6)

Pop 13,842 **Elev** 83 ft **Area code** 410
Zip 21001

This is the home of the 75,000-acre Aberdeen Proving Grounds, a federal reservation along Chesapeake Bay. Various types of army materiel, ranging from gunsights to tanks, are tested under simulated combat conditions.

What to See and Do

PECO Energy Company. Hydroelectric plant on the Susquehanna River. Limited area of plant is open for guided tours (Apr-Sept, Sat; rest of yr, by appt; closed hols). Contact the Conowingo Information Center, 7 mi NE on US 40 or I-95, then 11 mi NW on US 222 to Conowingo. Phone 410/457-5011. **FREE** Nearby is

Recreation area. Fourteen-mi-long man-made lake; swimming pool (fee), boating (ramps, marinas), fishing, fishermen's gallery (over 12 yrs only); picnicking, hiking. Phone 410/457-5011. **FREE**

US Army Ordnance Museum. Tanks, artillery, self-propelled artillery, extensive small arms, and ammunition collection. (Daily; closed hols) At Aberdeen Proving Ground, off I-95 exit 85, 3 mi E on MD 22, follow signs. Phone 410/278-3602. **FREE**

Motels/Motor Lodges

★ **DAYS INN.** *783 W Bel Air Ave (21001). 410/272-8500; fax 410/272-5782. www.daysinn.com.* 49 rms, 2 story. S $43; D $47; each addl $4; under 16 free. Crib free. Pet accepted; $5. TV; cable (premium). Pool. Complimentary continental bkfst. Restaurant nearby. Ck-out 11 am. Business servs avail. Refrigerators avail. Cr cds: A, DS, MC, V.
⊡ ⬚ ⬚ ⬚ ⬚

★★ **HOLIDAY INN CHESAPEAKE HOUSE.** *1007 Beards Hill Rd (21001). 410/272-8100; fax 410/272-1714; toll-free 800/465-4329. www.holiday-inn. com.* 122 rms, 5 story. S, D $95-$115;

each addl $10; suites $150; kit. units $105-$120; under 18 free; wkend rates. Pet accepted. TV; cable (premium), VCR avail. Indoor pool. Restaurant 6 am-2 pm, 5-10 pm; Sat, Sun from 7 am. Bar. Ck-out noon. Meeting rms. Sundries. Exercise equipt. Health club privileges. Some refrigerators. Balconies. Cr cds: A, C, D, DS, JCB, MC, V.
⊡ ⬚ ⬚ ⬚ ⬚ ⬚ ⬚ SC

★ **QUALITY INN AND SUITES.** *793 W Bel Air Ave (24382). 410/272-6000; fax 410/272-2287. www.qualityinn. com.* 124 rms, 2 story. Feb-Oct: S, D $49.95-$59.95; each addl $5; under 19 free; wkly, wkend rates; lower rates rest of yr. Crib free. TV; cable (premium), VCR avail. Pool; wading pool. Complimentary continental bkfst. Restaurant adj 6 am-2 pm, 5-10 pm. Ck-out noon. Coin lndry. Meeting rms. Business servs avail. Cr cds: A, C, D, DS, JCB, MC, V.
⊡ ⬚ ⬚ ⬚ SC

Annapolis

(D-6) *See also Baltimore, Baltimore/Washington International Airport Area*

Founded 1649 **Pop** 35,838 **Elev** 57 ft
Area code 410 and 443

Information Annapolis and Anne Arundel County Conference and Visitors Bureau, 26 West St, 21401; 410/268-TOUR. Information is also available at the Visitor Information Booth located at the city dock.

Web www.visit-annapolis.org

The capital of Maryland, gracious and dignified in the Colonial tradition, Annapolis has had a rich history for more than 300 years. Planned and laid out as the provincial capital in 1695, it was the first peacetime capital of the United States (Congress met here November 26, 1783 to August 13, 1784). In 1845 the US Naval Academy was established here at the Army's Fort Severn. Town life centers on sport and commercial water-oriented activ-

Annapolis Marina

ities, state government, and the academy. Every May, at commencement time, thousands of visitors throng the narrow brick streets.

What to See and Do

Boat Trips. Forty-min narrated tours of city harbor, USNA, and Severn River aboard *Harbor Queen* (Memorial Day-Labor Day, daily); 90-min cruises to locations aboard *Annapolitan II* and *Rebecca*, cruises to St. Michael's aboard the *Annapolitan II* (Memorial Day-Labor Day); 40-min cruises up Spa Creek, residential areas, city harbor, and USNA aboard the *Miss Anne* and *Miss Anne II* (Memorial Day-Labor Day). Some cruises early spring and late fall, weather permitting. Fees vary. From city dock at foot of Main St. Phone 410/268-7600.

Chesapeake Bay Bridge. The 7¼ mi link of US 50 across the Bay. Toll (charged eastbound only) ¢¢

Government House. (1868) This Victorian structure was remodeled in 1935 into a Georgian country house; furnishings reflect Maryland's history and culture. Tours by appt (Jan-mid-Apr, Tues and Thurs; rest of yr, Tues-Thurs). Between State and Church cirs. Phone 410/974-3531. **FREE**

Hammond-Harwood House. (1774) Georgian house designed by William Buckland; antique furnishings; garden. Matthias Hammond, a Revolutionary patriot, was its first owner.

Guided tours. (Daily; closed Jan 1, Thanksgiving, Dec 25) 19 Maryland Ave, at King George St, 1 blk W of US Naval Academy. Phone 410/269-1714. ¢¢

Historic Annapolis Foundation Welcome Center and Museum Store. This 1815 building stands on the site of a storehouse for Revolutionary War troops that burned in 1790. Audiocassette walking tours. Products reflecting Annapolis history. (Mon-Sat, also Sun afternoons; closed Thanksgiving, Dec 25) 77 Main St. Phone 410/268-5576.

London Town. (ca 1760) Once considered a site for Maryland's capital; the only surviving structure of the Lost Town is the William Brown House, a Georgian mansion on banks of South River. Has eight acres of woodland gardens. Museum and garden shop; boat docking. Special events. Guided tours. (Mon-Sat, also Sun afternoon; closed hols). 8 mi SE via MD 2S, (Mayo Rd) in Edgewater, at the end of Londontown Rd (#839). Phone 410/222-1919. ¢¢

Sailing Tours. Two-hr narrated trips through Chesapeake Bay aboard 74-ft sailing yacht *Woodwind*. (May-Sept, Tues-Sun four trips daily, Mon Sunset Sail only; Apr, Oct, Nov, schedule varies) Departs from Pusser's Landing next to City Dock. Phone 410/263-8619. ¢¢¢¢

St. John's College. (1784) 475 students. Nonsectarian liberal arts college. This 36-acre campus, one of the oldest in the country, is a National Historic Landmark. The college succeeded King William's School, founded in 1696. George Washington's two nephews and step-grandson studied here; Francis Scott Key was an alumnus. College Ave. Phone 410/626-2539. On campus are

Charles Carroll, Barrister House. (1722) Birthplace of the author of the Maryland Bill of Rights; moved in 1955 to the campus and restored; now an administration building. Not open to public. Phone 410/269-1737.

Elizabeth Myers Mitchell Art Gallery. Displays museum-quality traveling exhibitions. (Academic yr, Tues-Sun) Phone 410/626-2556. **FREE**

McDowell Hall. (begun 1742, finished 1789) Named for St. John's first president; originally built as the Governor's Mansion. Lafayette was feted here in 1824. Not open to public.

Sandy Point State Park. On 786 acres. The park's location on the Atlantic Flyway makes it a fine area for bird-watching; view of Bay Bridge and oceangoing vessels. Swimming in bay at two guarded beaches, two bathhouses, surf fishing, crabbing, boating (rentals, launches); concession. Standard fees. (See SPECIAL EVENTS) 7 mi E on US 50, at W end of Chesapeake Bay Bridge. Phone 410/974-2149.

HISTORY AND GOVERNMENT IN ANNAPOLIS

In the years just prior to the American Revolution, the colonial elite flocked to the bustling seaport of Annapolis, Maryland's capital on the Chesapeake Bay. This was the city's "golden age," and many, George Washington among them, were drawn by its spirited social life and elegant mansions built by wealthy tobacco planters. You can see some of the same sights Washington might have enjoyed on a one-hour, one-mile stroll through the city's well-preserved Historic District. Begin at the Visitor Center, 26 West Street, where tourist parking is available. From the center head east (left) on West Street; detour around St. Anne's Church (1859), noting its Tiffany windows; pause on School Street to view Government House, the Georgian-style Maryland Governor's residence (remodeled 1936); and then climb the stairs, as Washington surely did, to the Maryland State House on State Circle (1772), the oldest state capitol in continuous legislative use. Perched atop the city's highest hill, the State House provides a panoramic view of the bay. Inside, the Old Senate Chamber appears as it did on December 23, 1783, when Washington resigned his commission as the victorious commander of the Continental Army. At 21 State Circle, the John Shaw House (1720s) was the home of the city's premier cabinet maker, whose furniture is displayed in the State House. Continue east from State Circle on Maryland Avenue, lined with antique shops, to the Hammond-Harwood Home (1774) at No. 19. A house museum, this Georgian structure features what is considered by many to be the most beautiful doorway in America. Double back one block on Maryland Avenue, pausing briefly at the Chase-Lloyd House (1769), another elegant Georgian mansion where Francis Scott Key, author of the "Star-Spangled Banner," was married in 1802. Turn toward the harbor (left) onto Prince George Street. The William Paca House (1765) at No. 186 and its two-acre colonial garden, carefully restored for authenticity, are national treasures. Now a house museum, the Paca house was the home of Maryland's Revolutionary War governor and a signer of the Declaration of Independence. Built in the symmetrical five-part structure of the city's finest colonial homes, it is considered one of the best examples of a Georgian home in America. Neighboring Brice House (1767) at 42 East Street is another magnificent Georgian mansion built by a wealthy merchant. To conclude this tour, continue downhill on Prince George Street, and turn west (right) one block onto Randall Street to City Dark for refreshments at Middleton Tavern. Once an "Inn for Seafaring Men," it has been serving Annapolis visitors since 1754.

State House. (1772-1779) Oldest state house in continuous legislative use in US, this was the first peacetime capitol of the US. Here in 1784, a few weeks after receiving George Washington's resignation as commander-in-chief, Congress ratified the Treaty of Paris, which officially ended the Revolutionary War. Visitors Information Center. Guide service (closed Jan 1, Thanksgiving). (Daily; closed Dec 25) State Cir, center of town. Phone 410/974-3400. **FREE**

United States Naval Academy. (1845) 4,000 students. World-renowned school for naval officers; Leftwich Visitor Center provides guided walking tours, film, exhibits, gift shop (daily; closed Jan 1, Thanksgiving, Dec 25). The remains of John Paul Jones, removed from their original burial place in France, lie here beneath the chapel in a crypt similar to Napoleon's in Paris. Naval Academy Museum exhibits 300 yrs of American naval history. Sites incl Bancroft Hall, dormitory for all midshipmen; a bust of Tamanend; replica of figurehead of USS *Delaware,* renamed *Tecumseh.* Parades, concerts, and other events are held annually and during "Commissioning Week" (late May), culminated by midshipmen's graduation. Enter through Gate 1, King George St. Phone 410/263-6933. **FREE**

Walking Tours.

   Historic Annapolis Foundation. Self-guided audiocassette walking tours. Incl Historic District, State House, Old Treasury, US Naval Academy, and William Paca House. (Mar-Nov, daily) Tours leave from museum store, 77 Main St. Phone 410/267-7619. ¢¢

   Three Centuries Tours of Annapolis. Walking tours of US Naval Academy and Historic District conducted by guides in Colonial attire. Tour incl historic Maryland State House, St. John's College, Naval Academy Chapel, crypt of John Paul Jones, Bancroft Hall dormitory, and Armel-Leftwich Visitor Center. (Apr-Oct, daily) Morning tour leaves from Visitor Center at 26 West St; afternoon tour leaves from Visitor Information Booth on City Dock. Phone 410/263-5401. ¢¢¢

William Paca Garden. Restored two-acre pleasure garden originally developed in 1765 by William Paca, a signer of the Declaration of Independence and governor of Maryland during the Revolutionary War. Incl waterways, formal parterres, and a garden wilderness. (Mon-Sat, also Sun afternoons; closed Thanksgiving, Dec 25) 186 Prince George St. Also here is

   William Paca House. Paca built this five-part Georgian mansion in 1765. (Mon-Sat, also Sun afternoons; closed Thanksgiving, Dec 25) Phone 410/263-5553. ¢¢

Special Events

Maryland Renaissance Festival. Food, crafters, minstrels, dramatic productions. Usually last wk Aug-third wkend Oct. Phone 410/266-7303.

Maryland Seafood Festival. Sandy Point State Park. Food; entertainment. Usually wkend after Labor Day. Phone 410/974-2149.

US Sailboat Show. City dock and harbor. Features world's largest in-water display of sailboats; exhibits of related marine products. Early-mid-Oct. Phone 410/268-8828.

US Powerboat Show. City dock and harbor. Extensive in-water display of powerboats; exhibits of related marine products. Mid-Oct. Phone 410/268-8828.

Chesapeake Appreciation Days. Sandy Point State Park. Skipjack sailing festival honors state's oystermen. Usually last wkend Oct. Phone 410/974-2149.

Annapolis by Candlelight. For information, res contact Historic Annapolis Foundation. Usually early Nov. Phone 410/267-0432.

Christmas in Annapolis. Features decorated 18th-century mansions, parade of yachts, private home tours, pub crawls, concerts, holiday meals, First Night celebration, caroling by candlelight at the State House and other events. For free events calendar phone 410/268-8687. Thanksgiving-Jan 1.

Motels/Motor Lodges

★ **BEST WESTERN.** *2520 Riva Rd (21401). 410/224-2800; fax 410/266-5539. www.bestwestern.com.* 152 rms, 2 story. Mid-Mar-mid-Nov: S, D $59-

$119; suites $119-$129; lower rates rest of yr. Crib free. TV; cable (premium). Pool. Complimentary continental bkfst. Restaurant adj 11 am-10 pm. Bar. Ck-out 11 am. Meeting rms. Business servs avail. Coin lndry. Health club privileges. Game rm. Some refrigerators. Cr cds: A, D, DS, JCB, MC, V.

⭐ **COMFORT INN.** *76 Old Mill Bottom Rd (21401). 410/757-8500; fax 410/757-4409. www.comfortinn.com.* 60 rms, 2 story. Apr-Oct: S $65-$110; D $70-$120; each addl $5; under 18 free; lower rates rest of yr. Crib free. TV; cable (premium). Pool; lifeguard. Complimentary continental bkfst. Restaurant nearby. Ck-out 11 am. Coin lndry. Business servs avail. Cr cds: A, C, D, DS, ER, JCB, MC, V.

⭐⭐ **COURTYARD BY MARRIOTT.** *2559 Riva Rd (21401). 410/266-1555; fax 410/266-6376; toll-free 800/321-2211. www.courtyard.com.* 149 units, 3 story. S, D $109-$119; suites $129-$149; under 12 free. Crib free. TV; cable (premium). Indoor pool; whirlpool, lifeguard. Complimentary coffee in rms. Restaurant 6:30 am-1:30 pm; Sat, Sun from 7 am. Bar 4-10 pm. Ck-out noon. Coin lndry. Meeting rms. Business servs avail. In-rm modem link. Valet serv. Sundries. Exercise equipt. Refrigerator in suites. Cr cds: A, C, D, DS, MC, V.

Hotels

⭐⭐⭐ **LOEWS ANNAPOLIS HOTEL.** *126 West St (21401). 410/263-7777; fax 410/263-0084; toll-free 800/526-2593. www.loewsannapolis.com.* 217 rms, 6 story, 11 suites. S, D $119-$185; each addl $15; suites $185-$350; under 17 free. Crib free. Pet accepted. Valet parking $10. TV; cable (premium). Pool privileges. Restaurant (see also CORINTHIAN). Bar 11-2 am. Ck-out noon. Meeting rms. Business center. In-rm modem link. Concierge. Gift shop. Barber, beauty shop. Exercise equipt. Health club privileges. Refrigerators, minibars. Private patios, balconies. Luxury level. Cr cds: A, C, D, DS, MC, V.

⭐⭐⭐ **MARRIOTT ANNAPOLIS WATERFRONT.** *80 Compromise St (21401). 410/268-7555; fax 410/269-5864; res 800/228-9290. www.marriott.com.* 150 rms, 6 story. May-Sept: S, D $159-$269; varied rates rest of yr. Crib free. Garage $12. TV; cable (premium), VCR avail. Restaurant 6:30 am-11 pm. Bar 11-2 am. Ck-out 11 am. Meeting rms. Business servs avail. In-rm modem link. Exercise equipt. Some in-rm whirlpools; refrigerators, microwaves avail. Some balconies. On waterfront; 300 ft dockage. Cr cds: A, D, DS, MC, V.

⭐⭐ **RADISSON.** *210 Holiday Ct (21401). 410/224-3150; fax 410/224-3413; toll-free 800/333-3333. www.radisson.com.* 220 rms, 6 story. S $79-$119; D $89-$129; suites $139; under 18 free. Crib free. TV; cable (premium). Pool; lifeguard. Restaurant 6:30 am-2 pm, 5-10 pm. Bar 4 pm-midnight. Ck-out noon. Meeting rms. Business servs avail. In-rm modem link. Bellhops. Valet serv. Sundries. Health club privileges. Microwaves avail. Cr cds: A, C, D, DS, JCB, MC, V.

⭐⭐ **SHERATON BARCELO.** *173 Jennifer Rd (21401). 410/266-3131; fax 410/266-6247; toll-free 800/625-5144. www.sheraton.com.* 197 rms, 6 story. S $89-$139; D $99-$149; each addl $10; suites $109-$209; under 18 free; hol rates; higher rates special events. Crib free. TV; cable. Indoor pool; whirlpool, lifeguard. Coffee in rms. Restaurant 6:30 am-2:30 pm, 5-10 pm. Rm serv 5-10 pm. Bar 4 pm-midnight. Ck-out noon. Meeting rms. Business servs avail. In-rm modem link. Exercise equipt; sauna. Health club privileges. Some refrigerators; microwaves avail. Cr cds: A, C, D, DS, MC, V.

B&Bs/Small Inns

⭐⭐ **CHESAPEAKE BAY LIGHTHOUSE BED AND BREAKFAST.** *1423 Sharps Point Rd (21401). 410/757-0248; fax 410/757-0248.* 5 rms, 2 story. No rm phones. S, D $110-$210; each addl $10. Children over 12 only. TV in sitting rm. Complimentary continental bkfst. Restaurant nearby. Ck-out 11 am, ck-in 3-7 pm. Working lighthouse on Chesapeake Bay. Totally nonsmoking. Cr cds: DS, MC, V.

★★ **GIBSON'S LODGINGS.** *110 Prince George St (21401). 410/268-5555; fax 410/268-2775. www.avmcyber.com/gibson.* 20 rms, 13 share bath in 3 bldgs, 3 story. Some rm phones. S $58-$110; D $68-$125; each addl $15. TV in some rms; cable, VCR avail. Complimentary continental bkfst; afternoon refreshments. Restaurant nearby. Ck-out 11 am, ck-in 2 pm. Meeting rm. Business servs avail. Microwaves avail. Antiques; library. Totally nonsmoking. Cr cds: A, MC, V.

★★★ **GOVERNOR CALVERT HOUSE.** *58 State Cir (21401). 410/263-2641; fax 410/268-3813; toll-free 800/847-8882.* 51 rms, 4 story. S, D $125-$175; each addl $10; suites $185-$285; under 18 free; higher rates special events. Crib free. Valet parking $12. TV; cable (premium). Restaurant nearby. Ck-out noon, ck-in 3 pm. Meeting rms. Business servs avail. In-rm modem link. Lighted tennis privileges. Golf privileges. Health club privileges. Refrigerators, microwaves avail. 18th-century state house with modern addition; Colonial gardens, atrium. Cr cds: A, C, D, DS, JCB, MC, V.

★★ **MARYLAND INN.** *58 State Cir (21401). 410/263-2641; fax 410/268-3813; toll-free 800/847-8882.* 44 rms, 4 story. S $105-$135; D $105-$165; each addl $10; suites $145-$260; under 18 free; higher rates special events. Crib free. Valet parking $12. TV; cable (premium). Restaurant (see also TREATY OF PARIS). Bar; entertainment. Ck-out noon, ck-in 3 pm (at Governor Calvert House). Business servs avail. In-rm modem link. Bellhops. Lighted tennis, golf privileges. Health club privileges. Some refrigerators; microwaves avail. View of bay. Historic inn built 1772; many antique furnishings. Cr cds: A, C, D, DS, JCB, MC, V.

★★★ **PRINCE GEORGE INN.** *232 Prince George St (21401). 410/263-6418; fax 410/626-0009. www.princegeorgeinn.com.* 4 rms, 2 share bath, 3 story. No rm phones. S $90-$100; D $110-$115; under 8 free; wkends (2-day min). Parking $4. TV; cable, VCR. Complimentary full bkfst. Restaurant nearby. Ck-out noon, ck-in 4-6 pm. Refrigerators. Victorian townhouse built in 1884. Totally nonsmoking. Cr cds: DS, MC, V.

★★ **ROBERT JOHNSON HOUSE.** *23 State Cir (21401). 410/263-2641; fax 410/268-3613; toll-free 800/847-8882.* 29 rms, 4 story. S $105-$135; D $105-$165; each addl $10; suites $260; under 18 free; higher rates special events. Crib free. Valet parking $12. TV; cable (premium). Restaurant nearby. Ck-out noon, ck-in 3 pm (at Governor Calvert House). Business servs avail. In-rm modem link. Lighted tennis privileges. Golf privileges. Health club privileges. Refrigerators, microwaves avail. Consists of 18th-century mansion plus 2 connecting townhouses of the same period. Cr cds: A, C, D, DS, JCB, MC, V.

★★ **WILLIAM PAGE INN.** *8 Martin St (21401). 410/626-1506; fax 410/263-4841; toll-free 800/364-4160. www.williampageinn.com.* 5 rms, 2 share bath, 3 story. S, D $95-$195; wkly rates. Complimentary full bkfst. Restaurant nearby. Ck-out noon, ck-in 4-6 pm. Business servs avail. Former clubhouse (1908). Totally nonsmoking. Cr cds: MC, V.

Restaurants

★★★ **CAFE BRETTON.** *849 Baltimore-Annapolis Blvd, Severna Park (21146). 410/647-8222.* Hrs: 5-10 pm; early-bird dinner to 6 pm. Closed Sun, Mon; hols. Res required Fri, Sat. French menu. Bar. Wine list. Dinner $10.95-$26.95. Specializes in lamb shank, seafood. Own baking. Country French atmosphere with original artwork. Totally nonsmoking. Cr cds: A, DS, MC, V.

★★ **CAFE NORMANDIE.** *185 Main St (21401). 410/263-3382.* Hrs: 8 am-10 pm; Fri, Sat to 10:30 pm. French menu. Serv bar. Bkfst $3-$6, lunch $5.50-$15, dinner $8.95-$21. Specializes in seafood, Maryland crab dishes. French-style cafe. Cr cds: A, D, DS, MC, V.

D

★★ **CARROL'S CREEK.** *410 Severn Ave, Eastport (21403). 410/263-8102. www.carrollscreek.com.* Hrs: 11:30 am-4 pm, 5-10 pm; Sun brunch 10 am-2 pm. Res accepted Mon-Thurs; required hols. Bar. Lunch $4.95-$9.95, dinner $14-$22. Sun brunch $16.95. Specializes in local seafood. Own baking. Outdoor dining. On water. Cr cds: A, DS, MC, V.

D ➛

★★★ **CORINTHIAN.** *126 West St (21401). 410/263-1299.* Hrs: 6:30 am-2 pm, 5-10 pm; Sun brunch from 10 am. Res accepted Sat. Bar. Wine list. Bkfst $6.50-$14.95, lunch $6.95-$15.95, dinner $18.95-$28.95. Sun brunch $22. Child's menu. Specializes in fresh seafood, prime beef. Valet parking. Elegant atmosphere. Cr cds: A, D, DS, MC, V.

D SC ➛

★★ **FRED'S.** *2348 Solomon's Island Rd (21401). 410/224-2386.* Hrs: 11 am-10 pm; Fri, Sat to 11 pm; early-bird dinner Mon-Fri 4-6 pm, Sat, Sun noon-6 pm. Closed Thanksgiving, Dec 25. Res accepted. Continental menu. Bar. Lunch $4.50-$8.95, dinner $9.95-$33.95. Child's menu. Specializes in seafood, steak, Italian dishes. Victorian decor; antiques. Family-owned. Cr cds: A, D, MC, V.

D ➛

★★ **GRIFFIN'S.** *22 Market Space (21401). 410/268-2576. www.griffins-citydock.com.* Hrs: 11 am-midnight; Fri, Sat to 1 am; Sun brunch 11 am-1 pm. Closed Dec 25. Res accepted Mon-Thurs. Bar to 1:30 am. Lunch $6.95-$8.95, dinner $8.95-$12.95. Sun brunch $6.95-$9.95. Child's meals. Specializes in seafood, steak, pasta. Own desserts. Cr cds: A, C, D, DS, ER, MC, V.

D ➛

★★★ **HARRY BROWNE'S.** *66 State Cir (21401). 410/263-4332.* Hrs: 11 am-3 pm, 5:30-10 pm; wkends to 11 pm; Sun brunch 10 am-3 pm. Closed Jan 1, Dec 25. Res accepted. Continental menu. Bar. Wine cellar. Lunch $6.95-$12, dinner $17-$22. Specialties: crab cakes, rack of lamb. Enter-

tainment Mon, Fri, Sat. Valet parking Fri, Sat. Decorated with mirrors; pressed tin ceiling. Cr cds: A, DS, MC, V.

D

★★ **LEWNES' STEAKHOUSE.** *401 4th St (21403). 410/263-1617. www. lewnesssteakhouse.com.* Hrs: 5-10 pm; Fri, Sat to 10:30 pm. Closed Thanksgiving, Dec 25. Res required. Bar. A la carte entrees: dinner $15-$27. Specializes in prime steak, seafood. Street parking. 1950s steakhouse atmosphere; casual fine dining. Cr cds: D, MC, V.

D ➛

★★ **MIDDLETON TAVERN.** *2 Market Space (21401). 410/263-3323.* Hrs: 11:30-2 am; Sat, Sun from 10 am. Bar. Lunch $5.95-$10.95, dinner $11.95-$23.95. Specializes in seafood, crab dishes. Oyster bar. Entertainment. Outdoor dining. Restored building (1750), traditional tavern decor. Overlooks harbor. Family-owned. Cr cds: A, DS, MC, V.

➛

★★★ **NORTHWOODS.** *609 Melvin Ave (21401). 410/268-2609.* Hrs: 5:30-10 pm; Sun 5-9 pm. Closed hols. Res accepted. Continental menu. Wine list. Dinner $18.95-$23. Complete meals: dinner $26.95. Specializes in fresh seafood, Italian dishes. Outdoor dining. Casual elegance in romantic setting. Cr cds: A, C, D, DS, MC, V.

D

★★ **O'LEARY'S SEAFOOD.** *310 3rd St (21403). 410/263-0884.* Hrs: 5:30-10 pm; Fri, Sat 5-11 pm; Sun 5-10 pm. Closed Thanksgiving, Dec 24, 25. Res accepted. Bar. Dinner $10.95-$29.95. Child's menu. Specializes in seafood. Own desserts. Cr cds: A, C, D, DS, ER, MC, V.

★★★ **TREATY OF PARIS.** *58 State Cir (21401). 410/263-2641. www. annapolisinns.com.* Hrs: 7 am-2:30 pm, 5:30-10:30 pm; Fri, Sat to 11:30 pm; Sun to 9:30 pm; Sun brunch 10 am-2:30 pm. Closed Jan 1. Res accepted; required Fri, Sat. Continental menu. Bar 11-2 am; Sun to 1 am. Wine cellar. Bkfst $3.50-$9, lunch $6.95-$10, dinner $14-$22. Complete meals: dinner $20, $25. Sun brunch $18.95. Specializes in New American cuisine, fresh local seafood. Salad bar (lunch). Valet parking (dinner). Early American tavern atmosphere; fireplace. Cr cds: A, D, MC, V.

D SC

Baltimore (C-5)

Settled 1661 **Pop** 654,154 **Elev** 32 ft
Area code 410 and 443

Information Baltimore Area Convention & Visitors Association, 100 Light St, 12th floor, 21202; 410/659-7300 or 800/343-3468

Web www.baltimore.org

Suburbs Aberdeen, Cockeysville, Columbia, Ellicott City, Pikesville, Towson.

Metropolis of Maryland and one of America's great cities, Baltimore is a city of neighborhoods built on strong ethnic foundations, a city of historic events that helped shape the nation, and a city that has achieved an incredible downtown renaissance in the past 20 years. It is a major East Coast manufacturing center and, almost from its beginning, a world seaport. Several colleges and universities, foremost of which is Johns Hopkins, make their home here.

Lying midway between North and South and enjoying a rich cultural mixture of both, Baltimore is one of the nation's oldest cities. When British troops threatened Philadelphia during the Revolutionary War the Continental Congress fled to Baltimore, which served as the nation's capital for a little more than two months.

In October 1814 a British fleet attacked the city by land and sea. The defenders of Fort McHenry withstood the naval bombardment for 25 hours until the British gave up. Francis Scott Key saw the huge American flag still flying above the fort and was inspired to pen "The Star-Spangled Banner."

Rapid growth in the early 19th century resulted from the opening of the National Road and then the nation's first railroad, the Baltimore & Ohio.

Politics was a preoccupation in those days and the city hosted many national party conventions. At least seven presidents and three losing candidates were nominated here. Edgar Allan Poe's mysterious death in the city may have been at the hands of shady electioneers.

Untouched physically by the Civil War, effects came later when Southerners flooded in to rebuild their fortunes and commerce was disrupted by the loss of Southern markets. A disastrous fire in 1904 destroyed 140 acres of the business district but the city recovered rapidly and, during

Babe Ruth House

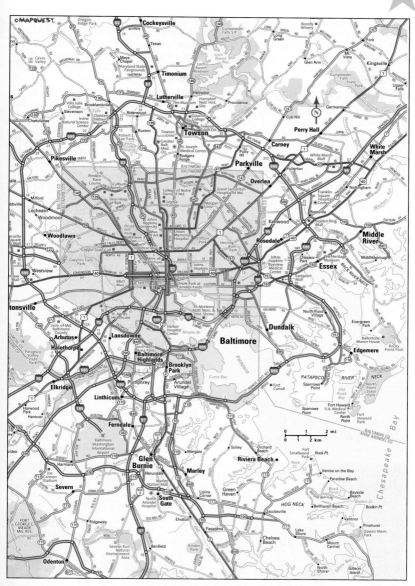

the two World Wars, was a major shipbuilding and naval repair center.

In the 1950s and early 1960s, Baltimore was the victim of the apathy and general decay that struck the industrial Northeast. But the city fought back, replacing hundreds of acres of slums, rotting wharves, and warehouses with gleaming new office plazas, parks, and public buildings. The Inner Harbor was transformed into a huge public area with shops, museums, restaurants, and frequent concerts and festivals. Millions of tourists and proud Baltimoreans flock downtown to enjoy the sights and activities.

Famous residents and native sons and daughters include Babe Ruth, Edgar Allan Poe, H. L. Mencken, Mother Elizabeth Ann Seton, Eubie Blake, Ogden Nash, Thurgood Marshall, Wallis Warfield Simpson, who became the Duchess of Windsor, and more recent sports legends Brooks Robinson, Johnny Unitas, Jim Palmer, and Cal Ripken.

Additional Visitor Information

For additional accommodations, see BALTIMORE/WASHINGTON INTERNATIONAL AIRPORT AREA, which follows BALTIMORE.

Maps, brochures, and calendars of events are available at the Baltimore Area Visitors Center, 301 E Pratt St, Constellation Pier, 21202; phone 410/837-INFO or 800/282-6632.

Transportation

Airport. See BALTIMORE/WASHINGTON INTERNATIONAL AIRPORT AREA.

Car Rental Agencies. See IMPORTANT TOLL-FREE NUMBERS.

Public Transportation. Bus and subway (Mass Transit Administration), phone 410/539-5000.

Rail Passenger Service. Amtrak 800/872-7245; MARC (commuter train serving Baltimore and Washington, D.C.) 800/325-RAIL or 410/291-4267.

What to See and Do

Babe Ruth Birthplace/Baseball Center. Renovated house where Babe Ruth was born. Features memorabilia of Babe Ruth, Orioles and Maryland baseball; 25-min movie of the "Sultan of Swat" and many other audio-visual displays. (Daily) 216 Emory St. Phone 410/727-1539. ¢¢¢

Baltimore Maritime Museum. USS *Torsk,* WWII submarine; Coast Guard cutter *Taney;* and lightship *Chesapeake.* (Daily) 802 S Caroline, Inner Harbor area. Phone 410/396-3453. ¢¢

Baltimore Museum of Art. Variety of collections, incl American paintings, period rms; African and Oceanian art. Noted for Cone collection of French post-impressionists, incl Matisse and Picasso; Cheney miniature rms; modern art wing; sculpture gardens; museum cafe and shop. (Wed-Sun; closed hols) 10 Art Museum Dr near N Charles and 31st sts. Phone 410/396-7100 or 410/396-7101. ¢¢¢

Baltimore Museum of Industry. Exhibits trace the growth of Baltimore as an industrial center. Turn-of-the-century machine shop, print shop, and garment loft. Hands-on exhibits; children's activities. Restored tugboat on waterfront behind museum. (Tues-Sun; limited hrs) 1415 Key Hwy. Phone 410/727-4808. ¢¢¢

Baltimore Streetcar Museum. Eleven electric streetcars and two horsecars used in city between 1859-1963; 1¼ mi rides (fee). (June-Oct, Sat and Sun

Nottoway Estate 1859

afternoons; rest of yr, Sun afternoons only; also open Memorial Day, July 4, Labor Day) 1901 Falls Rd, under North Ave Bridge. Phone 410/547-0264. ¢¢

Baltimore Zoo. Main zoo has collection of more than 1,500 animals. Incl three-acre African elephant park; six-acre African watering hole; hippo and African flamingo exhibit; eight-acre children's zoo (daily); track train and carousel (Apr-Sept; fee). Zoo (daily; closed Dec 25). Druid Hill Park. Phone 410/366-5466. ¢¢¢¢

B & O Railroad Museum. The museum incl the Mount Clare Station (1851), site of the nation's first passenger station, and the roundhouse (1884); original tracks and wooden turntable are fully preserved. Collection incl more than 120 full-size train cars. (Daily; closed major hols). 901 W Pratt St, at Poppleton St. Phone 410/752-2490. ¢¢¢

Edgar Allan Poe House

Basilica of the National Shrine of the Assumption. Now a co-cathedral, this was the first Roman Catholic cathedral in the US. Bishop John Carroll, head of the diocese of Baltimore from its establishment in 1789, blessed the cornerstone in 1806. The church was dedicated in 1821. Architectural design by B. H. Latrobe. Tours (by appt). (Daily) Cathedral and Mulberry sts, downtown. Phone 410/727-3565.

Battle Monument. (1815) Memorial to those who fell defending the city in the War of 1812. Calvert and Fayette sts.

Charles Center. Business area with European-style plazas, part of an overhead walkway system, shops, restaurants, and outdoor activities. Prize-winning office building by Mies van der Rohe borders center plaza. Bounded by Charles, Liberty, Saratoga, and Lombard sts, Downtown. Also here is

Baltimore Center for the Performing Arts—Morris Mechanic Theater. Hosts Broadway productions. Hopkins Plaza. Phone 410/625-4230.

Church Home and Hospital. Edgar Allan Poe died here in 1849. Broadway and Fairmount Ave.

City Court House. (1900) On steps is statue of Cecil Calvert, brother of Leonard and founder of Maryland as the second Lord Baltimore. St. Paul and Fayette sts, Downtown.

City Hall. Post-Civil War architecture, restored to original detail. 100 N Holliday St, Downtown. Tours by appt, Phone 410/396-3100. **FREE**

City of Baltimore Conservatory. This graceful building (ca 1885) houses a large variety of tropical plants. Special shows during Easter, Nov, and Christmas. (Thurs-Sun) Druid Hill Park. Phone 410/396-0180. **FREE**

Cylburn Arboretum. Marked nature trails. Nature museum, ornithological rm, horticultural library in restored mansion; shade and formal gardens, All-American Selection Garden, Garden of the Senses. (Daily) 4915 Greenspring Ave. Phone 410/396-0180. **FREE**

Edgar Allan Poe Grave. Baltimore's oldest cemeteries also contain the graves of many prominent early Marylanders. Tour of catacombs by appt (Apr-Nov, first and third Fri and Sat). At Westminster Hall and Bury-

Summertime at Inner Harbor

ing Ground and Catacombs, Fayette and Greene sts, Downtown. ¢¢

Edgar Allan Poe House. (ca 1830). Poe's home from 1832-1835. (Apr-July and Oct-mid-Dec, Wed-Sat, afternoons; Aug and Sept, Sat afternoon only) Also offered are tours of Westminster Cemetery and Catacombs (evenings, by appt; fee). 203 N Amity St, off 900 blk W Lexington St, Downtown. Phone 410/396-7932. ¢¢

Enoch Pratt Free Library. City's public library. H. L. Mencken and Edgar Allan Poe collections. (Sept-May, daily; rest of yr, Mon-Sat; closed hols) 400 Cathedral St, at Franklin St, Downtown. Phone 410/396-5430.

Federal Hill. View of city harbor and skyline. Named after a celebration that occurred here in 1788 to mark Maryland's ratification of the Constitution. Warren St and Battery Ave, Inner Harbor area.

Fell's Point. Shipbuilding and maritime center, this neighborhood dates back to 1730; approx 350 original residential structures. Working tugboats and tankers can be observed from docks. Broadway, S of Fleet St to the harbor.

First Unitarian Church. (1817) William Ellery Channing preached a sermon here that hastened the establishment of the Unitarian denomination. Example of Classic Revival architecture. Charles and Franklin

sts, in Mt Vernon Pl area. Phone 410/685-2330.

Fort McHenry National Monument and Historic Shrine. The flag flying over this five-pointed, star-shaped brick fort inspired Francis Scott Key to write the poem in 1814 that later became the lyrics to the national anthem. Named for James McHenry, Secretary of War (1796-1800). Replica flagpole on 1814 site. Restored powder magazine, guardrm, officers' quarters, and barracks all contain exhibits. Cannons of War of 1812 and Civil War periods. Guided activities (mid-June-Aug, daily). The Fort McHenry Guard, in period uniform, reenacts life at the garrison (mid-June-Aug, Sat and Sun afternoons). Military ceremony (July-Aug, some Sun eves). Visitor Center has exhibit area, film, gift shop. Special exhibits for visually and hearing impaired. (Daily; closed Jan 1, Dec 25) E end of Fort Ave. Phone 410/962-4299. ¢¢

> **Narrated cruises.** The *Baltimore Patriot* departs from Inner Harbor Finger Pier to Fort McHenry and Fell's Point (Memorial Day-Labor Day). Also departures from Fort McHenry and Fell's Point. For other tours contact Maryland Tours, Inc. Phone 410/962-4299. ¢¢¢

Gunpowder Falls State Park. Approx 16,000 acres, located in Gunpowder River Valley. **Hammerman Area,** E on US 40, right onto Ebenezer Rd, 5 mi to park entrance in Chase, is a developed day-use area. Offers swimming beach, windsurfing beach, boating, marina (Dundee Creek); picnicking, playground. Other areas offer hiking/biking trails, canoeing, trout fishing. Standard fees. Phone 410/592-2897.

Harbor cruises. Depart from Inner Harbor.

>   ***Baltimore Patriot.*** Ninety-min tours around Baltimore harbor. (Apr-Oct, daily)

>   **MV *Lady Baltimore.*** Round-trip cruises to Annapolis (June-Aug, Wed); also cruises to the Chesapeake & Delaware Canal (three selected Sun in Oct). *Bay Lady* has lunch and dinner cruises (Apr-Oct, daily; limited schedule rest of yr). West Bulkhead, 301 Light St. Phone 410/727-3113.

Harborplace. European-style marketplace comprised of two glass-enclosed pavilions; one featuring many eateries, incl waterside cafes and restaurants, the other housing dozens of specialty shops arranged in Parisian style along a colonnade. Overhead walkway leads to **The Gallery at Harborplace**, with many additional top-name shops and eateries. Free summer concerts along waterfront. (Daily; closed Thanksgiving, Dec 24) Light and Pratt sts, Inner Harbor area. Phone 410/332-4191.

Holocaust Memorial. Simple stone memorial to the victims of the Holocaust. Water and Gay sts, Downtown. Phone 410/752-2630.

Jewish Historical Society of Maryland. Buildings incl Lloyd St Synagogue (1845), the oldest in Maryland; B'nai Israel Synagogue (1876); Jewish Museum of Maryland. (Tues-Thurs and Sun afternoons; or by appt; closed Jewish hols) Research archives (Mon-Fri, by appt). 15 Lloyd St, Downtown. Phone 410/732-6400. ¢

Johns Hopkins Medical Institutions. (1889) Widely known as a leading medical school, research center, and teaching hospital. Victorian buildings. Broadway and Monument St. Phone 410/955-7894.

Johns Hopkins University. (1876) 4,600 students. Modern buildings in Georgian style on wooded 126-acre campus. Distinguished research school founded by wealthy merchant of the city. Charles and 34th sts, 2 mi N. Phone 410/516-8000. On grounds are

>   **Bufano Sculpture Garden.** A wooded retreat with animals sculpted by artist Beniamino Bufano. Dunning Park, behind Mudd Hall. **FREE**

>   **Evergreen House.** On 26 wooded acres; features Classical Revival architecture and formal garden. Library (35,000 volumes). Post-impressionist paintings, Japanese and Chinese collections, and Tiffany glass. Tours (daily). 4545 N Charles St, approx 2 mi N of Homewood campus. Phone 410/516-0341. ¢¢¢

>   **Homewood House Museum.** (1801) Former country home of Charles Carroll, Jr., whose father was a signer of the Declaration of Independence; period furnishings. (Tues-Sat, also Sun afternoons) Guided tours (hrly). 3400 N Charles St near 34th St. Phone 410/516-5589. ¢¢¢

Joseph Meyerhoff Symphony Hall. Permanent residence of the Baltimore Symphony Orchestra. 1212 Cathedral St. Phone 410/783-8000.

Lacrosse Hall of Fame Museum. Team trophies, display of lacrosse artifacts and memorabilia, incl rare photographs and art, vintage equipt and uniforms. Also historical video documentary. (Feb-May, Tues-Sat; June-Jan, Mon-Fri; closed hols) 113 W University Pkwy. Phone 410/235-6882. ¢¢

Lexington Market. In continuous operation since 1782, this famous indoor marketplace houses more than 140 stalls run by independent merchants. (Mon-Sat; closed hols) 400 W Lexington St, between Eutaw and Paca sts, Downtown. Phone 410/685-6169. **FREE**

Lovely Lane Museum. Permanent and changing exhibits of items of Methodist church history since 1760. Guided tours (Mon-Fri; also Sun after services and by appt; closed hols). 2200 St. Paul St. Phone 410/889-4458. **FREE**

Maryland Historical Society Library of Maryland. Original manuscript of "Star-Spangled Banner" is displayed; extensive displays of Maryland silver, furniture, and painting; changing exhibits; maritime museum. Also within the museum is the **Darnall Young People's Museum,** a gallery with "hands-on" exhibits. Museum and gallery (Oct-Apr, Tues-Sun; rest of yr, Tues-Sat). Library (Tues-Sat). Museum free on Wed. 201 W Monument St, between Park Ave and Howard St, in Mt Vernon Place area. Phone 410/685-3750. ¢¢

Maryland Institute, College of Art. (1826) 880 students. Institute hosts frequent contemporary art exhibitions. Cafeteria. Campus distinguished by recycled buildings and white marble Italianate main building. (Daily) Main building 1300 Mt Royal Ave, at Lanvale St. Phone 410/669-9200.

Maryland Science Center & Davis Planetarium. Home of the Maryland Academy of Sciences, the oldest scientific institution in the state. Features exhibits in areas such as energy, physics, the Chesapeake Bay, optical illusions, and television production. Planetarium. Incl IMAX theater. Science demonstrations. (Daily; closed Thanksgiving, Dec 25) 601 Light St, Inner Harbor area. Phone 410-685-5225 (recording). ¢¢¢¢

Minnie V. Chesapeake Bay skipjack built in 1906. Harbor tours under sail (open wkends). Docks near Pier 1, Pratt St, Inner Harbor area. Phone 410/685-9062.

Morgan State University. (1867) 5,100 students. The James E. Lewis Museum of Art has changing exhibits (Mon-Fri; wkends by appt; closed hols). Cold Spring Ln and Hillen Rd. Phone 443/885-3333.

Mother Seton House. Home of St. Elizabeth Ann Bayley Seton from 1808-1809. Here she established forerunner of the parochial school system, as well as an order of nuns that eventually became the Daughters & Sisters of Charity in the US and Canada. (Sat and Sun afternoons, also by appt; closed Jan 1, Easter, Dec 25) 600 N Paca St, Downtown. Phone 410/523-3443. **FREE**

Mount Clare Museum House. (1760) Oldest mansion in Baltimore, former home of Charles Carroll, barrister. 18th- and 19th-century furnishings. Guided tours on the hr. (Tues-Sun; closed hols) In Carroll Park at 1500 Washington Blvd. Phone 410/837-3262. ¢¢

Mount Vernon Place United Methodist Church. (ca 1850) Brownstone with balcony and grillwork extending entire width of house; spiral staircase suspended from three floors; library with century-old painting on ceiling; drawing rm. (Mon-Fri; closed hols and Mon after Easter) 10 E Mt Vernon Place. Phone 410/685-5290. **FREE**

National Aquarium

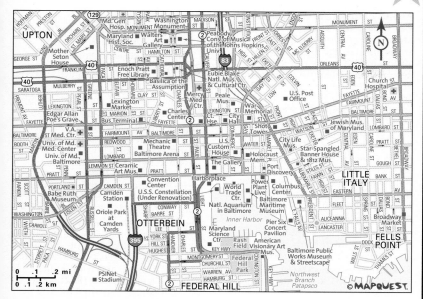

MPT (Maryland Public Television). Tours of state's television network studios. (By appt) Phone 410/356-5600. **FREE**

⭐ **National Aquarium.** One of most advanced facilities in US. Exhibits incl a South American rain forest, Atlantic coral reef, shark tank; houses 5,000 specimens of 500 different types of mammals, fish, birds, reptiles, amphibians, invertebrates, and plants. (Daily; closed Thanksgiving, Dec 25) Pier 3, 501 E Pratt St, Inner Harbor area. Phone 410/576-3800. ¢¢¢¢ Visitors cross an enclosed skywalk to reach the adj wing, which houses

Marine Mammal Pavilion. This unique structure features a 1,300-seat amphitheater surrounding a 1.2-million-gallon pool, which houses Atlantic bottlenose dolphins; underwater viewing areas enable visitors to observe the mammals from below the surface. (Daily) Special video programs about dolphins and whales; educational arcade with computerized video screens and other participatory exhibits around the pavilion's upper deck. Visitor service area located in the atrium. Gift shop. Cafe. A life-size replica of a humpback whale spans two levels of the atrium. Discovery Room houses a

collection of marine artifacts. Resource Center is an aquatic learning center for school visitors; library boasts extensive collection of marine science material. Pier 4.

Old Otterbein United Methodist Church. (1785-1786) Fine Georgian architecture; mother church of United Brethren. Tours of historic building (Apr-Oct, Sat). Conway and Sharp sts, Inner Harbor area. Phone 410/685-4703.

Old Town Mall. This 150-yr-old, brick-lined commercial area has been beautifully refurbished; closed to vehicular traffic. 400 and 500 blks of N Gay St. Nearby is

Stirling Street. First community urban "homesteading" venture in the US. Renovated homes date back to the 1830s. Original facades have been maintained; interior rehabilitation ranges in style from the antique to the avant-garde. 1000 blk of Monument St, 1 blk W of mall.

Otterbein "Homesteading." The original neighborhood dates back to 1785. Houses have been restored. Area around S Sharp St, Inner Harbor area.

Patterson Park. Defenses here helped stop British attack in 1814. Breastworks, artillery pieces are displayed. Baltimore St, Eastern and Patterson Park aves. Phone 410/396-7931.

Peabody Institute of the Johns Hopkins University. (1857) 550 students. Music conservatory founded by philanthropist George Peabody; now affiliated with Johns Hopkins. Research and reference collection in library accessible to the public (Mon-Fri; closed hols). The Miriam A. Friedberg Concert Hall seats 800. Orchestral, recital, and opera performances. In Mt Vernon Place area. (box office) Phone 410/659-8124.

Pier 6 Concert Pavilion. Summertime outdoor concerts and plays at the water's edge. Some covered seating. (June-Sept, eves) Pier 6, Inner Harbor area. Phone 410/625-3100. ¢¢¢¢

Professional sports.

Baltimore Orioles (MLB). Oriole Park at Camden Yards, 333 W Camden St. Phone 410/685-9800.

Baltimore Ravens (NFL). PSINet Stadium, 1101 Russell St. Phone 410/230-8000.

Public Works Museum & Streetscape. Museum exhibits the history and artifacts of public works. Located in historic sewage pumping station. Streetscape sculpture outside depicts the various utility lines and ducts under a typical city street, in a walk-through model. (Tues-Sun) 751 Eastern Ave, at Inner Harbor East. Phone 410/396-5565. ¢¢

Sherwood Gardens. More than six acres in size, the gardens reach their peak of splendor in late Apr and early May, when thousands of tulips, azaleas, and flowering shrubs bloom. Stratford Rd and Greenway, in the residential community of Guilford in northern Baltimore.

⭐ **Star-Spangled Banner Flag House and 1812 Museum.** The banner (30 by 42 ft) with 15 stars and 15 stripes that Key saw "by the dawn's early light" over Fort McHenry was hand-sewn here by Mary Young Pickersgill. The actual flag is in the Smithsonian. House (1793) is authentically restored and furnished in the Federal period. 1812 Museum contains relics, documents, weapons, memorabilia; audiovisual program; garden. Focal point of the garden is a stone map of the US; every state is represented by a stone native to and cut in the shape of that state. (Tues-Sat; closed hols) 844 E Pratt St, at Albemarle St, Downtown. Phone 410/837-1793. ¢¢

Theaters.

Cockpit in Court Summer Theatre. (See SPECIAL EVENTS)

Vagabond Players. Oldest continuously operating "little theater" in US. Recent Broadway shows, revivals, and original scripts are performed. (Fri-Sun) 806 S Broadway. (Box office) Phone 410/563-9135.

Top of the World. Observation deck and museum on the 27th floor of the World Trade Center, which was designed by I. M. Pei. Exhibits describe the city's history, famous residents, and the activities of the port. (Daily) World Trade Center, Pratt St, Inner Harbor area. ¢¢

University of Maryland at Baltimore. 5,476 students. The 32-acre downtown campus incl six professional schools; the University of Maryland Medical System, and the Graduate School. Davidge Hall (1812) is the oldest medical teaching building in continuous use in the Western Hemisphere. Lombard, Greene, and Redwood sts, Downtown. Phone 410/706-7820.

Walters Art Museum. City-owned fine arts collection of paintings, sculpture, arms, armor, jewelry, and manuscripts from antiquity through the 19th century. (Tues-Sun; closed hols) 600 N Charles St, at Centre St, in Mt Vernon Pl area. Phone 410/547-9000. ¢¢¢

Washington Monument. (1815-1842) First major monument to honor George Washington. Museum in base; view city from top. Other monuments nearby honor Lafayette, Chief Justice Roger Brooke Taney, philanthropist George Peabody, lawyer Severn Teackle Wallis, and Revolutionary War hero John Eager Howard. Charles and Monument sts, in Mt Vernon Pl area. Phone 410/396-1049.

Special Events

ACC Crafts Fair. Convention Center. Featuring more than 800 national artisans. Late Feb. Phone 410/649-7144.

Pimlico Race Course. Hayward and Winner aves, 2 mi W of Jones Falls Expy. Thoroughbred racing. **The Preakness**, the $500,000 middle jewel in Thoroughbred racing's Triple Crown, has been run here yearly since 1873 and is held the third Sat in May. All seats reserved Preakness Day. Late Mar-early June and early Aug-early Oct. Phone 410/466-2521.

Maryland House and Garden Pilgrimage. More than 100 homes and gardens throughout the state are open. To purchase tour book contact 1105-A Providence Rd, 21286. Late Apr-early May. Phone 410/821-6933.

Maryland Preakness Celebration. Statewide festival; events incl hot-air balloon festival, parade, steeplechase, celebrity golf tournament, block parties, and schooner race. Phone 410/837-3030. Ten days preceding Preakness Stakes (see SPECIAL EVENTS). Early to mid-May.

Showcase of Nations Ethnic Festivals. Various downtown locations. Presenting the food, music, and crafts of a different culture each wkend. June-Sept. Phone 410/752-8632.

Cockpit in Court Summer Theatre. 7201 Rossville Blvd, use Beltway (I-695) exit 34, in Baltimore County. Theater in residence at Essex Community College. Four separate theaters offer a diverse collection of plays, incl Broadway productions, contemporary drama, revues, and Shakespeare. Mid-June-mid-Aug. Phone 410/780-6369.

Harbor Expo. Middle Branch and Canton waterfront. Boat parades, seafood festival; entertainment; events. Mid-June. Phone 410/396-7931.

Artscape. Salute to the arts and culture.Three days July. Phone 410/396-4575.

New Year's Eve Extravaganza. Convention Center and Inner Harbor. Parties, entertainment, big bands, fireworks. Phone 410/649-7144.

Motels/Motor Lodges

★★ **BEST WESTERN HOTEL AND CONFERENCE CENTER.** *5625 O'Donnell St (21224). 410/633-9500; fax 410/633-4314; toll-free 800/633-9511. www.bestwestern.com.* 175 rms, 12 story. S, D $109-$129; under 12 free; each addl $10; suites $129-$229. Crib free. TV; cable (premium). Indoor pool; whirlpool; lifeguard. Coffee in rms. Restaurant 6:30 am-10 pm. Bar. Ck-out noon. Coin lndry. Valet serv. Meeting rms. Business

servs avail. In-rm modem link. Gift shop. Bus depot transportation. Exercise equipt; sauna. Game rm. Microwaves avail. Cr cds: A, C, D, DS, JCB, MC, V.

[D] [≊] [🐾] [SC] [≈] [🏃]

★ **CHRISTLEN MOTEL.** *8733 Pulaski Hwy (21237). 410/687-1740.* 28 rms. S $32-$38; D $38-$42; each addl $5. Crib $5. TV; cable (premium). Restaurant adj open 24 hrs. Ck-out 11 am. Some refrigerators. Cr cds: A, D, DS, MC, V.

[D] [≊] [🐾]

★ **DAYS INN INNER HARBOR HOTEL.** *100 Hopkins Pl (21201). 410/576-1000; fax 410/576-9437; toll-free 800/329-7466. www.daysinn.com.* 250 rms, 9 story. S $90-$120; D $100-$130; each addl $10; suites $140-$180; under 12 free; higher rates special events. Crib free. Garage $8.50. TV; cable (premium). Pool; poolside serv, lifeguard. Restaurant 6:30 am-10 pm. Bar. Coffee in rms. Ck-out 11 am. Meeting rms. Business center. In-rm modem link. Valet serv. Bellhops. Concierge. Sundries. Health club privileges. Some refrigerators; microwaves avail. Cr cds: A, C, D, DS, MC, V.

[D] [≊] [🐾] [SC] [≈] [🏃]

★★ **HAMPTON INN.** *8225 Town Ctr Dr (21236). 410/931-2200; fax 410/931-2215; res 800/426-7866. www.hamptoninn.com.* 127 rms, 4 story, 16 suites. S, D $89; suites $109; under 18 free. Crib $10. TV; cable (premium). Complimentary continental bkfst. Coffee in rms. Restaurant nearby. Ck-out noon. Meeting rms. Business center. In-rm modem link. Exercise equipt. Health club privileges. Indoor pool; lifeguard. Coin lndry. Valet serv. Wet bar in suites. Refrigerators, microwaves avail. Cr cds: A, D, DS, MC, V.

[D] [≈] [🏃] [≊] [🐾] [🏃]

★★ **HOLIDAY INN.** *1800 Belmont Ave (21244). 410/265-1400; fax 410/281-9569; toll-free 800/465-4329. www.holiday-inn.com.* 133 units, 2 story. S, D $89. Crib free. Pet accepted, some restrictions; $25. TV; cable (premium). Pool; lifeguard. Restaurant 6-10 am, 5-9:30 pm; Sat, Sun to 11 am. Bar 5 pm-midnight. Coffee, tea in rms. Ck-out noon.

Meeting rms. Business servs avail. In-rm modem link. Coin lndry. Valet serv. Sundries. Health club privileges $8. Some refrigerators; microwaves avail. Cr cds: A, C, D, DS, JCB, MC, V.

⊡ 🐾 ≊ 🏖 SC

★ ★ **HOLIDAY INN SELECT.** *2004 Greenspring Dr (21093). 410/252-7373; fax 410/561-0182; toll-free 800/289-4499. www.holiday-inn.com.* 245 rms, 5 story. S, D $139; each addl $10; suites $259-$368; family, wkly, wkend, hol rates. Crib free. TV; cable (premium). Indoor/outdoor pool; whirlpool. Restaurant 6 am-10 pm. Bars; entertainment. Coffee, tea in rms. Ck-out noon. Coin lndry. Meeting rms. Business servs avail. In-rm modem link. Bellhops. Concierge. Gift shop. Valet serv. Exercise equipt. Microwaves avail. Cr cds: A, C, D, DS, JCB, MC, V.

≊ 🕱 ⊡ ≊ 🏖 SC

Hotels

★ ★ ★ **BROOKSHIRE INNER HAR-BOR SUITE HOTEL.** *120 E Lombard St (21202). 410/625-1300; fax 410/649-2635; toll-free 800/647-0013. www.harbormagic.com.* 97 suites, 66 suites, 11 story. Apr-Oct: S, D $169-$249; suites $219-$309; each addl $20; children free; wkend rates. Valet parking $20. Crib free. Pet accepted, some restrictions; $100 deposit. TV; cable (premium), VCR avail. Complimentary full bkfst. Coffee in rms. Restaurant 6:30-10 am, 5-9 pm. Rm serv. Bar 5-10 pm. Ck-out noon. Meeting rms. Exercise equipt. In-rm modem link. Health club privileges. Valet serv. Bathrm phones, minibars; microwaves avail. Cr cds: A, D, DS, MC, V.

🕱 ⊡ ≊ 🏖 SC 🐾

★ **CLARION HOTEL PEABODY COURT.** *612 Cathedral St (21201). 410/727-7101; fax 410/789-3312. www.clarioninn.com.* 104 rms, 14 story. S, D $149-$169; each addl $10; suites $189-$500; under 18 free; wkend rates; package plans. Crib free. Parking $18/day. TV; cable (premium), VCR avail (movies). Pool privileges. Complimentary bkfst buffet. Restaurants 6:30-9:30 am; 11 am-2 pm; 5-10 pm; Sun to 9 pm. Bar. Coffee in rms. Ck-out 11 am. Meeting rms. Business servs avail. Valet serv. In-rm modem link. Bellhops.

Concierge. Health club privileges. Refrigerators. Some in-rm whirlpools. Restored hotel built in 1927. Marble floors, stairs in lobby. Period furnishings, artwork, crystal chandeliers. Cr cds: A, D, DS, MC, V.

⊡ ≊ 🏖 SC

★ ★ **DOUBLETREE INN AT THE COLONNADE.** *4 W University Pkwy (21218). 410/235-5400; fax 410/235-5572; toll-free 800/222-8733. www.doubletree.com.* 125 units, 3 story, 31 suites. S, D $145-$202; each addl $15; suites $167-$475; family rates; wkend plans. Crib free. Pet accepted. TV; cable (premium). Indoor pool; whirlpool, poolside serv, lifeguard. Coffee in rms. Restaurant 6 am-11 pm (see also POLO GRILL). Rm serv to 10 pm. Ck-out noon. Meeting rm. Business center. Valet serv. In-rm modem link. Gift shop. Barber, beauty shop. Exercise equipt. Some wet bars. Refrigerators, microwaves avail. Balconies. Biedermeier-inspired furnishings; extensive collection of 18th-century European masters. Adj Johns Hopkins University. Cr cds: A, C, D, DS, ER, JCB, MC, V.

⊡ 🐾 ≊ 🏖 SC 🕱

★ ★ ★ **HARBOR COURT.** *550 Light St (21202). 410/234-0550; fax 410/659-5925; res 800/824-0076. www.harborcourt.com.* 200 rms, 8 story, 25 suites. S, D $270-$340; suites $405-$2,000; under 18 free; wkend rates; some package plans. Crib free. Covered parking: self-park $19; valet $25. TV; cable (premium), VCR avail. Indoor pool; whirlpool, poolside serv, lifeguard. Restaurant 6:30 am-9 pm; Sun from 7 am (see also HAMPTON'S). Rm serv 24 hrs. Bar 11-2 am; entertainment Mon-Sat. Coffee in rms. Ck-out noon. Meeting rms. Business center. In-rm modem link. Concierge. Airport transportation. Tennis. Exercise rm; sauna. Massage. Racquetball. Lawn games. Bathrm phones, refrigerators. CD player in suites. Elegant retreat located on Inner Harbor; panoramic view of city. Cr cds: A, C, D, DS, MC, V.

🕱 ⊡ ≊ 🕱 ≊ 🏖 🕱

★ ★ ★ **HILTON HOTEL AND TOWERS.** *20 W Baltimore St (21201). 410/539-8400; fax 410/625-1060. www.hilton.com.* 419 rms, 23 story. S $189; D $209; each addl $15; suites $275-$400; kit. units $600-$800;

under 17 free; wkend rates. Crib free. Valet parking $15. TV; cable. Restaurants 6:30 am-10 pm. Bar 11-2 am. Ck-out noon. Meeting rms. In-rm modem link. Exercise equipt; sauna. Whirlpool. Health club privileges. Microwaves avail. Historic landmark; near harbor. Cr cds: A, C, D, DS, ER, MC, V.

D 🐟 🏊 🔥 SC

★ ★ **HOLIDAY INN INNER HAR-BOR.** *301 W Lombard St (21201). 410/685-3500; fax 410/727-6169; res 800/465-4329. www.holiday-inn.com.* 373 rms; 13 story. Apr-Sept: S, D $219; each addl $10; suites $275; under 19 free; lower rates rest of yr. Crib free. Garage parking $11/night. TV; cable (premium). Indoor pool; lifeguard. Complimentary coffee, tea in rms. Restaurant 6:30 am-11 pm. Rm serv. Bar 11-1 am. Ck-out noon. Coin lndry. Convention facilities. Business servs avail. In-rm modem link. Gift shop. Concierge. Exercise equipt; sauna. Cr cds: A, C, D, DS, JCB, MC, V.

🏊 🐟 D 🐟 🔥 SC

★ ★ ★ **HYATT REGENCY.** *300 Light St (21202). 410/528-1234; fax 410/685-3362; res 800/233-1234. www.hyatt.com.* 486 rms, 15 story. Memorial Day-late Oct: S, D $125-$363; each addl $25; suites $450-$1,000; under 18 free; wkend plan. Crib free. Garage $15, valet parking $20. TV; cable (premium). 2 pools, 1 indoor; whirlpool; sundeck; lifeguard; poolside serv. Supervised children's activies. Restaurant 6:30-1 am. Bar 11:30-2 am; entertainment Fri, Sat. Coffee in rms. Ck-out noon. Convention facilities. Business center. In-rm modem link. Valet serv. Bellhops. Concierge. Gift shop. Tennis. Exercise rm; sauna. Putting green. Basketball ½ court. Minibars; refrigerators avail. Luxury level. Cr cds: A, C, D, DS, ER, JCB, MC, V.

D 🐟 🐟 🔥 SC 🐟 🐟

★ ★ ★ **MARRIOTT INNER HARBOR BALTIMORE.** *110 S Eutaw St (21201). 410/962-0202; fax 410/625-7892. www.marriott.com.* 524 units, 10 story. S, D $229-$259; suites $284-$650; under 18 free; wkend rates. Crib free. Covered parking $8. TV; cable (premium), VCR avail. Indoor pool; whirlpool, lifeguard. Restaurant

6 am-10 pm. Bar noon-2 am; entertainment. Coffee in rms. Ck-out noon. Convention facilities. Business center. In-rm modem link. Valet serv. Coin lndry. Concierge. Gift shop. Exercise equipt; sauna. Minibars. Opp baseball stadium at Camden Yards. Luxury level. Cr cds: A, C, D, DS, JCB, MC, V.

D 🏊 🐟 🔥 🐟 🐟

★ ★ ★ **MARRIOTT WATERFRONT HOTEL BALTIMORE.** *700 Aliceanna St (21202). 410/385-3000; fax 410/895-1900; res 800/228-9290. www.marriott.com.* 750 rms, 32 story. S, D $249-$279; under 17 free. Crib avail. TV; cable (premium). Indoor pool; whirlpool. Restaurant 6:30 am-10 pm. Bar to midnight. Coffee in rms. Ck-out noon, ck-in 4 pm. Meeting rms. Business center. In-rm modem link. Concierge. Gift shop. Exercise equipt; sauna. Valet serv. Minibars; many refrigerators in suites. Luxury level. Cr cds: A, C, D, DS, MC, V.

D 🏊 🐟 SC 🐟 🐟

★ ★ **RADISSON CROSS KEYS.** *100 Village Sq (21210). 410/532-6900; fax 410/532-2403; res 800/333-3333. www.radisson.com.* 148 rms, 4 story. S, D $139-$189; each addl $15; suites $225-$425; under 17 free; wkend rates. Crib free. TV; cable (premium). Pool; poolside serv, lifeguard. Complimentary coffee in rms. Restaurant 6:30 am-11 pm. Bar 11 am-midnight. Ck-out noon. Meeting rms. Business servs avail. In-rm modem link. Exercise equipt. Shopping arcade. Barber, beauty shop. Tennis privileges. Health club privileges. Bathrm phones. Some private balconies. Cr cds: A, D, DS, MC, V.

🐟 D 🐟 🐟 🐟 🏊 🐟 🔥

★ ★ ★ **RENAISSANCE HARBOR-PLACE HOTEL.** *202 E Pratt St (21202). 410/547-1200; fax 410/539-5780; toll-free 800/535-1201. www.renaissancehotels.com.* 622 rms, 12 story. Mar-Nov: S, D $169-$249; each addl $20; suites $275-$3,000; under 18 free; wkend rates. Garage, valet parking avail. Crib free. TV; cable (premium), VCR avail. Heated indoor pool; whirlpool, poolside serv, lifeguard. Coffee in rms. Restaurant 6:30 am-11 pm. Rm serv 24 hrs. Bar 11-1:30 am; entertainment. Ck-out noon. Convention facilities. Business center. In-rm modem link. Concierge. Bellhops. Gift shop. Shopping arcade. Valet serv. Exercise equipt; sauna. Health club privileges. Minibars; bathrm phones. Luxury level. Cr cds: A, D, DS, JCB, MC, V.

🏋 🏃 D ⇌ ⇲ ♿

★★★ **SHERATON INNER HARBOR HOTEL.** *300 S Charles St (21201).* 410/962-8300; fax 410/962-8211; toll-free 800/325-3535. 337 rms, 15 story. Mar-June, Sept-Dec: S, D $199-$239; each addl $15; suites $425-$1,400; under 17 free; wkly, wkend rates; lower rates rest of yr. Crib free. Covered parking $14, valet parking $19. TV; cable (premium), VCR avail (movies). Heated indoor pool; lifeguard. Restaurant 7 am-10 pm. Rm serv. Bar 11:30-2 am. Coffee in rms. Ck-out noon. Convention facilities. Business center. In-rm modem link. Bellhops. Concierge. Valet serv. Gift shop. Exercise equipt; sauna. Health club privileges. Minibars; some bathrm phones. Refrigerators avail. Cr cds: A, C, D, DS, JCB, MC, V.

D ⇌ 🏋 🏃 ⇲ ♿ SC

★★ **TREMONT HOTEL.** *8 E Pleasant St (21202).* 410/576-1200; fax 410/244-1154; toll-free 800/873-6668. *www.tremontsuiteshotels.com.* 58 kit. suites, 13 story. S, D $159-$179; each addl $20; under 16 free; wkend rates. Crib free. Pet accepted; $5. Valet parking $14. Pool privileges. TV; cable, VCR avail. Complimentary continental bkfst. Restaurant 5-9 pm. Bar to 10 pm. Ck-out noon. Meeting rms. Business servs avail. Concierge. Valet serv. Health club privileges. Cr cds: A, C, D, DS, JCB, MC, V.

D ⇲ 🐾 ⇌

★★★ **WYNDHAM INNER HARBOR HOTEL.** *101 W Fayette St (21201).* 410/752-1100; fax 410/752-0832; toll-free 800/996-3426. *www.wyndham.com.* 707 rms in 2 bldgs, 23, 27 story. Apr-Nov: S, D $199-$269; each addl $20; suites $250-$1,500; under 17 free; wkend rates; package plans. Crib free. Garage; valet parking. TV; cable (premium). Pool; lifeguard, poolside serv. Coffee in rms. Restaurant 6:30 am-midnight. Bars noon-2 am. Ck-out noon. Convention facilities. Business center. In-rm modem link. Bellhops. Concierge. Gift shop. Valet serv. In-

rm modem link. Exercise equipt. Minibars; some refrigerators; microwaves avail. Cr cds: A, D, DS, MC, V.

D ⇲ ♿ SC ⇌ 🏋 🏃

B&Bs/Small Inns

★★★ **ABERCROMBIE BADGER BED AND BREAKFAST.** *58 W Biddle St (21201).* 410/244-7227; fax 410/244-8415. *www.badger-inn.com/index.htm.* 12 rms, 4 story. S $88; D $115-$155. TV; cable. Children over 10 yrs only. Complimentary continental bkfst. Restaurant 11 am-10 pm; Fri, Sat to midnight; closed Mon. Bar to midnight; Fri, Sat to 2 am. Ck-out 11 am, ck-in 4-6 pm. Business servs avail. Turn-of-the-century building; many antique furnishings. Totally nonsmoking. Cr cds: A, D, DS, MC, V.

⇲ ♿

★★★ **ADMIRAL FELL INN.** *888 S Broadway, Historic Fell's Point (21231).* 410/522-7377; fax 410/522-0707; toll-free 800/292-4667. *www.admiralfell.com.* 80 rms, 5 story. S $115-$145; D $135-$195; each addl $20; suites $220-$395; under 16 free; wkly rates. Pet accepted, some restrictions. TV; cable (premium). Complimentary continental bkfst. Dining rm noon-10 pm. Bar to 2 am. Ck-out 11 am; ck-in 4 pm. Meeting rms. Health club privileges. Some in-rm whirlpools. Cr cds: A, MC, V.

D 🐾 ⇲ ♿ SC

★★★ **CELIE'S WATERFRONT BED AND BREAKFAST.** *1714 Thames St (21231).* 410/522-2323; fax 410/522-2324; toll-free 800/432-0184. *www.baltimore-bed-breakfast.com.* 7 rms, 1 with shower only, 3 story. S $114-$212; D $132-$242; hol, wkend rates. Children over 10 yrs only. TV; cable, VCR. Complimentary continental bkfst, coffee in rms. Restaurant nearby. Ck-out 11 am, ck-in 3-6 pm. In-rm modem link. Health club privileges. Refrigerators; some in-rm whirlpools, fireplaces, balconies. On harbor; many antiques. Roof deck. Totally nonsmoking. Cr cds: A, DS, MC, V.

D ⇲ ♿

★★★ **HOPKINS INN.** *3404 St. Paul St (21218).* 410/235-8600; fax 410/235-7051. *www.bichotels.com/hopkinsinn.* 25 rms, 4 story. S $99-$129, D $109-$139;

each addl $10; wkly, monthly rates. Covered parking $6. TV; cable. Complimentary continental bkfst. Restaurant nearby. Ck-out 11 am, ck-in 3 pm. Meeting rms. Business servs avail. 1920s Spanish Revival building. Rms individually furnished in variety of styles. Totally nonsmoking. Cr cds: A, C, D, DS, JCB, MC, V.

★ ★ ★ **INN AT GOVERNMENT HOUSE.** *1125 N Calvert St (21202). 410/539-0566; fax 410/539-0567. www.baltimorecity.gov/visitor.* 18 rms, 4 story. S, D $125-$150; wkly rates; Preakness (2-day min). Complimentary continental bkfst; afternoon refreshments. Restaurant nearby. Ck-out noon, ck-in 3-8 pm. Business servs avail. Part of complex of several Federal and Victorian mansions and townhouses (1888). Totally nonsmoking. Cr cds: A, C, D, DS, MC, V.

★ ★ **INN AT HENDERSON'S WHARF.** *1000 Fell St (21231). 410/ 522-7777; fax 410/522-7087; toll-free 800/522-2088. www.hendersonswharf. com.* 38 rms. Apr-Nov: S, D $120-$160; kit. suites $400; under 18 free; higher rates special events; lower rates rest of yr. TV; cable (premium). Complimentary continental bkfst. Restaurant nearby. Ck-out noon, ck-in 3 pm. Coin lndry. Meeting rms. Business servs avail. In-rm modem link. Valet serv. Exercise equipt. Some refrigerators. On waterfront; dockage avail. 19th-century tobacco warehouse. Cr cds: A, C, D, MC, V.

★ ★ ★ **MR. MOLE BED AND BREAKFAST.** *1601 Bolton St (21217). 410/728-1179; fax 410/728-3379. www.mrmolebb.com.* 5 rms, 5 story, 2 suites. S, D $119-$175; suites $150-$175; 2-day min wkends. Garage parking. Children over 10 yrs only. Complimentary bkfst. Restaurant nearby. Ck-out 11 am, ck-in 4-6 pm. Business servs avail. In-rm modem link. Totally nonsmoking. Cr cds: A, D, DS, MC, V.

Restaurants

★ ★ **ANGELINA'S.** *7135 Harford Rd (21234). 410/444-5545. www.crab* cake.com. Hrs: 11:30 am-10 pm; Fri, Sat to 11 pm. Closed Mon; Thanksgiving, Dec 25. Italian, seafood menu. Bar. Lunch $4.95-$16.95, dinner $8.95-$29. Child's menu. Specializes in crab cakes, seafood. Entertainment Fri. Cr cds: A, DS, MC, V.

★ ★ ★ **ATLANTIC.** *2400 Boston St (21224). 410/675-4565. www.atlantic restaurant.com.* Specializes in fresh seafood. Hrs: 11 am-3 pm, 5:30-10 pm; Fri, Sat to 11 pm; brunch 11 am-3 pm. Closed hols. Res accepted. Parking. Wine list. Lunch $6.50-$16; dinner $17-$26. Sun brunch $6-$12. Child's menu. Entertainment. Cr cds: A, C, D, DS, MC, V.

★ **BERTHA'S.** *734 S Broadway (21231). 410/327-5795. www.berthas. com.* Hrs: 11:30 am-11 pm; Fri, Sat to midnight; Sun brunch to 2 pm. Closed hols. Res required for Scottish afternoon tea (Mon-Sat). Bar. Lunch, dinner $5.75-$27.90. Sun brunch $7.50-$8.25. Specializes in mussels, seafood. Eclectic decor. Historic 19th-century building. Entertainment. Cr cds: MC, V.

★ ★ ★ **BLACK OLIVE.** *814 S Bond St (21231). 410/276-7141. www.theblack olive.com.* Mediterranean menu. Specializes in whole fish on the grill, lamb. Hrs: 5:30-10 pm; Sun 5-9 pm. Closed hols. Res accepted. Wine list. Dinner $22-$36. Entertainment. Cr cds: A, C, D, DS, MC, V.

★ ★ ★ **BOCCACCIO.** *925 Eastern Ave (21231). 410/234-1322.* Hrs: 11:30 am-2:30 pm, 5-11 pm; Sat from 5 pm; Sun 3-10 pm. Closed Thanksgiving, Dec 25. Res required eves. Italian menu. Bar. Lunch $9.75-$15.75, dinner $13.50-$28.50. Specializes in veal, seafood, pasta. Formal decor. Cr cds: A, D, MC, V.

★ **CAFE HON.** *1002 W 36th St (21211). 410/243-1230. www.cafehon. com.* Hrs: 7 am-9 pm; Fri, Sat to 10 pm; Sun to 8 pm; Sat, Sun brunch 9 am-3 pm. Closed hols. Res accepted. Bar. Bkfst $1.25-$6.25, lunch, dinner $3.75-$14.95. Sun brunch $1.75-

$8.95. Child's menu. Specialties: crab cakes, meatloaf. Eclectic cafe reminiscent of 1930s Baltimore soda fountain. Totally nonsmoking. Cr cds: A, D, MC, V.
D

★ ★ ★ ★ **CHARLESTON.** *1000 Lancaster St (21202). 410/332-7373. www. charlestonrestaurant.com.* Baltimore's culinary leader, Cindy Wolf, has outdone herself with this casually upscale, contemporary American restaurant located in the Inner Harbor East Development. Southern-inspired culinary elements are elevated to fine-dining status with dishes such as roasted duck breast with pecan and onion stuffing and nectarine-armagnac sauce. Service is very civilized and the wine list is among the best the city has to offer. Specializes in duck breast, veal tenderloin, quail, foie gras. Hrs: 5:30-10 pm; Fri, Sat to 11 pm. Closed Sun, hols. Res accepted. Extensive wine list. Menu changes daily. A la carte entrees: dinner $26-$32; prix fixe $60. Entertainment. Cr cds: A, C, D, DS, MC, V.
D

★ ★ **CHIAPPARELLI'S OF LITTLE ITALY.** *237 S High St (21202). 410/ 837-0309. www.chiapparellis.com.* Hrs: 11 am-10 pm; Fri, Sat to midnight. Closed Thanksgiving, Dec 25. Res accepted. Italian menu. Bar. Lunch $6-$17, dinner $13-$28. Child's menu. Specialty: Momma Chiapparelli's ravioli. Valet parking $5. Built 1870; original brick walls, oak paneling. 7 dining rms on 2 levels. Family-owned. Cr cds: A, C, D, DS, MC, V.
⊟

★ ★ **CITY LIGHTS.** *301 Light St (21202). 410/244-8811. www.citylights seafood.com.* Hrs: 11:30 am-10 pm; Fri to 11 pm; Sat to midnight; Sun to 9 pm. Closed Thanksgiving, Dec 24, 25. Bar. Wine list. A la carte entrees: lunch, dinner $5.95-$23.95. Child's menu. Specializes in Chesapeake Bay seafood. Own desserts. Outdoor dining. Cr cds: A, C, D, DS, MC, V.
D

★ ★ ★ **DALESIO'S OF LITTLE ITALY.** *829 Eastern Ave (21202). 410/ 539-1965. www.dalesios.com.* Hrs: 11:30 am-3 pm, 5-10 pm; Sun 4-9 pm. Closed Thanksgiving. Res

accepted. Valet parking. Northern Italian menu. Bar. A la carte entrees: lunch $4.95-$10.95, dinner $14-$25. Specializes in Northern Italian spa cuisine. Wine list. Own cakes, pasta. Outdoor dining. Cr cds: MC, V.
D **⊟**

★ ★ **GERMANO'S TRATTORIA.** *300 S High St (21202). 410/752-4515. www.littleitalybaltimore.com.* Hrs: 11:30 am-11 pm; Fri, Sat to midnight. Closed Thanksgiving, Dec 25. Res accepted. Tuscan, regional Italian menu. Bar. Lunch $4.95-$11.95, dinner $12.50-$25.95. Child's menu. Wine list. Specializes in Tuscan cuisine and seafood. Cr cds: A, C, D, DS, ER, MC, V.
D

★ ★ ★ **HAMPTON'S.** *550 Light St (21202). 410/234-0550. www.harbor court.com.* Specializes in seafood, regional dishes. Own pastries. Hrs: 5:30-10 pm; Sun brunch 10:30 am-2 pm. Closed Mon. Res required. Serv bar. Extensive wine list. A la carte entrees: dinner $31-$41. Prix-fixe dinner: $68. Vegetarian prix-fixe dinner: $45. Sun brunch $23-$36. Valet parking. Jacket. Totally nonsmoking. Cr cds: A, D, DS, MC, V.
D

★ **HENNINGER'S TAVERN.** *1812 Bank St (21231). 410/342-2172. www. henningerstavern.com.* Hrs: 5-10 pm; Fri, Sat to 11 pm. Closed Sun, Mon; Jan 1, Dec 25. Bar to 1 am. A la carte entrees: dinner $16.50-$23.95. Specializes in seafood. Late 1800s atmosphere. Cr cds: A, D, MC, V.

★ ★ **IKAROS.** *4805 Eastern Ave (21224). 410/633-3750.* Hrs: 11 am-10 pm; Fri, Sat to 11 pm. Closed Tues; Thanksgiving, Dec 25. Greek, American menu. Serv bar. Lunch $4-$9, dinner $8-$15. Specializes in lamb, squid, fresh whole fish. Cr cds: A, D, DS, MC, V.
D **⊟**

★ ★ **JEANNIER'S.** *105 W 39th St (21211). 410/889-3303.* Hrs: noon-2:30 pm, 5:30-9:30 pm; Fri to 10 pm; Sat 5:30-10 pm; early-bird dinner 5:30-7 pm. Closed Sun; hols. French, continental menu. Bar noon-11 pm. A la carte entrees: lunch $6-$11, dinner $13.95-$25. Complete meals: dinner $14-$25. Specializes in seafood, country French cuisine.

Own desserts. Country chateau decor. Cr cds: A, D, MC, V.

D ⊒

★ ★ **JOHN STEVEN, LTD.** *1800 Thames St (21231). 410/327-5561. www.johnstevensltd.com.* Hrs: 11 am-11 pm; Fri, Sat to midnight. Sushi bar noon-1:30 am. Res accepted. Bar to 2 am; Sun from 10 am. A la carte entrees: lunch, dinner $6-$21. Specializes in seafood, sushi. Outdoor dining. Building built 1838. Cr cds: A, D, MC, V.

D ⊒

★ ★ ★ **JOY AMERICA CAFE.** *800 Key Hwy (21230). 410/244-6500.* Hrs: 11:30 am-2:30 pm, 5:30-10 pm; Sun brunch 11 am-4 pm. Closed Mon; Labor Day, Thanksgiving, Dec 25. Res accepted. Contemporary American menu. Bar. Lunch $9-$15, dinner $19-$28.50. Sun brunch $11.50-$14. Child's menu. Specialties: chicken and dried cherry dim sum, Thai-grilled rack of lamb. Outdoor dining. View of city and Inner Harbor. Totally nonsmoking. Cr cds: A, C, D, MC, V.

D ⊒

★ ★ **KAWASAKI.** *413 N Charles St (21201). 410/659-7600.* Hrs: 11:30-2:30 pm, 5-11 pm; Fri to midnight; Sat 5-midnight. Closed Sun; hols. Japanese menu. Bar. A la carte entrees: lunch, dinner $2.50-$9. Lunch $5.95-$9.50, dinner $9.50-$18. Specializes in Japanese seafood, sushi rolls. In townhouse; Japanese decor. Cr cds: A, D, MC, V.

D

★ ★ ★ **LA SCALA.** *1012 Eastern Ave (21202). 410/783-9209. www.lascala dining.com.* Hrs: 4:30-10 pm; Fri, Sat to 11 pm; Sun 2-10 pm. Closed Jan 1, Thanksgiving, Dec 25. Res accepted. Italian menu. Bar. Wine list. Dinner $11.95-$29.95. Specializes in veal, pasta, seafood. Contemporary decor. Cr cds: A, D, DS, MC, V.

⊒

★ ★ **MT. WASHINGTON TAVERN.** *5700 Newbury St (21209). 410/367-6903. www.mtwashingtontavern.com.* Hrs: 11:30 am-10 pm; Sun 10:30 am-10 pm; Sun brunch to 3 pm. Closed Dec 25. Res accepted. Bar. Lunch, dinner $6-$24.50. Sun brunch $4.95-

$12.95. Child's menu. Specializes in Angus beef, veal chops, shrimp. Entertainment Wed, Sat. Outdoor dining. Tavern atmosphere has varied dining areas. Cr cds: A, D, MC, V.

⊒

★ ★ **OBRYCKI'S CRAB HOUSE.** *1727 E Pratt St (21231). 410/732-6399. www.obryckis.com.* Hrs: 11:30 am-11 pm; Sun to 9:30 pm. Closed mid-Dec-Mar. Bar. Lunch $4.95-$13.50, dinner $6.50-$28.95. Child's menu. Specializes in crab. Parking. Family-owned. Cr cds: A, D, DS, MC, V.

D

★ ★ **PIERPOINT.** *1822 Aliceanna St (21231). 410/675-2080. www.pierpoint restaurant.com.* Hrs: 11:30 am-2 pm, 5-9:30 pm; Fri, Sat 5:30-10:30 pm; Sun 4-9 pm; Sun brunch 10:30 am-1:30 pm. Closed Mon; Jan 1, July 4, Dec 25. Res accepted. Bar. Wine list. A la carte entrees: lunch $5.95-$8.95, dinner $18.50-$25. Specializes in Maryland cuisine. Contemporary decor. Cr cds: A, C, D, DS, ER, MC, V.

⊒

★ ★ ★ **POLO GRILL.** *4 W University Pkwy (21218). 410/235-8200. www. polo-grill.com.* Hrs: 6:30-10 am, 11:30 am-4 pm, 5:30-11 pm; Fri to midnight; Sat 7-10:30 am, 11:30 am-4 pm, 5:30 pm-midnight; Sun 7-10:30 am, 11 am-2:30 pm, 5:30-10 pm; Sun brunch 11 am-2:30 pm. Res accepted. Bar. Wine list. A la carte entrees: lunch $5.95-$19.50, dinner $19.95-$43.95. Complete meals: bkfst $7.50-$7.95. Sun brunch $24.95, under 12 $12.95. Specializes in seafood, pasta. Valet parking. English hunt decor. Cr cds: A, C, D, DS, ER, MC, V.

D

★ ★ ★ **PRIME RIB.** *1101 N Calvert St (21202). 410/539-1804. www.theprime rib.com.* Hrs: 5 pm-11:30 pm; Sat to midnight; Sun 4-10:30 pm. Closed Thanksgiving. Res accepted. Bar. Wine list. A la carte entrees: dinner $20-$25. Specializes in steak, seafood, lamb. Pianist. Parking. Black lacquered walls. Paintings and prints displayed. Jacket. Family-owned. Cr cds: A, C, D, MC, V.

D

★ ★ **ROCCO CAPRICCIO.** *846 Fawn St (21202). 410/685-2710.* Hrs: 11:30

am-10:30 pm; Fri, Sat to 11:30 pm.
Closed Thanksgiving, Dec 25. Res
accepted. Northern Italian menu.
Bar. Lunch $6.25-$12, dinner $9.95-
$28. Child's menu. Specialties: fet-
tucine frutta de mare (white or red),
veal Capriccio. Own pasta. Cr cds: A,
DS, MC, V.

★★★ **RUBY LOUNGE.** *802 N
Charles St (21201). 410/539-8051.*
Hrs: 5:30-11 pm; Fri, Sat to midnight.
Closed Sun, Mon; also hols. Res
accepted. Bar. A la carte entrees: dinner $9.95-$15.95. Specializes in duck,
pork, seafood. Valet parking. Casual
decor. Cr cds: A, C, D, DS, MC, V.
D

★★ **RUTH'S CHRIS STEAK HOUSE.**
600 Water St (21202). 410/783-0033.
www.ruthschris.com. Hrs: 5-10 pm; Fri,
Sat to 11 pm. Closed Jan 1, Super
Bowl Sun, Thanksgiving, Dec 25. Res
accepted. Bar. Wine list. A la carte
entrees: dinner $17.95-$32.95. Specializes in steaks, seafood. Free valet
parking. Upscale furnishings. Cr cds:
A, D, DS, MC, V.
D

★★ **SOTTO SOPRA.** *405 N Charles
St (21201). 410/625-0534. www.sotto
soprainc.com.* Northern Italian menu.
Specializes in risotto. Hrs: 11:30 am-
2:30 pm, 5:30-10:30 pm; Fri, Sat to
11:30 pm; Sun to 9:30 pm. Res
accepted. Wine list. Lunch $8-$16;
dinner $16-$29. Entertainment. Cr
cds: A, MC, V.
D

★★★ **SPIKE AND CHARLIE'S.**
*1225 Cathedral St (21201). 410/752-
8144. www.spikeandcharlies.com.* New
American menu. Hrs: 5:30-10 pm;
Fri, Sat to midnight. Closed Mon;
hols. Res required. Bar. Dinner $7-
$24. Specializes in seafood, veal,
steak. Wine list. Own baking. Contemporary decor. Cr cds: MC, V.
D

★★ **TIO PEPE.** *10 E Franklin St
(21202). 410/539-4675.* Hrs: 11:30
am-2:30 pm, 5-10:30 pm; Fri to 11:30
pm; Sat 5-11:30 pm; Sun 4-10:30 pm.
Closed hols. Res required. Spanish,
continental menu. Bar. Wine cellar.
Lunch $9-$14, dinner $13.75-$24.
Specialties: shrimp in garlic sauce,
suckling pig. Spanish casa atmosphere. Jacket. Cr cds: A, C, D, DS, ER,
MC, V.
D

★★ **VELLEGGIA'S.** *829 E Pratt St
(21202). 410/685-2620.* Hrs: 11 am-
11 pm; Fri to midnight; Sat to 1 am.
Closed Dec 24, 25. Res accepted. Italian menu. Bar. A la carte entrees:
lunch $4.95-$9.95, dinner $9.25-
$19.95. Child's menu. Specializes in
veal, seafood. Own pasta. Family-
owned. Cr cds: A, C, D, DS, ER,
MC, V.
D

★ **WAYNE'S BAR-B-QUE.** *201 E
Pratt St (21202). 410/539-3810. www.
waynecooks.com.* Hrs: 8 am-11 pm;
Fri, Sat to midnight. Closed Thanksgiving, Dec 25. Res accepted. Bar to 2
am. A la carte entrees: bkfst $3.50-
$8.99, lunch, dinner $6.50-$23.99.
Child's menu. Specializes in barbecue
dishes, desserts. Outdoor dining.
View of harbor. Cr cds: A, DS, MC, V.
D SC

Baltimore/ Washington International Airport Area

*See also Baltimore; also see District of
Columbia*

Services and Information

Information. 410/859-7100.

Lost and Found. 410/859-7387.

Weather. 410/936-1212.

Cash Machines. Main Terminal, Pier C.

Airlines. Air Aruba, Air Canada, Air
Jamaica, America West, American,
British Airways, Continental, Delta,
El Al, Icelandair, Midway, Northwest,
Southwest, TWA, United, USAir.

Motels/Motor Lodges

★★ **BEST WESTERN BWI AIRPORT.**
*6755 Dorsey Rd, Elkridge (21075). 410/
796-3300; fax 410/379-0471; toll-free
800/780-7234. www.bestwestern.com.*
134 rms, 4 story. S, D $93; each addl
$5; under 12 free. Crib free. TV; cable
(premium), VCR avail. Heated indoor

pool; whirlpool. Complimentary coffee in lobby. Restaurant adj 7 am-11 pm; Sat, Sun 8 am-10 pm. Ck-out noon. Meeting rms. In-rm modem link. Valet serv. Fee airport transportation. Exercise equipt; sauna. Cr cds: A, D, DS, MC, V.

⊠ 🕱 D ⊠ ♨ SC

★★ **COURTYARD BY MARRIOTT.** *1671 W Nursery Rd, Linthicum Heights (21090). 410/859-8855; fax 410/859-5068; res 800/321-2211. www.court yard.com.* 149 rms, 3 story. Apr-Nov: S, D $154-$179; suites $160-$170; under 10 free; lower rates rest of yr. Crib avail. TV; cable (premium). Indoor pool; whirlpool, lifeguard. Complimentary coffee in rms, lobby. Restaurant 6:30-10:30 am, 5-10 pm; Sat, Sun 7 am-noon. Rm serv. Bar 4-10 pm. Ck-out noon. Meeting rms. Business servs avail. Coin lndry. Concierge. Free airport transportation. Exercise equipt. Some refrigerators. Cr cds: A, C, D, DS, JCB, MC, V.

D ⊠ ⊠ ♨ 🕱

★★ **DAYS INN.** *6600 Ritchie Hwy, Glen Burnie (21061). 410/761-8300; fax 410/760-4966; res 800/329-7466. www.daysinn.com.* 100 rms, 3 story. S, D $104-$114; each addl $10; under 18 free. Crib free. Pet accepted, some restrictions. TV; cable (premium). Pool; lifeguard. Complimentary continental bkfst. Restaurant 6 am-2 pm, 5-10 pm; Sat, Sun from 7 am. Rm serv. Bar 4 pm-midnight. Coffee in rms. Ck-out noon. Meeting rms. In-rm modem link. Valet serv. Health club privileges. Refrigerators, microwaves avail. Mall opp. Cr cds: A, C, D, DS, MC, V.

D ⤳ ⊠ ⊠ ♨

★ **FAIRFIELD INN.** *1734 W Nursery Rd, Linthicum Heights (21090). 410/859-2333; fax 410/859-2357. www.fair fieldinn.com.* 130 rms, 5 story. S, D $129; each addl $7; under 18 free. Crib free. TV; cable (premium). Pool; lifeguard. Complimentary continental bkfst. Restaurant nearby. Ck-out noon. Coin lndry. Valet serv. Business servs avail. In-rm modem link. Free airport, RR station transportation. Exercise equipt. Microwaves avail. Cr cds: A, C, D, DS, MC, V.

D ⊠ 🗙 ⊠ ♨

★★ **HAMPTON INN.** *829 Elkridge Landing Rd, Linthicum (21090). 410/ 850-0600; fax 410/691-2119; toll-free 800/426-7866. www.hamptoninn.com.* 139 rms, 5 story. S, D $94-$114; under 18 free. Crib free. Pet accepted. TV; cable (premium). Complimentary continental bkfst. Coffee in rms. Restaurant nearby. Ck-out noon. Meeting rms. Business servs avail. In-rm modem link. Valet serv. Free airport, RR transportation. Refrigerators, microwaves avail. Cr cds: A, C, D, DS, ER, JCB, MC, V.

D ⤳ 🗙 ⊠ ♨ SC

★★ **HAMPTON INN.** *6617 Governor Ritchie Hwy, Glen Burnie (21061). 410/ 761-7666; fax 410/761-0253; toll-free 800/426-7866. www.hamptoninn.com.* 115 rms, 5 story. S $104-$109; D $114-$119; suites $155; under 18 free; higher rates special events. Crib free. TV; cable (premium). Complimentary continental bkfst. Restaurant adj open 24 hrs. Rm serv. Coffee in rms. Ck-out noon. Meeting rms. Business servs avail. In-rm modem links. Valet serv. Sundries. Health club privileges. Refrigerators. Microwaves avail. Cr cds: A, C, D, DS, ER, JCB, MC, V.

D ⊠ ♨ SC

Hotels

★★ **EMBASSY SUITES.** *1300 Concourse Dr, Linthicum (21090). 410/850-0747; fax 410/850-0895. www.embassy suites.com.* 251 suites, 8 story. S $229.95-$259.95; D $249.95-$279.95; each addl $10; under 18 free; wknd rates. Crib free. TV; cable (premium). Indoor pool; whirlpool, lifeguard. Complimentary coffee in rms. Restaurant 6:30 am-10 pm; wkends to 11 pm. Rm serv. Bar 11-1 am. Complimentary bkfst. Ck-out noon. Convention facilities. Business center. In-rm modem link. Gift shop. Airport transportation. Valet serv. Exercise equipt; sauna. Health club privileges. Bathrm phones, refrigerators, microwaves. Some wet bars. Cr cds: A, C, D, DS, ER, JCB, MC, V.

⊠ 🕱 🕱 D ⊠ ♨ SC

★★★ **MARRIOTT BWI AIRPORT.** *1743 W Nursery Rd, Linthicum (21240). 410/859-8300; fax 410/691-4555; toll-free 800/228-9290. www.*

marriott.com. 310 rms, 10 story. S, D $235-$269; each addl $15; suites $255-$279; under 18 free. Crib free. TV; cable (premium). Indoor pool; whirlpool. Complimentary coffee in lobby, rms. Restaurant 6:30 am-10 pm. Bar 4 pm-1:30 am. Ck-out noon. Convention facilities. Business center. In-rm modem link. Coin lndry. Valet serv. Gift shop. Free airport transportation. Exercise equipt. Health club privileges. Massage. Luxury level. Cr cds: A, C, D, DS, MC, V.
🏊 🎿 🏃 Ⓓ 🛎 🐾 SC

★ ★ ★ **SHERATON INTERNATIONAL ON BWI AIRPORT.** *7032 Elm Rd, Baltimore (21240). 410/859-3300; fax 410/859-0565; res 800/325-3535. www.sheraton.com.* 201 rms, 2 story. S, D $199-$239; each addl $10; suites $219-$259; under 16 free; wkend rates. Crib free. TV; cable (premium). Pool; poolside serv, lifeguard. Coffee, tea in rms. Restaurant 6:30 am-10:30 pm. Rm serv 24 hrs. Bar noon-2 am; entertainment. Ck-out noon. Meeting rms. Business servs avail. In-rm modem link. Bellhops. Sundries. Gift shop. Airport transportation. Exercise equipt. Luxury level. Cr cds: A, C, D, DS, JCB, MC, V.
Ⓓ 🏊 🛎 🐾 🎿

Bethesda

(D-5) *Also see District of Columbia*

Pop 55,277 **Elev** 305 ft **Area code** 301
Information The Greater Bethesda-Chevy Chase Chamber of Commerce, Landow Building, 7910 Woodmont Ave, Suite 1204, 20814; 301/652-4900
Web www.bccchamber.org

A suburb of Washington, D.C., Bethesda is the home of both the National Institutes of Health, research arm of the Public Health Service, and Bethesda Naval Hospital.

What to See and Do

Cabin John Regional Park. This 551-acre park has playgrounds, miniature train ride; nature center; concerts (summer eves; free); tennis courts, game fields, ice rink, nature trails, picnicking. Fee for some activities. (Daily) Approx 3 mi N on MD 355 then W on Tuckerman Lane. Phone 301/299-0024.

Clara Barton National Historic Site. (see DISTRICT OF COLUMBIA) 3 mi W via MD 191, Goldsboro Rd in Glen Echo. Phone 301/492-6245.

National Library of Medicine. World's largest biomedical library; rare books, manuscripts, prints; medical art displays. (Mon-Sat; closed hols and Sat before Mon hols) Visitors center and guided tour (Mon-Fri, one departure each day). 8600 Rockville Pike. Phone 301/496-6308. **FREE**

Motels/Motor Lodges

★ ★ **AMERICAN INN OF BETHESDA.** *8130 Wisconsin Ave (20814). 301/656-9300; fax 301/656-2907. www.american-inn.com.* 76 rms, 5 story. S $126; D $136; each addl $5; under 18 free; wkend, wkly, monthly rates. Crib free. TV; cable (premium), VCR avail. Pool; lifeguard. Complimentary continental bkfst. Restaurant 11:30 am-10 pm; Fri, Sat to midnight; Sun to 10 pm. Ck-out 12:30 pm. Coin lndry. Meeting rms. Business center. Sundries. Valet serv. Health club privileges. Some refrigerators. Cr cds: A, C, D, DS, MC, V.
🏊 🛎 🐾 SC 🎿

★ ★ **HOLIDAY INN.** *5520 Wisconsin Ave, Chevy Chase (20815). 301/656-1500; fax 301/656-5045. www.holiday-inn.com.* 215 rms, 12 story. S, D $89-$159; each addl $10; suites $169; under 18 free. Crib free. Pet accepted, some restrictions; $50. TV; cable (premium), VCR avail. Pool. Complimentary coffee in rms. Restaurant 6:30 am-11 pm. Bar. Ck-out noon. Free lndry facilities. Meeting rms. Business center. In-rm modem link. Gift shop. Health club privileges. Bathrm phones; microwaves avail. Cr cds: A, D, DS, JCB.
🐾 🏃 Ⓓ 🏊 🎿 🛎 🐾

Hotels

★ ★ ★ **HYATT REGENCY.** *1 Bethesda Metro Ctr (20814). 301/657-1234; fax 301/657-6453; res 800/233-1234. www.hyatt.com.* 381 rms, 12 story. S $225; D $250; each addl $25; suites $200-$600; under 18 free; wkend rates. Crib free. Covered parking $10; valet $12. TV; cable (premium), VCR avail. Indoor pool; lifeguard. Restaurant 6:30 am-11:30 pm. Bar 11:30-12:30 am. Ck-out noon. Convention facilities. Business center. In-rm modem link. Gift shop. Exercise equipt; sauna. Bathrm phones. Private patios, balconies. 12-story atrium lobby; extensive collection of artwork. Luxury level. Cr cds: A, D, DS, MC, V.

⬛🔳🏃🛏🔥🏃

★★★ MARRIOTT BETHESDA .
5151 Pooks Hill Rd (20814). 301/897-9400; fax 301/897-0192; res 800/228-9290. www.marriott.com. 407 rms, 4-16 story. S $199; D $219; suites $300-$750; under 18 free; wkend plan. Crib free. TV; cable (premium), VCR avail. Indoor/outdoor pool; whirlpool, poolside serv, lifeguard. Coffee in rms. Restaurants 6:30 am-10 pm. Rm serv to 1 am. Bar 11-1 am; Fri, Sat to 2 am, entertainment Fri, Sat. Ck-out noon. Guest lndry. Convention facilities. Business center. In-rm modem link. Gift shops. Lighted tennis. Exercise equipt; sauna. Game rm. Microwaves avail. Some balconies. On 18 landscaped acres. Luxury level. Cr cds: A, D, DS, JCB, MC, V.

⬛⛷🛏🏃🔥🏃

All Suite

★★★ MARRIOTT SUITES BETHESDA.
6711 Democracy Blvd (20817). 301/897-5600; fax 301/530-1427. www.marriott.com. 274 suites, 11 story. Suites $190-$220; family rates. Crib free. TV; cable (premium), VCR avail. Indoor/outdoor pool; whirlpool, poolside serv, lifeguard. Complimentary coffee in rms. Restaurant 6:30 am-10:30 pm. Bar noon-midnight. Ck-out 11 am. Meeting rms. Business center. In-rm modem link. RR station transportation. Exercise equipt. Wet bars; microwaves avail. Balconies. Cr cds: A, D, DS, MC, V.

⬛🛏🏃🔥🏃

Extended Stay

★★ RESIDENCE INN BY MARRIOTT.
7335 Wisconsin Ave (20814). 301/718-0200; fax 301/718-0679; toll-free 800/331-3131. www.marriott.com. 187 kit suites, 13 story. S, D $189-$299; under 16 free; wkend, wkly, monthly rates. Crib free. Pet accepted; $100 and $5/day. Valet parking $12. TV; cable (premium), VCR avail (movies). Pool; lifeguard. Complimentary continental bkfst, coffee in rms. Restaurant adj 6:30 am-midnight. Ck-out noon. Coin lndry. Meeting rms. Business servs avail. Exercise equipt. Rec rm. Microwaves. Cr cds: A, C, D, DS, JCB, MC, V.

⬛🐕🛏🏃🔥 SC

Restaurants

★★★ ANDALUCIA DE BETHESDA.
4931 Elm St (20814). 301/907-0052. www.andalucia restaurant.com. Hrs: 11:30 am-2:30 pm, 5:30-10 pm; Fri, Sat to 11 pm; Sun 5-9:30 pm. Closed hols. Res accepted; required Fri, Sat dinner. Spanish menu. Bar. Wine list. Lunch $7.25-$10.95, dinner $13.95-$22.95. Specialties: zarzuela Mediterraneo, mero en salsa verde, paella para dos. Own desserts. Classical guitar Sun-Thurs. Totally nonsmoking. Cr cds: A, C, D, DS, MC, V.

⬛

★ AUSTIN GRILL.
7278 Woodmont Ave (20814). 301/656-1366. www. austingrill.com. Hrs: 11:30 am-11 pm; Mon to 10 pm; Fri to midnight; Sat 11 am-midnight; Sun 11 am-10 pm; Sat, Sun brunch to 3 pm. Closed Thanksgiving, Dec 24, 25. Tex-Mex menu. Bar. Lunch $6-$9, dinner $6-$14. Sat, Sun brunch $5-$7. Child's menu. Specializes in chicken, fresh seafood, vegetarian dishes. Outdoor dining. Contemporary Southwestern motif. Totally nonsmoking. Cr cds: D, MC, V.

⬛➖

★★ BACCHUS BETHESDA.
7945 Norfolk Ave (20814). 301/657-1722. Hrs: noon-2 pm, 6-10 pm; Fri to 10:30 pm; Sat 6-10:30 pm; Sun 6-10 pm. Closed Thanksgiving, Dec 25. Res accepted; required Fri, Sat. Lebanese menu. Serv bar. Lunch $4-$9, dinner $12.25-$16.25. Specialties: falafel, shish kebab. Valet parking (dinner). Outdoor dining. Cr cds: A, MC, V.

⬛

★ **BETHESDA CRAB HOUSE.** *4958 Bethesda Ave (20814). 301/652-3382.* Hrs: 9 am-midnight. Closed Dec 25. Res accepted. Wine, beer. A la carte entrees: lunch, dinner $10-$30. Specializes in spiced shrimp, steamed crab, crabcakes. Outdoor dining. Rustic decor; established 1961. Cr cds: MC, V.
⊟

★★ **BOMBAY DINING.** *4931 Cordell Ave (20814). 301/656-3373.* Hrs: 11:30 am-2:30 pm, 5:30-10 pm; Sat, Sun noon-3 pm, 5:30-10:30 pm. Res accepted. Indian menu. Bar. Lunch, dinner $7.95-$15.95. Sat, Sun brunch $9.95. Specializes in tandoori, curries, vegetables. Salad bar. Valet parking (wkends). Cr cds: A, DS, MC, V.
⊟

★★ **BUON GIORNO.** *8003 Norfolk Ave (20814). 301/652-1400.* Hrs: 11:30 am-2:30 pm, 5:30-10 pm; Fri to 10:30 pm; Sat 5:30-10:30 pm; Sun 5:30-10 pm. Closed Mon; Jan 1, Thanksgiving, Dec 25; also mid-Aug-mid-Sept. Res accepted; required Fri, Sat. Italian menu. Serv bar. Lunch $8.95-$10.95, dinner $12.95-$20.95. Specialties: trenette alla Genovese, pappardelle alla contadina, fresh fish. Own pasta. Valet parking (dinner). Totally nonsmoking. Cr cds: A, C, D, DS, MC, V.
D

★★★ **CAFE BETHESDA.** *5027 Wilson Ln (20814). 301/657-3383.* Hrs: 11:30 am-2 pm, 5:30-9 pm; Fri to 10 pm; Sat 5:30-10 pm; Sun 5:30-9 pm. Closed hols. Res accepted; required Fri, Sat. French menu. Wine, beer. Lunch $8-$12, dinner $14-$25. Specializes in rack of lamb, seafood, veal. Valet parking. Outdoor dining. Atmosphere of French country inn. Totally nonsmoking. Cr cds: A, D, DS, MC, V.

★★★ **CESCO TRATTORIA.** *4871 Cordell Ave (20814). 301/654-8333.* Hrs: 11:30 am-2 pm, 5:30-10 pm; Fri to 11 pm; Sat 5:30-11 pm; Sun 5-9 pm. Closed hols. Res accepted; required Fri, Sat dinner. Italian menu. Bar. Wine list. A la carte entrees: lunch $10-$13.95, dinner $11.95-$21.95. Specializes in fresh seafood, Tuscan cuisine, pasta. Own pasta. Valet parking (dinner). Outdoor din-

ing. Contemporary Italian trattoria atmosphere. Cr cds: A, MC, V.
D

★★ **COTTONWOOD CAFE.** *4844 Cordell Ave (20814). 301/656-4844. www.cottonwoodcafe.com.* Hrs: 11:30 am-10 pm; Fri, Sat to 11 pm; Sun from 5:30 pm. Closed hols. Res accepted. Southwestern menu. Bar. Lunch $5.95-$7, dinner $12.65-$20.95. Specializes in grilled meats, seafood. Valet parking (dinner). Southwestern atmosphere. Mural of adobe village. Cr cds: MC, V.
D ⊟

★★ **DELRAY VIETNAMESE GARDEN.** *4918 Delray Ave (20814). 301/986-0606.* Hrs: 11:30 am-2:30 pm, 5-10 pm; Sat, Sun 5-10 pm. Closed major hols. Res required Fri, Sat (dinner). Vietnamese menu. Bar. A la carte entrees: lunch $5.95-$12.75, dinner $7.95-$12.75. Specialties: pinecone fish, nid d'amour, curry. Valet parking wkends. Outdoor dining. Country inn decor. Cr cds: A, V.
D SC

★★ **FOONG LIN.** *7710 Norfolk Ave (20814). 301/656-3427.* Hrs: 11 am-10:30 pm; Fri, Sat to 11 pm. Closed Thanksgiving. Res accepted. Chinese menu. Bar. Lunch $3.95-$7.50, dinner $7.25-$19.95. Specialties: fresh fish, Peking duckling, crispy beef. Cr cds: A, MC.
D

★★ **FRASCATI.** *4806 Rugby Ave (20814). 301/652-9514.* Hrs: 11 am-2:30 pm, 4-10:30 pm; Sat from 5 pm; Sun 4-9:30 pm; early-bird dinner Tues-Fri, Sun 4-6:30 pm. Closed Mon; Jan 1, Easter, Dec 25. Res accepted; required Fri, Sat. Italian menu. Lunch $4.75-$6.95, dinner $9.75-$16.95. Child's menu. Specializes in fresh fish, veal, pasta. Outdoor dining. Totally nonsmoking. Cr cds: A, C, D, DS, MC, V.
D

★★ **HAANDI.** *4904 Fairmont Ave (20814). 301/718-0121. www.haandi. com.* Hrs: 11:30 am-2:30 pm, 5-10 pm; Fri, Sat to 10:30 pm. Res accepted. Indian menu. Bar. Lunch $4.95-$10.95, dinner $7.95-$14.95. Buffet: lunch $7.95. Specialties: tandoori dishes, vegetarian dishes, murg

makhini. Totally nonsmoking. Cr cds: A, C, D, DS, MC, V.
[D]

★★ **JEAN-MICHEL.** *10223 Old Georgetown Rd (20814). 301/564-4910.* Hrs: 11:30 am-2:30 pm, 5:30-10 pm; Sat from 5:30 pm; Sun 5:30-8:30 pm. Closed hols; also Sun July-Aug. Res accepted. French menu. Serv bar. Lunch $9.50-$13.25, dinner $12.95-$21.75. Specialties: mussels marinieres, venison with chestnut puree and cranberry jelly. French decor. Cr cds: A, C, D, MC, V.
[D]

★★★ **LA FERME.** *7101 Brookville Rd, Chevy Chase (20815). 301/986-5255. www.lafermerestaurant.com.* Hrs: noon-2 pm, 6-10 pm; Sat from 6 pm; Sun 5-9 pm. Closed Mon; Dec 25. Res accepted; required Fri, Sat dinner. French menu. Serv bar. Wine cellar. Lunch $7.25-$10.75, dinner $15.75-$22.75. Specialties: duck with turnips and apple cider; lobster, shrimp, scallops and grouper in saffron broth; boneless breast of chicken. Pianist. Outdoor dining. Country inn decor. Cr cds: A, C, D, DS, MC, V.
[D]

★★ **LA MICHE.** *7905 Norfolk Ave (20814). 301/986-0707. www. washingtonpost.com/yp/lamiche.* Hrs: 11:30 am-2 pm, 6-9:45 pm; Mon, Sat from 6 pm; Sun 5:30-8 pm. Closed hols. Res required Fri, Sat. French menu. Serv bar. A la carte entrees: lunch $6-$16, dinner $13-$24. Specialties: souffles, fricassee of lobster, grilled breast of duck. Valet parking (dinner). Outdoor dining. French country decor. Cr cds: A, C, D, MC, V.
[D]

★★★ **LE VIEUX LOGIS.** *7925 Old Georgetown Rd (20814). 301/652-6816.* Hrs: 5:30-10 pm; hrs vary Nov-Dec. Closed Sun; Jan 1, Dec 25. Res accepted; required Sat. French, American menu. Serv bar. Wine list. Lunch $7-$15, dinner $16-$24. Specialties: roasted Long Island duckling, grilled Norwegian salmon. Free valet parking. Outdoor dining. Rustic French inn atmosphere. Cr cds: A, D, DS, MC, V.
[D]

★ **MATUBA.** *4918 Cordell Ave (20814). 301/652-7449.* Hrs: 11:30 am-2:30 pm, 5-10 pm; Fri to 10:30 pm; Sat noon-3 pm, 5-10:30 pm; Sun 5-10 pm. Japanese menu. Wine, beer. Lunch $4.95-$9.95, dinner $6.95-$11.95. Specialties: sushi, chicken teriyaki. Casual decor. Totally non-smoking. Cr cds: A, C, D, DS, MC, V.
[D]

★★ **MONTGOMERY'S GRILLE.** *7200 Wisconsin Ave (20814). 301/654-3595.* Hrs: 11:30 am-10 pm; Thurs to 11 pm; Fri, Sat to midnight; Sun from 10 am; Sun brunch to 2 pm. Closed Thanksgiving, Dec 25. Bar to 12:30 am; Fri, Sat to 1:30 am. Lunch $5.95-$8.95, dinner $7.95-$14.95. Sun brunch $12.95. Child's menu. Specializes in pasta, fresh grilled seafood, crab cakes. Own baking. Outdoor dining. American pub atmosphere with antique bar, bronze-framed windows, hand-carved woodwork. Totally nonsmoking. Cr cds: A, C, D, DS, MC, V.

★★ **NAM'S.** *4928 Cordell Ave (20814). 301/652-2635.* Hrs: 11:30 am-2:30 pm, 5:30-11 pm; Sat 5-11 pm; Sun 5-9:30 pm. Closed Thanksgiving, Dec 25. Res accepted. Vietnamese menu. Bar. Lunch $5.50-$8.50, dinner $7.50-$10.95. Specializes in chicken, beef, pork. Contemporary decor. Cr cds: A, MC, V.

★★ **O'DONNELL'S.** *8301 Wisconsin Ave (20814). 301/656-6200. www. odonnellsrestaurants.com.* Hrs: 11:30 am-10 pm; Sun noon-9 pm. Closed Dec 25. Res accepted. Bar. Lunch $5.50-$12.95, dinner $13.95-$21.95. Child's menu. Specializes in seafood. Outdoor dining on patio. Nautical theme. Family-owned. Cr cds: A, D, DS, MC, V.
[D]

★ **ORIGINAL PANCAKE HOUSE.** *7703 Woodmont Ave (20814). 301/986-0285.* Hrs: 7 am-3 pm. Closed Dec 25. A la carte entrees: bkfst, lunch $3.95-$7.95. Child's meals. Specializes in crepes, waffles, pancakes. Casual dining. Cr cds: A, MC, V.
[D] [SC]

★ **RAKU.** *7240 Woodmont Ave (20814). 301/718-8680.* Hrs: 11:30 am-10 pm; Fri, Sat to 10:30 pm; Sun to 9 pm. Closed Thanksgiving, Dec

25. Pan-Asian menu. Serv bar. Lunch $2.35-$9.25. A la carte entrees: dinner $2.35-$13.25. Child's menu. Specializes in noodles, wraps, stir fry. Own desserts. Outdoor dining. Casual decor with Asian flair. Totally nonsmoking. Cr cds: A, MC, V.

★★ **RED TOMATO CAFE.** *4910 St Elmo Ave (20814). 301/652-4499. www.redtomato.com.* Hrs: 11:30 am-9:30 pm; Thurs to 10 pm; Fri, Sat to 11 pm; Sun 4:30-9 pm. Closed Jan 1, Thanksgiving, Dec 25. Res accepted Sun-Thurs. Italian, American menu. Serv bar. A la carte entrees: lunch $3.95-$10.95, dinner $5.95-$15.95. Specializes in pasta, pizza. Valet parking Thurs-Sat. Colorful, contemporary pizzeria; large mural, wood-burning pizza oven. Totally nonsmoking. Cr cds: A, D, DS, MC, V.
D

★★ **ROCK BOTTOM BREWERY.** *7900 Norfolk Ave (20814). 301/652-1311. www.rockbottom.com.* Hrs: 11-1 am; Fri, Sat to 2 am. Bar. Lunch $6.50-$9.95, dinner $8.50-$17.95. Specializes in enchiladas, hamburgers, pizza. Own baking. Musicians Sat, Sun. Valet parking (dinner). Outdoor dining. American brew pub atmosphere with open kitchen, microbrewery, wood-burning pizza oven. Cr cds: A, DS, MC, V.
D

★★ **RUTH'S CHRIS STEAKHOUSE.** *7315 Wisconsin Ave (20814). 301/652-7877. www.ruthschris.com.* Hrs: 5-10:30 pm; Sun 4-9:30 pm. Closed Thanksgiving, Dec 25. Res accepted; required Fri, Sat dinner. Bar to midnight. Wine list. A la carte entrees: dinner $18.95-$29.95. Specializes in beef, lobster, fresh seafood. Own desserts. Pianist Thurs-Sat. Valet parking. Intimate, clublike atmosphere; artwork. Totally nonsmoking. Cr cds: A, D, DS, MC, V.
D

★★★ **TARA THAI.** *4828 Bethesda Ave (20814). 301/657-0488.* Hrs: 11:30 am-3 pm, 5-10 pm; Fri to 11 pm; Sat noon-3:30 pm, 5-11 pm; Sun noon-3:30 pm, 5-10 pm. Closed July 4, Thanksgiving. Thai menu. Bar. Lunch $4.95-$7.95, dinner $6.95-$15.95. Specialties: grilled whole rockfish, crispy whole flounder.

Underwater theme. Totally nonsmoking. Cr cds: A, C, D, DS, MC, V.
D

★★ **TEL-AVIV CAFE.** *4869 Cordell Ave (20814). 301/718-9068.* Hrs: 11:30 am-midnight; Mon to 11 pm; Sat to 1 am; Sun 4:30-11 pm. Closed Yom Kippur, Passover. Mediterranean menu. Bar to 1 am; Fri, Sat to 2 am. Lunch, dinner $6.95-$15.95. Specialties: lamb shank, kafta kabob, kosher dishes. Own baking. Entertainment Tues, Sat. Outdoor dining. Contemporary Mediterranean decor. Cr cds: A, C, D, DS, MC, V.
D ▭

★★ **THYME SQUARE.** *4735 Bethesda Ave (20814). 301/657-9077.* Hrs: 11 am-10 pm; Fri, Sat to 11 pm. Closed Dec 24, 25. Res accepted; required Thurs-Sun dinner. Bar. Lunch $5.95-$10.95, dinner $6.95-$18.95. Specializes in seasonal American dishes, vegetarian dishes, fresh seafood. Contemporary decor with extensive murals; open kitchen. Totally nonsmoking. Cr cds: MC, V.
D

★★★ **TRAGARA.** *4935 Cordell Ave (20814). 301/951-4935. www.tragara. com.* Hrs: 11:30 am-2:30 pm, 5:30-10:30 pm; Sat from 5:30 pm; Sun 5-9 pm. Closed hols. Res accepted; required Fri, Sat. Italian menu. Lunch $8.95-$15.95. A la carte entrees: dinner $15.95-$25. Specialties: veal scaloppini, linguine with Maine lobster, lamb chops sauteed with herbs and mustard. Own baking, pastas. Valet parking (dinner). Italian marble, original paintings, chandelier. Cr cds: A, C, D, MC, V.
D

Boonsboro (Garrett County)

(B-4) *See also Frederick, Hagerstown*

Settled 1787 **Pop** 2,803 **Elev** 591 ft
Area code 301 **Zip** 21713

Information Hagerstown/Washington County Chamber of Commerce, 111 W Washington St; 301/739-2015

Web www.hagerstown.org

What to See and Do

Crystal Grottoes Caverns. Limestone caverns may be viewed from walkways. Picnicking. Guided tours (Apr-Oct, daily; rest of yr, by appt). 1 mi SW on MD 34. Phone 301/432-6336. ¢¢¢

Gathland State Park. On 140 acres. A site once owned by George Townsend, Civil War reporter. Monument built in 1896 to honor Civil War correspondents. Visitor center contains original papers. Picnicking, walking tour, winter sports. 8 mi S off MD 67, then 1 mi E, W of Burkittsville off MD 17. Phone 301/791-4767.

Washington Monument State Park. On 147 acres. A 34-ft tower of native stone (1827) was first completed monument to honor George Washington. Views of nearby battlefields, two states (PA and WV). History Center displays firearms and Civil War mementos (by appt). The Appalachian Trail leads through the park; hiking and picnicking. 3 mi SE off US 40A. Phone 301/791-4767. **FREE**

Restaurant

★★ **OLD SOUTH MOUNTAIN INN.** *6132 Old National Pike (Alt US 40), Boonsboro (21713). 301/371-5400. www.oldsouthmountaininn.com.* Hrs: 5-9 pm; Sat 11:30 am-2:30 pm, 4-10 pm; Sun 10:30 am-8 pm, brunch to 2 pm. Closed Mon; Dec 25. Res accepted; required Sat, Sun. Bar. Lunch $5-$11, dinner $14-$28. Sun brunch $12.95. Child's menu. Specialties: crab cakes, prime rib. Outdoor dining. Founded 1732; was once a stagecoach stop. Totally nonsmoking. Cr cds: A, C, D, MC, V.

[D]

Bowie

(D-5) *See also College Park, Silver Spring, also see District of Columbia*

Pop 50,269 **Elev** 150 ft **Area code** 301 and 204

Information Greater Bowie Chamber of Commerce, 6770 Race Track Rd, Hilltop Plaza, 20715; 301/262-0920. Information is also avail from Prince George's Conference & Visitors Bureau, 9475 Lottsford Rd, #130, Landover 20785; 301/925-8300

What to See and Do

Bel Air Mansion. Georgian-style home (ca 1745) was home of Governor Samuel Ogle in the 1700s; later owned by the Woodward family, prominent racehorse breeders in the first half of the 20th century. Tours. (Thurs-Sun afternoons, groups by appt) 12207 Tulip Grove Dr. Phone 301/262-6200. **DONATION**

Bel Air Stable. Part of famed Bel Air Stud, one of the premier Thoroughbred racing stables of the '30s, '40s, and '50s. Was home to two Triple Crown winners—Gallant Fox and Omaha—and the 1955 Horse of the Year, Nashua. (Thurs-Sun afternoons, groups by appt) 2835 Belair Dr. Phone 301/262-6200. **FREE**

Marietta House Museum. A modest Federal-style plantation house built by Gabriel Duvall, an associate justice of the US Supreme Court (1811-1835). Tours. (Fri-Sun; also by appt) 3 mi W in Glenn Dale, at 5626 Bell Station Rd. Phone 301/464-5291. ¢

Special Event

Heritage Day. Bel Air Mansion and Stable. Performance by Congress' Own Regiment; tour of stables and grounds; battle reenactments; demonstrations of Colonial crafts. Third Sun May. Phone 301/262-6200.

Motel/Motor Lodge

★ **FOREST HILLS MOTEL.** *2901 Crain Hwy, Upper Marlboro (20774). 301/627-3969; fax 301/627-4058.* 13

rms, shower only. Apr-Oct: S $42-$44; D $46-$49; under 13 free; lower rates rest of yr. Crib free. Pet accepted. TV. Complimentary coffee in rms. Ck-out 11 am. Some refrigerators. Picnic tables. Cr cds: A, D, DS, MC, V.

Cambridge

(E-7) *See also Easton, Salisbury*

Founded 1684 **Pop** 10,911 **Elev** 14 ft
Area code 410 **Zip** 21613
Information Dorchester County Visitors Center, 2 Rose Hill Pl; 410/228-1000 or 800/522-TOUR
Web www.tourdorchester.org

On the Eastern Shore, Cambridge is Maryland's second-largest deep-water port. Boating and fishing opportunities are found in the Choptank and Honga rivers and Chesapeake, Tar, and Fishing bays.

What to See and Do

Blackwater National Wildlife Refuge. Over 20,000 acres of rich tidal marsh, freshwater ponds, and woodlands. One of the chief wintering areas for Canada geese and ducks using the Atlantic Flyway; in fall, as many as 33,000 geese and 17,000 ducks swell the bird population. Also a haven for the bald eagle, the Delmarva fox squirrel, and the peregrine falcon. Scenic drive, woodland trails, photo blind. Visitor center (Daily; closed Thanksgiving, Dec 25). Golden Age, Golden Eagle, and Golden Access passports (see MAKING THE MOST OF YOUR TRIP). 12 mi S via MD 16, 335. Phone 410/228-2677. ¢

Old Trinity Church, Dorchester Parish. (ca 1675) One of the oldest churches in US still holding regular services; faithful restoration of interior. (By appt) 8 mi SW on MD 16 in Church Creek. Phone 410/228-2940. **FREE**

Special Events

National Outdoor Show. Goose and duck calling, log sawing, crab picking, trap setting contests; entertainment. Last wkend Feb. Phone 800/522-TOUR.

Antique Aircraft Fly-In. Dorchester Heritage Museum, 5 mi W on MD 343 at 1904 Horne Point Rd. Old and new planes on display. Third wkend May. Phone 410/228-5530, 410/228-1899, or 800/522-TOUR.

Chesapeake and Ohio Canal National Historical Park

As early as 1754 the enterprising George Washington, only in his twenties, proposed a system of navigation along the Potomac River valley. His Potowmack Canal Company, organized in 1785, cleared obstructions and built skirting canals to facilitate the transportation of goods from settlements beyond the Allegheny Mountains to the lower Potomac River towns.

The eventual inadequacy of these improvements and the renowned success of the Erie Canal spurred the formation in 1828 of the Chesapeake and Ohio Canal Company, whose purpose was to connect Georgetown with the Ohio Valley by river and canal. On July 4, 1828, President John Quincy Adams led the traditional groundbreaking ceremony declaring, "To subdue the earth is preeminently the purpose of this undertaking." Unfortunately, the earth was not easily subdued. President Adams bent his shovel after several attempts before breaking into an energetic frenzy and successfully getting a shovelful of dirt.

The difficulty of the groundbreaking ceremony foreshadowed the canal's short-lived future as a major transportation artery. Completed in 1850 as far as Cumberland, Maryland (184½ miles from Georgetown), the waterway was used extensively for the transportation of coal, flour, grain, and lumber. Financial and legal difficulties, the decline of commerce after the Civil War, the Baltimore & Ohio Railroad, and the advent of improved roads cut deeply

Mule-drawn canal boats

into the commerce of the waterway, and it gradually faded into obsolescence. The canal still had limited commercial use as late as 1924, when a flood destroyed many of the canal locks and nothing was restored.

The unfortunate demise of the C & O Canal is now a blessing for hikers, canoeists, and bikers, who can find access to the towpath along the banks of the waterway. Remaining as one of the least altered of old American canals, the Chesapeake and Ohio is flanked by ample foliage throughout most of its 20,239 acres.

Many points of interest can be seen along the waterway. Exhibits are offered in Cumberland, Georgetown, Hancock, and Williamsport and at a museum near the Great Falls of the Potomac. At the Great Falls there are interpretive programs, including self-guiding trails, picnic facilities, and a working lock. Mule-drawn canal boat rides are offered April-October at Georgetown and Great Falls (fee). Camping for hikers and bikers is available throughout the park.

For information about the canal contact the Chief of Visitor Services, C & O Canal National Historical Park, PO Box 4, Sharpsburg, MD 21782; 301/739-4200. Visitor centers are located in Cumberland, Georgetown, Great Falls, Hancock, and Williamsport.

Chesapeake Bay Bridge Area

The majestic twin spans of the Chesapeake Bay Bridge carry visitors to the Eastern Shore, a patchwork of small picturesque towns, lighthouses, and fishing villages tucked away from the city. Scenic rivers and bays, wildlife, gardens, and wildflowers fill the countryside. The main attractions of any visit, however, are the many fine inns and the restaurants specializing in local seafood.

What to See and Do

Wye Oak State Park. Official state tree of Maryland is in this 29-acre park; it is the largest white oak in the US (108 ft high, 28 ft around) and believed to be over 460 yrs old; a new tree has been started from an acorn. A restored 18th-century one-rm schoolhouse and the Old Wye Mill (late 1600s) are nearby. E on US 50 to Wye Mills. Phone 410/820-1668.

Motels/Motor Lodges

★ **COMFORT INN.** *3101 Main St, Grasonville (21638). 410/827-6767;*

fax 410/827-8626; toll-free 800/228-5150. www.comfortinn.com. 86 units, 4 story, 9 kit. suites. Apr-Nov: S $66-$126; D $76-$140; each addl $8; kit. suites $125-$200; under 18 free; higher rates special events; lower rates rest of yr. Crib free. TV; cable (premium). Indoor pool; whirlpool. Complimentary continental bkfst, coffee in rms. Restaurant nearby. Ck-out 11 am. Coin lndry. Meeting rms. Business servs avail. Exercise equipt; sauna. Refrigerators, microwaves. Cr cds: A, C, D, DS, ER, JCB, MC, V.

★★ **COMFORT SUITES.** *160 Scheeler Rd, Chestertown (21666). 410/810-0555; fax 410/810-0286. www. chestertown.com/comfortsuites.* 53 suites, 3 story. Apr-Nov: S, D $69.95-$109.95; under 18 free; lower rates rest of yr. Crib avail. TV; cable. Indoor pool. Complimentary continental bkfst. Restaurant nearby. Ck-out 11 am. Meeting rms. Business servs avail. Coin lndry. Health club privileges. Refrigerators, microwaves. Cr cds: A, C, D, DS, MC, V.

B&Bs/Small Inns

★★ **HUNTINGFIELD MANOR.** *4928 Eastern Neck Rd, Rock Hall (21661). 410/639-7779; fax 410/639-2924; toll-free 800/720-8788. www. huntingfield.com.* 6 rms, 2 story. No rm phones. S, D $85-$125; each addl $25; under 3 free. Pet accepted. Complimentary continental bkfst. Restaurant nearby. Ck-out noon, ck-in 2 pm. Telescope-type house on a working farm that dates back to the middle 1600s. Cr cds: A, MC, V.

★★★ **IMPERIAL HOTEL.** *208 High St, Chestertown (21620). 410/778-5000; fax 410/778-9662; toll-free 800/295-0014. www.imperialchestertown.com.* 13 rms, 3 story. S, D $125-$200; suites $200-$250; lower rates wkdays. Crib free. TV; cable (premium), VCR avail. Continental bkfst Tues-Sat. Dining rm 11:45 am-2:30 pm, 5:30-close; Sun brunch 11:30 am-3 pm; closed Mon. Ck-out 11 am, ck-in 3 pm. Meeting rms. Business servs avail. Refrigerator in suites. Built in 1903; Victorian furnishings. Cr cds: A, MC, V.

★★★ **INN AT MITCHELL HOUSE.** *8796 Maryland Pkwy, Chestertown (21620). 410/778-6500; fax 410/778-2861. www.chestertown.com/mitchell.* 5 rms, 2 story. No rm phones. S, D $90-$110; wkends (2-day min). Crib free. TV in parlor. Complimentary full bkfst. Dinner avail Fri, Sat 7 pm; res required. Ck-out noon, ck-in 3 pm. Manor house built in 1743 on ten acres. Totally nonsmoking. Cr cds: A, MC, V.

★★ **KENT MANOR INN.** *500 Kent Manor Dr, Stevensville (21666). 410/643-5757; fax 410/643-8315; toll-free 800/820-4511. www.kentmanor.com.* 24 rms, 3 story. S, D $135-$215; lower rates mid-wk. Crib $15. TV. Pool. Complimentary continental bkfst. Restaurant 11:30 am-9 pm; Fri, Sat to 9:30 pm; Sun brunch 10 am-2 pm, 4:30-8 pm. Ck-out 11 am, ck-in 3 pm. Meeting rms. Business servs avail. Built 1820; antiques. On Thompson Creek. Cr cds: A, D, DS, MC, V.

★★ **WHITE SWAN TAVERN.** *231 High St, Chestertown (21620). 410/778-2300; fax 410/778-4543. www. chestertown.com/whiteswan.* 6 rms, 2 story, 2 suites. No rm phones. S, D $100-$130; suites $140-$150; under 3 free. Crib free. TV in sitting rm. Complimentary continental bkfst. Restaurant nearby. Ck-out noon, ck-in 3 pm. Health club privileges. Refrigerators. Game rm. Former house and tavern built in 1733 and 1793; restored with antique furnishings; museum. Cr cds: MC, V.

Restaurants

★★ **FISHERMAN'S INN AND CRAB DECK.** *316 Main St, Kent Narrows (21638). 410/827-8807. www.fishermansinn.com.* Hrs: 11 am-10 pm. Closed Dec 24, 25. Bar. Lunch $4.95-$9.95, dinner $6.95-$21. Specializes in fresh seafood. 2 dining areas; fireplace; display of antique oyster plates. Scenic view of the Kent Narrows of the Eastern Bay. Family-owned. Cr cds: A, DS, MC, V.

★ **HARRIS CRAB HOUSE.** *433 Kent Narrows Way N, Grasonville (21638).*

410/827-9500. www.harriscrabhouse. com. Hrs: 11 am-10 pm; Fri, Sat to 11 pm. Closed Thanksgiving, Dec 25. Bar. Lunch, dinner $6-$21.95. Specialties: fresh seafood, barbecued ribs and chicken, steamed crabs. Outdoor dining. Gazebo. On waterfront; dockage. Cr cds: MC, V.

★ ★ ★ **NARROWS.** *3023 Kent Narrows Way S, Grasonville (21638). 410/827-8113.* Hrs: 11 am-9 pm; summer to 10 pm; Sun brunch to 2 pm. Closed Dec 24, 25. Res accepted. Regional Eastern Shore menu. Bar. Wine list. Lunch $6-$12, dinner $12.75-$25. Sun brunch $9.75. Child's menu. Specializes in seafood, traditional Maryland recipes. Waterfront dining. View of the Narrows. Cr cds: A, C, D, DS, MC, V.

★ ★ **OLD WHARF INN.** *Cannon St, Chestertown (21620). 410/778-3566.* Hrs: 11 am-9 pm; Sun from 10 am; Sun brunch to 3 pm. Closed Dec 25. Bar. Lunch $3-$8, dinner $7.25-$19.95. Sun brunch $2.50-$12.25. Child's menu. Specializes in fresh seafood, steak, salad. Outdoor dining. View of river. Cr cds: A, MC, V.

★ **WATERMAN'S CRAB HOUSE.** *21055 Sharp St, Rock Hall (21661). 410/639-2261.* Hrs: 11 am-9 pm; Fri, Sat to 10 pm. Closed Thanksgiving; also Dec-Feb. Bar. Lunch, dinner $8.99-$16.95. Child's menu. Specializes in seafood, crabs, ribs. Outdoor dining. On Rock Hall Harbor. Cr cds: A, DS, MC, V.

Cockeysville

(B-6) *See also Baltimore, Towson*

Pop 19,388 **Elev** 260 ft **Area code** 410 **Zip** 21030

Information Baltimore County Chamber of Commerce, 102 W Pennsylvania Ave, Suite 402, Towson 21204; 410/825-6200

What to See and Do

⭐ **Ladew Topiary Gardens.** Extensive topiary gardens on 22 acres; 15 garden rooms. Also here is the Manor House (fee), with English antiques, fox hunting memorabilia, paintings, unusual china, reconstructed Elizabethan rm; Oval Library housing more than 3,000 volumes; carriage museum; cafe; gift shop. (Mid-Apr-Oct, Tues-Sun) 3535 Jarrettsville Pike, 5 mi E on MD 143 to Sunnybrook, then 6 mi N on MD 146. Phone 410/557-9466. ¢¢¢

Special Event

Point-to-Point Steeplechase. Three well-known meets on consecutive wkends: **My Lady's Manor.** In Monkton. Mid-Apr. **Grand National.** In Butler; phone 410/666-7777. Mid-Apr. **Maryland Hunt Cup.** In Glyndon; Phone 410/666-7777. Late Apr. Phone 410/825-6200.

Motel/Motor Lodge

★ ★ **COURTYARD BY MARRIOTT.** *221 International Cir, Hunt Valley (21030). 410/584-7070; fax 410/584-8151; res 800/321-2211. www. courtyard.com.* 146 rms, 3 story, 12 suites. S $72; D $76; suites $92-$99. Crib free. TV; cable (premium). Complimentary coffee in rms. Restaurant 6:30-10:30 am, 5-9:30 pm. Rm serv from 5 pm. Bar 4-10 pm Mon-Fri. Ck-out noon. Meeting rms. Business servs avail. In-rm modem link. Valet serv. Sundries. Coin lndry. Exercise equipt. Indoor pool; whirlpool, lifeguard. Refrigerator in suites. Balconies. Cr cds: A, D, DS, MC, V.

Hotel

★ ★ ★ **MARRIOTT'S HUNT VALLEY INN.** *245 Shawan Rd, Hunt Valley (21031). 410/785-7000; fax 410/785-0341; toll-free 800/228-9290. www. marriott.com.* 390 rms, 4 story. Mar-Nov: S $129; D $149; suites $179-$350; under 12 free; wkend rates. Pet accepted, some restrictions. TV; cable (premium). Coffee in rms. Restaurant 6:30 am-10 pm; Fri to 11 pm; Sat 7 am-11 pm; Sun from 7 am. Bar 3 pm-1 am. Ck-out noon. Convention facilities. Business center. In-rm modem link. Bellhops. Valet serv. Concierge. Gift shop. Tennis. Exercise equipt. Heated indoor/outdoor pool; wading pool, whirlpool, poolside serv. Refrigerator in suites. Luxury level. Cr cds: A, C, D, DS, JCB, MC, V.

Restaurants

★ ★ ★ **THE MILTON INN.** *14833 York Rd, Sparks (21152). 410/771-4366.* Hrs: 5:30-9:30 pm; Sun 4-9 pm. Closed some major hols. Res accepted. Bar. Wine cellar. Complete meals: dinner $45. Child's menu. Specializes in seasonal dishes, fresh seafood, poultry. Outdoor dining. Main part of building ca 1820; one section was stagecoach stop ca 1740. English country decor. Cr cds: A, D, DS, MC, V.

★ ★ ★ ★ **THE OREGON GRILLE.** *1201 Shawan Rd, Hunt Valley (21030). 410/771-0505. www.theoregongrille. com.* This New American steakhouse is anything but a typical meat-and-potatoes destination with its 19th-century-farmhouse location and creative menu. Chef Mark Henry's inventively prepared steaks, chops, and seafood are easy to savor in the sensual surroundings of dark wood paneling, romantic booths, fireplaces, and live piano. Creativity aside, the simple drama of the dry-aged sirloin strip steak is worth every penny. American menu. Specializes in crab cakes, lamb, dry aged prime steak, veal. Own pastries. Hrs: 11:30 am-4 pm, 5-10 pm; Fri, Sat to 11 pm. Sun brunch 11 am-3 pm, dinner 4-10 pm. Res accepted. Wine cellar. A la carte entrees: lunch $7-$16, dinner $18-$32. Cr cds: A, C, D, DS, MC, V.

★ ★ **YORK INN.** *10010 York Rd (21030). 410/666-0006. www.yorkinn. com.* Hrs: 11-2 am; Sun brunch 9 am-2 pm. Closed Dec 25. Res accepted; required hols. Continental menu. Bar to 2 am. Lunch $5.95-$10.95, dinner $11.95-$25.95. Sun bkfst buffet $6.95. Child's menu. Specializes in seafood, steak. Casual dining. Cr cds: A, C, D, DS, ER, MC, V.

College Park

(D-5) *See also Bowie, Silver Spring; also see District of Columbia*

Pop 24,657 **Elev** 190 ft **Area code** 301 **Zip** 20740

Information Prince George's County Conference & Visitors Bureau, 9200 Basil Ct, #101, Largo 20774; 301/925-8300 or 888/925-8300

Web www.goprincegeorgescounty. com

What to See and Do

College Park Aviation Museum. World's oldest operating airport, started by Wilbur Wright in 1909 to train two military officers in the operation of aircraft. First airplane machine gun and radio-navigational aids tested here; first air mail and controlled helicopter flights. Museum (daily; closed hols). 1985 Corporal Frank Scott Dr. Phone 301/864-6029. ¢¢

Greenbelt Park. A 1,100-acre wooded park operated by the National Park Service. Nature trails, picnicking, camping (dump station, showers; seven-day limit Memorial Day-Labor Day; 14-day limit rest of yr). Self-registration; first-come, first-served. Standard fees. 6565 Greenbelt Rd, E off Kenilworth Ave, MD 201 exit 23. Phone 301/344-3948.

NASA/Goddard Visitor Center. Satellites, rockets, capsules, and exhibits in all phases of space research. (Mon-Fri) SE on I-95 to Baltimore-Washington Pkwy, exit 22A Greenbelt, then follow signs. Phone 301/286-8981. **FREE**

University of Maryland. (1865) 35,000 students. Tawes Fine Arts Theater has plays, musicals, concerts, dance, opera, and music festivals. Tours. Phone 301/405-1000.

Motels/Motor Lodges

★ ★ **COURTYARD BY MARRIOTT.** *6301 Golden Triangle Dr, Greenbelt (20770). 301/441-3311; fax 301/441-4978. www.courtyard.com.* 152 rms, 4 story, 12 suites. S, D $110; each addl $10; suites $124-$134; under 17 free;

wkend, wkly rates. Crib free. TV; cable (premium). Indoor pool; whirlpool, lifeguard. Complimentary coffee in rms. Restaurant 6:30-10 am, 5-10 pm; wkends 6:30 am-midnight. Bar 4-10 pm Mon-Thurs. Ck-out noon. Meeting rms. Business servs avail. Bellhops. Valet serv. Sundries. Coin lndry. Exercise equipt. Refrigerator in suites; microwaves avail. Some balconies. Cr cds: A, DS, MC, V.

D ▱ 🕅 ▨ 🔥

★★ **HOLIDAY INN.** *10000 Baltimore Ave (20740). 301/345-6700; fax 301/441-4923; toll-free 800/465-4329. www.holiday-inn.com.* 222 rms in 2 bldgs, 4 story. S, D $139; under 18 free. Crib free. TV; cable (premium). Indoor pool; whirlpool, lifeguard. Coffee in rms. Restaurant 6:30 am-10 pm. Bar 11 am-midnight. Ck-out noon. Coin lndry. Meeting rms. Business center. In-rm modem link. Exercise equipt; sauna. Health club privileges. Refrigerators, microwaves avail. Cr cds: A, C, D, DS, ER, MC, V.

D ▱ 🕅 ▨ 🔥 SC 🕅

Hotels

★★★ **MARRIOTT GREENBELT.** *5400 Ivy Ln, Greenbelt (20770). 301/441-3700; fax 301/441-3995; toll-free 800/228-9290. www.marriott.com.* 283 rms, 18 story. S, D $149-$179; kit. units (min stay) $139-$184; family, wkend rates. Crib free. TV; cable (premium), VCR avail. 2 pools, 1 indoor; whirlpool, poolside serv, lifeguard. Restaurant 6:30 am-10:30 pm. Bar. Ck-out noon. Coin lndry. Convention facilities. Business center. In-rm modem link. Gift shop. Lighted tennis. Exercise equipt; sauna. Refrigerators, microwaves avail. Luxury level. Cr cds: A, C, D, DS, ER, JCB, MC, V.

D 🏌 ▱ 🕅 ▨ 🔥 SC 🕅

★★ **SHERATON COLLEGE PARK.** *4095 Powder Mill Rd, Beltsville (20705). 301/937-4422; fax 301/937-4455.* 206 rms, 9 story. S, D $109-$129; each addl $7; suites $165; under 18 free; wkend rates; higher rates Cherry Blossom. Crib free. TV; cable (premium). Pool; lifeguard. Complimentary coffee in rms. Restaurant 6:30 am-10 pm; wkends from 7 am. Bar. Ck-out noon. Coin

lndry. Meeting rms. Business servs avail. In-rm modem link. Gift shop. Exercise equipt. Massage. Game rm. Refrigerator; microwaves avail. Cr cds: A, C, D, DS, JCB, MC, V.

D ▱ 🕅 ▨ 🔥 SC

Restaurants

★★ **ALAMO.** *5508 Kenilworth Ave, Riverdale (20737). 301/927-8787.* Hrs: 11 am-11 pm. Res accepted. Mexican menu. Bar. Lunch $5-$11, dinner $8.30-$12.95. Child's menu. Specializes in tostadas, tacos, enchiladas. Entertainment Fri, Sat. Mexican decor. Cr cds: A, MC, V.

D 🖼

★★ **CALVERT HOUSE INN.** *6211 Baltimore Ave, Riverdale (20737). 301/864-5220. www.calverthouseinn.com.* Hrs: 11 am-10 pm; Sat from 4 pm; Sun 4-9 pm; early-bird dinner 4-6 pm. Closed hols. Res accepted; required Fri, Sat dinner. Bar. Lunch $4.50-$10.95, dinner $6.95-$19.95. Child's menu. Specializes in fresh seafood, steak, crab cakes. Tavern atmosphere. Cr cds: A, DS, MC, V.

D 🖼

★★★ **CHEF'S SECRET.** *5810 Greenbelt Rd, Greenbelt (20770). 301/345-6101.* Hrs: 11:30 am-3 pm, 5-9 pm; Fri, Sat to 10 pm; Sun 4-9 pm; early-bird dinner 5-6 pm. Closed Labor Day, Dec 25. Res accepted. Continental menu. Serv bar. Lunch $7.95-$14.95, dinner $11.95-$17.95. Specializes in seafood, veal, steak. Own desserts. Cr cds: A, DS, MC, V.

D 🖼

★ **SANTA FE CAFE.** *4410 Knox Rd (20740). 301/779-1345. www.santafecafe.com.* Hrs: 11 am-midnight. Closed Sun; Thanksgiving, Dec 25. Res accepted. Southwestern, American menu. Bar to 1:30 am. Lunch, dinner $3.95-$9.95. Specializes in fajitas, buffalo wings, pizzas. Outdoor dining. Casual Southwestern decor; murals, buffalo heads, Native American rugs. Cr cds: A, D, DS, MC, V.

D 🖼

Columbia

(C-5) *See also Baltimore*

Pop 88,254 **Elev** 402 ft **Area code** 410 & 443

Information Howard County Tourism Council, 8267 Main St, PO Box 9, Ellicott City 21041; 410/313-1900 or 800/288-TRIP

Web www.visithowardcounty.com

A planned city built on a tract of land larger than Manhattan Island, Columbia is comprised of 11 villages surrounding a central downtown service area. Construction of the city began in 1966.

What to See and Do

African Art Museum of Maryland. Masks, sculptured figures, textiles, basketry, household items, and musical instruments displayed in a 19th-century manor. (Tues-Fri, also Sun afternoons; closed hols) 5430 Vantage Point Rd, in Historic Oakland at Town Center. Phone 410/730-7105. ¢

Howard County Center of African-American Culture. Contains artifacts and memorabilia depicting images of African Americans over the last 200 yrs. Extensive collection of spiritual, jazz, and rap music; more than 2,000 books and periodicals; hands-on exhibit for children. (Tues-Sun; closed hols) 5434 Vantage Point Rd. Phone 410/715-1921. ¢¢

Special Events

Wine in the Woods. Symphony Woods at Merriweather Post Pavilion. Two-day celebration featuring Maryland wines, gourmet food, entertainment, arts and crafts. Third wkend May. Phone 410/313-PARK.

Columbia Festival of Arts. Music, dance, theater, lakeside entertainment. Ten days in mid-June.

Symphony of Lights. Animated lighting displays along a 1½-mi park route. Late Nov-early Jan. Phone 410/313-1900.

Hotels

★ ★ ★ **HILTON HOTEL.** *5485 Twin Knolls Rd (21045). 410/997-1060; fax 410/997-0169; toll-free 800/445-8667. www.hilton.com.* 152 rms, 4 story. S, D $99-$129; each addl $10; suites $175-$250; under 18 free; wkend plans. Crib free. TV; cable (premium) VCR avail. Indoor pool; whirlpool. Coffee in rms. Restaurant 6:30 am-11 pm. Bar noon-midnight; Fri, Sat to 1 am. Ck-out 11 am. Meeting rms. Business servs avail. In-rm modem link. Exercise equipt; sauna. Microwaves avail. Cr cds: A, C, D, DS, ER, MC, V.

⊡ ⌣ 🏋 ⊠ 🐾 SC

★ ★ ★ **SHERATON HOTEL.** *10207 Wincopin Cir (21044). 410/730-3900; fax 410/730-1290; toll-free 800/325-3535. www.sheraton.com.* 289 rms, 3-10 story. S $115-$130; D $130-$145; each addl $10; suites $250-$375; under 12 free; wkend plan. Crib free. Pet accepted, some restrictions; $75 refundable. TV; cable (premium). Pool; poolside serv (in season), lifeguard. Coffee in rms. Restaurant 7 am-2:30 pm, 5:30-10:30 pm. Bar 4 pm-2 am. Ck-out noon. Lndry facilities. Meeting rms. Business servs avail. In-rm modem link. Gift shop. Tennis privileges. 18-hole golf privileges, greens fee $35-$44. Health club privileges. Some bathrm phones; microwaves avail. Overlooks Lake Kittamaqundi; boat rides, entertainment on lake (summer). Cr cds: A, C, D, DS, MC, V.

⊡ 🐾 🏋 ⌣ ⊠ 🐾 SC 🏌

Restaurants

★ ★ **CLYDE'S.** *10221 Wincopin Cir (21044). 410/730-2829. www.clydes. com.* Hrs: 11:30-2 am; Sun from 10 am; early-bird dinner Mon-Fri 4:30-6 pm; Sun brunch to 4 pm. Closed Dec 25. Res accepted (dinner). Bar. Lunch $7-$13, dinner $10-$18. Sun brunch $6-$11. Child's menu. Specializes in seasonal dishes, salmon, crab. Own baking. Outdoor dining. Bistro atmosphere; etched and stained glass; view of lake. Totally nonsmoking. Cr cds: A, C, D, DS, ER, MC, V.

⊡

★ ★ ★ **KING'S CONTRIVANCE.** *10150 Shaker Dr (21046). 410/995-0500.* Hrs: 11:30 am-2 pm, 5:30-9 pm; Fri, Sat 5:30-9:30 pm; Sun 4-8 pm. Res accepted; required Dec. Bar. Wine cellar. Lunch $8-$14, dinner $14-$26. Specializes in fresh seafood, rack of lamb. Own baking. Enclosed porch dining. Mansion built in 1900. Cr cds: A, D, DS, MC, V.

Crisfield

(F-7) *See also Pocomoke City*

Pop 2,723 **Elev** 4 ft **Area code** 410 **Zip** 21817

Information Crisfield Area Chamber of Commerce, 906 W Main St, PO Box 292; 410/968-2500

Web www.crisfield.org

What to See and Do

Janes Island State Park. These 3,147 acres are nearly surrounded by Chesapeake Bay and its inlets. Swimming, fishing, boat ramp (rentals); cabins, camping. Standard fees. Approx 2 mi NE via MD 413, then 1½ mi N on MD 358. Phone 410/968-1565.

Tangier Island Cruises. Trips to the fishing village of Tangier Island, VA. (Mid-may-Oct) 1001 W Main St. Phone 410/968-2338. ¢¢¢¢

Tyler's Cruises. The *Chelsea's Lane Tyler* and the *Capt Tyler* make approx one-hr cruises to Smith Island. Bus tour of the two villages comprising the island, with spare time to visit the rest of the island; lunch avail (fee). Tour length approx 4½ hrs. (Memorial Day wkend-mid-Oct) Somers Cove Marina. Phone 410/425-2771.

Special Event

National Hard Crab Derby & Fair. Cooking, crab picking, boat docking contests; crab racing; fireworks and parade. Fri-Sun, Labor Day wkend. Phone 410/968-2500.

Motel/Motor Lodge

★ ★ **PINES MOTEL.** *127 N Somerset Ave (21817). 410/968-0900; fax 410/968-0900. www.intercom.net/biz/pines.*

40 rms. July-Aug: S $50-$55; D $55-$70; each addl $5; kit. units $15 addl; under 11 free; higher rates: July 4, Labor Day, special events; lower rates rest of yr. TV; cable. Pool. Restaurant nearby. Ck-out 11 am. Gift shop. Picnic area. In scenic, wooded section. Cr cds: A, MC, V.
◿ ◿ ◿ **SC**

Cumberland (B-2)

Settled 1750 **Pop** 21,518 **Elev** 688 ft **Area code** 301 and 240 **Zip** 21502

Information Allegany County Convention & Visitors Bureau, 13 Canal St; 301/777-5132 or 800/425-2067

Web www.mdmountainside.com

Far to the west in the state, Cumberland is nestled between Pennsylvania and West Virginia. The Potomac River and its tributary, Wills Creek, flow peaceably by this onetime western outpost of the colonies.

British General Edward Braddock was sent here to conquer the French and Native Americans in 1755; unprepared for the wilderness, he met with defeat and death. George Washington, who defended the town in that period, felt the main east-west route would pass through Cumberland eventually. In 1833 the National Road (US 40 Alternate) made the town a supply terminus for overland commerce. The road was extended farther west, the B & O Railroad reached here in 1842, and eight years later came the Chesapeake and Ohio Canal (see CHESAPEAKE AND OHIO CANAL NATIONAL HISTORICAL PARK), bringing prosperous business. Today's economy no longer depends on industry alone but includes services and recreational facilities.

What to See and Do

Dans Mountain State Park. On 481 acres. Nearby Dans Rock affords a panoramic view of surrounding region from a height of 2,898 ft. Swimming pool (fee), fishing; picnicking, playground, hiking, sledding. 10 mi W on

I-68, then 8 mi S on MD 36, 2 mi SE of Lonaconing. Phone 301/463-5564.

Fort Cumberland Trail. Walking trail covers several city blks downtown around the site of Fort Cumberland. Incl boundary markers, narrative plaques.

George Washington's Headquarters. (ca 1755) His first military headquarters. Taped narration. In Riverside Park, Downtown, on Greene St. **FREE**

Gordon-Roberts House. (ca 1867) Restored 18-rm Victorian house with nine period rms; costumes; research room. (June-Oct, Tues-Sun; rest of yr, Tues-Sat) 218 Washington St, in Victorian Historic District. Phone 301/777-8678. ¢¢

Green Ridge State Forest. These 44,000 acres of forest land stretch across mountains of western Maryland and occupy portions of Town Hill, Polish Mtn, and Green Ridge Mtn. Abundant wildlife. Fishing, boat launch, canoeing; hiking trails, camping, winter sports. C & O Canal runs through here into 3,118-ft Paw-Paw Tunnel. 21 mi E off I-68 at exit 64. Phone 301/478-3124.

The Narrows. Picturesque 1,000-ft gap through Alleghenies (US 40A) used by pioneers on their way to the West.

Rocky Gap State Park. Mountain scenery around 243-acre lake with three swimming beaches. Swimming, fishing, boating (electric motors only; rentals); nature and hiking trails, picnicking, cafe, improved camping (res accepted one yr in advance), winter activities. Resort; 18-hole golf course. Standard fees. (See SPECIAL EVENTS) 6 mi E on I-68, exit 50. Phone 301/777-2138. ¢

Toll Gate House. (1836) Built to collect tolls from users of Cumberland Rd (National Rd); only remaining toll house in state; restored. (Late May-late Oct, Sat and Sun afternoons; other times by appt) Approx 6 mi W on US 40A, in La Vale. Phone 301/777-5905. ¢

Western Maryland Station Center. This 1913 railroad station houses Canal Place Authority, Industrial and Transportation Museum; C & O Canal National Historical Park Visitors Center and Allegany County Visitors Center. (Daily; closed hols)

Canal St. Phone 301/777-5905. **FREE** This is also the departure point for

Western Maryland Scenic Railroad. Excursion train makes scenic trip 17 mi to Frostburg and back. (May-Oct, Tues-Sun; Nov-mid-Dec, wkends) Phone 301/759-4400.

Special Events

Agricultural Expo and Fair. Allegany County Fairgrounds. Poultry, livestock, carnival, entertainment. Mid-July. Phone 301/729-1200.

Drumfest. Greenway Ave Stadium. Drum and bugle corps championship. Last Sat July. Phone 301/777-8325.

Rocky Gap Music Festival. Allegany College. Features bluegrass and country music; children's activities, crafts, workshops. Fri-Sun, First wknd Aug. Phone 888/762-5942.

Street Rod Roundup. 6 mi S on MD 220, at fairgrounds. Hundreds of pre-1950 hot rods on display and in competitions. Labor Day wknd. Phone 301/729-5555.

Motels/Motor Lodges

★ ★ **BEST WESTERN BRADDOCK MOTOR INN.** *1268 National Hwy, La Vale (21502). 301/729-3300; fax 301/729-3300; res 800/296-6006. www.bestwestern.com.* 108 rms, 1-2 story. S $49-$60; D $55-$66; each addl $6; suites $82-$102; under 18 free. TV; cable (premium), VCR avail (movies). Indoor pool; whirlpool, poolside serv. Restaurant 7 am-9 pm. Bar 4:30 pm-midnight; Fri, Sat to 1 am; closed Sun. Ck-out 11 am. Meeting rm. Business servs avail. In-rm modem link. Sundries. Airport transportation. Exercise equipt; sauna. Game rm. Cr cds: A, C, D, DS, MC, V.

🄳 ⌷ 🕅 ⊠ 🖲 SC

★ **DAYS INN & SUITES.** *11100 New Georges Creek Rd SW, Frostburg (21532). 301/689-2050; fax 301/689-2050; res 800/329-7466. www.daysinn. com.* 100 rms, 2 story. May-Oct: S $66-$78; D $71-$83; each addl $5; suites $86; under 18 free; wkly rates; lower rates rest of yr. Crib free. Pet accepted; $10. TV; cable. Complimentary continental bkfst. Restaurant nearby. Ck-out 11 am. Meeting rms. Business servs avail. In-rm modem link. 18-hole golf privileges.

X-country ski 15 mi. Exercise rm. Pool privileges. Some in-rm whirlpools. Picnic tables. Cr cds: A, C, D, DS, ER, JCB, MC, V.

★ ★ **HOLIDAY INN.** *100 S George St (21502).* 301/724-8800; fax 301/724-4001; res 800/465-4329. www.holiday-inn.com. 130 rms, 6 story. S, D $89; under 18 free. Crib free. Pet accepted. TV; cable (premium), VCR avail. Pool; lifeguard. Restaurant 6:30 am-2 pm, 5-10 pm; Sun from 7 am. Rm serv. Bar noon-midnight; Sun from 4 pm; entertainment. Ck-out noon. Meeting rms. Business center. In-rm modem link. Sundries. Airport transportation. Cr cds: A, C, D, DS, MC, V.

★ **SUPER 8 MOTEL.** *1301 National Hwy, La Vale (21502).* 301/729-6265; fax 301/729-6265; toll-free 800/800-8000. www.super8.com. 63 rms, 3 story. S $46.98; D $56.98; each addl $8; suites $64.98-$69.98; under 12 free. Crib free. TV; cable. Complimentary continental bkfst. Restaurant nearby. Ck-out 11 am. Meeting rms. Business servs avail. Cr cds: A, C, D, DS, MC, V.

B&B/Small Inn

★ ★ ★ **INN AT WALNUT BOTTOM.** *120 Greene St (21502).* 301/777-0003; fax 301/777-8288; toll-free 800/286-9718. www.iwbinfo.com. 12 rms, 4 share bath, 2-3 story, 2 suites. S, D $79-$120; each addl $15; suites $120-$180. Crib avail. TV; cable (premium). Complimentary full bkfst. Restaurant. Ck-out 11 am, ck-in 3 pm. Business servs avail. Health club privileges. Two buildings (1820, 1890). Antiques; period reproductions. Totally nonsmoking. Cr cds: A, DS, MC, V.

Restaurants

★ ★ ★ **AU PETIT PARIS.** *86 E Main St, Frostburg (21532).* 301/689-8946. www.aupetitparis.com. Hrs: 6-9:30 pm. Closed Sun, Mon; hols. Res accepted. French menu. Bar 5:30 pm-midnight. Wine list. Dinner $10.50-$35. Child's menu. Specialties: coq au vin, Dover

sole. Tableside preparation. Cr cds: A, D, DS, MC, V.

★ ★ **WARNER'S GERMAN RESTAURANT.** *McMullen Hwy (21505).* 301/729-2361. Hrs: 11 am-9 pm; Fri, Sat to 10 pm; Sun noon-7 pm. Closed Mon; Jan 1, July 4, Dec 25. German, American menu. Bar. Lunch $3.50-$7.95, dinner $8.95-$13.95. Child's menu. Specialties: sauerbraten, bratwurst, bienenstich. Outdoor dining. Old World Bavarian atmosphere; costumed waitresses. Family-owned. Totally nonsmoking. Cr cds: A, C, D, DS, MC, V.

Easton

(D-7) *See also Cambridge, St. Michael's*

Settled 1682 **Pop** 11,708 **Elev** 28 ft
Area code 410 **Zip** 21601
Information Talbot County Chamber of Commerce, PO Box 1366, Easton Plaza Ste 53; 410/822-4653
Web www.talbotchamber.org

What to See and Do

Academy Art Museum. Housed in renovated 1820s schoolhouse, Academy exhibits works of local and national artists in permanent collection. Also hosts over 250 visual and performing arts programs annually. (Mon-Sat) 106 South St. Phone 410/822-0455. ¢

Historical Society of Talbot County. A three-gallery museum in a renovated early commercial building; changing exhibits, museum shop. Historic houses: 1810 Federal town house, 1700s Quaker cabinetmaker's cottage, period gardens; tours. (Tues-Sat) 25 S Washington St. Phone 410/822-0773. ¢¢

Third Haven Friends Meeting House. (1682-1684) One of the oldest frame-construction houses of worship in US. (Daily) 405 S Washington St. Phone 410/822-0293. **FREE**

Tuckahoe State Park. A 60-acre lake and Tuckahoe Creek provide a secluded atmosphere in this 3,800-acre park. The Adkins Arboretum (500 acres) propagates trees, plants, and shrubs indigenous to Maryland. Fishing, boating; hunting, hiking, picnicking, camping (electric hook-ups, dump station). Standard fees. 5 mi N of Queen Anne, off MD 404. Phone 410/820-1668.

Special Events

Eastern Shore Chamber Music Festival. Various locations. World-class chamber music; young people's concert. Two wks June. Phone 410/819-0380.

Tuckahoe Steam and Gas Show and Reunion. 5 mi N via US 50, opp Woodlawn Memorial Park. Old steam and gas engines; antique tractors and cars. Demonstrations in soap and broom making; flour milling. Gas and steam wheat threshing; sawmill working; flea market, crafts, parade, entertainment. Phone 410/643-6123 or 410/820-9868 (during event). Usually wkend after July 4.

Waterfowl Festival. Downtown and various locations in and around town. Exhibits on waterfowl; pictures, carvings; food. First or second wkend Nov. Phone 410/822-4606.

Motels/Motor Lodges

★ **COMFORT INN.** 8523 Ocean Gtwy (21601). 410/820-8333; fax 410/820-8436; toll-free 800/228-5150. www.comfortinn.com. 84 units, 2 story, 15 suites. Mid-Apr-Nov: S, D $79-$99; each addl $8; suites $105; under 18 free; higher rates special events; lower rates rest of yr. Crib free. TV; cable (premium). Pool; whirlpool. Complimentary continental bkfst. Restaurant nearby. Ck-out 11 am. Meeting rms. Business servs avail. In-rm modem link. Sundries. Some refrigerators; microwaves avail. Picnic tables. Cr cds: A, C, D, DS, MC, V.
🄳 ➳ ⛱ 🔥 SC

★ **DAYS INN.** 7018 Ocean Gateway (21601). 410/822-4600; fax 410/820-9723; toll-free 800/329-7466. www.daysinn.com. 80 rms, 2 story. Apr-Nov: S $69-$89; D, suites $79-$102; under 18 free; higher rates Waterfowl Festival; lower rates rest of yr. Crib free. Pet accepted, some restrictions; $8. TV; cable (premium). Complimentary continental bkfst. Ck-out 11 am. Pool; wading pool. Some refrigerators. Cr cds: A, C, D, DS, ER, JCB, MC, V.
🄳 ➳ ⛱ 🔥 SC

★★ **HOLIDAY INN EXPRESS.** 8561 Ocean Gateway (21601). 410/819-6500; fax 410/819-6505; toll-free 877/327-8661. www.holiday-inn.com. 73 rms, 4 story. Apr-Nov: S, D $109-$129; each addl $8; under 18 free; lower rates rest of yr. Crib free. Pet accepted. TV; cable (premium). Indoor pool; whirlpool. Complimentary continental bkfst. Restaurant adj open 24 hrs. Ck-out 11 am. Meeting rms. Business servs avail. Exercise equipt. Cr cds: A, C, D, DS, MC, V.
🄳 ➳ ⛱ 🏋 🔥 SC

Hotel

★★★ **TIDEWATER INN AND CONFERENCE CENTER.** 101 E Dover St (21601). 410/822-1300; fax 410/820-8847; toll-free 800/237-8775. www.tidewaterinn.com. 114 rms, 4 story. June-Nov: S $90-$175; D $90-$190; each addl $10; under 13 free; wkly, wkend rates; package plans; higher rates Waterfowl Festival; lower rates rest of yr. Crib free. TV; cable (premium), VCR avail. Pool; poolside serv. Restaurant (see also HUNTER'S TAVERN). Bar 11-2 am; entertainment Fri, Sat, Sun brunch. Ck-out noon. Meeting rms. Business center. In-rm modem link. Free valet parking. Airport transportation. Health club privileges. Restored turn-of-the-century hotel. Cr cds: A, C, D, DS, MC, V.
🄳 ⛱ 🔥 SC 🏋

B&Bs/Small Inns

★★ **BISHOP'S HOUSE.** 214 Goldsborough St (21601). 410/820-7290; fax 410/820-7290. www.traveldata.com/inns/data/bishop.html. 5 rms, 3 story. No rm phone. No elvtr. 2-day min: S $110; D $120; lower rates mid-wk. Children over 13 yrs only. TV, cable (premium) in main rm. Complimentary full bkfst. Restaurant nearby. Ck-out 11 am, ck-in 4-5 pm. Tennis privileges. Golf privileges. Some whirlpools, fireplaces. Built in 1880; antiques, toys, porcelains. Totally nonsmoking. Cr cds: A, DS, MC, V.
🏋 🔥

★ ★ ★ **ROBERT MORRIS INN.** *314 N Morris St, Oxford (21654). 410/226-5111; fax 410/226-5744. www. robertmorrisinn.com.* 35 rms, 13 rms with showers only, 2-3 story, 2 kit. cottages. No rm phones. S, D $100-$240. Children over 10 yrs only. Dining rm 8-10 am, noon-9 pm; winter hrs vary. Bar noon-10 pm. Ck-out noon, ck-in 3 pm. Business servs avail. Golf privileges. Private patios, balconies. Historic house (1710) built by ships' carpenters. Private beach on river. Totally nonsmoking. Cr cds: A, MC, V.

Restaurant

★ ★ ★ **HUNTER'S TAVERN.** *101 E Dover St (21601). 410/822-1300. www. tidewaterinn.com.* Hrs: 7 am-10 pm; early-bird dinner Mon-Fri 4-6 pm; Sun brunch 9:30 am-2 pm. Res accepted (dinner). Bar; Fri, Sat 11-2 am. Bkfst $4.95-$10.50, lunch $6.95-$12.50, dinner $12.95-$24.95. Sun brunch $15.70-$18.80. Specializes in Chesapeake Bay seafood, prime rib, crab cakes. Valet parking. Outdoor dining. Waterfowl theme; carvings and murals. Cr cds: A, C, D, DS, ER, MC, V.

Elkton

(B-7) *See also Havre de Grace*

Pop 11,893 **Elev** 30 ft **Area code** 410 **Zip** 21921

Information Elkton Chamber of Commerce, 101 E Main St; 410/398-1640

What to See and Do

Elk Neck State Forest. Has 3,165 acres. Forest wildlife, particularly whitetail deer, can be seen; food plots have been established. Hunting, hiking, bridle trail, picnicking, primitive camping, shooting range, winter sports. Pets allowed. 4 mi W off MD 7, near North East. Phone 410/287-5675.

Elk Neck State Park. Park has 2,188 acres of sandy beaches, marshlands and heavily wooded bluffs. Swimming, fishing, boating (launch, rentals); miniature golf (fee), hiking and nature trails, picnicking, concession, winter sports, camping, cabins. Standard fees. 14 mi SW via US 40, MD 272, near North East. Phone 410/287-5333.

Motels/Motor Lodges

★ **ELKTON LODGE.** *200 Belle Hill Rd (21921). 410/398-9400; fax 410/398-9579.* 32 rms, 2 story. S $35-$40; D $42-$50; each addl $4; under 15 free. Crib $5. TV; cable (premium). Restaurant nearby. Ck-out 11 am. Refrigerators; some microwaves. Cr cds: A, C, D, DS, MC, V.

★ **SUTTON MOTEL.** *405 E Pulaski Hwy (21921). 410/398-3830.* 11 rms, shower only. No rm phones. S $31; D $34-$36; each addl $3. Crib $1. Pet accepted, some restrictions. TV. Restaurant nearby. Ck-out 11 am. Cr cds: A, DS, MC, V.

B&B/Small Inn

★ ★ **INN AT THE CANAL.** *104 Bohemia Ave, Chesapeake City (21915). 410/885-5995; fax 410/885-3585. www.innatthecanal.com.* 7 rms, 3 story. Apr-Nov: D $75-$130; each addl $25; 2-day min some hols; lower rates rest of yr. Children over 10 yrs only. TV; cable (premium). Complimentary full bkfst; afternoon refreshments. Restaurant nearby. Ck-out 11 am, ck-in 2 pm. Business servs avail. Lawn games. Mansion built 1870; antiques. Overlooks Chesapeake and Delaware Canal. Totally nonsmoking. Cr cds: A, C, D, DS, MC, V.

Restaurant

★ ★ **SCHAEFER'S CANAL HOUSE.** *208 Bank St, Chesapeake City (21915). 410/885-2200.* Hrs: 8 am-10 pm; wkend hrs may vary; Sun brunch 10 am-3 pm. Closed Dec 25. Res accepted Sun-Fri. Bar. Bkfst $3-$9, lunch $5-$24, dinner $18-$32. Sun brunch $14.95. Child's menu. Specializes in seafood. Outdoor dining. Nautical decor; view of canal. Cr cds: A, MC, V.

Ellicott City

(C-5) See also Baltimore

Settled 1772 **Pop** 56,397 **Elev** 233 ft
Area code 410
Information Howard County Tourism Council, 8267 Main St, PO Box 9, 21041; 410/313-1900 or 800/288-TRIP
Web www.visithowardcounty.com

The town was originally named Ellicott Mills for the three Quaker brothers who founded it as the site of their gristmill. Charles Carroll of Carrollton, whose Doughoregan Manor can still be seen nearby, lent financial help to the Ellicotts and the town eventually became the site of ironworks, rolling mills, and the first railroad terminus in the United States. The famous Tom Thumb locomotive race with a horse took place near here. Many of the town's original stone houses and log cabins, on hills above the Patapsco River, have been preserved.

What to See and Do

Ellicott City B & O Railroad Station Museum. Two restored buildings (ca 1830 and 1885) house historic rms, railroad displays and memorabilia, operating HO model railroad of the first 13 mi of the B & O track, photographs, dioramas. Full-size B & O caboose and museum store. Civil War reenactments of military and civilian life, June-Sept. (May-Sept, Mon, Wed-Sun; rest of yr, Mon, Fri-Sun) 2711 Maryland Ave, at Main St. Phone 410/461-1944. ¢¢

Patapsco Valley State Park. Four of the recreation areas located within the 15,000 acres sprawling along the Patapsco River are as follows. Area 1: Glen Artney via South St from MD 1, in Relay; Baltimore County. Fishing, picnicking. Area 2: Hilton Ave, via Rolling Rd, S of Frederick Rd, in Catonsville; Baltimore County. Picnicking, camping. Area 3: Hollofield, adj to US 40, near Ellicott City; Howard County. Scenic overlook, camping. Pets allowed in camping area. Area 4: McKeldin Area, off Marriottsville Rd; Carroll County. Fishing, picnicking. Hiking trails and pavilions available in all areas. Golden Age Passport (see MAKING THE MOST OF YOUR TRIP). NE and SE of town; 5 mi from I-695 exits 12 and 15, 50 yards from I-195 exit 1. Phone 410/461-5005. ¢¢

Special Events

Maryland Sheep and Wool Festival. In West Friendship. Sheep breeds and other wool-bearing animals; sheep dog demonstration. Crafters sell products related to sheep and wool; spinning, weaving, and sheep-shearing contests; wool dyeing; entertainment. First wkend May. Phone 410/442-1022.

Howard County Fair. In West Friendship. Rides, entertainment, concessions, 4-H exhibits, horse-pulling contests, and other events. Early-Aug. Phone 410/442-1022.

Hotel

★ ★ **TURF VALLEY HOTEL AND COUNTRY CLUB.** *2700 Turf Valley Rd (21042). 410/465-1500; fax 410/465-8280. www.turfvalley.com.* 223 rms, 7 story, 6 villas. Mar-Nov: S $120; D $135; each addl $15; suites $130-$415; villas $650-$700; under 12 free; wknd rates; lower rates rest of yr. Crib free. TV; cable (premium). Indoor/outdoor pool; whirlpool, poolside serv, lifeguard. Restaurant 6:30 am-10 pm. Bar 4:30-11 pm; Fri, Sat to 2 am; entertainment Fri-Sun. Ck-out noon. Convention facilities. Business servs avail. In-rm modem link. Gift shop. Tennis. 54-hole golf, greens fee $37-$52, pro, putting green, driving range. Exercise equipt; steam rm. Spa. Cr cds: A, D, DS, MC, V.

Restaurants

★ ★ **CRAB SHANTY.** *3410 Plumtree Dr (21042). 410/465-9660. www.crabshanty.com.* Hrs: 11:30 am-2:30 pm, 5-10 pm; Mon, Tues to 9 pm; Sun 2-9 pm. Bar. Lunch $2.95-$9.50, dinner $8.75-$18.95. Child's menu.

Specializes in seafood. Cr cds: A, D, DS, MC, V.

[D] [SC] [⊸]

★ **SIDESTREETS.** *8069 Tiber Alley (21043).* 410/461-5577. Hrs: 11:30 am-10 pm; Fri, Sat to 11 pm; Sun 11 am-9 pm; Sun brunch to 2 pm. Closed Thanksgiving, Dec 25. Res accepted Fri, Sat dinner. Seafood menu. Bar. Lunch, dinner $5.95-$19.95. Sun brunch $2.95-$7.95. Specializes in Chesapeake Bay seafood. Eclectic decor. Totally nonsmoking. Cr cds: A, DS, MC, V.

[D]

★★★ **TERSIGUEL'S.** *8293 Main St (21043).* 410/465-4004. *www. tersiguels.com.* Hrs: 11:30 am-2:30 pm, 5-9 pm; Fri to 10 pm; Sat 11:30 am-3:30 pm, 5-10 pm; Sun 11:30 am-3:30 pm, 5-9 pm. Closed Dec 25. Res accepted. French menu. Bar. Wine cellar. Lunch $8.95-$19.95, dinner $14.95-$26.95. Prix fixe: lunch $15.95-$25.95, dinner $27.95-$37.95. Specialities: rack of lamb, châteaubriand pour deux. Historic bldg; mementos from Brittany, France. Totally nonsmoking. Cr cds: A, C, D, DS, MC, V.

Emmitsburg

(B-4) *See also Frederick, Hagerstown, Thurmont*

Settled 1785 **Pop** 2,290 **Elev** 449 ft
Area code 301 **Zip** 21727
Information Tourism Council of Frederick County, 19 E Church St, Frederick 21701; 301/228-2888
Web www.visitfrederick.org

What to See and Do

Mount St. Mary's College and Seminary. (1808) 1,800 students. Oldest independent Catholic college in US. Liberal arts and sciences. 3 mi S on US 15. Phone 301/447-6122. Near the campus is the

National Shrine Grotto of Lourdes. Replica of the French shrine is ⅓ the size of the original; oldest replica in the Western Hemisphere.

Pangborn Memorial Campanile, constructed of native stone and located at the entrance, is 120 ft tall and is surmounted by a 25-ft bronze gold-leaf statue of the Blessed Virgin Mary. (Apr-Oct, daily; rest of yr, Tues-Sun) Phone 301/447-5318. **FREE**

🔲 **Seton Shrine Center.** National Shrine of St. Elizabeth Ann Seton, first US female saint, canonized 1975. Incl Stone House (1750), White House (1810), home in which Mother Seton died; video presentation, basilica, museum and cemetery. (Tues-Sun, or by appt; closed major hols; also last two wks Jan) 333 S Seton Ave. Phone 301/447-6606. **FREE**

B&B/Small Inn

★★ **ANTRIM 1844.** *30 Trevanion Rd, Taneytown (21787).* 410/756-6812; fax 410/756-2744; toll-free 800/858-1844. *www.antrim1844.com.* 21 rms, 2 with shower only, 3 story, 2 suites. No rm phones. S, D $150-$300; suites $300; ski, golf plans; 2-day min wkends, hols; higher rates Dec 31. Pool; whirlpools. Complimentary full bkfst. Complimentary coffee in rms. Restaurant (see ANTRIM 1844). Ck-out 11 am, ck-in 3 pm. Luggage handling. Business servs avail. Airport transportation. Tennis. Putting green. Croquet. Downhill ski 14 mi; x-country 15 mi. Lawn games. Many fireplaces, in-rm whirlpools. Some balconies. Antebellum plantation (1844) on 25 acres. Elegant antique furnishings, 3-story spiral staircase. Formal gardens and gazebo. Cr cds: A, D, DS, MC, V.

[D] [⊸] [⊸] [⊸] [⊸] [⊸] [⊸]

Restaurant

★★★ **ANTRIM 1844.** *30 Trevanion Rd, Taneytown (21787).* 410/756-6812. *www.antrim1844.com.* Sittings: 7-7:30 pm (hors d'oeuvres served at 6:30 pm). Closed Jan 1. Res required. French, American menu. Bar. Wine cellar. Prix fixe: $55. Specialties: wild rockfish with scallop mousse, black Angus tenderloin. Outdoor dining. Refined dining in elegant atmosphere; fireplace, piano. Cr cds: A, C, D, DS, MC, V.

[D]

Frederick

(C-4) *See also Hagerstown, Thurmont*

Settled 1745 **Pop** 52,767 **Elev** 290 ft
Area code 301 and 240 **Zip** 21701
Information Tourism Council of Frederick County, 19 E Church St; 301/663-8687 or 800/999-3613
Web www.visitfrederick.org

Home of dauntless Barbara Fritchie, who reportedly spoke her mind to Stonewall Jackson and his "rebel hordes," Frederick is a town filled with history. Named for Frederick Calvert, sixth Lord Baltimore, it is the seat of one of America's richest agricultural counties. Francis Scott Key and Chief Justice Roger Brooke Taney made their homes here. Court House Square was the scene of several important events during the Revolutionary War, including the famed protest against the Stamp Act, in which an effigy of the stamp distributor was burned.

During the Civil War, Frederick was a focal point for strategic operations by both sides. In the campaign of 1862 the Confederacy's first invasions of the North were made at nearby South Mountain and Sharpsburg, at Antietam Creek. Wounded men by the thousands were cared for here. Troop movements continued for the duration of the war; cavalry skirmishes took place in the streets. In July 1864, the town was forced to pay a $200,000 ransom to Confederate General Jubal Early before he fought the Battle of Monocacy a few miles south. Frederick today is an educational center, tourist attraction, location of Fort Detrick army installation, and home of diversified small industry. A 33-block area has been designated an Historic District.

What to See and Do

Barbara Fritchie House and Museum. Exhibits incl quilts, clothing made by Fritchie, her rocker and Bible, the bed in which she died, and other items; ten-min film; also garden. (Apr-Sept, Mon, Thurs-Sun; Oct-Nov, Sat and Sun) 154 W Patrick St. Phone 301/698-0630. ¢¢

Brunswick Museum. Furnishings and clothing interpret life in turn-of-the-century railroad town; large HO model train exhibit; gift shop. Special events held on selected wkends. (June-Sept, Thurs-Sun; Apr-May and Oct-late Dec, Sat and Sun; limited hrs) Phone 301/834-7100. ¢¢

Gambrill State Park. Park has 1,136 acres with two developed areas. Fishing; nature and hiking trails, picnicking, tent and trailer sites (standard fees). Tea room. Two overlooks. Phone 301/791-4767.

Historical Society of Frederick County Museum. House, built in early 1800s, shows both Georgian and Federal details; leaded side and fanlights, Doric columns inside, double porches in rear, and boxwood gardens. Portraits of early Frederick residents. Genealogy library (Tues-Sat). (Mon-Sat; also Sun afternoons) 24 E Church St. Phone 301/663-1188. ¢

Horse-drawn carriage tours. (Daily, by appt) Phone 301-694-RIDE

Monocacy National Battlefield. On July 9, 1864, Union General Lew Wallace with 5,000 men delayed General Jubal Early and his 23,000 Confederate soldiers for 24 hrs, during which Grant was able to reinforce, and save, Washington, D.C. New Jersey, Vermont, Pennsylvania, and Confederate monuments mark the area. 3 mi S on MD 355. Phone 301/662-3515. **FREE**

Mount Olivet Cemetery. (1852) Monuments mark graves of Francis Scott Key and Barbara Fritchie. Flag flies over Key's grave. S end of Market St.

Roger Brooke Taney Home (1799) **and Francis Scott Key Museum.** Chief Justice of the US from 1835-1864, Taney was chosen by Andrew Jackson to succeed John Marshall. He swore in seven presidents, incl Abraham Lincoln, and issued the famous Dred Scott Decision. He is buried in the cemetery of St. John's Catholic Church at E 3rd and East sts. (Apr-Oct, wkends) 121 S Bentz St. Phone 301/663-8687. ¢¢

Rose Hill Manor Children's Museum. Hands-on exhibits of 19th-century family life; carriage museum; Colonial herb and fragrant gardens; farm museum; blacksmith shop; log cabin.

CIVIL WAR SITES OF FREDERICK

A well-preserved city of elegant 18th- and 19th-century structures, Frederick should be placed on anyone's tour of important Civil War landmarks. It is an especially appropriate sequel to a visit to nearby Antietam National Battlefield, which has entered the history books as the site on September 17, 1862 of the single bloodiest day of the Civil War. At the end of the battle, thousands of Union wounded were transported to the small city, where 29 buildings were turned into makeshift hospitals. President Lincoln later praised townsfolk for their humanity. This heritage proved an important factor when Frederick was chosen from among 15 communities vying to be the site of the National Museum of Civil War Medicine. Begin an hour-long, one-mile walking tour of the city's Historic District at the museum at 48 East Patrick Street. The museum tells the story of radical improvements in medical treatment during the four years of the war, as the divided nation coped with the flood of ill or wounded soldiers on both sides of the Mason-Dixon line. As the museum points out, the use of ambulances and the technique of embalming both emerged during the war. From the museum, walk three blocks west (left) to the reconstructed Barbara Fritchie House & Museum at 154 West Patrick. Fritchie was immortalized in John Greenleaf Whittier's Civil War poem, "Shoot if you must, this old gray head, but spare your country's flag." According to legend, she waved a Union flag defiantly at "Stonewall" Jackson, who was leading a Confederate army through the city. In truth, she may have waved a flag, but to honor Union troops passing by later. Double back on Patrick Street to Court Street and walk north (left) one block to tour Courthouse Square. On Court Street, opposite City Hall, is the small office where Francis Scott Key, author of the "Star-Spangled Banner," practiced law. Revolutionary War General Lafayette was a guest at 103 Council Street during his ceremonial US tour in 1824. At 119 Record Street, Lincoln visited a wounded general and addressed a crowd from its steps after the Antietam battle. Head east (left) on West Church Street. At No. 108, you'll see a cast-iron model of the pet dog of John Tyler, a pioneer ophthalmologist. The statue was stolen by Confederates seeking to melt it into bullets, but later it was found near an Antietam battlefield. Conclude your tour two blocks east at the Historical Society of Fredericksburg at 24 East Church. A large 1820 home, it is maintained as a house museum furnished with local antiques—appropriately so, because nearby East Patrick Street has been dubbed "Antique Row" for its many antique shops.

(Apr-Oct, daily; Nov, Sat and Sun only) 1611 N Market St. Phone 301/694-1648. ¢¢

Schifferstadt. (1756) Fine example of German Colonial farmhouse architecture. Tours of architectural museum. Gift shop. (Apr-mid Dec, Tues-Sun; closed Thanksgiving) 1110 Rosemont Ave. Phone 301/663-3885. ¢

Trinity Chapel. (1763) Graceful Colonial church; Francis Scott Key was baptized here. Steeple houses town clock and ten-bell chimes; chimes play every Sat eve. W Church St, near N Market St. The chapel is now used as Sunday School for

Evangelical Reformed Church. United Church of Christ (1848). Opp Trinity Chapel. A Grecian-style building modeled after the Erechtheum, with two towers resembling Lanterns of Demos-

thenes. Here Stonewall Jackson slept through pro-Union sermon before Battle of Antietam; Barbara Fritchie was a member. Phone 301/662-2762.

Special Events

Beyond the Garden Gates Tour. Downtown. Tour historic and contemporary gardens. Late May. Phone 301/663-8687.

Lotus Blossom Festival. Lilypons Water Gardens, 6800 Lilypons Rd, 10 mi S via MD 85. Endless blooms of water lilies and lotus, water garden; arts and crafts, food, entertainment, lectures. First double-digit wkend July. Phone 800/999-5459.

Great Frederick Fair. Frederick county fair. Mid-late Sept. Phone 301/663-5895.

New Market Days. 8 mi E, in New Market. Nostalgic revival of the atmosphere of a 19th-century village; costumed guides, period crafts and events; held in New Market, the town dedicated to being the "Antiques Capital of Maryland." Last full wkend Sept. Phone 301/831-6755.

Fall Festival. Rose Hill Manor. Apple butter making, music, crafts demonstrations, tractor pull, hay rides, country cooking. Early Oct.

Motels/Motor Lodges

★ **DAYS INN.** *5646 Buckeystown Pike (21704). 301/694-6600; fax 301/831-4242; toll-free 800/329-7466. www. daysinn.com.* 119 rms, 2 story. Apr-Oct: S, D $56-$75; under 18 free; lower rates rest of yr. Crib free. TV; cable (premium). Pool. Playground. Complimentary continental bkfst. Ck-out noon. Meeting rm. Business servs avail. Sundries. Refrigerators, microwaves avail. Cr cds: A, C, D, DS, MC, V.

★★ **FAIRFIELD INN.** *5220 Westview Dr (21703). 301/631-2000; fax 301/631-2100. www.fairfieldinn.com.* 105 rms, 3 story. May-mid-Oct: S $69-$82; D $69-$87; higher rates special events. Crib free. TV; cable (premium). Complimentary continental bkfst. Ck-out noon. Business servs avail. Sundries. Exercise equipt. Indoor pool; whirlpool. Health club privileges. Some refrigerators, microwaves. Cr cds: A, D, DS, MC, V.

★★ **HAMPTON INN.** *5311 Buckeystown Pike (21704). 301/698-2500; fax 301/695-8735; toll-free 800/426-7866. www.hamptoninn.com.* 160 rms, 6 story. S, D $69-$100; suites $150; under 18 free. Crib free. Pet accepted, some restrictions; fee. TV; cable (premium). Pool; lifeguard. Complimentary continental bkfst. Restaurant 11:30 am-9 pm. Bar; entertainment. Ck-out noon. Coin lndry. Meeting rms. Business servs avail. In-rm modem link. Sundries. Valet serv. Exercise equipt. Health club privileges. Some refrigerators; microwaves avail. Cr cds: A, C, D, DS, MC, V.

B&Bs/Small Inns

★★ **CATOCTIN INN.** *3619 Buckeystown Pike, Buckeystown (21717). 301/874-5555; fax 301/831-8102. www.catoctininn.com.* 20 rms, 3 story, 3 cottages. S, D $85-$125; each addl $10; cottages $150; under 2 free; wkly rates; min stay hols; higher rates: wkends, fall foliage. Crib free. TV; cable (premium), VCR avail (movies). Complimentary full bkfst, coffee in rms. Restaurant nearby. Ck-out noon, ck-in by appt. Luggage handling. Meeting rms. Business servs avail. Lawn games. Refrigerators. Built 1780s; parlour with antique sofas, fireplaces. Cr cds: A, C, D, DS, MC, V.

★★★ **INN AT BUCKEYSTOWN.** *3521 Buckeystown Pike, Buckeystown (21717). 301/874-5755; fax 301/831-1355; toll-free 800/272-1190. www. innatbuckeystown.com.* 5 rms, 3 story. MAP: S, D $200-$225; suite $225; cottage $250-$300. Children over 12 yrs only. TV avail; cable (premium), VCR avail (movies). Whirlpool. Restaurant (public by res) 7:30 pm sitting; Wed-Sat. Setups. Ck-out noon, ck-in 4 pm. Meeting rm. Business servs avail. Downhill ski 20 mi; x-country ski 1 mi. Refrigerators avail; microwaves in cottages. Restored Victorian mansion (1897). Near river. Totally nonsmoking. Cr cds: A, MC, V.

★★★ **STONE MANOR.** *5820 Carroll Boyer Rd, Middletown (21769). 301/473-5454; fax 301/371-5622. www.stone manor.com.* 6 rms, 2 story, 5 suites. No rm phones. S, D $200; suites $125-$250. TV; VCR avail. Complimentary continental bkfst. Restaurant 11 am-2 pm, 6-9 pm; Sun 11 am-2 pm (brunch), 4-7 pm; closed Mon. Rm serv 24 hrs. Ck-out 11 am, ck-in 2 pm. Business servs avail. Lawn games. Fireplaces. Balconies. On pond. Stone building built in 1760s; on more than 100 acres of wooded area. Totally nonsmoking. Cr cds: A, DS, MC, V.

★★★ **TURNING POINT INN.** *3406 Urbana Pike (21704). 301/831-8232; fax 301/831-8092. www.turningpoint inn.com.* 5 rms, 2 with shower only, 3 story, 2 kit. cottages. S, D $75-$95;

kit. cottages $100-$150. TV; cable (premium). Complimentary full bkfst; afternoon refreshments. Dining rm 11:30 am-2 pm, 5:30-9 pm; wkend hrs vary; Tues-Sun. Ck-out 11 am, ck-in 3 pm. Business servs avail. Built in 1910; antiques. View of Sugarloaf Mtn and adj farmland. Cr cds: A, C, D, DS, MC, V.

Restaurants

★ ★ **BROWN PELICAN.** *5 E Church St (21701). 301/695-5833.* Hrs: 11:30 am-3 pm, 5-9:30 pm; Fri to 10 pm; Sat 5-10 pm; Sun 5-9:30 pm. Closed Jan 1, Thanksgiving, Dec 25; also Super Bowl Sun. Res accepted; required Fri, Sat. Continental menu. Bar. Lunch $5.75-$12.95, dinner $12.95-$23.95. Specializes in fresh seafood, pasta, veal. In basement of antebellum bank. Cr cds: A, C, D, DS, MC, V.

★ ★ **GABRIEL'S.** *4730 Ijamsville Rd, Ijamsville (21754). 301/865-5500. www.gabrielsinn.com.* Hrs: 6-10 pm; Sun 3-9:30 pm. Closed Mon-Wed; Jan 1. Res accepted; required Fri, Sat. French menu. Serv bar. Entrees: $16.95-$24.50. Specialties: beef Wellington, salmon coulibac, stuffed breast of chicken Marengo. French Provincial inn atmosphere; building constructed in 1862. Family-owned. Cr cds: D, DS, MC, V.

★ ★ **TAURASO'S.** *6 East St (21701). 301/663-6600.* Hrs: 11 am-10 pm; Fri, Sat to 11 pm. Closed Dec 25. Res accepted. Italian, American menu. Bar to midnight. Lunch $4.95-$8.95, dinner $7.95-$19.95. Specializes in fresh fish, veal, steak. Outdoor dining. In restored factory building (late 1800s). Cr cds: A, D, DS, MC, V.

Gaithersburg

(C-5) *See also Rockville*

Pop 52,613 **Elev** 508 ft **Area code** 301

Information Chamber of Commerce, 9 Park Ave, 20877; 301/840-1400

What to See and Do

Seneca Creek State Park. Stream valley park of 6,109 acres with 90-acre lake. Historic sites with old mills, an old schoolhouse, stone quarries. Fishing, boating (rentals); picnicking, disk golf, hiking, bicycle and bridle trails, winter sports. Standard fees. 2½ mi W of I-270 on MD 117. Phone 301/924-2127. ¢

Special Event

Montgomery County Agricultural Fair. One of the East Coast's leading county fairs; emphasis on agriculture, 4-H activities; animal exhibits, home arts; antique farm equipt; tractor pull, horse pull, demolition derby; rodeo; entertainment. Mid-late Aug. Phone 301/926-3100.

Motels/Motor Lodges

★ **COMFORT INN AT SHADY GROVE.** *16216 Frederick Rd (20877). 301/330-0023; fax 301/258-1950; toll-free 800/228-5150. www.comfortinn.com.* 127 rms, 7 story. Apr-Oct: S, D $49-$109; each addl $10; under 18 free; monthly rates; lower rates rest of yr. Crib free. Pet accepted, some restrictions. TV; cable (premium). Heated pool; lifeguard. Complimentary full bkfst. Coffee in rms. Restaurant adj 11 am-9 pm. Ck-out 11 am. Coin lndry. Meeting rms. Business center. In-rm modem link. Valet serv. Gift shop. Exercise equipt. Health club privileges. Some refrigerators; microwaves. Picnic tables. Cr cds: A, C, D, DS, ER, JCB, MC, V.

★ ★ **COURTYARD BY MARRIOTT.** *805 Russell Ave (20879). 301/670-0008; fax 301/948-4538; res 800/336-6880. www.marriott.com.* 203 rms, 7 story. S $105; D $115; each addl $10; suites $250; wkend rates. Crib free. TV; cable (premium), VCR avail. Pool; whirlpool, lifeguard. Coffee in rms. Restaurant 6-10 am, 5:30-9:30 pm; Sat 7-11 am; Sun 7 am-noon. Bar 5 pm-midnight. Ck-out noon. Coin lndry. Meeting rms. Business servs avail. In-rm modem link. Valet serv. Lighted tennis. Exercise equipt;

steam rm. Some refrigerators, microwaves. Some balconies. Cr cds: A, D, DS, MC, V.

🄳 🔁 🕅 ⛵ 🔥 ⛷

★★ **HAMPTON INN.** *20260 Goldenrod Ln, Germantown (20876). 301/428-1300; fax 301/428-9034. www.hampton inn.com.* 178 rms, 6 story, 16 kit. units. S, D $95-$105; kit. units $129; suites $199; under 18 free; wkend rates. Crib free. TV; cable (premium). Pool. Complimentary continental bkfst. Restaurant 11 am-11 pm. Ck-out noon. Coin lndry. Meeting rms. Business servs avail. Valet serv. Sundries. Exercise equipt; sauna. Health club privileges. Microwaves avail. Cr cds: A, DS, MC, V.

🄳 🔁 🕅 ⛵ 🔥

★★ **HOLIDAY INN.** *2 Montgomery Village Ave (20879). 301/948-8900; fax 301/258-1940; toll-free 800/465-4329. www.holiday-inn.com.* 301 rms, 2-8 story. S $114-$124; D $124-$149; suites $300-$350; kit. units $119-$139; under 18 free. Crib free. Pet accepted, some restrictions. TV; cable (premium). Indoor pool; whirlpool, poolside serv, lifeguard. Coffee in rms. Restaurant 6:30 am-10 pm. Rm serv to midnight. Bar noon-midnight. Ck-out noon. Coin lndry. Convention facilities. Business center. In-rm modem link. Bellhops. Gift shop. Exercise equipt. Game rm. Some refrigerators; microwaves avail. Balconies. Cr cds: A, C, D, DS, JCB, MC, V.

🄳 🍴 🔁 🕅 ⛵ 🔥 SC ⛷

Hotels

★★★ **HILTON HOTEL.** *620 Perry Pkwy (20877). 301/977-8900; fax 301/977-3450; res 800/599-5111. www.hilton.com.* 301 rms, 12 story. S, D $115-$155; suites $325; under 18 free; wkend rates. Crib free. Pet accepted, some restrictions. TV; cable (premium). Indoor/outdoor pool. Restaurant 6:30 am-11 pm; wkends from 7 am. Bars 11-1 am. Convention facilities. Business servs avail. In-rm modem link. Exercise equipt. Health club privileges. Refrigerators avail. Some private patios, balconies. Adj to Lake Forest shopping center. Cr cds: A, C, D, DS, ER, JCB, MC, V.

🄳 🍴 🔁 🕅 ⛵ 🔥 SC

★★★ **MARRIOTT WASHINGTON CENTER GAITHERSBURG .** *9751*

Washingtonian Blvd (20878). 301/590-0044; fax 301/212-6155; toll-free 800/228-9290. www.marriott.com. 284 rms, 11 story. S, D $164; suites $250; under 18 free; wkend rates. Crib free. TV; cable (premium). Indoor pool; whirlpool, poolside serv, lifeguard. Restaurant 6:30 am-11 pm; wkend hrs vary. Bar 4 pm-midnight. Ck-out noon. Convention facilities. Business center. In-rm modem link. Concierge. Gift shop. Exercise equipt; sauna. Health club privileges. Luxury level. Cr cds: A, C, D, DS, ER, JCB, MC, V.

🄳 🔁 🕅 ⛵ 🔥 SC ⛷

Restaurants

★ **CHRIS' STEAK HOUSE.** *201 E Diamond Ave (20877). 301/869-6116.* Hrs: 11 am-midnight. Closed Sun; hols. Bar. Lunch $3.95-$8.50, dinner $6.50-$18. Child's menu. Specializes in beef, pork, seafood. Football memorabilia. Cr cds: D, MC, V.

🄳 🍽

★★ **FLAMING PIT.** *18701 N Frederick Ave (20879). 301/977-0700.* Hrs: 11:30 am-10 pm; Fri to 11 pm; Sat 4-11 pm; Sun 5-10 pm; early-bird dinner Mon-Fri 4-7 pm. Closed hols. Res accepted; required Fri, Sat. Bar to midnight; Fri, Sat to 1 am. Lunch $6.95-$12.95, dinner $13.95-$29.95. Child's menu. Specializes in prime rib, lamb, fresh seafood. Pianist. Skylight; hanging baskets. Original antique fireplaces. Cr cds: A, C, D, DS, MC, V.

🄳 🍽

★★ **GOLDEN BULL GRAND CAFE.** *7 Dalamar St (20877). 301/948-3666.* Hrs: 11 am-3 pm, 4:30-10 pm; Fri, Sat to 11 pm; Sun noon-10 pm; early-bird dinner 4:30-6:30 pm, Sun noon-4 pm. Closed Dec 25. Bar 11 am-11 pm. Lunch $5.50-$10.95, dinner $9.95-$29.95. Child's menu. Specializes in beef, seafood. Salad bar. Cr cds: A, D, DS, MC, V.

🄳 🍽

★ **IL FORNO PIZZERIA.** *8941 Westland Dr (20877). 301/977-5900.* Hrs: 11 am-10 pm; Fri, Sat to 11 pm. Closed hols. Italian menu. Wine, beer. A la carte entrees: lunch $4.45-$7.95, dinner $10-$15.95. Specializes

in pizza, pasta. Outdoor dining. Casual decor. Cr cds: MC, V.
D

★★ **PEKING CHEERS.** *519 Quince Orchard Rd (20878). 301/216-2090. www.thepekingcheers.com.* Hrs: 11 am-10:30 pm; Fri, Sat to 11 pm. Res accepted. Chinese menu. Serv bar. Lunch $4.25-$5.50, dinner $5.95-$11.95. Specialties: Peking duck, sesame chicken, crispy beef. Casual decor; large murals. Totally nonsmoking. Cr cds: A, D, DS, MC, V.
D

★ **PEKING SUPREME.** *19204 Montgomery Village Ave, Montgomery Village (20886). 301/963-8088.* Hrs: 11:30 am-9:45 pm; Fri, Sat to 10:45 pm. Closed Thanksgiving. Chinese menu. Bar. Lunch $4.50-$5.50, dinner $6.95-$11.95. Specialties: Peking-style chicken, crispy beef. Art Deco decor. Cr cds: A, C, D, DS, MC, V.
D

★ **ROY'S PLACE.** *2 E Diamond Ave (20877). 301/948-5548. www.roysplacerestaurant.com.* Hrs: 11 am-11 pm; Fri, Sat to midnight; Sun from 11:30 am. Closed Thanksgiving, Dec 24, 25. Bar. A la carte entrees: lunch, dinner $4.50-$14. Specializes in extensive sandwich selection. 1920s tavern atmosphere; Tiffany-style lamps, beamed ceiling, period posters. Family-owned. Cr cds: A, D, DS, MC, V.
D

★★ **SIR WALTER RALEIGH.** *19100 Montgomery Village Ave (20886). 301/258-0576. www.sirwalterraleigh. com.* Hrs: 11:30 am-2 pm, 5-9 pm; Fri to 10 pm; Sat 5-10 pm; Sun 4-8:30 pm. Closed Dec 25. Bar. Lunch $7-$11, dinner $10.95-$19.95. Child's menu. Specializes in prime rib, seafood, crab cakes. Salad bar. Brick fireplaces. Cr cds: A, D, DS, MC, V.
D

Grantsville

(B-1) *See also Cumberland, Oakland (Garrett County)*

Pop 619 **Elev** 2,300 ft **Area code** 301 **Zip** 21536

Information Garrett County Chamber of Commerce, 15 Visitors Center Dr, McHenry 21541; 301/387-4386

Web www.garrettchamber.com

What to See and Do

Casselman Bridge and State Park. Single-span stone arch bridge over the Casselman River was built in 1813. Contact 349 Headquarters Ln. Phone 301/895-5453.

New Germany State Park. A 13-acre lake built on site of a once prosperous milling center. Swimming, fishing, boating; nature, hiking trails, winter sports, picnicking, playground, concession, improved campsites, cabins (fee). 5 mi S. Phone 301/895-5453. ¢

Savage River State Forest. Largest of Maryland's state forests comprises about 52,800 acres of near wilderness. A strategic watershed area, the northern hardwood forest surrounds the Savage River Dam. Fishing; hunting, hiking trails, winter sports, primitive camping (permit required). W and S via US 40 and I-68. Phone 301/895-5453.

Springs Museum. Depicts life of settlers of Casselman Valley; 18th-century farming tools, fossil collection, other exhibits. (Memorial Day-mid-Oct, Wed-Sat afternoons) 2 mi N via MD 669, PA 669 in Springs, PA. Phone 814/662-4158.

Spruce Forest Artisan Village. Original log cabins plus other historic buildings serve as studios for a potter, internationally recognized bird carver, weaver, spinner, stained-glass maker, and other artisans. Buildings (Mon-Sat). Special events (summer; fee). Restaurant. (See SPECIAL EVENTS) 1 mi E on US 40, near Penn Alps. Phone 301/895-3332. **FREE**

Special Events

Spruce Forest Summerfest and Quilt Show. Spruce Forest Artisan Village. More than 200 quilts on display; more than 70 craftspeople demonstrate their various skills. Phone 301/895-3332. Second full Thurs, Fri, and Sat wkend July.

Springs Folk Festival. On grounds of Springs Museum (see). Pennsylvania Dutch food, music. First Fri and Sat Oct. Phone 814/662-4158.

Restaurant

★ ★ **PENN ALPS.** *125 Casselman Rd, Gaithersburg (21536). 301/895-5985. www.pennalps.com.* Hrs: 7 am-8 pm; Sun brunch 10 am-3 pm. Closed Dec 24, 25. Complete meals: bkfst $2.50-$6.95, lunch $4-$7.95, dinner $8.75-$15.95. Sun brunch $8.95. Child's menu. Specializes in Dutch cooking. Salad bar. Colonial decor; 1818 stagecoach stop. Totally nonsmoking. Cr cds: A, DS, MC, V.

Hagerstown

(B-4) *See also Boonsboro (Garrett County), Frederick, Thurmont*

Settled 1762 **Pop** 36,687 **Elev** 552 ft
Area code 301 **Zip** 21740
Information Hagerstown/Washington County Tourism Office, 16 Public Sq; 301/791-3246 or 800/228-7829
Web www.marylandmemories.org

Within the city of Hagerstown there is a walking tour with points of interest marked on downtown sidewalks and walking paths in city parks. South Prospect Street is one of the city's oldest neighborhoods, listed on the National Register of Historic Places. The tree-lined street is graced by homes dating back to the early 1800s.

What to See and Do

Antietam National Battlefield. (see) 11 mi S on MD 65.

Fort Frederick State Park. Erected in 1756, during French and Indian War, the fort is considered a fine example of a pre-Revolutionary stone fort. Overlooks Chesapeake and Ohio Canal National Historical Park (see); barracks, interior, and wall of fort restored; military reenactments throughout yr. Fishing, boating (rentals); nature and hiking trails, picknicking (shelter), playground, unimproved camping. Museum, orientation film, historical programs. Standard fees. Winter hrs may vary. 18 mi W of jct I-81 and I-70 to Big Pool, then 1 mi SE via MD 56, unnumbered road. Phone 301/842-2155.

Greenbrier State Park. The Appalachian Trail passes near this 1,275-acre park and its 42-acre man-made lake. Swimming (Memorial Day-Labor Day, daily), fishing, boating (rentals; no gas motors); nature and hiking trails, picnicking. Standard fees. 6 mi E via US 40. Phone 301/791-4767.

Hagerstown Roundhouse Museum. Museum houses photographic exhibits of the seven railroads of Hagerstown; historic railroad memorabilia, tools, and equipt; archives of maps, books, papers, and related items. Gift shop. (Fri-Sun afternoons) (See SPECIAL EVENTS) 300 S Burhans Blvd, across the tracks from City Park. Phone 301/739-4665. ¢

Jonathan Hager House and Museum. (1739) Stone house in park setting; authentic 18th-century furnishings. (Apr-Dec, Tues-Sun) 110 Key St, in City Park. Phone 301/739-8393. ¢¢

Miller House. Washington County Historical Society Headquarters. Federal town house (ca 1820); three-story spiral staircase; period furnishings; garden; clock, doll, and Bell pottery collections; Chesapeake & Ohio Canal and Civil War exhibits; 19th-century country store display. (Apr-Dec, Wed-Sat; closed hols; also first two wks Dec) 135 W Washington St. Phone 301/797-8782. ¢¢

Washington County Museum of Fine Arts. Paintings, sculpture, changing exhibits; concerts, lectures. (Tues-Sun; closed hols) 91 Key St in City Park, S on US 11 (Virginia Ave). Phone 301/739-5727. **FREE**

Special Events

Hagerstown Railroad Heritage Days. Special events centered on the

Roundhouse Museum. Early May.
Phone 301/739-4665.

Halfway Park Days. Helicopter rides,
antique cars, dance bands, flea market, food. Late May. Phone 301/791-
3246.

Jonathan Hager Frontier Craft Day.
Colonial crafts demonstrated and
exhibited. Bluegrass music; food.
First wkend Aug.

Leitersburg Peach Festival. Peach-
related edibles, farmers market, bluegrass music. Second wkend Aug.

Williamsport C & O Canal Days. Arts
and crafts, Indian Village, National
Park Service activities; food. Late Aug.

**Alsatia Mummers Halloween Parade
Festival.** Sat, wkend closest to Halloween. Phone 301/791-3246.

Motels/Motor Lodges

★★ **CLARION INN.** *901 Dual Hwy
(21740). 301/733-5100; fax 301/733-
9192. www.clarion.com.* 210 rms, 5
story. S $62-$69; D $67-$74; each
addl $5; suites $95-$200; under 18
free. Crib free. TV; cable (premium).
Indoor pool. Restaurant 6:30 am-9:30
pm; Sun to 9 pm. Bar noon-2 am.
Ck-out 11 am. Coin lndry. Meeting
rms. Business servs avail. Free airport
transportation. Exercise equipt. Some
refrigerators, in-rm whirlpools. Cr
cds: A, C, D, DS, MC, V.

[D] [≈] [⊼] [≧] [▨] [SC]

★ **DAYS INN.** *900 Dual Hwy (21740).
301/739-9050; fax 301/739-8347; toll-
free 800/422-2754. www.daysinn.com.*
140 rms, 2 story. May-Oct: S $48-$58;
D $54-$65; each addl $5; under 18
free; wkend rates; lower rates rest of
yr. TV; cable (premium). Playground.
Pool. Complimentary continental
bkfst. Restaurant 6:30 am-2 pm, 5-9
pm. Bar 4:30-9:30 pm. Ck-out noon.
Coin lndry. Meeting rms. Business
servs avail. Refrigerators avail. Cr cds:
A, C, D, DS, JCB, MC, V.

[D] [≈] [≧] [▨] [SC]

★★ **FOUR POINTS BY SHERA-
TON.** *1910 Dual Hwy (21740). 301/
790-3010; fax 301/733-4559; toll-free
800/325-3535. www.fourpoints.com.*
108 rms, 2 story. S $60-$75; D $64-
$79; each addl $6; suites $150; under
18 free. Crib $6. Pet accepted; $50
deposit. TV; cable (premium). Pool;

whirlpool. Complimentary continental bkfst. Restaurant 6:30 am-10 pm;
Sat, Sun 7 am-9 pm. Bar 11-2 am.
Ck-out noon. Meeting rms. Business
servs avail. Bellhops. Valet serv. Sundries. Free airport transportation.
Exercise equipt; sauna. Microwaves
avail. Cr cds: A, C, D, DS, MC, V.

[D] [◥] [≈] [⊼] [≧] [▨] [SC]

★ **PLAZA HOTEL.** *1718 Underpass
Way (21740). 301/797-2500; fax 301/
797-6209; toll-free 800/826-4534.
www.plazahotelhagerstown.com.* 163
units, 6 story. S $64; D $70; each
addl $8; suites $90-$102; under 18
free. Crib free. TV; cable (premium),
VCR avail. Indoor pool; whirlpool.
Complimentary coffee in rms.
Restaurant 6:30 am-9 pm. Rm serv.
Bar 11 am-11 pm. Ck-out noon.
Meeting rms. Business servs avail. In-
rm modem link. Valet serv. Free airport transportation. Exercise equipt;
sauna. Refrigerators. Cr cds: A, C, D,
DS, JCB, MC, V.

[D] [≈] [⊼] [≧] [▨] [SC]

★★ **VENICE INN.** *431 Dual Hwy
(21740). 301/733-0830; fax 301/733-
4978.* 220 rms, 2-5 story. Apr-Oct: S
$58-$68; D $63-$73; each addl $6;
suites $125-$250; under 18 free;
lower rates rest of yr. Crib $6. Pet
accepted, some restrictions. TV; cable
(premium), VCR (movies). Pool.
Complimentary coffee in lobby.
Restaurant 6 am-10:30 pm. Bar;
entertainment Tues-Sat. Ck-out
noon. Meeting rms. Bellhops. Valet
serv. Beauty shop. Airport transportation. Game rm. Golf adj. Exercise
equipt. Refrigerators, microwaves
avail. Whirlpool in suites. Cr cds: A,
C, D, DS, MC, V.

[D] [◥] [≈] [⊼] [≧] [▨]

Restaurants

★ **JUNCTION 808.** *808 Noland Dr
(21740). 301/791-3639.* Hrs: 6 am-
8:30 pm. Closed Sun; also July 4, Dec
24-26. Res accepted. Bkfst $1.50-
$4.95, lunch $2.50-$4.25, dinner
$4.95-$10.95. Child's menu. Specialties: lasagne, Cajun steak. Own pies.
Located near railroad tracks. Rail-
road-theme decor and tapes of actual
trains; model trains circle the room

at the ceiling. Totally nonsmoking.
Cr cds: MC, V.
[D] [SC]

★★ **RED HORSE STEAK HOUSE.**
*1800 Dual Hwy (21740). 301/733-
3788.* Hrs: 4-10 pm; Sun to 9 pm.
Closed hols. Res accepted. Bar. Dinner $9.75-$19.95. Child's menu. Specializes in prime rib, broiled seafood,
steak. Open-hearth grill. Western-
style atmosphere. Family-owned. Cr
cds: D, MC, V.
[D]

★★ **RICHARDSON'S.** *710 Dual Hwy
(21740). 301/733-3660.* Hrs: 7 am-10
pm; Fri, Sat to 11 pm. Closed Dec 24
eve, Dec 25. Res accepted. Bar. Bkfst
$1.95-$4.95, lunch $2.95-$6.95, dinner $5.95-$14.95. Buffet: bkfst $4.95,
lunch $4.99, dinner $8.95-$18.95.
Child's menu. Specializes in fried
chicken, seafood, crab cakes. Salad
bar. Own pies, cakes. 3 dining areas;
railroad theme, memorabilia. Cr cds:
DS, MC, V.
[D] [⌐]

Havre de Grace

(B-7) *See also Aberdeen, Elkton*

Settled 1658 **Pop** 11,331 **Elev** 52 ft
Area code 410 and 443 **Zip** 21078
Information Chamber of Commerce,
224 N Washington St, PO Box 339;
410/939-3303 or 800/851-7756
Web www.hdgchamber.com

What to See and Do

Concord Point Lighthouse. (1827)
Built of granite, considered the oldest
continuously used lighthouse on the
East Coast. It was automated in
1928. (May-Oct, wkends and hols
only) At foot of Lafayette St. **FREE**

Decoy Museum. Houses a collection
of hand-carved waterfowl decoys and
interprets this art form as it applies
to the heritage of Chesapeake Bay.
(Daily; closed Jan 1, Thanksgiving,
Dec 25) (See SPECIAL EVENTS) Giles
and Market sts, at the bay. Phone
410/939-3739. ¢

Susquehanna State Park. A 2,639-
acre park. Fishing, boat launch;
nature, riding, and hiking trails; x-
country skiing, picnicking, camping

(May-Sept; fee). 3318 Rockchrome
Hill Rd. Phone 410/557-7994. In the
park is

Steppingstone Museum. Self-
guided tour of museum grounds
incl sites of a once working Harford County farm; farmhouse is
furnished as a turn-of-the-century
country home; nearby shops and
barn hold many displays and
exhibits of the 1880-1920 period;
demonstrations of rural arts and
crafts of the period. Also here are
blacksmith, woodworking, cooper,
and dairy shops. (May-first Sun
Oct, Sat and Sun afternoons) Special events held throughout the yr
(see SPECIAL EVENTS). 461 Quaker
Bottom Rd. Phone 410/939-2299.

Special Events

Decoy Festival. Decoys on display,
auction. Carving, gunning, and calling contests. Refreshments. Fri-Sun
first wkend May. Phone 410/939-
3739.

Fall Harvest Festival and Craft Show.
Steppingstone Museum. Features
activities related to the harvest and
preparation for winter: apple press-
ing, scarecrow stuffing, and other
events. Entertainment. Last full
wkend Sept. Phone 410/939-2299.

B&B/Small Inn

★★★ **VANDIVER INN.** *301 S Union
Ave (21078). 410/939-5200; fax
410/939-5202; toll-free 800/245-1655.*
www.vandiverinn.com. 9 rms, 3 story. S,
D $75-$105; wkly rates. TV in parlor.
Complimentary full bkfst. Ck-out 11
am, ck-in 4-7 pm. Some fireplaces.
Some balconies. Queen Anne-style
mansion (1886); antiques. Chesapeake
Bay 2 blks. Cr cds: A, DS, MC, V.
[D] [⌐] [🐾] [SC]

Restaurants

★★ **BAYOU.** *927 Pulaski Hwy (US
40) (21078). 410/939-3565.* Hrs:
11:30 am-10 pm. Closed Dec 24-26.
Res accepted; required hols. Lunch
$3-$6.25, dinner $7.50-$13.50.
Child's menu. Specializes in seafood,
veal. Cr cds: A, C, D, MC, V.
[D] [⌐]

★★ **CRAZY SWEDE.** *400 N Union
Ave (21078). 410/939-5440.* www.

crazyswederestaurant.com. Hrs: 11-2 am; Sun brunch 10 am-2:30 pm. Closed Thanksgiving, Dec 25. Res accepted; required Fri, Sat. Continental menu. Bar. Lunch $4.25-$6.95, dinner $11.95-$21. Sun brunch $3.50-$9. Child's menu. Specializes in seafood. Cr cds: A, MC, V.

La Plata

(E-5) *See also Waldorf; also see District of Columbia*

Pop 6,551 **Elev** 193 ft **Area code** 301 **Zip** 20646

Information Charles County Chamber of Commerce, 6360 Crain Hwy, phone 301/932-6500; or the Department of Tourism, 301/645-0558

Web www.ccc-md.org

What to See and Do

Doncaster Demonstration Forest. Heavily forested with yellow poplar, sweet gum, red and white oaks, and pine throughout its 1,477 acres. Hunting, 13 mi of hiking trails, bridle trails, picnic area, x-country skiing. 13 mi W on MD 6, near Doncaster. Phone 301/934-2282.

Port Tobacco. Infrared aerial photography and archaeological excavation revealed the site of one of the oldest continuously-inhabited English settlements in North America. Appearing as a Native American village on Captain John Smith's map of the area (1608), the area was colonized by the English as early as 1638. The town was chartered in 1727, and the first courthouse was erected in 1729. Among the remaining buildings are the Chimney House (1765) and Stagg Hall (1732), an original Colonial home still a private residence, Burch (Catslide) House (1700), the reconstructed Quenzel Store, and a Federal period courthouse, with the Port Tobacco Museum on the second floor; archeological items on display, replicas of Colonial houses; Civil War and John Wilkes Booth exhibits, 30-min audiovisual film *The Story of Port*

Tobacco. (Apr-Dec, Sat and Sun afternoons) 3 mi SW on MD 6. Phone 301/934-4313. ¢

Smallwood State Park. Restored home of Revolutionary General William Smallwood. Guided tour and historical program during summer. Marina. Boating (launch, rentals), fishing; hiking, picnicking. Retreat house. Park (daily). Standard fees. 16 mi W via MD 225, 224, near Rison. Phone 301/743-7613. ¢

Motel/Motor Lodge

★ ★ **BEST WESTERN.** *6900 Crain Hwy; Rte 301 (20646).* 301/934-4900; fax 301/934-5389; toll-free 800/780-7234. www.bestwestern.com. 73 rms, 2 story, 8 suites. S, D $57-$67; each addl $5; suites $90-$105; under 13 free. Crib free. TV; cable (premium), VCR avail. Pool. Complimentary continental bkfst. Restaurant adj 11 am-11 pm. Ck-out noon. Coin lndry. Meeting rm. Business servs avail. Exercise equipt. Refrigerators, microwaves. Picnic table. Cr cds: A, C, D, DS, MC, V.

Laurel

(C-5) *See also Bowie, College Park, Silver Spring*

Pop 19,960 **Elev** 160 ft **Area code** 240 and 301

Information Baltimore/Washington Corridor Chamber of Commerce, 312 Marshall Ave, Suite 104; 301/725-4000

Web www.laurel.md.us

What to See and Do

Montpelier Mansion. (ca 1780) Built and owned for generations by Maryland's Snowden family; Georgian architecture. George Washington and Abigail Adams were among its early visitors. On the grounds are boxwood gardens, an 18th-century herb garden, and a small summer house. Tours; purchase ticket in gift shop. (Mar-Nov, Sun afternoons; groups by appt; closed hols) Candlelight tours held in early Dec. 3 mi SE on MD 197 at Muirkirk. Phone 301/953-1376. ¢¢

National Wildlife Visitor Center. A 12,750-acre national wildlife refuge and research area. Interactive exhibits focus on global environmental issues, migratory birds, wildlife habitats, and endangered species. Tram tours avail of surrounding forests and lakes (weather permitting; fee). Trails. Gift shop. (Daily; closed Dec 25) 10901 Scarlet Tanager Loop. Phone 301/497-5760. **FREE**

Special Event

Thoroughbred racing. Laurel Race Course, on MD 198. Entrances accessible from northbound or southbound on US 1, I-95, or from Baltimore-Washington Pkwy, MD 198 exit. Phone 301/725-0400 or 800/638-1859 for current racing schedule.

Motels/Motor Lodges

★★ **COMFORT SUITES.** *14402 Laurel Pl (20707). 301/206-2600; fax 301/725-0056; res 800/221-2222. www.comfortinn.com.* 119 rms, 5 story. S, D $80-$100; each addl $10; suites $95-$125; under 18 free; wkly, wkend rates; higher rates: cherry blossom, Memorial Day wkend. Crib free. Pet accepted; $50 refundable. TV; cable (premium). Indoor pool; whirlpool, lifeguard. Complimentary continental bkfst, coffee in rms. Restaurant nearby. Ck-out noon. Coin lndry. Meeting rms. Business servs avail. Sundries. Valet serv. Airport transportation. Exercise equipt. Refrigerators, microwaves. Cr cds: A, C, D, DS, JCB, MC, V.
🄳 🔧 ⌨ 🏌 ⊠ 🐾

★★ **HOLIDAY INN.** *3400 Fort Meade Rd (20724). 301/498-0900; fax 301/498-3203; toll-free 800/477-7410. www.holiday-inn.com.* 166 rms, 2 story. S, D $84-$114; each addl $10; under 18 free. Crib free. TV; cable (premium), VCR avail. Pool; lifeguard. Complimentary coffee in rms. Restaurant 6:30 am-2 pm, 5-10 pm. Rm serv from 7 am. Bar 4 pm-midnight. Ck-out 11 am. Coin lndry. Meeting rms. Business servs avail. In-rm modem link. Valet serv. Exercise equipt. Health club privileges. Refrig-

erators, microwaves avail. Cr cds: A, C, D, DS, ER, JCB, MC, V.
🄳 ⌨ 🏌 ⊠ 🐾 **SC**

Leonardtown

(E-5) *See also St. Mary's City*

Pop 1,896 **Elev** 87 ft **Area code** 301 **Zip** 20650

Information St. Mary's County Division of Tourism, 23115 Leonard Hall Dr, PO Box 653; 301/475-4411 or 800/327-9023

Web www.co.saint-marys.md.us

What to See and Do

Calvert Marine Museum. Museum complex with exhibits relating to the culture and marine environment of Chesapeake Bay and Patuxent River estuary; fossils of marine life; estuarine biology displays, aquariums, touch-tank; maritime history exhibits, incl boat-building gallery. Also here is the restored Drum Point Lighthouse, built 1883; ½ mi S is the JC Lore Oyster House, with exhibits on the area's seafood industry. Gift shop. (Daily; closed Jan 1, Thanksgiving, Dec 25) 1 mi SE on MD 5, then 11 mi NE on MD 4, cross bridge and turn right on Solomons Island Rd; follow signs. Phone 410/326-2042. ¢¢

Old Jail Museum. Local historical exhibits housed in old jail; also a genealogy library for researchers. A cannon from Leonard Calvert's ship, the *Ark,* is mounted in front. (Tues-Sat; closed hols; also last wk Dec) 11 Court House Dr. Phone 301/475-2467. **FREE**

St. Clements Island-Potomac River Museum. Maryland colonists first landed on the island in 1634. Exhibits trace 12,000 yrs of local history and pre-history. Museum incl Little Red School House (ca 1821) and country store. Picnic area; fishing and crabbing. (Late Mar-Sept, Mon-Fri, also Sat, Sun afternoons; rest of yr, Wed-Sun afternoons; closed hols) 5 mi W via MD 234 to Clements, then 9 mi S on MD 242, in Colton Point. Phone 301/769-2222.

Sotterley Plantation. (ca 1715) Overlooks Patuxent River. Working plantation; house in original condition. Chinese Chippendale staircase, antiques, original pine paneling in three rms. Farming exhibit. (Grounds open May-Oct, Tues-Sun; individual tours of manor house on wkends; group tours by appt only) 9 mi E on MD 245. Phone 301/373-2280. ¢¢¢

Special Events

St. Mary's County Fair. Midway, seafood, horse shows. Late Sep. Phone 301/475-2707.

Blessing of the Fleet and Historical Pageant. St. Clements Island, Potomac River Museum. Celebration commemorates first Roman Catholic Mass held on Maryland soil and Governor Leonard Calvert's proclamation of religious freedom. Blessing of oyster and clam fishing fleets. Folk dances, historical exhibits, concerts. Boat rides to the island. First wkend Oct. Phone 301/769-2222.

St. Mary's County Oyster Festival. County Fairgrounds. National oyster shucking contest; oyster cook-off, seafood, and crafts. Third wkend Oct. Phone 301/863-5015.

Oakland (Garrett County) (B-1)

Settled 1851 **Pop** 1,930 **Elev** 2,384 ft
Area code 301 **Zip** 21550
Information Garrett County Chamber of Commerce, 200 S Third St; 301/387-4386
Web www.garrettchamber.com

What to See and Do

Backbone Mountain. Highest point in the state (3,360 ft). 8 mi S on US 219, then W on US 50.

Deep Creek Lake State Park. Approx 1,800 acres with 3,900-acre man-made lake. Swimming, bathhouse, fishing, boating (rowboat rentals); nature and hiking trails, picnicking (shelters), playground, concession, improved campsites (fee). From I-68,

10 mi SE off US 219. General information and camping reservations Phone 301/387-5563. ¢

Garrett State Forest. Approx 6,800 acres. The forest contains much wildlife. Fishing; hunting, hiking and riding trails, winter activities, primitive camping. Forestry demonstration area. 5 mi NW on County 20. Phone 301/334-2038. Within the forest are

> **Herrington Manor State Park.** Well-developed 365-acre park with housekeeping cabins, 53-acre lake. Swimming, fishing, boating (launch, rentals); hiking trails, concession, picnicking, x-country skiing (rentals). Interpretive programs (summer). No pets. Standard fees. Phone 301/334-9180.

> **Swallow Falls State Park.** Surrounding 257 acres, the Youghiogheny River tumbles along the park's boundaries, passing through shaded rocky gorges and over sunny rapids. Muddy Creek produces a 52-ft waterfall. Here the last remaining stand of virgin hemlock dwarfs visitors. Fishing; nature trails, hiking, picnicking, improved campsites. Pets at registered campsites only. Standard fees. Phone 301/334-9180.

Potomac State Forest. More than 10,685 acres for hiking, riding, and hunting. Primitive camping. Timber is harvested regularly here and the area is important in the management of watershed and wildlife programs. 9 mi SE off MD 560, along Potomac River. Phone 301/334-2038.

Special Events

Winterfest. Deep Creek Lake in McHenry. Ski races, parade, fireworks. Late Feb or early Mar.

McHenry Highland Festival. Deep Creek Lake. Traditional Scottish and Celtic festival. First Sat June.

Garrett County Fair. McHenry Fairgrounds. Early Aug. Phone 301/334-1948.

Autumn Glory Festival. Celebrates fall foliage. Features arts and crafts, five-string banjo contest, state fiddle contest, western Maryland tournament of bands, parades, antique show. Mid-Oct. Phone 301/334-1948.

Motels/Motor Lodges

★ **LAKE SIDE MOTOR COURT.** *19956 Garrett Hwy, Oakland (21550). 301/387-5566.* 10 rms, 1 cottage. Mid-June-Labor Day: S, D $64; each addl $4; cottage for 2-6, $468-$900/wk; MAP avail; lower rates May-mid-June, after Labor Day-Oct. Closed rest of yr. TV; cable. Pool privileges. Playground. Restaurant adj 7 am-2 pm, 5-9:30 pm. Ck-out 11 am. Refrigerators. Picnic area, grills. Overlooks lake; private swimming beach; dock. Cr cds: A, D, DS, MC, V.
▯ ▯ ▯

★ **WILL O' THE WISP.** *20160 Garrett Hwy, Oakland (21550). 301/387-5503; fax 301/387-4999. www.willothewisp. com.* 10 rms. May-Oct: S, D $62; each addl $4; cottage for 2-6, $468-$900/wk; MAP avail. Closed rest of yr. Crib free. TV. Pool privileges. Restaurant adj 7 am-2 pm, 5-9:30 pm. Ck-out 11 am. On lake; private beach, dock. Picnic tables. Cr cds: A, DS, MC, V.
▯ ▯ ▯ ▯ ▯

B&Bs/Small Inns

★ ★ ★ **CARMEL COVE BED AND BREAKFAST.** *105 Monastery Way, Swanton (21550). 301/387-0067; fax 301/387-2394. www.carmelcoveinn. com.* 10 rms, 5 with shower only, 2 story, 3 suites. S, D $80-$140; suites $120-$140; ski plans; package plans; wkends, hols (2-3 day min). Children over 12 yrs only. TV in common rm; cable (premium), VCR (movies). Complimentary full bkfst. Ck-out 11 am, ck-in 4-9 pm. In-rm modem link. Luggage handling. Concierge serv. Gift shop. Tennis. X-country ski 10 mi. Game rm. Rec rm. In-rm whirlpool, fireplace in suites. Some balconies. Picnic tables, grills. On lake. Built in 1945. Totally nonsmoking. Cr cds: DS, MC, V.
▯ ▯ ▯ ▯ ▯

★ ★ ★ **HALEY FARM BED AND BREAKFAST.** *16766 Garrett Hwy, Oakland (21550). 301/387-9050; res 888/231-3276. www.haleyfarm.com.* 10 rms, 2 story, 3 kit. suites. Rm phone in 4 suites only. S, D $130-$140; each addl $25; suites $165-$185; kit. units $195-$205; golf rates; package plans; wkends, hols (2-3 day min). Children over 12 yrs only. TV in suites; cable (premium), VCR (movies). Complimentary full bkfst; afternoon refreshments. Ck-out noon, ck-in 3 pm. Concierge serv. Gift shop. Downhill ski 5 mi; x-country ski on site. Bicycles. Sauna. Fireplaces; in-rm whirlpool, refrigerators in suite; microwaves avail. Some balconies. Picnic tables, grills. Built in 1923; formerly a working farm. Totally nonsmoking. Cr cds: A, DS, MC, V.
▯ ▯ ▯ ▯ ▯

Restaurant

★ ★ **POINT VIEW INN.** *609 Deep Creek Dr, McHenry (21541). 301/387-5555. www.pointviewinn.com.* Hrs: 8 am-10 pm; Sun to 9 pm. Closed Easter, Dec 25. Res accepted. Bar 11-2 am. Bkfst $3-$6, lunch $5.75-$8.50, dinner $7.50-$21.95. Child's menu. Specialities: crab cakes, prime rib. Entertainment wkends. Patio dining. Elevated dining areas with view of Deep Creek Lake. Cr cds: A, DS, MC, V.
▯

Ocean City (E-8)

Founded 1869 **Pop** 7,173 **Elev** 7 ft
Area code 410 **Zip** 21842
Information Chamber of Commerce, 12320 Ocean Gateway; 410/213-0552
Web www.oceancity.org

Deep-sea fishing is highly regarded in Maryland's only Atlantic Ocean resort. The white sand beach, three-mile boardwalk, amusements, golf courses, and boating draw thousands of visitors every summer.

What to See and Do

⬛ **Assateague Island National Seashore.** A 37-mi barrier strand that supports an intricate ecosystem, Assateague is also known for its population of ponies, Sika deer (miniature Asian elk) and, in autumn, the migratory peregrine falcon. Campground (fee; phone 410/641-3030); hike-in and canoe-in campsites and day-use facilities; conducted walks

Wild horses at Assateague Island National Seashore

and demonstrations in summer. Visitor center (daily; closed winter hols). 1 mi W on US 50, then 7 mi S on MD 611. Phone 410/641-1441. ¢¢ Also on the island is

Assateague State Park. Has 755 acres with two mi of ocean frontage and gentle, sloping beaches. Swimming, fishing, boat launch; picnicking, concession (summer), bicycle and hiking trails, camping (Apr-Oct). Standard fees (summer). For res, contact 7307 Stephen Decatur Hwy, Berlin 21811. Phone 410/641-2120. ¢

Special Events

Harness racing. Ocean Downs. 4 mi W on US 50. Nightly Tues-Sun. Children with adult only. Late July-Labor Day. Phone 410/641-0600.

Fishing contests and tournaments. Many held throughout the yr. For exact dates contact the Chamber of Commerce. Phone 410/213-0552.

Motels/Motor Lodges

★★ **BEST WESTERN FLAGSHIP OCEANFRONT.** *2600 Baltimore Ave (21842). 410/289-3384; fax 410/289-1743; res 800/837-3585. www.best western.com.* 93 rms, 3 story. Late June-late Aug (3-day min wkends): S, D $179-$189; under 13 free; lower

rates rest of yr. Closed 2 wks Dec and wkdays Dec 26-Feb 14. Crib free. TV; cable (premium), VCR (free movies). 2 pools, 1 indoor; wading pool, whirlpool, poolside serv. Dinner buffet avail May-Sept. Ck-out 11 am. Guest lndry. Business servs avail. Lighted tennis. Exercise equipt; sauna. Game rm. Rec rm. Many kit. units. Cr cds: A, C, D, DS, MC, V.

D 📠 🏊 🏋 🐾 SC

★★ **CASTLE IN THE SAND HOTEL.** *3701 Atlantic Ave (21842). 410/289-6846; fax 410/289-9446; toll-free 800/552-7263. www.castleinthe sand.com.* 36 rms, 5 story, 27 cottages, 108 kit. units. Early July-late Aug: S, D $165-$182; each addl $8; kit. units $165-$205; cottages $750-$1,295/wk; under 12 free; lower rates mid-Apr-early July and late Aug-late Oct. Closed rest of yr. Crib $5. TV; cable (premium). Pool; lifeguard. Supervised children's activities (June-Aug); ages 3-12. Restaurant 7:30 am-midnight. Bar 11-2 am; entertainment wkends. Ck-out 11 am. Meeting rm. Business servs avail. In-rm modem link. Bellhops. Free airport transportation. Game rm. Refrigerators. Some balconies. Cr cds: A, D, DS, MC, V.

D 🐾 🏊 🏋 🐾

★ **CAYMAN SUITES.** *12500 Coastal Hwy (21842). 410/250-7600; fax*

410/250-7603; toll-free 800/546-0042. www.caymansuites.com. 57 suites. July-Aug: suites $179-$209; each addl $10; under 16 free; wkly, mid-wk rates; lower rates rest of yr. Closed Jan, Feb. Crib $6. TV; cable (premium). Indoor pool. Complimentary coffee in lobby. Ck-out 11 am. Meeting rms. Business servs avail. Bellhops (in season). Exercise equipt. Microwaves. Balconies. Near beach. Cr cds: A, DS, MC, V.

⊡ ⇌ 🏋 ⊠ 🔥 SC

★ **COMFORT INN.** 507 Atlantic Ave (21842). 410/289-5155; fax 410/289-6547; toll-free 800/228-5150. www.comfortinnboardwalk.com. 84 kit. units in 2 bldgs, 5 story. June-Aug: S, D $164-$209; each addl $10; under 12 free; lower rates Mar-May, Sept-Nov. Closed rest of yr. Crib free. TV; cable (premium). 2 pools, 1 indoor. Complimentary continental bkfst. Restaurant nearby. Ck-out 11 am. Bellhops. Balconies. On ocean. Cr cds: A, C, D, DS, ER, JCB, MC, V.

⊡ ⇌ ⊠ 🔥 SC

★ **EXECUTIVE MOTEL.** 30th St and Baltimore Ave (21843). 410/289-3101; toll-free 800/638-1600. www.executive motel.com. 47 rms, 3 story. No elvtr. Memorial Day wkend, July-Labor Day (3-day min wkends): S, D $78-$88; each addl $6; under 6 free; lower rates late May-June, after Labor Day-mid-Sept. Closed rest of yr. Crib $6. TV; cable. Restaurant nearby. Ck-out 11 am. Refrigerators. Cr cds: MC, V.

⊡ 🔥

★ **GATEWAY RESORT HOTEL.** 4800 Coastal Hwy (21842). 410/524-6500; fax 410/524-5374; toll-free 800/382-2582. www.gatewayoc.com. 59 kit. units, 3 story. July-mid-Aug: S, D $195-$230; each addl $10; suites $1,195-$1,285/wk; under 6 free; higher rates hol wkends; lower rates rest of yr. Crib $10. TV; cable (premium). Pool; wading pool, whirlpool, lifeguard (summer). Playground. Complimentary coffee in rms. Restaurant 11-2 am. Bar; entertainment. Ck-out 11 am. Coin lndry. Business servs avail. Health club privileges. Lawn games. Balconies. Picnic tables. On ocean, swimming beach. Cr cds: A, C, D, DS, MC, V.

⇌ ⊠ 🔥

★★ **HOLIDAY INN OCEANFRONT.** 6600 Coastal Hwy (21842). 410/524-1600; fax 410/524-1135; res 800/837-3588. www.holiday-inn.com. 216 kit. units, 8 story. Memorial Day-Labor Day: S, D $160-$250; each addl $9; under 19 free; higher rates hol wkends; golf plans; lower rates rest of yr. Crib free. TV; cable (premium). 2 pools, 1 indoor; wading pools, whirlpool, poolside serv. Supervised children's activities (June-Aug); ages 5-9. Restaurant 7-11:30 am, 5-11 pm. Rm serv. Bar 5-midnight. Ck-out 11 am. Free lndry facilities. Meeting rms. Business servs avail. In-rm modem link. Bellhops. Tennis. Exercise equipt; sauna. Game rm. Balconies. Picnic tables. On ocean. Cr cds: A, DS, MC, V.

⊡ 🏌 ⇌ 🏋 ⊠ 🔥

★ **HOWARD JOHNSON OCEANFRONT.** 2401 Baltimore Ave (21842). 410/289-9101; fax 410/289-1722; res 800/926-1122. www.hojo.com. 72 units, 4 story, 26 kits. Late June-Aug: S, D $135-$175; each addl $10; kit. units $165-$185; under 18 free; lower rates Mar-June, Sept-Oct. Closed rest of yr. Crib free. TV; cable (premium). Heated pool; whirlpool. Complimentary coffee in lobby. Restaurant 7 am-6 pm. Ck-out 11 am. Business servs avail. Bellhops. Refrigerators. Balconies. On beach. Cr cds: A, DS, MC, V.

⊡ ⚓ ⇌ ⊠ 🔥

★ **NASSAU MOTEL.** 6002 Coastal Hwy (21842). 410/524-6451. 62 rms, 3 story, 42 kits. No elvtr. July-late Aug: S, D $102-$120; each addl $6; higher rates wkends; lower rates Apr-June, late Aug-Oct. Closed rest of yr. Crib $5. TV; cable (premium). Pool. Coffee in rms. Restaurant opp 6 am-11 pm. Ck-out 11 am. Refrigerators, microwaves. Grills. Sun deck. On ocean, beach. Cr cds: A, DS, MC, V.

⊡ ⇌ ⊠ 🔥

★★ **PHILLIPS BEACH PLAZA HOTEL.** 1301 N Atlantic Ave (21842). 410/289-9121; fax 410/289-3041; toll-free 800/492-5834. www.phillipsbeach plaza.com. 96 units, 5 story, 26 kits., 8 3-bedrm kit. suites. July-late Aug: S, D $119-$174; each addl $20; kit. units $154-$194; kit. suites $200-$230; $20 surcharge wkends; package plans; lower rates rest of yr. Crib $10. TV; cable. Restaurant 8 am-1 pm, 5-

9:30 pm. Bar 5 pm-2 am; entertainment 6-11 pm. Ck-out 11 am. Business servs avail. Bellhops. Shopping arcade. On ocean. Cr cds: A, C, D, DS, MC, V.

★ **QUALITY INN.** 3301 Atlantic Ave (21843). 410/289-1234; toll-free 800/228-5151. www.qualityinn.com. 109 units, 5 story, 92 kits., 15 suites. June-Aug: S, D $158-$235; suites $250-$330; lower rates rest of yr. Crib $5. TV; cable, VCR (movies). 2 pools, 1 indoor; wading pool, whirlpool. Restaurant 7:30 am-2 pm. Restaurant nearby. Ck-out 11 am. Sundries. Coin lndry. Business servs avail. Gift shop. Exercise equipt; sauna. Game rm. Some in-rm whirlpools. Balconies. Cr cds: A, C, D, DS, MC, V.

★ **QUALITY INN.** 5400 Coastal Hwy (21842). 410/524-7200; fax 410/723-0018; res 800/228-5151. www.quality inn.com. 126 kit. units, 3-5 story. Memorial Day-Labor Day: kit. units $79-$239; each addl $7; under 6 free; wkly rates; package plans; higher rates hols; lower rates rest of yr. Crib free. TV; cable (premium), VCR (movies). 2 pools, 1 indoor; wading pool, whirlpool. Playground. Restaurant 8 am-9 pm. Bar 11 am-11 pm. Ck-out 11 am. Free lndry facilities. Business servs avail. In-rm modem link. Bellhops (summer). Tennis. Exercise equipt; saunas. Game rm. Lawn games. Private patios, balconies. Picnic tables, grills. On ocean, swimming beach. Tropical atrium. Cr cds: A, D, DS, MC, V.

★★ **RAMADA LIMITED OCEAN-FRONT.** Oceanfront and 32nd St (21842). 410/289-6444; fax 410/289-0108; res 800/837-3589. www.ramada. com. 76 kit. units, 3 story. No elvtr. July-Aug: S, D $174-$189; each addl $7; surcharge off-season wkends; lower rates rest of yr. Crib free. TV; cable (premium), VCR (movies). Pool; wading pool. Complimentary continental bkfst. Complimentary coffee in lobby. Ck-out 11 am. Guest lndry. Balconies overlook beach. Picnic area. Cr cds: A, C, D, DS, ER, MC, V.

★ **SAFARI MOTEL.** 1-13th St (21842). 410/289-6411; toll-free 800/787-2183. 46 rms in 2 buildings, 3 and 4 story. July-Aug: S, D $119; under 14 free; lower rates mid-Apr-June, Sept-Oct. Closed rest of yr. Crib free. Pet accepted, some restrictions; $9/day. TV; cable (premium). Restaurant opp from 8 am. Ck-out 11 am. Bellhops. Balconies. On ocean. Cr cds: A, C, D, DS, MC, V.

★ **SAHARA MOTEL.** 19th St & Boardwalk (21842). 410/289-8101; fax 410/289-2894; toll-free 800/638-1600. www.saharamotel.com. 161 rms in 4 bldgs, 3 and 4 story, 5 kits. Elvtr in Tower bldg. Late June-mid-Sept: S, D $78-$140; each addl $6; kit. units $102-$138; lower rates late Apr-late June, late Sept. Closed rest of yr. Crib $6. TV. 2 pools. Restaurant 6 am-3 pm. Ck-out 11 am. Refrigerators. Some balconies. On beach. Cr cds: MC, V.

★ **TIDES.** 7100 Coastal Hwy (21843). 410/524-7100; fax 410/289-3039; toll-free 800/638-1600. www.bestmotels. com. 54 kit. units, 3 story. No elvtr. Late June-late Aug: S, D $99; each addl $6; under 6 free; higher rates: wkends and hols (3-day min), July-Aug wkdays (2-day min), Memorial Day and Labor Day; lower rates May-late June and Sept. Closed rest of yr. Crib $5. TV; cable. Pool. Coffee in rms. Restaurant nearby. Ck-out 11 am. Bellhops (in season). Some balconies. Cr cds: MC, V.

Hotels

★★★ **CLARION FONTAINEBLEAU.** 10100 Coastal Hwy (21842). 410/524-3535; fax 410/524-3834. www.clarion inn.com. 250 rms, 16 story, 8 kits. June-Aug: S, D $230-$300; each addl $15; suites, kit. units $350; studio rms $320; condos $1,600-$2,700/wkly; under 17 free; higher rates hol wkends (3-day min); lower rates rest of yr. Crib $15. Pet accepted; $20/day. TV; cable (premium), VCR avail. Heated pool; whirlpool, poolside serv in season, lifeguard. Coffee in rms. Restaurant 7 am-11 pm. Bar to 2 am; entertainment. Ck-out 11 am. Meeting rms.

Business center. In-rm modem link. Beauty shop. Airport, bus depot transportation. Tennis privileges. Golf privileges. Exercise equipt; sauna, steam rm. Game rm. Refrigerators. Balconies. On ocean, beach. Cr cds: A, C, D, DS, MC, V.

★ ★ ★ **COCONUT MALORIE HOTEL RESORT.** *200 59th St (21842). 410/723-6100; fax 410/524-9327; toll-free 800/767-6060. www. coconutmalorie.com.* 85 units, 5 story. 52 suites. Memorial Day-Labor Day: S, D $164-$290; each addl $15; wkly rates; lower rates rest of yr. Crib $15. TV; cable (premium), VCR avail. Pool; poolside serv. Complimentary coffee in rms. Restaurant adj 11 am-11 pm. Ck-out noon. Meeting rms. Business servs avail. In-rm modem link. Concierge. Health club privileges. Refrigerators; many bathrm phones. Balconies. Original Haitian art; antique collection. Footbridge over marsh to dining facilities. Cr cds: A, C, D, MC, V.

★ ★ ★ **THE LIGHTHOUSE CLUB HOTEL.** *56th St in the Bay (21842). 410/524-5400; fax 410/524-3928; res 888/371-5400. www.fagers.com.* 23 rms, 3 story. No elvtr. Mid-June-Labor Day (2-day min): S, D $184-$285; each addl $15; wkly rates; lower rates rest of yr. Crib $15. TV; cable (premium), VCR. Pool privileges. Complimentary continental bkfst, coffee in rms. Restaurant adj 11 am-11 pm. Bar 11-2 am; entertainment. Ck-out noon. Meeting rm. Business servs avail. In-rm modem link. Health club privileges. Bathrm phones, in-rm whirlpools, refrigerators, wet bars; some fireplaces. Balconies. Cr cds: A, C, D, DS, MC, V.

★ ★ ★ **PRINCESS ROYALE OCEANFRONT HOTEL.** *9100 Coastal Hwy (21842). 410/524-7777; fax 410/524-7787; toll-free 800/476-9253. www. princessroyale.com.* 310 kit. suites, 5 story. Mid-June-Labor Day: D $109-$299; under 12 free; wkly rates; golf plans; lower rates rest of yr. Crib $10. TV; cable. Indoor pool; whirlpool, poolside serv. Complimentary coffee in rms. Restaurant 7-2 am. Bar 11-2 am; entertainment. Ck-out 11 am. Coin lndry. Convention facilities.

Business center. Gift shop. Beauty shop. Lighted tennis. 18-hole golf privileges, pro, putting green, driving range. Exercise equipt; sauna. Health club privileges. Game rm. Some in-rm whirlpools. Balconies. On ocean; swimming beach, ocean deck, private boardwalk. Most suites with ocean view. Cr cds: A, C, D, DS, MC, V.

B&Bs/Small Inns

★ ★ ★ **BERLIN ATLANTIC.** *2 N Main St, Berlin (21811). 410/641-0189; fax 410/641-4928; toll-free 800/814-7672. www.atlantichotel.com.* 17 rms, 5 with shower only, 3 story. S, D $75-$140; golf plans. Crib free. TV; cable. Complimentary full bkfst. Dining rm 6-9 pm; Fri, Sat to 10 pm. Bar noon-1 am. Ck-out 11 am, ck-in 3 pm. 18-hole golf privileges, greens fee $30-$35, pro, putting green. Porch on each floor. Restored Victorian hotel (1895); antiques. 2nd-floor parlor. Cr cds: A, DS, MC, V.

★ ★ **MERRY SHERWOOD PLANTATION.** *8909 Worcester Hwy, Berlin (21811). 410/641-2112; fax 410/641-9528; toll-free 800/660-0358. www. merrysherwood.com.* 8 rms, 6 with bath. No rm phones. Mid-May-mid-Oct: S, D $150-$175; lower rates rest of yr. Children over 8 yrs only. Complimentary full bkfst; afternoon refreshments. Restaurant nearby. Ck-out 11 am, ck-in 2 pm. Some fireplaces. Built in 1859; on grounds of former plantation; large variety of trees and shrubs. Totally nonsmoking. Cr cds: MC, V.

Restaurants

★ ★ **BONFIRE.** *71st St (21842). 410/524-7171.* Hrs: 5-10 pm; from 4 pm in season; early-bird dinner 4-5 pm. Closed Mon-Thurs in winter. Res accepted. Bar to 2 am. Dinner $14.95-$26.95. Seafood buffet $21.95. Child's menu. Specializes in steak, prime rib, seafood. Cr cds: A, C, D, MC, V.

★ ★ **EMBERS.** *2305 Philadelphia Ave (21842). 410/289-3322. www.embers. com.* Hrs: 2-10 pm; also 8 am-noon

Memorial Day wkend-Labor Day. Closed Dec-Feb. Res accepted. Bar to 2 am. Buffet: bkfst $7.99. Dinner $14-$25. Seafood buffet $22.95. Child's menu. Specializes in fresh seafood, steak, prime rib. Family-owned. Cr cds: A, C, DS, MC, V.
D

★★★ **FAGER'S ISLAND.** *201 60th St (21842). 410/524-5500. www.fagers. com.* Hrs: 11 am-12am. Res accepted. Bar. Lunch $3.75-$10.95, dinner $17-$25. Specializes in seafood, beef, Pacific rim dishes. Entertainment. View of bay. Oudoor dining in season. Cr cds: A, D, DS, MC, V.
D

★★ **HANNA'S MARINA DECK.** *306 Dorchester St (21842). 410/289-4411. www.marinadeckrestaurant.com.* Hrs: 11 am-11 pm. Closed mid-Oct-Easter. Bar. Lunch $4.95-$7.95, dinner $7.95-$27.95. Child's menu. Specializes in fish, lobster. On waterfront. Cr cds: A, DS, V.
D

★★★ **HARRISON'S HARBOR WATCH.** *806 S Boardwalk (21842). 410/289-5121.* Hrs: 5-10 pm; July-Aug from 11:30 am. Closed Mon-Thurs Dec-Mar. Res accepted. Bar. Wine list. Dinner $8.95-$24.95. Child's menu. Specializes in fresh seafood, fish. Raw bar. Own breads. View of inlet overlooking Assateague Island. Cr cds: A, D, DS, MC, V.
D

★★★ **HOBBIT.** *81st St and Bay (21842). 410/524-8100.* Hrs: 11 am-midnight; early-bird dinner 5-6 pm. Closed Dec 24-25. Res accepted. Contemporary American menu. Bar. Wine list. Lunch $3.95-$10.95, dinner $15.95-$24.95. Child's menu. Specializes in beef, veal, seafood. Own baking. Outdoor dining. View of bay. Family-owned. Cr cds: A, DS, MC, V.
D

★★ **OCEAN CLUB.** *49th St (21842). 410/524-7500.* Hrs: 11-2 am; early-bird dinner 5-7 pm. Closed Dec 25; Mon, Tues off-season; also 2 wks in Jan. Res accepted. Bar. Bkfst $3.95-$9.95, lunch $4.25-$10, dinner $12.95-$26.95. Child's menu. Specializes in seafood. Entertainment Apr-Oct; rest of yr, Wed-Sun. Out-

door dining. On ocean. Cr cds: A, MC, V.
D

★★ **PHILLIPS CRAB HOUSE.** *2004 Philadelphia Ave (21842). 410/289-6821. www.phillipsoc.com.* Hrs: noon-10 pm. Closed Nov-Mar. Serv bar. Lunch, dinner $4-$25. Seafood buffet $21.95. Child's menu. Specializes in crab dishes, fresh seafood. Family-owned. Cr cds: A, D, DS, MC, V.
D

★★ **PHILLIPS SEAFOOD HOUSE.** *14101 Coastal Hwy (21842). 410/250-1200. www.phillipsseafoodhouse.com.* Hrs: noon-10 pm; Fri, Sat to 11 pm; off-season 5-9 pm. Closed last wk Nov-Feb. Bar to 2 am. Lunch $4.95-$8.95, dinner $8.95-$22.95. Child's menu. Specializes in fresh seafood, crab, lobster. Pianist exc Mon; off-season Thurs-Sun. Cr cds: A, D, DS, MC, V.
D

Pikesville

(X-0) *See also Baltimore*

Pop 29,123 **Area code** 410 **Zip** 21208

Motels/Motor Lodges

★ **COMFORT INN.** *10 Wooded Way (21208). 410/484-7700; fax 410/653-1516; res 800/732-2458. www.comfortinn.com.* 103 rms, 2-3 story. No elvtr. S, D $59-$89; under 18 free; wkly, monthly rates. Crib free. Pet accepted. TV; cable (premium). Pool; wading pool, lifeguard. Complimentary continental bkfst. Coffee in rms. Restaurant adj 6:30 am-11:30 pm. Ck-out 11 am. Coin lndry. Meeting rms. Business servs avail. In-rm modem link. Valet serv Mon-Fri. Health club privileges. Microwaves avail. Cr cds: A, C, D, DS, ER, JCB, MC, V.
D SC

★ **RAMADA INN.** *1721 Reisterstown Rd (21208). 410/486-5600; fax 410/484-9377; toll-free 800/272-7232. www.ramada.com.* 108 rms, 2 story. S, D

$69; under 18 free; higher rates Preakness. Crib free. Pet accepted. TV; cable (premium). Pool; poolside serv, lifeguard. Restaurant 6 am-1 pm, 5-10 pm; Sat, Sun from 7 am. Rm serv. Bar 5 pm-midnight. Ck-out noon. Meeting rms. Business servs avail. Valet serv. Health club privileges. Some refrigerators; microwaves avail. Cr cds: A, C, D, DS, ER, JCB, MC, V.

D ⊜ ⊠ ⊠ ⊠ SC

Hotel

★★★ **HILTON.** *1726 Reisterstown Rd (21208). 410/653-1100; fax 410/415-6232; toll-free 800/445-8667. www. hilton.com.* 171 rms, 5 story. S $99-$154; D $102-$164; each addl $15; suites $300-$399; wknd plans; family rates. Crib $10. TV; cable (premium), VCR avail (movies). Pool; lifeguard. Coffee in rms. Restaurant 7 am-11 pm. Bar 11-1 am. Ck-out noon. Meeting rms. Business servs avail. Bellhops. Valet serv. Gift shop. Barber, beauty shop. Airport transportation. Tennis privileges. Exercise equipt. Bathrm phones; microwaves avail. Cr cds: A, C, D, DS, ER, MC, V.

D ⊠ ⊠ ⊠ ⊠ SC

B&B/Small Inn

★★★ **GRAMERCY BED AND BREAKFAST.** *1400 Greenspring Valley Rd, Stevenson (21153). 410/486-2405; fax 410/486-1765; res 800/553-3404. www.gramercymansion.com.* 10 rms, 3 story, 2 suites. S, D $155-$260; each addl $25; suites $250. Crib $10. TV; VCR (movies). Pool. Complimentary full bkfst. Ck-out noon, ck-in 3 pm. Business servs avail. In-rm modem link. Tennis. Lawn games. Picnic tables. Mansion (1902) on 45-acre wooded estate. Flower, herb gardens. Totally nonsmoking. Cr cds: A, DS, MC, V.

⊠ ⊠ ⊠ ⊠

Restaurants

★★ **DUE.** *25 Crossroads Dr, Owings Mills (21117). 410/356-4147.* Hrs: 5:30-10 pm; Fri, Sat to 11 pm; Sun 5-9 pm. Closed hols. Res accepted. Italian menu. Bar. A la carte entrees: dinner $9.95-$24.95. Specializes in

pasta, veal, chicken. Comtemporary decor. Cr cds: A, C, D, MC, V.

D

★★★ **LINWOOD'S CAFE.** *25 Crossroads Dr, Owings Mills (21117). 410/356-3030.* Hrs: 11:30 am-3 pm, 5:30-10 pm; Fri, Sat to 11 pm; Sun 5-9 pm. Closed hols. Res accepted; required Fri, Sat. Bar. A la carte entrees: lunch $4.95-$14.95, dinner $9.95-$27.95. Specializes in chicken, seafood, steak. Formal decor. Cr cds: A, C, D, MC, V.

D

Pocomoke City

(F-7) *See also Crisfield*

Founded 1670 **Pop** 4,098 **Elev** 22 ft
Area code 410 and 443 **Zip** 21851
Information Pocomoke Chamber of Commerce, 144 Market St; 410/957-1919
Web chamber@pocomoke.com

Motel/Motor Lodge

★ **QUALITY INN.** *825 Ocean Hwy (21851). 410/957-1300; fax 410/957-9329; res 800/228-5151. www.quality inn.com.* 64 rms. Memorial Day-Labor Day: S $60-$75; D $65-$82; each addl $5; under 18 free; higher rates Pony Penning. Crib free. Pet accepted. TV; cable (premium). Pool; wading pool. Complimentary continental bkfst. Ck-out 11 am. Business servs avail. In-rm modem link. Some in-rm whirlpools, refrigerators. Picnic tables, grills. Cr cds: A, C, D, DS, ER, JCB, MC, V.

D ⊜ ⊠ ⊠ ⊠ ⊠

B&B/Small Inn

★★ **RIVER HOUSE INN.** *201 E Market St, Snow Hill (21863). 410/632-2722; fax 410/632-2866. www.river houseinn.com.* 8 rms, 2 with shower only, 3 story, 1 guest house. No elvtrs. No rm phones. Apr-Oct: S, D $100-$175; each addl $20; suite $100; guest house $160; under 16 free; golf rates; package plans; wkends (2-day min); lower rates rest of yr. Pet accepted, some restrictions. 18-hole golf privileges, greens fee, pro. Lawn games. Some refrigerators, microwaves. In-rm whirlpool in suite. Fireplaces. On river. Built in 1860. Totally nonsmoking. Cr cds: A, DS, MC, V.

Restaurant

★ **UPPER DECK.** *1245 Ocean Hwy (21851). 410/957-3166.* Hrs: 11 am-10 pm; Sun noon-9 pm. Res accepted. Bar to 11 am; Sun to 10 pm. Lunch $4.95-$5.95, dinner $7.50-$20. Child's menu. Specializes in local seafood, steak. Own desserts. Antiques. Cr cds: MC, V.

Rockville

(C-5) *See also Gaithersburg*

Pop 47,388 **Elev** 451 ft **Area code** 240 and 301

Information Chamber of Commerce, 250 Hungerford Dr, Suite L10, 20850; 301/424-9300

Web www.rockvillechamber.org

Second-largest city in the state of Maryland, Rockville is the seat of Montgomery County, located at the north edge of the District of Columbia. The Great Falls of the Potomac are nine miles south off MD 189. This series of small falls was pretty but unnavigable, so the Chesapeake and Ohio Canal (see CHESAPEAKE AND OHIO CANAL NATIONAL HISTORICAL PARK) was built from Washington, D.C., to Cumberland to simplify travel. Stone locks and levels are still visible. The graves of F. Scott and Zelda Fitzgerald are in St. Mary's Cemetery.

What to See and Do

Beall-Dawson House. (1815) Federal architecture; period furnishings; library; museum shop; 19th-century doctor's office. Tours guided by docents. (Tues-Sat; also first Sun of month; closed hols) 103 W Montgomery Ave. Phone 301/762-1492. ¢

Special Event

Hometown Holidays. Family entertainment. Memorial Day wkend. Phone 301/424-9300.

Motels/Motor Lodges

★★ **COURTYARD BY MARRIOTT.** *2500 Research Blvd (20850). 301/670-6700; fax 301/670-9023. www.courtyard.com.* 147 rms, 2 story, 13 suites. S, D $120-$135; suites $135-$145; under 12 free; wkly rates. Crib free. TV; cable (premium). Indoor pool; whirlpool, lifeguard. Complimentary coffee. Restaurant 6:30 am-2 pm, 5-10 pm; Sat 7-11 am; Sun 7 am-2 pm. Rm serv 5-10 pm. Bar 5-11 pm. Ck-out 1 pm. Coin lndry. Meeting rms. Business servs avail. In-rm modem link. Valet serv. Sundries. Exercise equipt. Balconies. Refrigerators avail. Cr cds: A, C, D, DS, MC, V.

★ **QUALITY SUITES.** *3 Research Ct (20850). 301/840-0200; fax 301/258-0160; toll-free 800/228-5151. www.qualityinn.com.* 124 rms, 3 story, 66 kit. suites. S, D $99.95-$129.95; each addl $10; kit. suites $109.95-$139.95; under 18 free; wkend rates. Crib free. TV; cable (premium), VCR avail. Complimentary full bkfst, coffee in rms. Restaurant nearby. Ck-out noon. Meeting rms. Business center. Valet serv. Sundries. Gift shop. Coin lndry. Exercise equipt. Pool; lifeguard. Refrigerators, microwaves, wet bars. Cr cds: A, C, D, DS, MC, V.

★★★ **WOODFIN SUITES HOTEL.** *1380 Piccard Dr (20850). 301/590-9880; fax 301/590-9614; toll-free 800/237-8811. www.woodfinsuiteshotel.com.* 203 suites, 3 story. S, D $165-$230; each addl $15; 2-bedrm suites $275; under 12 free. Crib free. Pet accepted, some restrictions. TV; cable (premium). Pool; whirlpool, lifeguard. Complimentary full bkfst. Restaurant 6-9 am, wkends 7-10 am. Bar 5-10 pm Mon-Thurs. Ck-out noon. Meeting rms. Business center. In-rm modem link. Valet serv. Sundries. Exercise equipt. Refrigerators, microwaves. Cr cds: A, C, D, DS, ER, JCB, MC, V.

Hotel

★ ★ **DOUBLETREE.** *1750 Rockville Pike (20852).* 301/468-1100; fax 301/468-0308; res 800/222-8733. *www.doubletreehotels.com.* 315 rms, 8 story. S, D $159-$169; each addl $10; suites $195-$325; under 19 free; wkly, wkend rates. Crib free. TV; cable (premium). Indoor/outdoor pool; whirlpool, lifeguard. Coffee in rms. Restaurant 6 am-11 pm. Bar from 11 am; Fri, Sat to 1 am. Ck-out noon. Convention facilities. Business center. In-rm modem link. Gift shop. Beauty shop. Covered valet parking. Exercise equipt: sauna. Game rm. Refrigerators, microwaves avail. 8-story atrium; 20-ft waterfall. Gazebo. Luxury level. Cr cds: A, D, DS, MC, V.
D ⊵ 🏌 ⊿ 🐾 🏃

Restaurants

★ **A AND J.** *1319-C Rockville Pike (20852).* 301/251-7878. Hrs: 11:30 am-9 pm; Fri, Sat to 9:30 pm. Chinese menu. A la carte entrees: lunch $4.85-$9, dinner $6.25-$9. Specializes in Northern Chinese dim sum. Casual decor. Totally nonsmoking. Cr cds: A, MC, V.

★ ★ **ADDIE'S.** *11120 Rockville Pike (20852).* 301/881-0081. Hrs: 11:30 am-2:30 pm, 5:30-9:30 pm; Fri to 10 pm; Sat noon to 3 pm, 5:30-10 pm. Closed Sun; Jan 1, Thanksgiving, Dec 25. Res accepted Mon-Thurs dinner. Regional American menu. Bar. Lunch $6.50-$10.95, dinner $11.95-$20. Child's menu. Specializes in seasonal American dishes. Own pastries. Outdoor dining. Eclectic decor; collection of whimsical clocks; woodburning grill. Cr cds: A, D, MC, V.
D

★ ★ **ANDALUCIA.** *12300 Wilkens Ave (20852).* 301/770-1880. Hrs: 11:30 am-2:30 pm, 5:30-10 pm; Sat 5:30-10:30 pm; Sun 4:30-9:30 pm. Closed Mon; Jan 1. Res accepted; required Fri, Sat dinner. Spanish menu. Serv bar. A la carte entrees: lunch $7.50-$10.95, dinner $12.50-$19.95. Specialties: paella Valenciana, zarzuela costa del sol, fresh seafood. Own desserts. Entertainment Thurs. Mediterranean decor; many plants. Totally nonsmoking. Cr cds: A, D, DS, MC, V.
D

★ ★ **BOMBAY BISTRO.** *98 W Montgomery Ave (20850).* 301/762-8798. *www.bombaybistro.com.* Hrs: 11 am-2:30 pm, 5-9:30 pm; Fri, Sat to 10 pm; Sun noon-3 pm, 5-9:30 pm. Closed Thanksgiving, Labor Day. Indian menu. Wine, beer. A la carte entrees: lunch, dinner $6.95-$15.95. Buffet lunch: $6.95-$8.95. Specializes in vegetarian, tandoori dishes. Casual decor. Cr cds: A, DS, MC, V.
D

★ ★ **COPELAND'S OF NEW ORLEANS.** *1584 Rockville Pike (20852).* 301/230-0968. Hrs: 11 am-midnight. Closed Dec 25. Bar. Lunch $6-$12, dinner $7-$15. Child's menu. Specializes in seafood, Creole and Cajun dishes. Art Deco decor. Cr cds: A, D, DS, MC, V.
D

★ ★ **IL PIZZICO.** *15209 Frederick Rd (20850).* 301/309-0610. Hrs: 11 am-2:30 pm, 5-9:30 pm; Fri to 10 pm; Sat 5-10 pm. Closed Sun; hols. Italian menu. Bar. Lunch $6.95-$10.95, dinner $8.95-$13.95. Specializes in pasta, seafood. Italian decor. Cr cds: A, MC, V.
D

★ ★ ★ **NORMANDIE FARM.** *10710 Falls Rd, Potomac (20854).* 301/983-8838. *www.popovers.com.* Hrs: 11:30 am-2:30 pm, 6-10 pm; Sun 5-9 pm; Sun brunch 11 am-2 pm. Closed Mon. Res accepted. French menu. Bar. Lunch $6.50-$12.50, dinner $14-$25. Sun brunch $18.50. Specializes in seafood, veal. Entertainment Thur-Sat. French Provincial decor. Cr cds: A, DS, MC, V.
D

★ ★ ★ **OLD ANGLER'S INN.** *10801 MacArthur Blvd, Potomac (20854).* 301/299-9097. *www.oldanglersinn.com.* Hrs: noon-2:30 pm, 6-10:30 pm. Closed Mon. Bar. Wine list. A la carte entrees: lunch $12-$16, dinner $22-$29. Prix fixe: dinner $55-$75. Specializes in seafood, lamb. Patio dining overlooking wooded area. Stone inn (1860); fireplace. Family-owned. Cr cds: A, MC, V.

★ **RED HOT & BLUE.** *16811 Crabbs Branch Way (20855).* 301/948-7333. *www.redhotandblue.com.* Hrs: 11 am-10 pm; Fri to 11 pm; Sat noon-11 pm; Sun from noon. Closed Thanksgiving, Dec 25. Bar. Lunch, dinner

$5.99-$13.99. Child's menu. Specializes in Memphis pit barbecue, ribs. Outdoor dining. Casual deéor; blues memorabilia. Totally nonsmoking. Cr cds: A, D, MC, V.

D

★ **RICCIUTI'S.** *3308 Olney-Sandy Spring Rd, Olney (20832). 301/570-3388. www.ricciutis.com.* Hrs: 11:30 am-9 pm; Fri, Sat to 10 pm; Sun 4-9 pm. Closed hols. Italian menu. Wine, beer. Lunch $3.95-$5.50, dinner $5.25-$10.75. Child's menu. Specialties: calzone, stromboli, chocolate pizza. Outdoor dining. Italian decor. Totally nonsmoking. Cr cds: A, DS, MC, V.

D

★ **SEVEN SEAS.** *1776 E Jefferson St (20852). 301/770-5020.* Hrs: 11:30-1 am. Closed Thanksgiving. Res accepted. Chinese, Japanese menu. Bar. Lunch $3.95-$6.50, dinner $7.25-$16.95. Specializes in Szechwan, Taiwan, Shanghai cuisine. Sushi bar. Chinese artwork. Cr cds: A, D, DS, MC, V.

D

★ **SILVER DINER.** *11806 Rockville Pike (20852). 301/770-1444. www.silverdiner.com.* Hrs: 7-2 am; Fri, Sat to 3 am; early-bird dinner Mon-Fri 4-6 pm. Closed Dec 25. Serv bar. Bkfst $3.99-$5.99, lunch $5.99-$7.99, dinner $5.99-$9.99. Child's menu. Specialties: meatloaf, chicken pot pie, turkey. 1950s-style diner; jukeboxes. Servers dressed in period clothing. Cr cds: A, C, D, DS, MC, V.

D SC

★★ **TASTE OF SAIGON.** *410 Hungerford Dr (20850). 301/424-7222. www.tasteofsaigon.com.* Hrs: 11 am-10 pm; Fri, Sat to 11 pm; Sun 11 am-9:30 pm. Closed Thanksgiving, Dec 25. Res accepted. Vietnamese menu. Bar. A la carte entrees: lunch $5.95-$14.95, dinner $7.95-$16.95. Specialties: black pepper soft shell crab and shrimp, pepper Saigon steak. Outdoor dining. Contemporary decor. Cr cds: A, D, DS, MC, V.

D SC ⊣

★★ **THAT'S AMORE.** *15201 Shady Grove Rd (20850). 301/670-9666. www.thatsamore.com.* Hrs: 11:30 am-10:30 pm; Fri to midnight; Sat 4 pm-midnight; Sun 4-9:30 pm. Closed Labor Day, Thanksgiving, Dec 25. Italian menu. Bar. A la carte entrees: lunch $5.95-$9.95, dinner $18-$22. Specializes in pasta, veal, chicken. Stained-glass windows. Early 20th-century mens' club atmosphere. Cr cds: A, D, DS, MC, V.

D SC ⊣

Unrated Dining Spot

HARD TIMES CAFE. *1117 Nelson St (20850). 301/294-9720. www.hardtimes.com.* Hrs: 11:30 am-10 pm; Fri, Sat to 11 pm; Sun noon-9 pm. Closed Thanksgiving, Dec 25. Bar. A la carte entrees: lunch, dinner $4.50-$6. Child's menu. Specializes in chili, vegetarian dishes. Cr cds: A, MC, V.

SC ⊣

St. Mary's City

(E-6) *See also Leonardtown, Waldorf*

Settled 1634 **Pop** 1,300 **Elev** 36 ft
Area code 240 and 301 **Zip** 20686
Information St. Mary's County Division of Tourism, 23115 Leonard Hall Dr, PO Box 653, Leonardtown 20650; 301/475-4411 or 800/327-9023
Web www.co.saint-marys.md.us

Maryland's first colonists bought a Native American village on this site upon their arrival in the New World under Leonard Calvert. The settlement was the capital and hub of the area until 1694, when the Colonial capital was moved to Annapolis. The town gradually disappeared. The city and county are still rich in historical attractions.

What to See and Do

Historic St. Mary's City. Outdoor museum at site of Maryland's first capital (1634) incl reconstructed State House (1676), replica of the original capitol building; other exhibits include the *Maryland Dove*, replica of a 17th-century ship, and archaeological exhibits. Also seasonal living history programs, a 17th-century tobacco plantation, reconstructed 17th-century inn; visitor center, outdoor cafe. Visitor center (daily; closed Jan 1, Thanksgiving, Dec 25); outdoor museum (fourth wkend Mar-Nov, Wed-Sun). MD 5 and Rosecroft Rd. Phone 301/862-0990. Also here is

Margaret Brent Memorial. Gazebo overlooking the river; memorial to the woman who, being a wealthy landowner, requested the right to vote in the Maryland Assembly in 1648, in order to settle Leonard Calvert's affairs after his death.

Leonard Calvert Monument. Monument to Maryland's first Colonial governor. Trinity Churchyard.

Point Lookout State Park. Site of Confederate Monument, the only memorial erected by US government to honor POWs who died in Point Lookout Prison Camp during Civil War (3,384 died here). Swimming, fishing, boating; hiking, picnicking, improved camping (Apr-Oct; self-contained camping units yr-round). Nature center. Civil War museum. Standard fees. (May-Sept, wkends) 13 mi S on MD 5. Phone 301/872-5688. ¢¢

Confederate Monument at Point Lookout State Park, St. Mary's City

Special Events

Maryland Days. Boat rides, seafood, 17th-century militia musters. Third wkend Mar.

Crab Festival. Steamed crabs, other seafood and nonseafood dishes. Arts and crafts, antique and classic car show. First Sun June.

Restaurant

★ **ALOHA.** *2025 MD 235, California (20619). 301/862-4838.* Hrs: 10:30 am-10 pm; Fri to 11 pm; Sat noon-11 pm; Sun noon-9:30 pm. Closed Thanksgiving, Dec 25. Chinese, Japanese menu. Bar. Lunch $4.25-$5.25, dinner $5.95-$19. Complete meals: lunch $4.95, dinner $7.25-$9.95. Buffet: lunch $5.99, dinner $7.99. Child's menu. Specializes in Szechwan, Hunan dishes. Sushi bar. Polynesian atmosphere. Cr cds: A, C, DS, MC, V.
D ◨

Unrated Dining Spot

EVANS SEAFOOD. *16680 Piney Point Rd, St. George Island (20674). 301/994-2299. www.evansseafood.com.* Hrs: 4-10 pm; Sat from noon; Sun noon-9 pm. Closed Mon. Bar. Lunch $5.50-$13.95, dinner $8.95-$21.95. Child's menu. Specializes in steak, seafood. View of the Potomac River. Family-owned. Cr cds: MC, V.
D ◨

St. Michael's (D-6)

Pop 1,193 **Elev** 7 ft **Area code** 410 **Zip** 21663

Information Talbot County Chamber of Commerce, PO Box 1366, Easton

Plaza Ste 53, Easton 21601; 410/822-4653

Web www.talbottchamber.org

Chartered in 1804, St. Michael's has become a boating and tourist center with its abundance of shops, marinas, restaurants, bed-and-breakfasts, and country inns. It is a town with many Federal- and Victorian-period buildings.

What to See and Do

Chesapeake Bay Maritime Museum. Waterside museum consists of nine buildings. Incl historic lighthouse, floating exhibits, boat-building shop with working exhibit, ship models, small boats; paintings; waterfowl exhibits; workboats and mechanical propulsion. Special events throughout the yr (see SPECIAL EVENT). (Daily) Mill St. Phone 410/745-2916. ¢¢¢

The Footbridge. Only remaining bridge of three that once connected the town with areas across the harbor. Joins Navy Point to Cherry St.

The *Patriot*. A one-hr narrated cruise on Miles River. Four trips daily. (Apr-Oct) Berthed at Chesapeake Bay Maritime Museum. Phone 410/745-3100.

St. Mary's Square. Public square laid out in 1770 by Englishman James Braddock. Several buildings date to the early 1800s, incl the Cannonball House and Dr. Miller's Farmhouse.

The Ship's Carpenter Bell was cast in 1842; across from the bell stand two cannons, one dating from the Revolution, the other from the War of 1812. Also here is

St. Mary's Square Museum. Mid-19th-century home of "half-timber" construction; one of the earliest buildings in St. Michael's. Exhibits of historical and local interest. (First wkend May-last wkend Oct, Sat and Sun; also by appt) Inquire about the town walking tour brochures. Contact the Town Office. Phone 410/745-9535.

Special Event

Mid-Atlantic Maritime Festival. Chesapeake Bay Maritime Museum. Nautical celebration with fly-fishing demonstration, skipjack races, boat building contest, boat parade, seafood festival cooking contest. Three days mid-May. Phone 410/745-2916 or 410/822-5553.

Motel/Motor Lodge

★★ **BEST WESTERN ST. MICHAEL'S MOTOR INN.** *1228 S Talbot St (21663). 410/745-3333; fax 410/745-2906; toll-free 800/528-1234. www.bestwestern.com.* 93 rms, 2 story. May-mid-Nov: S $75-$96; D $87-$107; each addl $8; under 18 free; lower rates rest of yr. TV; cable (premium). 2 pools. Complimentary con-

Chesapeake Bay Maritime Museum, St. Michael's

tinental bkfst. Restaurant adj 11 am-11 pm. Ck-out 11 am. Meeting rms. Business servs avail. Cr cds: A, C, D, DS, MC, V.

D 〰 ⊠ 🔥 SC

Hotel

★ ★ ★ **ST. MICHAEL'S HARBOUR INN AND MARINA.** *101 N Harbor Rd (21663). 410/745-9001; fax 410/745-9150; toll-free 800/332-8994. www.harbourinn.com.* 46 units, 3 story, 38 suites. May-Oct: S, D, suites $169-$429; under 18 free; higher rates wkends (2-day min); lower rates rest of yr. Crib $10. TV; cable (premium). Pool; whirlpool, poolside serv. Coffee in rms. Restaurant. Bar 11 am-10 pm. Ck-out noon. Coin lndry. Meeting rms. Business servs avail. Gift shop. Exercise equipt. Health club privileges. Refrigerator in suites; some in-rm whirlpools. Some balconies. Picnic tables. 60-slip marina. Cr cds: A, C, D, DS, MC, V.

D 〰 🔼 ⊠ 🔥

Resorts

★ ★ **HARBOURTOWNE GOLF RESORT AND CONFERENCE CENTER.** *Rte 33 and Martingham Dr, St. Michaels (21663). 410/745-9066; fax 410/745-9124; toll-free 800/446-9066. www.harbortowne.com.* 111 rms, 1-2 story. Mar-Nov: S, D $155-$175; each addl $10; suites $225-$250; under 12 free; golf plans; lower rates rest of yr. TV; cable (premium), VCR avail. Crib free. Pool; poolside serv, lifeguard. Dining rm 7 am-10 pm. Ck-out 11 am, ck-in 3 pm. Grocery, package store 3 mi. Meeting rms. Business center. In-rm modem link. Tennis. 18-hole golf, greens fee $55, pro, putting green, driving range. Exercise equipt. Bicycles. Paddle boats. Lawn games. Private patios, balconies. Refrigerators. Some fireplaces. Cr cds: A, C, D, DS, MC, V.

D ⬤ 🏌 〰 🔼 ⊠ 🔥 SC 🎿 🍴

★ ★ ★ ★ **THE INN AT PERRY CABIN.** *308 Watkins Ln (21663). 410/745-2200; fax 410/745-3348; toll-free 800/722-2949. www.perrycabin.com.* This colonial mansion is perched along Miles River, a tributary to Chesapeake Bay, and is surrounded by relaxing recreation options including sailing, golfing, and riding in horse-drawn carriages. The building's 1812 heritage is evident in the English and early-American antiques that fill the 35 uniquely themed guestrooms and six suites. 41 rms, 3 story, 6 suites. S, D $295-$695; suites $695. Children over 10 yrs only. TV; cable (premium), VCR avail (movies). Indoor pool; whirlpool. Complimentary full bkfst. Dining rm (see also THE DINING ROOM). Ck-out noon, ck-in 3 pm. Business center. In-rm modem link. Valet serv. Concierge serv. Tennis. Golf privileges. Exercise equipt; sauna, steam rm. Massage. Health club privileges. Rec rm. Lawn games. Dockage. Cr cds: A, C, D, MC, V.

D ⬤ 🏌 🏌 🏃 〰 🔼 ⊠ 🔥 🏃

B&Bs/Small Inns

★ **BLACK WALNUT POINT INN.** *Black Walnut Point Rd, Tilghman Island (21671). 410/886-2452; fax 410/886-2053.* 7 rms, 6 with shower only, 3 bldgs, main bldg 3 story. No rm phones. D $120-$135; each addl $20; kit. unit $150. Adults only. TV in sitting rm. Pool; whirlpool. Complimentary continental bkfst; afternoon refreshments. Ck-out 11 am, ck-in 2-7 pm. Business servs avail. Lighted tennis. Lawn games. Balconies. Picnic tables, grills. On Cheasapeake Bay. Built in 1843; hand-hewn beams. Cr cds: DS, MC, V.

⬤ 🏃 🏃 ⊠ 🔥

★ ★ ★ **CHESAPEAKE WOOD DUCK INN.** *Gibsontown Rd at Dogwood Harbor, Tilghman Island (21671). 410/886-2070; fax 410/886-2263; toll-free 800/956-2070. www.woodduckinn.com.* 7 rms, 2 with shower only, 3 story. No rm phones. No elvtr. Apr-Nov: S, D $125-$155; suites $165-$205; lower rates rest of yr. Children over 14 yrs only. TV; cable, in main rm; VCR. Complimentary full bkfst. Restaurant nearby. Ck-out 11 am, ck-in 4-7 pm. Business servs avail. Luggage handling. Water sport privileges. Built in 1890. Fireplace. Totally nonsmoking. Cr cds: MC, V.

⬤ ⊠ 🔥 SC

★ ★ ★ **LAZYJACK INN.** *5907 Tilghman Island Rd, Tilghman Island (21671). 410/886-2215; fax 410/886-2635. www.lazyjackinn.com.* 4 rms, 2 with shower only, 2 story. No rm phones. Apr-mid-Nov: S, D $130-

205; lower rates rest of yr. Children over 12 yrs only. Complimentary full bkfst; afternoon refreshments. TV, VCR in main rm. Restaurant nearby. Ck-out 11 am, ck-in 4-7 pm. Luggage handling. Some in-rm whirlpools. Historic waterfront bldg (1855); antiques. Private yacht for charter. Totally nonsmoking. Cr cds: A, MC, V.

★ ★ **PARSONAGE INN.** *210 N Talbot (21663). 410/745-5519; toll-free 800/394-5519. www.bestinns.net.* 8 rms, 7 with shower only, 2 story. No rm phones. May-Oct: D $110-$172; lower rates rest of yr. Crib free. TV in some rms. Complimentary full bkfst. Restaurant adj 5-10 pm. Ck-out 11 am, ck-in 2-7 pm. Health club privileges. Balconies. Picnic table, grill. Built 1883 as private residence; later used as parsonage. Restored and furnished with period reproductions. Unique architecture. Totally nonsmoking. Cr cds: MC, V.

★ ★ ★ **WADE'S POINT INN.** *Wades Point Rd (21663). 410/745-2500; fax 410/745-3443; res 888/923-3466. www.wadespoint.com.* 24 rms, 6 share bath, 12 A/C, 2-3 story, 4 kits. No rm phones. D $95-$230; each addl $10; kit. units $230; under 12 free. Crib free. Complimentary continental bkfst. Restaurant nearby. Ck-out 11 am, ck-in 2-8 pm. Business servs avail. Balconies. Picnic tables. Main building (1819) with new guest house (1989) built in same style. Both buildings surrounded by fields and Chesapeake Bay. Located on 120 acres; flower gardens, woods with nature trail. Totally nonsmoking. Cr cds: MC, V.

Restaurants

★ ★ **BAY HUNDRED RESTAURANT.** *6178 Tilghman Island Rd, Tilghman (21671). 410/886-2126.* Seafood menu. Specializes in seafood, clams. Hrs: 11 am-9 pm; Fri-Sun to 10 pm. Res accepted. Wine list. Lunch $6-$15; dinner $12-$24. Sun brunch $6-$12. Child's menu. Entertainment. Cr cds: A, DS, MC, V.

★ **BISTRO ST. MICHAELS.** *403 S Talbot St, St. Michaels (21663). 410/745-9111. www.stmichaels.com.* Mediterranean menu. Menu changes seasonally. Hrs: 5:30-9 pm; Sat, Sun 11:30 am-2 pm, 5:30-9 pm. Closed Tues, Wed. Res accepted. Wine list. Lunch $9; dinner $19-$24. Entertainment. Over 100 yrs old. Cr cds: A, D, DS, MC, V.

★ ★ **THE BRIDGE.** *6316 Tilghmand Island Dr, Tilghman (21671). 410/886-2330. www.bridgerestaurant.com.* Hrs: 11:30 am-9 pm; Fri-Sun to 9:30 pm. Closed Thanksgiving, Dec 25. Res required Fri-Sun (dinner). Bar to 2 am. Lunch, dinner $13.95-$19.95. Child's meals. Specializes in seafood, sandwiches, pizza. Parking. Outdoor dining. View of bay. Casual dining. Totally nonsmoking. Cr cds: A, MC, V.

★ **CHESAPEAKE LANDING SEAFOOD.** *23713 St. Michael's Rd, Mc Daniel (21663). 410/745-9600.* Hrs: 11 am-9 pm; early-bird dinner 4-6 pm (Mon-Fri). Closed Dec 25. Res accepted. Serv bar. Lunch $2.75-$8.25, dinner $8.95-$16.95. Child's menu. Specializes in seafood, steak, chicken. Parking. Totally nonsmoking. Cr cds: A, DS, MC, V.

★ ★ ★ ★ **THE DINING ROOM.** *308 Watkin Ln (21663). 410/745-2200. www.perrycabin.com.* Housed in The Inn at Perry Cabin, an 1812 colonial mansion on the Miles River, this restaurant offers gentle service and renowned cuisine. English-born chef Mark Salter highlights seasonal ingredients in creative continental dishes such as crab spring roll with pink grapefruit, avocado and toasted almonds. Take a step back in time for the classic afternoon tea. Hrs: 8-10:30 am, 12:30-2:30 pm, 6-10 pm; Sun brunch 11:30 am-2:30 pm; afternoon tea 3-5 pm. Res accepted. Serv bar. Wine list. A la carte entrees: bkfst $27.50, lunch $30. Prix fixe: 5-course dinner $69.50. Sun brunch $40. High tea $19.50. Specialtizes classic cuisine. Menu changes seasonally. Own herb garden. Own baking. Valet parking. English country-style dining rm with fireplace; French doors open to terrace overlooking

bay. Totally nonsmoking. Cr cds: A,
D, DS, MC, V.
D

★ ★ ★ **HARBOUR LIGHTS.** *101 N
Harbor Rd (21663). 410/745-5102.
www.harbourinn.com.* Hrs: 7 am-9 pm;
Oct-May to 10 pm. Closed Mon, Tues
(Dec-mid-Mar). Res accepted. Bar.
Wine list. Bkfst $5.95-$9.95, lunch
$5.95-$11.95, dinner $14.95-$22.95.
Specializes in seafood, steaks,
chicken. Cr cds: A, D, DS, MC, V.
D

★ **ST. MICHAEL'S CRAB HOUSE.**
*305 Mulberry St (21663). 410/745-
3737. www.stmichaelscrabhouse.com.*
Hrs: 11 am-10 pm; Fri, Sat to 11 pm.
Closed mid-Dec-early Mar. Res
accepted. Bar. Lunch $4.95-$10.95,
dinner $9.95-$17.95. Child's meals.
Specializes in fresh seafood, beef,
chicken. Outdoor dining. Overlooks
harbor. Cr cds: DS, MC, V.
D

★ ★ ★ **208 TALBOT.** *208 N Talbot St
(21663). 410/745-3838. www.208
talbot.com.* Hrs: 5-10 pm; Sun 5-9
pm; Sun brunch 11 am-2 pm. Closed
Mon, Tues; Dec 24, 25. Res accepted;
required wkends. Bar. Dinner $21-
$26. Prix fixe: Sat dinner $48. Sun
brunch $9.50-$15.50. Specializes in
fresh seafood, rack of lamb. Own
pastries, ice cream. Casual gourmet
dining in renovated mid-1800s brick
house; many antiques; original fireplace. Cr cds: DS, MC, V.
D

Salisbury

(E-7) *See also Ocean City*

Founded 1732 **Pop** 20,592 **Elev** 33 ft
Area code 410 and 443 **Zip** 21801
Information Wicomico County Con-
vention & Visitors Bureau, 8480
Ocean Hwy, Delmar 21875; 410/548-
4914 or 800/332-TOUR. Information
is also avail from the Chamber of
Commerce, 300 E Main St, PO Box
510, 21803; 410/749-0144
Web www.salisburyarea.com

"Central City of the Eastern Shore"
and of the Delmarva Peninsula, Salisbury has a marina on the Wicomico
River providing access to Chesapeake
Bay. It lies within 30 miles of duck
hunting and deep-sea fishing. Gasoline pumps, hydraulic lifts, canned
and frozen foods, seafood, and poultry come from this area.

What to See and Do

Mason-Dixon Line Marker. Bears
coats of arms of Lord Baltimore and
William Penn. 5 mi N on US 13, 13A,
then 7 mi W on MD 467.

Nassawango Iron Furnace. One of
the oldest industrial sites in Maryland and one of the earliest hot blast
mechanisms still intact. The stack
was restored in 1966; archaeological
excavations were made and a canal, a
dike, and a portion of the old waterwheel used in the manufacturing
process were found. The remains of
the area are undergoing restoration.
(Apr-Oct, daily) 16 mi S via MD 12 to
Old Furnace Rd. Phone 410/632-
2032. ¢¢ Surrounding the iron furnace is

Furnace Town. This 1840s industrial village occupies 22 acres
around the iron furnace and also
incl six historic structures; a working 19th-century blacksmith shop
and broom-making shop has
demonstrations on selected days; a
museum and company store;
archaeological excavations; a
nature trail and picnic area. Special
events take place throughout the
season. (Same days and fees as furnace)

Poplar Hill Mansion. (ca 1805).
Example of Georgian and Federal-
style architecture; Palladian and
bull's-eye windows; large brass box
locks on doors, woodwork, mantels,
and fireplaces. Period furniture;
country garden. (Usually Sun afternoons; Tues-Sat by appt, Phone
410/749-1776. ¢

Princess Anne. This town was the
home of Samuel Chase, signer of the
Declaration of Independence. Buildings of the Colonial and Federal periods are of architectural interest. 13
mi SW on US 13.

Salisbury Zoological Park. Natural
habitats for almost 400 mammals,
birds, and reptiles. Major exhibits
incl bears, monkeys, jaguars, bison,

waterfowl. Also exotic plants. (Daily) 755 S Park Dr. Phone 410/548-3188. **DONATION**

Ward Museum of Wildfowl Art. Displays incl the history of decoy and wildfowl carving in North America; wildfowl habitats; contemporary wildfowl art. Changing exhibits. Gift shop. (Mon-Sat, also Sun afternoons) 909 S Schumaker Dr, at Beaglin Park Dr. Phone 410/742-4988. **¢¢**

Motels/Motor Lodges

★ **COMFORT INN.** *2701 N Salisbury Blvd (21801). 410/543-4666; fax 410/749-2639; toll-free 800/638-7949. www.comfortinn.com.* 96 units, 2 story, 24 suites. Mid-May-mid-Sept: S $74.95-$97.95; D $85.95-$108.95; each addl $8; suites $97.95-$120.95; under 18 free; higher rates wkends; lower rates rest of yr. Crib avail. Pet accepted. TV; cable (premium). Pool privileges. Complimentary continental bkfst. Restaurant nearby. Ck-out 11 am. Meeting rm. Business servs avail. Lawn games. Refrigerator, wet bar avail. Picnic table, grills. Cr cds: A, C, D, DS, ER, JCB, MC, V.

D 🐾 ➳ 🖎 🐾 **SC**

★ **HOWARD JOHNSON.** *2625 N Salisbury Blvd (21801). 410/742-7194; fax 410/742-5194; toll-free 800/465-4329. www.hojo.com.* 123 rms, 2 story. Mid-June-mid-Sept: S $49-$99; D $49-$107; each addl $8; under 18 free; lower rates rest of yr. Crib free. Pet accepted, some restrictions. TV; cable (premium). Pool. Complimentary bkfst buffet. Restaurant 6:30-9:30 am. Bar 4:30 pm-midnight. Ck-out 11 am. Coin lndry. Meeting rms. Business servs avail. Health club privileges. Cr cds: A, C, D, DS, MC, V.

D 🐾 ➳ 🖎 🐾 **SC**

★★ **RAMADA INN CONFERENCE CENTER.** *300 S Salisbury Blvd (21801). 410/546-4400; fax 410/546-2528; res 888/800-7617. www.ramada.com.* 156 rms, 5 story. July-Aug: S, D $87-$135; each addl $10; under 18 free; lower rates rest of yr. Crib free. Pet accepted. TV; cable (premium). Indoor pool. Coffee in rms. Restaurant 6:30 am-2:30 pm, 5:30-10 pm; wkends from 7 am. Bar 4 pm-2 am; wkends from noon. Ck-out noon. Meeting rms. Business servs avail. Bellhops. Free airport transportation. Health club privileges. On river. Cr cds: A, C, D, DS, MC, V.

D 🐾 ➳ 🖎 🐾 **SC**

B&B/Small Inn

★★★ **WATERLOO COUNTRY INN.** *28822 Mt Vernon Rd, Princess Anne (21853). 410/651-0883; fax 410/651-5592. www.waterloocountryinn.com.* 5 rms, 3 story, 2 suites. Apr-Oct: S, D $125-$175; suites $205-$225; wkends, hols (2-day min); lower rates rest of yr. Closed Jan-Feb. Children over 9 yrs only. TV; cable. Complimentary full bkfst. Ck-out 11 am, ck-in 2 pm. Luggage handling. Golf privileges, greens fee $60, pro, putting green. Pool; whirlpool. In-rm whirlpool, fireplace in suites. Picnic tables. Built in 1750; on 317 acres. Totally nonsmoking. Cr cds: A, MC, V.

D 🐾 ➳ 🖎 🐾 🏌

Silver Spring

(C-5) *See also Bowie, College Park, Rockville; also see District of Columbia*

Pop 76,540 **Elev** 350 ft **Area code** 240 and 301

Information Chamber of Commerce, 8601 Georgia Ave, Suite 203, 20910; 301/565-3777

Web www.gsscc.org

What to See and Do

Brookside Gardens. A 50-acre display garden with two conservatories, flowering displays; variety of flowering plants in eight gardens; educational programs. (Daily; closed Dec 25) N on MD 97, right on Randolph Rd, right on Glenallan Ave, in Wheaton. Phone 301/949-8230. **FREE**

National Capital Trolley Museum. Rides on old-time American and European trolleys; exhibits depict history of streetcars. Special events during yr. (July-Aug, Sat-Sun and Wed; rest of yr, Sat and Sun only; also open Memorial Day, July 4, Labor Day) Northwest Branch Park, about 7 mi N on Bonifant Rd, just off MD 650 in Layhill. Phone 301/384-6088. ¢¢

Motel/Motor Lodge

★ ★ **COURTYARD BY MARRIOTT.** *12521 Prosperity Dr (20904). 301/680-8500; fax 301/680-9232; toll-free 800/321-2211. www.marriott.com.* 146 units, 3 story. S $114; D $124; suites $140-$150; wkly, wkend rates. Crib free. TV; cable (premium). Indoor pool; whirlpool, lifeguard. Complimentary coffee in rms. Restaurant 6:30-10 am, 5-10 pm; Sat, Sun 7 am-1 pm. Bar Mon-Fri 4-10 pm. Ck-out noon. Coin lndry. Meeting rms. Business servs avail. In-rm modem link. Valet serv. Sundries. Exercise equipt. Health club privileges. Refrigerators, microwaves avail. Cr cds: A, C, D, DS, ER, JCB, MC, V.

D 🏊 🕺 ➗ 🐾 SC

Restaurants

★ ★ **BLAIR MANSION INN.** *7711 Eastern Ave (20912). 301/588-6646. www.blairmansion.com.* Hrs: 11:30 am-9 pm; Sat from 5 pm; Sun from 2 pm. Closed Mon. Res accepted. Continental, American menu. Bar. Lunch $5.95-$9.95, dinner $9.95-$19.95. Specializes in poultry, beef, crab. Murder mystery dinners Thurs-Sun. 1890s Victorian mansion; gaslight chandelier, 7 fireplaces. Family-owned. Totally nonsmoking. Cr cds: A, DS, MC, V.

D

★ ★ **CRISFIELD.** *8606 Colesville Rd (20910). 301/588-1572.* Hrs: 11:30 am-10 pm; Fri to 11 pm; Sat 4-11 pm; Sun 2-9:30 pm. Closed Thanksgiving, Dec 25. Res accepted; required Fri, Sat. Bar. Lunch $5.95-$15.95, dinner $14.95-$17.95. Child's menu. Specializes in seafood, shrimp, crab. Art Deco decor. Cr cds: A, D, DS, MC, V.

D SC ➗

★ ★ ★ **MRS. K'S TOLL HOUSE.** *9201 Colesville Rd (20910). 301/589-3500. www.mrsks.com.* Hrs: 11:30 am-2:30 pm, 5-9 pm; Fri, Sat to 9:30 pm; Sun 11 am-9 pm; Sun brunch to 1 pm. Closed Mon; Dec 25. Serv bar. Complete meals: lunch $11.95, dinner $17.95-$25.50. Sun brunch $15.75. Specializes in regional American cuisine. Century-old tollhouse; antique china, glass. Gardens. Totally nonsmoking. Cr cds: A, C, D, DS, MC, V.

D

★ **VICINO.** *959 Sligo Ave (20910). 301/588-3372.* Hrs: 11:30 am-10:30 pm; Mon to 9:30 pm; Sun 1-9:30 pm. Closed hols. Italian menu. Wine, beer. A la carte entrees: lunch, dinner $6.50-$12. Child's menu. Specializes in pizza, pasta, seafood. Outdoor dining. Casual Italian neighborhood decor. Totally nonsmoking. Cr cds: A, MC, V.

Thurmont

(B-4) *See also Frederick, Hagerstown*

Settled 1751 **Pop** 5,588 **Elev** 523 ft **Area code** 301 **Zip** 21788

Information Tourism Council of Frederick County, 19 E Church St, Frederick 21701; 301/228-2888 or 800/999-3613

Web www.visitfrrederick.org

What to See and Do

Catoctin Mountain National Park. A 5,770-acre area on a spur of the Blue Ridge Mtns. Self-guided nature trails; restored whiskey still; fishing; picnicking, camping (mid-Apr-mid-Nov; fee), cabins (mid-Apr-Oct; fee). Park (daily). A unit of the National Park Service. 3 mi W on MD 77. Phone 301/663-9330. **FREE**

Cunningham Falls State Park. 4,950 acres in the Catoctin Mtns. Two recreation areas: Houck, 5 mi W of town, has swimming, fishing, boating (rentals); picnicking, camping, hiking trails that lead to 78-ft falls and scenic overlooks. Manor Area, 3 mi S of town on US 15, has picnicking, camping, playground. Trout fishing in Big Hunting Creek. Ruins of Iron Masters Mansion and the industrial village that surrounded it are also here. (See SPECIAL EVENTS) Standard fees. Phone 301/271-7574.

Special Events

Maple Syrup Demonstration. At Cunningham Falls State Park. Tree tapping, sap boiling; carriage rides; food;

children's storytelling corner. Usually second and third wkend Mar. Phone 301/271-7574.

Catoctin Colorfest. Fall foliage; arts and crafts show. Second wkend Oct. Phone 301/271-4432.

Motel/Motor Lodge

★ ★ ★ **COZY COUNTRY INN THURMONT.** *103 Frederick Rd (21788). 301/271-4301; fax 301/271-4301. www.cozyvillage.com.* 21 units, 3 with shower only, 2 story, 5 cottages. May-Oct: S, D $46-$130; each addl $5; cottages $46-$110; under 12 free; wkly rates. Crib avail. Pet accepted. TV; cable (premium), VCR avail. Complimentary continental bkfst Mon-Fri. Complimentary coffee in rms. Restaurant 11 am-9 pm; Sat, Sun from 8 am. Bar 11 am-10 pm. Meeting rms. Business servs avail. In-rm modem link. Gift shop. Downhill ski 12 mi; x-country ski 4 mi. Refrigerators; some minibars; microwaves avail. Balconies. Picnic tables. Near Camp David; visiting dignitaries have stayed here. Cr cds: A, DS, MC, V.

Restaurant

★ ★ **COZY.** *103 Frederick Rd (MD 806) (21788). 301/271-7373. www.cozyvilage.com.* Hrs: 11 am-8:45 pm; Fri to 9:15 pm; Sat 8 am-9:15 pm; Sun 8 am-8:45 pm. Closed Dec 24, 25. Res accepted. Bar. Buffet: bkfst $5.99, lunch $5.59-$15.25, dinner $8.50-$15.25. Lunch $4.29-$5.99, dinner $8.19-$12.79. Child's menu. Specializes in fresh fish, poultry, chicken. Own desserts. Outdoor dining. Family-owned. Cr cds: A, MC, V.

D

Towson

(C-6) *See also Baltimore*

Pop 51,793 **Elev** 465 ft **Area code** 410 and 443 **Zip** 21204
Information Baltimore County Chamber of Commerce, 102 W Pennsylvania Ave, Suite 402; 410/825-6200
Web www.baltcountycc.com

What to See and Do

Fire Museum of Maryland. More than 60 pieces of antique firefighting equipt; incl motorized and hand/horse-drawn units from 1822-1957. (May, Sept-Oct, wkends; June-Aug, daily) 1301 York Rd, 1 blk N of I-695 exit 26B, in Lutherville. Phone 410/321-7500. ¢¢

Hampton National Historic Site. Incl ornate Georgian mansion (ca 1790) (tours), formal gardens, and plantation outbuildings. Gift shop. (Daily; closed Jan 1, Thanksgiving, Dec 25) Tea rm open for luncheon (Daily; closed six wks mid-Jan-early Mar). 535 Hampton Ln, ½ mi off Dulaney Valley Rd; I-695 exit 27B. Phone 410/823-1309. ¢¢

Soldiers Delight Natural Environment Area. This 1,725-acre park has 19th-century chrome mines; restored log cabin; scenic overlook; hiking and nature trails, picnicking (at visitor center only). It is the only undisturbed serpentine barren in the state. Pets must be on leash. 7 mi W on I-695, then W on MD 26, then 5 mi N on Deerpark Rd to overlook. Phone 410/922-3044.

Towson State University. (1866) 15,000 students. On campus are three art galleries, incl Holtzman Art Gallery, with an extensive collection of art media (Sept-May, Tues-Sat). Concerts and sporting events are held in the Towson Center. York Rd. Phone 410-830-ARTS (information on entertainment and events).

Special Event

State Fair. Timonium Fairgrounds, 3 mi N on York Rd, in Timonium. Ten-day festival of home arts; entertainment, midway; agricultural demonstrations, Thoroughbred horse racing, livestock presentations. Phone 410/252-0200. Aug-Sept.

Motel/Motor Lodge

★ **DAYS INN.** *9615 Deereco Rd, Timonium (21093). 410/560-1000; fax 410/561-3918; toll-free 800/235-3297. www.daysinn.com.* 146 rms, 7 story.

Apr-Nov: S $49.95-$85; D $55-$90; each addl $5; suites $100-$140; family, hol rates; lower rates rest of yr. Crib avail. TV; cable (premium), VCR. Pool. Complimentary continental bkfst. Restaurant open 24 hrs. Rm serv 7 am-10 pm. Bar. Ck-out 11 am. Guest lndry. Meeting rms. Business servs avail. In-rm modem link. Exercise equipt. Game rm. Refrigerators; microwaves avail. Cr cds: A, D, DS, JCB, MC, V.

⊡ ⇔ ⟆ ⊠ ⚒ SC

Hotel

★ ★ ★ **SHERATON BALTIMORE NORTH HOTEL.** 903 Dulaney Valley Rd (21204). 410/321-7400; fax 410/296-9534; toll-free 800/433-7619. www.sheraton.com. 284 units, 12 story. S, D $109-$179; each addl $12; suites $350-$450; under 17 free; wkend plans; higher rates Preakness. Crib free. TV; cable (premium). Indoor pool; whirlpool, poolside serv, lifeguard. Coffee in rms. Restaurant 6:30 am-10:30 pm. Bar 11:30-1 am; entertainment. Ck-out noon. Convention facilities. Business center. In-rm modem link. Gift shop. Free valet parking. Exercise equipt; sauna. Health club privileges. Refrigerators, microwaves avail. Cr cds: A, C, D, DS, MC, V.

⊡ ⇔ ⟆ ⊠ ⚒ SC ⟆

Restaurants

★ ★ **CAFE TROIA.** 28 W Allegheny Ave (21204). 410/337-0133. www.cafetroia.com. Hrs: 11 am-3 pm, 5-10 pm; Mon 5-10 pm; Fri to 11 pm; Sat 5-11 pm; Sun 5-9 pm. Res accepted. Italian menu. Bar. Lunch $4-$12, dinner $9-$22. Specializes in regional Italian dishes. Outdoor dining. Cr cds: A, MC, V.

⊡

★ ★ ★ **LIBERATORE'S.** 9515 Derreco Rd, Timonium (21093). 410/561-3300. www.liberatores.com. Hrs: 11 am-10 pm; Fri, Sat to 11 pm; Sun 3-10 pm. Closed hols. Res accepted. Italian menu. Bar. A la carte entrees: lunch, dinner $3.95-$14.95. Specializes in pasta, chicken, seafood. Pianist Thurs-Sat. Italian decor. Cr cds: A, D, DS, MC, V.

⊡

★ ★ **PEERCE'S PLANTATION.** 12460 Dulaney Valley Rd, Phoenix (21131). 410/252-3100. Hrs: 11:30 am-3 pm, 5-10 pm; Fri, Sat to 11 pm; Sun 5-9 pm; Sun brunch 11:30 am-2 pm. Closed Dec 25. Res accepted. Continental menu. Bar 11:30-2 am. Lunch $6.25-$15, dinner $15.95-$25.95. Sun brunch $6.25-$12.95. Child's menu. Specialties: rack of lamb, filet Chesapeake. Valet parking. Outdoor dining. Antebellum decor. Scenic view of countryside overlooking Loch Raven Reservoir. Family-owned. Jacket. Cr cds: A, C, D, DS, MC, V.

⊡

★ ★ **ROTHWELL'S GRILLE.** 106 W Padonia Rd, Timonium (21093). 410/252-0600. Hrs: 11:30 am-midnight; Sat, Sun from 5 pm. Closed hols. Res accepted (dinner). Bar. Lunch $6-$12, dinner $9-$19. Specializes in fresh meats and fish cooked on wood burning grill. Own baking. Outdoor dining. Casual atmosphere. Cr cds: A, D, DS, MC, V.

⊡ ⇥

★ ★ **THAT'S AMORE.** 720 Kenilworth Dr (21204). 410/825-5255. www.thatsamore.com. Hrs: 11:30 am-10:30 pm; Fri to midnight; Sat 4 pm-midnight; Sun 4-9:30 pm. Closed Labor Day, Thanksgiving, Dec 25. Italian menu. Bar. A la carte entrees: lunch $3.50-$10.95, dinner $16-$22. Specializes in seafood. Outdoor dining. Italian vineyard setting. Cr cds: A, DS, MC, V.

⊡ ⇥

Waldorf

(D-5) See also La Plata

Pop 22,312 **Elev** 215 ft **Area code** 301
Information Tourism Director, PO Box 2150, La Plata 20646; 301/645-0558 or 800/766-3386
Web www.explorecharlescomd.com

What to See and Do

Cedarville State Forest. Incl 3,697 acres of woodland, once home of the Piscataway, who settled around the Zekiah Swamp. Fishing; hunting, nature and hiking trails, picnicking. Standard fees. Schedule varies. 4 mi E off US 301 on Cedarville Rd. Phone 301/856-8987.

Farmer's Market and Auction.
Nearby Amish farms offer fresh baked goods and produce (auction Wed) for sale; more than 90 shops. Antique dealers. (Wed and Sat) 13 mi SE on MD 5. Phone 301/884-3108.

❚ John Wilkes Booth Escape Route.
After shooting Abraham Lincoln on Apr 14, 1865, John Wilkes Booth fled south into Maryland to rendezvous with his accomplice, David Herold, at

Surratt House and Tavern. (1852) Where they recovered arms they had hidden there. Though she may have been innocent, Mary Surratt was hanged for conspiracy. Eight period rms, museum; guides in period costumes; Dec candlelight tours; special events and exhibits throughout the yr. (Mar-mid-Dec, Thurs-Sun) 9110 Brandywine Rd, Clinton (then Surrattsville). Phone 301/868-1121. ¢ Booth and Herold next stopped at

Dr. Samuel A. Mudd House Museum. (ca 1830) Where Dr. Mudd set Booth's broken leg, unaware that Booth had just shot the president. Mudd was convicted and imprisoned for life, but pardoned four yrs later by President Andrew Johnson. Tours conducted by costumed docents, some of whom are Dr. Mudd's descendants. (Apr-Nov, Sat-Sun afternoons and Wed 11 am-3 pm; closed Easter, Thanksgiving) From US 301, take MD 5, then left on MD 205, turn right on Poplar Hill Rd approx 4 mi, right on Dr. Samuel Mudd Rd, continue to house; sign at entrance. Phone 301/934-8464. ¢¢

Maryland Indian Cultural Center.
Exhibits reflect diverse tribal structures, art, lodging construction, and cultures of Native Americans. (Tues, Thurs, Sun afternoons) 16816 Country Ln. Phone 301/372-1932. **FREE**

Special Event

John Wilkes Booth Escape Route Tour. Day-long bus tour of Booth's route from Ford's Theatre, Washington, through southern Maryland to site of Garrett's farm, Virginia, with expert commentary. Mid-Apr and early Sept. Phone 301/868-1121.

Motels/Motor Lodges

★ **DAYS INN.** *US 301 (20603). 301/932-9200; fax 301/843-9816.* 100 rms, 3 story. S, D $65-$75; suite $119-$135. each addl $5; under 18 free. Crib free. Pet accepted; $10. TV; cable (premium). Complimentary continental bkfst. Coffee in rms. Restaurant adj 11 am-10 pm. Ck-out 11 am. Coin lndry. Meeting rm. Business servs avail. Some in-rm whirlpools, refrigerators. Cr cds: A, C, D, DS, MC, V.
🄳 🐾 ⛱ 🔥

★ ★ **HOLIDAY INN.** *45 St. Patrick's Dr (20603). 301/645-8200; fax 301/843-7945; res 800/645-8277. www.holiday-inn.com.* 192 rms, 3 story, 8 kit. units. S, D $69-$74; each addl $6; suites, kit. units $70-$90; under 19 free. Crib free. TV; cable (premium). Pool; lifeguard. Complimentary coffee in rms. Restaurant 6:30 am-10 pm. Bar noon-11 pm. Ck-out 11 am. Coin lndry. Meeting rms. Business servs avail. In-rm modem link. Bellhops. Valet serv. Beauty shop. Health club privileges. Refrigerators, microwaves avail. Cr cds: A, C, D, DS, JCB, MC, V.
🄳 ⛱ ⛱ 🔥 SC

★ **HOWARD JOHNSON EXPRESS INN.** *3125 Crain Hwy (20603). 301/932-5090; fax 301/932-5090; toll-free 800/826-4534. www.hojo.com.* 109 rms. S, D $55-$65; suites, kit. units $60-$65; under 18 free. Crib free. Pet accepted; $10. TV; cable (premium), VCR (movies). Pool. Complimentary continental bkfst. Coffee in rms. Restaurant adj 11 am-10 pm. Ck-out noon. Meeting rms. Business servs avail. Health club privileges. Refrigerators, microwaves avail. Picnic tables, grills. Cr cds: A, C, D, DS, JCB, MC, V.
🄳 🐾 ⛱ ⛱ 🔥 SC

Westminster

(B-5) *See also Baltimore, Frederick*

Founded 1764 **Pop** 16,731 **Elev** 717 ft
Area code 410 and 443

Westminster, a Union supply depot at the Battle of Gettysburg, saw scattered action before the battle. It is the county seat of Carroll County, first in the United States to offer complete rural free delivery mail service (started in 1899 with four two-horse wagons).

Motel/Motor Lodge

★ **COMFORT INN.** *451 WMC Dr (21158). 410/857-1900; fax 410/857-9584. www.bestwesternwestminster. com.* 101 rms, 1-2 story. May-June: S $69-$89; D $69-$159; each addl $10; under 18 free; wkly rates; monthly rates; higher rates: WMC parents wkend, graduation, Dec 31; lower rates rest of yr. Crib free. Pet accepted, some restrictions; $25 refundable. TV; cable. Pool; whirlpool. Complimentary continental bkfst. Ck-out 11 am. Meeting rms. Business servs avail. Valet serv. Tennis privileges. Golf privileges. Some in-rm whirlpools; microwaves avail. Cr cds: A, C, D, DS, ER, JCB, MC, V.
🄳 ⛷ 🏊 🚭 🐾 🆂🅲

Restaurants

★★ **JOHANSSON'S.** *4 W Main St (21157). 410/876-0101.* Hrs: 11 am-11 pm; Sat to midnight; Sun to 10 pm. Closed hols. Res accepted; required Fri, Sat dinner. Bar to 1 am. Lunch $5.95-$8.95, dinner $11.95-$17.95. Child's menu. Specializes in veal, beef, fresh seafood. Musicians Fri. Outdoor dining. English pub atmosphere, originally a nickel-and-dime store; colored glass artwork. Cr cds: A, DS, MC, V.
🄳

★★ **RUDY'S 2900.** *2900 Baltimore Blvd, Finksburg (21048). 410/833-5777. www.rudys2900.com.* Hrs: 11:30 am-2:30 pm, 5:30-10 pm; Fri to 11 pm; Sat 5:30-11 pm; Sun 4-9 pm. Closed Mon; hols. Res accepted; required Fri, Sat dinner. Continental menu. Bar to 10:30 pm. Lunch $5.95-$11.95, dinner $9.95-$24.95. Specialties: roast duckling with plum sauce, grilled pork chop with fennel-flavored sausage, grouper in potato crust with red wine butter. Own pastries. Vocalist Wed. European decor; French impressionist oil paintings. Cr cds: A, MC, V.
🄳

PENNSYLVANIA

From its easternmost tip near Bordentown, New Jersey, to its straight western boundary with Ohio and West Virginia, Pennsylvania's 300-mile giant stride across the country covers a mountain-and-farm, river-and-stream, mine-and-mill topography. Its cities, people, and resources are just as diverse. Philadelphia is a great city in the eastern part of the state, a treasure house of tradition and historical shrines; Pittsburgh is a great city in the western part, a mighty arsenal of industry. In this state are the Pennsylvania Dutch, their barns painted with vivid hex signs; here also are steel mills. Pennsylvania miners dig nearly all the anthracite coal in the United States and still work some of the oldest iron mines in the country. Oil employees work more than 19,000 producing wells, and 55,000 farm families make up 20 percent of the Pennsylvania work force.

Population: 11,881,643
Area: 44,892 square miles
Elevation: 0-3,213 feet
Peak: Mount Davis (Somerset County)
Entered Union: Second of original 13 states (December 12,1787)
Capital: Harrisburg
Motto: Virtue, liberty, and independence
Nickname: Keystone State
Flower: Mountain Laurel
Bird: Ruffed Grouse
Tree: Eastern Hemlock
Fair: (Pennsylvania State Farm Show), January 11-18, 2003, in Harrisburg
Time Zone: Eastern
Website: www.state.pa.us

Pennsylvania, the keystone of the original 13 states, remains one of the keystones in modern America. A leader in steel and coal production, the state also is a leader in cigar leaf tobacco, apples, grapes, ice cream, chocolate products, mushrooms (nearly ½ of the US total), and soft drinks, plus factory and farm machinery, electronics equipment, scientific instruments, watches, textile machines, railroad cars, ships, assorted metal products, and electrical machinery. This fifth most populous state is also a major factor in national politics.

Pennsylvania has been a keystone of culture. The first serious music in the colonies was heard in Bethlehem; today, it resounds throughout the state—Pittsburgh has an acclaimed symphony, as does Philadelphia. There are 140 institutions of higher learning (including the oldest medical school in the United States at the University of Pennsylvania), celebrated art galleries, and hundreds of museums.

Despite its size, all of Pennsylvania is within the motorist's grasp. Its 44,000 miles of state highways, including the 470-mile Pennsylvania Turnpike (pioneer of superhighways), plus 69,363 miles of other roads make up one of the largest road networks in the nation.

Swedes made the first settlement on this fertile land at Tinicum Island in the Delaware River in 1643. The territory became Dutch in 1655 and British in 1664. After Charles II granted William Penn a charter that made him proprietor of "Pennsilvania," this Quaker statesman landed here in 1682 and invested the land with his money, leadership, and fellow Quakers. The Swedes, Finns, and Dutch already in the new land were granted citizenship; soon came Welsh, Germans, Scots, Irish, and French Huguenots. Of these, the Germans left the strongest imprint on the state's personality. Commercial, agricultural, and industrial growth came quickly, and all these resources were contributed to the Revolution. In Pennsylvania, Washington camped at Valley Forge, the Declaration of Independence was signed, and the Constitution drafted.

With Philadelphia the capital of the new nation, tides of pioneers pushed west and north to develop far corners of the state. The Civil War brought fresh industrial development, and for the past century Pennsylvania has continued to develop at an ever-quickening industrial pace. Today the Keystone State is an empire of industry and a storehouse of historic traditions.

When to Go/Climate

Pennsylvania's lowlands and hill country enjoy typical east-coast seasonal temperatures—hot, humid summers; relatively mild winters; crisp falls; and wet springs. The mountains, however, experience short summers and cold, snowy winters.

AVERAGE HIGH/LOW TEMPERATURES (°F)

PHILADELPHIA

Jan 38/23	**May** 73/53	**Sept** 78/59
Feb 41/25	**June** 82/62	**Oct** 66/47
Mar 52/33	**July** 86/67	**Nov** 55/38
Apr 63/42	**Aug** 85/66	**Dec** 43/28

PITTSBURGH

Jan 34/19	**May** 71/48	**Sept** 74/54
Feb 37/20	**June** 79/57	**Oct** 63/42
Mar 49/30	**July** 83/62	**Nov** 50/34
Apr 60/39	**Aug** 81/60	**Dec** 39/24

Parks and Recreation Finder

Directions to and information about the parks and recreation areas below are given under their respective town/city sections. Please refer to those sections for details.

NATIONAL PARK AND RECREATION AREAS

Key to abbreviations. I.H.S. = International Historic Site; I.P.M. = International Peace Memorial; N.B. = National Battlefield; N.B.P. = National Battlefield Park; N.B.C. = National Battlefield and Cemetery; N.C.A. = National Conservation Area; N.E.M. = National Expansion Memorial; N.F. = National Forest; N.G. = National Grassland; N.H.P. = National Historical Park; N.H.C. = National Heritage Corridor; N.H.S. = National Historic Site; N.L. = National Lakeshore; N.M. = National Monument; N.M.P. = National Military Park; N.Mem. = National Memorial; N.P. = National Park; N.Pres. = National Preserve; N.R.A. = National Recreational Area; N.R.R. = National Recreational River; N.Riv. = National River; N.S. = National Seashore; N.S.R. = National Scenic Riverway; N.S.T. = National Scenic Trail; N.Sc. = National Scientific Reserve; N.V.M. = National Volcanic Monument.

Place Name	Listed Under
Allegheny N.F.	WARREN
Allegheny Portage Railroad N.H.S.	EBENSBURG
Delaware Water Gap N.R.A.	same
Edgar Allan Poe N.H.S.	PHILADELPHIA
Eisenhower N.H.S.	GETTYSBURG
Fort Necessity N.B.	UNIONTOWN
Friendship Hill N.H.S.	UNIONTOWN
Gettysburg N.M.P.	same
Hopewell Furnace N.H.S.	same
Independence N.H.P.	PHILADELPHIA
Johnstown Flood N.Mem.	JOHNSTOWN
Steamtown N.H.S.	SCRANTON

CALENDAR HIGHLIGHTS

JANUARY

Pennsylvania State Farm Show (Harrisburg). State fair. Phone 717/787-5373.

FEBRUARY

Chocolate Lovers' Extravaganza (Hershey). Hotel Hershey. Everything chocolate—tasting and sampling, chef-taught classes, decorating instruction, and more. For reservations, phone 800/533-3131.

MAY

Devon Horse Show (Philadelphia). Horse Show Grounds in Devon. One of America's leading equestrian events. More than 1,200 horses compete; country fair; antique carriage drive. Phone 610/964-0550.

JUNE

Three Rivers Arts Festival (Pittsburgh). Point State Park. Juried, original works of local and national artists; paintings, photography, sculpture, crafts, and videos; artists' market in outdoor plazas. Ongoing performances include music, dance, and performance art. Special art projects; film festival; food; children's activities. Phone 412/281-8723.

CoreStates US Pro Cycling Championship (Philadelphia). Longest single-day cycling event in the country—156 mi.

JULY

Civil War Heritage Days (Gettysburg). Lectures by historians; Civil War collectors' show; entertainment; Civil War book show; firefighters' festival; fireworks. Phone Convention & Visitors Bureau 717/334-6274.

Folk Festival (Kutztown). Festival grounds. Celebration of Pennsylvania Dutch folk culture; quilts, music, dancing, and food of Plain and Fancy Dutch. Craftspeople make baskets, brooms, rugs, toleware, and other handcrafts. Phone 215/679-9610.

AUGUST

Das Awkscht Festival (Allentown). Macungle Memorial Park. 2,500 antique, classic, and special-interest autos; arts and crafts; antique toy show, entertainment, food, fireworks. Phone 610/967-2317.

Musikfest (Bethlehem). Nine sites in downtown historic area. Nine-day festival celebrating Bethlehem's rich musical and ethnic heritage. More than 600 performances of all types of music from folk to rock. Phone 610/861-0678.

SEPTEMBER

Ligonier Highland Games and Gathering of the Clans of Scotland (Ligonier). Idlewild Park. Sports; massed pipe bands, Highland dancing competitions, Scottish fiddling; sheep dog, wool spinning, and weaving demonstrations; geneology booth, Scottish fair. Phone 724/238-3666.

Wine Country Harvest Festival (North East). Gravel Pit Park and Gibson Park. Arts and crafts, bands, buses to wineries, food. Phone 814/725-4262.

DECEMBER

Army-Navy Football Game (Philadelphia). John F. Kennedy Memorial Stadium or Veterans Stadium.

Thaddeus Kosciuszko N.Mem.   PHILADELPHIA
Valley Forge N.H.P.   same

STATE PARK AND RECREATION AREAS

Key to abbreviations. I.P. = Interstate Park; S.A.P. = State Archaeological Park; S.B. = State Beach; S.C.A. = State Conservation Area; S.C.P. = State Conservation Park; S.Cp. = State Campground; S.F. = State Forest; S.G. = State Garden; S.H.A. = State Historic Area; S.H.P. = State Historic Park; S.H.S. = State Historic Site; S.M.P. = State Marine Park; S.N.A. = State Natural Area; S.P. = State Park; S.P.C. = State Public Campground; S.R. = State Reserve; S.R.A. = State Recreation Area; S.Res. = State Reservoir; S.Res.P. = State Resort Park; S.R.P. = State Rustic Park.

Place Name	Listed Under
Bald Eagle S.P.	LOCK HAVEN
Bendigo S.P.	KANE
Black Moshannon S.P.	BELLEFONTE
Blue Knob S.P.	BEDFORD
Caledonia S.P.	CHAMBERSBURG
Canoe Creek S.P.	ALTOONA
Chapman S.P.	WARREN
Clear Creek S.P.	BROOKVILLE
Codorus S.P.	HANOVER
Cook Forest S.P.	CLARION
Fort Washington S.P.	FORT WASHINGTON
French Creek S.P.	POTTSTOWN
Gifford Pinchot S.P.	YORK
Gouldsboro S.P.	MOUNT POCONO
Greenwood Furnace S.P.	LEWISTOWN
Hickory Run S.P.	WHITE HAVEN
Hills Creek S.P.	MANSFIELD
Kettle Creek S.P.	LOCK HAVEN
Kinzua Bridge S.P.	KANE
Kooser S.P.	SOMERSET
Laurel Hill S.P.	SOMERSET
Little Pine S.P.	WILLIAMSPORT
McConnell's Mill S.P.	NEW CASTLE
Moraine S.P.	BUTLER
Ohiopyle S.P.	UNIONTOWN
Ole Bull S.P.	GALETON
Parker Dam S.P.	CLEARFIELD
Pine Grove Furnace S.P.	CARLISLE
Point S.P.	PITTSBURGH
Presque Isle S.P.	ERIE
Prince Gallitzin S.P.	ALTOONA
Promised Land S.P.	HAWLEY
Pymatuning S.P.	CONNEAUT LAKE
Raccoon Creek S.P.	AMBRIDGE
Reeds Gap S.P.	LEWISTOWN
Ridley Creek S.P.	MEDIA
S.B. Elliott S.P.	CLEARFIELD
Shawnee S.P.	BEDFORD
Sizerville S.P.	PORT ALLEGANY
Tobyhanna S.P.	MOUNT POCONO

Whipple Dam S.P.   STATE COLLEGE
Yellow Creek S.P.   INDIANA

Water-related activities, hiking, riding, various other sports, picnicking, and environmental interpretive centers, as well as camping, are available in many of these areas. More than 116 state parks and four environmental centers are scattered throughout the commonwealth. Fifty-seven campgrounds offer camping. Seven are open all year; the rest are open from second Friday April-third Sunday October or December. Occupancy is limited to two consecutive weeks; $9-$14 resident, $11-$16 nonresident/night (primitive areas); $11-$14 resident, $13-$16 nonresident/night (modern areas). Cabins (daily and weekly rentals spring, fall, and winter; one week only, Friday after Memorial Day-Friday before Labor Day). Boat launching (yearly) $10 resident, $15 nonresident. No pets allowed in overnight areas. Write to Bureau of State Parks, PO Box 8551, Harrisburg 17105-8551, for detailed information. Cabin reservations are made by calling the park directly. For other state park information, phone 888/PA-PARKS.

SKI AREAS

Place Name	Listed Under
Alpine Mountain Ski Area	STROUDSBURG
Big Boulder Ski Area	WHITE HAVEN
Blue Knob Ski Area	BEDFORD
Blue Mountain Ski Area	ALLENTOWN
Boyce Park Ski Area	PITTSBURGH
Camelback Ski Area	TANNERSVILLE
Doe Mountain Ski Area	ALLENTOWN
Elk Mountain Ski Center	CARBONDALE
Hidden Valley Ski Area	SOMERSET
Jack Frost Ski Area	WHITE HAVEN
Montage Ski Area	SCRANTON
Mount Airy Lodge Ski Area	MOUNT POCONO
Mount Tone Ski Resort	CARBONDALE
Mount View Ski Area	EDINBORO
Seven Springs Mountain Resort Ski Area	DONEGAL
Shawnee Mountain Ski Area	SHAWNEE ON DELAWARE
Ski Denton/Denton Hill Ski Area	GALETON
Ski Liberty Ski Area	GETTYSBURG
Ski Roundtop Ski Area	YORK
Ski Sawmill Resort	WELLSBORO
Spring Mountain Ski Area	LIMERICK
Tanglwood Ski Area	HAWLEY

FISHING

Pennsylvania is one of the country's leading states in the amount of waters open to public and private fishing. There are nearly 5,000 miles of trout streams stocked annually and many thousands of miles of warm-water streams plus thousands of acres of lakes with walleye, panfish, muskellunge, and bass. Nonresident fishing license is $35; three-day tourist license is $15; seven-day tourist license is $30. A $5.50 trout/salmon stamp also is required (for trout fishing only). Write to Pennsylvania Fish and Boat Commission, PO Box 67000, Harrisburg 17106-7000, or phone 717/705-7800, for the annual "Summary of Fishing Regulations and Laws" as well as maps and other useful information.

HUNTING

A license is required to hunt, take, trap, or kill any wild bird or animal in the state. Nonresident hunting license, $101; children 12-16, $41. The license tag must be displayed on the back of outer garment, between the shoulders, at all times. For big-game and turkey hunting and small-game hunting in the fall, 250 square inches of fluorescent orange must be worn on the head, chest, and back combined. For the "Official Digest, Pennsylvania Hunting and Trapping Regulations," contact the Pennsylvania Game Commission, 2001 Elmerton Ave, Harrisburg 17110-9797, phone 717/787-4250.

Driving Information

Safety belts are mandatory for all persons in front seat of vehicle. Children under four years must be in an approved passenger restraint anywhere in vehicle: age four and older may use a regulation safety belt; ages one-three may use a regulation safety belt in back seat only. Children under four years must use an approved safety seat in front seat; under age one must use an approved safety seat anywhere in the vehicle. For further information phone 717/787-6853.

INTERSTATE HIGHWAY SYSTEM

The following alphabetical listing of Pennsylvania towns in *Mobil Travel Guide* shows that these cities are within ten miles of the indicated Interstate highways. A highway map should, however, be checked for the nearest exit.

Highway Number	Cities/Towns within ten miles
Interstate 70	Bedford, Breezewood, Donegal, Greensburg, New Stanton, Somerset, Washington.
Interstate 78	Allentown, Bethlehem, Easton, Hamburg, Kutztown, Lebanon, Shartlesville.
Interstate 79	Conneaut Lake, Edinboro, Erie, Harmony, Meadville, Mercer, Pittsburgh, Washington.
Interstate 80	Bellefonte, Bloomsburg, Brookville, Clarion, Clearfield, Danville, Du Bois, Hazleton, Lewisburg, Lock Haven, Mercer, Mount Pocono, Sharon, Shawnee on Delaware, Stroudsburg, Tannersville, White Haven.
Interstate 81	Ashland, Carlisle, Chambersburg, Harrisburg, Hazleton, Scranton, Wilkes-Barre.
Interstate 83	Harrisburg, York.
Interstate 84	Milford, Scranton.
Interstate 90	Erie, North East.
Interstate 95	Bristol, Philadelphia.

Additional Visitor Information

A free visitors guide is available by calling 800/VISIT-PA, at the Pennsylvania Office of Travel, Tourism, and Film Promotion, Department of Community & Economic Development, PO Box 61, Warrendale 15086.

There are 14 state-run traveler information centers in Pennsylvania; visitors who stop by will find information and brochures most helpful in planning stops at points of interest. Their locations are as follows: I-79 Edinboro (southbound), 1 mi S of the Edinboro exit; I-81 Greencastle (northbound), 1 mi N of the Pennsylvania/Maryland border; I-95 Linwood (northbound), ½ mi N of the Pennsylvania/Delaware border; I-70 Warfordsburg (westbound), 1 mi from the Pennsylvania/Maryland border; I-80 West Middlesex (eastbound), ½ mi E of the Pennsylvania/Ohio border; Neshaminy Welcome Center, Mile Marker 351 (westbound) on the Pennsylvania Turnpike, 7 mi W of the Pennsylvania/New Jersey border, located inside the plaza building; I-78 Easton (westbound), 1 mi W of the Pennsylvania/New Jersey border; Sideling Hill Welcome Center, Mile Marker 172 (eastbound and westbound) on the Pennsylvania Turnpike, 10 mi E of the Breezewood exit, located inside the plaza building; I-81 Lenox (southbound), 4 mi S of the Lenox exit 64; I-83 Shrewsbury (northbound), ½ mi N of the Pennsylvania/Maryland border; Zelienople Welcome Center, Mile Marker

21 (eastbound), 21 mi E of the Pennsylvania/Ohio border, located inside the plaza building; I-79 northbound, N of Pennsylvania/West Virginia line; I-70 Washington County, E of Pennsylvania/West Virginia line.

Ride with Me—Pennsylvania, Interstate 81 is a 90-min audio cassette tape that provides information on points of interest along I-81, from New York to Maryland. Topics such as the history of the Pennsylvania Dutch, notable battlegrounds and areas related to the Civil War, and anthracite coal miners are discussed. Contact RWM Associates, PO Box 1324, Bethesda, MD 20817, phone 301/299-7817.

BUCKS COUNTY (APPROX 75 MI)

Over the years, literary references to Bucks County, just north of Philadelphia, have been plentiful, and with good reason. This woodland retreat along the Delaware River has been favored by notable Manhattanite literati for decades, including Broadway's Moss Hart and George S. Kaufman and the acerbic writer Dorothy Parker. Though estate-sized homes are popping up everywhere in this privileged realm, the rumpled landscape still retains the look of a Currier and Ives print. Stately old fieldstone houses stand beneath towering trees, and stalks of ripening corn march across the fields. In fall, pumpkins peek from among patches of vines. Nearby, the wide and peaceful Delaware flows quietly past. A one-day, 75-mile loop drive out of New Hope provides a rewarding glimpse of Bucks County's scenic and cultural appeal. Begin in New Hope, a small town noted as a romantic weekend getaway destination. A colonial-era ferry crossing on the main road between Philadelphia and New York, the town is dotted with old stone structures sandwiched between the river and the Delaware Canal. The shops they house are well worth a look; several feature exquisite hand-made crafts of local and national artisans. Many visitors come simply to stroll the old streets and enjoy the cafes, pubs, and ice cream parlors. You can hike or bicycle on the canal tow path. If you're in town on Saturday or Tuesday morning, drop by Rice's Market on Greenhill Road, a ten-minute drive northwest of New Hope. Set in a 30-acre field, the market is the next best thing to an old-fashioned county fair. More than 200 vendors haul in booths selling merchandise of all kinds—produce, plants and flowers, crafts, furniture pieces, clothing, you name it—often at bargain prices. To see more of the county, return to New Hope and take River Road (State Route 32) north. The road winds alongside the Delaware River for about 25 miles to Kintnersville, providing gorgeous river views the entire way. Quaint river towns, mostly a cluster of old homes, dot the route. In places, the road narrows as it skirts a stone wall. The stretch of road between New Hope and Lumberville passes a river setting that in the early years of the century drew a number of landscape artists, who formed a colony of Pennsylvania Impressionists in the hamlet of Phillips Mill. You can't miss it; River Road makes a sharp turn here. Today, their work can be seen in a permanent exhibit called "Visual Heritage of Bucks County" at the James A. Michener Art Museum in Doylestown, ahead on this drive. In Kintnersville, take Route 611, the Lackawanna Trail, south to Doylestown. Visit the Michener Museum, which also features a diverting exhibit detailing the Broadway and Hollywood legends who have lived in the county. Save plenty of time for the three fantastical castlelike structures that archeologist and historian Henry Chapman Mercer bequeathed his hometown. Turrets, towers, and parapets adorn the buildings, all built between 1908 and 1916 in a free-form style of reinforced concrete. The Moravian Pottery and Tile Works, which resembles a Spanish-colonial mission, houses Mercer's innovative tile factory. Good-quality artistic tiles are still made here by hand. On the same 70-acre, parklike grounds stands Fonthill, Mercer's 44-room mansion, a fairy-tale creation of strange nooks and crannies adorned with decorative tiles from his factory and around the world. A mile away, the seven-story Mercer Museum houses an important collection of furnishings, folk art, and implements of early America. Conclude this drive by returning to New Hope via Routes 202 and 179.

Laurel Highlands (Approx 150 mi)

As the name suggests, the Laurel Highlands–spread across the Allegheny Mountains in southwestern Pennsylvania–is a region of lofty wooded ridges, slender farm valleys, splashing streams, and quiet lakes, many boasting swimming beaches. Here and there you come upon covered bridges. George Washington once trod these hills, acquiring the military skills he would need as the Revolutionary War commander. Early on, the beauty of the setting drew many travelers–and continues to do so. Today the Highlands serve as a year-round playground, where you can raft, kayak, fish, swim, and bicycle. This two-day, 150-mile drive meanders through this appealing setting while visiting several important historic sites. This is a one-way trip between Bedford in the east and Uniontown in the west. You can drive in either direction; we'll begin at Bedford, just off the Pennsylvania Turnpike. Stop in Bedford at the Old Bedford Village, which preserves more than 40 original farm buildings and other structures from bygone days in a villagelike cluster. One that catches the eye is the eight-sided frame schoolhouse built nearby in 1851. Called an Eight Square, the octagon shape had a specific purpose: it gave every student an equal share of window light and proximity to the pot-bellied stove in the center. In summer, crafters demonstrate blacksmithing, barrel-making, broom-making, and other pioneer skills. From Bedford, take I-99 north to State Route 56 northwest to Johnstown. Two sites here capture the horror of the Johnstown Flood of 1889, which struck the small steel-manufacturing city with a sudden ferocity that left 2,200 people dead. Just east of the city, the National Park Service operates the Johnstown Flood National Memorial. It overlooks the dry basin of what was once a man-made lake that emptied when heavy rains collapsed an earthen dam. In Johnstown itself, the Johnstown Flood Museum illustrates the damage wrought by the flood and Johnstown's determination to rebuild. Ahead on the drive, two reconstructed 18th-century forts, Fort Ligonier in Ligonier and Fort Necessity National Battlefield near Farmington, recount British colonial efforts to wrest the Ohio River Valley west of the Alleghenies from French control. Both forts played a role in the ultimate defeat of the French at Fort Duquesne, which became the site of Pittsburgh. Ligonier is the most imposing of the two forts, but Fort Necessity may be more memorable. To reach it, take Route 271 west from Johnstown to Ligonier, and plan to spend the night there. To reach Fort Necessity, jog two miles southeast on US 30 to Route 381 to Farmington, and turn right on US 40. At Fort Necessity, a modest ring of stakes thrusting from the earth marks the site of George Washington's only military surrender, a lesson that surely must have aided him two decades later as commander of the Continental Army. The route from Ligonier to Farmington edges past Fallingwater, architect Frank Lloyd Wright's masterpiece on Bear Run. The structure, stair-stepping down a wooded mountainside, combines architecture and nature in a glorious piece of artwork. A stop here is a must, but allow at least three hours to take an escorted tour and to walk the grounds. Exhibits at the Entrance Pavilion explain the construction of the house, built in 1936 as a mountain retreat for a wealthy Pittsburgh department store owner. Inside the house, you'll learn about Wright's daring use of new construction materials and his fascination with the possibilities of space, as well as his idiosyncrasies. Short in stature, Wright designed the house with surprisingly low ceilings. A couple of miles down the road, the village of Ohiopyle is a center for whitewater rafting. Sign up for thrills, or watch helmet-clad rafters arriving or departing on upper and lower stretches of the Youghiogheny River (also called the "Yock"). From Fort Necessity, continue west on US 40 to Uniontown to conclude this tour.

Allentown

(D-7) *See also Bethlehem, Easton, Kutztown, Quakertown (Bucks County)*

Founded 1762 **Pop** 106,632 **Elev** 364 ft **Area code** 484 and 610
Information Lehigh Valley Convention & Visitors Bureau, PO Box 20785, Lehigh Valley 18002-0785; 610/882-9200

Allentown, situated in the heart of Pennsylvania Dutch country, is conveniently accessible via a network of major highways. Allentown was originally incorporated as Northamptontown. The city later took the name of its founder, William Allen, a Chief Justice of Pennsylvania. Allentown was greatly influenced by the Pennsylvania Germans who settled the surrounding countryside and helped the city become the business hub for a rich agricultural community.

What to See and Do

Cedar Crest College. (1867) 1,700 women. An 84-acre campus that includes nationally registered William F. Curtis Arboretum (tours); chapel with stained-glass windows portraying outstanding women in history; art galleries, sculpture gardens, museum, and theater. Campus tours. 100 College Dr. Phone 610/437-4471.

Dorney Park and Wildwater Kingdom. Theme park/water park featuring more than 100 rides and attractions, antique wooden carousel, four world-class roller coasters, including Steel Force—the longest, tallest, fastest steel roller coaster on the East Coast; 11 water slides; Berenstain Bear Country; midway games and entertainment; public picnic facility adjacent to the park. **Wildwater Kingdom** is one of the top seasonal water parks in the country. Dorney Park (May-Oct). Water park (mid-May-Sept). Operating hrs may vary. 3830 Dorney Park Rd. Phone 610/395-3724. ¢¢¢¢

Frank Buchman House. Constructed in 1892, this three-story row house, typical of Allentown's inner city, is an example of Victorian architecture; period rooms. (Sat and Sun afternoons; also by appt) 117 N 11th St. Phone 610/435-4664. **FREE**

George Taylor House and Park. (1768) House of a signer of the Declaration of Independence; 18th-century restoration period rooms; museum; walled garden. Guided tours. (June-Oct, Sat and Sun afternoons; also by appt) 4 mi N off US 22, at Lehigh and Poplar sts in Catasauqua. Phone 610/435-4664. ¢

Haines Mill Museum. (ca 1760) Operating gristmill (reconstructed 1909); exhibits portray the development and importance of the gristmill in rural America. (May-Sept, Sat and Sun afternoons; also by appt; closed hols) 3 mi W via Hamilton St, at 3600 Dorney Park Rd (Cetronia). Phone 610/435-4664. **FREE**

Lehigh County Museum. Exhibits illustrate economic, social, and cultural history of the county. (Mon-Sat, Sun afternoons; closed hols) Old Courthouse, 5th and Hamilton sts. Phone 610/435-4664. **FREE**

Liberty Bell Shrine. Reconstructed Zion's church has shrine in basement area where Liberty Bell was hidden in 1777; contains a full-size replica of the original bell; a 46-ft mural depicts the journey of the bell; other historical exhibits, art collection. (Mon-Sat afternoons; closed hols) 622 Hamilton, at Church St. Phone 610/435-4232. **FREE**

Lock Ridge Furnace Museum. Exhibits on the development of the US iron and steel industry; emphasis on the anthracite-coal-heated iron industry. Located in a reconstructed 19th-century iron furnace. (May-Sept, Sat and Sun afternoons; also by appt) 525 Franklin St. Phone 610/435-4664. **FREE**

Muhlenberg College. (1848) 2,000 students. Founded by the Lutheran Church to honor patriarch of Lutheranism in America. On campus is the Gideon F. Egner Memorial Chapel, an example of Gothic architecture. Also here is the Center for the Arts, a dramatic building designed by renowned architect Philip Johnson, which houses the Muhlenberg Theater Association. Campus tours. 2400 W Chew St. Phone 484/664-3100.

Saylor Park Cement Industry Museum. Outdoor historic site featuring remains of cement kilns. (Daily, yr round) 245 N 2nd in Coplay. Phone 610/435-4664. **FREE**

Ski areas.

Bear Creek Ski Area. Four chairlifts, one handle tow, T-bar, two rope tows; 15 slopes; patrol, school, rentals, snowmaking; night skiing and snowboarding; tubing park; restaurant, cafeteria, bar; nursery. Longest run 1½ mi; vertical drop 500 ft. (Dec-mid-Mar, daily) 12 mi SW, 4½ mi off PA 100, just N of Hereford. Phone 610/682-7100. ¢¢¢¢

Blue Mountain. Seven chairlifts, T-bar; school, rentals, snowmaking; cafeteria, bar, lodge. Vertical drop 1,082 ft. Also 27 trails with day and night skiing. (Dec-Apr, daily) 17 mi N via PA 145, Treichlers exit, at "Y" turn right to Cherryville, and on to Danielsville, to top of Blue Mtn. Phone 610/826-7700 or 800/SKI-BLUE. ¢¢¢¢

Trexler-Lehigh County Game Preserve. A 1,200-acre zoo, petting farm, and wilderness tour that is home to more than 350 animals. Scenic overlooks; picnic area. (Mid-Apr-Oct, daily) 4 mi W on US 22, then 6 mi N on US 309, at 5150 Game Preserve Rd, near Schnecksville. Phone 610/799-4171. ¢¢

Trexler Memorial Park. Spring outdoor bulb display (Apr-May). **Gross Memorial Rose Garden** (at peak second wk June) and **Old-Fashioned Garden**, Cedar Pkwy (June-Aug). **Trout Nursery** and Fish-for-Fun stream, Lehigh Pkwy; picnic areas. **West Park**, 16th and Turner. Band concerts (June-Aug). Cedar Crest Blvd and Broadway. Phone 610/437-7628. **FREE**

Trout Hall. (1770) Oldest house in city, Georgian Colonial; restored. Period rooms, museum. Guided tours (Apr-May and Sept-Nov, Sat and Sun afternoons; June-Aug, Tues-Sun afternoons; also by appt; closed hols) 414 Walnut St. Phone 610/435-4664. ¢

Troxell-Steckel House and Farm Museum. (1756) Stone house is an example of German medieval architecture. Period rooms; museum. Swiss-style bank barn adj has exhibits of farm implements, carriages, and sleighs. Guided tours. (June-Oct, Sat and Sun afternoons; also by appt) 6 mi N on PA 145, then 1 mi W on PA 329, at 4229 Reliance St in Egypt. Phone 610/435-4664. ¢

Special Events

Mayfair Festival of the Arts. Allentown parks. Family arts festival with 150 free musical performances; crafts and food. Phone 610/437-6900. Mon and Thurs-Sun, Memorial Day wknd.

Das Awkscht Fescht. Macungie Memorial Park. 2,500 antique, classic, and special-interest autos; arts and crafts; antique toy show, entertainment, food, fireworks. Phone 610/967-2317 (festival) or 610-966-4289 (park office). First wknd Aug. Phone 610/966-4289.

Great Allentown Fair. Fairgrounds. 17th and Chew sts. Farm and commercial exhibits, rides, games, food, entertainment. Phone 610/435-SHOW. Late Aug-early Sept.

Drum Corps International-Eastern Regional Championship. J. Birney Crum Stadium, 21st and Linden sts. Drum and bugle corps competition. Phone 610/966-5344. Sept.

Motels/Motor Lodges

★ **ALLENWOOD MOTEL.** *1058 Hausman Rd (18104). 610/395-3707; fax 610/530-8166.* 21 rms. S, D, studio rms $45-$50; each addl $5. Crib free. Pet accepted. TV; cable. Restaurant nearby. Ck-out 11 am. Cr cds: A, DS, MC, V.
⬛ ⬛ ⬛

★★ **COMFORT SUITES.** *3712 Hamilton Blvd (18103). 610/437-9100; fax 610/437-0221; toll-free 800/228-5150. www.comfortsuites.com.* 122 suites, 4 story. Suites $105-$130; each addl $10; under 18 free. Crib free. TV; cable. Complimentary continental bkfst. Restaurant 7-2 am. Bar; entertainment Thurs-Sat. Ck-out noon. Meeting rms. Business servs avail. In-rm modem link. Sundries. Free airport, RR station, bus depot transportation. Exercise equipt. Refrigerators. Cr cds: A, C, D, DS, ER, JCB, MC, V.
⬛ ⬛ ⬛ ⬛ SC

★ **DAYS INN.** *1151 Bulldog Dr (18104). 610/395-3731; fax 610/395-9899; res 888/395-5200. www.daysinn.com.* 282 rms, 2 story. May-Oct: S

$79.95; D $109; each addl $6; suites
$109-$129; under 18 free; wkly rates;
package plans; higher rates local fes-
ivals; lower rates rest of yr. Crib free.
TV; cable. Pool; poolside serv, lifeguard. Playground. Restaurant 6:30
am-10 pm. Bar 2 pm-1 am. Ck-out
noon. Coin lndry. Convention facili-
ies. Business servs avail. Sundries.
Free airport, bus depot transporta-
ion. Game rm. Lawn games. Some
efrigerators. Some balconies. Cr cds:
A, C, D, DS, MC, V.

D ⌷ ⌷ ⌷ SC

★★ **HAMPTON INN.** *7471 Keebler
Way (18106). 610/391-1500; fax
610/391-0386; toll-free 800/426-7866.
www.hamptoninn.com.* 124 rms, 5
story. S, D $89-$129; under 18 free;
higher rates special events. Crib free.
TV; cable. Complimentary continen-
al bkfst. Restaurant nearby. Ck-out
noon. Meeting rms. Business servs
avail. Free airport transportation.
Exercise equipt; sauna. Cr cds: A, C,
D, DS, MC, V.

D ⌷ ⌷ ⌷ SC

★★ **SUPER 8.** *1715 Plaza Ln (18104).
610/435-7880; fax 610/432-2555; toll-
free 800/800-8000. www.super8.com.* 82
rms, 4 story. S, D $74-$95; each addl
$5; under 18 free. Crib free. Pet
accepted; $5. TV; cable. Complimen-
ary continental bkfst. Restaurant
nearby. Ck-out 11 am. Business servs
avail. Cr cds: A, C, D, DS, MC, V.

D ⌷ ⌷ ⌷ SC

Hotels

★★★ **HILTON HOTEL.** *904 Hamilton Mall (18101). 610/433-2221; fax
610/433-6455; toll-free 800/999-7784.*
224 rms, 9 story. S $125; D $135;
each addl $10; suites $145-$250;
under 18 free; wkend rates. Crib free.
TV; cable. Heated pool; lifeguard.
Restaurant 6:30 am-10 pm. Bar 11-2
am. Ck-out 11 am. Meeting rms.
Business servs avail. In-rm modem
ink. Free airport transportation.
Exercise equipt; sauna. Cr cds: A, C,
D, DS, ER, JCB, MC, V.

D ⌷ ⌷ ⌷ ⌷ SC

★★★ **SHERATON INN.** *3400 Airport
Rd (18109). 610/266-1000; fax
610/266-1888; toll-free 800/325-3535.*
147 rms, 3 story, 30 suites. S $99; D
$109; each addl $10; suites $115-

$145; under 13 free; higher rates
NASCAR races. Crib free. Pet accepted.
TV; cable (premium), VCR avail.
Indoor pool; whirlpool, lifeguard.
Complimentary coffee in rms. Restau-
rant 6:30 am-10 pm. Bar 11-2 am,
entertainment Tues-Sun. Ck-out
noon. Meeting rm. Business servs
avail. In-rm modem link. Bellhops.
Sundries. Valet serv. Free airport trans-
portation. Exercise equipt; sauna.
Some refrigerators. Cr cds: A, D, DS,
MC, V.

D ⌷ ⌷ ⌷ ⌷ ⌷ ⌷ SC

B&B/Small Inn

★★★ **THE GLASBERN INN.** *2141
Pack House Rd, Fogelsville (18051).
610/285-4723; fax 610/285-2862.
www.glasbern.com.* 24 rms, 2 story, 17
suites. S $100-$155; D $120-$355;
each addl $20; suites, kit. units $120-
$355; special wkends, hols (2-day
min). Crib avail. TV; cable. VCR
(movies). Heated pool. Complimentary full bkfst. Dining rm (public by
res) 6-8 pm. Ck-out noon, ck-in 4
pm. Meeting rm. Business servs avail.
Exercise equipt. Many whirlpools,
fireplaces. Farmhouse, barn, gate
house and carriage house built in late
1800s; antiques. Cr cds: A, MC, V.

D ⌷ ⌷ ⌷ ⌷ ⌷

Restaurants

★★★ **APPENNINO.** *3079 Willow St
(18104). 610/799-2727.* Hrs: 5:30-10
pm. Closed Sun; hols. Res accepted.
Northern Italian menu. Bar. Wine
list. A la carte entrees: dinner $17-
$30. Specialties: veal Valdostana, filet
of sole in green sauce with shrimp.
Own desserts. Restored hotel (1800s);
imported Italian lamps, chandeliers,
and tapestry on chairs. Jacket. Cr cds:
A, DS, MC, V.

D ⌷

★★ **BAY LEAF.** *935 W Hamilton St
(18103). 610/433-4211.* Hrs: Mon-Fri
11:30 am-2 pm, 5-10 pm. Sat from
5:00 pm. Closed Sun; hols. Res
accepted. Bar. A la carte entrees:
lunch $7.95, dinner $13.95-$24.95.
Specializes in seafood, steak, lamb.
Street parking. Thai pictures. Cr cds:
A, MC, V.

D ⌷

★ ★ ★ **THE FARMHOUSE.** *1449 Chestnut St, Emmaus (18049). 610/967-6225. www.thefarmhouse.com.* Hrs: from 5 pm. Closed Sun, Mon. Res accepted. Contemporary American menu. Bar 5-11 pm. Wine list. A la carte entrees: dinner $16-$23. Specialties: creme brulee, saffron risotto. Parking. Outdoor dining. In 1830 farmhouse. Cr cds: A, D, DS, MC, V.

★ ★ **FEDERAL GRILL.** *536 E Hamilton St (18101). 610/776-7600. www.federalgrill.com.* Hrs: 11 am-midnight; Sat, Sun brunch 11 am-3 pm. Closed hols. Res required Fri, Sat. Bar. A la carte entrees: lunch $5-$15, dinner $13-$24. Brunch $8-$15. Specializes in seafood, pasta. Parking. Outdoor dining. Cigar bar. Cr cds: A, D, DS, MC, V.

Altoona

(D-3) *See also Ebensburg*

Founded 1849 **Pop** 49,523 **Elev** 1,170 ft **Area code** 814
Information Allegheny Mountains Convention & Visitors Bureau, One Convention Center Dr, 16602; 814/943-4183 or 800/842-5866
Web www.alleghenymountains.com

The rough, high Alleghenies ring this city, which was founded by the Pennsylvania Railroad. Altoona expanded rapidly after 1852, when the difficult task of spanning the Alleghenies with track, linking Philadelphia and Pittsburgh, was completed. The railroad shops still offer substantial employment for residents of the city and Blair County, but new and diversified industries now provide the economic base.

What to See and Do

Allegheny Portage Railroad National Site. View authentic Lemon House and original rehabbed Engine House; learn how canal boats were taken over the Allegheny Mountains before the Horseshoe Curve was built. (Daily; closed Dec 25) In Cresson. Phone 814/886-6150. ¢¢

Baker Mansion Museum. (1844-1848) Stone Greek Revival house of early ironmaster; now occupied by Blair County Historical Society. Hand-carved Belgian furniture of the period; transportation exhibits, gun collection, clothing, housewares. (Memorial Day-Labor Day, Tues-Sun; mid-Apr-Memorial Day and Labor Day-Oct, Sat and Sun; closed hols) 3500 Oak Ln. Phone 814/942-3916. ¢¢

Canoe Creek State Park. Approx 950-acre park features 155-acre lake. Swimming beach, fishing, boating (launches, rentals); hiking, picnicking (res for pavilion), x-country skiing, sledding, ice boating, ice skating, cabins. Standard fees. 12 mi E via US 22. Phone 814/695-6807.

Delgrossos Park. More than 30 rides and attractions including antique carousel, miniature golf, and pony rides. Also here are arcade games, picnic pavilions, and restaurant. (May-Sept, Tues-Sun) 10 mi N on US 220 in Tipton. Phone 814/684-3538. ¢¢¢

Fort Roberdeau. Reconstructed Revolutionary War fort with horizontal logs; contains lead smelter, blacksmith shop, lead miners' hut, barracks, storehouse, officers' quarters, powder magazine. Costumed guides; wkend reenactments. Visitor center. Picnicking, nature trails. (Mid-May-early Oct, Tues-Sun) 8 mi NE via US 220, Kettle St exit onto PA 1013. Phone 814/946-0048. ¢¢

Horseshoe Curve Visitors Center. World-famous engineering feat, carrying main-line Conrail and Amtrak trains around western grade of 91 ft per mi. Curve is 2,375 ft long and has a central angle of 220 degrees. Funicular runs between interpretive center and observation area. Gift shop. (Apr-Dec, daily) 5 mi W via well-marked, unnumbered road. Phone 814/946-0834. ¢¢

Lakemont Park. An amusement park with more than 30 rides and attractions; home of the nation's oldest wooden roller coaster; water park, miniature golf, entertainment. (May-Sept, daily) 700 Park Ave, Frankstown Rd and I-99. Phone 814/949-7275. ¢¢¢

Prince Gallitzin State Park. Approx 6,200 acres; 26 mi of shoreline on

1,600-acre lake. Swimming beach, fishing, boating (rentals, mooring, launching, marina); hiking trails, horseback riding, x-country skiing, snowmobiling, ice skating, ice fishing, picnicking, snack bar, store, laundry facilities, tent and trailer sites, cabins. Standard fees. 8 mi NW on PA 36, then 1¼ mi NW off PA 53, then W on PA 1026. Phone 814/674-1000.

Railroader's Memorial Museum. Exhibits feature railroad artifacts, art, and theme displays. Railroad rolling stock, steam and electric locomotive collections. (Daily) 1300 9th Ave. Phone 814/946-0834. ¢¢¢

Wopsononock Mountain. Lookout provides view of six-county area from height of 2,580 ft; offers one of the best views in the state. 6 mi NW on Juniata Gap Rd.

Special Events

Blair County Arts Festival. Penn State Altoona Campus. Arts, crafts, hobbies on display. Mid-May.

Keystone Country Festival. Lakemont Park. Arts and crafts, continuous music; food. Contact Convention and Visitors Bureau for details. Wkend after Labor Day.

Railfest. 1300 9th Ave. A celebration of Altoona's rich rail heritage. Phone 814/946-0834. Oct 2-3.

Motel/Motor Lodge

★ **RAMADA INN.** 1 Sheraton Dr (16601). 814/946-1631; fax 814/946-0785. www.ramada.com. 215 rms, 2-3 story. S, D $55-$85; each addl $5; suites $80-$140; under 18 free; some wkend rates; higher rates: football games, ski season. Crib $5. Pet accepted. TV; cable (premium), VCR avail. Indoor pool; wading pool, whirlpool, lifeguard. Complimentary continental bkfst. Restaurants 6:30 am-2:30 pm, 5:30-10 pm; Sat to 11 pm. Bar 11-2 am. Ck-out noon. Meeting rms. Business center. In-rm modem link. Bellhops. Valet serv. Gift shop. Airport transportation. 18-hole golf privileges. Downhill ski 20 mi. Exercise equipt. Rec rm. Microwaves avail. Cr cds: A, C, D, DS, JCB, MC, V.
🅳 🐾 🏊 ⛷ 🏌 🎿 🐾 SC 🏃 🎿

Restaurants

★ ★ ★ **ALLEGRO.** 3926 Broad Ave (16601). 814/946-5216. Hrs: 4-9:30 pm; Sat to 10 pm. Closed Sun; hols. Res accepted. Italian, American menu. Bar. Wine list. Dinner $10.95-$25.50. Child's menu. Specializes in veal, seafood. Own baking, sauces, pasta. Cr cds: A, C, D, DS, MC, V.
🅳 SC 🖃

★ ★ **HOUSE OF CHANG PEKING II.** 601 Logan Blvd (16602). 814/942-3322. Hrs: 11:30 am-10 pm; Sun to 9 pm. Closed Thanksgiving, Dec 25. Chinese menu. Bar. Lunch $4.45-$6.25, dinner $6.50-$16.50. Buffet: lunch (Sun) $7.45. Child's menu. Specialties: Peking shrimp, subgum wonton. Asian decor. Cr cds: A, MC, V.
SC 🖃

Ambridge

(D-1) See also Beaver Falls, Pittsburgh

Founded 1901 **Pop** 7,769 **Elev** 751 ft **Area code** 724 **Zip** 15003

Information Beaver County Recreation & Tourism Department, Brady's Run Park, RD 1, Box 526, Beaver Falls, PA, 15010; 724/891-7030

Web www.co.beaver.pa.us

Founded by and taking its name from the American Bridge Company, this city rests on part of the site of Old Economy Village. In 1825, under the leadership of George Rapp, the Harmony Society established a communal pietistic colony that for many decades was important in the industrial life and development of western Pennsylvania. Despite its spiritual emphasis, Old Economy Village enjoyed a great material prosperity; farms were productive, craft shops were busy, and factories made textiles widely acclaimed for their quality. Surplus funds financed railroads and industrial enterprises throughout the upper Ohio Valley. After celibacy was adopted and unwise investments were made, the community's productivity decreased. Officially dissolved in 1905, the remains of the community were taken over by the Commonwealth of Pennsylvania in 1916.

What to See and Do

⭐ **Old Economy Village.** Seventeen original Harmony Society buildings located on six acres, restored and filled with furnishings of the community. Included are the communal leader's 32-room Great House, the Feast Hall, the Grotto in the Gardens, wine cellars, a five-story granary, shops, dwellings, and community kitchens. Cobblestone streets link the buildings. Special festivals and events. (Tues-Sun; closed hols) 14th and Church sts. Phone 724/266-4500.

Raccoon Creek State Park. Approx 7,300 acres. Swimming beach, fishing, boating (rentals, mooring, launching); hunting, hiking, horseback riding, x-country skiing, sledding, snowmobiling, ice-skating, ice fishing, snack bar, tent and trailer sites. Nature and historical centers. Standard fees. 9 mi W on PA 151, then 7 mi S on PA 18, near Frankfort Springs. Phone 724/899-2200.

Special Event

Nationality Days. Ethnic cultural displays, foods; native music, dancing. Mid-May.

Ashland

(C-7) *See also Hazleton*

Pop 3,283 **Elev** 1,000 ft
Area code 717 **Zip** 17921
Information Schuylkill County Visitors Bureau, 91 S Progress Ave, Pottsville 17901; 717/622-7700 or 800/765-7282
Web www.schuylkill.org

What to See and Do

Museum of Anthracite Mining. Museum on geology and technology of mining "hard" coal. (May-Oct, Mon-Sat, also Sun afternoons; rest of yr, Tues-Sat, also Sun afternoons; closed hols) Pine and 17th sts. Phone 570/875-4708. ¢¢

Pioneer Tunnel Coal Mine and Steam Lokie Ride. Tour and explanation of mining in original coal mine tunnel; indoor temperature 52°F. Narrow-gauge steam train ride; picnic park.

(call for hrs) 19th and Oak sts. Phone 717/875-3850. ¢¢¢

Beaver Falls

(D-1) *See also Ambridge, Harmony*

Founded 1806 **Pop** 9,920 **Elev** 800 ft
Area code 724 **Zip** 15010
Information Beaver County Recreation & Tourism Department, Brady's Run Park, RD 1, Box 526, Beaver Falls, PA, 15010; 724/891-7030
Web www.co.beaver.pa.us

Founded as Brighton, the town changed its name for the falls in the Beaver River. The plates from which US currency is printed are made in Beaver Falls. Geneva College (1848) is located here.

Motels/Motor Lodges

★ **BEAVER VALLEY MOTEL.** *7257 Big Beaver Blvd (15010). 724/843-0630; fax 724/843-1610; toll-free 800/400-8312. www.bvmotel.com.* 27 rms. S $39.60-$44; D $47-$52; each addl $6; kit. units $225/wk; under 18 free; Crib free. TV; cable (premium). Complimentary coffee in lobby. Ck-out 11 am. Business servs avail. Cr cds: A, DS, MC, V.
🄳 ⊠ 🖪 🆂🅲

★ **CONLEY INN.** *Big Beaver Blvd; Rural Rte 18 (15010). 724/843-0630; fax 724/843-9039; res 800/345-6819.* 56 rms. S $45; D $55; each addl $10; under 12 free; wkly, monthly rates. Pet accepted. TV; cable. Restaurant 5:30-10 pm. Bar. Ck-out 11 am. Meeting rms. Business servs avail. Refrigerators. Cr cds: A, C, D, DS, MC, V.
🅟 ⊠ 🖪 🆂🅲

★★ **HOLIDAY INN.** *7195 Eastwood Rd (15010). 724/846-3700; fax 724/846-7008; res 800/613-1490. www.holiday-inn.com.* 156 rms, 3 story. S, D $89; under 18 free. Crib free. Pet accepted. TV. Indoor pool; whirlpool, poolside serv, lifeguard. Coffee in rms. Restaurant 6:30 am-2 pm, 5-10 pm. Bar 11-2 am. Ck-out noon. Meeting rms. Business servs avail. In-rm modem link. Valet serv.

Sauna. Miniature golf. Game rm. Cr cds: A, C, D, DS, JCB, MC, V.

Restaurant

★ ★ ★ **WOODEN ANGEL.** *308 Leopard Ln, Beaver (15009). 724/774-7880. www.wooden-angel.com.* Hrs: 11:30 am-11 pm; Sat from 5 pm. Closed Sun, Mon; hols exc Mother's Day. Res accepted. Bar. Wine cellar. Lunch $6.75-$15.75, dinner $16-$28. Specializes in rack of lamb, fresh seafood. Own baking. Cr cds: A, C, D, DS, MC, V.

Bedford (E-3)

Settled 1751 **Pop** 5,417 **Elev** 1,106 ft
Area code 814 **Zip** 15522
Information Bedford County Conference & Visitors Bureau, 141 S Juliana St; 814/623-1771 or 800/765-3331
Web www.bedfordcounty.net

Fort Bedford was a major frontier outpost in pre-Revolutionary War days. After the war it became an important stopover along the route of western migration and has remained so up until the present. Garrett Pendergrass, the second settler here, built Pendergrass's Tavern, which figures in a number of novels by Hervey Allen.

What to See and Do

Bedford County Courthouse. Federal-style building constructed in 1828 has unique hanging spiral staircase; oldest courthouse still in operation in PA. (Mon-Fri; closed hols) S Juliana St. Phone 814/623-4807. **FREE**

Fort Bedford Park and Museum. Log blockhouse, erected during Bedford's bicentennial. Contains large-scale replica of original fort, displays of colonial antiques and relics, Native American artifacts. (May-late Oct, daily) Fort Bedford Dr, N end of Juliana St, park along Raystown River. Phone 814/623-8891.

Old Bedford Village. More than 40 authentic log and frame structures (1750-1851) house historical exhibits; crafts demonstrations; operating pioneer farm. Many special events throughout the yr. 1 mi N on US Business 220 N. (Memorial Day wkend-Labor Day) Phone 814/623-1156. ¢¢¢

Skiing. Blue Knob Ski Area. Two triple, two double chairlifts; three platter pulls; patrol, school, rentals; snowmaking; bar, cafeteria; nursery. Longest run approx two mi; vertical drop 1,072 ft. (Dec-Mar, daily) Half-day rates avail. Phone 814/239-5111. ¢¢¢¢

State parks.

Blue Knob. Approx 6,000 acres. Swimming pool, fishing; hunting, hiking, x-country skiing, snowmobiling, sledding, picnicking, playfield, camping (mid-Apr-mid-Oct). Standard fees. 10 mi N on US 220, then 8 mi NW on PA 869. Phone 814/276-3576.

Shawnee. Approx 450-acre lake surrounded by 3,840 acres. Swimming beach, fishing, boating (rentals, mooring, launching); hunting, x-country skiing, snowmobiling, sledding, ice skating, ice fishing, picnicking, playfield, snack bar, camping; tent and trailer sites. Standard fees. 8 mi W on US 30. Phone 814/733-4218.

Special Events

Civil War Reenactment. Old Bedford Village. Early Sept.

Fall Foliage Festival Days. Entertainment, ethnic foods, antique cars, more than 350 craft booths. First two full wkends Oct.

Motels/Motor Lodges

★ ★ **BEST WESTERN.** *4517 Business 220 (15522). 814/623-9006; fax 814/623-7120; toll-free 800/752-8592. www.bestwestern.com.* 105 rms, 2 story. Apr-Oct: S $49.95; D $59.95; suites $67.95; each addl $10; under 18 free; lower rates rest of yr. Crib free. Pet accepted, some restrictions; $50. TV; cable (premium), VCR avail (movies). Pool; whirlpool, lifeguard. Restaurant 6:30-11 am, 5-10 pm; Sat, Sun 6:30 am-10 pm. Bar 5 pm-midnight. Ck-out noon. Meeting rms. Gift shop. Exercise equipt; sauna. Game rm. Cr cds: A, C, D, DS, MC, V.

★ **ECONO LODGE.** *141 Hillcrest Dr (15522). 814/623-5174; fax 814/623-5455. www.hotelchoice.com.* 32 rms, 2 story. May-Oct: S $42-$58; D $46-$65; each addl $6; under 18 free; ski plans; higher rates special events; lower rates rest of yr. Crib free. Pet accepted. TV; cable (premium). Bar 4 pm-midnight. Ck-out 11 am. Downhill ski 15 mi. Game rm. Cr cds: A, C, D, DS, JCB, MC, V.

★ **QUALITY INN.** *4407 Business 220 (15522). 814/623-5188; fax 814/623-0049; toll-free 800/228-5050. www.qualityinn.com.* 66 rms. May-Nov: S $57-$63; D $63-$69; each addl $6; under 18 free; lower rates rest of yr. Crib $4. Pet accepted, some restrictions. TV; cable (premium). Pool. Complimentary continental bkfst. Restaurant 7 am-10 pm. Bar 11 am-11 pm. Ck-out 11 am. Meeting rms. Business servs avail. Downhill ski 20 mi. Cr cds: A, C, D, DS, ER, JCB, MC, V.

Restaurant

★ ★ **ED'S STEAK HOUSE.** *4476 Business 220 (15522). 814/623-8894.* Hrs: 7 am-9 pm; Fri, Sat to 10 pm. Closed Thanksgiving, Dec 25. Res accepted. Bar. Bkfst $2.59-$4.59, lunch $2.99-$5.99, dinner $6.59-$14.99. Child's menu. Specializes in steak, seafood. Family-owned. Cr cds: A, MC, V.

Bellefonte

(C-4) See also State College

Settled 1770 **Pop** 6,395 **Elev** 809 ft
Area code 814 **Zip** 16823

Information Bellefonte Intervalley Area Chamber of Commerce, Train Station, 320 W High St; 814/355-2917

Web www.bellefontechamber.org

When the exiled French minister Talleyrand saw the Big Spring here in 1794, his exclamation—"Beautiful fountain"—gave the town its name. Bellefonte is perched on seven hills at the southeast base of Bald Eagle Mountain.

What to See and Do

Black Moshannon State Park. Approx 3,450 acres. Swimming beach, fishing, boating (rentals, mooring, launching); hunting, hiking, x-country skiing, snowmobiling, ice skating, ice fishing, ice boating, picnicking, snack bar, tent and trailer sites, cabins. Interpretive program. Standard fees. N via PA 144/150, SW via US 220, then approx 12 mi W on PA 504. Phone 814/342-5960.

Centre County Library and Historical Museum. Local historical museum includes central Pennsylvania historical and genealogical books, records. (Mon-Sat; closed hols) 200 N Allegheny St. Phone 814/355-1516. **FREE**

Restaurant

★ ★ **GAMBLE MILL TAVERN.** *160 Dunlap St (16823). 814/355-7764. www.gamblemill.com.* Hrs: 11:30 am-2 pm, 5-8 pm. Closed Sun; Thanksgiving, Dec 25. Res accepted. Continental menu. Bar. A la carte entrees: lunch $6-$10, dinner $12.50-$24. Specializes in fresh seafood, veal, duck. Own desserts. Restored mill (1786); rustic early-American decor. Cr cds: DS, MC, V.

Bethlehem

(D-7) See also Allentown, Easton, Quakertown (Bucks County)

Founded 1741 **Pop** 71,329 **Elev** 340 ft
Area code 484 and 610

Information Bethlehem Tourism Authority, 52 W Broad St, 18018; 610/868-1513 or 800/360-8687

Web www.bethtour.org

The city is famous throughout the world for Bethlehem Steel products and is also well known for its Bach Festival, for Lehigh University (1865), Moravian College (1807), Musikfest, its historic district, and as "America's Christmas city."

Moravians, members of a very old Protestant denomination that came here to the banks of the Lehigh River, assembled on Christmas Eve 1741 in the only building, a log house that was part stable. Singing a hymn that praised Bethlehem, they found a name for their village. The musical heritage, too, dates from this moment; string quartets and symphonies were heard here before any other place in the colonies.

The opening of the Lehigh Canal in 1829 started industrialization of the area and development of the borough of South Bethlehem (1865), which was incorporated into the city of Bethlehem in 1917.

What to See and Do

Apothecary Museum. Original fireplace (1752), where prescriptions were compounded; collection of artifacts includes retorts, grinders, mortars and pestles, scales, blown-glass bottles, labels, and a set of Delft jars (1743); herb and flower garden. (By appt) 424 Main St, in rear; entry gate next to book shop. Phone 610/867-0173. ¢

Brethren's House. (1748) Early residence and shop area for single men of the Moravian Community. Used as a general hospital by the Continental Army during the Revolutionary War. Now serves Moravian College as its Center for Music and Art. Church and Main sts. Phone 610/861-3916.

Central Moravian Church. (1806) Federal-style with hand-carved detail, considered foremost Moravian church in the US. Noted for its music, including a trombone choir in existence since 1754. Main and W Church sts.

God's Acre. (1742-1910) Old Moravian cemetery following Moravian tradition that all gravestones are laid flat, indicating that all are equal in the sight of God. Market St.

Hill-to-Hill Bridge. Joins old and new parts of the city and provides excellent view of historic area, river, and Bethlehem Steel plant. Main St, PA 378 over Lehigh River.

Historic Bethlehem Inc's 18th-Century Industrial Quarter. Guided tours (July-Aug, Sat; late Nov-late Dec, wkends). (See SPECIAL EVENTS) Ohio Rd and Main St (pedestrian entrance); Old York Rd and Union Blvd (parking lot entrance). Phone 610/691-0603. Tours ¢¢ Tour of area includes

Goundie House. (1810) Restored Federal-style brick house has period-furnished rooms and interpretive exhibits. 501 Main St.

Luckenbach Mill. (1869) Restored gristmill contains contemporary craft gallery and museum shop; also the offices of Bethlehem Area Chamber of Commerce and Historic Bethlehem Inc. Interpretive display here is included in guided tour.

Springhouse. (1764) Reconstruction on site of original spring that served Moravian community as a water source from the time of settlement in 1741 until 1912.

Tannery. (1761) Exhibits Moravian crafts, trades, and industries. Includes a working model of the original oil mill.

Waterworks. (1762) with reconstructed 18-ft wooden waterwheel and pumping mechanisms.

Kemerer Museum of Decorative Arts. Exhibits incl art, Bohemian glass, toys, prints, china; regional German folk art from 1750-1900; Federal furniture; period room settings. (Tues-Sun; closed hols) 427 N New St. Phone 610/691-0603. ¢¢

Lost River Caverns. Stalagmites, stalactites, other formations. Picnic area; Gilman Museum with rocks and minerals, ancient and modern armor; also jungle garden (free). Thirty-min guided tours. (Daily; closed Jan 1, Thanksgiving, Dec 25) Durham St, 3 mi SE via PA 412 in Hellertown. Phone 610/838-8767. ¢¢¢

Moravian Museum (Gemein Haus). (1741) This five-story log building is the oldest structure in the city; docents interpret the history and culture of early Bethlehem and the Moravians. 45-min tour. (Tues-Sun; closed hols including Good Friday, Holy Saturday, also Jan) 66 W Church St. Phone 610/867-0173.

Old Chapel. (1751) Once called the "Indian chapel" because so many Native Americans attended the services, this stone structure, the second church for the Moravian congregation, is still used frequently. May be toured only in combination with Moravian Museum community walking tour. Heckewelder Place, adj to Moravian Museum.

Special Events

Shad Festival. Historic Bethlehem Inc's 18th-century Industrial Quarter. Old-fashioned planked shad bake (res required for dinner), exhibits, demonstrations. Phone 610/691-0603. First Sun May.

Bach Festival. Packer Church, Lehigh University campus. One of the country's outstanding musical events. Famous artists and the Bach Choir of Bethlehem participate. Phone 610/866-4382. Mid-late May.

Moravian College Alumni Association Antiques Show. Johnston Hall, Moravian College Campus. Phone 610/861-1366. Early June.

Musikfest. Nine-day festival celebrating Bethlehem's rich musical and ethnic heritage. More than 600 performances (most free) of all types of music including folk, big-band, jazz, Bach, country-western, chamber, classical, gospel, rock, swing; held at nine different sites in downtown historic area. Also children's activities. Phone 610/861-0678. Late Aug.

Christmas. Bethlehem continues more than two centuries of Christmas tradition with candlelight, music, and a number of special events. Moravians sing their own Christmas songs intermingled with Mozart and Handel. A huge "Star of Bethlehem" shines from the top of South Moutain and the Hill-to-Hill Bridge has special lighting. The community "Putzes," a Moravian version of nativity scenes, are open to the public daily. Thousands of people post their Christmas cards from Bethlehem. Night Light Tours of city's Christmas displays and historical areas are offered (Dec) by the Bethlehem Tourism Authority. Res suggested. Phone 610/868-1513 or 800/360-8687. Thanksgiving-Jan 1.

Live Bethlehem Christmas Pageant. Scores of volunteers (garbed in biblical costumes) and live animals (including camels, horses, donkey and sheep) join together to re-create the nativity story; narrated. Phone 610/867-2893. First wkend Dec.

Motels/Motor Lodges

★ **COMFORT INN.** *3191 Highfield Dr (18020). 610/865-6300; fax 610/865-5074; toll-free 800/732-2500. www.comfortinn.com.* 116 rms, 2½ story. S $59-$80; D $66-$86; each addl $6; under 18 free; ski plan. Crib free. Pet accepted. TV; cable, VCR (movies $5). Complimentary continental bkfst. Restaurant adj. Bar noon-2 am; entertainment Fri, Sat. Ck-out noon. Business servs avail. Valet serv. Cr cds: A, C, D, DS, ER, JCB, MC, V.
[D] [🐾] [◨] [♿] [SC] [✈]

★ ★ **HOLIDAY INN.** *3560 Bath Pike; Rtes 512 and 22 (18017). 610/866-5800; fax 610/867-9120; toll-free 888/222-8512. www.holiday-inn.com.* 192 rms, 2 story. S $110-$115; D $120-$125; each addl $10; under 18 free. Crib free. TV; cable. Pool; wading pool, lifeguard. Restaurant 6:30 am-10 pm. Bar 11-2 am. Ck-out noon. Meeting rms. Business center. In-rm modem link. Valet serv. Gift shop. Free airport, bus depot transportation. Exercise equipt. Cr cds: A, C, D, DS, MC, V.
[D] [🛏] [🏋] [◨] [♿] [SC] [🏃]

B&B/Small Inn

★ ★ ★ **WYDNOR HALL INN.** *3612 Old Philadelphia Pike (18015). 610/867-6851; fax 610/866-2062; toll-free 800/839-0020.* 5 rms, 3 story, 2 suites. No elvtr. S $100-$130; D $110-$140; each addl $10; suites $120-$130; wkend rates; wkend, hols (1-3 day min); higher rates special events. TV. Complimentary continental bkfst. Ck-out 11 am, ck-in 2-8 pm. Built in 1895. European-style inn; antiques. Totally nonsmoking. Cr cds: A, C, DS, MC, V.
[◨] [♿]

Restaurants

★ ★ **CAFE.** *221 W Broad St (18018). 610/866-1686.* Hrs: 11 am-2 pm, 5-9 pm. Closed Mon, Sun. Res required Fri, Sat (dinner). International menu. Lunch $6-$7, dinner $14-$21. Specializes in fresh seafood, Thai cuisine,

French pastries. Piano Fri, Sat. Totally nonsmoking. Cr cds: A, D, DS, MC, V.
D

★★★ **CAFE LUIGI.** *2915 Schoen-ersville Rd (18017).* 610/694-8853. Hrs: 4-10 pm. Closed Mon, Sun; hols. Res required Fri, Sat. Italian menu. Setups. A la carte entrees: dinner $11.95-$19.95. Child's menu. Specialties: pasta alla basta, penne alla Dante, chicken alla cognac. Parking. Pictures. Totally nonsmoking. Cr cds: A, DS, MC, V.
D

★★ **CANDLELIGHT INN.** *4431 Easton Ave (18020).* 610/691-7777. Hrs: 11 am-10 pm; Sat from 4 pm; Sun from 10 am. Res accepted. Continental menu. Bar. Lunch $5.95-$8.95, dinner $8.95-$19.95. Child's menu. Specializes in prime rib, steak, seafood. Contemporary decor. Cr cds: A, DS, MC, V.
D ⊒

★★ **EASTERN CHINESE.** *3926 Linden St (18020).* 610/868-0299. Hrs: 11 am-10 pm. Closed Thanksgiving. Res required Fri, Sat (dinner). Chinese menu. Bar. Lunch $6-$8, dinner $10-$15. Specializes in chicken, seafood, beef. Parking. Chinese decor. Cr cds: A, DS, MC, V.
D ⊒

★★★ **INN OF THE FALCON.** *1740 Seidersville Rd (18015).* 610/868-6505. *www.innofthefalcon.com.* Hrs: 5-9:30 pm. Closed Sun; hols. Res required. International menu. Bar. Wine list. A la carte entrees: dinner $15-$24. Specialties: seafood strudel, salmon chaine, filet nouveau. Parking. Building built in 1800s. Antiques, fireplaces. Cr cds: A, MC, V.
D ⊒

★★★ **MAIN STREET DEPOT.** *61 W Lehigh St (18018).* 610/868-7123. Hrs: 11:30 am-2 pm, 4:30-9:30 pm. Closed Sun; hols. Res required Fri, Sat (dinner). Bar to midnight. A la carte entrees: lunch $4.50-$7, dinner $15-$27. Specialties: veal a la Jessica, Norwegian chicken, salmon Adria. Parking. 1873 Victorian railway station; old train pictures, gas chandeliers. Family-owned since 1979. Cr cds: A, MC, V.
D ⊒

★★ **MINSI TRAIL INN.** *626 Stefko Blvd (18018).* 610/691-5613. *www.minsitrail.com.* Hrs: 11 am-9 pm; Sun brunch 11 am-3 pm. Closed hols. Res required Fri, Sat (dinner). Greek, American menu. Bar. A la carte entrees: lunch $5.95-$9.95, dinner $8.95-$18.95. Sun brunch $10.95. Child's menu. Specializes in seafood, veal, beef. Parking. Totally nonsmoking. Cr cds: A, MC, V.
D

Bird-in-Hand

(E-6) *See also Ephrata, Lancaster*

Pop 700 **Elev** 358 ft **Area code** 717 **Zip** 17505
Information Pennsylvania Dutch Convention and Visitors Bureau, 501 Greenfield Rd, Lancaster 17601; 717/299-8901 or 800/723-8824
Web www.800padutch.com

This Pennsylvania Dutch farming village got its name from the signboard of an early inn.

What to See and Do

Amish Village. Reconstructed and original buildings include blacksmith shop, schoolhouse, operating smokehouse; livestock. Guided tours of Amish farmhouse. (Mar-Dec, daily; rest of yr, most wkends; closed wk of Thanksgiving, also Dec 25) 1 mi W on PA 340, then 3 mi S on PA 896. Phone 717/687-8511. ¢¢¢

Bird-in-Hand Farmers' Market. Indoor market with a wide variety of Pennsylvania Dutch foods and gifts. (July-Oct, Wed-Sat; Apr-June and Nov, Wed, Fri, and Sat; rest of yr, Fri and Sat; closed Jan 1, Thanksgiving, Dec 25) On PA 340 and Maple Ave. Phone 717/393-9674.

Folk Craft Center & Museum. Early 18th-century buildings display tools, household implements, stoneware pottery, toys, Stiegel glass, quilts, coverlets, and early Pennsylvania Dutch memorabilia; log cabin loom house (1762); herb and ornamental gardens; turn-of-the-century woodworking and print shops; audiovisual presentation. (Apr-Nov, daily) 1½ mi

W on PA 340, then N on Mt Sidney Rd, in Witmer. Phone 717/397-3609.

DONATION

The People's Place. Arts and heritage center features three-screen documentary on the Amish; interpretive museum with hands-on exhibits; Amish quilt museum. Also bookstore, art gallery. 5 mi E on PA 340, on Main St in Intercourse. (Mon-Sat; closed Jan 1, Thanksgiving, Dec 25) Phone 717/768-7171.

Weavertown One-Room Schoolhouse. Life-size animated re-creation of activities at a one-room schoolhouse. (Early April-Oct, daily; Mar and Nov, wkends) 1 mi E via PA 340. Phone 717/768-3976. ¢¢

Motel/Motor Lodge

★ ★ ★ **BIRD-IN-HAND FAMILY INN.** *2740 Old Philadelphia Pike, Bird-In-Hand (17505). 717/768-8271; fax 717/768-1117; toll-free 800/665-8780. www.bird-in-hand.com.* 100 rms, 1-2 story. May-Nov: S $60-$88; D $74-$90; each addl $8; under 16 free; higher rates wkends; lower rates rest of yr. Crib $6. TV; cable, VCR avail (movies). 2 pools, 1 indoor. Playground. Complimentary coffee in rms. Restaurant 6 am-9 pm. Ck-out 11 am. Coin lndry. Meeting rms. Business servs avail. In-rm modem link. Sundries. Lighted tennis. Game rm. Refrigerators; microwaves avail. Picnic tables. Cr cds: A, D, DS, MC, V.
D 🏃 ☒ ☒ 🏔

B&B/Small Inn

★ ★ ★ **VILLAGE INN.** *2695 Old Philadelphia Pike, Bird-In-Hand (17505). 717/293-8369; fax 717/768-1117; toll-free 800/914-2473. www.bird-in-hand. com/villageinn.* 11 units, 6 suites, 3 story. Mid-June-Nov: S, D $79-$99; each addl $10; suites $109-$139; under 4 free; lower rates rest of yr. Closed early Dec-early Feb. Crib free. TV; cable. Pool privileges. Complimentary continental bkfst. Restaurant nearby. Ck-out noon, ck-in 3 pm. Tennis privileges. Built 1734 as inn on Old Philadelphia Pike. Victorian interior ambience. Cr cds: A, DS, MC, V.
🏃 ☒ 🏔

Restaurants

★ ★ **AMISH BARN.** *3029 Old Philadelphia Pike (17505). 717/768-8886. www.amishbarnpa.com.* Hrs: winter 8 am-7 pm; summer to 9 pm. spring/fall 8 am-8 pm. Closed Jan 1, Dec 25. Res accepted exc hols. Pennsylvania Dutch menu. A la carte entrees: bkfst $3-$5.25, lunch $3.95-$6, dinner $9.95-$16.95. Child's menu. Specialties: apple dumplings, chicken corn soup. Courtyard patio dining. Rustic Amish decor. Family-owned. Cr cds: A, C, DS, MC, V.
D SC ⌐

★ **PLAIN AND FANCY FARM.** *3121 Old Philadelphia Pike (17505). 717/768-4400. www.plainandfancyfarm.com.* Hrs: 11:30 am-8 pm; Sun noon-7 pm. Res accepted. Pennsylvania Dutch cuisine. Closed Dec 24, 25. Complete meals: lunch, dinner $15.95-$16.95. Child's menu. Specializes in family-style food. Authentic Amish homestead. Buggy rides avail 8 am-dusk. Variety of specialty shops. Family-owned. Totally nonsmoking. Cr cds: A, C, DS, MC, V.
D

Bloomsburg

(C-6) *See also Danville*

Settled 1802 **Pop** 12,375 **Elev** 530 ft **Area code** 570 **Zip** 17815

Information Columbia-Montour Visitors Bureau, 121 Papermill Rd; 570/784-8279 or 800/847-4810

Web www.cmtpa.org

Situated on the north bank of the Susquehanna River, Bloomsburg is the seat of Columbia County. The town was a center of mining, transportation, and industry during the 19th and early 20th centuries. Although manufacturing continues to be the largest employer here, Bloomsburg retains the relaxed atmosphere of earlier days with its lovely scenery and many covered bridges. In nearby Orangeville, nine miles west on PA 487, Fishing Creek offers trout, bass, and pickerel.

The only incorporated town in the state (all the others are boroughs or cities), Bloomsburg has silk and rayon manufacturers; it also produces architectural aluminum, processed foods, and electronic products. During the Civil War, Union troops came here to crush the "Fishing Creek Confederacy," a group of alleged draft dodgers who were reportedly building fortifications; no fort was found, and the men were released. One of the "Molly Maguire" murder trials was held here. (The Molly Maguires was a miners' society seeking improved conditions through force and violence.)

What to See and Do

Bloomsburg University of Pennsylvania. (1839) 6,600 students. On campus are Carver Hall (1867); the Harvey A. Andruss Library (1966); Haas Center for the Arts (1967) with 2,000-seat auditorium and art gallery; McCormick Center for Human Services (1985); Redman Stadium and Nelson Field House. Tours (academic yr, Mon-Fri). E 2nd St. Phone 570/389-4316.

Columbia County Historical Society. Museum and Edwin M. Barton Library with local history exhibits, pioneer items. (Apr-Oct, Thurs-Sat; closed hols) 6 mi N on PA 487; 410 Main St, in Orangeville. Phone 570/784-1600. ¢

Historic District. More than 650 structures spanning architectural styles from Georgian to art deco. Center of town. Phone 570/784-7703.

Twin covered bridges. Believed to be only twin covered bridges in US. More than 20 other covered bridges are in the area. 10 mi N on PA 487.

Special Events

Bloomsburg Fair. Fairgrounds, W side of town. Fair held since 1854. Agricultural and industrial exhibits; harness racing. Eight days late Sept.

Bloomsburg Theatre Ensemble. Alvina Krause Theatre, 226 Center St. Three to four wks of performances for each of six plays. Contact BTE, PO Box 66; 717/784-8181. Main stage Oct-June (special performances rest of yr).

Covered Bridge & Arts Festival. I-80, exit 35. Tours of covered bridges; apple butter boil; weaving; old-fashioned arts and crafts. Early Oct.

Motels/Motor Lodges

★ **BUDGET HOST PATRIOT INN.** *6305 Columbia Blvd (17815). 570/387-1776; fax 570/387-9611; toll-free 800/873-1180. www.budgethost.com.* 48 rms. S $42-$48; D $48-$55; each addl $6; under 18 free. Crib free. TV; cable, VCR avail (movies). Restaurant adj 11 am-9 pm. Bar from 4 pm. Ck-out noon. Meeting rms. Business servs avail. Health club privileges. Some refrigerators. Cr cds: A, C, D, DS, MC, V.

D ⊠ 🖈 SC

★ ★ **INN AT BUCKHORN.** *5 Buckhorn Rd (17815). 570/784-5300; fax 570/387-0367; toll-free 888/754-6600. www.pavisnet.com/innatbuckhorn.* 120 rms, 2 story. S $45-$65; D $50-$70; each addl $5; under 18 free. Crib $5. Pet accepted. TV; cable. Coffee in lobby. Restaurant adj 6 am-10 pm. Bar 7-2 am, Sun from 11 am. Ck-out 11 am. Business servs avail. Sundries. Balconies. Cr cds: A, C, D, DS, MC, V.

D 🖈 ⊠ 🖈

B&Bs/Small Inns

★ ★ ★ **INN AT TURKEY HILL.** *991 Central Rd (17815). 570/387-1500; fax 570/784-3718. www.innatturkeyhill.com.* 18 rms, 2 story. S $87, D $92; each addl $15; suites $115-$185; under 12 free. Pet accepted; $15. TV; cable. Complimentary continental bkfst. Dining rm 5-9 pm. Bar. Ck-out noon, ck-in 2 pm. Business servs avail. In-rm modem link. Airport, bus depot transportation. Fireplace in some rms. Elegant antiques. Old homestead (1839); guest rooms overlook landscaped courtyard; gazebo, lily pond. Cr cds: A, C, D, DS, MC, V.

D 🖈 ⊠ 🖈 SC

★ ★ **MAGEE'S MAIN STREET INN.** *20 W Main St (17815). 570/784-3200; fax 570/784-5517; toll-free 800/331-9815. www.magees.com.* 43 rms, 3 story. S $57-$79; D $66-$87; each addl $3.95-$7.95; under 6 free. Pet accepted. TV; cable. Complimentary full bkfst. Dining rm 7 am-midnight. Bar 11-1 am, Sun to 11 pm. Ck-out noon. Meeting rms. Business servs avail. Cr cds: A, C, D, DS, MC, V.

D 🖈 🖈 🖈 ⊠ 🖈

Bradford

(A-3) *See also Kane, Warren*

Settled 1827 **Pop** 9,175 **Elev** 1,442 ft
Area code 814 **Zip** 16701
Information Bradford Area Chamber of Commerce, 10 Marilyn Horne Way, PO Box 135; 814/368-7115
Web www.bradfordpa.com

When oil was discovered here the price of land jumped from about six cents to $1,000 an acre; wells appeared on front lawns, in backyards, even in a cemetery. An oil exchange was established in 1877, two years after the first producing well was brought in. Diversified industry now provides the city's economic base. A Ranger District office of the Allegheny National Forest (see WARREN) is located here.

What to See and Do

Bradford Landmark Society. Headquartered in restored bakery; local history exhibits, period rooms. (Mon, Wed, and Fri; closed hols) 45 E Corydon St. Phone 814/362-3906. **FREE**

Crook Farm. (1848) Original home of Erastus and Betsy Crook; being restored to the 1870s period. (May-Sept, Tues-Fri afternoons, also Sat by appt; closed hols) (See SPECIAL EVENT) On Seaward Ave extension near the Tuna Crossroad. Phone 814/362-3906. ¢

> **Carpenter Shop.** (ca 1870) Reconstruction of original; old hand tools.

> **Old Barn.** (ca 1870) Identical to the original; moved to Crook Farm in 1981 and rebuilt on the site of the original barn.

> **Old One-Room Schoolhouse #8.** (1880) Authentic structure where classes are still held occasionally.

Special Event

Crook Farm Country Fair. Crook Farm. Arts and crafts, exhibits, entertainment, food. Last wkend Aug. Phone 914/362-3906.

Motels/Motor Lodges

★ **DE SOTO HOLIDAY HOUSE.** *515 South Ave (16701). 814/362-4511; fax 814/362-1699.* 70 rms, 2-3 story. No elvtr. S $39-$49; D $47-$53; each addl $4. Crib free. TV; cable. Heated pool; whirlpool. Sauna. Playground. Restaurant 7 am-10 pm; Sun to 8 pm. Bar 11-2 am; entertainment. Ck-out noon. Meeting rms. Business servs avail. Sundries. Rec rm. Driving range, miniature golf, batting cages. Cr cds: A, C, D, DS, MC, V.

★ **HOWARD JOHNSON MOTOR LODGE.** *100 S Davis St (16701). 814/362-4501; fax 814/362-2709; toll-free 800/654-2000. www.hojo.com.* 120 rms, 3 story. S $64-$74; D $69-$79; each addl $10; under 12 free. Crib free. TV; cable (premium). Heated pool; lifeguard. Restaurant 6:30 am-2 pm, 5-10 pm. Bar 3 pm-1 am. Ck-out noon. Meeting rms. Business servs avail. Valet serv. Health club privileges. Cr cds: A, C, D, DS, JCB, MC, V.

B&B/Small Inn

★★★ **GLENDORN - A LODGE IN THE COUNTRY.** *1032 W Corydon (16701). 814/362-6511; fax 814/368-9923; toll-free 800/843-8568. www.glendorn.com.* 12 units, 2 story (main lodge), 4 suites, 6 cabins. AP: S $285-$485; D $345-$545; each addl $100; cabins $445-$1,545; wkend rates; hols (2-day min). Closed Jan. Children over 12 yrs only. TV. Heated pool. Sittings: 9:30 am bkfst, 1 pm lunch, 7:30 pm dinner. Ck-out 2 pm, ck-in 11 am. Luggage handling. Business servs avail. Tennis. Golf privileges. X-country ski on site. Exercise equipt. Game rm. Lawn games. Some refrigerators. Cr cds: A, MC, V.

Breezewood

(E-4) *See also Bedford, Chambersburg*

Pop 180 **Elev** 1,356 ft **Area code** 814
Zip 15533

Motels/Motor Lodges

★★ **BEST WESTERN PLAZA MOTOR LODGE.** *16407 Lincoln Hwy (15533). 814/735-4352; fax 814/735-*

3036; toll-free 800/780-7234. www. bestwestern.com. 89 rms, 2 story. S $37-$42; D $43-$52; each addl $7. Crib $7. TV; cable (premium). Pool. Restaurant 7 am-10 pm. Ck-out 11 am. Meeting rm. Cr cds: A, C, D, DS, MC, V.

★ **QUALITY INN BREEZE MANOR.** 16621 Lincoln Hwy (15533). 814/735-4311; fax 814/735-3433; res 800/228-5151. www.qualityinn.com. 50 rms, 1-2 story. May-Nov: S $43-$76; D $48-$76; each addl $5; family rates; lower rates rest of yr. Crib $5. TV; cable (premium). Heated pool; wading pool, lifeguard. Playground. Restaurant opp open 24 hrs. Ck-out noon. Coin lndry. Business servs avail. Sundries. Cr cds: A, C, D, DS, ER, JCB, MC, V.

★ **RAMADA INN.** US Rte 30 & I-70 (15533). 814/735-4005; fax 814/735-3228; toll-free 814/535-4025. www. ramada.com. 125 rms, 2 story. Apr-Oct: S $57; D $79; under 18 free; lower rates rest of yr. Crib avail. Pet accepted, some restrictions. TV; cable (premium), VCR avail (movies). Indoor pool. Playground. Restaurant 6:30 am-10 pm. Rm serv. Bar 4 pm-midnight. Ck-out noon. Meeting rms. Business center. In-rm modem link. Gift shop. Golf privileges. Exercise equipt. Game rm. Some in-rm whirlpool. Picnic tables. Cr cds: A, C, D, DS, JCB, MC, V.

Bristol (Bucks County)

(E-8) See also Philadelphia

Settled 1697 **Pop** 9,923 **Elev** 20 ft
Area code 215 & 267 **Zip** 19007
Information Bucks County Conference and Visitors Bureau, Inc, 152 Swamp Rd, Doylestown 18901; 215/345-4552 or 800/836-BUCKS
Web www.buckscountycvb.org

Bristol, founded in 1681, was the main thoroughfare from Philadelphia to New York. It has been frequented by famous visitors including Joseph Bonaparte, brother of Napoleon, and General Lafayette. There are homes dating from the 1700s; most of these have been restored.

What to See and Do

Grave of Captain John Green. Grave of US Navy captain who piloted the *Columbia* around the world in 1787-1789 on first such voyage by vessel flying American flag. St. James Protestant Episcopal Church Burial Ground. Cedar and Walnut sts.

Historic Fallsington. Restored 17th-, 18th-, and 19th-century buildings. Guided tours of 17th-century log house, Burges-Lippincott house, tavern. Also museum store. (See SPECIAL EVENT) (Mid-May-Oct, daily; closed hols) 4 Yardley Ave, Fallsington, 5 mi N of PA Tpke, off PA 13. Phone 215/295-6567. ¢¢

Pennsbury Manor. Reconstruction of William Penn's 17th-century country manor; formal and kitchen gardens; livestock. Craft demonstrations; hands-on workshops. (Tues-Sun; closed some hols) 5 mi NE at 400 Pennsbury Memorial Rd, off Bordentown Rd. Phone 215/946-0400. ¢¢

Sesame Place. Family theme park combines fun with learning. More than 50 outdoor physical play activities develop skills and coordination with kid-powered units. The indoor interactive and science galleries offer games to challenge the mind. Sesame Food Factory: visible kitchen-in-the-round serves wholesome favorites. Mr. Hooper's Emporium: complete shop for all Sesame Street items. Sesame Island area with Caribbean theme; water activities including Big Bird's Rambling River and Sky Splash. Musical revue with Sesame Street characters. (May-Labor Day, daily; after Labor Day-late Oct, wkends only) Approx 7 mi N, near Oxford Valley Mall (Langhorne), just N of Philadelphia off I-95 between Philadelphia and Trenton, NJ. Phone 215/752-7070. ¢¢¢¢

Special Event

Fallsington Day. In Fallsington. Outdoor fair; restored buildings open; colonial craft demonstrations; entertainment. Second Sat Oct.

Brookville

(C-2) See also Clarion

Settled 1830 **Pop** 4,230 **Elev** 1,269 ft
Area code 814 **Zip** 15825
Information Brookville Area Chamber of Commerce, 70 Pickering St; 814/849-8448

What to See and Do

Clear Creek State Park. Approx 1,600 acres. Swimming beach, fishing, canoeing; hiking trails, x-country skiing, picnicking, playing field, camping, cabins (dump station). Nature center; interpretive activities. Standard fees. 8 mi N on PA 36, then 4 mi NE on PA 949. Contact Park Manager, RD 1, Box 82, Sigel 15860; Phone 814/752-2368.

Special Event

Western Pennsylvania Laurel Festival. Phone 814/849-2024. Third wk June.

Motels/Motor Lodges

★ **DAYS INN.** *US 322 & I-80, exit 13 (15825). 814/849-8001; fax 814/849-9647; toll-free 800/329-7466. www. daysinn.com.* 118 rms, 3 story. S $40-$60; D $45-$85; each addl $5; under 18 free; higher rates hunting season. Crib free. Pet accepted. TV; cable. Heated pool; wading pool, whirlpool, poolside serv, lifeguard. Restaurant 6-10 am, 4:30-10 pm; winter from 7 am. Bar 5 pm-midnight; closed Sun. Ck-out noon. Coin lndry. Business servs avail. X-country ski 17 mi. Game rm. Cr cds: A, D, DS, MC, V.

★★ **HOLIDAY INN EXPRESS.** *235 Allegheny Blvd (15825). 814/849-8381; fax 814/849-8386. www.holiday-inn. com.* 68 rms, 3 story. S $50-$60; D $57-$67; each addl $7; under 12 free; higher rates hunting season. Crib

free. Pet accepted. TV; cable (premium). Complimentary continental bkfst. Restaurant adj 11 am-11 pm. Ck-out noon. Coin lndry. Meeting rm. Business servs avail. Sundries. Private patios, balconies. Cr cds: A, C, D, DS, MC, V.

Restaurant

★★ **MEETING PLACE.** *209 Main St (15825). 814/849-2557.* Hrs: 11 am-8:30 pm; Sun to 2 pm. Closed hols. Res accepted. Bar. Bkfst $2-$5, lunch $2.75-$7, dinner $4.95-$12. Child's menu. Specializes in salads, chicken, seafood. Restored Victorian building (1871); casual dining. Cr cds: A, D, DS, MC, V.

Bucks County

Bucks County's great natural resources, location, and waterway transportation were known to the Leni-Lenape centuries ago. Dutch explorers, followed by Swedes, English Quakers, and Germans, began to take possession of the area in the 1600s. William Penn established his country estate in this area in the 17th century.

The county's historic importance is highlighted in the central section—it was here that General George Washington crossed the Delaware River with the Continental Army during the Revolutionary War. More recently, artists and writers have settled in and around New Hope, giving rise to the village's fame as an art center. Bucks County's scenic beauty and rich history make it a popular tourist spot.

Following are the places in Bucks County included in the *Mobil Travel Guide*. For full information on any one of them, see the individual alphabetical listing: Bristol, Doylestown, New Hope, Quakertown, Washington Crossing Historic Park.

Laughlin Grist Mill

Bushkill

(C-8) *See also Milford*

Pop 900 **Elev** 365 ft **Area code** 570
Zip 18324

Information Pocono Moutains Vacation Bureau, 1004 Main St, Strouds-burg 18360; 570/424-6050; for free brochure phone 800/POCONOS

Web www.poconos.org

What to See and Do

Bushkill Falls. Largest series of falls in Pocono Moutains. Main falls have 100-ft drop. Scenic gorge. Fishing, boating; picnicking. Wildlife exhibit of mounted animals and birds of Pennsylvania. (Apr-mid-Nov, daily) 2 mi N off US 209 on local road. Phone 570/588-6682. ¢¢¢

Delaware Water Gap. (see) 3 E Main St. Phone 315/386-8133. ¢¢

Pocono Indian Museum. Traces history of the Delaware through displays of artifacts, weapons, and tools. Gift shop. (Daily; closed Thanksgiving, Dec 25) 3 mi S on US 209. Phone 570/588-9338. ¢¢

Butler

(D-1) *See also Harmony, Pittsburgh*

Settled 1793 **Pop** 15,121 **Elev** 1,077 ft
Area code 724 **Zip** 16003

Information Butler County Chamber of Commerce, PO Box 1082; 724/283-2222

Web www.butlercountychamber.com

This is a manufacturing city nestled amid rolling hills that were owned by Robert Morris of Philadelphia, financier of the Revolutionary War.

The city and county are named for General Richard Butler, who died in the St. Clair Indian Expedition. During the 1930s, the Butler-based American Austin Company—later called American Bantam Company—pioneered the development of small, lightweight cars in America and invented the prototype of the jeep.

What to See and Do

Cooper Cabin. (ca 1810) A family homestead on four acres with heirlooms and memorabilia; spinning house, spring house, tool shed. Self-guided nature trail and herb garden; live history demonstrations and tours. (Call for hrs and events) 199 Cooper Rd, in Cabot. Phone 724/283-8116. ¢

Jennings Environmental Education Center. Blazing Star, a relict prairie wildflower, blooms profusely here late July-early Aug. Trails, guided walks, interpretive center; picnicking. (Memorial Day-Labor Day, daily; rest of yr, Mon-Fri, some Sun) 12 mi N, at jct PA 8, 528, 173. Phone 724/794-6011. **FREE**

Moraine State Park. A 3,225-acre lake in a 16,180-acre park. Swimming beaches, fishing, boating (rentals, mooring, launching, marina); hunting, hiking, bicycle trails (rentals), horseback riding, x-country skiing, snowmobiling, sledding, ice skating, ice fishing, ice boating, picnicking, playground, snack bar, restaurant, cabin rentals. Waterfowl observation area; interpretive programs. Pontoon boat tours. 12 mi NW on US 422. Phone 724/368-8811. **FREE**

Motels/Motor Lodges

★ ★ **CONLEY RESORT INN.** *740 Pittsburgh Rd (16002). 724/586-7711; fax 724/586-2944; toll-free 800/344-7303. www.conleyresort.com.* 56 rms, 3 story. No elvtr. S $62-$65; D $84-$99; each addl $10; under 18 free; golf plans. Crib free. TV. Indoor pool; whirlpool, lifeguard. Sauna. Restaurant 7 am-10 pm. Bar 11-2 am; Sun to midnight. Ck-out 1 pm. Meeting rms. Business servs avail. Sundries. Rec rm. Tennis. 18-hole golf, greens fee $20-$32, putting green. X-country ski on site. Game rm. 150-ft indoor water slide. Cr cds: A, DS, MC, V.
🏊 D 🏌️ 🎿 ≈ 🐾

★ **DAYS INN.** *139 Pittsburgh Rd (16001). 724/287-6761; fax 724/287-4307; toll-free 800/329-7466. www. daysinn.com.* 139 rms, 2 story. S $56-$72; D $62-$77; each addl $6; family rates; golf package plan. Crib free. Pet accepted. TV; cable. Indoor pool; whirlpool, lifeguard. Coffee in rms. Restaurant 6 am-10 pm. Bar 3 pm-2 am; Sun 1 pm-midnight; entertainment. Ck-out 11 am. Coin lndry. Meeting rms. Business servs avail. Valet serv. Sundries. Exercise equipt. Game rm. Cr cds: A, D, DS, MC, V.
🐾 ≈ 🏌️ 🎿 🐾 **SC**

★ **MCKEE'S MOTEL.** *930 New Castle Rd (16001). 724/865-2272.* 22 rms. S $29.68-$33.92; D $41; kit. units $49; under 5 free; wkly rates. TV; cable. Ck-out 11 am. Cr cds: A, DS, MC, V.
🎿 🐾

B&B/Small Inn

★ ★ ★ **APPLEBUTTER INN.** *666 Centreville Pike, Slippery Rock (16057). 724/794-1844; fax 724/794-3319; res 888/275-3466. www.pathway.net/apple butterinn.* 11 rms, 2 story. S $59-$79; D $79-$125; each addl $15; higher rates wkends. Adults only. TV. Complimentary full bkfst. Ck-out 11 am, ck-in 3-8 pm; Fri, Sat 3-10 pm. Sitting rm. Massage. Restored brick farmhouse (1844) furnished with antiques; addition 1988. Totally non-smoking. Cr cds: A, MC, V.
D 🎿 🐾

Canadensis (C-7)

Pop 1,200 **Area code** 570 **Zip** 18325

What to See and Do

Holley Ross Pottery. Twenty-min guided tours with demonstration of pottery making (Mon-Fri). Swinging bridge, park, sawdust trails. (May-mid-Dec, daily) S on PA 390, NW on PA 447, on PA 191 N in La Anna. Phone 570/676-3248. **FREE**

Resort

★ ★ ★ **SKYTOP LODGE.** *1 Skytop, Mt Pocono (18357). 570/595-7401; fax 570/595-9618; toll-free 800/345-7759. www.skytop.com.* 185 rms, 1-4 story,

0 cottages. Rates: S, D $395-$650, ratuity/svc charge $30; under 18 ree; family, wkend, hol rates; ski, olf plans; wkends, hols (3-day min); igher rates some hols; lower rates est of yr. Crib free. 2 pools, 1 ndoor; wading pool, whirlpool, oolside serv, lifeguard. Playground. upervised children's activities; ages -10. Dining rm. Box lunches, pic-ics. Bar noon-midnight. Ck-out 1 m, ck-in 4 pm. Gift shop. Grocery, oin lndry 3-5 mi. Bellhops. Valet erv. Meeting rms. Business servs vail. Sports dir. Tennis, pro. 18-hole olf, pro, greens fee $40, putting reen, driving range. Downhill/x-ountry ski on site. Boats. Sleighing, oboganing. Hiking. Bicycle rentals. awn games. Soc dir. Rec rm. Game m. Exercise rm; sauna, steam rm. Massage. Fishing guides, clean and tore. Refrigerators in cottages. Picnic ables. On beach. Cr cds: A, C, D, DS, MC, V.

&Bs/Small Inns

★★★ CRESCENT LODGE. *191 aradise Valley, Mt Pocono (18326). 70/595-7486; fax 570/595-3452; ll-free 800/392-9400. www.crescent dge.com.* 12 lodge rms, 4 motel ms, 9 suites, 6 cottages (some with it.). Mid-June-mid-Sept: S, D $85-185; each addl $15; suites $172-275; kit. cottages $1,000-$1,150/wk; P, MAP, wkly rates; ski plans; lower ates rest of yr. TV; cable. Heated ool. Complimentary continental kfst (exc summer). Restaurant. Bar. k-out 11 am, ck-in 2 pm. Business ervs avail. Free bus depot trans-ortation. Gift shop. Tennis. Down-ill/x-country ski 5 mi. Fitness trail. awn games. Some refrigerators; vhirlpool in suites. Varied accom-odations. Private patios. Picnic ables. Same owners for over 40 yrs. r cds: A, D, DS, MC, V.

★★ PINE KNOB INN. *RR 447 8325). 570/595-2532; fax 570/595-429; toll-free 800/426-1460. ww.pineknobinn.com.* 28 units, 19 aths. No rm phones. MAP: S $79-95; D $168-$200. TV in library; able. Ck-out 11 am, ck-in 2 pm. ennis. Downhill/x-country ski 5 mi.

Lawn games. Pre-Civil War period inn (1847); antiques. Cr cds: A, DS, MC, V.

★ PUMP HOUSE INN. *Rte 390 N (18325). 570/595-7501.* 8 rms, 2 story. S, D $65-$100; each addl $5; suites $85-$100. Complimentary continental bkfst. Restaurant (see also PUMP HOUSE INN). Ck-out 11 am, ck-in 2 pm. Built as stagecoach stop in 1842; furnished in country decor; antiques. Cr cds: C, D, MC, V.

Restaurant

★★★ PUMP HOUSE INN. *Rte 390 N (18325). 570/595-7501.* Hrs: 5-9 pm; Sun 2:30-8:30 pm. Closed Mon; Dec 25. Res accepted. French, Ameri-can menu. Bar. Wine list. Dinner $13.95-$24.95. Specialties: roast rack of lamb, shrimp in beer batter, choco-late mousse. Own breads. Country inn (1842). Cr cds: D, MC, V.

Carbondale

(B-7) *See also Hawley, Scranton*

Founded 1822 **Pop** 9,804 **Elev** 1,070 ft **Area code** 570 **Zip** 18407

Information Northeast Pennsylvania Convention and Visitors Bureau, 99 Glenmaura Natl Blvd, Scranton, 18507; 800/229-3526

Web www.visitnepa.org

Carbondale, located in the heart of the northeast Pocono area, has excel-lent sports facilities. There are 33 lakes within an eight-mile radius and 201 more lakes within 25 miles. One of the first railroad lines in the coun-try was built to haul coal from Car-bondale.

What to See and Do

Merli-Sarnoski Park. Covers 850 acres of woodlands with 40-acre lake. Swimming beach (lifeguards), fishing (seasonal), boating (launch); hiking trails, picnicking. Winter activities including x-country skiing, ice-skating, ice fishing. (Daily) Extra ½ mi off PA 106. Phone 570/876-1714.

Ski areas.

Elk Mountain Ski Center. At an elevation of 2,693 ft, this is eastern Pennsylvania's highest mountain. Quad, five double chairlifts; patrol, school, rentals; cafeteria, restaurant, bar. Longest run two mi; vertical drop 1,000 ft. (Early Dec-late Mar, daily) Half-day rate. NW on PA 106, E on PA 374. ¢¢¢¢¢

Mount Tone Ski Resort. Triple chairlift, T-bar, rope tow, mighty mite; school, rentals; snowmaking; cafeteria; lodge. Vertical drop 450 ft. (Late Dec-mid-Mar) Two mountains, ten trails; also night skiing, x-country trails. N via PA 171, E via PA 370 to Lakewood, then S on PA 247 to Lake Como, follow signs. Phone 570/798-2707. ¢¢¢¢¢

Carlisle

(E-5) *See also Harrisburg*

Settled 1720 **Pop** 17,970 **Elev** 478 ft
Area code 717 **Zip** 17013
Information Greater Area Chamber of Commerce, 212 N Hanover St, PO Box 572; 717/243-4515
Web www.carlislechamber.org

In the historically strategic Cumberland Valley, Carlisle was a vital point for Native American fighting during the Revolutionary and Civil wars.

Carlisle Barracks is one of the oldest military posts in America. Soldiers mounted guard here as early as 1750 to protect the frontier. From here began British campaigns that drove the French from the Ohio Valley and, in 1763, the march to relieve Fort Pitt. In 1794 President Washington reviewed troops assembled to march against the "Whiskey Rebels." Troops went from the Barracks to the Mexican and Civil wars. The famous Carlisle Indian Industrial School, the first nonreservation school, was here until 1918. The Barracks was reopened in 1920 as the Medical Field Service School. It is now the home of the US Army War College.

George Ross, James Wilson, and James Smith, all signers of the Declaration of Independence, lived in Carlisle, as did Molly Pitcher.

What to See and Do

Carlisle Barracks. Army War College, senior school in US Army's educational system. Includes the US Army Military History Institute and Hessian Powder Magazine Museum (1777), built by prisoners captured at the Battle of Trenton. The Carlisle Indian Industrial School (1879-1918) was one of the first institutions of higher learning for Native Americans. Also includes the Omar Bradley Museum, containing a collection of personal and military memorabilia of the five-star general. Jim Thorpe and other famous Native American athletes studied here. Military History Institute and the Omar Bradley Museum (Mon-Fri; closed federal hols). Post/grounds (daily; closed federal hols). 1 mi N on US 11. Phone 717/245-3611. **FREE**

Cumberland County Historical Society and Hamilton Library Association. Woodcarvings, furniture, silver, tools, redware, ironware, tall-case clocks, coverlets, paintings by local artisans; mementos of the Carlisle Indian School; special exhibits and programs. Library contains books, tax lists, early photographs, genealogical material. (Tues-Sat, Mon eves; closed hols) 21 N Pitt St. Phone 717/249-7610. **FREE**

Dickinson College. (1773) 1,900 students. Tenth college chartered in US; President James Buchanan was a graduate. On campus is "Old West" (1804), a building registered as a National Historic Landmark that was designed by Benjamin Henry Latrobe, one of the designers of the Capitol in Washington. Tours of campus. W High St (US 11). Phone 717/243-5121. Also here is

The Trout Gallery. Permanent and temporary exhibits. (Sept-mid-June, Tues-Sat) Emil R. Weiss Center for the Arts. Phone 717/245-1711. **FREE**

Grave of "Molly Pitcher". (Mary Ludwig Hays McCauley) Soldiers in the Battle of Monmouth (June 1778) gave Molly her nickname because of her devotion to her husband and others who were fighting by bringing hem pitchers of water. When her husband was wounded, Molly took his place at a cannon and continued fighting for him. In Old Graveyard, E South St.

Huntsdale Fish Hatchery. Springs and mountain stream fill tanks and ponds of brown, rainbow, and palomino trout, muskellunge, and walleye; visitor center. (Daily) 10 mi SW in Huntsdale. Phone 717/486-3419. **FREE**

Pine Grove Furnace State Park. Pre-Revolutionary iron, slate, and brick works were in this area. Approx 696 acres. Swimming beaches, fishing, boating (rentals, mooring, launching); hunting, hiking, bicycling (rentals), x-country skiing, ice skating, ice fishing, picnicking, snack bar, store, tent and trailer sites. Visitor center. Lodging avail 10 mi SW on I-81, exit 11, then 8 mi S on PA 233. Phone 717/486-7575.

Special Events

Summerfair. Downtown Carlisle. Early July.

Art Festival and Octoberfest. Oct.

Motels/Motor Lodges

★ ★ **APPALACHIAN TRAIL INN.** 1825 Harrisburg Pike (17013). 717/245-2242; fax 717/258-4881; toll-free 800/445-6715. 200 rms, 2 story. Apr-Oct: S $42-$52; D $47-$57; each addl $5; suites $85-$125; under 12 free; higher rates car shows; lower rates rest of yr. Crib free. TV; cable (premium). Restaurant 5-2 am. Ck-out noon. Business servs avail. Downhill ski 16 mi. Picnic tables. Cr cds: A, D, DS, MC, V.
⊠ D ⊠ 🐾

★ ★ **BEST WESTERN.** 1245 Harrisburg Pike (17013). 717/243-5411; fax 717/243-0778; toll-free 800/304-1082. www.bestwestern.com. 130 rms, 2 story. S $46.50-$64.50; D $63.50-$77.50; each addl $7; suites $68.50-$140; under 18 free. Crib free. TV; cable (premium), VCR avail (movies). Pool; lifeguard. Restaurant 6:30 am-9 pm. Bar 5 pm-1 am. Ck-out noon. Meeting rms. Valet serv. Sundries. Health club privileges. Microwaves avail. Cr cds: A, C, D, DS, ER, MC, V.
D ⊠ ⊠ 🐾 SC

★ **CLARION INN AND CONVENTION CENTER.** 1700 Harrisburg Pike (17013). 717/243-1717; fax 717/243-6648; toll-free 800/692-7315. www.clarioncarlisle.com. 270 rms. S $62; D $67; each addl $5; suites $110-$173; under 18 free. Crib $10. Pet accepted. TV; cable (premium), VCR avail (movies). Indoor pool; whirlpool. Sauna. Restaurant 7 am-9 pm. Bar 11-2 am. Ck-out 11 am. Meeting rms. Business servs avail. In-rm modem link. Sundries. Gift shop. Tennis. Refrigerators; microwaves avail. Cr cds: A, C, D, DS, ER, MC, V.
D 🐾 ⊠ ⊠ 🐾 SC

★ **DAYS INN.** 101 Alexander Spring Rd (17013). 717/258-4147; fax 717/258-1207; toll-free 800/329-7466. www.daysinn.com. 130 rms, 3 story. S $55-$80; D $60-$80; suites $85-$125; each addl $5; under 18 free; higher rates special events. Crib free. TV; cable, VCR avail (movies). Pool; lifeguard. Complimentary continental bkfst. Restaurant nearby. Ck-out noon. Coin lndry. Meeting rm. Business servs avail. Sundries. Airport transportation. Exercise equipt. Game rm. Some refrigerators. Cr cds: A, C, D, DS, JCB, MC, V.
D ⊠ 🏋 ⊠ 🐾 SC

★ ★ **HOLIDAY INN.** 1450 Harrisburg Pike (17013). 717/245-2400; fax 717/245-9070; toll-free 800/465-4329. 100 rms, 2 story. S, D $79; each addl $10; under 18 free; higher rates special events. Crib free. Pet accepted. TV; cable (premium), VCR avail. Pool; lifeguard. Restaurant 6:30 am-2 pm, 5-10 pm. Bar 11 am-midnight. Ck-out noon. Coin lndry. Meeting rms. Business servs avail. In-rm modem link. Valet serv. Health club privileges. Cr cds: A, D, DS, JCB, MC, V.
D 🐾 ⊠ ⊠ 🐾 SC

★ **QUALITY INN.** 1255 Harrisburg Pike (17013). 717/243-6000; fax 717/258-4123; res 800/228-5151. www.qualityinn.com. 96 rms, 2 story. S, D $62.99; each addl $5; under 18 free; higher rates special events. Crib free. Pet accepted. TV; cable (premium). Pool; wading pool. Complimentary continental bkfst. Coffee in rms. Restaurant adj open 24 hrs. Bar 5 pm-midnight. Ck-out noon. Coin lndry. Meeting rm. Business servs

avail. Valet serv. Refrigerators, microwaves avail. Cr cds: A, D, DS, MC, V.

★ **SUPER 8 MOTEL.** *1800 Harrisburg
Pike (17013). 717/249-7000; fax
717/249-9070; toll-free 800/800-8000.
www.super8.com.* 112 rms, 2 story, 16
kits. S $40-$80; D $45-$90; kits. $58;
under 12 free; higher rates special
events. Crib free. TV; cable. Complimentary coffee in lobby. Restaurant
nearby. Ck-out 11 am. Coin lndry.
Microwaves avail. Cr cds: A, D, DS,
MC, V.

Resort

★ ★ ★ **ALLENBERRY RESORT INN.**
*1559 Boiling Springs Rd, Boiling Springs
(17007). 717/258-3211; fax 717/960-
5293; toll-free 800/430-5468. www.
allenberry.com.* 69 rms in lodges, 1
cottage (3-bedrm). S $89; D $109;
each addl $15; suites $225; cottage
$295; under 17 free; package plans.
Crib free. TV. Pool; wading pool,
whirlpool, lifeguard. Dining rm 8-10
am, 11 am-2 pm, 5-9 pm. Bar 11 am-
midnight. Ck-out noon. Meeting
rms. Business servs avail. Airport
transportation. Lighted tennis. Professional theater. On 57 wooded
acres, 200-yr-old trees; several remodeled limestone buildings date from
1785, 1812. On Yellow Breeches
Creek. Cr cds: A, DS, MC, V.

Restaurants

★ ★ **BOILING SPRINGS TAVERN.**
*Front and First sts, Boiling Springs
(17007). 717/258-3614.* Hrs: 11:30
am-10 pm. Closed Sun, Mon; hols.
Res accepted. Continental menu. Bar.
Lunch $5.95-$11.95, dinner $11-$22.
Child's menu. Specializes in fresh
seafood, aged Western steak. Old
stone structure (1832), originally an
inn. Colonial decor. Cr cds: A, MC, V.

★ ★ ★ **CALIFORNIA CAFE.** *38 W
Pomfret St (17013). 717/249-2028.
www.calcaf.com.* Hrs: 11 am-9 pm.
Closed Memorial Day wknd, Dec 25.
Res accepted. French, California
menu. Serv bar. Lunch $4.45-$9.45.
Complete meals: dinner $14.95-
$22.95. Specialties: escalope de veau
aux artichauts, poulet grille chasseur.

1859 fire station building; French
and Florentine artwork in addition to
artwork from local gallery. Cr cds: A,
D, DS, MC, V.

Chambersburg

(E-4)

Settled 1730 **Pop** 17,862 **Elev** 621 ft
Area code 717 **Zip** 17201
Information Chamber of Commerce,
75 S Second St; 717/264-7101. Information is also available at the Visitors Station, 1235 Lincoln Way E;
717/261-1200
Web www.chambersburg.org

Named for Colonel Benjamin Chambers, a Scottish-Irish pioneer, this is
an industrial county seat amid peach
and apple orchards. John Brown had
his headquarters here. During the
Civil War, Confederate cavalry
burned down the town, destroying
537 buildings after the citizens
refused to pay an indemnity of
$100,000.

What to See and Do

Caledonia State Park. Confederate
General Jubal A. Early came through
here during the Civil War and
destroyed an iron furnace, which
had been producing arms for the
Union armies. Approx 1,100 acres.
Swimming pool (fee), fishing; nature
and hiking trails, bicycling, 18-hole
golf course, x-country skiing, picnicking, playground, snack bar, tent
and trailer sites. Standard fees. (See
SPECIAL EVENTS) 10 mi E on US 30.
Phone 717/352-2161.

Capitol Theatre. This 1927 movie
house presents performances ranging
from classical concerts to big bands;
theatrical presentations. Features a
1928 Moller pipe organ. Call for performances and fees. 159 S Main St.
Phone 717/263-0202.

The Old Jail. Jail complex (1818)
restored and renovated for use as the
Kittochtinny Historical Society's
Museum and Library. An 1880 cell
block houses community cultural

activities, art and historical exhibits; other events. Also on grounds are Colonial, Fragrance, and Japanese gardens; 19th-century barn; agricultural museum. Cultural programs (May-Oct). Tours (May-Nov, Thurs-Sat). 175 E King St. Phone 717/264-6364. **FREE**

Special Events

Totem Pole Playhouse. Caledonia State Park. Resident professional theater company performs dramas, comedies, and musicals in 453-seat proscenium theater. Tues-Sun eves; matinees Wed, Sat-Sun. Phone 717/352-2164. June-Aug.

ChambersFest. Caledonia State Park. Civil War festival with crafts, food, reenactments, parade of pets. Phone 717/264-7101. July.

Franklin County Fair. Arts and crafts displays, needlework, home and dairy products, state turkey-calling contest, tractor pull, agricultural and livestock exhibits, entertainment. Phone 717/369-4100. Third full wk Aug.

Motels/Motor Lodges

★ **DAYS INN.** 30 Falling Spring Rd (17201). 717/263-1288; fax 717/263-6514. www.daysinn.com. 107 rms, 3 story. Apr-Oct: S $46-$60; D $51-$65; each addl $7; suites $70-$85; under 17 free; lower rates rest of yr. Crib free. Pet accepted. TV; cable (premium). Complimentary continental bkfst. Restaurant adj 6 am-11 pm. Ck-out 11 am. Business servs avail. Downhill ski 15 mi. Cr cds: A, D, DS, MC, V.
🐾 D 🐾 ⊠ 🔥

★★ **HAMPTON INN.** 955 Lesher Rd (17201). 717/261-9185; fax 717/261-1984; toll-free 800/426-7866. www.hamptoninn.com. 124 rms, 3 story. May-Oct: S, D $64-$72; under 18 free; higher rates special events; lower rates rest of yr. Crib free. TV; cable (premium). Complimentary continental bkfst. Coffee in rms. Restaurant adj 6 am-11 pm. Ck-out noon. Meeting rms. Business servs avail. In-rm modem link. Sundries. Exercise equipt. Refrigerators. Cr cds: A, C, D, DS, MC, V.
D 🐓 ⊠ 🔥 SC

★ **QUALITY INN AND SUITES.** 1095 Wayne Ave (17201). 717/263-3400; fax 717/263-8386; toll-free 800/465-4329. www.qualityinn.com. 139 rms, 2 story. Apr-Oct: S $59; D $66; each adl $7; under 19 free; wkend rates; golf plan; lower rates rest of yr. Crib free. Pet accepted, some restrictions. TV; cable, VCR avail. Pool; poolside serv, lifeguard. Restaurant 6 am-2 pm, 5-10 pm. Bar. Ck-out noon. Meeting rms. Business servs avail. Some in-rm modem links. Bellhops. Sundries. Valet serv. 18-hole golf privileges. Health club privileges. Cr cds: A, D, DS, JCB, MC, V.
D 🐾 ⊠ 🍴 ⊠ 🐾 SC

★ **TRAVELODGE.** 565 Lincoln Way E (17201). 717/264-4187; fax 717/264-2446; res 800/578-7878. www.travelodge.com. 52 rms, 3 story. S $39-$49; D $45-$57; each addl $7; under 18 free. Crib free. Pet accepted, some restrictions. TV; cable (premium). Coffee in rms. Restaurant 6 am-2 pm, 4:30-9:30 pm. Bar 11 am-2 pm, 4:30-9:30 pm. Ck-out noon. Meeting rm. Health club privileges. Refrigerators avail. Some balconies. Cr cds: A, DS, MC, V.
D 🐓 ⊠ 🔥

B&Bs/Small Inns

★★★ **MERCERSBURG INN.** 405 S Main St, Mercersburg (17236). 717/328-5231; fax 717/328-3403. www.mercersburginn.com. 15 rms, 3 story. S, D $120-$235; each addl $25. TV in game rm. Complimentary full bkfst. Restaurant (see also MERCERSBURG INN). Ck-out 11 am, ck-in 3 pm. Some fireplaces. Some balconies. Totally nonsmoking. Cr cds: DS, MC, V.
⊠ 🔥

★★ **PENN NATIONAL INN AND GOLF CLUB.** 3809 Anthony Hwy, Fayetteville (17237). 717/352-2400; fax 717/352-3926; toll-free 800/231-0080. www.penngolf.com. 48 rms, 4 in manor house, 2 story. Mid-Apr-Oct: S $80-$100; D $90-$110; each addl $10-$15; under 18 free; golf plan; monthly rates; lower rates rest of yr. Crib free. Pet accepted, some restrictions. TV; cable. Heated pool. Playground. Coffee in rms. Restaurant (Apr-Oct) 7 am-7 pm. Ck-out 11 am, ck-in 2 pm. Business servs avail. Tennis. 18-hole golf course, greens fee $25-$45, putting green, driving range. Refrigerators; microwaves avail. Georgian-style manor house built 1847, additions built 1989. Cr cds: A, DS, MC, V.

🏋️ 🄳 🐾 🛖 🐟 ⛵ 🛄 🦌 SC

Restaurants

★★ **COPPER KETTLE.** *1049 Lincoln Way E (US 30) (17201).* 717/264-3109. Hrs: 5-9:30 pm; Fri, Sat to 10 pm. Closed Sun; hols. Res accepted; required Fri, Sat. Bar to midnight. Dinner $8-$21.50. Child's menu. Specializes in seafood, steak, prime rib. Early American decor; antiques. Cr cds: A, D, DS, MC, V.

🄳 ➡️

★★★ **MERCERSBURG INN.** *405 S Main St, Mercersburg (17236).* 717/328-5231. *www.mercersburginn.com.* Sitting: 5:30-8:30 pm. Closed Sun-Wed; Dec 24-25. Res required. Bar. Complete meals: 5-course dinner $45. Specialties: pan-seared venison with red currant glace de veau, cornbread crusted salmon chive ravioli, lobster ravioli. Cr cds: C, DS, MC, V.

Chester

(E-7) *See also Kennett Square, King of Prussia, Media, Philadelphia, West Chester*

Settled 1643 **Pop** 41,856
Area code 484, 610
Information Delaware County Convention & Tourist Bureau, 200 E Estate St, Suite 100, Media 19063; 610/565-3679 or 800/343-3983
Web www.delcocvb.org

The oldest settlement in the state, Chester was established by the Swedish Trading Company as Upland. William Penn came to Upland in 1682 to begin colonization of the land granted to him by King Charles II. He renamed the settlement in honor of Chester, a Quaker center in Cheshire, England. The first Assembly here adopted Penn's Framework of Government, enacted the first laws, and organized the county of Chester—from which Delaware

County broke off in 1789. On the Delaware River, 15 miles southwest of Philadelphia, Chester is a busy port and home of shipyards where every type of vessel has been built for the navy and merchant marine.

What to See and Do

Caleb Pusey Home, Landingford Plantation. (1683) Built for manager and agent of Penn's mill; only remaining house in state visited by William Penn. Period furniture. Also on 27 acres of original plantation are a log house (1790), stone schoolhouse-museum (1849), and herb garden. (May-Sept, Sat and Sun afternoons; also by appt; closed hols) 15 Race St, in Upland, 2 mi W. Phone 610/874-5665. **FREE**

Morton Homestead. (ca 1655) Two-part log house built by ancestors of John Morton, signer of Declaration of Independence. Contemporary outdoor exhibits on Pennsylvania's Swedish Period, log-house construction, Morton family. (Wed-Sat) 4 mi NE on US 13, then SW on PA 420, at 100 Lincoln Ave in Prospect Park. Phone 610/583-7221. **FREE**

Penn Memorial Landing Stone. Marks spot where William Penn first landed Oct 28, 1682. Front and Penn sts.

Swarthmore College. (1864) 1,320 students. Coeducational; on wooded 330-acre campus are Friends Historical Library and Peace Collection, an art gallery, concert hall, performing arts center, observatory, terraced grass amphitheater, Friends Meeting House, Scott Arboretum, a collection of trees, shrubs, and herbaceous plants throughout campus. Symposia, exhibits, music, and dance programs are open to the public. 4 mi N on PA 320, in Swarthmore. Phone 610/328-8000.

Widener University. (1821) 7,000 students. On campus are Old Main, a national historic landmark, and the University Art Museum, with a permanent collection of 19th- and 20th-century American Impressionist and European academic art as well as contemporary exhibits (Sept-May, Tues-Sat; June and Aug, Mon-Thurs; closed July). Also here is Wolfgram Memorial Library. Campus tours. 14th and Walnut sts. Phone 610/499-4000.

Clarion (C-2)

Founded 1839 **Pop** 8,491 **Elev** 1,491 ft **Area code** 814 **Zip** 16214
Information Clarion Area Chamber of Business and Industry, 41 S Fifth Ave; 814/226-9161
Web www.clarionpa.com

Once the forests were so thick and tall here that, according to tradition, the wind in the treetops sounded like a distant clarion. That's how the town, county, and river got their names. Today many campers and sports and outdoors enthusiasts enjoy the beauty and recreation that the Clarion area offers.

What to See and Do

Clarion County Historical Society. Museum housed in mid-19th century Sutton-Ditz house. Contains exhibits on county industry and business; Victorian bedroom and parlor; genealogical and historical library (researchers may call ahead for appt other than regular hrs); changing exhibits. (Apr-Dec, Tues, Thurs, and Fri afternoons; closed hols) 18 Grant St. Phone 814/226-4450. **FREE**

Cook Forest State Park. Approx 6,700 acres. Swimming pool (fee), fishing; hunting, hiking, bicycling, horseback riding, x-country skiing (rentals), snowmobiling, sledding, ice-skating, picnicking, tent and trailer sites, cabins (rentals). Nature and historical center. Standard fees. 11 mi NE on Clarion to Cook Forest Rd, then 3 mi S on PA 36. Phone 814/744-8407.

Tionesta Reservoir. (see WARREN) 5 mi NW on US 322, then 20 mi NW on PA 66, in Allegheny National Forest.

Special Events

Spring Fling. Concerts, food concessions, games, entertainment. Early May.

Autumn Leaf Festival. Parade, carnival, autorama, scholarship pageants, concerts, flea market, craft shows. Sept 25-Oct 3.

Motels/Motor Lodges

★ **DAYS INN.** *24 United Dr (16214). 814/226-8682; fax 814/226-8372. www.daysinn.com.* 150 rms, 2 story. S $46-$56; D $51-$61; each addl $5; under 18 free; tennis, golf, ski plans; higher rates: Autumn Leaf Festival, hunting season. Crib free. Pet accepted. TV; cable (premium). Heated pool; lifeguard. Complimentary continental bkfst. Restaurant 6 am-2 pm, 5-10 pm. Bar 5 pm-2 am; entertainment. Ck-out noon. Coin lndry. Meeting rms. Business servs avail. Sundries. Golf privileges. Health club privileges. Cr cds: A, C, D, DS, MC, V.
🔲 🔦 ⏰ ➤ ⇛ 🔥 🏃

★★ **HOLIDAY INN.** *45 Holiday Inn Dr (16214). 814/226-8850; fax 814/226-9055; toll-free 800/596-1313. www.holiday-inn.com.* 122 rms, 2 story. S, D $69-$94; suites $149; under 20 free. Crib free. Pet accepted. TV; cable (premium), VCR avail (movies). Indoor pool; lifeguard. Sauna. Coffee in rms. Restaurant 6:30 am-10 pm. Bar 4 pm-1 am. Ck-out noon. Meeting rms. Business servs avail. In-rm modem link. Airport transportation. 18-hole golf privileges, greens fee $14-$28, putting green. Game rm. Indoor balconies. Cr cds: A, D, DS, MC, V.
🔲 🔦 ➤ ⇛ 🔥 ⏰

★ **SUPER 8.** *I-80 and Rte 68 (16214). 814/226-4550; fax 814/227-2337; toll-free 800/800-8000. www.super8.com.* 99 rms, 9 kits. S, D $45-$90; each addl $5; under 18 free; wkly, monthly rates (winter). Crib free. Pet accepted. TV; cable (premium), VCR avail (movies). Pool. Complimentary continental bkfst. Coffee in rms. Restaurant adj open 24 hrs. Ck-out noon. Business servs avail. In-rm modem link. Cr cds: A, C, D, DS, MC, V.
🔲 🔦 ➤ ⇛ 🔥 **SC**

Clearfield (Clearfield County) (C-3)

Settled 1805 **Pop** 6,631 **Elev** 1,109 ft
Area code 814 **Zip** 16830
Information Clearfield Chamber of Commerce, 125 E Market St, PO Box 250; 814/765-7567

The old and important Native American town of Chinklacamoose occupied this site until it was burned in 1757. Coal and clay mining and more than 20 diversified plants producing school supplies, firebrick, fur products, precision instruments, electronic products, and sportswear now occupy what used to be cleared fields. Easy access to other parts of the state and rich river bottom land led to the establishment of the county seat here.

What to See and Do

State parks.

   Parker Dam. Approx 950 acres in Moshannon State Forest. Swimming beach, fishing, boating (launch, rentals); hiking, x-country skiing, snowmobiling, sledding, ice-skating, ice fishing, snack bar, tent and trailer sites (electric hookups), cabins. Nature center. Standard fees. 14 mi NW on PA 153, 6 mi off I-80 exit 18, then 2 mi E on unnumbered road. Phone 814/765-0630.

   S. B. Elliott. Approx 300 acres in the heart of the Moshannon State Forest; entirely wooded; display of mountain laurel in season. Fishing in small mountain streams surrounding the park. Hiking, snowmobile trails, tent and trailer sites, cabins. Standard fees. 9 mi N, off PA 153, just N of I-80 exit 18. Phone 814/765-7271.

Special Events

Central Counties Concerned Sportsmen Annual Show. Clearfield County Fairgrounds. Phone 814/765-9495. Fri-Sun mid-Mar.

Laurel Tour. Late June-early July.

High Country Arts & Craft Fair. S. B. Elliott State Park. Phone 814/765-9804. Sun after July 4.

Clearfield County Fair. Phone 814/765-4629. Late July-early Aug.

Motel/Motor Lodge

★ **DAYS INN.** *PA 879 & I-80, Clearfield (16830).* 814/765-5381; fax 814/765-7885. www.daysinn.com. 119 rms, 2 story. S $40-$60; D $46-$80; each addl $6; under 18 free; higher rates special events. Crib free. Pet accepted. TV, VCR avail (movies). Pool; lifeguard. Complimentary continental bkfst. Ck-out noon. Meeting rms. Business servs avail. In-rm modem link. Exercise equipt. Some refrigerators. Cr cds: A, D, DS, MC, V.
🄳 🔌 ⚓ 🕺 🔜 🔥

Conneaut Lake

(B-1) *See also Edinboro, Meadville*

Pop 708 **Elev** 1,100 ft **Area code** 814
Zip 16316
Information Crawford County Convention & Visitors Bureau, 211 Chestnut St, Meadville 16335; 814/333-1258 or 800/332-2338
Web www.visitcrawford.org

Located on the largest natural lake in Pennsylvania (929 acres), this resort town has swimming, boating, and excellent fishing for perch, muskellunge, walleye, bass, and crappie.

What to See and Do

Conneaut Cellars Winery. Tours and tastings. (Daily) 12005 Conneaut Lake Rd. Phone 814/382-3999. **FREE**

Pymatuning Spillway. Part of Pymatuning State Park. When fish are fed bread, they flock so thickly that ducks walk on them. NW via US 6 on N end of reservoir. Phone 724/932-3141. **FREE**

Pymatuning State Park. Approx 21,100 acres with 17-mi lake. Swimming beach, fishing, boating (rentals, mooring, launching, marina); hunting, hiking, x-country skiing, snowmobiling, sledding, ice-skating, picnicking, playground, tent and trailer areas along shore, cabins.

Waterfowl museum and refuge; fish hatchery. Standard fees. SW via US 322, 1 mi W of Jamestown. Phone 724/932-3141.

Wildlife Learning Center. Part of Pennsylvania Game Commission; birds and animals indigenous to Pymatuning Reservoir area; bald eagle's nest visible from museum. Educational and interpretive programs. (Apr-mid Oct, Wed-Sun) 9 mi W on US 285, then N on Hartstown-Linesville Rd. Phone 814/683-5545. **FREE**

Connellsville

(E-2) See also New Stanton, Uniontown

Pop 9,146 **Elev** 885 ft **Area code** 724 **Zip** 15425
Information Greater Connellsville Chamber of Commerce, 923 W Crawford Ave; 724/628-5500

Located in an area visited by George Washington and where he owned land, the region has many references to him in place names. The restored Crawford Cabin near the river was the home of Colonel William Crawford, surveyor of these properties and Washington's surveying pupil.

Northwest of town in Perryopolis are many historic restorations. The town square is named for Washington, who some believe planned the design of the town.

What to See and Do

⭐ **Fallingwater (Kaufmann Conservation on Bear Run).** One of the most famous structures of the 20th century, Fallingwater, designed by Frank Lloyd Wright in 1936, is cantilevered on three levels over a waterfall; interior features Wright-designed furniture, textiles, and lighting, as well as sculpture by modern masters; extensive grounds are heavily wooded and planted with rhododendron, which blooms in early July. Visitor center with self-guided orientation program; concession; gift shop. Guided tours (Mid-Mar-Nov, Tues-Sun; winter, Sat-Sun). No children under six; child-care center. No pets. Res required. 8 mi E on PA 711, then 8 mi S on PA 381, near Mill Run. Phone 724/329-8501.

Linden Hall. (1913) Conference and convention center in mountaintop mansion, situated in picturesque Laurel Highlands. Swimming, fishing; golf, tennis, walking trail. Guided tours of mansion (Mar-Dec, Mon-Fri; wkends by appt). 4 mi S on PA 201, then 1 mi N on PA 819, left

Fallingwater (Kaufmann Conservation on Bear Run)

on River Rd in Dawson. Phone
724/529-7543. ¢¢¢

Motel/Motor Lodge

★ **MELODY MOTOR LODGE.** *1607
Morrell Ave (15425). 724/628-9600.* 46
rms. S, D $34-$47; higher rates Labor
Day wkend. Crib $5. Pet accepted,
some restrictions. TV; cable. Restaurant adj 6 am-10 pm. Ck-out 11 am.
Picnic tables. Cr cds: A, DS, MC, V.
◨ ⊠ ⊠

B&B/Small Inn

★ ★ **NEWMYER HOUSE.** *507 S
Pittsburgh St (15425). 724/626-0141.
www.bbonline.com/pa/newmyer.* 4 rms,
1 with shower only, 3 story. No rm
phones. S, D $125; each addl $10;
June-Labor Day wkends (2-day min).
Children over 12 yrs only. TV in
common rm; cable, VCR avail
(movies). Complimentary full bkfst.
Ck-out 11 am, ck-in 3 pm. Down-
hill/x-country ski 20 mi. Many fireplaces. Restored Queen Anne-style
mansion built in 1892; antiques. Cr
cds: MC, V.
⊠ ⊠ ⊠

Coraopolis (D-1)

(see Pittsburgh International Airport
Area)

Cornwall

(E-6) *See also Ephrata, Hershey, Lancaster, Lebanon, Manheim*

Settled 1732 **Pop** 3,486 **Elev** 680 ft
Area code 717 **Zip** 17016

Information Pennsylvania Rainbow
Region Vacation Bureau, 625
Quentin Rd, PO Box 329, Lebanon
17042; 717/272-8555

Web www.parrvb.com

The Cornwall Ore Banks were a
major source of magnetic iron ore for
nearly 250 years.

What to See and Do

Cornwall Iron Furnace. In operation
1742-1883. Open pit mine; 19th-
century Miners Village still occupied.
Furnace building houses "great
wheel" and 19th-century steam
engine. Visitor center, exhibits, book
store. (Tues-Sun; closed Jan 1,
Thanksgiving, Dec 25) Rexmont Rd
at Boyd St. Phone 717/272-9711. ¢¢

Historic Schaefferstown. An 18th-
century farm established by Swiss-
German settlers. Village square with
authentic log and stone and half-
timber buildings; site of first waterworks in US (1758), still in
operation. Schaeffer Farm Museum
has Swiss Bank House and Barn
(1737); early farm tools; colonial
farm garden. The museum north of
the square has antiques and artifacts
of settlers. (See SPECIAL EVENT)
House and museum (open during
festivals; also June-Sept, by appt). 6
mi SE of Lebanon at jct PA 419, 501,
897. Phone 717/949-2244. ¢¢

Special Event

Historic Schaefferstown Events.
Events during the yr include **Cherry
Fair,** fourth Sat June; **Folk Festival,**
mid-July; **Harvest Fair** & **Horse Plow-
ing Contest,** second wkend Sept.

Danville

(C-6) *See also Bloomsburg, Lewisburg*

Pop 4,897 **Elev** 490 ft **Area code** 570
Zip 17821

Information Danville Area Chamber
of Commerce, 206 Walnut St;
570/275-5200

Web www.danvillepa.org

What to See and Do

Joseph Priestley House. (1798)
American house of the 18th-century
Englishman and Unitarian theolo-
gian who, in 1774, isolated the ele-
ment oxygen. (Tues-Sat; closed hols)
SW via US 11 in Northumberland at
472 Priestley Ave. Phone 570/473-
9474. ¢¢

PP & L Montour Preserve. Fishing,
boating (no gasoline motors) on 165-
acre Lake Chillisquaque. Hiking and
nature trails, picnicking. Birds of

prey exhibit in visitor center; scheduled programs (Daily, fee for some). From I-80 exit 33, then PA 54 W to Washingtonville, and NE on local roads. Phone 570/437-3131. **FREE**

Motel/Motor Lodge

★ ★ **QUALITY INN.** *15 Valley West Rd (17821). 570/275-5100; fax 570/275-1886. www.qualityinn.com.* 77 rms, 2 story. Apr-Oct: S $45-$55; D $50-$65; each addl $5; under 18 free; lower rates rest of yr. Crib free. TV; cable. Pool. Restaurant adj open 24 hrs. Ck-out noon. Coin lndry. Meeting rms. Business servs avail. In-rm modem link. Game rm. Cr cds: A, MC, V.

B&B/Small Inn

★ ★ ★ **PINE BARN INN.** *1 Pine Barn Pl (17821). 570/275-2071; fax 570/275-3248; toll-free 800/627-2276. www.pinebarninn.com.* 65 rms, 1-2 story. S $42-$65; D $46-$75; each addl $2; under 16 free. Crib $5. TV; cable. Restaurant (see also PINE BARN INN). Rm serv. Bar 11 am-midnight, Sun 1-8 pm. Ck-out 1 pm. Meeting rms. Business servs avail. Valet serv. Gift shop. Geisinger Medical Center adj. Cr cds: A, C, D, DS, MC, V.

Restaurant

★ ★ **PINE BARN INN.** *1 Pine Barn Pl (17821). 570/275-2071. www.pinebarninn.com.* Hrs: 7 am-10 pm; Sun 8 am-8 pm; Sun brunch 11 am-2 pm. Closed hols. Res accepted. Bar 11 am-midnight; Sun 1-8 pm. Bkfst $3.50-$6.50, lunch $4.50-$9.50, dinner $12-$26. Sun brunch $5-$13. Child's menu. Specializes in New England seafood, steak. Salad bar. Outdoor dining. Converted 19th-century barn. Fireplace. Family-owned. Cr cds: A, D, DS, MC, V.

Delaware Water Gap

(C-8) *See also Milford, Pocono Moutains, Stroudsburg*

It is difficult to believe that the quiet Delaware River could carve a path through the Kittatinny Mountains, which are nearly ¼ of a mile high at this point. Conflicting geological theories account for this natural phenomenon, which is part of a national recreation area. The prevailing theory is that the mountains were formed after the advent of the river, rising up from the earth so slowly that the course of the Delaware was never altered.

Despite the speculation about the origin of the gap, there is no doubt about the area's recreational value. A relatively unspoiled area along the river boundary between Pennsylvania and New Jersey, stretching approximately 35 miles from Matamoras to an area just south of I-80, the site of the Delaware Water Gap is managed by the National Park Service.

Trails and overlooks (year-round) offer scenic views. Also here are canoeing and boating, hunting and fishing; camping is nearby at the Dingmans Campground within the recreation area. Swimming and picnicking at Smithfield and Milford beaches. Dingmans Falls and Silver Thread Falls, two of the highest waterfalls in the Poconos, are near here (see MILFORD). Several 19th-century buildings are in the area, including Millbrook Village (several buildings open May-October) and Peters Valley (see BRANCHVILLE, NJ). The visitor center is located off I-80 in New Jersey, at Kittatinny Point (Apr-Nov, daily; rest of year, Sat and Sun only; closed Jan 1, Dec 25), phone 908/496-4458 or 717/588-2451. Park headquarters are in Bushkill, PA. Phone 717/588-2451.

Denver/ Adamstown

(E-6) *See also Ephrata, Lancaster, Reading*

Pop 3,332 **Elev** Denver 380 ft; Adamstown 500 ft **Area code** 717 **Zip** Denver 17517; Adamstown 19501 **Information** Pennsylvania Dutch Convention and Visitors Bureau, 501 Greenfield Rd, Lancaster 17601; 717/299-8901 or 800/PADUTCH **Web** www.800padutch.com

Located near a Pennsylvania Turnpike exit, Denver and Adamstown are in the center of an active antique marketing area, which preserves its Pennsylvania German heritage.

What to See and Do

Stoudt's Black Angus. More than 350 dealers display quality antiques for sale. (Sun) Along PA 272 from PA Tpke exit 21 to just beyond Adamstown. Phone 717/484-4385.

Special Event

Bavarian Summer Fest. Oompah bands, schuhplattler dance groups; Oktoberfest atmosphere. Includes special events, German folklore, German food, displays, shops. SW via PA 272 in Adamstown at Black Angus Bier Garten. Phone 717/484-4385 (wkends). Fri-Sun, early Aug-Labor Day; Sun only Oct.

Motels/Motor Lodges

★★★ **BLACK HORSE LODGE & SUITES.** *2180 N Reading Rd, Denver (17517). 717/336-7563; fax 717/336-1110; toll-free 800/610-3805. www. blackhorselodge.com.* 74 rms, 2 story. Mid-Apr-mid-Nov: S $59-$129; D $69-$139; under 13 free; suites $100-$250; wkly, monthly rates; golf plans; lower rates rest of yr. Crib free. Pet accepted, some restrictions. TV; cable. Pool. Complimentary full bkfst, coffee in rms. Restaurant (see also BLACK HORSE). Bar to 11 pm. Ck-out noon. Coin lndry. Business servs avail. Golf privileges. Many refrigerators; some bathrm phones; microwaves avail. Private patios, balconies. Picnic tables, grills. Cr cds: A, C, D, DS, MC, V.

★★ **HOLIDAY INN.** *1 Denver Rd, Denver (17517). 717/336-7541; fax 717/336-0515; toll-free 800/437-5711. www.holiday-inn.com.* 110 rms, 2 story. June-Oct: S, D $89; each addl $8; under 18 free; higher rates special events; lower rates rest of yr. Crib free. TV; cable (premium), VCR avail (movies). Pool; poolside serv, lifeguard. Restaurant 6:30 am-2 pm, 5-10 pm. Bar 5-10 pm. Ck-out noon. Coin lndry. Meeting rms. Business servs avail. In-rm modem link. Valet serv. Golf privileges. Cr cds: A, C, D, DS, JCB, MC, V.

B&B/Small Inn

★★★ **INNS OF ADAMSTOWN.** *62 W Main St, Adamstown (19501). 717/484-0800; fax 717/484-1384; res 800/594-4808. www.adamstown.com.* 4 rms, 2 with shower only, 2 story. Rm phones avail. S $63-$108; D $70-$130; wkends (2-day min). Children over 12 yrs only. TV in some rms; cable. Complimentary continental bkfst; afternoon refreshments. Restaurant nearby. Ck-out 10 am, ck-in 3-6 pm. Luggage handling. Valet serv. Concierge serv. Health club privileges. Some in-rm whirlpools, fireplaces. Patio. Picnic tables. Built in 1925; Victorian decor; antiques, family heirlooms. Totally nonsmoking. Cr cds: MC, V.

Restaurant

★★★ **BLACK HORSE.** *2180 N Reading Rd, Denver (17517). 717/336-6555. www.blackhorselodge.com.* Hrs: 5-10 pm; Sun 11:30 am-9 pm. Closed Dec 25. Res accepted. Bar 4-11 pm; Sun 11 am-10 pm. Wine cellar. Dinner $14-$30. Child's menu. Specializes in certified Angus beef, fresh seafood, gourmet desserts. Own pasta. Casual yet elegant decor with stained-glass windows, antique chandeliers, artwork. Cr cds: A, C, D, DS, MC, V.

Donegal

(E-2) *See also Connellsville, Greensburg, Ligonier, Somerset*

Pop 165 **Elev** 1,814 ft **Area code** 724 **Zip** 15628

What to See and Do

Skiing. Seven Springs Mountain Resort Ski Area. Three quad, five triple chair-lifts; two rope tows, six-passenger high-speed chair; patrol, school, rentals; snowmaking; cafeteria, restaurant, bar; lodge. Longest run 1¼ mi; vertical drop 750 ft. Night skiing. (Dec-Mar, daily) Alpine slide (May-Sept, daily). Hotel and conference center; summer activities include 18-hole golf, tennis, rope course, horseback riding, swimming. 12 mi SE of PA Tpke exit 9 on Champion-Trent Rd. Phone 800/452-2223. ¢¢¢¢¢

Motel/Motor Lodge

★ **DAYS INN.** *Rte 31 (15628).* 724/593-7536; fax 724/593-6165; toll-free 800/329-7466. www.daysinn.com. 50 rms, 20 with shower only. S, D $59-$72; each addl $6; under 12 free; higher rates special events. TV; cable (premium). Heated pool. Complimentary continental bkfst. Restaurant nearby. Ck-out 11 am. Downhill/x-country ski 9 mi. Lawn games. Picnic tables. Cr cds: A, MC, V.

⊠ ⊠ ⊠ ⊠ SC

Resort

★★★ **SEVEN SPRINGS MOUN-TAIN RESORT.** *Rd 1, County Line Rd, Champion (15622).* 814/352-7777; fax 814/352-7911; toll-free 800/452-2223. www.7springs.com. 385 rms in 10-story lodge; 20 kit. chalets, cabins, 1-4 bedrm, 2 story. Lodge: S, D $155; each addl $50; under 17 free; suites $420; kit. chalets $525; package plans; cabins for 6-25, $520-$895/wk; also daily rates (2-day min); wkend rates. Crib free. Maid serv avail in chalets, cabins $5/bed. TV; VCR avail. Heated indoor/outdoor pools (open to public); wading pool, pool-side serv, lifeguard. Playground. Free supervised children's activities. Dining rm 7 am-10 pm (see also HELEN'S). Snack bar; box lunches. Bar 11-2 am. Ck-out noon, ck-in 5 pm. Coin lndry. Convention facilities. Business servs avail. Bellhops. Shopping arcade. Beauty shop. Airport transportation. Sports dir. Tennis. Golf, greens fee $65.90, pro, putting green, driving range. Miniature golf. Downhill ski on site. Outdoor games. Hay rides. Mountain bikes avail. Soc dir; dancing, entertainment. Rec rm. Bowling. Indoor roller skating. Exercise equipt; sauna, steam rm. Wet bar in suites. Many private patios, balconies. Cr cds: DS, MC, V.

🎿 D 🏂 ⛷ 🏊 🚴 🏋 🎾 🛷 ⛸

Restaurants

★★★ **HELEN'S.** *RD 1, Champion (15622).* 814/352-7777. www.7springs.com. Hrs: 6-10 pm; also lunch during ski season. Res required. Continental menu. Bar. A la carte entrees: dinner $19-$30. Specialties: Dover sole, chicken Frangelica, lamb Helena. Totally nonsmoking. Cr cds: DS, MC, V.

D

★★★ **NINO BARSOTTI'S.** *PA 31, Mt Pleasant (15666).* 724/547-2900. Hrs: 11 am-3 pm, 5-10 pm; Sat to 11 pm; Sun to 9 pm; Sun brunch 11:30 am-2 pm. Closed Mon; hols. Res accepted Fri, Sat. Italian, American menu. Bar. Lunch $4.95-$9.45, dinner $7.45-$23.45. Sun brunch $7.95. Child's menu. Specializes in fresh seafood, steak. Own desserts. Salad bar. Own pasta. Valet parking. Family-owned. Cr cds: A, D, DS, MC, V.

D 🍽

Downingtown

(E-7) *See also King of Prussia, West Chester*

Settled 1702 **Pop** 7,589 **Elev** 244 ft **Area code** 484 and 610 **Zip** 19335 **Information** Chester County Conference and Visitors Bureau, 400 Exton

Sq Pkwy, Exton, 19341; 610/280-6145 or 800/228-9933
Web www.brandywinevalley.com

Settled by emigrants from Birmingham, England, Downingtown honors Thomas Downing, who erected a log cabin here in 1702. The borough was first called Milltown, after the mill built here by Roger Hunt in 1765. The town, with its many historically interesting homes, retains much of its colonial charm. Jacob Eichholtz, a leading early-American portrait artist, was born here.

What to See and Do

Hibernia County Park. Once the center of an iron works community, it is now the largest of the county parks, encompassing 800 acres of woodlands and meadows. The west branch of the Brandywine Creek, Birch Run, and a pond are stocked with trout; hiking trails, picnicking, tent and trailer camping (dump station). Park features Hibernia Mansion; portions of house date from 1798, period furnishings. Tours of mansion (Memorial Day-Labor Day, Sun; fee). From US 30 Bypass take PA 82 approx 2 mi N to Cedar Knoll Rd, then left 1¼ mi to park entrance on left. Phone 610/384-0290. **FREE**

Historic Yellow Springs. From its beginnings as a fashionable spa, this historic village has been everything from a Revolutionary War hospital to an art school. Countryside covers 145 acres with buildings, medicinal herb garden, and mineral springs. Events and educational programs throughout the yr (some fees). Self-guided tour. Office (Mon-Fri). 10 mi NE via PA 113, NW on Yellow Springs Rd. Phone 610/827-7414.

Valley Forge National Historical Park. (see) 10 mi E on I-76.

Special Events

Old Fiddlers' Picnic. Hibernia County Park. Second Sat Aug.

Hibernia Mansion Christmas Tours. Hibernia County Park. First wk Dec.

Motel/Motor Lodge

★★ **BEST WESTERN.** *815 N Pottstown Pike, Exton (19341). 610/363-1100; fax 610/524-2329; toll-free* *800/780-7234. www.bestwestern.com.* 225 rms, 4 story. S, D $109; under 18 free. Crib free. Pet accepted. TV; cable (premium). 2 pools, 1 indoor; poolside serv, lifeguard. Coffee in rms. Restaurant (see also ARTHUR'S). Bar 2 pm-2 am. Ck-out 11 am. Coin lndry. Meeting rms. Business servs avail. In-rm modem link. Valet serv. Gift shop. Airport transportation. Health club privileges. Refrigerators, microwaves avail. Picnic tables. Cr cds: A, C, D, DS, ER, JCB, MC, V.

⬛ 🐾 ⛱ ⛷ 🎿 SC

Hotel

★★★ **SHERATON GREAT VALLEY HOTEL.** *707 Lancaster Pike (19355). 610/524-5500. www.sheraton.com.* 198 rms, 5 story. S, D $195-$250; under 17 free. Crib avail. TV; cable (premium). Pool; whirlpool. Restaurant 6:30 am-10 pm. Bar to midnight. Ck-out noon. Meeting rms. Business center. In-rm modem link. Concierge. Exercise equipt. Minibars; many refrigerators in suites. Cr cds: A, D, DS, MC, V.

⛱ 🏋 🎿 🚶 ⬛ 🎿

Restaurants

★★ **ARTHUR'S.** *815 N Pottstown Pike, Exton (19341). 610/363-1100. www.bestwestern.com.* Hrs: 6:30 am-2 pm, 5:30-10 pm; Sat 7 am-2 pm, 5:30-10 pm; Sun 7 am-1 pm. Res accepted. Bar 11:30-2 am. A la carte entrees: bkfst $3.50-$7, lunch $4.95-$9, dinner $7.99-$20. Lunch buffet $7.99. Child's menu. Specialties: salmon Rockefeller, filet of tenderloin. Jazz Mon. Parking. Outdoor dining. Family-owned since 1971. Cr cds: A, DS, MC, V.

⬛ ⬛

★★★ **VICKERS.** *192 E Welsh Pool Rd, Lionville (19341). 610/363-7998.* Hrs: 11:30 am-2:30 pm, 5:30-9:30 pm; Fri to 10 pm; Sat 5:30-10 pm. Closed Sun; hols. Res accepted; required Sat. French, continental menu. Bar. Lunch $6.50-$14.95, dinner $19.95-$29.95. Specialties: beef Wellington, Dover sole, rack of lamb. Own desserts. Pianist Fri, Sat. Authentic farmhouse, built 1823. Cr cds: A, D, DS, MC, V.

⬛ ⬛

Doylestown (Bucks County)

(D-8) *See also Philadelphia, Quakertown (Bucks County)*

Settled 1735 **Pop** 8,227 **Elev** 340 ft
Area code 215 **Zip** 18901
Information Bucks County Conference and Visitors Bureau, 152 Swamp Rd; 215/345-4552 or 800/836-2825
Web www.buckscountycvb.org

Doylestown is the county seat of historic and colorful Bucks County.

What to See and Do

Covered bridges. Descriptive list, map of 11 bridges in Bucks County may be obtained at Bucks County Tourist Commission.

James A. Michener Art Museum. Changing exhibitions of 20th-century American art, contemporary crafts, and sculpture garden. Located in restored old Bucks County jail. (Tues-Sun; closed hols) 138 S Pine St. Phone 215/340-9800. ¢¢

Mercer Mile. Three reinforced-concrete structures built between 1910-1916 within a one-mi radius by Dr. Henry Chapman Mercer, archaeologist, historian, world traveler, and tile maker. They include

   Fonthill Museum. Concrete castle of Henry Chapman Mercer (1856-1930) displays his collection of tiles and prints from around the world. Guided tours (times vary). Phone 215/348-9461. ¢¢¢

   Mercer Museum of the Bucks County Historical Society. Collection of over 50,000 early-American artifacts and tools. Changing exhibits gallery. (Daily; closed Jan 1, Thanksgiving, Dec 25) 84 S Pine St. Phone 215/345-0210. ¢¢¢

   Moravian Pottery and Tile Works. Restored and established as a living history museum; tiles are hand-crafted on premises. Video and self-guided tour explain ceramic process and history of Mercer's work, which appears in buildings all over the country. (Daily; closed hols) 130 Swamp Rd. Phone 215/345-6722. ¢¢

⭐ **Pearl S. Buck House.** (1835) House of Pulitzer and Nobel Prize winning author Pearl S. Buck. Original furnishings include desk at which *The Good Earth* was written; memorabilia, Chinese artifacts. Picnicking on grounds. Gift shop. One-hr guided tours (Mar-Dec, Tues-Sun; closed hols). 520 Dublin Rd, 8 mi NW via PA 611, 313 in Hilltown Township. Phone 215/249-0100. ¢¢¢

Motel/Motor Lodge

★ **COMFORT INN.** *678 Bethlehem Pike, Montgomeryville (18936). 215/361-3600; fax 215/361-7949; toll-free 800/228-5150. www.comfortinn.com.* 84 rms, 3 story. S $90.95-$129.95; D $95.95-$129.95; each addl $5; suites $124.95-$129.95; under 18 free. Crib free. TV; cable, VCR avail (movies). Complimentary continental bkfst. Coffee in rms. Restaurant nearby. Ck-out 11 am. Coin lndry. Meeting rm. Business servs avail. In-rm modem link. Valet serv. Health club privileges. Microwaves avail. Refrigerator, wet bar in suites. Cr cds: A, C, D, DS, MC, V.
D 🛄 🐾 SC

B&Bs/Small Inns

★★ **THE INN AT FORDHOOK FARM.** *105 New Britain Rd, Doylestown (18901). 215/345-1766; fax 215/345-1791. www.fordhook.com.* 6 rms, 3 story. S, D $100-$300; each addl $20; wkends (2-day min). Children over 12 yrs only. 2 TVs; VCR avail (movies). Complimentary full bkfst. Ck-out 11 am, ck-in 3 pm. Meeting rms. Business servs avail. X-country ski on site. Lawn games. Balconies. On 60 acres of woods and meadows; many antiques. Totally nonsmoking. Cr cds: A, MC, V.
🐾 🛄 🐾

★★★ **PINE TREE FARM BED AND BREAKFAST.** *2155 Lower State Rd, Doylestown (18901). 215/348-0632.* 4 rms, 3 story. S, D $175-$195; wkends (2-day min), hols (3-day min). Children over 16 yrs only. Pool. Complimentary full bkfst; afternoon refreshments. Ck-out 11 am, ck-in 4 pm. Tennis. Solarium. 16-acre country estate built 1730; antiques. Totally nonsmoking. Cr cds: A, MC, V.

★★ **SIGN OF THE SORREL HORSE.** *4424 Old Easton Rd, Doylestown (18901). 215/230-9999; fax 215/230-8053. www.sorrelhorse.com.* 5 rms, 2 with shower only, 2 story, 2 suites. No rm phones. S, D $85-$175; wkends (2-day min). Complimentary continental bkfst, coffee in rms. Restaurant (see also SIGN OF THE SORREL HORSE). Ck-out 11 am, ck-in 4 pm. Luggage handling. Free airport, RR station transportation. Lawn games. Picnic tables. On river. Built as a gristmill (1714); antiques. Totally nonsmoking. Cr cds: A, C, D, MC, V.

Restaurants

★★ **BLACK WALNUT.** *80 W State St, Doylestown (18901). 215/348-0708. www.blackwalnutcafe.com.* Hrs: noon-2:30 pm, 5:30-9 pm; Fri to 9:30 pm; Sat 5:30-9:30 pm; Sun 5-8:30 pm. Closed Mon; also hols. Res required Sat (dinner). Continental menu. A la carte entrees: dinner $16-$29. Specialties: foie gras, galette of goat cheese, beef tenderloin with 1,000 peppercorns. Parking. Outdoor dining. In historic 1846 town; garden. Totally nonsmoking. Cr cds: A, DS, MC, V.

★★ **KNIGHT HOUSE.** *96 W State St, Doylestown (18901). 215/345-8746.* Hrs: 11:30 am-2 pm, 5:30-9:30 pm; Sat 5:30-9:30 pm; Res accepted. French, American menu. Bar. A la carte entrees: lunch $7-$12, dinner $17-$29. Sun brunch $15.95. Specialties: New Zealand rack of lamb, Norwegian salmon, Peking duck breast. Outdoor dining. Intimate dining. Cr cds: A, MC, V.

★ **LOS SARAPES.** *17 Moyer Rd, Chalfont (18914). 215/822-8858. www.lossarapes.com.* Hrs: 11 am-9 pm; Fri, Sat to 10 pm; Sun from 4 pm. Closed Mon; hols. Res accepted. Mexican menu. Bar. Lunch, dinner $4.50-$14. Specialties: tampiquena, mole poblano, pescado a la Veracruzana. Own desserts. Outdoor dining. Casual Mexican decor.

Totally nonsmoking. Cr cds: A, DS, MC, V.

★★★ **SIGN OF THE SORREL HORSE.** *4424 Old Easton Rd, Doylestown (18901). 215/230-9999. www.sorrelhorse.com.* Hrs: 5:30-9:30 pm. Closed Mon, Tues; Dec 25; also 2 wks Mar. Res accepted. French, American menu. Bar. A la carte entrees: dinner $15.95-$28. Prix fixe: dinner $55. Specialties: Swedish elk, kangaroo, ostrich. Outdoor dining. Guest rms avail. Located in historic grist-mill (1714). Cr cds: A, MC, V.

Du Bois

(C-3) *See also Clearfield (Clearfield County)*

Settled 1865 **Pop** 8,123 **Elev** 1,420 ft **Area code** 814 **Zip** 15801
Information Du Bois Area Chamber of Commerce, 31 N Brady St; 814/371-5010

At the entrance to the lowest pass of the Allegheny Range, Du Bois is a transportation center—once the apex of huge lumbering operations. Destroyed by fire in 1888, the town was rebuilt on the ashes of the old community and today ranks as one of the 12 major trading centers in the state.

Motels/Motor Lodges

★★ **BEST WESTERN INN & CONFERENCE CENTER.** *82 N Park Pl (15801). 814/371-6200; fax 814/371-4608. www.bestwestern.com.* 60 rms, 3 story. S $47-$57; D $53-$63; each addl $6; under 18 free. Crib free. TV; cable. Playground. Complimentary continental bkfst. Restaurant nearby. Ck-out 11 am. Business servs avail. Sundries. Golf privileges. Health club privileges. Picnic tables. Cr cds: A, C, D, DS, MC, V.

★★ **HAMPTON INN.** *RR 8 Box 3A (15801). 814/375-1000; fax 814/375-4668; toll-free 800/426-7866. www.hamptoninn.com.* 96 rms, 3 story. S $59-$64; D $64; kit. suite $95; under

8 free; wkly, wkend, hol rates; ski,
olf plans; Penn State football games
2-day min). Crib free. TV; cable (pre-
nium), VCR avail. Indoor pool;
whirlpool. Complimentary continen-
al bkfst, coffee in rms. Restaurant
dj open 24 hrs. Ck-out noon. Meetng rms. Business servs avail. Valet
erv. Downhill/x-country ski 1 mi.
xercise equipt. Health club privi-
eges. Refrigerators avail. Cr cds: A,
C, D, DS, MC, V.

★ ★ **HOLIDAY INN.** *US 219 & I-80
15801). 814/371-5100; fax 814/375-
230; res 800/959-3412. www.holiday-
nn.com.* 160 rms, 2 story. S $72-$77;
) $78-$84; each addl $6; studio rms
75; under 18 free. Pet accepted. TV;
able (premium), VCR avail. Pool;
ading, poolside serv, lifeguard.
Complimentary coffee in rms.
Restaurant 7 am-2 pm, 5-10 pm. Bar
pm-1 am. Ck-out noon. Coin
ndry. Meeting rms. Business servs
vail. In-rm modem link. Bellhops.
ree airport transportation. Health
lub privileges. Cr cds: A, C, D, DS,
CB, MC, V.

★ **RAMADA INN.** *I-80 and Rte 255
15801). 814/371-7070; fax 814/371-
055; res 800/272-6232. www.ramada.
om.* 96 rms, 2-3 story. No elvtr. S
53-$65; D $59-$75; each addl $10;
uites $80-$150; under 18 free. Crib
ree. Pet accepted. TV; cable (pre-
nium), VCR avail. Indoor pool; pool-
ide serv. Restaurant 6:30 am-1:30
m, 5:30-10 pm. Bar 5 pm-2 am;
ntertainment Mon-Sat. Ck-out
oon. Meeting rms. Business servs
vail. Airport transportation. Golf
rivileges, pro. Health club privileges.
Cr cds: A, C, D, DS, JCB, MC, V.

B&B/Small Inn

★ ★ ★ **TOWNE HOUSE INN.** *138
Center St, Saint Marys (15857).
14/781-1556; fax 814/834-4449; toll-
ree 800/851-1180. www.townehouse
nn.com.* 57 rms, 3 story. S $48-$90;
) $53-$97; each addl $7. Crib $7.
V; cable (premium). Complimentary
ontinental bkfst, coffee in rms.
Restaurant 6:30 am-2 pm, 5-9 pm;
at from 5 pm; closed Sun. Ck-out 11

am. Meeting rms. Business servs
avail. In-rm modem link. Exercise
equipt. Fireplaces. Picnic tables.
Stained glass, antiques in 7 historic
(1890s) townhouses. Cr cds: A, D,
DS, MC, V.

Easton

(D-8) *See also Allentown, Bethlehem*

Founded 1752 **Pop** 26,263 **Elev** 300 ft
Area code 484 and 610 **Zip** 18042
Information Two Rivers Area Cham-
ber of Commerce, 1 S 3rd St, PO Box
637, 18044-0637; 610/253-4211
Web www.eastonareachamber.org

Named by Thomas Penn, one of the
proprietors, for the English birthplace
of his bride, Easton today is the gateway to the great industrial Lehigh
Valley. Lafayette College, with its
beautiful campus, and the historic
Great Square are of interest. Easton,
the seat of Northampton County, is
part of a larger metropolitan area, the
Lehigh Valley, which also includes
Allentown and Bethlehem.

What to See and Do

Canal Museum. Exhibits include photographs, models, documents, and
artifacts from the era of mule-drawn
canal boats in the 1800s; electronic
map and audiovisual programs.
Changing exhibits. (Memorial Day-
Labor Day, daily; rest of yr, Tues-Sun;
closed Jan 1, Thanksgiving, Dec 25)
PA 611, 1 mi S of US 22, Two Rivers
Landing. Phone 610/250-6700. ¢¢

The Crayola Factory. See how
crayons and markers are created.
Visit Crayola Hall of Fame; enjoy
dozens of interactive exhibits featuring the wonders of light and color.
Same location and schedule as Canal
Museum. Phone 610/515-8000.

"The Great Square." Center of business district. Now called Center Sq.
Dominated by Soldiers' and Sailors'
Monument. Bronze marker shows
replica of Old Courthouse, which
stood until 1862 on land rented from

the Penns for one red rose a year. From Old Courthouse steps, the Declaration of Independence was read on July 8, 1776, when the Easton Flag, the first Stars and Stripes of the united colonies, was unfurled here.

Hugh Moore Park. Restored Lehigh Canal, locks, and locktender's house; mule-drawn canal boat rides (early May-Labor Day, daily; early-late Sept, wkends) Also hiking, picnicking; boat rentals in park. Park (daily). S 25th St, 2 mi S of US 22. Phone 610/250-6700. **FREE**

Lafayette College. (1826) 2,000 students. Bronze statue of Lafayette by Daniel Chester French in front of college chapel; American historical portrait collection in Kirby Hall of Civil Rights. Tour of campus. N side of town. Phone 610/250-5000.

Northampton County Historical Society. Changing exhibits; library; museum. (By appt) 101-107 S 4th St, diagonally opp Parsons-Taylor House. Phone 610/253-1222. ¢

Restaurants

★ ★ **MANDARIN TANG.** *25th St Shopping Center (18045). 610/258-5697.* Hrs: 11:30 am-10 pm; Fri, Sat to 11 pm. Res accepted Fri-Sun. Chinese menu. Lunch $3.95-$5.50, dinner $5-$16.95. Specialties: mandarin orange beef, General Tso's chicken. Chinese decor. Cr cds: A, DS, MC, V.

★ ★ **PEARLY BAKER'S ALE HOUSE.** *11 Center Sq (18042). 610/253-9949.* Hrs: 11:30 am-10 pm. Closed Mon; hols. Res required Fri, Sat (dinner). International menu. Bar to 2 am. A la carte entrees: lunch $6-$9, dinner $14-$19. Child's menu. Entertainment Fri. Specializes in international cuisine. Outdoor dining. Austrian chandelier in main dining rm. Cr cds: A, MC, V.
[D] [⟶]

Ebensburg

(D-3) *See also Altoona, Johnstown*

Pop 3,091 **Elev** 2,140 ft
Area code 814 **Zip** 15931

Information Johnstown/Cambria County Convention & Visitors Bureau, 416 Main St, Suite 200, Johnstown 15901-1608; 814/536-7993 or 800/237-8590
Web www.visitjohnstownpa.com

What to See and Do

Allegheny Portage Railroad National Historic Site. Remains of railroad built 1831-1834 to link east and west divisions of the Pennsylvania Mainline Canal. Cars were pulled up ten inclined planes by ropes powered by steam engines. Horses or locomotives pulled the cars over the level stretches of the 36-mi route across the Alleghenies from Hollidaysburg to Johnstown. The Skew Arch Bridge, an engine house exhibit, and the Lemon House, an historic tavern, help tell the story of the Allegheny Portage Railroad. A visitor center (daily; closed Dec 25) has exhibits and a 20-min film. There are ranger-led programs (summer, daily) and costumed demonstrations (summer); picnic area (daily); hiking and x-country trails. 12 mi E on US 22. Phone 814/886-6150. ¢¢

Portage Station Museum. This historic station was once a stop on the Pennsylvania Railroad. The first floor, with its original lighting fixtures, oak wainscoting, and woodwork, contains the Master's Office and waiting room. Exhibits on the second floor include artifacts from the newly renovated Mainline Mining Museum. (Wed, Sat and Sun afternoons). 400 Lee St, in Portage. Phone 814/736-8918. **FREE**

Edinboro

(B-1) *See also Erie, Meadville*

Pop 6,950 **Elev** 1,210 ft
Area code 814 **Zip** 16412

This is a resort town on Edinboro Lake and the home of Edinboro State College.

What to See and Do

Skiing. Mountain View Ski Area. Two T-bars, Pomalift; patrol, school, rentals; snowmaking; cafeteria. Longest run 2,500 ft; vertical drop

320 ft. (Dec-Mar, daily) Half-day and eve rates. 4 mi E on US 6 N, then 3 mi S on PA 86, in Cambridge Springs. Phone 814/734-1641. ¢¢¢¢

Motel/Motor Lodge

★ **RAMADA INN.** *401 W Plum St (16412). 814/734-5650; fax 814/734-7532; res 888/449-0344. www.ramada. com.* 105 rms, 2 story. S, D $80-$90; each addl $10; package plans. Crib free. Pet accepted. TV. Indoor pool. Sauna. Restaurant 6 am-10 pm. Bars 11:30-2 am; entertainment. Ck-out noon. Coin lndry. Meeting rms. Business servs avail. 18-hole golf adj, greens fee $18-$24, putting green. Downhill ski 7 mi. Cr cds: A, C, D, DS, MC, V.

🄳 ◀ 👆 🐾 🏊 🏂 SC 🗝

B&B/Small Inn

★ ★ ★ **RIVERSIDE INN.** *1 Fountain Ave, Cambridge Spgs (16403). 814/398-4645; fax 814/398-8161; toll-free 800/964-5173. www.theriversideinn.com.* 74 rms, 3 story. S $50-$70; D $65-$95; each addl $10; suites $100; under 5 free. Closed Jan-mid-Apr. TV in suites and sitting rm. Pool. Complimentary full bkfst. Dining rm 11:30 am-2 pm, 5:30-8:30 pm; Fri, Sat to 10 pm; Sun 11 am-2 pm, 5:30-8:30 pm. Dinner theater on wkends, matinees wkdays. Bar. Ck-out 11 am, ck-in 3 pm. Business servs avail. Tennis privileges. Golf privileges. Lawn games. Victorian inn (1885) overlooking French Creek. Cr cds: DS, MC, V.

🄳 👆 ⛷ 🏊 🏂 🗝

Ephrata

(E-6) *See also Bird-in-Hand, Denver/Adamstown, Lancaster, Lebanon, Reading*

Settled 1732 **Pop** 13,213 **Elev** 380 ft
Area code 717 **Zip** 17522
Information Chamber of Commerce, 77 Park Ave, Suite 1; 717/738-9010
Web www.ephrata-area.org

What to See and Do

Ephrata Cloister. Buildings stand as a monument to an unusual religious experiment. In 1732 Conrad Beissel, a German Seventh-Day Baptist, began to lead a hermit's life here; within a few years he established a religious community of recluses, with a Brotherhood, a Sisterhood, and a group of married "householders." The members of the solitary order dressed in concealing white habits; the buildings (1735-1749) were without adornment, the halls were narrow, the doorways were low, and board benches served as beds and wooden blocks as pillows. Their religious zeal and charity, however, proved to be their undoing. After the Battle of Brandywine, the cloistered community nursed the Revolutionary sick and wounded, but contracted typhus, which decimated their numbers. Celibacy also contributed to the decline of the community, but the Society was not formally dissolved until 1934. An orientation exhibit and video prepare each visitor for their relaxing journey back through time. Surviving and restored buildings include the Sisters' House, Chapel, Almonry, and eight others. Craft demonstrations (summer). (Mon-Sat; closed hols) 632 W Main St. Phone 717/733-6600. ¢¢¢

Museum and Library of the Historical Society of Cocalico Valley. Italianate Victorian mansion contains period displays; historical exhibits; genealogical and historical research library (fee) on Cocalico Valley area and residents. (Mon, Wed, Thurs, Sat) 249 W Main St. Phone 717/733-1616. **FREE**

Special Event

Street Fair. One of largest in state. Last full wk Sept.

B&Bs/Small Inns

★ ★ **THE INNS AT DONECKERS.** *318-324 N State St (17522). 717/738-9502; fax 717/738-9554; toll-free 800/377-2206. www.doneckers.com.* 40 rms, 3 story, 2 carriage house suites. S $65-$81; D $75-$99; each addl $10; suites $149-$195; package plans. Crib $8. TV in sitting rm; cable. Complimentary continental bkfst. Restaurant nearby. Ck-out 11 am, ck-in 3 pm. Health club privileges. Microwaves avail. Restored clockmaker's house (1777). Antiques. Hand-cut stenciling. Cr cds: A, C, D, DS, MC, V.

★ ★ **SMITHTON BED & BREAK-FAST COUNTRY INN.** *900 W Main St (17522). 717/733-6094; toll-free 877/755-4590. www.historicsmithton inn.com.* 8 rms, 3 story. S $75-$115; D $85-$155; each addl $20-$35; suites $145-$180. Complimentary full bkfst. Restaurant nearby. Ck-out noon, ck-in 3:30 pm. Concierge. Some in-rm whirlpools. Historic stone inn (1763); fireplaces, antiques. Totally nonsmoking. Cr cds: MC, V.

Restaurant

★ ★ ★ **DONECKERS.** *333 N State St (17522). 717/738-9501. www.doneckers. com.* Hrs: 11 am-10 pm. Closed Wed, Sun; hols. Res accepted. Bar. Wine list. French, American menu. A la carte entrees: lunch $6.95-$13.75, dinner $7.50-$29. Child's menu. Specialties: Dover sole with strawberry sauce, steak au poivre. Own baking. Elegant French decor. Cr cds: A, C, D, DS, MC, V.

Erie

(A-1) *See also North East*

Settled 1753 **Pop** 103,717 **Elev** 744 ft
Area code 814
Information Erie Area Chamber of Commerce, 109 Boston Store Pl, 16501-2312; 814/454-7191
Web www.eriechamber.com

Third-largest city in the state and only Great Lakes port in Pennsylvania, Erie has a fine natural harbor on Lake Erie, which is protected and bounded by Presque Isle peninsula, the site of many historic events. Greater Erie is also one of the nation's mighty industrial centers, with more than 750 highly diversified manufacturing firms and several large industrial parks. The lake and city take their name from the Eriez tribe, who were killed by the Seneca about 1654.

On the south shore of Presque Isle Bay, Commodore Oliver Hazard Perry built his fleet, floated the ships across the sandbars, and fought the British in the Battle of Lake Erie (1813). Fort Presque Isle, built by the French in 1753 and destroyed by them in 1759, was rebuilt by the English, burned by Native Americans, and rebuilt again in 1794 by Americans.

What to See and Do

Bicentennial Tower. Commemorating Erie's 200th birthday, this 187-ft tower features two observation decks with aerial view of city, bay, Lake Erie. Concessions in tower lobby. (Apr-Sept, daily; rest of yr, call for schedule; closed hols) Free admission Tues. Erie's Bayfront, at the foot of State St. Phone 814/455-6055. ¢

Erie Art Museum. Temporary art exhibits in a variety of media; regional artwork and lectures in the restored Greek Revival Old Customs House (1839). Art classes, concerts, lectures, and workshops are also offered. (Tues-Sat, also Sun afternoons; closed hols) Free admission Wed. 411 State St. Phone 814/459-5477. ¢

Erie Zoo. Zoo houses more than 300 animals, including gorillas, polar bears, and giraffes; children's zoo (May-Sept); one-mi tour of grounds on Safariland Express Train (fee). Indoor ice rink (Sept-Mar) 423 W 38th St, 3 mi N of I-90 State St exit 7. Phone 814/868-3651. ¢¢

Firefighters Historical Museum. More than 1,300 items of firefighting memorabilia are displayed in the old #4 Firehouse. Exhibits include fire apparatus dating from 1823, alarm systems, uniforms, badges, ribbons, helmets, nozzles, fire marks and fire extinguishers; fire safety films are shown in the Hay Loft Theater. (May-Oct, Sat and Sun) 428 Chestnut St. Phone 814/456-5969. ¢¢

Gridley's Grave. Final resting place of Captain Charles Vernon Gridley, to whom, at the Battle of Manila Bay in 1898, Admiral Dewey said, "You may fire when ready, Gridley." Gridley died in Japan; his body was returned here for burial. Four old Spanish cannons from Manila Harbor, built in 1777, guard the grave. Offers view of peninsula, Lake Erie and entrance to Erie Harbor from cliff by Gridley Circle. Lakeside Cemetery, 1718 E Lake Rd. Phone 814/459-8200.

Land Lighthouse. (1867) The first lighthouse on the Great Lakes was constructed on this site in 1813. Foot of Lighthouse St. Phone 814/452-3937.

Misery Bay. State monument to Perry; named after Perry defeated British and the fleet suffered cold and privations of a bitter winter. NE corner of Presque Isle Bay.

Presque Isle State Park. Peninsula stretches seven mi into Lake Erie and curves back toward city. Approx 3,200 acres of recreation and conservation areas. Swimming, fishing, boating (rentals, mooring, launching, marina); hiking, birding, trails, x-country skiing, ice skating, ice fishing, ice boating, picnicking, concessions. Visitor center, environmental education, and interpretive programs. N off PA 832. Phone 814/833-7424.

Waldameer Park & Water World. Rides, midway, kiddieland, water park, picnic area, food, dance pavilion. (Memorial Day-Labor Day, Tues-Sun; open Mon hols) 220 Peninsula Dr, at entrance to Presque Isle State Park. Phone 814/838-3591. ¢¢¢¢

Watson-Curtze Mansion. Housed in 1890s Victorian mansion. Museum features regional history and decorative arts exhibits; restored period rooms; changing exhibits (Tues-Sat afternoons; closed hols). Also planetarium with shows (Sat afternoons). 356 W 6th St. Phone 814/871-5790. ¢¢

Wayne Memorial Blockhouse. Replica of blockhouse in which General Anthony Wayne died Dec 15, 1796, after becoming ill on a voyage from Detroit. He was buried at the foot of the flagpole; later, his son had the body disinterred and the remains moved to Radnor. (Memorial Day-Labor Day, daily) On grounds of State Soldiers' and Sailors' Home, 560 E 3rd St. Phone 814/871-4531. **FREE**

Motels/Motor Lodges

★ ★ ★ **BEL AIRE HOTEL COMPLEX.** *2800 W 8th St (16505). 814/833-1116; fax 814/838-3242; toll-free 800/888-8781. www.bel-airehotel.com.* 151 rms, 3 story. Mid-June-mid-Sept: S, D $95-$100; each addl $10; suites $125-$200; under 19 free; lower rates rest of yr. Crib $10. TV; cable. Indoor pool; whirlpool, lifeguard. Complimentary coffee in rms. Restaurant 6 am-11 pm. Bar 11-2 am; Sun to midnight. Ck-out noon. Meeting rms. In-rm modem link. Valet serv. Sundries. Exercise equipt; sauna. Private patios, balconies. Cr cds: A, C, D, DS, MC, V.

Duck pond at Presque Isle State Park, Erie

★ **COMFORT INN.** *8051 Peach St (16509). 814/866-6666; fax 814/864-1367; res 800/221-2222. www.comfort inn.com.* 110 rms, 2 story, 50 suites. Mid-May-Sept: S $80-$99; D $90-$120; each addl $6; suites $95-$125; under 18 free; higher rates hol wkends; lower rates rest of yr. Crib free. TV; cable (premium), VCR (movies). Heated pool; whirlpool, lifeguard. Complimentary continental bkfst. Coffee in rms. Restaurant adj 6 am-midnight. Ck-out noon. Meeting rm. Business servs avail. In-rm modem link. Free airport transportation. Exercise equipt. Refrigerator, wet bar in suites. Some balconies. Cr cds: A, C, D, DS, JCB, MC, V.
D ≈ ⛷ ≊ ⚲ SC

★ **ECONO LODGE.** *8050 Peach St (16509). 814/866-5544; fax 814/864-6218; toll-free 800/638-7949. www.econolodge.com.* 97 rms, 3 story. Late May-Oct: S $79-$109; D $89.95-$149; each addl $10; higher rates special events; lower rates rest of yr. Crib free. TV; cable, VCR (movies). Indoor pool; whirlpool. Complimentary continental bkfst. Restaurant adj 7-2 am. Ck-out noon. Meeting rms. Business servs avail. In-rm modem link. Sundries. Free airport transportation. Exercise equipt. Some refrigerators, wet bars. Cr cds: A, C, D, DS, JCB, MC, V.
D ≈ ⛷ ≊ ⚲ SC

★★ **GLASS HOUSE INN.** *3202 W 26th St (16506). 814/833-7751; fax 814/833-4222; toll-free 800/956-7222. www.glasshouseinn.com.* 30 rms. June-Labor Day: S, D $65-$92; each addl $7; family rates; lower rates rest of yr. Crib $4. TV; cable (premium), VCR avail (movies). Heated pool. Complimentary continental bkfst. Restaurant nearby. Ck-out 11 am. In-rm modem link. Sundries. Gift shop. Downhill/x-country ski 20 mi. Cr cds: A, C, D, DS, MC, V.
⛷ ≈ ≊ ⚲

★★ **HAMPTON INN.** *3041 W 12th St (16505). 814/835-4200; fax 814/835-5212; toll-free 800/426-7866. www.hamptoninn.com.* 100 rms, 3 story. S $71-$105; D $78-$105; under 18 free. Crib avail. TV; cable (premium). Heated pool. Complimentary continental bkfst. Restaurant nearby 7 am-10:30 pm. Ck-out noon. Busi-

ness servs avail. Valet serv. Cr cds: A, C, D, DS, MC, V.
D ≈ ≊ ⚲ SC

★★ **HOLIDAY INN.** *18 W 18th St (16501). 814/456-2961; fax 814/456-7067; res 800/832-9101. www.holiday-inn.com.* 133 rms, 4 story. Memorial Day-Labor Day: S, D $69-$94; each addl $6; under 18 free; lower rates rest of yr. Crib free. TV; cable (premium). Heated pool; poolside serv. Complimentary full bkfst. Coffee in rms. Restaurant 6:30 am-10 pm. Bar 11:30-2 am. Ck-out noon. Coin lndry. Meeting rms. Business center. In-rm modem link. Bellhops. Valet serv. Free airport transportation. Exercise equipt. Health club privileges. Cr cds: A, D, DS, JCB, MC, V.
D ≈ ⛷ ≊ ⚲ SC ⛷

★ **MOTEL 6.** *7875 Peach St (16509). 814/864-4811; fax 814/868-1277; toll-free 800/542-7674. www.motel6.com.* 83 rms, 2 story. Late May-Sept: S $59-$89; D $69-$99; each addl $10; under 18 free; package plan; some lower rates rest of yr. Crib free. Pet accepted. TV; cable. Indoor pool; wading pool. Complimentary coffee. Restaurant nearby. Ck-out noon. Business servs avail. Coin lndry. Valet serv. Free airport transportation. Exercise equipt; sauna. Private patios, balconies. Cr cds: A, C, D, DS, ER, JCB, MC, V.
D ≈ ≊ ⛷ ≊ ⚲ SC

★ **QUALITY INN.** *8040 Perry Hwy (16509). 814/864-4911; fax 814/864-3743; toll-free 800/550-8040. www.qualityinn.com.* 107 rms, 2 story. S, D $49-$109; each addl $6; under 18 free. Crib free. Pet accepted. TV; cable. Heated pool. Restaurant 6:30 am-10 pm. Bar 11-1 am. Ck-out 11 am. Meeting rms. Business center. In-rm modem link. Bellhops. Valet serv. Free airport, RR station transportation. Health club privileges. Cr cds: A, C, D, DS, JCB, MC, V.
D ≈ ≊ ✈ ≊ ⚲ SC ⛷

★ **RAMADA INN.** *6101 Wattsburg Rd (16509). 814/825-3100; fax 814/825-0857; res 800/374-1875. www.ramada.com.* 122 rms, 2 story. July-Sept: S, D $80-$90; each addl $8; suites $90-$120; under 18 free; ski, wkend plans; lower rates rest of yr. Crib free. TV; cable (premium), VCR (movies). Heated pool; wading pool, whirlpool, lifeguard. Restaurant 6:30 am-1 pm,

5-10 pm. Bar 5 pm-2 am. Ck-out noon. Meeting rms. Business center. In-rm modem link. Sundries. Downhill ski 15 mi. Exercise equipt. Game rm. Cr cds: A, C, D, DS, JCB, MC, V.

★ **SUPER 8.** *8040 B Perry Hwy (16509). 814/864-9200; fax 814/864-3743; res 800/800-8000. www.super8. com.* 93 rms, 4 story. Apr-Oct: S, D $39-$89; under 18 free; family rates; package plans; higher rates special events; lower rates rest of yr. Crib free. Pet accepted, some restrictions. TV; cable (premium). Complimentary continental bkfst. Restaurant adj 6:30 am-10 pm. Ck-out 11 am. Business servs avail. In-rm modem link. Bellhops. Valet serv. Coin lndry. Airport transportation. Pool privileges. Game rm. Some refrigerators, microwaves. Cr cds: A, D, DS, ER, MC, V.

Restaurant

★ ★ **PUFFERBELLY.** *414 French St (16507). 814/454-1557.* Hrs: 11:30 am-9:30 pm; Fri, Sat to 11 pm; Sun to 8 pm; Sun brunch to 3 pm. Closed hols. Res accepted. Bar. Lunch $3.95-$6, dinner $8.95-$15.95. Sun brunch $9.95. Specializes in regional cuisine, steak, seafood. Outdoor dining. Restored firehouse (1907). Cr cds: A, DS, MC, V.

Fort Washington (E-8)

Pop 3,680 **Elev** 250 ft **Area code** 215 **Zip** 19034
Information Valley Forge Convention & Visitors Bureau, 600 W Germantown Pike, Suite 130, Plymouth Meeting 19462; 610/834-1550
Web www.valleyforge.org

What to See and Do

Fort Washington State Park. Commemorates the site of Washington's northern defense line against the British in 1777. Fishing; hiking, ball fields, picnicking. 500 Bethlehem Pike. Phone 215/646-2942.

The Highlands. (1796) Late-Georgian mansion on 43 acres built by Anthony Morris, active in both state and federal government. Formal gardens and crenellated walls built ca 1845. Tours. (Mon-Fri) 7001 Sheaff Ln. Phone 215/641-2687. ¢¢

Hope Lodge. (ca 1745) Colonial Georgian mansion; headquarters for Surgeon General John Cochran after Battle of Germantown. Historic furnishings, paintings, ceramics. (Tues-Sun; closed hols) 1 mi S, 553 Bethlehem Pike. Phone 215/646-1595. ¢¢

Restaurant

★ ★ **PALACE OF ASIA.** *285 Commerce Dr (19034). 215/646-2133. www.palaceofasia.citysearch.com.* Hrs: 11:30 am-11 pm; Sat, Sun brunch to 3:30 pm. Closed Dec 24. Res required Fri-Sun dinner. Indian menu. Bar. Lunch $6.25-$7.95, dinner $7.95-$15.95. Sat, Sun brunch $3.50-$8.25. Specializes in vegetarian and curry dishes. Own baking. Authentic Indian atmosphere. Cr cds: A, DS, MC, V.

Franklin (Venango County)

(C-2) *See also Meadville, Oil City, Titusville*

Settled 1787 **Pop** 7,212 **Elev** 1,020 ft **Area code** 814 **Zip** 16323
Information Franklin Area Chamber of Commerce, 1259 Liberty St; 814/432-5823
Web www.franklin-pa.org

A series of French and British forts was erected in this area. The last one, Fort Franklin, was razed by local settlers who used the stone and timber in their own buildings. Old Garrison took its place in 1796 and later served as the Venango County Jail. In 1859, James Evans, a blacksmith, made tools to drill an oil well that brought an oil boom to the area. For years, oil was dominant in the area's industries.

What to See and Do

DeBence Antique Music World. Features nickelodeons, band organs, calliopes, German organs, a variety of music boxes, many other items. Unique "see and hear" museum. Guided tours. (Mid-Mar-Dec, Tues-Sun; closed hols) 1261 Liberty St. Phone 814/432-5668. ¢¢¢

Hoge-Osmer House. (ca 1865) Museum owned by Venango County Historical Society; houses displays of materials and artifacts relating to Venango County history; period furnishings, research library. House open (May-Dec, Tues-Thurs and Sat; rest of yr, Sat; closed hols). Inquire for genealogy library hrs. Corner of South Park and Elk sts. Phone 814/437-2275. **FREE**

Pioneer Cemetery. (1795-1879) Self-guided walking tour booklets can be purchased at the Chamber of Commerce. Otter and 15th sts.

Venango County Court House. (1868). Unique styling; contains display of Native American artifacts. (Mon-Fri; closed hols) 1168 Liberty St. Phone 814/432-9500.

Special Events

Franklin Silver Cornet Band Concerts. City Park. Thurs, mid-June-Aug.

Rocky Grove Fair. July.

Applefest. Apple pie-baking contest; arts and crafts; entertainment; classic car show. Kids Korner. Five-km race; horse-drawn buggy rides. Phone 814/432-5823. First full wkend Oct.

B&B/Small Inn

★ ★ **QUO VADIS BED & BREAKFAST.** *1501 Liberty St, Franklin (16323). 814/432-4208; fax 814/797-1162; toll-free 800/360-6598.* 6 rms, 3 story. S, D $60-$80; each addl $10; wkly rates. TV in sitting rm. Complimentary full bkfst. Restaurant nearby. Ck-out 11 am, ck-in 4-9 pm. Victorian mansion (1867); detailed woodwork, heirloom

antiques. Totally nonsmoking. Cr cds: A, DS, MC, V.

Galeton

(B-4) *See also Wellsboro*

Pop 1,325 **Elev** 1,325 ft
Area code 814 **Zip** 16922
Information Potter County Recreation, PO Box 245, Coudersport 16915; 814/435-2290 or 888-POTTER2

What to See and Do

Ole Bull State Park. At upper reaches of the Kettle Creek. Site of unsuccessful effort by the famous Norwegian violinist, Ole Bornemann Bull, to establish a colony called "New Norway." Approx 125 acres. Swimming beach, fishing; hunting, hiking, x-country skiing, snowmobiling, tent and trailer sites (electric hookups). Interpretive program. Standard fees. 18 mi SW on PA 144. Phone 814/435-5000.

Pennsylvania Lumber Museum. Exhibits on lumbering and its techniques, forest industries, and products; reconstructed lumber camp and sawmill; restored locomotive and log-loader; nature trails, picnicking. Slide show in visitor center. (Apr-Nov, daily; closed hols) (See SPECIAL EVENTS) 10 mi W on US 6. Phone 814/435-2652. ¢¢

Skiing. Ski Denton/Denton Hill. Double, triple chairlifts; two Pomalifts; patrol, school, rentals, snowmaking; cafeteria, restaurant, lodge, cabins. Longest run one mi; vertical drop 650 ft. (Dec-Mar, daily) 100 mi of x-country trails; night skiing; camping. (See SPECIAL EVENTS) 10 mi W on US 6. Phone 814/435-2115. ¢¢¢¢

Special Events

Bark Peeler's Convention. On grounds of Pennsylvania Lumber Museum. Re-creation of old-time festival held by lumber camp workers celebrating the end of the work yr. Features many demonstrations, including cross-cut sawing, hewing, bark peeling; entertainment; period music; exhibits. Phone 814/435-2652. July 4-5.

Woodsmen's Carnival. Cherry Springs State Park, 12 mi SW on West Branch Rd. Horse-pulling and wood-cutting competitions; food; displays. Phone 814/435-5010. First full wkend Aug.

Bowhunter's Festival. Denton Hill. Wkend late Aug.

Germania Old Home Day. Food, dancing, events, games, entertainment. 7 mi SE via PA 144 in Germania. Phone 814/435-8881. Early Sept.

Gettysburg

(E-5) *See also Hanover, York*

Founded 1798 **Pop** 7,490 **Elev** 560 ft
Area code 717 **Zip** 17325
Information Convention & Visitors Bureau, 35 Carlisle St; 717/334-6274
Web www.gettysburg.com

Because of the historical nature of this area and the many attractions in this town, visitors may want to stop in at the Gettysburg Convention & Visitors Bureau for complete information about bus tours, guide service (including a tape-recorded and self-guided tour) and help in planning their visit here.

What to See and Do

A. Lincoln's Place. Live portrayal of the 16th president; 45 min. (Mid-June-Labor Day, Mon-Fri) 571 Steinwehr Ave. Phone 717/334-6049. ¢¢¢

Eisenhower National Historic Site. (see GETTYSBURG NATIONAL MILITARY PARK)

General Lee's Headquarters. Robert E. Lee planned Confederate strategy for the Gettysburg battle in this house; contains collection of historical items from the battle. (Mid-Mar-mid-Nov, daily) 401 Buford Ave. Phone 717/334-3141. ¢¢

Gettysburg Battle Theatre. Battle-field diorama with 25,000 figures; 30-min film and electronic maps program showing battle strategy.

(Mar-Nov, daily) 571 Steinwehr Ave. Phone 717/334-6100. ¢¢¢

Gettysburg College. (1832) 2,000 students. Liberal arts; oldest Lutheran-affiliated college in US. Pennsylvania Hall was used as Civil War hospital; Eisenhower House and statue on grounds. Tour of campus. 3 blks NW of Lincoln Sq off US 15 Business. Phone 717/337-6000.

Gettysburg Scenic Rail Tours. A 22-mi round trip to Aspers on steam train. Also charter trips and special runs. (June, Thurs-Sun; July-Aug, Tues-Sun; Sept Sat-Sun afternoons) Washington St. Phone 717/334-6932. ¢¢¢

Ghosts of Gettysburg Candlelight Walking Tours. Armed with tales from Mark Nesbitt's *Ghosts of Gettysburg* books, knowledgeable guides lead 1¼-hr tours through sections of town that were bloody battlefields 130 yrs ago. (June-Oct, daily eves; Apr, May, Nov, wkend eves) Tours depart from gallery at 271 Baltimore St. Phone 717/337-0445. ¢¢¢

Hall of Presidents and First Ladies. Costumed life-size wax figures of all the presidents; reproductions of their wives' inaugural gowns; "The Eisenhowers at Gettysburg" exhibit. (Mid-Mar-Nov, daily) 789 Baltimore St, adj to National Cemetery. Phone 717/334-5717. ¢¢¢

Land of Little Horses. A variety of performing horses—all in miniature. Continuous entertainment; indoor arena; exotic animal races. Saddle and wagon rides. Picnic area, snack bar, gift shop. (May-late Aug, daily; Apr, Sept, Oct, wkends) 5 mi W off US 30, on Knoxlyn Rd to Glenwood Dr; follow signs. Phone 717/334-7259. ¢¢¢

Lincoln Room Museum. Preserved bedroom in Wills House; collection of Lincoln items; huge plaque inscribed with Gettysburg Address, audiovisual display. (Apr-Nov, daily) 12 Lincoln Sq. Phone 717/334-8188. ¢¢

The Lincoln Train Museum. Museum features more than 1,000 model trains and railroad memorabilia; Lincoln Train Ride—simulated trip of 15 min. (Mar-Nov, daily) ½ mi S via US 15 on Steinwehr Ave. Phone 717/334-5678. ¢¢¢

GETTYSBURG: A TOWN GRIPPED BY WAR

A three-day Civil War battle in July 1863 unfolded about a mile outside Gettysburg, which was a small rural community at the time. The town also suffered from the battle, and the impact can be seen in a one-hour, one-mile walking tour that visits several of the well-preserved buildings that witnessed the conflict. Begin at Lincoln Square, the commercial heart of Gettysburg. Abraham Lincoln stayed at the David Wills House, now a small museum at No.12, the night before he gave the "Gettysburg Address" dedicating the nearby National Cemetery. Just outside the door is a life-size statue of Lincoln in somber attire appearing to help a visiting tourist casually dressed in a colorful sweater and cords. Among the townsfolk, it is called the "Perry Como statue," because that's who the tourist looks like. Head south on Baltimore Street to Nos. 242-246, the Jennie Wade Birthplace. Wade, the only civilian to be killed in the battle, is believed to have been shot by a Confederate sharpshooter while baking bread and biscuits for Union troops in her sister's nearby house. That house, on Baltimore Street next to the Holiday Inn, is a museum, the Jennie Wade House. Between the two homes, stop at the Schriver House at 309 Baltimore. Built for George Schriver and his family, its garret was occupied by Confederate sharpshooters who poked still-visible holes in the wall for their rifles. Now a museum, the Schriver House details life in the town during and immediately after the battle. Across the street at No. 304, formerly the Methodist parsonage, note the shell near the second-story window in front. The parson's daughter, Laura, was said to have narrowly escaped injury when a shell crashed through the brick wall into her room. Later, the shell was placed in the hole to mark the spot. Return to Lincoln Square via Washington Street. At the corner of West Middle Street, pause in front of the Michael Jacobs House at No. 101. A meteorologist, Jacobs recorded the weather throughout his life, leaving important details to posterity of weather and cloud conditions during the battle.

Lutheran Theological Seminary.
(1826) 250 students. Oldest Lutheran seminary in US; cupola on campus used as Confederate lookout during battle. Old Dorm, now home of Adams County Historical Society, served as hospital for both Union and Confederate soldiers. Confederate Ave, 1 mi W of Lincoln Sq on US 30. Phone 717/334-6286.

National Civil War Wax Museum. Highlights Civil War era and Battle of Gettysburg. (Mar-Dec, daily; rest of yr, Sat and Sun; closed Jan 1, Thanksgiving, Dec 25) 297 Steinwehr Ave. Phone 717/334-6245. ¢¢

Schriver House. Built prior to the Civil War, this two-story brick house was used by Confederate sharpshooters, who knocked still-visible holes in the garret walls through which to aim their weapons. Private owners have restored and furnished the house as a period museum; the 30-min guided tour details the Schriver family's experience during the battle, as well as the experience of other townspeople. (Apr-Nov, daily; Dec-Mar, wkends) 309 Baltimore St. Phone 717/337-2800. ¢¢¢

Skiing. Ski Liberty. Two quad, three double chairlifts; J-bar, handle tow; patrol, school, rentals; snowmaking; cafeteria, restaurant, bar; nursery, lodge. Longest run approx one mi; vertical drop 600 ft. (Dec-Mar, daily) 9 mi W on PA 116, in Carroll Valley. Phone 717/642-8282. ¢¢¢¢

Soldiers' National Museum. Dioramas of major battles, with sound; Civil War collection. (Mar-Nov, daily; schedule may vary) 777 Baltimore St. Phone 717/334-4890. ¢¢

Special Events

Apple Blossom Festival. South Mountain Fairgrounds, 8 mi NW. May 1-2.

Civil War Heritage Days. Lectures by historians; Civil War collectors' show; entertainment; Civil War book show; firefighters' festival; fireworks. June 26-July 4.

Apple Harvest Festival. South Mountain Fairgrounds. Demonstrations; arts and crafts; guided tours of orchard, mountain areas. First and second wkends Oct.

Motels/Motor Lodges

★ **BEST INN.** *301 Steinwehr Ave (17325). 717/334-1188; fax 717/334-1188; toll-free 800/237-8466. www. gettysburg.com.* 77 rms, 2 story. Apr-Oct: S, D $59-$99; under 18 free; lower rates rest of yr. Crib free. Pet accepted, some restrictions. TV; cable (premium), VCR avail. Pool; lifeguard. Coffee in rms. Restaurant adj 6:30 am-11 pm. Bar 4 pm-1 am; closed Sun. Ck-out noon. Sundries. Free bus depot transportation. Downhill ski 9 mi; x-country ski adj. Private patios. Sun deck. Cr cds: A, C, D, DS, MC, V.

D ⬛ ⬛ ⬛ ⬛ ⬛ SC

★★ **BEST WESTERN INN.** *1 Lincoln Sq (17325). 717/337-2000; fax 717/337-2075; toll-free 800/780-7234. www.bestwestern.com.* 83 rms, 6 story, 23 suites. Mid-June-Oct: S, D $88-$125; each addl $5; suites $125-$150; under 16 free; higher rates: graduation, homecoming; lower rates rest of yr. Crib free. TV; cable, VCR avail (movies). Pool; whirlpool, poolside serv, lifeguard. Restaurant 7-10:30 am, 5-9 pm. Bar from 5 pm. Ck-out 11 am. Meeting rms. Business center. In-rm modem link. Free garage parking. Tennis privileges. Downhill ski 8 mi. Some refrigerators. Established 1797. Cr cds: A, D, DS, MC, V.

D ⬛ ⬛ ⬛ ⬛ ⬛ SC ⬛

★★ **COLLEGE MOTEL.** *345 Carlisle St (17325). 717/334-6731; toll-free 800/367-6731. www.gettysburg.com.* 21 rms. Mid-June-Labor Day: S, D $76; each addl $10; higher rates: wkends, graduation, parents' wkend; lower rates rest of yr. TV; cable. Pool; lifeguard. Restaurant nearby. Ck-out 11 am. Cr cds: A, MC, V.

⬛ ⬛ SC

★ **COLONIAL MOTEL.** *157 Carlisle St (17325). 717/334-3126; toll-free 800/336-3126. www.gettysburg.com.* 30 rms, 2 story. Early June-early Sept: S, D $68-$82; each addl $5; under 17 free; higher rates special events; lower rates rest of yr. Crib free. TV; cable (premium). Complimentary coffee in lobby. Restaurant nearby. Ck-out 11 am. Cr cds: A, MC, V.

⬛ SC

★ **COMFORT INN.** *871 York Rd (17325). 717/337-2400; fax 717/337-0831; toll-free 800/221-2222. www. gettysburg.com.* 81 rms, 2 story. June-Aug: S $77-$82; D $87-$90; each addl $6; under 18 free; higher rates: antique car show, college events; lower rates rest of yr. Crib free. TV; cable (premium). Indoor pool; whirlpool. Complimentary continental bkfst. Restaurant nearby. Ck-out 11 am. Business servs avail. In-rm modem link. Some in-rm whirlpools; refrigerator in suites. Cr cds: A, C, D, DS, ER, JCB, MC, V.

D ⬛ ⬛ ⬛ SC

★★ **CROSS KEYS MOTOR INN RESTAURANT.** *6110 York Rd, New Oxford (17350). 717/624-7778; fax 717/624-7941.* 64 rms, 4 story. Apr-Sept: S $39-$63; D $49-$73; each addl $5; under 12 free; wkly rates; higher rates special events; lower rates rest of yr. Crib free. TV; cable, VCR avail (movies). Restaurants 6 am-10 pm; Fri, Sat to 11 pm. Bar 4 pm-2 am. Ck-out 11 am. Meeting rms. Business servs avail. Gift shop. Golf privileges. Downhill ski 15 mi. Some in-rm whirlpools. Cr cds: A, DS, MC, V.

⬛ ⬛ ⬛ ⬛ SC

★ **DAYS INN.** *865 York Rd (17325). 717/334-0030; fax 717/337-1002; toll-free 800/329-7466. www.daysinn gettysburg.com.* 112 rms, 5 story. Apr-Oct: S $59-$98; D $69-$108; each addl $5; under 18 free; ski plans; higher rates special events; lower rates rest of yr. Crib free. TV; cable (premium), VCR avail. Heated pool; lifeguard. Complimentary coffee in lobby. Restaurant adj 6 am-11 pm. Ck-out noon. Coin lndry. Meeting rms. Business servs avail. In-rm modem link. Valet serv. Sundries. Downhill ski 10 mi. Exercise equipt. Game rm. Microwaves avail. Cr cds: A, C, D, DS, JCB, MC, V.

D ⬛ ⬛ ⬛ ⬛ ⬛ SC

★★ **HOLIDAY INN EXPRESS.** *869 York Rd (15628). 717/337-1400; fax 717/337-0159; toll-free 800/465-4329. www.gettysburg.com.* 51 rms, 2 story. Apr-Oct: S $79-$99; D $89-$109; each addl $10; suites $109-$129; under 19 free; higher rates special events; lower rates rest of yr. Crib free. TV; cable (premium). Indoor pool; lifeguard, whirlpool. Complimentary continental bkfst. Restaurant adj open 24 hrs. Ck-out 11 am. In-rm modem link. Downhill ski 8 mi. Picnic tables. Cr cds: A, C, D, DS, MC, V.

★ **HOMESTEAD MOTOR LODGE.** *1650 York Rd (17325). 717/334-3866. www.gettysburg.com.* 10 rms. June-Oct: S, D $45-$65; each addl $8; lower rates Apr-May, Nov. Closed rest of yr. TV. Restaurant nearby. Ck-out 10 am. Downhill ski 8 mi. Totally nonsmoking. Cr cds: A, DS, MC, V.

★ **QUALITY INN.** *401 Buford Ave (17325). 717/334-3141; fax 717/334-1813; toll-free 800/228-5050. www.gettysburg.com.* 41 rms. June-early Sept: S, D $69-$89; each addl $5; under 17 free; lower rates rest of yr. Crib $3. TV; VCR avail. Pool. Restaurant 7 am-9 pm. Bar from noon. Ck-out noon. Business servs avail. Downhill ski 6 mi. General Lee's Headquarters (museum) adj. Cr cds: A, C, D, DS, ER, JCB, MC, V.

★ **QUALITY INN MOTOR LODGE.** *380 Steinwehr Ave (17325). 717/334-1103; res 800/228-5151. www.gettysburg qualityinn.com.* 109 rms, 2 story. Apr-Oct: S, D $69-$107; suite $97-$135; under 16 free; lower rates rest of yr. Crib free. Pet accepted, some restrictions. TV; cable (premium), VCR avail. 2 pools, 1 indoor; lifeguard. Coffee in rms. Restaurant opp 6 am-11 pm. Bar 6 pm-1 am. Ck-out noon. Coin lndry. Meeting rm. Gift shop. Free bus depot transportation. Putting green. Downhill/x-country ski 8 mi. Exercise equipt; sauna. Balconies. Cr cds: A, C, D, DS, MC, V.

★ **RED CARPET INN.** *2450 Emmitsburg Rd (17325). 717/334-1345; fax 717/334-5026; toll-free 800/336-1345. www.reservahost.com.* 25 rms. Apr-early Nov: S, D $35-$69; suites $58-$85; higher rates: spring, fall wkends, college, area events; lower rates rest of yr. Crib $5. TV; cable (premium). Pool. Complimentary coffee. Restaurant nearby. Ck-out 11 am. Microwaves avail. Picnic tables, grills. Cr cds: A, C, D, DS, ER, MC, V.

B&Bs/Small Inns

★ ★ ★ **BALADERRY INN.** *40 Hospital Rd (17325). 717/337-1342; fax 717/337-1342; toll-free 800/220-0025. www.baladerryinn.com.* 8 rms, 7 with shower only, 2 story. S $84-$102; D $94-$112; each addl $15; wkends Apr-Nov (2-day min). Children over 14 yrs only. TV in common area; VCR. Complimentary full bkfst. Ck-out 11 am, ck-in 2 pm. Tennis. Golf privileges. Downhill ski 10 mi; x-country ski adj. Built in 1812; used as a field hospital during the Civil War battle of Gettysburg. Restored; furnished with antiques and reproductions. Cr cds: A, C, D, DS, MC, V.

★ ★ ★ **BATTLEFIELD BED AND BREAKFAST INN.** *2264 Emmitsburg Rd (17325). 717/334-8804. www.gettysburgbattlefield.com.* 8 rms, 2 story. No rm phones. Apr-Nov: S, D $147-$172; each addl $10; suite $193-$218; hols, wkends (2-day min); lower rates rest of yr. Crib free. TV in sitting rm; VCR. Complimentary full bkfst; afternoon refreshments. Ck-out 11:30 am, ck-in 2:30 pm. Luggage handling. Concierge serv. Business servs avail. Downhill ski 10 mi. Lawn games. Carriage rides. Fireplaces. Restored 1809 farmhouse famous for living history activities. Totally nonsmoking. Cr cds: A, C, D, DS, MC, V.

★ ★ **BRAFFERTON INN.** *44 York St (17325). 717/337-3423. www.gettysburg.com.* 10 rms, 2 story, 2 suites. No rm phones. S, D $75-$125; each addl $10; suites $120-$125; higher rates special events. TV in suites. Complimentary full bkfst. Restaurant nearby. Ck-out 11 am, ck-in 2 pm. First house built in town (1786); antiques. Cr cds: A, DS, MC, V.

★ ★ ★ **FARNSWORTH HOUSE INN.** *401 Baltimore St (17325). 717/334-8838; fax 717/334-5862. www.gettysburgaddress.com.* 9 rms, 2 story. No rm phones. Apr-Oct: S $85; D $95; each addl $10. TV in some rms, sitting rm; cable. Complimentary full bkfst. Restaurant (see also FARNSWORTH HOUSE). Ck-out 11 am, ck-in 3 pm. Business servs avail. Concierge serv. Luggage handling.

Downhill ski 7 mi; x-country ski ¼ mi. Some in-rm whirlpools. Historic house (1810), restored to its 1863 appearance. The uppermost level of the inn was once used by Confederate sharpshooters; more than 100 bullet holes still remain in the south wall of the inn. Daily tours. Cr cds: A, DS, MC, V.

★★★ **GASLIGHT INN.** *33 E Middle St (17325). 717/337-9100; fax 717/337-1100; toll-free 800/914-5698.* 9 rms, 8 with shower only, 3 story. S, D $100-$175; each addl $20; hol wkends (2-day min). Children over 10 yrs only. TV; cable, VCR (free movies). Complimentary full bkfst; afternoon refreshments. Dining rm 6-8 pm (by res only). Restaurant nearby. Ck-out 11 am, ck-in 3 pm. Concierge serv. Luggage handling. Business servs avail. In-rm modem link. Tennis privileges. Golf privileges. Downhill ski 6 mi; x-country ski 1 mi. Health club privileges. Balconies. Italianate house (1872) with original exterior trim. Rms decorated and named in theme of flowers. Cr cds: A, DS, MC, V.

★★ **GETTYSTOWN INN BED & BREAKFAST.** *89 Steinwehr Ave (17325). 717/334-2100; fax 717/334-5905. www.dobbinhouse.com.* 5 rms, 2 story, 1 suite. No rm phones. Mar-Nov: S $79-$99, D $85-$105; each addl $6; suite $105; under 12 free; wkly rates; higher rates: hols (2-day min), special events; lower rates rest of yr. TV in some rms; cable. Complimentary full bkfst. Restaurant (see also DOBBIN HOUSE). Ck-out 10 am, ck-in 2 pm. Downhill ski 7 mi; x-country ski 1 mi. Refrigerators. Renovated 1860s home; antiques. Overlooks site of Abraham Lincoln's Gettysburg Address. Totally nonsmoking. Cr cds: A, MC, V.

★★ **THE HERR TAVERN AND PUBLICK HOUSE.** *900 Chambersburg Rd (17325). 717/334-4332; fax 717/334-3332; toll-free 800/362-9849. www.herrtavern.com.* 16 rms, 3 story. S, D $90-$170. Children over 12 yrs only. TV; cable, VCR (movies). Complimentary full bkfst. Restaurant (see also HERR TAVERN & PUBLICK HOUSE). Ck-out 11 am, ck-in 4 pm.

Luggage handling. Downhill ski 5 mi. Some in-rm whirlpools. Built in 1815, antiques; served as Confederate hospital. Totally nonsmoking. Cr cds: DS, MC, V.

All Suite

★★★ **JAMES GETTYS HOTEL.** *27 Chambersburg St (17325). 717/337-1334; fax 717/334-2103; toll-free 800/900-5275. www.jamesgettyshotel. com.* 11 kit. suites, 4 story. Mid-Mar-Nov: kit. suites $125-$145; each addl $15; under 12 free; lower rates rest of yr. Crib free. TV; cable, VCR avail. Complimentary continental bkfst, coffee in rms. Restaurant adj 11:30 am-5 pm. Ck-out 11 am, ck-in 3 pm. Business servs avail. Luggage handling. Concierge serv. Gift shop. Guest lndry. Downhill ski 10 mi; x-country ski 1 mi. Refrigerators, microwaves, wet bars. Built in 1804. Totally nonsmoking. Cr cds: A, DS, MC, V.

Restaurants

★★★ **DOBBIN HOUSE.** *89 Steinwehr Ave (17325). 717/334-2100. www.dobbinhouse.com.* Hrs: 11:30 am-11 pm. Closed Jan 1, Thanksgiving, Dec 25. Res accepted. American menu. Bar. Lunch $4.95-$15.95, dinner $18.25-$36.95. Child's menu. Specializes in onion soup, duck, seafood Isabella. Own baking. Oldest building in Gettysburg; built 1776. Totally nonsmoking. Cr cds: A, DS, MC, V.

★★★ **FARNSWORTH HOUSE.** *401 Baltimore St (17325). 717/334-8838. www.farnsworthhousedining.com.* Hrs: 5-9 pm. Closed Jan 1, Thanksgiving, Dec 25. Res accepted. Bar to midnight. Dinner $12.95-$18. Child's menu. Specialties: peanut soup, game pie, pumpkin fritters. Outdoor dining. Built in 1810; tour avail. Cr cds: A, DS, MC, V.

★ **GINGERBREAD MAN.** *217 Steinwehr Ave (17325). 717/334-1100.* Hrs: 11 am-11 pm; Sun to 10 pm. Closed hols. Varied menu. Bar. Lunch $4.50-

$8.95, dinner $6.95-$18.95. Child's menu. Specializes in NY-style deli sandwiches, Mexican dishes, fresh Maryland crabcakes. Casual, lively atmosphere. Cr cds: A, D, DS, MC, V. D —

★★ **THE HERR TAVERN & PUB-LICK HOUSE.** *900 Chambersburg Rd (17325). 717/334-4332. www.herr tavern.com.* Hrs: 11 am-9 pm; Sun from 5 pm. Closed Jan 1, Dec 24, 25. Res accepted. Continental menu. Bar. Lunch $3.49-$8.49, dinner $13-$20. Specialties: blackened prime rib, chicken Chesapeake, seafood pasta. Child's menu. Restored antebellum tavern with period art and antiques. Cr cds: A, DS, MC, V. D —

Gettysburg National Military Park

(E-5) *See also Gettysburg, Hanover*

The hallowed battlefield of Gettysburg, scene of one of the most decisive battles of the Civil War and immortalized by Lincoln's Gettysburg Address, is preserved by the National Park Service. The town itself is still a college community, as it was more than a hundred years ago on July 1-3, 1863, when General Robert E. Lee led his Confederate Army in its greatest invasion of the North. The defending Northerners under Union General George Meade repulsed the Southern assault after three days of fierce fighting, which left 51,000 men dead, wounded, or missing.

The Gettysburg National Military Park has more than 35 miles of roads through 5,900 acres of the battlefield area. There are more than 1,300 monuments, markers, and tablets of granite and bronze; 400 cannons are also located on the field.

Visitors may wish to tour the battlefield with a Battlefield Guide, licensed by the National Park Service (two-hour tour; fee). The guides escort visitors to all points of interest and sketch the movement of troops and details of the battle. Or visitors may wish to first orient themselves

at the Electric Map at the Visitor Center; then using the park folder, the battlefield can be toured without a guide. Audio cassettes are also available for self-guided tours.

The late President Dwight D. Eisenhower's retirement farm, a National Historic Site, adjoins the battlefield. It is open to the public on a limited-tour basis. All visitors must obtain tour tickets at the tour information center, located at the lobby of the Visitor Center-Electric Map building. Transportation to the farm is by shuttle (fee). For further information contact Gettysburg National Military Park, 97 Taneytown Rd, Gettysburg 17325; 717/334-1124.

What to See and Do

The Angle. Spot where Pickett's Charge was repulsed on July 3, referred to as "high water mark" of the Confederacy.

Culp's Hill. Site of longest sustained fighting during battle.

Cyclorama Center. Adj to visitor center. Instructive film and exhibits: 356-ft Cyclorama painting of Pickett's Charge. (Daily) ¢¢

Devil's Den. Stronghold of Confederate sharpshooters following its capture during action on the second day.

East Cemetery Hill. Rallying point for Union forces on first day of battle. Scene of fierce fighting on evening of second day.

Eisenhower National Historic Site. Farm and home of the 34th President of the United States and his wife, Mamie. Tour of grounds and home (1½-2 hrs). Self-guided tours explore the farm and skeet range. Reception Center houses exhibits and bookstore; 11-min video is shown. Access to site is by shuttle only, from the National Park Service Visitor Center at 97 Taneytown Rd. (Daily; closed Jan 1, Thanksgiving, Dec 25) 97 Taneytown Rd. Phone 717/338-9114. ¢¢

The Eternal Light Peace Memorial. On Oak Ridge. Erected in 1938 and dedicated by President Roosevelt to "peace eternal in a nation united."

The Gettysburg National Cemetery. Site of Lincoln's Gettysburg Address.

Little Round Top. Key Union position during second and third days of battle.

Gettysburg National Military Park

Memorials to State Units. Includes Pennsylvania State Monument, with names of more than 34,500 Pennsylvanian soldiers who participated in the battle.

Seminary Ridge. Main Confederate battle line.

Visitor Center-Electric Map-Gettysburg Museum of the Civil War. Visits to the park should begin here. Park information, including a self-guided auto tour, and guides may be obtained at the center. Story of battle told on 750-square-ft electric map surrounded by 525 seats (every 45 min; fee). Gettysburg Museum of the Civil War has an extensive collection of Civil War relics (free). (Daily; closed Jan 1, Thanksgiving, Dec 25) On PA 134. Electric map. ¢¢ Obtain tickets here for

The Wheatfield and Peach Orchard. Scene of heavy Union and Confederate losses on the second day of fighting.

Whitworth Guns on Oak Hill. Only breech-loading cannon used here.

Gibsonia (D-1)

(see Pittsburgh)

Greensburg

(E-2) *See also Connellsville, Donegal, Ligonier, New Stanton*

Founded 1785 **Pop** 15,889 **Elev** 1,099 ft **Area code** 724 **Zip** 15601

Information Laurel Highlands Visitors Bureau, 120 E Main St, Ligonier 15658; 724/238-5661

Web www.laurelhighlands.org

Greensburg was named for Revolutionary General Nathanael Greene.

What to See and Do

Bushy Run Battlefield. Here Colonel Henry Bouquet defeated united Native American forces during Pontiac's War on Aug 5 and 6, 1763. The battle lifted the siege of Fort Pitt and was the turning point of the war. Picnicking, park (free), hiking trails. Visitor center exhibits depict battle (Wed-Sun; closed hols). NW on PA 993. Phone 724/527-5584. ¢¢

Historic Hanna's Town. Costumed tour guide tells story of Hanna's Town, site of first court west of Alleghenies. Includes reconstructed courthouse, tavern, jail, and stockaded fort; picnic area. (June-Aug,

Tues-Sun; May, Sept and Oct, wkends only) 3 mi NE via US 119. Phone 724/836-1800. ¢¢

Lincoln Highway Heritage Corridor. A 140-mi stretch of US 30 extending from Greensburg to Chambersburg. Pass through and explore countless historical and recreational areas. Driving guide avail (fee) from Lincoln Highway Heritage Corridor, PO Box 386. Phone 724/668-8330. ¢

Westmoreland County Courthouse. Building in style of Italian Renaissance; restored in 1982. (Mon-Fri; closed hols) Main and Pittsburgh sts. Phone 724/830-3000.

Westmoreland Museum of American Art. 18th-, 19th-, and early 20th-century American paintings, sculpture, furniture and decorative arts. 19th-and early 20th-century southwestern Pennsylvania paintings. Extensive toy collection. Lectures, guided tours. (Wed-Sun; closed hols) 221 N Main St. Phone 724/837-1500. **DONATION**

Motels/Motor Lodges

★ **COMFORT INN.** *1129 E Pittsburgh St (15601). 724/832-2600; fax 724/834-3442; toll-free 800/228-5150. www.comfortinn.com.* 77 rms, 3 story. S $66-$110; D $76-$110; each addl $5; suites $81-$147; under 18 free; higher rates special events. Crib free. TV; cable (premium), VCR avail (movies). Heated pool. Complimentary continental bkfst. Restaurant nearby. Ck-out 11 am. Meeting rm. Business servs avail. Valet serv. Health club privileges. Some in-rm whirlpools, refrigerators, wet bars; microwaves avail. Cr cds: A, C, D, DS, ER, JCB, MC, V.

D ⇌ ⤫ 🐾 **SC**

★★ **FOUR POINTS BY SHERATON.** *100 Sheraton Dr (Rte 30E) (15601). 724/836-6060; fax 724/834-5640. www.sheraton.com.* 146 rms, 2 story. S $66-$80; D $71-$85; each addl $5; suites $110-$250; under 17 free; package plans. Crib free. TV; cable (premium), VCR avail. Indoor pool. Sauna. Restaurant 6:30 am-2 pm, 5-10 pm. Bar 11-2 am; entertainment. Ck-out noon. Meeting rms. Business servs avail. Bellhops. Valet serv. Sundries. Free RR station, bus depot transportation. 9-hole golf course, greens fee, pro shop, putting green. Exercise equipt. Some refriger-

ators. Shopping mall opp. Cr cds: A, C, D, DS, JCB, MC, V.

🍴 **D** ⇌ ⤫ ⛳ 🐾 **SC**

★ **KNIGHTS INN.** *1215 S Main St (15601). 724/836-7100; fax 724/837-5390; toll-free 800/843-5644. www.knightsinn.com.* 110 rms, 10 suites, 11 kits. May-Oct: S $47.95-$57.95; D $56.95-$73.95; each addl $7; kit. units $63.95-$75.95; under 18 free; lower rates rest of yr. Crib free. TV; cable (premium), VCR avail. Pool. Complimentary coffee in lobby. Restaurant adj 6 am-11 pm. Ck-out noon. Meeting rm. In-rm modem link. Coin lndry. Refrigerators, microwaves avail. Cr cds: A, C, D, DS, MC, V.

⇌ ⛳ 🐾 **SC**

★★★ **MOUNTAIN VIEW INN.** *1001 Village Dr (15601). 724/834-5300; fax 724/834-5304; toll-free 800/537-8709. www.mountainviewinn.com.* 97 rms. S $59-$135; D $69-$135; suites $150-$275. TV; cable (premium), VCR avail. Pool. Complimentary continental bkfst. Coffee in rms. Restaurant 7 am-2 pm, 5-9 pm; wkend hrs vary. Rm serv 7:30 am-11 pm. Bar 11 am-midnight; Fri, Sat to 1 am; Sun noon-8 pm. Ck-out 11 am. Meeting rms. Business servs avail. In-rm modem link. Sundries. Exercise equipt. Health club privileges. Antique decor; English and herb gardens; gazebo. Cr cds: A, C, D, DS, MC, V.

D ⇌ ⤫ ⛳ 🐾 **SC**

Restaurant

★★ **CARBONE'S.** *US 119, Crabtree (15624). 724/834-3430. www.carbone pasta.com.* Hrs: 4:30-9 pm; Fri, Sat to 10 pm. Closed Sun; hols. Res accepted. Italian, American menu. Dinner $8.95-$16.95. Child's menu. Specialties: angel pie, antipasto, braciole. Mediterranean decor. Family-owned. Cr cds: A, D, DS, MC, V.

D **SC** ⊣

Hamburg

(D-7) *See also Kutztown, Reading, Shartlesville*

Founded 1779 **Pop** 4,114 **Elev** 373 ft
Area code 484 and 610 **Zip** 19526

Information Reading/Berks County
Visitors Bureau, 352 Penn St, Reading
19602; 610/375-4085 or 800/443-6610
Web www.readingberkspa.com

Situated on the banks of the
Schuylkill River, Hamburg is a center
for one of the finest farming sections
in Pennsylvania. The town's industries include the manufacture of
brooms, iron and steel castings,
knitwear, and soft-drink products.

What to See and Do

Blue Rocks. Covers 125 acres; pool,
fishing (stocked pond); picnicking,
two pavilions; hiking, Appalachian
Trail; camping, trailer facilities (fee;
hookups addl). Game rm. 5 mi E on
I-78 to Lenhartsville, then 2 mi N on
PA 143. Phone 610/756-6366. ¢

Hawk Mountain Sanctuary. Hawk
and eagle flights visible with binocu-
lars from lookouts mid-Aug-mid-Dec;
museum, bookstore. (Daily; closed
Jan 1, Thanksgiving, Dec 25) 11 mi
N via PA 61 and 895; follow signs.
Phone 610/756-6961. ¢¢

**Wanamaker, Kempton & Southern,
Inc.** A six-mi, 40-min round trip on
steam or deisel train along the Onte-
launee Creek at the foot of Hawk
Mountain. Model railroad (Sun),
antique shop. Snack bar, picnic area.
Steam train (July-Aug and Oct, Sat
and Sun afternoons; May and June,
Sun afternoons). Diesel train (June
and Sept, first and third Sat afternoons only). Also special events
throughout the yr. 5 mi E on I-78 to
Lenhartsville exit, then 5 mi N on PA
143 to Kempton. Phone 610/756-
6469. ¢¢

Hanover

(E-5) *See also Gettysburg, York*

Founded 1763 **Pop** 14,535 **Elev** 609 ft
Area code 717 **Zip** 17331
Information Hanover Area Chamber
of Commerce, 146 Carlisle St;
717/637-6130
Web www.hanoverchamber.com

Known in early days as "McAllister-
stown" (for founder Colonel Richard
McAllister) and "Rogue's Harbor" (for
lack of law enforcement), Hanover is
in the rich Conewago Valley. Here,
on June 30, 1863, Confederate General J.E.B. Stuart's cavalry tangled
with Union forces under Generals
Kilpatrick and Custer. The battle pre-
vented Stuart from reaching Gettysburg in time to function as "the eyes
of Lee's army."

Among the products of the town's
diversified industry are books, wire-
cloth, yarns, furniture, industrial
machinery, textiles, and foods,
including snack foods.

What to See and Do

Codorus State Park. Approx 3,300
acres. Swimming pool, fishing in
1,275-acre Lake Marburg, boating
(rentals, mooring, launching,
marina); hunting, hiking, bridle
trails, x-country skiing, snowmobiling, sledding, ice-skating, ice boating, ice fishing, picnicking,
mountain biking, snack bar, tent and
trailer sites. Standard fees. 3 mi E on
PA 216. Phone 717/637-2816.

Conewago Chapel. (1741) Oldest
stone Catholic church in the US. Designated Sacred Heart Basilica in 1962.
Cemetery dates from 1752. (Daily) 30
Basilica Dr, 2 mi W on PA 116, then
2 mi N. Phone 717/637-2721. **FREE**

Neas House Museum. Neas House
(ca 1783), restored Georgian mansion, serves as local history museum.
(May-Nov, Tues-Fri) Special events
(spring, summer, late Dec). 113 W
Chestnut St. Phone 717/632-3207.
FREE

Utz Quality Foods, Inc. Producers of
potato chips and snack foods. Glass-
enclosed tour gallery overlooks production area; push-to-talk audio
program and closed-circuit TV monitors. (Mon-Thurs; closed hols) 900
High St. Phone 717/637-6644. **FREE**

B&B/Small Inn

★ ★ ★ **BEECHMONT BED AND
BREAKFAST INN.** *315 Broadway
(17331). 717/632-3013; fax 717/632-
2769; toll-free 800/553-7009. www.
thebeechmont.com.* 7 rms, 2 story, 3
suites. S, D $80-$95; suites $115-
$135. Children over 12 yrs only.

Complimentary full bkfst; afternoon refreshments. Restaurant nearby. Ck-out 11 am, ck-in 3 pm. Microwaves avail. Federal period house (1834); landscaped courtyard. Cr cds: A, DS, MC, V.

Harmony

(D-1) *See also Butler, Pittsburgh*

Founded 1804 **Pop** 937 **Elev** 925 ft
Area code 724 **Zip** 16037
Information Butler County Chamber of Commerce, 112 Woody Dr, PO Box 1082, Butler, 16003; 724/283-2222
Web www.butlercountychamber.com

First settlement of George Rapp's Harmony Society, Harmony served the colony only until 1814. More than 100 of the original group are buried in Harmonists Cemetery, southeast of town. Several of the Rappite Society's sturdy brick houses still stand in the village.

What to See and Do

Harmony Museum. (1809) Exhibits depict early life under Harmonists and Mennonites; regional history. The Harmony Society was one of America's most successful experiments in communal living. Harmony was the society's first home (1804). Tour. (Tues-Sun afternoons) 218 Mercer St. Phone 724/452-7341. ¢¢

Special Events

Dankfest. Pioneer craft festival held on grounds of Harmony Museum (see). Crafts, entertainment, tours, refreshments. Contact museum for schedule. Late Aug. Phone 722/452-7341.

Christmas Open House. Candlelight tour of Harmony Museum, Wagner House and Ziegler log house. Entertainment, refreshments. Contact museum for schedule. Early Dec.

Harrisburg

(E-5) *See also Carlisle, Hershey, York*

Settled 1718 **Pop** 48,950 **Elev** 360 ft
Area code 717
Information Capital Regional Chamber of Commerce, 3211 N Front St, 17110-1342, phone 717/232-4099; or the Harrisburg-Hershey-Carlisle Tourism & Convention Bureau, 25 N Front St, 17101, phone 717/231-7788
Web www.harrisburgregional chamber.org

This midstate metropolis is graced by what many consider the finest capitol building in the nation. Its riverside park (known as City Island), Italian Lake, unique museum, and beautiful Forum are the showplaces; commerce, industry, and politics keep the city going.

The site was viewed in 1615 by Etienne Brulé on a trip down the Susquehanna, but more than a century passed before John Harris, the first settler, opened his trading post here. His son established the town in 1785. It became the seat of state government in 1812; the cornerstone of the first capitol building was laid in 1819.

What to See and Do

Capitol Hill buildings. N 3rd and Walnut sts. Phone 717/787-6810. Clustered in a 45-acre complex, the major buildings are

> **The Capitol.** (dedicated 1906) Italian Renaissance building covers two acres, has 651 rooms; 26,000-ton, 272-ft dome, imitating that of St. Peter's in Rome, dominates city skyline. Includes murals by Abbey and Okley. Tours (daily; closed hols). Main entrance, 3rd and State sts. **FREE**

> **Finance Building.** Ceiling murals by Maragliotti, Eugene Savage; mural in south vestibule illustrates *The Collection of Taxes*. (Mon-Fri)

> **Forum Building.** Includes auditorium below constellation-bedecked ceiling; walls review man's progress through time. Main lobby boasts a

Maragliotti ceiling. General and law libraries.

North Office Building. Map inscribed on main lobby floor shows state highways, seals of Pennsylvania cities.

South Office Building. Colorful murals by Edward Trumbull depict *Penn's Treaty with the Indians* and *The Industries of Pittsburgh*.

The State Museum of Pennsylvania. A six-story circular building housing four stories of galleries, authentic early country store, Native American life exhibit, technological and industrial exhibits, collection of antique autos and period carriages; planetarium; natural history and geology exhibits and one of the world's largest framed paintings, Rothermel's *The Battle of Gettysburg*. Planetarium has public shows (Sat and Sun; fee). (Tues-Sun; closed hols) N of Capitol Building, 3rd and North sts. Phone 717/787-4978. **FREE**

Dauphin County Courthouse. Seven imposing courtrooms; outline map on floor of main foyer pictures borough and township boundaries. (Mon-Fri; closed hols) Front and Market sts. Phone 717/255-2741.

Fort Hunter Park. Historic 37-acre property; site of British-built fort erected in 1754 to combat mounting threats prior to the French and Indian War. In 1787 the land was purchased and became a farm that eventually grew into a self-sufficient village. The Pennsylvania Canal runs through the park; on the grounds are historic buttonwood trees dating from William Penn's time; a 19th-century boxwood garden; herb gardens; paths along the banks of the Susquehanna River; picnic area. Also here are an ice house, springhouse (ca 1800), Centennial barn (1876), and corncrib (1880). Also on the grounds, but not open to the public because of restoration, are the old tavern (1800), and stone stable. 6 mi N on N Front St. Outstanding feature of park is

   Fort Hunter Mansion. Federal-style stone mansion, built in three sections. Front stone portions were built in 1786 and 1814; rear wooden portion built in 1870. Spacious mansion displays period fur-

nishings, clothing, toys, and other artifacts. Guided tours. (May-Dec, Tues-Sun) 5300 N Front St, in park. Phone 717/599-5751. ¢¢

Indian Echo Caverns. Stalagmite and stalactite formations. Picnicking, playground. (Daily, schedule varies; closed Jan 1, Thanksgiving, Dec 25) 10 mi E on US 322, 422, in Hummelstown. Phone 717/566-8131. ¢¢¢

Italian Lake. Bordered with flowers, shrubs, and shade trees in summer. N 3rd and Division sts.

John Harris Mansion. Home of city's founder, now Historical Society of Dauphin County headquarters. Stone house has 19th-century furnishings, library (Mon-Thurs; fee), collection of county artifacts. Tours (Mon-Thurs and by appt). 219 S Front St. Phone 717/233-3462. ¢¢

Penn National Race Course. Live yr-round Thoroughbred racing (Wed, Fri-Sun). Nationwide simulcasts (daily). Terrace dining room; gift shop. NE via I-81, exit 28, in Grantville. Phone 717/469-2211. ¢¢

Reservoir Park. View of east end of city, five nearby counties. Walnut and N 19th sts.

Riverfront Park. Four mi along Susquehanna River, with park promenade flanking Front St, concrete walk along river.

Rockville Bridge. (1902) A 3,810-ft stone-arch bridge; 48 spans carry four tracks of Penn Central Railroad main line. 4 mi N on US 22.

Special Events

Pennsylvania State Farm Show. State fair. Phone 717/787-5373. Jan 8-13. 2301 N Cameron.

Eastern Sports & Outdoor Show. Phone 717/630-2268. Early-mid-Feb.

Kipona. Boating and water-related activites. Labor Day wkend.

Pennsylvania National Horse Show. Phone 717/975-3677. Ten days mid-Oct.

Motels/Motor Lodges

★ ★ **BAYMONT INN.** *200 N Mountain Rd (17112).* 717/540-9339; fax 717/540-9486; toll-free 800/428-3438. *www.baymontinns.com.* 66 rms, 3 story, 8 suites. Apr-Oct: S $57.95-

$70.95; D $63.95-$76.95; suites $66.95-$80.95; under 19 free; lower rates rest of yr. Crib free. Pet accepted. TV; cable (premium), VCR avail. Complimentary continental bkfst, coffee in rms. Restaurant nearby. Ck-out noon. Coin lndry. Meeting rms. Business center. In-rm modem link. Sundries. Refrigerator, microwaves in suites. Cr cds: A, C, D, DS, MC, V.

🄳 🏊 🖫 🛁 🆂🅲 🏃

★★ **BEST WESTERN COUNTRY OVEN.** *300 N Mountain Rd (17112). 717/652-7180; fax 717/541-8991; toll-free 800/780-7234. www.bestwestern. com.* 49 rms, 2 story. S $50-$80; D $50-$85; each addl $3; under 13 free. Crib $5. Pet accepted. TV; cable (premium). Restaurant 6:30 am-9 pm. Bar 11 am-11 pm. Ck-out 11 am. Business servs avail. In-rm modem link. Sundries. Microwaves avail. Cr cds: A, C, D, DS, MC, V.

🏊 🖫 🛁 🆂🅲

★ **COMFORT INN EAST.** *4021 Union Deposit Rd (17109). 717/561-8100; fax 717/561-1357; toll-free 800/253-1409. www.harrisburgpacomfortinn.com.* 115 rms, 5 story. June-Oct: S, D $79-$109; under 18 free; higher rates car shows; lower rates rest of yr. Crib free. Pet accepted. TV; cable (premium). Heated pool; lifeguard. Complimentary continental bkfst. Coffee in rms. Restaurant adj 6 am-10 pm. Ck-out noon. Coin lndry. Meeting rms. Business servs avail. Free airport, RR station transportation. Health club privileges. Microwaves avail. Cr cds: A, C, D, DS, ER, JCB, MC, V.

🄳 🏊 🖙 🖫 🛁 🆂🅲

★★ **CROWNE PLAZA.** *23 S 2nd St (17101). 717/234-5021; fax 717/234-6797. www.crowneplaza.com.* 261 rms, 10 story. S $75-$95; D $85-$105; each addl $10; studio rms $78-$90; suites $145; under 19 free. TV; cable (premium), VCR avail (movies). Indoor pool. Restaurant 6:30 am-2 pm, 5-10 pm. Bar 4:30 pm-1 am. Ck-out noon. Meeting rms. Business servs avail. In-rm modem link. Gift shop. Airport transportation. Exercise equipt. Microwaves avail. Rooftop patio. Cr cds: A, C, D, DS, ER, JCB, MC, V.

🄳 🖙 🏃 🖫 🛁 🆂🅲

★ **DAYS INN.** *3919 N Front St (17110). 717/233-3100; fax 717/233-6415; toll-free 800/329-7466. www. daysinn.com.* 116 rms, 3 story. S $54.99-$69.99; D $54.99-$74.99; each addl $5; under 12 free; higher rates: car shows, farm show. Crib free. TV; cable. Pool; lifeguard. Playground. Complimentary continental bkfst. Restaurant nearby. Ck-out noon. Coin lndry. Business servs avail. In-rm modem link. Exercise equipt. Refrigerators, microwaves avail. Picnic tables. Cr cds: A, C, D, DS, JCB, MC, V.

🄳 🖙 🏃 🖫 🛁 🆂🅲

★★ **HAMPTON INN.** *4950 Ritter Rd, Mechanicsburg (17055). 717/691-1300; fax 717/691-9692. www.hamptoninn. com.* 129 rms, 4 story. S $79-$84; D $88-$93; under 18 free; ski plan. Crib free. TV; cable (premium), VCR avail. Heated pool; whirlpool, lifeguard. Complimentary continental bkfst. Restaurant adj 11 am-11 pm. Ck-out 11 am. Coin lndry. Meeting rms. Business center. In-rm modem link. Downhill ski 20 mi. Exercise equipt. Health club privileges. Microwaves avail. Cr cds: A, D, DS, MC, V.

🖂 🄳 🖙 🏃 🖫 🛁 🏃

★★ **HAMPTON INN.** *4230 Union Deposit Rd (17111). 717/545-9595; fax 717/545-6907; toll-free 800/426-7866. www.hampton-inn.com.* 145 rms, 5 story. S $68-$80; D $75-$86; under 18 free; higher rates auto shows. Crib avail. TV; cable (premium). Heated pool; whirlpool, lifeguard. Complimentary continental bkfst. Restaurant adj open 24 hrs. Ck-out noon. Coin lndry. Meeting rms. Business servs avail. Valet serv. Golf privileges. Downhill ski 15 mi. Exercise equipt. Health club privileges. Microwaves avail. Cr cds: A, D, DS, MC, V.

🄳 🖂 🖫 🛁 🆂🅲 🍴

★★ **HOLIDAY INN.** *5401 Carlisle Pike, Mechanicsburg (17055). 717/697-0321; fax 717/697-5917; toll-free 800/772-7829. www.holiday-inn.com.* 218 rms, 2 story. Feb-Oct: S $93; D $103; each addl $10; suites $125-$200; under 18 free; wkly rates; higher rates special events; lower rates rest of yr. Crib free. Pet accepted, some restrictions; $50 deposit. TV; cable (premium). Complimentary continental bkfst, coffee in rms. Restaurant 6:30 am-9 pm. Bar

5 pm-2 am; entertainment. Ck-out noon. Meeting rms. Business servs avail. Coin lndry. Exercise equipt. Miniature golf. Heated indoor/outdoor pool; lifeguard. Some in-rm whirlpools; microwaves avail. Picnic tables, grills. Cr cds: A, C, D, DS, JCB, MC, V.

★ ★ HOLIDAY INN. *4751 Lindle Rd (17111).* 717/939-7841; *fax* 717/939-9317; *toll-free* 800/637-4817. *www.holiday-inn.com.* 300 rms, 4 story. S $109-139; D $121-$151; each addl $12; under 19 free. Crib free. TV; cable (premium). 2 pools, 1 indoor; whirlpool, poolside serv, lifeguard. Restaurant 7 am-2 pm, 5-10 pm. Rm serv 7 am-10 pm. Bar 11-2 am. Ck-out 10 am. Valet serv. Convention facilities. Business servs avail. Free airport transportation. Lighted tennis. Putting green. Exercise equipt; sauna. Health club privileges. Game rm. Private patios, balconies. Cr cds: A, C, D, DS, MC, V.

★ ★ HOLIDAY INN. *148 Sheraton Dr, New Cumberland (17070).* 717/774-2721; *fax* 717/774-2485. *www.holilday-inn.com.* 196 rms, 2 story. May-Oct: S, D $59-$99; each addl $10; suites $160; under 18 free; family, wkend, hol rates; ski plans; higher rates special events; lower rates rest of yr. Crib free. Pet accepted, some restrictions; $10. TV; cable (premium). Indoor pool; whirlpool. Restaurant 6:30 am-2 pm, 5-9 pm; Fri, Sat to 10 pm. Bar 5 pm-2 am; entertainment. Ck-out 11 am. Meeting rms. Business center. In-rm modem link. Bellhops. Valet serv. Coin lndry. Free airport, RR station transportation. Exercise equipt. Health club privileges. Game rm. Refrigerators, microwaves avail. Some balconies. Picnic tables, grills. Luxury level. Cr cds: A, C, D, DS, JCB, MC, V.

★ HOWARD JOHNSON MOTOR LODGE. *473 Eisenhower Blvd (17111).* 717/564-6300; *fax* 717/564-4840; *res* 800/446-4656. *www.hojo.com.* 176 rms, 2 story. S $55-$79; D $62-$89; each addl $8; under 17 free; higher rates Hershey Antique Auto Show. Crib free. TV; cable (premium). Pool; wading pool. Restaurant 5 am-midnight. Bar from 11 am. Ck-out

noon. Meeting rms. Business center. Valet serv. Sundries. Free airport, RR station transportation. Exercise equipt. Microwaves avail. Private patios, balconies. Cr cds: A, C, D, DS, MC, V.

★ RED ROOF INN. *400 Corp Cir (17110).* 717/657-1445; *fax* 717/657-2775; *toll-free* 800/843-7663. *www.redroof.com.* 110 rms, 2 story. S $34-$44; D $44-$62; under 18 free. Crib free. Pet accepted. TV; cable (premium). Complimentary coffee in lobby. Restaurant nearby. Ck-out noon. Business servs avail. In-rm modem link. Cr cds: A, C, D, DS, MC, V.

Hotels

★ ★ ★ HILTON HOTEL. *1 N 2nd St (17101).* 717/233-6000; *fax* 717/233-6271. *www.hilton.com.* 341 rms, 15 story. S, D $99-$164; each addl $10; suites $200-$500; wkend rates. Crib avail. TV; cable (premium). Indoor pool. Restaurant 6:30 am-11 pm. Bar 11-1 am; entertainment. Ck-out noon. Convention facilities. Business servs avail. In-rm modem link. Concierge. Valet parking. Free airport transportation. Exercise equipt. Health club privileges. Minibars, refrigerators; microwaves avail. Luxury level. Cr cds: A, D, DS, MC, V.

★ ★ ★ MARRIOTT HARRISBURG. *4650 Lindle Rd (17111).* 717/564-5511; *fax* 717/564-6173; *res* 800/228-9290. *www.marriott.com.* 348 rms, 10 story. S, D $80-$159; each addl $14; suites $225-$235; under 18 free. Crib free. TV; cable (premium), VCR avail. Indoor/outdoor pool; whirlpool, poolside serv, lifeguard. Restaurant 6 am-midnight. Bar to 2 am; entertainment. Ck-out 11 am. Convention facilities. Business servs avail. In-rm modem link. Bellhops. Valet serv. Sundries. Gift shop. Free airport transportation. Exercise equipt; sauna. Game rm. Balconies. Luxury level. Cr cds: A, D, DS, ER, JCB, MC, V.

★ ★ RADISSON PENN HARRIS HOTEL. *1150 Camp Hill Byp, Camp Hill (17011).* 717/763-7117; *fax*

717/763-7120; res 800/333-3333.
www.radisson.com. 250 rms, 2-3 story.
No elvtr. S $69-$119; D $79-$139;
each addl $10; suites $225-$400;
under 18 free. Crib free. Pet accepted.
TV; cable (premium). Pool; poolside
serv, lifeguard. Coffee in rms. Restaurant 6:30 am-10 pm. Bar noon-2 am.
Ck-out 11 am. Convention facilities.
Business center. In-rm modem link.
Valet serv. Bellhops. Free airport
transportation. Exercise equipt. Some
refrigerators. Cr cds: A, C, D, DS,
MC, V.

★★★ **FOUR POINTS BY SHERA-
TON.** 800 E Park Dr (17111).
717/561-2800; fax 717/561-8398; toll-
free 800/644-3144. www.fourpoints.
com. 174 rms, 3 story. S $86-$105; D
$96-$115; each addl $10; suites $165-
$275; under 18 free. Crib free. Pet
accepted, some restrictions. TV; cable
(premium). Heated pool; whirlpool,
lifeguard. Restaurant 6:30 am-10 pm.
Bar 11-2 am. Ck-out noon. Meeting
rms. Business servs avail. In-rm
modem link. Bellhops. Valet serv.
Shopping arcade. Free airport transportation. Golf privileges. Exercise
rm; sauna. Game rm. Cr cds: A, C, D,
DS, ER, JCB, MC, V.

★★ **WYNDHAM GARDEN HOTEL.**
765 Eisenhower Blvd (17111).
717/558-9500; fax 717/558-8956; res
800/253-0238. www.wyndham.com.
167 rms, 6 story. May-Oct: S, D $89-
$119; each addl $10; suites $150;
under 19 free; ski plans; wkend rates;
higher rates car shows; lower rates
rest of yr. Crib free. Pet accepted. TV;
cable (premium). Heated pool; lifeguard. Coffee in rms. Restaurant 6
am-2:30 pm, 5-10 pm. Bar 4 pm-
midnight. Ck-out noon. Meeting
rms. Business servs avail. In-rm
modem link. Free airport, RR station,
bus depot transportation. Downhill
ski 20 mi. Exercise equipt. Health
club privileges. Refrigerator in suites;
microwaves avail. Cr cds: A, C, D,
DS, ER, JCB, MC, V.

Restaurants

★★★ **ALFRED'S VICTORIAN
RESTAURANT.** 38 N Union St, Middletown (17057). 717/944-5373. Hrs:
11:30 am-2 pm, 5-10 pm; Sat from 5

pm; Sun 3-9 pm. Closed hols. Res
accepted. Italian, continental menu.
Bar. Wine list. Lunch $7.95-$17.95,
dinner $12.95-$37.95. Specializes in
homemade pastas, hand-cut steaks,
seafood, steak Diane. Own baking,
pasta. Tableside cooking. Patio dining.
Victorian mansion; antique chandeliers, furnishings; floor-to-ceiling
windows; fireplaces. Family-owned.
Cr cds: A, D, DS, MC, V.

★★ **MANADA HILL INN.** 128 N Hershey Rd (17112). 717/652-0400. Hrs:
4-9 pm; Fri-Sat to 10 pm; Sun 11 am-
8 pm; Sun brunch to 2:30 pm. Closed
Dec 25. Continental menu. Bar to 11 pm. Dinner $8.25-
$19.95. Sun brunch $11.50. Child's
menu. Specializes in fresh seafood,
prime rib. Restored house; artwork,
antique brass chandeliers. 3 dining
rms. Cr cds: A, C, D, DS, MC, V.

Hawley

(B-8) *See also Milford, Scranton*

Settled 1827 **Pop** 1,303 **Elev** 920 ft
Area code 570 **Zip** 18428
Information Pocono Mtns Vacation
Bureau, 1004 Main St, Stroudsburg
18360; 570/424-6050; for brochures
phone 800/POCONOS
Web www.poconos.org

A major attraction in this Pocono
resort area is man-made Lake Wallenpaupack, offering summer recreation
on the lake as well as winter recreation nearby.

What to See and Do

Claws 'N Paws Wild Animal Park. A
zoo in the woods with more than
100 species of exotic animals. Petting
zoo with tame deer, lambs, and
goats. Farmyard area. Parrot, reptile
shows; zookeeper talks (schedule
varies). Picnicking, snack bar. (May-
Oct, daily) 12 mi W via PA 590, near
Lake Wallenpaupack. Phone
570/698-6154. ¢¢¢

Gravity Coach. Car used on Pennsylvania Gravity Railroad (22 inclined
planes between Hawley and Scranton, 1850-1885). W of town on US 6.

Lake Wallenpaupack. One of the largest man-made lakes in state (5,600 acres), formed by damming of Wallenpaupack Creek. Swimming beach (Memorial Day-day before Labor Day; fee), fishing, boating, water sports; ice fishing, camping. Information center, ½ mi NW on US 6 at PA 507 (Daily; closed Easter, Thanksgiving, Dec 25). Phone 570/226-2141. **FREE**

PPL. Hydroelectric facilities, dam; recreation area. Superintendent's office has information on campgrounds, hiking trails, picnic groves (Mon-Fri); observation point. (Daily) Approx 1½ mi E on US 6. Phone 570/226-3702. **FREE**

Promised Land State Park. Approx 2,950 acres. Swimming beach, fishing, boating (rentals, mooring, launch); hiking, x-country skiing, snowmobiling, ice skating, ice fishing, picnicking, snack bar, tent and trailer sites, cabins. Nature center, interpretive program. 12 mi S on PA 390. Phone 570/676-3428. ¢¢¢¢

Skiing. Tanglwood. Two double chairlifts, two rope tows, beginner lift; patrol, school, rentals, snowmaking; cafeteria, bar; nursery. Longest run one mi; vertical drop 415 ft. Night skiing. (Early Dec-late Mar, daily) Half-day rates. 4 mi S via PA 390, off I-84 in Tafton. Phone 570/226-7669 or 888/226-SNOW. ¢¢¢¢

Motel/Motor Lodge

★ **GRESHAM'S LAKE VIEW MOTEL.** *Rte 6 (18428).* 570/226-4621; *fax 570/226-4621.* 21 rms, 2 story. S, D $68-$73; each addl $5; under 5 free; wkly rates; ski plans; lower rates off-season. Crib free. TV; cable. Complimentary coffee in lobby. Restaurant nearby. Ck-out 11 am. Downhill/x-country ski 2½ mi. Balconies. Overlooks Lake Wallenpaupack. Cr cds: A, DS, MC, V.
🄳 ⬥ ⬧ ⬧ ⬧

B&Bs/Small Inns

★ **FALLS PORT INN & RESTAU-RANT.** *330 Main Ave (18428).* 570/226-2600; *fax 570/226-6409.* 9 rms, 5 share bath, 2 story. No rm phones. May-Labor Day: S, D $75-$95; under 2 free; wkend, hol rates (2-day min); ski plans; lower rates rest of yr. Crib free. 2 TVs; cable, VCR avail. Complimentary continental bkfst. Restaurant 11:30 am-9 pm. Ck-out 11 am, ck-in 1 pm. Downhill/x-country ski 9 mi. Built in 1902 as an inn. Cr cds: A, MC, V.
⬧ ⬧ ⬧

★ ★ ★ **ROEBLING INN ON THE DELAWARE.** *155 Scenic Dr, Lackawaxen (18435).* 570/685-7900; *fax 570/685-1718.* *www.roeblinginn.com.* 6 rms, 2 story, 4 rms with shower only, 1 rm with kit. July-Aug, AP: S $70-$90, D $75-$95, each addl $10, kit. unit $85-$105. Wkly rates. Min stay wkends, hols. Lower rates rest of yr. TV; cable. Complimentary full bkfst. Restaurant nearby 7 am-9 pm. Ck-out 11:30 am, ck-in 2:30 pm. Luggage handling. Business servs avail. Tennis privileges 1 mi. Downhill/x-country ski 5 mi. Refrigerators. On river. Cr cds: A, DS, MC, V.
⬧ ⬧ ⬧ ⬧

★ ★ ★ **SETTLERS INN AT BINGHAM PARK.** *4 Main Ave (18428).* 570/226-2993; *fax 570/226-1874;* toll-free 800/833-8527. *www.thesettlersinn.com.* 18 rms, 2 story, 5 suites. S $58-$75; D $83-$113; each addl $15; suites $113-$153; under 12 free. Crib $10. Complimentary full bkfst. Restaurant (see also THE SETTLERS INN). Ck-out noon, ck-in 1 pm. Business servs avail. In-rm modem link. Airport transportation. Downhill ski 8 mi; x-country ski 1 mi. Golf course nearby. Bingham Park opp. Tudor-revival manor (1927); stone fireplace, sitting rooms with many antiques. Totally nonsmoking. Cr cds: A, DS, MC, V.
⬧ ⬧ ⬧ ⬧ SC ⬧

Restaurants

★ **EHRHARDT'S LAKESIDE.** *PA 507 (18428).* 570/226-2124. *www.ehrhardts.com.* Hrs: 11 am-10 pm; Sun from 9 am; Sun brunch to 12:30 pm. Closed Thanksgiving, Dec 25. Res accepted. Bar. Lunch $2.50-$10, dinner $9-$20. Sun brunch $7.95. Child's menu. Specializes in steak, seafood. Tri-level dining area; overlooks lake. Cr cds: A, DS, MC, V.
🄳 ⬧

★ ★ ★ **THE SETTLERS INN.** *4 Main Ave (18428).* 570/226-2993. *www.*

thesettlersinn.com. Hrs: 11:30 am-2 pm, 5-9 pm; Sun brunch to 2 pm. Closed Dec 23-25. Res accepted wkends and July-Aug. Bar. A la carte entrees: lunch $5-$11, dinner $13-$20. Sun brunch $5.95-$10.95. Child's menu. Specializes in pheasant, seafood, trout. Pianist Fri, Sat. Dining rm of Tudor-style hotel constructed in 1920s. Cr cds: A, DS, MC, V.

Hazleton

(C-7) *See also Ashland, Bloomsburg, Jim Thorpe, Wilkes-Barre*

Settled 1809 **Pop** 23,329 **Elev** 1,660 ft
Area code 570 **Zip** 18201
Information Greater Hazleton Chamber of Commerce, 1 S Church St, Suite 200; 570/455-1508
Web www.hazletonchamber.org

On top of Spring Mountain, Hazleton calls itself the highest city in Pennsylvania. Rich agricultural land surrounds Hazleton, and its early and rapid economic growth was spurred by the rich anthracite coal reserves found in the area. Although coal dominated the town's economy during the 19th century, today there are many diversified industries located here, producing building materials, textiles, office furniture, business forms, foods and food containers, boxes, heavy fabricated steel, plastics, electronic parts, and other products.

What to See and Do

Eckley Miners' Village. (Pennsylvania Anthracite Museum Complex) Mining coal patch town (1850s) portrays life in the anthracite region until about 1940. Walking tour (Memorial Day-Labor Day; fee). (Daily; closed hols) 10 mi NE off PA 940, near Freeland. Phone 570/636-2070. ¢¢

National Shrine of the Sacred Heart. Large outdoor shrine includes stations of the cross and crucifixion scene; picnic area. (Mar-Oct, daily) 1½ mi NE on US 309, PA 940, in Harleigh section of Hazleton. Phone 570/455-1162. **FREE**

Motels/Motor Lodges

★★ **BEST WESTERN GENETTI MOTOR LODGE.** *PA 309, RR1 (18201).* 570/454-2494; fax 570/455-7793; toll-free 800/780-7234. *www. bestwestern.com.* 89 rms, 3 story. June-Oct: S $55-$65; D $65-$75; each addl $7; suites $130-$150; under 12 free; higher rates special events; lower rates rest of yr. Crib free. TV; cable, VCR avail (movies). Heated pool; lifeguard. Playground. Complimentary continental bkfst. Ck-out 11 am. Coin lndry. Business servs avail. Valet serv. Sundries. Bus depot transportation. Cr cds: A, C, D, DS, MC, V.

★ **RAMADA INN.** *Rte 309 N (18201).* 570/455-2061; fax 570/455-9387. 107 rms, 2 story. S, D, studio rms $72; under 18 free. Crib free. Pet accepted. TV; cable. Pool; lifeguard. Restaurant 6 am-10 pm. Bar 5 pm-2 am. Ck-out noon. Meeting rms. Business servs avail. In-rm modem link. Bellhops. Sundries. Cr cds: A, D, DS, MC, V.

Restaurant

★ **TOM'S KITCHEN.** *PA 93, Conyngham (18219).* 570/788-3808. Hrs: 7 am-8 pm; Sun from 8 am. Closed hols. Bkfst $3.45-$4.25, lunch $2.75-$3.75, dinner $5.25-$9.95. Child's menu. Specialties: roast turkey platter, stuffed breast of chicken. Family-style restaurant. Family-owned. Totally nonsmoking.

Hershey

(E-6) *See also Cornwall, Harrisburg, Lebanon*

Founded 1903 **Pop** 12,771 **Elev** 420 ft
Area code 717 **Zip** 17033
Information Hersheypark, 100 W Hersheypark Dr; 800/HERSHEY (information) or 800/533-3131
Web www.800hershey.com

One of America's most fascinating success stories, this planned community takes its name from founder M.

S. Hershey, who established his world-famous chocolate factory here in 1903, then built a town around it. The streets have names like Chocolate and Cocoa, and streetlights are shaped like chocolate kisses. But there's more than chocolate here. Today, Hershey is known as one of the most diverse entertainment and resort areas in the eastern United States. Hershey is also known as the "golf capital of Pennsylvania" and has a number of well-known golf courses.

What to See and Do

Founders Hall. Campus center of Milton Hershey School, noted for its striking rotunda. (Daily; closed hols) 801 Spartan Ln. Phone 717/520-2000.

Hershey Gardens. From mid-June to first frost, 8,000 rose plants bloom on 23 acres. Tulip garden (mid-Apr-mid-May); chrysanthemums and annuals; butterfly house featuring 400-500 butterflies; six theme gardens. (Mid-Apr-Oct, daily) Hotel Rd. Phone 717/534-3492. ¢¢¢

Hershey Museum. Pennsylvania German, Native American, Eskimo collections; displays of Stiegel glass; "Apostolic Clock" depicting life of Christ; Milton Hershey history. (Daily; closed Jan 1, Thanksgiving, Dec 25) Near entrance to Hersheypark. Phone 717/534-3439. ¢¢ Adj is

Hersheypark Arena. Capacity 10,000; professional hockey, basketball, ice skating, variety shows, concerts. 100 Hershey Park Dr. Phone 717/534-3911.

Hersheypark. 110-acre theme park including Rhine Land, Tudor Sq, Dutch crafts barn; more than 60 rides including six roller coasters; live family shows. (Mid-May-Labor Day, daily; May and Sept, selected wkends) Entrance on Hersheypark Dr (PA 39). ¢¢¢¢ Also here is

ZooAmerica. An 11-acre environmental zoo depicting five climatic regions of North America; home to more than 200 animals. (Daily; closed hols) Combination admission with Hersheypark avail. Park Ave. Phone 717/534-3860. ¢¢¢

Hersheypark Stadium/Star Pavilion. Stadium seats 25,000, Star Pavilion seats 7,200; sports and entertainment events. Phone 717/534-3911.

★ **Hershey's Chocolate World.** Tour via automated conveyance; simulates steps of chocolate production from cacao bean plantations through chocolate making in Hershey. Also tropical gardens, shopping village. (Daily; closed Dec 25) Entrance adj to Hersheypark. Phone 717/534-4900. **FREE**

Seltzer's Lebanon Bologna Company. Outdoor wooden smokehouses since 1902. (Mon-Sat; closed hols) 230 N College St, 3 blks N of US 422, in Palmyra. Phone 717/838-6336. **FREE**

Special Events

Chocolate Lovers' Weekend. Feb.

Hersheypark Balloonfest. Oct. Phone 717/534-3900.

Antique Automobile Club. National fall rally. Second wkend Oct.

Christmas in Hershey. Mid-Nov-Dec.

Motels/Motor Lodges

★ **ADDEY'S INN OF HERSHEY.** *150 E Governor Rd (17033). 717/533-2591; fax 717/533-2591. www.go2pa.com/addeys_inn.* 12 rms. May-Labor Day: S, D $89; each addl $5; lower rates rest of yr. Crib $5. TV; cable (premium). Complimentary coffee in lobby. Ck-out 11 am. Picnic tables. Cr cds: A, DS, MC, V.
🖼 🐾 **SC**

★★ **BEST WESTERN INN.** *150 E Governor Rd (17033). 717/533-5665; fax 717/533-5675; toll-free 800/780-7234. www.bestwestern.com.* 123 rms, 3 story. No elvtr. May-Aug: S, D $99-$159; each addl $10; under 17 free; wkly rates; higher rates special events; lower rates rest of yr. Crib $2. TV; cable (premium), VCR avail (movies). Heated pool; whirlpool. Complimentary continental bkfst. Restaurant nearby. Ck-out noon. Coin lndry. Meeting rms. Business servs avail. In-rm modem link. Valet serv. Game rm. Refrigerators; microwaves avail. Cr cds: A, D, DS, ER, MC, V.
D 🐝 🖼 🐾 **SC**

★ **DAYS INN.** *350 W Chocolate Ave (17033). 717/534-2162; fax 717/533-6409; toll-free 800/329-7466. www.*

daysinn.com. 75 rms, 4 story. Late June-Aug: S $119-$139; D $129-$149; each addl $6; under 18 free; higher rates antique car shows; lower rates rest of yr. Crib free. TV; cable, VCR avail (movies). Complimentary continental bkfst. Restaurant opp 11:30 am-10 pm. Ck-out 11 am. Valet serv. Free RR station, bus depot transportation. Health club privileges. Some refrigerators; microwaves avail. Cr cds: A, C, D, DS, JCB, MC, V.
[D] [icons] SC

★★ **HOLIDAY INN.** *604 Station Rd, Grantville (17028). 717/469-0661; fax 717/469-7755; toll-free 800/465-4329. www.stayholiday.com.* 195 rms, 4 story. Memorial Day-mid-Oct: S $119-$179; D $129-$189; each addl $10; suites $195-$295; under 19 free; lower rates rest of yr. Crib free. Pet accepted. TV; cable. 2 pools, 1 indoor; whirlpool. Restaurant 6:30 am-10 pm. Bar 11-2 am; entertainment. Ck-out noon. Coin lndry. Meeting rms. Business center. In-rm modem link. Bellhops. Valet serv. Gift shop. Airport, RR station, bus depot transportation. Exercise equipt; sauna. Lawn games. Microwaves avail. Balconies. Cr cds: A, C, D, DS, ER, JCB, MC, V.
[D] [icons] SC [icon]

★★ **MILTON MOTEL.** *1733 E Chocolate Ave (17033). 717/533-4533; fax 717/533-0369. www.miltonmotel.com.* 34 rms, 2 story. Mid-May-Labor Day: S $49-$76; D $66-$99; each addl $5; wkly rates Sept-May; higher rates hol wkends; lower rates rest of yr. Crib $6. TV; cable (premium), VCR avail. Heated pool. Restaurant adj 11-2 am. Ck-out 11 am. Business servs avail. In-rm modem link. Game rm. Refrigerators, microwaves avail. Cr cds: A, D, DS, MC, V.
[icons] SC

★ **RODEWAY INN & SUITES.** *43 W Areba Ave (17033). 717/533-7054; fax 717/533-3405; toll-free 800/638-7949. www.rodeway.com.* 22 rms, 2 story, 11 kits. Mid-June-early Sept: S $79-$119; D $89-$129; each addl $10; kits. $125-$198; under 18 free; lower rates rest of yr. Crib free. TV; cable. Indoor pool. Complimentary continental bkfst, coffee in rms. Restaurant nearby. Ck-out 11 am. Business servs avail. In-rm modem link. Refrigera-

tors; microwaves avail. Cr cds: A, C, D, DS, MC, V.
[icons] SC

★ **SIMMONS MOTEL.** *355 W Chocolate Ave (17033). 717/533-9177; fax 717/533-3605. www.simmonsmotel. com.* 32 rms, 2 story. June-Oct: S $55-$85; D $65-$95; each addl $5; apts (1-3 bedrm) $110-$185; kit. units $95-$110; wkly, family rates; higher rates antique car show; lower rates rest of yr. Crib free. TV; cable (premium), VCR avail. Complimentary coffee in lobby. Restaurant nearby. Ck-out 11 am. Business servs avail. Health club privileges. Many refrigerators; microwaves avail. Picnic tables, grills. Cr cds: A, DS, MC, V.
[icons] SC

★★ **SPINNERS MOTOR INN.** *845 E Chocolate Ave (17033). 717/533-9157; fax 717/534-1189. www.spinnersinn. com.* 52 rms, 6 with shower only, 2 story. May-mid-Oct: S $65-$95; D $69-$109; each addl $5; suites $89-$139; under 2 free; golf plans; wkends, hols (2-day min); higher rates special events; lower rates rest of yr. Crib $6. TV; cable (premium), VCR avail (movies). Heated pool. Complimentary continental bkfst. Restaurant (see also CATHERINE'S AT SPINNERS). Bar. Ck-out 11 am. Business servs avail. Game rms. Some refrigerators, microwaves. Some balconies. Picnic tables. Cr cds: A, C, D, DS, MC, V.
[D] [icons] SC

★★ **WHITE ROSE MOTEL.** *1060 E Chocolate Ave (17033). 717/533-9876; fax 717/533-6923. www.800hershey. com.* 24 rms, 2 story. July-Aug: S, D $108; under 18 free; lower rates rest of yr. Crib $5. TV; cable (premium). Heated pool; lifeguard. Coffee in rms. Restaurant nearby. Ck-out 11 am. Business servs avail. In-rm modem link. Gift shop. Health club privileges. Refrigerators. Private patios, balconies. Picnic tables. Totally nonsmoking. Cr cds: A, DS, MC, V.
[D] [icons] SC

Hotel

★★★ **HERSHEY LODGE & CONVENTION CENTER.** *W Chocolate Ave & University Dr (17033). 717/534-8600; fax 717/534-8666; toll-free 800/437-7439. www.800hershey.*

com/~herco. 665 rms, 1-2 story. May-Labor Day: S $130-$157; D $136-$163; each addl $15; suites $250-$650; under 18 free; package plans; lower rates rest of yr. Crib free. TV; cable (premium). 2 pools, 1 indoor; wading pool, whirlpool, poolside serv, lifeguard. Playground. Free supervised children's activities (May-early Sept, late Nov-Jan 1). Complimentary coffee in rms. Restaurant 7 am-10 pm; also dining rm. Bar 11-2 am; entertainment. Ck-out 11 am. Convention facilities. Business servs avail. In-rm modem link. Valet serv. Sundries. Gift shop. Free airport transportation. Lighted tennis. 18-hole golf privileges, greens fee $60-$120, miniature golf. Exercise equipt; sauna. Rec rm. Cinema. Cr cds: A, C, D, DS, ER, JCB, MC, V.

Resort

★★★★ **THE HOTEL HERSHEY.** *One Hotel Rd (17033). 717/533-2171; fax 717/534-8887; toll-free 800/533-3131. www.hersheypa.com.* This central Pennsylvania resort has a romantic, European-style facade and a palace-like decor. Recreation options are family oriented and include Hershey-park and golf plans. In conjunction with The Hershey Lodge and Convention Center, this property is one of the region's largest meeting and convention locations, with 125,000 square feet of space and over 900 rooms. 234 rms, 5 story. MAP, Apr-Oct: S $231-$293; D $289-$351; each addl $75; under 3 free; EP avail; package plans; lower rates rest of yr. Crib free. Valet parking. TV; cable, VCR avail. Indoor, outdoor pools, wading pool, whirlpool, lifeguard. Restaurants 7 am-11 pm. Rm serv 24 hrs. Bar 11-1 am; Sat entertainment. Ck-out noon, ck-in 4 pm. Conference facilities. Business center. Bellhops. Valet serv. Gift shop. Fitness center. Spa, sauna. Massage. 2 tennis courts. Basketball court. 9-hole golf, greens fee $19-$22, putting green. Nature trails. Bicycle rentals. Lawn games. Carriage rides. X-country ski on site. Extensive gardens, landscaping; scenic hilltop location. Cr cds: A, C, D, DS, MC, V.

B&B/Small Inn

★★ **PINEHURST INN BED AND BREAKFAST.** *50 NE Dr (17033). 717/533-2603; fax 717/534-2639; toll-free 800/743-9140.* 15 rms, some share bath, 2 story. No rm phones. S, D $45-$75; each addl $5; (2-day min) hols. TV in sitting rm. Complimentary full bkfst. Ck-out 11 am. Airport transportation. Health club privileges. Brick mansion built by Milton Hershey for orphaned boys. Totally nonsmoking. Cr cds: MC, V.

Restaurants

★★ **CATHERINE'S AT SPINNER'S.** *845 E Chocolate Ave (17033). 717/533-9050. www.spinnersinn.com.* Hrs: 4-10 pm. Closed Sun, Mon; hols. Res accepted. Bar. Dinner $10-$24. Child's menu. Specializes in steak, fresh seafood, pasta. Own baking. Elegant decor with chandelier, portraits of historical figures. Cr cds: A, C, D, DS, MC, V.

★★★ **CIRCULAR DINING ROOM.** *Hotel Rd (17033). 717/533-8800. www.hersheypa.com.* Contemporary American menu. Specializes in classic American dishes. Hrs: 7 am-2 pm, 5-10 pm. Res accepted. Wine list. Bkfst, lunch $7.95-$9.95; dinner $24-$35. Child's menu. Entertainment. Jacket. Cr cds: A, D, DS, MC, V.

★★ **DIMITRI'S.** *1311 E Chocolate Ave (17033). 717/533-3403.* Hrs: 4-11 pm. Closed hols. Res accepted. Greek, continental menu. Bar to 2 am. Lunch $3.95-$7.95, dinner $6.95-$21.95. Child's menu. Specializes in seafood, steak. Cr cds: A, DS, MC, V.

★★ **UNION CANAL HOUSE.** *107 S Hanover St (17033). 717/566-0054. www.unioncanalhouse.com.* Hrs: 5-10 pm. Closed Sun; hols. Res accepted. Continental menu. Bar. Dinner $8.95-$29.95. Child's menu. Specialties: roast duckling, Angus beef, lump crab cakes. Three dining areas; fireplace, memorabilia from 1800s. Family-owned. Cr cds: A, D, DS, MC, V.

Honesdale

(B-8) *See also Hawley, Scranton*

Founded 1826 **Pop** 4,874 **Elev** 980 ft
Area code 570 **Zip** 18431
Information Wayne County Chamber of Commerce, 303 Commercial St; 570/253-1960 or 800/433-9008
Web www.waynecountycc.com

Named in honor of Philip Hone, a mayor of New York City and first president of the Delaware & Hudson Canal Company, Honesdale was for many years the world's largest coal storage center, shipping millions of tons of anthracite. A gravity railroad brought coal here in winter; in spring it was reshipped by canal boats to tidewater. The *Stourbridge Lion,* first steam locomotive to operate in the United States (1829), was used by the Delaware & Hudson Canal Company, but when the rail bed proved too weak, mule power replaced the steam engine. Today, Honesdale manufactures textile products, business forms, and furniture, and is surrounded by dairy farms in the beautiful rolling countryside.

What to See and Do

Replica of the *Stourbridge Lion*. (Original is in Smithsonian Institution) First steam locomotive to operate in the US (1829). Main St.

Stourbridge Rail Excursions. Scenic rail excursions from Honesdale to Lackawaxen, centering on the change of seasons, with entertainment and activities. Contact the Chamber of Commerce for schedule, fees.

Triple W Riding Stable. A 181-acre horse ranch in the NE range of Pocono Moutains. Variety of trail rides for beginners or advanced riders; ½- and full-day trips; overnight camping trips. Hay and sleigh rides (seasonal; by appt). (Daily) US 6 through Hawley, left at post office, 3½ mi to "Triple W" sign, turn right. Phone 570/226-2620. ¢¢¢¢¢

Wayne County Historical Society Museum. Delaware and Hudson-Canal exhibit, Native American exhibit. (Jan-Feb, Sat; Mar-Dec,

Wed-Sat; closed Jan 1, Thanksgiving, Dec 25) 810 Main St. Phone 570/253-3240. ¢

Special Event
Wayne County Fair. Exhibits, livestock, horse racing. First full wk Aug.

Hopewell Furnace National Historic Site

(E-7) *See also Pottstown, Reading*

(15 mi SE of Reading via US 422, PA 82 to Birdsboro, then SE on Birdsboro-Warwick Rd/PA 345; 10 mi NE of Tpke Morgantown Interchange)

Hopewell, an early industrial community, was built around a charcoal-burning cold-blast furnace, which made pig iron and many other iron products from 1771-1883. Nearby mines and forests supplied ore and charcoal for the furnace. The National Park Service has restored the buildings, and interpretive programs emphasize the community's role in the history of American industry. Hopewell is surrounded by the approximately 7,330-acre French Creek State Park (see POTTSTOWN).

The Visitor Center has a museum and audiovisual program on iron-making and community life. Self-guided tour includes: charcoal house, where fuel for furnace was stored; anthracite furnace ruin; waterwheel and blast machinery; casting house, where 16 molders produced up to 5,000 stoves annually; cold-blast charcoal-burning furnace; blacksmith shop; tenant houses; barn for horses and mules transporting charcoal, ore, iron products to market; office store, which was source of staples, clothing, and house furnishings; spring-house, which supplied "refrigeration"; ironmaster's house, home of proprietor or manager. Stove molding and casting demonstrations (late June-Labor Day; fee). Captioned slide program for the hearing impaired; Braille map and large-print pamphlets for the visually impaired; wheelchair access. (Daily; closed winter holidays) Contact the Superintendent, 2 Mark Bird Lane, Elverson 19520; 610/582-8773 or 610/582-2093 (TDD). ¢¢

Huntingdon

(D-4) *See also Altoona, Orbisonia*

Founded 1767 **Pop** 6,918 **Elev** 643 ft
Area code 814 **Zip** 16652
Information Raystown County Visitors Bureau, 241 Mifflin St; 814/643-3577 or 888/RAYSTOWN
Web www.raystown.org

Founded on the site of an Oneida village in the Juniata Valley, Huntingdon was first called Standing Stone—for a 14-foot etched stone pillar venerated by Native Americans.

What to See and Do

Indian Caverns. A one-mi guided tour; extensive scenic beauty and authentic Native American history; relic room contains artifacts, tablet of picture writing; picnic area. (Apr-Oct, daily) 13 mi NW via US 22, PA 45 in Spruce Creek. Phone 814/632-7578. ¢¢¢

Lincoln Caverns. The one-hr tour of two caves includes Frozen Niagara, Diamond Cascade; visitor center and gift shop. (Apr-Nov, daily; Mar and Dec, wkends only) 3 mi W on US 22. Phone 814/643-0268. ¢¢¢

Raystown Lake. Large man-made lake, with 110 mi of shoreline. Swimming, fishing, boating; hunting, hiking, picnicking, camping. Restaurant. Observation area. Fee for some activities. 7 mi S on PA 26, follow signs to Hesston. Phone 814/658-3405.

Swigart Auto Museum. Changing exhibits of American steam, gas, electric autos. Large collection of nameplates, license plates, and auto memorabilia; picnic area. (Memorial Day-Oct, daily) 4 mi E on US 22. Phone 814/643-0885. ¢¢

Special Event

Hartslog Day. 7 mi NW via US 22, in Alexandria. Heritage festival includes crafts, food, music, games. Second Sat Oct.

Motels/Motor Lodges

★ **DAYS INN.** *US 22 & S 4th St (16652). 814/643-3934; fax 814/643-3005. www.daysinn.com.* 76 rms, 3 story. S $44-$56; D $49-$61; each addl $5; under 13 free; higher rates special events. Crib free. Pet accepted; $5. TV; cable. Restaurant 6 am-10 pm; Fri, Sat to 11 pm. Bar 4:30 pm-2 am. Ck-out 11 am. Meeting rms. Business servs avail. In-rm modem link. Valet serv. Sundries. Microwaves avail. Cr cds: A, C, D, DS, MC, V.
D 🐾 🚳 🛁 **SC**

★★ **HUNTINGDON MOTOR INN.** *US 22 (16652). 814/643-1133; fax 814/643-1331.* 48 rms, 2 story. S $37-$40; D $46-$52; each addl $4. Crib free. Pet accepted, some restrictions. TV; cable. Restaurant 7 am-9 pm. Bar 4:30 pm-2 am. Ck-out 11 am. Meeting rms. Business servs avail. In-rm modem link. Microwaves avail. Balconies. Cr cds: A, C, D, DS, MC, V.
D 🐾 🚳 🔥

Indiana

(D-3) *See also Johnstown*

Founded 1805 **Pop** 14,895 **Elev** 1,310 ft **Area code** 724 **Zip** 15701
Information Indiana County Tourist Bureau, 2334 Oakland Ave, Suite 7; 724/463-7505
Web www.indiana-co-pa-tourism.org

Named after the Native American population in the area, this borough was established on 250 acres donated for a county seat by George Clymer of Philadelphia, a signer of the Declaration of Independence. Indiana University of Pennsylvania (1875) is located here. This is also the birthplace of actor Jimmy Stewart.

What to See and Do

County parks. Blue Spruce. Covers 420 acres. Fishing for bass, perch, catfish, and crappie; boating (rowboat, canoe rentals); winter sports area, picnicking, grills, playground. (Daily) 6 mi N off PA 110. **Pine Ridge.** Covers 630 acres. Trout fishing; hiking, picnicking. Nature study. (Daily) SW via US 22 near Blairsville. **Hemlock Lake.** Covers 200 acres. Fishing; small game hunting, hiking, ice-skating. Nature study, photography. W on PA 286 near Rossiter. (Daily) Phone 724/463-8636.

Jimmy Stewart Museum. Highlights the namesake's accomplishments on film, radio, and TV. His roles as a military hero, civic leader, family man, and world citizen are woven into displays, film presentations, and gallery talks. Fifty-seat vintage theater. (Daily) Indiana Public Library Building, third floor, corner of 9th and Philadelphia sts. Phone 724/349-6112. ¢¢

Yellow Creek State Park. Approx 3,000 acres. Swimming beach, fishing, boating; hunting, hiking, x-country skiing, snowmobiling, sledding, ice-skating, ice fishing, ice boating, picnicking, playground. Standard fees. 12 mi E via US 422. Phone 724/357-7913.

Motels/Motor Lodges

★ ★ **BEST WESTERN INN.** *1545 Wayne Ave (15701). 724/349-9620; fax 724/349-2620; res 888/299-9620. www.bestwestern.com.* 107 rms, 2 story. S $55-$65; D $60-$70; each addl $5; under 12 free; higher rates special university events. Crib free. TV; cable (premium). Heated pool. Coffee in rms. Restaurant 6:30 am-1:30 pm; Sun from 8 am. Ck-out noon. Meeting rms. In-rm modem link. Cr cds: A, C, D, DS, MC, V.
D ≈ ⊠ 🐾 SC

★ ★ **HOLIDAY INN.** *1395 Wayne Ave (15701). 724/463-3561; fax 724/463-8006; res 800/477-3561. www.holiday-inn.com.* 159 rms, 2 story. S, D $69-$94; suites $199; family, wkend rates; golf plans; higher rates university events. Crib free. Pet accepted. TV; cable (premium). Indoor pool; whirlpool, poolside serv. Coffee in rms. Restaurant 6:30 am-10 pm; Sat, Sun from 7 am. Bar 4 pm-2 am; entertainment. Ck-out noon. Meeting rms. Business servs avail. In-rm modem link. Miniature golf. Game rm. Sauna. Health club privileges. Cr cds: A, C, D, DS, MC, V.
D 🐾 ≈ ⊠ 🐾 SC

Jenkintown

(E-8) *See also Ft Washington, Philadelphia, Willow Grove*

Pop 4,478 **Elev** 250 ft **Area code** 215 **Zip** 19046

Information Valley Forge Convention & Visitors Bureau, 600 W Germantown Pike, Suite 130, Plymouth Meeting 19462; 610/834-1550

Web www.valleyforge.org

What to See and Do

Abington Art Center. Contemporary art, sculpture garden (daily, dawn to dusk), gallery and gallery shop. (Tues-Sat) Located in historic Alverthorpe Manor. 515 Meetinghouse Rd. Phone 215/887-4882. **FREE**

Beth Sholom Synagogue. The only synagogue designed by Frank Lloyd Wright. (By appt) Old York and Foxcroft rds, one mi S, in Elkins Park. Phone 215/887-1342. ¢¢

Restaurant

★ ★ **STAZI MILANO.** *Township Line & Greenwood Ave (19046). 215/885-9000. www.stazimilano.com.* Hrs: 11:30 am-3 pm, 4-9:30 pm; Fri, Sat 5-10:30 pm; Sun 4-9 pm; early-bird dinner Mon-Thurs 4-6 pm. Italian menu. Bar to midnight; Fri, Sat to 1 am. Lunch $6.95-$10.95, dinner $6.95-$17.95. Specializes in pasta, beef, chicken. In 1931 RR station; mahogany railings. Cr cds: A, D, MC, V.
D ⊠

Jim Thorpe

(C-7) *See also Hazleton*

Settled 1815 **Pop** 4,804 **Elev** 600 ft
Area code 570 **Zip** 18229

Information Carbon County Tourist Promotion Agency Information Center, PO Box 90; 570/325-3673 or 888/JIM-THORPE

The twin towns, Mauch Chunk (Bear Mountain) and East Mauch Chunk, built on the sides of a narrow gorge of the Lehigh River, merged in 1954 and adopted the name of Jim Thorpe, the great Native American athlete. This, together with a "nickel-a-week" plan whereby each man, woman, and child paid five cents to promote the community and attract industry, gave the area (formerly dependent on coal mining) a new lease on economic life. Little has changed in appearance after more than a century; a walking tour will reveal 19th-century architecture.

What to See and Do

Asa Packer Mansion. Former showplace home of founder of Lehigh Valley Railroad and Lehigh University, one of state's wealthiest men. Packer's house, treasures, and money were left to the borough. (June-Nov, daily; Apr-May, wkends; first two weeks in Dec) Packer Hill. Phone 570/325-3229. ¢¢ Adj is

Jim Thorpe Memorial. A 20-ton granite mausoleum built in memory of the 1912 Olympic champion. 1 mi E on PA 903.

Old Jail Museum. Built in 1871, the Old Jail, which was an active prison until Jan 1995, contains 28 original cells, warden's living quarters, and 16 dungeon cells. Famous for hangings of Molly Maguires; one Molly, to claim his innocence, placed his hand on his cell wall and said his hand print would remain forever as a sign of his innocence. The hand print is still on the wall of Cell 17. (Late May-early Nov) 128 W Broadway. Phone 570/325-5259. ¢¢

Stone Row. Sixteen town houses built by Asa Packer for the engineers on his railroad; reminiscent of Philadelphia's Elfreth's Alley. Some are stores open to the public. Race St, downtown. Also here is

St. Mark's Church. Has Tiffany windows and copy of reredos from Windsor Castle. (June-Oct, Wed-Sat afternoons) Phone 570/325-2241.

Whitewater rafting. On upper and lower gorges of Lehigh River.

Jim Thorpe River Adventures, Inc. (Mar-Nov, daily) 1 Adventure Ln, NE via PA 903. Phone 570/325-2570. ¢¢¢¢

Pocono Whitewater Adventures. Also bike tours. (Mar-Nov, daily) 8 mi NE of Jim Thorpe Bridge on PA 903. Phone 570/325-3655. ¢¢¢¢

Special Events

Laurel Blossom Festival. Arts and crafts, entertainment, food, steam train rides. Second wkend June.

Fall Foliage Festival. Arts and crafts, food, entertainment. Scenic three-hr train rides. Second wkend Oct.

B&B/Small Inn

★★★ **HARRY PACKER MANSION.** *Packer Hill (18229).* 570/325-8566. *www.murdermansion.com.* 13 rms, 2 share bath, 2 with shower only, 3 story, 3 suites. S, D $75-$150; package plans; wkends, hols (2-day min); higher rates special events. Children over 12 yrs only. Pet accepted. TV in some rms; VCR (movies). Complimentary full bkfst; afternoon refreshments. Ck-out 11 am, ck-in 4 pm. Luggage handling. Valet serv. Concierge serv. Built in 1871; a second empire mansion used as a model for the haunted mansion in Disney World. Cr cds: A, MC, V.

Johnstown

(E-3) *See also Ebensburg, Ligonier*

Settled 1800 **Pop** 23,906 **Elev** 1,180 ft
Area code 814

Information Greater Johnstown/Cambria County Convention & Visitors

Bureau, 416 Main St, 15901; 814/536-7993 or 800/237-8590

Web www.visitjohnstownpa.com

On May 31, 1889, a break in the South Fork Dam that impounded an old reservoir ten miles to the east poured a wall of water onto the city in the disastrous "Johnstown Flood." The death toll rose to 2,209 and property damage totaled $17 million. The city has been flooded 22 times since 1850, most recently in 1977.

Founded by a Swiss Mennonite, Joseph Johns, the city today is the center of Cambria County's iron and steel industry, producing iron and steel bars, railroad cars, parts, and railroad supplies.

What to See and Do

Conemaugh Gap. Gorge, seven mi long and 1,700 ft deep, cuts between Laurel Hill Ridge and Chestnut Ridge. Located at the W end of the city.

Grandview Cemetery. The 777 unidentified victims of the 1889 flood are buried under blank headstones in the "Unknown Plot." 1 mi W on PA 271, in Westmont. Phone 814/535-2652.

Inclined Plane Railway. Joins Johnstown and Westmont. Ride is on steep (72% grade) passenger incline with 500-ft ascent. Counterbalanced cable cars take 50 passengers and two automobiles each. (Daily; closed Jan 1, Dec 25) Vine St and Roosevelt Blvd. Phone 814/536-1816. ¢¢

Johnstown Flood Museum. Museum depicts history of Johnstown, with permanent exhibits on 1889 Johnstown Flood; Academy Award-winning film, photographs, artifacts, memorabilia. (Daily; closed hols) 304 Washington St. Phone 814/539-1889. ¢¢

Johnstown Flood National Memorial. Commemorates 1889 Johnstown Flood; preserved remnants of the South Fork Dam. Visitor center with exhibits, 30-min movie (daily; closed Dec 25). Jct US 219, PA 869. Phone 814/495-4643. ¢

Motels/Motor Lodges

★ **COMFORT INN.** *455 Theatre Dr (15904). 814/266-3678; fax 814/266-9783; toll-free 800/228-5150. www.comfortinn.com.* 117 rms, 5 story, 27 suites. S $57-$63; D $63-$69; each addl $6; suites $84-$91; kit. units $94-$99; under 18 free; monthly rates; higher rates special events. Crib free. Pet accepted; $6. TV; cable, VCR (movies). Indoor pool; whirlpool, lifeguard. Complimentary continental bkfst. Restaurant nearby. Ck-out noon. Coin lndry. Meeting rms. Business center. In-rm modem link. Sundries. Free airport transportation. Exercise equipt. Health club privileges. Refrigerator, wet bar in suites; microwaves avail. Picnic table, grill. Cr cds: A, C, D, DS, ER, JCB, MC, V.

[D] [symbols] SC [symbol]

★ **SLEEP INN.** *453 Theatre Dr (15904). 814/262-9292; fax 814/262-0486. www.sleepinn.com.* 62 rms, 58 with shower only, 3 story. S $49-$55; D $55-$61; under 18 free; wkly rates; higher rates: Labor Day, sporting events. Crib free. Pet accepted, some restrictions; $6. TV; cable (premium). Complimentary continental bkfst. Restaurant adj 11 am-9 pm. Ck-out noon. Meeting rm. Business servs avail. In-rm modem link. Airport transportation. Refrigerators, microwaves avail. Cr cds: A, C, D, DS, ER, JCB, MC, V.

[D] [symbols] SC

Hotel

★★ **HOLIDAY INN.** *250 Market St (15901). 814/535-7777; fax 814/539-1393; toll-free 800/443-5663. www.holiday-inn.com.* 164 rms, 6 story. S, D $72-$89; suites $238-$290; under 18 free. Crib free. Pet accepted, some restrictions. TV; cable (premium). Indoor pool; whirlpool, poolside serv, lifeguard. Coffee in rms. Restaurant 7 am-10 pm. Bar 4 pm-midnight. Ck-out noon. Meeting rms. Business center. In-rm modem link. Airport transportation. Exercise equipt; sauna. Health club privileges. Cr cds: A, C, D, DS, JCB, MC, V.

[D] [symbols] SC [symbol]

Restaurant

★★ **SURF N' TURF.** *100 Valley Pike (15905). 814/536-9250.* Hrs: 4-10 pm; Sun 11 am-8 pm. Closed Dec 25. Bar. Dinner $8.95-$32.95. Child's menu.

specializes in seafood, steak. Salad bar. Pianist Sat. Cr cds: A, D, DS, MC, V.
D **SC** **⊡**

Kane

(C-2) *See also Clarion, Warren*

Settled 1864 **Pop** 4,126 **Elev** 2,000 ft
Area code 814 **Zip** 16735
Information Seneca Highlands Tourist Association, jct PA 770 W and US 219, PO Box H, Custer City 16725; 814/368-9370

Situated on a lofty plateau, Kane offers hunting, fishing, and abundant winter sports. Summers are cool and winters are bracing. Allegheny National Forest is to the north, west, and south; there are scenic drives through 4,000 acres of virgin timber. General Thomas L. Kane of "Mormon War" fame settled here and laid out the community, which prospered as a lumber and railroad town. General Ulysses Grant was once arrested here for fishing without a license.

What to See and Do

Bendigo State Park. Approx 100 acres. Swimming pool, fishing; sledding. Standard fees. 9 mi SE on PA 321, then 7 mi S on US 219, then 3 mi NE on unnumbered road. Phone 814/965-2646.

Kinzua Bridge State Park. An approx 300-acre park surrounds Kinzua Bridge. When built in 1882, it was the highest railroad bridge in the world, taking its 2,053-ft span 301 ft above the Kinzua Creek. Overlooks, picnicking. (Daily) 12 mi E via US 6 in Mt Jewett. Phone 814/965-2646. **FREE**

Thomas L. Kane Memorial Chapel. (1878) Built as a chapel for the new town under the direction of General Kane, a Civil War hero and humanitarian who championed the persecuted Mormons. Visitor center includes film of General Kane's life; small museum. (Tues-Sat) 30 Chestnut St. Phone 814/837-9729. **FREE**

Twin Lakes. Swimming (fee), fishing; hiking, picnicking, camping (fee). 8 mi S of E Kane on PA 321, then 2 mi

N on Forest Rd 191, in Allegheny National Forest. Phone 814/723-5150.

Kempton (D-7)

(see Hamburg)

Kennett Square

(E-7) *See also West Chester; also see Wilmington, DE*

Settled 1705 **Pop** 5,273 **Elev** 370 ft
Area code 484 and 610 **Zip** 19348
Information Chester County Conference and Visitors Bureau, 400 Exton Sq Pkwy, Exton, 19341; 610/280-6145 or 800/228-9933; or the Southeastern Chester County Chamber of Commerce, 206 E State St, PO Box 395, phone 610/444-0774
Web www.brandywinevalley.com

What to See and Do

Barns-Brinton House. (1714) Authentically restored 18th-century tavern, now a house museum furnished in the period. Guides in Colonial costume offer interpretive tours; domestic art demonstrations. (May-Sept, Sat-Sun; also by appt) 5½ mi NE on US 1, in Chadds Ford. Phone 610/388-7376. **¢¢**

Brandywine Battlefield. Includes Lafayette's quarters and Washington's headquarters. Here, and around Chadds Ford, the Battle of the Brandywine (1777) took place—a decisive battle for Washington. Visitor center with exhibits; tours of historic buildings; museum shop. Picnicking. (Tues-Sun; closed hols)
2 mi W of jct US 1 and 202, near Chadds Ford. Phone 610/459-3342. **¢¢**

Brandywine River Museum. Converted 19th-century gristmill houses largest collection of paintings by Andrew Wyeth and other Wyeth family members; also collections of American illustration, still life, and landscape painting. Nature trail, wildflower gardens; restaurant, museum shop, guided tours. (Daily; closed Dec

25) 7 mi NE on US 1, in Chadds Ford. Phone 610/388-2700. ¢¢¢

Chaddsford Winery. Tours of boutique winery, housed in renovated old barn; view of production process; tasting room. Tours; tastings. (Schedule varies) 5 mi NE on US 1, in Chadds Ford. Phone 610/388-6221. ¢¢

John Chads House. Stone building (ca 1725) is fine example of early 18th-century Pennsylvania architecture; authentically restored and furnished as a house museum. Narrated tours by guides in Colonial costume; baking demonstrations in beehive oven. (May-Sept, Sat-Sun; also by appt) 7 mi NE via US 1, then ¼ mi N on PA 100, in Chadds Ford. Phone 610/388-7376. ¢

⭐ **Longwood Gardens.** Longwood was the estate of Pierre S. du Pont, chairman of the board of both Du Pont Chemicals and General Motors, who designed the 1,050 acres of gardens around Peirce's Park, a grove of trees planted in 1798. Estate includes the original grove; the Peirce-du Pont House (1730); a variety of exterior gardens, including the rose, peony, wisteria, idea, hillside, heath, water lily, and topiary gardens; the Italian Water Garden; Open Air Theatre and Main Fountain Garden, which together feature more than 1,700 water jets; and the neoclassical conservatories, nearly four acres under glass, housing indoor gardens that are among the most spectacular in the world. Display of color-illuminated fountains (Memorial Day wkend-Sept, Tues, Thurs and Sat eves). Orchestral concerts, plays, holiday displays, horticultural lectures (schedules at visitor center). Restaurant (see TERRACE); picnic areas; museum shop. (Daily) 3 mi NE on US 1. Phone 610/388-1000. ¢¢¢¢

Motel/Motor Lodge

⭐⭐⭐ **MENDENHALL HOTEL.** Rte 52, Mendenhall (19357). 610/388-2100; fax 610/388-1184. www.mendenhallinn. com. 70 rms, 3 story. S $105; D $115; each addl $20; suites $150-$199; under 12 free. Crib free. TV; cable (premium), VCR avail (free movies). Complimentary continental bkfst. Bar from 11:30 am. Ck-out noon. Meeting rms. Business center. In-rm modem link. Bellhops. Valet serv. Concierge. Airport transportation. Exercise

equipt. Bathrm phones, minibars. Cr cds: A, C, D, DS, MC, V.

[D] [🚶] [🔗] [🐾] [SC] [🚶]

B&Bs/Small Inns

⭐⭐⭐ **BRANDYWINE RIVER HOTEL.** US 1 and SR 100, Chadds Ford (19317). 610/388-1200; fax 610/388-1200. 40 rms, 2 story, 10 suites. S, D $125-$169; each addl $10; suites $149-$169. Crib free. Pet accepted, some restrictions. TV; cable. Complimentary continental bkfst; afternoon refreshments. Restaurant adj 11:30 am-10 pm. Ck-out 11 am, ck-in 2 pm. Meeting rms. Business servs avail. Airport, RR station, bus depot transportation. Exercise equipt. Bathrm phones; refrigerator in suites. Specialty shops on site. Cr cds: A, C, D, DS, MC, V.

[D] [🐾] [🚶] [🔗] [🐾] [SC]

⭐⭐⭐ **FAIRVILLE INN.** 506 Kennett Pike, Mendenhall (19317). 610/388-5900; fax 610/388-5902; toll-free 877/285-7772. www.innbook.com. 15 rms, 2 story. S, D $135-$195; each addl $15. Adults only. TV; cable. Complimentary continental bkfst. Ck-out 11 am, ck-in after 3 pm. Business servs avail. Some fireplaces. Private patios, balconies. Built in 1826; antiques, period decor. View of surrounding countryside. Totally nonsmoking. Cr cds: A, DS, MC, V.

[D] [⚡] [🔗] [🐾]

⭐⭐ **SCARLETT HOUSE BED AND BREAKFAST.** 503 W State St (19348). 610/444-9592; fax 610/925-0373; toll-free 800/820-9592. www.bedandbreakfast.com. 4 rms, 2 with bath, 2 story, 1 suite. Rm phones avail. S, D $85-$135; suite $135; golf packages. TV; cable (premium). Complimentary full bkfst. Restaurants nearby. Ck-out 11 am, ck-in 4-6 pm. Street parking. American Foursquare house built in 1910; Victorian decor. 3 sitting rms. Fireplaces. Totally nonsmoking. Cr cds: A, DS, MC, V.

[🔗] [🐾]

Restaurants

⭐⭐ **KENNETT SQUARE INN.** 201 E State St (19348). 610/444-5687. www.kennettinn.com. Hrs: 11:30 am-2:30 pm, 5:30-10 pm; Sun 5-9 pm; Mon, Tues to 9 pm. Closed Jan 1, Dec 25. Res accepted. Bar 11:30-2

am. Lunch $4.50-$10, dinner $10.95-$25.95. Specializes in fresh mushroom dishes. Pianist Sat. Restored country inn (1835). Cr cds: A, C, D, MC, V.
D

★ ★ ★ **MENDENHALL INN.** *PA 52, Mendenhall (19357).* 610/388-1181. *www.mendenhallinn.com.* Hrs: 11:30 am-2:30 pm, 5-10 pm; Sun 4-8 pm; Sun brunch 10 am-2 pm. Closed Dec 25. Res required. Continental menu. Bar. Wine cellar. Lunch $6-$15, dinner $18-$29. Sun brunch $22.95. Child's menu. Specializes in veal, seafood, wild game. Pianist, harpist. Valet parking. Country inn; colonial decor. Cr cds: A, D, DS, MC, V.
D

★ ★ ★ **TERRACE.** *Longwood Gardens (19348).* 610/388-6771. *www.longwoodgardens.org.* Hrs: 11 am-4 pm, 5-9 pm; wkend hrs vary; Dec to 7:30 pm. Cafeteria 10 am-4 pm; wkend hrs vary; Jan, Feb 10 am-3 pm; Dec 10 am-8 pm. Dining rm closed Jan-Mar. Res accepted. Bar. Lunch $6.95-$13.95, dinner $9.95-$18.95. Child's menu. Specialties: crab cakes, mushroom strudel. Salad bar. Cafeteria avg ck: lunch, dinner $8. Outdoor dining. Admission to Longwood Gardens required. Cr cds: A, C, D, DS, MC, V.
D

King of Prussia

(E-7) *See also Norristown, Philadelphia, West Chester*

Settled early 1700s **Pop** 18,511
Elev 200 ft **Area code** 484 and 610
Zip 19406
Information Valley Forge Convention & Visitors Bureau, 600 W Germantown Pike, Suite 130, Plymouth Meeting 19462; 610/834-1550
Web www.valleyforge.org

Originally named Reeseville for the Welsh family that owned the land, the town changed its name to that of the local inn, which is still standing. The area around the town is full of historic interest.

What to See and Do

Harriton House. (1704) Early American domestic architecture of the Philadelphia area. Originally 700-acre estate, now 16½ acres. House of Charles Thomson, Secretary of the Continental Congresses; restored to early 18th-century period. Nature park. (Wed-Sat; Sun by appt; closed hols) 6 mi SE via Old Gulph Rd to Harriton Rd, in Bryn Mawr. Phone 610/525-0201. ¢

Mill Grove. (1762) Includes 175-acre wildlife sanctuary, developed around the first American home of ornithologist John James Audubon, now a museum. Prints, includes complete elephant folio. Hiking trails. (Tues-Sat, also Sun afternoons; closed Jan 1, Thanksgiving, Dec 25) 5 mi NW via US 422 and Audubon Rd, N of Valley Forge National Historic Park, on Pawlings Rd, in Audubon. Phone 610/666-5593. **FREE**

Swiss Pines. Japanese gardens featuring azalea and rhododendron collection; ponds, waterfalls, winding pathway; herb and groundcover garden. Children under 12 yrs not permitted. (Mid-Apr-Nov, Mon-Fri, also Sat mornings; closed hols and inclement weather) 6 mi SW via PA 202, Great Valley exit, on Charlestown Rd in Malvern. Phone 610/933-6916. **FREE**

Valley Forge National Historical Park. (see) Just W of town.

Motels/Motor Lodges

★ ★ **BEST WESTERN INN.** *127 S Gulph Rd; Rte 202 N (19406).* 610/265-4500; fax 610/354-8905; res 800/780-7234. *www.bestwestern.com.* 168 units, 2 story. S, D $95-$115; each addl $10; under 12 free. Crib free. TV; cable (premium). Pool. Complimentary continental bkfst. Restaurants adj. Ck-out noon. Coin lndry. Business servs avail. In-rm modem link. Valet serv. Airport transportation. Health club privileges. Some bathrm phones. Private patios, balconies. Cr cds: A, C, D, DS, MC, V.
D

★ **COMFORT INN.** *550 W Dekalb Pike (19406).* 610/962-0700; fax 610/962-0218; toll-free 800/222-0222. *www.comfortinn.com.* 121 rms, 5 story. S, D $85-$139; under 18 free; wkend rates. Crib free. TV; cable (premium), VCR avail. Complimentary continental bkfst. Ck-out noon. Coin lndry. Meeting rm. Business servs avail. Concierge. Airport transportation. Exercise equipt. Bathrm phones, minibars. Cr cds: A, C, D, DS, ER, JCB, MC, V.

D 🏃 🏊 🐾 SC

★★ **COURTYARD BY MARRIOTT VALLEY FORGE.** *1100 Drummers Ln, Wayne (19087).* 610/687-6700; fax 610/687-1149; res 800/320-5748. *www.courtyard.com.* 150 rms, 2 story. S, D $79-$144; suites $169; under 16 free; wkly, wkend rates. TV; cable (premium). Indoor pool; whirlpool. Complimentary coffee in rms. Restaurant 5-10 pm Mon-Th; 7-11 am Sat, Sun. Rm serv Sun-Thurs. Bar 5-10 pm. Ck-out 1 pm. Coin lndry. Meeting rms. Business center. In-rm modem link. Valet serv. Sundries. Exercise equipt. Refrigerator, microwaves avail. Many balconies. Cr cds: A, D, DS, MC, V.

D 🏊 🏃 🐾 🏃

★★ **HOLIDAY INN.** *260 Mall Blvd (19406).* 610/265-7500; fax 610/265-4076; toll-free 800/465-4329. *www.holiday-inn.com.* 225 rms, 5 story. S, D $135; each addl $10; under 19 free. Crib free. TV; cable (premium). Restaurant 6:30 am-9:30 pm. Bar 11-2 am. Ck-out 11 am. Meeting rms. Business center. In-rm modem link. Bellhops. Valet serv. Gift shop. Barber, beauty shop. Health club privileges. Pool privileges. Microwaves avail. Cr cds: A, C, D, DS, ER, JCB, MC, V.

D 🏊 🐾 SC 🏃

★★ **HOMEWOOD SUITES.** *12 E Swedesford Rd, Malvern (19355).* 610/296-3500; fax 610/296-1941; res 800/225-5466. *www.homewoodsuites. com.* 123 suites, 4 story. May-Nov: suites $134-$194; under 18 free; lower rates rest of yr. Crib avail. Pet accepted, some restrictions; $150. TV; cable (premium), VCR. Complimentary continental bkfst, coffee in rms. Rm serv to 10 pm. Ck-out noon. Meeting rms. Business servs avail. In-rm modem link. Bellhops. Valet serv.

Sundries. Coin lndry. Exercise equipt. Indoor pool; whirlpool, lifeguard. Refrigerators, microwaves. Picnic tables, grills. Cr cds: A, C, D, DS, JCB, MC, V.

D 🐾 🏊 🏃 🐾 🔥 SC

★ **MCINTOSH INN.** *260 N Gulph Rd (19406).* 610/768-9500; fax 610/768-0225; toll-free 800/444-2775. *www. mcintoshinn.com.* 210 rms, 7 story. S $64.95; D $64.95-$74.95; each addl $5. Crib free. TV; cable (premium). Complimentary continental bkfst. Restaurant adj open 24 hrs. Ck-out 11 am. Business servs avail. In-rm modem link. Valet serv Mon-Fri. Refrigerators, microwaves avail. Cr cds: A, D, MC, V.

D 🏃 🐾

Hotels

★★★ **HILTON.** *251 W Dekalb Pike (19406).* 610/337-1200; fax 610/337-2224; res 800/879-8372. *www.hilton. com.* 340 rms, 9 story. S, D $110-$139; each addl $10; suites $139-$500; under 18 free; wkend rates. Crib free. TV; cable (premium), VCR avail. Indoor/outdoor pool; whirlpool, lifeguard. Restaurants 6:30 am-11 pm. Bars 11:30-2 am. Ck-out noon. Meeting rms. Business center. In-rm modem link. Concierge. Gift shop. Garage parking. Airport, bus depot transportation. Exercise equipt; sauna. Luxury level. Cr cds: A, C, D, DS, ER, JCB, MC, V.

D 🏊 🏃 🐾 🔥 SC 🏃

★★★ **RADISSON VALLEY FORGE HOTEL.** *1160 1st Ave (19406).* 610/337-2000; fax 610/768-3222; res 800/333-3333. *www.radisson.com.* 489 rms, 15 story. S, D $140-$180; each addl $12; suites $175-$275. Crib. TV; cable (premium), VCR avail. Heated pool; whirlpool, poolside serv, lifeguard. Coffee in rms. Restaurant 6:30 am-11:30 pm; wkends to midnight. Bars 11-2 am; entertainment. Ck-out noon. Convention facilities. Business center. In-rm modem link. Concierge. Airport, RR station, bus depot transportation. Exercise equipt; sauna. Wet bar in suites; microwaves avail. Cr cds: A, C, D, DS, ER, JCB, MC, V.

D 🏊 🏃 ✈ 🐾 🐾 SC 🏃

★★★ **WAYNE HOTEL.** *139 E Lancaster Ave, Wayne (19087).* 610/687-

5000; fax 610/687-8387; toll-free 800/962-5850. *www.waynehotel.com*. 38 rms, 6 story. S, D $125-$159; each addl $10; suites $159-$189; under 12 free; wkend rates. Crib free. TV; cable (premium). Pool. Complimentary continental bkfst. Restaurant (see also TAQUET). Bar 11:30 am-midnight. Ck-out noon. Meeting rms. Business servs avail. In-rm modem link. Concierge. Airport, RR station transportation. Health club privileges. Microwaves avail. Restored Victorian building (1906) with ornate furnishings, antiques. Cr cds: A, D, DS, MC, V.

D ⊵ ⊠ ⚒ SC

★★ **WYNDHAM.** *888 Chesterbrook Blvd, Wayne (19087). 610/647-6700; fax 610/889-9420; res 800/996-3426. www.wyndham.com.* 229 suites, 5 story. Suites $149-$199; each addl $20; under 16 free; wkend rates. Crib free. TV; cable (premium), VCR avail. Indoor pool; whirlpool, lifeguard. Coffee in rms. Restaurant (see also TOWN AND COUNTRY GRILLE). Bar 11:30 am-midnight; wkends to 1 am. Ck-out noon. Meeting rms. Business servs avail. In-rm modem link. Gift shop. Airport, RR station, bus depot transportation. Tennis privileges. Exercise equipt; sauna. Refrigerators, bathrm phones; microwaves avail. Cr cds: A, D, DS, MC, V.

🏊 D ⊵ 🏋 ⊠ ⚒

Restaurants

★★ **BARON'S INNE.** *499 N Gulph Rd (19406). 610/265-2550. www.barons inne.com.* Hrs: 11 am-2:30 pm, 5-10 pm. Closed Sun; hols; also first wk in July. Res accepted. Bar 11 am-10 pm; Sat 5-10 pm. A la carte entrees: lunch $7-$13, dinner $16-$25. Specializes in steak, seafood. Piano Fri, Sat. Parking. Antique chandeliers and furniture. Cr cds: A, C, D, DS, MC, V.

D

★★ **LOTUS INN.** *402 W Swedesford Rd, Berwyn (19312). 610/725-8888.* Hrs: 11:30 am-10 pm; Fri to 11 pm; Sat noon-11 pm; Sun from noon; Sun brunch to 3 pm. Closed Thanksgiving. Res accepted; required Fri-Sun. Chinese, Japanese menu. Bar. Lunch $5.95-$14.95, dinner $5.95-$18.95. Sun brunch $9.95. Child's

menu. Specialties: sushi, sashimi, General Tso's chicken. Oriental decor; sushi bar. Cr cds: A, D, DS, MC, V.

⊟

★★★ **110 RESTAURANT AND BAR.** *110 N Wayne Ave, Wayne (19087). 610/687-8333.* Hrs: 11:30 am-2 pm; Sat from 5:30 pm; Sun brunch 11 am-2 pm. Closed hols. Res accepted. Classical French menu. Bar 6 pm-midnight. Wine cellar. A la carte entrees: dinner $18-$28. Sun brunch $12.50-$18.75. Specializes in seafood, lamb, game. Own pastries. Formal atmosphere. Cr cds: A, DS, MC, V.

D

★★★ **TAQUET.** *139 E Lancaster Ave, Wayne (19087). 610/687-5005. www.taquet.com.* Hrs: 11:30 am-2:30 pm, 5:30-10 pm; Fri, Sat to 10:30 pm. Closed Sun; Jan 1, Dec 25. Res accepted. French menu. Bar. Wine list. Lunch $10-$22.50, dinner $12.75-$24.75. Specializes in venison, seasonal fish, duck. Outdoor dining. Victorian decor. Chef-owned. Cr cds: A, D, DS, MC, V.

D

★★★ **TOWN AND COUNTRY GRILLE.** *888 Chesterbrook Blvd, Wayne (19087). 610/647-6700.* Hrs: 7 am-2 pm, 5-10 pm; Fri, Sat to 11 pm. Res accepted. Bar. A la carte entrees: bkfst, lunch $6.95-$10.95, dinner $13.95-$22.95. Buffet: bkfst, lunch $8.95-$9.95. Sun brunch $11.95. Child's menu. Specializes in pasta, grilled steak, seafood. Salad bar (lunch buffet). Country furnishings. View of Valley Forge National Park. Cr cds: A, D, DS, MC, V.

D ⊟

★★★ **VILLA STRAFFORD.** *115 Strafford Ave, Wayne (19087). 610/964-1116.* Hrs: 11:30 am-2:30 pm, 5:30-9:30 pm. Closed Sun; Jan 1. Res accepted. Continental menu. Bar. Wine cellar. A la carte entrees: lunch $9-$14, dinner $16.95-$27.95. Specialties: rack of lamb, Dover sole. Own pasta, desserts. Jazz Fri-Sat. Mansion built in 1909. Cr cds: A, D, DS, MC, V.

D ⊟

★ ★ **WILD ONION.** *900 Conestoga Rd, Rosemont (19010). 610/527-4826. www.thewildonion.com.* Hrs: 11:30 am-11 pm. Res accepted. Bar to 2 am. Lunch $5.25-$7.95, dinner $8.95-$18.95. Child's menu. Specializes in fresh seafood, in-season produce. Cr cds: A, D, DS, MC, V.
D

Kulpsville

(E-7) *See also Norristown, Philadelphia*

Pop 1,200 **Elev** 290 ft **Area code** 215 **Zip** 19443
Information Valley Forge Country Convention & Visitors Bureau, 600 W Germantown Pike, Suite 130, Plymouth Meeting 19462; 610/834-1550
Web www.valleyforge.org

What to See and Do

Morgan Log House. (1695) Built by the grandfather of General Daniel Morgan and Daniel Boone, this is the oldest and finest surviving medieval-style log house in the country. Partially restored; authentic early 18th-century furnishings. It exhibits fine, early antiques, including 18th century Pennsylvania furniture. Guided tours (Apr-Dec, wkends; other times by appt). E on PA 63, then N on Troxel Rd, E on Snyder Rd and N on Weikel Rd; house is on Weikel Rd, between Snyder and Allentown rds. Phone 215/368-2480. ¢¢

Restaurant

★ ★ **MAINLAND INN.** *17 Main St (19451). 215/256-8500.* Hrs: 11:30 am-2:30 pm, 5:30-9 pm; Fri to 9:30 pm; Sat 5:30-9:30 pm; Sun (brunch) 11 am-2 pm, 5-8 pm. Closed hols. Res accepted. Bar. A la carte entrees: lunch $7-$14, dinner $18-$25. Sun brunch $16.95. Specializes in seafood, lamb, game (in season). Parking. Cr cds: A, D, MC, V.

Kutztown

(D-7) *See also Allentown, Hamburg, Pennsylvania Dutch Area, Reading*

Founded 1771 **Pop** 5,067 **Elev** 417 ft
Area code 484 and 610 **Zip** 19530

Home of a popular folk festival, Kutztown is named for its founder, George Kutz. The town's population includes many descendants of the Pennsylvania Germans.

What to See and Do

Crystal Cave Park. Discovered in 1871; crystal formations, stalactites, stalagmites, natural bridges—all enhanced by indirect lighting. Also museum (July-Sept); nature trail; miniature golf (July-Sept; fee); theater. Cafe, rock shop, gift shop. Tours (Mar-Nov, daily). 3 mi NW off US 222. Phone 610/683-6765. ¢¢¢

Special Event

Folk Festival. Festival grounds. Celebration of Pennsylvania Dutch folk culture; quilts, music, dancing, and food of Plain and Fancy Dutch. Craftspeople make baskets, brooms, rugs, toleware and other handcrafts. Phone 610/683-8707. Late June-early July. Phone 215/679-9610.

Restaurant

★ ★ **NEW SMITHVILLE COUNTRY INN.** *10425 Old Rte 22 (19530). 610/285-2987.* Hrs: 11 am-11 pm; Sun 8 am-10 pm. Closed Memorial Day, Labor Day. Res accepted. Bar. Bkfst $2.25-$6.75, lunch $4.95-$7.25, dinner $9.25-$14.50. Child's menu. Specializes in prime rib, soups, salads. Originally a post office and general store; fireplace, antiques. Cr cds: A, MC, V.

Lancaster

(E-6) *See also Bird-in-Hand, Cornwall, Ephrata, Lebanon, Reading, Wrightsville (York County), York*

Settled 1721 **Pop** 56,348 **Elev** 380 ft
Area code 717

Information Pennsylvania Dutch Convention & Visitors Bureau, 501 Greenfield Rd, 17601; 717/299-8901 or 800/723-8824

Web www.800padutch.com

Lancaster blends the industrial modern, the colonial past, and the Pennsylvania Dutch present. It is the heart of the Pennsylvania Dutch Area (see), one of the East's most colorful tourist attractions. To fully appreciate the area visitors should leave the main highways and travel on country roads, which Amish buggies share with automobiles. Lancaster was an important provisioning area for the armies of the French and Indian and Revolutionary wars. Its crafters turned out fine guns, which brought the city fame as the "arsenal of the Colonies." When Congress, fleeing Philadelphia, paused here on September 27, 1777, the city was the national capital for one day. It was the state capital from 1799-1812.

What to See and Do

Amish Farm and House. Typical Amish farm in operation. Lecture on the Amish and tour through early 19th-century stone buildings furnished and decorated as old-order Amish household; waterwheels, windmill, hand-dug well, carriages, spring wagon, sleighs. (Daily; closed Dec 25) 4½ mi E via US 30. Phone 717/394-6185. ¢¢

⭐ **Bube's Brewery.** Historic brewery built before the Civil War is the only brewery left in the country that has remained intact since the mid-1800s; now operates as a restaurant (see CATACOMBS AT BUBE'S BREWERY). Guided tours take visitors 43 ft below the street into the brewery's aging vaults and passages, built from a cave and later part of the Underground Railroad; narrator tells history of brewery and explains methods of producing beer in a Victorian-age brewery. Tours (Memorial Day-Labor Day, daily). Restaurant open all yr (free tour included with res for Catacombs at Bube's Brewery restaurant). 102 N Market St, in Mount Joy. Phone 717/653-2056. **FREE**

Candy Americana Museum. Antique candy production equipt, confectionery molds, unusual candy containers; outlet store. (Mon-Sat; call for hrs) 5 mi N via PA 501 at Wilbur Chocolate Company, 48 N Broad St, in Lititz. Phone 717/626-3249. **FREE**

Choo-Choo Barn, Traintown, USA. A 1,700-square-ft layout of Lancaster County in miniature, featuring 20 operating trains and more than 150 animated and automated figures and vehicles. Gift shop. Picnicking. (Apr-Dec, daily; closed hols) E via US 30, then SE on PA 741, in Strasburg. Phone 717/687-7911. ¢

Dutch Wonderland. Family fun park with rides, botanical gardens, diving shows, shops. Monorail (fee). (Memorial Day-Labor Day, daily; Mid-May-Memorial Day and after Labor Day-Oct, Sat and Sun) 4 mi E via US 30. Phone 717/291-1888. ¢¢¢¢ Adj is

National Wax Museum of Lancaster County. Figures re-create Lancaster County's history from the 1700s to present. (Daily; closed Dec 25) Phone 717/393-3679. ¢¢

Franklin and Marshall College. (1787) 1,810 students. Liberal arts college. Rothman Gallery showcases Pennsylvania-German artifacts: quilts, Fraktur, and stoneware. More than 200 varieties of trees, plants, and shrubs on grounds. Tours of campus. College Ave. Phone 717/291-3981. Also here are

Joseph R. Grundy Observatory. Holds 11-inch refractor and 16-inch reflecting telescope demonstrations. Phone 717/291-4136. **FREE**

North Museum of Natural History and Science. General science and natural history; planetarium shows (Sat and Sun); children's Discovery Room; film series; monthly art exhibits. (Tues-Sun) Phone 717/291-3941. ¢

Fulton Opera House. (1852) One of the oldest American theaters; many legendary people have performed here. It is believed that more than one ghost haunts the theater's Victorian interior. Professional regional theater; home of community theater, opera and symphony organizations. 12 N Prince St. Phone 717/394-7133. ¢¢¢¢

Hans Herr House. (1719) Example of medieval Germanic architecture;

served as an early Mennonite meetinghouse and colonial residence of the Herr family. Mennonite rural life exhibit; blacksmith shop. House tours. (Apr-Nov, Mon-Sat; rest of yr by appt; closed hols) 1849 Hans Herr Dr, in Willow St. Phone 717/464-4438. ¢¢

Heritage Center Museum of Lancaster County. (1795) Houses examples of early Lancaster County arts and crafts. Furniture, tall clocks, quilts, needlework, silver, pewter, Fraktur, rifles. (Mid-Apr-early Jan, Tues-Sat) Penn Sq. Phone 717/299-6440. **FREE**

Historic Rock Ford. (1794) Preserved home of General Edward Hand, Revolutionary War commander, member of Continental Congress. (Apr-Oct, Tues-Fri and Sun) 2 mi S on Rock Ford Rd, off S Duke St at Lancaster County Park. Phone 717/392-7223. ¢¢

James Buchanan's Wheatland. (1828) Residence of President James Buchanan from 1848-1868; restored Federal mansion with period rooms containing American Empire and Victorian furniture and decorative arts. Guided tours (Apr-Oct, daily; Nov, Fri-Mon). Christmas candlelight tours (early Dec). 1120 Marietta Ave, 1½ mi W on PA 23. Phone 717/392-8721. ¢¢¢

Landis Valley Museum. Interprets Pennsylvania German rural life. Largest collection of Pennsylvania German objects in US; craft and living history demonstrations (May-Oct; see SPECIAL EVENTS); farmsteads, tavern, country store among other exhibit buildings. (Mar-Dec, daily; closed hols) 2451 Kissel Hill Rd, 2½ mi N, off PA 272. Phone 717/569-0401. ¢¢

Mennonite Information Center. Tourist information; interpretation of Mennonite and Amish origins, beliefs. Free video. (Mon-Sat; closed Jan 1, Thanksgiving, Dec 25) E on US 30, 2209 Millstream Rd. Phone 717/299-0954. **FREE** Also here is

Hebrew Tabernacle Reproduction. Tours (Mon-Sat; closed Jan 1, Thanksgiving, Dec 25). Phone 717/299-0954. ¢¢

Mill Bridge Village. Restored historic colonial mill village with operating water-powered gristmill (1738); covered bridge; country crafts including broommaking, quilting, candlemak-

ing, blacksmithing; quilt log cabin; Amish kitchen exhibit; music boxes and nickelodeons; horse-drawn hay and carriage rides; 1890s playground; picnicking. Amish house and schoolhouse tour avail. Oktoberfest (Oct wkends). Camp resort (early Apr-Oct, daily; fee). Village (early Apr-Nov, daily). S Ronks Rd, 4 mi E of jct US 30E, PA 462 in Strasburg. Phone 717/687-8181. ¢¢¢

Muddy Run LLC. Covers 700 acres with 100-acre lake for boating (rentals; no power boats), fishing; picnicking, playgrounds, snack bar, concession, camping. Park (Apr-early Nov). 11 mi S on PA 272, then 3½ mi SW on PA 372. Phone 717/284-4325.

National Toy Train Museum. Trains from the 1880s to present; live operating layouts; movies; rare, unusual and specialty trains. (May-Oct, daily; Apr and Nov-Dec, Sat and Sun) E via US 30, PA 896, PA 741, to Paradise Ln, in Strasburg. Phone 717/687-8976. ¢¢

Robert Fulton Birthplace. Robert Fulton, a great inventor and accomplished artist, is best known for having built the steamboat *Clermont,* which, in 1807, successfully made a trip up the Hudson River against winds and strong current. This little stone house, where Fulton was born, was nearly destroyed by fire about 1822; now refurbished. (Memorial Day-Labor Day, Sat and Sun) 14 mi S via PA 222. Phone 717/548-2679. ¢

Sightseeing tours.

Abe's Buggy Rides. A tour through Amish country in an Amish family carriage. (Mon-Sat) 6 mi E on PA 340, at 2596 Old Philadelphia Pike, Bird-in-Hand. Phone 717/392-1794. ¢¢¢

Amish Country Tours. Tours of Amish farmlands and Philadelphia. Phone 717/768-3600. ¢¢¢¢

Brunswick Tours. Private guide and auto tape tours. 2102 Lincoln Hwy E. Phone 717/397-7541. ¢¢¢¢

Historic Lancaster Walking Tour. A 90-min tour of historic downtown area. Costumed guide narrates 50 points of architectural or historic interest covering six square blks. (Apr-Oct, two tours daily Fri and Sat, one tour daily Mon-Thurs and Sun; rest of yr, by appt) 100 S Queen St. Phone 717/392-1776. ¢¢

Strasburg Railroad. Railroad runs 4½ mi to Paradise. Picnic stop. This 160-yr-old line uses late 19th-century coaches, various steam locomotives. Apr-Oct, daily; winter, wkends) 8 mi SE via US 30, PA 896, PA 741, in Strasburg. Phone 717/687-7522. ¢¢ Adj is

Railroad Museum of Pennsylvania. More than 50 locomotives, freight and passenger cars dating from 1825; audiovisual exhibits; railroading memorabilia. Picnicking. (Apr-Oct, daily; rest of yr, Tues-Sun; closed hols) Phone 717/687-8628. ¢¢¢

Sturgis Pretzel House. First US commercial pretzel bakery (1861), restored as museum. Early equipt (also modern plant); pretzel-making demonstrations, visitors may try twisting pretzels; outlet store. (Mon-Sat; closed Jan 1, Thanksgiving, Dec 25) 9 mi N via PA 501, 772 at 219 E Main St, in Lititz. Phone 717/626-4354. ¢

Twin Brook Winery. Estate winery housed in a restored 19th-century barn offers wine tasting, tours of wine-making facilities, visits to the vineyard; picnic areas. Outdoor concerts (late June-mid-Sept, Sat eves; fee); special events throughout the yr. (Apr-Dec, Mon-Sat, also Sun afternoons; rest of yr, Tues-Sat, also Sun afternoons) 17 mi E via US 30, S on PA 41, E on Strasburg Rd, located in Gap at 5697 Strasburg Rd. Phone 717/442-4915.

The Watch and Clock Museum. National Association of Watch and Clock Collectors living museum of timepieces and related tools and memorabilia. Over 8,000 items representing the 1600s to the present. Extensive research library. Special exhibitions. (May-Sept, Tues-Sat, also Sun afternoons; winter schedule varies; closed hols) 12 mi W via US 30, at 514 Poplar St in Columbia. Phone 717/684-8261. ¢¢

Special Events

Sheep Shearing. Amish Farm and House. Phone 717/394-6185. Last Thurs and Fri Apr, first Fri Oct.

Old Fashioned Sunday. At Wheatland. Festivities include entertainment, magic show, and 19th-century activities. Phone 717/392-8721. Mid-May.

Music at Gretna. 15 mi N via PA 72, in Mt Gretna. Chamber music and jazz; well-known artists. Phone 717/964-3836. Mid-June-early Sept.

Harvest Days. Landis Valley Museum. Demonstrations of more than 80 traditional craft and harvest-time activities. Phone 717/569-0401. Columbus Day wkend.

Victorian Christmas Week. On grounds of Wheatland. Phone 717/392-8721. Early Dec.

Motels/Motor Lodges

★ ★ **BEST WESTERN EDEN RESORT INN AND CONFERENCE CENTER.** *222 Eden Rd (17601). 717/569-6444; fax 717/569-4208; toll-free 800/780-7234. www.edenresort. com.* 276 rms, 3 story. June-Nov: S, D $125-$139; each addl $10; suites $129-$249; under 18 free; varied lower rates rest of yr. Crib free. Pet accepted. TV; cable (premium). 2 pools, 1 indoor; whirlpool, poolside serv, lifeguard. Playground. Restaurant 6:30 am-11 pm; wkends to midnight. Bar 11-2 am; entertainment. Ck-out noon. Meeting rms. Business center. In-rm modem link. Valet serv. Free airport transportation. Gift shop. Lighted tennis. Exercise equipt; saunas. Lawn games. Microwaves avail. Some balconies. Cr cds: A, C, D, DS, MC, V.

[D] [🐾] [🎿] [≈] [🏊] [🖿] [🦺] [SC] [🏃]

★ ★ **COUNTRY LIVING INN.** *2406 Old Philadelphia Pike (17602). 717/295-7295; fax 717/295-0994. www.countrylivinginn.com.* 34 rms, 2 story. July-Oct: S, D $79-$99; each addl $8; higher rates hol wkends; lower rates rest of yr. Crib free. TV; cable (premium). Restaurant nearby. Ck-out noon. Whirlpool in suite. Cr cds: MC, V.

[🖿] [🦺]

★ ★ **GARDEN SPOT MOTEL.** *2291 Lincoln Hwy E (17602). 717/394-4736; fax 717/299-6339.* 19 rms. S $35-$55; D $40-$62; each addl $5; under 5 free; higher rates hols. Closed Dec-Mar. Crib $4. TV; cable. Restaurant 7:30-11 am. Ck-out 11:30 am. Gift shop. Cr cds: A, DS, MC, V.

[🖿] [🦺]

★★ **HERSHEY FARM MOTOR INN.**
*240 Hartman Bridge Rd, Ronks (17572).
717/687-8635; fax 717/687-8638; toll-
free 800/827-8635. www.hersheyfarm.
com.* 59 rms, 2 story. June-Aug: S $84;
D $89; each addl $8; suites $104-
$109; under 16 free; wkly rates; lower
rates rest of yr. Crib free. TV; cable
(premium). Complimentary full bkfst.
Restaurant adj 8 am-7 pm; Sat, Sun to
8 pm. Ck-out 11 am. Meeting rms.
Business servs avail. Gift shop. Pool.
Playground. Some in-rm whirlpools;
refrigerators avail. Some balconies. Cr
cds: DS, MC, V.

★★ **HOLIDAY INN.** *521 Greenfield
Rd (17601). 717/299-2551; fax
717/397-0220; toll-free 800/465-4329.
www.holiday-inn.com.* 189 rms, 4
story. Early May-Nov: S, D $79-$109;
under 18 free; lower rates rest of yr.
Crib free. TV; cable (premium). 2
pools, 1 indoor. Restaurant 6:30 am-2
pm, 5-10 pm. Bar 4 pm-2 am. Ck-out
noon. Meeting rms. Business servs
avail. In-rm modem link. Valet serv.
Sundries. Tennis. Exercise equipt.
Health club privileges. Microwaves
avail. Cr cds: A, C, D, DS, ER, JCB,
MC, V.

★ **HOWARD JOHNSON INN.** *2100
Lincoln Hwy (17602). 717/397-7781;
fax 717/397-6340; res 800/446-4656.
www.hojo.com.* 112 rms, 2 story. June-
Oct: S $48-$75; D $68-$88; each addl
$7; higher rates hols; lower rates rest
of yr. Crib free. TV; cable (premium).
Indoor pool. Complimentary continental bkfst. Coffee in rms. Restaurant 11 am-midnight. Bar from 11
am. Ck-out 11 am. Meeting rms.
Business servs avail. Shopping
arcade. Private patios, balconies. Cr
cds: A, C, D, DS, MC, V.

★ **KELLER INN.** *30 Keller Ave (17601).
717/299-5700; fax 717/295-1907; toll-
free 800/329-7466. www.kellerinn.com.*
193 rms, 2-3 story. S $76-$81; D $88-
$91; each addl $10; under 12 free.
Crib free. TV; cable (premium). 2
pools, 1 indoor; wading pool, lifeguard. Playground. Restaurant 7-11
am, 5-9 pm. Bar noon-midnight. Ck-
out noon. Coin lndry. Meeting rms.
Business servs avail. Tennis. Game rm.

Some refrigerators. Balconies. Cr cds:
A, C, D, DS, MC, V.

★★ **RAMADA INN.** *1492 Lititz Pike
(17601). 717/393-0771; fax 717/299-
6238; res 800/228-2828. www.ramada.
com.* 160 rms, 2 story. May-Oct: S, D
$95; under 12 free; hols (2-day min
stay); lower rates rest of yr. Crib free.
TV; cable. Pool. Restaurant 6 am-2
pm, 5-10 pm, Sat, Sun 7 am-2 pm.
Bar 5 pm-midnight. Ck-out noon.
Meeting rms. Business servs avail. In-
rm modem link. Bellhops. Valet serv.
Sundries. Health club privileges.
Game rm. Some refrigerators. Balconies. Cr cds: A, C, D, DS, ER, JCB,
MC, V.

★ **RAMADA INN.** *2250 Lincoln Hwy
E (17602). 717/393-5499; fax
717/293-1014; toll-free 800/867-2623.
www.ramada.com.* 166 rms, 5 story.
Mid-June-Oct: S, D $84-$129; each
addl $10; under 18 free; lower rates
rest of yr. Crib free. Pet accepted,
some restrictions. TV; cable. 2 pools,
1 indoor. Sauna. Playground. Ck-out
11 am. Coin lndry. Meeting rms.
Business servs avail. In-rm modem
link. Free airport transportation. Tennis. 27-hole golf privileges, pro,
putting green, driving range. Health
club privileges. Game rm. Lawn
games. Refrigerators. Balconies. Picnic tables. Cr cds: A, C, D, DS, ER,
JCB, MC, V.

★★ **ROCKVALE VILLAGE INN.** *24 S
Willowdale Dr (17602). 717/293-9500;
fax 717/293-8558; toll-free 800/524-
3817. www.rockvaleinn.com.* 113 rms,
2 story. Late June-Nov: S, D $79-
$109; each addl $8; under 12 free;
lower rates rest of yr. Crib free. TV;
cable (premium). Pool; lifeguard.
Restaurant 7 am-2 pm. Bar noon-
midnight. Ck-out 11 am. Meeting
rm. Business servs avail. Cr cds: A, C,
DS, MC, V.

★★ **WESTFIELD MOTOR INN.**
*2929 Hempland Rd (17601). 717/397-
9300; fax 717/295-9240; toll-free
800/547-1395. www.westfieldinn.com.*
84 rms, 2 story. S, D $49-$79; each
addl $5; suites $79-$89; under 18
free. Crib free. TV; cable, VCR avail.
Pool; lifeguard. Complimentary continental bkfst. Restaurant nearby. Ck-

out 11 am. Coin lndry. Business servs avail. Some refrigerators; microwaves avail. Cr cds: A, C, D, DS, MC, V.

D ⛵ 🏊 🐾 SC

Hotels

★ ★ **BRUNSWICK HOTEL.** *N Queen St (17608). 717/397-4801; fax 717/397-4991; toll-free 800/233-0182. www.hotelbrunswick.com.* 222 rms, 7 story. S $62-$78; D $72-$86; each addl $6; under 17 free; monthly, wkly, wkend rates; golf plan; lower rates Nov-Apr. Crib free. Pet accepted; $100. TV; cable, VCR avail (movies). Indoor pool; lifeguard. Restaurant 7 am-1:30 pm, 5:30-9 pm. Bar; entertainment. Ck-out noon. Coin lndry. Meeting rms. Business servs avail. Free garage parking. Exercise equipt. Refrigerators avail. Cr cds: A, D, DS, MC, V.

D 🐾 🏊 🏋 🍴 🐾

★ ★ ★ **HILTON GARDEN INN.** *101 Granite Run Dr (17601). 717/560-0880; fax 717/560-5400; toll-free 800/445-8667. www.hilton.com.* 156 rms, 2 story. May-Oct: S $119-$149; D $124-$154; family rates; lower rates rest of yr. TV; cable (premium). Indoor pool; whirlpool, lifeguard. Complimentary coffee in rms. Restaurant 6:30 am-2 pm, 5-10 pm. Bar 11:30 am-midnight. Coin lndry. Meeting rms. Business center. In-rm modem link. Sundries. Exercise equipt. Cr cds: A, C, D, DS, MC, V.

D 🏊 🍴 🐾 🐾 SC 🍴

Resort

★ ★ **WILLOW VALLEY RESORT.** *2416 Willow St Pike (17602). 717/464-2711; fax 717/464-4784; toll-free 800/444-1714. www.willowvalley.com.* 352 rms, 5 story. Mid-June-early Sept, hol wkends: S, D $109-$149; each addl $10; ages 6-12, $5; under 6 free; lower rates rest of yr. Crib free. TV; cable, VCR avail (movies). 3 pools, 2 indoor; whirlpool, lifeguard. Playgrounds. Coffee in rms. Restaurants 6 am-9 pm. Ck-out noon. Free guest lndry. Meeting rms. Business servs avail. Shopping arcade. Free airport, RR station, bus depot transportation. Lighted tennis. 9-hole golf, putting green. Exercise equipt; sauna. Game rm. Some private patios, balconies.

Country view; large landscaped grounds. Cr cds: A, D, DS, MC, V.

D 🏌 🏊 🏋 🐾 🐾 SC 🍴

B&Bs/Small Inns

★ ★ **ALDEN HOUSE BED AND BREAKFAST.** *62 E Main St, Lititz (17543). 717/627-3363; fax 717/627-5428; res 800/584-0753. www.alden house.com.* 5 rms, shower only, 3 story, 3 suites. No rm phones. S $75; D $85; each addl $20; suites $105-$120; wkends (2-day min); higher rates special events. Children over 10 yrs only. TV; cable. Complimentary full bkfst. Restaurant nearby. Ck-out 11 am, ck-in after 3 pm. Luggage handling. Concierge serv. Microwaves avail. Some balconies. Built in 1850. Totally nonsmoking. Cr cds: MC, V.

🐾 🐾

★ ★ **AUSTRALIAN WALKABOUT INN BED AND BREAKFAST.** *837 Village Rd (17537). 717/464-0707; fax 717/464-2501. www.bbonline.com/pa/ walkabout/index.html.* 5 rms, 3 story, 3 suites. No rm phones. May-Nov: S $89-$135; D $99-$149; each addl $25; suites $139-$199; lower rates rest of yr. Adults only. TV; cable (premium). Whirlpools. Complimentary full bkfst. Ck-out 10 am, ck-in 3-8 pm. Lawn games. Some balconies. Picnic tables. Brick house with wraparound porch built in 1925. Totally nonsmoking. Cr cds: A, MC, V.

🐾 🐾

★ ★ **GENERAL SUTTER INN.** *14 E Main St, Lititz (17543). 717/626-2115; fax 717/626-0992. www.general sutterinn.com.* 16 rms, 3 story. S, D $75-$100. Crib $5. Pet accepted. TV; cable. Dining rm 7 am-9 pm; Sun 8 am-8 pm. Bar 11 am-11 pm. Ck-out noon, ck-in 3 pm. Spacious bricklined patio. Built in 1764; antique country and Victorian furniture. Fireplace in parlor. Cr cds: A, DS, MC, V.

🐾 🐾 🐾

★ ★ ★ **HISTORIC STRASBURG INN.** *1 Historic Dr Rte 896, Strasburg (17579). 717/687-7691; fax 717/687-6098; toll-free 800/872-0201. www. 800padutch.com/strasinn.html.* 101 rms in 5 bldgs, 2 story. Apr-Nov: S, D $119-$129; each addl $15; suites $159-$199; under 12 free; lower rates rest of yr. Crib $7. Pet accepted; $15. TV; cable, VCR avail (movies). Heated pool; whirlpool. Playground. Complimentary full bkfst. Restaurant (see also WASHINGTON HOUSE). Bar 11:30 am-11 pm. Ck-out noon. Meeting rms. Business servs avail. Gift shop. Exercise equipt; sauna. Lawn games. Balconies. Hot air balloon rides on property (58 acres). Cr cds: A, C, D, DS, MC, V.

★★★ **KING'S COTTAGE BED & BREAKFAST.** *1049 E King St (17602). 717/397-1017; fax 717/397-3447; toll-free 800/747-8717. www.bbonline.com/pa/kingscottage/.* 9 rms. Rm phones avail. S, D $100-$135. Children over 12 yrs only. TV; cable in library. Complimentary full bkfst; afternoon refreshments. Restaurant nearby. Ck-out 11 am, ck-in 4 pm. Restored Spanish/mission-style house (1913); library, antiques, fireplaces. Totally nonsmoking. Cr cds: DS, MC, V.

★★ **O'FLAHERTY'S DINGELDEIN HOUSE.** *1105 E King St (17602). 717/293-1723; fax 717/293-1947; res 800/779-7765. www.800padutch.com/ofhouse.html.* 5 rms, 2 share bath, 3 story, 1 suite. No rm phones. S, D $80-$100; each addl $15; suite $110; wkends, hols (2-, 3-day min). Crib free. TV in common rm; cable (premium), VCR avail (movies). Complimentary full bkfst; afternoon refreshments. Ck-out 11 am, ck-in 2:30 pm. Luggage handling. Free airport, RR station transportation. Playground. Dutch Colonial mansion built in 1912. Totally nonsmoking. Cr cds: DS, MC, V.

★★ **SWISS WOODS BED & BREAKFAST.** *500 Blantz Rd, Lititz (17543). 717/627-3358; fax 717/627-3483; toll-free 800/594-8018. www.swisswoods.com.* 7 rms, 2 story, 1 suite. Apr-Dec: S, D $125-$185; each addl $15; suite $165; wkends, hols (2-, 3-day min); lower rates rest of yr. Children over 12 yrs only. TV in suite and common rm; VCR avail. Complimentary full bkfst, coffee in rms. Ck-out 11 am, ck-in 3-7 pm. Luggage handling. Concierge serv. Gift shop. Some in-rm whirlpools; refrigerator, fireplace in suite. Some balconies. Picnic tables. Built to resemble Swiss chalet. Totally nonsmoking. Cr cds: A, DS, MC, V.

Restaurants

★★ **CATACOMBS AT BUBE'S BREWERY.** *102 N Market St, Mount Joy (17552). 717/653-2056. www.bubesbrewery.com.* Hrs: 11 am-2 pm, 5:30-9 pm; Fri, Sat to 10 pm; Sun 4:30-9 pm. Closed hols. Res accepted. Continental menu. Bar. Lunch $2.95-$7.45. Complete meals: dinner $15.95-$26.95. Specializes in shrimp, roast duck. Entertainment Fri, Sat. Outdoor dining. In old Victorian hotel and brewery (1876); dining areas are located in original bottling plant, original dining rms of the hotel portion (Victorian decor) and below ground, in the cellars (medieval atmosphere, costumes, entertainment). Guided tours. Cr cds: A, DS, MC, V.

★★ **D & S BRASSERIE.** *1679 Lincoln Hwy E (17602). 717/299-1694. www.dandsbrasserie.com.* Hrs: 11:30 am-midnight; Sat 4 pm-1 am; Sun 4-10 pm. Closed Thanksgiving, Dec 25. Res accepted. Continental menu. Bar. Lunch $3.75-$8.95, dinner $8.95-$33. Specializes in prime rib, pasta, seafood. Outdoor dining. House built in 1925; original woodwork, fireplaces. Cr cds: A, D, DS, MC, V.

★★★ **GROFF'S FARM RESTAURANT.** *650 Pinkerton Rd, Mount Joy (17552). 717/653-2048. www.groffsfarmrestaurant.com.* Hrs: 11:30 am-1:30 pm, 5-7:30 pm; Sat 11:30 am-1:30 pm, sittings 5 and 8 pm; Sun brunch 10 am-2 pm. Closed Dec 24-26; also wkdays Jan-mid-Feb. Res required. Serv bar. Wine list. A la carte entrees: lunch $2.50-$7.50, dinner $12.50-$25. Complete meals: dinner $16-$24. Child's menu. Specialties: chicken Stoltzfus, home-cured ham. Own pastries. Located in farmhouse built in 1756. Family-owned. Cr cds: DS, MC, V.

★★★ **HAYDN ZUG'S.** *1987 State St, East Petersburg (17520). 717/569-5746.* Hrs: 11:30 am-2 pm, 5-9 pm; Sat from 5 pm. Closed Sun, Mon; hols. Res accepted. Bar 5-9 pm. Wine cellar. A la carte entrees: lunch $4.25-$10.95, dinner $10.75-$27.95. Specialties: cheesy chowder, grilled lamb tenderloin, Norwegian chicken. Own pastries. Colonial setting. Family-operated. Cr cds: A, C, D, MC, V.

★ ★ ★ **LOG CABIN.** *11 Lehoy Forest Dr, Leola (17540). 717/626-1181. www.logcabinrestaurant.com.* Hrs: 5-10 pm; Sun 4-9 pm. Closed hols. Res accepted. Bar. Wine cellar. Dinner $15-$35. Child's menu. Specializes in charcoal-broiled steak, fresh seafood. Own baking. Log cabin in woods; paintings, fireplace. Entry through covered "kissing" bridge. Cr cds: A, D, MC, V.

★ ★ ★ **OLDE GREENFIELD INN.** *595 Greenfield Rd (17601). 717/393-0668. www.theoldegreenfieldinn.com.* Hrs: 11 am-2 pm, 5-10 pm; Mon from 5 pm; Sat 8 am-2 pm (brunch), 5-10 pm; Sun 8 am-2 pm (brunch). Closed some major hols. Res accepted. Bar. Wine cellar. Bkfst $4.95-$9.95, lunch $4.95-$8.45, dinner $10.95-$20.95. Sat, Sun brunch $4.95-$12.95. Child's menu. Specializes in steak, seafood, pasta. Own baking, pasta. Pianist Fri, Sat, hols. Outdoor dining. In restored stone farmhouse; dining avail on balcony and in wine cellar. Cr cds: A, D, DS, MC, V.

★ ★ **WASHINGTON HOUSE.** *1 Historic Dr, Strasburg (17579). 717/687-9211.* Hrs: 7 am-2 pm, 5-9:30 pm; Sun 7 am-9:30 pm. Res accepted. French menu. Bar 11:30 am-10 pm. A la carte entrees: lunch $5.25-$12.50, dinner $19.95-$26.95. Buffet: bkfst $6.95, lunch $9.95. Sun brunch $16.95. Child's menu. Specialties: crab cakes, medallions de filet, grillade de boeuf. Outdoor dining. Colonial decor. Cr cds: A, D, DS, MC, V.

Lebanon

(E-6) See also Cornwall, Ephrata, Hershey, Lancaster, Pennsylvania Dutch Area

Founded 1756 **Pop** 24,461 **Elev** 460 ft
Area code 717 **Zip** 17042
Information Pennsylvania Rainbow Region Vacation Bureau, 625 Quentin Rd, PO Box 329; 717/272-8555

This industrial city, steeped in German traditions, is the marketplace for colorful Lebanon County. Many Hessians were confined here after the Battle of Trenton. Today Lebanon bologna factories and food processing are important to the city's economy. Master planning for redevelopment of city and county combines with the traditional atmosphere to make this a charming community.

What to See and Do

Coleman Memorial Park. This 100-acre former estate has swimming pool (Memorial Day-Labor Day, daily; fee); tennis courts, athletic fields, picnic facilities. Fee for some activities. Park (daily). 2 mi N on PA 72, W Maple St. Phone 717/228-4470. **FREE**

The Daniel Weaver Company. Manufacturers, since 1885, of Weaver's Famous Lebanon Bologna and other wood-smoked gourmet meats; smoked in 100-yr-old outdoor smokehouses. Samples. Tours. (Mon-Sat) 15th Ave and Weavertown Rd. Phone 717/274-6100. **FREE**

Fort Zeller. One of state's oldest existing forts; originally built of logs, rebuilt of stone in 1745; has 12-ft-wide Queen Anne fireplace in kitchen. (By appt) 11 mi E on US 422, then S on PA 419, in Newmanstown. Phone 610/589-4301. **DONATION**

Middlecreek Wildlife Management Area. A 6,254-acre tract provides refuge for waterfowl, forest, and farmland wildlife. Permit and open hunting areas, inquire at visitor center for regulations. Fishing, boating (Feb-Nov); hiking, picnicking. Visitor center (Mar-Nov, Tues-Sun). 11 mi SE on PA 897 to Kleinfeltersville, then 1 mi S. Phone 717/733-1512. **FREE**

Stoevers Dam Recreational Area. A 153-acre park with 52-acre lake for fishing, boating (electric motors only), canoeing; 1½ mi trail for jogging, hiking, and bicycling; primitive camping (permit only; fee). Nature trails; nature barn (Apr-Oct, Tues-Sun; winter, by appt). Community park (daily). 2 mi N on PA 343, Miller St. Phone 717/228-4470. **FREE**

Stoy Museum of the Lebanon County Historical Society. Local historical museum containing 30 permanent room and shop displays on three floors of house built in 1773 and used as first county courthouse; research library. Tours. (Mon-Fri, Sun; closed Mon and Sun of hol wkends) 924 Cumberland St. Phone 717/272-1473. ¢¢

Motels/Motor Lodges

★ ★ **LANTERN LODGE MOTOR INN.** *411 N College St, Myerstown (17067). 717/866-6536; fax 717/866-8857; toll-free 800/262-5564. www. thelanternlodge.com.* 80 rms, 2 story. S $54-$66; D $60-$90; each addl $10; suites $110-$225; cottage $150-$200. Crib free. TV; cable, VCR avail. Playground. Complimentary coffee in rms. Restaurant 7 am-10 pm. Ck-out 11 am. Meeting rms. Business servs avail. Bellhops. Barber, beauty shop. Valet serv. Sundries. Tennis. Early-American decor. Cr cds: A, C, D, DS, MC, V.

🄳 ⊠ 🄰 🅕

★ **QUALITY INN.** *625 Quentin Rd (17042). 717/273-6771; fax 717/273-4882; res 800/228-5151. www.quality inn.com.* 56 hotel rms, 74 motel rms, 5 story. Late May-Oct: S $78-$110; D $83-$120; each addl $7; under 18 free; lower rates rest of yr. Crib free. TV; cable. Pool; lifeguard. Restaurant 6 am-9 pm. Bar 11-2 am; entertainment. Ck-out noon. Meeting rms. Business servs avail. Sundries. Barber. Game rm. Cr cds: A, C, D, DS, ER, JCB, MC, V.

🄳 ⊷ ⊠ 🄰 🆂🅒

B&B/Small Inn

★ ★ **SWATARA CREEK INN.** *10463 Jonestown Rd, Annville (17003).* *717/865-3259. www.swataracreek inn.com.* 10 rms, 2 with shower only, 3 story, 1 suite. No rm phones. Apr-Nov: S $45-$70; D $55-$80; suite $115; family rates; Hershey car show (3-day min); lower rates rest of yr. Complimentary full bkfst, coffee in sitting rm. Restaurant nearby. Ck-out 11 am, ck-in 3 pm. Concierge serv. Gift shop. Refrigerator on 2nd floor. Some balconies. Picnic tables. Victorian mansion built in 1860; country setting. Cr cds: A, D, DS, MC, V.

🄳 ⊠ 🄰 🆂🅒

Lewisburg

(C-5) *See also Danville, Williamsport*

Settled 1785 **Pop** 5,620 **Elev** 460 ft
Area code 570 **Zip** 17837
Information Susquehanna Valley Visitors Bureau, Rural Rte 3, 219-D Hafer Rd; 570/524-7234 or 800/525-7320
Web www.svvb.com

Home of Bucknell University (1846), this college community also has light industry. The Native American village of Old Muncy Town was located nearby before the region was opened by Ludwig (Lewis) Doerr.

What to See and Do

Fort Augusta. (1757) Museum collection of Northumberland County Historical Society. (Mon, Wed, Fri, afternoons) 9 mi SE on PA 147, in Sunbury, at 1150 N Front St. Phone 570/286-4083. **FREE**

Packwood House Museum. A three-story, 27-room log and frame building begun in the late 18th century. Former hostelry houses a wide-ranging collection of Americana, period furnishings, textiles, and decorative arts. Changing exhibits; museum shop. Tours. (Tues-Sun; closed hols) 15 N Water St. Phone 570/524-0323. ¢¢

Slifer House Museum. Elaborate three-story, 20-room Victorian mansion. First and second floors have been restored, complete with Victorian parlor, dining room, library, and five bedrooms. Gift shop. (Apr-late Dec, Tues-Sun; rest of yr, Tues-Fri afternoons, also by appt; closed hols)

1 mi N, on grounds of Riverwoods. Phone 570/524-2245. ¢¢

Motels/Motor Lodges

★ ★ **BEST WESTERN CUPBOARD INN.** *Rte 15 N (17837). 570/524-5500; fax 570/524-4291; res 800/780-7234. www.bestwestern.com.* 106 rms, 3 story. S $68-$99; D $75-$105; each addl $6; suites $105-$149; under 18 free; higher rates university events. Crib free. TV; cable. Heated pool; lifeguard. Complimentary continental bkfst. Restaurant adj 7 am-9 pm. Ck-out 11 am. Coin lndry. Meeting rms. Business servs avail. Exercise equipt. Game rm. Refrigerator in suites. Cr cds: A, C, D, DS, JCB, MC, V.

★ **DAYS INN.** *US Rte 15 (17837). 570/523-1171; fax 570/524-4667; toll-free 800/329-7466. www.daysinn.com.* 108 rms, 2 story. S $55-$69; D $61-$69; each addl $6; under 16 free. Crib free. TV; cable, VCR avail (movies). Pool; lifeguard. Restaurant adj open 24 hrs. Ck-out noon. Business servs avail. In-rm modem link. Exercise equipt. Cr cds: A, C, D, DS, MC, V.

Restaurant

★ ★ **COUNTRY CUPBOARD.** *Hafer Rd (US 15) (17837). 570/523-3211.* Hrs: 7 am-9 pm. Closed Dec 25. Res accepted Mon-Fri. Bkfst $2.25-$5.50, lunch, dinner $4.99-$10.99. Buffet: bkfst (Sat, Sun), lunch (Mon-Sat) $5.99, dinner $8.99-$10.99. Child's menu. Specializes in poultry, ham. Country dining. Totally nonsmoking. Cr cds: DS, MC, V.

Lewistown (D-4)

Settled 1754 **Pop** 9,341 **Elev** 520 ft
Area code 717
Information Juniata Valley Area Chamber of Commerce, 3 W Monument Sq, 17044; 717/248-6713

Surrounded by rich farmland and beautiful forested mountain ranges, Lewistown lies in the scenic Juniata River Valley in the heart of central Pennsylvania. Lewistown retains the charm of its rustic surroundings, which yearly attract thousands of sportsmen and outdoor enthusiasts to the area's fine hunting, fishing, and camping facilities. A large Amish population that thrives on the farmland of the Kishacoquillas Valley has contributed greatly to the area's culture and heritage.

What to See and Do

Brookmere Farm Vineyards. In 19th-century stone and wood barn. Winery tour, wine tasting; picnicking. (Mon-Sat, also Sun afternoons; closed hols) Approx 5 mi N via US 322, then SW on PA 655, near Belleville. Phone 717/935-5380. **FREE**

Greenwood Furnace State Park. Remains of Greenwood Works, last iron furnace to operate in area (ca 1833-1904); restored stack. Approx 400 acres. Swimming beach, fishing; hiking, snowmobiling, ice skating, ice fishing, picnicking, playground, snack bar, store, tent and trailer sites. Visitor center, interpretive program. Standard fees. 5 mi N on US 322, then 9 mi W on PA 655, then NW on PA 305. Phone 814/667-1800.

Reeds Gap State Park. Approx 200 acres. Swimming pool, fishing; hiking, picnicking, snack bar. Tent sites only. 8 mi N off US 322 and unnumbered road. Phone 717/667-3622.

Motel/Motor Lodge

★ **CLARION INN.** *13015 Furguson Valley Rd, Burnham (17009). 717/248-4961; fax 717/242-3013; toll-free 800/252-7466. www.clarioninn.com.* 119 rms, 2 story. S, D $59; each addl $5; under 18 free. Crib free. Pet accepted. TV; cable (premium). Pool; poolside serv, lifeguard. Restaurant 6 am-2 pm, 5-10 pm. Bar 4 pm-midnight. Ck-out noon. Meeting rms. In-rm modem link. Valet serv. Cr cds: A, C, D, DS, MC, V.

Ligonier

(E-2) *See also Donegal, Greensburg, Johnstown*

Founded 1816 **Pop** 1,695 **Elev** 1,200 ft **Area code** 724 **Zip** 15658
Information Ligonier Valley Chamber of Commerce, Town Hall, 120 E Main St; 724/238-4200
Web www.ligonier.com

Fort Ligonier, built in 1758 by the British, was the scene of one of the key battles of the French and Indian War. It also served as a supply base during Pontiac's War in 1763.

What to See and Do

Compass Inn Museum. A 1799 stage-coach stop; original log and stone inn authentically restored and furnished; log barn houses Conestoga wagon and stagecoach; cookhouse with beehive oven and fireplace; blacksmith shop contains working forge. (May-Oct, Tues-Sun) 3 mi E on US 30, in Laughlintown. Phone 724/238-4983. ¢¢

Fort Ligonier. Reconstructed 18th-century British fort; includes buildings with period furnishings. Museum houses outstanding French and Indian War collection, 18th-century artifacts; introductory film. (May-Oct, daily) (See SPECIAL EVENTS) S Market St, on US 30, PA 711. Phone 724/238-9701. ¢¢

Idlewild Park. Amusement rides; entertainment; picnicking; children's play area; water park. (Memorial Day-late Aug, Tues-Sun) 2 mi W on US 30. Phone 724/238-3666. ¢¢¢ Adj is

Story Book Forest. Children's park with animals, people, and buildings portraying nursery rhymes. (Memorial Day-late Aug, Tues-Sun) Phone 724/238-3666.

St. Vincent Archabbey and College. (1846) 1,200 students. Includes Benedictine monastery, seminary, and coeducational liberal arts college. St. Vincent Theatre has performances in theater-in-the-round; for schedule phone 412/537-8900. Free self-guided tape tours. 8 mi W on US 30, in Latrobe. Phone 724/537-4560.

Special Events

Ligonier Ice Fest. Professional ice sculptures on the Diamond and in front of businesses; collegiate ice-carving competition. Super Bowl wkend Jan. Phone 724/238-4200.

Mountain Playhouse. 11 mi SE on US 30, then ½ mi N on US 985, in Jennerstown. Phone 814/629-9201. Broadway shows in restored gristmill (1805). Matinees and eve performances. Late May-mid-Oct.

Ligonier Highland Games and Gathering of the Clans of Scotland. Idlewild Park. Sports; massed pipe bands, Highland dancing competitions, Scottish fiddling; sheep dog, wool spinning, and weaving demonstrations; genealogy booth, Scottish fair. Phone 724/238-3666. First Sat after Labor Day.

Fort Ligonier Days. Living history program of the French and Indian War. Parade, 150 juried crafters, food, and special events. Usually second wkend Oct. Phone 724/238-4200.

Motel/Motor Lodge

★ **RAMADA INN.** *216 W Loyalhanna St (15658). 724/238-9545; fax 724/238-9803; toll-free 800/272-6232. www.ramada.com.* 66 rms, 3 story. S, D $65-$95; each addl $6; suites $95-$150; under 12 free; ski plans. Crib free. TV; cable (premium), VCR avail. Pool. Restaurant 6:30 am-10 pm. Bar 4 pm-2 am. Ck-out noon. Meeting rms. Business servs avail. In-rm modem link. Health club privileges. Cr cds: A, MC, V.
[D] [≈] [≥] [🖐] [SC]

Limerick

(E-7) *See also Norristown, Pottstown, Reading*

Pop 800 **Elev** 302 ft **Area code** 484 and 610 **Zip** 19468
Information Valley Forge Convention & Visitors Bureau, 600 W Germantown Pike, Suite 130, Plymouth Meeting 19462; 610/834-1550
Web www.valleyforge.org

What to See and Do

Skiing. Spring Mountain Ski Area.
Triple, three double chairlifts; two
rope tows; patrol, school, rentals;
snowmaking; cafeteria, lodge.
Longest run ½ mi; vertical drop 420
ft. Also camping avail (fee; hookups).
(Mid-Dec-mid-Mar, daily) 6 mi N, off
PA 29 in Spring Mount. Phone
610/287-7900. ¢¢¢¢

Restaurant

★ ★ ★ **GYPSY ROSE.** *505 Bridge Rd
(PA 113), Collegeville (19426). 610/489-
1600. www.gypsyroserestaurant.com.*
Hrs: 11:30 am-10 pm; Fri, Sat to 11
pm; Sun 11 am-9 pm; Sun brunch to
2 pm. Closed hols. Res accepted. Bar
11-2 am. Lunch $7-$12, dinner $7-
$22. Sun brunch $13. Child's menu.
Specialties: chicken Philadelphia,
Maryland crab cakes. Own baking.
Outdoor dining. Farmhouse (1725);
views of creek and landscaped garden.
Cr cds: A, D, DS, MC, V.
🅓 🆂🅒 🅓

Lock Haven

(C-5) *See also Williamsport*

Founded 1833 **Pop** 9,149 **Elev** 564 ft
Area code 570 **Zip** 17745

Information Clinton County Tourist
Promotion Agency, Court House
Annex, 151 Susquehanna Ave;
570/893-4037

Founded on the site of pre-Revolutionary Fort Reed, the community
takes its name from two sources. The
lock of the Pennsylvania Canal once
crossed the West Branch of the
Susquehanna River here, and the
town was once a "haven" for the rafts
and lumberjacks of nearby logging
camps. Near the geographic center of
the state, the town today is a center
of commerce and small industry.

What to See and Do

Bucktail Natural Area. Scenic area
extends from mountain rim to
mountain rim for 75 mi from Lock
Haven north to Renovo and west to
Emporium. Connecting the three

towns and weaving through the park
is PA 120, an outstanding drive
through mountain scenery. Historic
site west of Renovo commemorates
Bucktail Trail, which served pioneers
and Civil War volunteers. Fishing.

Bull Run School House. (1899) Only
remaining one-room schoolhouse in
county; fully restored with all of its
original equipt, including double
desks, schoolmaster's and recitation
desks, Waterbury clock, bell. (Hrs
vary; Phone 570/893-4037. **FREE**

The Heisey Museum. Victorian house
museum; early 1800s kitchen; ice
house containing logging, farming,
and canal artifacts. (Tues-Fri; also by
appt) 362 E Water St. Phone
570/748-7254. **DONATION**

Hyner View. At 2,000 ft, "Laurel
Drive to the top of the world" provides panoramic view of valley, river,
highway and forest. Site of state and
national hang gliding competitions.
22 mi NW on PA 120.

State parks.

Bald Eagle. A 1,730-acre lake on
approx 5,900 acres. Swimming
beach, fishing, boating (rentals,
mooring, launching, marina);
hunting, hiking, sledding, ice skating, ice boating, picnicking, playground, snack bar, store, tent and
trailer sites. Standard fees. 13 mi
SW off PA 150. Phone 814/625-
2775.

Kettle Creek. Approx 1,600 acres.
Winds through beautiful valley
developed as tourist area. Swimming beach, fishing, boating
(mooring, launching); hunting,
hiking, bridle trail, snowmobiling,
sledding, ice skating, picnicking,
playground, tent and trailer sites
(electric hookups). Standard fees.
35 mi NW on PA 120 to Westport,
then 7 mi N on PA 4001. Phone
570/923-6004.

Special Event

Flaming Foliage Festival. 29 mi NW
on PA 120, in Renovo. Includes
parade, craft show, and contest for
festival queen. Phone 570/923-2411.
Second wkend Oct.

B&B/Small Inn

★★ **VICTORIAN INN BED AND BREAKFAST.** *402 E Water St (17745). 570/748-8688; fax 570/748-2444; toll-free 888/653-8688.* 12 rms, 2 with shower only, 2 share bath, 2 story. S $55-$60; D $60-$65; each addl $10. Adults only. Pet accepted. TV. Complimentary full bkfst. Restaurant nearby. Ck-out 1 pm, ck-in 2 pm. Health club privileges. Built in 1859; garden atrium. Cr cds: A, C, D, DS, MC, V.

Manheim

(E-6) *See also Cornwall, Lancaster, Lebanon*

Founded 1762 **Pop** 4,784 **Elev** 400 ft
Area code 717 **Zip** 17545
Information Manheim Area Chamber of Commerce, 210 S Charlotte St; 717/665-6330
Web www.manheimchamber.com

Baron Henry William Stiegel founded Manheim and started manufacturing the flint glassware that bore his name. In 1770 he owned the town; by 1774 he was in debtor's prison, the victim of his own generosity and his poor choice of business associates. After his imprisonment, he made a meager living teaching here.

What to See and Do

❖ **Mount Hope Estate & Winery.** Restored sandstone mansion was originally built in the Federal style (ca 1800), then increased its size to 32 rooms with an extension built in 1895, which changed the house's style to Victorian. Turrets, winding walnut staircase, hand-painted 18-ft ceilings, Egyptian marble fireplaces, grand ballroom, crystal chandeliers; greenhouse, solarium, gardens. Wine tasting in billiards room. (Daily; closed Jan 1, Thanksgiving, Dec 25) (See SPECIAL EVENTS) ½ mi S of exit 20 at jct PA 72 and PA Tpke. Phone 717/665-7021. **FREE**

Zion Lutheran Church. (1891) Victorian-Gothic structure built on site of original church; Stiegel donated the ground (1772) in exchange for one red rose from the congregation every yr. (Mon-Fri) 2 S Hazel St, 1 blk E of PA 72. Phone 717/665-5880.

Special Events

Rose Festival. Celebration during which Stiegel descendant accepts annual rent of one red rose for church grounds. Second Sun June.

Pennsylvania Renaissance Faire. Mt Hope Estate & Winery. A 16th-century village is created in the acres of gardens surrounding the mansion. Eleven stages including a jousting arena with capacity of 6,000. Highlights include medieval jousting tournament, trial and dunking, human chess match, knighthood ceremonies. Wkends, Aug-mid-Oct.

Mansfield

(B-5) *See also Wellsboro*

Pop 3,411 **Elev** 1,120 ft
Area code 570 **Zip** 16933
Information Wellsboro Area Chamber of Commerce, 114 Main St, PO Box 733, Wellsboro 16901; 570/724-1926
Web www.wellsboropa.com

What to See and Do

Cowanesque Lake. Same facilities as Tioga-Hammond Lakes (see). (May-Sept) 15 mi N on US 15 to Lawrenceville, then 3½ mi W on Bliss Rd. Phone 570/835-5281.

Hills Creek State Park. Approx 400 acres. Swimming beach; fishing for muskellunge, largemouth bass, walleye in Hills Creek Lake; boating (rentals, mooring, launching); hiking, sledding, ice-skating, ice fishing, picnicking, playground, snack bar, tent and trailer sites, cabins. Interpretive program. Standard fees. 6 mi W, then N on unnumbered road. Phone 570/724-4246.

Tioga-Hammond Lakes. Twin lakes and dams for flood control and recreation. Swimming, fishing, boating; hunting, trails, picnicking, camping (fee; some sites free). (Late Apr-Dec)

10 mi N on US 15, then 7 mi SW on PA 287. Phone 570/835-5281.

Motel/Motor Lodge

★ **COMFORT INN.** *300 Gateway Dr (16933). 570/662-3000; fax 570/662-2551; toll-free 800/822-5470. www. comfortinn.com.* 100 rms, 2 story. S $49-$75; D $59-$85; each addl $6; under 18 free; golf plans; higher rates seasonal events. Crib avail. Pet accepted. TV; cable. Complimentary continental bkfst. Ck-out noon. Business servs avail. Exercise equipt. Cr cds: A, C, D, DS, ER, JCB, MC, V.

D 🐾 🏋 🖎 🐾 SC

Meadville

(B-1) *See also Conneaut Lake, Franklin (Venango County)*

Settled 1788 **Pop** 13,685 **Elev** 1,100 ft
Area code 814 **Zip** 16335
Information Crawford County Convention & Visitors Bureau, 211 Chestnut St; 814/333-1258 or 800/332-2338
Web www.visitcrawford.org

David Mead—Revolutionary War ensign, tavernkeeper, and major general in the War of 1812—and his brothers established Mead's Settlement in 1788. Colonel Lewis Walker started manufacture of hookless slide fasteners here; since 1923 these fasteners (now known as "zippers") have been the leading local industry. The city is also a major producer of yarn and thread and is home to many tool-and-die manufacturers.

What to See and Do

Allegheny College. (1815) 1,850 students. Bentley Hall (1820) is a fine example of Federalist architecture. Also on campus are Bowman, Penelec, and Megahan Art Galleries (phone 814/332-4365 for schedule). Library has colonial, Ida Tarbell, and Lincoln collections. Tours of campus. N Main St. Phone 814/332-3100.

Baldwin-Reynolds House Museum. (1841-1843) Restored mansion of Henry Baldwin, congressman and US Supreme Court justice. First and second floors refurbished in period; basement exhibits 19th-century kitchen and Land Office. Also on grounds is 1890 doctor's office. Elaborate landscaping on three-acre grounds feature pond and icehouse. Tours (Late May-Labor Day, Wed-Sun). 639 Terrace St. Phone 814/724-6080. ¢¢

Colonel Crawford Park. Within park is Woodcock Creek Lake. Swimming (fee), fishing, boating; hunting, nature trail, picnicking, camping (fee). Park (Memorial Day-Labor Day, daily). 6 mi NE via PA 86, PA 198. Phone 814/724-6879. **FREE**

Erie National Wildlife Refuge. Over 250 species of birds, as well as woodchuck, white-tailed deer, fox, beaver, and muskrat are found on this 8,777-acre refuge. Fishing and hunting permitted, regulations at refuge office; nature and ski trails, overlook, photo blind. Office, 10 mi E on the outskirts of the village of Guys Mills (Mon-Fri). Refuge (daily). 10 mi E on PA 27. Phone 814/789-3585. **FREE**

Special Event

Crawford County Fair. Third wk Aug. Phone 814/337-2154.

Motel/Motor Lodge

★ **DAYS INN.** *18360 Conneaut Lake Rd (16335). 814/337-4264; fax 814/337-7304; toll-free 800/329-7466. www.daysinn.com.* 163 rms, 2 story. S $65-$85; D $70-$86; each addl $6; under 18 free; higher rates special events. Crib free. Pet accepted. TV; cable (premium), VCR avail (movies). Indoor pool; whirlpool. Restaurant 7 am-2 pm, 5-10 pm; Sun 7 am-2 pm. Bar 3 pm-2 am. Ck-out 11 am. Coin lndry. Meeting rms. Business servs avail. Cr cds: A, D, DS, JCB, MC, V.

🐾 🏊 🖎 🐾 SC

Media

(E-7) *See also Chester, Kennett Square, King of Prussia, Philadelphia, West Chester*

Pop 5,533 **Area code** 484 & 610

Information Delaware County Convention & Visitors Bureau, 200 E State St, Suite 100, 19063; 610/565-3679 or 800/343-3983

What to See and Do

Franklin Mint Museum. Houses original works by Andrew Wyeth and Norman Rockwell; collectibles on display include books, dolls, jewelry, furniture; artworks in porcelain, bronze, pewter, crystal, and precious metals; one of the world's largest private mints. (Daily; closed hols) 4 mi SW on US 1. Phone 610/459-6168. **FREE**

Newlin Mill Park. Park with operating stone gristmill (1704), furnished miller's house (1739), springhouse, blacksmith shop; milling exhibit. Tours, picnicking, fishing, nature trails. (Daily) 7 mi SW via US 1, in Glen Mills. Phone 610/459-2359. ¢

Ridley Creek State Park. Approx 2,600 acres of woodlands and meadows. Fishing; hiking, bicycling, sledding, picnicking, playground. S on US 1, then N on PA 352. Phone 610/892-3900. Within park is

Colonial Pennsylvania Plantation. A 200-yr-old farm is a living history museum that re-creates the life of a typical farm family of the late 1700s. Period tools and methods are used to perform seasonal and daily chores. Tours (Tues-Fri, by appt). Visitors may participate in some activities. (Mid-Apr-Nov, Sat and Sun) Phone 610/566-1725. ¢¢

Tyler Arboretum. Approx 650 acres of ornamental and native plants. Outdoor "living museum" with a 20-mi system of trails; special fragrant garden and bird garden; notable trees planted in the 1800s; bookstore. Guided walks and educational programs each wk. Phone 610/566-5431. ¢¢

Restaurant

★ ★ **D'IGNAZIO'S TOWNE HOUSE.** *117 Veterans Sq (19063). 610/566-6141. www.townehouse.com.* Hrs: 11:30 am-3 pm, 4:30-10 pm; Fri, Sat to 10:30 pm; Sun 4-8:30 pm. Closed hols. Res accepted. Bar to midnight; Fri, Sat to 1 am; Sun 4-9 pm. Wine cellar. A la carte entrees: lunch $6-$12, dinner $10-$20. Child's menu. Specializes in prime rib, seafood, Italian specialties. Pianist Tues-Sat.

Singing maître'd. Many stone fireplaces; extensive collection of memorabilia, antiques and personal photographs. Family-owned. Cr cds: A, C, D, DS, MC, V.
[D] [≒]

Mercer

(C-1) *See also Franklin (Venango County)*

Settled 1795 **Pop** 2,391 **Elev** 1,270 ft
Area code 724 **Zip** 16137
Information Mercer Area Chamber of Commerce, PO Box 473; 724/662-4185

What to See and Do

Magoffin House Museum. (1821) Houses collection of Native American artifacts, pioneer tools, furniture, children's toys, clothing; military items. Some original furnishings; memorabilia. Special collection of artifacts from John Goodsell's trip to the North Pole with Peary in 1908-1909, as well as early maps, historic records; restored print shop. Office of Mercer County Historical Society is located in the **Anderson House,** just off Court House Square. (Tues-Sat; closed hols) 119 S Pitt St. Phone 724/662-3490. **FREE**

Wendell August Forge, Inc. Creators of hand-hammered aluminum, bronze, copper, pewter, sterling silver, and glass and crystal items hand-cut on stone wheel lathe; also limited-edition collectors' items. Gift shop. Self-guided tours (15-30 min). (Daily; closed hols) 10 mi SE on PA 58, in Grove City at 620 Madison Ave. Phone 724/458-8360. **FREE**

Special Event

Penn's Woods West-Folk & Arts Festival. Mercer Area High School, W Butler St. Fine arts and country crafts. 130 artisans, live entertainment and demonstrations, children's activities, home-cooked food. Phone 412/662-1490. Mid Feb.

Motel/Motor Lodge

★ **HOWARD JOHNSON INN.** *835 Perry Hwy (16137). 724/748-3030; fax*

*724/748-3484; res 800/446-4656.
www.hojo.com.* 102 rms, 2 story. S
$67; D $71-$74; each addl $6; suites
$105-$125; under 18 free; higher
rates special events. Crib free. Pet
accepted. TV; cable (premium), VCR
avail. Heated pool; lifeguard. Playground. Coffee in rms. Restaurant 6
am-midnight. Bar. Ck-out noon.
Coin lndry. Meeting rms. Business
servs avail. In-rm modem link. Bellhops. Bus depot transportation. Exercise equipt; sauna. Private patios;
balconies. Amish craft shop in lobby.
Cr cds: A, D, DS, MC, V.

D ⬆ ⬱ ⛩ ⬲ ⬳

Restaurant

★ ★ **CHADAGAN'S.** *8399 Sharon
Mercer Rd (16137). 724/662-4533.
www.chadagans.com.* Hrs: 3-10 pm;
Fri, Sat 11:30 am-11 pm; Sun 11 am-
8 pm. Closed Mon; hols. Bar. Complete meals: dinner $6.95-$13.95.
Child's menu. Specializes in seafood,
prime rib. Rustic atmosphere; in converted barn (1872). Cr cds: A, DS,
MC, V.

D SC ⬲

Milford

(C-8) *See also Bushkill, Delaware Water
Gap*

Settled 1733 **Pop** 1,104 **Elev** 503 ft
Area code 570 **Zip** 18337
Information Pocono Mtns Vacation
Bureau, 1004 Main St, Stroudsburg
18360; 570/424-6050; for free
brochures phone 800/POCONOS
Web www.poconos.org

The borough of Milford was settled
by Thomas Quick, a Hollander. Noted
forester and conservationist Governor
Gifford Pinchot lived here. His house,
Grey Towers, is near the town.

What to See and Do

**Canoeing, rafting, kayaking, and tub-
ing. Kittatinny Canoes.** Trips travel
down the Delaware River. Camping.
(Mid-Apr-Oct, daily) S to Dingmans
Ferry via US 209, then ½ mi E via PA
739 S, at Dingmans Ferry toll bridge.
Phone 570/828-2338.

**Dingmans Falls and Silver Thread
Falls.** Part of Delaware Water Gap
National Recreation Area (see). Two
of the highest waterfalls in the
Pocono Moutains; many rhododen-
drons bloom in July. 8 mi S and W
on US 209 near Dingmans Ferry.
Phone 570/588-2451. **FREE**

Grey Towers. (1886) A 100-acre estate
originally built as summer house for
philanthropist James W. Pinchot;
became residence of his son, Gifford
Pinchot, "father of American conservation," governor of Pennsylvania
and first chief of USDA Forest Service. Now site of Pinchot Institute
for Conservation Studies. Tours.
(Memorial Day wkend-Labor Day
wkend, daily; after Labor Day-
Veterans Day, afternoons Mon and
Fri-Sun; rest of yr, by appt; occasionally closed for conferences. Phone
570/296-6401. **DONATION**

Motels/Motor Lodges

★ ★ **BEST WESTERN INN.** *120 Rte
6; Rte 209, Matamoras (18336).
570/491-2400; fax 570/491-2422; toll-
free 800/308-2378. www.bestwestern.
com.* 108 rms, 4 story. May-Oct: S
$69-$75; D $77-$85; each addl $6;
suites $115-$125; under 12 free;
lower rates rest of yr. Crib free. Pet
accepted. TV; cable. Indoor pool; lifeguard. Sauna. Restaurant 6:30 am-9
pm; Fri, Sat to 10 pm; Sun from 7
am. Bar 4-11 pm; entertainment. Ck-
out 11 am. Coin lndry. Meeting rms.
Business servs avail. In-rm modem
link. Sundries. Gift shop. Game rm.
Lawn games. Cr cds: A, C, D, DS,
MC, V.

D ⬆ ⬱ ⬲ ⬳ SC

★ ★ **MYER MOTEL.** *600 Rtes 6 and
209 (18337). 570/296-7223; toll-free
800/764-6937. www.myermotel.com.*
19 cottages, 1 kit. S $40-$50; D $45-
$70; each addl $5; kit. unit $90. Crib
free. Pet accepted, some restrictions.
TV; cable. Restaurant nearby. Ck-out
11 am. Lawn games. Refrigerators.
Picnic tables, grills. Cr cds: A, C, D,
DS, MC, V.

⬆ ⬲ ⬳ SC

B&Bs/Small Inns

★ **BLACK WALNUT BED & BREAKFAST COUNTRY INN.** *179 Fire Tower Rd (18337).* 570/296-6322; fax 570/296-7696. 12 rms, 8 with bathrm, 2 story. No A/C. D $60-$100; hols (2-day min). TV in sitting rm; movies. Dining rm 8:30-10 am; 5:30-9 pm; closed Mon-Thurs. Ck-out 11 am, ck-in 3 pm. Rec rm. Tudor-style stone house; marble fireplace; some antiques. 160-acre estate on the bank of a 5-acre stocked pond; paddleboats, rowboats. Cr cds: A, MC, V.

★ ★ ★ **CLIFF PARK INN.** *155 Cliff Park Rd (18337).* 570/296-6491; fax 570/296-3982; toll-free 800/225-6535. *www.cliffparkinn.com.* 18 rms, 1-3 story. S $82.50-$140; D $95-$205; EP, MAP avail; wkend rates. Dining rm 8-10 am, noon-3 pm, 6-9 pm. Business servs avail. In-rm modem link. 9-hole golf, greens fee $6-$13, pro, putting green, rentals. X-country ski; rentals. Hiking trails. Near Delaware River. Classic country inn; originally a farmhouse built 1820. Some fireplaces. Screened porches. Cr cds: A, C, D, DS, MC, V.

★ ★ **PINE HILL FARM BED AND BREAKFAST.** *181 Pine Hill Farm Rd (18337).* 570/296-5261. *www.pinehill farm.com.* 3 rms in main house, 2 story, 2 suites in adj cottage. No rm phones. S $75-$100; D $85-$110; each addl $25; suites $100-$110; hols (2-night min). Adults only. TV in some rms and sitting rm. Complimentary full bkfst. Ck-out 11 am, ck-in 3 pm. Bellman. X-country ski on site. Main house was the original farmhouse (ca 1870); fireplace, many antique furnishings. Located atop hill overlooking the Delaware River. Includes 268 acres of fields and forests, with 5 mi of 1800s logging trails for walking, birdwatching. Cr cds: DS, MC, V.

Monroeville (D-2)

(see Pittsburgh)

Mount Pocono

(C-7) *See also Pocono Moutains*

Pop 2,742 **Elev** 1,840 ft
Area code 570 **Zip** 18344
Information Pocono Mtns Vacation Bureau, Inc, 1004 Main St, Stroudsburg 18360; 570/424-6050; for brochures phone 800/POCONOS
Web www.poconos.org

One of the many thriving resort communities in the heart of the Pocono Mountains, Mount Pocono offers recreation year-round in nearby parks, lakes, and ski areas.

What to See and Do

Gouldsboro State Park. Approx 2,800 acres; 250-acre lake. Swimming beach, fishing, boating (rentals, mooring, launching); hunting, hiking, ice skating, ice fishing. 10 mi N on PA 611 and I-380, then NE on PA 507. Phone 570/894-8336.

Memorytown, USA. Old-time village including hex shop, country store, store with artifacts; ice-cream parlor; paddleboats; entertainment; lodging, restaurant, and tavern. Summer festivals. Fee for some activities. (Daily) 2 mi E via PA 940. Phone 570/839-1680. **FREE**

Pocono Knob. Excellent view of surrounding countryside. 1½ mi E on Knob Rd.

Skiing. Mount Airy Lodge Ski Area. Two double chairlifts; patrol, school, rentals, snowmaking; cafeteria, restaurant, bar, nursery, lodge. Longest run 1,800 ft; vertical drop 250 ft. Also x-country trails. (Mid-Dec-late Mar) Just E of town via PA 940 to PA 611. Phone 800/441-4410. ¢¢¢¢

Tobyhanna State Park. Approx 5,440 acres with 170-acre lake. Swimming beach; fishing, hunting; boating (rentals, mooring, launching). Hiking, biking; x-country skiing. Snowmobiling, ice skating, ice fishing. Tent and trailer sites. Standard fees. 5 mi N on PA 611, then NE on PA 423. Phone 570/894-8336.

Motels/Motor Lodges

★★ **MEMORYTOWN.** *HC 1 Box 10 (18344).* 570/839-1680; fax 570/839-5846. 30 rms, all with shower only. No A/C. No rm phones. May-Oct: S $109; D $118-$138; each addl $70; family rates; package plans; hols (2-day min); higher rates special events; lower rates rest of yr. Pet accepted. TV; cable. Complimentary continental bkfst; full bkfst wkends. Restaurant 11 am-8 pm. Ck-out 11 am, ck-in 3 pm. Gift shop. Downhill ski 10 mi; x-country ski on site. Playground. Game rm. Lawn games. Some fireplaces. Picnic tables. On lake. Built in 1890; antiques. Country store, farmhouse on premises. Cr cds: A, D, DS, MC, V.

⊕ 🐾 ⛷ ⤨ ⊠ 🔥

★ **SUPER 8 MOTEL.** *Rte 611, Mt Pocono (18344).* 570/839-7728; fax 570/839-7728; res 800/800-8000. *www.super8.com.* 37 rms. May-Sept: S $58-$135; D $65-$135; each addl $5; lower rates rest of yr. Crib free. TV; cable. Pool; whirlpool. Playground. Restaurant 6 am-10 pm. Ck-out 11 am. Business servs avail. Sundries. Downhill ski 5 mi. Private patios, picnic tables. Cr cds: A, D, DS, MC, V.

⤨ ⊠ 🔥 ⊕

Resorts

★★★ **CAESARS PARADISE STREAM.** *Rte 940 (18344).* 570/839-8881; fax 570/839-1842; res 800/233-4141. *www.caesarsparadisestream.com.* 164 rms. MAP: D $260-$335; wkly rates. Couples only. TV; cable, VCR avail (movies $5). 2 pools, 1 indoor; whirlpool, poolside serv, lifeguard. Rm serv limited hrs. Snack bar. Bar noon-2 am. Ck-out 11 am, ck-in 3 pm. Business servs avail. Concierge. Grocery, package store. Sundries. Bus depot transportation. Tennis. Miniature golf. Bicycles. Boats, paddleboats. Snowmobiles available. Lawn games. Soc dir; entertainment. Game rm. Exercise equipt; sauna. Hiking trails. Archery. Some fireplaces. Cr cds: A, D, DS, MC, V.

D 🐾 ⛷ ⤨ 🏊 👤 🔥

★★★ **POCONO MANOR INN AND GOLF CLUB.** *Rte 314, Pocono Manor (18349).* 570/839-7111; fax 570/839-0708; toll-free 800/233-8150. *www.poconomanor.com.* 190 rms in inn, 65 in 2 lodges. MAP: S $119; D $198; each addl $50; under 8 free; higher rates special events. Crib $7. Serv charge. TV. Indoor/outdoor pool; poolside serv, lifeguard. Free supervised children's activities. Dining rm (public by res) 7:30-9 am, noon-1 pm, 6:30-8:30 pm. Box lunches, snacks. Bar 11-2 am. Ck-out 11 am, ck-in 4 pm. Business servs avail. In-rm modem link. Bellhops. Grocery, package store 2 mi. Bus depot transportation. Sports dir. Tennis, pro. 36-hole golf, pro, putting green, driving range. Trapshooting. Artificial ice rink, sleigh rides. Indoor, outdoor games. Bicycles. Soc dir. Entertainment. Rec rm; library. Exercise equipt; sauna. Extra fee for some activities. On 3,100-acre mountain estate. Cr cds: A, D, MC, V.

⤨ 🏌 🏊 👤 ⊠ SC 🎿

B&Bs/Small Inns

★★★ **FRENCH MANOR.** *Rte 191 S Huckleberry Rd, South Sterling (18460).* 570/676-3244; fax 570/676-9786; toll-free 800/523-8200. *www.thesterlinginn.com.* 9 rms, 3 story. No rm phones. S, D $165-$180. Adults only. TV in sitting rm. Indoor pool privileges. Dining rm (public by res; jacket required) 8:30-10 am, noon-2 pm, 6-9 pm. Ck-out 11 am, ck-in 2 pm. Airport, bus depot transportation. X-country ski on premises. French chateau-style; Spanish slate roof; patio; 38-ft high dining rm with beamed ceilings; Great Hall has 2 floor-to-ceiling fireplaces. Antiques. Cr cds: A, DS, MC, V.

⛷ 🔥

★★★ **STERLING INN.** *PA 191, South Sterling (18460).* 570/676-3311; fax 570/676-9786; toll-free 800/523-8200. *www.sterlinginn.com.* 54 units, 3 story, 16 suites, 4 cottages. MAP: S $75-$95, D $140-$160; suites, cottages $190-$220; family, wkly rates; ski, golf plans; lower rates mid-wk. Crib $10. TV in some rms; cable. Indoor pool; whirlpool. Dining rm 8-10 am, noon-1:30 pm, 6-8:30 pm. Ck-out 11 am, ck-in 2 pm. Business servs avail. Airport, bus depot transportation. Tennis. Downhill ski 10 mi; x-country ski on site, rentals. Sleigh rides. Rec rm. Lawn games. On lake. Built in 1850s;

country and Victorian suites. Some fireplaces. Cr cds: A, DS, MC, V.
D 🛏 🏊 ⛳ 🛫 ♿

Restaurants

★ **TAVERN BY THE LAKE.** *HC 1, Box 10, Mt Pocono (18344)*. 570/839-1680. Hrs: 11 am-8 pm; Fri to midnight; Sat to 2 am. Res required Sat (dinner). Bar. A la carte entrees: lunch, dinner $5.50-$16.95. Specializes in chili, beef, chicken. Country music Fri-Sun. Parking. Outdoor dining. Cr cds: A, D, DS, MC, V.
🍴

★ **TOKYO TEAHOUSE.** *RR 940, Mt Pocono (18346)*. 570/839-8880. Hrs: 11:30 am-10 pm. Closed Tues in July, Aug. Res accepted. Japanese menu. Lunch $4.95-$7, dinner $7.25-$19.95. Specialties: sushi, steak takiki. Cr cds: D, DS, MC, V.
D 🍴

New Castle

(C-1) *See also Beaver Falls, Harmony*

Settled 1798 **Pop** 26,309 **Elev** 860 ft
Area code 724
Information Lawrence County Tourist Promotion Agency, Celli Central Station, 229 S Jefferson, 16101; 724/654-8408
Web www.lawrencecounty.com/tourism

At the junction of the Shenango, Mahoning, and Beaver rivers, this was long an important Native American trading center; the Delawares used it as their capital. Today the fireworks and plastics industries have become an integral part of the community.

What to See and Do

Greer House. Turn-of-the-century restored mansion houses the Lawrence County Historical Society. Museum has extensive Shenango and Castleton china collections, Sports Hall of Fame, fireworks room. Archives; workshops and speakers. (Tues-Sat; also by appt) 408 N Jefferson. Phone 724/658-4022. **DONATION**

Hoyt Institute of Fine Arts. Cultural arts center housed in two early 20th-century mansions on four acres of landscaped grounds; permanent art collection, changing exhibits, period rooms, performing arts programs, classes. Tours. (Tues-Sat; closed major hols) 124 E Leasure Ave. Phone 724/652-2882. **DONATION**

Living Treasures Animal Park. Pet and feed over 100 species from around the world. (Memorial Day-Labor Day, daily; May, Sept, Oct, wkends) On US 422. Phone 724/924-9571. ¢¢¢

McConnell's Mill State Park. Approx 2,500 acres. Century-old mill surrounded by beautiful landscape and scenery. Fishing, hunting; whitewater rafting, hiking. Picnicking, store. Historical center, interpretive program. Standard fees. 12 mi E via US 422. Phone 724/368-8091.

Scottish Rite Cathedral. On hillside; six 32-ft columns dominate city's skyline. Large auditorium; cathedral; ballroom. Local Masonic headquarters. Tours (by appt). Highland and Lincoln aves. Phone 724/654-6683. ¢

Motel/Motor Lodge

★ **COMFORT INN.** *1740 New Butler Rd (16101)*. 724/658-7700; fax 724/658-7727; res 800/228-5150. www.comfortinn.com. 79 rms, 2 story, 13 suites. S $66-$72; D $78-$88; each addl $6; suites $96-$124; under 18 free; wkly, wkend rates; higher rates: July 4, Dec 31. Crib free. Pet accepted, some restrictions; $6/day. TV; cable. Complimentary continental bkfst. Restaurant nearby. Ck-out noon. Meeting rm. Business servs avail. Valet serv. Exercise equipt; sauna. Some refrigerators. Cr cds: A, C, D, DS, ER, MC, V.
D 🐾 🏋 🛏 ♿

New Hope

(D-8) *See also Doylestown (Bucks County)*

Founded 1681 **Pop** 2,252 **Elev** 76 ft
Area code 215 and 267 **Zip** 18938
Information Information Center, 1 W Mechanic St, PO Box 633, phone; 215/862-5880 or Bucks County Con-

erence and Visitors Bureau, Inc, 152
Swamp Rd, Doylestown 18901, phone
215/345-4552 or 800/836-2825

Web www.buckscountycvb.org

The river village of New Hope was
originally the largest part of a 1,000-
acre land grant from William Penn
to Thomas Woolrich of Shalford,
England. In the 20th century the
area gained fame as the home of
artists and literary and theatrical
personalities.

What to See and Do

Bucks County River Country. On the
Delaware River; two- to four-hr canoeing, rafting, tubing, and kayaking
trips; one-day outings to full vacation
trips. (May-Oct) Bucks County River
Country, PO Box 6, Point Pleasant
18950. Phone 215/297-5000. ¢¢¢¢

Coryell's Ferry. Passenger and charter
rides aboard the *Major William C.
Barnett*, a 65-ft Mississippi-style sternwheel riverboat, on the Delaware
River. (Memorial Day-Labor Day,
daily; call for extended season) 22 S
Main St. Phone 215/862-2050. ¢¢¢

Ghost Tours. Follow a lantern-led
walk to learn about the area's ghosts.
(Oct, Fri and Sat eves; June-Sept, Sat
eve only) Main and Ferry sts. Phone
215/957-9988. ¢¢¢

New Hope & Ivyland Railroad. A
nine-mi, 50-min narrated train ride
through Bucks County. Reading Rail-
road passenger coaches from the
1920s depart from restored 1890
New Hope Station. Gift shop. (Early
Apr-Nov, daily; Dec, special Santa
Train Fri-Sun; rest of yr, wkends) W
Bridge St, adj to Delaware Canal.
Phone 215/862-2332. ¢¢¢

Parry Barn. (1784). Owned by New
Hope Historical Society; operated as
commercial art gallery. S Main St,
opp mansion. **FREE**

Parry Mansion Museum. (1784).
Restored stone house built by Benjamin Parry, prosperous merchant
and mill owner. Eleven rooms on
view, restored and furnished to
depict period styles from late 18th-
to early-20th centuries. (May-Dec,
Fri-Sun; also by appt) S Main and
Ferry sts. Phone 215/862-5652. ¢¢

Peddler's Village. An 18th-century-
style village featuring over 70 spe-

cialty shops, eight restaurants, 60-
room inn (see B&Bs/SMALL INNS),
festivals and craft competitions
throughout the yr (see SPECIAL
EVENTS). Forty-two acres with landscaped gardens and walkways. (Daily)
5 mi S on US 202 in Lahaska. Phone
215/794-4000. Also in village is

> **Carousel World.** Learn about his-
> tory of the carousel in turn-of-the-
> century park. Antique carousel
> rides. Gift shop. (Daily) Phone
> 215/794-8960. ¢

Washington Crossing Historical Park.
(see). 7 mi S on PA 32.

Special Events

Teddy Bear's Picnic. Peddler's Village.
Teddy bear vendors, parades, competitions. "Bear clinic" for hurt bears.
Appraisals. Music. Phone 215/794-
4000. July 18-19.

Scarecrow Festival. Peddler's Village.
Scarecrow making, pumpkin painting. Jack-o-lantern and gourd art contest. Square dancing, entertainment.
Phone 215/794-4000. Sept 19-20

New Hope Arts and Crafts Festival.
Contemporary and traditional crafts.
Painting, photography, sculpture.
Phone 215/862-5880. Oct 2-3.

B&Bs/Small Inns

★ ★ ★ **AARON BURR HOUSE.** *80
W Bridge St (18938). 215/862-2343;
fax 215/862-3937. www.new-hope-
inn.com.* 5 rms, 2 story, 2 suites. S, D
$80-$150; each addl $20; suite $160-
$205; wkly rates; lower rates mid-wk.
Pet accepted. TV in sitting rm; cable,
VCR avail. Swimming privileges.
Complimentary full bkfst; afternoon
refreshments. Restaurant nearby. Ck-
out 11 am, ck-in 2 pm. Meeting rm.
Business servs avail. Concierge. Free
bus depot transportation. Downhill
ski 2 mi; x-country ski adj. Tennis
privileges. Golf privileges. Health
club privileges. Lawn games. Fireplace in suites. Built in 1873; some
antiques. Screened flagstone patio.
Totally nonsmoking. Cr cds: MC, V.
🛏 D 🐾 ⚕ ➤ ✕ 🎿 ⛷ SC

★ ★ ★ **BARLEY SHEAF FARM BED
& BREAKFAST.** *5281 York Rd, Holi-
cong (18928). 215/794-5104; fax
215/794-5332. www.barleysheaf.com.*
15 rms, 3 story. Rm phones avail.

July-Oct, wkends: D $140-$255; each addl $20; lower rates rest of yr. TV in sitting rm; cable, VCR avail. Pool. Complimentary full bkfst; afternoon refreshments. Ck-out 11 am, ck-in 2 pm. Meeting rms. Business servs avail. In-rm modem link. Lawn games. Thirty-acre farmhouse; built in 1740. Totally nonsmoking. Cr cds: A, MC, V.

★★ **CENTRE BRIDGE INN.** *2998 N River Rd (18938).* 215/862-2048; fax 215/862-3244. *www.centrebridgeinn. com.* 9 rms, 2 story. No rm phones. D $80-$150; each addl $15. TV; cable. Complimentary continental bkfst. Restaurant (see also CENTRE BRIDGE INN). Bar. Ck-out noon, ck-in 3 pm. Business servs avail. Sitting rm and terrace overlook river. Fireplace; antiques. Cr cds: A, MC, V.

★★★ **EVERMAY ON THE DELAWARE.** *889 River Rd, Erwinna (18920).* 610/294-9100; fax 610/294-8249. *www.evermay.com.* 16 rms, 4 story. No elvtrs. S $95-$150; D $115-$195; suite $250; guest house $150; wkends (2-day min). Children over 13 yrs only. TV in common rm; cable, VCR avail. Complimentary continental bkfst. Restaurant (see also EVERMAY). Ck-out noon, ck-in 2 pm. Business servs avail. In-rm modem link. X-country ski on-site. Game rm. Rec rm. Lawn games. Some fireplaces. On river. Built in 1790; classic Federal structure with Victorian antiques. On 25 acres. Totally nonsmoking. Cr cds: MC, V.

★★★ **FOX AND HOUND BED AND BREAKFAST.** *246 W Bridge St (18938).* 215/862-5082; fax 215/862-5082; res 800/862-5082. *www.fox houndinn.com.* 8 rms, 3 story. Some rm phones. S, D $65-$170; wkend rates. Children over 12 yrs only. Pet accepted. TV avail; cable. Complimentary continental bkfst; full bkfst on wkends. Restaurant nearby. Ck-out 11 am, ck-in 1:30 pm. Business servs avail. Luggage handling. Free bus depot transportation. Health club privileges. Picnic tables. Stone manor house built in 1850. Cr cds: A, MC, V.

★★★ **GOLDEN PHEASANT INN.** *763 River Rd, Erwinna (18920).* 610/294-9595; fax 610/294-9882; res 800/830-4474. *www.goldenpheasant. com.* 6 rms, 3 with shower only, 2 story, kit. suite. No rm phones. MAP: S, D $85-$155; each addl $10; suite $125-$155; wkly rates; hols (3-day min). Pet accepted; $10. Complimentary continental bkfst. Coffee in rms. Restaurant (see also GOLDEN PHEASANT INN). Ck-out 11 am, ck-in 2 pm. Meeting rms. Cr cds: A, C, D, DS, MC, V.

★★★ **GOLDEN PLOUGH INN.** *SR 202, Lahaska (18931).* 215/794-4004; fax 215/794-4008. *www.peddlers village.com.* 65 units in 7 bldgs, 2-3 story, 24 suites. S, D $109-$325; each addl $15; suites $225-$325. Crib free. TV; cable. Complimentary continental bkfst, coffee in rms. Restaurant (see also SPOTTED HOG). Ck-out 11 am, ck-in 3 pm. Meeting rms. Business servs avail. In-rm modem link. Health club privileges. Refrigerators; some in-rm whirlpools. Some balconies. Country decor; antiques. Cr cds: A, C, D, DS, MC, V.

★★★ **HOLLILEIF BED & BREAKFAST.** *677 Durham Rd (SR 413), Newtown (18940).* 215/598-3100. *www.bbhost.com/hollileif.* 5 rms, 3 story. No rm phones. D $85-$160; each addl $20. TV in some rms; cable, VCR avail (free movies). Complimentary full bkfst; afternoon refreshments. Ck-out 11:30 am, ck-in 3 pm. Business servs avail. Lawn games. 18th-century house; antiques, fireplace. Totally nonsmoking. Cr cds: A, DS, MC, V.

★★ **HOTEL DU VILLAGE.** *2535 N River Rd (18938).* 215/862-9911; fax 215/862-9788. *www.hotelduvillage. com.* 20 rms, 2 story. No rm phones. S, D $85-$100; each addl $5; wkly rates. Pool. Complimentary continental bkfst. Dining rm. Bar. Ck-out 11 am, ck-in after 2 pm. Tennis. Small Tudor-style country inn on spacious grounds; former estate. Cr cds: A, D.

★ **INN AT PHILLIPS MILL.** *2590 N River Rd (18938).* 215/862-2984; fax 215/862-0530. 4 rms, 3 story, 1 suite.

D $80; suite $90. Closed Jan. Pool. Dining rm (see also INN AT PHILLIPS MILL). Ck-out 1 pm, ck-in 2 pm. Gift shop. Built in 1750 as stone barn; antiques, fireplaces. Cr cds: A, MC, V.
≈ ⊠ ⚲

★ ★ ★ **INN TO THE WOODS.** *150 Glenwood Dr, Washington Crossing (18977). 215/493-1974; fax 215/493-7592; toll-free 800/982-7619. www.inn-bucks.com.* 6 rms, 3 story, 1 suite. S, D $95-$210; each addl $25; suite $140-$210; wkend plans (2-day min). Children over 10 yrs only. TV; cable, VCR avail (movies). Complimentary full bkfst; afternoon refreshments. Ck-out 11 am, ck-in 2 pm. Luggage handling. Concierge serv. Business servs avail. In-rm modem link. X-country ski 1 mi. Whirlpool. Some fireplaces. On 10 acres of forest with hiking trails. Totally nonsmoking. Cr cds: A, DS, MC, V.
≈ ⊠ ⚲

★ **LOGAN INN.** *10 W Ferry St (18938). 215/862-2300; fax 215/862-3931. www.loganinn.com.* 16 rms, 10 with shower only, 3 story. S, D $75-$150; each addl $17; under 3 free; wkly, wkday rates; hols (3-day min). Crib avail. TV; cable. Complimentary continental bkfst. Restaurant 11 am-11 pm. Ck-out noon, ck-in 3-10 pm. Downhill/x-country ski 5 mi. On canal; built in 1722. One of the oldest inns in US. Cr cds: A, D, DS, MC, V.
🐾 ⤫ ⊠ ⚲

★ ★ **MANSION INN.** *9 S Main St (18938). 215/862-1231; fax 215/862-0277. www.themansioninn.com.* 9 rms, 3 story, 5 suites. No elvtr. D $160-$225; suites $205-$305; min stay 2-3 days. Children over 16 yrs only. TV; cable (premium). Pool. Complimentary full bkfst. Complimentary coffee delivered to rms. Restaurant nearby. Ck-out 11 am, ck-in 2 pm. Business servs avail. In-rm modem link. Luggage handling. Concierge serv. X-country ski 15 mi. Health club privileges. Some in-rm whirlpools, fireplaces. Built (1865); Victorian decor. Totally nonsmoking. Cr cds: A, MC, V.
≈ ⊠ ⚲ ⤫

★ ★ ★ **PINEAPPLE HILL BED AND BREAKFAST.** *1324 River Rd (18938). 215/862-1790; toll-free 888/866-8404.* *www.pineapplehill.com.* 8 rms, 3 with shower only, 3 story, 3 suites. May-Dec: S $75-$135; D $85-$145; each addl $30; suites $115-$165; wkly rates; wkends (2-day min); package plans; lower rates rest of yr. TV; cable, VCR avail (movies). Pool. Complimentary full bkfst; afternoon refreshments. Complimentary coffee in rms. Ck-out 11 am, ck-in 3 pm. Luggage handling. Concierge serv. Business servs avail. X-country ski on site. Health club privileges. Lawn games. Balconies. Picnic tables. On river. Built in 1790. Totally nonsmoking. Cr cds: A, DS, MC, V.
🐾 ⛷ ⤫ ≈ ⊠ ⚲ SC

★ ★ ★ **1740 HOUSE.** *3690 River Rd, Lumberville (18933). 215/297-5661; fax 215/297-5956. www.1740house.com.* 24 rms. Wkends (Sat 2-day min), hols (3-4-day min): D $113; lower rates wkdays. Pool. Complimentary buffet bkfst. Ck-out noon, ck-in 2 pm. Meeting rms. Business servs avail. Balconies. Overlooks Delaware River.
D ≈ ⊠ ⚲

★ ★ ★ **TATTERSALL INN.** *16 Cafferty N River Rd, Point Pleasant (18950). 215/297-8233; fax 215/297-5093; toll-free 800/297-4988. www.bbhost.com/tattersall_inn.* 6 rms, 2 story, 2 suites. S $60-$99; D $70-$130; each addl $15; suites $99-$130. TV in sitting rm. Complimentary full bkfst; afternoon refreshments. Restaurant nearby. Ck-out noon, ck-in 2 pm. Business servs avail. Some fireplaces. House (1740); porches, marble fireplace, antiques. Cr cds: A, DS, MC, V.
🐾 ⊠ ⚲ SC

★ ★ ★ **WEDGWOOD INN.** *111 W Bridge St (18938). 215/862-2570; fax 215/862-3937. www.1870wedgwoodinn.com.* 12 rms, 2 story. Some rm phones. S $75-$120; D $105-$175; each addl $20; suites $150-$225. Pet accepted. Swimming privileges. Complimentary full bkfst; afternoon refreshments. Ck-out 11 am, ck-in 3 pm. Concierge serv. Meeting rm. Business servs avail. Health club privileges. Tennis privileges. Golf privileges. Lawn games. Some fireplaces; microwaves avail. Picnic tables, grills. Carriage rides. Built 1870; antiques, large Wedgwood collection. Totally nonsmoking. Cr cds: A, MC, V.

★ ★ ★ **WHITEHALL INN.** *1370 Pineville Rd (18938). 215/598-7945; fax 215/598-0378; res 888/379-4483. www.innbook.com/whitehal.html.* 5 rms, 3 story, 1 suite. No rm phones. S, D $140-$195; suite $195; wkends, hols (2-3-day min). Complimentary full bkfst; afternoon refreshments. Ck-out 11 am, ck-in after 3 pm. Business servs avail. Luggage handling. Concierge serv. 18-hole golf privileges, pro, putting green, driving range. Downhill ski 7 mi; x-country ski on-site. Health club privileges. Pool. Lawn games. Many fireplaces. Picnic tables. Built in 1794; set on 12 rolling acres. Antiques. Totally nonsmoking. Cr cds: A, C, D, DS, MC, V.

Restaurants

★ ★ **BOURBON STREET.** *1600 River Rd (18938). 215/862-9477.* Hrs: 5-10 pm; Fri to 11 pm; Sat noon-11 pm; Sun noon-9 pm. Closed Tues; Jan 1, Thanksgiving, Dec 25. Res accepted; required Sat dinner. Contemporary American menu. Bar. A la carte entrees: lunch, dinner $13.95-$21.95. Child's menu. Specialties: Thai chicken curry, grilled salmon, seared sea scallops. Own pastries, ice cream. Cabaret Fri. Outdoor dining. Contemporary decor with local artists' works; woodburning oven. Cr cds: A, MC, V.

★ ★ **CENTRE BRIDGE INN.** *2998 N River Rd (18938). 215/862-9139. www.centrebridgeinn.com.* Hrs: 5:30-9:30 pm; Fri, Sat to 10 pm; Sun brunch 11:30 am-2:30 pm; dinner 3:30-9 pm. Closed Dec 25. Res accepted Fri-Sun. Continental menu. Bar. Dinner $18.95-$26.95. Sun brunch $20. Specializes in lamb, salmon, crab cakes. Entertainment Sat. Valet parking Sat. Outdoor dining. Stone fireplace. Patio overlooks canal, river. Cr cds: MC, V.

★ ★ **COCK N' BULL.** *US 202 and 263, Lahaska (18931). 215/794-4010. www.peddlersvillage.com.* Hrs: 11 am-3 pm, 5-9 pm; Fri to 10 pm; Sat 4-10 pm; Sun 4-8 pm; Sun brunch 9:30 am-2:30 pm. Closed Jan 1, Dec 25. Res accepted (dinner). Bar. Lunch $4.95-$10.95, dinner $11.25-$24.95. Sun brunch $14.95. Specialties: country chicken pie, beef Burgundy. Salad bar. Family-owned. Cr cds: A, C, D, DS, MC, V.

★ ★ ★ **CUTTALOSSA INN.** *3498 River Rd (PA 32), Lumberville (18933). 215/297-5082. www.cuttalossainn.com* Hrs: 11 am-2 pm, 5:30-9 pm; Fri, Sat 5:30-10 pm. Closed Sun; Jan 1, Dec 24, 25. Bar. Complete meals: lunch $6-$15, dinner $18-$28. Specializes in seafood. Entertainment in summer Tues-Sun. Outdoor dining. Built 1750; overlooks waterfall and wooden bridge. Cr cds: A, MC, V.

★ ★ ★ **EVERMAY.** *889 River Rd, Erwinna (18920). 610/294-9100. www.evermay.com.* Hrs: 7:30-11 pm. Closed Mon-Thurs. Res required. Bar. Wine cellar. Complete meal: $62. Specialties: poached Norwegian salmon with citrus beurre blanc, contrefilet of beef with port wine reduction. Menu changes daily. Jacket. Cr cds: MC, V.

★ ★ ★ **GOLDEN PHEASANT INN.** *763 River Rd (PA 32), Erwinna (18920). 610/294-9595. www.goldenpheasant. com.* Hrs: 5:30-10 pm; Sun 11 am-9 pm. Sun brunch 11 am-3 pm. Closed Mon. Res accepted. French menu. Bar. Wine cellar. A la carte entrees: dinner $18.95-$24.95. Sun brunch $18.95. Specialties: roast lamb, crabmeat Brittany, steak au poivre. Own baking. Restored 1857 inn; dining rm in solarium, overlooks canal. Cr cds: A, C, D, DS, MC, V.

★ ★ **INN AT PHILLIPS MILL.** *2590 N River Rd (18938). 215/862-9919.* Hrs: 5:30-9:30 pm; Fri, Sat to 10 pm. Closed Dec 25; also Jan. Res accepted, required Sat. French country menu. Setups. A la carte entrees: $14.50-$24. Specialties: sole bonne femme, filet de boeuf rochambeau, Muscovy duck with cranberry sauce. Entertainment Fri, Sun. Outdoor dining in garden setting. Jacket.

★ ★ ★ **JEAN PIERRE'S.** *101 S State St, Newtown (18940). 215/968-6201. www.jeanpierres.com.* Hrs: 11:30 am-2 pm, 5:30-9:30 pm; Sun 11:30 am-2 pm (brunch), 4:30-8 pm. Closed Mon; Jan 1, Dec 25. Res accepted. French menu. Wine cellar. Prix fixe: lunch $19.50. A la carte entrees: dinner $22-$29. Specializes in imported fish, rack of lamb, fresh game. Own pastries. Built in 1747. Fireplaces. Cr cds: A, D, DS, MC, V. 🗺

★ ★ **JENNY'S.** *US 202 and 263, Lahaska (18931). 215/794-4000. www.peddlersvillage.com.* Hrs: 11 am-9 pm; Mon to 3 pm; Fri, Sat to 10 pm; Sun 4:30-8 pm; Sun brunch 10 am-3 pm. Closed Dec 25. Res accepted. Continental menu. Bar. A la carte entrees: lunch $4.95-$9.95, dinner $15.95-$24.95. Sun brunch $5.25-$9.95. Specialties: lobster ravioli, filet Chesterfield, mushrooms Pennsylvania. Jazz, blues Fri, Sat. Cr cds: A, D, DS, MC, V. D 🗺

★ ★ ★ **ODETTE'S.** *S River Rd (18938). 215/862-2432. www.odettes.com.* Hrs: 11:30-2 am; Sun brunch 10:30 am-1:30 pm. Res accepted; required hols. Continental menu. Bar. Wine list. A la carte entrees: lunch $7.50-$10, dinner $15-$24. Sun brunch $15.95. Child's menu. Specializes in veal chops, salmon. Pianist. Valet parking. Built in 1794 as bargeman's inn; overlooks Delaware River; memorabilia of Odette Myrtil Logan of South Pacific fame. Cr cds: A, D, DS, MC, V. D 🗺

★ **SPOTTED HOG.** *US 202 and 263 (18931). 215/794-4000. www.peddlersvillage.com.* Hrs: 7 am-11 pm; Sun to 9 pm. Closed Thanksgiving, Dec 25. Bar to midnight; Fri, Sat to 1 am; Sun to 10 pm. A la carte entrees: bkfst $2.95-$7.25, lunch, dinner $3.25-$18.95. Child's menu. Specializes in stir-fry, pizza, calzones. Cr cds: A, C, D, DS, MC, V. D 🗺

New Stanton

(E-2) *See also Connellsville, Greensburg*

Pop 1,906 **Elev** 980 ft **Area code** 724 **Zip** 15672

Information Laurel Highlands Visitors Bureau, Town Hall, 120 E Main St, Ligonier 15658; 724/238-5661

Web www.laurelhighlands.org

What to See and Do

L.E. Smith Glass Co. Reproductions of several styles of antique handcrafted glass. Tours. Children under six yrs not admitted on tour. (Mon-Fri; closed first two wks July) 6 mi SE via US 119, PA 31, in Mt Pleasant, 1900 Liberty St. Phone 724/547-3544. **FREE**

Motels/Motor Lodges

★ **DAYS INN.** *127 W Byers Ave (15672). 724/925-3591; fax 724/925-9859; toll-free 800/329-7466. www.days inn.com.* 135 rms, 3 story. S $47-$55; D $49-$60; each addl $6; under 18 free. Crib free. TV; cable (premium). Pool; lifeguard. Restaurant 6-11 am, 4-10 pm; Sat, Sun from 7 am. Bar 4 pm-midnight; entertainment. Ck-out 11 am. Coin lndry. Meeting rms. Business servs avail. Sundries. Exercise equipt. Microwaves avail. Cr cds: A, DS, MC, V. D 🗺 🏋 🗺 🗺 SC

★ **HOWARD JOHNSON INN.** *112 W Byers Ave (15672). 724/925-3511; toll-free 800/446-4656.* 87 rms, 2 story. Mid-May-Sept: S $38-$79; D $45-$79; each addl $5; under 18 free; lower rates rest of yr. Crib free. TV; cable (premium), VCR avail (movies). Heated pool. Playground. Complimentary continental bkfst. Coffee in rms. Restaurant adj open 24 hrs. Ck-out noon. Business servs avail. In-rm modem link. Valet serv. Refrigerators, microwaves avail. Cr cds: A, C, D, DS, MC, V. D 🗺 🗺 🗺 SC

Norristown

(E-7) *See also King of Prussia, Kulpsville, Philadelphia*

Founded 1704 **Pop** 31,282 **Elev** 130 ft
Area code 484 and 610
Information Valley Forge Convention and Visitors Bureau, 600 W Germantown Pike, Suite 130, Plymouth Meeting 19462; 610/834-1550
Web www.valleyforge.org

William Penn, Jr., owner of the 7,600-acre tract around Norristown, sold it to Isaac Norris and William Trent for 50 cents an acre in 1704. It became a crossroads for colonial merchants and soldiers; Washington's army camped nearby. Dutch, German, Swedish, Welsh, and English immigrants left their mark on the city. Today Norristown, still a transportation hub, houses many industries and serves as a county government center.

What to See and Do

Elmwood Park Zoo. Features extensive North American waterfowl area; cougars, bobcats, bison, elk; outdoor aviary; birds of prey; children's zoo barn; museum with exhibit on animal senses. (Daily; closed Jan 1, Thanksgiving, Dec 25) Harding Blvd, off US 202. Phone 610/277-3825. ¢¢

Peter Wentz Farmstead. Restored and furnished mid-18th-century country mansion, twice used by Washington during the Pennsylvania campaign. More than 70 acres with demonstration field and crops of the period. Slide presentation; reconstructed 1744 barn with farm animals. (Tues-Sun; closed hols) 10 mi NW via US 202, W via PA 73 on Schultz Rd, in Worcester. Phone 610/584-5104. **FREE**

Valley Forge National Historical Park. (see) NW on US 422 to Trooper, then S.

Hotel

★ ★ ★ **SHERATON BUCKS COUNTY HOTEL.** *400 Oxford Valley Rd (19047). 215/547-4100. www.sheraton.com.* 187 rms, 15 story. S, D $225-$275; under 17 free. Crib avail. TV; cable (premium). Indoor pool; whirlpool. Restaurant 6:30 am-10 pm. Bar to midnight. Ck-out noon, ck-in 3 pm. Meeting rms. Business center. In-rm modem link. Concierge. Exercise equipt. Minibars; many refrigerators in suites. Cr cds: A, D, DS, MC, V.

B&B/Small Inn

★ ★ ★ **WILLIAM PENN INN.** *US 202 & Sumneytown Pike, Gwynedd (19436). 215/699-9272; fax 215/699-4808. www.philanet.com/wmpenn/.* 4 rms, 2 story, 3 suites. S, D $115-$150; suites $135-$180. TV; cable (premium). Complimentary continental bkfst. Restaurant (see also WILLIAM PENN INN). Rm serv 5-10 pm. Ck-out 11 am, ck-in 1 pm. Business servs avail. In-rm modem link. Luggage handling. Refrigerators, minibars. Continuous operation since 1714; antiques. Totally nonsmoking. Cr cds: A, C, D, DS, MC, V.

Restaurants

★ ★ ★ **THE JEFFERSON HOUSE.** *2519 DeKalb Pike (19401). 610/275-3407. www.thejeffersonink.com.* Hrs: 11:30 am-2:30 pm, 4:30-10 pm; Sun noon-8 pm; Sun brunch to 4 pm; early-bird dinner Mon-Sat 4-6 pm. Closed hols. Res accepted. Contemporary American menu. Bar to 2 am. Wine cellar. Lunch $5.50-$16.95, dinner $12.50-$32. Child's menu. Specializes in pastas, prime meats. Jazz, blues Fri in season. Manor house set on extensive, landscaped grounds; former Buckland estate. Family-owned. Cr cds: A, D, MC, V.

★ ★ **WILLIAM PENN INN.** *US 202 and Sumneytown Pike, Gwynedd (19436). 215/699-9272. www.philanet.com/wmpenn.* Hrs: 11:30 am-3 pm, 5-10 pm; Fri, Sat to 11 pm; Sun 2-8 pm; early-bird dinner Mon-Sat 5-6:30 pm; Sun brunch 10:30 am-2 pm. Closed Dec 25. Res accepted. Continental menu. Bar. Lunch $5.25-$15, dinner $18-$30. Sun brunch $17.95. Specializes in seafood, roast rack of lamb, prime rib. Own pastries. Salad

bar. Harpist, pianist Tues-Sun. Originally built as a tavern (1714);
antiques. Guest rms avail. Cr cds: A,
C, D, DS, MC, V.
D ➡

North East

A-2) *See also Erie*

Settled 1794 **Pop** 4,601 **Elev** 801 ft
Area code 814 **Zip** 16428

Information Chamber of Commerce,
21 S Lake St; 814/725-4262

When Pennsylvania bought from the
federal government the tract containing North East in 1778, the state
gained 46 miles of Lake Erie
frontage, a fine harbor, and some of
the best Concord grape country in
the nation.

What to See and Do

Winery tours.

Heritage Wine Cellars. Guided
tours; wine tastings. (Daily; closed
some hols) 12162 E Main Rd.
Phone 814/725-8015. **FREE**

Mazza Vineyards. Guided tours;
wine tastings. (Daily; closed some
hols) 11815 E Lake Rd. Phone
814/725-8695. **FREE**

Penn-Shore Vineyards and Winery.
Guided tours; wine tastings. (Daily;
closed some hols) 10225 E Lake
Rd. Phone 814/725-8688. **FREE**

Special Events

Cherry Festival. Concessions, rides,
games, parade. Mid-July.

Wine Country Harvest Festival.
Gravel Pit Park and Gibson Park. Arts
and crafts, bands, buses to wineries,
food. Phone 814/725-4262. Last full
wkend Sept.

Oil City

C-2) *See also Franklin (Venango
County), Titusville*

Pop 11,504 **Elev** 1,000 ft
Area code 814 **Zip** 16301

Spreading on both sides of Oil Creek
and the Allegheny River, Oil City was
born of the oil boom. Oil refining
and the manufacture of oil machinery are its major occupations today.
Nearby are natural gas fields. Seven
miles northwest stood the famous
oil-boom town of Pithole. In 1865 it
expanded from a single farmhouse to
a population of more than 10,000 in
five months as its first oil well
brought in 250 barrels a day.

Motel/Motor Lodge

★ ★ **HOLIDAY INN.** *1 Seneca St
(16301). 814/677-1221; fax 814/677-
0492. www.holiday-inn.com.* 106 rms,
5 story. S, D $65; each addl $5; suites
$75-$99; family rates. Crib free. Pet
accepted. TV; cable. Heated pool.
Coffee in rms. Restaurant 6:30 am-2
pm, 5-9 pm. Bar 5 pm-2 am, Sun
from 1 pm. Ck-out noon. Meeting
rms. Business servs avail. In-rm
modem link. Bellhops. Valet serv. X-
country ski 2 mi. Health club privileges. Cr cds: A, D, DS, MC, V.
D 🐾 ➖ ➤ ➤ 🐾

Orbisonia

(E-4) *See also Chambersburg, Huntingdon*

Pop 425 **Elev** 640 ft **Area code** 814
Zip 17243

What to See and Do

East Broad Top Railroad. The oldest
surviving narrow-gauge railroad east
of the Rockies. Train ride (70 min);
fascinating old equipment, bldgs.
Picnic area. (June-Oct, wkends only)
On US 522. Phone 814/447-3011. ¢¢
Opp is

Rockhill Trolley Museum. Old-time
trolleys; car barn and restoration
shop tours. A two-mi ride on
Shade Gap Electric Railway. Gift
shop. (Memorial Day-Oct, wkends)
½ mi W off US 522, on PA 994, in
Rockhill Furnace. Phone 814/447-
9576. ¢¢

Pennsylvania Dutch country

Pennsylvania Dutch Area

(D-7) *See also Allentown, Bird-in-Hand, Ephrata, Kutztown, Lancaster, Lebanon, Manheim, Reading*

Information Pennsylvania Dutch Convention & Visitors Bureau, 501 Greenfield Rd, Lancaster 17601; 717/299-8901 or 800/PADUTCH. There is also a downtown visitor center at 100 S Queen St in the Lancaster Chamber of Commerce & Industry Bldg which provides brochures, maps, and other general information; also another on US 272 near PA Tpke Exit 21
Web www.800padutch.com

From the Rhineland and Palatinate of Germany came great migrations of settlers to Pennsylvania in the 18th century, first near Philadelphia and then moving west. Because they retained their customs and speech and developed beautiful and bountiful farms, the Pennsylvania Dutch (corruption of the German *Deutsch*) country is one of the state's greatest tourist attractions. There are all degrees of conservatism among these descendants of German immigrants, ranging from the Amish to the Brethren, but all share tremendous vigor, family devotion, love of the Bible, and belief in thrift and hard work.

Many of the "plain people" - the Amish, Old Order Mennonites, and Bretren (Dunkards) - live today much as they did a century ago. Married men wear beards, black coats, and low-crowned black hats; women wear bonnets and long, simple dresses. They drive horses and buggies instead of cars, work long hours in the fields, shun the use of modern farm machinery, and turn to the Bible for guidance. Despire their refusal to use machinery they are master farmers. (They were among the first to rotate crops and practice modern fertilization methods.) Their harvests are consistently among the best in the country.

Many of the Amish regard photographs as "graven images"; visitors should not take pictures of individuals without their permission.

Philadelphia (E-8)

Founded 1682 **Pop** 1,517,550 **Elev** 45 ft **Area code** 215 and 267

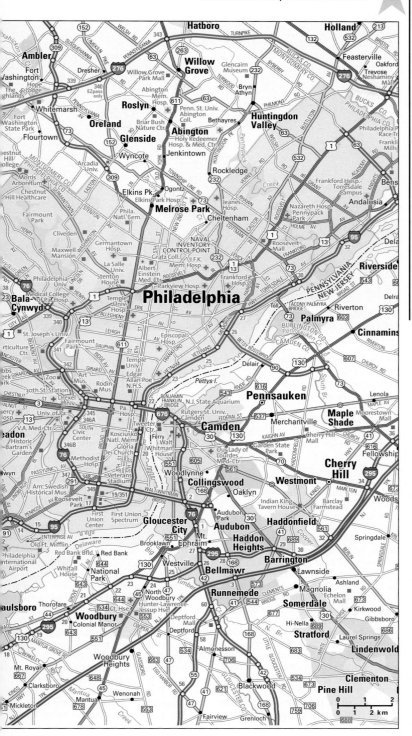

Philadelphia City Hall

Information Convention & Visitors Bureau, 1515 Market St, 19102; 215/636-3300
Web www.pcvb.org

Suburbs Bristol, Chester, Fort Washington, Jenkintown, Kennett Square, King of Prussia, Media, Norristown, West Chester, Willow Grove; also Wilmington, DE and Camden, NJ.

The nation's first capital has experienced a rebirth in the past few decades. Philadelphia has successfully blended its historic past with an electricity of modern times, all the while keeping an eye on the future. In the mid-18th century it was the second-largest city in the English-speaking world. Now, at the dawn of the 21st century, Philadelphia is the second-largest city on the East Coast and the fifth largest in the country. Here, in William Penn's City of Brotherly Love, the Declaration of Independence was written and adopted, the Constitution was molded and signed, the Liberty Bell was rung, Betsy Ross was said to have sewn her flag, and Washington served most of his years as president.

This is the city of "firsts," including the first American hospital, medical college, women's medical college, bank, paper mill, steamboat, zoo, sugar refinery, daily newspaper, US mint, and public school for black children (1750).

The first Quakers, who came here in 1681, lived in caves dug into the banks of the Delaware River. During the first year 80 houses were raised; by the following year William Penn's "greene countrie towne" was a city of 600 buildings. The Quakers prospered in trade and commerce and Philadelphia became the leading port in the colonies. Its leading citizen for many years was Benjamin Franklin—statesman, scientist, diplomat, writer, inventor, and publisher.

The fires of colonial indignation burned hot and early in Philadelphia. Soon after the Boston Tea Party, a protest rally of 8,000 Philadelphians frightened off a British tea ship. In May 1774, when Paul Revere rode from Boston to Philadelphia to report Boston's harbor had been closed, all of Philadelphia went into mourning. The first and second Continental Congresses convened here, and Philadelphia became the headquarters of the Revolution. After the Declaration of Independence was composed and accepted by Congress the city gave its men, factories, and hipyards to the cause. But British General Howe and 18,000 soldiers poured in on September 26, 1777, to spend a comfortable and social winter here while Washington's troops endured the bitter cold at Valley Forge. When the British evacuated the city, Congress returned. Philadelphia continued as the seat of government until 1800, except for a short period when New York City held the honor. The Constitution of the United States was written here and President George Washington graced the city's halls and streets.

Since those historic days Philadelphia has figured importantly in the politics, economy, and culture of the country. Here national conventions have nominated presidents. During our wars the city has served as an arsenal and a shipyard. More than 1,400 churches and synagogues grace the city. There are over 25 colleges, universities, and professional schools in Philadelphia as well. Fine restaurants are in abundance, along with exciting nightlife to top off an evening. Entertainment is offered by the world-renowned Philadelphia Orchestra, theaters, college and professional sports, outstanding parks, recreation centers, and playgrounds. Shoppers may browse major department stores, hundreds of specialty shops, and antique shopping areas.

For ten blocks between the Delaware River and 9th Street lies a history-rich part of Philadelphia. Here are the shrines of American liberty: Independence Hall, the Liberty Bell Pavilion, and many other historical sites in and around Independence National Historical Park.

Additional Visitor Information

There is also a visitor center at 3rd and Chestnut sts, operated by the National Park Service. (Daily) Phone 215/597-8975 or 215/597-8974 for information on park attractions.

The Visitors Center of the Philadelphia Convention and Visitors Bureau, 16th St and John F. Kennedy Blvd, 19102, has tourist information and maps (daily; closed Thanksgiving, Dec 25). Phone 215/636-1666 or 800/537-7676.

Transportation

Car Rental Agencies. See IMPORTANT TOLL-FREE NUMBERS.

Public Transportation. Subway and elevated trains, commuter trains, buses, trolleys (SEPTA), phone 215/580-7800.

Rail Passenger Service. Amtrak 800/872-7245.

Airport Information

Philadelphia International Airport. Information 215/937-6800 or 800/PHL-GATE; lost and found 215/937-6888; weather 215/936-1212.

What to See and Do

Academy of Music. (1857). City's opera house, concert hall; home of Philadelphia Orchestra, Philly Pops, Opera Company of Philadelphia and Pennsylvania Ballet (see SEASONAL EVENTS). Broad and Locust sts. Phone 215/893-1935.

Academy of Natural Sciences Museum. (1812). Dinosaurs, Egyptian mummies, animal displays in natural habitats, live animal programs, hands-on children's museum. (Daily; closed Jan 1, Thanksgiving, Dec 25) 1900 Benjamin Franklin Pkwy. Phone 215/299-1000. ¢¢¢

African-American Museum Philadelphia. Built to house and interpret African-American culture. Changing exhibits; public events including lectures, workshops, films and concerts. (Tues-Sun; closed Jan 1, Thanksgiving, Dec 25) 701 Arch St. Phone 215/574-0380. ¢¢¢

American Swedish Historical Museum. From tapestries to technology, the museum celebrates Swedish influence on American life. Special exhibits on the New Sweden Colony. Research library, collections. (Tues-Sun; closed hols) 1900 Pattison Ave. Phone 215/389-1776. ¢¢

Arch Street Meetinghouse. (1804) Perhaps the largest Friends meetinghouse in the world. Exhibits, slide show, tours. (Daily exc Sun; closed Jan 1, Thanksgiving, Dec 25) 320 Arch St. Phone 215/627-2667.
DONATION

Atwater Kent Museum. Artifacts depicting Philadelphia's history; 321

Saturday Evening Post covers produced by artist and illustrator Norman Rockwell between 1916 and 1975. (Mon, Wed-Sun) 15 S 7th St. Phone 215/685-4830.

Balch Institute for Ethnic Studies. A multicultural library, archive, museum and education center that promotes intergroup understanding using education; 300 yrs of US immigration are documented here. Features "Peopling of Pennsylvania," as well as changing exhibits. (Mon-Sat; closed hols) 18 S 7th St. Phone 215/925-8090. ¢¢

Betsy Ross House. Where the famous seamstress is said to have made the first American flag. Upholsterer's shop, memorabilia. Flag Day ceremonies, June 14. (Apr-Oct, daily; Tues-Sun rest of yr; closed Jan 1, Thanksgiving, Dec 25) 239 Arch St. Phone 215/686-1252. **DONATION**

Betsy Ross House

Burial Ground of Congregation Mikveh Israel. (1738) Graves of Haym Salomon, Revolutionary War financier, and Rebecca Gratz, probable model for "Rebecca" of Sir Walter Scott's *Ivanhoe*. Spruce and 8th sts.

Christ Church. (Episcopal) Patriots, Loyalists, and heroes have worshiped here since 1695. Sit in pews once occupied by Washington, Franklin, and Betsy Ross. (Mar-Dec, daily; rest of yr, Wed-Sun; closed Jan 1, Thanksgiving, Dec 25) 2nd St between Market and Arch sts. Phone 215/922-1695. **FREE**

Christ Church Burial Ground. Resting place of Benjamin Franklin, his wife, Deborah, and six other signers of the Declaration of Independence. (Call for hours) 5th and Arch sts. Phone 215/922-1695.

City Hall. Tours avail. (Mon-Fri; closed hols) Broad and Market sts. Phone 215/686-2840.

Civil War Library and Museum. Four-story brick 19th-century town house filled with 18,000 books and periodicals dealing with events leading up to the American Civil War, the war itself, and early Reconstruction. Unique collection of arms, uniforms, flags of the period, memorabilia and artifacts begun in 1888 by former officers of the Union Army. Exhibits on Lincoln, Grant, and Meade; also the Navy Room and the Armory. (Thurs-Fri; closed hols) 1805 Pine St. Phone 215/735-8196. ¢¢

Edgar Allan Poe National Historic Site. Where Poe lived before his move to New York in 1844. The site is the nation's memorial to the literary genius of Edgar Allan Poe. Exhibits, slide show, tours, and special programs. (June-Oct, daily; rest of yr, Wed-Sun; closed Jan 1, Dec 25) 532 N 7th, at Spring Garden St. Phone 215/597-8780. **FREE**

Elfreth's Alley. Oldest continuously residential street in America, with 30 houses dating from 1728-1836 (see SPECIAL EVENTS). At #126 is the mid-18th-century **Museum House;** period furnishings, historical exhibit. (Mar-Oct, Mon-Sat, Sun afternoons; Nov-Feb, Thurs-Sat, Sun afternoons) Off 2nd St between Arch and Race sts. Phone 215/574-0560. ¢

★ **Fairmount Park.** Covers 8,700 acres. Begins at Philadelphia Museum of Art, extends NW on both sides of Wissahickon Creek and Schuylkill River. Phone 215/685-0000. In park are

Boat House Row. Used by collegiate and club oarsmen. Schuylkill River is scene of many nationally important crew competitions; crews practice all spring and summer during early morning and afternoon. On E bank of river. Phone 215/978-6919.

Colonial Mansions. Handsome 18th-century dwellings in varying architectural styles, authentically preserved and furnished, incudes Mount Pleasant (1761) (daily exc Mon); Cedar Grove (1756) (daily exc Mon); Strawberry Mansion (1797) (Tues-Sun); Sweetbriar (1797) (Mon, Wed-Sun); Lemon Hill (1799) (Wed-Sun); Woodford (1756) (Tues-Sun); Laurel Hill (1760) (Wed-Sun). Further details and guided tours from Park Houses office at Philadelphia Museum of Art. Phone 215/684-7922. ¢

Japanese Exhibition House. Re-creates a bit of Japan, complete with garden, pond, bridge. (May-Labor Day, Tues-Sun; Labor Day-Oct, Sat and Sun) Fairmount Park Horticulture Center. Phone 215/878-5097. ¢

Philadelphia Zoo. America's first zoo. More than 2,000 animals, many in natural surroundings; Treehouse (fee); waterfowl collection; bear country; five-acre African plains exhibit; reptile house; bird house; carnivore kingdom; children's zoo. Picnic areas; concession. Guided tours by appt. Main zoo (daily; closed Jan 1, Thanksgiving, Dec 24, 25, 31). 3400 W Girard Ave. Phone 215/243-1100. ¢¢¢

Robin Hood Dell East. (See SPECIAL EVENTS)

Fireman's Hall Museum. Collection of antique fire-fighting equipment; displays and exhibits of fire department history since its beginning in 1736; library. (Tues-Sat; closed hols) 147 N 2nd St. Phone 215/923-1438. **DONATION**

Fort Mifflin. Site of a seven-wk siege during the Revolutionary War. Served as a military installation until 1959. Guided tours (Daily). From the airport, follow Island Ave toward the Delaware River, follow brown and white signs. Phone 215/685-4167. ¢¢¢

Franklin Institute Science Museum. **Science Center** includes exhibits on trains, shipmaking, astronomy, bioscience, communications, aviation, and electricity; highlights include a Baldwin #60,000 locomotive and a giant walk-through heart. **Mandell Futures Center** is dedicated to the science and technology shaping the 21st century; it explores such areas as space, earth, health, and computers. Also here are **Benjamin Franklin National Memorial, Fels Planetarium**, and the four-story screen of the **Tuttleman Omniverse Theater** (30-40-min films). (Daily; closed hols) 20th St and Ben Franklin Pkwy. Phone 215/448-1200. ¢¢

Free Library. Large central library with over nine million indexed items in all fields. Rare books, maps, theater scripts, and orchestral scores; automobile reference collections; changing exhibits. (Memorial Day-Labor Day, Mon-Sat; rest of yr, daily; closed hols) Logan Sq, 19th and Vine sts. Phone 215/686-5322. **FREE**

Elfreth's Alley

Liberty Bell

Germantown. Includes

Cliveden. (1767) A 2½-story stone Georgian house of individual design built as summer home by Benjamin Chew, Chief Justice of colonial Pennsylvania. On Oct 4, 1777, British soldiers used house as a fortress to repulse Washington's attempt to recapture Philadelphia. Used as Chew family residence for 200 yrs; many original furnishings. A National Trust for Historic Preservation property. (Apr-Dec, Thurs-Sun afternoons; closed Easter, Thanksgiving, Dec 25) 6401 Germantown Ave, between Johnson and Cliveden sts. Phone 215/848-1777. ¢¢

Deshler-Morris House. (1772-1773) Residence of President Washington in the summers of 1793, 1794; period furnishings, garden. (Wed-Sun afternoons, or by appt; closed hols) 5442 Germantown Ave. Phone 215/596-1748. ¢

Stenton House. (1723-1730) Mansion built by James Logan, secretary to William Penn. Excellent example of Pennsylvania colonial architecture, furnished with 18th- and 19th-century antiques. General Washington spent Aug 23, 1777, here and General Sir William Howe headquartered here for the Battle of Germantown. Colonial barn, gardens, kitchen. (Apr-Dec, Tues-Sat afternoons; rest of yr, by appt; closed hols) 18th St between Courtland St and Windrim Ave. Phone 215/329-7312. ¢¢

Gloria Dei Church National Historic Site ("Old Swedes"). (1700) State's oldest church. Memorial to John Hanson, president of the United States under Articles of Confederation. (Daily) Columbus Blvd and Christian St, 8 blks S of Chestnut. Phone 215/389-1513.

Haverford College. (1833) 1,138 students. Founded by members of the Society of Friends. The 204-acre campus includes Founders Hall; James P. Magill Library; Arboretum; Morris Cricket Library and Collection (by appt only; phone 610/896-1162). Tours of arboretum and campus. 10 mi W on US 30, in Haverford. Phone 610/896-1000.

Historical Society of Pennsylvania. Museum exhibit features first draft of Constitution, 500 artifacts and manuscripts, plus video tours of turn-of-the-century urban and suburban neighborhoods. Research library and archives house historical and genealogical collections. (Tues-Sat; closed hols) 1300 Locust St. Phone 215/732-6200. ¢¢

Historic Bartram's Garden. Pre-Revolutionary home of John Bartram, the royal botanist to the colonies under George III, naturalist and plant explorer. The 18th-century stone farmhouse (fee), barn, stable and cider mill overlook the Schuylkill River. Museum shop. (Apr-Dec, daily; rest of yr, Wed-Fri afternoons; closed hols) 54th St and Lindbergh Blvd. Phone 215/729-5281. ¢

⭐ **Independence National Historical Park.** The park has been called "America's most historic square mile." The Independence Visitor Center at 6th and Marker sts has a tour map, information on all park activities and attractions and a 30-min film entitled *Independence.* Phone 215/597-8974. Unless otherwise indicated, all historic sites and museums in the park are open daily and are free. In the park are

Independence Square. Known as State House Yard in colonial times. Bounded by Chestnut, Walnut, 5th, and 6th sts. Contains Independence Hall, Congress Hall, Old City Hall, and Philosophical Hall.

Declaration House. Reconstructed house on site of writing of Declaration of Independence by Thomas Jefferson; two rooms Jefferson rented have been reproduced. Short orientation and movie about Jefferson, his philosophy on the common man and the history of the house. 701 Market St.

Liberty Bell Pavilion. The Liberty Bell, created to commemorate the 50th anniversary of the Charter of Privileges granted by William Penn to his colony in 1701, bears the inscription, "Proclaim liberty throughout all the land unto all

the inhabitants thereof" (Leviticus, chapter 25). It was rung at public occasions thereafter, including the first reading of the Declaration of Independence on July 8, 1776, and was last rung formally on Washington's birthday in 1846. The bell got its name from 19th-century antislavery groups who adopted it as a symbol of their cause. The Liberty Bell faces

Independence Hall. (1732) Site of the adoption of the Declaration of Independence. First used as the Pennsylvania State House, it housed the Second Continental Congress, 1775-1783, and the Constitutional Convention in 1787—when the Constitution of the United States was written. Admission by tour only. Chestnut St between 5th and 6th sts. Beside Independence Hall is

Congress Hall. Congress met here during the last decade of the 18th century. House of Representatives and Senate chambers are restored. 6th and Chestnut sts. On the other side of Independence Hall is

Old City Hall. (1789) Built as City Hall, but was also home of first US Supreme Court, 1791-1800. Exterior restored. Interior depicts the judicial phase of the building. Chestnut and 5th sts. Nearby is

Philosophical Hall. (1785-1789) Home of the American Philosophical Society, oldest learned society in America (1743), founded by Benjamin Franklin. Not open to

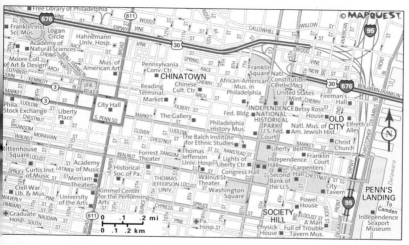

public. 5th St side of Sq. Across 5th St is

Library Hall. Reconstruction of Library Company of Philadelphia (1789-1790) building is occupied by library of American Philosophical Society. Open to scholars. (Mon-Fri) 5th and Library sts. To the NE is

Franklin Court. The site of Benjamin Franklin's house has been developed as a tribute to him; area includes working printing office and bindery, underground museum with multimedia exhibits, an archaeological exhibit and the B. Franklin Free Post Office. Between Market and Chestnut sts, in block bounded by 3rd and 4th sts. One-half blk S is

Carpenters' Hall. (1770) Constructed as guild hall; meeting site of First Continental Congress (1774). Historical museum since 1857; still operated by Carpenters Co. Contains original chairs; exhibits of early tools. 320 Chestnut St. Adj is

First Bank of the United States

New Hall Military Museum. This reconstruction houses the US Marine Corps Memorial Museum, featuring exhibits on the early history of the Marines, and the Army-Navy Museum. 4th and Chestnut sts, in Carpenters' Court. Also in Carpenters' Court is

Museum Shop (Pemberton House). Reconstruction of Quaker merchant's house; now shop with items relating to historic sites. Nearby is

The First Bank of the United States. (1797-1811) Organized by Alexander Hamilton; country's oldest bank building; exterior restored. Closed to public. 3rd St between Walnut and Chestnut sts. Walk approx $^{1}/_{2}$ blk S to

Bishop White House. (1786-1787) House of Bishop William White, first Episcopal Bishop of Pennsylvania. Restored and furnished. Tours. Free tickets at park's Visitor Center. 309 Walnut St. ¢ One blk W is

Todd House. (1775) House of Dolley Payne Todd, who later married

James Madison and became First Lady; 18th-century furnishings depict middle-class Quaker family life. Tours. Free tickets at park's Visitor Center. 4th and Walnut sts. Retrace steps 1 blk to

The Merchant's Exchange. Designed by William Strickland, one of the East's finest examples of Greek Revival architecture. Exterior restored; now houses regional offices of the National Park Service. Closed to public. 3rd and Walnut sts. Proceed E on Dock St. to

Thaddeus Kosciuszko National Memorial. House of Polish patriot during his second visit to US (1797-1798). He was one of the 18th century's greatest champions of American and Polish freedom and one of the first volunteers to come to the aid of the American Revolutionary Army. Exterior and second-floor bedroom have been restored. (Daily) 3rd and Pine sts.

Independence Seaport Museum. Ship models, figureheads, whaling equipment, paintings. Exhibits illustrate maritime history of Delaware Bay and River, Olympia exhibit; special exhibits. Waterfront facility at Penn's Landing houses boat building workshop and small gallery. (Daily; closed hols) 211 S Columbus Blvd. Phone 215/925-5439. ¢¢¢

John Heinz National Wildlife Refuge at Tinicum. Largest remaining fresh-water tidal wetland in the state, pro-ecting more than 1,000 acres of wildlife habitat. Area was first diked by Swedish farmers in 1643; Dutch farmers and the colonial government added dikes during the Revolution-ary War. More than 280 species of birds and 13 resident mammal species. Hiking, bicycling, nature observation, canoeing on Darby Creek, fishing. (Daily) S via I-95, W PA 291 exit, right on Bartram Ave, left on 84th St, left on Lindbergh Blvd, at 86th and Lindbergh Blvd. Phone 215/365-3118. **FREE**

Morris Arboretum of the University of Pennsylvania. (1887). Public gar-den with more than 14,000 acces-sioned plants on 166 acres; special garden areas such as Swan Pond, Rose Garden and Japanese gardens. Tours (Sat and Sun afternoon; one each day) (Daily; closed major hols) Approx 12 mi NW in Chestnut Hill; entrance on Northwestern Ave, between Stenton and Germantown aves. Phone 215/247-5777. ¢¢

Mütter Museum. In the College of Physicians of Philadelphia. Medical antiques and memorabilia; anatomi-cal and pathological specimens and models. (Daily; closed hols) 19 S 22nd St. Phone 215/563-3737. ¢¢¢

Mummer's Museum. Participatory exhibits and displays highlighting the history and tradition of the Mummer's Parade (see SPECIAL EVENTS). Costumes and videotapes of past parades. Free outdoor string band concerts (May-Sept, Tues eves, weather permitting); 20 string bands, different every wk. (Sept-June, Tues-Sat, also Sun afternoons; rest of yr, Mon-Sat; closed hols) 1100 S 2nd St Phone 215/336-3050. ¢¢

Museum of American Art of the Pennsylvania Academy of the Fine Arts. Oldest art museum and school in US; housed in restored Victorian building by architect Frank Furness. Outstanding permanent collection of three centuries of American art; rotating exhibits. Guided tours (Tues-Sun; closed hols). 118 N Broad St. Phone 215/972-7600. ¢¢¢

National Museum of American Jewish History. The museum presents expe-riences and educational programs that preserve, explore, and celebrate the history of Jews in America. (Daily exc Sat; limited hrs Fri and Sun; closed Jan 1, Thanksgiving, also Jew-ish hols) Independence Mall East, 55 N 5th St. Phone 215/923-3811. ¢¢

Old Pine Street Presbyterian Church. (1768). Colonial church and grave-yard, renovated in 1850s in Greek Revival style.(Daily) 412 Pine St, at 4th St. Phone 215/925-8051.

Old St. George's United Methodist Church. (1769) Oldest Methodist Church in continuous service in US. Colonial architecture; collection of Methodist memorabilia; has only Bishop Asbury bible and John Wesley chalice cup in America. (Daily) 235 N 4th St. Phone 215/925-7788.

Old St. Mary's Church. (1763). Com-modore John Barry, "father of the US Navy," is interred in graveyard behind the city's first Catholic cathedral. (Daily) 252 S 4th St, between Locust and Spruce sts. Phone 215/923-7930.

Penn's Landing. Columbus Blvd and Spruce St. Here are

Gazela of Philadelphia. (1883) Por-tuguese square-rigger, tall ship. (call for hrs) Columbus Blvd. Phone 215/218-0110.

USS *Olympia*. Commodore Dewey's flagship during Spanish-American War; restored. Naval museum has weapons, uniforms, ship models, naval relics of all periods. Also here is WWII subma-rine, USS *Becuna*. (Daily; closed hols) Columbus Blvd and Walnut St. Phone 215/925-5439. ¢¢¢

Pennsylvania Hospital. (1751) First in country, founded by Benjamin Franklin. 8th and Spruce sts.

Pentimenti Gallery. Exhibiting works of art in all modes ranging from figu-rative to abstract by local, regional and international artists. (Wed-Sat) 133 N 3rd St. Phone 215/625-9990.

Performing arts.

The Opera Company of Philadel-phia. Academy of Music. Phone 215/928-2100. Oct-Apr.

Pennsylvania Ballet. Performs at Merriam Theatre and at Academy of Music. Phone 215/551-7000.

Philadelphia Orchestra. Kimmel Center. Phone 215/893-1900. Sept-May. Also Mann Music Center late June-late July.

Philadelphia Theatre Company. Plays and Players Theatre, 1714 Delancey St. Four contemporary American plays per season. Phone 215/568-1920. Oct-June.

Philadelphia History Museum—The Atwater Kent. Hundreds of fascinating artifacts, toys and miniatures, maps, prints, paintings, and photographs reflecting the city's social and cultural history. (Wed-Mon; closed hols) 15 S 7th St. Phone 215/685-4830. ¢¢

Philadelphia Museum of Art. Over 200 galleries with collections of paintings, graphics, sculpture; period rooms, medieval cloister, Indian temple,

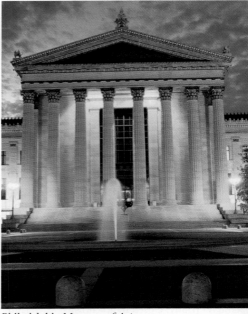

Philadelphia Museum of Art

Chinese palace hall, Japanese teahouse; armor collection. American wing includes rural Pennsylvania Dutch crafts, Shaker furniture and paintings of early American artists such as Gilbert Stuart and Thomas Eakins. Free guided tours. (Tues-Sun, also Wed, Fri eves; closed hols) 26th St and Benjamin Franklin Pkwy. Phone 215/763-8100. ¢¢¢

Please Touch Museum for Children. Unique museum designed especially for children under seven yrs old. Hands-on exhibits include "Sendak," "SuperMarket Science," "Studio PTM," and "Science Park." (Daily; closed Jan 1, Thanksgiving, Dec 25) 210 N 21st St. Phone 215/963-0667. ¢¢¢

Professional sports.

Philadelphia Eagles (NFL). NovaCare Complex, Broad St. Phone 215/463-2500.

Philadelphia Flyers (NHL). First Union Center, 3601 S Broad St. Phone 215/336-2000.

Philadelphia Phillies (MLB). Veterans Stadium, Broad St and Pattison Ave. Phone 215/463-6000.

Philadelphia 76ers (NBA). First Union Center, Broad St and Pattison Ave. Phone 215/339-7676.

Rodin Museum. Largest collection of Rodin sculpture outside Paris. (Tues-Sun; closed hols) 22nd St and Franklin Pkwy. Phone 215/563-1948. **DONATION**

St. Peter's Church. 1761 Episcopal. Georgian colonial architecture; numerous famous people buried in churchyard. 3rd and Pine sts.

Schuylkill Center for Environmental Education. A 500-acre natural area with more than seven mi of trails; discovery room; gift shop/bookstore. (Daily; closed hols) 9 mi NW, at 8480 Hagy's Mill Rd. Phone 215/482-7300. ¢¢

Sesame Place. (See BRISTOL) 20 mi NE via I-95 to Levittown exit (25E). Follow signs for the Oxford Valley Mall on the US 1 Bypass.

Shopping.

Antique Row. Dozens of antique, craft and curio shops. From 9th to 17th sts along Pine St.

The Bourse. (1893-1895) Restored Victorian building houses shops and restaurants. 5th St, across from Liberty Bell Pavilion.

The Gallery. Concentration of 250 shops and restaurants in four-level mall with glass elevators, trees, fountains, and benches. 10th and Market sts. Phone 215/925-7162.

Italian Market. Historical outdoor food mall sells fresh food, cookware, and clothing. Also here are restaurants and South Philly cheesesteak sandwiches. (Daily) 9th St between Christian and Wharton sts.

Jeweler's Row. Largest jewelry district in the country other than New York City. More than 300 shops, including wholesalers and diamond cutters. 7th and Sansom sts.

Shops at the Bellevue. Beaux Arts architecture of the former Bellevue Stratford Hotel has been preserved and transformed; it now contains offices, a hotel and a four-level shopping area centered around an atrium court. (Mon-Sat) Broad St at Walnut. Phone 215/875-8350.

South Street. Nearly 150 hip shops, boutiques, and galleries line either side of the street. Broad St at Walnut.

Sightseeing tours.

Centipede Tours. Candlelight strolls (90 min) through historic Philadelphia and Society Hill areas led by guides in 18th-century dress; begins and ends at City Tavern. (Mid-May-mid-Oct, Fri-Sat) Res preferred. 1315 Walnut St. Phone 215/735-3123. ¢¢

Gray Line bus tours. Contact 3101 E Orthodox St, 19137. Phone 215/744-1100.

Philadelphia Carriage Company. Guided tours via horse-drawn carriage covering Society Hill and other historic areas; begin and end on 5th St at Chestnut. (Daily, weather permitting; closed Dec 25) 500 N 13th St. Phone 215/922-6840. ¢¢¢¢

Society Hill Area. This historic area, the name of which is derived from the Free Society of Traders, was created by William Penn as the city's original land company and has undergone extensive renewal of its historic buildings. Area bounded approx by Front, Walnut, 7th and Lombard sts. In this area are

Athenaeum of Philadelphia. Landmark example of Italian Renaissance architecture (1845-1847); restored building has American neoclassical-style decorative arts, paintings, sculpture; research library; furniture and art from the collection of Joseph Bonaparte, King of Spain and older brother of Napoleon; changing exhibits of architectural drawings, photos, and rare books. Tours by appt. (Mon-Fri; closed hols) 219 S 6th St. Phone 215/925-2688. **FREE**

Physick House. (1786) House of Dr. Philip Sung Physick, "father of American surgery," from 1815-1837. Restored Federal-style house with period furnishings; garden. (Thurs-Sun afternoons) 321 S 4th St. Phone 215/925-7866. ¢¢

Powel House. (1765) Georgian town house of Samuel Powel, last colonial mayor of Philadelphia and first mayor under the new republic. Period furnishings, silver and porcelain; garden. Tours (Thurs-Sun afternoons; closed hols). 244 S 3rd St. Phone 215/627-0364. ¢¢

Temple University. (1884) 33,000 students. Undergraduate, professional and research school. Walking tours of campus. Cecil B. Moore Ave and Broad St. Phone 215/204-7000.

University of Pennsylvania. (1740) 23,000 students. On campus are the restored Fisher Fine Arts Library (phone 215/898-8325), Annenberg Center for performing arts (phone 215/898-6791); University Museum of Archaeology and Anthropology and Institute of Contemporary Art, located at 36th and Sansom sts (Wed-Sun; phone 215/898-7108; fee). Chestnut to Pine sts and 32nd to 40th sts. Phone 215/898-5000. Also here is

University of Pennsylvania Museum of Archaeology and Anthropology. World-famous archaeological and ethnographic collections developed from the museum's own expeditions, gifts and purchases; features Chinese, Near Eastern, Greek, ancient Egyptian, African, Pacific, and North, Middle, and South American materials; library. Restaurant, shops. (Tues-Sun; closed hols, also Sun in summer)

Tomb of Unknown Soldier

33rd and Spruce sts. Phone 215/898-4000. ¢¢

US Mint. Produces coins of all denominations. Gallery affords visitors an elevated view of the coinage operations. Medal making may also be observed. Audiovisual, self-guided tours. Rittenhouse Room on the mezzanine contains historic coins, medals, and other exhibits. (July-Aug, daily; rest of yr, Mon-Fri; closed Jan 1, Thanksgiving, Dec 25) On Independence Mall at 5th and Arch sts. Phone 215/408-0114. **FREE**

Wagner Free Institute of Science. Victorian science museum with more than 50,000 specimens illustrating the various branches of the natural sciences. Dinosaur bones, fossils, reptiles, and rare species are all mounted in the Victorian style. Reference library and research archives. (Tues-Fri) Montgomery and 17th sts. Phone 215/763-6529. **FREE**

Walnut Street Theatre. (1809) America's oldest theater. The Walnut Mainstage offers musicals, classical and contemporary plays. Two studio theaters provide a forum for new and avant-garde works. 9th and Walnut sts. Phone 215/574-3550.

Washington Square. Walnut St from 6th St, where hundreds of Revolutionary War soldiers and victims of the yellow fever epidemic are buried. Life-size statue of Washington has

tomb of Revolutionary War's Unknown Soldier at its feet. Across the street is

Philadelphia Savings Fund Society Building. (1816) Site of oldest savings bank in US. Not open to public. Walnut and 8th sts.

Special Events

Mummer's Parade. An eight-hr spectacle along Broad St. Jan 1. Phone 215/336-3050.

PECO Energy Jazz Festival. Jazz concerts around the city. Phone 800/537-7676. Four days mid-Feb.

American Music Theater Festival. Repertory includes new opera, musical comedy, cabaret-style shows, revues and experimental works. Mainstage productions Mar-June. Phone 215/893-1570.

The Book and the Cook. Sample fine cuisine as world-famous cookbook authors team up with the city's most respected chefs to create culinary delights. Wine tastings, market tours, film festival. Phone 215/686-3662. Mar.

Philadelphia Flower Show. Philadelphia Convention Center. Sponsored by the Philadelphia Horticultural Society, it's the largest indoor flower show in America. Phone 215/988-8879. First wk Mar.

Philadelphia Open House. House and garden tours in different neighborhoods; distinguished selection of over 150 private homes, gardens, historic sites. Many tours include lunches, candlelight dinners or high teas. Phone 215/928-1188. Late Apr-mid-May.

Devon Horse Show. Approx 20 mi NW via US 30, at Horse Show Grounds, in Devon. One of America's leading equestrian events. More than 1,200 horses compete; country fair; antique carriage drive. Phone 610/964-0550. Nine days beginning Memorial Day wkend.

Mann Center for the Performing Arts. 52nd St and Parkside Ave, West Fairmount Park. Philadelphia Orchestra performs late June-July, Mon, Wed, and Thurs. Also popular music attractions. Phone 215/546-7900. June-Sept.

Elfreth's Alley Fete Days. Homes open to public, costumed guides, demonstrations of colonial crafts; food, entertainment. Second wkend June. Phone 215/574-0560.

Head House Open Air Craft Market. Pine and 2nd sts, in Society Hill area in Head House Sq. Crafts demonstrations, children's workshops. Sat and Sun, June-Aug.

CoreStates US Pro Cycling Championship. At 156 mi, it's the longest (and richest) single-day cycling event in the country. Mid-June.

Robin Hood Dell East. 33rd and Ridge sts, in Fairmount Park. Top stars in outdoor popular music concerts. Phone 215/685-9560. July-Aug.

Thanksgiving Day Parade. Giant floats; celebrities. Phone 215/878-9700.

Fairmount Park Historical Christmas Tours. Period decorations in 18th-century mansions. Phone 215/684-7922. Early Dec.

Army-Navy Football Game. John F. Kennedy Memorial Stadium or Veterans Stadium. First Sat Dec.

Horse racing. Flat racing at Philadelphia Park, Richlieu and Street rds in Bensalem. For schedule phone 215/639-9000.

Motels/Motor Lodges

★★ **BEST WESTERN CENTER CITY HOTEL.** 501 N 22nd St (19130).

215/568-8300; fax 215/557-0259; res 800/780-7234. www.bestwestern.com. 183 rms, 3 story. S $109-$119; D $119-$139; each addl $10; suites $150; under 18 free. Pet accepted, some restrictions. TV; cable (premium). Pool; lifeguard. Restaurant 6:30 am-10 pm. Bar 11-2 am. Ck-out noon. Meeting rms. Business servs avail. In-rm modem link. Valet serv. Gift shop. Exercise equipt. Cr cds: A, D, DS, MC, V.

★★ **BEST WESTERN HOTEL.** 11580 Roosevelt Blvd (19116). 215/464-9500; fax 215/464-8511. www.bestwestern.com. 100 rms, 2 story. S, D $70-$125; under 18 free. Crib free. TV; cable (premium). Pool; lifeguard. Playground. Complimentary continental bkfst. Bar from 5 pm. Ck-out 11 am. Coin lndry. Meeting rms. Business servs avail. Exercise equipt. Lawn games. Refrigerators. Many balconies. Picnic tables. Cr cds: A, C, D, DS, JCB, MC, V.

★ **COMFORT INN.** 100 N Christopher Columbus Blvd (19106). 215/627-7900; fax 215/238-0809; toll-free 800/228-5150. www.comfortinn.com. 185 rms, 10 story. S, D $99-$169; each addl $10; suites $159-$199; under 18 free; higher rates hols. Crib free. TV. Complimentary continental bkfst. Coffee in rms. Restaurant nearby. Bar 5 pm-2 am. Ck-out 11 am. Meeting rms. Business servs avail. In-rm modem link. Airport, RR station, bus depot transportation. Health club privileges. View of Delaware River. Cr cds: A, C, D, DS, ER, JCB, MC, V.

★★ **HOLIDAY INN EXPRESS.** 1305 Walnut St (19107). 215/735-9300; fax 215/732-2682; toll-free 800/465-4329. www.holiday-inn.com. 166 rms, 20 story. S, D $115-$145; each addl $10; under 19 free. Crib $10. Garage $15. TV; cable (premium). Pool. Complimentary continental bkfst. Ck-out 1 pm. Meeting rms. Business servs avail. In-rm modem link. Health club privileges. Cr cds: A, C, D, DS, JCB, MC, V.

★ **RODEWAY INN.** *1208 Walnut St (19107). 215/546-7000; fax 215/546-7573; toll-free 800/887-1776. www. rodeway.com/hotel/pa271.* 25 rms, 22 with shower only, 7 story, 6 suites. S, D $69-$189; each addl $10; suites $125. Crib free. Parking adj $9. TV; cable. Complimentary continental bkfst; afternoon refreshments. Restaurant nearby. Ck-out noon, ck-in 3 pm. Luggage handling. Business servs avail. In-rm modem link. Health club privileges. Built in 1890s; Early-American decor. Walking distance from Pennsylvania Convention Center. Cr cds: A, C, D, DS, MC, V.

⊠ 🔥

Hotels

★ ★ **ADAM'S MARK HOTEL.** *4000 City Line Monument Rd (19131). 215/581-5000; fax 215/581-5069; toll-free 800/444-2326. www.adamsmark. com.* 515 rms, 23 story. S, D $99-$224; each addl $25; suites $179-$925; under 18 free; wkend, wkly rates. Crib $15. TV. Indoor/outdoor pool; whirlpool, poolside serv. Restaurant (see also MARKER RESTAURANT & LOUNGE). Bars; entertainment. Ck-out noon. Convention facilities. Business center. In-rm modem link. Shopping arcade. Barber, beauty shop. Airport, RR station, bus depot transportation. Exercise equipt; sauna, steam rm. Refrigerators. Gift shop. Cr cds: A, C, D, DS, MC, V.

D ⊠ 🏋 ✈ ⊠ 🔥 SC 🏋

★ ★ **CLUB HOTEL BY DOUBLE-TREE.** *9461 Roosevelt Blvd (19114). 215/671-9600; fax 215/464-7759; toll-free 800/354-4332. www.doubletree hotels.com.* 188 rms, 6 story. S, D $89-$119; suites $175; under 17 free; wkend rates. Crib free. TV; cable. Indoor pool. Restaurant 6 am-10 pm. Bar 5-11 pm. Ck-out 11 am. Coin lndry. Meeting rms. Business center. In-rm modem link. Sundries. Gift shop. Exercise equipt. Some refrigerators; microwaves avail. Cr cds: A, C, D, DS, MC, V.

D ⊠ ⊠ 🏋 🔥 SC 🏋

★ ★ **CROWNE PLAZA.** *1800 Market St (19103). 215/561-7500; fax 215/561-4484. www.crowneplaza.com.* 445 rms, 25 story. S $149-$215; D $195-$225;

each addl $10; suites $475; under 19 free; wkend rates. Crib free. Pet accepted. Garage fee. TV; cable (premium). Pool. Restaurant 6-2 am. Bar from 11 am. Ck-out noon. Coin lndry. Convention facilities. In-rm modem link. Concierge. Gift shop. Airport transportation. Exercise equipt. Health club privileges. Microwaves avail. Cr cds: A, C, D, DS, ER, JCB, MC, V.

D 🔦 ⊠ 🏋 ⊠ 🔥 SC

★ ★ **DOUBLETREE GUEST SUITES.** *640 W Germantown Pike, Plymouth Meeting (19462). 610/834-8300; fax 610/879-4242. www.doubletree.com.* 252 suites, 7 story. S, D $230-$250; family, wkend rates. Crib $10. TV; cable (premium), VCR avail. Indoor pool; whirlpool, wading pool, poolside serv. Restaurant 6:30 am-10 pm. Bar. Ck-out noon. Coin lndry. Meeting rms. Business servs avail. In-rm modem link. Gift shop. Airport, RR station, bus depot transportation. Exercise equipt; sauna. Bathrm phones, refrigerators, minibars; microwaves. Some private patios, balconies. Cr cds: A, C, D, DS, ER, JCB, MC, V.

D ⊠ 🏋 ⊠ 🔥 🔥

★ ★ **DOUBLETREE HOTEL.** *Broad and Locust sts (19107). 215/893-1600; fax 215/893-1663; toll-free 800/222-8733. www.doubletree.com.* 434 rms, 26 story. S $160-$195; D $185-$209; each addl $10; suites $239-$339; under 18 free; wkend rates; higher rates New Year's hols. Crib free. Garage $15, valet $19. TV; cable (premium), VCR avail. Indoor pool; whirlpool. Coffee in rms. Restaurant 6:30 am-11 pm; Fri, Sat to midnight. Bar to 1 am. Ck-out noon. Convention facilities. Business servs avail. In-rm modem link. Concierge. Gift shop. Airport transportation. Exercise equipt; sauna, steam rm. Health club privileges. Luxury level. Cr cds: A, C, D, DS, MC, V.

D ⊠ 🏋 ⊠ 🔥 SC

★ ★ ★ ★ **FOUR SEASONS HOTEL PHILADELPHIA.** *1 Logan Sq (19103). 215/963-1500; fax 215/963-9506; toll-free 800/332-3442. www.fourseasons. com.* Surrounded by museums in the city's cultural center, this 365-room hotel is steps from the financial, retail, and commercial districts and is filled with beautiful reproductions of

Federal-period furnishings. Views from the public spaces and many rooms include Calder's Swann Fountain, the Museum of Art, and the copper-domed cathedral. Dine in the magnificent Fountain Restaurant or outdoors at the Courtyard cafe. 365 rms, 8 story. S $310-$420; D $330-$420; each addl $30; suites $400-$2,600; under 18 free; wkend rates. Pet accepted. Garage $24. TV; cable (premium), VCR avail. Indoor pool; whirlpool, poolside serv, lifeguard. Restaurants 6:30-1 am; Sat, Sun from 7 am (see FOUNTAIN RESTAURANT and SWANN CAFE; and see SWANN LOUNGE, Unrated Dining). Rm serv 24 hrs. Bar 11-2 am; pianist. Ck-out 1 pm. Convention facilities. Business center. In-rm modem link. Concierge. Exercise rm; sauna. Massage. Minibars; microwaves avail. Some balconies. Cr cds: A, C, D, DS, ER, JCB, MC, V.

⊠ 🏊 🏃 ⊠ 🔥 🏃

★★★ **HILTON AIRPORT.** *4509 Island Ave (19153). 215/365-4150; fax 215/365-6382; res 800/445-8667. www.hilton.com.* 330 rms, 9 story. S, D $109-$149; suites $325; studio rms $150; under 18 free; wkend rates. Crib free. Pet accepted, some restrictions. TV; cable (premium). Indoor pool; whirlpool. Restaurant 6 am-11 pm. Rm serv 24 hrs. Bar 11-2 am. Ck-out noon. Meeting rms. Business center. In-rm modem link. Gift shop. Free airport transportation. Exercise equipt. Luxury level. Cr cds: A, C, D, DS, MC, V.

D ⊠ 🏃 ✈ ⊠ 🔥 🏃 ⌂

★★ **HOLIDAY INN.** *400 Arch St (19106). 215/923-8660; fax 215/923-4633; res 800/843-2355. www.holiday-inn.com.* 364 rms, 8 story. S, D $99-$169; suites $199-$250; under 12 free; wkend rates. Garage $10. Crib free. TV; cable (premium). Rooftop pool. Restaurant 6:30 am-10 pm. Bar 11-1 am, Sun from noon. Ck-out 11 am. Coin lndry. Meeting rms. Business center. Sundries. Health club privileges. Cr cds: A, C, D, DS, JCB, MC, V.

D ⊠ ⊠ 🔥 **SC** 🏃

★★★ **HYATT REGENCY PHILADELPHIA AT PENN'S LANDING.** *200 S Columbus Blvd (19106). 215/928-1234. www.hyatt.com.* 350 rms, 22 story. S, D $210-$235; under

17 free. Crib avail. TV; cable (premium). Indoor pool; whirlpool. Restaurant 6:30 am-10 pm. Bar to midnight. Ck-out noon, ck-in 3 pm. Meeting rms. Business center. In-rm modem link. Concierge. Exercise equipt. Minibars; many refrigerators in suites. Cr cds: A, D, DS, MC, V.

⊠ 🏃 🐾 🏃 ⊠

★★★ **KORMAN COMMUNITIES BUTTONWOOD SQUARE.** *2001 Hamilton St (19130). 215/569-7000; fax 215/496-0138; res 888/456-7626. www.kormancommunities.com.* 150 suites, 25 story. S $109-$169, D $139-$189; under 18 free; wkend rates. Crib free. TV; cable (premium). Pool; whirlpool, poolside serv, lifeguard. Complimentary coffee. Restaurant 6:30-2 am. Bar. Ck-out 11 am. Convention facilities. Business servs avail. In-rm modem link. Gift shop. Barber, beauty shop. Free garage parking. Exercise equipt. Microwaves. Landscaped Japanese sculpture garden. In museum district. Cr cds: A, D, MC, V.

D ⊠ 🏃 ⊠ 🐾 **SC**

★★★ **LATHAM HOTEL.** *135 S 17th St (19103). 215/563-7474; fax 215/568-0110; toll-free 800/LATHAM1. www.lathamhotel.com.* 139 rms, 14 story. S, D $195-$245; each addl $10; suites $219-$329; under 18 free; wkend, hol rates. Crib free. Valet parking $14. TV; cable (premium), VCR avail (movies). Pool privileges. Restaurant 6:30 am-10:30 pm. Bar 11:30-2 am. Ck-out noon. Meeting rms. Business center. In-rm modem link. Concierge. Exercise equipt. Health club privileges. Many minibars. European ambience in intimate, boutique-style hotel. Cr cds: A, C, D, DS, MC, V.

D 🏃 ⊠ 🐾 **SC** 🏃

★★★ **LOEWS PHILADELPHIA HOTEL.** *1200 Market St (19107). 215/627-1200; fax 215/231-7312; toll-free 800/23-LOEWS. www.loewshotels. com.* 583 rms, 32 story. S, D $250-$325; under 17 free; suites $275-$1,500. Crib avail. TV; cable (premium). Indoor pool; whirlpool. Restaurant 6:30 am-10 pm. Bar to midnight. Ck-out noon, ck-in 3 pm. Meeting rms. Business center. In-rm modem link. Concierge. Exercise rm;

sauna. Spa. Minibars; many refrigerators in suites. Cr cds: A, D, DS, MC, V.

★ ★ ★ MARRIOTT PHILADELPHIA.

1201 Market St (19107). 215/625-2900; fax 215/625-6000; toll-free 800/228-9290. www.marriott.com. 1,408 rms, 20 story, 76 suites. S $189-$230; D $210-$309; suites $450-$5,000; under 12 free; wkend, hol rates. Valet parking $23. TV; cable (premium), VCR avail. Indoor pool; wading pool, whirlpool. Restaurants 6:30-1:30 am. Bar 11-2 am. Ck-out noon. Coin lndry. Convention facilities. Business center. In-rm modem link. Concierge. Shopping arcade. Beauty shop. Exercise equipt; sauna. Refrigerator in suites; microwaves avail. Connected to shopping mall. Luxury level. Cr cds: A, C, D, DS, JCB, MC, V.

★ ★ ★ MARRIOTT PHILADELPHIA AIRPORT.

One Arrivals Rd (19153). 215/492-9000; fax 215/492-6799. www.marriott.com. 419 rms, 15 story. S, D $195-$250; under 17 free. Crib avail. TV; cable (premium). Indoor pool; whirlpool. Restaurant 6:30 am-10 pm. Bar to midnight. Ck-out noon, ck-in 3 pm. Meeting rms. Business center. In-rm modem link. Concierge. Exercise equipt. Cr cds: A, D, DS, JCB, MC, V

★ ★ ★ MARRIOTT PHILADELPHIA WEST.

111 Crawford Ave, West Conshohocken (19428). 610/941-5600; fax 610/941-4425; toll-free 800/237-3639. www.marriott.com. 286 rms, 17 story. S $179-$189; D $199-$209; each addl $30; suites $375; wkend, hol rates. Crib free. TV; cable (premium), VCR avail. Indoor pool; whirlpool, poolside serv, lifeguard. Restaurant 6 am-11 pm. Bar. Ck-out noon. Convention facilities. Business servs avail. In-rm modem link. Concierge. Gift shop. Airport, RR station transportation. Exercise rm; sauna. Microwaves avail. 1 blk from Schuylkill River. Atrium deck. Luxury level. Cr cds: A, C, D, DS, MC, V.

★ ★ ★ OMNI HOTEL AT INDEPENDENCE PARK.

4th and Chestnut sts (19106). 215/925-0000; fax 215/925-1263. www.omnihotels.com. 150 rms, 14 story. S $250; D $270; each addl $20; suites from $340; under 18 free; wkend rates. Garage, valet parking (fees). TV; cable (premium), VCR avail. Indoor pool; whirlpool. Restaurant (see also AZALEA). Rm serv 24 hrs. Bar 3-11 pm; entertainment Tues-Sat. Ck-out 11 am. Meeting rms Business center. In-rm modem link. Concierge. Gift shop. Exercise equipt, sauna. Bathrm phones, minibars; microwaves avail. Cr cds: A, C, D, DS, ER, JCB, MC, V.

★ ★ ★ PARK HYATT PHILADELPHIA AT THE BELLEVUE.

Broad and Walnut sts (19102). 215/893-1234; fax 215/732-8518; toll-free 800/228-9000. www.hyatt.com. 172 rms, 5 story. S $225-$325; D $250-$350; suites $350-$1,800; under 18 free; special plans. Crib free. Garage $14, valet $21. TV; cable (premium), VCR. Indoor pool privileges; whirlpool. Sauna. Restaurants 7 am-11 pm (see also THE FOUNDERS). Rm serv 24 hrs. Bar 11-1 am. Ck-out 11 am. Business center. In-rm modem link. Concierge. Shopping arcade. Barber, beauty shop. Health club privileges. Massage. Bathrm phones, minibars. Conservatory atrium. Cr cds: A, C, D, DS, MC, V.

★ ★ ★ PENN'S VIEW HOTEL.

14 N Front St (19106). 215/922-7600; fax 215/922-7642; toll-free 800/331-7634. www.pennsviewhotel.com. 52 rms, 5 story. S, D $165-$250; under 12 free; wkend rates. Crib free. TV; cable. Complimentary continental bkfst. Dining rm (see also RISTORANTE PANORAMA). Ck-out noon, ck-in 3 pm. Meeting rms. Business servs avail. In-rm modem link. Concierge. Airport, RR station, bus depot transportation. Health club privileges. Some in-rm whirlpools, fireplaces. Overlooks Delaware River. Built 1828; Old World elegance. Cr cds: A, C, D, ER, JCB, MC, V.

★ ★ RADISSON HOTEL.

US 1 at Old Lincoln Hwy, Trevose (19053). 215/638-8300; fax 215/638-4377; res 800/333-3333. www.radisson.com. 282 rms, 6 story. S, D $109-$159; suites $250; under 18 free; family rates. TV; cable.

Complimentary coffee in rms. Restaurant 6:30 am-10 pm; Sun 7 am-noon, 5-10 pm. Bar noon-2 am. Ck-out noon. Convention facilities. Business servs avail. In-rm modem link. Concierge. Gift shop. Barber, beauty shop. Coin lndry. Exercise equipt. Indoor/outdoor pool; poolside serv, lifeguard. Some refrigerators. Atrium. Cr cds: A, D, DS, MC, V.

⬛ 🏊 🅇 ⬛ 🔥

★★★ **RADISSON PLAZA - WAR-WICK HOTEL.** 1701 Locust St (19103). 215/735-6000; fax 215/790-7766; toll-free 800/333-3333. www.radisson.com. 545 rms, 21 story, 20 kits. S $165-$185; D $195-$200; each addl $15; suites $185-$390; studio rms $185; apt $195; under 12 free; wkend rates. Crib free. Garage (fee). TV; cable (premium), VCR avail. Restaurant 6:30 am-midnight. Bar 11-2 am. Ck-out noon. Meeting rms. Business servs avail. In-rm modem link. Concierge. Barber, beauty shop. Health club privileges. Cr cds: A, C, D, DS, JCB, MC, V.

⬛ ⬛ 🔥 SC

★★★ **RADNOR HOTEL.** 591 E Lancaster Ave, St. Davids (19087). 610/688-5800; fax 610/341-3299; toll-free 800/537-3000. www.radnorhotel.com. 171 rms, 4 story. S $139; D $149; each addl $10; suites $199; under 16 free. Crib free. TV; cable (premium), VCR avail. Pool; wading pool, lifeguard. Restaurant 6:30 am. Bar 11-2 am; entertainment wkends. Ck-out noon. Meeting rms. Business center. In-rm modem link. Airport transportation. Exercise equipt. Health club privileges. Game rm. Microwaves avail. Luxury level. Cr cds: A, C, D, DS, ER, JCB, MC, V.

⬛ 🏊 🅇 ⬛ 🔥 SC 🔥

★★★ **RENAISSANCE PHILADEL-PHIA AIRPORT.** 500 Stevens Dr (19113). 610/521-5900; fax 610/521-4362. www.renaissancehotels.com. 351 rms, 12 story. S, D $129-$215; suites $175; under 18 free; wkend packages. Crib free. TV; cable. Indoor pool; whirlpool, poolside serv. Restaurant 6:30 am-2 pm, 5-11 pm. Bars 2 pm-midnight. Ck-out noon. Meeting rms. Business center. In-rm modem link. Gift shop. Free airport transportation. Exercise equipt. Game rm.

Microwaves avail. Atrium. Cr cds: A, C, D, DS, ER, JCB, MC, V.

⬛ 🏊 🅇 ✈ ⬛ 🔥 🔥

★★★★ **THE RITTENHOUSE HOTEL.** 210 W Rittenhouse Sq (19103). 215/546-9000; fax 215/732-3364; toll-free 800/635-1042. www.rittenhousehotel.com. A striking bronze statue beckons visitors into the brick-entry courtyard of this regal hotel. Located at the city's center in a charming residential neighborhood steps from business and shopping districts, the decor of this property carries a comfortable, residential feel. Accommodations are spacious with lush mahogany and fine fabric furnishings and floor-to-ceiling windows overlooking Rittenhouse Square and the city lights. 198 rms, 9 story. S, D $240-$425; suites $500-$2,000; wkend rates. Crib free. Pet accepted. Garage; valet parking $25. TV; cable (premium), VCR (movies avail). Indoor pool; poolside serv. Restaurants. Rm serv 24 hrs. Bar; entertainment. Ck-out 1 pm. Meeting rms. Business center. In-rm modem link. Concierge. Barber, beauty shop. Tennis privileges. Golf privileges. Exercise rm; sauna, steam rm. Massage. Bathrm phones, minibars; microwaves avail. Cr cds: A, C, D, MC, V.

⬛ 🏌 🅇 🏌 🏊 🅇 ⬛ 🔥 🔥

★★★★ **THE RITZ-CARLTON, PHILADELPHIA.** Ten Avenue of the Arts (19102). 215/735-7700; fax 215/568-0942. www.ritzcarlton.com. Housed in two beautifully restored neoclassical turn-of-the-century structures, this hotel features a breathtaking lobby with large white marble columns, a beautiful oculus, a lounge, bar, and restaurant, and live music all day. Elegant accommodations are in an adjacent 30-story tower with views of downtown Philadelphia, and feature feather beds, crisp Frette linens, marble baths, and 24-hour in-room dining. Guests may choose to indulge in the many spa services offered, including massages, body wraps, and body scrubs, or reserve a butler-drawn bath with an accompanying food and beverage presentation. 331 rms, 31 story. S, D $250-$375; suites $450-$750. Crib avail. TV; cable (premium). Restaurant 6:30 am-10 pm. Bar to 2 am. Ck-out noon, ck-in 3 pm. Meeting rms. Business center. In-rm modem link. Concierge. Exercise equipt. Minibars; many refrigerators in suites. Cr cds: A, D, DS, MC, V.

★★★ **SHERATON PHILADELPHIA AIRPORT HOTEL.** *4101 Island Ave (19079). 215/492-0400; fax 215/365-6035. www.fourpoints.com.* 177 rms, 5 story. S, D $169; each addl $20; under 18 free. Crib free. TV; cable (premium), VCR avail. Pool. Coffee in rms. Restaurant 6 am-2 pm, 5 pm-midnight; Sat to noon. Bar 1 pm-midnight. Ck-out noon. Coin lndry. Meeting rms. Business servs avail. Valet serv. Free airport transportation. Health club privileges. Refrigerators, microwaves avail. Cr cds: A, C, D, DS, MC, V.

★★★ **SHERATON RITTENHOUSE SQUARE.** *227 S 18th St (19103). 215/546-9400; fax 215/875-9457; toll-free 800/325-3535. www.sheratonrittenhouse.com.* 193 rms, 16 story, 4 suites. Mar-June, Sep-Nov: S, D $279; suites $450-$575; under 17 free; lower rates rest of yr. Crib avail. Valet parking avail. TV; cable (premium), VCR avail. Complimentary continental bkfst, coffee in rms. Restaurant 6:30 am-1 pm. Rm serv 24 hrs. Bar. Ck-out noon, ck-in 3 pm. Meeting rms. Business center. Bellhops. Valet serv, coin lndry. Gift shop. Free airport transportation. Exercise equipt. Golf, 18 holes. Tennis. Supervised children's activities. Cr cds: A, C, D, DS, MC, V.

★★★ **SHERATON SOCIETY HILL HOTEL.** *One Dock St (19106). 215/238-6000; fax 215/238-6652; res 888/345-7333. www.sheraton.com.* 365 units, 4 story. S, D $119-$345; suites $450-$3,000; under 17 free; wkend rates. Crib free. Covered parking (fee). TV; cable (premium), VCR avail. Indoor pool; whirlpool, wading pool, poolside serv. Coffee in rms. Restaurants 6:30 am-2 pm, 5-10 pm. Rm serv 24 hrs. Bar noon-2 am. Ck-out noon. Convention facilities. Business servs avail. In-rm modem link. Concierge. Shopping arcade. Exercise rm; sauna. Massage. Mini-bars; some refrigerators. Cr cds: A, C, D, DS, ER, JCB, MC, V.

★★★ **SHERATON UNIVERSITY CITY HOTEL.** *36th and Chestnut sts (19104). 215/387-8000. www.sheraton. com.* 374 rms, 15 story. S, D $139-$165; under 17 free. Crib avail. TV; cable (premium). Pool; whirlpool. Restaurant 6:30 am-10 pm. Bar to midnight. Ck-out noon, ck-in 3 pm. Meeting rms. Business center. In-rm modem link. Concierge. Exercise equipt. Minibars; many refrigerators in suites. Cr cds: A, D, DS, MC, V.

★★★ **SOFITEL.** *120 S 17th St (19103). 215/569-8300; fax 215/569-1462; toll-free 800/SOFITEL. www. sofitel.com.* 306 rms, 14 story. S, D $225-$375; under 17 free. Crib avail. Pet accepted. TV; cable (premium). Pool; whirlpool. Restaurant 6:30 am-10 pm. Bar to midnight. Ck-out noon, ck-in 3 pm. Meeting rms. Business center. In-rm modem link. Concierge. Exercise equipt. Minibars; many refrigerators in suites. Cr cds: A, D, DS, ER, JCB, MC, V.

★★★ **THE WESTIN PHILADEL-PHIA.** *99 S 17th St (19103). 215/563-1600; fax 215/567-2822; toll-free 800/937-8461. www.westin.com.* 290 rms, 15 story, 16 suites. S $350; D $370; suites $480; each addl $20; under 12 free. Crib avail. Valet parking avail. TV; cable (premium). Complimentary coffee in rms. Restaurant 6:30 am-10 pm. Rm serv 24 hrs. Bar. Ck-out noon, ck-in 3 pm. Conference center. Business center. Bellhops. Concierge serv. Valet serv. Gift shop. Health club privileges. Cr cds: A, C, D, DS, ER, JCB, MC, V.

★★ **WYNDHAM FRANKLIN PLAZA HOTEL.** *2 Franklin Plaza (19103). 215/448-2000; fax 215/448-2864; res 800/822-4200. www.wyndham.com.* 758 rms, 26 story. S, D $189-$209; each addl $20; suites $400-$1,300; under 18 free; wkend rates. Crib free. Garage $17. TV; cable (premium). Indoor pool; whirlpool, poolside serv. Complimentary coffee in rms. Restaurant 6 am-11 pm. Bars 11-1 am. Ck-out noon. Convention facilities.

Business center. In-rm modem link. Barber, beauty shop. Tennis. Exercise rm; sauna, steam rm. Massage. Refrigerators avail. Cr cds: A, C, D, DS, ER, MC, V.

D ⊷ 🏋 ⊷ 🔥 🏃 🖨

B&Bs/Small Inns

★ **LA RESERVE CENTER CITY BED & BREAKFAST.** *1804 Pine St (19103). 215/735-1137; fax 215/735-0582; toll-free 800/354-8401. www.centercity bed.com.* 8 rms, 5 share bath, 4 story, 3 suites. No rm phones. S, D $60-$100; suites $95. Crib avail. TV in common rm; cable (premium), VCR avail (movies). Complimentary full bkfst. Restaurant nearby. Ck-out, ck-in times vary. Business servs avail. Luggage handling. Concierge serv. Street parking. Many fireplaces; microwaves avail. Built in 1868. Victorian decor; antiques. Totally non-smoking. Cr cds: A, MC, V.

⊷ 🦽

★★ **TEN-ELEVEN CLINTON.** *1011 Clinton St (19107). 215/923-8144; fax 215/923-5757.* 8 rms, 3 story, 7 kit. units. No elvtrs. S, D, kit. units $125-$175; each addl $15; wkends (2-day min). Crib free. Pet accepted, some restrictions. TV; cable, VCR (movies). Complimentary continental bkfst, coffee in rms. Restaurant nearby. Ck-out noon, ck-in 3 pm. Business servs avail. In-rm modem link. Luggage handling. Concierge serv. Coin lndry. Street parking. Health club privileges. Some fireplaces, balconies. Built in 1836; enclosed courtyard. Totally non-smoking. Cr cds: A, MC, V.

🔥 ⊷ 🦽 **SC**

★★ **THOMAS BOND HOUSE.** *129 S 2nd St (19106). 215/923-8523; fax 215/923-8504; toll-free 800/845-2663. www.bnbinns.com.* 12 rms, 4 story, 2 suites. No elvtr. S, D $95-$175; each addl $15; suites $175. TV. Complimentary continental bkfst; afternoon refreshments. Restaurants nearby. Ck-out noon, ck-in 3-9 pm. Business servs avail. Airport transportation. Health club privileges. Library/sitting rm; antiques. Restored guest house (1769) built by Dr. Thomas Bond, founder of the country's first public

hospital. Individually decorated rms. Cr cds: A, D, DS, MC, V.

⊷ 🦽 **SC**

Restaurants

★★ **ARROYO GRILLE.** *1 Leverington Ave, Manayunk (19127). 215/487-1400. www.arroyogrille.com.* Hrs: 11-2 am; Sun brunch to 3 pm. Closed Thanksgiving. Res accepted. Southwestern menu. Bar. A la carte entrees: lunch $7-$13, dinner $15-$21. Sun brunch $17.95. Child's menu. Specializes in smokehouse barbecue, margaritas. Own baking, pasta. Musicians Wed-Sun. Parking. Outdoor dining. Southwestern decor with woodburning fireplace; two-level dining area. Cr cds: A, DS, MC, V.

D

★★★ **AZALEA.** *4th and Chestnut (19106). 215/931-4270.* Hrs: 6:30-10:30 am, 11:30 am-2 pm, 5:30-9 pm; Fri to 9:30 pm; Sat 7-11 am, 5:30-10 pm; Sun 7-9:30 am, 10 am-2 pm. Res accepted. Bar. Wine list. A la carte entrees: bkfst $5.50-$15, lunch $7-$30, dinner $21.50-$34. Sun brunch $23.95. Specialties: Norwegian salmon, duck. Valet parking. Cr cds: A, D, DS, MC, V.

D

★ **BERLENGAS.** *4926 N 5th St (19120). 215/324-3240.* Hrs: noon-midnight. Closed Wed. Res required Fri-Sun dinner. Portuguese menu. Bar 10 am-midnight. A la carte entrees: lunch, dinner $10-$25. Specializes in seafood. Jacket. Intimate atmosphere. Cr cds: MC, V.

⊷

★★★ **BLUE ANGEL.** *706 Chestnut St (19106). 215/925-6889. www.citysearch. com.* Menu changes seasonally. Hrs: 11:30 am-3 pm, 5-11 pm; Fri, Sat to midnight; Sun to 10 pm. Closed hols. Res accepted. Wine, beer. Lunch $9-$17; dinner $14-$27. Brunch $8-$17. Entertainment. Cr cds: A, D, MC, V.

D ⊷

★★ **BOOKBINDER'S 15TH STREET SEAFOOD HOUSE.** *215 S 15th St (19102). 215/545-1137.* Hrs: 11:30 am-10 pm; Sat 4-11 pm; Sun 4-9 pm; Mon 4:30-10 pm. Closed Thanksgiving, Dec 25. Res accepted. Bar. Lunch $10-$60, dinner $20-$60.

Child's menu. Specializes in snapper turtle soup, baked crab. Own pastries. Family-owned since 1893. Cr cds: A, C, D, DS, MC, V.

D ⊟

★★★★ **BRASSERIE PERRIER.** *1619 Walnut St (19102). 215/568-3000. www.brasserieperrier.com.* Offering modern French cuisine with Italian and Asian influences, this brasserie is much more relaxed than its sister property Le Bec Fin. Plush banquettes with silver leaf ceilings and light cherry wood are enhanced with lighting to make this a warm and inviting spot to dine. Haitian, French, Asian menu. Hrs: 11:30 am-2:30 pm, 5:30-11 pm. Closed hols. Res required. Bar to 1 am. Wine cellar. Dinner $21-$34. Complete meal: 3-course lunch $26. Valet parking. Totally nonsmoking. Cr cds: A, D, DS, MC, V.

D ⊟

★★ **BRIDGET FOY'S SOUTH STREET GRILL.** *200 South St (19147). 215/922-1813. www.bridgetfoys.com.* Hrs: 11:30 am-midnight; Fri, Sat to 1 am. Closed Thanksgiving, Dec 25. Res accepted. Bar to 2 am. A la carte entrees: lunch $10-$12.95, dinner $12-$20. Specializes in grilled fish, meat. Outdoor dining. Cr cds: A, D, DS, MC, V.

⊟

★★★ **BUDDAKAN.** *325 Chestnut St (19106). 215/574-9440. www. buddakan.com.* Specializes in aged beef, sesame-crusted tuna, angry lobster. Hrs: 11:30 am-2 pm, 5-11 pm; Fri, Sat to midnight. Res required. Wine, beer. Lunch $14-$18; dinner $15-$28. Jacket. Cr cds: A, C, D, MC, V.

D ⊟

★★★ **CIRCA.** *1518 Walnut St (19102). 215/545-6800. www.circa restaurant.com.* Hrs: 11:30 am-2:30 pm, 5-10 pm; Thurs, Sat to 11 pm; Mon from 5 pm; Sun 4:30-9 pm. Closed Jan 1, Dec 25. Res accepted. Bar. Wine list. Lunch $7-$13, dinner $16-$29. Menu changes seasonally. Valet parking. Former bank lobby; cathedral ceilings. Seating in authentic bank vault. Cr cds: A, D, MC, V.

D ⊟

★★ **CITY TAVERN.** *138 S 2nd St (19106). 215/413-1443. www.city tavern.com.* Hrs: 11:30 am-9 pm; Fri, Sat to 10 pm. Res accepted. Bar. Lunch $9.95-$14.95, dinner $17.95-$24.95. Child's menu. Specializes in fresh fish, poultry, meats. Entertainment Sat. Outdoor dining (in season). Historical colonial tavern (1773). Cr cds: A, D, DS, MC, V.

★★ **COYOTE CROSSING.** *800 Spring Mill Ave, Conshohocken (19428). 610/825-3000. www.coyotecrossing.com.* Hrs: 11:30 am-2:30 pm, 5-9:30 pm; Fri, Sat to 10:30 pm; Sun to 9:30 pm. Closed Jan 1, July 4, Dec 25. Southwestern, Mexican menu. Bar. A la carte entrees: lunch $6.75-$12 dinner $11.95-$19. Specialties: homemade stuffed crêpes, filet mignon, enchiladas. Own baking. Outdoor dining. Modern Southwestern decor. Cr cds: A, MC, V.

D ⊟

★★ **CUVEE NOTREDAME.** *1701 Green St (19130). 215/765-2777. www.cuveenotredame.com.* Hrs: 11:30-2 am; Sun brunch 11:30 am-2:30 pm. Closed Thanksgiving, Dec 25. Res accepted. Belgian menu. Bar. A la carte entrees: lunch $5-$10, dinner $16-$22. Sun brunch $15. Child's menu. Specializes in mussels, duck. Outdoor dining. Belgian atmosphere. Cr cds: A, D, DS, MC, V.

D ⊟

★★ **DARK HORSE.** *Head House Sq (19147). 215/928-9307. www.dickens inn.com.* Hrs: 11:30 am-3 pm, 5-10 pm; Sat to 10:30 pm; Sun 4:30-9 pm; Sun brunch 11 am-2:30 pm. Closed Mon; Jan 1, Dec 25. Res accepted. Continental menu. Bar 11:30-2 am; Mon from 5 pm. A la carte entrees: lunch $8-$12, dinner $17-$20. Sun brunch $8-$12. Child's menu. Specializes in fish and chips. In historic Harper House (1788); Victorian decor; artwork imported from England. Cr cds: A, C, D, DS, MC, V.

D ⊟

★★★ **DEUX CHEMINEES.** *1221 Locust St (19107). 215/790-0200. www.deuxchem.com.* Hrs: 5:30-8:30 pm; Sat to 9 pm. Closed Sun, Mon; hols. Res accepted. French menu. Serv bar. Wine cellar. Prix fixe: dinner $85. Specialties: rack of lamb, crab soup. Menu changes daily. Own baking. Chef-owned. Totally non-smoking. Cr cds: A, D, MC, V.

★ **DIMITRI'S.** *795 S 3rd St (19147). 215/625-0556.* Hrs: 5:30-11 pm; Sun 5-10 pm. Closed Easter, Thanksgiving, Dec 24, 25. Mediterranean menu. Setups. A la carte entrees: $13.50-$17.50. Specializes in seafood, lamb. Cr cds: A, D, MC, V.

★★ **DINARDO'S.** *312 Race St (19106). 215/925-5115. www.dinardos.com.* Hrs: 11 am-10 pm; Fri, Sat to 11 pm; Sun 3-9 pm. Closed Easter, Thanksgiving, Dec 25. Bar. Lunch $7-$10, dinner $15-$25. Child's menu. Specializes in seafood. Historic bldg (1740). Cr cds: A, C, D, MC, V.

D ⊒

★★ **FELICIA'S.** *1148 S 11th St (19147). 215/755-9656.* Hrs: 11:30 am-10:30 pm. Closed Mon; most major hols. Res accepted; required Fri-Sun. Italian menu. Bar. Lunch $20, dinner $36. Specialties: ricotta gnocci, veal chop. Own desserts. Valet parking. Cr cds: A, D, DS, MC, V.

D ⊒

★★ **FORK.** *306 Market St (19106). 215/625-9425. www.forkrestaurant. com.* Hrs: 11:30 am-2:30 pm, 5:30-10:30 pm; Fri, Sat to 11:30 pm. Sat 5:30-11:30 pm; Sun 11 am-2:30 pm. Closed hols. Res accepted. Contemporary American menu. Bar 11:30-2 am. A la carte entrees: lunch $7-$12, dinner $16-$22. Sun brunch $7-$12. Child's menu. Specialties: Greek marinated lamb chops, Chilean sea bass with dill pinenut crust. Street parking. Outdoor dining. Modern American bistro atmosphere. Cr cds: A, D, DS, MC, V.

D ⊒

★★★ **THE FOUNDERS.** *Broad and Walnut sts (19102). 215/790-2814. www.hyatt.com.* Hrs: 6:30 am-10:30 pm; Sun, Mon 6:30 am-2:30 pm; Sun brunch 10:30 am-2 pm. Res accepted. French menu. Bar 11-2 am. Wine cellar. Complete meals: bkfst $9.50-$12.50, dinner $45-$70. A la carte entrees: lunch $9.50-$16.50, dinner $24-$36. Sat, Sun brunch $34.50. Specialties: whole fish in salt crust, citrus pernot coulis, pistachio-crusted pork loin. Entertainment. Valet parking. Rotunda with sweeping views of city. Elegant turn-of-the-century decor. Jacket (dinner). Cr cds: A, D, DS, MC, V.

D

★★★★ **FOUNTAIN RESTAURANT.** *1 Logan Sq (19103). 215/963-1500. www.fourseasons.com.* This silky-beige, wood-paneled dining room is luxuriously refined and filled with fresh flowers and unique touches such as the elegant, antique service plates. The menu items, which change daily, highlight the freshest local ingredients of the season such as pan-seared duck breast with pumpkin and duck rillette and cider vinegar sauce. Visit for the outstanding Sunday brunch. Continental menu with French Provençal influence. Own baking. Hrs: 6:30 am-2:30 pm, 6-10:30 pm; Sun brunch 11 am-2:30 pm. Res accepted. Bar to 2 am. Wine cellar. A la carte entrees: bkfst $12-$20, lunch $22-$35, dinner $32-$45. Prix fixe: 4-course dinner $110. Sun brunch $36-$45. Child's menu. Entertainment. Valet parking. Jacket (dinner). Cr cds: A, D, DS, MC, V.

D

★★ **ITALIAN BISTRO.** *211 S Broad St (19107). 215/731-0700. www.italian bistro.com.* Hrs: 11 am-11 pm; wkends 12:30 pm-midnight. Closed Thanksgiving, Dec 25. Res accepted. Bar. Complete meals: lunch $8-$12, dinner $8-$18. Child's menu. Specializes in northern Italian dishes, brick oven pizza. Own pasta, desserts. Cr cds: A, D, DS, MC, V.

D ⊒

★★★★ **JAKE'S RESTAURANT.** *4365 Main St, Manayunk (19127). 215/483-0444. www.jakes-restaurant. com.* Offering a trendy, eclectic menu for over a decade, owner/chef Bruce Cooper still draws followers to his stylishly hip space. Sink into plush banquettes and feast on an ingenious blend of comfort food and fusion flavors beneath a metal-mesh ceiling and bright yellow walls. Followers boast that the sauteed veal tournedos and lobster-mashed potatoes with chive-butter sauce is a sublime dish. Continental menu. Specializes in crab cakes, veal, lobster. Hrs: 5:30-9:30 pm; Fri, Sat 5-10:30 pm; Sun 5-9 pm. Sun brunch 10:30 am-2:30 pm. Res accepted. Lunch $2.50-$16, dinner $22-$32. Totally nonsmoking. Cr cds: A, C, D, MC, V.

D

★★ **JOSEPH POON.** *1002 Arch St (19107). 215/928-9333. www.joseph poon.com.* Hrs: 11:30 am-10:30 pm; Fri to 11:30 pm; Sat 2:30-11:30 pm; Sun 2:30-10 pm. Closed Mon; Thanksgiving, Dec 25; also Chinese New Year's. Res accepted. Bar. A la carte entrees: lunch $10, dinner $20. Specializes in duck, lobster, fish. Parking. Cr cds: A, D, DS, MC, V.

D

★★★ **KANSAS CITY PRIME.** *4417 Main St, Manayunk (19127). 215/482-3700. www.kansascityprime.com.* Hrs: 5:30-11 pm; Fri, Sat to midnight; Sun 5-10 pm. Closed Thanksgiving. Res accepted. Bar to 2 am. A la carte entrees: dinner $27-$33. Specializes in aged prime beef, grilled seafood. Entertainment Tues-Sat. Contemporary decor. Cr cds: A, D, DS, MC, V.

D ⬛

★★ **KNAVE OF HEARTS.** *230 South St (19147). 215/922-3956.* Hrs: 5:30-10:30 pm; Fri, Sat to 11:30 pm; Sun 5-10 pm; Sun brunch 11 am-3:30 pm. Closed Dec 25. Res accepted. Bar. A la carte entrees: lunch $5-$9, dinner $13-$18. Sun brunch $12.50. Specialties: chicken coco loco, grilled tuna, filet mignon. Cr cds: A, MC, V.

⬛

★★★★ **LA FAMIGLIA.** *8 S Front St (19106). 215/922-2803. www.la-famiglia.com.* Occupying the shell of a Colonial tea warehouse since 1976, this Society Hill Italian restaurant is just one of the Sena-family operations. The classic menu includes items such as Vitello Papa Sena's, a combination of veal picante, involtino, and Capri. The dining room is elegant, filled with paintings and family collectibles, and the wine cellar is one of the finest in the country. Italian menu. Specializes in veal, fresh fish, pasta. Own pasta, desserts. Hrs: noon-2 pm, 5:30-9:30 pm; Sat 5:30-10 pm; Sun 5-9 pm. Closed Mon; hols; also last wk Aug. Res required. Bar. Wine cellar. A la carte entrees: lunch $22, dinner $18-$45. Built in 1878 in one of the city's first blocks of

buildings. Valet parking. Jacket. Cr cds: A, D, DS, MC, V.

★★★ **LE BAR LYONNAIS.** *1523 Walnut St (19102). 215/567-1000. www.lebecfin.com.* Hrs: 11:30 am-1:30 pm, 6-9 pm; Sat 6-9:30 pm. Closed Sun; hols. French bistro menu. Bar. A la carte entrees: lunch, dinner $12-$25. Prix fixe: lunch $40, dinner $120. Specialties: escargots au champagne, galette de crabe, thon au poivres. Valet parking (dinner). Elegant bistro atmosphere; original art. Cr cds: A, D, DS, MC, V.

★★★★★ **LE BEC-FIN.** *1523 Walnut St (19102). 215/567-1000. www.lebecfin.com.* World-renowned chef Georges Perrier has overseen this grand dame of classic French cuisine since 1970. Dining here is a bit of a step back in time with its rich, saucy dishes and extravagant, triple-tiered dessert cart tempting diners with 40 house-made specialties. Overall, it's an impressive dining experience in a beautiful Louis XVI-style space filled with period furnishings, fireplaces, and sparkling chandeliers. French menu. Specializes in seasonal dishes. Own baking. Sittings: 11:30 am, 1:30 pm, 6 pm, 9 pm; Fri 11:30 am, 1:30 pm, 6 pm, 9:30 pm; Sat 6 pm, 9:30 pm. Closed hols. Res accepted. Bar to 1 am. Wine cellar. Prix fixe: lunch $40, dinner $120. Valet parking (dinner). Chef-owned. Jacket. Cr cds: A, D, DS, MC, V.

D

★ **MANAYUNK BREWING CO.** *4120 Main St, Manayunk (19127). 215/482-8220. www.manayunk brewery.com.* Specializes in cedar plank salmon with cherry sauce, baby back ribs. Hrs: 11 am-11 pm; Sun to 3 pm. Res accepted. Wine list. Lunch $10-$15; dinner $17-$23. Child's menu. Entertainment: jazz. On the river. Cr cds: A, DS, MC, V.

D ⬛

★★★ **MARKER RESTAURANT & LOUNGE.** *City Ave and Monument Rd (19131). 215/581-5010. www.adams mark.com.* Hrs: 11 am-2 pm, 5:30-10 pm; Sun brunch 10:30 am-2:30 pm. Closed hols. Res accepted. Contemporary American menu. Lunch $10-

$15; dinner $21-$26. Sun brunch $32.50. Own baking, pasta. Pianist. Formal French and English decor with stained glass, tapestries, stone fireplace and gold-plated chandelier. Jacket. Cr cds: A, D, DS, MC, V.

D—¾

★★ **MICHAEL'S.** *824 S 8th St (19147). 215/922-3986. www.michaels ristorante.com.* Hrs: 5-11 pm; Sun 3-10 pm. Closed Mon. Res accepted. Italian menu. Bar. A la carte entrees: dinner $13-$24. Specialties: veal chop, gnocchi. Valet parking. Exposed brick, stucco walls; statuary in alcoves. Bronze, glass chandeliers. Cr cds: A, MC, V.

—¾

★★★ **MONTE CARLO LIVING ROOM.** *150 South St (19147). 215/925-2220.* Hrs: 6-10:30 pm; Fri, Sat 5:30-11 pm; Sun 5-9 pm. Closed major hols. Res accepted. Northern Italian menu. Bar. Wine cellar. A la carte entrees: dinner $16-$30. Degustation dinner $65. Specializes in fresh fish, veal, beef. Daily menu. Own pastries. Mediterranean decor. Jacket. Cr cds: A, D, MC, V.

—¾

★★★ **MOONSTRUCK.** *7955 Oxford Ave (19111). 215/725-6000.* Hrs: 5-9 pm; Fri, Sat to 10 pm; Sun 4:30-8 pm. Closed Jan 1, July 4, Dec 25. Italian menu. Wine cellar. Dinner $18-$25. Specializes in veal dishes, seafood. Own pasta, pastries. Parking. Cr cds: A, MC, V.

—¾

★ **NAIS CUISINE.** *13-17 W Benedict Ave, Haverstown (19083). 610/789-5983.* Hrs: 5-9 pm; wkends to 10 pm. Res accepted; required Fri, Sat. French menu with Thai influence. A la carte entrees: $14.25-$24.75. Specialties: roast duckling, steamed salmon stuffed with crab meat, snow pea salad. Cr cds: A, D, DS, MC, V.

D—¾

★★★ **OPUS 251.** *251 S 18th St (19103). 215/735-6787. www.opus251. citysearch.com.* Hrs: 11 am-2:30 pm, 5-10 pm; Fri, Sat to 11 pm; Sun 4:30-8:30 pm; Sun brunch 11 am-2:30 pm. Closed Mon; Memorial Day, Thanksgiving, Dec 25. Res

accepted. Bar. Wine cellar. Lunch $15, dinner $30. Sun brunch $8-$17. Own baking, ice cream. Outdoor dining. Casually elegant dining in Philadelphia Art Alliance; arched windows, European garden. Cr cds: A, D, MC, V.

★★★ **OVERTURES.** *609 E Passyunk Ave (19147). 215/627-3455.* Hrs: 6-10:30 pm. Closed Mon; hols. Res required. Mediterranean menu. Setups. A la carte entrees: $16-$30. Prix fixe: $50. Specialties: sauteed veal sweetbreads in port, rack of lamb. Own desserts. Cr cds: A, D, DS, MC, V.

D

★★ **THE PALM.** *200 S Broad St (19102). 215/546-7256. www.thepalm. com.* Hrs: 11:30 am-11 pm; Sat from 5 pm; Sun 4:30-9 pm. Closed hols. Res accepted. Bar. A la carte entrees: lunch $10-$25, dinner $19-$60. Specializes in fresh seafood, prime aged beef, lamb chops. Valet parking. Counterpart of famous New York restaurant. Caricatures of celebrities. Cr cds: A, D, DS, MC, V.

D—¾

★★ **PALOMA.** *6516 Castor Ave (19149). 215/533-0356. www.paloma restaurant.com.* Hrs: 5-10 pm; Fri, Sat to 9:30 pm; Sun to 8 pm. Closed Mon; Dec 25. Res accepted. French/Mexican menu. Bar. Dinner $14-$33. Child's menu. Specialties: lobster chili rellenos, wild mushroom flan, two bean soup, rack of lamb tapatia. Own baking. Intimate atmosphere with modern European decor. Cr cds: A, D, DS, MC, V.

D

★★★ **PASION!.** *211 S 15th St (19102). 215/875-9895. www.pasion restaurant.com.* Specializes in ceviches, parrillada (mixed grill). Hrs: 11:30 am-2:30 pm, 5-10 pm; Fri, Sat to 11 pm; Sun 5-9 pm. Closed hols. Res accepted. Wine list. Dinner $18-$29. Cr cds: A, D, DS, MC, V.

D

★★ **PHILADELPHIA FISH.** *207 Chestnut St (19106). 215/625-8605. www.philadelphiafish.com.* Hrs: 11:30 am-10:30 pm; Fri to midnight; Sat noon-midnight; Sun 4-10:30 pm. Closed Thanksgiving, Dec 25. Res

accepted. Seafood menu. Bar to 2 am. A la carte entrees: lunch $9-$10, dinner $16-$22. Child's menu. Specialties: grilled whole fish, mahi mahi. Street parking. Outdoor dining. Cr cds: A, DS, MC, V.
D

★★ **PLOUGH & THE STARS.** *123 Chestnut St (19106). 215/733-0300. www.ploughstars.com.* Hrs: 11:30-2 am. Res accepted. Contemporary Irish menu. Bar. A la carte entrees: lunch $6.50-$9, dinner $14.75-$19.75. Child's menu. Specialties: striped bass, duck with pear, warm sea scallop salad. Irish music Sun. Street parking. Outdoor dining. Irish atmosphere. Cr cds: A, D, DS, MC, V.
D

★★ **POD.** *3636 Sansom St (19104). 215/387-1803. www.podphilidelphia. com.* Pan-Asian menu. Specializes in sushi, edamame ravioli, lobster rolls. Hrs: 11:30 am-11 pm; Fri 11:30 am-midnight; Sat 4 pm-midnight; Sun 4-10 pm. Res accepted. Wine list. Bar. Lunch $9-$15; dinner $20-$40. Conveyor belt sushi bar. Cr cds: A, D, MC, V.
D

★★ **RANGOON BURMESE RESTAURANT.** *112 N 9th St (19107). 215/829-8939. www.chinatown.com.* Hrs: 11:30 am-9 pm; Fri to 10 pm; Sat 1-10 pm; Sun from 1 pm. Closed Thanksgiving. Res accepted. Burmese menu. Bar. Lunch $9.50-$12.50, dinner $9.50-$21.50. Specializes in salads, curry dishes, appetizers. Authentic Burmese atmosphere. Totally nonsmoking. Cr cds: MC, V.
D

★★★ **RISTORANTE PANORAMA.** *14 N Front St (19106). 215/922-7800. www.pennsviewhotel.com.* Hrs: noon-2:30 pm, 5:30-10 pm; Fri to 11 pm; Sat 5:30-11 pm; Sun 5-9 pm. Closed hols. Res accepted. Northern Italian menu. Bar. Wine list. A la carte entrees: lunch, dinner $8.50-$26.95. Specializes in veal, seafood. Own pasta. Parking. Cr cds: A, MC, V.
D

★★★ **ROCOCO.** *123 Chestnut St (19106). 215/629-1100.* Hrs: 5-10 pm; Fri, Sat to midnight. Closed

Sun; Dec 25. Res accepted. American menu. Bar to 2 am. Wine cellar. Dinner $10-$28. Specializes in seafood, beef, lamb. Valet parking. European decor in converted bank bldg; cathedral ceiling. Cr cds: A, D, DS, MC, V.
D

★★★ **ROUGE 2003.** *205 S 18th St (19103). 215/732-6622.* American/French menu. Specializes in burgers, fresh fish, mussels. Hrs: 11:30-1 am; Sat, Sun from 10 am. Bar to 2 am. Closed Thanksgiving, Dec 25. Wine list. A la carte entrees: lunch, dinner $12-$30. Cr cds: A, D, MC, V.

★★★ **THE SALOON.** *750 S 7th St (19148). 215/627-1811.* Hrs: 11:30 am-2 pm, 5-10 pm; Sat to midnight. Closed Sun; hols. Res accepted. Italian menu. Bar. Wine list. A la carte entrees: lunch, dinner $18-$28. Specializes in veal, steak, seafood. Parking. Family-owned. Cr cds: A.
D

★★ **SERRANO.** *20 S 2nd St (19106). 215/928-0770. www.tinangel.com.* Hrs: 5-10:30 pm; Fri, Sat to 11:30 pm; Sun 4-10 pm. Closed hols. Res accepted. International menu. Bar. A la carte entrees: dinner $10-$20. Specialties: Vietnamese happy family, Malaysian pork chops. Own desserts. Entertainment Wed-Sat. Theatrical decor with puppets and tapestries from around the world. Cr cds: A, D, DS, MC, V.
D

★★ **SONOMA.** *4411 Main St, Manayunk (19127). 215/483-9400. www. sonomarestaurant.com.* Hrs: 11-2 am; early-bird dinner Sun-Thurs 5-6 pm; Sun brunch to 4 pm. California/Italian menu. Bar to 2 am. Lunch $7-$10, dinner $14-$24. Sun brunch $6-$10. Child's menu. Specialties: caesar salad, award-winning, secret recipe chicken. Own baking, pasta. Valet parking. Outdoor dining. Modern, eclectic decor; revolving art display. Cr cds: A, DS, MC, V.
D

★ **SOUTH STREET DINER.** *140 South St (19147). 215/627-5258.* Open 24 hrs. Closed Dec 25. Bar. Bkfst $4.50-$7, lunch $5-$7.50, dinner $8.50-$10.50. Child's menu. Specializes in bkfst dishes, Greek dishes, meats. Own pasta. Outdoor dining. Patio and sports bar. Cr cds: A, DS, MC, V.

D⍗

★★ **STEPHEN'S.** *1415 City Line Ave, Wynnewood (19096).* 610/896-0275. Hrs: 11:30 am-2:30 pm, 5-10 pm; Fri, Sat 5-11 pm; Sun from 4 pm. Closed Jan 1, Dec 25. Res accepted; required Fri, Sat. Northern Italian menu. Bar. A la carte entrees: lunch $7-$25; dinner $7-$25. Specialties: grilled Dover sole, double veal chop. Own pasta. Valet parking. Display of wine bottles; original art. Cr cds: A, MC, V.

D⍗

★★★★ **STRIPED BASS.** *1500 Walnut St (19102).* 215/732-4444. *www. mealticket.org.* Housed in a former brokerage house space, this seafood-only establishment has received national acclaim for its innovative presentations as well as its dramatic dining room. An energetic crowd dines beneath 28-foot ceilings, towering marble columns, palm trees, and expansive windows. It's all very grand and glamorous with a jumping exhibition kitchen and a highly sought-after chef's table. Specializes in fresh seafood, shellfish. Menu changes daily. Hrs: 11:30 am-2:30 pm, 5-11 pm; Fri to 11:30 pm; Sat 5-11:30 pm; Sun 11 am-2:30 pm, 5-10 pm. Closed hols. Res required. Bar. Wine cellar. Prix fixe: lunch $26, 5-course dinner $85. A la carte entrees: dinner $30-$50. Valet parking. Cr cds: A, MC, V.

D

★★★ **SUSANNA FOO.** *1512 Walnut St (19102).* 215/545-2666. *www.susannafoo.com.* Chinese, French menu. Specialties: crispy duck, soft-shell crabs, hundred-corner crab cake. Hrs: 11:30 am-2:30 pm, 5-10 pm; Fri, Sat to 11 pm; Sun 5-9 pm. Closed hols. Res accepted; required Sat. Bar. Wine cellar. Lunch $24.95. A la carte entrees: dinner $17-$35. Valet parking. Jacket. Cr cds: A, MC, V.

D

★★★ **SWANN CAFE.** *1 Logan Sq (19103).* 215/963-1500. *www.four seasons.com.* Hrs: 11:30-2 am; Sun 10-1 am; Sun brunch to 3 pm. Res accepted. Continental menu with French influences. Bar. Wine cellar. A la carte entrees: lunch $15-$22 , dinner $14-$35. Sun brunch $52. Child's menu. Specialties: steak pomfrite; osso bucco; shrimp, crab and scallop salad. Own baking, pasta. Entertainment. Valet parking. Outdoor dining. Intimate atmosphere; luxurious decor uses mahogany, silk, and large chandeliers. Cr cds: A, D, DS, MC, V.

D⍗

★★★ **TANGERINE.** *232 Market St (19106).* 215/627-5116. *www.tangerine restaurant.com.* Mediterrean menu. Specializes in filet mignon au poivre, shrimp/scallop afrique, and pistachio-crusted duck breast. Hrs: 5-11 pm; Fri, Sat 5 pm-midnight. Res accepted. Wine list. Bar. Dinner $18-$28. Cr cds: A, D, MC, V.

D

★★★ **TOSCANA CUCINA RUSTICA.** *24 N Merion Ave, Bryn Mawr (19010).* 610/527-7700. Hrs: 5:30-10 pm; Fri to 11 pm; Sat 5:30-11 pm; Sun from 5:30 pm. Closed Thanksgiving, Dec 25. Res accepted. Tuscan Italian menu. Bar. Wine cellar. A la carte entrees: dinner $15-$30. Specializes in grilled meats, wafer-thin-crusted brick-oven pizza. Own baking, pasta. Wine list offers over 550 selections. Totally nonsmoking. Cr cds: A, D, DS, MC, V.

★★ **UMBRIA.** *7131 Germantown Ave (19119).* 215/242-6470. Hrs: 6-9 pm. Closed Sun-Tues; hols. Res accepted. Eclectic menu. A la carte entrees: dinner $19.95-$26.95. Specialties: filet au poivre, curried lamb, soft shelled crabs in season. Blackboard menu changed daily. Totally nonsmoking. Cr cds: A, MC, V.

★★★ **VETRI.** *1312 Spruce St (19107).* 215/732-3478. *www.vetri ristorante.com.* Italian cuisine. Specialties: homemade pasta, fresh fish, onion crêpe in white truffle sauce. Hrs: 6 pm-midnight. Closed Sun, hols. Dinner $25-$32. Res required. Cr cds: A, DS, MC, V.

★★ **WHITE DOG CAFE.** *3420 Sansom St (19104).* 215/386-9224. *www. whitedog.com.* Hrs: 11:30 am-2:30 pm, 5:30-10 pm; Fri, Sat 5:30-11 pm; Sun 5-10 pm; Sat, Sun brunch

11 am-2:30 pm. Closed Thanksgiving, Dec 25. Res accepted. Bar. A la carte entrees: lunch $7-$12, dinner $16-$24. Sat, Sun brunch $7-$11. Child's menu. Specializes in beef, chicken. Own desserts. Outdoor dining. Former house (ca 1870) of author Madame Blavatsky, founder of the Theosophical Society. Cr cds: A, D, DS, MC, V.

★★ **ZOCALO.** *3600 Lancaster Ave (19104). 215/895-0139.* Hrs: noon-10 pm; Fri to 11 pm; Sat 5:30-11 pm; Sun 4-9 pm. Closed hols. Res accepted. Contemporary Mexican menu. Bar. Lunch $5-$12, dinner $14-$20. Specializes in handmade corn tortillas. Parking. Outdoor dining. Cr cds: A, D, DS, MC, V.

Unrated Dining Spots

FAMOUS 4TH STREET DELICATESSEN. *700 S 4th St (19147). 215/922-3274. www.famouscookies. com.* Hrs: 7:30 am-6 pm; Sun to 4 pm. Closed Rosh Hashana, Yom Kippur. Delicatessen fare. A la carte entrees: bkfst $2-$9, lunch $3.50-$10. Specializes in chocolate chip cookies, fresh roasted turkey, corned beef. Antique telephones. Family-owned more than 80 yrs. Cr cds: A, D, DS, MC, V.

GENO'S. *1219 S 9th St (19147). 215/389-0659.* Specializes in cheesesteak sandwiches. Hrs: open 24 hrs. Closed hols. Lunch, dinner $5.50. Entertainment.

THE RESTAURANT SCHOOL. *4207 Walnut St (19104). 215/222-4200. www.phillyrestaurants.com.* Hrs: 5:30-10 pm. Closed Sun, Mon; also during student breaks. Res accepted. Continental menu. Bar. Complete meals: dinner $13.50. Seasonal menu. Own baking. Parking. Bakery shop on premises. Unique dining experience in a "restaurant school." Consists of 2 buildings: a restored 1856 mansion is linked by a large atrium dining area to a new building housing the kitchen and classrooms. Cr cds: A, DS, MC, V.

ROLLER'S. *8705 Germantown Ave (19118). 215/242-1771.* Hrs: 11:30 am-2:30 pm, 5:30-9 pm; Fri to 10 pm; Sat noon-2:30 pm, 5:30-10 pm; Sun 5-9 pm; Sun brunch 11 am-2:30 pm. Closed Mon; hols. Bar. Lunch $6-$11, dinner $11-$28. Sun brunch $6-$11. Specializes in fresh fish, veal, duck. Parking. Outdoor dining. Modern cafe atmosphere. Totally nonsmoking.

SASSAFRAS. *48 S 2nd St (19106). 215/925-2317.* Hrs: noon-midnight; Fri, Sat to 1 am, Sun to 9 pm. Closed major hols. Bar. A la carte entrees: dinner $6-$19. Specializes in burgers, dumplings. Cr cds: A, MC, V.

SWANN LOUNGE. *1 Logan Sq (19103). 215/963-1500. www.fourseasons.com.* Hrs: 11:30 am-2 pm; tea 3-4:15 pm; Sun brunch 10:30 am-2 pm; Viennese buffet Fri, Sat 9 pm-1 am. Closed Mon. Res accepted. Bar 11:30-1 am; Fri, Sat to 2 am. Buffet: bkfst $9.75-$14, lunch $19.50-$21. Afternoon tea $22-$29. Sun brunch $62. Viennese buffet $15. Specializes in English tea service with sandwiches and cakes. Entertainment. Valet parking. Outdoor dining (lunch). Elegant atmosphere. Cr cds: A, D, DS, MC, V.

Pittsburgh

(D-1) See also Ambridge, Beaver Falls, Connellsville, New Stanton, Washington

Settled 1758 **Pop** 334,563 **Elev** 760 ft **Area code** 412

Information Greater Pittsburgh Convention & Visitors Bureau, 425 6th Ave. 30th Floor 15219; 800/366-0093

Web www.visitpittsburgh.com

Pittsburgh has had a remarkable renaissance to become one of the most spectacular civic redevelopments in America, with modern buildings, clean parks, and community pride. In fact, it has been named "all-American city" by the National

Pittsburgh Skyline

Civic League. The new Pittsburgh is a result of a rare combination of capital-labor cooperation, public and private support, enlightened political leadership, and imaginative, venturesome community planning. Its $1-billion international airport was designed to be the most user-friendly in the country.

After massive war production, Pittsburgh labored to eliminate the 1930s image of an unsophisticated mill town. During the 1950s and 1960s Renaissance I began, a $500-million program to clean the city's air and develop new structures such as Gateway Center, the Civic Arena, and Point State Park. The late 1970s and early 1980s ushered in Renaissance II, a $3-billion expansion program reflecting the movement away from industry and toward high technology.

Today Pittsburgh has completed this dramatic shift from industry to a diversified base including high technology, health care, finance, and education, and continues its transition to a services-oriented city.

Pittsburgh's cultural personality is expressed by the Pittsburgh Symphony Orchestra, Pittsburgh Opera, Pittsburgh Ballet, Phipps Conservatory, and the Carnegie Museums of Pittsburgh, which include the Museum of Natural History and Museum of Art. The city has 25 parks, 45 "parklets," 60 recreation centers, and 27 swimming pools.

Born of frontier warfare in the shadow of Fort Pitt, the city is named after the elder William Pitt, the great British statesman. Its strategic military position was an important commercial asset and Pittsburgh soon became a busy river port and transit point for the western flow of pioneers.

Industry grew out of the West's need for manufactured goods; foundries and rolling mills were soon producing nails, axes, frying pans, and shovels. The Civil War added tremendous impetus to industry, and by the end of the war, Pittsburgh was producing half the steel and one-third of the glass made in the country. Such captains of industry and finance as Thomas Mellon, Andrew Carnegie, and Henry Clay Frick built their industrial empires in Pittsburgh. The American Federation of Labor was born here (1881); the city has been the scene of historic clashes between labor and management.

World War I brought a fresh boom to the city, as well as changes in its industrial character. It was a vast arsenal for the Allies during World War II.

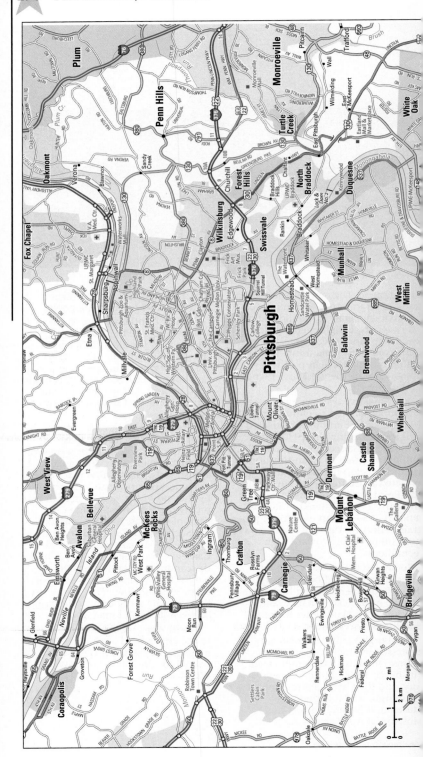

Additional Visitor Information

For additional accommodations, see PITTSBURGH INTERNATIONAL AIRPORT AREA, which follows PITTSBURGH.

For additional information about Pittsburgh contact the Greater Pittsburgh Convention and Visitors Bureau, 425 6th Ave, 30th Floor, 15219 (Mon-Fri); 412/281-7711 or 800/366-0093. A Visitor Information Center is along Liberty Ave, adj to 4 Gateway Center (Mar-Dec, daily; rest of yr, Mon-Sat). Other centers can be found in the Carnegie Library's Mt Washington branch and on the University of Pittsburgh's campus, Log Cabin, Forbes Ave. For a schedule of events in Pittsburgh, 24-hr visitor information, phone 800/366-0093.

Transportation

Airport. See PITTSBURGH INTERNATIONAL AIRPORT AREA.

Car Rental Agencies. See IMPORTANT TOLL-FREE NUMBERS.

Public Transportation. Subway and surface trains, buses (Port Authority of Allegheny County). Phone 412/442-2000.

Rail Passenger Service. Amtrak 800/872-7245.

What to See and Do

Alcoa Building. Pioneer in aluminum for skyscraper construction, exterior work was done from inside; no scaffolding was required. Draped in aluminum waffle, 30 stories high; considered to be one of the country's most daring experiments in skyscraper design. 425 6th Ave.

Allegheny County Courthouse. One of the country's outstanding Romanesque buildings, the two-square-city-blk structure was designed by Henry Hobson Richardson in 1884. (Mon-Fri; closed hols) Grant St and 5th Ave. **FREE**

Andy Warhol Museum. The most comprehensive single-artist museum in the world. More than 500 works. (Tues-Sun) 117 Sandusky St. Phone 412/237-8300. ¢¢

Benedum Center for the Performing Arts. Expansion and restoration of the Stanley Theater, a movie palace built in 1928. Gilded plasterwork, 500,000-piece crystal chandelier, and a nine-story addition to backstage area make this an exceptional auditorium with one of the largest stages in the country. The center is home to Pittsburgh Ballet Theatre, the Pittsburgh Dance Council, the Pittsburgh Opera, and Civic Light Opera. Free guided tours (by appt). Penn and 7th aves, at 719 Liberty Ave. Phone 412/456-6666.

Boyce Park Ski Area. Beginner-intermediate slopes; two double chairlifts; two surface lifts; patrol, school, rentals, snowmaking; cafeteria. Longest run, ¼ mi; vertical drop, 160 ft. Night skiing. (Dec-Mar, daily) 18 mi E on I-376 to Plum exit (16B); follow signs to park. ¢¢¢

Carnegie Mellon University. (1900) 7,900 students. Founded by Andrew Carnegie. Composed of seven colleges. Tours of campus. Adj to Schenley Park. Phone 412/268-2000 or 412/268-5052.

⭐ **The Carnegie Museums of Pittsburgh.** Public complex built by industrialist Andrew Carnegie. (Daily exc Mon; closed hols) 4400 Forbes Ave. Phone 412/622-3360. ¢¢
Includes

Library of Pittsburgh. Central branch contains more than 4½ million books. Houses first department of science and technology established in a US public library.

Museum of Art. Possibly America's first modern art museum, as Carnegie urged the gallery to exhibit works dated after 1896. Collection of Impressionist and Post-Impressionist paintings; Hall of Sculpture; Hall of Architecture; films, videos.

Museum of Natural History. Houses one of the most complete collections of dinosaur fossils. Exhibits include Dinosaur Hall, Polar World, Hillman Hall of Minerals and Gems, the Walton Hall of Ancient Egypt; changing exhibits.

Music Hall. Home to Mendelssohn Choir, Pittsburgh Chamber Music Society, and River City Brass Band. Elaborate gilt and marble foyer; walls of French eschallion, 24 pillars made of green stone, and a gold baroque ceiling.

The Carnegie Science Center. Learning and entertainment complex has over 40,000 square ft of exhibit galleries that demonstrate how human activities are affected by science and technology. USS *Requin*, moored in front of the center, is a WWII diesel-electric submarine; tours (40 min) demonstrate the electronic, visual and voice communication devices on board. Henry Buhl Jr. Planetarium and Observatory is a technologically sophisticated interactive planetarium with control panels at every seat. Also here are 350-seat OMNIMAX Theater and Health Sciences Amphitheater. Restaurant, gift shop. (Daily; closed Dec 25) One Allegheny Ave, on Ohio River. Phone 412/237-3400. ¢¢¢

County parks. South Park. 12 mi S on PA 88. **North Park,** 14 mi N on PA 19. **Boyce Park,** 14 mi E on I-376, US 22. **Settler's Cabin Park,** 9 mi W on I-279, US 22. Swimming; fishing; boating, bicycling (rentals), ball fields; golf, tennis, x-country skiing, ice-skating (winter, daily). Picnicking. Parks open daily. Fees for activities. Attractions for each park vary. Phone 412/350-2455.

⭐ **Fallingwater.** (See CONNELLSVILLE) 27 mi S on PA 51, 10 mi E on PA 201 to Connellsville, 8 mi E on PA 711, then 8 mi S on PA 381, near Mill Run.

⭐ **The Frick Art and Historical Center.** Museum complex built on grounds of estate once belonging to industrialist Henry Clay Frick; gardens, carriage house museum, greenhouse, cafe, and restored children's playhouse that now serves as a visitor's center. (Tues-Sun; closed hols) 7227 Reynolds St. For tour schedule and info, phone 412/371-0600. **FREE** Also on grounds are

    Clayton, the Henry Clay Frick Home. A restored four-story Victorian mansion with 23 rms; only remaining house of area in East End once known as "millionaire's row." Some original decor and personal mementos of the Fricks. Tours; res recommended. 7227 Reynolds St. ¢¢

    The Frick Art Musuem. Collection of Helen Clay Frick, daughter of Henry Clay Frick, includes Italian Renaissance, Flemish, and French 18th-century paintings and decora-

tive arts. Italian and French furniture, Renaissance bronzes, tapestries, Chinese porcelains. Also changing exhibits; concerts, lectures. 7227 Reynolds St. Phone 412/371-0600. **FREE**

Frick Park. Covers 476 acres, largely in natural state; nature trails wind through ravines and over hills; also nature center (2005 Beechwood Blvd), tennis courts, picnic areas, playgrounds. Park (daily). Beechwood Blvd and English Ln. Phone 412/422-6536. **FREE**

Gateway Center. Complex includes four skyscrapers of Trizec Properties, Inc. Gateway Center Plaza, a two-acre open-air garden over underground parking garage, has lovely walks, three fountains, more than 90 types of trees, and 100 varieties of shrubs and seasonal flowers. (Mon-Fri; closed hols) Covers 23 acres adj to Point State Park. Phone 412/392-6000.

Hartwood. (1929) A 629-acre re-creation of English country estate; Tudor mansion with many antiques; formal gardens, stables. Tours (Tues-Sun; closed hols). Also music and theater events during summer. 12 mi N via PA 8, at 215 Saxonburg Blvd. Phone 412/767-9200. ¢¢

⭐ **Inclines.** (Hill-climbing trolleys) Travel to top of Mt Washington for excellent view of Golden Triangle, where the Allegheny and Monongahela rivers join to form the Ohio River.

    Duquesne Incline. Built 1877; restored and run by community effort; observation deck. (Daily) Free parking at lower station. Lower station, W Carson St, opp the fountain, SW of Fort Pitt Bridge; upper station, 1220 Grandview Ave, in restaurant area. Phone 412/381-1665. ¢

    Monongahela Incline. Panoramic views from observation deck. (Daily) Station on W Carson St near Station Sq and Smithfield St Bridge. Phone 412/442-2000. ¢

James L. Kelso Bible Lands Museum. Artifacts and displays from the ancient Near East, especially Palestine. (Call for hrs) 616 N Highland, on grounds of Pittsburgh Theological Seminary. Phone 412/362-5610. **FREE**

Kennywood Park. Combines modern rides with rides from traditional

OAKLAND, THE CITY BEAUTIFUL

Once known as the "Forge of the Universe," industrial Pittsburgh was a smoky, pulsating mill town that fed the fortunes of such corporate giants as Carnegie, Westinghouse, and Mellon. Since then, the city has cleansed its air and its reputation to rank as one of America's most delightful big cities. Before this renaissance, Pittsburgh's 19th-century elite created a second city just three miles east of downtown called Oakland. A sparkling cultural and educational center, it was an antidote to the blue-collar grime from which many of them profited. Under the patronage of Andrew Carnegie and others Oakland became, as historians have described it, "The City Beautiful," a lavish fantasy of parks and monumental structures housing museums and universities. This one-hour, one-mile tour is an introduction to this rich heritage bequeathed to the public. To explore it fully might take days. Begin on the steps of The Carnegie at 4400 Forbes Avenue. An immense gray building, it is shared by the Museum of Art and the Museum of Natural History. Born to a poor family in Scotland in 1835, founder Carnegie came to the United States with his parents at age 12. Starting his career as a telegraph messenger, he went on to make a fortune in steel. A generous man, he gave The Carnegie to the city. For the Museum of Art, he sought contemporary artworks, thus creating what is considered the first museum of modern art in America. It boasts a fine collection of impressionists. Acquiring Jurassic Age fossils, Carnegie put the Museum of Natural History in the paleontology business. The Hall of Dinosaurs is particularly impressive. Across Forbes Avenue is the Foster Memorial, where composer Stephen Collins Foster is cited for the "beautiful ideals" given voice in his enduring music. Soaring above the memorial is the University of Pittsburgh's 42-story Tower of Learning, one of the largest academic buildings in the world. It was built in the early 1930s as a symbol of power and achievement. A ten-minute walk away in adjacent Schenley Park is Phipps Conservatory on Schenley Drive (west from the Carnegie), an elegant Beaux-Art greenhouse that is believed to be the largest in the country. When it opened in 1893, it was one of the nation's first large-scale enclosed botanical gardens. Conclude your tour by strolling among its many exhibits, from tropical flowers to a major assortment of bonsai.

streetcar parks, popular at the turn of the 20th century. **Lost Kennywood**, with lagoon, Victorian-era buildings, shopping. Gardens, picnic groves. (Mid-May-Labor Day, daily) 8 mi SE on PA 837, 4800 Kennywood Blvd, in W Mifflin. Phone 412/461-0500. ¢¢¢¢

Mellon Arena. This $22-million all-weather amphitheater accommodates 17,500 people. Retractable roof can fold up within 2½ min. In Golden Triangle, 66 Mario Lemieux Pl.

Museum of Photographic History. Photo gallery and museum. Selections from 100,000 antique photographic images. (Mon-Sat; closed hols) 531 E Ohio. Phone 412/231-7881. ¢¢

National Aviary. The Aviary is home to one of the world's premier bird collections and is the only indoor bird facility independent of a larger zoo in North America. A veritable jungle of

colorful, amusing and exotic birds. (Daily; closed Dec 25) Allegheny Commons West, approx 1 mi W of downtown. Phone 412/323-7235. ¢¢

Pittsburgh Children's Museum. Hands-on exhibits. Hands-on silkscreen studio; storytelling; regularly scheduled puppet shows; live performances; two-story climber. (Memorial Day-Labor Day, daily; rest of yr, Tues-Sat, also Sun afternoons) 10 Childrens Way. Phone 412/322-5058. ¢¢

The Pittsburgh Zoo. Over 70 acres containing over 6,000 animals, children's farm (late May-Oct), discovery pavilion, reptile house, tropical and Asian forests, African savanna, and aqua zoo. Merry-go-round and train rides (fee). Highland Park covers 75 acres and has tennis courts, picnic grounds, shelters (some require permit), twin reservoirs, swimming pool (fee). (Daily; closed Dec 25) NE on

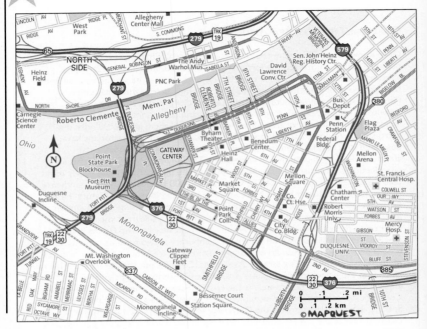

Highland Ave in Highland Park area. Phone 412/665-3639. ¢¢¢

Point State Park. "Point" where the Allegheny and Monongahela rivers meet to form the Ohio; 36 acres. Giant fountain symbolizes joining of rivers. There are military drills with fifes and drums, muskets and cannon (May-Labor Day; some Sun afternoons). Foot of Fort Duquesne and Fort Pitt blvds. Phone 412/471-0235. In the park are

> **Block House of Fort Pitt.** Last remaining building of original fort (1767). (Wed-Sun) **FREE**

> **Fort Pitt Museum.** Built on part of original fort. Exhibits on early Pittsburgh and Fort Pitt; military struggles between France and Britain for western Pennsylvania and the Old Northwest Territory. (Wed-Sun; closed hols) 101 Commonwealth Pl. Phone 412/281-9284. ¢¢

PPG Place. Designed by Philip Johnson, this is Pittsburgh's most popular Renaissance II building. PPG Place consists of six separate buildings designed in a postmodern, Gothic skyscraper style. Shopping and a food court can be found in Two PPG Place. Market Sq.

Professional sports.

> **Pittsburgh Penguins (NHL).** Mellon Arena, 66 Mario Lemieux Pl. Phone 412/323-1919.

> **Pittsburgh Pirates (MLB).** PNC Park, 115 Federal St. Phone 412/323-5000.

> **Pittsburgh Steelers (NFL).** Phone 412/432-7800.

Riverview Park. Covers 251 acres. Swimming pool (mid-June-Labor Day, daily, fee); tennis courts (Apr-Nov, daily), picnic shelter (May-Sept, permit required). Also playgrounds, parklet; nature, jogging trail. Fee for some activities. 2 mi N on US 19. **FREE** In the park is

> **Allegheny Observatory.** Slides, tour of building. Maintained by University of Pittsburgh. Children under 12 yrs only with adult. Res required. (Apr-Oct, Thurs-Fri; closed hols) Center of park, entrance on Riverview Ave off US 19. Phone 412/321-2400. **FREE**

Rodef Shalom Biblical Botanical Garden. The natural world of ancient Israel is re-created here in settings that specialize in plants of the Bible. A waterfall, desert, and stream all help simulate the areas of the Jordan, Lake Kineret, and the Dead Sea. Tours (by appt). Special programs nd exhibits. (June-mid-Sept, Mon-Thurs, Sat-Sun; Sat hrs limited) 4905 th Ave. Phone 412/621-6566. **FREE**

Sandcastle Water Park. The city's town-by-the-riverside water park has 5 slides, adult and kiddie pools; boardwalk; food. (First Sat June-Labor Day, daily; closed hols) Approx 5 mi E of downtown via I-376 & PA 837. Phone 412/462-6666. ¢¢¢¢

Schenley Park. Covers 456 acres; picnic areas; 18-hole golf course, lighted tennis courts; swimming pool; ice-skating (winter); softball fields, running track; nature trails; bandstand (summer; free). Fee for some activities. (Daily) Forbes Ave, adj Carnegie-Mellon University. Phone 412/687-1800. **FREE** Also in park is

Phipps Conservatory. Constantly changing array of flowers; tropical gardens; outstanding orchid collection. Children's Discovery Garden with interactive learning opportunities. Seasonal flower shows (see SPECIAL EVENTS). (Tues-Sun) Phone 412/622-6914. ¢¢

The Senator John Heinz Regional History Center. In Chatauqua Ice Warehouse (1898). Preserves 300 yrs of region's history with artifacts and extensive collection of archives, photos. Houses the Historical Society of Western Pennsylvania. Library (Tues-Sat). (Daily; closed Jan 1, Thanksgiving, Dec 25) 1212 Smallman St. Phone 412/454-6000. ¢¢

Sightseeing tours.

Guided Bus and Walking Tours. Offered through the Pittsburgh History and Landmarks Foundation. Phone 412/471-5808. ¢¢¢

Sightseeing USA/Lenzner Coach USA. Contact 110 Lenzner Ct, Sewickley 15143. Phone 412/741-2720.

Soldiers and Sailors Memorial Hall and Military History Museum. Auditorium has Lincoln's Gettysburg Address inscribed above stage; flags, weapons, uniforms, memorabilia from US wars. (Tues-Fri, also Sat and Sun afternoons; closed hols) 4141 5th Ave at Bigelow Blvd. Phone 412/621-4253. ¢¢

Station Square. This 40-acre area features shopping, dining, and entertainment in and among the historic buildings of the P & LE Rail-road. Shopping in warehouses that once held loaded railroad boxcars. (Daily; closed hols) 450 Landmarks Building, 1 Station Sq, along Monongahela River across from downtown, via Smithfield St Bridge. Phone 412/471-5808.

Tour-Ed Mine and Museum. Complete underground coal mining operation; sawmill; furnished log house (1789); old company store; historical mine museum; shelters; playground. (May-Labor Day wk, daily) 20 mi NW via PA 28 (Allegheny Valley Expy) to Tarentum, then ¼ mi W via Red Belt W. Phone 724/224-4720. ¢¢

Two Mellon Bank Center. Formerly the Union Trust Building, its Flemish-Gothic style was modeled after a library in Louvain, Belgium. Interior has a glass rotunda. Grant St and 5th Ave.

University of Pittsburgh. (1787) 33,000 students. Tours of Nationality Rooms in Cathedral of Learning (wknds; fee). Campus of 70 building on 125 acres. 5th Ave and Bigelow Blvd. Phone 412/624-4141. Buildings include

Cathedral of Learning. (1935) Unique skyscraper of classrms, stretching its Gothic-Moderne architecture 42 floors high (535 ft); vantage point on 36th floor. Surrounding a three-story Gothic commons room are an Early-American Room and 24 Nationality Rooms, each reflecting the distinctive culture of the ethnic group that created and furnished it. Tours (Daily; closed hols). Phone 412/624-6000. ¢

Heinz Chapel. Tall stained-glass windows; French Gothic architecture. (Mon-Fri, Sun; closed hols) E of Cathedral of Learning. Phone 412/624-4157. **FREE**

Henry Clay Frick Fine Arts Building. Glass-enclosed cloister; changing exhibits; art reference library. (Sept-mid-June, daily; rest of yr, Mon-Fri; closed university hols, also Dec 24-Jan 2) Schenley Plaza. Phone 412/648-2400. **FREE**

Stephen Foster Memorial. Auditorium/theater. Collection of the Pittsburgh-born composer's music and memorabilia. Said to be one of the most elaborate memorials ever built to a musician. (Mon-Sat, also

Sun afternoons; closed hols) Phone 412/624-4100.

USX Tower. Once known as the US Steel Building, it is 64 stories high and the tallest building in Pittsburgh. Ten exposed triangular columns and an exterior paneling of steel make up its construction. Grant St and 7th Ave.

Special Events

Folk Festival. Pittsburgh Expo Mart, Monroeville. Food of many nations; arts and crafts; folk music, dancing. Memorial Day wkend.

Three Rivers Arts Festival. Point State Park, Gateway Center, USX Tower, PPG Place. Juried, original works of local and national artists: paintings, photography, sculpture, crafts and videos; artists' market in outdoor plazas. Ongoing performances incl music, dance and performance art. Special art projects; film festival; food; children's activities. Phone 412/281-8723. Early-mid-June.

Pittsburgh/Shop 'N Save Three Rivers Regatta. Point State Park. Water, land, and air events; water shows and speedboat races. Last wkend July and first wkend Aug.

Pittsburgh Irish Festival. I. C. Light Amphitheatre, Station Square. Irish foods, dances and entertainment. Phone 412/422-1113. Early or mid-Sept.

Pittsburgh Public Theater. City's largest resident professional company. 621 Penn Ave. Phone 412/316-1600. Sept-June.

Pittsburgh Symphony Orchestra. Classical, pops, and family concerts. Heinz Hall for the Performing Arts, 600 Penn Ave. Phone 412/392-4900. Sept-May.

Phipps Conservatory Flower Shows. Schenley Park. Phone 412/622-6914. Spring, summer, fall, and hols.

Motels/Motor Lodges

★★ **BEST WESTERN PARKWAY CENTER.** 875 Greentree Rd (15220). 412/922-7070; fax 412/922-4949; res 800/780-7234. www.bestwestern.com. 138 rms, 6 story, 44 kits. S, D $69-$108; kit. units $118; under 12 free; wkend rates. Crib free. TV; cable (premium). Indoor pool; lifeguard. Complimentary bkfst. Ck-out noon. Coin lndry. Meeting rms. Business servs avail. In-rm modem link. Valet serv. Sundries. Free airport transportation. Exercise equipt; sauna. Rec rm. Microwaves avail. Cr cds: A, C, D, DS, ER, MC, V.
🄳 🏊 🏋 📶 ♿ SC

★★ **COUNTRY INN & SUITES.** 5311 Campbells Run Rd (15205). 412/788-8400; fax 412/788-2577. www.countryinns.com. 152 rms, 3 story, 26 suites. S, D $79-$94; each addl $10; suites $109-$114; under 18 free; lower rates Fri, Sat. Crib free. TV; cable (premium). Heated pool; whirlpool. Complimentary buffet bkfst. Restaurant adj 11 am-11 pm. Ck-out noon. Meeting rms. Business servs avail. In-rm modem link. Free airport transportation. Exercise equipt. Some microwaves; refrigerator in suites. Cr cds: A, C, D, DS, MC, V.
🄳 🏊 🏋 📶 ♿

★★ **HAMPTON INN.** 1550 Lebanon Church Rd (15236). 412/650-1000; fax 412/650-1001; res 800/426-7866. www.hamptoninn.com. 70 rms, 3 story. S, D $94; under 18 free; higher rates: hols, football games. Crib free. TV; cable (premium). Restaurant nearby. Ck-out noon. Meeting rms. Business servs avail. In-rm modem link. Heated pool; lifeguard. Some in-rm whirlpools, refrigerators, microwaves. Cr cds: A, C, D, DS, JCB, MC, V.
🄳 🏊 📶 ♿ SC

★★ **HAMPTON INN.** 555 Trumbull Dr (15205). 412/922-0100; fax 412/921-7631; res 800/426-7866. www.hamptoninn.com. 132 rms, 6 story. June-Nov: S $79-$99; D $79; under 18 free; wkend rates; lower rates rest of yr. Crib free. Pet accepted. TV; cable (premium). Complimentary continental bkfst. Coffee in rms. Restaurant nearby. Ck-out noon. Meeting rms. Business servs avail. In-rm modem link. Valet serv. Free airport transportation. Health club privileges. Picnic tables. Cr cds: A, C, D, DS, ER, JCB, MC, V.
🄳 🐾 📶 ♿

★★ **HAWTHORN SUITES.** 700 Mansfield Ave (15205). 412/279-6300; fax 412/279-4993; res 800/527-1133. www.hawthornsuitespittsburgh.com. 151 suites, 2 story. S $79-$119; D $109-$149; wkly, monthly rates. Crib free. Pet accepted, some restrictions;

$50 and $6/day. TV; cable (premium). Pool; whirlpool, lifeguard. Complimentary full bkfst. Ck-out noon. Meeting rms. Business servs avail. Airport, RR station, bus depot transportation. Health club privileges. Refrigerators, microwaves, fireplaces. Private patios, balconies. Picnic tables, grills. Chalet-style buildings. Cr cds: A, C, D, DS, JCB, MC, V.

⬜ 🔖 🏊 🚬 🔥 SC

★★ **HOLIDAY INN.** *401 Holiday Dr (15220). 412/922-8100; fax 412/922-6511; toll-free 800/465-4329. www.holiday-inn.com.* 200 rms, 4 story. S, D $104-$148; each addl $10; under 18 free. Crib free. Pet accepted. TV; cable, VCR avail. Heated pool; poolside serv, lifeguard. Restaurant 6:30 am-10 pm; Fri, Sat to 11 pm. Bar 11-2 am; Sun from 1 pm; entertainment. Ck-out noon. Meeting rms. Business servs avail. In-rm modem link. Valet serv. Sundries. Free airport transportation. Tennis privileges. Golf privileges. Exercise equipt. Health club privileges. Private patios. Cr cds: A, C, D, DS, JCB, MC, V.

⬜ 🔖 🏊 🎾 🚬 🔥 SC 🎿

★★ **HOLIDAY INN.** *915 Brinton Rd (15221). 412/247-2700; fax 412/371-9619; toll-free 800/465-4323. www.holiday-inn.com.* 177 rms, 11 story. Apr-Oct: S, D $89.95-$120; suites $150; under 18 free; wkend, hol rates; lower rates rest of yr. Crib free. Pet accepted. TV; cable (premium). Indoor pool; lifeguard. Coffee in rms. Restaurant 6:30 am-10 pm. Bar 5 pm-1 am; entertainment Fri, Sat. Ck-out noon. Coin lndry. Meeting rms. Business servs avail. Valet serv. Health club privileges. Some refrigerators; microwaves avail. Cr cds: A, D, DS, ER, JCB, MC, V.

⬜ 🔖 🏊 🚬 🔥 SC

★★ **HOLIDAY INN.** *4859 McKnight Rd (15237). 412/366-5200; fax 412/366-5682; toll-free 800/465-4329. www.holiday-inn.com.* 147 rms, 7 story, 19 suites. S, D $99-$109; each addl $10; suites $109-$139; under 18 free. Crib free. TV; cable (premium). Heated pool; poolside serv, lifeguard. Complimentary coffee in rms. Restaurant 6:30 am-10 pm; Sun from 7 am. Bar 11 am-11 pm; entertainment Sat. Ck-out noon. Coin lndry.

Meeting rms. Business servs avail. In-rm modem link. Valet serv. Sundries. Health club privileges. Refrigerator in suites; microwaves avail. Cr cds: A, C, D, DS, MC, V.

⬜ 🏊 🚬 🔥 SC

★★ **HOLIDAY INN.** *180 Gamma Dr (15238). 412/963-0600; fax 412/963-7852. www.holiday-inn.com.* 223 rms, 2 story. S, D $109; suites $150; under 18 free. TV; cable (premium). Heated pool; pooside serv, lifeguard. Coffee in rms. Restaurant 6 am-10 pm; Sat, Sun from 7 am. Rm serv. Bar 11-2 am; Sun 1 pm-1 am. Ck-out noon. Meeting rms. Business servs avail. In-rm modem link. Bellhops. Airport transportation. Exercise equipt. Refrigerator in suites; microwaves avail. Cr cds: A, C, D, DS, JCB, MC, V.

⬜ 🏊 🎾 🔥

★★ **HOLIDAY INN.** *2750 Mosside Blvd, Monroeville (15146). 412/372-1022; fax 412/373-4065; toll-free 800/465-4329. www.holiday-inn.com.* 188 rms, 4 story. S, D $109.95-$115.95; under 19 free; package plans. Crib free. Pet accepted. TV; cable (premium). Pool. Complimentary coffee in rms. Restaurant 6:30 am-2 pm, 5-10 pm. Bar 11-2 am. Ck-out noon. Coin lndry. Meeting rms. Business servs avail. In-rm modem link. Valet serv. Sundries. Exercise equipt. Health club privileges. Some in-rm whirlpools; microwaves avail. Cr cds: A, C, D, DS, ER, MC, V.

⬜ 🔖 🏊 🎾 🚬 🔥 SC

★ **RAMADA.** *699 Rodi Rd (15235). 412/244-1600; fax 412/829-2334; toll-free 800/272-6232. www.ramada.com.* 152 rms, 3 story. No elvtr. S $112-$122; D $122-$132; each addl $10; under 18 free; wkend plan. Crib free. TV; cable. 2 heated pools, 1 indoor; whirlpool, poolside serv, lifeguard. Sauna. Restaurant 6:30 am-2 pm, 5:30-10 pm; Fri, Sat 6-11 pm. Rm serv 7 am-11 pm. Bar 4:30 pm-midnight; Fri to 1 am; Sat noon-1 am; Sun 4:30-11 pm; entertainment Sat. Ck-out 11 am. Meeting rms. Business servs avail. In-rm modem link. Sundries. Airport transportation. Health club privileges. Private patios, balconies. Cr cds: A, C, D, DS, JCB, MC, V.

⬜ 🏊 🚬 🔥 SC

★★ **RAMADA PLAZA SUITES AND CONFERENCE CENTER.** *1 Bigelow Sq (15219). 412/281-5800; fax 412/281-4208; res 800/225-5858. www.ramada.com.* 308 kit. suites, 20 story. S, D $99-$189; under 16 free; package plans. Crib free. TV; cable, VCR avail. Complimentary coffee in rms. Restaurant 6:30-1 am; wkends 7 am-midnight. Bar 11-1 am. Ck-out noon. Convention facilities. In-rm modem link. Grocery store. Beauty shop. Coin lndry. Exercise rm; sauna. Indoor pool. Cr cds: A, C, D, DS, JCB, MC, V.
🄳 ≈ 🏃 ☒ 🐾 SC

★ **RED ROOF INN.** *6404 Steubenville Pike (15205). 412/787-7870; fax 412/787-8392. www.redroof.com.* 120 rms, 2 story. S, D $45.99-$59.99; under 18 free. Crib free. Pet accepted, some restrictions. TV; cable (premium). Complimentary morning coffee. Restaurant adj open 24 hrs. Ck-out noon. Business servs avail. Cr cds: A, C, D, DS, MC, V.
🄳 🐾 ☒ 🐾

Hotels

★★ **FOUR POINTS BY SHERATON HOTEL.** *1 Industry Ln (15275). 724/695-0002; fax 724/695-7262. www.sheraton.com.* 140 rms, 4 story. S $109; D $119; each addl $10; suites $109-$119; under 18 free; wkend, hol rates. Crib free. TV; cable (premium). Pool; wading pool, lifeguard. Complimentary coffee in rms. Restaurant 6:30 am-2 pm, 5-10 pm. Bar 4 pm-midnight. Ck-out noon. Meeting rms. Business center. In-rm modem link. Free airport transportation. Exercise equipt. Some refrigerators. Cr cds: A, C, D, DS, ER, JCB, MC, V.
🄳 ≈ 🏃 ☒ 🐾 SC 🏃

★★★ **HILTON HOTEL.** *600 Commonwealth Pl (15222). 412/391-4600; fax 412/594-5161. www.hilton.com.* 713 rms, 24 story. S $154-$219; D $134-$254; each addl $20; suites $350-$1,500; studio rms $109; under 12 free; wkend plans. Crib free. Pet accepted, some restrictions. TV; cable (premium). Coffee in rms. Restaurant 6:30 am-11:30 pm. Bars 11-2 am. Ck-out noon. Meeting rms. Business center. In-rm modem link. Concierge. Garage; valet parking. Airport transportation. Exercise equipt.

Minibars; some bathrm phones, refrigerators. Luxury level. Cr cds: A, C, D, DS, ER, JCB, MC, V.
🄳 🏃 ≈ 🐾 🏃

★★★ **MARRIOTT PITTSBURGH CITY CENTER.** *112 Washington Pl (15219). 412/471-4000. www.marriott. com.* 402 rms, 11 story. S, D $195-$250; under 17 free. Crib avail. TV; cable (premium). Indoor pool. Restaurant 6:30 am-10 pm. Bar to midnight. Ck-out noon, ck-in 3 pm. Meeting rms. Business center. In-rm modem link. Concierge. Exercise equipt. Many refrigerators in suites. Cr cds: A, D, DS, MC, V.
≈ 🏃 🐾 🏃

★★★ **OMNI WILLIAM PENN HOTEL.** *530 William Penn Pl (15219). 412/281-7100; fax 412/553-5252; res 412/553-5100. www.omnihotels.com.* 596 rms, 24 story. S, D $204-$214; each addl $20; suites $400-$2,200; under 18 free; wkend rates. Crib free. Valet parking $19.50. TV; cable (premium), VCR avail. Restaurant 6:30 am-10 pm (see also TERRACE ROOM, Unrated Dining). Rm serv 24 hrs. Bar 11-2 am. Ck-out noon. Convention facilities. Business center. Gift shop. Airport, RR station, bus depot transportation. Exercise equipt. Health club privileges. Historic, landmark hotel. Cr cds: A, C, D, DS, JCB, MC, V.
🄳 🏃 ≈ 🐾 🏃

★★ **RADISSON HOTEL GREEN TREE.** *101 Radisson Dr (15205). 412/922-8400; fax 412/922-8981; res 800/525-5902. www.radisson.com.* 467 rms, 7 story. S, D $109-$129; suites $150-$275; wkend rates; package plans. Crib free. Pet accepted. TV; cable (premium), VCR avail. 3 pools, 1 indoor; whirlpool, poolside serv, lifeguard. Restaurant 6:30 am-midnight. Bar 11-2 am; entertainment. Ck-out noon. Meeting rms. Business servs avail. In-rm modem link. Bellhops. Valet serv. Sundries. Gift shop. Barber, beauty shop. Free airport transportation. Exercise equipt; sauna. Health club privileges. Rec rm. Many minibars. Luxury level. Cr cds: A, C, D, DS, ER, MC, V.
🄳 🐾 ≈ 🏃 ☒ 🐾 SC

★★★ **RENAISSANCE PITTS-BURGH HOTEL.** *107 6th St (15222). 412/562-1200; fax 412/992-2010. www.renaissancehotels.com.* 300 rms, 14 story. S, D $159-$250; under 17 free. Crib avail. TV; cable (premium). Restaurant 6:30 am-11 pm. Bar to midnight. Ck-out noon, ck-in 4 pm. Meeting rms. Business center. In-rm modem link. Concierge. Exercise equipt. Minibars; many refrigerators in suites. Cr cds: A, D, DS, MC, V.

★ ★ ★ **SHERATON HOTEL.** *7 Station Square Dr (15219). 412/261-2000; fax 412/261-2932; res 800/255-7488. www.sheraton.com.* 292 rms, 15 story. S $149-$170; D $149-$185; each addl $15; suites $225-$600; under 18 free; wkend rates. Crib free. TV; cable (premium), VCR avail. Indoor pool; whirlpool, lifeguard. Coffee in rms. Restaurant 6 am-midnight. Bar 11-2 am; entertainment. Ck-out noon. Meeting rms. Business center. In-rm modem link. Shopping arcade. RR station, bus depot transportation. Exercise equipt. Health club privileges. On riverfront. Luxury level. Cr cds: A, C, D, DS, ER, JCB, MC, V.

★ ★ ★ **WESTIN CONVENTION CENTER HOTEL.** *1000 Penn Ave (15222). 412/281-3700; fax 412/227-4500; res 888/625-5144. www.westin.com.* 616 rms, 26 story. S $125-$180; D $145-$215; each addl $20; suites $350-$1,500; family rates; wkend rates. Crib free. Pet accepted. TV; cable (premium). Indoor pool; whirlpool. Coffee in rms. Restaurants 6:30 am-2:30 pm, 5-10:30 pm; Fri, Sat to 11 pm. Rm serv 24 hrs. Bar 11-1 am. Ck-out noon. Convention facilities. Business center. In-rm modem link. Concierge. Shopping arcade. Exercise rm; sauna, steam rm. Refrigerators; many bathrm phones. Cr cds: A, C, D, DS, ER, JCB, MC, V.

B&Bs/Small Inns

★ ★ ★ **APPLETREE BED AND BREAKFAST.** *703 S Negley Ave (15232). 412/661-0631; fax 412/661-7525. www.appletreeb-b.com.* 8 rms, 3 story, suite. MAP: S, D $140-$190; each addl $15; suite $190; wkend plans; hols (2-3 day min). Children over 12 yrs only. TV; VCR. Complimentary full bkfst. Ck-out 11 am, ck-in 3-6 pm. Concierge serv. Luggage handling. Business servs avail. In-rm

modem link. Health club privileges. Fireplaces. Historic building (1884). Totally nonsmoking. Cr cds: A, DS, MC, V.

★ ★ ★ **INN AT OAKMONT.** *300 Rte 909, Oakmont (15139). 412/828-0410; fax 412/828-1358. www.pittsburghbnb. com.* 8 rms, 1 with shower only, 2 story. S $105; D $135-$155; each addl $10. TV; VCR avail. Complimentary full bkfst. Coffee in library. Restaurant nearby. Ck-out 11 am, ck-in 2 pm. Concierge serv. Business servs avail. Exercise equipt. Balconies. Many antiques. Totally nonsmoking. Cr cds: A, DS, MC, V.

★ ★ ★ **PRIORY INN.** *614 Pressley St (15212). 412/231-3338; fax 412/231-4838. www.thepriory.com.* 24 rms, 3 story. S, D $112; each addl $12; suites $134-$155; lower rates wkends. TV; cable. Complimentary continental bkfst; refreshments. Ck-out 11 am, wkends noon, ck-in 3 pm. Meeting rms. Business servs avail. Previously a haven for Benedictine monks (1888). European-style inn with fountain and floral arrangements in courtyard. Cr cds: A, C, D, DS, MC, V.

Restaurants

★ **BENIHANA.** *2100 Greentree (15220). 412/276-2100. www.benihana. com.* Hrs: 11:30 am-2 pm, 5:30-10 pm; Fri to 10:30 pm; Sat 4-10:30 pm; Sun noon-9 pm. Res required. Japanese menu. Bar. Lunch $7-$13, dinner $15-$31. Child's menu. Specializes in hibachi chicken, steak, seafood. Japanese garden. Cr cds: A, D, DS, MC, V.

★ ★ ★ **CAFE ALLEGRO.** *51 S 12th St (15203). 412/481-7788. www.cafe allegropittsburgh.com.* Hrs: 5-10 pm; Fri, Sat to 11 pm. Closed major hols. Res accepted. Italian menu. Bar. Wine list. Dinner $18-$26. Specialties: pasta del sole, seafood arrabbiata, grilled veal medallions. Valet parking. Ambience of Riviera cafe; artwork. Cr cds: A, D, MC, V.

★ ★ **CAFE AT THE FRICK.** *7227 Reynolds St (15208). 412/371-0600. www.frickart.org.* Hrs: 11 am-5 pm; Sun noon-6 pm; high tea from 3 pm. Closed Mon; hols. Lunch $7.95-$10. Specializes in salads, desserts. Outdoor dining. View of garden and Frick estate. Totally nonsmoking. Cr cds: A, D, DS, MC, V.
D

★ ★ ★ **CARLTON.** *500 Grant St (15219). 412/391-4099. www.thecarlton restaurant.com.* Hrs: 11:30 am-2:30 pm, 5-10 pm; Fri to 11 pm; Sat 5-11 pm. Closed Sun; major hols. Res accepted. Continental menu. Bar. Wine list. Lunch $10.95-$15.95, dinner $19.95-$32.95. Child's menu. Specializes in charcoal-grilled seafood, prime steak, veal. Own pastries. Parking. Cr cds: A, D, DS, MC, V.
D

★ ★ ★ **CARMASSI'S TUSCANY GRILL.** *711 Penn Ave (15222). 412/281-6644. www.carmassis.com.* Hrs: 11 am-10 pm; Sat from 4:30 pm; Sun 4:30-8 pm. Closed hols. Res accepted. Northern Italian menu. Bar. Lunch $12-$13, dinner $19-$35. Specialties: veal a'la lucca, penne arrabiatta. Italian art on display. Cr cds: A, D, DS, MC, V.
D

★ ★ ★ **CASBAH.** *229 S Highland Ave (15206). 412/661-5656. www.big burrito.com.* Hrs: 11:30 am-2:30 pm, 5-11 pm; Sat 5-11 pm; Sun 11 am-2 pm, 5-10 pm. Closed hols. Res accepted. Mediterranean menu. Bar. Wine list. Lunch $5.50-$12, dinner $15-$25. Specialties: lamb mixed grill, roasted vegetable tagine, Mahi Mahi and grape leaves. Cr cds: A, D, DS, MC, V.
D

★ ★ **CHEESE CELLAR CAFE & BAR.** *25 Station Sq (15219). 412/471-3355.* Hrs: 11 am-11 pm; Fri, Sat to midnight; Sun 10 am-10 pm. Closed Thanksgiving, Dec 25. Res accepted Sun-Thurs. Continental menu. Bar to 2 am. Sun bkfst $5.95-$6.50; lunch $6.95-$10.95, dinner $12.95-$18.95. Child's menu. Specialty: cheese and chocolate fondue. Outdoor dining. Rustic decor. Cr cds: A, D, DS, MC, V.
D

★ ★ **CHINA PALACE.** *5440 Walnut St (15232). 412/687-7423.* Hrs: 11:30 am-10 pm; Fri, Sat to 11 pm; Sun 2-9 pm. Closed July 4, Labor Day, Thanksgiving. Chinese menu. Bar. Lunch $5.50-$6.25, dinner $5.50-$26. Specialties: crispy walnut shrimp, orange beef, lemon chicken. Cr cds: A, D, DS, MC, V.
D

★ ★ **THE CHURCH BREW WORKS.** *3525 Liberty Ave (15201). 412/688-8200. www.churchbrew.com.* Hrs: 11:30 am-midnight; Fri, Sat to 1 am; Sun noon-10 pm. Closed Thanksgiving, Dec 25. Regional American menu. Bar. Lunch $7-$15, dinner $7-$25. Specialties: buffalo steak, wood-fired oven pizza, Pittsburgh pierogie. Outdoor dining. Brew-pub in 1902 church; vaulted ceiling, stained-glass windows. Cr cds: A, D, DS, MC, V.
D

★ ★ ★ **CLIFFSIDE.** *1208 Grandview Ave (15211). 412/431-6996.* Hrs: 5-9:30 pm; Fri, Sat to 11 pm. Closed major hols. Res accepted. Continental menu. Bar. Dinner $18-$25. Specializes in fresh seafood, chicken, veal. Pianist. Valet parking. Contemporary decor in older building (1897). Cr cds: A, D, DS, MC, V.

★ ★ ★ **COMMON PLEA.** *308 Ross St (15219). 412/281-5140. www.common plea.citysearch.com.* Hrs: 11:30 am-2:30 pm, 5-10 pm; Sat 5-10 pm. Closed Mon; hols. Res accepted. Bar. Wine list. Complete meals: lunch $10, dinner $20. Specializes in seafood, veal, chicken. Own baking. Valet parking (dinner). Courtroom decor. Family-owned. Cr cds: A, D, MC, V.

★ ★ ★ **D'IMPERIO'S.** *3412 Wm Penn Hwy (15235). 412/823-4800.* Hrs: 11:30 am-3 pm, 5-10 pm; Mon, Sat from 5 pm. Closed Sun; hols. Res accepted. Italian, American menu. Bar. Dinner $13-$38. Child's menu. Specialties: shrimp Sorrento, lobster sausage, veal Genovese. Pianist Fri, Sat. Parking. Different displays of artwork in each dining rm. Cr cds: A, D, DS, MC, V.
D

★ ★ **GEORGETOWN INN.** *1230 Grandview Ave (15211). 412/481-4424.* Hrs: 11 am-3 pm, 5 pm-midnight; Fri,

Sat to 1 am; Sun 4-10 pm. Closed hols. Res accepted. Bar. Lunch $7-$8, dinner $18-$31.95. Specializes in steak, fresh seafood. Panoramic view of city. Cr cds: A, D, DS, MC, V.
D **⛟**

★ ★ ★ **GRAND CONCOURSE.** *1 Station Sq (15219). 412/261-1717. www.muer.com.* Hrs: 11:30 am-2:30 pm, 4:30-10 pm; Sat 4:30-11 pm; Sun 4:30-9 pm; early-bird dinner 4:30-6 pm; Sun brunch 10 am-2:30 pm. Closed Dec 25. Res accepted. Continental menu. Bar 11:30-2 am; Sun 11 am-10 pm. Wine list. Lunch $7-$20, dinner $25-$30. Sun brunch $18.95. Child's menu. Specializes in seafood, steak, pasta. Own baking, pasta. Pianist. Converted railroad station. Braille menu. Outdoor dining. Cr cds: A, D, DS, MC, V.
D **SC**

★ ★ **INDIA GARDEN.** *328 Atwood St (15213). 412/682-3000. www.india garden.net.* Hrs: 11:30 am-1 pm, 3 pm-1 am. Res accepted. Northern Indian menu. Setups. A la carte entrees: $7.95-$13.95. Buffet: lunch $8.95. Specialties: tandoori chicken, chicken tekka masala, vegetable korma. Indian decor, chairs. Cr cds: A, D, DS, MC, V.
D

★ ★ **JIMMY TSANG'S.** *5700 Centre Ave (15206). 412/661-4226.* Hrs: 11:30 am-10 pm; Fri, Sat to 11 pm; Sun 3:30-9 pm; early-bird dinner Mon-Sat 3-6 pm. Closed July 4, Thanksgiving. Chinese menu. Bar. A la carte: lunch $7-$9, dinner $9-$12. Specialties: Peking duck, honey chicken, Mongolian beef. Oriental decor, artwork. Cr cds: A, D, DS, MC, V.
D **⛟**

★ ★ **KAYA.** *2000 Smallman St (15222). 412/261-6565. www.bigburrito.com.* Hrs: 11:30 am-11 pm; Fri, Sat to midnight; Sun to 9 pm. Closed hols. Carribean menu. Bar. Lunch $3.50-$10, dinner $3.50-$19. Specialties: Jamaican jerk chicken wings, grilled alligator, salmon. Outdoor dining. Cr cds: A, D, DS, MC, V.
D **SC**

★ ★ **LE MONT.** *1114 Grandview Ave (15211). 412/431-3100. www.lemont pittsburgh.com.* Hrs: 5-11:30 pm; Sun

4-10 pm. Closed major hols. Res accepted. Contemporary American menu. Bar to midnight. Wine list. A la carte entrees: dinner $27-$50. Specializes in variety of wild game dishes, flaming desserts. Own baking. Pianist Fri, Sat. Valet parking. Atop Mt Washington; panoramic view of city. Cr cds: A, D, DS, MC, V.
D **⛟**

★ ★ ★ **LE POMMIER.** *2104 E Carson St (15203). 412/431-1901. www.le pommier.com.* Hrs: 11 am-2 pm, 5:30-10:30 pm; Sat 5:30-10:30 pm. Closed Sun; hols. Res accepted. French menu. Bar. Wine cellar. A la carte entrees: lunch $6-$12, dinner $16-$28. Specializes in seasonal French country fare. Own baking. Valet parking Fri, Sat. Located in oldest storefront in area (1863). Outdoor dining in season. Country French decor. Cr cds: A, D, DS, MC, V.
D **⛟**

★ ★ ★ **LONDON GRILLE.** *1500 Washington Rd, Mt Lebanon (15228). 412/563-3400.* Hrs: 11:30 am-10 pm; Fri, Sat to 11:30 pm; Sun noon-9 pm. Closed Dec 25. British menu. Bar. Wine list. Lunch $7.95-$11.95; dinner $17.95-$25.95. Specialties: prime rib, beef Wellington. Patio dining. 4 dining rms. Cr cds: A, C, D, DS, MC, V.
D **⛟**

★ **MAX & ERMA'S.** *5533 Walnut St (15232). 412/681-5775. www.maxand ermas.com.* Hrs: 11:30 am-10 pm; Fri, Sat to midnight. Closed Thanksgiving, Dec 25. Bar. Lunch, dinner $7-$15. Specializes in steak, ribs, pasta. Cr cds: A, DS, MC, V.
D **⛟**

★ ★ **MAX'S ALLEGHENY TAVERN.** *537 Suismon St (15212). 412/231-1899. www.maxsalleghenytavern.com.* Hrs: 11 am-midnight; Sun to 10 pm. Closed hols. German menu. Bar. A la carte entrees: lunch $4.25-$7.95, dinner $5.95-$13.95. Specialties: jagerschnitzel, kase spatzle, sauerbraten. Tavern with German memorabilia and collection of photographs. Cr cds: A, D, DS, MC, V.
D **⛟**

★ ★ **MONTEREY BAY FISH GROTTO.** *1411 Grandview Ave (15211). 412/481-4414. www.monterey*

bayfishgrotto.com. Menu changes daily. Hrs: 11 am-3 pm, 5-10 pm; Fri, Sat to 11 pm; Sun 5-9 pm. Res accepted. Wine list. Lunch $7.95-$16.95; dinner $14.95-$28.95. Child's menu. Entertainment. Cr cds: A, D, DS, MC, V.

★★ 1902 LANDMARK TAVERN. *24 Market Sq (15222). 412/471-1902.* Hrs: 11:30 am-11 pm; Fri, Sat to 11 pm. Closed Sun; hols. Res accepted. American menu. Bar to 2 am. Lunch $7.95, dinner $18.95. Specializes in steak, fresh seafood. Restored tavern (1902); ornate tin ceiling, original tiles. Cr cds: A, D, DS, MC, V.

★★ PASTA PIATTO. *736 Bellefonte St (15232). 412/621-5547.* Hrs: 11:30 am-3 pm, 4:30-10 pm; Wed, Thurs to 10:30 pm; Fri, Sat to 11 pm; Sun 4-9 pm. Closed hols. Northern Italian menu. Bar. Lunch $6-$12, dinner $12-$22. Child's menu. Specializes in homemade pasta, veal, seafood. Cr cds: A, MC, V.

★★ PENN BREWERY. *800 Vinial St Troy Hill (15212). 412/237-9402. www.pennbrew.com.* Hrs: 11 am-midnight; Fri, Sat to 1 am. Closed Sun; hols. German menu. Bar. Lunch $5-$12, dinner $8-$15. Child's menu. Specialties: Wiener schnitzel, sauerbrauten, chicken Berlin. Entertainment Tues-Sat. Outdoor dining. Restored 19th-century brewery, German beer hall-style communal dining. Cr cds: A, DS, MC, V.

★★★ PICCOLO MONDO. *661 Andersen Dr (15220). 412/922-0920. www.piccolo-mondo.com.* Hrs: 11:30 am-10 pm; Sat to 4-11 pm. Closed Sun exc Mother's Day; some hols. Res accepted. Northern Italian menu. Bar. Wine list. Lunch $7.50-$13, dinner $14-$24. Child's menu. Specializes in fresh fish, veal. Own desserts. Parking. Jacket. Cr cds: A, D, DS, MC, V.

★★★ POLI. *2607 Murray Ave (15217). 412/521-6400. www.polisince1921.com.* Hrs: 11:30 am-11 pm; Sun 1-9 pm; early-bird dinner Tues-Fri 3-5:30 pm. Closed Mon; Thanksgiving, Dec 25. Bar. Lunch $6-$10, dinner $15-$20.

Child's menu. Specializes in fresh seafood, Italian cuisine. Own baking. Valet parking. Family-owned. Cr cds: A, D, DS, MC, V.

★ PRIMANTI BROTHERS. *46 18th St (15222). 412/263-2142. www. primantibros.com.* Hrs: open 24 hrs. Closed Dec 25. Italian, American menu. Wine, beer. Prices: $3.75-$4.25. Specializes in deli sandwiches with fries and cole slaw inside, soups. Family-owned. Cr cds: A, MC, V.

★★★ RICO'S. *1 Rico Ln (15237). 412/931-1989. www.ricosrestaurant. com.* Hrs: 11:45 am-2:45 pm, 4-10:30 pm; Fri, Sat 4-11:30 pm. Closed Sun; hols. Italian, American menu. Bar to midnight. Wine cellar. Lunch $8.50-$13.50, dinner $16.50-$32. Specializes in fresh seafood, veal. Valet parking. Old World atmosphere; Italian lithographs. Jacket. Cr cds: A, D, DS, MC, V.

★★ SEVENTH STREET GRILLE. *130 7th St (15222). 412/338-0303. www.seventhstreetgrille.com.* Hrs: 11:30 am-9 pm; Fri, Sat to 11 pm; Sun to 8 pm. Closed hols. Res accepted. Continental menu. Bar. Lunch $8-$10, dinner $16-$18. Specializes in grilled seafood, prime rib. Cr cds: A, D, DS, MC, V.

★★ SOBA LOUNGE. *5847 Ellsworth Ave (15232). 412/362-5656. www. bigburrito.com.* Hrs: 5-10 pm; Fri, Sat to 11 pm. Closed Thanksgiving. Res accepted. Pan-Asian menu. Bars. Dinner $15-$30. Specialties: pork and vegetarian dumplings, wok-seared salmon, zaru soba noodles. Own noodles. Outdoor dining. Three dining levels; eclectic decor with original artwork. Cr cds: A, D, DS, MC, V.

★★★ STEELHEAD GRILL. *112 Washington Place (15219). 412/394-3474. www.steelhead-grill.com.* Menu changes seasonally. Hrs: 6:30 am-2 pm, 5-10 pm; Sat, Sun 6:30 am-2 pm, 5-11 pm. Res accepted. Wine list. Lunch $5-$11; dinner $15-$31. Child's menu. Entertainment. Cr cds: A, C, D, DS, ER, JCB, MC, V.

★★ **SUSHI TWO.** *2122 E Carson St (15203). 412/431-7874. www.sushi2-go.com.* Hrs: 11:30 am-3 pm, 5-10 pm; Fri to 11:30 pm; Sat 11:30 am-11 pm; Sun 1-9 pm. Closed Thanksgiving. Res accepted. Japanese menu. Bar. Lunch $5.95-$11.50, dinner $10.95-$40.95. Specializes in traditional Japanese dishes. Valet parking Fri, Sat. Contemporary Japanese decor. Cr cds: A, D, DS, MC, V.
D ⊟

★★ **TAMBELLINI.** *860 Saw Mill Run Blvd (15226). 412/481-1118. www.tambellini.com.* Hrs: 11:30 am-10 pm. Closed Sun; Jan 1, Thanksgiving, Dec 25. Res accepted. Continental menu. Bar. Lunch $7.95-$9.50, dinner $14.50-$18.95. Complete meals: dinner $21.95. Child's menu. Specializes in seafood, pasta, steak. Valet parking (dinner). Modern decor. Cr cds: A, D, DS, MC, V.
D ⊟

★ **TESSARO'S.** *4601 Liberty Ave (15224). 412/682-6809.* Hrs: 11 am-midnight. Closed Sun; hols. Mexican, American menu. Bar. Lunch $6-$8, dinner $12-$20. Specializes in hamburgers, fresh seafood. Casual decor has pressed tin ceiling (ca early 1900s), paddle ceiling fans, fireplaces. Cr cds: A, C, D, DS, MC, V.
D ⊟

★ **THAI PLACE.** *5528 Walnut St (15232). 412/687-8586.* Hrs: 11 am-10 pm; Fri, Sat to 11 pm; Sun noon-9:30 pm; Mon from 4:30 pm. Thai menu. Bar. A la carte entrees: lunch $5.95-$7.95, dinner $7.95-$16.95. Specializes in authentic Thai cuisine. Asian art. Cr cds: A, D, DS, MC, V.
D

★★ **TIN ANGEL.** *1200 Grandview Ave (15211). 412/381-1919.* Hrs: 5-10 pm. Closed Sun; hols. Res accepted. Bar. Wine list. Complete meals: $36-$59. Specializes in steak and seafood. Panoramic view of city. Cr cds: A, D, DS, MC, V.
⊟

VERMONT FLATBREAD CO. *701 Penn Ave (15222). 412/434-1220.* Hrs: 11 am-10 pm; Fri, Sat to 11 pm. Closed Sun. Bar. Lunch $5.95-$7.50, dinner $5.95-$8.25. Child's menu. Specialties: maple-sugar flatbread,

Italian grilled sandwich, sweet stuffed peppers with chorizo sausage. Own baking, pasta. Street parking. Rustic Vermont decor with skylights. Cr cds: A, D, DS, MC, V.
D ⊟

Unrated Dining Spots

DAVE AND ANDY'S ICE CREAM PARLOR. *207 Atwood St (15213). 412/681-9906.* Hrs: 11:30 am-10 pm; Sat, Sun from noon. Closed hols. Specialties: homemade ice cream (fresh daily), homemade cones. 1930s look; some counters.
D

TERRACE ROOM. *530 Wm Penn Pl (15219). 412/281-7100. www.omni hotels.com.* Hrs: tea time 2:30-5:30 pm. English custom tea serv. Bar. A la carte items also avail. Specializes in tea, finger sandwiches, pastries. Pianist. Parking avail opp Lobby room; Georgian decor. Cr cds: A, D, DS, MC, V.
D ⊟

Pittsburgh International Airport Area

(D-1) *See also Pittsburgh*

Services and Information

Information. 412/472-3525 or 412/472-3526.

Lost and Found. 412/472-3500.

Weather. 412/936-1212.

Cash Machines. Landside Terminal, entrance; Airside Terminal, throughout concourses in Passenger Service Centers.

Airlines. American, British Airways, Continental, Delta, Northwest, TWA, United, USAir.

Motels/Motor Lodges

★★ **AIRPORT PLAZA HOTEL.** *1500 Beers School Rd, Coraopolis (15108). 412/264-7900; fax 412/262-3229. www.plazaairport.com.* 193 rms, 2 story. S, D $59; under 18 free. Pet accepted; $50 refundable. TV; cable (premium). Complimentary continental bkfst. Restaurant adj open 24 hrs. Ck-out noon. Meeting rms. Business servs avail. In-rm modem link. Sundries. Free airport transportation. Exercise equipt. Some refrigerators. Some balconies. Cr cds: A, C, D, DS, MC, V.

★★ **HAMPTON INN.** *1420 Beers School Rd, Coraopolis (15108). 412/264-0020; fax 412/264-3220; toll-free 800/426-7866. www.hamptoninn.com.* 129 rms, 5 story. S, D $79-$99; under 18 free. Crib free. Pet accepted. TV; cable (premium). Complimentary continental bkfst. Coffee in rms. Restaurant adj 6 am-10 pm. Ck-out noon. Meeting rms. Business servs avail. Valet serv. Free airport transportation. Health club privileges. Cr cds: A, C, D, DS, ER, MC, V.

★ **LA QUINTA INN.** *1433 Beers School Rd, Coraopolis (15108). 412/269-0400; fax 412/269-9258; res 800/687-6667. www.laquinta.com.* 127 rms, 3 story. S $84.99; D $94.99; suites $94.99-$104.99; under 18 free. Crib free. Pet accepted. TV; cable. Complimentary continental bkfst. Coffee in rms. Restaurant adj 6 am-11 pm. Ck-out noon. Coin lndry. Business servs avail. In-rm modem link. Valet serv. Sundries. Free airport transportation. Cr cds: A, D, DS, MC, V.

★ **RED ROOF INN.** *1454 Beers School Rd, Coraopolis (15108). 412/264-5678; fax 412/264-8034. www.redroof.com.* 119 rms, 3 story. S $49.99-$59.99; D $54-$64; each addl $6; under 18 free. Crib free. Pet accepted. TV; cable (premium). Restaurant opp 6 am-10 pm. Ck-out noon. Coin lndry. Meeting rm. Business servs avail. Valet serv. Free airport transportation. Cr cds: A, D, DS, MC, V.

Hotels

★★ **CROWNE PLAZA.** *1160 Thorn Run Rd, Coraopolis (15108). 412/262-2400; fax 412/264-9373. www.crownplaza.com.* 193 rms, 9 story. S $69-$129; D $69-$139; each addl $10; suites $109-$150; under 18 free; wkend rates. Crib free. TV; cable (pre-

mium). Pool; lifeguard. Coffee in rms. Restaurant 6:30 am-1:30 pm, 5-10 pm; Sat, Sun 7 am-11 pm. Bar 11-2 am; entertainment wkends. Ck-out noon. Meeting rms. Business center. In-rm modem link. Concierge. Airport transportation. Exercise equipt. Luxury Level. Cr cds: A, C, D, DS, MC, V.

★★★ **HYATT REGENCY PITTS-BURGH INTERNATIONAL AIR-PORT.** *1111 Airport Blvd, Pittsburgh (15231). 724/899-1234. www.hyatt.com.* 336 rms, 11 story. S, D $79-$179; under 17 free. Crib avail. TV; cable (premium). Indoor pool. Restaurant 6:30 am-10 pm. Bar to midnight. Ck-out noon, ck-in 3 pm. Meeting rms. Business center. In-rm modem link. Concierge. Exercise equipt. Minibars; many refrigerators in suites. Cr cds: A, D, DS, MC, V.

Restaurant

★★★ **HYEHOLDE.** *190 Hyeholde Dr, Moontownship (15108). 412/264-3116.* Hrs: 11:30 am-2 pm, 5-10 pm; Sat from 5 pm. Closed Sun exc Mother's Day; hols. Res accepted. Continental menu. Serv bar. Wine list. Complete meals: lunch $9.50-$13, dinner $19.50-$36. Specializes in lamb, fresh trout. Own baking. Valet parking. Patio dining. Herb garden. Country French decor; fireplaces; estate grounds. Cr cds: A, C, D, DS, MC, V.

Pocono Mountains

See also Bushkill, Canadensis, Hawley, Milford, Mount Pocono, Shawnee on Delaware

(Northeast Pennsylvania resort area)

Information Pocono Mountains Vacation Bureau, 1004 Main St, Stroudsburg 18360; 717/424-6050; for free brochures phone 800/POCONOS

Web www.poconos.org

The Pocono Mountains area in northeast Pennsylvania extends

orth from Wind Gap and Delaware
Water Gap into Pike, Carbon, Mon-
oe, and Wayne counties. Within its
,400 square miles almost every form
f recreation can be found.

This scenic country with 500
akes, including Lake Wallenpaupack
see HAWLEY), has hundreds of
ccommodations and is a well-estab-
shed resort area. Visitors, many of
whom return year after year, take
dvantage of the large plush resorts,
maller family-run resorts, house-
eeping cottage resorts, camping
esorts, country inns, and bed &
reakfasts. There is primitive,
orested country for those who wish
o rough it. For the hunter there are
eer, bear, wildcat, and fox. For the
eshwater angler there are black
ass, trout, pickerel, and walleye.

Summer offers boating, swimming,
iking, horseback riding, mountain
iking, golf, theaters, and a host of
ther diversions. In the autumn
here is a magnificent display of
oliage as well as heritage festivals
nd country fairs. The first snowfall
rings skiing, snowboarding, snow
ubing, ice-skating, sleigh rides,
oboganing, and snowmobiling.

The name "Pocono" was probably
aken from the Native American
ocohanne, meaning a stream
etween the mountains. Settled in
he mid-1700s, the Poconos yielded
on and, later, coal. The lakes and
orest still retain their charm. The
and "between the mountains" is as
viting as it always has been.

Port Allegany

-3) *See also Bradford*

ettled 1816 **Pop** 2,355 **Elev** 1,481 ft
rea code 814 **Zip** 16743
formation Chamber of Commerce,
2 Church St; 814/642-2181

ative Americans called this spot
canoe place" because here on the
ortage route between the Allegheny
nd Susquehanna headwaters they
aused to build canoes. Early settlers
ollowed their route. Soon after the
own was established, lumbering
perations reached their peak; later

industrial expansion included coal
mining and tanning. In the late
1890s, the borough became the center of a boom resulting from the discovery of natural gas and glass sand.

What to See and Do

Eldred World War II Museum.
Exhibits include battle maps, posters,
dioramas with narrative, periscope,
video history. Centerpiece is
"Remembering the Women Behind
the Front Lines" exhibit. Library.
(Tues, Thurs, Sat, Sun) 15 mi N on PA
155, 5 mi N on PA 446, in Eldred.
Phone 814/225-2220. **FREE**

Sizerville State Park. Approx 385
acres. Swimming pool; fishing, hunting; x-country skiing, snowmobiling.
Picnicking, playground, snack bar.
Tent and trailer sites. Standard fees.
19 mi S on PA 155, in Sizerville.
Phone 814/486-5605.

Motel/Motor Lodge

★ **MIDTOWN MOTEL.** *111 N Main St
(16743).* 814/642-2575. 25 rms, 2
story. S $40-$49; D $44-$54; each addl
$5. Crib $5. TV; cable (premium).
Restaurant opp 6 am-11 pm. Ck-out
11 am. Cr cds: A, D, DS, MC, V.
D ⊗ 🖈

Pottstown

(E-7) *See also Limerick, Norristown,
Reading*

Settled 1701 **Pop** 21,859 **Elev** 160 ft
Area code 610 **Zip** 19464

Information TriCounty Area Chamber of Commerce, 135 High St;
610/326-2900

Web www.tricopa.com

An iron forge operating in 1714 at
Manatawny Creek, about three miles
north of Pottstown, was the first
industrial establishment in the state.
The borough was established by John
Potts, an ironmaster, on land
William Penn had earlier deeded to
his son, John. Today the community
is the commercial and cultural hub

for an area with a population of 130,000. Nearly 200 modern industries are located here.

What to See and Do

Boyertown Museum of Historic Vehicles. Collection of over 100 antique autos, trucks, sleighs, buggies, and bicycles. Also include the Hill, which was among the first gasoline-powered cars. (Tues-Sun) 7 mi N via PA 100, 73, in Boyertown, on Walnut St. Phone 610/367-2090. ¢¢

French Creek State Park. Approx 7,330 acres, two lakes. Boating (rentals, mooring, launching), fishing, swimming pool, ice fishing; hiking trails, playground, disc golf. Picnicking. Tent and trailer sites, cabins. Standard fees. 9 mi W on PA 724, then 4 mi S on PA 345. Phone 610/582-9680. Also here is

Hopewell Furnace National Historic Site. (see)

Merritt's Museum of Childhood. Antique toys, costumed figures, furnishings; gift shop in lobby. (Mon, Wed-Sun; closed hols) 1 mi W on US 422, in Douglassville. Phone 610/385-3408. ¢¢ Admission includes

Mary Merritt Doll Museum. Antique dolls and toys dating from 1725 to 1900. (Mon, Wed-Sun; closed hols) Phone 610/385-3809.

Pottsgrove Manor. (1752) Newly restored house of John Potts, 18th-century ironmaster and founder of Pottstown; outstanding example of early Georgian architecture and furniture. Includes recently discovered slave quarters and Potts's office. Slide orientation. Museum shop. (Tues-Sun; closed hols) W King St and PA 100. Phone 610/326-4014. **FREE**

Ringing Rocks Park. Roller skating (Fri-Sun; fee); nature trails, picnicking, interesting rock formations. (Daily) 3 mi N off PA 663. Phone 610/323-6560. **FREE**

Special Event

Duryea Day Antique & Classic Auto Show. Boyertown Community Park. Antique autos, trucks and other vehicles; displays, arts and crafts, flea market with automotive memorabilia, activities, Pennsylvania Dutch food. Labor Day wkend.

Motels/Motor Lodges

★ **COMFORT INN.** *Rte 100 and Shoemaker Rd (19464). 610/326-5000; fax 610/970-7230; res 800/879-2477. www.pottstowncomfortinn.com.* 121 rms, 4 story. S, D $79-$109; each addl $7; under 18 free; golf plans; wkend rates. Crib free. Pet accepted. TV; cable (premium). Heated pool; lifeguard. Complimentary continental bkfst. Restaurant adj 6 am-11 pm. Rm serv. Ck-out noon. Coin lndry. Meeting rms. Business servs avail. In-rm modem link. Free bus depot transportation. Health club privileges. Refrigerators, microwaves avail Cr cds: A, C, D, DS, ER, JCB, MC, V.

[icons: D, pet, pool, no-smoking, health-club, SC]

★ ★ **HOLIDAY INN EXPRESS.** *1600 Industrial Hwy (19464). 610/327-3300, fax 610/327-9447; toll-free 800/386-0031. www.hiexpottstownpa.com.* 120 rms, 4 story. S, D $69; each addl $5; suites $122; under 19 free; wkly, hol rates; higher rates special events. Crib free. Pet accepted. TV; cable (premium), VCR avail (movies). Pool. Complimentary continental bkfst, coffee in rms. Restaurant adj open 24 hrs. Rm serv 24 hrs. Ck-out noon. Meeting rms. Business servs avail. In-rm modem link. Sundries. Valet serv. Health club privileges. Refrigerators, microwaves avail. Cr cds: A, D, DS, MC, V.

[icons: D, pet, pool, no-smoking, health-club]

B&B/Small Inn

★ ★ ★ **TWIN TURRETS INN.** *11 E Philadelphia Ave, Boyertown (19512). 610/367-4513; fax 610/369-7898; toll-free 877/877-7897. www.netjunction. com/twinturrets.* 10 rms, 3 story. S, D $95-$120; each addl $15; wkly rates. Children over 12 yrs preferred. TV; cable (premium), VCR avail. Complimentary full bkfst; afternoon refreshments. Restaurant nearby. Ck-out 11 am, ck-in 1 pm. Luggage handling. Business center. Health club privileges. Original Boyer mansion built in 1850; antiques and original art. Flower gardens with fountain. Totally nonsmoking. Cr cds: A, DS, MC, V.

[icons: no-smoking, health-club, SC, jogging]

Restaurants

★ ★ ★ **CAB FRYE'S TAVERN.** *914 Gravel Pike; Rte 29, Palm (18070).*

215/679-9935. www.cabfryes.com. Hrs: 11:30 am-2 pm, 5-10 pm; Mon, Tues, Sat from 5 pm. Closed Sun; hols. Res required Fri, Sat (dinner). Continental menu. Bar from 4 pm. Wine cellar. A la carte entrees: lunch $5-$10, dinner $13-$22. Child's menu. Specialties: Scottish lobster, Dover sole, wild game. Parking. Outdoor dining. Old stage coach stop; countryside atmosphere. Antiques. Cr cds: A, DS, MC, V.

D ⌐¬

★ ★ ★ **COVENTRY FORGE INN.** *3360 Coventryville Rd (19465).* *610/469-6222.* Hrs: 5:30-9 pm; Sat 5-10 pm. Res accepted. Closed Mon, Sun exc Mother's Day; Jan 1, Dec 25. French menu. Bar. Wine cellar. A la carte entrees: dinner $16.95-$25.95. Prix fixe: (Sat) dinner $39.50. Specialties: carre d'agneau Provençal, escalopes de veau. Own baking. Built in 1717; antiques. Cr cds: A, DS, MC, V.

★ ★ ★ **GRACIE'S 21ST CENTURY CAFE.** *Nana Tawny Rd, Pine Forge (19548). 610/323-4004. www.gracies21stcentury.com.* Hrs: 5:30-10:30 pm. Closed Mon, Tues, Sun; hols. Res required Sat (dinner). Contemporary American menu. Bar from 5:30 pm. Wine cellar. A la carte entrees: dinner $21.50-$31.50. Specialties: rasta pasta, quail in rose petal sauce, sushi-quality seared tuna. Jazz Fri, Sat. Valet parking. Outdoor dining. Ultramodern facility. Cr cds: A, MC, V.

D ⌐¬

Quakertown (Bucks County)

(D-7) *See also Allentown, Bethlehem, Doylestown (Bucks County), Pottstown*

Founded 1715 **Pop** 8,931 **Elev** 500 ft
Area code 215 **Zip** 18951
Information Upper Bucks County Chamber of Commerce, 2170 Portzer Rd; 215/536-3211 or Bucks County Conference and Visitors Bureau, 152

Swamp Rd, Doylestown 18901, phone 215/345-4552 or 800/836-2825
Web www.ubcc.org

Once a station on the Underground Railroad, Quakertown today still retains some of its colonial appearance. In 1798, angered by what they considered an unfair federal tax and incited by one John Fries, Quakertown housewives started greeting tax assessors with pans of hot water. The "hot water" rebellion cooled down when federal troops arrived, but the town switched political parties (from Federalist to Jeffersonian) almost en masse.

What to See and Do

Mennonite Heritage Center. An interpretive video and exhibits including quilts, Pennsylvania German Fraktur, furniture, books, deeds, and clothing show the history of local Mennonites through three centuries. (Tues-Sun) 4 mi S of PA 309 on PA 113, in Harleysville, 565 Yoder Rd. Phone 215/256-3020. **Donation**

Restaurants

★ **LA PIAZZA CAFE.** *1408 W Broad St, Quakertown (18951). 215/536-2452.* Hrs: 11 am-11 pm. Closed hols. Res required Fri, Sat (dinner). Italian menu. A la carte entrees: lunch $5.95, dinner $7.50-$12.95. Buffet: lunch $7.95, dinner $10.95. Child's menu. Specializes in chicken, pizza, pasta. Parking. Cr cds: A, D, DS, MC, V.

D ⌐¬

★ ★ ★ **WASHINGTON HOUSE.** *136 N Main St, Sellersville (18960). 215/257-3000. www.washington-house. com.* Hrs: 11:30 am-2:30 pm, 5-9 pm; Fri to 10:30 pm; Sat noon-2 pm, 5-10:30 pm; Sun (brunch) 10 am-2 pm, 4-8 pm; early-bird dinner 5-6 pm; Sun from 4 pm. Closed hols. Res accepted. Bar to midnight. A la carte entrees: lunch $6-$12, dinner $12-$20. Sun brunch $13.95-$15.95. Child's menu. Specializes in fresh fish, chicken, beef. Harpist Mon (eve). Parking. Restored Victorian bldg. Antiques, artwork. Romantic atmosphere. Cr cds: A, MC, V.

D

Reading

(D-7) *See also Denver/Adamstown, Hamburg, Kutztown, Lancaster, Pottstown*

Founded 1748 **Pop** 81,207 **Elev** 260 ft
Area code 484 and 610
Information Reading & Berks County Visitors Bureau, 352 Penn St 19602; 610/375-4085 or 800/443-6610
Web www.readingberkspa.com

A city of railroads and industry famous for its superb pretzels, Reading (RED-ing) was the second community in the United States to vote a Socialist government into office; however, the city has not had such a government for many years. Love of music and the thrift and vigor of the "Dutch" are reflected in the character of this unofficial capital of Pennsylvania Dutch land.

William Penn purchased the land now occupied by Reading from the Lenni-Lenape Native Americans and settled his two sons, Thomas and Richard, on it. They named it Reading (fern meadow) for their home in England. During the Revolution the citizens of Reading mustered troops for the Continental army, forged cannon, and provided a depot for military supplies and a prison for Hessians and British. The hundreds of skilled German craftspeople, plus canal and railroad transportation, ignited Reading's industrial development. Today some of the world's leading industries continue to headquarter here.

What to See and Do

Berks County Heritage Center. Historical interpretive complex. Here are the Gruber Wagon Works (1882), where finely crafted wagons were produced for farm and industry; Wertz's Red Bridge (1867), the longest single-span covered bridge in the state; Deppen Cemetery, with graves of Irish workers who died of "swamp fever" while building the Union Canal; C. Howard Hiester Canal Center, with its collection of canal artifacts. Tours of wagon works and canal center; orientation slide program. (May-Oct, Tues-Sun) 4 mi N via PA 183, then W onto Red Bridge Rd, in Bern Twp. Phone 610/374-8839. ¢¢

Conrad Weiser Homestead. (1729) Restored and furnished house of colonial "ambassador" to the Iroquois nation; springhouse; gravesite; visitor center; picnicking in 26-acre park. (Wed-Sun) 14 mi W via US 422. Phone 610/589-2934. ¢¢

Daniel Boone Homestead. Birthplace of Daniel Boone in 1734. Approx 570 acres; includes Boone House, barn, blacksmith shop and sawmill. Picnicking. Nature trails. Youth camping. Visitor's center. (Tues-Sun; closed some hols) 7 mi E on US 422 to Baumstown, then N on Boone Rd. Phone 610/582-4900. ¢¢

Historical Society of Berks County. Local history exhibits; decorative arts, antiques, transportation displays. (Tues-Sat; closed hols) 940 Centre Ave. Phone 610/375-4375. ¢¢

Koziar's Christmas Village. Valley set aglow with over 500,000 Christmas lights; Wishing Well Lane; two barns filled with handmade items, decorations; theme exhibits, Santa's Post Office. (Thanksgiving-Dec) 12 mi N via PA 183, in Bernville, 782 Christmas Village Rd. Phone 610/488-1110. ¢¢¢

Mid-Atlantic Air Museum. Aviation museum dedicated to the preservation of vintage aircraft; planes are restored to flying condition by volunteers. Collection of 40 airplanes and helicopters; 20 on public display, including Martin 4-0-4 airliners, B-25 bomber and others. (Daily; closed Jan 1, Thanksgiving, Dec 25) Reading Regional Airport, at PA 183 and Van Reed Rd. Phone 610/372-7333. ¢¢

Outlet Shopping. More than 300 factory outlet stores can be found at five different shopping complexes. Contact Visitors Bureau. Phone 610/375-4085.

Reading Public Museum and Art Gallery. In 25-acre Museum Park with stream. Exhibits of art and science. (Tues-Sun; closed Dec 25) 500 Museum Rd. Phone 610/371-5850. ¢¢ Adj is

Planetarium. Changing exhibits. Star and laser light shows. Phone 610/371-5854. ¢¢

Motels/Motor Lodges

★ ★ **BEST WESTERN INN.** *4635 Perkiomen Ave (19606). 610/779-2345; fax 610/779-8348; res 800/780-7234. www.bestwestern.com.* 71 rms, 2 story. May-Nov: S $58-$83; D $63-$88; each addl $5; under 18 free; lower rates rest of yr. Crib $5. Pet accepted, some restrictions; $5. TV; cable. Pool; lifeguard. Restaurant (see also ANTIQUE AIRPLANE). Bar 11-2 am. Ck-out noon. Coin lndry. Meeting rms. Business servs avail. Valet serv. Sundries. Health club privileges. Lawn games. Microwaves avail. Balconies. Cr cds: A, D, DS, MC, V.

★ **COMFORT INN.** *2200 Stacy Dr (19605). 610/371-0500; fax 610/478-9421; toll-free 800/228-5150. www.comfortinn.com.* 60 rms, 2 story. Apr-Oct: S $55-$70; D $55-$75; each addl $5; under 18 free; wkly rates; higher rates: car shows, antique shows; lower rates rest of yr. Crib free. TV; cable (premium), VCR. Complimentary continental bkfst. Restaurant nearby. Ck-out 11 am. Meeting rms. Business servs avail. In-rm modem link. Valet serv. Free airport transportation. Exercise equipt. Some refrigerators; microwaves avail. Cr cds: A, C, D, DS, ER, JCB, MC, V.

★ **ECONO LODGE INN OUTLET VILLAGE.** *635 Spring St, Wyomissing (19610). 610/378-5105; fax 610/373-3181. www.econolodge.com.* 84 rms, 4 story. Mar-Nov: S D $58-$85; each addl $5; under 18 free; higher rates: Keystone Nationals, Antique Wkends; lower rates rest of yr. Crib free. Pet accepted; $5/day. TV; cable (premium). Complimentary continental bkfst. Restaurant adj 7 am-10 pm. Ck-out 11 am. Business servs avail. Sundries. Coin lndry. Exercise equipt. Many refrigerators, microwaves. Cr cds: A, D, DS, MC, V.

★ ★ **HOLIDAY INN.** *6170 Morgantown Rd, Morgantown (19543). 610/286-3000; fax 610/286-1920; toll-free 800/339-0264. www.holiday-inn.com.* 191 rms, 4 story. S $79-$99; D $89-$109; each addl $5; under 18 free. Crib $10. Pet accepted, some restrictions. TV; cable (premium). Indoor pool; whirlpool. Coffee in rms. Restaurant 6:30 am-2 pm, 5-10 pm; Sat, Sun from 5 pm. Bar 5 pm-1 am. Ck-out noon. Meeting rms. Business center. In-rm modem link. Sundries. Exercise equipt. Some refrigerators. Cr cds: A, C, D, DS, JCB, MC, V.

★ ★ **INN AT READING.** *1040 N Park Rd, Wyomissing (19610). 610/372-7811; fax 610/372-4545; toll-free 800/383-9713. www.innatreading.com.* 250 rms, 1-2 story. S, D $79-$129; suites $99-$129; each addl $10; under 18 free; some wknd rates. Crib free. TV; cable (premium). Pool; poolside serv, lifeguard. Restaurant 6:30 am-10 pm. Bar 11-1 am; entertainment. Ck-out 11 am. Meeting rms. Business center. In-rm modem link. Bellhops. Valet serv. Free airport, bus depot transportation. Exercise equipt. Refrigerators. Picnic tables. Cr cds: A, C, D, DS, MC, V.

★ **RAMADA INN AT THE OUTLETS.** *2545 N 5th St (19605). 610/929-4741; fax 610/929-5237; toll-free 888/929-9234. www.ramada.com.* 138 rms, 2 story. S $55-$175; D $60-$175; each addl $10; under 18 free; some wkend rates. Crib free. TV; cable (premium). Pool. Coffee in rms. Restaurant 6:30-10:30 am, 5-9 pm. Bar 5-11:30 pm. Ck-out noon. Meeting rms. Business servs avail. In-rm modem link. Valet serv. Sundries. Refrigerators, microwaves. Cr cds: A, C, D, DS, MC, V.

Hotel

★ ★ **READING INN.** *1741 W Papermill Rd, Wyomissing (19610). 610/376-3811; fax 610/375-7562.* 254 rms, 5 story. S, D $79-$139; each addl $10; suites $185-$195; studio rms $140-$150; under 18 free; some wkend rates. Crib free. Pet accepted; $50. TV; cable (premium), VCR avail. Indoor pool; whirlpool, poolside serv, lifeguard. Coffee in rms. Restaurant 6:30 am-10:30 pm. Bar 11:30-2 am; entertainment. Ck-out noon. Meeting rms. Business servs avail. In-rm modem link. Bellhops. Gift shop. Free airport, bus depot transportation. Putting green. Exercise equipt; sauna. Massage. Health club privileges. Some bathrm phones; microwaves avail. Cr cds: A, C, D, DS, JCB, MC, V.

Restaurants

★ ★ **ALPENHOF BAVARIAN.** *903 Morgantown Rd (19607). 610/373-1624.* Hrs: 11:30 am-2 pm, 5-8:30 pm; Mon to 2 pm; Sat to 9 pm; Sun 11:30 am-7 pm. Closed Jan 1, Dec 25. Res accepted. German, American menu. Bar. Lunch $3.45-$6.95, dinner $8.75-$19.95. Specialties: schnitzel, sauerbraten. Outdoor dining. Bavarian Gasthaus with authentic decor. Family-owned. Cr cds: A, MC, V.

★ ★ **ANTIQUE AIRPLANE.** *4635 Perkiomen Ave (19606). 610/779-2345.* Hrs: 7 am-3 pm, 5-9:30 pm; Sun to 1 pm. Closed Jan 1, Dec 25. Res accepted. Bar. Bkfst $2.95-$4.95, lunch $3.99-$5.95, dinner $6.95-$17.95. Child's menu. Specializes in seafood, steak. Salad bar. Casual elegance; aviation theme. Cr cds: A, D, DS, MC, V.

★ ★ ★ **GREEN HILLS INN.** *2444 Morgantown Rd (19607). 610/777-9611.* Hrs: 5-9 pm. Closed Sun. Res accepted. French menu. Wine cellar. A la carte entrees: dinner $16.95-$27.95. Specialties: herb-crusted rack of lamb, boneless squab with honey ginger glaze, warm Valrhona chocolate souffle. Family-owned. Cr cds: A, D, MC, V.

Scranton

(C-7) *See also Carbondale, Pocono Mountains, Wilkes-Barre*

Settled 1771 **Pop** 76,415 **Elev** 754 ft
Area code 570
Information Northeast Pennsylvania Convention and Visitors Bureau Montage Mountain Rd; 570/963-6363 or 800/22-WELCOME
Web www.visitnepa.org

The first settlers here found a Monsey Native American village on the site. In 1840 George and Seldon Scranton built five iron furnaces using the revolutionary method of firing with anthracite coal instead of charcoal. Manufacture of iron and steel remained an important industry until 1901, when the mills moved to Lake Erie to ease transportation problems.

After World War II Scranton thoroughly revamped its economy when faced with depletion of the anthracite coal mines, which for more than a century had fired its forges. Scranton's redevelopment drew nationwide attention and served as a model for problem cities elsewhere. Today Scranton is the home of electronic and printing industries and is host to several major trucking firm terminals.

What to See and Do

Catlin House. (1912) Headquarters of Lackawanna Historical Society; period furnishings (colonial-1900s), historic exhibits, antiques; research library (fee). Tours avail (fee). (Tues-Fri, also Sat afternoons; closed hols) 232 Monroe Ave. Phone 570/344-3841. **FREE**

Lackawanna County Stadium. Open-air stadium/civic arena seats 11,000. Home of AAA baseball, high school and college football and marching band competitions. (Apr-Nov) Exit 51 off I-81, Montage Mountain Rd. Phone 570/969-2255.

Montage Ski Area. Quad, double, three triple chairlifts; school, rentals; snowmaking; bar, restaurant; lodge. Vertical drop 1,000 ft. Night skiing. More than 130 acres of trails set in 400 acres of mountainside. (Early Dec-late Mar, daily) Summer activities include water slides, batting cages, amphitheater (June-Labor Day). S on I-81, exit 51, follow signs. Phone 570/969-7669. ¢¢¢¢

Nay Aug Park. More than 35 acres with memorials to pioneer days. Picnicking, swimming pool (fee), walking trail, refreshment stands, and the "Pioneer," a gravity railroad car dating back to 1850; wkend concerts (summer). (Daily) Arthur Ave and Mulberry St in E Scranton. Phone 570/348-4186. In park is

   Anthracite Heritage Museum. History and culture of anthracite region. Other affiliated parts of the complex are the Iron Furnaces; Museum of Anthracite Mining (see ASHLAND), with emphasis on the technology of the industry, and the 19th-century miners' village of Eckley, near Hazleton (see). (Daily; closed some hols) Keyser Ave in McDade Park. Phone 570/963-4804. ¢¢

Everhart Museum. Permanent collections include 19th- and 20th-century American art; Dorflinger glass; Native American, Asian, and primitive art; natural history displays, include Dinosaur Hall. Gift shop. (Tues-Sun; closed hols) Phone 570/346-7186. ¢¢

Lackawanna Coal Mine Tour. Underground coal mine 300 ft below ground shows world of anthracite miners. Conditions are authentic (damp, dark, slippery, and cold); dress appropriately. Above-ground facilities include a "shifting shanty" exhibit room with photo-mural graphic displays, mine artifacts and video presentations; gift shop; restaurant. (Apr-Nov, daily; closed Thanksgiving) McDade Park. Phone 570/963-8002. ¢¢¢

Scranton Iron Furnaces. Partially restored site of four anthracite-fired iron furnaces built 1848-1857 and used until 1902. Visitor center, outdoor exhibits. Self-guided tours (daily). Guided tours (late May-early Sept, Mon-Thurs). 159 Cedar Ave. Phone 570/963-3208. **FREE**

Steamtown National Historic Site. Site with large collection of steam locomotives and other memorabilia located in an authentic freight yard. Steam train ride through yard (Memorial Day-Dec; daily). 25-mi train excursion (July 4-mid-Oct, Sat and Sun). 150 S Washington Ave (mailing address), Lackawanna and Cliff sts (location). ¢¢¢

Motels/Motor Lodges

★ **CLARION INN.** *300 Meadow Ave (18505). 570/344-9811; fax 570/344-7799; toll-free 800/347-1551. www.clarioninn.com.* 125 rms, 6 story. S $59-$69; D $69-$79; each addl $10; suites $135-$150; under 13 free; higher rates special events. Crib free.

TV; cable (premium). Pool; lifeguard. Restaurant 6 am-10 pm. Bar 11-2 am; entertainment Tues-Sun. Ck-out noon. Meeting rms. Business servs avail. Valet serv. Free airport, bus depot transportation. Cr cds: A, C, D, DS, MC, V.

D ⌂ ⌂ ⌂ SC

★ **DAYS INN.** *1226 O'Neill Hwy, Dunmore (18512). 570/348-6101; fax 570/348-5064; toll-free 888/246-3297. www.daysinn.com.* 90 rms, 4 story. S $59.99-$83.99; D $61.99-$99.99; suites $78.99-$99.99; under 17 free; wkend, hol rates; higher rates Pocono NASCAR. Crib free. Pet accepted; $3. TV; cable (premium), VCR avail. Complimentary continental bkfst. Restaurant adj open 24 hrs. Ck-out 11 am. Business servs avail. Valet serv. Refrigerators. Cr cds: A, C, D, DS, MC, V.

D ⌂ ⌂ ⌂

★★ **HAMPTON INN.** *22 Montage Mountain Rd (18507). 570/342-7002; fax 570/342-7012; toll-free 800/426-7866. www.hamptoninn.com.* 129 rms, 4 story. S $72-$82; D $77-$87; suites $90-$175; under 19 free; wkend rates; ski plans; higher rates: NASCAR, hols. Crib free. TV; cable (premium). Indoor pool; whirlpool. Complimentary continental bkfst. Ck-out noon. Meeting rms. Business servs avail. Valet serv. Sundries. Free airport, bus depot transportation. Downhill ski 2 mi. Exercise equipt. Picnic tables. Cr cds: A, C, D, DS, MC, V.

D ⌂ ⌂ ⌂ ⌂ ⌂ ⌂ SC

★★ **HOLIDAY INN.** *200 Tigue St, Dunmore (18512). 570/343-4771; fax 570/343-5171. www.holiday-inn.com.* 139 rms, 2-3 story. S, D $79-$89; each addl $10; suites $145-$175; under 18 free; some wkend rates; ski plan. Crib free. Pet accepted. TV; cable. Pool. Restaurant 6:30 am-10 pm. Bar noon-2 am. Ck-out noon. Meeting rms. Business servs avail. In-rm modem link. Valet serv. Cr cds: A, D, DS, MC, V.

D ⌂ ⌂ ⌂

★★★ **INN AT NICHOLS VILLAGE.** *1101 Northern Blvd, Clarks Summit (18411). 570/587-1135; fax 570/586-7140; toll-free 800/642-2215. www.nicholsvillage.com.* 135 rms, 4 story. S,

D $98-$150; each addl $10; under 18 free. Crib free. TV; cable. Indoor pool; lifeguard. Restaurant 6 am-10 pm. Bar 5-11 pm. Ck-out noon. Meeting rms. Business servs avail. In-rm modem link. Sundries. Free airport transportation. Exercise equipt; sauna. Rec rm. 12 acres include over 1,000 rhododendrons; forestland. Cr cds: A, C, D, DS, MC, V.

D ⇔ 🏂 🖎 🔥 SC

Hotel

★ ★ **RADISSON HOTEL.** *700 Lackawanna Ave (18503). 570/342-8300; fax 570/342-0380; toll-free 800/333-3333. www.radisson.com.* 145 rms, 6 story. S $99; D $109; each addl $10; suites $119-$300; studio rms $109; package plans. Crib free. TV; cable. Restaurant 7 am-10 pm. Bar 11-2 am. Ck-out noon. Meeting rms. Business servs avail. In-rm modem link. Gift shop. Free airport, bus depot transportation. Downhill/x-country ski 4 mi. Exercise equipt; sauna, steam rm. Whirlpool. Some refrigerators, in-rm whirlpools. Located in historic Lackawanna RR station building. Cr cds: A, C, D, DS, JCB, MC, V.

D ⊁ 🏂 🖎 🔥 SC

Resort

★ ★ **SHADOWBROOK RESORT.** *615 Rte 6 E, Tunkhannock (18657). 570/836-2151; fax 570/836-5655; toll-free 800/955-0295. www.shadowbrook resort.com.* 73 rms, 2 story. S $50-$85; D $60-$95; each addl $12; kit. units $80-$90; under 12 free. Crib $8/day. TV; cable (premium). Pool; poolside serv, lifeguard. Complimentary continental bkfst. Restaurant 6 am-10 pm. Rm serv 5-8 pm. Box lunches, picnics. Bar 11-2 am; entertainment Wed, Fri-Sun. Ck-out noon, ck-in 2 pm. Gift shop. Grocery, coin lndry 2 mi. Meeting rms. Business servs avail. Sports dir. 18-hole golf, pro. Hiking. Game rm. Exercise rm; sauna, steam rm. Some refrigerators. Balconies. Picnic tables. Cr cds: A, C, D, DS, MC, V.

🏌 ⇔ 🏂 🖎 🔥 SC 🏋

Restaurants

★ **COOPER'S SEAFOOD HOUSE.** *701 N Washington Ave (18509). 570/346-6883. www.coopers-seafood.*

com. Hrs: 11 am-midnight. Closed hols. Bar 4 pm-1 am; Sun to 11 pm. Complete meals: lunch $5.99-$9.99, dinner $9.99-$28.99. Child's menu. Specializes in seafood. Pianist, vocalist Tues-Sun. Nautical decor. Cr cds: D, MC, V.

D ⊒

★ **FIREPLACE.** *1111 PA 6W, Tunkhannock (18657). 570/836-9662.* Hrs: 11 am-10 pm; Fri, Sat to 11 pm. Closed Dec 25. Bar. A la carte entrees: lunch, dinner $2-$21.95. Child's menu. Specializes in beef, chicken. Cr cds: A, D, DS, MC, V.

⊒

Shamokin Dam

(D-6)

Settled 1790 **Pop** 1,502 **Elev** 500 ft
Area code 570 **Zip** 17876

Motel/Motor Lodge

★ **INN OF SHAMOKIN DAM.** *Rte 11 & Rte 15 (17876). 570/743-1111; fax 570/743-1190.* 151 rms, 2 story. S $50-$60; D $55-$70; each addl $5; under 18 free. Crib free. Pet accepted. TV; cable. Pool; lifeguard. Restaurant 7 am-9 pm. Bar from 5 pm; Ck-out noon. Meeting rms. Business servs avail. In-rm modem link. Valet serv. Sundries. Cr cds: A, C, D, DS, MC, V.

D 🐾 ⇔ 🖎 🔥

B&B/Small Inn

★ ★ ★ **INN AT OLDE NEW BERLIN.** *321 Market St, New Berlin (17855). 570/966-0321; fax 570/966-9557; toll-free 800/797-2350. www.newberlin-inn. com.* 5 rms, 3 with shower only, 2 story. MAP: S, D $85-$175; each addl $20; higher rates special events. Crib $5. Complimentary full bkfst. Restaurant 10 am-2 pm, 4:30-8:30 pm; closed Mon, Tues. Ck-out noon, ck-in 3 pm. Gift shop. Garden setting. Cr cds: DS, MC, V.

D 🖎 🔥

Sharon

(C-1) *See also Mercer*

Settled 1802 **Pop** 16,328 **Elev** 998 ft
Area code 724 **Zip** 16146
Information Mercer County Convention & Visitors Bureau, 50 N Water Ave, 16146; 724/748-5315 or 800/637-2370
Web www.mercercountypa.org

In the heart of the rich Shenango Valley, Sharon is a busy industrial city that started with a lonely mill on the banks of the Shenango River. Steel, fabrication of steel products, and manufacture of electric transformers are a major part of the economic base. The Shenango Dam and its reservoir are northeast of town, near Sharpsville, and offer many recreational activities.

What to See and Do

Shenango Lake. Swimming, waterskiing; fishing, hunting; boating (ramps). Picnicking. More than 300 tent and trailer sites (mid-May-Labor Day; rest of Sept, reduced number of sites; electric hookups addl). 6 mi N of I-80, PA 18. Phone 724/646-1115.

Special Event

The Small Ships Review. Downtown. Parade of ships, entertainment, fireworks, food. Phone 724/981-3123. July.

B&B/Small Inn

★ ★ ★ **TARA COUNTRY INN.** 2844 *Lake Rd, Clark (16113).* 724/962-2992; *fax* 724/962-3250; *toll-free* 800/782-2803. www.tara-inn.com. 27 rms, 2 story. MAP: S, D $180-$450; wkly rates; package plans; higher rates Sat. Adults only. TV; cable. 2 pools, 1 indoor. Dining rms 11 am-8 pm. Ck-out noon, ck-in 3 pm. Meeting rm. Business center. In-rm modem link. Croquet court. Some in-rm whirlpools. Antebellum mansion dates from 1854; formal gardens. Cr cds: A, DS, MC, V.
D 🐾 ⇌ ⇜ 🐾 🚶

Restaurants

★ ★ **HOT ROD CAFE MONTI-CELLO.** 101 Chestnut St (16146). 724/981-3123. www.quakersteak andlube.com. Hrs: 4 pm-2 am. Hot Rod Cafe closed Mon. Bar. Dinner $8.99-$15.99. Child's menu. Specializes in char-grilled steak. Entertainment Thurs-Sun. Outdoor dining. 3 dining rooms in a converted, restored railroad depot. Family-owned. Cr cds: A, D, DS, MC, V.
D ⇌

★ **QUAKER STEAK & LUBE.** 101 *Chestnut St (16146).* 724/981-7221. www.quakersteakandlube.com. Hrs: 11-1 am; Thurs-Sat to 2 am; Sun noon-1 am. Bar. Lunch $3.99-$12, dinner $5.50-$18. Child's menu. Specializes in chicken wings, steak, hamburgers. Outdoor dining. Former gas station; vintage automobiles, license plates, memorabilia. Casual dining. Cr cds: A, D, DS, MC, V.
D ⇌

Shartlesville

(D-7) *See also Hamburg, Reading*

Pop 300 **Elev** 560 ft **Area code** 610
Zip 19554

What to See and Do

Roadside America. This miniature "village" consists of O-gauge trains, villages, and scenes, with 66 miniature displays re-creating 200 yrs of life in rural America. Started in 1903, displays now cover 6,000 square ft. (Daily; closed Dec 25) Just off US 22, Shartlesville exit I-78. 109 Roadside Dr. Phone 610/488-6241. ¢¢

Restaurants

★ **BLUE MOUNTAIN FAMILY RESTAURANT.** I-78 (19554). 610/488-0353. Hrs: 6:30 am-10 pm. Closed Jan 1, Dec 25. Res accepted. Continental menu. Bar. Bkfst $1.95-$4.95, lunch $2.75-$6.95, dinner $5.95-$12.95. Child's menu. Specializes in fresh seafood, Greek, Italian dishes. Salad bar. Own baking. Cr cds: A, DS, MC, V.

★ **HAAG'S HOTEL.** *Main and Third sts (19554).* 717/362-3476. Hrs: 7:30 am-7:30 pm. Closed Dec 25. Res accepted. Bar 11:00-midnight. Complete meals: bkfst $1.75-$6.50, lunch $4.75-$7, dinner $7-$13. Buffet: bkfst $6.50, lunch, dinner $13. Specializes in Pennsylvania Dutch cooking, family-style dinners. Own pies. In former hotel (1914); Early American decor. Cr cds: MC, V.

Shawnee on Delaware

(C-8) *See also Bushkill, Stroudsburg*

Pop 400 **Elev** 320 ft **Area code** 717 **Zip** 18356

Information Pocono Mountains Vacation Bureau Inc, 1004 Main St, Stroudsburg 18360; 717/424-6050; for free brochures phone 800/POCONOS

Web www.poconos.org

What to See and Do

Delaware Water Gap. (see) Phone 315/229-5261.

Shawnee Place Play & Water Park. Kids can jump in a pool of plastic balls, swing on a cable glide, climb on cargo nets, glide down waterslides, and splash in a wading pool. Magic shows, picnics, video games, snack bar. (Mid-June-early Sept, daily; Late May-mid-June, wkends only). I-80, exit 52, Rte 209 N and follow signs. Phone 570/421-7231. ¢¢¢

Skiing. Shawnee Mountain Ski Area. Quad, triple, seven double chairlifts; patrol, school, rentals; snowmaking; cafeteria, bar; nursery. Twenty-three slopes and trails; longest run one mi; vertical drop 700 ft. (late Nov-Mar, daily) Night skiing. Half-day rates. 6 mi N on I-80, exit 52, follow signs. ¢¢¢¢

Resort

★ ★ **SHAWNEE INN.** *1 River Rd (18356).* 570/424-4000; fax 570/424-9168; toll-free 800/742-9633. *www. shawneeinn.com.* 103 rms, 3 story. MAP, May-Oct: S $129; D $179; suites $50 addl; kit. units (Nov-Apr) $120; EP: S, D $89-$115; under 8 free; some wkly, wkend rates; higher rates Christmas hols; lower rates rest of yr. Crib free. Serv charge 10%. TV; cable, VCR avail. 4 pools, 1 indoor; wading pool, lifeguard. Playground. Supervised child's activities. Dining rm 7 am-9 pm. Snack bar. Picnics. Bar hrs vary. Ck-out noon, ck-in 4 pm. Coin lndry. Grocery, package store 4 mi. Meeting rms. Lighted tennis, pro (summer). 27-hole golf, pro, putting green, driving range, miniature golf. Downhill/x-country ski 3 mi. Lawn games. Soc dir; entertainment. Rec rm. Game rm. Cr cds: A, C, D, DS, MC, V.

Somerset

(E-3) *See also Johnstown, Ligonier*

Settled 1773 **Pop** 6,762 **Elev** 2,190 ft **Area code** 814 **Zip** 15501

Information Somerset County Chamber of Commerce, 601 N Center Ave; 814/445-6431

Web www.shol.com/smrst/somrst. htm

Somerset, a county seat, is also the marketing place for farms, lumber mills and coal mines in the area. James Whitcomb Riley described the countryside in his poem *'Mongst the Hills of Somerset.* The county offers fishing, swimming, boating, hiking, biking, camping, skiing, and ice-skating.

What to See and Do

Mount Davis. Highest point in state (3,213 ft). 26 mi S on US 219 to Salisbury, then W on unnumbered road. Phone 724/238-9533.

Skiing. Hidden Valley Ski Area. Six chairlifts, beginner's lift; patrol, school, rentals; snowmaking; cafeteria, restaurant, bars; nursery. Longest run 5,280 ft; vertical drop 610 ft; 28 slopes (Dec-Mar, daily). 30 mi of x-country trails (rentals). Night skiing. Shuttle service. Conference center, lodging. Yr-round facilities, activities. 12 mi W of PA Tpke Somerset exit 10; 8 mi E of PA Tpke Donegal exit 9, on PA 31. Phone 814/443-8000. ¢¢¢¢¢

Somerset Historical Center. Museum exhibits on rural life; outdoor display includes log house, log barn, covered bridge, sugarhouse. Bus tour (fee). (Tues-Sat; closed hols) 5 mi N on PA 985. Phone 814/445-6077. ¢¢

State parks.

    Kooser. Approx 220 acres. Four-acre lake with fishing, swimming beach (Memorial Day-Labor Day); x-country skiing, sledding. Picnicking. Tent and trailer sites, cabins. Standard fees. 9 mi NW on PA 31. Phone 814/445-8673.

    Laurel Hill. Approx 3,900 acres. Swimming beach, snack bar, boating (mooring, launching); hunting, hiking; snowmobiling, ice fishing. Picnicking. Tent and trailer sites. Standard fees. 8 mi W on PA 31, then SW on unnumbered road. Phone 814/445-7725.

Special Events

Maple Festival. Festival Park in Meyersdale. Phone 814/634-0213. Apr.

Somerfest. Laurel Arts/Phillip Dressler Center for the Arts. German festival: dancing, competitions, entertainment, food, tours. Phone 814/443-2433. Mid-July.

Farmers' and Threshermen's Jubilee. 9 mi SW via PA 281, in New Centerville. Equipment demonstrations; tractor-pulling, horseshoe-pitching, tobacco-spitting contests; antique car show and flea market; food. Phone 814/926-3142. Early Sept.

Mountain Craft Days. Somerset Historical Center. More than 150 traditional craft demonstrations; antique exhibits; entertainment. Phone 814/445-6077. Early Sept.

Springs Folk Festival. On PA 669, in Springs. Crafts demonstrations include bread baking, wheat weaving, basket and broom making, candle dipping, quilt stitching; entertainment featuring banjo and

fiddle music; pioneer exhibits on forest trail; maple sugaring, apple butter boiling, log hewing; museum adj with antique tools, furnishings, historical artifacts. Phone 814/662-4158 or 814/662-4298. Early Oct.

Motels/Motor Lodges

⭐ **A-1 ECONOMY INN.** *1138 North Center Ave (15501). 814/445-4144; fax 814/445-3763. www.a-1economy inn.com.* 19 rms. S $35-$45; D $40-$95; each addl $5; under 12 free; higher rates: special events, ski season. TV; cable (premium), VCR. Indoor pool. Playground. Complimentary continental bkfst. Restaurant nearby. Ck-out 11 am. Coin lndry. Exercise equipt. Game rm. Refrigerators, microwaves. Cr cds: A, DS, MC, V.
🏊 🏋 🛏 🐾 SC

⭐ **BUDGET HOST INN.** *799 N Center Ave (15501). 814/445-7988; toll-free 800/283-4678.* 28 rms, 2 story. S $33-$35; D $45-$55; each addl $5. Crib $4. Pet accepted. TV; cable (premium). Complimentary coffee in lobby. Restaurant nearby. Ck-out 11 am. Downhill ski 10 mi; x-country ski 13 mi. Cr cds: A, C, D, DS, MC, V.
🏄 🛫 🛏 🐾 SC

⭐ **DOLLAR INN.** *1146 N Center Ave (15501). 814/445-2977; fax 814/443-6205; toll-free 800/250-1505.* 16 rms. S $25-$40; D $30-$50; each addl $5; under 10 free; wkly, wkend rates; higher rates special events. Crib $5. Pet accepted, some restrictions; $5. TV; cable (premium). Complimentary coffee in lobby. Restaurant nearby. Ck-out 11 am. Business servs avail. Some refrigerators. Cr cds: A, D, DS, MC, V.
🏄 🛏 🐾 SC

⭐ **KNIGHTS INN.** *585 Ramada Rd (15501). 814/445-8933; fax 814/443-9745; res 800/843-5644. www.knights inn.com.* 112 rms, 10 kit. units. S $39.95-$59.95; D $46.95-$69.95; each addl $10; kit. units $43.95-$52.95; under 18 free; wkly rates; higher rates Dec-Mar wkends. Crib free. Pet accepted, some restrictions. TV; cable (premium), VCR avail (movies). Pool. Complimentary coffee in lobby. Restaurant nearby. Ck-out noon. Coin lndry. Business servs avail. Downhill ski 15 mi. Cr cds: A, C, D, DS, MC, V.

⬛🔲🟦🔳🔥

★ **RAMADA INN.** *215 Ramada Rd (15501). 814/443-4646; fax 814/445-7539. www.ramada.com.* 152 rms, 2 story. S $64-$78; D $74-$88; each addl $10; suites $95-$125; under 18 free; some wkend rates. Crib free. Pet accepted. TV; cable (premium). Indoor pool; whirlpool, poolside serv, lifeguard. Sauna. Restaurant 6:30 am-2 pm, 5-10 pm; Sun 7-11 am. Bar 2 pm-2 am; Sun to 9 pm; entertainment Tues-Sat. Ck-out noon. Meeting rms. Business servs avail. Bellhops. Valet serv. Sundries. Downhill/x-country ski 12 mi. Health club privileges. Game rm. Cr cds: A, D, DS, MC, V.

🔲⬛🔲🟦🔳🔥

Resort

★★★ **HIDDEN VALLEY RESORT CONFERENCE CENTER.** *1 Craighead Dr, Hidden Valley (15502). 814/443-6454; fax 814/443-1907; toll-free 800/458-0175. www.hiddenvalleyresort.com.* 206 units, some A/C, 2-3 story. Mid-Dec-mid-Mar: S $120-$180; D $222-$350; each addl $30; under 13 free; ski, golf packages; MAP avail; lower rates rest of yr. Crib free. TV; cable (premium). 4 pools, 1 indoor; whirlpool, lifeguard. Playground. Supervised children's activities (June-Sept). Dining rms 7 am-10 pm. Bars 11-1 am; entertainment. Ck-out noon, ck-in 4 pm. Grocery. Package store. Convention facilities. Business servs avail. Bellhops. Valet serv. Gift shop. Airport transportation. Sports dir. Lighted tennis, pro. 18-hole golf, greens fee $49-$59, pro, putting green, driving range. Boats. Downhill/x-country ski on site. Hiking. Soc dir. Exercise equipt; sauna. Fireplaces; microwaves avail. Balconies. Picnic tables. Located in scenic Laurel Highlands mountain area. Cr cds: A, C, D, DS, MC, V.

⬛🔲🟦🔳🟦🔲🔳🔥🆂🅲

B&Bs/Small Inns

★★★ **BAYBERRY INN BED AND BREAKFAST.** *611 N Center Ave (15501). 814/445-8471.* 11 rms, shower only, 2 story. No A/C. No rm phones. S $40-$50; D $45-$55; each

addl $10; suite $75; min stay some hol wkends. Children over 12 yrs only. TV in sitting rm; VCR. Complimentary continental bkfst; afternoon refreshments. Restaurant nearby. Ck-out 11 am, ck-in 3 pm. Luggage handling. Concierge serv. Downhill/x-country ski 18 mi. Brick house built 1902. Cr cds: A, DS, MC, V.

🔲🔳🔥🔲

★★★ **INN AT GEORGIAN PLACE.** *800 Georgian Place Dr (15501). 814/443-1043; fax 814/443-6220. www.theinnatgeorgianplace.com.* 11 rms, 3 story, 2 suites. S, D $95-$145; each addl $10; suites $170-$185. Children over 5 yrs only. Pet accepted, some restrictions. TV; cable (premium), VCR (movies). Complimentary full bkfst. Restaurant noon-4 pm. Ck-out noon, ck-in 3 pm. Business servs avail. Luggage handling. Valet serv. Concierge serv. Downhill/x-country ski 12 mi. Some fireplaces. Georgian mansion built in 1915; chandeliers, marble foyer. Cr cds: A, D, DS, MC, V.

🔲🔲🔳🔥🔲

Restaurants

★ **COUNTRY COTTAGE.** *2817 New Centerville Rd, New Centerville (15557). 814/926-4078.* Hrs: 10:30 am-9 pm. Closed hols. Res accepted. Bkfst $2.50-$4.25, lunch $2.50-$4.50, dinner $4.95-$6.95. Child's menu. Specialties: pot pies, roast turkey, grilled chicken salad. Own pies. Country decor; gift shop with local products and crafts. Cr cds: A, D, MC, V.

⬛🆂🅲🔳

★★ **OAKHURST TEA ROOM.** *2409 Glades Pike (15501). 814/443-2897.* Hrs: 11 am-10 pm; Sun to 8 pm. Closed Mon; Dec 25. Bar. Lunch $3-$7. Complete meals: lunch, dinner $10.95-$28.95. Buffet (Tues-Sat): lunch $6.95, dinner $10.95. Sun brunch $8.95. Child's menu. Specializes in waffles, own noodles in chicken broth. Salad bar. Outdoor dining. Early American decor. Fireplace. Family-owned. Cr cds: A, D, MC, V.

⬛🆂🅲🔳

★★ **PINE GRILL.** *800 N Center Ave (15501). 814/445-2102.* Hrs: 7 am-10 pm. Closed Dec 25. Res accepted. Bar. Bkfst $1.50-$4.50, lunch $3-

$14.50. Child's menu. Specializes in fresh seafood, grilled steak, gourmet pasta. Early-American decor; artwork. Opened 1941. Cr cds: A, MC, V.
D

State College

(D-4) *See also Bellefonte*

Settled 1859 **Pop** 38,420 **Elev** 1,154 ft
Area code 814
Information Centre County Convention & Visitors Bureau, 800 E Park Ave, 16803; 814/231-1400 or 800/358-5466
Web www.visitpennstate.org

The home of Pennsylvania State University and principally concerned with services to this institution, this borough is near the geographic center of the state. In the beautiful Nittany Valley, State College is surrounded by farmland famous for its production of oats and swine. Iron ore was discovered just east of town in 1790, and many iron furnaces later sprang up.

What to See and Do

Columbus Chapel—Boal Mansion Museum. The mansion has been the Boal family home since 1789 and includes original furnishings, china, tools, and weapons. Colonel Theodore Davis Boal, who outfitted his own troop for WWI, lived here. The 16th-century chapel belonged to the family of Christopher Columbus in Spain and was brought here in 1909 by Boal relatives. It contains religious items and Renaissance and baroque art, as well as an admiral's desk and explorer's cross that belonged to Columbus himself. Summer concerts on grounds. (May-early-Oct, Tues-Sun) 4 mi E on US 322, in Boalsburg. Phone 814/466-6210. ¢¢

Mount Nittany Vineyard & Winery. Stone-faced, chalet-style building nestled on southern slopes of Mt Nittany. Tasting room offers variety of wines and view of large pond, vineyard and mountains. Group tastings (by appt). (Fri-Sun; closed hols, also Jan) 7 mi E on US 322, E on PA 45, N on Linden Hall Rd. Phone 814/466-6373. **FREE**

Penn's Cave. A one-hr, one-mi boat trip through cavern; stalactites, stalagmites; plus ride-through wildlife park. Picnic area; visitor center; gift shop; snack bar. (Mid-Feb-Nov, daily) NE on PA 26, SE on PA 144, then 5 mi E of Centre Hall on PA 192. Phone 814/364-1664. ¢¢¢

Pennsylvania Military Museum. On grounds of 28th Division Shrine; dioramas; battle exhibits and equipment from the Revolutionary War to the present. Audiovisual program; military bookstore. (Tues-Sun; closed hols) 4 mi E on US 322, in Boalsburg. Phone 814/466-6263. ¢¢

Pennsylvania State University. (1855) 41,000 students. Approx 760 major buildings on a 15,984 campus; it is the land grant institution of Pennsylvania. On US 322 in University Park. Phone 814/865-4700. On campus are

"Ag Hill," The College of Agriculture. Showplace for state's dairy industry includes the dairy center, off Park Rd near stadium, with five herds of cows, automatic milking equipt (daily). The creamery, Curtain Rd, has retail salesroom for cheeses, milk, cream, ice cream (Daily; closed hols). Also test flower gardens off Park Rd near East Halls (July-Sept). **FREE**

Earth and Mineral Sciences Museum. Exhibitions of ores, gems and fossils; automated displays; art gallery. (Mon-Fri; closed hols) Steidle Building on Pollock Rd. Phone 814/865-6427. **FREE**

Old Main. (1929) Present building, on site of original Old Main (1863), uses many of the original stones; topped by lofty bell tower. Here are Henry Varnum Poor's land grant frescoes. (Mon-Fri; closed hols) E of Mall near Pollock Rd. Phone 814/865-2501. **FREE**

Whipple Dam State Park. Approx 250 acres. Swimming beach, fishing, boating (launching; mooring); hunting, hiking, snowmobiling, ice-skating, ice fishing. Picnicking, snack bar. Standard fees. 10 mi S on PA 26, then 1 mi E on unnumbered road. Phone 814/667-3808.

Special Events

Memorial Day Celebration. In Boalsburg. Celebrate the holiday in the birthplace of Memorial Day. Phone 814/231-1400.

Central Pennsylvania Festival of the Arts. Open-air display of visual and performing arts; indoor exhibits; demonstrations of arts and crafts; food booths. Phone 814/237-3682. Mid-July.

Centre County Grange Fair. PA 144S, at Grange Park in Centre Hall. Exhibits, livestock show, rides, concessions, entertainment. Phone 814/364-9674. Last wk Aug.

Motels/Motor Lodges

★★★ **AUTOPORT MOTEL & RESTAURANT.** *1405 S Atherton St (16801). 814/237-7666; fax 814/237-7456; toll-free 800/932-7678. www.autoport.statecollege.com.* 86 rms, 3 story, 12 kit. units. S $55-$65; D $59-$69; each addl $5; suites $69-$85; under 16 free; wkly, wkend rates; higher rates special events. Crib free. TV; cable (premium), VCR avail (movies). Heated pool; lifeguard. Restaurant 6 am-11 pm; dining rm 11:30 am-2 pm, 5-10 pm. Bar 11-2 am; Sun to midnight; entertainment Wed-Sat. Ck-out 11 am. Coin lndry. Meeting rms. Business servs avail. In-rm modem link. Sundries. Downhill ski 4 mi. Rms vary. Cr cds: A, D, DS, MC, V.

D ⊠ ⊠ ⊠ ⊠

★ **DAYS INN.** *240 S Pugh St (16801). 814/238-8454; fax 814/237-1607; toll-free 800/258-3297. www.daysinn.com.* 184 rms, 6 story. S $59-$115; D $69-$115; each addl $10; suites $150; under 18 free; some wkend rates; higher rates special events. Crib free. Pet accepted, some restrictions; $10. TV; cable. Indoor pool; lifeguard. Complimentary continental bkfst Mon-Fri. Restaurant 6:30 am-midnight; Sun from 7 am. Bar 11-2 am; entertainment. Ck-out noon. Meeting rms. Business center. In-rm modem link. Bellhops. Valet serv. Sundries. Free airport transportation. Exercise rm; sauna. Rec rm. Game rm. Refrigerators avail. Cr cds: A, C, D, DS, MC, V.

⊠ ⊠ ⊠ ⊠ ⊠ SC ⊠

★★ **HAMPTON INN.** *1101 E College Ave (16801). 814/231-1590; fax 814/238-7320; res 800/426-7866. www.hamptoninn.com.* 121 rms, 3 story. S $59-$74; D $66-$81; suites $71-$78; under 18 free; ski, golf plans. Crib free. TV; cable (premium). Heated pool; lifeguard. Complimentary continental bkfst. Restaurant adj. Meeting rm. Valet serv. Sundries. Airport transportation. Downhill/x-country ski 5 mi. Picnic tables. Cr cds: A, D, DS, MC, V.

D ⊠ ⊠ ⊠

★ **RAMADA INN.** *1450 S Atherton St (16801). 814/238-3001; fax 814/237-1345; toll-free 888/298-2054. www.ramada.com.* 288 rms, 2 story. S $72-$79; D $78-$85; each addl $7; suites $175; under 19 free. Crib free. Pet accepted. TV; cable (premium). 2 pools; lifeguard. Restaurant 7 am-10 pm; Fri, Sat to 11 pm. Bar 11 am-midnight. Ck-out noon. Meeting rms. Business servs avail. In-rm modem link. Exercise equipt. Health club privileges. Game rm. Microwaves avail. Cr cds: A, C, D, DS, JCB, MC, V.

D ⊠ ⊠ ⊠ ⊠ ⊠ SC

★ **RODEWAY INN.** *1040 N Atherton St (16803). 814/238-6783; fax 814/238-4519; toll-free 800/228-2000. www.rodeway.com.* 29 rms, 3 with shower only, 2 story. S $39-$69; D $44-$69; each addl $5; under 16 free; wkly rates; higher rates special events. Crib $6. TV; cable. Complimentary coffee in lobby. Restaurant nearby. Ck-out 11 am. Some refrigerators. Cr cds: A, C, D, DS, JCB, MC, V.

⊠ ⊠ SC

★ **STEVENS MOTEL.** *1275 N Atherton St (16803). 814/238-2438; fax 814/238-7548.* 18 rms, 17 with shower only, 2 story. S $33-$38; D $38-$48; each addl $4; family rates; higher rates special events (2-day min). Crib $4. TV; cable (premium). Complimentary coffee in lobby. Restaurant adj 6 am-midnight. Ck-out 11 am. Downhill ski 4 mi; x-country ski 1 mi. Cr cds: A, D, DS, MC, V.

⊠ ⊠ ⊠ SC

Hotel

★★★ **ATHERTON HOTEL.** *125 S Atherton St (US 322 Business) (16801).*

814/231-2100; fax 814/237-1130; toll-free 800/832-0132. www.atherton.state college.com. 150 rms, 7 story. S $75-$95; D $85-$105; each addl $10; suites $165; under 18 free; higher rates special events. Crib free. TV; cable (premium). Restaurant 5 am-10 pm. Bar 2 pm-2 am. Ck-out noon. Meeting rms. Business servs avail. In-rm modem link. Valet serv. Free garage parking. Free airport, bus depot transportation. Tennis privileges. Golf privileges. Downhill ski 6 mi. Health club privileges. Some in-rm whirlpools; refrigerator, microwave in suites. Cr cds: A, C, D, DS, ER, MC, V.

🐕 D ➢ ✂ ⊠ 🔥 SC

Resort

★★★ **TOFTREES RESORT.** *1 Country Club Ln (16803). 814/234-8000; fax 814/238-4404; toll-free 800/458-3602. www.toftrees.com.* 113 units, 3 story, 22 suites. Apr-mid-Oct: S $99-$150; D $125-$170; each addl $15; suites $150-$250; AP, MAP avail; golf plans; some wkend rates; lower rates rest of yr. Crib avail. TV; cable (premium), VCR avail. Heated pool; lifeguard. Dining rms 6:30 am-10 pm. Bar from 11 am; entertainment. Ck-out noon, ck-in 3 pm. Business servs avail. In-rm modem link. Free airport transportation. Tennis, pro. 18-hole golf, pro, putting green, driving range. Exercise equipt. Refrigerators; microwaves avail. Balconies. Mediterranean decor. Cr cds: A, C, D, DS, MC, V.

D ✂ ⊠ 🐕 🏃 ⊠ 🔥 SC

B&Bs/Small Inns

★★★ **CARNEGIE HOUSE.** *100 Cricklewood Dr (16803). 814/234-2424; fax 814/231-1299; toll-free 800/229-5033. www.cmagic.com/ch/.* 22 rms, 2-3 story. S, D $125-$175; suites $250-$275; under 6 free. TV; cable (premium), VCR. Complimentary continental bkfst. Dining rm 6:30-10 am, 11:30 am-1:30 pm, 5:30-9 pm. Ck-out 11 am, ck-in 3 pm. Business servs avail. In-rm modem link. Luggage handling. Gift shop. Free airport transportation. Downhill ski 6 mi; x-country ski adj. Minibar; some microwaves. Decor and

ambiance is reminiscent of Scotland. Cr cds: A, MC, V.

D ➢ ⊠ 🔥

★★★ **NITTANY LION INN.** *200 W Park Ave (16803). 814/865-8500; fax 814/865-8501; toll-free 800/233-7505. www.pshs.psu.edu.* 237 rms, 3 story. S $85-$95; D $95-$105; each addl $10; suites $160-$190; under 12 free; golf plan. Crib free. TV; cable, VCR avail. Dining rm 6:45 am-9 pm. Bar 11:30-1 am. Ck-out noon, ck-in 3 pm. Meeting rms. Business servs avail. In-rm modem link. Valet serv. Free airport transportation. Exercise equipt. Cr cds: A, D, DS, MC, V.

D 🏃 ⊠ 🔥

Restaurants

★★ **TAVERN.** *220 E College Ave (16801). 814/238-6116. www.thetavern. com.* Hrs: 5-10:30 pm; Sun to 8:30 pm. Closed hols. Res accepted Sun-Thurs. Bar 4 pm-12:30 am. Dinner $6.95-$16.95. Child's menu. Specializes in fresh veal dishes, fresh seafood. Classical music. Colonial decor; large collection of original Pennsylvania prints. Cr cds: A, C, D, DS, MC, V.

D ➥

★★★ **VICTORIAN MANOR.** *901 Pike St, Lemont (16851). 814/238-5534.* Hrs: 5-9 pm. Closed Mon; Jan 1, Memorial Day, Labor Day, Dec 25. Res accepted; required wkends. Continental menu. Wine list. Dinner $11.95-$28.45. Prix fixe: 3-course dinner $16.50. Specialties: rack of lamb, filet of salmon. Own pastries. Historic building (1891). Victorian decor. Totally nonsmoking. Cr cds: A, MC, V.

D

Stroudsburg

(C-8) *See also Easton, Pocono Mountains*

Settled 1769 **Pop** 5,756 **Elev** 430 ft
Area code 570 **Zip** 18360
Information Pocono Mountains Vacation Bureau, Inc, 1004 Main St;

phone 570/424-6050; for free brochures phone 800/POCONOS

Web www.poconos.org

This is a center for the Pocono Mountains resort area and the surrounding rural community. It is the Monroe County seat.

What to See and Do

Canoeing. Canoe trips on the Delaware River; equipt provided; also transportation to and from the river. (May-Oct) Contact Chamberlain Canoes, PO Box 155, Minisink Hills 18341; Phone 570/421-0180. ¢¢¢¢

Delaware Water Gap. (see) Phone 315/379-9241.

Quiet Valley Living Historical Farm. A log house (1765) with kitchen and parlor added 1892; 12 other original or reconstructed buildings. Demonstrations of seasonal farm activities. Farm animals, garden, gift shop. Guided tours with costumed guides, 1½-2 hrs. (Late June-Labor Day, Tues-Sun) 3½ mi SW on US 209 Business, then 1½ mi S (follow signs). Phone 570/992-6161. ¢¢

Skiing. Alpine Mountain Ski Area. Two quad, one double chairlift; patrol, school, rentals; snowmaking; lodge, restaurant, bar; child-care center. Vertical drop 500 ft. Twenty-one trails and slopes. Night skiing. (Dec-Mar, daily) 6 mi N via PA 191, 447N, just outside Analomink. Phone 570/595-2150 or 800/233-8240. ¢¢¢¢

Stroud Mansion. (18th century) Built by founder of city; houses Historical Society of Monroe County. Historical artifacts, genealogical records. Tours. (Tues-Fri, also Sun afternoons; closed hols) 9th and Main sts. Phone 570/421-7703. ¢

Motels/Motor Lodges

★ ★ **BEST WESTERN POCONO INN.** 700 Main St (18360). 570/421-2200; fax 570/421-5561; res 800/780-7234. www.bestwestern.com. 90 rms, 4 story. S, D $74-$109; each addl $10; higher rates special events. Crib free. TV; cable, VCR avail (movies). Indoor pool; whirlpools. Restaurant. Bar 11:30-2 am; entertainment. Ck-out 11 am. Meeting rms. Business servs avail. Game rm. Cr cds: A, DS, MC, V.
D ⊠ ⊠ ⊠

★ **BUDGET MOTEL.** I-80 exit 51, East Stroudsburg (18301). 570/424-5451; fax 570/424-0389; toll-free 800/233-8144. www.reservns@postoffice.ptd.net. 115 rms, 2-3 story. No elvtr. S $33.90-$48; D $48-$66; higher rates: special events, hols, some wkends. Crib free. Pet accepted; $20 deposit. TV; cable, VCR avail (movies). Restaurant 7-11 am, 5-10 pm. Bar 4 pm-midnight. Ck-out 11 am. Business servs avail. In-rm modem link. Game rm. Cr cds: A, C, D, DS, MC, V.
D ⊠ ⊠ ⊠

★ ★ **FOUR POINTS BY SHERATON** 1220 W Main St (18360). 570/424-1930; fax 570/424-5909; toll-free 800/777-5453. www.sheraton.com. 133 rms, 2 story. S, D $85-$99; each addl $10; suites $120-$130; under 18 free; some wkend rates. Crib free. TV; cable. Pool; poolside serv. Sauna. Restaurant 7 am-10 pm. Bars 11-2 am; entertainment. Ck-out 11 am. Meeting rms. Business servs avail. In-rm modem link. Bellhops. Sundries. Game rm. Balconies. Cr cds: A, D, DS MC, V.
⊠ ⊠ ⊠ SC

★ ★ **SHANNON INN.** US Rte 209 and State Rte 447 (18301). 570/424-1951; fax 570/424-7782; toll-free 800/424-8052. 120 rms, 2 story. S $60-$90; D $65-$95; each addl $5; under 18 free; hols (2-day min); higher rates NASCAR races. Crib free. TV; cable. Indoor pool. Complimentary continental bkfst. Restaurant 4 pm-2 am. Bar; entertainment Fri, Sat. Ck-out 11 am. Coin lndry. Meeting rms. Business servs avail. In-rm modem link. Valet serv. Sundries. Downhill/x-country ski 4 mi. Some refrigerators. Picnic tables. Cr cds: A, D, DS, MC, V.
⊠ ⊠ ⊠ ⊠ SC

Resort

★ ★ ★ **CAESARS POCONO PALACE RESORT.** Rte 209, Marshalls Creek (18335). 570/588-6692; fax 570/588-0754; res 800/233-4141. www.caesarspoconosresorts.com. 189 units, 155 suites. MAP: S, D, suites $195-$350; wkly rates. Adults only. TV; cable, VCR avail (movies $5). 2 pools, 1 indoor; whirlpool. Dining rm 8:30-11 am; 6-8 pm. Rm serv 11-2 am. Bar from 11:30 am; entertainment. Ck-out 11 am, ck in 3 pm. Business servs avail. Gift shop. 9-hole golf, pro, putting green, driving ange. Marina; paddle boats, water-kiing. Downhill ski 3 mi; x-country on site. Snowmobiles, ice-skating. Softball field. Volleyball. Archery. Lawn games. Rec rm. Game rm. Exer-ise equipt; sauna. Refrigerators. Some balconies. On lake. Cr cds: A, C, D, DS, MC, V.

Restaurants

★ **ARLINGTON DINER.** *834 N 9th t (18360).* 570/421-2329. Hrs: 6 am-0 pm; Fri, Sat to 11 pm; Sun 7 am-0 pm. Closed Jan 1, Thanksgiving, Dec 25. Bkfst $2.50-$6.40, lunch $3-6, dinner $5.75-$11.50. Child's menu. Specializes in pudding, home-made pies. Cr cds: A, MC, V.

★ **BEAVER HOUSE.** *1001 N 9th St 18360). 570/424-1020. www.beaver house.com.* Hrs: 11:30 am-9:30 pm; Sat to 10:30 pm; Sun noon-8 pm. Closed Dec 25. Res accepted. Bar. Complete meals: lunch $4.95-$8.95, dinner $12.50-$31.95. Specializes in seafood, prime rib. Many antiques; Tiffany lamps, trophies, bottles, stained glass, clocks. Family-owned. Cr cds: A, D, DS, MC, V.

★ **BROWNIE'S IN THE BURG.** *700 Main St (18360). 570/421-2200.* Hrs: 1 am-10 pm; Fri, Sat to 11 pm. Bar. Lunch $3.95-$9.95, dinner $8.95-23.95. Specialties: captain's seafood platter, Kansas City steak. Salad bar. Family-owned. Cr cds: A, D, DS, MC, V.

★ **LEE'S.** *PA 611, Bartonsville (18321). 570/421-1212.* Hrs: noon-9 pm; Sat 2-0 pm; Sun 1-9:30 pm. Closed Thanksgiving. Res required Fri-Sun. Chinese, Japanese menu. Bar. A la carte entrees: lunch, dinner $6.50-12.95. Specializes in steak dishes. Salad bar. Sushi bar. Asian decor. Cr cds: A, D, DS, MC, V.

★ ★ **STONEBAR INN.** *PA 209 18360). 570/992-6634. www.stonebar nn.com.* Hrs: 5-10 pm; Fri, Sat to 11

pm; Sun from 4 pm. Closed hols. Res required Fri, Sat. Bar. A la carte entrees: dinner $12.95-$25.95. Child's menu. Specializes in beef, seafood, game. Guitarist Wed. Park-ing. Outdoor dining. Fireside dining. Intimate dining; Tiffany-style lamps. Cr cds: A, D, MC, V.

Unrated Dining Spot

DANSBURY DEPOT. *50 Crystal St, East Stroudsburg (18360). 570/476-0500. www.dansburydepot.com.* Hrs: 11 am-10 pm; Fri, Sat to 11 pm; Sun to 9 pm. Closed Thanksgiving, Dec 25. Continental menu. Bar. Lunch $4-$6, dinner $8-$14. Child's menu. Specializes in steak, seafood. Con-verted railroad station depot and freight house, built in 1864. Display of railroad memorabilia. Small trains move around the rm, overhead on the walls. Cr cds: A, C, D, DS, MC, V.

Tannersville

(C-8) *See also Pocono Moutains, Strouds-burg*

Pop 1,200 **Elev** 890 ft **Area code** 570 **Zip** 18372

Information Pocono Moutains Vaca-tion Bureau Inc, 1004 Main St, Stroudsburg 18360; 570/424-6050; for free brochures phone 800/POCONOS

Web www.poconos.org

What to See and Do

Skiing. Camelback Ski Area. Two quad, three triple, seven double chairlifts, surface lift; patrol, school, rentals; snowmaking; cafeteria, restaurant, bar; nursery. Longest run one mi; vertical drop 800 ft. Night skiing. (Late Nov-late Mar, daily) Thirty-three trails. Alpine slide, water slides, swimming pool, bumper boats, entertainment (mid-June-Labor Day, daily; mid-May-mid-June and Labor Day-Oct, wkends only). Single and combination tickets. 3½ mi W off I-80, exit 45, in Big Pocono State Park. Phone 570/629-1661. ¢¢¢¢

Resort

★ ★ **CAESAR'S POCONO RESORTS.** *Rte 611, Brookdale Rd, Scotrun (28374). 570/839-8844; fax 570/839-2414; toll-free 800/233-4141. www.caesarspoconoresorts.com.* 127 rms in 8 bldgs, 1-2 story. June-Sept, MAP: S $106-$215; D $190-$250; each addl $55; suites $230-$360; under 5 free; wkly plans; hol plans (3-day min); higher rates hols and theme wkends; lower rates rest of yr. Crib free. TV; cable, VCR avail (movies). 2 pools, 1 indoor; wading pool, whirlpool, poolside serv, lifeguard. Playground. Supervised children's activities (seasonal); from 5 yrs. Complimentary coffee in lobby. Restaurant 8:30-11:30 am, 5:30-8 pm. Box lunches, picnics. Bar noon-2 am; entertainment. Ck-out 11 am, ck-in 3 pm. Gift shop. Grocery. Coin lndry. Meeting rms. Business servs avail. Valet serv. Sports dir. Lighted tennis. 9-hole golf privileges, putting green, driving range. Beach, boats. Downhill ski 3 mi; x-country ski 17 mi. Snowmobiles, sleighing, tobogganing. Hiking. Bicycles. Lawn games. Soc dir. Rec rm. Game rm. Exercise rm; sauna. Massage. Some refrigerators. Balconies. Picnic tables. On lake. Cr cds: A, C, D, DS, MC, V.

Titusville

(B-2) *See also Franklin (Venango County), Meadville, Oil City*

Settled 1796 **Pop** 6,146 **Elev** 1,199 ft **Area code** 814 **Zip** 16354
Information Titusville Area Chamber of Commerce, 202 W Central Ave; 814/827-2941

Titusville spreads from the banks of Oil Creek, so called because of the oil that appeared on its surface. Edwin L. Drake drilled the first successful oil well in the world on August 27, 1859. Overnight, Titusville became the center of the worldwide oil industry.

What to See and Do

Drake Well Museum. Site of world's first oil well; operating replica of Drake derrick and engine house; picnic area. Museum contains dioramas, working models, life-size exhibits depicting history of oil. (May-Oct, daily; Nov-Apr, Tues-Sat, also Sun afternoons) 1 mi SE of PA 8. Phone 814/827-2797. ¢¢

Resort

★ ★ **CROSS CREEK RESORT.** *Rte 8 S (16354). 814/827-9611; fax 814/827-2062; toll-free 800/461-3173. www.crosscreekresort.com.* 94 rms, 1-2 story. May-Oct: S $95-$110; D $100-$120; each addl $10; suites $120-$140; under 12 free; golf plan; lower rates rest of yr. Crib free. TV; cable. Heated pool; lifeguard. Restaurant 7 am-2 pm, 6-10 pm. Bar 11-2 am; entertainment. Ck-out 2 pm. Meeting rms. In-rm modem link. Gift shop. Tennis. 27-hole golf, greens fee $28-$33, putting green. Some private patios, balconies. Cr cds: A, D, DS, MC, V.

Towanda

(C-7) *See also Mansfield, Scranton*

Settled 1794 **Pop** 1,131 **Elev** 737 ft **Area code** 570 **Zip** 18848
Information Endless Mountains Visitors Bureau, 712 Rte 6E, Tunkhannock 18657-9232; 570/836-5431 or 800/769-8999
Web www.endlessmountains.org

On the north branch of the Susquehanna River, Towanda takes its name from a Native American word meaning "where we bury the dead."

In 1793 the Asylum Company purchased 1,600 acres of these wild valleys as a refuge for Marie Antoinette of France, should she escape to America. "La Grande Maison," a queenly house, was built. French noblemen settled here and a thriving community (called Azilum) was planned. The colony was unsuccessful and most of its founders returned to France. Many

of their descendants, however, still live in Bradford County.

What to See and Do

David Wilmot's Burial Place. Congressman (1845-1851), senator (1861-1863), leader of the Free Soil Party, Wilmot introduced the Wilmot Proviso in Congress, which would have required the US to outlaw slavery in any lands purchased from Mexico. This was an important factor in the dissension between North and South that led to the Civil War. Riverside Cemetery, William St between Chestnut and Walnut sts.

French Azilum. Site of colony for refugees from the French Revolution (1793-1803). Three cabins with crafts, tool exhibits; log cabin museum (1793); Laporte House (1836), built by son of one of colony's founders, reflects elegant French influence. Special events. Guided tours. (June-Aug, Wed-Sun; May, Sept-Oct, Sat and Sun) 8 mi SE via US 6, PA 187. Phone 570/265-3376. ¢¢

Tioga Point Museum. Mementos of French Azilum; Civil War, Stephen Foster, and Native American exhibits; historical displays of early canals and steam railroad. (Tues, Thurs and Sat; closed hols) 17 mi N off US 220, on PA 199, Spalding Memorial Building, 724 S Main St in Athens. Phone 570/888-7225. **DONATION**

Valley Railroad Museum. Century-old Lehigh Valley passenger station houses museum with displays of railroad memorabilia and railroad exhibit of Lehigh Valley in miniature; gift shop. (Tues-Sun; closed hols) 15 mi N off US 220, in Sayre on S Lehigh Ave. Phone 570/888-1881. ¢¢

Motels/Motor Lodges

★★ **BEST WESTERN GRAND VICTORIA INN.** 255 Spring St, Sayre (18840). 570/888-7711; fax 570/888-0541; toll-free 800/627-7972. www.bestwestern.com. 100 rms, 4 story. S $83-$86; D $93-$96; each addl $10; suites $154; under 12 free; wknd package. Crib $10. TV; cable. Indoor pool; whirlpool; lifeguard. Complimentary coffee in rms. Restaurant 6:30 am-9 pm; Fri, Sat to 10 pm. Bar;

entertainment Fri, Sat. Ck-out 11 am. Meeting rms. Business servs avail. In-rm modem link. Sundries. Lighted tennis. 18-hole golf privileges. Exercise rm; sauna, steam rm. Balconies. Cr cds: A, C, D, DS, MC, V.

★ **TOWANDA MOTEL & RESTAURANT.** 383 York Ave (18848). 570/265-2178; fax 570/265-9060. 48 rms. S $39-$65; D $43-$70; each addl $5; under 12 free. Crib $3.50. Pet accepted. TV; cable. Pool. Restaurant 6 am-9:30 pm; Sat, Sun from 7 am. Bar 3 pm-2 am. Ck-out noon. Meeting rms. Business servs avail. Sundries. Cr cds: A, DS, MC, V.

Uniontown

(E-2) *See also Connellsville*

Settled 1768 **Pop** 12,422 **Elev** 999 ft
Area code 724 **Zip** 15401
Information Laurel Highlands Visitors Bureau, 120 E Main St, Ligonier 15658; 724/238-5661
Web www.laurelhighlands.org

Coal and its byproducts made Uniontown prosperous, but with the decline in coal mining the city has developed a more diversified economic base. First known as Union, this city has been the Fayette County seat since 1784. General Lafayette and his son, George Washington de Lafayette, came on a visit after the Revolutionary War and were welcomed by Albert Gallatin, one-time senator and secretary of the Treasury. Uniontown was a hotbed of the Whiskey Rebellion, and federal troops were sent here in 1794.

What to See and Do

Braddock's Grave. Granite monument marks burial place of British General Edward Braddock, who was wounded in battle with French and Native American forces on July 9, 1755, and died four days later. Also nearby is

Fort Necessity National Battlefield. (1754) The site of Washington's first major battle and the opening battle of the French and Indian War (1754). This land was known as the Great Meadows. A portion was later purchased by Washington, who owned it until his death. A replica of the original fort was built on the site following an archaeological survey in 1953. Picnic area (mid-spring-late fall). 11 mi SE on US 40. Phone 724/329-5512. ¢¢ Nearby and included in the admission fee is

Visitor Center. Exhibits on battle at Great Meadows; audiovisual program. (Daily; closed Dec 25) Overlooking Fort Necessity is

Friendship Hill National Historic Site. Preserves the restored home of Albert Gallatin, a Swiss immigrant who served his adopted country, in public and private life, for nearly seven decades. Gallatin made significant contributions to our young Republic in the fields of finance, politics, diplomacy and scholarship. He is best known as the Treasury Secretary under Jefferson and Madison. Exhibits, audiovisual program, and audio tour provide info on Albert Gallatin. (Daily; closed Dec 25) 15 mi S on US 119 to PA 166. Phone 724/329-5512. **FREE**

Jumonville Glen. Site of skirmish between British and French forces that led to the battle at Fort Necessity. (Mid-Apr-mid-Oct) 7 mi from Ft Necessity, 2½ mi N of US 40 on Summit Rd.

Laurel Caverns. Colored lighting; unusual formations. Indoor miniature golf. Repelling (fee). Guided tours. Exploring trips. (May-Oct, daily) 5 mi SE on US 40, then 5 mi S on unmarked road. Phone 724/438-3003. ¢¢¢¢

Ohiopyle State Park. Approx 18,700 acres of overlooks, waterfalls. Fishing, whitewater boating; hunting, hiking, bicycling, x-country skiing, snowmobiling, sledding. Picnicking, playground, snack bar. Tent and trailer sites. Nature center, interpretive program. Standard fees. 10 mi SE on US 40, then 6 mi NE off PA 381. Phone 724/329-8591.

River tours. Whitewater rafting on the Youghiogheny River; some of the wildest and most scenic in the eastern US. Cost includes equipment and professional guides. Age limits are imposed because of level of difficulty.

Laurel Highlands River Tours. For info contact PO Box 107, Dept PM, Ohiopyle 15470; Phone 724/329-8531. ¢¢¢¢

Mountain Streams & Trails Outfitters. Also on the Youghiogheny, Big Sandy, Cheat, and Tygart's Valley rivers. Contact Manager, PO Box 106, Ohiopyle 15470. Phone 724/329-8810. Also rentals of whitewater rafts, canoes, trail bikes; for info contact Ohiopyle Recreational Rentals, PO Box 4, Ohiopyle 15470. Phone 724/329-8810 or 800/723-8669. ¢¢¢¢

White Water Adventurers. Contact Director, PO Box 31, Ohiopyle 15470; ¢¢¢¢

Wilderness Voyageurs. Trips on the lower and middle Youghiogheny. Also bicycle, canoe rentals; kayak and canoe lessons. Contact PO Box 97, Ohiopyle 15470. Phone 800/272-4141. ¢¢¢¢

Motels/Motor Lodges

★ ★ **HOLIDAY INN.** *700 W Main St (15401).* 724/437-2816; *fax 724/437-3505; res 800/258-7238. www.holiday-inn.com.* 179 rms, 2 story. S $75-$99; D $77-$99; suites $145-$175; under 18 free; package plans; higher rates Labor Day wknd. Crib free. Pet accepted, some restrictions. TV; cable (premium), VCR avail. Indoor pool; whirlpool, poolside serv, lifeguard. Sauna. Coffee in rms. Restaurant 6:30 am-2 pm, 4:30-10 pm. Rm serv from 7 am. Bar 3 pm-2 am; entertainment. Ck-out 11 am. Meeting rms. Business servs avail. In-rm modem link. Valet serv. Sundries. Lighted tennis. Miniature golf. Rec rm. Game rm. Lawn games. Microwaves avail. Some balconies. Cr cds: A, C, D, DS, JCB, MC, V.

D 🐾 🎣 ⇌ 🏊 🐾 SC

★ ★ **LODGE AT CHALK HILL.** *Rte 40E, Chalkhill (15421).* 724/438-0168; *fax 724/438-1685; toll-free 800/833-4283. www.thelodgeatchalkhill.com.* 60 units, 6 suites, 6 kit. units. May-Nov: S $60-$73; D $72-$78; each addl $10; suites $143-$167; kit. units $77-$93; under 14 free; higher rates: July 4, Memorial Day, Labor Day, Dec 31; lower rates rest of yr. Crib free. Pet accepted, some restrictions. $10. TV;

cable (premium), VCR avail. Complimentary continental bkfst. Restaurant opp 7 am-9 pm. Ck-out noon. Meeting rms. Business servs avail. Balconies. Picnic tables. On Lake Lenore. Cr cds: A, DS, JCB, MC, V.

Resorts

★ ★ ★ **NEMACOLIN WOODLANDS RESORT.** *1001 Lafayette Dr, Farmington (15437). 724/329-8555; fax 724/329-6153; toll-free 800/422-2736. www.nemacolin.com.* 220 rms, 4 and 5 story, 60 condo units (1-2 bedrm). May-Oct: S, D $215; each addl $25; suites $345-$1,500; kit. condos $245; under 17 free; AP, MAP avail; wkly rates; golf plans; lower rates rest of yr. Crib free. TV; cable (premium), VCR avail. 4 pools, 2 indoor; whirlpools, poolside serv, lifeguard. Playground. Supervised children's activities; ages 4-12. Dining rm 6 am-midnight. Box lunches, snack bar, picnics. Rm serv 24 hrs. Bar noon-2 am; entertainment. Ck-out noon, ck-in 3 pm. Lndry facilities in condos. Convention facilities. Business servs avail. In-rm modem link. Bellhops. Valet serv. Concierge. Gift shop. Sports dir. Lighted tennis, pro. Two 18-hole golf courses, greens fee (incl cart) $69-$109, pro, 2 putting greens, driving range. Boats. Downhill/x-country ski on site. Sleighing, tobogganing. Equestrian center; surrey rides all yr. Hiking. Bicycle rentals. Miniature golf. Lawn games. Social dir. Rec rm. Game rm. Exercise rm; saunas. Massage. Bathrm phones, minibars; many refrigerators; some wet bars. Microwave in condos. Balconies. Private collection of art and antiques. Situated on 1,250 acres with 7 lakes; landing strip. Cr cds: A, C, D, MC, V.

★ ★ ★ **SUMMIT INN RESORT.** *101 Skyline Dr, Farmington (15437). 724/438-8594; fax 724/438-3917; res 800/433-8594. www.summitinnresort. com.* 100 rms, 3 story. No elvtr. July-Labor Day: S $82-$110; D $92-$120; suites $135-$185; family rates; golf plan, MAP avail (2-day min); some wkend rates; lower rates mid-Apr-June, after Labor Day-early Nov. Closed rest of yr. Crib $10. TV; cable,

VCR avail (movies). Indoor/outdoor pool; whirlpool, lifeguard. Dining rm (public by res) 8-11 am, noon-3 pm, 5-9 pm. Box lunches, snacks. Bar 11-1 am. Ck-out noon, ck-in 4 pm. Business servs avail. Grocery, package store 3 mi. Gift shop. Tennis. 9-hole golf, greens fee $8.50, pro, putting green. Exercise equipt. Rec rm. Soc dir; entertainment. Picnic tables, grills. Built in 1907. Atop Mt Summit. Cr cds: A, DS, MC, V.

B&B/Small Inn

★ ★ ★ **INNE AT WATSON'S CHOICE.** *234 Balsinger Rd (15401). 724/437-4999; res 888/820-5380. www.watsonschoice.com.* 7 rms, shower only, 2 story. S, D $89-$125; each addl $20; wkly rates; wkends, hols (2-day min). Adults only. TV in common rm; cable (premium), VCR avail (movies). Complimentary full bkfst, coffee in rms. Ck-out 11 am, ck-in after 3 pm. Luggage handling. Concierge serv. Gift shop. Guest lndry. Golf privileges. Downhill ski 10 mi; x-country ski 10 mi. Many fireplaces. Picnic tables, grills. Built in 1820; German architecture. Totally nonsmoking. Cr cds: A, DS, MC, V.

Restaurants

★ ★ ★ **CHEZ GERARD AUTHENTIC FRENCH RESTAURANT.** *1187 National Pike, US 40E, Hopwood (15445). 724/437-9001. www.chez gerard.net.* Hrs: 11:30 am-2 pm, 5:30-9 pm; Sun brunch 11:30 am-2 pm. Closed Tues; hols. Res accepted. French menu. Bar. Wine list. Lunch $6-$10, dinner $10-$22. Prix fixe: lunch $16.50, dinner $35-$47. Sun brunch $18. Child's menu. Specialties: champagne gratined onion soup, Dover sole meuniere, creme brulee. Own baking. Outdoor dining. Renovated 1790 stone house with country French decor, fireplaces. Cr cds: A, MC, V.

★ ★ ★ **COAL BARON.** *Rte 40 (15401). 724/439-0111. www.coal baron.com.* Hrs: 4-11 pm; Sun noon-8 pm. Closed Mon; Dec 24-25. Res accepted. Continental menu. Bar.

Wine list. Complete meals: dinner $14-$20.95. Child's menu. Specialties: veal saltimbocca, entrecôte maître d'hôtel, seafood. Own baking. Valet parking. Jacket. Cr cds: A, D, DS, MC, V.

D ⊟

★ ★ **SUN PORCH.** *US 40E, Hopwood (15445). 724/439-5734.* Hrs: 11 am-8 pm; Sat 4-9 pm. Closed Mon; Dec 24, 25. Res accepted. Lunch $4.50-$8, dinner $7-$12. Buffet: dinner $8.50-$10.50. Child's menu. Specializes in fresh seafood, beef, poultry. Salad bar. Many plants; atmosphere of a country garden. Cr cds: D, DS, MC, V.

D SC ⊟

Valley Forge National Historical Park

(E-7) *See also King of Prussia, Philadelphia*

_____

(3 mi N of PA Tpke, interchange 24)
Information Superintendent, PO Box 953, Valley Forge 19482; 610/783-1077
Web www.nps.gov/vato

From December 19, 1777, to June 19, 1778, General George Washington and his Continental Army were camped here. Of the 12,000 soldiers Washington brought to Valley Forge, 2,000 would die of disease in camp; however, due to an active recruiting that took place, the overall numbers of the army grew to 20,000. The national park is a 3,600-acre memorial to their trial and success. The park itself is scenic any time of the year. A marked tour route offers the visitor a chance to see the primary encampment facilities; other roads provide a beautiful drive and a chance to view other historical features. (Daily; closed Dec 25)

What to See and Do

National Memorial Arch. Built in 1917 to commemorate Washington's army. Inscribed in the arch is a quote from General Washington: "Naked and starving as they are, we cannot enough admire the incomparable patience and fidelity of the soldiery."

Soldier Life Program. Interpreters present programs detailing camp life of the Continental Army soldier (offered at various times during the yr).

Tours.

   Auto Tape Tour. Self-guided tour dramatizes Washington's winter encampment. (Two-hr tape rental, May-Oct, daily) Bookstore. Phone 610/783-5788. ¢¢

   Bus Tour. Narrated tour (approx 90 min) includes stops at historic sites. (June-Labor Day, tour departures every ½-hr; Labor Day-Oct, wkends only) Tours leave from Visitor Center. Phone 610/783-5788. ¢¢

Visitor Center. Information, exhibits, audiovisual program, tour maps. Bus tours depart from here. (Daily) Jct PA 23 and N Gulph Rd, just inside park. Phone 610/783-1077.

Washington Headquarters. Park staff will provide info about the house where Washington lived for six months and which served as military headquarters for the Continental Army during that time. (Daily) Fee charged Apr-Nov ¢

Washington Memorial Chapel. Private property within park boundaries. Stained-glass windows depict the story of the New World, its discovery and development; hand-carved oak choir stalls, Pews of the Patriots, and Roof of the Republic bearing the State Seal of all the states. Also part of the chapel is the 58 cast-bell Washington Memorial National Carillon, with bells honoring states and territories. On PA 23. Phone 610/783-0120. **FREE**

Restaurants

★ ★ ★ **KENNEDY-SUPPLEE MANSION.** *1100 W Valley Forge Rd, Valley Forge (19406). 610/337-3777. www.kennedysupplee.com.* Hrs: 11:30 am-2 pm, 5:30-11 pm; Sat from 5:30 pm. Closed Sun; hols. Res accepted. Continental menu. Bar; pianist Fri, Sat. A la carte entrees: lunch $8-$16, dinner $22-$30. Specializes in French, northern Italian cuisine. Valet parking. 8 dining rooms in mansion (1850s). Crystal chandeliers, original artwork. Jacket (dinner). Cr cds: A, DS, MC, V.

D

★★★ **KIMBERTON INN.** *Kimberton Rd, Kimberton (19442). 610/933-8148. www.kimbertoninn.com.* Hrs: 5:30-9:30 pm; Sun to 8:30 pm; Sun brunch 11 am-2 pm. Res accepted. Continental menu. Bar. Wine list. Dinner $17.95-$21.95. Sun brunch $17.95. Specializes in fresh seafood. Own desserts. Harpist or pianist. Tavern (1796) on 4½ acres of gardens. Cr cds: A, C, D, DS, MC, V.

D

★★ **SEVEN STARS INN.** *263 Hoffecker Rd, Phoenixville (19460). 610/495-5205. www.sevenstarsinn.com.* Hrs: 4:30-10 pm; wkends to 11 pm; Sun 3-7 pm. Closed Mon; most major hols. Res accepted. Bar. Wine list. Complete meals: dinner $19.95-$27.95. Child's menu. Specializes in prime rib, seafood, veal. Colonial inn decor. Cr cds: A, DS, MC, V.

D ⊟

Warren (B-2)

Founded 1795 **Pop** 10,259 **Elev** 1,200 ft **Area code** 814 **Zip** 16365

Information Warren County Chamber of Commerce, 308 Market St, PO Box 942,; 814/723-3050; or Travel Northern Alleghenies, 315 Second St, at the point, PO Box 804, 814/726-1222

Web www.warrenpachamber.com

At the junction of the Allegheny and Conewango rivers, Warren is the headquarters and gateway of the famous Allegheny National Forest. Named for General Joseph Warren, American patriot killed in the Battle of Bunker Hill, the town was once the point where great flotillas of logs were formed for the journey to Pittsburgh or Cincinnati.

What to See and Do

Allegheny National Forest. More than 510,000 acres S and E on US 6, 62, located in Warren, Forest, McKean and Elk counties. Black bear, whitetail deer, wild turkey, a diversity of small birds and mammals; streams and reservoirs with trout, walleye, muskellunge, northern pike and bass; rugged hills, quiet valleys, open meadows, dense forest. These lures, plus swimming, boating, hiking, camping, and picnicking facilities, draw more than two million visitors a yr. Hundreds of campsites; fees are charged at some recreation sites. For

Allegheny National Forest

info contact Supervisor, US Forest Service, PO Box 847, phone 814/723-5150. In forest are

Buckaloons Recreation Area. Site of former Native American village on the banks of the Allegheny River. Boat launching; picnicking, camping (fee). Seneca Interpretive Trail. 6 mi W on US 6. Phone 814/362-4613.

Kinzua Dam and Allegheny Reservoir. Dam (179 ft high, 1,897 ft long) with 27-mi-long lake. Swimming, fishing, boating (ramps, rentals; fees); picnicking, overlooks, camping (fee). Kinzua Dam Visitor Center has displays. Kinzua Point Information Center, 4 mi NE of dam, phone 814/726-1291. Some fees. 3 mi SE on US 6, then 6 mi E on PA 59. *(It is possible that the PA 59 bridge, 1½ mi E of Kinzua Dam, will be closed; phone ahead for information.)* Phone 814/726-0661.

Chapman State Park. Approx 800 acres. Lake and creek stocked with trout and bass. Swimming beach, fishing, boating (rentals, mooring, launching); hunting, hiking, x-country skiing, snowmobiling, sledding, ice-skating, ice fishing. Picnicking, snack bar. Tent and trailer sites avail (some with electric; fee). Interpretive program. 7 mi SE on US 6, then W at light in Clarendon. Phone 814/723-0250.

Washington (E-1)

Founded 1781 **Pop** 15,268 **Elev** 1,120 ft **Area code** 724 **Zip** 15301

Information Washington County Tourism Promotion Agency, Franklin Mall, 1500 W Chestnut St; 724/228-5520 or 800/531-4114

Web www.washpatourism.org

Originally a Native American village known as Catfish Camp, the village of Bassettown became Washington during the Revolution. During the Whiskey Rebellion the town was a center of protest against the new federal government's tax; arrival of federal troops quieted the rebellious farmers. Washington and Jefferson College (1781) is located here.

What to See and Do

David Bradford House. (1788) Restored frontier home of a leader of the Whiskey Rebellion. (May-mid-Dec, Wed-Sat, limited hrs, also Sun afternoons) 175 S Main St. Phone 724/222-3604.

LeMoyne House. (1812) Abolitionist's home, built by the LeMoyne family, was a stop on the underground railroad; period furnishings, paintings, library; gardens; museum shop. Administered by Washington County Historical Society. (Jan-Feb, Tues-Fri; Mar-Dec, Tues-Sat) 49 E Maiden St. Phone 724/225-6740. ¢¢

Magna Entertainment Corporation. Harness racing. Parimutuel betting. (Tues, Thurs-Sat eves) Simulcasts (daily). 4 mi N on US 19. Phone 724/225-9300.

Meadowcroft Museum of Rural Life. A 200-acre outdoor museum complex that preserves the history of life on the land in Western Pennsylvania. General store, restored log houses, one-rm schoolhouse, blacksmith shop, and archaeology exhibit. (May-Oct, Wed-Sun) 19 mi NW via PA 18, 50, in Avella. Phone 724/587-3412. ¢¢

Pennsylvania Trolley Museum. Museum displays include more than 35 trolley cars dating from 1894. Scenic trolley ride; car barn and trolley-restoration shop; visitor center and gift shop with exhibit, video presentation, and picnic area. (June-Aug, daily; Apr-May and Sept-Dec, wkends) I-79 N, exit 41 (Meadowlands), follow signs. Phone 724/228-9256. ¢¢

Motels/Motor Lodges

★ **ECONO LODGE.** *1385 W Chestnut St (15301). 724/222-6500; fax 724/222-6501. www.econolodge.com.* 62 rms, 1-2 story. S $40-$60; D $48-$68; each addl $6; under 18 free; higher rates special events. Crib free. TV; cable (premium). Complimentary continental bkfst. Restaurant adj open 24 hrs. Ck-out 11 am. Business servs avail. Bellhops. Airport transportation. Picnic tables. Cr cds: A, C, D, DS, MC, V.
D ⊠ 🐾 SC

★★ **HOLIDAY INN MEADOWLANDS.** *340 Racetrack Rd (15301). 724/222-6200; fax 724/228-1977; toll-free 800/465-4329. www.holiday-inn.*

com. 138 rms, 7 story. S, D $99-$109; each addl $6; under 18 free. Crib free. Pet accepted, some restrictions. TV; cable (premium), VCR avail. Pool; whirlpool, poolside serv; lifeguard. Restaurant 6:30 am-10 pm. Bars 11-2 am; entertainment. Ck-out noon. Meeting rms. Business servs avail. In-rm modem link. Airport transportation. Exercise equipt; sauna. Microwaves avail. Private patios. Meadows Racetrack adj. Cr cds: A, C, D, DS, ER, JCB, MC, V.

★ **MOTEL 6.** *1283 Motel 6 Dr (15301). 724/223-8040; fax 724/228-6445; res 800/466-8356. www.motel6.com.* 102 rms. S $35.99; D $42.39; each addl $6; under 18 free. Crib free. Pet accepted. TV; cable (premium). Pool. Complimentary coffee in lobby. Restaurant adj open 24 hrs. Ck-out noon. Cr cds: A, C, D, DS, MC, V.

★ **RED ROOF INN.** *1399 W Chestnut St (15301). 724/228-5750; fax 724/228-5865; res 800/843-7663. www.redroof.com.* 110 rms, 2 story. May-Oct: S $35.99-$45.99; D $42.99-$64.99; each addl $6; under 18 free; lower rates rest of yr. Crib free. Pet accepted, some restrictions. TV; cable (premium). Complimentary coffee in lobby. Restaurant adj open 24 hrs. Ck-out noon. Cr cds: A, C, D, DS, MC, V.

Washington Crossing Historic Park (Bucks County)

(E-8) *See also Doylestown (Bucks County), New Hope, Philadelphia*

(Two sections: Bowman's Hill, 2 mi S of New Hope on PA 32, and Washington Crossing, 7 mi S of New Hope on PA 32)

Information Superintendent, PO Box 103, Washington Crossing, 18977; 215/493-4076

In a blinding snowstorm on Christmas night 1776, George Washington

and 2,400 soldiers crossed the Delaware River from the Pennsylvania shore and marched to Trenton, surprising the celebrating Hessian mercenaries and capturing the city. Washington's feat was a turning point of the Revolutionary War. Park (Tues-Sun; closed hols). ¢¢

What to See and Do

Bowman's Hill.

Memorial Flagstaff. Marks graves of unknown Continentals who died during encampment.

Wildflower Preserve. Adj park; two mi of native wildflower trails. (Daily) Phone 215/862-2924.

Washington Crossing.

Area of Embarkation. Marked by tall granite shaft supporting Washington's statue.

Concentration Valley. Where Washington assembled troops for raid on Trenton.

McConkey Ferry Inn. (1752) At Washington Crossing; restored as historic house. Sold in 1777 to Benjamin Taylor, whose descendents established the 19th-century village of Taylorsville.

Memorial Building. Near Point of Embarkation. Houses copy of Emanuel Leutze's painting, *Washington Crossing the Delaware.* Movie shown five times a day. Phone 215/493-4076.

Special Event.

The Crossing. Reenactment of Washington's crossing of the Delaware River, Christmas night in 1776. Phone 215/493-4076. Dec.

Wellsboro

(B-5) *See also Galeton, Mansfield*

Settled 1799 **Pop** 3,328 **Elev** 1,311 ft **Area code** 570 **Zip** 16901

Information Wellsboro Area Chamber of Commerce, 114 Main St, PO Box 733; 570/724-1926

Web www.wellsboropa.com

Wellsboro is the gateway to Pennsylvania's "canyon country." Settled largely by New Englanders, it is sustained by an assortment of industries. The area yields coal, natural gas, hardwoods, maple syrup, and farm products.

What to See and Do

Auto tours. There are more than a million acres of forests, mountains, and streams to be explored. The Wellsboro Area Chamber of Commerce has published a map of three tours.

Red Arrow Tour. Follows PA 660 SW 10 mi from Wellsboro to Leonard Harrison State Park. Lookout Point, near the parking area, has large picnic area nearby. Path winds one mi from park to bottom of gorge, through shady glens, past waterfalls.

White Arrow Tour. Leads from the Switchbacks (1½ mi W of Bradley Wales Park), three mi S to Leetonia, once a prosperous lumber village, now occupied by State Forest Rangers; then W and N to Cushman View, Wilson Point Rd, Lee Fire Tower, Cedar Run Mountain Rd and US 6; approx 75 mi.

Yellow Arrow Tour. Leads from Leonard Harrison State Park, back on PA 660, NW on PA 362, then ¼ mi W on US 6 to Colton Point Rd for views of the canyon and Four Mile Run Country. At Colton Point State Park (observation points, picnic shelters, fireplaces) the arrows follow Pine Creek S on old lumbering railroad tracks, converted into roadways called the "Switchbacks," to Bradley Wales Park overlooking Tiadaghton, the next lookout point on Pine Creek. From here continue S on W Rim Rd to Blackwell. From Blackwell, NE on PA 414 to Morris, then N on PA 287 to Wellsboro—a circle of 65 mi.

Robinson House Museum. (ca 1820) Houses turn-of-the-century artifacts; genealogical library. (Mon-Fri afternoons) 120 Main St. Contact Tioga County Historical Society, PO Box 724; Phone 570/724-6116. **FREE**

Skiing. Ski Sawmill Family Resort. Chairlift, three T-bars; patrol, school, rentals; snowmaking; cafeteria, restaurant, bar. Longest run 3,250 ft; vertical drop 515 ft. (Dec-Mar, daily) Yr-round activities. Oregon Hill Rd, 16 mi S via PA 287. Phone 570/353-7521 or 800/532-SNOW. ¢¢¢¢

Special Event

Pennsylvania State Laurel Festival. Week-long event includes parade of floats, marching musical and precision units, antique cars, laurel queen contestants; crowning of the queen; arts and crafts; children's pet and hobby parade, exhibits and displays. Mid-June.

Motels/Motor Lodges

★ **CANYON MOTEL.** *18 East Ave (16901). 570/724-1681; fax 570/724-1681; toll-free 800/255-2718. www.canyonmotel.com.* 28 rms. S $28-$45; D $32-$49; each addl $5; under 12 free; golf, ski package plans. Crib $5. Pet accepted. TV; cable. Heated pool; lifeguard. Playground. Complimentary continental bkfst. Restaurant nearby. Ck-out 11 am. Business servs avail. In-rm modem link. Downhill/x-country ski 17 mi. Refrigerators. Picnic tables, grills. Cr cds: A, C, D, DS, MC, V.
🅳 🐾 🏊 🖙 🐾 SC

★★ **PENN WELLS LODGE.** *4 Main St (16901). 570/724-3463; fax 570/724-2270; toll-free 800/545-2446. www.pennwells.com.* 55 rms, 2 story. S $53-$61; D $61-$69; each addl $5; under 18 free. Crib $5. TV; cable. Indoor pool; whirlpool, lifeguard. Playground. Restaurant nearby. Ck-out noon. Business servs avail. Downhill/x-country ski 17 mi. Exercise rm; sauna. Community-owned. Cr cds: A, D, DS, MC, V.
🅳 🖙 🏋 🖙 🐾

★ **SHERWOOD MOTEL.** *2 Main St (16901). 570/724-3424; fax 570/724-5658; toll-free 800/626-5802. www.sherwoodmotel.org.* 42 rms, 1-2 story. S $37; D $49-$54; each addl $5; under 10 free; golf, ski package plans. Crib $5. Pet accepted; $5. TV; cable. Heated pool; lifeguard. Playground. Complimentary coffee. Restaurant nearby. Ck-out 11 am. Business servs avail. In-rm modem link. Downhill/x-country ski 17 mi. Refrigerators. Cr cds: A, DS, MC, V.
🅳 🐾 🖙 🖙 🐾

Hotel

★ **PENN WELLS HOTEL & LODGE.**
*62 Main St (16901). 570/724-2111; fax
570/724-3703; toll-free 800/545-2446.
www.pennwells.com.* 73 rms. Late May-
Oct, hunting season: S $30-$40; D
$40-$49; each addl $5; suites $55-
$60; under 18 free; golf plans; lower
rates rest of yr. Crib $5. TV; cable.
Indoor pool; whirlpool. Playground.
Restaurant 7 am-1:30 pm, 5-10 pm.
Bar 11:30-1 am; entertainment Fri,
Sat. Ck-out noon. Meeting rms. Business servs avail. Downhill/x-country
ski 17 mi. Exercise rm; sauna. Built in
1869; high ceilings, oak and cherry
woodwork, antiques, early Americana. Community-owned. Cr cds: A,
DS, MC, V.

B&B/Small Inn

★★ **KALTENBACH'S BED AND
BREAKFAST.** *Stony Fork Rd (16901).
570/724-4954; res 800/722-4954.
www.kaltenbachsinn.com.* 10 rms, 2
suites, 1 rm with shared bath. 5 rm
phones. S $35; D $70; suites $125;
under age 6 free; golf, ski plans;
wknds, hols (2-day min); lower rates
Jan-April. TV; cable (premium). Playground. Complimentary full bkfst;
afternoon refreshments. Restaurant
nearby 11 am-10 pm. Ck-out 11 am,
ck-in noon. 18-hole golf privileges 2
mi, greens fee $35, putting green,
driving range, pro. Downhill ski 12
mi; x-country ski 20 mi. Totally nonsmoking. Cr cds: A, C, D, DS, MC, V.

West Chester

(E-7) *See also Chester, Kennett Square,
King of Prussia, Media, Philadelphia*

Founded 1788 **Pop** 17,861 **Elev** 459 ft
Area code 484 and 610
Information Chester County Tourist
Bureau, 601 Westtown Rd, Suite 170,
19382; 610/344-6365 or 800/228-9933
Web www.brandywinevalley.com

In the heart of three Pennsylvania
Revolutionary War historic sites—
Brandywine, Paoli, and Valley
Forge—West Chester today is a university and residential community
with fine examples of Greek Revival
and Victorian architecture.

What to See and Do

Brinton 1704 House. Stone house
built by Quaker farmer William Brinton, authentically restored and furnished. (May-Oct, Sat, Sun; also by
appt) 5 mi S just off US 202, Oakland
Rd, in Dilworthtown. Phone
302/478-2853. ¢

Motels/Motor Lodges

★ **ABBEY GREEN MOTOR LODGE.**
*1036 Wilmington Pike (19382).
610/692-3310; fax 610/431-0811.
www.abbeygreen.com.* 6 rms. S $49-
$59; D $59-$69; each addl $5; cottages with kit. $59-$69; wkly rates.
Crib free. Pet accepted. TV; cable
(premium). Restaurant nearby. Ck-
out 11 am. Business servs avail. Gift
shop. Refrigerators; some fireplaces;
microwaves avail. Picnic tables, grill.
Cr cds: A, C, D, DS, MC, V.

★★ **BEST WESTERN.** *Rtes 322 and
1, Concordville (19331). 610/358-
9381; fax 610/358-9381; res 800/522-
0070. www.concordville.com.* 116 rms,
5 story, 25 suites. S $110; D $125;
each addl $15; suites $160-$195;
under 12 free. Crib free. TV; cable,
VCR avail. Indoor pool; whirlpool;
lifeguard. Complimentary continental bkfst. Restaurant (see also YE
OLDE CONCORDVILLE INN). Bar.
Ck-out noon. Meeting rms. Business
servs avail. In-rm modem link. Gift
shop. Beauty shop; spa. Valet serv.
Exercise rm; sauna. Refrigerator in
suites, mini bars. Cr cds: A, C, D,
MC, V.

★★ **HOLIDAY INN.** *943 S High St
(19382). 610/692-1900; fax 610/692-
5598; toll-free 800/465-4329.
www.holiday-inn.com.* 143 rms, 3
story. S, D $85-$105; each addl $10;
suites $109-$129; kit. suites $129-
$149; under 17 free. Crib free. TV;
cable (premium), VCR avail. Pool;
lifeguard. Restaurant 6:30 am-10 pm.

Bar 4 pm-2 am. Ck-out noon. Coin lndry. Meeting rms. Business servs avail. In-rm modem link. Valet serv. Airport transportation. Lawn games. Exercise equipt. Microwaves avail. Cr cds: A, C, D, DS, MC, V.

B&B/Small Inn

★ ★ ★ **DULING-KURTZ HOUSE & COUNTRY INN.** *146 S Whitford Rd, Exton (19341). 610/524-1830; fax 610/524-6258. www.duling-kurtz.com.* 15 rms, 3 story, 5 suites. S, D $55-$120; each addl $25; suites $79-$120; higher rates Fri, Sat and hols. TV; cable (premium). Complimentary continental bkfst. Restaurant (see also DULING-KURTZ HOUSE). Rm serv. Ck-out 11 am, ck-in 3 pm. Business servs avail. Built in 1783; period furniture, antiques, sitting rm. Cr cds: A, C, D, DS, MC, V.

Restaurants

★ ★ ★ **DULING-KURTZ HOUSE.** *146 S Whitford Rd, Exton (19341). 610/524-1830. www.duling-kurtz.com.* Hrs: 11:30 am-10 pm; Sat from 5 pm; Sun 3-9 pm. Res accepted. French, continental menu. Bar. Wine list. A la carte entrees: lunch $6.95-$13.95, dinner $16.50-$29.75. Specialties: hickory smoked buffalo, lobster crepes, Oyster Lafayette. Valet parking Fri, Sat. 7 dining rms. Country inn atmosphere; formal gardens with gazebo. Fireplaces. Cr cds: A, C, D, DS, MC, V.

★ ★ ★ **YE OLDE CONCORDVILLE INN.** *US 1 and US 322, Concordville (19331). 610/459-2230. www.concordville.com.* Hrs: 11 am-10 pm; Sun to 8 pm; early-bird dinner 4-5:30 pm. Closed Dec 25. Res accepted. Continental menu. Bar to 2 am. Wine cellar. Lunch $5.50-$9.95; dinner $14.95-$24.95. Child's menu. Specialties: crab imperial, crab cakes, prime rib. Outdoor dining. Family-owned. Cr cds: A, C, D, DS, MC, V.

Unrated Dining Spot

THE DILWORTHTOWN INN DINING ROOM. *1390 Old Wilmington Pike (19382). 610/399-1390. www.dilworthtown.com.* Hrs: 5:30-10 pm; Sun 3-9 pm. Closed Jan 1, Dec 25. Res required. Bar. Wine cellar. Dinner $18-$25. Specializes in seafood, game, beef. Outdoor dining. Entertainment Fri, Sat. Fifteen dining rms in restored Colonial house (1758). Authentic period decor. Cr cds: A, D, DS, MC, V.

West Middlesex

(C-1)

Pop 929 **Elev** 840 ft **Area code** 724 **Zip** 16159

Motel/Motor Lodge

★ ★ **HOLIDAY INN.** *3200 S Hermitage Rd, Hermitage (16159). 724/981-1530; fax 724/981-1518; toll-free 800/465-4329. www.holiday-inn.com.* 180 rms, 3 story. S, D $79.95; under 19 free; golf plans. Crib free. Pet accepted. TV; cable (premium). Heated pool; poolside serv, lifeguard. Playground. Restaurant 6:30 am-10 pm; Dec-Mar 6:30 am-2 pm, 5-10 pm. Bar 11-2 am; entertainment. Ck-out 11 am. Coin lndry. Meeting rms. Business servs avail. In-rm modem link. Valet serv. Game rm. Cr cds: A, C, D, DS, ER, JCB, MC, V.

Hotel

★ ★ **RADISSON HOTEL SHARON.** *I-80 and Rte 18 (16159). 724/528-2501; fax 724/528-2306; res 800/358-7260. www.radisson.com.* 153 rms, 3 story. S $80-$90; D $88-$98; each addl $8; suites $150-$200; under 12 free; wkend rates. Crib free. Pet accepted. TV; cable. Indoor pool; whirlpool, poolside serv, lifeguard. Restaurant 6:30 am-10 pm. Bar 11-2 am; entertainment Wed, Fri, Sat. Ck-out 11 am. Coin lndry. Meeting rms. Business servs avail. Bellhops. Valet serv. Gift shop. Sundries. Exercise equipt; sauna. Game rm. In-rm whirlpools; refrigerator in suites. Cr cds: A, C, D, DS, MC, V.

Restaurant

★ ★ **THE TAVERN.** *108 N Market St, New Wilmington (16142). 724/946-2020. www.newcastlenews.com.* Hrs: 11:30 am-2 pm, 5-8 pm; Sun noon-6:30 pm. Closed Tues; July 4, Thanksgiving, Dec 25. Res required. Complete meals: lunch $9-$13, dinner $11-$18.50. Specialties: stuffed pork chops, creamed chicken and biscuits, baked chicken. Country decor; built in 1840. Cr cds: A, DS, MC, V.

White Haven

(C-7) See also Hazleton, Jim Thorpe, Pocono Moutains, Wilkes-Barre

Pop 1,182 **Elev** 1,221 ft
Area code 570 **Zip** 18661
Information Pocono Mountains Vacation Bureau, 1004 Main St, Stroudsburg 18360; 570/424-6050; for free brochures phone 800/POCONOS
Web www.poconos.org

What to See and Do

Hickory Run State Park. Approx 15,500 acres of scenic area. Swimming beach, fishing; hunting, hiking, x-country skiing, snowmobiling, sledding, ice-skating, ice fishing. Picnicking, playground, snack bar, store. Tent and trailer sites. Standard fees. 6 mi S on PA 534 off I-80 exit 41. Phone 570/443-0400.

Ski areas.

Big Boulder. Five double, two triple chairlifts; patrol, school, rentals; snowmaking; cafeteria, bar; nursery, lodge. Night skiing. Longest run approx ¾ mi; vertical drop 475 ft. (Dec-Mar, daily) 1 mi E off PA 903 in Lake Harmony. Phone 570/722-0100. ¢¢¢¢

Jack Frost. Two triple, five double chairlifts; patrol, school, rentals; snowmaking; cafeteria, restaurant, bar; nursery. Longest run approx ½ mi; vertical drop 600 ft. (Dec-Mar, daily) Half-day rate. 6 mi E on PA 940. Phone 570/443-8425. ¢¢¢¢

Motels/Motor Lodges

★ **COMFORT INN.** *Rte 940 (18661). 570/443-8461; fax 570/443-7988. www.comfortinn.com.* 123 rms, 6 story. S, D $70; each addl $10; under 18 free; ski plans. Crib free. TV; cable. Pool. Restaurant adj 6 am-midnight. Bar 11-2 am. Ck-out noon. Meeting rms. Business servs avail. Downhill/x-country ski 4 mi. Hiking trails. Game rm. Cr cds: A, C, D, DS, MC, V.

★ **POCONO RAMADA INN.** *Rte 940, Lake Harmony (18624). 570/443-8471; fax 570/443-0326; res 800/272-6232. www.poconoramada.com.* 138 rms, 4 story, 2 suites. Jan-Feb and mid-June-Columbus Day: S $90-$120; D $95-$130; each addl $10; under 18 free; higher rates NASCAR races; lower rates rest of yr. Crib free. Pet accepted; $50 deposit. TV; cable. Indoor pool; poolside serv, lifeguard. Sauna. Complimentary coffee in lobby. Restaurant 7 am-10 pm. Bar 4 pm-midnight. Ck-out noon. Meeting rm. Business servs avail. Gift shop. Valet serv. Coin lndry. Airport transportation. Golf privileges, greens fee $40, pro, putting green, driving range. Downhill/x-country ski 4 mi. Game rm. Lawn games. Some refrigerators. Picnic tables. Cr cds: A, D, DS, MC, V.

Resort

★ ★ ★ **MOUNTAIN LAUREL RESORT AND SPA.** *I-80 at PA Tpke NE exit (18661). 570/443-8411; fax 570/443-5518. www.mountainlaurel resort.com.* 250 rms, 3 story. MAP: S $134; D $188/person; each addl $10; suites $150; under 13 free; golf plan; some wkend rates; higher rates hols. Crib free. TV; cable, VCR avail (movies). 2 pools, 1 indoor; whirlpool, poolside serv, lifeguard. Playground. Supervised children's activities. Dining rm 6-9 pm. Box lunches, snacks, picnics. Bar 11-2 am; entertainment. Ck-out noon, ck-in 4 pm. Coin lndry. Meeting rms. Business center. Airport, RR station, bus depot transportation. Sports dir. 4 lighted tennis courts. 18-hole golf, greens fee from $44 (incl cart), driving range, putting green, miniature golf. Archery. Downhill ski 5 mi. Soc dir; entertainment. Nursery. Movies. Game rm. Exercise rm; sauna. Picnic tables. Cr cds: A, MC, V.

🏇 D ♨ 🏌 🏂 🎿 ➳ 🏋 ➷ 🔥 🏃

Restaurant

★ ★ ★ **POWERHOUSE.** *I-80 exit 40 (18661). 570/443-4480. www. powerhouseeatery.com.* Hrs: 4-10 pm; Sun noon-10 pm. Closed Dec 24, 25. Res accepted. Italian, American menu. Bar. Prices: $11.95-$15.95. Specialties: veal marsala, shrimp and crab fracaise. Located in old power plant. Cr cds: A, D, MC, V.

D ➷

Wilkes-Barre

(C-7) *See also Hazleton, Pocono Moutains, Scranton, White Haven*

Founded 1769 **Pop** 43,123 **Elev** 550 ft **Area code** 570

Information Northeast Pennsylvania Convention & Visitors Bureau, 99 Glenmaura National Blvd, Scranton, 18507; 800/22WELCOME

Web www.visitnepa.org

Named in honor of two members of the British Parliament who championed individual rights and supported the colonies, Wilkes-Barre (WILKS-berry) and the Wyoming Valley were settled by pioneers from Connecticut. Pennsylvania, and Connecticut waged the Pennamite-Yankee War, the first phase ending in 1771 with Connecticut in control of the valley. It was later resumed until Connecticut relinquished its claims in 1800. Wilkes-Barre was burned by the Native Americans and Tories during the Revolution and again by Connecticut settlers protesting the Decree of Trenton (1782), in which Congress favored Pennsylvania's claim to the territory. Discovery of anthracite coal in the valley sparked the town's growth after Judge Jesse Fell demonstrated that anthracite could be burned in a grate without forced draft.

Motels/Motor Lodges

★ ★ **BEST WESTERN EAST MOUNTAIN INN.** *2400 E End Blvd (18702). 570/822-1011; fax 570/822-6072; toll-free 800/780-7234. www.bestwestern. com.* 156 rms, 7 story, 24 suites. S $87-$92; D $92-$97; each addl $5; suites $115-$120; under 13 free; ski, golf plans; higher rates special events. Crib free. TV; cable, VCR avail (movies). Indoor pool; whirlpool, poolside serv, lifeguard. Restaurant 6 am-11 pm. Bar 11-1 am; entertainment Tues-Sun. Ck-out noon. Coin lndry. Meeting rms. Business servs avail. In-rm modem link. Free airport, RR station, bus depot transportation. Tennis privileges. Downhill ski 10 mi. Exercise equipt; sauna. Game rm. Refrigerator, wet bar in suites. Balconies. Cr cds: A, C, D, DS, ER, MC, V.

D ➳ 🏋 ➳ 🏋 ➷ 🔥 SC

★ ★ **BEST WESTERN GENETTI HOTEL AND CONFERENCE CENTER.** *77 E Market St (18701). 570/823-6152; fax 570/820-8502; toll-free 800/833-6152. www.bestwestern.com.* 72 rms, 5 story, 16 suites. Apr-Dec: S $74-$79; D $79-$89; each addl $10; suites $89-$99; under 12 free; higher rates NASCAR races; lower rates rest of yr. Crib free. Pet accepted; $25. TV; cable, VCR avail (movies). Pool; poolside serv. Complimentary coffee in lobby. Restaurant 7 am-2 pm, 5-9 pm. Bar 4 pm-2 am; entertainment. Ck-out 11 am. Coin lndry. Meeting rms. Business servs avail. Bellhops. Valet serv. Downhill/x-country ski 12 mi. Cr cds: A, C, D, DS, MC, V.

🔺 ➳ ➳ ➷ 🔥

★ ★ **HAMPTON INN.** *1063 Hwy 315 (18702). 570/825-3838; fax 570/825-8775; toll-free 800/426-7866. www. hamptoninn.com.* 123 rms, 5 story. May-Oct: S $55-$65; D $65-$75; under 18 free; ski plans; higher rates: car races, Dec 31; lower rates rest of yr. Crib free. Pet accepted. TV; cable. Complimentary continental bkfst. Restaurant adj 7 am-11 pm. Ck-out noon. Meeting rm. Business servs avail. In-rm modem link. Valet serv Mon-Fri. Downhill ski 10 mi. Cr cds: A, C, D, DS, ER, MC, V.

D 🔺 ➳ ➷ 🔥 SC

★ ★ **HOLIDAY INN.** *880 Kidder St (18702). 570/824-8901; fax 570/824-*

9310; toll-free 888/466-9272. 120 rms,
2 story. S, D $69-$120; each addl
$10; studio rms $75; package plans.
Pet accepted. TV; cable. Pool; wading
pool, poolside serv. Restaurant 6:30-1
am. Bar noon-2 am. Ck-out noon.
Meeting rms. Business servs avail. In-
rm modem link. Bellhops. Sundries.
Downhill ski 10 mi. Cr cds: A, C, D,
DS, ER, JCB, MC, V.

Resort

★ ★ ★ **THE WOODLANDS INN
AND RESORT.** *1073 Hwy 315 (18702).*
570/824-9831; fax 570/824-8865; toll-
free 800/762-2222. www.woodlandresort.
com. 179 rms, 9 story, 25 apts. S $69-
$107; D $79-$107; each addl $10;
package plans; wkend rates. Crib $5.
TV; cable. 2 pools, 1 indoor; whirlpool, poolside serv, lifeguard. Restaurant 7 am-11 pm. Rm serv. Bar 11-2
am; entertainment, dancing. Ck-out
noon. Meeting rms. Business servs
avail. Bellhops. Sundries. Barber,
beauty shop. Free airport transportation. Lighted tennis. Exercise rm;
sauna. Game rm. Rec rm. Lawn
games. Private patios, balconies. Cr
cds: A, D, DS, MC, V.

B&B/Small Inn

★ ★ **PONDA - ROWLAND BED
AND BREAKFAST.** *RR 1 Box 349,*
Dallas (84532). 570/639-3245; fax
570/639-5531; toll-free 888/855-9966.
www.pondarowland.com. 5 rms, 2
story. No rm phones. S, D $70-$95;
each addl $25; under 3 free; hols (2-
day min). Crib free. 2 cable TVs.
Playground. Complimentary full
bkfst, coffee in rms. Ck-out noon, ck-
in 1 pm. Business servs avail. Refrigerators. Picnic tables. On 130-acre
farm. Country antiques. Totally nonsmoking. Cr cds: A, DS, MC, V.

Restaurant

★ ★ ★ **SABER ROOM.** *94 Butler St*
(18702). 570/829-5743. Hrs: 11 am-
2:30 pm, 5-11 pm; Sat from 5 pm.
Closed Sun, Easter, July 4. Res
accepted, required hols. Continental
menu. Bar. Wine list. A la carte

entrees: lunch $3.95-$8.95, dinner
$10.95-$21.95. Specializes in veal,
seafood. Family-owned. Cr cds: A,
DS, MC, V.

Williamsport

(C-5) *See also Lewisburg, Lock Haven*

Settled 1795 **Pop** 30,706 **Elev** 528 ft
Area code 570 **Zip** 17701
Information Lycoming County
Tourist Promotion Agency, 454 Pine
St; 800/358-9900

Now famous as the birthplace of Little League baseball, Williamsport
once was known as the "lumber capital of the world." In 1870, a log
boom extended seven miles up the
Susquehanna River; 300 million feet
of sawed lumber were produced each
year. When the timber was
exhausted the city developed diversified industry and remained prosperous. The historic district of
Williamsport, known as "millionaire's row," includes homes of former
lumber barons.

What to See and Do

Hiawatha. Sightseeing trips down
Susquehanna River aboard replica of
an old-fashioned paddlewheel riverboat. Public cruises (May-Oct, Tues-
Sun). I-180 Reach Rd exit, in
Susquehanna State Park. Phone
800/248-9287.

**Little League Baseball International
Headquarters.** Summer baseball
camp and Little League World Series
Stadium are here. (Mon-Fri; closed
hols) 1 mi S on US 15. Phone
570/326-1921. **FREE** Adj is

Little League Baseball Museum.
(Memorial Day-Labor Day, daily;
rest of yr, Mon, Thurs-Sun; closed
Jan 1, Thanksgiving, Dec 25) 1 mi S
on US 15. Phone 570/326-3607. ¢¢

Little Pine State Park. Approx 2,000
acres. Swimming beach; fishing,
hunting; boating (ramps, mooring);
x-country skiing, snowmobiling,
sledding, ice skating, ice fishing. Pic-

nicking, playground, store. Tent and trailer sites (electric hook-ups). Interpretive program. 15 mi SW via US 220, then 13 mi N via PA 44 and Legislative Rte 4001. Phone 570/753-6000.

Thomas T. Thaber Museum of the Lycoming County Historical Society. Exhibits on regional history from 10,000 B.C. to present. Exhibits include Native American, frontier era; canals, steam fire engine, and hose cart; military history; general store, blacksmith shop, woodworker's shop, gristmill, crafts and industry; Victorian parlor and furnished period rooms; wildlife, sports, and Little League; lumber business. (May-Oct, daily; rest of yr, Tues-Sun; closed hols) 858 W 4th St. Phone 570/326-3326. ¢¢ Within museum is

> **Shempp Toy Train Collection.** Extensive toy train collection. More than 350 train sets on display, including the entire Lionel collection. Two detailed running displays allow visitors to start trains, blow whistles. Twelve unique trains including an American Flyer #3117 and Lionel "Super #381."

Special Events

Victorian Sunday. House tours, flower show, entertainment. Second Sun June.

Lycoming County Fair. 20 mi SE via US 220, at Hughesville Fairgrounds. More than 50 acres of amusements, commercial displays, livestock judging, demolition derbies, grandstand entertainment, food. Mid-July.

Little League World Series. Teams from all over the world compete. Third wk Aug.

Motels/Motor Lodges

★ **ECONO LODGE.** 2019 E 3rd St (17701). 570/326-1501; fax 570/326-9776; res 800/553-2666. www.econo lodge.com. 99 rms, 2 story. S $45-$50; D $50-$55; each addl $5; higher rates Little League World Series. Crib free. Pet accepted. TV; cable (premium). Complimentary coffee in lobby. Restaurant 6 am-8 pm. Bar 6 pm-2 am; entertainment Tues-Sat. Ck-out noon. Meeting rms. Business servs

avail. Valet serv. Cr cds: A, C, D, DS, MC, V.

D 🐾 ✈ ⊠ 🔥

★ ★ **HOLIDAY INN.** 1840 E 3rd St (17701). 570/326-1981; fax 570/323-9590; toll-free 800/369-4572. www.holiday-inn.com. 170 rms, 2 story. S, D $64-$79; each addl $10; under 18 free; higher rates Little League World Series. Crib free. Pet accepted, some restrictions. TV; cable. Pool; lifeguard. Restaurant 6:30-1 am. Bar 11-1:30 am. Ck-out 11 am. Coin lndry. Meeting rms. Business servs avail. In-rm modem link. Cr cds: A, C, D, DS, JCB, MC, V.

D 🐾 ⊠ 🔥

★ **QUALITY INN.** 234 Montgomery Pike (17701). 570/323-9801; fax 570/322-5231; toll-free 800/221-2222. www.qualityinn.com. 115 rms, 3 story. No elvtr. S $55; D $61; each addl $7; suites $85-$90; under 18 free. Crib $4. TV; cable. Pool; poolside serv, lifeguard. Restaurant 6:30 am-1:30 pm, 5-10 pm. Bar 4:30 pm-2 am; entertainment Wed, Fri, Sat. Ck-out noon. Business servs avail. Valet serv. Sundries. Airport, bus depot transportation. Game rm. Cr cds: A, C, D, DS, ER, JCB, MC, V.

D ⊠ 🔥 SC

Hotels

★ ★ ★ **GENETTI HOTEL & SUITES.** 200 W 4th St (17701). 570/326-6600; fax 570/326-5006; toll-free 800/321-1388. www.genetti.com. 206 rms, 10 story, 42 suites. S $29.95-$59, D $35.95-$65.95, each addl $6, suites $75.95-$139; under 10 free; higher rates Little League World Series. Wkly rates; golf plans. Crib free. Pet accepted. TV; cable (premium), VCR avail. Pool; poolside serv. Restaurant 6:30 am-10 pm. Bar 11-2 am; entertainment Fri, Sat. Ck-out 11 am. Meeting rm. Business servs avail. Barber, beauty shop. Coin lndry. Free airport transportation. Downhill ski, 20 mi. Exercise equipt. Some refrigerators. Cr cds: A, C, D, DS, MC, V.

D 🐾 ⊠ 🏋 🔥 ▶

★ ★ **RADISSON.** 100 Pine St (17701). 570/327-8231; fax 570/322-2957; toll-free 800/325-3535. www.radisson.com. 148 rms, 5 story. S, D $85-$95; suites $150; under 18 free. Crib free. Pet accepted. TV; cable. Indoor pool.

Restaurant 6:30 am-10 pm. Bar 11:30-2 am; DJ Tues-Sat. Ck-out noon. Meeting rms. Business servs avail. Bellhops. Free airport transportation. Downhill/x-country ski 18 mi. Some refrigerators. Whirlpool in suites. Cr cds: A, C, D, DS, MC, V.

D 🔯 ➤ ⌧ ⬚ ♨ SC

Willow Grove

(E-8) *See also Philadelphia*

Pop 35 **Elev** 310 ft **Area code** 215 and 267 **Zip** 19090

What to See and Do

Bryn Athyn Cathedral. Outstanding example of Gothic architecture. Free guided tours (Apr-Nov, Tues-Sun). 3 mi N of PA Tpke, exit 27 on PA 611N, then 4 mi E on County Line Rd to PA 232, in Bryn Athyn. Phone 215/947-0266. On grounds adj is

Glencairn Museum. Romanesque building features medieval sculpture and one of the largest privately owned collections of stained glass in the world; also Egyptian, Greek, Roman, ancient Near East, and Native American collections. (Mon-Fri by appt) 1001 Cathedral Rd, at PA 232. Phone 215/938-2600. ¢¢

Graeme Park. (1722) A fine example of Georgian architecture; stone house built by Sir William Keith, colonial governor of colony 1717-1726. Tours. (Wed-Sun; closed hols) 5 mi N on PA 611. Phone 215/343-0965. ¢¢

Motels/Motor Lodges

★★ **COURTYARD BY MARRIOTT.** 2350 Easton Rd (19090). 215/830-0550; fax 215/830-0572; res 800/321-2211. www.courtyard.com. 149 rms, 3 story. S, D $159; suites $170-$180; wkly, wkend rates. Crib free. TV; cable (premium), VCR avail (movies). Indoor pool; whirlpool. Complimentary coffee in rms. Restaurant 6:30-10 am; Sat, Sun 7-11:30 am. Bar 5-10 pm Mon-Sat. Ck-out noon. Coin lndry. Meeting rms. Business servs avail. In-rm modem link. Valet serv. Airport transportation. Exercise

equipt. Refrigerators; microwaves avail. Cr cds: A, C, D, DS, MC, V.

D ⇌ ⌧ ⬚ ♨ SC

★★ **HAMPTON INN.** 1500 Easton Rd (19090). 215/659-3535; fax 215/659-4040. www.hamptoninn.com. 150 rms, 5 story. S, D $119-$139; under 18 free; wkend rates. Crib free. TV; cable (premium). Complimentary continental bkfst. Restaurants nearby. Ck-out noon. Meeting rms. Business servs avail. In-rm modem link. Valet. Airport transportation. Exercise equipt; sauna. Health club privileges. Some refrigerators; microwaves avail. Cr cds: A, C, D, DS, MC, V.

D ⌧ ⬚ ♨ SC

B&B/Small Inn

★★★ **JOSEPH AMBLER INN.** 1005 Horsham Rd, North Wales (19454). 215/362-7500; fax 215/361-5924. www.philanet.com/jai. 37 rms, 2-3 story. S $88-$190; D $98-$200; each addl $15. TV; VCR avail. Complimentary full bkfst. Restaurant (see also JOSEPH AMBLER INN). Ck-out 11 am, ck-in 3 pm. Business center. In-rm modem link. Private parking. Some in-rm whirlpools. Four bldgs built 1734-1820; antiques. Cr cds: A, C, D, DS, MC, V.

D ⬚ ♨ 🚶

Restaurants

★★ **CASABLANCA.** 1111 Easton Rd, Warrington (18976). 215/343-7715. Hrs: 5-1 am. Res required. Moroccan menu. Setups. Complete meal: 7-course dinner $22. Child's menu. Specialties: Moroccan salad platter, cous cous with mint tea, rabbit. Belly dancers Fri-Sun. Parking. Traditional Moroccan atmosphere. Cr cds: A, D, DS, MC, V.

D

★★★ **JOSEPH AMBLER INN.** 1005 Horsham Rd, Montgomeryville (19454). 215/362-7500. www.josephamblerinn. com. Hrs: 6-10 pm; Sat from 5 pm; Sun 5-9 pm. Res accepted. Bar 5-11 pm. Dinner $18.95-$26.95. Specialties: rack of lamb, crab cakes, salmon en croute. Entertainment Fri. Outdoor dining. In 1820s stone barn. Cr cds: A, D, DS, MC, V.

D ⇌

★★ **OTTO'S BRAUHAUS.** *233 Easton Rd, Horsham (19044). 215/675-1864.* Hrs: 7 am-10 pm; early-bird dinner 3-5:30 pm. Closed Dec 25. Res accepted. German, American menu. Bar 11 am-midnight. Bkfst $3-$8, lunch $5-$11, dinner $9-$20. Child's menu. Specialties: sauerbraten, Wiener schnitzel. Own desserts. Outdoor dining. Musicians Fri, Sat (summer). Large German beer garden. Cr cds: A, C, D, DS, MC, V. **D**

Wrightsville (York County)

(E-6) *See also Bird-in-Hand, Lancaster, Pennsylvania Dutch Area, York*

Pop 2,223 **Elev** 306 ft **Area code** 717 **Zip** 17368

Information York County Visitors Information Center, 1618 Toronita St, York 17402; 717/848-4000 or 800/673-2429

Web www.yorkpa.org

What to See and Do

Donegal Mills Plantation & Inn. (1800) Historic village and resort dating from 1736. Mansion, bake house, gardens; restaurant and lodging (yr-round). Plantation tours (Mar-Dec, Sat and Sun afternoons). 5 mi N via US 30, PA 441, 772, in Mt Joy (Lancaster Co). Phone 717/653-2168. ¢¢

York

(E-6) *See also Hanover, Harrisburg, Lancaster, Pennsylvania Dutch Area, Wrightsville (York County)*

Founded 1741 **Pop** 40,862 **Elev** 400 ft **Area code** 717

Information Convention and Visitors Bureau, 1 Market Way East, PO Box 1229, 17405, phone 800/673-2429; or the Visitors Information Center, 1618 Toronita St, 17402, phone 717/843-6660

Web www.yorkpa.org

York claims to be the first capital of the United States. The Continental Congress met here in 1777 and adopted the Articles of Confederation, using the phrase "United States of America" for the first time. The first Pennsylvania town founded west of the Susquehanna River, York was and is still based on an agricultural and industrial economy. The city is dotted with 17 historical markers and 35 brass or bronze tablets marking historical events or places. There are more than ten recreation areas in the county.

What to See and Do

Bob Hoffman Weightlifting Hall of Fame. Weightlifting section honors Olympic weightlifters, powerlifters, bodybuilders and strongmen; displays include samples of Iron Game artifacts, memorabilia and photos. (Mon-Sat; closed hols) 4 mi N via I-83, exit 11; at York Barbell Co corporate headquarters. Phone 717/767-6481. **FREE**

Central Market House. Opened in March 1888. Over 70 vendors offer fresh produce, homemade baked goods, regional handcrafts and specialty items. (Tues, Thurs, Sat; closed hols) 34 W Philadelphia St. Phone 717/848-2243. **FREE**

Fire Museum of York County. Turn-of-the-century firehouse preserves two centuries of firefighting history; from leather bucket brigades to hand-drawn hose carts and pumps, horse-drawn equipt and finally to motorized equipt; artifacts and memorabilia; fire chief's office and firefighter's sleeping quarters are re-created, complete with brass slide pole. (Apr-Oct, Sat and second Sun every month; also by appt; closed hols) 757 W Market St. Phone 717/843-0464. ¢

Friends Meeting House. (1766) Original virgin pine paneling; restored. Regular meetings are still held here. (By appt) 135 W Philadelphia St. Phone 717/843-2285. **FREE**

Gifford Pinchot State Park. Approx 2,300 acres; 340-acre lake. Fishing, boating (rentals, mooring, launching); hunting, hiking, x-country skiing, ice-skating, ice fishing, ice boating. Picnicking, store. Tent and trailer sites, cabins. Nature center, interpretive center. Standard fees. 14

mi NW on PA 74 to Rossville, then NE on PA 177. Phone 717/432-5011.

Harley-Davidson, Inc. Guided tour through motorcycle assembly plant and the Rodney Gott Antique Motorcycle Museum. Children under 12 and cameras not permitted on plant tour. Plant and museum combination tour (Mon-Fri); museum tour (Sat). 1425 Eden Rd, 2 mi E on US 30. Schedule may vary. Phone 717/848-1177. **FREE**

Historical Society of York County. Includes library with genealogical records (Tues-Sat; fee for nonmembers). Museum features exhibits on the history of York County. Combination ticket for all historic sites maintained by the society. (Daily; closed hols) 250 E Market St. Phone 717/848-1587. ¢ Sites include

> **Bonham House.** (ca 1875) Historic house reflects life in late 19th century. (By appt; closed most hols) 152 E Market St. Phone 717/848-1587. ¢

> **General Gates' House.** (1751) It was here that Lafayette gave a toast to Washington, marking the end of a movement to replace him. Also here are **Golden Plough Tavern** (1741), one of the earliest buildings in York, which reflects the Germanic background of many of the settlers in its furnishings and half-timber architecture, and the **Bobb Log House** (1811), furnished with painted and grained furniture. (Tues-Sat; closed hols) 157 W Market St (enter on N Pershing Ave). ¢¢

Skiing. Ski Roundtop. Triple, two double chairlifts, two quad, two J-bars, one magic carpet, two tubing lifts; patrol, school, rentals; snowmaking; cafeteria; nursery. Longest run 4,100 ft; vertical drop 600 ft. (Mid-Nov-mid-Mar, daily) 12 mi NW on PA 74, then ½ mi N on PA 177 to Mt Airy Rd, then to Roundtop Rd, follow signs. Phone 717/432-9631. ¢¢¢¢

Warrington Friends Meeting House. (1769; expanded in 1782) Fine example of early Quaker meeting house. 14 mi NW on PA 74.

York County Colonial Court House. Replica of 1754 original. Exhibits include multimedia presentation of Continental Congress's adoption of the Articles of Confederation, audio-visual story of 1777-1778 historic events; original printer's copy of Articles of Confederation, historic documents and artifacts. Tours. (Daily) W Market and Pershing Aves. Phone 717/848-1587. ¢

Special Event

River Walk Art Festival. Along Codorus Creek at York County Colonial Court House. Late Aug.

Motels/Motor Lodges

★ ★ **BEST WESTERN INN.** *1415 Kenneth Rd (17404). 717/767-6931; fax 717/767-6938; toll-free 800/780-7234. www.bestwestern.com.* 105 rms, 3 story. S $57-$83; D $68-$93; each addl $5; under 18 free. Crib free. TV; cable (premium), VCR avail (movies). Complimentary continental bkfst. Restaurant adj 11 am-midnight. Ck-out noon. Meeting rms. In-rm modem link. Health club privileges. Some refrigerators; microwaves avail. Cr cds: A, C, D, DS, JCB, MC, V.
D ⬚ ⬚ SC

★ **BUDGET HOST INN.** *1162 Haines Rd (17402). 717/755-1068; fax 717/757-5571; toll-free 800/283-4678. www.budgethost.com.* 40 rms, 1-2 story. S $34-$35; D $36-$50; each addl $4; under 12 free. Crib $2. TV; cable, VCR avail (movies $5). Coffee in rms. Restaurant adj open 24 hrs. Ck-out 11 am. Some refrigerators; microwaves avail. Cr cds: A, D, DS, MC, V.
⬚ ⬚

★ ★ **HAMPTON INN.** *1550 Mt Zion Rd (17402). 717/840-1500; fax 717/840-1567; toll-free 800/426-7866. www.hampton-inn.com.* 144 rms, 5 story. S $79-$83; D $87-$91; suites, kit. units $95-$103; under 18 free. Crib free. TV; cable (premium), VCR avail. Heated pool. Coffee in rms. Complimentary continental bkfst. Restaurant adj 6 am-10 pm. Ck-out 11 am. Coin lndry. Meeting rms. In-rm modem link. Sundries. Exercise equipt. Refrigerator in suites. Picnic tables. Cr cds: A, D, DS, MC, V.
D ⬚ ⬚ ⬚ ⬚ SC

★ ★ **HOLIDAY INN.** *2000 Loucks Rd (17404). 717/846-9500; fax 717/764-*

5038; toll-free 800/465-4329. www. holiday-inn.com. 181 rms, 2 story. S, D $72-$98; under 18 free. Crib $10. Pet accepted. TV; cable (premium). 2 pools, 1 indoor; whirlpool, poolside serv, lifeguard. Playground. Restaurant 6:30 am-9:30 pm. Bar 3 pm-2 am. Ck-out 11 am. Meeting rms. Business servs avail. Bellhops. Valet serv. Miniature golf. Exercise equipt; sauna. Cr cds: A, C, D, DS, JCB, MC, V.

D ◗ ⇌ ⊼ ⊰ ⟲ SC

★ ★ **HOLIDAY INN.** 334 Arsenal Rd (17402). 717/845-5671; fax 717/845-1898. www.holiday-inn.com. 100 rms, 2 story. S, D $69-$79; under 18 free. Crib free. TV; cable (premium). Pool. Restaurant 6 am-2 pm, 5:30-10 pm. Bar 5 pm-midnight. Ck-out noon. Meeting rms. Business servs avail. Valet serv. Sundries. Health club privileges. Microwaves avail. Cr cds: A, D, DS, MC, V.

D ⇌ ⊰ ⟲

★ ★ **QUALITY INN.** 2600 E Market St (17402). 717/755-1966; fax 717/755-6936; toll-free 800/228-5151. www.qualityinn.com. 110 rms, 2 story. S, D, studio rms $69-$79; under 18 free. Crib free. TV; cable (premium). Pool; lifeguard. Restaurant 6 am-2 pm, 5:30-10 pm. Rm serv 7:30 am-9:30 pm. Bar 4 pm-midnight. Ck-out noon. Business servs avail. In-rm modem link. Valet serv. Sundries. Free airport transportation. Health club privileges. Refrigerators, microwaves avail. Cr cds: A, C, D, DS, JCB, MC, V.

D ⇌ ⊰ ⟲ SC

Hotel

★ ★ ★ **YORKTOWNE HOTEL.** 48 E Market St (17405). 717/848-1111; fax 717/854-7678; toll-free 800/233-9324. www.yorktowne.com. 122 rms, 8 story. S $52-$89; D $59-$96; each addl $7; suites $95-$225. Crib free. TV; cable (premium). Restaurants 6:30-2 am. Bar from 11 am. Ck-out noon. Meeting rms. Business servs avail. In-rm modem link. Gift shop. Barber. Free valet parking. Airport transportation. Exercise equipt. Health club privileges. Some in-rm whirlpools; microwaves avail. Cr cds: A, D, DS, MC, V.

D ⊼ ⊰ ⟲ SC

Restaurants

★ ★ ★ **ACCOMAC INN.** 6330 S River Dr (17368). 717/252-1521. www. accomac.com. Hrs: 5:30-9:30 pm; Sun 4-8:30 pm; Sun brunch 11 am-2:30 pm. Closed Dec 25. Res accepted; required wkends. Continental, French menu. Bar. Wine list. Dinner $16-$32. Sun brunch $22.95-$28.95. Specialties: roast duckling, steak Diane. Own pastries. Porch dining. Reconstructed historic building (1775) on banks of river. Cr cds: A, MC, V.

D

★ ★ **SAN CARLO'S.** 333 Arsenal Rd US 30 (17402). 717/854-2028. Hrs: 4-9:30 pm; Fri, Sat to 10 pm. Res accepted. Continental menu. Bar. Dinner $9.95-$18.95. Child's menu. Specializes in fresh seafood, prime rib, veal. Entertainment. Renovated 175-yr-old barn; original fieldstone walls. Cr cds: A, MC, V.

D ⊰

VIRGINIA

Settled by Elizabethans and named for their Virgin Queen, the first of the Southern states still retains a degree of the graceful courtliness that reached its peak just before the Civil War. Evidence of strong ties with the past are apparent in the Old Dominion. More than 1,600 historical markers dot its 55,000 miles of paved roads. More than 100 historic buildings are open all year; hundreds more welcome visitors during the statewide Historic Garden Week (usually the last week in April).

Permanent English settlement of America began in Jamestown in 1607 and started a long line of Virginia "firsts": the first legislative assembly in the Western Hemisphere (1619); the first armed rebellion against royal government (Bacon's Rebellion, 1676); the first stirring debates, in Williamsburg and Richmond, which left pre-Revolutionary America echoing Patrick Henry's inflammatory "Give me liberty, or give me death!" Records show that America's first Thanksgiving was held December 4, 1619, on the site of what is now Berkeley Plantation.

To Virginia the nation owes its most cherished documents—Thomas Jefferson's Declaration of Independence, George Mason's Bill of Rights, James Madison's Constitution. From here came George Washington to lead the Revolution and to become the first of eight US presidents to hail from Virginia.

Population: 6,377,000
Area: 40,767 square miles
Elevation: 0-5,729 feet
Peak: Mount Rogers (Between Smyth, Grayson Counties)
Entered Union: Tenth of original 13 states (June 25, 1788)
Capital: Richmond
Motto: Thus always to tyrants
Nickname: Old Dominion
Flower: American Dogwood
Bird: Cardinal
Fair: September-October, 2003, in Richmond
Time Zone: Eastern
Website: www.virginia.org

Potomac River

Ironically, the state so passionately involved in creating a new nation was very nearly the means of its destruction. Virginia was the spiritual and physical capital of the Confederacy; the Army of Northern Virginia was the Confederacy's most powerful weapon, General Robert E. Lee its greatest commander. More than half the fighting of the Civil War took place in Virginia; and here, in the courthouse of the quaint little village of Appomattox, the war finally came to an end.

When chartered in 1609, the Virginia territory included about 1/10 of what is now the United States; the present state ranks 36th in size, but the remaining area is remarkably diverse. Tidewater Virginia—the coastal plain—is low, almost flat, arable land cut by rivers and bays into a magnificent system of natural harbors. It was vital to commerce and agriculture in the early days. Today it is still important commercially (the Hampton Roads port is one of the world's great naval and shipbuilding bases) and a perennial lure to vacationers as well.

Inland lies the gentle rolling Piedmont, covering about half the state. Here is Virginia's leading tobacco area; it also produces apples, corn, wheat, hay, and dairy products. The world's largest single-unit textile plant is in Danville; the Piedmont also manufactures shoes, furniture, paper products, clay, glass, chemicals, and transportation equipment.

West of the Piedmont rise the Blue Ridge Mountains; high, rugged upland plateaus occur to the south. Further west is the Valley of Virginia, a series of fertile valleys. Best known is the Shenandoah, which contains some of the richest—and once bloodiest—land in the nation. Civil War fighting swept the valley for four years; Winchester changed hands 72 times.

To the southwest are the Appalachian Plateaus, a rugged, forested region of coal mines. Here the splendid outdoor drama, *Trail of the Lonesome Pine,* romanticized by the novelist John Fox, is performed.

For the vacationer today, the state offers colonial and Civil War history at every turn, seashore and mountain recreation year-round, such natural oddities as caverns in the west and the Dismal Swamp in the southeast, and the Skyline Drive (see SHENANDOAH NATIONAL PARK), one of the loveliest scenic drives in the East.

When to Go/Climate

Virginia summers can be hot and humid, marked by brief, powerful thunderstorms; winter snows are common in the mountains. Moderate temperatures, light rainfall, verdant flowering gardens, and brilliant foliage make spring and fall the best seasons to visit.

AVERAGE HIGH/LOW TEMPERATURES (°F)

RICHMOND

Jan 46/26	**May** 78/54	**Sept** 81/59
Feb 49/28	**June** 85/63	**Oct** 71/47
Mar 60/36	**July** 88/68	**Nov** 61/38
Apr 70/45	**Aug** 87/66	**Dec** 50/30

ROANOKE

Jan 44/25	**May** 76/53	**Sept** 79/57
Feb 47/27	**June** 83/60	**Oct** 68/45
Mar 58/36	**July** 86/65	**Nov** 58/37
Apr 67/44	**Aug** 85/64	**Dec** 48/29

Parks and Recreation Finder

Directions to and information about the parks and recreation areas below are given under their respective town/city sections. Please refer to those sections for details.

NATIONAL PARK AND RECREATION AREAS

Key to abbreviations. I.H.S. = International Historic Site; I.P.M. = International Peace Memorial; N.B. = National Battlefield; N.B.P. = National Battlefield Park; N.B.C. = National Battlefield and Cemetery; N.C.A. = National Conservation Area; N.E.M. = National Expansion Memorial; N.F. = National Forest; N.G. = National Grassland; N.H.P. = National Historical Park; N.H.C. = National Heritage Corridor; N.H.S. = National Historic Site; N.L. = National Lakeshore; N.M. = National Monument; N.M.P. = National Military Park; N.Mem. = National Memorial; N.P. = National Park; N.Pres. = National Preserve; N.R.A. = National Recreational Area; N.R.R. = National Recreational River; N.Riv. = National River; N.S. = National Seashore; N.S.R. = National Scenic Riverway; N.S.T. = National Scenic Trail; N.Sc. = National Scientific Reserve; N.V.M. = National Volcanic Monument.

Place Name	Listed Under
Appomattox Court House N.H.P.	same
Assateague Island N.S.	CHINCOTEAGUE
Blue Ridge Parkway	same
Booker T. Washington N.M.	same
Cape Henry Memorial	same
Colonial N.H.P.	same
Colonial Parkway	same
Fredericksburg & Spotsylvania N.M.P.	same
George Washington Birthplace N.M.	same
Jamestown	same
Manassas N.B.P.	same
Patrick Henry N. Mem.	BROOKNEAL
Petersburg N.B.	same
Prince William Forest Park	TRIANGLE
Richmond N.B.P.	same
Robert E. Lee N.Mem.	ARLINGTON COUNTY
Shenandoah N.P.	same
Washington and Jefferson N.F.	HARRISONBURG
Yorktown N.B.	YORKTOWN

STATE PARK AND RECREATION AREAS

Key to abbreviations. I.P. = Interstate Park; S.A.P. = State Archaeological Park; S.B. = State Beach; S.C.A. = State Conservation Area; S.C.P. = State Conservation Park; S.Cp. = State Campground; S.F. = State Forest; S.G. = State Garden; S.H.A. = State Historic Area; S.H.P. = State Historic Park; S.H.S. = State Historic Site; S.M.P. = State Marine Park; S.N.A. = State Natural Area; S.P. = State Park; S.P.C. = State Public Campground; S.R. = State Reserve; S.R.A. = State Recreation Area; S.Res. = State Reservoir; S.Res.P. = State Resort Park; S.R.P. = State Rustic Park.

Place Name	Listed Under
Breaks I.P.	same
Chippokes Plantation S.P.	SURRY
Claytor Lake S.P.	RADFORD
Douthat S.P.	CLIFTON FORGE
Fairy Stone S.P.	MARTINSVILLE
First Landing/Seashore S.P.	VIRGINIA BEACH
Grayson Highlands S.P.	ABINGDON
Grist Mill Historical S.P.	MOUNT VERNON
Holliday Lake S.P.	APPOMATTOX COURT HOUSE N.H.P.
Hungry Mother S.P.	MARION

CALENDAR HIGHLIGHTS

APRIL

International Azalea Festival (Norfolk). Downtown and Norfolk Botanical Garden. To honor NATO. Parade, coronation ceremony, air show (held at Norfolk Naval Air Station), events, concerts, fair, ball, entertainment. Phone 757/664-6620.

Garden Week (Charlottesville). Some fine private homes and gardens in the area are open. Phone Garden Club of Virginia/Richmond headquarters 804/644-7776.

Garden Week in Historic Lexington (Lexington). Tour of homes and gardens in the Lexington and Rockbridge County areas. Phone 540/463-3777.

MAY

Jamestown Weekend (Jamestown, Colonial National Historical Park). Original Jamestown site. Commemorates arrival of first settlers in 1607; special tours and activities. Phone 757/229-1733.

JUNE

Natural Chimneys Jousting Tournament (Harrisonburg). Natural Chimneys Regional Park. America's oldest continuous sporting event, held annually since 1821. "Knights" armed with lances charge down an 80-yard track and attempt to spear three small rings suspended from posts. Phone 540/350-2510.

Red Cross Waterfront Festival (Alexandria). Commemorates Alexandria's maritime heritage. Features "tall ships," blessing of the fleet, river cruises, races, arts and crafts, exhibits, food, variety of music; fireworks. Phone 703/549-8300.

JULY

Pony Penning (Chincoteague). The "wild" ponies are rounded up on Assateague Island, then swim the inlet to Chincoteague, where foals are sold at auction before the ponies swim back to Assateague. Carnival amusements. Phone Chincoteague Chamber of Commerce, 757/336-6161.

SEPTEMBER

Publick Times (Williamsburg). Colonial Williamsburg. Re-creation of colonial market days; contests, crafts, auctions, military encampment. Phone 757/220-7645 or 800/246-2099.

Virginia State Fair (Richmond). Animal and 4-H contests, music, horse show, carnival. Phone 804/228-3200.

OCTOBER

Blue Ridge Folklife Festival (Martinsville). Blue Ridge Farm Museum. Gospel, blues, and string band music; traditional regional crafts; regional foods; quilt show, antique autos, steam and gas-powered farm equipment. Sports events including horse-pulling and log-skidding contests, coon dog swimming and treeing contests. Phone 540/365-4415.

DECEMBER

Christmas Candlelight Tour (Fredericksburg). Historic homes open to the public; carriage rides; Christmas decorations and refreshments of the colonial period. Phone Visitor Center, 540/373-1776 or 800/678-4748.

Natural Tunnel S.P.	BIG STONE GAP
New Market Battlefield S.H.P.	NEW MARKET
Occoneechee S.P.	CLARKSVILLE
Pocahontas S.P.	RICHMOND
Sailor's Creek Battlefield Historic S.P.	FARMVILLE
Sky Meadows S.P.	FRONT ROYAL
Staunton River S.P.	SOUTH BOSTON
Twin Lakes S.P.	KEYSVILLE
Westmoreland S.P.	MONTROSS
York River S.P.	WILLIAMSBURG

Water-related activities, hiking, various other sports, picnicking, and visitor centers, as well as camping, are available in many of these areas. State park facilities and services are operated on a seasonal basis. Parking for noncampers, $1.50-$2.50/car/day, Memorial Day-Labor Day. Admission to State Historical Parks $1.25; children $1. Swimming, boat rentals, cafes, and concessions, Memorial Day-Labor Day; fees for activities. Pets are allowed in camping and cabins, but must be kept inside at night. At all other times pets must be on a leash not longer than six feet. Facilities for the disabled at many parks.

Tent and trailer campgrounds are available in 19 state parks generally from Mar-Nov; maximum stay is two weeks. $11/site/night, $19.25 at Seashore (up to six persons, one vehicle); electricity and water $15/site/night where available. Reservations may be made 180 days-one week in advance (see below for addresses). Seven parks offer housekeeping cabins (May-September). Douthat (see CLIFTON FORGE) has a guest lodge for 15. Reservations for campsites are accepted beginning late March. Campsite and cabin reservations may be made by phoning 800/933-PARK or 804/225-3867. Booklets with details on each park may be obtained from the Virginia Department of Conservation & Recreation, 203 Governor St, Suite 213, Richmond 23219. A campground directory is available from Virginia Tourism Corporation, 901 E Byrd St, Richmond 23219, phone 804/786-4484.

SKI AREAS

Place Name	Listed Under
Bryce Resort	BASYE
Homestead Ski Area	HOT SPRINGS
Wintergreen Resort	CHARLOTTESVILLE

FISHING AND HUNTING

Saltwater fishing on ocean, bay, river, or creek is a major sport. Virginia is blessed with many miles of shoreline: 120 miles on the Atlantic Ocean, 300 miles on Chesapeake Bay, and 1,300 miles of tidal shores. There is no closed season for saltwater fishing except for striped bass. There are some species size and bag limits. No license is required to fish in ocean waters or seaside of the eastern shore, but a license is required to fish in the Chesapeake and tidal tributaries. Information concerning size limits and bag limits on saltwater game fish may be obtained from the Virginia Marine Resources Commission, PO Box 756, Newport News 23607, phone 800/937-9247. The Commonwealth of Virginia sponsors an annual Saltwater Fishing Awards Program (see VIRGINIA BEACH), open to the public. Contact Virginia Saltwater Fishing Tournament, 968 S Oriole Dr, Suite 102, Virginia Beach 23451, phone 757/491-5160.

Freshwater fishing is excellent in many of the state's large reservoirs and rivers for such species as largemouth and smallmouth bass, landlocked striped bass, muskie, and a wide variety of panfish. Lake Anna, Smith Mountain Lake, Lake Gaston, James River, Lake Moomaw, and Buggs Island Lake are nationally known for excellent bass and landlocked striped bass fishing. Nonresident license: $30; $30 additional for license for trout in designated stocked waters. Five-day license to fish statewide, $6; other special fees. Fishing in a national forest requires an additional fishing/hunting stamp, $3.

Hunting for upland game and migratory waterfowl in season. Nonresident license: $60; thee-day license: $30; bear, deer, turkey, $60 additional; nonresident muzzleloader license, $25; nonresident special archery license to hunt during special archery season, $25. Hunting in a national forest requires an additional fishing/hunting stamp, $3. There is a 50¢ issuance fee for all licenses. For fishing and hunting regulations and information contact Department of Game and Inland Fisheries, 4010 W Broad St, Richmond 23230, or phone 804/367-1000.

Driving Information

Safety belts are mandatory for all persons in front seat of vehicle. Children under four years must be in an approved safety seat anywhere in vehicle. For further information phone 804/367-0538.

INTERSTATE HIGHWAY SYSTEM

The following alphabetical listing of Virginia towns in *Mobil Travel Guide* shows that these cities are within ten miles of the indicated Interstate highways. A highway map should, however, be checked for the nearest exit.

Highway Number	Cities/Towns within ten miles
Interstate 64	Ashland, Charlottesville, Chesapeake, Clifton Forge, Covington, Hampton, Jamestown, Lexington, Newport News, Norfolk, Portsmouth, Richmond, Staunton, Virginia Beach, Waynesboro, Williamsburg, Yorktown.
Interstate 66	Alexandria, Arlington County, Fairfax, Falls Church, Front Royal, Manassas, McLean.
Interstate 77	Wytheville.
Interstate 81	Abingdon, Blacksburg, Bristol, Front Royal, Harrisonburg, Lexington, Marion, Natural Bridge, New Market, Radford, Roanoke, Salem, Staunton, Strasburg, Winchester, Woodstock, Wytheville.
Interstate 85	Petersburg, South Hill.
Interstate 95	Alexandria, Arlington County, Ashland, Emporia, Fairfax, Falls Church, Fredericksburg, Hopewell, McLean, Mount Vernon, Petersburg, Richmond, Springfield, Triangle.

Additional Visitor Information

Recreational and tourist information, including travel guides, brochures, and maps, is available from the Virginia Tourism Corporation, 901 E Byrd St, Richmond 23219, phone 800/932-5827. Virginia Department of Transportation, 1401 E Broad St, Richmond 23219, phone 804/786-2838, offers an official state map.

There are ten welcome information centers in Virginia at the following locations: the northern end of the state, on I-81 in Clear Brook, and on I-66 in Manassas; at the northeastern side, on I-95 in Fredericksburg; around the bay area on the eastern side, on US 13 in New Church; around the southerly border, on I-95 in Skippers, and on I-85 in Bracey; in the southwestern part of the state, on I-81 in Bristol, and I-77 in Lambsburg; and on the western side, on I-64 in Covington, and on I-77 in Rocky Gap.

GEORGE WASHINGTON'S PLANTATIONS (APPROX 170 MI)

Ask any historically knowledgeable American to name George Washington's home, and the answer you would expect is Mount Vernon, just south of Alexandria, Virginia, but this is only partly correct. In his youth, Washington lived on two other plantations—both of which, like Mount Vernon, honor the country's first president. Each unique home tells a different aspect of his life. All three can be visited in a one-day, 170-mile round-trip. Make sure to get an early start, and begin in Alexandria, a Potomac River port long before the capital at Washington D.C. was conceived. Paralleling the Potomac, the scenic Mount Vernon Parkway winds south for about ten miles to Mount Vernon, a sprawling estate Washington inherited at the age of 20 from a half-brother. Here you can tour his stately white mansion, enjoy the Potomac views as he surely did, walk among the 18th-century farm fields and gardens, and pay homage at his and Martha's tombs. At Mount Vernon, you'll learn about Washington the farmer, the soldier, and the statesman, an imposing man of laudable qualities. Plan to spend much of the morning at the estate. About noon, head south to Washington's two childhood homes to get to know the youth who became the "father of his country." Your first stop is Popes Creek Plantation, which is officially called George Washington Birthplace National Monument. From Mount Vernon, take State Route 235 west to US 1 south and follow the signs to I-95 south to Fredericksburg—about 40 miles. In Fredericksburg, take State Route 3 east for about 36 miles. Make a left turn onto State Route 204, which ends at the plantation in about two miles. This is where Washington was born on February 22, 1732. Unlike Mount Vernon, nothing remains of the original house except a few foundation bricks and grand Potomac River views. And yet the 550-acre park—recreated in part as a colonial farm with fields, pastures, and livestock—does a fine job of exploring Washington's origins. His great-grandfather John, an English seaman, settled in the area in 1657, prospered, and was eventually buried in the park. You can tour Memorial House, a colonial-style farmhouse similar to one that might have stood on the property in 1732. Nearby are other reconstructed period farm buildings and a large herb garden. Walking trails trace the river's shoreline past a grove of towering cedars, and a shaded picnic area is provided. Packing a picnic is a good idea since the park has no food service. Plan on staying about 90 minutes here, giving yourself time to return to Fredericksburg and Ferry Farm, where Washington's family moved when he was six. At the city outskirts, bear right onto Business Route 3. A sign to Ferry Farm will indicate a U-Turn at a stoplight. It is at Ferry Farm that Washington might have chopped down a cherry tree—wild cherries still grow on the property—and where he might have tossed a coin across the Rappahannock River. Archeological digs, sometimes open to visitors, are underway, and a small museum describes the life of Washington as a lad on these hilly, wooded acres. Return to Alexandria via Route 3 and I-95 north. Conclude your day there with dinner in early-American style at Gadsby's Tavern, built in 1792.

NORTHERN VIRGINIA WINE COUNTRY (APPROX 150 MI)

Fifteen years ago, a tour of Virginia's Wine Country would have struck wine connoisseurs as preposterous. But that was then. The state now counts more than 60 wineries, many of them producing award-winning vintages. Even California, home to some of America's most notable wines, is taking notice because several of Virginia's winemakers are producing new and different wines from grapes not yet grown on the West Coast. In recent years, wine-tasting has become an inviting pastime for weekenders. Fortunately, many of the wineries are clustered conveniently to make a visit to three or four in half a day quite practical, though many visitors combine a sampling tour with a stay in a country inn that serves Virginia wines. Part of the fun of visiting Virginia's wineries is that they tend to be located in out-of-the-way corners of the countryside. To get to them, you have to negotiate winding back roads over which you might not otherwise travel. This one-day, 150-mile tour from Fairfax County (a Washington D.C. suburb) traverses the scenic foothills of the Blue Ridge Mountains. Here and there it edges Shenandoah National Park, where a detour of a few miles will take you to one of the lofty overlooks along Skyline Drive, the famed ridge-top parkway. Begin the tour on I-66 west just north of Fairfax City. Near Manassas, stop at the Visitor Information Center to pick up the latest edition of Virginia Wineries Festival and Tour Guide. It lists the operating hours of the tasting rooms, many of which are open daily, some only on weekends. If Civil War history interests you, stop briefly at Manassas National Battlefield Park, which commemorates the first major clash between the North and South. At Gainesville, head south on US 29 past Culpeper to the village of Leon; the Prince Michel Vineyards will be on the right. A visit begins with a self-guided tour of the wine-making facility. This French-owned facility produces a very nice Chardonnay. Its gourmet restaurant, serving lunch and dinner, overlooks acres of vineyards draped across rolling hills. From St. Michel, continue south on US 29 to Madison, and turn right onto State Route 231 north. For about 20 miles, this stretch of the road is a Virginia Scenic Byway. On your left, the high, forested ridge rising overhead is Shenandoah National Park. On both sides of the road, stately plantation homes carry descriptive names. Just south of Sperryville, pick up US 522 north. In Sperryville, browse the sprawling Sperryville Antiques Market and stop for a bite—or at least a peek—at The Appetite Repair Shop, a cafe in used-auto motif. A "Sub in a Hub" is a sandwich served in a hub cap. Continue north on US 522 toward Front Royal, turning right at Route 635. For about a mile, the road glides beneath towering trees; Oasis Winery is on the right. Oasis is best known for its sparkling wines. After your visit to Oasis, return to US 522 and continue north to Front Royal. Head east (right) on Route 55 to Linden. Turn right onto Route 638 and proceed two miles to Linden. Perched atop a small hill, its outdoor deck offers gorgeous Blue Ridge views. Linden is one of Virginia's finest wineries, and one of the prettiest. Linden's Seyval, a dry white wine, is popular with wine fanciers looking for something new. Return to Route 55 and turn west (left) one mile to the entrance to I-66. Take I-66 east back to Fairfax City.

Abingdon

(F-2) *See also Bristol, Marion*

Settled ca 1770 **Pop** 7,780 **Elev** 2,069 ft **Area code** 540 **Zip** 24210
Information Abingdon Convention & Visitors Bureau, 335 Cummings St; 800/435-3344
Web www.abingdon.com

Daniel Boone passed through this area in 1760 and dubbed it Wolf Hill after a pack of wolves from a nearby cave disturbed his dogs. Wolf Hill had long been a crossing for buffalo and Native Americans; Boone later used it for his own family's westward migration. Later, Black's Fort was built here and the community adopted that name. Now known as Abingdon, this summer resort in the Virginia Highlands just north of Tennessee is the Washington County seat, Virginia's largest burley tobacco market, and a livestock auction center.

What to See and Do

Grayson Highlands State Park. Within this 4,935-acre park are rugged peaks, some more than 5,000 ft; alpine scenery. Hiking, horse trails, picnicking, camping, visitor center, interpretive programs, pioneer life displays (June-Aug). Adj to Mount Rogers National Recreation Area (see MARION). (Daily) Standard fees. 35 mi SE on US 58. Phone 276/579-7092.

White's Mill. Old gristmill and general store, still in operation. (Wed-Sat) 12291 White's Mill Rd. Phone 276/676-0285. ¢

Special Events

Barter Theatre. Main St, on US 11 off I-81, in former Town Hall. America's oldest, longest-running professional repertory theater. Founded during the Depression on the theory that residents would barter their abundant crops for first-rate professional entertainment. Designated State Theatre of Virginia in 1946. Phone 540/628-3991. Barter Players

perform Mar-Dec. Children's theater June-Aug.

Virginia Highlands Festival. Exhibits, demonstrations of rustic handicrafts; plays, musical entertainment; historical reenactments; historic house tours, antique market. Early-mid-Aug.

Motels/Motor Lodges

★ **ALPINE MOTEL.** *882 E Main St (24212). 540/628-3178; fax 540/628-4247.* 19 rms. S, D $38-$56; each addl $5; under 12 free; higher rates special events. Crib $2. TV; cable. Restaurant nearby. Ck-out 11 am. Business servs avail. View of mountains. Cr cds: A, DS, MC, V.
[icons]

★ **COMFORT INN.** *170 Old Jonesboro Rd (24210). 540/676-2222; res 800/228-5150. www.comfortinn.com.* 80 rms, 2 story. S, D $55-$150; each addl $6; under 18 free; higher rates special events. Crib free. TV; cable (premium), VCR avail. Pool. Complimentary continental bkfst. Ck-out noon. Business servs avail. Cr cds: A, C, D, DS, ER, JCB, MC, V.
[icons]

★★ **EMPIRE MOTOR LODGE ABINGDON.** *887 Empire Dr SW (24210). 540/628-7131; fax 540/628-7158.* 105 rms, 2 story. S, D $38-$48; each addl $2; under 12 free; higher rates special events. Crib $5. TV; cable (premium). Restaurant 7 am-10 pm. Ck-out 11 am. Business servs avail. Balconies. Cr cds: A, MC, V.
[icons]

B&B/Small Inn

★★★ **THE MARTHA WASHINGTON INN.** *150 W Main St (24210). 540/628-3161; fax 540/628-8885; toll-free 800/533-1014. www.camberley hotels.com.* 61 rms. S, D $149-$159; each addl $10; suites $185-$300; under 12 free; higher rates special events. Crib free. TV; cable (premium), VCR avail. Pool privileges. Dining rm (see THE DINING ROOM). Bar 5 pm-midnight. Ck-out 11 am, ck-in 3 pm. Meeting rms. Business servs avail. Airport transportation. Tennis privileges. Golf privileges. Health club privileges. Cr cds: A, C, D, DS, MC, V.

Restaurants

★ ★ **THE DINING ROOM.** *150 W Main St (24210).* 540/628-9151. Hrs: 6:30-10 am, 11:30 am-2 pm, 5-9 pm; Fri to 10 pm; Sat 7-10 am, 11:30 am-2 pm, 5-10 pm; Sun 7-10 am, 5-9 pm; Sun brunch 11:30 am-2 pm. Res accepted. Bar. Bkfst $4-$8, lunch $6-$9.95, dinner $15-$25. Sun brunch $16.95. Specialties: Virginia trout, tenderloin of beef. Own baking. Cr cds: A, C, D, DS, MC, V.

★ ★ **THE TAVERN.** *222 E Main St (24210).* 540/628-1118. Hrs: 11 am-10 pm. Closed Dec 25. Res accepted. Continental menu. Bar. Lunch $5.95-$7.25, dinner $14.95-$25.95. Specialties: Kassler rippchen, Wiener schnitzel, stuffed filet mignon. Two-story building (1779); Colonial decor with fireplace in each of the three dining rms. Cr cds: A, DS, MC, V.

Alexandria

(C-7) *See also Arlington County (Ronald Reagan Washington-National Airport Area), Fairfax, Falls Church; also see District of Columbia*

Settled 1670 **Pop** 128,283 **Elev** 52 ft **Area code** 703

Information Convention/Visitors Association, 421 King St, 22314-3209; 703/838-4200

Web www.funside.com

A group of English and Scottish merchants established a tobacco warehouse at the junction of Hunting Creek and the "Potowmack" River in the 1740s. The little settlement prospered and 17 years later surveyor John West, Jr. and his young assistant, George Washington, arrived and "laid off in streets and 84 half-acre lots" the town of Alexandria. Among the first buyers on the July morning in 1749 when

the lots were offered for public sale were Lawrence Washington and his brother Augustus, William Ramsay, the Honorable William Fairfax, and John Carlyle. Erecting handsome town houses, these gentlemen soon brought a lively and cosmopolitan air to Alexandria with parties, balls, and horse racing. It was also the home town of George Mason and Robert E. Lee and home to George Washington.

In 1789 Virginia ceded Alexandria to the District of Columbia, but in 1846 the still Southern-oriented citizens asked to return to the Old Dominion, which Congress allowed.

In the Civil War Alexandria was cut off from the Confederacy when Union troops occupied the town to protect Potomac River navigation. Safe behind Union lines, the city escaped the dreadful destruction experienced by many other Southern towns. After the war, even with seven railroads centering here for transfer of freight, Alexandria declined as a center of commerce and was in trade doldrums until about 1914, when the Alexandria shipyards were reopened and the Naval Torpedo Station was built. Today it has developed into a trade, commerce, transportation, and science center. More than 250 national associations are based here.

What to See and Do

Alexandria Black History Resource Center. Photographs, letters, documents, and artifacts relate history of African Americans in Alexandria. (Tues-Sat; closed hols) 638 N Alfred St. Phone 703/838-4356. **DONATION**

The Athenaeum. Greek Revival structure (1851) built as bank, now houses Fine Arts Association. Art shows, dance performances. (Wed-Fri and Sat-Sun afternoons; closed hols) 201 Prince St. Phone 703/548-0035.

Doorways to Old Virginia. Offers guided walking tours of historic district. (Mar-Oct, Fri-Sun, eves) Departs from Ramsay House. Phone 703/548-0100. ¢¢¢

Fort Ward Museum and Historic Site. Restored Union Fort from Civil War; museum contains Civil War collection. Museum (Tues-Sun; closed Jan 1, Thanksgiving, Dec 25). Park, picnicking (daily to sunset). 4301 W

Braddock Rd. Phone 703/838-4848.
FREE

George Washington Masonic National Memorial. American Freemasons' memorial to their most prominent member, this 333-ft-high structure houses a large collection of objects that belonged to George Washington, which were collected by his family or the masonic lodge where he served as the first master. Guided tours explore a replica of Alexandria-Washington Lodge's first hall, a library, museum, and an observation deck on the top floor. (Daily; closed Jan 1, Thanksgiving, Dec 25) 101 Callahan Dr, W end of King St. Phone 703/683-2007. **FREE**

Gunston Hall. (1755-1759) The 550-acre estate of George Mason, framer of the Constitution, father of the Bill of Rights. Restored 18th-century mansion with period furnishings; reconstructed outbuildings; display of historic livestock on working farm; museum; boxwood gardens on grounds; nature trail; picnic area; gift shop. (Daily; closed Jan 1, Thanksgiving, Dec 25) 18 mi S on US 1, then 4 mi E on VA 242 in Lorton at 10709 Gunston Rd. Phone 703/550-9220. ¢¢¢

King Street. Street is lined with trendy restaurants, shops, and fine antique stores. In Old Town.

Mount Vernon. (see) 9 mi S on Mt Vernon Memorial Hwy.

Pohick Bay Regional Park. Near Gunston Hall. Activities in this 1,000-acre park incl swimming (Memorial Day-Labor Day), boating (ramp, rentals, fee); 18-hole golf, miniature and Frisbee golf, camping (seven-day limit; electric hookups avail; fee), picnicking. Park (all yr). Fee charged for activities. 6501 Pohick Bay Dr, in Lorton. Phone 703/339-6104. ¢¢¢

Pohick Episcopal Church. (1774) The colonial parish church of Mt Vernon and Gunston Hall. Built under supervision of George Mason and George Washington; original walls; interior fully restored. (Daily) 9301 Richmond Hwy, 16 mi S on US 1 in Lorton. Phone 703/550-9449. **FREE**

Sightseeing boat tours. Tours of Alexandria waterfront. Contact the Potomac Riverboat Company. Phone 703/684-0580. ¢¢¢

Torpedo Factory Arts Center. Renovated munitions plant houses artists' center with more than 160 professional artists of various media. Studios, cooperative galleries, school. Also home of Alexandria Archaeology offices, lab, museum; phone 703/838-4399. (Daily; closed hols) 105 N Union St. Phone 703/838-4565. **FREE**

⭐ **Walking tour of historic sites.** Start at Visitors Center in **Ramsay House** (ca 1725). Oldest house in Alexandria and later used as a tavern, grocery store, and cigar factory. Here vistors can obtain special events information and a free visitors guide, as well as purchase "block tickets" good for reduced admission to three of the city's historic properties. Guided walking tours, depart from here (spring-fall, weather permitting). The Bureau also issues free parking permits, tour and highway maps, and hotel, dining, and shopping information. (Daily; closed Jan 1, Thanksgiving, Dec 25) 221 King St, at Fairfax St. Phone 703/838-4200. 1 blk N on Fairfax St is

Carlyle House. (1753) This stately stone mansion built in Palladian style was the site of a 1755 meeting between General Edward Braddock and five British colonial governors to plan the early campaigns of the French and Indian War. (Tues-Sun; closed hols) 121 N Fairfax St. Phone 703/549-2997. ¢¢ 1-½ blks S on Fairfax St is

Stabler-Leadbeater Apothecary Museum. (1792) Largest collection of apothecary glass in its original setting in the country; more than 1,000 apothecary bottles. Original building is now a museum of early pharmacy; collection of old prescriptions, patent medicines, scales, other 18th-century pharmacy items. George Washington, Robert E. Lee, and John Calhoun were regular customers. (Daily; closed Jan 1, Thanksgiving, Dec 25) 105 S Fairfax St. Phone 703/836-3713. 2 blks S on Fairfax St is

Old Presbyterian Meeting House. (1774) Tomb of the unknown soldier of the Revolution is in churchyard. (Mon-Fri) 321 S Fairfax St.

Phone 703/549-6670. **FREE** ½ blk N, then 3 blks W on Duke St is

Lafayette House. Fine example of Federal architecture. House was loaned to Lafayette for his last visit to America (1825). (Private) 301 St. Asaph St. Walk 2 blks N to Prince St, then left on Prince St to SW corner of Prince and Washington sts to

The Lyceum. Museum, exhibitions; Virginia travel information (limited). (Daily; closed Jan 1, Thanksgiving, Dec 25) 201 S Washington St. Phone 703/838-4994. **FREE** 2 blks N on Washington St is

Christ Church. (1773) Washington and Robert E. Lee were pewholders. Fine Palladian window; interior balcony; wrought-brass and crystal chandelier brought from England. Structure is extensively restored but changed little since it was built. Exhibit, gift shop at Columbus St entrance. (Mon-Sat, also Sun afternoons; closed hols; also for weddings, funerals) 118 N Washington St. Phone 703/549-1450. 1 blk E on Cameron St is

Home of General Henry "Light Horse Harry" Lee. (Private) 611 Cameron St. 3 blks N, 1 blk W, left on Washington St is

Lee-Fendall House. (1785) Built by Phillip Richard Fendall and lived in by Lee family for 118 yrs. Both George Washington and Revolutionary War hero "Light Horse Harry" Lee were frequent visitors to the house. Remodeled in 1850, the house is furnished with Lee family belongings. (Tues-Sun, wkend hrs may vary; closed hols) 614 Oronoco St. Phone 703/548-1789. ¢¢ Proceed N, turn right on Oronoco St, ½ blk E to

Boyhood Home of Robert E. Lee. Federalist architecture. Famous guests incl Washington and Lafayette. (Now a private residence) 607 Oronoco St. 3 blks E, then 3 blks S on Royal St is

Gadsby's Tavern Museum. (1770, 1792) Famous hostelry frequented by Washington and other patriots. Combines two 18th-century buildings; interesting architecture. (Tues-Sun; closed hols) 134 N Royal St. Phone 703/838-4242. ¢¢

Special Events

George Washington Birthday Celebrations. Events incl race, Revolutionary War reenactment; climaxed by birthday parade on federal holiday. Feb.

House tours. Fine Colonial and Federalist houses are opened to the public: Historic Garden Week (Apr); Hospital Auxiliary Tour of Historic Houses (Sept); Scottish Christmas Walk (Dec). Tickets, addl information at Alexandria Convention/Visitors Association. Phone 703/838-4200.

Red Cross Waterfront Festival. Commemorates Alexandria's maritime heritage. Features "tall ships," blessing of the fleet, river cruises, races, arts and crafts, exhibits, food, variety of music; fireworks. Phone 703/549-8300. June.

Virginia Scottish Games. Athletic competition, Highland dance and music, antique cars, displays, food. Phone 703/838-4200. Fourth wkend July.

Scottish Christmas Walk. Parade, house tour, concerts, greens and heather sales, dinner/dance to emphasize city's Scottish origins. First Sat Dec. Phone 800/388-9119.

Motels/Motor Lodges

★★ **BEST WESTERN.** 615 1st St (22314). 703/739-2222; fax 703/549-2568; toll-free 800/528-1234. www.bestwestern.com. 151 rms, 2 story. Apr-June, Sept-Oct: S $89; D $99; each addl $10; kits. $109; under 18 free; wkend, hol rates; lower rates rest of yr. Crib free. Pet accepted; $50 deposit and $10/day. TV; cable (premium). Pool; lifeguard. Complimentary continental bkfst. Restaurant adj 6:30 am-11 pm. Ck-out noon. Meeting rms. Business servs avail. In-rm modem link. Sundries. Valet serv. Free airport transportation. Health club privileges. Cr cds: A, C, D, DS, MC, V.

D 🐾 ⇌ ✈ ⇘ 🐾 SC

★★ **BEST WESTERN MOUNT VERNON.** 8751 Richmond Hwy (22309). 703/360-1300; fax 703/799-7713; toll-free 800/528-1234. www.bestwestern.com. 132 rms, 5 story. Mar-Oct: S $77-$82; D $82-$87; each addl $5; suites $110-$120; under 18 free; lower rates rest of yr. Crib free. TV; cable (premium). Complimentary continental bkfst. Restaurant nearby. Ck-out 11 am. Meeting rm. Business servs avail. Valet serv. Exercise equipt. Some refrigerators; microwaves avail. Cr cds: A, C, D, DS, MC, V.

⬛ 🧘 🛏 🐾 **SC**

★★ **COMFORT INN.** *7212 Richmond Hwy (22306). 703/765-9000; fax 703/765-2325; res 800/433-2546. www.comfortinn.com.* 92 rms, 2 story. S $50-$65; D $55-$75; each addl $7; under 17 free; package plans. Crib free. Pet accepted, some restrictions. TV; cable (premium). Pool; lifeguard. Complimentary continental bkfst. Restaurant nearby. Ck-out noon. Meeting rm. Business servs avail. In-rm modem link. Valet serv. Sundries. Refrigerators, microwaves avail. Cr cds: A, C, D, DS, MC, V.

⬛ 🐕 🛏 🛏 🐾 **SC**

★★ **COURTYARD BY MARRIOTT.** *2700 Eisenhower Ave (22314). 703/329-2323; fax 703/329-6853; res 800/321-2211. www.marriott.com.* 176 rms, 8 story. Apr-May, Oct-Nov: S $169; D $179; suites $220; under 12 free; higher rates Cherry Blossom Festival; lower rates rest of yr. Crib free. TV; cable (premium). Complimentary coffee in rms. Restaurant 6:30-10 am, 5-10 pm; Sat, Sun 7-11 am, 5-10 pm. Rm serv from 5 pm. Bar 4 pm-midnight. Ck-out noon. Meeting rms. Business servs avail. Valet serv. Sundries. Free RR station transportation. Exercise equipt. Whirlpool. Some refrigerators, microwaves. Some balconies. Cr cds: A, C, D, DS, JCB, MC, V.

⬛ 🧘 🛏 🐾

★★ **EXECUTIVE CLUB SUITES.** *610 Bashford Ln (22314). 703/739-2582; fax 703/548-0266; toll-free 800/535-2582. www.dcexcclub.com.* 78 kit. suites, 3 story. No elvtr. S, D $190-$220; wkend, hol rates. Crib free. Pet accepted, some restrictions. TV; cable (premium). Pool; lifeguard. Complimentary continental bkfst, coffee in rms. Restaurant nearby. Ck-out noon. Coin lndry. Meeting rms. Business center. In-rm modem link. Valet serv. Sundries. Free airport transportation. Exercise equipt; sauna. Microwaves. Picnic tables. Cr cds: A, D, DS, MC, V.

🐕 🛏 🧘 ✈ 🛏 🐾

★★ **HAMPTON INN.** *4800 Leesburg Pike (22302). 703/671-4800; fax 703/671-2442; toll-free 800/426-7866.* 130 rms, 4 story. S $95; D $95-$105. Crib free. TV; cable (premium). Pool. Complimentary continental bkfst. Coffee in rms. Ck-out noon. Business servs avail. In-rm modem link. Valet serv. Exercise equipt. Health club privileges. Cr cds: A, C, D, DS, MC, V.

⬛ 🛏 🧘 🛏 🐾 **SC**

★★ **HOLIDAY INN.** *2460 Eisenhower Ave (22314). 703/960-3400; fax 703/329-0953; toll-free 800/465-4329. www.holiday-inn.com.* 197 rms, 10 story. Mar-early July, mid-Sept-mid-Nov: S $94-$120; D $104-$130; suite $250; each addl $10; under 18 free; wkend, hol rates; lower rates rest of yr. Crib free. TV; cable (premium). Indoor pool. Restaurant 6:30 am-10 pm. Bar 11 am-midnight; entertainment Fri, Sat. Ck-out noon. Coin lndry. Meeting rms. Business servs avail. In-rm modem link. Gift shop. Free airport, RR station transportation. Exercise equipt. Game rm. Refrigerators avail. Cr cds: A, C, D, DS, JCB, MC, V.

⬛ 🛏 🧘 🛏 🐾 **SC**

★★ **HOLIDAY INN.** *480 King St (22314). 703/549-6080; fax 703/684-6508; res 800/368-5047. www.holiday-inn.com.* 227 rms, 6 story. Mar-June, Sept-Oct: S $149-$199; D $169-$209; each addl $20; suites $275-$350; under 18 free; wkend rates; lower rates rest of yr. Crib free. Pet accepted, some restrictions. Garage $7/day. TV; cable (premium). Indoor pool; lifeguard. Complimentary coffee in rms. Restaurant 6:30 am-11 pm. Bars 11 am-midnight. Ck-out noon. Coin lndry. Meeting rms. Business center. In-rm modem link. Concierge. Gift shop. Free airport transportation. Exercise equipt; sauna. Refrigerators, minibars, microwaves avail. Some balconies. Cr cds: A, C, D, DS, ER, JCB, MC, V.

⬛ 🐕 🛏 🧘 🛏 🐾 **SC** 🧘

★★ **HOLIDAY INN AND SUITES.** *625 1st St (22314). 703/548-6300; fax 703/548-8032; toll-free 800/465-4329.* 161 rms, 4 story, 17 suites. S, D $149; each addl $10; suites $159-$199; under 18 free; wkend rates. Crib free. TV; cable (premium). Indoor/outdoor pool; whirlpool. Coffee in rms.

Restaurant 6:30 am-10 pm. Bar 11 am-midnight. Ck-out noon. Coin lndry. Meeting rm. Business center. In-rm modem link. Bellhops. Free airport transportation. Exercise rm. Microwave, wet bar in suites; refrigerators avail. Cr cds: A, C, D, DS, JCB, MC, V.

⬛ 🏊 🧍 ✈️ 🛢 🔥 SC 🏃

★★ **HOMEWOOD SUITES HOTEL.** 4850 Leesburg Pike (22302). 703/671-6500; fax 703/671-9322; toll-free 800/225-4663. www.homewoodsuites. com. 105 rms, 5 story. S $129-$139, D $135-$155. Crib free. TV; cable (premium). Pool; whirlpool. Complimentary continental bkfst. Restaurant nearby. Ck-out noon. Meeting rms. Business center. Valet serv. Coin lndry. Exercise equipt. Health club privileges. Game rm. Gift shop. Cr cds: A, C, D, DS, MC, V.

⬛ 🏊 🧍 🛢 🔥 🏃

★★ **RADISSON.** 901 N Fairfax St (22314). 703/683-6000; fax 703/683-5750. www.radisson.com. 258 rms, 12 story. S, D $139-$179; each addl $10; under 18 free; wkend rates. Crib free. TV; cable (premium). Pool; lifeguard. Coffee in rms. Restaurant 6 am-10 pm. Bar 11-1 am. Ck-out noon. Business servs avail. In-rm modem link. Gift shop. Free airport transportation. Health club privileges. Refrigerators, microwaves avail. Cr cds: A, C, D, DS, MC, V.

⬛ 🏊 🛢 🔥 SC

★ **RED ROOF INN.** 5975 Richmond Hwy (22303). 703/960-5200; fax 703/960-5209; res 800/843-7663. www.redroof.com. 115 rms, 3 story. Apr-Oct: S, D $69.99-$78.99; each addl $5; under 18 free; higher rates special events; lower rates rest of yr. Crib free. Pet accepted, some restrictions. TV; cable (premium). Complimentary coffee in lobby. Restaurant nearby. Ck-out noon. Business servs avail. In-rm modem link. Coin lndry. Valet serv. Cr cds: A, D, DS, MC, V.

⬛ 🐾 🛢 🔥

★★ **TRAVELERS MOTEL.** 5916 Richmond Hwy (22303). 703/329-1310; fax 703/960-9211; toll-free 800/368-7378. 30 rms. S $58-$66; D $59.99-$73.99; each addl $5. Crib free. TV; cable (premium). Pool; lifeguard. Complimentary coffee in lobby. Restaurant opp 6 am-11 pm.

Ck-out 11 am. Business servs avail. Cr cds: A, C, D, DS, MC, V.

⬛ 🏊 🛢 🔥 SC

Hotels

★★ **HILTON ALEXANDRIA MARK CENTER.** 5000 Seminary Rd (22311). 703/845-1010; fax 703/845-7662; toll free 800/333-3333. www.hilton.com. 495 rms, 30 story. S, D $125-$195; each addl $20; suites $250-$800; under 16 free; wkly rates; wkend packages. Crib free. Covered parking $4/day, valet parking $10. TV; cable (premium), VCR avail (free movies). Indoor/outdoor pool; whirlpool. Coffee in rm. Restaurant 6 am-11 pm. Bars 11-1 am. Ck-out noon. Convention facilities. Business center. In-rm modem link. Gift shop. Barber, beauty shop. Free airport transportation. Tennis. Exercise equipt; sauna. Game rm. Refrigerators; some bathrm phones. Whirlpool in some suites. Located on 50 wooded acres with nature preserve. Luxury level. Cr cds: A, C, D, DS, ER, JCB, MC, V.

⬛ 🏌 🏊 🧍 🛢 🔥 SC 🏃

★★★★ **MORRISON HOUSE.** 116 S Alfred St (22314). 703/838-8000; fax 703/684-6283; toll-free 800/367-0800. www.morrissonhouse.com. Located in the heart of old Alexandria, this house offers a comfortable stay for those who prefer a small property to a chain hotel. The rooms are well appointed with excellent quality wood furniture in a classical style. The restaurant Elysium is considered one of the best in the area. 45 rms, 5 story. S, D $195-$315; suites $315-$515; wkend rates. Crib free. Covered parking $10/day. TV; cable (premium), VCR avail (movies $5). Dining rm (see also ELYSIUM). Afternoon tea 3-5 pm. Rm serv 24 hrs. Bar 11:30 am-11 pm; Fri, Sat to midnight; entertainment Thurs-Sat. Ck-out noon, ck-in after 3 pm. Meeting rms. Business servs avail. In-rm modem link. Butlers. Health club privileges. Bathrm phones. Cr cds: A, C, D, MC, V.

⬛ 🛢 🔥

★★ **WASHINGTON SUITES.** 100 S Reynolds St (22304). 703/370-9600; fax 703/370-0467; res 877/736-2500. www.washingtonsuiteshotel.com. 225 kit. suites, 9 story. S, D $125-$260; each addl $10; under 18 free; wkend rates. Crib $10. Pet accepted; $10/day. TV; cable (premium). Pool; lifeguard. Complimentary continental bkfst. Restaurant 6:30-9:30 am, 5-10 pm. Bar from 5 pm. Ck-out noon. Coin lndry. Meeting rms. Business center. Exercise equipt. Health club privileges. Microwaves. Some balconies. Cr cds: A, C, D, DS, MC, V.

All Suite

★★★ **SHERATON SUITES.** *801 N Saint Asaph St (22314). 703/836-4700; fax 703/548-4514; toll-free 800/325-3535. www.sheraton.com.* 247 suites, 10 story. Apr-May: S, D $220; under 12 free; wknd, hol rates; lower rates rest of yr. Crib free. Pet accepted. Garage parking $7. TV; cable (premium). Indoor pool; whirlpool, lifeguard. Complimentary coffee in rms. Restaurant 6:30 am-11 pm; wknds from 7 am. Bar. Ck-out 1 pm. Guest lndry. Meeting rms. Business servs avail. In-rm modem link. Gift shop. Free airport transportation. Exercise equipt. Refrigerators; microwaves avail. Luxury level. Cr cds: A, C, D, DS, ER, JCB, MC, V.

Restaurants

★★ **BILBO BAGGINS.** *208 Queen St (22314). 703/683-0300.* Hrs: 11:30 am-10:30 pm; Sun 11 am-9:30 pm; early-bird dinner Mon-Thurs 5:30-6 pm; Sun brunch 11 am-2:30 pm. Closed Dec 25. Res accepted. Continental menu. Bar. Lunch $6.95-$9.95, dinner $10.95-$17.95. Sun brunch $7.95-$9.95. Specialties: Bilbo's bread, Bilbo's salad. Own baking. Upstairs in 1898 structure; stained glass, skylights. Cr cds: A, DS, MC, V.

★★ **BLUE POINT GRILL.** *600 Franklin St (22314). 703/739-0404. www.suttongourmet.com.* Hrs: 11:30 am-10 pm; Fri, Sat to 11 pm; Sun 11 am-3 pm (brunch), 5-9 pm. Closed 3-5:30 pm Oct-May; also Dec 25. Res accepted. A la carte entrees: lunch $7-$15, dinner $13.95-$20.95. Sun brunch $8.50-$11.95. Specializes in fresh seafood. Parking. Outdoor dining. Cafe atmosphere; adj to gourmet

Sutton Place Market. Cr cds: A, DS, MC, V.

★★ **CALVERT GRILLE.** *3106 Mt Vernon Ave (22305). 703/836-8425. www.calvertgrille.qpg.com.* Hrs: 11-12:30 am; Fri to 2 am; Sat from 9:30 am; Sun 9:30 am-9 pm; Sat, Sun brunch to 2 pm. Closed Thanksgiving, Dec 25. Bar. Bkfst $2.95-$6.50, lunch $5.25-$8.95, dinner $5.95-$11.95. Sat, Sun brunch $6.95-$12.95. Child's menu. Specializes in babyback ribs, crab cakes, regional dishes. Family-friendly atmosphere. Cr cds: A, D, DS, MC, V.

★★ **CHART HOUSE.** *1 Cameron St (22314). 703/684-5080. www.charthouse.com.* Hrs: 5-10 pm; Fri, Sat to 11 pm; Sun 10:45 am-2:15 pm, 4-10 pm. Closed Dec 25. Res accepted; required Fri-Sun. Contemporary American menu. Bar. Dinner $14.95-$32.95. Sun brunch $16.95-$23. Child's menu. Specializes in grilled fresh seafood, aged beef. Views of the Capitol, Potomac River. Cr cds: A, D, DS, MC, V.

★★★ **CHEZ ANDRE.** *10 E Glebe Rd (22305). 703/836-1404.* Hrs: 11 am-2:30 pm, 5-9:30 pm; Sat from 5 pm. Closed Sun; hols. Res accepted; required Fri, Sat. French menu. Serv bar. Lunch $8.95-$15.50, dinner $13.95-$21.95. Prix fixe (Mon, Tues): dinner $24.95. Specialties: salmon Hollandaise, coquilles St. Jacques, duck a l'orange. Parking. French country decor. Family-owned. Cr cds: A, D, MC, V.

★★ **COPELAND'S OF NEW ORLEANS.** *4300 King St (22302). 703/671-7997.* Hrs: 11 am-10 pm; Fri, Sat to midnight; Sun brunch to 3 pm. Closed Thanksgiving, Dec 25. Cajun, Creole, American menu. Bar. Lunch $6.99-$7.95, dinner $6.99-$15.95. Sun brunch $7.95-$10.95. Child's menu. Specializes in seafood. Parking. Outdoor dining. Cr cds: A, D, DS, MC, V.

★★ **EAST WIND.** *809 King St (22314). 703/836-1515.* Hrs: 11:30

am-2:30 pm, 5:30-10 pm; Fri to 10:30 pm; Sat 5:30-10:30 pm; Sun 5:30-9:30 pm. Closed hols. Res accepted. Vietnamese menu. Bar. Lunch $5.95-$7.95, dinner $7.95-$15.50. Specialty: charbroiled shrimp and scallops. Own desserts. Original Vietnamese paintings and panels. Cr cds: A, D, DS, MC, V.
◰

★ ★ **ECCO CAFE.** *220 N Lee St (22314). 703/684-0321. www.eccocafe. com.* Hrs: 11 am-11 pm; Mon to 10 pm; Fri, Sat to midnight; Sun 4-10 pm; Sun brunch 11:30 am-3 pm. Closed Thanksgiving, Dec 25. Res accepted Sun-Thurs. Italian, American menu. Bar. A la carte entrees: lunch $6.95-$9.95, dinner $10.95-$16.95. Sun brunch $7.95-$11.95. Specializes in beef, chicken, pasta. Own baking, pasta. Jazz Sun. In restored 1890s warehouse bldg; eclectic decor. Cr cds: A, D, DS, MC, V.
D

★ ★ ★ **ELYSIUM.** *116 S Alfred St (22314). 703/838-8000. www.morrison house.com.* Hrs: 6-10 pm; Fri, Sat to 11 pm; Sun brunch noon-2:30 pm. Closed Mon; Jan 1. Res required Fri, Sat. Bar 11:30 am-midnight. Wine list. Prix fixe: dinner $35-$55; Sun brunch $25. Specializes in New American cuisine. Formal Federal period dining rm. Cr cds: A, D, MC, V.
D

★ **FACCIA LUNA.** *823 S Washington St (22314). 703/838-5998. www.faccia luna.com.* Hrs: 11:30 am-11 pm; Fri, Sat to midnight; Sun from noon. Closed hols. Italian menu. Bar. Lunch $4.95-$7, dinner $7-$12. Child's menu. Specializes in pizza, fresh pasta, grinders. Own pasta. Outdoor dining. Contemporary American trattoria with woodburning oven. Totally nonsmoking. Cr cds: A, MC, V.
D ◰

★ ★ **FISH MARKET.** *105 King St (22314). 703/836-5676.* Hrs: 11:15-2 am; Sun to midnight. Closed Thanksgiving, Dec 25. Bar. Lunch $3.95-$12.95, dinner $4.25-$16.25. Specializes in Chesapeake Bay-style seafood. Ragtime pianist. Outdoor dining. In restored 18th-century warehouse built of bricks carried to

New World as ballast in ship's hold; nautical decor. Cr cds: A, D, MC, V.
◰

★ ★ **GADSBY'S TAVERN.** *138 N Royal St (22314). 703/548-1288. www. gadsbys.org.* Hrs: 11:30 am-3 pm, 5:30-10 pm; Sun brunch 11 am-3 pm. Closed Jan 1, Dec 25. Res accepted; required Fri, Sat. Lunch $6.95-$8.95, dinner $14.95-$22.95. Sun brunch $6.75-$9.95. Child's menu. Specialties: Sally Lunn bread, George Washington's favorite duck, English trifle. Strolling minstrels. Outdoor dining. Built 1792; Georgian architecture; Colonial decor and costumes. Gadsby's Tavern Museum adj. Totally nonsmoking. Cr cds: A, D, MC, V.
D

★ ★ ★ **GERANIO.** *722 King St (22314). 703/548-0088.* Hrs: 11:30 am-2:30 pm, 6-10:30 pm; Sat from 6 pm; Sun 5:30-9:30 pm. Closed hols. Res accepted; required Fri, Sat. Italian menu. Serv bar. Lunch $6.95-$10.25, dinner $11.75-$15.50. Specializes in veal, seafood, pasta. Rustic Mediterranean decor. Fireplace, ceramic chandeliers. Cr cds: A, D, MC, V.
D

★ ★ ★ **IL PORTO.** *121 King St (22314). 703/836-8833. www.ilporto. com.* Hrs: 11:15 am-midnight. Res accepted. Northern Italian menu. Bar from 6 pm. Lunch $3.50-$9.50, dinner $9-$16.75. Child's menu. Specialties: pasta de Venezia, chicken Angelica. Extensive dessert menu. In 18th-century building originally a marine warehouse. Cr cds: A, D, MC, V.
D

★ ★ ★ **LA BERGERIE.** *218 N Lee St (22314). 703/683-1007. www.labergerie. com.* Hrs: 11:30 am-2:30 pm; 5:30-10:30 pm. Closed Sun exc Mother's Day; hols. Res accepted; required Fri, Sat. French, American menu. Serv bar. Lunch $10.95-$14.95, dinner $14.95-$24.95. Specializes in fresh seafood. Own pastries. Restored 1890s warehouse. Cr cds: A, D, DS, MC, V.
D

★ ★ **LANDINI BROTHERS.** *115 King St (22314). 703/836-8404. www.landini brothers.com.* Hrs: 11:30 am-11 pm; Sun 3-10 pm. Closed hols. Res accepted; required Fri, Sat. Italian

menu. Bar. A la carte entrees: lunch $9-$13, dinner $13.50-$24.95. Specializes in veal, pasta, fresh fish. 1790s building. Cr cds: A, D, DS, MC, V.
D 🗺

★ ★ ★ **LE GAULOIS.** *1106 King St (22314).* 703/739-9494. Hrs: 11:30 am-10:30 pm; Fri, Sat to 11 pm. Closed Sun; hols. Res accepted. French menu. Serv Bar. A la carte entrees: lunch $4.75-$12.50, dinner $5.75-$19.75. Specialty: pot au feu Gaulois. Outdoor dining. French provincial decor; fireplace. Cr cds: A, D, DS, MC, V.
D 🗺

★ ★ **LE REFUGE.** *127 N Washington St (22314).* 703/548-4661. Hrs: 11:30 am-2:30 pm, 5:30-10 pm; early-bird dinner 5:30-7 pm. Closed Sun; hols. Res accepted; required Fri, Sat. French menu. Serv bar. Lunch $7.95-$12.95, dinner $13.95-$19.95. Complete meals: lunch $10.95. Specialties: bouillabaisse, salmon en croûte, veal Normande. Country French decor. Cr cds: A, D, DS, MC, V.

★ **MANGO MIKE'S.** *4580 Duke St (22304).* 703/823-1166. www.mango mikes.com. Hrs: 11 am-10 pm; Thurs-Sat to 11 pm; Sun from 10 am; Sun brunch to 2 pm. Closed Thanksgiving, Dec 25. Caribbean menu. Bar to 2 am. Lunch $4.95-$10.95, dinner $9.95-$13.95. Sun brunch $9.95. Child's menu. Specialties: jerk chicken, mango barbecue ribs. Own desserts. Caribbean drummer Sun. Outdoor dining. Informal Caribbean atmosphere. Cr cds: A, D, DS, MC, V.
D

★ ★ **MONROE'S.** *1603 Commonwealth Ave (22301).* 703/548-5792. Hrs: 5-10 pm; Fri, Sat to 11 pm; Sun 5-9 pm; Sun brunch 9:30 am-2 pm. Closed hols. Res accepted; required Fri, Sat. Italian menu. Bar. Dinner $8.50-$16.95. Sun brunch $3.95-$10.95. Child's menu. Specialties: tonno alla livornese, bowtie pasta with crab meat, aged Angus beef. Own pastries. Outdoor dining. Contemporary trattoria with large murals. Totally nonsmoking. Cr cds: A, DS, MC, V.
D

★ ★ **R.T.'S.** *3804 Mt Vernon Ave (22305).* 703/684-6010. www.rts.com.

Hrs: 11 am-10:30 pm; Fri, Sat to 11 pm; Sun 4-9 pm. Closed hols. Res accepted. Creole/Cajun menu. Bar. Lunch $5.95-$10.95, dinner $12.95-$19.95. Child's menu. Specialties: Jack Daniels shrimp, Acadian peppered shrimp, she-crab soup. Cr cds: A, D, DS, MC, V.
D 🗺

★ ★ **SANTA FE EAST.** *110 S Pitt St (22314).* 703/548-6900. www.santafe east.com. Hrs: 11:30 am-10 pm; Fri, Sat to 11 pm; Sun 11 am-10 pm. Closed July 4, Thanksgiving, Dec 25. Res accepted; required Fri, Sat. Southwestern menu. Bar. A la carte entrees: lunch $5.95-$9.95, dinner $8.95-$18.75. Sun brunch $5.25-$7.25. Specialties: chipotle chicken, enchilada Santa Fe, salmon a la plancha. Outdoor dining. Native American art, artifacts. Fountain in courtyard. Fireplaces. In historic (1790) building. Cr cds: A, D, DS, MC, V.
D 🗺

★ ★ **SCOTLAND YARD.** *728 King St (22314).* 703/683-1742. www. scotlandyardrestaurant.com. Hrs: 6-8 pm. Closed Mon; Thanksgiving. Res accepted; required Fri, Sat. Scottish menu. Serv bar. A la carte entrees: dinner $12.95-$18.95. Complete meal: dinner $28.95. Specializes in salmon, lamb, venison. Old Scottish inn (1792); tin ceiling, fireplace. Totally nonsmoking. Cr cds: A, MC, V.
D

★ **SOUTH AUSTIN GRILL.** *801 King St (22314).* 703/684-8969. www. austingrill.com. Hrs: 11:30 am-11 pm; Mon to 10 pm; Fri to midnight; Sat 11 am-midnight; Sun 11 am-10 pm; Sat, Sun brunch to 3 pm. Closed Thanksgiving, Dec 24, 25. Tex-Mex menu. Bar. Lunch, dinner $6.95-$13.95. Sat, Sun brunch $4.95-$6.95. Child's meals. Specializes in beef, chicken. Own baking. Colorful decor with memorabilia of Austin, TX. Cr cds: A, D, DS, MC, V.
D 🗺

★ ★ **TAVERNA CRETEKOU.** *818 King St (22314).* 703/548-8688. Hrs: 11:30 am-2:30 pm, 5-10:30 pm; Sat noon-11 pm; Sun 5-9:30 pm; Sun brunch 11 am-3 pm. Closed Mon; hols. Res accepted; required Fri, Sat. Greek menu. Serv bar. A la carte

entrees: lunch $6.25-$8.95, dinner
$11.95-$21.95. Sun brunch $14.95.
Specializes in seafood, lamb. Entertainment Thurs. Outdoor dining.
Mediterranean decor; brick patio,
arbor. Cr cds: A, MC, V.

★ ★ **TEMPO.** *4231 Duke St (22304).*
703/370-7900. Hrs: 11:30 am-2:30
pm, 5:30-10 pm; Sun to 9 pm; Sun
brunch to 2:30 pm. Closed hols. Res
accepted; required Fri, Sat dinner.
Italian, French menu. Bar. Lunch
$8.95-$10.95, dinner $11.95-$16.95.
Sun brunch $5.95-$10.95. Specialties:
linguini with lobster, lamb chops
with fresh herbs. Outdoor dining.
Modern decor with cathedral windows, original artwork. Cr cds: A, D,
DS, MC, V.

D **SC**

★ ★ **THAI HUT.** *408 S Van Dorn St
(22304).* *703/823-5357.* Hrs: 11 am-
10 pm; Fri to 11 pm; Sat noon-11
pm; Sun noon-9:30 pm. Closed
Thanksgiving, Dec 25. Thai menu. A
la carte entrees: lunch, dinner $6.95-
$11.95. Complete meals (Mon-Fri):
lunch $5.95. Specialties: curries, pad
Thai, drunken noodles. Parking.
Modern decor; Thai artwork. Cr cds:
A, D, MC, V.

D

★ ★ **UNION STREET PUBLIC
HOUSE.** *121 S Union St (22314).*
703/548-1785. Hrs: 11:30 am-10:30
pm; Fri, Sat to 11:30 pm; Sun brunch
11 am-3 pm. Closed Thanksgiving,
Dec 25. Bar to 1:15 am. Lunch, dinner $5.50-$16.95. Sun brunch $4.95-
$8.95. Child's menu. Specialties:
pasta jambalya, linguine with lobster
and smoked scallops, aged Angus
beef. Oyster raw bar. In sea captain's
house and warehouse (ca 1870). Cr
cds: A, D, DS, MC, V.

★ ★ **VILLA D'ESTE.** *600 Montgomery
St (22314).* *703/549-9477.* Hrs: 11:30
am-2:30 pm, 5-10 pm; Fri, Sat to
10:30 pm; Sun 5-9 pm. Closed hols.
Res accepted; required Fri, Sat. Italian
menu. Bar. Wine list. A la carte
entrees: lunch $10.95-$13.95, dinner
$13.75-$18.75. Specialties: osso buco,
lamb shank, veal. Own baking, pasta.
Elegant, modern decor. Cr cds: A,
MC, V.

D

★ ★ **WHARF.** *119 King St (22314).*
703/836-2834. www.wharfrestaurant.
com. Hrs: 11 am-10:30 pm; Fri, Sat to
11 pm. Closed Jan 1, Thanksgiving,
Dec 25. Res accepted. Bar. Lunch:
$5.95-$9.95, dinner $14.95-$21.95.
Child's menu. Specializes in Maine
lobster, Chesapeake Bay seafood. Late
18th-century building. Cr cds: A, D,
DS, MC, V.

Unrated Dining Spot

HARD TIMES CAFE. *1404 King St
(22314).* *703/683-5340. www.hard*
times.com. Hrs: 11 am-10 pm; Fri, Sat
to 11 pm; Sun noon-10 pm. Closed
hols. A la carte entrees: lunch, dinner
$3.95-$5.75. Specializes in Texas,
Cincinnati and vegetarian-style chili.
Country, western music on juke box.
Housed in former church; rustic
decor; collection of state flags. Cr
cds: A, MC, V.

D

Appomattox Court House National Historical Park

See also Lynchburg

(3 mi NE of Appomattox on VA 24)

What to See and Do

⭐ **Appomattox Courthouse Building.**
Reconstructed building houses visitor
center, museum; audiovisual slide
program (every half hr, second floor).
Self-guided tour of village begins
here and incl

Clover Hill Tavern and outbuildings.
(1819) Oldest structure in village;
bookstore, restrms.

Confederate Cemetery.

County jail. (1870) Furnished.

McLean House and outbuildings.
Reconstruction of house where
Generals Lee and Grant met on
Apr 9, 1865. East from house, past
the courthouse and about 100

yards along Stage Rd past county jail, is

Meek's Store and Meek's Storehouse. With period furnishings.

Stacking of Arms. On the fourth anniversary of the firing on Fort Sumter, which triggered the outbreak of war, Confederate soldiers laid down their weapons here.

Woodson Law Office. With period furnishings.

Holliday Lake State Park. Approx 250 acres in Buckingham-Appomattox State Forest. Swimming beach, bathhouse, fishing, boating (launch, rentals) on 150-acre lake; hiking trails, picnicking, concession, tent and trailer sites. Visitor center, interpretive programs. Standard fees. Park (daily); most activities, incl camping (Memorial Day-Labor Day). 9 mi NE of Appomattox on VA 24, then 6 mi SE via VA 626, 692. Phone 434/248-6308.

Arlington County (Ronald Reagan Washington-National Airport Area)

(C-7) *See also Alexandria, Fairfax, Falls Church, McLean; also see District of Columbia*

Originally a part of the District of Columbia laid out for the capital in 1791, Arlington County, across the Potomac River from Washington, was returned to Virginia in 1846. The community is the urban center of northern Virginia.

Services and Information

Airlines. America West, American, American Eagle, Continental, Delta, Midwest Express, Northwest, TWA, United, USAir.

Transportation

Car Rental Agencies. See IMPORTANT TOLL-FREE NUMBERS.

Public Transportation. Subway trains and buses (Metro Transit System), phone 202/962-1234. Information 202/637-7000.

Rail Passenger Service. Amtrak 800/872-7245.

Airport Information

Ronald Reagan Washington-National Airport. Information 703/417-8000; lost and found 703/417-8560; weather 202/936-1212; cash machines at Main Terminal, main level near Travelers Aid.

What to See and Do

⭐ **Arlington National Cemetery.** The most famous of US national cemeteries was established in 1864. Here are interred more than 200,000 men and women who served their country; two presidents, William Howard Taft and John F. Kennedy; Senator Robert F. Kennedy; and Jacqueline Kennedy Onassis. Guided "tourmobiles" leave from visitor center (fare incl on/off privileges), Phone 703/979-0690. ¢¢¢ Here are

Arlington House, the Robert E. Lee Memorial. National memorial to Robert E. Lee. Built between 1802 and 1818 by George Washington Parke Custis, Martha Washington's grandson and foster son of George Washington. In 1831 his daughter, Mary Anna Randolph Custis, married Lieutenant Robert E. Lee; six of the seven Lee children were born here. As executor of the Custis estate, Lee took extended leave from the US Army and devoted his time to managing and improving the estate. It was the Lee homestead for 30 yrs before the Civil War. On Apr 20, 1861, following the secession of Virginia, Lee made his decision to stay with Virginia. Within a month the house was vacated. Some of the family possessions were moved for safekeeping, but most were stolen or destroyed when Union tropps occupied the house during the Civil War. In 1864, when Mrs. Lee could not appear personally to pay property tax, the estate was confiscated by the federal government; a 200-acre section was set aside for a national cemetery. (There is some evidence that indicates this was done to ensure the Lee family could never again live on the estate.) G. W. Custis Lee, the general's son, later regained title to the property through a Supreme Court decision and sold it to the US government in 1883 for $150,000. Restoration of the house to its 1861 appearance was begun in 1925. The Classic Revival house is furnished with authentic pieces of the period, incl some Lee family originals. From the grand portico with its six massive, faux-marble Doric columns there is a panoramic view of Washington, D.C. (Daily; closed Jan 1, Dec 25) Phone 703/557-0613.

Arlington National Cemetery

Memorial Amphitheatre. This impressive white marble edifice is used for ceremonies such as Memorial Day, Easter sunrise, and Veterans Day services.

Tomb of the Unknowns. On Nov 11, 1921, the remains of an unknown American soldier of WWI were entombed here. A memorial was erected in 1932 with the inscription "Here rests in honored glory an American soldier known but to God." On Memorial Day 1958, an unknown warrior who died in WWII and another who died in the Korean War were laid beside him. On Memorial Day 1984, an unknown soldier from the Vietnam War was interred here. Sentries stand guard 24 hrs a day; changing of the guard is every hr on the hr Oct-Mar, every 30 min Apr-Sept.

Fashion Centre at Pentagon City. Upscale, 160-store shopping mall with restaurants, movie theaters, and adjoining 360-rm hotel; features 115,000-square-ft glass ceiling in atrium. Off I-395 at jct S Hayes St and Army-Navy Dr, S of the Pentagon. Phone 703/415-2130.

Iwo Jima Statue. Marine Corps War Memorial depicts raising of the flag on Mt Suribachi, Iwo Jima, Feb 23, 1945; this is the largest sculpture ever cast in bronze. Sunset Parade concert with performances by US Marine Drum and Bugle Corps, US Marine Corps Color Guard, and the Silent Drill Team (late May-late Aug, Tues evenings). On Arlington Blvd, near Arlington National Cemetery.

⭐ **The Newseum.** This 72,000-square-ft interactive museum of news takes visitors behind the scenes to see and experience how and why news is made. Be a reporter or newscaster; relive great news stories through multimedia exhibits; see today's news as it happens on a blk-long video wall. (Wed-Sun; closed hols) 1101 Wilson Blvd. Phone 888/703-2843. **FREE** On grounds is

Freedom Park. Nearly 1,000 ft in length, park occupies never-used bridge. Features memorial to journalists killed in line of duty and various icons of freedom.

The Pentagon. With some six million square ft of floor area, this is one of the largest office buildings in the world; houses offices of the Department of Defense. Guided tour (1½ hr) with a walk of about 1½ mi incl movie, Hall of Heroes, Flag Corridor, *Time/Life* Art Collection (Mon-Fri; closed hols). Tour window located on concourse near the Metrorail subway or by entering at Corridor One, South Parking entrance. A valid picture ID must be presented at tour registration; visitors must stay on the tour once it begins. Cameras are allowed. Accommodations for the disabled avail with 48-hr advance notice. Bounded by Jefferson Davis Hwy, Washington Blvd, and I-395. Phone 703/695-1776. **FREE**

Special Events

Memorial Day Service. Arlington National Cemetery. Presidential wreath laying ceremony at Tomb of the Unknowns; music. Memorial Day.

Arlington County Fair. Countywide fair; arts, crafts, international foods, children's activities. Phone 703/228-6400. Aug. Phone 703/920-4556.

Army Ten-miler. America's largest ten-mi road race, attracting thousands of military and civilian runners. Phone 202/685-3361. Early Oct.

Motels/Motor Lodges

★★ **BEST WESTERN KEY BRIDGE.** 1850 Fort Myer Dr, Arlington (23692). 703/522-0400; fax 703/524-5275; res 800/539-2743. www.bestwestern.com. 178 rms, 11 story. S $129; D $139; suites $149-$169; under 12 free. Crib free. Pet accepted. TV; cable (premium). Pool. Restaurant 6:30 am-2 pm, 5-10 pm. Ck-out noon. Meeting rms. Business servs avail. Exercise equipt. Health club privileges. Some refrigerators; microwaves avail. Cr cds: A, C, D, DS, MC, V.
D ✦ ≈ ⏃ ⊠ SC

★ **COMFORT INN BALLSTON.** 1211 N Glebe Rd, Arlington (22201). 703/247-3399; fax 703/524-8739; toll-free 800/228-5150. www.comfortinn. com. 126 rms, 3 story. Mar-Oct: S, D $120; suites $135; under 18 free; wkend rates; lower rates rest of yr. Crib free. TV; cable (premium). Pool

privileges. Complimentary continental bkfst. Restaurant 6:30 am-10:30 pm. Bar 4-11 pm. Ck-out 11 am. Meeting rms. Business servs avail. In-rm modem link. Valet serv (Mon-Fri). Sundries. Gift shop. Garage parking. Refrigerators avail. Cr cds: A, C, D, DS, ER, JCB, MC, V.
≈ D ⊠ ▨ SC

★★ **COURTYARD BY MARRIOTT.** 2899 Jefferson Davis Hwy, Arlington (22202). 703/549-3434; fax 703/549-7440; toll-free 800/321-2211. www. courtyard.com. 272 rms, 14 story. S, D $154-$169; each addl $15; suites $200-$250; under 12 free. Crib free. Garage parking $9. TV; cable (premium), VCR avail. Indoor pool; whirlpool, lifeguard. Complimentary coffee in rms. Restaurant 6-10 am, 5 pm-midnight; wkends 7 am-noon, 5 pm-midnight. Rm serv 5-10 pm. Bar 4 pm-midnight. Ck-out 1 pm. Coin lndry. Meeting rms. Business servs avail. In-rm modem link. Valet serv. Sundries. Free airport transportation. Exercise equipt. Health club privileges. Some refrigerators, wet bars; microwaves avail. Cr cds: A, C, D, DS, ER, JCB, MC, V.
D ≈ ⏃ ✈ ⊠ ▨ SC

★★ **COURTYARD BY MARRIOTT.** 1533 Clarendon Blvd, Arlington (22209). 703/528-2222; fax 703/528-1027; toll-free 800/321-2211. www. marriott.com. 162 rms, 10 story, 18 suites. Apr-June, Aug-Oct: S $154; D $164; each addl $10; suites $174-$184; under 12 free; wkend rates; lower rates rest of yr. Crib free. Garage parking $6.50 Sun-Thurs; Fri, Sat free. TV; cable (premium). Indoor pool; whirlpool, lifeguard. Complimentary coffee in rms. Restaurant 6:30-10 am, 5-11 pm. Rm serv from 5 pm. Bar from 5 pm. Ck-out noon. Business servs avail. Valet serv. Sundries. Coin lndry. Exercise equipt. Health club privileges. Some refrigerators; microwaves avail. Many balconies. Cr cds: A, C, D, DS, MC, V.
D ≈ ⏃ ⊠ ▨ SC

★ **DAYS INN.** 2000 Jefferson Davis Hwy, Arlington (22202). 703/920-8600; fax 703/920-2840; toll-free 800/329-7466. www.daysinn.com. 247 rms, 8 story. Mar-June, Sept-Nov: S $127-$160; D $137-$170; each addl $10; under 16 free; wkend, hol rates; lower rates rest of yr. Crib free. TV; cable (premium). Pool; lifeguard. Complimentary coffee in rms. Restaurant 6 am-2 pm, 5-10 pm; wkends 7 am-noon, 5-10 pm. Bar 4:30-10 pm. Ck-out 11 am. Meeting rms. Business servs avail. In-rm modem link. Bellhops. Gift shop. Valet serv. Garage parking. Free airport transportation. Exercise equipt. Cr cds: A, C, D, DS, JCB, MC, V.

D ➤ 🛬 🛪 🛬 🔥 SC

★ ★ ★ **EXECUTIVE CLUB SUITES.** *108 S Courthouse, Arlington (22204). 703/522-2582; fax 703/486-2694; res 800/535-2582.* 74 kit. suites, 2-3 story. Mar-Sept: kit. suites: $159-$179; wkend, wkly, hol rates; higher rates Cherry Blossom Festival; lower rates rest of yr. Crib free. Pet accepted, some restrictions; $250 deposit ($25 nonrefundable). TV; cable (premium), VCR avail. Pool; whirlpool, lifeguard. Complimentary continental bkfst, coffee in rms. Ck-out noon. Meeting rms. Business servs avail. Valet serv. Sundries. Coin lndry. Free airport transportation. Exercise equipt; sauna. Refrigerators, microwaves. Picnic tables, grills. Cr cds: A, D, DS, MC, V.

🐾 ➤ 🛬 🛬 🔥

★ ★ **HOLIDAY INN.** *2650 Jefferson Davis Hwy, Arlington (22202). 703/684-7200; fax 703/684-3217; res 800/465-4329. www.holiday-inn.com.* 279 rms, 11 story. Apr-July, Sept-Oct: S $89-$159; D $89-$169; under 10 free; suites $210-$230; under 18 free; wkend rates; lower rates rest of yr. Crib free. Garage, in/out parking $9. TV; cable. Complimentary coffee in rms. Restaurant 6 am-11 pm. Bar 4-11 pm. Ck-out noon. Meeting rms. Business center. In-rm modem link. Gift shop. Coin lndry. Free airport, RR station transportation. Exercise equipt. Health club privileges. Pool; lifeguard. Balconies. Cr cds: A, C, D, DS, ER, MC, V.

D ➤ 🛬 🛬 🔥 🏃

★ **QUALITY HOTEL.** *1200 N Court House Rd, Arlington (22201). 703/524-4000; fax 703/522-6814; res 888/987-2555. www.qualityhotelarlington.com.* 392 rms, 1-10 story. S $69.95-$125.95; D $75.95-$135.95; each addl $10; suites $109.95-$169.95; under 18 free; package plans. Crib free. Pet accepted, some restrictions. TV; cable

(premium). Pool; lifeguard. Coffee in rms. Restaurant 6:30 am-2 pm, 5-9:30 pm. Bar 4-10 pm. Ck-out noon. Coin lndry. Convention facilities. Business servs avail. In-rm modem link. Concierge. Gift shop. Exercise equipt; sauna. Microwaves avail. Balconies. Luxury level. Cr cds: A, C, D, DS, ER, JCB, MC, V.

D 🐾 ➤ 🛬 🛬 🔥 SC

★ **QUALITY INN IWO JIMA.** *1501 Arlington Blvd, Arlington (22209). 703/524-5000; fax 703/522-5484; res 800/424-1501. www.qualityinn.com.* 141 rms, 1-3 story. Mar-Nov: S, D $95-$105; each addl $10; wkend, family rates; higher rates special events; lower rates rest of yr. Crib free. TV; cable (premium), VCR avail. Indoor pool; poolside serv, lifeguard. Restaurant (in season) 6:30 am-10 pm; Sat, Sun from 7 am. Bar. Ck-out noon. Coin lndry. Meeting rms. Business servs avail. In-rm modem link. Bellhops. Sundries. Exercise equipt. Health club privileges. Refrigerators, microwaves avail. Some balconies. Cr cds: A, C, D, DS, ER, JCB, MC, V.

D ➤ 🛬 🛬 🔥 SC

Hotels

★ ★ **CROWNE PLAZA WASHING-TON-NATIONAL AIRPORT.** *1489 Jefferson Davis Hwy, Arlington (22202). 703/416-1600; fax 703/416-1615. www.basshotels.com/crowneplaza.* 308 rms, 11 story. S, D $189; each addl $10; suites $199-$209; under 18 free; wkend, hol rates. Crib free. Pet accepted, some restrictions; $25 deposit. Garage $8/day. TV; cable (premium). Pool; lifeguard. Coffee in rms. Restaurant 6 am-10 pm; Sat, Sun from 7 am. Bar 11 am-midnight. Ck-out noon. Meeting rms. Business center. In-rm modem link. Gift shop. Free airport transportation. Exercise equipt. Refrigerators avail. Cr cds: A, C, D, DS, JCB, MC, V.

D 🐾 ➤ 🛬 🛪 🛬 🔥 SC 🏃

★ ★ **DOUBLETREE HOTEL.** *300 Army Navy Dr, Arlington (22202). 703/416-4100; fax 703/416-4126; toll-free 800/222-8733. www.doubletree. com.* 632 rms, 15 story, 265 suites. S, D $190; suites $200-$375; under 18 free; wkend rates. Crib free. Pet accepted, some restrictions. Garage $10; valet $12. TV; cable (premium).

Indoor pool; lifeguard. Coffee in rms. Restaurant 6:30 am-11 pm. Bar 11-2 am; entertainment. Ck-out noon. Convention facilities. Business center. In-rm modem link. Concierge. Gift shop. Free airport transportation. Exercise rm; sauna. Health club privileges. Bathrm phones; some refrigerators; microwaves avail. Some balconies. Luxury level. Cr cds: A, C, D, DS, ER, JCB, MC, V.

$\boxed{D}$ 🐾 ⇌ ✕ 🔁 🔥 **SC** 🏃

★ ★ ★ **HILTON AND TOWERS.** 950 N Stafford St, Arlington (22203). 703/528-6000; fax 703/812-5127; toll-free 800/468-3571. www.hilton.com. 209 rms, 7 story. S $180-$200; D $200-$220; suites $240; under 18 free; wkend rates. Crib free. TV; cable (premium). Indoor pool; whirlpool; lifeguard. Restaurant 6:30 am-10 pm. Bar 4 pm-midnight. Ck-out 1 pm. Meeting rms. Business servs avail. In-rm modem link. Concierge. Gift shop. Health club privileges. Metro stop in building. Luxury level. Cr cds: A, C, D, DS, ER, JCB, MC, V.

$\boxed{D}$ ⇌ 🔁 🔥 **SC**

★ ★ ★ **HYATT.** 1325 Wilson Blvd, Arlington (22209). 703/525-1234; fax 703/875-3393; toll-free 800/233-1234. www.hyatt.com. 302 rms, 16 story. S $195; D $225; each addl $25; suites $275-$575; under 12 free; wkend rates. Crib free. Pet accepted, some restrictions. Garage $10/day (Sun-Thurs). TV; cable (premium), VCR avail. Restaurant 6:30 am-midnight. Bars 11:30 am-midnight. Ck-out noon. Free guest lndry. Meeting rms. Business center. In-rm modem link. Gift shop. Exercise equipt. Health club privileges. Metro adj. Cr cds: A, C, D, DS, ER, JCB, MC, V.

$\boxed{D}$ 🐾 ✕ 🔁 🔥 **SC** 🏃

★ ★ ★ **HYATT REGENCY.** 2799 Jefferson Davis Hwy, Arlington (22202). 703/418-1234; fax 703/418-1289; toll-free 800/233-1234. www.hyatt.com. 685 rms, 20 story. S $189; D $214; each addl $25; suites $350-$725; under 18 free; wkend rates. Crib free. Garage; valet $10/day. TV; cable (premium), VCR avail. Pool; whirlpool, poolside serv, lifeguard. Complimentary coffee in rms. Restaurant 6-2 am. Bar 3 pm-1 am. Ck-out noon. Convention facilities. Business center. In-rm modem link. Concierge.

Gift shop. Free airport transportation. Exercise equipt; saunas. Health club privileges. Some refrigerators, wet bars; microwaves avail. Some balconies. Cr cds: A, C, D, DS, ER, JCB, MC, V.

$\boxed{D}$ ⇌ ✕ ✕ 🔁 🔥 **SC** 🏃

★ ★ ★ **MARRIOTT CRYSTAL CITY.** 1999 Jefferson Davis Hwy, Arlington (22202). 703/413-5500; fax 703/413-0192; res 800/331-3131. www.marriott.com. 345 rms, 12 story. S $189; D $209; suites $250-$400; under 18 free; wkend rates. Crib free. Valet parking $15/day. TV; cable (premium), VCR avail. Indoor pool; whirlpool, lifeguard. Complimentary coffee in rms. Restaurant 6:30 am-10:30 pm; Sat, Sun from 7 am. Bar 11:30 am-midnight. Ck-out 1 pm. Coin lndry. Convention facilities. Business center. In-rm modem link. Concierge. Gift shop. Free airport transportation. Exercise equipt; sauna. Health club privileges. Luxury level. Cr cds: A, C, D, DS, JCB, MC, V.

$\boxed{D}$ ⇌ ✕ ✕ 🔁 🔥 🏃

★ ★ ★ **MARRIOTT CRYSTAL GATEWAY.** 1700 Jefferson Davis Hwy, Arlington (22202). 703/920-3230; fax 703/271-5212; toll-free 800/228-9290. www.marriott.com. 700 units, 16 story. S, D $192-$220; suites $199-$700; under 18 free; wkend rates. Crib free. Pet accepted, some restrictions. Garage $12. TV; cable (premium). Indoor/outdoor pool; whirlpool, lifeguard. Restaurant 6:30-2 am. Bar 11-2 am. Ck-out 1 pm. Convention facilities. Business center. In-rm modem link. Concierge. Free airport transportation. Tennis privileges. Exercise equipt; sauna. Health club privileges. Original artwork. Luxury level. Cr cds: A, C, D, DS, ER, JCB, MC, V.

$\boxed{D}$ 🐾 🤸 ⇌ ✕ ✕ 🔁 🔥 **SC** 🏃

★ ★ ★ **MARRIOTT KEY BRIDGE.** 1401 Lee Hwy, Arlington (22209). 703/524-6400; fax 703/524-8964; res 800/228-9290. www.marriott.com. 584 rms, 2-14 story. S, D $199-$209; suites $225-$500; wkend rates. Crib free. Garage $8/day. TV; cable (premium), VCR avail. Indoor/outdoor pool; whirlpool, poolside serv, lifeguard. Coffee in rms. Restaurant (see also J.W.'S STEAKHOUSE). Bar noon-2 am; entertainment Thurs-Sat. Ck-out 1 pm. Convention facilities. Business center. In-rm modem link. Concierge. Gift shop. Barber, beauty shop. Exercise equipt; sauna. Health club privileges. Refrigerators, microwaves avail. Some balconies. Overlooks Washington across Potomac River. Luxury level. Cr cds: A, D, DS, MC, V.

D ⌖ 🛉 ⌖ 🐾 🏃

★ ★ ★ ★ **THE RITZ-CARLTON, PENTAGON CITY.** *1250 S Hayes St, Arlington (22202). 703/415-5000; fax 703/415-5061; res 800/241-3333. www.ritzcarlton.com.* The Persian carpets, fine art, and 18th-century antiques of this quiet hotel contrast with its surroundings. Guest rooms are lavishly appointed with silk drapes and Federal-style furnishings and have panoramic views of the nation's capital and the Potomac River. 366 rms, 18 story. S, D $279; each addl $20; suites $379-$2,200; under 18 free; wkend rates. Crib free. Valet parking $24. TV; cable (premium), VCR avail (movies). Indoor pool; whirlpool; lifeguard. Afternoon tea 3-5 pm. Restaurant. Bar; entertainment. Ck-out noon. Convention facilities. Business center. In-rm modem link. Concierge serv. Shopping arcade. Tennis privileges. Golf privileges. Exercise rm; sauna, steam rm. Massage. Bathrm phones, minibars; microwaves avail. Luxury level. Cr cds: A, C, D, DS, JCB, MC, V.

D 🛉 ⌖ ⌖ 🛉 ⌖ 🐾 🏃

★ ★ ★ **SHERATON CRYSTAL CITY HOTEL.** *1800 Jefferson Davis Hwy, Arlington (22202). 703/486-1111; fax 703/769-3970; res 800/862-7666. www.sheraton.com.* 197 rms, 15 story. S $145-$195; D $145-$200; each addl $20; under 18 free; wkend rates. Crib free. TV; cable (premium). Pool; lifeguard. Coffee in rms. Restaurant 6:30 am-10 pm; Sat, Sun from 7 am. Bar 11 am-midnight; entertainment, pianist. Ck-out 1 pm. Meeting rms. Business center. In-rm modem link. Gift shop. Free airport transportation. Exercise equipt; sauna. Refrigerators; some bathrm phones. Luxury level. Cr cds: A, C, D, DS, MC, V.

D ⌖ 🛉 ⌖ 🐾 SC 🏃

All Suite

★ ★ **EMBASSY SUITES.** *1300 Jefferson Davis Hwy, Arlington (22202).*

703/979-9799; fax 703/920-5947; res 800/362-2779. www.embassysuites. com. 267 suites, 11 story. Feb-June, Sept-Nov: S $179-$209; D $189-$219; each addl $10; under 12 free; wkend rates; lower rates rest of yr. Crib free. Parking $10. TV; cable (premium). Heated pool; lifeguard. Complimentary full bkfst, coffee in rms. Restaurant 11 am-2 pm, 5-10 pm. Rm serv to midnight. Bar to midnight. Ck-out noon. Meeting rms. Business servs avail. In-rm modem link. Gift shop. Free airport transportation. Exercise equipt. Health club privileges. Refrigerators. Atrium lobby. Cr cds: A, C, D, DS, ER, JCB, MC, V.

D 🛉 ⌖ 🛉 ⌖ 🐾 🐾

Extended Stay

★ ★ **RESIDENCE INN BY MARRIOTT.** *550 Army Navy Dr, Arlington (22202). 703/413-6630; fax 703/418-1751; res 800/214-6847. www.residenceinn.com.* 299 kit. suites, 17 story. Kit. suites $170-$235; wkend, wkly rates. Crib free. Garage parking $10/day. TV; cable (premium). Indoor pool; whirlpool; lifeguard. Complimentary continental bkfst, coffee in rms. Restaurant nearby. No rm serv. Ck-out noon. Meeting rms. Business servs avail. No bellhops. Concierge. Coin lndry. Free airport transportation. Exercise equipt. Health club privileges. Refrigerators, microwaves. Picnic tables. Cr cds: A, C, D, DS, JCB, MC, V.

D ⌖ 🛉 ⌖ 🐾

Restaurants

★ ★ **ALPINE.** *4770 Lee Hwy, Arlington (22207). 703/528-7600.* Hrs: 11:30 am-11 pm; Sun noon-10 pm. Closed hols. Res accepted. Italian, continental menu. Bar. Lunch $7.45-$10.75, dinner $10.95-$17.95. Specializes in veal, pasta dishes, seafood. Own pasta. Parking. Family-owned. Cr cds: A, D, MC, V.

D ⌖

★ ★ **BISTRO BISTRO.** *4021 S 28th St, Arlington (22206). 703/379-0300. www.bistro-bistro.com.* Hrs: 11 am-10 pm; Fri, Sat to 11 pm; early-bird dinner Mon-Thurs 5-6:30 pm; Sun brunch 10:30 am-3 pm. Closed Thanksgiving, Dec 24, 25. Res accepted. Bar to 1:30 am. A la carte entrees: lunch $5.75-$10.95, dinner $9.95-$16.95. Sun brunch $6-$12. Specializes in pasta, seafood. Outdoor dining. Bistro atmosphere, eclectic decor. Cr cds: A, D, DS, MC, V.

[D] [=]

★ **CAFE DALAT.** *3143 Wilson Blvd, Arlington (22201).* 703/276-0935. Hrs: 11 am-9:30 pm; Fri, Sat to 10:30 pm. Closed July 4, Thanksgiving, Dec 25; also Chinese New Year. Vietnamese menu. Serv bar. Lunch $4.25, dinner $7.50-$8.95. Buffet: lunch $4.95. Specialties: sugarcane shrimp, grilled lemon chicken. Own desserts. Totally nonsmoking. Cr cds: MC, V.

★★ **CARLYLE GRAND CAFE.** *4000 S 28th St, Arlington (22206).* 703/931-0777. www.carlylegrand-gar.com. Hrs: 11:30 am-11 pm; Fri, Sat to midnight; Sun brunch 10:30 am-2 pm. Closed Thanksgiving, Dec 25. Bar. Lunch $5.95-$11.75, dinner $8.95-$18.95. Sun brunch $4.95-$11.95. Specialties: lobster pot stickers, baby-back ribs, smoked salmon filet. Outdoor dining. Totally nonsmoking. Cr cds: A, MC, V.

★ **COWBOY CAFE.** *4792 Lee Hwy, Arlington (22207).* 703/243-8010. www.washingtonpost.com/cowboycafe. Hrs: 11 am-11 pm; Fri to midnight; Sat 9 am-midnight; Sun 9 am-9 pm. Bar to midnight; Fri, Sat to 1 am; Sun 11 am-9 pm. Bkfst $2.99-$6.50, lunch, dinner $2.75-$8.25. Specializes in hamburgers, bkfst dishes. Musicians Thurs-Sat. Casual, Western decor. Cr cds: A, D, DS, MC, V.

[D] [=]

★ **FACCIA LUNA.** *2909 Wilson Blvd, Arlington (22201).* 703/276-3099. www.faccialuna.com. Hrs: 11 am-11 pm; Fri, Sat to midnight; Sun noon-11 pm. Closed Thanksgiving, Dec 24, 25. Italian menu. Bar. Lunch $4.95-$5.95, dinner $7.75-$14.95. Child's menu. Specializes in pasta, pizza. Outdoor dining. Upscale trattoria. Cr cds: A, MC, V.

[D] [=]

★★ **J.W.'S STEAKHOUSE.** *1401 Lee Hwy, Arlington (22209).* 703/524-6400. Hrs: 5-10 pm; Fri to 11 pm; Sat 6-11 pm; Sun 5:30-9:30 pm; Sun brunch 10 am-2:30 pm. Closed Jan 1. Res accepted; required July 4. Bar. Wine list. A la carte entrees: dinner

$18.95-$28.95. Sun brunch $25.95-$27.95. Specializes in seafood, steak, certified Angus beef. Parking. View of Washington across Potomac. Cr cds: A, D, DS, MC, V.

[D]

★★ **KABUL CARAVAN.** *1725 Wilson Blvd, Arlington (22209).* 703/522-8394. Hrs: 11:30 am-2:30 pm, 5:30-11 pm; Sat, Sun from 5:30 pm. Closed Thanksgiving, Dec 25. Res accepted. Afghan menu. Serv bar. Prix fixe dinners for 2-4: $55.95-$115.95. Lunch $7.95-$11.95, dinner $10.95-$16.95. Specialties: sauteed pumpkin with yogurt and meat sauce, orange pallow, eggplant and shish kabob. Outdoor dining. Walls covered with Afghan clothing, pictures, rugs, artifacts, jewelry. Cr cds: A, MC, V.

[D] [=]

★★ **LA COTE D'OR CAFE.** *6876 Lee Hwy, Arlington (22213).* 703/538-3033. Hrs: 11:30 am-3 pm, 5:30-11 pm; Sun brunch 11 am-3 pm. Closed Jan 1, Dec 25. Res accepted. French menu. Bar. Lunch $5.95-$12.95, dinner $18.75-$22.95. Sun brunch $7.95-$11.50. Specializes in seafood, veal. Outdoor dining. French decor. Cr cds: A, D, MC, V.

[D] [=]

★★ **LITTLE VIET GARDEN.** *3012 Wilson Blvd, Arlington (22201).* 703/522-9686. Hrs: 11 am-2:30 pm, 5-10 pm; Sat, Sun 11 am-10 pm. Closed Thanksgiving, Dec 25. Vietnamese menu. Bar. Lunch $4.95-$6.95, dinner $6.95-$11.95. Specialties: Viet Garden steak, grilled jumbo shrimp. Parking. Outdoor dining. Cr cds: A, MC, V.

[D]

★ **MATUBA.** *2915 Columbia Pike, Arlington (22204).* 703/521-2811. Hrs: 11:30 am-2 pm, 5:30-10 pm; Fri, Sat 5:30-10:30 pm; Sun 5:30-10 pm. Res accepted. Japanese menu. Lunch $4.95-$8.50, dinner $7-$12.50. Specializes in seafood, poultry. Japanese decor. Cr cds: A, MC, V.

[D]

★★ **QUEEN BEE.** *3181 Wilson Blvd, Arlington (22201).* 703/527-3444. Hrs: 11 am-10 pm. Vietnamese menu. Serv bar. Lunch $3.95-$7.50, dinner

$6.50-$9.95. Specialties: spring roll, Hanoi beef noodle soup, Hanoi-style grilled pork. Totally nonsmoking. Cr cds: A, C, D, MC, V.

D

★ **RED HOT AND BLUE.** *1600 Wilson Blvd, Arlington (22209). 703/276-8833. www.redhotandblue.com.* Hrs: 11 am-10 pm; Fri, Sat to 11 pm. Closed Thanksgiving, Dec 25. Bar. Lunch, dinner $4.69-$11.99. Specializes in Memphis pit barbecue dishes. Memphis blues memorabilia. Cr cds: A, D, DS, MC, V.

D

★ ★ ★ **RITZ-CARLTON, THE GRILL.** *1250 S Hayes St, Arlington County (22202). 703/412-2760. www. ritzcarlton.com.* Hrs: 6:30 am-10:30 pm; Fri, Sat to 11 pm; Sun brunch 11 am-2:30 pm. Res accepted. Bar. Wine list. Bkfst $5-$15, lunch $10-$25, dinner $22-$32. Buffet: bkfst $12-$17. Sun brunch $45. Tea 3-5 pm; $14-$26. Child's menu. Specializes in seasonal, Mid-Atlantic cuisine including macrobiotic daily specials and cuisine vitale. Pianist Fri, Sat eves. Valet parking. English club-like decor and atmosphere. Fireplace. Cr cds: A, D, DS, MC, V.

D

★ ★ **R.T.'S SEAFOOD KITCHEN.** *2300 Clarendon Blvd, Arlington (22201). 703/841-0100.* Hrs: 11 am-10:30 pm; Fri, Sat to 11 pm; Sun 4-9:30 pm. Closed Jan 1, July 4, Thanksgiving, Dec 25. Cajun menu. Bar to midnight. Lunch $7.95-$10.95, dinner $11.95-$17.95. Child's menu. Specializes in Cajun-style seafood. Outdoor dining. Contemporary decor. Cr cds: A, D, DS, MC, V.

D

★ **SILVER DINER.** *3200 Wilson Blvd, Arlington (22201). 703/812-8667.* Hrs: 7 am-midnight; Thurs to 1 am; Fri, Sat to 3 am; Sat, Sun brunch 7 am-2 pm. Closed Dec 25. Wine, beer. Bkfst $2.99-$7.99, lunch $4.99-$7.99, dinner $4.99-$11.99. Sat, Sun brunch $5.99-$7.99. Child's menu. Specializes in classic diner food. Own desserts. Reminiscent of 1950s-style diner. Cr cds: A, D, DS, MC, V.

D SC

★ ★ **TIVOLI.** *1700 N Moore St, Arlington (22209). 703/524-8900. www.erols. com/tivolirestaurant.* Hrs: 11:30 am-2:30 pm, 5:30-10 pm; Sat from 5:30 pm; early-bird dinner Mon-Sat 5:30-6:30 pm. Closed Sun; hols. Res accepted; required Fri, Sat. Italian menu. Bar 11:30 am-midnight. Lunch $8.50-$11.50; dinner $12.50-$23.50. Specializes in pasta, seafood, veal. Contemporary decor. Cr cds: A, D, DS, MC, V.

D

★ ★ **TOM SARRIS' ORLEANS HOUSE.** *1213 Wilson Blvd, Arlington (22209). 703/524-2929.* Hrs: 11 am-11 pm; Sat from 4 pm; Sun 4-10 pm. Res accepted. Bar. Lunch $4.25-$7.95, dinner $8.95-$14.95. Child's menu. Specializes in prime rib, NY steak, seafood. Salad bar. Parking. New Orleans atmosphere; fountains, iron railings, Tiffany lampshades. Family-owned. Cr cds: A, D, DS, MC, V.

D

★ **VILLAGE BISTRO.** *1723 Wilson Blvd, Arlington (22209). 703/522-0284.* Hrs: 11:30 am-2:30 pm, 5-10:30 pm; Fri, Sat to 11 pm; Sun 5-10 pm; early-bird dinner 5-7 pm. Closed Thanksgiving, Dec 25. Res accepted; required Fri, Sat. Continental menu. Bar. Lunch $5.50-$12.95, dinner $7.95-$18.95. Specializes in seafood, pasta. Parking. Outdoor dining. Monet prints on walls. Cr cds: A, DS, MC, V.

D

★ ★ **WOO LAE OAK.** *1500 S Joyce St, Arlington (22202). 703/521-3706. www.woolaeoak.com.* Hrs: 11:30 am-10:30 pm. Closed Jan 1. Res accepted. Korean menu. Lunch, dinner $8-$20. Specializes in barbecued dishes prepared tableside. Parking. Large, open dining rm; Korean decor. Cr cds: A, MC, V.

D

Ashland

(D-6) *See also Richmond*

Founded 1858 **Pop** 6,619 **Elev** 221 ft
Area code 804 **Zip** 23005

Information Ashland/Hanover Visitor Information Center, 112 N Railroad Ave; 804/752-6766 or 800/897-1479

Web www.vatc.org

Ashland was founded when the president of the Richmond, Fredericksburg, and Potomac Railroad bought land here. He dug a well, struck mineral water, and started a health resort—Slash Cottage (wilderness acres were called "slashes"). A thriving village grew up and took the name of Henry Clay's Kentucky estate. In 1866 the railroad company gave land to the Methodist Church and induced the church to move Randolph-Macon College here. A section of early 1900s houses along the railroad tracks has been set aside as a historic district.

What to See and Do

Paramount's Kings Dominion. A 400-acre family theme park consisting of six theme areas, incl Water Werks; Action Epic Theatre; the Anaconda, a looping roller coaster that passes through an underwater tunnel; also Shockwave stand-up roller coaster; The Outer Limits roller coaster; 33-story likeness of the Eiffel Tower with panoramic view; whitewater raft ride; live entertainment; shops. (June-Labor Day, daily; late Mar-May, after Labor Day-early Oct, wkends only) 1 mi E on VA 54, then 7 mi N on I-95 in Doswell. Phone 804/876-5000. ¢¢¢¢

Patrick Henry Home "Scotchtown". (1719) Also girlhood home of Dolley Madison; fine Colonial architecture. (May-Oct, Wed-Sat; Apr, wkends; also by appt) 11 mi NW via VA 54, 671, County 685 (Scotchtown Rd), left onto Chiswell Ln. Phone 804/227-3500. ¢¢

Randolph-Macon College. (1830) 1,100 students. Coeducational, liberal arts, Methodist-affiliated college. Historic buildings incl Washington-Franklin Hall, Old Chapel, and Pace Hall. 1 mi W of I-95. Phone 804/752-7305. **FREE**

Motels/Motor Lodges

★★ **BEST WESTERN.** *10296 Sliding Hill Rd (23005). 804/550-2805; fax 804/550-3843; toll-free 800/528-1234.*

www.bestwestern.com. 93 rms, 2 story. Apr-mid-Oct: S $38-$68; D $51-$68; each addl $5; under 12 free; higher rates special events; lower rates rest of yr. Crib free. TV; cable. Pool. Restaurant 6:30 am-9 pm. Ck-out noon. Coin lndry. Meeting rms. Business servs avail. Exercise equipt. Some balconies. Cr cds: A, C, D, DS, MC, V.

⊠ ✗ ⊠ 🔥 SC

★ **COMFORT INN.** *101 N Cottage Green Dr (23005). 804/752-7777; fax 804/798-0327; res 800/228-5150. www.comfortinn.com.* 126 rms, 2 story. Memorial Day-Labor Day: S, D $59-$89; each addl $5; suites $120; under 18 free; lower rates rest of yr. Crib free. TV; cable. Pool. Complimentary continental bkfst. Restaurant adj open 24 hrs. Ck-out noon. Coin lndry. Business servs avail. Exercise equipt; sauna. Some refrigerators. Cr cds: A, C, D, DS, ER, JCB, MC, V.

D ⊠ ✗ ⊠ 🔥

★★ **QUALITY INN.** *810 England St (23005). 804/798-4231; fax 804/798-9074. www.qualityinn.com.* 56 rms, 2 story. S, D $45-$98; under 18 free; higher rates some wkends. Crib free. TV; cable (premium). Pool; wading pool. Restaurant 6 am-10 pm. Bar. Ck-out 11 am. Coin lndry. Meeting rms. Business servs avail. Valet serv. Exercise equipt. Private patios, balconies. Cr cds: A, C, D, DS, ER, JCB, MC, V.

D ⊠ ✗ ⊠ 🔥 SC

B&B/Small Inn

★★★ **HENRY CLAY INN.** *114 N Railroad Ave (23005). 804/798-3100; fax 804/752-7555; toll-free 800/343-4565. www.henryclayinn.com.* 15 rms, 3 story, 1 suite. S, D $90-$115; each addl $15; suite $145; higher rates special events. Crib $15. TV; cable. Complimentary continental bkfst. Dining rm 7-9 am; wkends also 11 am-2:30 pm, 6-9 pm. Ck-out 11 am, ck-in 2 pm. Business servs avail. In-rm modem link. Gift shop. Balconies. Authentic reproduction of Georgian Revival inn. Totally non-smoking. Cr cds: A, MC, V.

D ⊠ 🔥 SC

Restaurants

★ ★ **IRONHORSE.** *100 S Railroad Ave (23005). 804/752-6410.* Hrs: 11:30 am-2:30 pm, 5:30-9 pm; Mon to 2:30 pm; Fri, Sat to 10 pm. Closed Sun; hols; also wk after Jan 1 and wk after July 4. Res accepted. Bar to midnight. Entertainment. Lunch $4.95-$8.95, dinner $13.95-$18.95. Specializes in Angus beef, barbecue shrimp, crab cakes. Railroad memorabilia. Cr cds: DS, MC, V.

D ⊒

★ **SMOKEY PIG.** *212 S Washington Hwy (23005). 804/798-4590.* Hrs: 11 am-9 pm; Sun from noon. Closed Mon; hols. Bar. Lunch $3.45-$13.99, dinner $3.88-$16.95. Child's menu. Specializes in pit-cooked meats, seafood, ribs. Cr cds: A, MC, V.

D ⊒

Basye

See also Luray, New Market, Woodstock

Pop 200 **Elev** 1,354 ft **Area code** 540
Zip 22810
Information Bryce Resort, PO Box 3; 540/856-2121
Web www.bryceresort.com

What to See and Do

Bryce Resort. On VA 263.

Summer. Fishing, swimming, boating; horseback riding, golf, tennis, hiking, grass skiing. Fee for activities. Phone 540/856-2121.

Winter. Skiing. Two double chairlifts, three surface lifts; patrol, school, rentals; snowmaking; ski shop; restaurant, cafeteria, bar. Longest run 2,750 ft; vertical drop 500 ft. Night skiing. (Mid-Dec-mid-Mar, daily) Phone 540/856-2121.
¢¢¢¢

Motel/Motor Lodge

★ ★ **BEST WESTERN.** *250 Con-ickville Blvd, Mount Jackson (22842). 540/477-2911; fax 540/477-2392; toll-free 800/528-1234. www.bestwestern. com.* 98 rms, 2 story. June-Oct: S $60; D $70; each addl $4; lower rates rest of yr. Crib free. Pet accepted. TV; cable. Pool; wading pool. Play-

ground. Restaurant 6 am-midnight. Bar 5-10 pm. Ck-out 11 am. Meeting rms. Business servs avail. Sundries. Gift shop. Tennis. Game rm. Cr cds: A, C, D, DS, MC, V.

D ⊸ ⟆ ⇞ ⇞ ⟆ SC

B&B/Small Inn

★ ★ ★ **WIDOW KIP'S COUNTRY INN.** *355 Orchard Dr, Mt Jackson (22842). 540/477-2400; toll-free 800/478-8714. www.widowkips.com.* 5 rms, showers only; 2 cottages. No rm phones. S $55-$75; D $65-$85; each addl $15, lower rates mid-wk. Pet accepted in cottages. TV in sitting rm, cottages; cable (premium). Pool. Complimentary full bkfst. Picnic lunches avail. Ck-out 11 am, ck-in 3 pm. Some fireplaces. Bicycles. Grill. Federal-style saltbox house (1830) on 7 acres. Victorian furnishings, handmade quilts. Totally nonsmoking. Cr cds: MC, V.

⇞ ⟆ ⇞ ⇞ ⟆ SC

Big Stone Gap

See also Breaks Interstate Park, Wise

Founded 1888 **Pop** 4,856 **Elev** 1,488 ft **Area code** 540 **Zip** 24219
Information Lonesome Pine Tourist Information Center, 619 Gilley Ave, PO Box 236; 540/523-2060

This rugged mountain country gave John Fox, Jr. his inspiration for *Trail of the Lonesome Pine* and *Little Shepherd of Kingdom Come.* The town lies at the junction of three forks of the Powell River, which cuts a pass through Stone Mountain.

What to See and Do

John Fox, Jr., House & Museum. Occupied from 1888 by the author of *Trail of the Lonesome Pine* and *Little Shepherd of Kingdom Come,* best-selling novels of the early 1900s. Memorabilia and original furnishings. Guided tours (June-Sept, Tues-Sun; Oct, wkends). 117 Shawnee Ave. Phone 276/523-2747.

June Tolliver House. Heroine in *Trail of the Lonesome Pine* lived here; period furnishings; now an arts and crafts center; restored 1890 house. (June-late Dec, Tues-Sun) Jerome St and Clinton Ave, jct US 23, 58A. Phone 276/523-1235. **FREE**

Natural Tunnel State Park. Consists of 648 acres. Giant hole chiseled through Purchase Ridge by Stock Creek; pinnacles or "chimneys." Railroad and stream are accommodated in this vast tunnel—100 ft or more in diameter, 850 ft long. Tunnel, visitor center with exhibits. Swimming, pool, fishing; hiking, picnicking, concession, camping, tent and trailer sites (Memorial Day-Labor Day). Interpretive programs. Chairlift. Park (daily); tunnel and most activities (Memorial Day-Labor Day; daily). Standard fees. 18 mi SE, off US 23. Phone 276/940-2674.

Southwest Virginia Museum. Four-story mansion contains exhibits dealing with life in southwestern Virginia during original coal boom of the 1890s; also Native Americans of the area and early pioneers. (Memorial Day-Labor Day, daily; Mar-late May and early Sept-Dec, Tues-Sun; closed Thanksgiving, Dec 25) W 1st St and Wood Ave. Phone 540/523-1322. ¢¢

Special Event

Trail of the Lonesome Pine. June Tolliver Playhouse, adj to June Tolliver House. Outdoor musical drama. For reserved seats phone 540/523-1235. Thurs-Sat, late June-Labor Day.

Blacksburg

E-4) *See also Radford, Roanoke, Salem*

Founded 1798 **Pop** 39,573 **Elev** 2,080 ft **Area code** 540 **Zip** 24060

Information Blacksburg Regional Chamber of Commerce, 1995 S Main St, Suite 901; 540/522-4503 or 800/288-4061

Web www.blacksburg-chamber.com

The Washington and Jefferson national forests, which lie to the northwest, provide a colorful backdrop of azaleas, flowering dogwood, and redbud in spring and brilliant hardwoods in fall. Virginia Polytechnic Institute and State University is a source of employment for the town. The forests' Blacksburg Ranger District office is located here.

What to See and Do

Mountain Lake. A resort lake, particularly inviting in late June and early July, when azaleas and rhododendron are in bloom. 20 mi NW on US 460, VA 700.

Smithfield Plantation. (1773) Restored pre-Revolutionary house; original woodwork. Home of Colonel William Preston and three governors. Architectural link between Tidewater and Piedmont plantations of Virginia and those of the Mississippi Valley. Grounds restored by Garden Club of Virginia. (Apr-Nov, Thurs-Sun afternoons) ¼ mi W off US 460 bypass, at VA Tech exit. Phone 540/231-3947. ¢¢

Motels/Motor Lodges

★ ★ **BEST WESTERN.** *900 Plantation Rd (24060). 540/552-7770; fax 540/552-6346; toll-free 800/528-1234. www.bestwestern.com.* 104 rms, 1-2 story. S $49-$54; D $64-$68; each addl $6; suites $139; under 18 free; higher rates university events. Crib free. TV; cable, VCR avail. Pool; poolside serv. Playground. Restaurant 7 am-10 pm. Bar 4:30 pm-2 am. Ck-out noon. Meeting rms. Business servs avail. Valet serv. Sundries. Tennis. Golf privileges. X-country ski 15 mi. Lawn games. Picnic tables, grills. On 13 acres. Cr cds: A, C, D, DS, MC, V.
⬛ ⬛ ⬛ ⬛ ⬛ ⬛ ⬛ ⬛

★ **COMFORT INN.** *3705 S Main St (24060). 540/951-1500; fax 540/951-1530; toll-free 800/228-5150. www.comfortinn.com.* 80 rms, 4 story. S $57-$65; D $62-$67; each addl $5; suite $85; under 18 free; higher rates special events. Crib free. Pet accepted. TV; cable (premium), VCR avail. Pool. Complimentary continental bkfst. Restaurant adj 6 am-10 pm. Ck-out 11 am. Business servs avail. In-rm modem link. Valet serv. Exercise equipt. Microwaves avail. Cr cds: A, C, D, DS, ER, JCB, MC, V.

★ **DAYS INN.** 3705 S Main St, Christiansburg (24068). 540/382-0261; fax 540/382-0365; toll-free 800/329-7466. www.daysinn.com. 122 rms, 2 story. S $46-$84; D $54-$84; each addl $5; under 18 free; higher rates: special events. Crib free. Pet accepted. TV; cable (premium). Pool. Playground. Complimentary continental bkfst. Ck-out noon. In-rm modem link. Cr cds: A, D, DS, MC, V.

★★ **FOUR POINTS BY SHERATON.** 900 Price's Fork Rd (24060). 540/552-7001; fax 540/552-0827; toll-free 800/325-3535. www.sheraton.com. 148 rms, 2 story. S, D $89-$169; each addl $10; suites $199; under 18 free. Crib free. TV; cable (premium). 2 pools, 1 indoor; wading pool. Complimentary coffee in lobby. Restaurant 7 am-2 pm, 5-9 pm. Bar noon-2 am; entertainment. Ck-out noon. Meeting rms. Business servs avail. In-rm modem link. Valet serv. Health club privileges. Tennis. Cr cds: A, C, D, DS, ER, JCB, MC, V.

★★ **HAMPTON INN.** 50 Hampton Blvd, Christiansburg (24073). 540/382-2055; fax 540/382-4515; res 800/426-7866. www.hamptoninn.com. 125 rms, 2 story. S $57; D $70; under 18 free; higher rates: wkends, univ graduation, football games. Crib free. TV; cable (premium). Pool. Restaurant opp 6 am-10 pm. Ck-out 11 am. Coin lndry. Business servs avail. Microwave avail. Cr cds: A, C, D, DS, ER, MC, V.

★ **RAMADA.** 3503 Holiday Ln (24060). 540/951-1330; fax 540/951-4847; res 888/298-2054. www.ramada.com. 98 rms, 2 story. S $55-$65; D $60-$70; each addl $5; suites $135; under 12 free; higher rates: univ graduation, football games. Crib free. Pet accepted. TV; cable (premium). Pool; wading pool. Restaurant 6:30 am-2 pm, 5-10 pm. Bar. Ck-out noon. Coin lndry. Meeting rm. Business servs avail. Valet serv. Sundries. X-country ski 20 mi. Some

in-rm steam baths. Cr cds: A, C, DS, MC, V.

B&B/Small Inn

★★★ **OAKS VICTORIAN INN.** 311 E Main St, Christiansburg (24073). 540/381-1500; fax 540/381-3036; toll-free 800/336-6257. www.bbhost.com/theoaksinn. 7 rms, 3 story. S $85-$125; D $115-$150; lower rates Jan-Mar. Children over 14 yrs only. TV; cable (premium). Whirlpool. Complimentary full bkfst; afternoon refreshments. Restaurant nearby. Ck-out noon, ck-in 4 pm. Business servs avail. In-rm modem link. Valet serv. Airport transportation. Health club privileges. Refrigerators; some fireplaces. Balconies. Queen Anne/Victorian residence (1889); period furnishings. Surrounded by 300-yr-old white oak trees. Totally nonsmoking. Cr cds: A, DS, MC, V.

Blue Ridge Parkway

See also Roanoke, Waynesboro

Elev 649-6,050 ft; avg 3,000 ft

Winding 469 mountainous miles between the Shenandoah and Great Smoky Mountains national parks (about 217 miles are in Virginia), the Blue Ridge Parkway represents a different concept in highway travel. It is not an express highway (speed limit 45 miles per hr) but a road intended for leisurely travel. All towns are bypassed. Travelers in a hurry would be wise to take state and US routes, where speed limits are higher.

The parkway follows the Blue Ridge Mountains for about 355 miles, then winds through the Craggies, Pisgahs, and Balsams to the Great Smokies. Overlooks, picnic and camp sites, visitor centers, nature trails, fishing streams and lakes, and points of interest are numerous and well-marked.

Accommodations are plentiful in cities and towns along the way. Food availability is limited on the parkway.

The parkway is open all year, but the best time to drive it is between April and November. Some sections are closed by ice and snow for periods in winter and early spring. Fog may be present during wet weather. The higher sections west of Asheville to Great Smoky Mountains National Park and north of Asheville to Mount Mitchell may be closed January through March due to hazardous driving conditions.

For maps, pamphlets and detailed information contact Superintendent, 199 Hemphill Road, Asheville, NC 28803; 828/298-0398.

What to See and Do

Camping. Tent and trailer sites at **Otter Creek, Peaks of Otter, Roanoke Mtn, Rocky Knob, Doughton Park, Julian Price Memorial Park, Linville Falls, Crabtree Meadows,** and **Mt Pisgah.** (May-Oct) 14-day limit, June-Labor Day. No electricity; pets on leash only; water shut off with first freeze, usually late Oct. Fee/site/night. Primitive winter camping at Linville Falls when roads are passable.

Craft demonstrations and sales.

Folk Art Center. Craft Guild Headquarters, sales, parkway travel information, park ranger. (Daily) Mi 382.

Northwest Trading Post. Country store sells native handicrafts. Mi 258.6.

Parkway Craft Center. (See BLOWING ROCK, NC) Mi 294.

Fishing. Rainbow, brook, brown trout and smallmouth bass in streams and lakes. State licenses required.

Horseback Riding. 20 mi of trails in Moses H. Cone Memorial Park (Mi 292.7). Horses for hire at Blowing Rock, NC.

Interpretive programs. Outdoor talks (mid-June-Labor Day) at Otter Creek (mi 60.8), Peaks of Otter (mi 86), Rocky Knob (mi 169), Doughton Park (mi 241.1), Price Park (mi 297.1), Linville Falls (mi 316.3), Crabtree Meadows (mi 340), and Mt

Pisgah (mi 408.6). Obtain schedules at Parkway Visitor Centers.

Self-guided trails. Moderate grades. Walks take from five min to one hr. Trails on the parkway incl

Cascades Trail. Leads to waterfall. Mi 272.

Cone Park Trail. Manor house wild garden. Mi 294.

Craggy Gardens Trail. Traverses high mountain "gardens." Mi 364.6.

Elk Run Trail. Forest, plant, animal community. Mi 86.

Flat Rock Trail. Magnificent valley and mountain views. Mi 308.3.

Greenstone Trail. Of geologic interest. Mi 8.8.

Linville Falls Trail. Views of falls, Linville River Gorge. Mi 317.5.

Mabry Mill Trail. Old-time mountain industry. Mi 176.

Mountain Farm Trail. Typical mountain farm, reconstructed. Mi 5.8.

Richland Balsam Trail. Spruce-fir forests. Highest spot on parkway. Mi 431.

Rocky Knob Trail. Leads to overlook of Rock Castle Gorge. Mi 168.

Trail of the Trees. Leads to overlook of James River. Mi 63.6.

⭐ **Visitor Centers.** Exhibits, travel information, interpretive publications. Centers (daily during peak travel season) incl

Craggy Gardens Visitor Center. 5,892-ft elevation. Natural history exhibits, naturalist. (Mid-June-Labor Day, daily; May-mid-June, early Sept-Oct, wkends) Mi 364.6.

Cumberland Knob Contact Station. Visitor information, publications, park ranger. Mi 218.

Humpback Rocks Visitor Center. Pioneer mountain farm, park ranger. Mi 5.8.

James River Wayside. Story of James River and Kanawha Canal, park ranger. Mi 63.6.

Linn Cove Information Center. Mi 304.

Mabry Mill. Old-time mountain industry, incl tannery exhibits, picturesque mill, blacksmith shop. Mi 176.

Museum of North Carolina Minerals. (Daily, winter hrs vary; closed hols) Mi 331.

Peaks of Otter Visitor Center. Wildlife exhibits, park ranger. Mi 86.

Rocky Knob Information Station. Information, exhibits, park ranger. Mi 170.

Waterrock Knob Information Center. Panoramic views, visitor information, exhibits, publications. Mi 451.

Motel/Motor Lodge

★ ★ ★ **PEAKS OF OTTER LODGE.** *Blue Ridge Pkwy, Bedford (24523). 540/586-1081; fax 540/586-4420; toll-free 800/542-5927. www.peaksofotter.com.* 63 rms, 2 story. Mar-Nov: S $67; D $72; each addl $6.25; suites $85-$100; under 16 free; MAP rest of yr. Crib free. TV in lobby. Restaurant (see also PEAKS OF OTTER). Bar 5-11 pm. Ck-out noon. Meeting rm. Business servs avail. Sundries. Gift shop. Private patios, balconies. Located on a lake; surrounded by mountain peaks. Scenic view. Cr cds: MC, V.
🄳 ⬥ ⬛ 🔥

Resort

★ ★ ★ **DOE RUN LODGE RESORT AND CONFERENCE CENTER.** *Blue Ridge Pkwy, Fancy Gap (24343). 540/398-2212; fax 540/398-2833; res 800/325-6189. www.doerunlodge.com.* 47 kit. suites, 1-2 story. No elvtr. May-Oct: kit. suites $119-$250; each addl $18; under 15 free; package plans; lower rates rest of yr. Crib free. Pet accepted; $45 deposit. TV; VCR (movies $3). Heated pool; poolside serv. Sauna. Complimentary coffee in rms. Restaurant (see also HIGH COUNTRY). Bar; entertainment Fri, Sat. Ck-out noon. Meeting rms. Business servs avail. Sundries. Lighted tennis. 18-hole golf privileges, greens fee, pro, putting green, driving range. Lawn games. Balconies. Picnic tables. Cr cds: A, MC, V.
🄳 🄳 ⬛ 🔥 **SC**

B&B/Small Inn

★ ★ **THE OSCEOLA MILL COUNTRY INN.** *Hwy 56, Steele's Tavern (24476). 540/377-6455; fax 540/377-*

5148. 12 rms, 1-2 story, 1 cottage. No rm phones. S, D $89-$109; each addl $20; cottage $149-$169; wkly rates. Pool. Complimentary full bkfst. Ck-out 11 am, ck-in 2 pm. Business servs avail. In renovated 1849 mill, mill store and restored 1873 miller's house. Totally nonsmoking. Cr cds: MC, V.
🄳 ⬛ 🔥

Restaurants

★ ★ **HIGH COUNTRY.** *Blue Ridge Pkwy, Fancy Gap (24328). 540/398-2212. www.doerunlodge.com.* Hrs: 8 am-10 pm; Sun brunch 11:30 am-2:30 pm. Closed Mon; Dec 25. Res accepted. Bar noon-midnight; closed Sun. Complete meals: bkfst $4.25-$12.95. Lunch $4.95-$16.95, dinner $13.95-$25. Specializes in beef, chicken. Entertainment Fri, Sat. Panoramic view of countryside. Cr cds: A, MC, V.
⬛

★ ★ **PEAKS OF OTTER.** *Mile Post 86, Bedford (24523). 540/586-9263. www.peaksotter.com.* Hrs: 7:30-10:30 am, 11:30 am-2:30 pm, 5-8:30 pm; Sun brunch noon-8:30 pm. Bar 5-11 pm. Bkfst $3-$7.95, lunch $4.50-$8.95, dinner $4.70-$16.95. Sun brunch $10.55. Child's menu. Specialties: prime rib au jus, barbecued "little pig" ribs, whole rainbow trout. Salad bar. Panoramic view of mountains, lake. Rustic decor. Family-owned. Cr cds: MC, V.
🄳

Booker T. Washington National Monument

See also Roanoke

(Approx 18 mi S on VA 116 from Roanoke to Burnt Chimney, then continue 6 mi E on VA 122)

The 1861 property inventory of the Burroughs plantation listed, along with household goods and farm implements, the entry "1 Negro boy

(Booker)—$400." Freed in 1865, the boy and his family moved to Malden, West Virginia. There, while working at a salt furnace and in coal mines, the youngster learned the alphabet from *Webster's Blueback Spelling Book*. Later, by working at the salt furnace before school, then going to work at the mine after school, he got the rudiments of an education. When he realized that everyone else at the school roll call had two names, he chose Washington for his own.

At age 16 he started the 500-mile trip from Malden to Hampton Institute, where he earned his way. He taught at Malden for two years, attended Wayland Seminary, and returned to Hampton Institute to teach. In July 1881 he started Tuskegee Institute in Alabama with 30 pupils, two run-down buildings, and $2,000 for salaries. When Washington died in 1915 the Institute had 107 buildings, more than 2,000 acres, and was assessed at more than $500,000.

The 224-acre monument includes most of the original plantation. A ¼-mile self-guided plantation trail passes reconstructed farm buildings, a slave cabin, crops and animals of the period; there is also a 1½ mile self-guided Jack-O-Lantern Branch nature trail. Picnic facilities. Visitor Center has an audiovisual program, exhibits depicting his life (daily; closed January 1, Thanksgiving, December 25). Phone 540/721-2094. **FREE**

Breaks Interstate Park

See also Wise

(8 mi N of Haysi, VA, and 7 mi SE of Elkhorn City, KY, on KY-VA 80)

The "Grand Canyon of the South," where the Russell Fork of the Big Sandy River plunges through the mountains, is the major attraction of this 4,600-acre park on the Virginia-Kentucky border. From the entrance, a paved road winds through an ever-green forest and then skirts the canyon rim. Overlooks provide a spectacular view of the Towers, a ½-mile long, ⅓-mile wide pyramid of rocks; the five-mile long, 1,600-foot deep, 250 million-year-old gorge; odd rock formations, caves, springs, and a profusion of rhododendron.

The visitor center houses natural and historical exhibits and a coal exhibit (April-October, daily). Laurel Lake is stocked with bass and bluegill. Picnicking, swimming pool, pedal boats; hiking and bridle trails, playground. Camping (April-October, fee); cottages (all year), restaurant, gift shop, conference center. Facilities (April-mid-December, daily); park (all year, daily). For details contact Breaks Interstate Park, PO Box 100, Breaks, 24607; phone 540/865-4413 or 800/982-5122. Memorial Day-Labor Day, per car ¢; Rest of year **FREE**

Motel/Motor Lodge

★★ **BREAKS INTERSTATE.** *Rte 1, Breaks (24607).* 540/865-4414; fax 540/865-5561; toll-free 800/982-5122. *www.breakspark.com.* 34 rms, 1-2 story. Apr-Dec: S $66.03; D $74.55; each addl $8; cottages $350/wk. Closed late Dec-Mar. Crib free. TV; cable. Pool; wading pool, lifeguard. Restaurant 7 am-9 pm. Ck-out 11 am. Meeting rm. Sundries. Gift shop. Balconies. Picnic tables, grills. Bicycle rentals. Woodland setting; overlooks Breaks Canyon. Hiking trails, picnic shelters. Cr cds: A, DS, MC, V.

⒟ 🐾 ⛷ ☰ ⊠ 🐾 **SC**

Bristol

(F-2) *See also Abingdon*

Founded 1771 **Pop** 17,367 **Elev** 1,680 ft **Area code** 540 (VA); 423 (TN) **Zip** 24201 (VA); 37620 (TN)

Information Chamber of Commerce, 20 Volunteer Pkwy, TN, or PO Box 519, VA 24203; 423/989-4850

Web www.bristolchamber.org

Essentially a city in two states, Bristol is actually two cities—Bristol, Tennessee and Bristol, Virginia—sharing the same main street and the same personality. Each has its own government and city services. Together they constitute a major shopping center. Named for the English industrial center, Bristol is an important factory town in its own right. These cities carry on the pioneer tradition of an ironworks established here about 1784 which made the first nails for use on the frontier.

What to See and Do

Bristol Caverns. Unusual rock formations seen from lighted, paved walkways winding through caverns and along an underground river. Guided tours every 20 min. Picnic area. (Daily; closed Easter, Dec 25) 5 mi SE on US 435, off I-81. Phone 423/878-2011. ¢¢¢

Rocky Mount Historic Site. Features the 2½-story log house (1770) that served from 1790 to 1792 as capitol under William Blount, governor of the Territory of the United States South of the River Ohio. Restored to its original simplicity; 18th-century furniture. On grounds are restored log kitchen, slave cabin, barn, blacksmith shop, and smokehouse. (Daily; closed Thanksgiving, Dec 21-Jan 5; also wkends Jan, Feb) 11 mi SW on US 11 E. Phone 423/538-7396. ¢¢

Special Event

Bristol Motor Speedway. 5 mi S on US 11 E. Phone 423/764-1161. Apr, June, and Aug.

Motels/Motor Lodges

★ **BUDGET HOST.** *1209 W State St (24201).* 540/669-5187; fax 540/466-5848. *www.budgethost.com.* 24 rms. S, D $28.50-$80; each addl $4; under 12 free; wkly rates. TV; cable (premium). Restaurant nearby. Ck-out 11 am. Business servs avail. Cr cds: A, DS, MC, V.
≊ 🐾

★ **COMFORT INN.** *2368 Lee Hwy (24201).* 540/466-3881; fax 540/466-6544; res 800/221-2222. *www.comfort inn.com.* 60 rms, 2 story. Apr-Oct: S, D $65-$195; each addl $5; suites $125-$225; under 18 free; higher rates special events; lower rates rest of yr. Crib free. TV; cable (premium).

Pool. Complimentary continental bkfst. Restaurant nearby. Ck-out 11 am. Business servs avail. Cr cds: A, C, D, DS, JCB, MC, V.
D ≊ ≊ 🐾 SC

★ **LA QUINTA INN.** *1014 Old Airport Rd (24201).* 540/669-9353; fax 540/669-6974. *www.laquinta.com.* 123 rms, 4 story. June-Sept: S $59-$79; D $69-$89; each addl $10; suites $95-$105; under 18 free; higher rates races; lower rates rest of yr. Crib free. Pet accepted. TV; cable (premium), VCR avail. Complimentary continental bkfst, coffee in rms. Restaurant nearby. Ck-out noon. Meeting rms. Business servs avail. In-rm modem link. Pool. Cr cds: A, D, DS, MC, V.
D 🐾 ≊ ≊ 🐾

★ **RAMADA INN.** *2221 Euclid Ave (24201).* 540/669-7171. *www.ramada. com.* 123 rms, 2 story. S, D $55-$95; each addl $4; under 18 free; higher rates special events. TV; cable. Pool. Restaurant 7 am-2 pm, 5-9 pm. Bar from 5 pm. Ck-out noon. Meeting rms. Business servs avail. Sundries. Microwaves avail. Cr cds: A, C, D, DS, MC, V.
D ≊ ≊ 🐾

★ **RED CARPET INN.** *15589 Lee Hwy (24202).* 540/669-1151. 60 rms, 2 story. June-Oct: S, D $48-$74; each addl $5; higher rates special events; lower rates rest of yr. Crib free. Pet accepted, some restrictions. TV; cable (premium). Pool. Ck-out noon. Microwaves avail. Cr cds: A, D, DS, MC, V.
D 🐾 🐾 🛆 ≊ ≊ 🐾

★ **SUPER 8.** *2139 Lee Hwy (24201).* 540/466-8800; res 800/800-8000. *www.super8.com.* 62 rms, 3 story. S, D $46-$64; each addl $6; under 12 free; higher rates races. Crib free. Pet accepted. TV; cable. Complimentary coffee in lobby. Restaurant nearby. Ck-out 11 am. Business servs avail. Some refrigerators, microwaves. Picnic tables. Cr cds: A, D, DS, MC, V.
D 🐾 ≊ 🐾

Restaurants

★ **ATHENS STEAK HOUSE.** *105 Goodson St (24201).* 540/466-8271. Hrs: 4-10:30 pm. Closed Sun; hols. Greek, American menu. Bar. Dinner

$7.95-$20.45. Specializes in lobster tail, steak. Cr cds: MC, V.

D ⬛

★ ★ **VINEYARD.** *603 Gate City Hwy (24201).* 540/466-4244. Hrs: 7 am-10 pm; Fri, Sat to 11 pm. Closed July 4, Dec 24, 25. Res accepted wkends. Italian, American menu. Bar. Bkfst $3.95-$6.95, lunch $4.95-$7.95. Complete meals: dinner $8.25-$25. Specializes in fresh seafood, veal. Salad bar. Cr cds: A, D, DS, MC, V.

D ⬛

Brookneal

See also Lynchburg, South Boston

Settled ca 1790 **Pop** 1,259 **Elev** 560 ft **Area code** 804 **Zip** 24528

What to See and Do

Patrick Henry National Memorial (Red Hill). Last home and burial place of Patrick Henry. Restoration of family cottage, cook's cabin, smokehouse, stable, kitchen. Patrick Henry's law office. Museum and gift shop on grounds. Interpretive video. (Daily; closed Jan 1, Thanksgiving, Dec 25) 3 mi E on VA 40, 2 mi S on VA 600 and 619. Phone 434/376-2044. ¢¢¢

Cape Charles

See also Hampton, Newport News, Norfolk, Portsmouth, Virginia Beach

Pop 1,134 **Elev** 10 ft **Area code** 757 **Zip** 23310

Information Chesapeake Bay Bridge & Tunnel District, Public Relations Department, PO Box 111; 757/331-2960, ext 20

Web www.cbbt.com

The Chesapeake Bay Bridge-Tunnel (17.6 miles long) leads from Cape Charles (12 miles south of the town) to Virginia Beach/Norfolk. There is a scenic stop, gift shop, restaurant, and

fishing pier (bait available). **Note:** Noncommercial vehicles entering with compressed gas containers are limited to *(a)* two nonpermanently-mounted containers with a maximum individual capacity of 105 pounds water or 45 pounds LP gas each, or one container with a maximum capacity of 60 pounds LP gas; or *(b)* not more than two permanently-mounted containers with a total capacity of 200 gallons water when LP gas is used as a motor fuel. One-way passenger car toll ¢¢¢

B&B/Small Inn

★ ★ **WILSON-LEE HOUSE BED AND BREAKFAST.** *403 Tazewell Ave (23310).* 757/331-1954; fax 757/331-8133. www.wilsonleehouse.com. 6 rms, 4 with shower only. S, D $85-$120; each addl $20; package plans; hols 2-day min. Children over 12 yrs only. Cable TV in common rm, VCR avail (movies). Complimentary full bkfst. Restaurant nearby. Ck-out 11 am, ck-in 4-6 pm. Business servs avail. Luggage handling. Street parking. Built in 1906. Totally nonsmoking. Cr cds: A, MC, V.

⬛ ⬛ ⬛

Restaurants

★ ★ ★ **EASTVILLE MANOR.** *6058 Willow Oak Rd, Eastville (23347).* 757/678-7378. www.eastvillemanor.com. Hrs: 5:30-9 pm. Closed Sun, Mon; also Tues Sept-May. Res accepted. Contemporary American menu. Wine list. A la carte entrees: dinner $11.95-$17.95. Child's menu. Specializes in fresh seafood, beef tenderloin, pasta. Menu changes monthly. Own baking. In 1886 farmhouse; polished wood floors, chandeliers, antiques; landscaped grounds. Cr cds: MC, V.

D

★ **LITTLE ITALY.** *10027 Rogers Dr, Nassawadox (23413).* 757/442-7831. Hrs: 11 am-8 pm, Fri, Sat to 9 pm; summer hrs vary. Closed Sun; hols. Res accepted. Italian menu. Bar. Lunch, dinner $2.99-$12.99. Child's menu. Specialties: lasagna, cannolli, tiramisu. Street parking. Former country grocery store.

D ⬛

Ash Lawn

Cape Henry Memorial

See also Norfolk, Virginia Beach

(10 mi E of Norfolk on US 60)

The first English settlers of Jamestown landed here on April 26, 1607. They claimed the land for England, stayed four days, named their landing spot for Henry (then Prince of Wales and oldest son of King James I), and put up a cross.

A cross put up by the Daughters of the American Colonists in 1935 marks the approximate site of the first landing. An interpretive display describes the Battle of the Capes, a sea battle fought between England and France in 1781 and a prelude to the Battle of Yorktown. Nearby is Cape Henry Lighthouse, first lighthouse in the United States authorized and built by the federal government (1791). The memorial is in Fort Story Military Reservation.

Charlottesville

(D-6) *See also Waynesboro*

Founded 1762 **Pop** 45,049 **Elev** 480 ft
Area code 804
Information Charlottesville/Albemarle Convention & Visitors Bureau, jct I-64 and VA 20, PO Box 178, 22902; 804/977-1783
Web www.charlottesvilletourism.org

Thomas Jefferson was born here, as was the University of Virginia, which he founded and designed. Ash Lawn-Highland, which was James Monroe's home, and Monticello are southeast of the city.

In the gently rolling terrain of Albemarle County, Charlottesville is almost at the center of Virginia; it is the trading center for a widespread area. In colonial times tobacco was the dominant product. Today wheat, beef and dairy herds, riding and race horses, peaches, frozen foods, electronic products, light industry, and mountains of native Albemarle pippin apples invigorate the economy.

What to See and Do

Albemarle County Courthouse.
North wing was used in 1820s as a
"common temple" shared by Episco-
palian, Methodist, Presbyterian, and
Baptist sects, one Sun a month to
each but with all who wished attend-
ing each Sun. Jefferson, Monroe, and
Madison worshiped here. Court Sq.

⭐ **Ash-Lawn Highland.** (1799) Built
on a site personally selected by
Thomas Jefferson, this 535-acre
estate was the home of President
James Monroe (1799-1823). The
estate is now owned by Monroe's
alma mater, the College of William
and Mary. This early 19th-century
working plantation offers guided
tours of the house with Monroe possessions, spinning and weaving
demonstrations, old boxwood gardens, peacocks, picnic spots. Special
events incl Summer Music Festival
(June-Aug) of arts, eve concerts, children's shows (Sat), Plantation Days
Weekend, spring and Christmas programs. (Daily; closed Jan 1, Thanksgiving, Dec 25) 4¼ mi SE on County
795. Phone 434/293-9539. ¢¢¢

Historic Michie Tavern. (ca 1784)
Located near Jefferson's Monticello.
Visitors dine on hearty Midday Fare
in the Tavern's Ordinary where
servers in period attire greet them.
Afterwards, a tour of the original
Tavern features living history where
guests participate in 18th century

activities including a lively Virginia
dance. (Daily; closed Jan 1, Dec 25) 1
mi S on VA 20. Phone 434/977-1234.
¢¢¢

⭐ **Monticello.** Located on a mountaintop, this is one of the most beautiful estates in Virginia and is
considered a classic of American
architecture. Monticello was
designed by Thomas Jefferson and
built over the course of 40 yrs, sym-
bolizing the pleasure he found in
"putting up and pulling down." Jefferson moved into the first completed outbuilding of his new home
in 1771, though construction continued until 1809. Most of the interior
furnishings are original. Tours of the
restored orchard, vineyard, 1,000-ft-
long vegetable garden, and Mulberry
Row, once the site of plantation
workshops. Jefferson died at Monticello on July 4, 1826 and was buried
in the family cemetery. The Thomas
Jefferson Memorial Foundation
maintains the house and gardens.
(Daily; closed Dec 25) 2 mi SE on VA
53. Phone 434/984-9822. ¢¢¢¢
Approx 2 mi W of here is

Monticello Visitors Center. Personal and family memorabilia;
architectural models and drawings;
*Thomas Jefferson: The Pursuit of Lib-
erty,* a 35-minute film, shown twice
daily. (Daily; closed Dec 25) On VA
20S at I-64. Phone 434/984-9822.
FREE

Monticello

Monuments.

George Rogers Clark Memorial. Brother of William Clark and soldier on the frontier, this intrepid explorer who opened up the Northwest Territory was an Albemarle County native son. W Main St, E of university.

Lewis and Clark Monument. Memorial to Jefferson's secretary, Meriwether Lewis, who explored the Louisiana Territory with his friend William Clark. Midway Park, Ridge, and Main sts.

Robert E. Lee Monument. Jefferson St between 1st and 2nd sts.

Stonewall Jackson on Little Sorrel. By Charles Keck. Adj to courthouse.

Shenandoah National Park. (see) 20 mi W on VA 250 to Afton, then N on Skyline Dr.

Skiing. Wintergreen Resort. Quad, three triple, double chairlifts; patrol, school, rentals, snow making; lodge (see RESORTS); nursery. Twenty runs; longest run 1½ mi; vertical drop 1,003 ft. (Dec-Mar, daily) Night skiing. Summer activities incl fishing, boating; golf, tennis, horseback riding. W on US 250 to VA 151, then S to VA 664, turn right, follow signs (approx 4½ mi). Phone 434/325-2200. ¢¢¢¢

University of Virginia. (1819) 18,100 students. Founded by Thomas Jefferson and built according to his plans. Handsome red brick buildings with white trim, striking vistas, smooth lawns, and ancient trees form the grounds of Jefferson's "academical village." The serpentine walls, one brick thick, which Jefferson designed for strength and beauty, are famous. Room 13, West Range, occupied by Edgar Allan Poe as a student, is displayed for the public. Walking tours start at the Rotunda (daily; closed three wks mid-Dec-early Jan). W end of Main St. Phone 434/924-1019. **FREE**

Walking tour. The Charlottesville/ Albemarle Information Center, located on VA 20 S in the Monticello Visitors Center Building, has information for a walking tour of historic Charlottesville. Phone 434/977-1783.

Special Events

Founder's Day. (Jefferson's Birthday) Commemorative ceremonies. Apr 13.

Dogwood Festival. Parade, lacrosse and golf tournaments, carnival. Nine days mid-Apr.

Garden Week. Some fine private homes and gardens in the area are open. Mid-Apr.

Motels/Motor Lodges

★ **BEST WESTERN.** *1613 Emmet St (22906). 434/296-5501; fax 434/977-6249; toll-free 800/528-1234. www. bestwestern.com.* 104 rms, 1-2 story. Mar-Oct: S $68; D $76; each addl $6; under 18 free; family, wkly rates; higher rates graduation; lower rates rest of yr. Crib free. Pet accepted, some restrictions. TV; cable (premium). Complimentary coffee in rms. Restaurant adj 6-10 am. Ck-out noon. Meeting rms. Business servs avail. Bellhops. Sundries. Pool; wading pool. Refrigerators, microwaves avail. Cr cds: A, C, D, DS, MC, V.

[D] [🛎] [⊠] [✕] [🐾] [SC]

★ ★ **BEST WESTERN CAVALIER INN.** *105 Emmet St N (22903). 434/296-8111; fax 434/296-3523; res 800/528-1234. www.bestwestern.com.* 118 rms, 5 story. S $63-$79; D $73-$89; each addl $8; suites $125; under 18 free; 2-day packages; higher rates univ events. Crib free. Pet accepted. TV; cable (premium). Pool. Complimentary continental bkfst. Coffee in rms. Ck-out noon. Meeting rms. Business center. Bellhops. Valet serv. Free airport, RR station, bus depot transportation. Univ of VA opp. Cr cds: A, C, D, DS, MC, V.

[D] [⊠] [✕] [🏃]

★ ★ **COURTYARD BY MARRIOTT.** *638 Hillsdale Dr (22901). 434/973-7100; fax 434/973-7128; res 800/321-2211. www.courtyard.com.* 150 rms, 2-3 story. Mar-late Nov: S, D $79-$109; under 18 free; wkly rates; higher rates graduation; lower rates rest of yr. Crib free. TV; cable (premium), VCR avail. Indoor pool; whirlpool. Complimentary coffee in rms. Bar 5-10 pm. Ck-out noon. Coin lndry. Meeting rms. Business servs avail. In-rm modem link. Sundries. Free airport transportation. Exercise equipt. Some refrigerators; microwaves avail. Balconies. Picnic tables. Cr cds: A, D, DS, MC, V.

[D] [⊠] [🏃] [✕] [🐾]

★ **DAYS INN.** *1600 Emmet St N (22901). 434/293-9111; fax 434/977-2780; toll-free 800/329-7466. www. daysinn.com.* 129 rms, 2 story. S $60-$68; D $52-$90; each addl $10; under 18 free; higher rates special univ events. Crib free. Pet accepted; $10/day. TV; cable (premium). Pool; wading pool. Restaurant 7 am-10 pm; Fri, Sat to 11 pm. Bar 10-1 am. Ck-out noon. Meeting rms. Business servs avail. In-rm modem link. Bellhops. Valet serv. Free airport, RR station, bus depot transportation. Exercise equipt. Health club privileges. Cr cds: A, C, D, DS, JCB, MC, V.

D ⬤ ≈ 🏃 ⛵ 🐾 SC

★★ **ENGLISH INN OF CHARLOTTESVILLE.** *2000 Morton Dr (22903). 434/971-9900; fax 434/977-8008; toll-free 800/786-5400. www. wytestone.com.* 67 units, 3 story, 21 suites. S $69; D $74; each addl $6; suites $75-$80; under 18 free; higher rates: univ graduation, sports events. Crib free. TV; cable (premium). Indoor pool. Complimentary bkfst buffet. Ck-out noon. Meeting rms. Business servs avail. Exercise equipt. Free airport, RR station, bus depot transportation. Sauna. Refrigerator in suites. Cr cds: A, C, D, DS, MC, V.

D ≈ ⛵ 🐾 SC 🏃

★★ **HAMPTON INN.** *2035 India Rd (22901). 434/978-7888; fax 434/973-0436.* 123 rms, 5 story. S, D $75-$98; under 18 free; higher rates university graduation. Crib free. TV; cable (premium). Pool. Complimentary continental bkfst, coffee. Restaurant nearby. Ck-out noon. Meeting rm. Business servs avail. Bellhops. Sundries. Free airport, RR station, bus depot transportation. Health club privileges. Cr cds: A, C, D, DS, MC, V.

D ≈ ⛵ 🐾

★★ **HOLIDAY INN.** *1200 5th St SW (22902). 434/977-5100; fax 434/293-5228; toll-free 800/465-4329.* 131 rms, 6 story. S, D $65-$80; each addl $10; suites $115-$125; under 18 free; wkend rates; higher rates univ events. Crib free. Pet accepted. TV; cable (premium). Pool; wading pool. Complimentary coffee in rms. Restaurant 6:30-10:30 am, 5-10 pm. Bar to 11 pm. Ck-out noon. Meeting rms. Coin lndry. Business servs avail.

Bellhops. Exercise rm. Game rm. Refrigerators avail. Cr cds: A, D, DS, MC, V.

D ≈ ⛵ 🐾 SC 🏃 🐾

★ **RAMADA INN.** *2097 Inn Dr (22911). 434/977-3300; res 800/272-6232. www.ramada.com.* 100 rms, 2 story. Apr-Nov: S $50-$55; D $55-$70; each addl $10; under 17 free; higher rates special events; lower rates rest of yr. Crib free. TV; cable (premium), VCR avail. Complimentary continental bkfst, coffee in rms. Restaurant 7 am-10 pm. Bar 5-10 pm. Ck-out 11 am. Meeting rms. Business servs avail. Bellhops. Sundries. Coin lndry. Pool. Playground. Game rm. Exercise equipt. Some in-rm whirlpools, refrigerators, microwaves. Picnic tables, grills. Cr cds: A, C, D, DS, JCB, MC, V.

D ≈ ⛵ 🐾 SC 🏃

Hotels

★★ **DOUBLETREE.** *990 Hilton Heights Rd (22901). 434/973-2121; fax 434/978-7735; res 800/222-8733. www.doubletree.com.* 240 units, 9 story. S, D $99-$149; each addl $10; suites $229-$299; family, wkend rates. Crib free. Pet accepted; $25. TV; cable (premium), VCR avail. Indoor/outdoor pool; whirlpool, poolside serv. Coffee in rms. Restaurant 6:30 am-10:30 pm. Bar 5:30 pm-11 pm. Rm serv 6:30 am-11 pm. Ck-out noon. Convention facilities. Business servs avail. In-rm modem link. Free airport, RR station, bus depot transportation. Tennis. Exercise equipt. Refrigerators avail. Cr cds: A, C, D, DS, MC, V.

D 🏈 ≈ 🏃 ⛵ 🐾 🐾

★★★ **OMNI CHARLOTTESVILLE HOTEL.** *235 W Main St (22902). 434/971-5500; fax 434/979-4456; res 800/843-6664. www.omnihotels.com.* 204 rms, 7 story. S, D $120-$160; each addl $15; under 18 free; suites $199-$250; wkend rates; higher rates univ events. Crib free. Pet accepted, some restrictions. TV; cable (premium). 2 pools, 1 indoor; whirlpool. Coffee in rms. Restaurant 6:30 am-10 pm. Bar 11-1 am. Ck-out noon. Convention facilities. Gift shop. Free covered parking. Exercise rm; sauna. Cr cds: A, C, D, DS, MC, V.

D 🐾 ≈ 🏃 ⛵ 🐾 SC

Resorts

★ ★ ★ **BOAR'S HEAD INN.** *W Rte 250 (22903). 434/296-2181; fax 434/972-6024; toll-free 800/476-1988. www.boarsheadinn.com.* 171 rms. Apr-Nov: S, D $185-$225; each addl $10; suites $360-$500; under 18 free; lower rates rest of yr. Crib $10. TV; cable (premium), VCR avail. 3 pools; poolside serv, lifeguard. Supervised children's activities (mid-June-Labor Day); ages 5-16. Dining rm (see also OLD MILL ROOM). Bar 2 pm-midnight. Ck-out noon, ck-in 4 pm. Convention facilities. Business center. In-rm modem link. Valet serv Mon-Fri. Concierge. Gift shop. Free airport transportation. Lighted outdoor, indoor tennis, pro. 18-hole golf, driving range. Bicycles. Hot-air ballooning. Exercise equipt; sauna. Some refrigerators. Some private patios, balconies. Two ponds with ducks, swans, and geese. Local landmark; 1834 gristmill. Flower gardens. Local winery tours. Cr cds: A, D, DS, MC, V.

★ ★ ★ ★ **KESWICK HALL AT MON-TICELLO.** *701 Club Dr, Keswick (22947). 434/979-3440; fax 434/977-4171. www.orient-expresshotels.com.* Reminiscent of an Italian villa, this luxury hotel stands atop the rolling hills of Virginia countryside overlooking its golf course and semiresidential acreage. Take in breathtaking views from a private terrace, enjoy afternoon tea in the historic parlor, or relax with a book in the cool, Mediterranean lobby. The staff, correct and obliging, maintains the estate with European charm. 48 rms, 1-3 story, 6 suites. Mar-June, Sept-Nov: S, D $250-$595; each addl $50; suites $595; golf plan; special events (2-day min); lower rates rest of yr. Children over 8 yrs only. TV; cable (premium); VCR avail. Indoor/outdoor pool; whirlpool. Complimentary full bkfst; afternoon refreshments. Restaurant (see THE RESTAURANT). Rm serv 24 hrs. Ck-out noon, ck-in 3 pm. Concierge serv. Business servs avail. Free airport, RR station transportation. Lighted tennis privileges, pro. 18-hole golf, greens fee $40-$100, pro, putting green, driving range. Exercise rm; sauna. Exercise rm. Rec rm. Lawn games. Many balconies. Picnic tables. English country house (1912) on 600-acre estate; designs by Laura Ashley. Cr cds: A, C, D, DS, MC, V.

★ ★ ★ **WINTERGREEN RESORT.** *Rte 664, Wintergreen (22958). 434/325-2200; fax 434/325-8003; toll-free 800/266-2444. www.wintergreenresort.com.* 315 kit. units, 2-3 story. Dec-Mar: S, D $137-$191; lower rates rest of yr; family, golf, ski, tennis plans; lower rates rest of yr. Crib avail. TV; cable (premium), VCR avail (movies). 6 pools, 1 indoor; wading pool, whirlpools, lifeguards. Playground. Supervised children's activities (ages 3-12). Restaurants. Box lunches, snack bar, picnics. Bar. Ck-out 11 am, ck-in 4 pm. Convention facilities. Business center. Shopping arcade. Airport, RR station transportation. Indoor tennis, pro. Two 18-hole golf courses, greens fee $55-$99, pro, putting green, driving range. Downhill ski on site. Rowboats, canoes. Nature programs. Bicycles. Entertainment, movies. Exercise rm. Some fireplaces. Private patios, balconies. Picnic tables. Cr cds: A, MC, V.

B&Bs/Small Inns

★ ★ ★ ★ **THE CLIFTON COUNTRY INN.** *1296 Clifton Inn Dr (22911). 434/971-1800; fax 434/971-7098; res 888/971-1800. www.cliftoninn.com.* The elegantly landscaped grounds, distinctively appointed rooms, and gracious service of this 1799 country inn exude Southern gentility. All 14 rooms are antique-filled with wood-burning fireplaces and views of the inn's manicured grounds and private lake. The Virginia Historic Landmark property also boasts some of the best dining in the Charlottesville area with a prix fixe menu featuring fresh, local ingredients. 14 rms, 1-2 story, 8 suites. Apr-Nov: S, D $150-$265; each addl $75-$133; suites $225-$315; wkends (2-day min); lower rates rest of yr. Complimentary full bkfst, coffee in rms. Restaurant 6:30-11 pm. Ck-out 11 am, ck-in 3-5 pm. Business servs avail. Lighted tennis. Pool; whirlpool. Lawn games. Fireplaces. 18th-century manor built 1799. Totally nonsmoking. Cr cds: A, DS, MC, V.

★ ★ ★ **INN AT MONTICELLO.** *Rte 20 S; 1188 Scottsville Rd (22902). 434/979-3593; fax 434/296-1344. www.innatmonticello.com.* 5 rms, 2 story. No rm phones. S $85; D $150-$175; each addl $25; wkends (2-day min). Children over 12 yrs only. Complimentary full bkfst; afternoon refreshments. Ck-out 11 am, ck-in 3 pm. Business servs avail. Country manor (mid-1800s) filled with period antiques and reproductions. Totally nonsmoking. Cr cds: A, MC, V.

★ ★ ★ **PROSPECT HILL PLANTATION INN.** *2887 Poindexter Rd, Louisa (23093). 540/967-0844; fax 540/967-0102; toll-free 800/277-0844. www.prospecthill.com.* 13 rms, 2 with shower only, 2 story, 6 suites. No rm phones. MAP: S $200-$300; D $285-$380; each addl $50; suites $325-$420; under 5 free. Closed Dec 24 eve, Dec 25. Pool. Complimentary full bkfst; afternoon refreshments. Dining rm, 1 sitting: 7 pm; Fri, Sat 8 pm. Ck-out 11 am, ck-in 3 pm. Meeting rm. Business servs avail. Bellhop. Lawn games. Many refrigerators; some in-rm whirlpools. Plantation house built 1732; many antique furnishings; tree-shaded lawns, veranda, gazebo. Cr cds: A, C, D, DS, JCB, MC, V.

★ ★ ★ **SILVER THATCH INN.** *3001 Hollymead Dr (22911). 434/978-4686; fax 434/973-6156. www.silverthatch.com.* 7 rms, 4 with shower only, 2 story. No rm phones. S, D $130-$170; each addl $25; 2-day min wkends Apr-Nov. Children over 12 yrs only. Pool. Complimentary full bkfst; refreshments. Dining rm Tues-Sat 5:30-9 pm. Ck-out 11 am, ck-in 3 pm. Business servs avail. Original building dates to 1780 (built by captured Hessian soldiers), additions in 1812 and 1937. Rms named for Virginia-born presidents. Totally nonsmoking. Cr cds: A, C, D, MC, V.

★ ★ **200 SOUTH STREET INN.** *200 W South St (22902). 434/979-0200; fax 434/979-4403. www.southstreetinn.com.* 20 rms, 4 story. S, D $125-$220; each addl $20; under 16 free. Crib free. TV. Complimentary continental bkfst. Restaurant nearby. Ck-out 11 am, ck-in 2 pm. Business servs avail.

Health club privileges. Some in-rm whirlpools, fireplaces. Built 1856; antiques. Cr cds: A, C, D, MC, V.

Restaurants

★ ★ **ABERDEEN BARN.** *2018 Holiday Dr (22901). 434/296-4630. www.aberdeenbarn.com.* Hrs: 5 pm-midnight; Sun to 10 pm. Closed Thanksgiving, Dec 25. Res accepted. Bar. Dinner $15.95-$33.95. Child's menu. Specializes in prime rib, steak, seafood. Entertainment. Open charcoal hearth. Family-owned. Cr cds: A, D, MC, V.

★ ★ **BERTINE'S NORTH CARIBBEAN.** *206 S Main St, Madison (22727). 540/948-3463.* Hrs: 6-9 pm. Closed Tues-Thurs; also Easter, Dec 25. Res accepted. Caribbean menu. Wine, beer. Dinner $9.85-$21. Specialties: jerk chicken, steak on a hot rock, blackened swordfish. Outdoor dining. Caribbean decor. Cr cds: DS, MC, V.

★ ★ **C & O.** *515 E Water St (22902). 434/971-7044. www.candorestaurant.com.* Hrs: 5 pm-2 am. Closed hols. Res accepted. French, eclectic cuisine. Bar. A la carte entrees: dinner $14-$25. Specializes in regional fresh cooking. Own baking. Cr cds: A, MC, V.

★ ★ **CARMELLO'S.** *400 Emmet St (22903). 434/977-5200.* Hrs: 5-10 pm; Mon to 9 pm. Closed hols. Res accepted. Northern Italian menu. Bar. Dinner $9.50-$25. Specializes in veal, pasta, chicken. Cr cds: A, C, D, DS, MC, V.

★ ★ **HARDWARE STORE.** *316 E Main St (22902). 434/977-1518.* Hrs: 11 am-9 pm; Fri, Sat to 10 pm; winter hrs vary. Closed Sun; hols. Res accepted. Eclectic menu. Lunch, dinner $6-$18. Specializes in burgers, chicken, sandwiches. Outdoor dining. In 1890s hardware store; vintage signs displayed. Cr cds: A, D, MC, V.

★ ★ **IVY INN.** *2244 Old Ivy Inn (22903). 434/977-1222. www.ivyinn*

restaurant.com. Hrs: 5-9:30 pm. Closed Sun. Res required. Dinner $18-$27. Sun brunch $8-$13. Specializes in regional cuisine. Outdoor dining. Victorian-style house (1804); fireplaces. Totally nonsmoking. Cr cds: A, D, MC, V.

★ ★ **L'AVVENTURA.** *220 W Market St (22902). 804/977-1912. www. vinegarhilltheatre.com.* Northern Italian menu. Specializes in osso bucco, grilled rainbow trout, crab and linguine. Hrs: 5:30-10 pm. Closed Sun, Mon, Thanksgiving, Dec 25. Res accepted. Wine list. Dinner $13-$20. Entertainment. Cr cds: A, MC, V. D

★ ★ **MAHARAJA.** *139 Zan Rd (22901). 434/973-0440.* Hrs: noon-2 pm, 5-10 pm; Mon from 5 pm. Closed Dec 25. Res accepted. Indian menu. Bar. Buffet: lunch $6.99. A la carte entrees: dinner $11.90-$13.90. Specializes in vegetarian dishes, chicken, seafood. Own baking. Outdoor dining. Casual decor; Indian pictures, urns. Totally nonsmoking. Cr cds: A, C, D, DS, MC, V. D

★ ★ ★ **OLD MILL ROOM.** *US 250 W (22905). 804/972-2230. www.boars headinn.com.* Hrs: 7-10 am, 11:30 am-1:30 pm, 6-9:30 pm; Sat, Sun 7-10:30 am, 11:30 am-1:30 pm; 6-9 pm; Sun brunch 11:30 am-2 pm. Res accepted. Contemporary American menu. Bar 4 pm-midnight. Extensive wine list. Bkfst $4.95-$11, lunch $6.50-$15, dinner $21-$33. Sun brunch $15.95. Child's menu. Salad bar. Own baking. Jazz Tues-Sat evening; harpist Sun. Valet parking. Outdoor dining. 19th-century decor with mahogany woodwork, fireplaces, framed artwork. Cr cds: A, D, DS, MC, V. D

★ ★ ★ **THE RESTAURANT.** *701 Club Dr, Keswick (22947). 434/979-3440. www.orient-expresshotels.com.* Hrs: 6:30-9:30 pm; Sun 11:30 am-2:30 pm (brunch). Res required. Continental menu. Wine cellar. Dinner $21-$33. Sun brunch $25. Own baking. Entertainment Fri-Sun. Valet parking. Elegant dining in Victorian setting; murals, fireplaces, antiques. Totally nonsmoking. Cr cds: A, D, JCB, MC, V. D

★ ★ **ROCOCO'S.** *2001 Commonwealth Dr (22901). 434/971-7371. www.rococos.com.* Hrs: 11 am-4 pm; Sat 5-10 pm; Sun 11 am-3 pm. Closed Dec 25. Italian menu. Lunch $8-$9, dinner $14-$24. Sun brunch $7-$10. Child's menu. Specializes in pasta, pizza, mesquite-grilled seafood. Cr cds: A, D, DS, MC, V. D

★ ★ **SCHNITZELHOUSE.** *2208 Fontaine Ave (22903). 434/293-7185.* Hrs: 5-9:30 pm. Closed Sun, Mon; hols; 1 wk Jan, also 1 wk July. Res accepted. Swiss, German menu. Bar. Complete meals: dinner $12.95-$29. Child's menu. Specializes in veal. Parking. Alpine decor. Cr cds: A, MC, V.

Chesapeake

(F-8) *See also Norfolk, Portsmouth, Virginia Beach*

Pop 199,184 **Elev** 12 ft **Area code** 757
Information Public Communications Dept, 306 Cedar Rd, PO Box 15225, 23328; 757/382-6241
Web www.chesapeake.va.us

This city is located in the heart of the Hampton Roads area, at the northeastern boundary of the Great Dismal Swamp National Wildlife Refuge (see).

What to See and Do

Northwest River Park. Approx eight mi of hiking/nature trails wind through this 763-acre city park. Fishing, boating, canoeing (ramp, rentals); picnicking (shelters), playground, nine-hole miniature golf, camping, tent and trailer sites (Apr-Dec, daily; fee; hookups, dump station). Shuttle tram. (Daily; closed Jan 1, Dec 25) Fragrance trail for the visually impaired. 1733 Indian Creek Rd, off Battlefield Blvd (VA 168). Phone 757/421-3145. **FREE**

Special Event

Chesapeake Jubilee. City Park. National and regional entertainment, carnival, food booths, fireworks. Third wkend May.

Motels/Motor Lodges

★★ **COMFORT SUITES.** *1550 Crossways Blvd (23320). 757/420-1600; fax 757/420-0099; res 800/228-5150. www.comfortinn.com.* 123 suites, 3 story. Apr-Oct: S, D $65-$100; each addl $7; under 18 free; higher rates: Labor Day, Jubilee; lower rates rest of yr. Crib free. TV; cable (premium), VCR (movies $5). Pool; whirlpool. Complimentary continental bkfst. Coffee in rms. Ck-out 11 am. Meeting rm. Business servs avail. Exercise equipt; sauna. Refrigerators, microwaves. Cr cds: A, D, DS, MC, V.
D ⇔ 🏋 ⊠ 🔥

★ **DAYS INN.** *1433 N Battlefield Blvd (23320). 757/547-9262; fax 757/547-4334; res 800/329-7466. www.daysinn.com.* 90 rms, 2 story. May-Sept: S, D $55-$95; each addl $5; under 12 free; wkly rates (off season); lower rates rest of yr. TV; cable (premium), VCR avail (movies). Pool. Complimentary continental bkfst. Restaurant adj open 24 hrs. Ck-out 11 am. Business servs avail. Health club privileges. Some refrigerators, microwaves. Cr cds: A, C, D, DS, MC, V.
D ⇔ ⊠ 🔥

★★ **FAIRFIELD INN.** *1560 Cross Ways Blvd (23320). 757/420-1300; fax 757/366-0608. www.fairfieldinn.com.* 113 rms, 3 story. May-Aug: S $52-$70; D $56-$72; under 18 free; higher rates special events. Crib free. TV; cable (premium). Pool. Complimentary continental bkfst. Restaurant nearby. Ck-out noon. Meeting rm. Business center. In-rm modem link. Exercise equipt. Cr cds: A, C, D, DS, MC, V.
D ⇔ 🏋 ⊠ 🔥 🏃

★★ **HAMPTON INN.** *701A Woodlake Dr (23320). 757/420-1550; fax 757/424-7414. www.hamptoninn.com.* 119 rms, 4 story. Memorial Day-Labor Day: S, D $65-$85; higher rates summer wkends; lower rates rest of yr. Crib free. TV; cable (premium). Pool. Complimentary continental bkfst. Coffee in rms. Restaurant adj 6:30 am-10 pm. Ck-out noon. Meeting rm. Business servs avail. In-rm modem link. Health club privileges.

Microwaves avail. Cr cds: A, C, D, DS, MC, V.
D ⇔ ⊠ 🔥

★★ **HOLIDAY INN.** *725 Woodlake Dr (23320). 757/523-1500; fax 757/523-0683; toll-free 800/465-4329. www.holiday-inn.com.* 230 units, 7 story. S, D $74-$109; each addl $10; suites $89-$119; under 18 free; higher rates: special events, hols, wkends. TV; cable (premium). Indoor pool; whirlpool. Coffee in rms. Restaurant 6:30 am-10:30 pm. Bar 11 am-midnight. Ck-out noon. Guest lndry. Meeting rms. Business servs avail. In-rm modem link. Bellhops. Sundries. Free airport transportation. Exercise equipt; sauna. Some refrigerators; microwaves avail. Cr cds: A, C, D, DS, JCB, MC, V.
D ⇔ 🏋 ⊠ 🔥 SC

★ **SUPER 8 MOTEL.** *3216 Churchland Blvd (23321). 757/686-8888. www.super8.com.* 59 rms, 3 story. May-Sept: S $44.88-$50.88; D $56.88-$68.88; each addl $6; suites $68.88-$76.88; under 16 free; wkly rates; higher rates special events; lower rates rest of yr. Crib free. Pet accepted, some restrictions. TV; cable (premium). Complimentary continental bkfst. Restaurant opp 6 am-midnight. Ck-out 11 am. Meeting rms. Business servs avail. In-rm modem link. Cr cds: A, C, D, DS, JCB, MC, V.
D 🐾 ⊠ 🔥 SC

★★ **WELLESLEY INN.** *721 Conference Center Dr (23320). 757/366-0100; fax 757/366-0396; res 800/444-8888.* 106 rms, 4 story. S $80-$110; D $85-$110; each addl $10; suites $100-$140; under 18 free. Pet accepted; $5. TV; cable (premium). Pool. Complimentary continental bkfst. Coffee in rms. Restaurant adj 6:30 am-10:30 pm. Ck-out 11 am. Meeting rms. Business servs avail. In-rm modem link. Valet serv. Coin lndry. Health club privileges. Refrigerators, microwaves. Cr cds: A, C, D, DS, ER, JCB, MC, V.
D 🐾 ⇔ ⊠ 🔥 SC

Restaurants

★★ **KYOTO.** *1412 Greenbriar Pkwy (23320). 757/420-0950.* Hrs: 11 am-2 pm, 5-10 pm; Sun 4-9 pm. Closed July 4, Thanksgiving, Dec 25. Res accepted. Japanese menu. Bar. Lunch $4.50-$13, dinner $8.95-$20.95. Child's menu. Specialties: teppanyaki, Kyoto special, sukiyaki. Sushi bar. Original Asian art. Cr cds: A, D, DS, MC, V.

D ➡

★ ★ **LOCKS POINTE.** *136 N Battlefield Blvd (23320).* 757/547-9618. *www.lockspointe.com.* Hrs: 11:30 am-3 pm, 5-10 pm; Sat from 5 pm; Sun 10:30 am-9 pm; Sun brunch to 3 pm. Closed Mon; Dec 24, 25. Res accepted. Bar 4 pm-1:30 am. Lunch $4.50-$6.95, dinner $8.95-$21.95. Sun brunch $7.95. Child's menu. Specializes in fresh seafood. Entertainment wkends. Outdoor dining. On Intracoastal Waterway; dockage. Cr cds: A, MC, V.

D

★ **TABOO.** *1036 Volvo Pkwy (23320).* 757/548-1996. Hrs: 11 am-10 pm; Fri to 11 pm; Sat 4-11 pm. Closed Sun; hols. Res accepted. Bar. Lunch $5.95-$9.95, dinner $8.95-$19.95. Child's menu. Specializes in crab cakes, black Angus steaks, wood-fired pizzas. Own breads. Colorful, contemporary decor. Cr cds: A, DS, MC, V.

D ➡

Chesapeake and Ohio Canal National Historical Park

(see Maryland)

Chincoteague

Founded 1662 **Pop** 4,317 **Elev** 4 ft
Area code 757 **Zip** 23336
Information Chamber of Commerce, 6733 Maddox Blvd, PO Box 258; 757/336-6161
Web www.chincoteaguechamber.com

Chincoteague oysters, wild ponies, and good fishing are the stock in trade of this small island, connected with Chincoteague National Wildlife Refuge by a bridge and to the mainland by 10 miles of highway (VA 175, from US 13), causeways, and bridges.

The oysters, many of them grown on the hard sand bottoms off Chincoteague from seed or small oysters brought from natural beds elsewhere, are among the best in the East. Clams and crabs are also plentiful. Commercial fishing has always been the main occupation of the islanders, but now, catering to those who fish for fun is also important economically.

Chincoteague's wild ponies are actually small horses but when full-grown somewhat larger and more graceful than Shetlands. They are thought to be descended from horses that swam ashore from a wrecked Spanish galleon, their limited growth caused by generations of marsh grass diet.

What to See and Do

🌟 **Assateague Island.** Accessible by bridge from town. Incl Chincoteague National Wildlife Refuge and Virginia unit of Assateague Island National Seashore. A 37-mi barrier island, Assateague's stretches of ocean and sand dunes, forest, and marshes create a natural environment unusual on the East coast. Sika deer, a variety of wildlife and countless birds, incl the peregrine falcon (autumn), can be found here, but wild ponies occasionally roaming the marshes offer the most exotic sight for visitors. Nature and auto trails; interpretive programs. Swimming (bathhouse), lifeguards in summer, surf fishing; camping, hike-in and canoe-in camp sites and day-use facilities. Picnicking permitted in designated areas; cars are limited to designated roads. No pets allowed. Obtain information at Toms Cove Visitor Center (spring-fall, daily) and at Chincoteague Refuge Visitor Center (daily). Access for disabled to all facilities. Contact the Chief of Interpretation, Assateague Island National Seashore, Rte 611, 7206 National Seashore Ln, Berlin, MD 21811; phone 410/641-1441 or 410/641-3030 (camping). (See OCEAN CITY, MD) Also contact Refuge Manager, Chincoteague National Wildlife Refuge, PO Box 62, 23336; 757/336-6122. ¢¢

NASA Visitor Center. Showcases world of past, present, and future flight. Features moon rock brought from *Apollo 17* mission; scale models of space probes, satellites, and aircraft; displays of current and future NASA projects; full-scale aircraft and rockets; films on space and aeronautics. Model rocket demonstrations (Mar-Nov, first Sat; June-Aug also third Sat, weather permitting). Picnic facilities. Gift shop. (July 4-Labor Day, daily; Sept-Nov and Mar-June, Mon and Thurs-Sun; closed hols) 5 mi S on VA 175 on Wallops Island. Phone 757/824-1344. **FREE**

Oyster and Maritime Museum of Chincoteague. Museum contains diorama, aquarium, shellfish industry interpretation. Also has the Wyle Maddox Library. (May-Aug, daily; Sept-Oct, Sat and Sun) 7125 Maddox Blvd. Phone 757/336-6117. ¢¢

Refuge Waterfowl Museum. Rotating displays of antique decoys and hunting tools. Decoy making and waterfowl art. Call ahead for hrs. (Daily; closed Dec 25) 7059 Maddox Blvd. Phone 757/336-5800. ¢¢

Sightseeing tours. Captain Barry's Back Bay Cruises & Expeditions. Incl Bird Watch Cruise, Back Bay Expedition, Champagne Sunset Cruise, Moonlight Excursions, and Fun Cruise. Trips vary from one to four hrs. Res recommended. Phone 757/336-6508. ¢¢¢¢

Special Events

Easter Decoy & Art Festival. Easter wkend. Phone 757/336-6161.

Chincoteague Power Boat Regatta. Late June. Phone 757/336-6161.

Pony Penning. The "wild" ponies are rounded up on Assateague Island, then swim the inlet to Chincoteague, where foals are sold at auction before the ponies swim back to Assateague. Carnival amusements. Last Wed and Thurs July. Phone 757/336-6161.

Oyster Festival. Columbus Day wkend.

Waterfowl Week. National Wildlife Refuge open to vehicles during peak migratory waterfowl populations. Late Nov.

Motels/Motor Lodges

★ **BIRCHWOOD.** *3650 Main St (23336).* 757/336-6133; fax 757/336-6535. 41 rms. Apr-Nov: S, D $43-$89; each addl $5; kits. $58-$97. Closed rest of yr. Crib $5. TV; cable. Pool. Playground. Complimentary coffee in lobby. Ck-out 11 am. Coin lndry. Refrigerators. Cr cds: A, DS, MC, V.
[icons]

★ **COMFORT INN.** *25297 Lankford Hwy, Onley (23418).* 757/787-7787; fax 757/787-4641. www.comfortinn.com. 80 units, 2 story, 10 suites. Mid-May-mid-Sept: S $62; D $69; each addl $5; suites $69-$83; under 18 free; lower rates rest of yr. Crib free. TV; cable. Pool. Complimentary continental bkfst. Restaurant adj 11 am-9:30 pm. Ck-out 11 am. Business servs avail. In-rm modem link. Exercise equipt. Refrigerators; microwaves avail. Cr cds: A, D, DS, MC, V.
[icons]

★ ★ **DRIFTWOOD MOTOR LODGE.** *7105 Maddox Blvd (23336).* 757/336-6557; fax 757/336-6558; toll-free 800/553-6117. www.driftwood motorlodge.com. 53 rms, 3 story. Mid-June-early Sept: S, D $86-$91; each addl $7; under 12 free; wkend, hol rates; lower rates rest of yr. Crib $6. TV; cable (premium). Pool. Complimentary coffee in lobby. Restaurant nearby. Ck-out 11 am. Business servs avail. Refrigerators. Private patios, balconies. Picnic tables. At entrance to Assateague National Seashore. Cr cds: A, C, D, DS, MC, V.
[icons]

★ ★ ★ **ISLAND MOTOR INN.** *4391 Main St (23336).* 757/336-3141; fax 757/336-1483; toll-free 800/832-2925. 60 units, 3 story, 16 suites. Mid-June-Labor Day: S, D $92-$150; suites $133-$150; under 16 free; lower rates rest of yr. Crib $5. TV; cable (premium). 2 pools, 1 indoor; whirlpool. Restaurant 6:30-11:30 am. Ck-out 11 am. Guest lndry. Meeting rms. Business servs avail. In-rm modem link. Sundries. Exercise rm. Refrigerators. Bathrm phone in suites. Balconies. Picnic tables, grills. On bay. Cr cds: A, C, D, DS, MC, V.
[icons]

★ **LIGHTHOUSE INN.** *4218 Main St N (23336). 757/336-5091; toll-free 800/505-5257.* 17 rms, 1-2 story. June-Aug: S, D $59-$75; each addl $6; min stays hols, special events; lower rates rest of yr. Crib $6. TV; cable. Pool; whirlpool. Complimentary coffee in rms. Restaurant nearby. Ck-out 11 am. Health club privileges. Refrigerators, microwaves. Picnic tables, grill. Cr cds: MC, V.

⊠ ⊠ ⊠ SC

★ **MARINER MOTEL.** *6273 Maddox Blvd (23336). 757/336-6565; fax 757/336-5351; toll-free 800/221-7490. www.esva.net/~motel.* 92 rms, 2 story. Mid-June-mid-Sept: S, D $54-$95; each addl $5; suites $95; under 12 free; wkly rates; hols 2-day min; higher rates special events; lower rates rest of yr. Closed Dec-Feb. Crib $5. TV; cable. Complimentary continental bkfst. Restaurant adj 5-10 pm. Ck-out 11 am. Meeting rms. Business servs avail. Sundries. Coin lndry. Pool. Playground. Many refrigerators; some microwaves. Picnic tables, grills. Cr cds: A, D, DS, MC, V.

D ⊠ ⊠ ⊠ ⊠

★★ **REFUGE INN.** *7058 Maddox Blvd (23336). 757/336-5511; fax 757/336-6134; toll-free 800/544-8469. www.refugeinn.com.* 70 units, 2 suites, 2 story, 1 cottage. June-Aug: S, D $92-$202; each addl $10; under 12 free; higher rates special events; lower rates rest of yr. Crib $5. TV; cable. Indoor/outdoor pool; whirlpool. Sauna. Ck-out 11 am. Coin lndry. Business servs avail. Meeting rm. Gift shop. Bicycle and beach gear rentals. Exercise equipt; sauna. Refrigerators; some in-rm whirlpools. In-rm coffee. Picnic tables, grill, playground. Near wildlife refuge and national seashore. Chincoteague ponies on grounds. Cr cds: A, D, MC, V.

D ⊠ ⊼ ⊠ ⊠

★ **SEA SHELL.** *3720 Willow St (23336). 757/336-6589; fax 757/336-0641.* 46 rms, 1-2 story. Mid-June-early Sept: S, D $66-$74; each addl $4; suites; kit. cottages $550-$600/wk; 2-day min wkends, 3-day min hols; lower rates Apr-mid-June, mid-Sept-Oct, Thanksgiving. Closed rest of yr. Crib $3. TV; cable. Pool. Complimentary coffee in rms. Restaurant nearby. Ck-out 11 am. Business servs avail. Refrigerators;

microwaves avail. Picnic tables. Cr cds: A, DS, MC, V.

D ⊠ ⊠ ⊠

★ **SUNRISE MOTOR INN.** *4491 Chicken City Rd (23336). 757/336-6671; fax 757/336-3752; toll-free 800/673-5211.* 24 units, 2 kits. Mid-June-early Sept: S $66; D $70; each addl $5; kit. units $540-$575/wk; under 12 free; lower rates mid-Mar-mid-June, early Sept-Nov. Closed rest of yr. Crib free. TV; cable. Pool. Playground. Complimentary coffee in lobby. Restaurant nearby. Ck-out 11 am. Business servs avail. Refrigerators. Picnic tables, grills. Cr cds: A, C, D, DS, MC, V.

D ⊠ ⊠

★★ **WATERSIDE MOTOR INN.** *3761 S Main St (23336). 757/336-3434; fax 757/336-1878. www.intercom.net/ local/chincoteague/hot/water.html.* 45 rms, 3 story. Mid-June-mid-Sept (2-day min): S, D $95-$150; each addl $5; suites (3-day min) $155; under 12 free; lower rates rest of yr. Crib $5. TV; cable (premium). Heated pool; whirlpool. Complimentary coffee in rms. Restaurant nearby. Ck-out 11 am. Coin lndry. Business servs avail. Sundries. Tennis. Exercise equipt. Refrigerators; microwaves avail. Balconies. Picnic tables, grills. On saltwater river; marina. Cr cds: A, C, D, DS, MC, V.

D ⊠ ⊁ ⊠ ⊼ ⊠ ⊠

B&Bs/Small Inns

★★★ **CEDAR GABLES SEASIDE INN.** *6095 Hopkins Ln (23336). 757/336-6860; fax 757/336-1291; res 888/491-2944. www.intercom.net/ user/cdrgbl.* 4 rms, 3 story, 2 suites. Memorial Day-Labor Day: S, D $150-$175; each addl $25; suites $175; wkends 2-day min, hols 3-day min; lower rates rest of yr. Children over 14 yrs only. TV; cable (premium), VCR (movies). Complimentary full bkfst; refreshments. Complimentary coffee in rms. Ck-out 11 am, ck-in 3 pm. Business servs avail. In-rm modem link. Luggage handling. Gift shop. Heated pool; whirlpool. Bathrm phones, in-rm whirlpools, refrigerators, balconies. Many balconies. Picnic tables, grills. On channel. Contemporary seaside location. Cr cds: A, DS, MC, V.

⊠ ⊠ ⊠ ⊠ SC

★ ★ ★ **CHANNEL BASS INN.** *6228 Church St (23336). 757/336-6148; fax 757/336-6599; res 800/249-0818. www. channelbass-inn.com.* 6 rms, 3 story. June-Sept: S, D $99-$175; suites $175; wkly rates; lower rates mid-Mar-May, Oct, Dec. Closed rest of yr. Children over 8 yrs only. Complimentary full bkfst; afternoon refreshments. Ck-out 11 am, ck-in 2 pm. Built 1892. Assateague Wildlife Refuge nearby. Totally nonsmoking. Cr cds: A, MC, V.
⊠ 🐾 SC

★ ★ **THE GARDEN AND THE SEA INN.** *4188 Nelson Rd, New Church (23415). 757/824-0672; toll-free 800/824-0672. www.gardenandseainn.com.* 6 rms in 2 bldgs. No rm phones. July-Sept: D $75-$165; under 6 free; wkends (2-day min); wkday rates; lower rates mid-Mar-June, Oct-Nov. Closed rest of yr. Pet accepted. Complimentary continental bkfst; afternoon refreshments. Restaurant (see also THE GARDEN AND THE SEA INN). Ck-out 11 am, ck-in 3 pm. Business servs avail. Luggage handling. Concierge serv. Some in-rm whirlpools. Patio and garden. Built as Bloxom's Tavern (1802) and adj farmhouse. Cr cds: A, DS, MC, V.
D 🐾 ⊠ 🐾

★ ★ **MISS MOLLY'S INN.** *4141 Main St (23336). 757/336-6686; fax 757/336-0600; toll-free 800/221-5620. www.missmollys-inn.com.* 7 rms, 2 share bath, 3 story. Memorial Day-Sept: S $89-$145; D $99-$155; each addl $20; lower rates Mar-late May, Oct-Dec. Closed rest of yr. Children over 8 yrs only wkends. Complimentary full bkfst; afternoon refreshments. Restaurant nearby. Ck-out 11 am, ck-in 2 pm. Business servs avail. Near saltwater bay. In historic building (1886); library, sitting rm; antiques. Marguerite Henry stayed here while writing Misty of Chincoteague. Cr cds: A, DS, MC, V.
⊠ 🐾

★ ★ **SPINNING WHEEL BED AND BREAKFAST.** *31 N St, Onancock (23417). 757/787-7311; fax 757/787-8555.* 5 rms, all with shower only, 3 story. No rm phones. S, D $75-$95; each addl $10. Closed Nov-Mar. Children over 12 yrs only. Complimentary full bkfst. Ck-out 11 am, ck-in 3

pm. Luggage handling. 18-hole golf privileges, pro, putting green, driving range. Built in 1890s. Folk Victorian inn; antiques. Cr cds: DS, MC, V.
🏌 ⊠ 🐾

★ ★ **WATSON HOUSE.** *4240 Main St (23336). 757/336-1564; fax 757/336-5776; toll-free 800/336-6787. www. chincoteauge.com/b-b/watson.* 6 rms, 5 with shower only, 2 story. No rm phones. Memorial Day-Labor Day: S $79-$99; D $89-$109; each addl $15; higher rates: wkends (2-day min), hols (3-day min); lower rates Mar-late May, early Sept-Thanksgiving. Closed rest of yr. Children over 9 yrs only. Complimentary full bkfst; afternoon refreshments. Restaurant nearby. Ck-out 11 am, ck-in 2 pm. Business servs avail. Bicycles. Health club privileges. Victorian residence (1874). Totally nonsmoking. Cr cds: MC, V.
⊠ 🐾

Restaurants

★ **DON'S SEAFOOD.** *4113 Main St, Chincoteague Island (23336). 757/336-5715.* Hrs: 7 am-9 pm. Closed mid-Jan-late Mar. Bar 10 am-10 pm. Bkfst $2.95-$3.95, lunch $3.95-$4.95, dinner $9.95-$15.95. Child's menu. Specialties: crab cakes, crab imperial, flounder. Salad bar. Entertainment Wed, Fri, Sat in summer. Parking. Vew of channel. Family-owned since 1973. Cr cds: D, DS, MC, V.
D ⊠

★ ★ **THE GARDEN AND THE SEA INN.** *4188 Nelson Rd, New Church (23415). 757/824-0672. www.garden andseainn.com.* Hrs: 6-9 pm. Closed Mon-Wed; also Dec-Mar. Res accepted. Wine list. A la carte entrees: dinner $14.75-$23. Complete meals: dinner $27.50-$33. Specializes in Northern French cuisine, seafood. Intimate dining rm in historic country inn. Cr cds: A, DS, MC, V.
D

★ **LANDMARK CRAB HOUSE.** *6162 N Main St, Chincoteague Island (23336). 757/336-5552.* Hrs: 5-10 pm; early-bird dinner 4:30-6 pm. Closed Mon (Sept-May); also Dec 25. Res required Fri, Sat. Seafood menu. Bar to 2 am. Dinner $12.95-$21.95. Child's menu. Specializes in seafood, steaks. Salad bar. Piano bar Fri, Sat. Parking. Outdoor dining. On waterfront. Cr cds: A, DS, MC, V.

★ **STEAMERS SEAFOOD.** *6251 Maddoc Blvd (23336). 757/336-5478.* Hrs: 5-9 pm. Closed Nov-Apr. Wine, beer. Dinner $10.95-$19.95. Child's menu. Specializes in steamed crabs and shrimp. Nautical theme. Cr cds: DS, MC, V.

Clarksville

See also South Boston, South Hill

Pop 1,329 **Elev** 359 ft **Area code** 804 **Zip** 23927

Information Clarksville Lake Country Chamber of Commerce, 105 2nd St, PO Box 1017; 804/374-2436

Web www.kerrlake.com/chamber

What to See and Do

Occoneechee State Park. Approx 2,700 acres under development; long shoreline on John H. Kerr Reservoir (Buggs Island Lake). Fishing, boat launching; hiking, picnic shelters, tent and trailer sites (hookups, season varies). Amphitheater; interpretive programs. Standard fees. (Daily) 1½ mi E on US 58. Phone 434/374-2210.

Prestwould. (1795) Manor house built by Sir Peyton Skipwith; rare French scenic wallpaper; original and period furnishings; restored gardens. (April 15th-Oct, daily; rest of yr, by appt) 2 mi N on US 15. Phone 434/374-8672. ¢¢

Special Events

Native American Heritage Festival and Powwow. Occoneechee State Park. Native American music, dances, crafts. Phone 804/374-2436. Second wkend May.

Virginia Lake Festival. Juried arts and crafts show, beach music, dancers, gymnasts. Fun Run, antique car show, sailboat race, hot-air balloons. Food vendors. Phone 804/374-2436. Third wkend July.

Motels/Motor Lodges

★ **LAKE MOTEL.** *101 Virginia Ave (23927). 804/374-5500; fax 804/374-0108. www.conradusa.com/lakemotel.* 84 rms, 2 story, 3 suites. Mid-May-mid-Sept: S, D $53-$68; each addl $5; suites $65-$90; under 12 free; lower rates rest of yr. Pet accepted. TV; cable. Pool. Restaurant adj 6 am-10 pm. Bar 5 pm-1 am. Ck-out 11 am. Meeting rm. Business servs avail. Free airport transportation. Refrigerators avail. Picnic tables, grills. On lake; swimming. Cr cds: A, MC, V.

★ **QUALITY INN ON THE LAKE.** *103 2nd St (23927). 804/374-5023; fax 804/374-0900; res 800/228-5151.* 50 rms, 2 story, 8 suites. Feb-Oct: S, D $69-$79; each addl $5; suites $79-$95; under 18 free; wkends, hols (2-3 days min); higher rates lake festival; lower rates rest of yr. Crib $5. Pet accepted; $10. TV; cable (premium). Complimentary continental bkfst, coffee in rms. Restaurant nearby. Ck-out 11 am. Meeting rms. Business servs avail. In-rm modem link. Valet serv. Sundries. Pool. Refrigerators, microwaves. On lake. Cr cds: A, C, D, DS, MC, V.

Clifton Forge

See also Covington, Lexington, Warm Springs

Settled 1878 **Pop** 4,289 **Elev** 1,079 ft **Area code** 540 **Zip** 24422

Information Alleghany Highlands Chamber of Commerce, 501 E Ridgeway St; 540/862-4969

Web members.aol.com/ahchamber

The town, named after a tilt-hammer forge that operated profitably for almost a hundred years, is at the southern tip of the Shenandoah Valley just west of the Blue Ridge Parkway.

What to See and Do

C & O Historical Society Archives. Incl C & O Railroad artifacts, old blueprints for cars and engines, books, models, collection of photos. (Mon-Sat; closed hols) 312 E Ridgeway St, opp terminal building. Phone 540/862-2210. **FREE**

Douthat State Park. Nearly 4,500 acres, high in the Allegheny Mtns, with 50-acre lake. Swimming beach, bathhouse, trout fishing (fee/day), boating (Memorial Day-Labor Day; rentals, some electric and water hook-ups, launching, electric motors only); hiking, self-guided trails, picnicking, restaurant, concession, camping (fee), tent and trailer sites (Mar-Sept; no hookups), cabins (all yr). Visitor center, interpretive programs. Standard fees. (Daily) 8 mi N on VA 629. Phone 862/720-0540. **FREE**

Iron Gate Gorge. Perpendicular walls of rock rise from banks of Jackson River. James River Division of C & O Railroad and US 220 pass through gorge. Restored chimney of old forge is here. 2 mi S on US 220.

B&B/Small Inn

★ ★ **LONGDALE INN.** *6209 Longdale Furnace Rd (24422).* 540/862-0892; fax 540/862-3554. 10 rms, 3 with shower only, 4 share bath, 3 story, 2 suites. No A/C. Rm phones avail. S, D $75-$95; each addl $25; suites $95-$120; wkly rates. Crib $25. Pet accepted. TV in common rm; VCR. Complimentary full bkfst. Ck-out 11 am, ck-in 3 pm. Business servs avail. Gift shop. X-country ski 2 mi. Playground. Game rm. Lawn games. Many fireplaces. Picnic tables, grills. Virginia countryside setting; Victorian inn built in 1873. Totally non-smoking. Cr cds: A, DS, MC, V.

Colonial National Historical Park

Made up of four independent areas—Cape Henry Memorial, Colonial Parkway, Jamestown (see all three), and Yorktown Battlefield (see YORKTOWN)—this is where America as we know it began. Jamestown, Yorktown, and Williamsburg (not a National Park Service area) are connected by the Colonial Parkway. Each of these areas is described in this book under its own name. Abundant in natural as well as historical wealth, the park boundaries enclose more than 9,000 acres of forest woodlands, marshes, shorelines, fields, and a large variety of wildlife.

Colonial Parkway

See also Colonial National Historical Park, Jamestown (Colonial National Historical Park), Williamsburg, Yorktown

The Colonial Parkway is a 23-mile link between the three towns that formed the "cradle of the nation"—Jamestown, Williamsburg, and Yorktown. It starts at the Visitor Center at Jamestown, passes through Williamsburg (the Colonial Williamsburg Information Center is near the north underpass entrance), and ends at the Visitor Center in Yorktown.

At turnouts and overlooks along the route, information signs note such historic spots as Glebeland, Kingsmill, Indian Field Creek, Powhatan's Village, Fusilier's Redoubt, and others. A free picnic area is provided during the summer at Ringfield Plantation, midway between Williamsburg and Yorktown.

The parkway is free to private vehicles. Commercial vehicles are not permitted. Speed limit is 45 miles per hour. There are no service stations.

Covington

(D-4) *See also Clifton Forge, Hot Springs*

Founded 1833 **Pop** 6,303 **Elev** 1,245
ft **Area code** 540 **Zip** 24426
Information Alleghany Highlands
Chamber of Commerce, 501 E Ridgeway St, Clifton Forge 24422;
540/862-4969
Web members.aol.com/ahchamber

Named for its oldest resident, Covington developed from a small village
on the Jackson River. It is located in
the western part of Virginia known as
the Allegheny Highlands. The James
River Ranger District office of the
Washington and Jefferson national
forests is located here.

What to See and Do

Humpback Bridge. Erected in 1857,
this 100-ft-long structure was made
of hand-hewn oak held together
with locustwood pins. In use until
1929, it is now maintained as part of
a five-acre state highway wayside and
is the only surviving curved-span
covered bridge in the US. 3 mi W
just off US 60/I-64.

Lake Moomaw. The 12-mi-long lake
has a rugged shoreline of more than
43 miles set off by towering mountains. Surrounded by the Gathright
Wildlife Management Area and portions of the Washington and Jefferson national forests. Boating,
swimming, fishing, waterskiing; picnicking, camping (fee). Visitor center.
(Apr-Oct, daily) 13 mi N via US 220,
VA 687, follow signs to Gathright
Dam. Phone 540/962-2214. ¢

Motels/Motor Lodges

★★ **BEST WESTERN MOUNTAIN
VIEW.** *820 E Madison St (24426).*
*540/962-4951; fax 540/965-5714; toll-
free 800/465-4329. www.bestwestern.
com.* 79 rms, 2 story. S $52-$69; D
$66-$79; each addl $8; under 18 free.
Crib free. Pet accepted; $10. TV;
cable (premium). Pool; wading pool.
Coffee in rms. Restaurant 6 am-2 pm,
5-10 pm. Ck-out 11 am. Meeting
rms. Business servs avail. In-rm

modem link. Bellhops. Valet serv.
Some refrigerators. Cr cds: A, C, D,
DS, ER, JCB, MC, V.
⊡ ⊠ ⊠ ⊠ ⊠ SC

★ **COMFORT INN.** *203 Interstate Dr
(24426). 540/962-2141; fax 540/965-
0964; res 800/228-5160.* 99 units, 2
story, 32 suites. S $67-$76; D $76-
$86; each addl $9; suites $76-$86;
under 18 free. Crib free. Pet accepted;
$10. TV; cable (premium), VCR
(movies $4). Pool; whirlpool. Restaurant 7 am-midnight. Bar 4 pm-2 am.
Ck-out 11 am. Business servs avail.
Guest lndry. Sundries. Some refrigerators. Cr cds: A, C, D, DS, ER, JCB,
MC, V.
⊡ ⊠ ⊠ ⊠ ⊠ SC

B&B/Small Inn

★★★ **MILTON HALL BED AND
BREAKFAST INN.** *207 Thorny Ln
(24426). 540/965-0196; fax 540/962-
8232.* 6 rms, 2 with shower only, 2
story, 1 suite. Some rm phones. S $75;
D $85; each addl $10; suite $130-
$140; under 10 free. Pet accepted. TV
in some rms, sitting rm; cable (premium). Complimentary full bkfst. Ck-
out noon, ck-in 2 pm. Lawn games.
Historic country manor house (1874)
on 44 acres adj George Washington
National Forest. Cr cds: DS, MC, V.
⊠ ⊠ SC

Culpeper

(D-6) *See also Orange, Warrenton*

Founded 1748 **Pop** 9,664 **Elev** 430 ft
Area code 540 **Zip** 22701
Information Chamber of Commerce,
133 W Davis St; 540/825-8628

Volunteers from Culpeper, Fauquier,
and Orange counties marched to
Williamsburg in 1777 in answer to
Governor Patrick Henry's call to
arms. Their flag bore a coiled rattlesnake with the legends "Don't
Tread on Me" and "Liberty or
Death."

In the winter of 1862-1863,
churches, homes, and vacant buildings in Culpeper were turned into

hospitals for the wounded from the battles of Cedar Mountain, Kelly's Ford, and Brandy Station. Later, the Union Army had headquarters here.

Today Culpeper is a light industry and trading center for a five-county area, with a healthy agriculture industry.

What to See and Do

Dominion Wine Cellars. Tours and tasting. (Daily; closed hols) Winery Ave, 2 mi S on VA 3. Phone 540/825-3772. **FREE**

Motels/Motor Lodges

★ **COMFORT INN.** *890 Willis Ln (22701). 540/825-4900; fax 540/825-4904; toll-free 800/228-5150. www.comfortinn.com.* 49 rms, 2 story. Apr-Oct: S $65; D $74; each addl $7; under 18 free. Crib free. Pet accepted, some restrictions; $5. TV; cable (premium). Pool. Complimentary continental bkfst, coffee in rms. Ck-out 11 am. Business servs avail. In-rm modem link. Refrigerators, microwaves avail. Cr cds: A, C, D, DS, JCB, MC, V.

 🐾 ➯ 🛏 🔥 **SC**

★★ **HOLIDAY INN.** *791 James Madison Rd S (22701). 540/825-1253; fax 540/825-7134; toll-free 800/465-4329. www.holiday-inn.com.* 159 rms, 2 story. S, D $74; under 19 free. Crib free. Pet accepted, some restrictions. TV; cable (premium). Pool; wading pool. Complimentary coffee in rms. Restaurant 6 am-2 pm, 5-10 pm. Rm serv. Bar 2 pm-12:30 am. Ck-out noon. Coin lndry. Meeting rms. Business servs avail. In-rm modem link. Valet serv. Sundries. Refrigerators avail. Cr cds: A, C, D, DS, JCB, MC, V.

🅳 🐾 ➯ 🛏 🔥 **SC**

B&B/Small Inn

★★★ **FOUNTAIN HALL BED AND BREAKFAST.** *609 S East St (22701). 540/825-8200; fax 540/825-7716; toll-free 800/298-4748. www.fountainhall.com.* 6 rms, 2 story, 2 suites. S, D $85-$150; suites $150; Oct, some hols (2-day min). Crib $10. TV; cable (premium); VCR in common rm. Complimentary continental bkfst; afternoon refreshments. Ck-out 11

am, ck-in 2 pm. Business servs avail. In-rm modem link. Health club privileges. Lawn games. Some fireplaces, in-rm whirlpools. Balconies. Picnic tables. Colonial Revival house (1859). Totally nonsmoking. Cr cds: A, C, D, DS, MC, V.

🅳 🔥

Guest Ranch

★★ **GRAVES' MOUNTAIN LODGE.** *VA 670, Syria (22743). 540/923-4231; fax 540/923-4312. www.gravesmountain.com.* 40 rms, 13 cottages, 8 kits. AP, mid-Mar-Nov: S $57-$92; D $65-$98/person; kit. cottages $110-$230; higher rates Oct. Closed rest of yr. Crib free. Pet accepted. Pool; wading pool, lifeguard. Playground. Dining rm (public by res) 8:30-9:30 am, 12:30-1:30 pm, 6:30-7:30 pm. Box lunches. Ck-out 11 am, ck-in 3 pm. Coin lndry. Grocery ¼ mi. Meeting rms. Business servs avail. Tennis. Golf privileges, greens fee $45. Lawn games. Rec rm. Some fireplaces; refrigerators, microwaves avail. Picnic tables, grills. Cr cds: DS, MC, V.

🅳 🐾 🦌 🔥 🎿 ➯ 🛏 🔥 🎣

Restaurant

★★★ **PRINCE MICHEL.** *US 29 S HCR 4, Box 77, Leon (22725). 540/547-9720. www.princemichel.com.* Hrs: noon-2 pm, 6-9 pm; Sun 11 am-2:30 pm. Closed Mon-Wed; hols; also Dec 25-mid-Jan, mid-June-mid-July. Res accepted. French menu. Serv bar. Wine list. Complete meal: lunch $25-$35; dinner $70, Sat $80. Specialties: venison in red wine sauce, medallions of lamb, hot foie gras with apples. Outdoor dining. Parking. Located at vineyard. Cr cds: A, DS, ER, MC, V.

🅳

Danville

(F-5) *See also Martinsville, South Boston*

Founded 1792 **Pop** 48,411 **Elev** 500 ft
Area code 804

Information Danville Area Chamber of Commerce, 635 Main St, PO Box 1538, 24543; 804/793-5422
Web www.danvillechamber.com

This textile and tobacco center blends the leisurely pace of the Old South with the modern tempo of industry. It is one of the nation's largest brightleaf tobacco auction markets. Dan River, Inc houses the largest single-unit textile mill in the world; other major industries are also located here. Nancy Langhorne, Viscountess Astor, the first woman to sit in the British House of Commons, was born in Danville in 1879.

What to See and Do

⊠ **Chatham.** Founded in 1777, this county seat of Pittsylvania County has many historically interesting houses, schools, and public buildings: **Hargrave Military Academy** (1909) with the Owen R. Cheatham Chapel and Yesteryear Hall (museum); **Chatham Hall** (1894) with Renaissance Chapel, stained-glass windows of women, and St. Francis mural in Commons Building; **Old Clerk's Office** (1813) restored as museum; **Courthouse** (1853) in Greek Revival style with delicate plaster ceiling frescoes and portraits; **Emmanuel Episcopal Church** (1844) with Gothic interior and signed Tiffany windows; and **Sims-Mitchell House** (1860s). Also of interest are the Educational and Cultural Center with planetarium and museum; antique shops, restaurants, trolley diners, and many private houses, several of which offer overnight accommodations. 17 mi N via US 29. Self-guided walking tour information for town and county may be obtained at the Chamber of Commerce, 38 Main St, Chatham 24531. Phone 434/432-1650.

Danville Museum of Fine Arts and History. Home of Major W. T. Sutherlin; built 1857. President Jefferson Davis and his cabinet fled to Danville after receiving news of General Lee's retreat from Richmond. It was during this time that the Sutherlin mansion served as the last capitol of the Confederacy. Victorian restoration in historical section of house (parlor, library, and Davis bedrm). Rotating art exhibits by national and regional artists. (Tues-Fri, also Sat and Sun afternoons; closed hols, also Dec 24-Jan 2) 975 Main St. Phone 434/793-5644. **FREE**

Danville Science Center. Hands-on museum for the entire family. Located in a restored Victorian train station. (Daily; closed Thanksgiving, Dec 25) 677 Craghead St. Phone 434/791-5160. ¢¢

Tobacco auctions. Several huge warehouses ring with the chants of tobacco auctioneers. (Aug-early-Nov, Mon-Thurs; closed Labor Day, Columbus Day, Veterans Day) Phone 434/793-5422. **FREE**

"Wreck of the Old 97" Marker. Site of celebrated train wreck (Sept 27, 1903), made famous by a folk song. On Riverside Dr (US 58) between N Main and Locust Ln overpass.

Special Events

Festival in the Park. Arts, crafts, entertainment. Phone 804/799-5200. Third wkend May.

Danville Harvest Jubilee. Celebration of tobacco harvest season. Phone 804/799-5200. Mid-Sept.

Motels/Motor Lodges

★ ★ **HOLIDAY INN EXPRESS.** *2121 Riverside Dr (24540). 804/793-4000; fax 804/799-5516. www.holiday-inn.com.* 98 rms, 3 story. S $58-$60; D $64-$66; each addl $6; under 16 free. Crib free. TV; cable (premium). Pool. Complimentary continental bkfst. Restaurant adj 6 am-10 pm. Ck-out noon. Meeting rm. Business servs avail. Health club privileges. Golf privileges. Bathrm phones; some refrigerators. Deck overlooking river. Cr cds: A, C, D, DS, MC, V.
🄳 🏊 🖎 🐾 🍴

★ **HOWARD JOHNSON.** *100 Tower Dr (24540). 804/793-2000; fax 804/792-4621; res 800/446-4656. www.hojo.com.* 118 rms, 6 story, 20 suites. S $69-$74; D $77-$82; each addl $8; suites $89-$97; under 18 free. Crib avail. TV; cable (premium). Pool. Coffee in rms. Restaurant 6:30 am-midnight. Bar from 11 am. Ck-out noon. Coin lndry. Meeting rms. Business servs avail. Valet serv. Health club privileges. Cr cds: A, D, DS, MC, V.
🄳 🏊 🖎 🔥

★ **INNKEEPER MOTOR LODGE.**
3020 Riverside Dr (24541). 804/799-1202; fax 804/799-9672; toll-free 800/466-5337. 118 rms, 2 story. S $40.99-$52.99; D $50.99-$70.99; each addl $5. Crib free. TV; cable (premium). Pool; whirlpool. Complimentary continental bkfst. Restaurant adj 6 am-midnight. Ck-out noon. Business servs avail. Health club privileges. Cr cds: A, C, D, DS, MC, V.

D ⇔ ⊠ ⚲

★ **STRATFORD INN.** *2500 Riverside Dr (24540). 804/793-2500; fax 804/793-6960.* 151 rms, 2 story. S, D $58-$75; each addl $7; suites $93-$165; under 18 free. Crib free. Pet accepted. TV; cable (premium). Heated pool; wading pool, whirlpool. Complimentary full bkfst. Restaurant 6 am-2 pm, 5-10 pm. Bar to midnight. Ck-out noon. Coin lndry. Meeting rms. Business servs avail. In-rm modem link. Valet serv. Sundries. Exercise equipt. Health club privileges. Cr cds: A, D, DS, MC, V.

D ⋪ ⇔ ⤨ ⊠ ⚲ SC

Dulles International Airport Area

See also Fairfax

Services and Information

Information. 703/419-8000.
Lost and Found. 703/572-2954.
Weather. 703/260-0307.

Airlines. Aeroflot, Air Canada, Air France, All Nippon, American, ANA, British Airways, Continental, Continental Express, Delta, Delta Connection, Japan Airlines, KLM, Lufthansa, Northwest, Qantas, Saudi Arabia Airways, Swissair, TACA, Transbrasil, TWA, United, United Express, USAir, Western Pacific.

What to See and Do

Reston Town Center. A 20-acre urban development incorporating elements of a traditional town square. Incl more than 50 retail shops and restau-

rants, movie theater complex, office space, and hotel. (See SPECIAL EVENTS) Adj Dulles Toll Rd (VA 267) at Reston Pkwy in Reston. Phone 703/709-8500.

Special Events

Northern Virginia Fine Arts Festival. Reston Town Center (see). Art sale, children's activity area, barbecue. Mid-May.

Summer Concerts. Reston Town Center (see). Sat eves June-Aug; also Thurs eves July.

Taste of the Town. Selected restaurants offer sample-size specialties. Last wkend June.

Oktoberfest. Reston Town Center (see). Biergarten with authentic German music, food. Mid-Sept.

Fountain Square Ice Rink. Reston Town Center (see). Outdoor public ice rink. Mid-Nov-mid-Mar.

Fountain Square Holiday Celebration. Reston Town Center (see). Choral groups, puppeteers, magicians, ice shows, dancers, parade. Thanksgiving-Dec 24.

Motels/Motor Lodges

★ **COMFORT INN DULLES AIRPORT.** *200 Elden St, Herndon (20170). 703/437-7555; fax 703/437-7572; toll-free 800/228-5160. www.comfortinn.com.* 103 rms, 3 story. S, D $119-$169; under 19 free; wkend plans. TV; cable (premium). Complimentary continental bkfst, coffee in rms. Restaurant adj 11 am-10 pm. Ck-out 11 am. Meeting rm. Business servs avail. Valet serv. Free airport transportation. Exercise equipt. Refrigerators; microwaves avail. Cr cds: A, C, D, DS, ER, JCB, MC, V.

D ⚲ ⤨ ⊠ ⚲ SC

★ ★ **COURTYARD BY MARRIOTT.** *533 Herndon Pkwy, Herndon (22070). 703/478-9400; fax 703/478-3628; toll-free 800/321-2211. www.courtyard.com/iadhc.* 146 rms, 3 story. S $129; D $139; suites $149; under 16 free; wkend rates. Crib free. TV; cable (premium). Indoor pool; whirlpool, lifeguard. Complimentary coffee in rms. Restaurant 6-10 am, 5-10 pm; wkends 7-11 am, 5-10 pm. Bar 5-10 pm. Ck-out noon. Coin lndry. Meeting rms. Business servs avail. In-rm modem link. Sundries. Valet serv. Free airport transportation. Exercise equipt. Refrigerators, microwaves avail. Cr cds: A, C, D, DS, MC, V.

⬛ 🛏 🏋 🔄 🔥 SC

★★ **COURTYARD BY MARRIOTT.** *3935 Centerview Dr, Chantilly (20151). 703/709-7100; fax 703/709-8672; toll-free 800/321-2211. www.courtyard. com.* 149 rms, 3 story. S $105; D $125; suites $129; under 12 free; wkly rates; higher rates special events. Crib free. TV; cable (premium). Indoor pool; whirlpool, lifeguard. Complimentary coffee in rms. Restaurant 6-10 am; Sat, Sun 7 am-noon. Restaurant opp 11 am-midnight. Rm serv 5-10 pm. Ck-out noon. Coin lndry. Meeting rms. Business servs avail. In-rm modem link. Valet serv. Sundries. Free airport transportation. Exercise equipt. Microwaves avail. Balconies. Picnic tables. Cr cds: A, C, D, DS, MC, V.

⬛ 🛏 🏋 🔄 🔥 SC

★ **DAYS INN.** *2200 Centreville Rd, Herndon (20170). 703/471-6700; fax 703/742-8965; toll-free 800/329-7466. www.daysinn.com.* 205 rms, 4 story. Apr-June, Sept-Oct: S, D $74-$139; each addl $10; under 18 free; wknd, monthly rates; lower rates rest of yr. Crib free. TV; cable (premium). Pool; whirlpool, lifeguard. Complimentary continental bkfst. Restaurant 6-1 am. Bar. Ck-out noon. Business servs avail. In-rm modem link. Bellhops. Sundries. Gift shop. Free airport transportation. Exercise equipt. Cr cds: A, C, D, DS, JCB, MC, V.

⬛ 🛏 🏋 ✈ 🔄 🔥 SC

★★ **HOLIDAY INN.** *1000 Sully Rd, Sterling (20166). 703/471-7411; fax 703/709-0785; res 800/465-4329. www. holiday-inn.com.* 296 rms, 2 story. S, D $160; suites $179-$209; each addl $10; under 18 free; wknd rates. Crib free. Pet accepted, some restrictions. TV; cable (premium). Indoor pool; whirlpool, lifeguard. Restaurant 6:30 am-10:30 pm. Rm serv to midnight. Bars 11-1:30 am, Sun to midnight; entertainment. Ck-out noon. Coin lndry. Meeting rms. Business center. In-rm modem link. Bellhops. Gift shop. Valet serv. Free airport transportation. Exercise equipt; sauna. Refrigerators, microwaves avail.

Game rm. Cr cds: A, C, D, DS, MC, V.

⬛ 🛏 🛟 🏋 🔄 🏃 🔄 🏃

★★ **HOLIDAY INN EXPRESS.** *485 Elden St, Herndon (20170). 703/478-9777; fax 703/471-4624. www. holiday-inn.com.* 115 rms, 4 story. S, D $99-$129; each addl $6; under 19 free. Crib free. Pet accepted, some restrictions. TV; cable (premium). Complimentary continental bkfst, coffee in rms. Restaurant nearby. Ck-out 11 am. Meeting rm. Business center. Valet serv. Free airport transportation. Exercise equipt. Refrigerators, microwaves avail. Cr cds: A, C, D, DS, JCB, MC, V.

⬛ 🛏 🏋 🔄 🔥 🏃

Hotels

★★★ **HYATT.** *2300 Dulles Corner Blvd, Herndon (20171). 703/713-1234; fax 703/713-3410; res 800/233-1234. www.hyatt.com.* 317 rms, 14 story. S $189; D $214; suites $300-$700; wkly, wkend rates. Crib free. TV; cable (premium), VCR avail. Indoor pool; whirlpool, lifeguard. Restaurant 6 am-midnight. Bar from noon; pianist. Ck-out noon. Business center. In-rm modem link. Gift shop. Free airport transportation. Exercise equipt; sauna. Refrigerators, microwaves avail. Cr cds: A, D, DS, MC, V.

⬛ 🛏 🏋 ✈ 🔄 🔥 🏃

★★★ **HYATT REGENCY.** *1800 President's St, Reston (22190). 703/709-1234; fax 703/709-2291; toll-free 800/233-1234. www.hyatt.com.* 514 rms, 12 story. S $215; D $235; each addl $25; suites $275-$550; under 18 free; wknd rates. Crib free. Garage parking; valet (fee). TV; cable (premium), VCR avail. Indoor pool; whirlpool, poolside serv, lifeguard. Restaurant (see also MARKET STREET BAR AND GRILL). Bar 11:30-2 am; entertainment Fri-Sun. Ck-out noon. Convention facilities. Business center. In-rm modem link. Concierge. Shopping arcade. Free airport transportation. Tennis privileges. Golf privileges. Exercise rm; sauna. Luxury level. Cr cds: A, C, D, DS, ER, JCB, MC, V.

⬛ 🏌 🛏 🏋 ✈ 🔄 🔥 SC 🏃 ⛷

★★★ **MARRIOTT SUITES WASH-INGTON DULLES.** *13101 Worldgate Dr, Herndon (20170). 703/709-0400; fax 703/709-0426; toll-free 800/228-*

9290. www.marriott.com. 253 suites, 11 story. S $175; D $190; under 18 free; wkend rates. Crib free. TV; cable (premium), VCR avail. Indoor/outdoor pool; whirlpool, lifeguard. Complimentary coffee in lobby. Restaurant 6:30 am-10:30 pm. Bar to 11 pm. Ck-out noon. Free guest lndry. Meeting rms. Business servs avail. In-rm modem link. Free garage parking. Free airport transportation. Exercise equipt; sauna. Health club privileges. Refrigerators, wet bars; microwaves avail. Cr cds: A, C, D, DS, ER, JCB, MC, V.

★ ★ ★ **MARRIOTT WASHINGTON DULLES AIRPORT.** 45020 Aviation Dr, Dulles (20166). 703/471-9500; fax 703/661-8714; res 800/228-9290. www.marriott.com. 367 rms, 3 story. S $154; D $169; each addl $15; suites $275-$300; under 18 free; wkend plans. Crib free. TV; cable (premium), VCR avail. 2 pools, 1 indoor; whirlpool, poolside serv. Restaurant 6 am-midnight; Sat, Sun from 6:30 am. Bar 11:30-1 am. Ck-out noon. Coin lndry. Convention facilities. Business center. In-rm modem link. Concierge. Gift shop. Free airport transportation. Lighted tennis. Exercise equipt. Lawn games. Microwaves avail. Picnic area. On 21 acres with small lake; attractive landscaping. Luxury level. Cr cds: A, C, D, DS, JCB, MC, V.

★ ★ ★ **SHERATON RESTON.** 11810 Sunrise Valley, Reston (20191). 703/620-9000. www.sheraton.com. 301 rms, 5 story. S, D $195-$250; under 17 free. Crib avail. TV; cable (premium). Pool; whirlpool. Restaurant 6:30 am-10 pm. Bar to midnight. Ck-out noon, ck-in 3 pm. Meeting rms. Business center. In-rm modem link. Concierge. Exercise equipt. Minibars; many refrigerators in suites. Cr cds: A, D, DS, MC, V.

Resort

★ ★ ★ **MARRIOTT CONFERENCE CENTER WESTFIELDS .** 14750 Conference Center Dr, Chantilly (20151). 703/818-0300; fax 703/818-3655; res 800/228-9290. www.marriott.com. 340 rms, 4 story. S $195; D $215; each addl $20; suites $295-$695; under 12 free; MAP, AP avail; wkend rates. Crib free. Pet accepted, some restrictions; $50 deposit. TV; cable (premium), VCR avail. 2 pools, 1 indoor; whirlpool, poolside serv, lifeguard. Complimentary coffee in lobby. Restaurant (see also PALM COURT). Rm serv 6-1 am. Box lunches, picnics. Bar 11-1 am; entertainment. Ck-out 1 pm, ck-in 3 pm. Bellhops. Valet serv. Concierge. Gift shop. Convention facilities. Business center. In-rm modem link. Valet parking. Free airport transportation. Sports dir. Lighted tennis, pro. 18-hole golf, greens fee $85. Hiking. Bicycles. Lawn games. Basketball. Exercise rm; sauna, steam rm. Massage. Health club privileges. Minibars; some in-rm whirlpools; refrigerators avail. Balconies. Picnic tables. Cr cds: A, D, DS, MC, V.

Extended Stay

★ ★ **RESIDENCE INN BY MARRIOTT.** 315 Elden St, Herndon (20170). 703/435-0044; fax 703/437-4007; res 800/331-3131. www.residenceinn.com. 168 kit. units, 2 story. S, D $135-$174; wkend rates. Crib free. Pet accepted; $100 nonrefundable and $6/day. TV; cable (premium), VCR avail (movies). Pool; whirlpool, lifeguard. Playground. Complimentary continental bkfst, coffee in rms. Restaurant opp 6:30 am-10 pm. Ck-out noon. Coin lndry. Business servs avail. In-rm modem link. Valet serv. Sundries. Lighted tennis. Health club privileges. Microwaves. Picnic tables, grills. Cr cds: A, C, D, DS, JCB, MC, V.

Restaurants

★ ★ **CLYDE'S.** 11905 Market St, Reston (20190). 703/787-6601. www.clydes.com. Hrs: 11 am-midnight; Fri, Sat to 1 am; Sun 10 am-10 pm; early-bird dinner Mon-Fri 4:30-6 pm; Sun brunch to 4 pm. Closed Dec 25. Contemporary American menu. Bar to 2 am. Lunch $4.95-$10.95, dinner $4.95-$18.50. Sun brunch $4.95-$10.95. Specializes in aged beef, fresh seafood, hamburgers. Own baking, ice cream. Outdoor dining. Contemporary pub decor; toys, art and artifacts reminiscent of youth. Cr cds: A, D, MC, V.

D ⬛

★ ★ **FORTUNE.** *1428 N Point Village Ctr, Reston (20194). 703/318-8898.* Hrs: 11 am-10:30 pm; Fri, Sat to 11:30 pm. Res accepted; required Fri, Sat dinner. Chinese menu. Serv bar. A la carte entrees: lunch $1.95-$5.50, dinner $6.25-$20. Specializes in dim sum, seafood, traditional Hong Kong dishes. Chinese decor. Cr cds: DS, MC, V.

D

★ ★ **IL CIGNO.** *1617 Washington Plaza N, Reston (20190). 703/471-0121. www.ilcigno.com.* Hrs: 11:30 am-2:30 pm, 5:30-10 pm. Sun 5-9 pm. Closed hols. Res accepted; required Fri, Sat. Northern Italian menu. Bar. Lunch $8.95-$17.95, dinner $13.95-$25.95. Specializes in fish, veal, pasta. Own baking, pasta, ice cream. Outdoor dining overlooking Lake Anne. Split-level dining rm with original art. Cr cds: A, C, D, MC, V.

D ⬛

★ ★ ★ **MARKET STREET BAR AND GRILL.** *1800 Presidents St, Reston (20190). 703/709-6262. www.msbg. net.* Hrs: 6:30 am-2:30 pm, 5:30-10 pm; Fri, Sat to 10:30 pm; Sun to 9:30 pm. Res accepted; required Fri, Sat. Contemporary American, Asian menu. Bar. A la carte entrees: bkfst $4.50-$7.95, lunch $6.95-$14.95, dinner $13.75-$22.75. Sun brunch $17.95. Specializes in seasonal cuisine. Entertainment Fri-Sun. Valet parking. Outdoor dining. Bistro decor. Cr cds: A, D, DS, MC, V.

D

★ ★ ★ **PALM COURT.** *14750 Conference Ctr Dr, Chantilly (20151). 703/818-3522.* Hrs: 7 am-2 pm, 6-10 pm; Sun brunch 10 am-2 pm. Res accepted; required Fri, Sat, Sun brunch. Continental menu. Bar 11-1 am. Bkfst $4.75-$9.95, lunch $6.95-$15.95. A la carte entrees: dinner $21-$29.95. Prix fixe (Mon-Sat): $40. Sun brunch $30. Child's menu. Specializes in fresh seafood, game. Pianist. Valet parking. Formal decor. Cr cds: A, D, DS, MC, V.

D SC

★ ★ ★ **RUSSIA HOUSE.** *790 Station St, Herndon (20170). 703/787-8880.*

Hrs: 11:30 am-2:30 pm, 5:30-10 pm; Sat 5:30-10:30 pm; Sun 5-9 pm. Closed hols. Res accepted; required Fri, Sat. Continental, Russian menu. Bar. Wine list. Lunch $8-$12.95, dinner $14-$21.95. Complete meals (wkends): dinner $25-$45. Specializes in fresh seafood, beef, veal. Pianist, violinist Fri, Sat. Parking. Modern decor highlighted by Russian artwork. Cr cds: A, MC, V.

D

★ ★ **SIAM ASIAN BISTRO.** *328 Elden St, Herndon (20170). 703/742-8881.* Hrs: 11:30 am-10 pm; Fri to 10:30 pm; Sat noon-10:30 pm; Sun noon-9:30 pm; early-bird dinner Sun-Thurs 4:30-6:30 pm. Closed Dec 25. Res accepted; required Fri, Sat dinner. Asian, Thai menu. Bar. Lunch $6.95-$7.95, dinner $9.95-$12.95. Specialties: pad Thai, Thai curry. Own desserts. Outdoor dining. Contemporary Thai decor with light woods, etched glass. Cr cds: A, D, DS, MC, V.

D ⬛

★ ★ **SWEETWATER TAVERN.** *14250 Sweetwater Ln, Centreville (22020). 703/449-1100. www.sweetwater1-gar. com.* Hrs: 4:30-11 pm; Mon to 10 pm; Fri, Sat noon-1 am; Sun noon-10 pm; early-bird dinner Mon-Thurs to 6 pm. Closed Thanksgiving, Dec 25. Bar. Lunch $4.95-$9.95, dinner $4.95-$16.95. Child's menu. Specializes in hickory-fired Angus beef, fresh seafood, chops. Own baking. Microbrewery. Totally nonsmoking. Cr cds: A, MC, V.

D

★ **TORTILLA FACTORY.** *648 Elden St, Herndon (20172). 703/471-1156.* Hrs: 11 am-10 pm; Mon to 9 pm; Fri, Sat to 10:30 pm; Sun noon-9 pm. Closed hols. Res accepted. Mexican menu. Serv bar. Lunch $4.75-$6.95, dinner $5-$11.25. Child's menu. Specialties: carne machaca, chimichangas. Own tortillas. Folk music Tues. Cr cds: A, D, DS, MC, V.

D SC ⬛

★ **WINFIELD'S.** *5127 Westfield Blvd, Centreville (20120). 703/803-1040.* Hrs: 11 am-midnight; Fri, Sat to 1:30 am; Sun to 9 pm. Closed hols. Res accepted; required Fri, Sat dinner. Bar. Lunch $5.25-$8.50, dinner $7.95-$14.95; Child's menu. Specializes in fresh seafood, steaks. Outdoor dining. Sports bar; informal dining. Cr cds: A, D, MC, V.

Emporia (F-6)

Pop 5,665 **Elev** 110 ft **Area code** 804
Zip 23847

Motels/Motor Lodges

★ ★ **BEST WESTERN INN.** *1100 W Atlantic St (23847). 804/634-3200; fax 804/634-5459; toll-free 800/528-1234. www.bestwestern.com.* 99 rms, 2 story. Apr-Sept: S, D $45-$75; each addl $5; under 18 free; lower rates rest of yr. Crib free. Pet accepted. TV; cable (premium). Pool. Complimentary continental bkfst. Restaurant opp 6 am-10 pm. Ck-out 11 am. Meeting rms. Business servs avail. In-rm modem link. Exercise equipt. Some refrigerators, microwaves. Cr cds: A, C, D, DS, MC, V.

★ **COMFORT INN.** *1411 Skippers Rd (23847). 804/348-3282; toll-free 800/228-5150. www.comfortinn.com.* 96 rms, 2 story. S $48.95-$62.95; D $56.95-$62.95; each addl $4; family rates. Crib $2. Pet accepted. TV; cable (premium). Heated pool. Playground. Complimentary continental bkfst. Restaurant adj 6 am-11 pm; Fri, Sat 5 am-midnight. Business servs avail. In-rm modem link. Cr cds: A, C, D, DS, ER, MC, V.

★ **DAYS INN.** *921 W Atlantic St (23847). 804/634-9481; fax 804/348-0746. www.daysinn.com.* 122 rms, 2 story. June-Sept: S $45-$55; D $65-$75; each addl $6; under 18 free; lower rates rest of yr. Crib free. Pet accepted. TV; cable (premium). Complimentary full bkfst. Restaurant nearby. Ck-out noon. Business servs avail. Sundries. Coin lndry. Pool. Cr cds: A, C, D, DS, MC, V.

★ ★ **HAMPTON INN.** *1207 W Atlantic St (23847). 804/634-9200; fax*

804/348-0071; toll-free 800/426-7866. www.hamptoninn.com. 115 rms, 2 story. S $59-$65; D $69-$77; under 18 free. Crib free. Pet accepted. TV; cable (premium). Pool. Complimentary continental bkfst. Coffee in rms. Restaurant nearby. Ck-out 11 am. Cr cds: A, C, D, DS, MC, V.

Fairfax

(C-7) See also Alexandria, Arlington County (Ronald Reagan Washington-National Airport Area), Falls Church, McLean; also see District of Columbia

Pop 21,498 **Elev** 447 ft **Area code** 703
Information Fairax County Convention & Visitors Bureau, 8300 Boone Blvd, Suite 450, Tyson's Corner-Vienna 22182; 703/790-3329, 703/550-2450 (visitor center), or 800/7-FAIRFAX
Web www.visitfairfax.org

What to See and Do

County parks. For additional information contact Fairfax County Park Authority, 12055 Government Center Pkwy, Suite 927, 22035. Phone 703/324-8700.

> **Burke Lake.** Consists of 888 acres. Fishing, boating (ramp, rentals); picnicking, playground, concession, miniature train, carousel (summer, daily; early May and late Sept, wkends), 18-hole and par-three golf, camping (May-Sept; seven-day limit). Beaver Cove Nature Trail; fitness trail. Fee for activities. (Daily) 6 mi S on VA 123, in Fairfax Station. Phone 703/323-6601. ¢¢

> **Lake Fairfax.** Pool, boat rentals, fishing, excursion boat; picnicking, carousel, miniature train (late May-Labor Day, daily), camping (Mar-Dec; seven-day limit; electric addl fee). Fee for activities. (Daily) On VA 606 near Leesburg Pike in Reston. Phone 703/471-5415.

George Mason University. (1957) 24,000 students. State-supported, started as branch of University of

Virginia. Performing Arts Center features concerts, theater, dance; Fenwick Library maintains largest collection anywhere of material pertaining to Federal Theatre Project of the 1930s. Research Center for Federal Theatre Project contains 7,000 scripts, incl unpublished works by Arthur Miller, sets and costume designs, and oral history collection of interviews with former Federal Theatre personnel. (Mon-Fri; closed hols) 4400 University Dr. Phone 703/993-1000.

Regional parks. Contact Northern Virginia Regional Park Authority, 5400 Ox Rd, Fairfax Station 22039. Phone 703/352-5900.

Algonkian. An 800-acre park on the Potomac River; swimming (Memorial Day-Labor Day, fee), fishing, boating (ramp); golf, miniature golf, picnicking, vacation cottages, meeting and reception areas. 6 mi NE on VA 123 to VA 7, then 9 mi NW to Cascades Pkwy N, then 3 mi N near Sterling. Phone 703/450-4655. **FREE**

Bull Run. Consists of 1,500 acres. Themed swimming pool (Memorial Day-Labor Day, daily; fee); camping (one to four persons, fee; electricity avail; res accepted, phone 703/631-0550); concession, picnicking, playground, miniature golf, Frisbee golf, public shooting center, nature trail. (Mid-Mar-Dec) From Beltway I-66 W, exit at Centreville, W on US 29 3 mi to park sign. Per vehicle/for day use (non-residents only) ¢¢

Meadowlark Botanical Gardens. Lilac, wildflower, herb, hosta, native plants, and landscaped gardens on 95 acres. Incl three ponds; water garden; gazebos; trails. Visitor center. (Daily) Children under 7 free. 6 mi N off VA 123. Phone 703/255-3631. Apr 1-Oct 31 only. ¢¢

Sully. (1794) Restored house of Richard Bland Lee, brother of General "Light Horse Harry" Lee; some original furnishings; kitchen-washhouse, log house store, smokehouse on grounds. Guided tours. (Mon, Wed-Sun; closed Jan 1, Thanksgiving, Dec 25) 10 mi W on US 50, then N on VA 28 (Sully Rd), near Chantilly. Phone 703/437-1794. ¢¢

Special Events

Wolf Trap Farm Park for the Performing Arts. In Vienna, 8 mi NE on VA 123, then W on US 7 to Towlston Rd (Trap Rd), then follow signs. Varied programs incl ballet, musicals, opera, classical, jazz, and folk music. Filene Center open theater seats 3,800 under cover and 3,000 on lawn. Picnicking on grounds, all yr. Also free interpretive children's programs, July-Aug. For schedules and prices contact Wolf Trap Foundation, 1624 Trap Rd, Vienna 22182. Phone 703/255-1900. Late May-Sept.

Antique Car Show. Sully. Four hundred antique cars, flea market, and music. June.

Quilt Show. Sully. Quilts for sale, quilting demonstrations, and antique quilts on display. Sept.

Barns of Wolf Trap. ¾ mi S of Wolf Trap Farm Park on Trap Rd. A 350-seat theater with chamber music, recitals, mime, jazz, folk, theater, and children's programs. For schedule contact the Barns, 1635 Trap Rd, Vienna 22182. Phone 703/938-2404. Late Sept-early May.

Motels/Motor Lodges

★ **COMFORT INN.** *11180 Main St (22030). 703/591-5900; fax 703/273-7915; res 800/223-1223. www.comfort inn.com.* 205 rms, 6 story, 90 kit. units. Mid-Mar-mid-Nov: S, D $89-$109; kit. units $89-$129; under 18 free; higher rates special events; lower rates rest of yr. Crib free. TV; cable (premium), VCR avail (movies). Complimentary continental bkfst, coffee in rms. Restaurant 11 am-10 pm. Bar to 11 pm. Ck-out 11 am. Meeting rms. Business servs avail. Bellhops. Valet serv. Sundries. Gift shop. Coin lndry. Free airport, RR station transportation. Exercise equipt. 2 pools, 1 indoor; lifeguard. Game rm. Some in-rm whirlpools; microwaves avail. Cr cds: A, C, D, DS, JCB, MC, V.

D ⟲ 🏋 ⟲ 🐾 SC

★ ★ **COURTYARD BY MARRIOTT.** *11220 Lee-Jackson Hwy (22030). 703/273-6161; fax 703/273-3505. www.courtyard.com.* 144 rms, 3 story. S, D $109-$119; suites $134-$154; under 13 free; package plans. Crib free. TV; cable (premium), VCR avail. Indoor pool; whirlpool, lifeguard.

Complimentary coffee in rms. Restaurant 6:30-10 am; Sat 7-11 am; Sun 7 am-noon. Bar 5-10 pm. Ck-out noon. Coin lndry. Meeting rms. Business servs avail. In-rm modem link. Valet serv. Sundries. Exercise equipt. Health club privileges. Some refrigerators; microwaves avail. Private patios, balconies. Cr cds: A, C, D, DS, JCB, MC, V.

D ⇌ ⽊ ⊠ ⦿ SC

★ ★ **HAMPTON INN.** 10860 Lee Hwy (22030). 703/385-2600; fax 703/385-2742. www.hamptoninn.com. 86 rms, 5 story. S, D $82-$99; under 18 free. Crib free. TV; cable (premium). Complimentary continental bkfst, coffee in rms. Restaurant adj 7 am-11 pm. Ck-out noon. Meeting rms. Business servs avail. In-rm modem link. Exercise equipt. Health club privileges. Some refrigerators, wet bars; microwaves avail. Cr cds: A, C, D, DS, MC, V.

D ⽊ ⊠ ⦿ SC

★ ★ **HOLIDAY INN.** 11787 Lee Jackson Memorial Hwy (22033). 703/352-2525; fax 703/352-4471; res 800/465-4329. www.holiday-inn.com. 312 rms, 6 story. S, D $129-$149; each addl $10; under 19 free; package plans. Crib free. Pet accepted. TV; cable (premium), VCR avail. Indoor pool; lifeguard. Complimentary coffee in rms. Restaurant 6:30 am-midnight. Bar; entertainment. Ck-out noon. Coin lndry. Convention facilities. Business center. In-rm modem link. Concierge. Gift shop. Exercise equipt; sauna. Health club privileges. Game rm. Refrigerators avail. Balconies. Luxury level. Cr cds: A, D, DS, MC, V.

D 🐾 ⇌ ⽊ ⊠ ⦿

Hotel

★ ★ ★ **HYATT FAIR LAKES.** 12777 Fair Lakes Cir (22033). 703/818-1234; fax 703/818-3140; toll-free 800/233-1234. www.hyatt.com. 316 rms, 14 story. S, D $169-$199; each addl $25; suites $199-$475; under 18 free; wkend rates. Crib free. TV; cable (premium), VCR avail. Indoor pool; whirlpool, lifeguard. Restaurant 6:30 am-11 pm; Fri, Sat to midnight. Bar 11:30-1 am; entertainment. Ck-out noon. Convention facilities. Business

center. In-rm modem link. Free airport, RR station transportation. Exercise equipt; sauna. Health club privileges. Refrigerators, microwaves avail. Cr cds: A, C, D, DS, ER, JCB, MC, V.

D ⇌ ⽊ ⊠ ⦿ SC ⽊

B&B/Small Inn

★ ★ ★ **BAILIWICK INN.** 4023 Chain Bridge Rd (22030). 703/691-2266; fax 703/934-2112; toll-free 800/366-7666. www.bailiwickinn.com. 14 rms, some with shower only, 4 story. No elvtr. S, D $140-$310. TV; VCR avail. Complimentary full bkfst. Restaurant (see also BAILWICK INN). Ck-out 11 am, ck-in 2 pm. Health club privileges. Some in-rm whirlpools, fireplaces. Restored private residence (1800); antiques. The first Civil War skirmish occured here in June of 1861. Totally nonsmoking. Cr cds: A, MC, V.

D ⊠ ⦿ SC

Restaurants

★ ★ **ARTIE'S.** 3260 Old Lee Hwy (22030). 703/273-7600. www.arties-gar.com. Hrs: 11:30 am-11 pm; Fri, Sat to midnight; Sun 10:30 am-10 pm; Sun brunch to 3 pm; early-bird dinner Mon-Thurs 5-6 pm. Closed Thanksgiving, Dec 25. Bar. Lunch $7.25-$10.25, dinner $8.95-$16.50. Sun brunch $7.25-$9.95. Specializes in steak, seafood, pasta. Parking. Cr cds: A, MC, V.

D

★ ★ ★ **BAILIWICK INN.** 4023 Chain Bridge Rd (22030). 703/691-2266. www.bailiwickinn.com. Hrs: Wed, Thurs, Sun seatings 6:30, 7:30, 8:30 pm; Fri, Sat seatings 6, 8:30 pm; Fri lunch noon-2 pm. Closed Mon, Tues. Res required. American menu with Mediterranean influence. A la carte entrees: lunch $12-$18. Complete meals: dinner $45; Fri, Sat $55. Specializes in chicken, beef, seafood. Menu changes biweekly. Parking. Patio dining overlooking English garden. In restored inn (1800). Totally nonsmoking. Cr cds: A, MC, V.

SC

★ **BLUE OCEAN.** 9440 Main St (22031). 703/425-7555. Hrs: 11:30 am-2:30 pm, 5-10 pm; Fri to 10:30 pm; Sat noon-2:30 pm, 5-10:30 pm;

Sun from 5 pm. Closed hols. Res accepted. Japanese menu. Serv bar. Lunch $7.95-$9.95, dinner $9.50-$17.95. Specialties: sushi, teriyaki, sukiaki. Salad bar. Authentic Japanese decor; sushi bar. Cr cds: A, MC, V.

★ ★ **BOMBAY BISTRO.** *3570 Chain Bridge Rd (22030). 703/359-5810. www.bombaybistro.com.* Hrs: 11:30 am-2:30 pm, 5-10 pm; Fri, Sat to 10:30 pm; Sat, Sun brunch noon-3 pm. Closed Thanksgiving. Indian menu. Bar. A la carte entrees: lunch, dinner $5.95-$11.95. Buffet (Mon-Fri) $6.95. Sat, Sun brunch $8.95. Specializes in tandoori, vegetarian dishes. Outdoor dining. Indian decor. Cr cds: A, D, DS, MC, V.

★ ★ **CONNAUGHT PLACE.** *10425 North St (22030). 703/352-5959. www.connaughtplacerestaurant.com.* Hrs: 11:30 am-2:30 pm, 5-10 pm; Sat noon-3 pm, 5-10 pm; Sun noon-3 pm, 5-9 pm. Closed Thanksgiving, Dec 25. Res accepted. Indian menu. Bar. Lunch $5-$11, dinner $6.95-$16.95. Buffet $7.95-$8.95. Sat, Sun brunch $8.95. Specializes in seafood, vegetarian dishes. Sitar Fri, Sat. Middle Eastern decor. Cr cds: A, D, MC, V.

★ ★ **HEART-IN-HAND.** *7145 Main St, Clifton (20124). 703/830-4111. www.heartinhandrestaurant.com.* Hrs: 11 am-2:30 pm, 6-9:30 pm; Sun 5-8 pm; Sun brunch 11 am-2:30 pm. Closed Jan 1, July 4, Dec 25. Res accepted. Lunch $5.95-$12.95, dinner $14.95-$22.95. Sun brunch $6.95-$12.95. Specialties: beef Wellington, rack of lamb. Own ice cream. Parking. Outdoor dining. Converted general store (ca 1870). Antique decor; original floors, ceiling fans, antique quilts. Totally non-smoking. Cr cds: A, D, DS, MC, V.

★ ★ ★ **HERMITAGE INN.** *7134 Main St, Clifton (20124). 703/266-1623. www.hermitageinnrestaurant.com.* Hrs: 11:30 am-2:30 pm, 5:30-9 pm; Tues from 5:30 pm; Fri, Sat to 10 pm; Sun from 11 am. Closed Mon. Res accepted. French, Mediterranean menu. Serv bar. Lunch $5.50-$11.50. Prix fixe: dinner $28-$39. Sun

brunch $17.95. Specialties: paella, crepes Homard, châteaubriand. Own pastries. Outdoor dining. Located in 1869 clapboard hotel. Cr cds: A, C, D, DS, MC, V.

★ **P. J. SKIDOO'S.** *9908 Lee Hwy (22030). 703/591-4515. www.pjskidoos. com.* Hrs: 11-2 am; Sun 10 am-9 pm. Closed Thanksgiving, Dec 25. Bar. Lunch, dinner $5.50-$12.95. Sun brunch $8.95. Child's menu. Specializes in prime rib, fresh seafood, chicken. Entertainment Tues, Thurs-Sat. Parking. 1890s saloon atmosphere. Cr cds: A, MC, V.

Unrated Dining Spot

THE ESPOSITO'S/PIZZA 'N PASTA. *9917 Lee Hwy (22030). 703/385-5912.* Hrs: 11:30 am-10 pm; Fri to 11 pm; Sat from noon; Sun noon-10 pm. Closed Jan 1, Thanksgiving, Dec 25. Southern Italian menu. Wine, beer. A la carte entrees: lunch, dinner $3.50-$11.50. Lunch $5.50-$12.95, dinner $6.25-$13.95. Specialties: pollo Cardinale, fettucine alla Romano. Own pasta. Parking. Pizza baked in wood-burning oven imported from Italy. Italian trattoria decor. Cr cds: A, D, DS, MC, V.

Falls Church

See also Alexandria, Arlington County (Ronald Reagan Washington-National Airport Area), Fairfax, McLean; also see District of Columbia

Pop 10,377 **Elev** 340 ft **Area code** 703

Information Greater Falls Church Chamber of Commerce, 417 W Broad St, PO Box 491, 22040-0491; 703/532-1050

Web www.fallschurchchamber.org

Falls Church is a pleasant, cosmopolitan suburb of Washington, D.C. just over the Arlington County line, graced with many interesting old houses. This was a crossover point between the North and the South through which pioneers, armies, adventurers, and merchants passed.

What to See and Do

The Falls Church. (1769) Episcopal. This building replaced the original wooden church built in 1732. Served as a recruiting station during the Revolutionary War; abandoned until 1830; used during the Civil War as a hospital and later as a stable for cavalry horses. Restored according to original plans with gallery additions in 1959. (Mon-Fri, Sun; closed hols) Worship services Wed noon and Sun at 8 am and noon. 115 E Fairfax St at Washington St, on US 29. Phone 703/532-7600. **FREE**

Fountain of Faith. Memorial dedicated to the four chaplains—two Protestant, one Jewish, one Catholic—who were aboard the USS *Dorchester* when it was torpedoed off Greenland in 1943. They gave their life jackets to four soldiers on deck who had none. In National Memorial Park. Phone 703/560-4400.

Motel/Motor Lodge

★ **QUALITY INN.** 6650 Arlington Blvd (22042). 703/532-8900; fax 703/532-7121; res 800/228-5151. www.qualityinn.com. 121 rms. Mar-Sept: S $67-$83; D $70-$85; each addl $5; suites $95; under 18 free; lower rates rest of yr. Crib free. TV; cable (premium). Pool; lifeguard. Restaurant 6:30 am-10 pm; Sat, Sun from 7 am. Ck-out noon. Meeting rms. Business servs avail. Some refrigerators. Cr cds: A, C, D, DS, MC, V.

Hotel

★★★ **MARRIOTT FAIRVIEW PARK.** 3111 Fairview Park Dr (22042). 703/849-9400; fax 703/849-8692; toll-free 800/228-9290. www.marriott.com. 394 rms, 15 story. S $189; D $199; suites $250-$500; under 16 free. Crib free. TV; cable (premium), VCR avail. Indoor/outdoor pool; whirlpool, poolside serv, lifeguard. Coffee in rms. Restaurant 6:30 am-10 pm; Fri, Sat 7 am-11 pm. Bar 11-2 am. Ck-out noon. Coin lndry. Convention facilities. Business center. In-rm modem link. Concierge. Gift shop. Exercise

equipt; sauna. Some bathrm phones. Some balconies. Luxury level. Cr cds: A, C, D, DS, ER, JCB, MC, V.

Restaurants

★★ **BANGKOK STEAKHOUSE.** 926 W Broad St #A (22046). 703/534-0095. Hrs: 11 am-10 pm; wkends to 11 pm. Res accepted. Thai, Laotian menu. Lunch $3.95-$8.95, dinner $6.50-$9.25. Lunch buffet $5.95. Specialties: spicy Thai beef noodle, tom yam gung, kaeng seafood combo. Parking. Asian decor. Cr cds: A, D, DS, MC, V.

★★★ **DUANGRAT'S.** 5878 Leesburg Pike (22041). 703/820-5775. Hrs: 11:30 am-2:30 pm, 5-10 pm; Fri to 11 pm; Sat 11:30 am-11 pm; Sun 11:30 am-10 pm. Res accepted. Thai menu. Bar. Lunch $6.95-$8.95, dinner $9.95-$18.95. Specialties: pad Thai noodles, Thai curry, crispy fish with chili sauce. Parking. Display of Thai headdresses and masks. Cr cds: A, D, MC, V.

★★★ **HAANDI.** 1222 W Broad St (VA7) (22046). 703/533-3501. www. haandi.com. Hrs: 11:30 am-2:30 pm, 5-10 pm; wkends to 10:30 pm. Closed Dec 25. Res accepted Sun-Thur. Northern Indian menu. Serv bar. Lunch $5.95-$10.95, dinner $7.95-$14.95. Specializes in barbecued meats, chicken, vegetarian dishes. Parking. Totally nonsmoking. Cr cds: A, C, D, DS, ER, MC, V.

★★ **PANJSHIR.** 924 W Broad St (22046). 703/536-4566. www.enterit. com/panjshir566.htm. Hrs: 11 am-2 pm, 5-10 pm; Sun 5-9 pm. Closed July 4, Thanksgiving, Dec 25. Afghan menu. Bar. Lunch $6.50-$7.25, dinner $9.95-$13.25. Specializes in kebab, palows, vegetarian dishes. Parking. Totally nonsmoking. Cr cds: A, MC, V.

★★ **PEKING GOURMET INN.** 6029 Leesburg Pike (VA 7) (22041). 703/671-8088. pekinggourmet.com. Hrs: 11 am-10:30 pm; Fri, Sat to midnight. Closed Thanksgiving. Res accepted; required Fri, Sat. Northern Chinese menu. Serv bar. Lunch $6.25-$13.45, dinner $8.45-$24.95. Specialties: Peking duck, beef Szechuan, striped bass Peking-style. Parking. Asian antiques and screens; 300 yr-old jade Buddha; original artwork. Favorite of Washington politicians. Cr cds: A, MC, V.

D

★★ **PILIN THAI.** *116 W Broad St (VA 7) (22046).* 703/241-5850. Hrs: 11:30 am-10 pm; Fri, Sat to 11 pm; Sun 5-9 pm. Closed hols. Res accepted; required Fri, Sat dinner. Thai menu. Bar. Lunch $4.95-$6.95, dinner $7.95-$13.95. Specialties: spicy, crispy catfish; pad Thai; pad gra prow talay. Parking. Cr cds: A, D, DS, MC, V.

★★ **SECRET GARDEN BEEWON.** *6678 Arlington Blvd (22042).* 703/533-1004. Hrs: 11-1 am. Closed Jan 1. Res accepted; required Fri, Sat. Korean, Japanese menu. Serv bar. Lunch $5.50-$11.95, dinner $8.95-$18. Complete meals: lunch (Mon-Fri) $5.95-$9.95. Specialties: bulgogi, heamul chongol. Sushi bar. Parking. Tableside preparation. Traditional Korean decor. Cr cds: A, C, D, DS, MC, V.

⊒

★ **SIR WALTER RALEIGH INN.** *8120 Gatehouse Rd (22042).* 703/560-6768. Hrs: 11:30 am-2 pm, 5-9 pm; Fri to 10 pm; Sat 5-10 pm; Sun 4-8:30 pm; early-bird dinner 5-6 pm, Sun 4-5 pm. Closed Dec 25. Bar. Lunch $5.75-$10.95, dinner $7.95-$17.95. Child's menu. Specializes in steak, seafood. Salad bar. Parking. Cr cds: A, C, D, DS, MC, V.

D

Farmville

(E-6) See also Keysville

Pop 6,845 **Elev** 304 ft **Area code** 804 **Zip** 23901

Longwood College's Jeffersonian buildings provide architectural interest in downtown Farmville.

What to See and Do

Sailor's Creek Battlefield Historic State Park. Site of last major battle of Civil War on Apr 6, 1865, preceding Lee's surrender at Appomattox by three days. Auto tour. 9 mi E on US 460, then 7 mi NE on VA 307 and 2 mi N on VA 617. Phone 804/392-3435. **FREE**

Motels/Motor Lodges

★ **COMFORT INN.** *US 15 & US 460 Bypass (23901).* 804/392-8163; fax 804/392-1966; toll-free 800/228-5150. www.comfortinn.com. 51 rms, 2 story. S $53-$59; D $56-$62; each addl $6; under 18 free; higher rates special events. TV; cable (premium), VCR avail. Pool. Ck-out noon. Business servs avail. Cr cds: A, C, D, DS, ER, MC, V.

D ➔ ⊒ 🔥 SC

★ **DAYS INN.** *2011 S Main St (23901).* 804/392-6611; fax 804/392-9774. www.daysinn.com. 60 rms, 2 story. S $53; D $59; under 18 free; family, wkend, wkly rates; higher rates: homecoming wkend, graduation. Crib free. TV; cable (premium). Complimentary continental bkfst. Restaurant opp 11 am-9 pm. Ck-out 11 am. Business servs avail. Valet serv. Sundries. Pool. Picnic tables, grills. Cr cds: A, C, D, DS, JCB, MC, V.

D ➔ ⊒ 🔥

Fredericksburg

(D-6) See also Triangle

Settled 1727 **Pop** 19,279 **Elev** 61 ft **Area code** 540

Information Visitor Center, 706 Caroline St, 22401; 540/373-1776 or 800/678-4748.

Web www.fredericksburgvirginia.net

One of the seeds of the American Revolution was planted here when a resolution declaring independence from Great Britain was passed on April 29, 1775. Here is where George Washington went to school, where his sister Betty lived, and his mother, Mary Ball Washington, lived and

FREDERICKSBURG'S PRESIDENTIAL LEGACY

Midway between Washington and Richmond, the old colonial river port of Fredericksburg earned the dubious nickname of "battlefield city" in the Civil War, as the site of four major battles between 1862 and 1864. As a result, many visitors overlook its colonial antecedents and its unique status as the hometown of both George Washington and James Monroe, who were born not far away. This one-hour, one-mile stroll down its quiet tree-shaded streets is an introduction to this presidential legacy. Begin by visiting the Fredericksburg Visitor Center at 706 Caroline Street. Walk north along Caroline Street, the Historic District's attractive main street, which is lined with interesting shops and cafes. At George Street, turn left one block to Charles Street, and then go right to 908 Charles, the James Monroe Museum. As a young man, Monroe practiced law in an office on this site. The museum displays rich pieces of furniture he took with him to the White House as the country's fifth president. Continue north on Charles Street to Lewis Street and turn left onto Washington Avenue. Turn right a half block to Kenmore Plantation, the lovely mansion and garden at 2101 Washington. Built in 1752, it was the home of Betty Lewis, who was George Washington's sister, and her husband Fielding Lewis, a financier and gun manufacturer who aided the Revolutionary cause. The house is particularly noted for its richly decorated, hand-molded ceilings. From Kenmore, retrace your steps on Lewis Street for three blocks to Charles Street. At 1200 Charles Street stands the Mary Washington House, which George Washington bought for his mother in 1772 so she could be more easily looked after by daughter Betty. Though busy George, who lived 40 miles north at Mount Vernon, was a dutiful son, his mother often accused him of neglect, a story told at the museum. Continue east on Lewis to Caroline Street, and turn north (left) to the Rising Sun Tavern at 1306, the tour's conclusion. Built in 1760 as a private home by Charles Washington, George's younger brother, it has been restored to the 18th-century tavern it became in 1792.

died. James Monroe practiced law in town. Guns for the Revolution were manufactured here, and four of the most savage battles of the Civil War were fought nearby.

Captain John Smith visited the area in 1608 and gave glowing reports of its possibilities for settlement. In 1727, the General Assembly directed that 50 acres of "lease-land" be laid out and the town called Fredericksburg, after the Prince of Wales.

Ships from abroad sailed up the Rappahannock River to the harbor—ampler then than now—to exchange their goods for those brought from "upcountry" by the great road wagons and river carriers. The town prospered.

The Civil War left Fredericksburg ravaged. Situated midway between Richmond and Washington, it was recurringly an objective of both sides; the city changed hands seven times and the casualties were high.

Even so, many buildings put up before 1775 still stand. Proudly aware of their town's place in the

country's history, the townspeople keep Fredericksburg inviting with fresh paint, beautiful lawns, and well-kept gardens.

What to See and Do

Belmont (The Gari Melchers Estate and Memorial Gallery). Residence from 1916 to 1932 of American-born artist Gari Melchers (1860-1932), best known for his portraits of the famous and wealthy, incl Theodore Roosevelt, William Vanderbilt, and Andrew Mellon, and as an important impressionist artist of the period. The artist's studio comprises the nation's largest collection of his works, housing more than 1,800 paintings and drawings. The site is a registered National and State Historic Landmark and incl a 27-acre estate, frame house built in the late 18th century and enlarged over the years, and a stone studio built by Melchers. Owned by the state of Virginia, Belmont is administered by Mary Washington College. (Daily; closed hols)

224 Washington St. Phone 540/654-1843. ¢¢¢

George Washington Birthplace National Monument. (see)

George Washington's Ferry Farm. Site of George Washington's boyhood home. Once a tobacco plantation, it now serves as an archaeological dig and nature preserve. Guided tours. (Daily) 1 mi E on VA 3. Phone 540/370-0732. ¢

Mary Washington College. (1908) 3,700 students. Coeducational liberal arts and sciences institution incl historic preservation, computer science, and business administration. Incl 275 acres of open and wooded campus; red brick, white-pillared buildings. President of the college occupies Brompton (private), house built in 1830 on land sold to Fielding Lewis in 1760 and expanded by a later owner, Colonel John Lawrence Marye. Campus tours. College Ave. Phone 540/654-1000.

⭐ **Walking or driving tour of Fredericksburg.** Begin at

Visitor Center. Orientation film; information; obtain walking tour brochure and combination tickets here. 706 Caroline St. 3 blks N begin at

Hugh Mercer Apothecary Shop. This 18th-century medical office and pharmacy offers exhibits on the medicine and methods of treatment used by Dr. Hugh Mercer before he left to join the Revolutionary War as brigadier general. Authentic herbs and period medical instruments. (Daily; closed hols) 1020 Caroline St. Phone 540/373-3362. ¢ Follow Caroline St 3 blks N to

Rising Sun Tavern. (ca 1760) Washington's youngest brother Charles built this tavern, which became a social and political center and stagecoach stop. Restored and authentically refurnished as an 18th-century tavern; costumed tavern staff, English and American pewter collection. (Daily; closed hols) 1306 Caroline St. Phone 540/371-1494. ¢¢ W to Princess Anne St, 4 blks S is the

Fredericksburg Area Museum (Town Hall). (1814) Museum and cultural center interpret the history of Fredericksburg area from its first settlers to the 20th century. Changing exhibits. Children's events. (Daily; closed Jan 1, Thanksgiving, Dec 25) 907 Princess Anne St. Phone 540/371-3037. ¢¢ Behind Town Hall to the S on Princess Anne St is

St. George's Episcopal Church and Churchyard. Patrick Henry, uncle of the orator, was the third rector. Headstones in the churchyard bear the names of illustrious Virginians. (Daily) NE corner of Princess Anne and George sts. Phone 540/373-4133. 1 blk S to Hanover St is

Rising Sun Tavern

Kenmore

Fredericksburg Masonic Lodge #4, AF and AM. Washington was initiated into this Lodge Nov 4, 1752; the building, dating from 1812, contains relics of his initiation and membership; authentic Gilbert Stuart portrait; 300-yr-old Bible on which Washington took his Masonic oath. (Mon-Sat, also Sun afternoons; closed Jan 1, Thanksgiving, Dec 25) Princess Anne and Hanover sts. Phone 540/373-5885. ¢ Across the street is the

Presbyterian Church. (1833) Cannonballs in the front pillar and other damages inflicted in 1862 bombardment. Pews were torn loose and made into coffins for soldiers. Clara Barton, founder of the American Red Cross, is said to have nursed wounded here. A plaque to her memory is in the churchyard. Open on request (Mon-Fri, Sun). SW corner of Princess Anne and George sts. Phone 540/373-7057. 1 blk W on George St is

Masonic Cemetery. One of nation's oldest Masonic burial grounds. George and Charles sts. Just N on Charles St is

James Monroe Museum. As a young lawyer James Monroe lived and worked in Fredericksburg from 1786 to 1789, and even served on Fredericksburg's City Council.

Museum houses one of the nation's largest collections of Monroe memorabilia, articles, and original documents. Incl are the desk bought in France in 1794 during his yrs as ambassador and used in the White House for signing of the Monroe Doctrine, formal attire worn at Court of Napoleon, and more than 40 books from Monroe's library; also garden. The site is a National Historic Landmark owned by Commonwealth of Virginia and administered by Mary Washington College. (Daily; closed hols) 908 Charles St. Phone 540/654-1043. ¢¢ Continue N on Charles St to

Old Slave Block. Circular block of sandstone about three ft high from which ladies mounted their horses and slaves were auctioned in antebellum days. William and Charles sts. 2 blks N on Charles St is

Mary Washington House. Bought by George for his mother in 1772; she lived here until her death in 1789. Here she was visited by General Lafayette. Some original furnishings. Boxwood garden. (Daily; closed hols) 1200 Charles St. Phone 540/373-1569. ¢¢ On Charles St is

St. James House. Frame house built in 1760s, antique furnishings, porcelain and silver collections; landscaped gardens. (Open Historic

Garden Week in Apr and first wk in Oct; other times by appt) 1300 Charles St. Phone 540/373-1569. ¢¢ Walk back 1 blk to Lewis St and 2 blks W to

Kenmore. (1752) Considered one of finest restorations in Virginia; former home of Colonel Fielding Lewis, commissioner of Fredericksburg gunnery, who married George Washington's only sister, Betty. On an original grant of 863 acres, Lewis built a magnificent home; three rms have full decorative molded plaster ceilings. Diorama of 18th-century Fredericksburg. (Daily; closed Jan, Feb, hols) 1201 Washington Ave. Phone 540/373-3381. ¢¢¢ 2-½ blks N is

Mary Washington Monument. Where Mrs. Washington often went to rest and pray and where she is buried. Near "Meditation Rock." 5 blks S on Washington Ave is

Confederate Cemetery. There are 2,640 Confederate Civil War soldiers buried here, some in graves marked "Unknown." Washington Ave between Amelia and William sts.

Special Events

Historic Garden Week. Private homes open. Usually third wk Apr.

Market Square Fair. Entertainment, crafts demonstrations, food. Mid-May.

Quilt Show. Exhibits at various locations. Demonstrations and sale of old and new quilts. Sept.

Christmas Candlelight Tour. Historic homes open to the public; carriage rides; Christmas decorations and refreshments of the Colonial period. First wkend Dec.

Motels/Motor Lodges

★ ★ **BEST WESTERN.** *3000 Plank Rd (22401). 540/786-7404; fax 540/785-7415; toll-free 800/528-1234. www. bestwestern.com.* 76 rms, 2-3 story. Mar-Oct: S $48-$55; D $55-$63; each addl $4; under 12 free; higher rates special events. Crib $2. Pet accepted, some restrictions. TV; cable (pre-

mium). Complimentary continental bkfst. Restaurant nearby. Ck-out noon. Coin lndry. Business servs avail. Sundries. Valet serv. Health club privileges. Refrigerators avail. Cr cds: A, C, D, DS, MC, V.
⊡ 🔧 ⊠ 🛄 SC

★ **COMFORT INN.** *5422 Jefferson Davis Hwy (22407). 540/898-5550; fax 540/891-2861; toll-free 800/221-2222. www.comfortinn.com.* 125 rms, 5 story. Mid-Mar-Aug: S, D $62-$74; each addl $6; under 18 free; lower rates rest of yr. Crib free. TV; cable (premium). Indoor pool; whirlpool. Complimentary continental bkfst. Restaurant adj 6 am-10 pm. Ck-out

Confederate Cemetery

noon. Meeting rms. Business servs avail. In-rm modem link. Sundries. Valet serv. 18-hole golf privileges, greens fee, pro, putting green, driving range. Exercise equipt; sauna. Cr cds: A, C, D, DS, ER, JCB, MC, V.
🏌 ⊡ ⊠ 🏋 ⊠ 🛄 SC

★ ★ **HOLIDAY INN.** *5324 Jefferson Davis Hwy (22408). 540/898-1102; fax 540/898-2017; toll-free 800/465-4329. www.holiday-inn.com.* 195 rms, 2 story. S, D $65-$100; each addl $6;

under 18 free. Crib free. Pet accepted. TV; cable (premium). Indoor pool; whirlpool. Coffee in lobby. Restaurant 6:30 am-1 pm, 5-9:30 pm. Bar 4 pm-2 am; entertainment Wed-Sat. Ck-out noon. Coin lndry. Meeting rms. Business servs avail. In-rm modem link. Bellhops. Sundries. Valet serv. Exercise equipt. Game rm. Cr cds: A, C, D, DS, JCB, MC, V.

🄳 ⊶ ≈ 🛅 ⊠ 🔥 SC

★ ★ **HOLIDAY INN NORTH.** *564 Warrenton Rd (22405). 540/371-5550; fax 540/373-3641; res 800/465-4329. www.holiday-inn.com.* 150 rms, 2 story. June-Aug: S $52; D $67; each addl $5; under 18 free; lower rates rest of yr. Crib free. TV; cable (premium). 2 pools, 1 indoor; whirlpool. Coffee in rms. Restaurant 6-10 am, 5-9:30 pm. Bar 4 pm-2 am; entertainment Fri, Sat. Ck-out noon. Coin lndry. Meeting rms. Business servs avail. Valet serv. Sundries. Exercise equipt. Refrigerators avail. Cr cds: A, D, DS, MC, V.

🄳 ⊶ ≈ 🛅 ⊠ 🔥

★ **RAMADA INN.** *2802 Plank Rd (22404). 540/786-8361; fax 540/786-8811; toll-free 800/272-6232. www.ramada.com.* 129 rms, 2 story. S $45-$57; D $50-$62; each addl $5; suites $75-$100; under 18 free. Crib free. Pet accepted; $25 refundable. TV; cable. Pool. Complimentary coffee in lobby. Restaurant 6 am-10 pm. Rm serv 11 am-9 pm. Ck-out 1 pm. Meeting rms. Business servs avail. In-rm modem link. Valet serv. Sundries. Health club privileges. Cr cds: A, C, D, DS, ER, JCB, MC, V.

🄳 ⊶ ≈ ⊠ 🔥 SC

★ **SUPER 8 NORTH.** *557 Warrenton Rd (22405). 540/371-8900; fax 540/372-6958; res 800/800-8000. www.super8.com.* 80 rms, 3 story, 10 kit. units. S, D $62.96-$69.95; each addl $5; kit. units $69.95; under 18 free; wkly rates. Crib free. TV; cable (premium). Indoor pool; whirlpool. Complimentary continental bkfst. Restaurant adj open 24 hrs. Ck-out 11 am. Business servs avail. In-rm modem link. Exercise equipt; sauna. Some in-rm whirlpools. Cr cds: A, D, DS, MC, V.

🄳 ⊠ 🔥 ≈ 🛅

Hotel

★ ★ ★ **SHERATON INN.** *2801 Plank Rd (22404). 540/786-8321; fax 540/786-3957; res 800/682-1049. www.sheratoninn.com/fredericksburg.* 195 rms, 3 story. S, D $79-$129; each addl $10; suites $150-$275; under 18 free. Crib free. Pet accepted. TV; cable (premium). Pool; wading pool, poolside serv, lifeguard. Complimentary coffee in rms. Restaurant 6:30 am-10 pm. Bar 11:30-2 am; entertainment Mon-Sat. Ck-out noon. Meeting rms. Business servs avail. Bellhops. Valet serv. Sundries. Gift shop. Airport transportation. Tennis. Golf privileges. Exercise equipt. Health club privileges. Lawn games. Private patios, balconies. Refrigerators avail. Picnic tables. Cr cds: A, C, D, DS, ER, JCB, MC, V.

🛅 🄳 ⊶ 🏌 ≈ 🛅 ⊠ 🔥 SC

B&Bs/Small Inns

★ ★ **FREDERICKSBURG COLONIAL INN.** *1707 Princess Anne St (22401). 540/371-5666.* 39 rms, 2 story. S, D $55; each addl $6; suites $75-$85; under 12 free. Crib free. TV; cable. Complimentary continental bkfst. Ck-out 11 am, ck-in 2 pm. Meeting rms. Health club privileges. Refrigerators. Built 1928; antiques. Totally non-smoking. Cr cds: A, MC, V.

🄳 ⊠ 🔥 SC

★ ★ **KENMORE INN.** *1200 Princess Anne St (22401). 540/371-7622; fax 540/371-5480. www.kenmoreinn.com.* 12 rms, 2 story. S $85-$115; D $100-$130; each addl $10; suite $175. Crib free. TV in lounge; cable. Complimentary continental bkfst. Dining rm 11:30 am-2:30 pm, 5:30-9:30 pm. Bar 11:30 am-11 pm; Fri, Sat to midnight. Ck-out noon, ck-in 2 pm. Business servs avail. In-rm modem link. Health club privileges. Fireplace, canopy bed in some rms. Refrigerators avail. Structure built late 1700s; in historic district. Cr cds: A, C, D, MC, V.

🄳 ⊠ 🔥 SC

★ ★ **RICHARD JOHNSTON INN.** *711 Caroline St (22401). 540/899-7606.* 7 rms, 3 story, 2 suites. No rm phones. S, D $95-$125; suites $145. Complimentary continental bkfst. Ck-out 11 am, ck-in 2-8 pm. Built 1787;

antiques. In historic district. Totally nonsmoking. Cr cds: A, MC, V.

Restaurants

★ ★ **LA PETITE AUBERGE.** *311 William St (22401). 540/371-2727.* Hrs: 11:30 am-2:30 pm, 5:30-10 pm; early-bird dinner Mon-Thurs 5:30-7 pm. Closed Sun; major hols. Res accepted. French, American menu. Bar. Wine list. A la carte entrees: lunch $6.50-$13.95, dinner $9.95-$19.95. Specializes in fresh seafood, seasonal specialties, beef. Outdoor dining. French cafe decor. Cr cds: A, MC, V.

D

★ **OLDE MUDD TAVERN.** *5414 Mudd Tavern Rd, Thornburg (22565). 540/582-5250.* Hrs: 4-9 pm; Sun noon-8 pm. Closed Mon, Tues; Jan 1, Dec 25; also 1st wk July. Res accepted. Serv bar. Dinner $14-$20. Child's menu. Specializes in fresh vegetables, seafood, steak. Own baking. Entertainment Sat. Early American decor. Cr cds: MC, V.

D SC

★ ★ ★ **RENATO.** *422 William St (22401). 540/371-8228. www.renatos1. com.* Hrs: 11:30 am-2 pm, 4:30-10 pm; Sat, Sun from 4:30 pm. Closed hols. Italian menu. Bar. Lunch $5.95-$10.95, dinner $9.95-$24.95. Specializes in seafood, poultry, pasta. Antique chandeliers; fireplace. Cr cds: A, MC, V.

D

Fredericksburg and Spotsylvania National Military Park

(D-6) *See also Fredericksburg*

(Visitor Center on Old US 1 in Fredericksburg)

(see)

What to See and Do

Chancellorsville Visitor Center. Slide program, museum with exhibits; dioramas. (Daily; closed Jan 1, Dec 25) 7 mi W of I-95 on VA 3. Phone 540/786-2880. ¢¢

Chatham Manor. Georgian brick manor house, owned by a wealthy planter, was converted to Union headquarters during two of the battles of Fredericksburg. The house was eventually used as a hospital where Clara Barton and Walt Whitman nursed the wounded. (Daily; closed Jan 1, Dec 25) Phone 540/371-0802. ¢¢

Fredericksburg Visitor Center. Information and directions for various parts of park. Tours should start here. (Daily; closed Jan 1, Dec 25) Lafayette Blvd (US 1) and Sunken Rd. Phone 540/373-6122. ¢¢ Center incl

Fredericksburg National Cemetery. More than 15,000 Federal interments; almost 13,000 unknown.

Museum. Slide program, diorama, exhibits. (Same days as Visitor Center) ¢¢ Across Sunken Rd is

Old Salem Church. (1844) Building used as a field hospital and refugee center. Scene of battle on May 3-4, 1863. 1 mi W of I-95 on VA 3.

Stonewall Jackson Shrine. Plantation office where on May 10, 1863, Confederate General Jackson, ill with pneumonia and with his shattered left arm amputated, murmured, "Let us cross over the river, and rest under the shade of the trees," and died. (Mid-June-Labor Day, daily; Apr-mid-June, after Labor Day-Oct, Mon, Tues, Fri-Sun; rest of yr, Mon, Sat-Sun) 12 mi S on I-95 to Thornburg exit, then 5 mi E on VA 606 to Guinea. Phone 804/633-6076. ¢¢

Front Royal

(C-6) *See also Winchester, Woodstock*

Founded 1788 **Pop** 13,589 **Elev** 567 ft **Area code** 540 **Zip** 22630

Information Chamber of Commerce of Front Royal-Warren County, 414 E

Main St; 540/635-3185 or 800/338-2576
Web www.frontroyal.com

Once known as Hell Town for all the wild and reckless spirits it attracted, Front Royal was a frontier stop on the way to eastern markets. The present name is supposed to have originated in the command, "Front the royal oak," given by an English officer to his untrained mountain militia recruits.

Belle Boyd, the Confederate spy, worked here extracting military secrets from Union officers. It is said that she invited General Nathaniel Banks, whose regiment was occupying the town, and his officers to a ball once. Later she raced on horseback to tell General Jackson what she had learned. The next morning (May 23, 1862), the Confederates attacked and captured nearly all of the Union troops, providing Jackson one of his early victories in the famous Valley Campaign.

Front Royal was a quiet little village until the entrance to Shenandoah National Park (see) and the beginning of Skyline Drive opened in 1935, just one mile to the south. With millions of motorists passing through every year, the town has grown rapidly. The production of automotive finishes, limestone, and cement contributes to the town's economy, but the tourism industry remains one of its largest.

What to See and Do

Belle Boyd Cottage. Relocated to its present site, the two-story cottage has been restored to reflect life in Front Royal between 1840 and 1860. For a two-yr period during the Civil War, Belle Boyd stayed in this cottage while visiting relatives and used the opportunity to spy on Union troops occupying the town. This modest dwelling was also used to house wounded soldiers of both armies. (Mid-Apr-Oct, Mon-Fri, wkends by appt; closed hols) 101 Chester St, behind Ivy Lodge. Phone 540/636-1446. ¢

Skyline Caverns. Extensive, rare, intricate flowerlike formations of calcite (anthodites); sound and light presentation; 37-ft waterfall; clear stream stocked with trout (observation only). Electrically lighted; 54°F yr-round. Miniature train provides trip through surrounding wooded area (Mar-mid-Nov, daily, weather permitting). Snack bar; gift shop. Cavern tours start every few minutes. (Daily) 1 mi S on US 340. Phone 540/635-4545. ¢¢¢

Sky Meadows State Park. A 1,862-acre park. Fishing pond; hiking and bridle trails, picnicking, primitive walk-in camping. Visitor center; programs. (Daily) Standard fees. 20 mi E on US 66, 7 mi N on VA 17. Phone 540/592-3556. ¢¢

Warren Rifles Confederate Museum. Historic relics and memorabilia of War between the States. (Mid-Apr-Oct, daily; rest of yr, by appt) 95 Chester St. Phone 540/636-6982. ¢¢

Special Events

Warren County Garden Tour. Garden Club sponsors tours of historic houses and gardens. Last wk Apr.

Virginia Mushroom and Wine Festival. Mushrooms, wine, and cheese. Entertainment. Third Sat May.

Warren County Fair. Entertainment, livestock exhibits and sale, contests. First wk Aug.

Festival of Leaves. Arts and crafts, demonstrations; historic exhibits; parade. Second wkend Oct.

Motel/Motor Lodge

★ **QUALITY INN.** *10 S Commerce Ave (22630).* 540/635-3161; fax 540/635-6624; res 800/821-4488. *www.qualityinn.com.* 107 rms, 3 story. Sept-Oct: S $58-$85; D $68-$85; each addl $9; under 18 free; higher rates special events; lower rates rest of yr. Crib free. TV; cable (premium), VCR avail (movies). Pool. Complimentary coffee in rms. Restaurant 6 am-9 pm; wkends to 10 pm. Ck-out 11 am. Meeting rms. Business servs avail. In-rm modem link. Gift shop. Lawn games. Refrigerators, microwaves avail. Cr cds: A, C, D, DS, ER, MC, V.
D ⌖ ⌖ ⌖ SC

B&B/Small Inn

★ ★ ★ **CHESTER HOUSE.** *43 Chester St (22630).* 540/635-3937; fax 540/

*636-8695; toll-free 800/621-0441. www.
chesterhouse.com.* 6 rms, 2 share bath,
1 with shower only, 2 story, 1 suite.
S, D $65-$130; suite $165-$190; special events (2-day min). Children
over 12 yrs only. TV in lounge. Complimentary full bkfst; refreshments.
Restaurant nearby. Ck-out 11 am, ck-
in 3 pm. Business servs avail. Luggage handling. Health club privileges.
Lawn games. Guest refrigerator. Picnic tables. Formal gardens with
fountain and statuary. Georgian-
style mansion built 1905. Cr cds: A,
MC, V.

Galax

(F-3) *See also Wytheville*

Settled 1904 **Pop** 6,837 **Elev** 2,382 ft
Area code 540 **Zip** 24333
Information Galax-Carroll-Grayson
Chamber of Commerce, 405 N Main
St; 540/236-2184

Galax is named for the pretty ever-
green with heart-shaped leaves that
florists use in various arrangements.
It grows in the mountainous regions
around Galax and is gathered for sale
all over the United States. Nearby are
three mountain passes: Fancy Gap,
Low Gap, and Piper's Gap.

What to See and Do

Jeff Matthews Memorial Museum.
Two authentically restored log cabins
(1834 and 1860s). Relocated to present site and furnished with items
used in the period in which the cabins were inhabited. Also houses collection of photos of Civil War
veterans, artifacts and memorabilia
of the area; covered wagon; farm
implements. Restored log cabin used
as a blacksmith's shop. (Wed-Sun,
Phone 276/236-7874. **FREE**

Recreation. Swimming, boating, fishing on New River; hunting and hiking. Canoeing and other activities
can be found at

    Cliffview Trading Post. Bike rentals
    (Tues-Sat; closed Thanksgiving, Dec
    25) and horse rentals (Apr-Nov,

Tues-Sat); trail rides in New River
Trail State Park. Cliffview Rd.
Phone 276/238-1530.

Special Event

Old Fiddler's Convention. Felts Park.
Folk songs, bands, and dancing. Second wk Aug.

George Washington Birthplace National Monument

See also Fredericksburg, Montross

*(38 mi E of Fredericksburg on VA 3, then
2 mi E on VA 204)*

George Washington, first child of
Augustine and Mary Ball Washington, was born February 11, 1732 (celebrated February 22 according to the
new-style calendar) at his father's
estate on Popes Creek on the south
shore of the Potomac. The family
moved in 1735 to Little Hunting
Creek Plantation (later called Mount
Vernon), then in 1738 to Ferry Farm
near Fredericksburg.

    The 538-acre monument includes
much of the old plantation land.
(Daily; closed January 1, December
25)

What to See and Do

Family burial ground. Site of 1664
home of Colonel John Washington,
first Washington in Virginia and
great-grandfather of the first president. Washington's ancestors are
buried here. 1 mi NW on Bridges
Creek. Phone 804/224-1732.

Memorial House. Original house
burned (1779) and was never rebuilt.
The Memorial House is not a replica
of the original; it represents a com-
posite of typical 18th-century Virginia plantation house. Bricks were
handmade from nearby clay. Furnishings are typical of the times.
Phone 804/224-1732. Near house is

Colonial farm. "Living" farm designed to show 18th-century Virginia plantation life; livestock, colonial garden, several farm buildings, furnished colonial kitchen, household slave quarters, and spinning and weaving rm. Phone 804/224-1732.

Picnic area. ¼ mi N of house. Phone 804/224-1732.

Visitor Center. Orientation film; museum exhibits. Phone 804/224-1732. ¢

Gloucester

See also Newport News, Williamsburg, Yorktown

Founded 1769 **Pop** 900 **Elev** 70 ft **Area code** 804 **Zip** 23061
Information Chamber of Commerce, PO Box 296; 804/693-2425.

In the spring, acres of daffodil blooms make this area a treat for the traveler. This elm-shaded village is the commercial center of Gloucester (GLOSS-ter) County. There are many old landmarks and estates nearby, including the birthplace of Walter Reed, at the junction of VA 614 and 616.

What to See and Do

County Courthouse. (18th century) Part of Gloucester Court House Circle Historic District. Portraits of native sons in the courtrm; plaques memorializing Nathaniel Bacon, leader in the rebellion of 1676, first organized resistance to British authority, and Major Walter Reed, surgeon and conqueror of yellow fever. (Mon-Fri; closed hols) On US 17 Business. Phone 804/693-4042. **FREE** Nearby are Debtors Prison, the pre-Revolutionary Botetourt Building, and the

Roswell Historic Ruins. Three-story Georgian mansion's brickwork was put in place over 250 yrs ago. Majestic ruins hint at projecting pavilions, arched windows, and stone-capped chimney stacks. Tours by appt. (Apr-Oct, Sun; win-

ter by appt) Phone 804/693-2585. **FREE**

Virginia Institute of Marine Science, College of William and Mary. Small marine aquarium and museum display local fishes, and invertebrates; marine science exhibits, bookstore. (Mon-Fri; closed hols) Gloucester Point. Phone 804/684-7000. **FREE**

Restaurant

★★ **SEAWELL'S ORDINARY.** *3968 George Washington Hwy (23131). 804/642-3635. www.seawellsordinary. com.* Hrs: 11:30 am-3 pm, 5-9:30 pm; Sun brunch 11:30 am-3 pm. Closed Mon; Dec 25. Res accepted. Continental menu. Bar. Lunch $4-$12.95, dinner $10.95-$18.95. Sun brunch $8.95-$14.95. Specializes in regional French dishes. Outdoor dining. Built in 1712; became country tavern (1757); was frequented by Washington, Jefferson, Lafayette. Cr cds: A, D, MC, V.

Great Dismal Swamp National Wildlife Refuge

See also Chesapeake, Portsmouth

Harriet Beecher Stowe found Virginia's Dismal Swamp a perfect setting for her antislavery novel *Dred* (1856); modern hunters, fishermen, and naturalists find the area fits their ambition just as well. From its northern edge just southwest of Norfolk, the swamp stretches almost due south like a great ribbon, 25 miles long and 11 miles wide. Centuries of decaying organic matter have created layers of peat so deep that fires would sometimes smolder under the surface for weeks.

Creation of the refuge began in 1973 when the Union Camp Corporation donated 49,100 acres of land to the Nature Conservancy, which in turn conveyed it to the Department of Interior. The refuge was officially established through the Dismal Swamp Act of 1974 and is managed for the primary purpose of protecting and preserving a unique ecosystem. The refuge now consists of over 107,000 acres of forested wetlands that have been greatly altered by drainage and logging operations.

Near the center is Lake Drummond, 3,100 acres of juniper water, which is water that combines the juices of gum, cypress, and maple with a strong infusion of juniper or white cedar. The chemical mix added by the tree resins results in a water that remains sweet, or fresh, indefinitely. In the days of long sailing voyages, when ordinary water became foul after a few weeks, this "dark water" was highly valued.

The Great Dismal Swamp has also been commercially exploited for its timber, particularly cypress and cedar. A company organized by George Washington and several other businessmen bought a large piece of the swamp and used slave labor to dig the Dismal Swamp Canal, which both facilitated drainage of timber land and provided a transportation route in and out of the swamp.

Animal and bird life continues to abound in this eerie setting. There are white-tailed deer and rarely observed black bear, foxes, bobcats—and a large number of snakes, including copperheads, cottonmouths, and rattlesnakes. Birding is popular in the swamp from April-June; the peak of spring migration is mid-April-mid-May.

For further information contact Refuge Manager, PO Box 349, Suffolk 23439-0349. Phone 757/986-3705.

Hampton

(E-8) *See also Newport News, Norfolk, Portsmouth, Virginia Beach*

Settled 1610 **Pop** 146,437 **Elev** 12 ft
Area code 757
Information Hampton Visitor Center, 710 Settlers Landing Rd, 23669; 757/727-1102 or 800/800-2202
Web www.hampton.va.us/tourism

Hampton is the oldest continuously English-speaking community in the United States (Jamestown, settled in 1607, is a national historical park, but not a town). The settlement began at a place then called Kecoughtan, with the building of Fort Algernourne as protection against the Spanish. In the late 1600s and early 1700s the area was harassed by pirates. Finally in 1718, the notorious brigand Blackbeard was killed by Lieutenant Robert Maynard and organized piracy came to an end here.

Hampton was shelled in the Revolutionary War, sacked by the British in the War of 1812, and burned in 1861 by retreating Confederates to prevent its occupation by Union forces. Only the gutted walls of St. John's Church survived the fire. The town was rebuilt after the Civil War by its citizens and soldiers. Computer technology, manufacturing, aerospace research, and commercial fishing are now big business here.

Langley Air Force Base, headquarters for the Air Combat Command, Fort Monroe, headquarters for the US Army's Training and Doctrine Command, and the NASA Langley Research Center are located here.

What to See and Do

Air Power Park and Aviation History Center. Over 50 indoor and outdoor exhibits feature real fighter aircraft, missiles, and rockets; local aviation history and model aircraft exhibits. Picnicking, playground. (Daily; closed Jan 1, Thanksgiving, Dec 25) 413 W Mercury Blvd, US 258. Phone 757/727-1163. **FREE**

Bluebird Gap Farm. This 60-acre farm incl barnyard zoo; indigenous wildlife such as deer and wolves; antique and modern farm equipt and farmhouse artifacts. Picnicking, playground. (Wed-Sun; closed hols) 60 Pine Chapel Rd. Phone 757/727-6739. **FREE**

Buckroe Beach. Swimming; public park, concerts. Lifeguards (Memorial Day-Labor Day). 4 mi E on VA 351, foot of E Pembroke Ave on Chesapeake Bay. Phone 757/727-6347. **FREE**

Fort Monroe. First fort here was a stockade called Fort Algernourne (1609); the second, Fort George, though built of brick, was destroyed by hurricane in 1749; present fort was completed about 1834. 3 mi SE via Mercury Blvd, Ingalls Rd. **FREE** Here are

Casemate Museum. Provides insight on heritage of the fort, Old Point Comfort, and the Army Coast Artillery Corps. Museum offers access to a series of casemates and a walking tour of the fort. Jefferson Davis casemate contains cell in which the Confederacy's president was confined on false charges of plotting against the life of Abraham Lincoln. Museum features Civil War exhibits, military uniforms, and assorted artwork, incl three original Remington drawings, along with audiovisual programs. Scale models of coast artillery guns and dioramas represent the role of the coast artillery from 1901 to 1946. (Daily; closed Jan 1, Thanksgiving, Dec 25) Phone 757/788-3391. **FREE**

Chapel of the Centurion. (1858) One of the oldest churches on the Virginia peninsula. Woodrow Wilson worshiped here occasionally.

Hampton Carousel. (1920) Completely restored in 1991, antique carousel is housed in its own pavilion and features 48 hand-carved horses. (Apr-Sept, Mon-Sat, also Sun afternoons; Oct-Nov, daily, weather permitting; Dec 1-15, wkends) 602 Settlers Landing Rd, Downtown, on waterfront. Phone 757/727-6381. ¢

Hampton University. (1868) 6,100 students. Founded by Union Brigadier General Samuel Chapman Armstrong, chief of the Freedman's Bureau, to prepare the youth of the South, regardless of color, for the work of organizing and instructing schools in the Southern states; many blacks and Native Americans came to be educated. Now Virginia's only coeducational, nondenominational, four-yr private college. The Hampton choir is famous. It "sang up" a building, Virginia-Cleveland Hall, in 1870 on a trip through New England and Canada, raising close to $100,000 at concerts. E end of Queen St, ¼ mi off I-64 exit 267. Phone 757/727-5253. On campus are

Emancipation Oak. The Emancipation Proclamation was read here.

Museum. Collection of ethnic art; Native American and African artifacts; contemporary African-American works; paintings by renowned artists. (Daily; closed school hols) Huntington Building. **FREE**

Miss Hampton II Harbor Cruises. Narrated three-hr cruise incl a stop at Fort Wool, a Civil War island fortress. (Apr-Oct) 764 Settlers Landing Rd. Phone 757/722-9102. ¢¢¢¢

St. John's Church. (1728) **and Parish Museum.** Fourth site of worship of Episcopal parish established in 1610. Bible dating from 1599; communion silver from 1618; Colonial Vestry Book; taped historical message. (Daily) W Queens Way and Franklin St. Phone 757/722-2567.

Settlers Landing Monument. Marks approx site of first settlers' landing near Strawberry Banks in 1607. Painting by Sidney King depicts visit to Kecoughtan by colonists en route to Jamestown. (Daily) ½ mi S, on grounds of the Veterans Affairs Medical Center between Hampton River and Mill Creek, off I-64 exit 268. **FREE**

Virginia Air and Space Center and Hampton Roads History Center. Exhibits show the historical link between Hampton Roads' seafaring past and spacefaring future. Exhibits incl 19 full-sized air- and spacecraft, the Apollo 12 Command Module, a moon rock, and rare NASA artifacts. Films shown in 283-seat IMAX theater (daily). Gift shop. (Daily; closed Thanksgiving, Dec 25) Downtown, off I-64 exit 267. Phone 757/727-0900 or 800/296-0800. ¢¢¢

Special Events

Hampton Jazz Festival. Hampton Coliseum. Phone 757/838-4203 (box office). Three days late June.

Hampton Cup Regatta. Inboard hydroplane races. Phone 800/800-2202. Mid-Aug.

Hampton Bay Days. Arts and crafts, rides, science exhibits; entertainment. Phone 757/727-6122. Mid-Sept.

Motels/Motor Lodges

★★ **COURTYARD BY MARRIOTT.** *1917 Coliseum Dr (23666). 757/838-3300; fax 757/838-6387; res 800/321-2211. www.courtyard.com.* 146 rms, 3 story. June-Sept: S, D $75-$85; each addl $10; suites $90-$119; under 18 free; higher rates jazz festival; lower rates rest of yr. Crib avail. TV; cable (premium). Heated pool; whirlpool. Complimentary coffee in rms. Bar Mon-Thurs 6-10 pm. Ck-out noon. Coin lndry. Business servs avail. In-rm modem link. Valet serv. Sundries. Exercise equipt. Refrigerator avail in suites. Cr cds: A, MC, V.

★★ **HAMPTON INN.** *1813 W Mercury Blvd (23666). 757/838-8484; fax 757/826-0725; res 800/426-7866. www.hamptoninn.com.* 131 rms, 6 story. S, D $79-$99. Crib free. Pet accepted, some restrictions. TV; cable (premium). Pool privileges. Complimentary continental bkfst, coffee in rms. Restaurant adj 6 am-10 pm. Ck-out noon. Business servs avail. In-rm modem link. Exercise equipt. Cr cds: A, C, D, DS, MC, V.

★★ **HOLIDAY INN.** *1815 W Mercury Blvd (23666). 757/838-0200; fax 757/838-4964; res 800/465-4329. www.holiday-inn.com.* 320 rms, 2-4 story. S, D $89-$130; suites $125-$225; wkend rates; higher rates Jazz Festival. Crib free. TV; cable (premium). 2 pools, 1 indoor; whirlpool. Coffee in rms. Restaurant 6 am-10 pm. Rm serv to 11 pm. Bar 11 am-midnight. Ck-out 11 am. Coin lndry. Convention facilities. Business center. In-rm modem link. Bellhops. Valet serv. Free airport transportation. Exercise equipt; sauna. Game rm. Some refrigerators. Balconies. Cr cds: A, DS, ER.

★★ **RADISSON.** *700 Settlers Landing (23669). 757/727-9700; fax 757/722-4557; res 800/333-3333. www.radisson.com.* 172 rms, 9 story. S, D $89-$125; each addl $10; suites $185-$450; under 18 free; wkend rates; higher rates special events. Crib free. TV; cable (premium). Pool; whirlpool, poolside serv. Restaurant 6:30 am-10 pm. Bar 11-2 am. Coffee in rms. Ck-out noon. Meeting rms. Business servs avail. In-rm modem link. Gift shop. Free airport, RR station, bus depot transportation. Exercise equipt. Some refrigerators. On Hampton River. Luxury level. Cr cds: A, D, DS, MC, V.

Restaurant

★ **SAMMY AND NICK'S.** *2718 W Mercury Blvd (23666). 757/838-9100.* Hrs: 11 am-11 pm. Sat, Sun from 7 am. Closed Thanksgiving, Dec 25. Res accepted. Bar. Bkfst $2-$6.45, lunch, dinner $2.95-$12.95. Child's menu. Specializes in prime rib, steak. Cr cds: A, D, DS, MC, V.

Harrisonburg

(D-5) *See also Luray, New Market, Staunton*

Founded 1780 **Pop** 40,468 **Elev** 1,352 ft **Area code** 540

Information Harrisonburg-Rockingham Convention and Visitors Bureau, 10 E Gay St, 22802; 540/434-2319

Web www.hrcvb.org

Originally named Rocktown due to the limestone outcroppings prevalent in the area, Harrisonburg became the county seat of Rockingham County when Thomas Harrison won a race against Mr. Keezle of Keezletown, three miles east. They had raced on horseback to Richmond to file their respective towns for the new county seat. Harrisonburg is noted for good hunting and fishing, recreational opportunities, beautiful scenery, and turkeys. The annual production of more than five million turkeys, most of them processed and frozen, has made Rockingham County widely known. This is a college town with three 4-year universities. Much of the Washington and Jefferson national forests are here.

What to See and Do

Caverns. There are several caverns within 24 mi of Harrisonburg. They incl

Grand Caverns Regional Park. Known for its immense underground chambers and spectacular formations. Visited by Union and Confederate troops during the Civil War. Unique shield formations. Electrically lighted; 54°F. Park facilities incl swimming pool; tennis courts, miniature golf, picnic pavilions, hiking and bicycle trails. Guided tours. (Apr-Oct, daily; Mar, wkends) 12 mi S on I-81, then 6 mi E on VA 256 in Grottoes. Phone 540/249-5705. ¢¢¢

Shenandoah Caverns. (See NEW MARKET) 24 mi N on US 11.

Eastern Mennonite University. (1917) 1,350 students. Many Mennonites live in this area. On campus is an art gallery, planetarium (shows by appt, free), natural history museum, and the Menno Simons Historical Library, containing many 16th-century Mennonite volumes (school yr, Mon-Sat). Campus tours. 2 mi NW on VA 42. Phone 540/432-4000.

Fishing.

Lake Shenandoah. 3 mi E.

Shenandoah River. Good bass fishing.

Silver Lake. 5 mi SW on VA 42 in Dayton.

George Washington and Jefferson National Forests. Consist of approx nearly two million acres. Swimming; fishing for trout, bluegill, and bass; hunting for deer, bear, wild turkey, and small game; riding trails, camping, picnicking. Scenic drives past Crabtree Falls, hardwood forests, and unusual geologic features. Overlooks of Shenandoah Valley. Part of Appalachian Trail crosses forest. Fees are charged at some recreation sites. Trails for the visually impaired. 10 mi W on US 33. Contact Forest Headquarters, 5162 Valleypointe Pkwy, Roanoke 24019-3050. Phone 540/265-5100. **FREE**

James Madison University. (1908) 15,000 students. Interesting old bluestone buildings. Campus tours through Visitor Center phone 540/568-5681. S Main St. Phone 540/568-3621. On campus is

Miller Hall Planetarium and Sawhill Art Gallery. Phone 540/568-3621. **FREE**

Lincoln Homestead. Brick house, the rear wing of which was built by Abraham Lincoln's grandfather, and where his father was born. Main portion of the house was built about 1800 by Captain Jacob Lincoln. (Private) 9 mi N on VA 42.

Natural Chimneys Regional Park. Seven colorful and massive rock towers rise 120 ft above the plain. Pool; picnic facilities, camping (fee; limited Nov-Feb), bicycle and nature trails, playground. Park (daily). 15 mi SW off VA 42 in Mt Solon. Phone 540/350-2510. ¢¢

Shenandoah National Park. (see) 24 mi E on US 33.

Shenandoah Valley Folk Art and Heritage Center. Featured is the Stonewall Jackson Electric Map that depicts his Valley Campaign of 1862. The 12-ft vertical relief map fills an entire wall and lets visitors see and hear the campaign, battle by battle. Also displays of Shenandoah Valley history, artifacts. (Mon-Sat; closed hols) 115 Bowman Rd. Phone 540/879-2681. ¢¢

Virginia Quilt Museum. Resource center for the study of quilts and quilting. (Mon, Thurs-Sat, also Sun afternoons; closed hols) 301 S Main St. Phone 540/433-3818. ¢¢

Special Events

Natural Chimneys Jousting Tournament. Natural Chimneys Regional Park. America's oldest continuous sporting event, held annually since 1821. "Knights" armed with lances charge down an 80-yard track and attempt to spear three small rings suspended from posts. Each knight is allowed three rides at the rings, thus a perfect score is nine rings. Ties are run off using successively smaller rings. Third Sat June and Aug.

Rockingham County Fair. Mid-Aug.

Motels/Motor Lodges

★ **COMFORT INN.** *1440 E Market St (22801). 540/433-6066; fax 540/433-0793; res 800/228-5150. www.comfort inn.com.* 60 rms, 2 story. S, D $70-$80; each addl $10; under 18 free. Crib free. Pet accepted, some restrictions. TV; cable (premium). Pool. Complimentary continental bkfst, coffee in rms. Ck-out noon. Business servs avail. Cr cds: A, D, DS, MC, V.

🄳 🐾 📶 📶 🔥

★ **DAYS INN.** *1131 Forest Hill Rd (22801). 540/433-9353; fax 540/433-5809; res 800/457-2792. www.daysinn. com.* 89 rms, 4 story. June-Oct: S $55; D $68; each addl $5; under 17 free; ski plan; higher rates special events, wkends (2-day min); lower rates rest of yr. Crib free. Pet accepted; $5/day. TV; cable (premium). Indoor pool; whirlpool. Complimentary continental bkfst. Restaurant adj 11 am-11 pm. Ck-out 11 am. Meeting rms. Business servs avail. Sundries. Valet serv. 27-hole golf privileges, greens fee $30, pro, putting green, driving range. Downhill ski 12 mi. Health club privileges. Refrigerators, microwaves avail. Cr cds: A, C, D, DS, MC, V.

🄳 🐾 🏊 📶 📶 🔥 SC 🎿

★★ **FOUR POINTS BY SHERA-TON.** *1400 E Market St (22801). 540/433-2521; fax 540/434-0253; res 800/708-7037. www.fourpoints.com.* 140 rms, 5 story. S, D $99-$109; each addl $10; under 18 free. Crib free. Pet accepted. TV; cable (premium). Indoor pool; wading pool, whirlpool, poolside serv. Restaurant 6:30-2 pm, 5-10 pm. Bar 11-2 am; entertainment. Ck-out noon. Meeting rms. Business servs avail. In-rm modem link. Bellhops. Valet serv. Exercise equipt; sauna. Health club privileges. Some bathrm phones; refrigerators, microwaves avail. Cr cds: A, C, D, DS, ER, JCB, MC, V.

🄳 🐾 📶 🏋 📶 📶 SC

★★ **HAMPTON INN.** *85 University Blvd (22801). 540/432-1111; fax 540/432-0748; toll-free 800/426-7866. www. hamptoninn.com.* 164 rms, 4 story. May-Oct: S, D $68-$78; under 19 free; higher rates university events; lower rates rest of yr. Crib free. TV; cable (premium). Pool. Complimentary continental bkfst, coffee in rms. Restaurant nearby. Ck-out noon. Meeting rms. Business servs avail. In-rm modem link. Valet serv. Sundries. Health club privileges. Refrigerators, microwaves avail. Cr cds: A, C, D, DS, MC, V.

🄳 📶 📶 🔥 SC

★ **HOWARD JOHNSON.** *605 Port Republic Rd (22801). 540/434-6771; fax 540/434-0153; res 800/446-4656.* *www.hojo.com.* 134 rms, 2 story. Mar-Nov: S $44.95-$54.95; D $44.95-$59.95; each addl $5; higher rates some university events; lower rates rest of yr. Crib free. Pet accepted. TV; cable (premium). Pool; wading pool. Restaurant 6 am-9 pm. Ck-out noon. Business servs avail. Refrigerators avail. Private patios, balconies. Cr cds: A, D, DS, MC, V.

🄳 🐾 📶 📶 🔥

★★ **VILLAGE INN.** *4979 S Valley Pike (22801). 540/434-7355; toll-free 800/736-7355. www.shenandoah.org/ villageinn.* 36 rms. S $43; D $49-$59; each addl $5; kit. units $64. Crib free. Pet accepted. TV; cable (premium), VCR avail (movies). Pool. Playground. Restaurant 7-10 am, 5:30-9 pm; closed Sun. Ck-out noon. Meeting rm. Business servs avail. Sundries. Health club privileges. Lawn games. Many in-rm whirlpools. Picnic tables. Cr cds: A, C, D, DS, MC, V.

🄳 🐾 📶 📶 🔥

⛽

Hopewell

(E-7) *See also Petersburg, Richmond, Surry, Williamsburg*

Founded 1613 **Pop** 22,354 **Elev** 50 ft **Area code** 804 **Zip** 23860

Information Hopewell Area-Prince George Chamber of Commerce, 210 N 2nd Ave; 804/458-5536

The second permanent English settlement in America has been an important inland port since early times, having a fine channel 28 feet deep and 300 feet wide. It was the birthplace of statesman John Randolph of Roanoke. Edmund Ruffin, an early agricultural chemist who fired the first shot at Fort Sumter, was born near here.

"Cittie Point," at the junction of the James and Appomattox rivers, finally became one of Virginia's big cities during World War I when an E. I. du Pont de Nemours Company dynamite plant on Hopewell Farm supplied guncotton to the Allies.

What to See and Do

City Point Unit of Petersburg National Battlefield. (see) Grant's headquarters during the siege of Petersburg and largest Civil War supply depot. Incl Appomattox Manor, home to one family for 340 yrs; Grant's headquarters were on the front lawn. Many other buildings. (Daily; closed hols) Jct Cedar Ln and Pecan Ave. Phone 804/458-9504. ¢

Flowerdew Hundred. Outdoor museum on the site of an early English settlement on the south bank of the James River. Originally inhabited by Native Americans, settled by Governor George Yeardley in 1618. Thousands of artifacts dating from the prehistoric period through the present have been excavated and are on exhibit in the museum. A replicated 19th-century detached kitchen and working 17th-century-style windmill are open to visitors. Exhibits, interpretive tours. Picnicking. (Apr-Nov, Sat & Sun; rest of the wk by appt; rest of yr, by appt) 10 mi SE on VA 10. Phone 804/541-8897. ¢¢

Merchants Hope Church. (1657) Given the name of a plantation that was named for a barque plying between Virginia and England. The exterior has been called the most beautiful colonial brickwork in America. Oldest operating Protestant church in the country. (Open by request) 6 mi E on VA 10, then ½ mi S on VA 641. Phone 804/458-6197. **DONATION**

Special Events

Prince George County Heritage Fair. Flowerdew Hundred. Arts and crafts; educational exhibits and demonstrations; music, food, children's rides, hayrides. Last wkend Apr.

Hooray for Hopewell Festival. Downtown. Arts and crafts, food, entertainment, children's rides. Third wkend Sept.

Motels/Motor Lodges

★★ **HOLIDAY INN EXPRESS.** 4911 Oaklawn Blvd (23860). 804/458-1500; fax 804/458-9151. www.holiday-inn. com. 115 rms, 2 story, 50 kit. suites. S $50-$75; D $50-$95; each addl $5; kit. suites $62-$100; under 18 free; higher rates special events. Crib free. TV; cable, VCR avail (movies). Pool; whirlpool. Complimentary continental bkfst. Restaurant nearby. Ck-out 11 am. Coin lndry. Business servs avail. Exercise equipt; sauna. Refrigerators. Cr cds: A, C, D, DS, ER, JCB, MC, V.
D ⇌ 👤 ⇲ 🔥 🐾

★ **INNKEEPER.** 3952 Courthouse Rd (23860). 804/458-2600; fax 804/458-1915; toll-free 800/466-6337. 104 rms, 3 story. S $52.99-$79.99; D $55.99-$79.99; each addl $5. Crib free. TV; cable. Complimentary continental bkfst. Restaurant adj 6:30 am-11 pm. Ck-out noon. Coin lndry. Meeting rms. Business servs avail. In-rm modem link. Refrigerators; microwaves avail. Cr cds: A, C, D, DS, MC, V.
D ⇌ ⇲ 🐾 SC

Hot Springs

See also Clifton Forge, Covington, Warm Springs

Pop 300 **Elev** 2,238 ft **Area code** 540 **Zip** 24445

A Ranger District office of the Washington and Jefferson national forests is located here.

What to See and Do

Skiing. The Homestead. Double chairlift, T-bar, J-bar, baby rope tow; patrol, school, rentals; snowmaking; cafeteria, bar. Ice curling, ice-skating rink (Thanksgiving-Mar). On US 220. Phone 800/838-1766. ¢¢¢¢

Motel/Motor Lodge

★ **ROSALOE MOTEL.** 590 N Rte 220 (24445). 540/839-5373; fax 540/839-4625. www.rosaloe.com. 14 rms, 6 kits. S $60; D $80; each addl $4; family rates. Crib free. Pet accepted; $10. TV; cable (premium). Complimentary coffee in rms. Restaurant nearby. Ck-out 11 am. Downhill ski 3 mi. Refrigerators; microwaves avail. Cr cds: A, C, D, DS, MC, V.
🏊 🐾 🔄

Resort

★ ★ ★ ★ **THE HOMESTEAD** . *US 220 (24445). 540/839-1766; fax 540/839-7556; toll-free 800/838-1766. www.thehomestead.com.* This premier Allegheny Mountain resort, built in the Georgian architectural style around seven natural-mineral springs, has welcomed guests since 1766. There are over 500 luxurious rooms and suites energetically decorated with patterned carpets and floral draperies in addition to fine dining, a full-service spa, and championship golf. The 60,000-square-foot conference center also makes this an ideal group destination. 513 units, 4-12 story. Apr-Oct: S, D $212-$306; suites $372-$810; family rates; MAP avail; ski, golf, tennis plans; some seasonal rates; some lower rates rest of yr. Serv charges: 15 percent for daily housekeeping and 15 percent at all dining outlets. Crib free. TV; cable. 2 pools, 1 indoor; lifeguard. Supervised child's activities; ages 3-12. Dining rm 7-10 am, 11:30 am-4 pm, 6-9:30 pm. Afternoon tea. Box lunches, snack bar. Rm serv 7 am-midnight. Bar 11 am-midnight. Ck-out noon, ck-in 4 pm. Convention facilities. Business center. Valet serv. Gift shops. Airport, railroad station, bus depot transportation. Sports pros. Tennis. Three 18-hole golf courses, greens fee $100-$150, cart $15/person, putting greens, driving range. Downhill/x-country ski on site. Snowboarding. Skating. Hiking, horseback trails. Skeet and trap shooting. Lawn games. Game rm. Movies. Bowling. Exercise equipt. Spa, mineral pool. Microwaves avail. Cr cds: A, C, D, DS, MC, V.

B&B/Small Inn

★ ★ **VINE COTTAGE INN.** *US 220 (24445). 540/839-2422; toll-free 800/410-9755.* 15 rms, 7 share bath, 3 story. No elvtrs. No rm phones. S, D $65-$90; each addl $15-$20; hols 2-day min. Closed 2 wks in Mar. Crib $15. Pet accepted, some restrictions; $15. Cable TV in common rm, VCR avail. Complimentary full bkfst. Restaurant nearby 11 am-10 pm. Ck-out noon, ck-in 3 pm. Luggage handling. Downhill ski 1 mi. Built in 1894; family-oriented Victorian inn.

Totally nonsmoking. Cr cds: A, C, D, DS, MC, V.

Restaurants

★ **COUNTRY CAFE.** *Rte 220 S (24445). 540/839-2111.* Hrs: 7 am-9 pm; Sun to 2 pm. Closed Mon; hols. Res accepted. Wine, beer. Bkfst $3-$6, lunch $4-$5, dinner $7-$15. Child's menu. Specializes in prime rib. Own baking. Country decor with woodburning kitchen stove. Cr cds: MC, V.

★ ★ **SAM SNEAD'S TAVERN.** *Main St (24445). 540/839-7666. www.thehomestead.com.* Hrs: 5:30-9:30 pm; Sun to 9 pm. Closed Mon-Wed (Jan-Mar). Res required. Dinner $7.95-$29. Specializes in fresh mountain trout, Black Angus steaks. Outdoor dining. Rustic decor. Cr cds: A, MC, V.

Irvington

See also Lancaster

Pop 673 **Elev** 31 ft **Area code** 804 **Zip** 22480

What to See and Do

Historic Christ Church. (1735) Built by Robert Carter, ancestor of eight governors of Virginia, two presidents, three signers of the Declaration of Independence, a chief justice, and many others who served the country with distinction. Restored; original structure and furnishings, triple-decker pulpit. Built on site of earlier wooden church (1669); family tombs. Tours. (Apr-Nov, daily) 2½ mi W, off VA 200. Phone 804/438-6855. **FREE** On the grounds is

    Carter Reception Center. Narrated video presentation; museum with artifacts from Corotoman, home of Robert Carter, and from the church construction; photographs of the restoration. Guides. (Apr-Nov, daily) **FREE**

Motel/Motor Lodge

★ **WHISPERING PINES MOTEL.** *Rte 3, White Stone (22578). 804/435-1101.* 29 rms. S, D $59-$69; each addl $5. Crib $5. TV; cable. Pool; wading pool. Restaurant nearby. Ck-out 11 am. Sundries. Picnic tables. On wooded grounds. Cr cds: A, MC, V.

Resort

★★ **THE TIDES.** *480 King Carter Dr (22480). 804/438-6000; fax 804/438-5222; toll-free 800/843-3746. www.the-tides.com.* 60 units. Mid-Mar-Dec: S, D $108-$198; each addl $30; cottages to 2 persons $300; under 18 free; AP, MAP avail; golf plans; higher rates some wkends. Closed rest of yr. Crib free. Pet accepted, some restrictions; $10. TV; cable (premium), VCR avail (free movies). 2 pools, 1 saltwater, 1 heated; poolside serv. Playground. Free supervised children's activities (late June-Labor Day); ages 5-12. Coffee in rms. Dining rm 8-9:30 am, noon-2 pm, 6-10 pm. Bar noon-11 pm. Ck-out 1 pm, ck-in after 3:30 pm. Coin lndry. Meeting rms. Business servs avail. Bellhops. Valet serv. Gift shop. Lighted tennis. 45-hole golf, greens fee $25-$40, pro, putting greens, driving range. Exercise equipt; sauna. Marina, cruises, boat rental. Bicycles. Lawn games. Game rm. Rec rm. Refrigerators. Balconies. Cr cds: A, C, D, DS, MC, V.

Jamestown (Colonial National Historical Park)

See also Colonial Parkway, Newport News, Surry, Williamsburg, Yorktown

On May 13, 1607, in this unpromising setting, the first permanent English settlement in the New World was founded. From the beginning, characteristics of the early United States were established—self-government, industry, commerce, and the plantation system. The 104 men and boys who landed here that day and the people who followed them forecast the varied origins of the American populace. There were English, Germans, Africans, French, Italians, Poles, and Irish.

The *Susan Constant* (120 tons), the *Godspeed* (40 tons), and the *Discovery* (20 tons) brought the settlers here after a landing at Cape Henry. Thus, 20 years after the tragic failure to establish a colony at Roanoke Island and 13 years before the Pilgrims landed at Plymouth, Massachusetts, the English succeeded in settling in America.

The landing was not auspicious. Captain John Smith, ablest man in the group, was in chains; most of the others possessed a singular ineptitude for existing in a strange, hostile wilderness. Smith's ability and driving personality soon made him the acknowledged leader. For about a year he kept the bickering at a minimum, and the establishment of a colony was well under way.

The London Company, under whose patronage the colonists had set forth, continued to send "gentlemen" and adventurers to reinforce the colony. The second such shipment (September 1608) elicited the famous "Smith's rude answer" to company demands for gold and assorted riches. He wrote in part, "I entreat you rather send but thirty carpenters, husbandmen, gardeners, fishermen, blacksmiths, masons, and diggers up of trees, roots...than a thousand of such as we have: for except we be able both to lodge them and feed them, the most will consume with want of necessaries before they can be made good for anything."

Good for anything or not, this little band made glass in 1608, introduced the first commercial tobacco cultivation in 1612, and produced the country's first representative legislative body in 1619. In the earliest years, clapboards (some of which were shipped back to England) were made here, and later bricks, fishing nets, pottery, a variety of tools, and other items needed in the colony.

The first Africans were brought to the colony in 1619 on a Dutch privateer. They were probably indentured servants, pledged to work until their passage had been paid off. This was a common arrangement at the time.

There was not an easy day for any of the colonists for years. Crops failed and rats ate the corn. Until John Rolfe married Pocahontas, daughter of Chief Powhatan, in 1614, the Native Americans were suspicious and unfriendly. Disease plagued the settlers. The winter of 1609-1610 was called the "starving time." The 350-person colony was reduced to about 60 emaciated, defeated survivors who decided to give up and return to England. The June 1610 arrival of Lord de la Warre with reinforcements and supplies dissuaded them. Then the colony began to build and hope returned.

When Jamestown became a Royal Colony in 1624, feeling against personal (and often high-handed) government began to mount. By 1676 there was open revolt, led by Nathaniel Bacon, the younger. Bacon's forces finally burned the town, calling it a "stronghold of oppression." It was partially rebuilt but decline was inevitable, in part due to the damp, unhealthy climate of the area. The statehouse burned in 1698 and in 1699 the government moved to Middle Plantation and renamed it Williamsburg. By Revolutionary War days Jamestown was no longer an active community. About the same time, the James River washed away the sandy isthmus and the site became an island.

Nothing of the 17th-century settlement remains above ground except the Old Church Tower. Since 1934, however, archaeological exploration by the National Park Service has made the outline of the town clear. Cooperative efforts by the Park Service and the Association for the Preservation of Virginia Antiquities (which owns 22.5 acres of the island, including the Old Church Tower) have exposed foundations and restored streets, property ditches, hedgerows, fences, and the James Fort site from 1607. Markers, recorded messages, paintings, and monuments are everywhere. Entrance station (daily; closed December 25). Contact the Superin-tendent, PO Box 210, Yorktown 23690; phone 757/898-3400. Jamestown Island entrance fee $5/adult (over age 16); Golden Access, Age, and Eagle passports accepted (see MAKING THE MOST OF YOUR TRIP).

What to See and Do

Confederate Fort. (1861) One of two Civil War fortifications on the island. Near Old Church Tower.

Dale House. Archaeological laboratory. A viewing area is open to the public.

First landing site. Fixed by tradition as point in river, about 200 yards from present seawall, upriver from Old Church Tower.

Glasshouse. Colonists produced glass here in 1608. Demonstration exhibits, glassblowing (daily; closed Dec 25).

James Fort site. Excavation of first fort (1607) can be viewed between seawall and Old Church Tower.

Jamestown Settlement. Living history museum re-creates the first permanent English settlement in New World. Recalls early-17th-century Jamestown with full-scale reproductions of ships which arrived in 1607 and the triangular James Fort. Powhatan Indian Village depicts Native American culture encountered by English colonists. Museum complex features orientation film, changing gallery, and three exhibit galleries focusing on the history of Jamestown and the Powhatan. Food service avail. Combination ticket with Yorktown Victory Center (see YORKTOWN) avail. (Daily; closed Jan 1, Dec 25) Adj to historic Jamestown. Phone 757/253-4838. ¢¢¢

Memorial Church. Built in 1907 by the National Society of the Colonial Dames of America over foundations of original church. Within are two foundations alleged to be of earlier churches, one from 1617 that housed first assembly.

"New Towne." Area where Jamestown expanded around 1620 may be toured along "Back Streete" and other original streets. Section incl reconstructed foundations indicating sites of Country House, Governor's House, homes of Richard Kemp, builder of one of the first

Jamestown Memorial Church Tower

brick houses in America, Henry Hartwell, a founder of College of William and Mary, and Dr. John Pott and William Pierce, who led the "thrusting out" of Governor John Harvey in 1635.

Old Church Tower. Only standing ruin of the 17th-century town. Believed to be part of first brick church (1639). Has three-ft-thick walls of handmade brick.

Tercentenary Monument. Erected by US (1907) to commemorate 300th Jamestown anniversary. Other monuments incl Captain John Smith statue (by William Couper), Pocahontas Monument (by William Ordway Partridge), House of Burgesses Monument (listing members of first representative legislative body in America). Located near Jamestown Visitor Center.

Trails. Three- and five-mi auto drives provide access to entire area. Visitor center has 45-min auto drive and town site tape tours avail.

Visitor Center. Guide leaflets, introductory film and exhibits. Post office. (Daily; closed Dec 25)

Special Events

Jamestown Weekend. Jamestown, the original town site. Commemorates arrival of first settlers in 1607; special tours and activities. Mid-May.

First Assembly Day. Jamestown, the original town site. Commemorates first legislative assembly in 1619. Late July.

Keysville

Pop 817 **Elev** 642 ft **Area code** 804 **Zip** 23947

What to See and Do

Twin Lakes State Park. More than 250 acres of state forest; two lakes. Swimming, bathhouse, fishing, boating (rentals, launching, electric motors only); hiking, bicycle, and self-guided trails; picnicking, playground, concession, camping, hookups, tent and trailer sites, cabins (Mar-Dec); pavilion. Standard fees. 15 mi NE on US 360, then 1½ mi NW off VA 613. Phone 434/392-3435.

Motel/Motor Lodge

★ **SHELDON'S MOTEL.** *1450 Four Locust Hwy (23947).* 804/736-8434;

fax 804/736-9402. www.sheldons hospitality.com. 40 rms, 2 story. S $35.95-$50; D $41.95-$50; each addl $6. Crib $6. Pet accepted. TV; cable (premium). Restaurant 6:30 am-10 pm. Ck-out noon. Business servs avail. Some refrigerators; microwaves avail. Cr cds: A, DS, MC, V.

Lancaster

(B-2) *See also Irvington*

Pop 150 **Elev** 89 ft **Area code** 804
Zip 22503

The family of Mary Ball Washington, mother of George Washington, were early settlers of this area. Washington's maternal ancestors are buried in the churchyard of St. Mary's Whitechapel Church five miles west of Lancaster.

What to See and Do

Lancaster County Courthouse Historic District. Sycamore trees surround this area around the antebellum courthouse (1860). Marble obelisk is one of the first monuments erected to Confederate soldiers (1872).

Mary Ball Washington Museum and Library Complex. Contains the Old Clerk's Office (1797), the Old Jail (1819), Lancaster House (1800), the headquarters and main museum building. Also Virginia genealogical research center. (Wed-Sat, Tues by appt) Phone 804/462-7280. ¢

St. Mary's Whitechapel Church. (1740-1741) Church where Mary Ball and her family worshiped; many of the tombstones bear the Ball name. 5 mi W on VA 622.

B&B/Small Inn

★ ★ **INN AT LEVELFIELD.** *10155 Mary Ball Rd (22503). 804/435-6887; fax 804/435-7440.* 4 rms, 2 story. No rm phones. S $55; D $95; each addl $15. Pool. Complimentary full bkfst. Ck-out 11 am, ck-in 2 pm. Business servs avail. Lawn games. Antiques; hand-made quilts. Antebellum landmark homestead (1857) with double-tiered portico and four massive

chimneys; 1,000-ft entrance drive. Located on 54 acres with 12 acres of lawn and 42 acres of timberland bounded by stream. Cr cds: A, MC, V.

Leesburg

(C-6) *See also Arlington County (Ronald Reagan Washington-National Airport Area), McLean; also see District of Columbia*

Founded 1758 **Pop** 28,311 **Elev** 352 ft
Area code 703
Information Loudoun Tourism Council, 108-D South St SE, 20175; 703/771-2170 or 800/752-6118
Web www.visitloudoun.org

Originally named Georgetown for King George II of England, this town was later renamed Leesburg, probably after Francis Lightfoot Lee, a signer of the Declaration of Independence and a local landowner. Leesburg is located in a scenic area of rolling hills, picturesque rural towns, and Thoroughbred horse farms, where point-to-point racing and steeplechases are popular.

What to See and Do

Ball's Bluff Battlefield. One of the smallest national cemeteries in US marks site of third armed engagement of Civil War. On Oct 21, 1861, four Union regiments suffered catastrophic losses while surrounded by Confederate forces; the Union commander, a US senator and presidential confidant, was killed here along with half his troops, who were either killed, wounded, captured, or drowned while attempting to recross the Potomac River. Oliver Wendell Holmes, Jr., later to become a US Supreme Court justice, was wounded here. N via US 15.

Loudoun Museum. Century-old restored building contains exhibits and memorabilia of the area; audiovisual presentation "A Special Look at Loudoun." Brochures, information about Loudoun County; walking tours; self-guided tour booklets (fee).

(Daily; closed Thanksgiving, Dec 25; also Jan) 16 Loudoun St SW. Phone 703/777-7427. ¢

Morven Park. Originally the residence of Thomas Swann, early Maryland governor, the estate was enlarged upon by Westmoreland Davis, governor of Virginia from 1918 to 1922. The 1,200-acre park incl a 28-rm mansion, boxwood gardens, Winmill Carriage Museum with more than 70 horse-drawn vehicles, Museum of Hounds and Hunting with video presentation and artifacts depicting the history of fox hunting, and Morven Park International Equestrian Center (see SPECIAL EVENTS). (Apr-Nov, Fri-Mon afternoons) Old Waterford Rd, 1 mi N of Leesburg. Phone 703/777-2414. ¢¢¢

Oatlands. (1803) A 261-acre estate; Classical Revival mansion, built by George Carter, was the center of a 5,000-acre plantation; house was partially remodeled in 1827, which was when the front portico was added. Most of the building materials, incl bricks and wood, came from or were made on the estate. Interior furnished with American, English, and French antiques; reflects period between 1897 and 1965 when the house was owned by Mr. and Mrs. William Corcoran Eustis, prominent Washingtonians. Formal garden has some of the finest boxwood in US. Farm fields provide equestrian area for races and horse shows. (Early Apr-Dec, daily; closed Thanksgiving, Dec 24, 25) 6 mi S on US 15. Phone 703/777-3174.

Vineyard and Winery Tours. For a list of area winery tours contact the Loudoun Tourism Council, 108-D South St SE; Phone 800/752-6118.

Waterford. Eighteenth-century Quaker village, designated a National Historic Landmark, has been restored as a residential community. An annual homes tour (first full wkend Oct) has craft demonstrations, exhibits, traditional music. Waterford Foundation has brochures outlining self-guided walking tours. 3 mi NW on VA 7, ¼ mi on VA 9, then 2 mi N on VA 662. Phone 703/771-2170. ¢

Special Events

Loudoun Hunt Pony Club Horse Trials. Held at Morven Park International Equestrian Institute, Morven Park. Competition in combined training: dressage, x-country, and stadium jumping. Phone 703/777-2890. Late Mar.

Homes and Gardens Tour. Sponsored by Garden Club of Virginia. Late Apr.

Sheep Dog Trials. Oatlands. May.

Wine Festival. Morven Park. Many wineries participate; incl seminar for home/commercial wine growers; grape-stomping, waiters' race, jousting tournament, music, wine tastings, awards presentations. Phone 202/537-0961. Mid-July.

August Court Days. Reenactment of the opening of the 18th-century judicial court. Festivities resemble a country fair with craft demonstrations, games, entertainers on the street. Phone 703/771-2170 or 800/752-6118. Third wkend Aug.

Christmas at Oatlands. Candlelight tours, 1800s decorations, refreshments. Mid-Nov-Dec, Sat eves.

Motels/Motor Lodges

★ **DAYS INN.** *721 E Market St (20176). 703/777-6622; fax 703/777-4119; toll-free 800/329-7466. www. daysinn.com.* 81 rms, 2 story. Mar-Oct: S, D $65; each addl $6; under 12 free; lower rates rest of yr. Crib free. Pet accepted, some restrictions; $6. TV; cable (premium). Complimentary continental bkfst. Restaurant nearby. Ck-out noon. Coin lndry. Business servs avail. Cr cds: A, C, D, DS, JCB, MC, V.
D ⮌ ⋈ 🐾 SC

★ ★ **HOLIDAY INN.** *1500 E Market St (20176). 703/771-9200; fax 703/ 771-1575; res 888/850-8545. www. holiday-inn.com.* 126 rms, 2 story. S, D $99-$159; each addl $10; suites $159; under 16 free. Crib free. Pet accepted. TV; cable (premium). Pool. Coffee in rms. Restaurant 6:30 am-2 pm, 5-10 pm. Bar 4 pm-midnight. Ck-out noon. Coin lndry. Meeting rms. Business servs avail. Free airport transportation. Exercise equipt. Colonial mansion (1773). Cr cds: A, C, D, DS, ER, JCB, MC, V.
D ⮌ ≈ 🏋 ⋈ 🐾 SC

Resort

★ ★ ★ **LANSDOWNE CONFER-ENCE RESORT.** *44050 Woodridge Pkwy (20176). 703/729-8400; fax 703/729-4096; toll-free 800/541-4801. www.lansdowneresort.com.* 305 units, 9 story. S $149-$209; D $169-$229; suites $275-$700; under 18 free; wkend rates; golf plans. Crib free. TV; cable (premium). 2 pools, 1 indoor; whirlpool, poolside serv, lifeguard. Supervised children's activities; ages 3-12. Restaurant 6 am-midnight. Bar; entertainment Wed-Sun. Ck-out noon. Convention facilities. Business center. In-rm modem link. Concierge. Gift shop. Airport transportation. Lighted tennis. 18-hole golf, pro, greens fee $85-$95, putting green, driving range. Racquetball. Exercise rm; sauna, steam rm. Massage. Lawn games. Bicycle rentals. Refrigerators avail. Balconies. Picnic tables. Cr cds: A, C, D, DS, MC, V.

B&Bs/Small Inns

★ ★ **LEESBURG COLONIAL INN.** *19 S King St (20176). 703/777-5000; toll-free 800/478-8502. www.leesburg colonialinn.com.* 10 rms, 3 story. S $58-$150; D $68-$150; under 10 free. Crib free. Pet accepted, some restrictions. TV; cable. Complimentary full bkfst; afternoon refreshments in library. Restaurant (see also LEESBURG COLONIAL INN). Rm serv. Ck-out noon, ck-in 2 pm. Luggage handling. Free airport transportation. Tennis privileges. Golf privileges. Health club privileges. Picnic tables. Historic building (1759) built of same stone as Capitol in DC. Fireplaces; some in-rm whirlpools. Cr cds: A, C, D, DS, MC, V.

★ ★ **LITTLE RIVER INN.** *39307 John Mosby Hwy, Aldie (20105). 703/327-6742; fax 703/327-6645. www.aldie. com.* 9 units, 3 share bath, 2 story, 3 cottages. Some rm phones. S $65-$80; D $65-$95; each addl $20; cottages $145-$190. Children under 10 yrs in cottages only. Complimentary full bkfst. Pool privileges. Ck-out noon, ck-in 3 pm. Meeting rm. Private patios, balconies. Picnic tables. Built 1810; antiques. In foothills of Bull Run Mnts. Cr cds: A, MC, V.

★ ★ ★ **NORRIS HOUSE INN.** *108 Loudoun St SW (20175). 703/777-1806; fax 703/771-8051; toll-free 800/644-1806. norrishouse.com.* 6 rms, all share bath, 3 story. Rm phones avail. S $75-$90; D $90-$105; each addl $25; higher rates wkends (2-day min). Children wkdays only. Complimentary full bkfst; afternoon refreshments. Restaurant nearby. Ck-out noon, ck-in 4-8 pm. Business servs avail. Airport transportation. Lawn games. Picnic tables. Built 1760. Veranda overlooking gardens. Antique furnishings; most rms with fireplace. Totally nonsmoking. Cr cds: A, C, D, DS, MC, V.

Restaurants

★ ★ **GREEN TREE.** *15 S King St (20175). 703/777-7246.* Hrs: 11:30 am-10 pm; Sun brunch 11:30 am-4 pm. Res accepted. Serv bar. Lunch $6.95-$11.95, dinner $14.95-$24.95. Sun brunch $14.95. Specialties: Robert's Delight (beef dish), Jefferson's Delight (calf's liver soaked in milk). Own baking. Authentic 18th-century recipes. Windows open to street. Fireplaces. Strolling musician Fri-Sat. Cr cds: A, C, D, DS, MC, V.

★ ★ **LAUREL BRIGADE INN.** *20 W Market St (20176). 703/777-1010. www.laurelbrigade.com.* Hrs: 11:30 am-2 pm, 5:30-8:30 pm; Fri, Sat to 9 pm; Sun 8 am-11 am, noon-7 pm. Closed Mon. Res accepted; required hols. Serv bar. Lunch $4-$10, dinner $9.50-$20. Complete meals: lunch $11-$14.50, dinner $12.50-$25. Child's menu. Specializes in chicken, beef, seafood. Outdoor dining. Oldest section dates from 1759; Colonial decor, stone walls, fireplace. Family-owned. Cr cds: A, DS, MC, V.

★ ★ **LEESBURG COLONIAL INN.** *19 S King St (20175). 703/777-5000. www.leesburgcolonialinn.com.* Hrs: 11:30 am-10 pm. Res accepted. Continental menu. Bar. Lunch $5.95-$10.95, dinner $15.95-$18.95. Child's menu. Specializes in beef, seafood. Outdoor dining. Colonial decor. Cr cds: A, C, D, DS, MC, V.

Lexington

(D-5) *See also Clifton Forge, Natural Bridge*

Founded 1777 **Pop** 6,867 **Elev** 1,060 ft **Area code** 540 **Zip** 24450

Information Visitors Bureau, 106 E Washington St; 540/463-3777

Web www.lexingtonvirginia.com

Lexington was home to two of the greatest Confederate heroes: Robert E. Lee and Thomas J. "Stonewall" Jackson. Both are buried here. Sam Houston, Cyrus McCormick, and James Gibbs (inventor of the sewing machine) were born nearby.

Set in rolling country between the Blue Ridge and Allegheny mountains, this town is the seat of Rockbridge County. Lexington is known for attractive homes, trim farms, fine old mansions, and two of the leading educational institutions in the Commonwealth: Washington and Lee University and Virginia Military Institute.

What to See and Do

Goshen Pass. Scenic mountain gorge formed by Maury River. Memorial to Matthew Fontaine Maury is here. 19 mi NW on VA 39.

Lexington Carriage Company. Approx 45-min narrated horse-drawn carriage tours of historic Lexington. Groups of ten or more by appt only. (Apr-Oct, daily, weather permitting) Tours depart across street from Visitor Center. 106 E Washington St. Phone 540/463-5647. ¢¢¢

Stonewall Jackson House. Only home owned by Confederate General Stonewall Jackson, restored to its appearance of 1859-1861. Many of the furnishings were once owned by Jackson. Interpretive slide presentation and guided tours (½ hr). Restored gardens; shop. (Daily; closed hols) 8 E Washington St. Phone 540/463-2552. ¢¢

Stonewall Jackson Memorial Cemetery. General Jackson and more than 100 other Confederate soldiers are buried here. E side of S Main St.

Virginia Horse Center. Sprawling across nearly 400 acres, the Center provides a versatile site for numerous horse-related functions yr-round: shows, clinics, auctions, festivals. Fees vary. VA 11 N to VA 39 W. For schedule of events, contact PO Box 1051. Phone 540/463-2194.

Virginia Military Institute. (1839) 1,300 cadets. State military, engineering, sciences, and arts college. Coeducational since 1997. Stonewall Jackson taught here, as did Matthew Fontaine Maury, famed naval explorer and inventor. George Catlett Marshall, a general of the army and author of the Marshall Plan, was a graduate. Mementos of these men on display in VMI museum (daily; closed Jan 1, Thanksgiving, Dec 24-31). Dress parade (most Fri afternoons, weather permitting). On US 11. Phone 540/464-7207. **FREE** Located on the S end of the parade ground is

George C. Marshall Museum. (1964) Displays on life and career of the illustrious military figure and statesman (1880-1959); WWI electric map and recorded narration of WWII; Marshall Plan; gold medallion awarded with his Nobel Prize for Peace (1953). (Daily; closed Jan 1, Thanksgiving, Dec 25) Faces parade ground. Phone 540/463-7103. ¢¢

Washington and Lee University. (1749) 2,137 students. Liberal arts university situated on an attractive campus with white colonnaded buildings; also incl Washington and Lee Law School. Founded as Augusta Academy in 1749; became Liberty Hall in 1776; name changed to Washington Academy in 1798 after receiving 200 shares of James River Canal Company stock from George Washington, and then to Washington College. General Robert E. Lee served as president from 1865-1870; soon after Lee's death in 1870 it became Washington and Lee University. W Washington St. Phone 540/463-8400. On campus is

Lee Chapel. Robert E. Lee is entombed here. Also houses Lee family crypt and museum, marble "recumbent statue" of Lee, portions of art collection of Washington and Lee families. Lee's office remains as he left it. (Daily; closed hols) **FREE**

Special Events

Garden Week in Historic Lexington. Tour of homes and gardens in the Lexington, Rockbridge County area. Phone 540/463-3777. Late Apr.

Lime Kiln Arts Theater. 14 S Randolph St. Professional theatrical productions and concerts in outdoor theater. Phone 540/463-3074. Memorial Day-Labor Day.

Holiday in Lexington. Parade, plays, children's events. Phone 540/463-3777. Early Dec.

Motels/Motor Lodges

★★ **BEST WESTERN INN.** *Willow Springs Rd (24450). 540/464-1500; res 800/919-9675. www.bestwestern.com.* 100 rms, 3 story, 10 suites. Apr-Oct: S $69.95-$87.95; D $79.95-$92.95; each addl $8, suites $92.95; under 12 free; higher rates special events; lower rates rest of yr. Crib free. Pet accepted, some restrictions. TV; cable (premium). Indoor/outdoor pool. Complimentary coffee in rms. Restaurant 7 am-10 pm. Bar to midnight. Ck-out 11 am. Coin lndry. Meeting rms. Business servs avail. In-rm modem link. Health club privileges. Refrigerator, microwave in suites. Cr cds: A, DS, MC, V.
🄳 🔧 🌊 🔜 🔥

★ **COMFORT INN VIRGINIA HORSE CENTER.** *US 11 and I-64 (24450). 540/463-7311; fax 540/463-4590; toll-free 800/628-1956. www.comfortinn.com.* 80 rms, 4 story. Apr-Nov: S $64.95-$76.95; D $64.95-$85; each addl $5; under 18 free; lower rates rest of yr. Crib free. Pet accepted. TV; cable (premium). Indoor pool. Complimentary continental bkfst. Restaurant adj 6 am-11 pm. Ck-out 11 am. Coin lndry. Business servs avail. Sundries. Cr cds: A, C, D, DS, ER, JCB, MC, V.
🄳 🔧 🌊 🔜 🔥 **SC**

★ **DAYS INN.** *325 W Midland Tr (24450). 540/463-2143; fax 540/463-2143; res 800/329-7466. www.daysinn.com.* 53 rms, 10 kit. units. S $47.95-$57.95; D $55.95-$65.95; each addl $5. Crib free. Pet accepted, some

restrictions. TV; cable (premium). Ck-out 11 am. Business servs avail. Some bathrm phones, refrigerators. Picnic tables. View of mountains. Cr cds: A, C, D, DS, MC, V.
🄳 🔧 🐾 🔜 🔜 🔥

★★ **HOLIDAY INN EXPRESS.** *US 11 and I-64 (24450). 540/463-7351; fax 540/463-7351; toll-free 800/465-4329. www.holiday-inn.com.* 72 rms, 2 story. S $75; D $85; each addl $10; under 18 free. Crib free. Pet accepted. TV; cable (premium). Complimentary continental bkfst. Ck-out 11 am. Business servs avail. In-rm modem link. View of mountains. Cr cds: A, C, D, DS, ER, JCB, MC, V.
🄳 🔧 🔜 🔥 **SC**

★ **HOWARD JOHNSON INN.** *2836 N Lee Hwy (24450). 540/463-9181; fax 540/464-3448; toll-free 800/654-2000. www.hojo.com.* 100 rms, 5 story. S $50-$65; D $55-$75; each addl $7; under 18 free; higher rates special events. Crib free. Pet accepted. TV; cable (premium). Pool. Restaurant 6 am-8 pm. Ck-out noon. Coin lndry. Meeting rm. Business servs avail. Gift shop. Balconies. Private patios. On hill; panoramic view of mountains. Cr cds: A, C, D, DS, ER, JCB, MC, V.
🄳 🔧 🔜 🔜 🔥 **SC**

★ **RAMADA INN.** *US 11 and I-64 (24450). 540/463-7311; fax 540/464-3639; res 888/298-2054. www.ramada.com.* 80 rms, 4 story. May-Oct: S $60; D $70; each addl $6; under 19 free; wkly, wkend rates; higher rates special events; lower rates rest of yr. Crib free. Pet accepted. TV; cable (premium). Indoor pool. Restaurant 6 am-2 pm, 5-10 pm. Bar 5-10 pm. Ck-out noon. Meeting rms. Business servs avail. Sundries. Cr cds: A, D, DS, MC, V.
🄳 🔧 🔜 🔜 🔥

★ **TRAVELODGE.** *2809 N Lee Hwy (24450). 540/463-9131; fax 540/463-7448; toll-free 800/521-9131. www.travelodge.com.* 150 rms, 3 story. May-Oct: S, D $50-$85; each addl $5; under 18 free; lower rates rest of yr. Crib free. TV; cable (premium). Pool. Coffee in rms. Restaurant adj 6 am-9 pm. Ck-out 11 am. Meeting rms. Microwaves avail. Cr cds: A, C, D, DS, MC, V.
🄳 🔜 🔜 🔥 **SC**

B&Bs/Small Inns

★★ **ALEXANDER WITHROW INN.** *3 W Washington St (24450). 540/463-2044; fax 540/463-7262. www.lexingtonhistoricinns.com.* 16 units, 4 story. S $85-$130; D $100-$145; each addl $15; family rates. Crib $5. TV; cable. Pool privileges. Complimentary continental bkfst; afternoon refreshments. Restaurant opp 5:30-9 pm. Ck-out noon, ck-in 2 pm. Business servs avail. Tennis privileges. Refrigerators. Private patios, balconies. Picnic tables. Built 1809; antiques. Cr cds: DS, MC, V.

★★★ **HUMMINGBIRD INN.** *30 Wood Ln, Goshen (24439). 540/997-9065; fax 540/997-0289; res 800/397-3214. www.hummingbirdinn.com.* 5 rms, 2 story. No rm phones. May-Nov: S $75-$105; D $80-$110; wkend rates; MAP avail; wkends (2-day min); lower rates rest of yr. Children over 12 yrs only. Pet accepted; $20. TV in common rm. Complimentary full bkfst. Restaurant nearby. Ck-out 11 am, ck-in 4 pm. Business servs avail. Rec rm. Lawn games. Some in-rm whirlpools, fireplaces. Picnic tables. On river. Victorian Carpenter Gothic villa built in 1780; wraparound verandas. Totally nonsmoking. Cr cds: A, DS, MC, V.

★★★ **INN AT UNION RUN.** *325 Union Run (24450). 540/463-9715; fax 540/463-3526; res 800/528-6466. www.unionrun.com.* 8 rms, 2 story. Apr-Nov: S $75-$90; D $85-$125; each addl $20; lower rates rest of yr. Children over 10 yrs only. TV in common rm; cable (premium). Complimentary full bkfst. Restaurant 5-9 pm; closed Sun, Mon. Ck-out 11 am, ck-in 3 pm. Business servs avail. Lawn games. Many in-rm whirlpools. Some balconies. Picnic tables. Federal manor house built in 1883. View of mountains. Cr cds: A, MC, V.

★★ **MAPLE HALL COUNTRY INN.** *3111 N Lee Hwy (24450). 540/463-6693; fax 540/463-2114. www.lexingtonhistoricinns.com.* 21 rms, 9 with shower only, 3 story. S $85-$155; D $100-$165; each addl $15; child under 12, $5. Crib avail. TV in parlor; cable, VCR avail. Pool. Complimentary continental bkfst; afternoon refreshments. Dining rm 5:30-9 pm. Ck-out noon, ck-in 2 pm. Meeting rms. Business servs avail. Tennis. Lawn games. Plantation house built 1850; period furnishings. Cr cds: DS, MC, V.

★★★ **STEELES TAVERN MANOR.** *US 11, Steeles Tavern (24476). 540/377-6444; fax 540/377-5937; res 800/743-8666. www.steelestavern.com.* 5 rms, 2 story. No rm phones. S, D $135-$165; each addl $20. Children over 13 yrs only. TV; VCR (movies). Complimentary full bkfst; afternoon refreshments. Complimentary coffee in rms. Ck-out 11 am, ck-in 3 pm. Business servs avail. Luggage handling. Valet serv. In-rm whirlpools; some fireplaces. Picnic tables. Restored 1916 manor; antiques. On 55 acres. Panoramic view. Cr cds: DS, MC, V.

Restaurants

★ **REDWOOD.** *898 N Lee Hwy (24450). 540/463-2168.* Hrs: 7 am-10 pm. Closed Dec 25. Bkfst $2.50-$4.50, lunch $3-$6, dinner $4.50-$9. Child's menu. Specializes in seafood, steak, chicken. Family restaurant with home-style cooking; casual atmosphere. Cr cds: DS, MC, V.

★★★ **WILLSON-WALKER HOUSE.** *30 N Main St (24450). 540/463-3020. www.willsonwalker.com.* Hrs: 11:30 am-2:30 pm, 5:30-9 pm. Closed Sun, Mon; Jan 1, Thanksgiving, Dec 24, 25; also Sat lunch Dec-Mar. Res accepted. Serv bar. Wine list. Lunch $5-$8, dinner $10-$20. Child's menu. Specializes in pasta, veal, fresh seafood. Outdoor dining. In restored Greek Revival house (1820) located in downtown historic district; period antiques. Cr cds: A, MC, V.

Luray

See also Basye, Front Royal, Harrisonburg, New Market

Founded 1812 **Pop** 4,871 **Elev** 789 ft
Area code 540 **Zip** 22835
Information Page County Chamber of Commerce, 46 E Main St; 540/743-3915
Web www.luraypage.com

The name of this town is of French origin; its fame comes from the caverns discovered here in 1878. Situated at the junction of US 211 and US 340, Luray is nine miles away from, and within sight of, Shenandoah National Park (see) and Skyline Drive. Headquarters of the park are here. There are three developed recreation areas north and west of town in Washington and Jefferson national forests.

What to See and Do

⭐ **Luray Caverns.** One of the largest caverns in the east. Huge underground rms (one is 300 ft wide, 500 ft long, with a 140-ft ceiling) connected by natural corridors and paved walkways are encrusted with colorful rock formations, some delicate as lace, others massive. In one chamber is the world's only "stalacpipe" organ, which produces music of symphonic quality from stone formations. Indirect lighting permits taking of color photos within caverns. Temperature is 54°F. One-hr guided tours start about every 20 min. (Daily) W edge of town on US 211. Phone 540/743-6551. ¢¢¢ Fee incl

  Car and Carriage Museum. Exhibits incl 140 restored antique cars, carriages, and coaches featuring history of transportation from 1625.

Luray Singing Tower. Houses 47-bell carillon; largest bell weighs 7,640 lbs. Features 45-min recitals by celebrated carillonneur. (June-Aug, Tues, Thurs, and Sun eves; Mar-May and Sept-Oct, wkend afternoons) In park adj to caverns. Phone 540/743-6551. **FREE**

Luray Zoo. Features large reptile collection, exotic animals, and tropical birds; petting zoo; live animal shows; life-sized dinosaur reproductions. Gift shop. (Mid-Apr-Oct, daily) ½ mi W on US 211. Phone 540/743-4113. ¢¢

Massanutten One-room School. Restored and furnished as it was in the 1800s. Period displays and pictures. (By appt) In Lawn Park. Contact Chamber of Commerce. **FREE**

Shenandoah National Park. (see) 9 mi E on US 211, then S on Skyline Dr.

Special Events

Mayfest Street Festival. Entertainment, crafts. Third Sat May.

Page County Heritage Festival. Arts and crafts exhibits. Self-guided tour of churches and old homes. Columbus Day wkend.

Motels/Motor Lodges

⭐⭐ **BEST WESTERN INN.** *410 W Main St (22835). 540/743-6511; fax 540/743-2917; res 800/526-0942. www.bestwestern.com.* 40 rms, 2 story. Apr-Nov: S, D $43-$94.50; each addl $5; under 18 free; lower rates rest of yr. Crib $4. Pet accepted; $20/day. TV; cable (premium). Pool. Playground. Complimentary coffee in rms. Restaurant 6 am-2 pm, 5-9 pm. Ck-out noon. Business servs avail. Lawn games. Cr cds: A, C, D, DS, MC, V.
🐾 🏊 📶 🐕 **SC**

⭐⭐ **BIG MEADOWS LODGE.** *Skyline Dr (22835). 540/999-2221; fax 540/999-2011; res 800/999-4714. www.visitshenandaoh.com.* 92 units: 62 motel rms, 20 lodge rms, 10 cabins. No A/C. Mid-May-Nov 1: lodge S, D $65-$80; motel S, D $85-$95; cabins $70-$80; suites $130-$140; each addl $5; under 16 free. Closed rest of yr. Crib free. TV in some rms. Playground. Restaurant 7:30-10 am, noon-2 pm, 5:30-8:30 pm. Box lunches. Bar 4-11 pm; entertainment. Ck-out noon. Business servs avail. Gift shop. Private patios, balconies. Panoramic view of Shenandoah Valley. Cr cds: A, DS, MC, V.
D 🐾 📶 🏊 🐕

⭐⭐⭐ **CABINS AT BROOKSIDE.** *2978 US 211 E (22835). 540/743-5698; fax 540/743-1326; toll-free 800/299-2655. www.brooksidecabins.com.* 9 cottages. No rm phones. Feb-Nov: S $75-$145; D $135-$150; each addl $5-

$10; kit. suite $150-$185; lower rates rest of yr. Crib avail. Complimentary coffee in rms. Restaurant adj 7 am-8:30 pm. Ck-out noon. Sundries. Some fireplaces, in-rm whirlpools; refrigerators avail. Cr cds: A, C, D, DS, MC, V.

D 🔥

★ **LURAY CAVERNS MOTEL.** *832 W Main (22835). 540/743-4531; fax 540/743-7088. www.luraycaverns.com.* 64 rms. S, D $57-$74; each addl $7; under 16 free; TV; cable. Pools. Restaurants nearby. Business servs avail. Tennis privileges. Golf privileges. Views of Blue Ridge Mtns. Cr cds: A, DS, MC, V.

D 🔥 🔥 🔥

★★ **MIMSLYN INN.** *401 W Main St (22835). 540/743-5105; fax 540/743-2632; toll-free 800/296-5105. www.svta.org/mimslyn.* 49 rms, 2 with shower only, 3 story, 11 suites. Mid-June-Oct: S $94; D $104; suites $144-$164; under 18 free; lower rates rest of yr. Crib free. Pet accepted; $10 deposit. TV; cable. Restaurant 7-10 am, 11:30 am-2 pm, 5-9 pm. Ck-out noon. Business servs avail. Gift shop. Health club privileges. Art gallery, antique shop. Built 1930 in style of antebellum mansion. Cr cds: A, DS, MC, V.

🔥 🔥 SC

★ **RAMADA INN.** *138 Whispering Hill Rd (22835). 540/743-4521; fax 540/743-6863; toll-free 800/272-6232. www.ramada.com.* 101 rms, 2 story. Apr-Oct: S, D $69-$130; each addl $5; under 16 free; lower rates rest of yr. Crib free. TV; cable, VCR avail (movies). Pool. Complimentary coffee. Restaurant 6:30 am-2 pm, 5-9 pm. Bar 5 pm-1 am; entertainment wkends. Ck-out noon. Meeting rms. Business servs avail. Health club privileges. Miniature golf. Game rm. Some in-rm whirlpools; refrigerators, microwaves avail. Picnic tables. Cr cds: A, C, D, DS, JCB, MC, V.

D 🔥 🔥 🔥 SC

★★ **SKYLAND LODGE.** *Skyline Dr (22835). 540/999-2211; fax 540/999-2231; toll-free 800/999-4714.* 177 rms. No A/C. Apr-Nov: S, D $48-$105; each addl $5; suites $112-$160; under 16 free. Closed rest of yr. Crib free. TV avail. Playground. Coffee in

rms. Restaurant 7:30 am-8:30 pm. Box lunches avail. Bar 3-11:30 pm. Ck-out noon. Meeting rms. Business servs avail. Sundries. Gift shop. Private patios. Balconies. Cr cds: A, DS, MC, V.

D 🔥 🔥 🔥 🔥 🔥

B&Bs/Small Inns

★★★ **JORDAN HOLLOW FARM INN.** *326 Hawksbill Park Rd, Stanley (22851). 540/778-2285; fax 540/778-1759; res 888/418-7000. www.jordan hollow.com.* 20 rms in 2 buildings, 1-2 story. S $85-$130; D $110-$154; each addl $25; under 6 free. Crib free. TV in some rms; cable. Complimentary full bkfst. Dining rm 8:30-10 am, 5:30-9:30 pm. Bar. Ck-out noon, ck-in 3 pm. Business servs avail. Some in-rm whirlpools. Converted 45-acre horse farm; sun deck with view of Blue Ridge Mtns. Totally nonsmoking. Cr cds: C, D, DS, MC, V.

🔥 🔥 🔥

★★★ **MAYNEVIEW BED AND BREAKFAST.** *439 Mechanic St (22835). 540/743-7921; fax 540/743-1191. www.mountain-lodging.com/mayne_view.htm.* 5 rms, 1 with shower only, 3 story, 1 cottage. No rm phones. No elvtr. S, D $100-$135; cottage (2-day min) $175-$195; under 4 free. Complimentary full bkfst; afternoon refreshments. Restaurant nearby. Ck-out noon, ck-in 3 pm. Luggage handling. Whirlpool. Underground Railroad stop during the Civil War. Victorian bldg (1865). Cr cds: A, DS, MC, V.

🔥 🔥 SC

★★★ **WOODRUFF HOUSE BED AND BREAKFAST.** *330 Mechanic St (22835). 540/743-1494; fax 540/743-1722. www.bbonline.com/va/woodruff.* 6 rms in 2 bldgs, 2 with shower only, 3 story. No rm phones. MAP: S, D $98-$195; higher rates Oct. Children over 10 yrs only. Complimentary coffee in rms. Ck-out noon, ck-in 3 pm. Luggage handling. Health club privileges. Some in-rm whirlpools. Victorian house (1830, 1890); antiques. Totally nonsmoking. Cr cds: DS, MC, V.

🔥 🔥

Restaurants

★ **BROOKSIDE.** *2978 US 211 E (22835). 540/743-5698. www. brooksidecabins.com.* Hrs: 7 am-8:30 pm; Fri, Sat to 9 pm. Closed mid-Dec-mid-Jan. Res accepted. Wine, beer. Bkfst $3-$6, lunch $3.50-$7.50, dinner $7.50-$14.95. Buffet: bkfst (Sat, Sun) $5.95, lunch $5.95, dinner $8.45-$9.45. Child's menu. Specializes in steak, spaghetti, seafood. Salad bar. Own baking. Cr cds: A, D, DS, MC, V.

D ⮐

★★ **PARKHURST.** *2547 US 211 W (22835). 540/743-6009.* Hrs: 11 am-10 pm; winter hrs vary. Closed hols. Bar. A la carte entrees: dinner $14.95-$17.95. Specializes in steak, fowl, seafood. View of Blue Ridge Mtns. Cr cds: A, C, D, DS, MC, V.

D

Lynchburg (E-5)

Settled 1757 **Pop** 65,269 **Elev** 795 ft
Area code 804
Information Visitors Information Center, 12th and Church sts, 24504; 804/847-1811 or 800/732-5821

Lynchburg is perched on hills overlooking the James River, which was for many years its means of growth. Today the city is home to more than 3,000 businesses and diversified industries. Educational institutions located here include Lynchburg College, Randolph-Macon Women's College, and Liberty University.

One of the first buildings in the town was a ferry house built by John Lynch. The same enterprising young man later built a tobacco warehouse, probably the first one in the country. During the Civil War, Lynchburg was important as a supply base and hospital town. In June 1864 General Jubal A. Early successfully defended the town from an attack by Union forces. More than 2,200 Confederates are buried in the Confederate Cemetery, located in the Old City Cemetery.

What to See and Do

Anne Spencer House. House of noted poet, only black woman and only Virginian to be incl in *Norton Anthology of Modern American and British Poetry.* On grounds is Spencer's writing cottage "Edan Kraal." Many dignitaries have visited here. Museum with artifacts, memorabilia, period antique furnishings; formal garden. (House by appt; gardens daily) 1313 Pierce St. Phone 434/845-1313. ¢¢

Appomattox Court House National Historical Park. (see) 21 mi E on US 460.

Blackwater Creek Natural Area. Ruskin Freer Nature Preserve (115 acres) incl trails with plants; athletic area; bikeway winds past wildflower area and historical sites, ending downtown; Creekside Trunk Trail, natural grass trail with typical Piedmont species of plants, moist ravines, north-facing rocky bluffs. (Daily) In center of city. **FREE**

Fort Early. Defense earthwork for Lynchburg's closest battle during the Civil War. Confederates under General Jubal A. Early turned back forces under General David Hunter in 1864. (Daily) Memorial and Fort aves. **FREE**

Jefferson's Poplar Forest. Designed and built by Thomas Jefferson as a personal retreat; begun in 1806. Restoration in progress; house unfurnished. (Apr-Nov, daily; closed Thanksgiving) SW of Lynchburg on US 221, then left on VA 811 and left again on VA 661 in Bedford County. Phone 434/525-1806. ¢¢¢

Old Court House Museum. (1855) Restored to original Greek Revival appearance. Three galleries have exhibits on early history of the area, highlighting Quaker settlement and role of tobacco; restored mid-19th-century courtrm. (Daily; closed hols) 901 Court St. Phone 434/847-1459. ¢

Pest House Medical Museum. The 1840s white frame medical office of Quaker physician Dr. John Jay Terrell has been joined with Pest House quarantine hospital to typify the standard of medicine during late 1800s. Original medical instruments incl operating table, hypodermic needle, clinical thermometer, and chloroform mask. Period furnishings on one side duplicate Dr. Terrell's office during the Civil War; other side represents quarantine hospital for Confederate soldiers in which Dr. Terrell volunteered to assume responsibility. Window displays with audio description. Tours (by appt). (Daily) Old City Cemetery, 4th and Taylor sts. Phone 434/847-1465. **FREE**

Point of Honor. (1815) Restored mansion on Daniel's Hill above the James River, built by Dr. George Cabell, Sr., physician to Patrick Henry. Federalist style with octagon bay facade and finely crafted interior woodwork; period furnishings; gardens and grounds being restored. (Daily; closed hols) 112 Cabell St. Phone 804/847-1459. ¢¢

Randolph-Macon Women's College. (1891) 748 women. A 100-acre campus on historic Rivermont Ave near James River. First college for women in the South granted a Phi Beta Kappa chapter. Campus is interesting mixture of architecture incl Vincent Kling design for Houston Chapel. Tours (by appt). 2500 Rivermont Ave. Phone 434/947-8000. On campus is

Maier Museum of Art. Collection is representative of 19th- and 20th-century American painting. Artists incl Thomas Hart Benton, Edward Hicks, Winslow Homer, James McNeil Whistler, Mary Cassatt, and Georgia O'Keeffe. Changing exhibits. (Academic yr, Tues-Sun afternoons) Phone 804/947-8136. **FREE**

Riverside Park. (Daily) Rivermont Ave. **FREE** In park is

Packet Boat Marshall. Mounted on a stone base, boat carried remains of Stonewall Jackson home to Lexington; for many yrs packets were principal mode of transportation along the James River and Kanawha Canal.

South River Meeting House. Completed in 1798, the stone building remained the site of Quaker worship and activity until the 1840s. John Lynch, founder of Lynchburg, and other early leaders of community are buried in adj historic cemetery. (Daily; closed hols) 5810 Fort Ave. Phone 804/239-2548. **FREE**

Motels/Motor Lodges

★ ★ **BEST WESTERN.** *2815 Candlers Mountain Rd (24502). 804/237-2986; toll-free 800/528-1234. www.bestwestern.com.* 87 rms, 2-3 story. S $59; D $69; each addl $8; under 12 free; higher rates: homecoming, graduation. Crib free. TV; cable (premium). Pool. Complimentary continental bkfst, coffee in rms. Restaurant adj 11 am-midnight. Ck-out 11 am. Meeting rms. Business servs avail. In-rm modem link. Valet serv. Sundries. Health club privileges. Microwaves avail. Cr cds: A, C, D, DS, MC, V.

[D] [≈] [≈] [≈] [SC]

★ **COMFORT INN.** *3125 Albert Lankford Dr (24501). 804/847-9041; fax 804/847-8513; res 800/228-5150. www.comfortinn.com.* 120 rms, 5 story. S $71-$85; D $76-$90; each addl $5; suites $151-$170; under 18 free; higher rates: homecoming, graduation. Crib free. Pet accepted. TV; cable (premium), VCR avail. Complimentary full bkfst, coffee in rms. Restaurant nearby. Ck-out noon. Meeting rms. Business servs avail. Free airport, RR station transportation. Health club privileges. Pool. Some refrigerators, microwaves. Balconies. Picnic tables, grills. Cr cds: A, D, DS, JCB, MC, V.

[D] [≈] [≈] [⊀] [≈] [≈]

★ **DAYS INN.** *3320 Candlers Mt Rd (24502). 804/847-8655; fax 804/846-3297; res 800/787-3297. www.daysinn.com.* 131 rms, 5 story. S, D $64-$74; each addl $8; under 17 free. Crib free. TV; cable (premium). Pool. Playground. Restaurant 6 am-2 pm, 5 pm-midnight. Ck-out noon. Meeting rms. Business servs avail. In-rm modem link. Valet serv. Sundries. Free airport, RR station, bus depot transportation. Health club privileges. Microwaves avail. Private patios, balconies. Cr cds: A, C, D, DS, JCB, MC, V.

[D] [≈] [≈] [≈] [SC]

★ **ECONO LODGE INN.** *2400 Stadium Dr (24501). 804/847-1045; fax 804/846-0086. www.econolodge.com.* 48 rms, 2 story. S $39.95-$55; D $55-$80. Crib free. TV; cable (premium). Continental bkfst. Restaurant nearby.

Ck-out 11 am. Business servs avail. Cr cds: A, C, D, DS, JCB, MC, V.

★ ★ **HAMPTON INN.** *5604 Seminole Ave (24502). 804/237-2704; fax 804/239-9183; res 800/426-7866. www.hamptoninn.com.* 65 rms, 2 story. S $61-$67; D $71-$77; under 18 free; higher rates Randolph-Macon graduation. Crib avail. TV; cable (premium). Complimentary continental bkfst. Restaurant adj 10:30 am-midnight. Ck-out noon. Business servs avail. Health club privileges. Sundries. Cr cds: A, D, DS, MC, V.

★ ★ **HOLIDAY INN.** *5600 Seminole Ave (24501). 804/237-7771; fax 804/239-0659; res 800/465-4329. www.holiday-inn.com.* 104 rms, 3 story. S $49.99-$55.99; D $54.99-$59.99; each addl $5; under 16 free. Crib free. TV; cable (premium). Pool. Complimentary continental bkfst. Restaurant nearby. Ck-out noon. Meeting rm. Valet serv. Health club privileges. Microwaves avail. Cr cds: A, C, D, DS, JCB, MC, V.

★ ★ **HOLIDAY INN SELECT.** *601 Main St (24505). 804/528-2500; fax 804/528-0062. www.holiday-inn.com.* 243 units, 8 story. S, D $72; each addl $10; suites $85-$110; under 17 free. Crib free. Pet accepted. TV; cable (premium). Pool; poolside serv. Restaurant 6:30 am-10 pm. Bar 3 pm-1 am. Ck-out noon. Meeting rms. Business servs avail. In-rm modem link. Free airport, RR station, bus depot transportation. Exercise equipt. Some bathrm phones, refrigerators; microwaves avail. Cr cds: A, C, D, DS, JCB, MC, V.

★ **HOWARD JOHNSON.** *US 29 N, Madison Heights (24572). 804/845-7041; fax 804/845-4718; res 800/446-4656. www.hojo.com.* 70 rms, 2 story. S, D $46-$77; each addl $7; under 18 free. Crib free. TV; cable (premium). Pool; wading pool. Restaurant 6 am-10 pm. Ck-out noon. Coin lndry. Business servs avail. Valet serv. Sundries. Free airport transportation. Microwaves avail. Private patios, balconies. Cr cds: A, C, D, DS, MC, V.

Hotel

★ ★ ★ **HILTON.** *2900 Candlers Mtn Rd (24502). 804/237-6333; fax 804/237-4277; res 800/221-4982. www.hilton.com.* 168 rms, 5 story. S $85-$120; D $105-$140; each addl $20; suites $186; family rates. Crib free. TV; cable (premium). Indoor pool; whirlpool. Restaurant 6:30 am-2 pm, 5:30-10 pm. Bar 11-1:30 am; entertainment. Ck-out 11 am. Meeting rms. Business center. Bellhops. Valet serv. Sundries. Gift shop. Free airport transportation. Exercise equipt; sauna. Bathrm phone in suites. Microwaves avail. Cr cds: A, C, D, MC, V.

B&Bs/Small Inns

★ ★ ★ **1880'S MADISON HOUSE.** *413 Madison St (24504). 434/528-1503. www.madisonhousebb.com.* 4 rms, 2 story. S $79-$99; D $89-$119; each addl $10; suite $109-$119. TV; cable (premium). Complimentary full bkfst. Ck-out 11 am, ck-in 3-6 pm. Free airport, RR station transportation. Some fireplaces. Victorian mansion (1880); antiques. Library features antiques, Civil War collection. Totally nonsmoking. Cr cds: A, MC, V.

★ ★ ★ **LYNCHBURG MANSION BED AND BREAKFAST.** *405 Madison St (24504). 804/528-5400; fax 804/847-2545; toll-free 800/352-1199. www.bbonline.com/va/lynchburg.* 5 rms, 2 story. S $104-$139; D $109-$144; each addl $25; under 8 free. TV; cable. Complimentary full bkfst. Ck-out 11 am, ck-in 3-6 pm. Some refrigerators, fireplaces. Picnic tables. Spanish/Georgian mansion built 1914; individually decorated rms incl Gilliam Room (traditional English-manor style) and Bowen Room (Country-French style). Back porch overlooks landscaped grounds. Totally nonsmoking. Cr cds: A, D, MC, V.

Restaurants

★ ★ **CROWN STERLING.** *6120 Fort Ave (24502). 804/239-7744.* Hrs: 5:30-10 pm. Closed Sun; hols. Res accepted. Bar from 5 pm. Dinner $12-$24. Specializes in steak. Salad bar. Parking. Colonial decor. Cr cds: A, D, DS, MC, V.

★ ★ **JEANNE'S.** *9789 Richmond Hwy (24504).* 804/993-2475. Hrs: 11:30 am-2:30 pm, 4:30-9 pm; wkends to 10 pm; Sun noon-9 pm; Jan-Mar noon-2 pm, 5-9 pm. Closed July 4; also late Dec. Lunch $3.95-$9.95, dinner $6.95-$20.95. Child's menu. Specializes in steak, seafood. Salad bar. Own desserts. Parking. Rustic redwood overlooking lake, dining on deck. Cr cds: A, C, D, DS, MC, V.
D

★ ★ **LANDMARK STEAKHOUSE.** *6113 Fort Ave (24502).* 804/237-1884. Hrs: 5:30-10 pm; Sat, Sun from 5:30 pm. Closed Mon; hols. Bar. Dinner $6.95-$25.95. Child's menu. Specialties: prime rib, filet mignon. Salad bar. Piano bar. Parking. Cr cds: A, MC, V.
D

★ ★ ★ **SACHIKO'S PORTERHOUSE.** *126 Old Graves Mill Rd (24502).* 804/237-5655. Hrs: 5:30-10 pm. Closed Sun; hols. Res accepted. Bar. Dinner $10.95-$25. Specializes in New American cuisine. Own baking. Parking. Fireplaces. Cr cds: A, MC, V.
D

★ **T. C. TROTTER'S.** *2496 Rivermont Ave (24503).* 804/846-3545. Hrs: 11:30 am-10 pm. Closed Mon; Thanksgiving, Dec 25. Res accepted. Bar to 2 am. Lunch $6.95-$9.95, dinner $6.95-$19.95. Child's menu. Specializes in fajitas, steak, seafood. Outdoor dining. Cr cds: A, D, DS, MC, V.

Manassas

(C-6) *See also Arlington County (Ronald Reagan Washington-National Airport Area), Fairfax, Falls Church, Triangle; also see District of Columbia*

Pop 35,135 **Elev** 321 ft **Area code** 703

Information Prince William County/Manassas Conference & Visitors Bureau, 14420 Bristow Rd, 20112; 703/792-4254 or 800/432-1792
Web www.visitpwc.com

Though the Native Americans who had lived in this area for thousands of years were driven out under a treaty in 1722, settlement remained concentrated along the Potomac River until the coming of the railroad in 1858. The Manassas rail junction was vital to the South, and many troops were stationed along this line of communication. Control of this junction led to two major battles nearby (see MANASSAS (BULL RUN) NATIONAL BATTLEFIELD PARK).

What to See and Do

The Manassas Museum. Museum features collections dealing with Northern Virginia Piedmont history from prehistoric to modern times, with special emphasis on Civil War. (Tues-Sun; closed hols) 9101 Prince William St. Phone 703/368-1873. ¢¢

Special Event

Prince William County Fair. Carnival, entertainment, tractor pull, exhibits, contests. Phone 703/368-0173. Mid-Aug.

Motels/Motor Lodges

★ ★ **BEST WESTERN.** *10820 Balls Ford Rd (20109).* 703/361-8000; fax 703/361-8000; toll-free 800/528-1234. www.bestwestern.com. 121 rms, 2 story. S $54-$89; D $64-$89; each addl $10; under 18 free. Crib free. Pet accepted; $10/day. TV; cable (premium). Pool. Complimentary continental bkfst. Restaurant 5-10 pm; closed Sun. Bar to midnight, Fri, Sat to 2 am; entertainment Tues-Sat. Ckout 11 am. Meeting rms. Business servs avail. In-rm modem link. Valet serv. Sundries. Health club privileges. Refrigerators, microwaves avail. Cr cds: A, C, D, DS, MC, V.
D

★ ★ **BEST WESTERN INN.** *8640 Mathis Ave (20110).* 703/368-7070; fax 703/368-7292; res 800/528-1234. www.bestwestern.com. 60 rms, 2 story. Apr-Oct: S, D $59-$79; under 18 free;

higher rates: special events, hol wkends; lower rates rest of yr. Crib free. TV; cable (premium). Complimentary continental bkfst. Restaurant adj 4 pm-2 am. Ck-out 11 am. Coin lndry. Business servs avail. Whirlpool. Sauna. Refrigerators, microwaves; some in-rm whirlpools. Cr cds: A, C, D, DS, MC, V.

D ⌖ ⌖

★ ★ **COURTYARD BY MARRIOTT.** *10701 Battleview Pkwy (20109). 703/ 335-1300; fax 703/335-9442; toll-free 800/321-2211. www.marriott.com.* 149 rms, 3 story. S, D $89-$98; each addl $5; suites $100-$115; under 18 free. Crib free. TV; cable (premium). Indoor pool; whirlpool. Complimentary coffee in rms. Restaurant 6:30-10 am, 5-10 pm; Sat, Sun 7 am-noon. Bar. Ck-out noon. Coin lndry. Meeting rms. Business servs avail. In-rm modem link. Valet serv. Sundries. Exercise equipt. Health club privileges. Refrigerators, microwaves avail. Balconies. Cr cds: A, C, D, DS, MC, V.

D ⌖ ⌖ ⌖ ⌖ SC

★ **DAYS INN.** *10653 Balls Ford Rd (20109). 703/368-2800; fax 703/368-0083; toll-free 800/329-7466. www. daysinn.com.* 120 rms, 2 story. S $56; D $62; each addl $6; under 18 free. Crib free. TV; cable (premium). Pool. Complimentary continental bkfst. Ck-out 11 am. Coin lndry. Business servs avail. Health club privileges. Refrigerators avail. Cr cds: A, C, D, DS, MC, V.

D ⌖ ⌖ ⌖ SC

★ ★ **HOLIDAY INN.** *10800 Vandor Ln (20109). 703/335-0000; fax 703/ 361-8440. www.holiday-inn.com.* 158 rms, 5 story. S $125; D $130; under 12 free. Crib free. Pet accepted, some restrictions; deposit. TV; cable (premium). Pool. Complimentary coffee. Restaurant 6-11 am, 6-11 pm. Bar 4-11 pm; Fri, Sat to midnight. Ck-out noon. Coin lndry. Meeting rms. Business servs avail. In-rm modem link. Valet serv. Exercise equipt. Health club privileges. Refrigerators, microwaves avail. Near Manassas (Bull Run) Battlefield. Cr cds: A, C, D, DS, MC, V.

D ⌖ ⌖ ⌖ ⌖ ⌖

★ **RED ROOF INN.** *10610 Automotive Dr (20109). 703/335-9333; fax 703/335-9342; res 800/733-7663.*

www.redroof.com. 119 rms, 3 story. S $52.99-$68.99; D $57.99-$72.99; under 18 free; higher rates: Cherry Blossom, hol wkends. Crib free. Pet accepted, some restrictions. TV; cable (premium). Complimentary coffee in lobby. Restaurant adj 6-2 am. Ck-out noon. Business servs avail. Sundries. Cr cds: A, C, D, DS, MC, V.

D ⌖ ⌖ ⌖

★ **SUPER 8 MOTEL.** *8691 Phoenix Dr (22110). 703/369-6323; fax 703/ 369-9206; toll-free 800/800-8000. www. super8.com.* 78 rms, 3 story. S $42-$50; D $47-$55; each addl $5; under 18 free. Crib free. TV; cable (premium). Complimentary continental bkfst, coffee in rms. Restaurant adj 6 am-11 pm. Ck-out 11 am. Business servs avail. Some in-rm whirlpools; microwaves avail. Cr cds: A, C, D, MC, V.

D ⌖ ⌖ SC

Restaurants

★ ★ ★ **CARMELLO'S AND LITTLE PORTUGAL.** *9108 Center St (20110). 703/368-5522. www.carmellos.com.* Hrs: 11:30 am-2:30 pm, 5-10 pm; Sat from 5 pm, Sun 4-9 pm. Closed most major hols. Res accepted. Northern Italian, Portuguese menu. Bar. Lunch $7-$11, dinner $12-$20. Child's menu. Specializes in fresh seafood, veal, chicken. Own pasta. Pianist Sat. Located in two-story brick storefront. Cr cds: A, C, D, DS, MC, V.

D

★ ★ **HERO'S AMERICAN.** *9412 Main St (20110). 703/330-1534. herosmanassas.com.* Hrs: 11 am-10 pm; Thurs-Sat to 12:30 am; Sun from noon. Contemporary American menu. Bar to 1:30 am. Lunch, dinner $5.25-$18.95. Specializes in fresh seafood, hamburgers, sandwiches. Salad bar. Own desserts, ice cream. Jazz Sat. Outdoor dining. Contemporary Amer pub; two-level dining; jazz memorabilia. Cr cds: A, D, DS, MC, V.

D ⌖

★ ★ ★ **PANINO.** *9116 Mathis Ave (20110). 703/335-2566.* Hrs: 11:30 am-2:30 pm, 5:30-10 pm; Sat from 5:30 pm. Closed Sun; hols. Res accepted; required Fri, Sat dinner. Northern Italian menu. Serv bar. Wine list. Lunch $8.50-$12.50, dinner $9-$19. Specialties: homemade

Tuscan bread, seafood ravioli, osso buco. Own baking. Contemporary Italian decor; extensive art collection. Cr cds: A, D, DS, MC, V.

D

Manassas (Bull Run) National Battlefield Park

See also Falls Church, Manassas

(26 mi SW of Washington, D.C., at jct US 29, VA 234)

This 5,000-acre park was the scene of two major Civil War battles. More than 26,000 men were killed or wounded here in struggles for control of a strategically important railroad junction.

The first major land battle of the war (July 21, 1861) was fought here between poorly trained volunteer troops from both North and South. The battle finally resolved itself into a struggle for Henry Hill, where "Stonewall" Jackson earned his nickname. With the outcome in doubt, Confederate reinforcements arrived by railroad from the Shenandoah Valley and turned the battle into a rout.

Thirteen months later (August 28-30, 1862), in the second battle of Manassas, Robert E. Lee outmaneuvered and defeated Union General John Pope and cleared the way for a Confederate invasion of Maryland.

Contact Park Superintendent, 6511 Sudley Rd, Manassas 22110; phone 703/361-1339. Park (daily; closed Dec 25). ¢¢

What to See and Do

Chinn House Ruins. The house served as a field hospital in both engagements and marked the left of the Confederate line at First Manassas; also the scene of Longstreet's counterattack at Second Manassas.

Dogan House. An original structure at Groveton, a village around which the battle of Second Manassas was fought.

Stone Bridge. Where Union artillery opened the Battle of First Manassas; it afforded an avenue of escape for the Union troops after both First and Second Manassas.

Stone House. Originally a tavern (ca 1848), used as field hospital in both battles. (Summer, daily) Phone 703/361-1339.

Unfinished Railroad. Fully graded railroad bed, never completed, behind which Stonewall Jackson's

Stone Bridge

men were positioned during the second battle.

Visitor Center. Hill affords view of much of the first battlefield. Information; self-guided tours start here (walking tour of First Manassas, directions for driving tour of Second Manassas). Markers throughout park explain various aspects of battles. Ranger-conducted tours (summer). On Henry Hill, just N of I-66 off VA 234. Phone 703/361-1339. In same building is

> **Battlefield Museum.** Exhibits reflect incidents of battles; audiovisual presentations offer orientation. (Daily; closed Dec 25)

Marion

(F-3) *See also Abingdon, Wytheville*

Founded 1835 **Pop** 6,349 **Elev** 2,178 ft **Area code** 540 **Zip** 24354
Information Chamber of Commerce of Smyth County, 124 W Main St, PO Box 924; 540/783-3161
Web www.swanva.net/smythcoc.htm

This popular vacation spot is surrounded by Washington and Jefferson national forests, abounding in game and birds, near a state park, and high enough to promise an invigorating climate. The seat of Smyth County, it was named for General Francis Marion, known during the American Revolution as the "Swamp Fox."

What to See and Do

George Washington and Jefferson National Forests. (See HARRISONBURG) SE of town via VA 16 is the

> **Mount Rogers National Recreation Area.** A 140,000-acre area that incl Mt Rogers, the state's highest point (5,729 ft), mi-high open meadows known as "balds," and a great variety of animals and plants. Swimming, fishing; hunting, camping (fee at some areas), four visitor centers, approx 400 mi of hiking, bicycle, and bridle trails. Mount Rogers Scenic Byway (auto); Virginia Creeper Trail (hikers, bicycles, horses) follows an abandoned rail-

road grade through spectacular river gorges. Adj to New River Trails State Park (see ABINGDON). Visitor Center (Daily all yr) (Mid-May-Mid-Sept, daily; rest of yr, Mon-Fri) Some fees. Phone 276/783-5196.

Hungry Mother State Park. More than 2,180 acres amid the mountains with a 108-acre lake; panoramic views. Swimming beach, bathhouse, fishing, boating (rentals, launching, electric motors only); hiking, self-guided trails, picnicking, restaurant, concession, tent and trailer sites (electrical hookups, late Mar-Dec), cabins (yr round). Hilltop visitor center, interpretive programs. Standard fees. 3 mi N on VA 16. Phone 276/781-7400. ¢

Special Events

Whitetop Ramp Festival. Mid-May.

Hungry Mother Arts and Crafts Festival. Hungry Mother State Park. Mid-July.

Chilhowie Apple Festival. Mid-Sept.

Motel/Motor Lodge

★ ★ **BEST WESTERN INN.** *1424 N Main St (24354). 540/783-3193; fax 540/783-3193; toll-free 800/528-1234. www.bestwestern.com.* 79 rms, 1-2 story. S $54-$68, D $59-$72; under 18 free. Crib free. TV; cable (premium). Pool. Complimentary continental bkfst. Restaurant 5:30-9:30 pm. Bar 5 pm-midnight; closed Sun. Ck-out noon. Meeting rms. Business servs avail. Valet serv. Some microwaves. Cr cds: A, C, D, DS, JCB, MC, V.
🛰 ⬊ 🐾 🔥 **SC**

B&B/Small Inn

★ **FOX HILL INN.** *8568 Troutdale Hwy, Troutdale (24378). 540/677-3313; toll-free 800/874-3313. www.bbonline.com/va/foxhill.* 8 rms, 2 story. No A/C. No rm phones. S, D $75; each addl $10; under 18 free; wkly rates. Crib free. TV in sitting rm. Complimentary full bkfst. Restaurant nearby. Ck-out 10 am, ck-in 3 pm. X-country ski 5 mi. Situated on mountaintop with panoramic view. On 70 acres of woods and pasture; wildlife, farm animals; hiking trails. Cr cds: DS, MC, V.
🛰 ⬊ 🔥

Martinsville

(F-4) *See also Danville*

Founded 1793 **Pop** 15,416 **Elev** 1,020 ft **Area code** 540

Information Martinsville-Henry County Chamber of Commerce, 115 Broad St, PO Box 709, 24114; 540/632-6401

Web www.neocomm.net/~mhccoc

Martinsville was named for Joseph Martin, a pioneer who settled here in 1773. Henry County takes its name from Patrick Henry, who lived here. When Henry County Court first opened in October 1776, 640 residents pledged an oath of allegiance to the United States; 40 refused to renounce allegiance to England. Located near the beautiful Blue Ridge Mountains, this community is home to Bassett Furniture and E. I. du Pont de Nemours.

What to See and Do

Blue Ridge Farm Museum. Presents the heritage of mountain region through reconstructed farmsteads and "folklife galleries." Authentic buildings from 1800 German heritage farm, incl log house, kitchen, blacksmith shop, and barn. Costumed interpreters demonstrate farm and household chores. Special events (fees). (Mid-May-mid-Aug, wkends; rest of yr, by appt) VA 40 in Ferrum. Phone 540/365-4415. ¢¢

Fairy Stone State Park. Consists of 4,570 acres, with a 168-acre lake adjoining Philpott Reservoir. Nestled in the foothills of the Blue Ridge Mtns, this park is named for the "fairy stones" (staurolites) found near the southern tip of its boundary. Swimming beach, bathhouse, fishing, boating (launch, rentals, electric motors only); hiking and bicycle trails, picnic shelters, concession, cafe, tent and trailer sites (dump station, electrical hookups), cabins (Mar-Dec). Visitor center, eve programs. Standard fees. (Daily) 21 mi NW via US 220/VA 57, VA 346. Phone 276/930-2424.

Philpott Lake. State's fourth-largest lake, formed by Philpott Dam, a US Army Corps of Engineers project. Swimming, skin diving, waterskiing, boating, fishing; hunting, hiking, picnicking; four camping areas (Apr-Oct), one area free, some fees. Just NE of Fairy Stone State Park. Phone 276/629-2703.

Virginia Museum of Natural History. State museum focuses on preservation, study, and interpretation of Virginia's natural heritage. Features visual and hands-on exhibits; incl a computer-animated triceratops dinosaur and a life-size ground sloth model. Special events during the yr incl Earth Day (Apr) and Virginia Indian Festival (Sept). (Mon-Sat; closed hols) 1001 Douglas Ave. Phone 276/666-8600. **FREE**

Special Events

Stock car races. Martinsville Speedway. 3 mi S. Phone 540/956-3151. Miller Genuine Draft 300, mid-Mar. Hanes 500, late Apr. Goody's 500, late Sept. Taco Bell 300, mid-Oct.

Blue Ridge Folklife Festival. Held at Blue Ridge Farm Museum. Gospel, blues, and string band music; traditional regional crafts; regional foods; quilt show, antique autos, steam and gas-powered farm equipt. Sports events incl horse-pulling and log-skidding contests, coon dog swimming and treeing contests. Phone 540/365-4415. Late Oct.

Motels/Motor Lodges

★ ★ **BEST WESTERN INN.** *1755 Virginia Ave (24112). 540/632-5611; fax 540/632-1168; toll-free 800/528-1234. www.bestwestern.com.* 97 rms, 2 story, 20 suites. S $48; D $54; each addl $10; suites $49-$59; under 12 free; package plans. Crib free. Pet accepted. TV, cable (premium). Pool; wading pool. Complimentary coffee in rms. Restaurant 6 am-10 pm; Sat, Sun from 7 am. Bar 4 pm-midnight. Ck-out noon. Coin lndry. Meeting rms. Business servs avail. In-rm modem link. Valet serv. Sundries. Exercise equipt. Microwave avail. Cr cds: A, C, D, DS, ER, MC, V.

⬜ 🐾 ≈ 🏋 🔌 🔥 SC

★ ★ **DUTCH INN.** *2360 Virginia Ave, Collinsville (24078). 540/647-3721; fax 540/647-4857; toll-free 800/800-3996. www.dutchinns.com.* 150 rms, 2 story. S $48-$60; D $56-$66; each addl $6; suites $88-$125; studio rms $55-$75; under 16 free; higher rates race wks. Crib free. Pet accepted. TV; cable (premium). Pool; whirlpool, poolside serv. Restaurant 6 am-10:30 pm. Rm serv. Bar 4 pm-midnight; Fri, Sat to 2 am. Ck-out noon. Meeting rms. Business servs avail. In-rm modem link. Valet serv. Sundries. 18-hole golf privileges. Exercise equipt; sauna. Many bathrm phones, refrigerators; microwaves avail. Cr cds: A, C, D, DS, MC, V.

McLean

See also Arlington County (Ronald Reagan Washington-National Airport Area), Fairfax, Falls Church, Tyson's Corner; also see District of Columbia and Rockville, MD

Pop 38,929 **Elev** 300 ft **Area code** 703

Information Fairfax County Convention and Visitors Bureau, 8300 Boone Blvd, Suite 450, Tyson's Corner 22182; 703/790-3329 or 800/7-FAIRFAX

Web www.visitfairfax.org

What to See and Do

Claude Moore Colonial Farm. At Turkey Run. Demonstration of 1770s low-income working farm; costumed interpreters work with crops and animals using 18th-century techniques. (Apr-mid-Dec, Wed-Sun weather permitting; closed Thanksgiving) 2 mi E on VA 193 (Georgetown Pike). Phone 703/442-7557. ¢

Colvin Run Mill Historic Site. Tours of historical gristmill. General store, miller's house exhibit, barn and grounds (free). (Mar-Dec, Mon and Wed-Sun; rest of yr, wkends; closed Jan 1, Thanksgiving, Dec 25) 3 mi W via VA 123, then 5 mi NW via VA 7, on Colvin Run Rd in Great Falls. Phone 703/759-2771. ¢¢

Evans Farm. Approx 25 acres of farmland. Colonial atmosphere; 18th-century-style building with restaurant. Collection of early American cooking utensils; Robert E. Lee memorabilia. Country store, handcraft and doll shop, old mill. Farm animals for children to feed. (Daily; closed Dec 25) Chain Bridge Rd, on VA 123, 1 mi E of I-495 McLean-VA 123N exit 11. Phone 703/356-8000. **FREE**

Motel/Motor Lodge

★ ★ **HOLIDAY INN.** *1960 Chain Bridge Rd (22102). 703/893-2100; fax 703/356-8218; res 800/465-4329.* 316 rms, 9 story. S, D $179-$194; each addl $15; family rates; wkend rates. Crib free. TV; cable (premium). Indoor pool; whirlpool. Restaurant 6:30 am-10 pm. Bar; entertainment. Ck-out 1 pm. Conference facilities. Business center. In-rm modem link. Gift shop. Airport transportation. Exercise equipt. Balconies. Cr cds: A, DS, MC, V.

Restaurants

★ ★ **CAFE OGGI.** *6671 Old Dominion Dr (22101). 703/442-7360. www. cafeoggi.com.* Hrs: 11:30 am-2:30 pm, 5:30-10 pm; Sat, Sun from 5:30 pm. Closed hols. Res accepted; required Fri, Sat dinner. Italian menu. Serv bar. A la carte entrees: lunch $6.95-$11.95, dinner $9.95-$19.95. Specializes in fresh seafood, veal. Own baking, pasta. Cr cds: A, D, DS, MC, V.

★ ★ **CAFE TAJ.** *1379 Beverly Rd (22101). 703/827-0444.* Hrs: 11:30 am-2:30 pm, 5:30-10 pm; Fri, Sat to 10:30 pm. Closed July 4. Res accepted. Indian menu. Bar. Lunch $8.95-$10.95, dinner $8.95-$14.95. Lunch buffet (Mon-Fri) $8.99. Specialties: tandoori chicken tikka, prawns masala. Outdoor dining. Modern decor. Cr cds: A, C, D, DS, MC, V.

★ ★ **DA DOMENICO.** *1992 Chain Bridge Rd (22102). 703/790-9000.* Hrs: 11:30 am-11 pm; Sat from 5 pm. Closed Sun; hols. Res accepted; required Fri, Sat. Northern Italian menu. Bar. Lunch $7.95-$9.95, dinner $9.95-$23.95. Specializes in veal chops, seafood, fresh pasta. Parking.

Italian garden decor. Cr cds: A, D,
DS, MC, V.
🖪

★★★ **DANTE.** *1148 Walker Rd,
Great Falls (22066). 703/759-3131.
www.dante.com.* Hrs: 11:30 am-2:30
pm, 5:30-10:30 pm; Sat from 5:30
pm; Sun 4-9 pm. Closed hols. Res
accepted; required Fri, Sat. Northern
Italian menu. Bar. Wine list. A la
carte entrees: lunch $9.25-$14.50,
dinner $14.50-$22.95. Child's menu.
Specialties: grilled Dover sole, grilled
veal chops. Own pasta, bread. Parking. Patio dining. Converted country
house. Cr cds: A, C, D, DS, MC, V.
🅳

★★★ **IL BORGO.** *1381 Beverly Rd
#A (22101). 703/893-1400. www.
ilborgo.net.* Hrs: 11 am-midnight; Sat
from 5 pm; Sun 4-10:30 pm. Closed
hols. Res accepted; required Fri, Sat
dinner. Italian menu. Bar. Wine list.
Lunch $5.75-$13.50, dinner $12-
$17.50. Specializes in veal, pasta,
seafood. Own pastas, desserts. Cr cds:
A, C, D, DS, MC, V.
🅳

★★ **J GILBERT'S STEAKHOUSE.**
*6930 Old Dominion Dr (22101). 703/
893-1034.* Hrs: 11 am-10 pm; Fri, Sat
to 10:30 pm; Sun 10:30 am-9 pm;
early-bird dinner 4-6 pm; Sun
brunch 10:30 am-2 pm. Closed Dec
25. Bar to midnight. Lunch $5.99-
$10.95, dinner $5.99-$18.95. Child's
menu. Specializes in steak, pasta,
seafood. Outdoor dining. Parking.
Fireplaces. Cr cds: A, D, DS, MC, V.
🅳 🖪

★★ **J. R.'S GOODTIMES.** *8130 Watson St (22102). 703/821-0546. www.
jrsbeef.com.* Hrs: 11:30 am-3 pm, 5-
10:30 pm; Fri to 11 pm; Sat 5-11 pm;
Sun 5-9 pm. Closed July 4, Thanksgiving, Dec 24, 25. Res accepted;
required Fri, Sat. Bar. Lunch $5.95-
$9.50, dinner $13.50-$19.95. Special-
izes in sirloin, prime aged beef, fresh
seafood. Parking. Western-style chop
house. Cr cds: A, D, DS, MC, V.
🅳 🖪

★★ **KAZAN.** *6813 Redmond Dr
(22101). 703/734-1960.* Hrs: 11 am-
2:30 pm, 5-10 pm; Sat 5-10:30 pm.
Closed Sun. Res accepted. Turkish
menu. Serv bar. Lunch $6.95-$11.95,

dinner $11.95-$19.95. Child's menu.
Specializes in seafood, lamb. Middle
Eastern decor. Totally nonsmoking.
Cr cds: A, D, MC, V.
🅳

★★★ **L'AUBERGE CHEZ FRAN-
COIS.** *332 Springvale Rd, Great Falls
(22066). 703/759-3800. www.lauberge
chezfrancois.com.* Hrs: 5:30-9:30 pm;
Sun 1:30-8 pm. Closed Mon; Jan 1,
July 4, Dec 25. Res required. French
menu. Serv bar. Wine cellar. Table
d'hôte: dinner $36-$44. Prix fixe:
dinner $25-$26 (Tue-Thur, Sun). Specialties: salmon souffle de l'Auberge;
le saute gourmandise Papa Ernest; la
choucroute royale garnie comme en
Alsace. Own baking, ice cream. Outdoor dining. Chef-owned. Jacket.
Totally nonsmoking. Cr cds: A, C, D,
DS, MC, V.
🅳

★★ **PULCINELLA.** *6852 Old Dominion Dr (22101). 703/893-7777. www.
pulcinella.com.* Hrs: 11:30 am-10:45
pm; Sat, Sun from noon. Closed
Thanksgiving, Dec 25. Italian menu.
Bar. Lunch $4.25-$13.95, dinner
$6.50-$16.50. Specializes in pasta,
chicken. Italian decor. Cr cds: A, D,
MC, V.
🅳 🖪

★★★ **SERBIAN CROWN.** *1141
Walker Rd, Great Falls (22066). 703/
759-4150. www.serbiancrown.com.*
Hrs: 5:30-10 pm; Thurs, Fri noon-
2:30 pm; Sun 4-9 pm. Res accepted;
required Fri-Sun. Russian, Serbian
menu. Bar. Wine list. A la carte
entrees: lunch $8.95-$19.50, dinner
$17.50-$26. Prix fixe: dinner $26,
$39. Specialty: kulebiaka. Extensive
vodka selection. Own pastries. Piano
bar Tue, Fri, Sat. Gypsy music Wed-
Sun. Parking. Intimate atmosphere;
antique Russian paintings. Enclosed,
heated terrace dining. Family-owned.
Cr cds: A, C, D, DS, MC, V.
🅳

★★ **TACHIBANA.** *6715 Lowell Ave
(22101). 703/847-1771.* Hrs: 11:30
am-2 pm, 5-10 pm; Fri to 10:30 pm;
Sat noon-2:30 pm, 5-10:30 pm; Sun
12:30-3 pm, 4:30-9 pm. Closed hols.
Res accepted Mon-Thurs. Japanese
menu. Serv bar. Lunch $6.50-$15,
dinner $8.95-$30. Complete meals:
dinner $16.50-$30. Specialties: sushi,

sashimi, soft-shell crab tempura (in season). Parking. Circular dining rm. Totally nonsmoking. Cr cds: A, C, D, DS, MC, V.

Monterey

See also Staunton, Warm Springs

Pop 158 **Elev** 2,881 ft **Area code** 540 **Zip** 24465

Information Highland County Chamber of Commerce, PO Box 223; 540/468-2550

Special Event

Highland County Maple Festival. Tours of sugar camps producing maple syrup and maple sugar products. Juried craft show; food, entertainment. Phone 540/468-2550. Mar 13-14 and 20-21.

B&B/Small Inn

★ ★ **HIGHLAND INN.** *Main St (24465). 540/468-2143; fax 540/468-3143; res 888/466-4682. www. highland-inn.com/.* 17 rms, 3 story. No A/C. S, D $55-$95; suites $79-$95. TV; cable (premium). Dining rm Wed-Sat 6-8 pm; Sun (brunch)11:30 am-2 pm. Bar Mon-Sat 5-8 pm. Ckout 11 am, ck-in after 2 pm. Meeting rm. Business servs avail. Guest parlor. Porches. Victorian building furnished with period antiques. Built 1904. Cr cds: A, DS, MC, V.

Montross

Pop 315 **Elev** 149 ft **Area code** 804 **Zip** 22520

What to See and Do

Stratford Hall Plantation. Boyhood home of Richard Henry Lee and Francis Lightfoot Lee and birthplace of General Robert E. Lee. Center of restored, working plantation is monumental Georgian house built circa 1735, famous for its uniquely grouped chimney stacks. Interiors span approx 100-yr period and feature a Federal-era parlor and neoclassical paneling in the Great Hall. Flanking dependencies incl kitchen, plantation office, and gardener's house. Boxwood garden; 18th- and 19th-century carriages; working mill; visitor center with museum, video presentations. Plantation luncheon (daily). (Daily; closed Jan 1, Thanksgiving, Dec 25) 6 mi N on VA 3 to Lerty, then E on VA 214. Phone 804/493-8038. ¢¢¢

Westmoreland State Park. Approx 1,300 acres on Potomac River. Sand beach, swimming pool, bathhouse, fishing, boating (ramp, rentals); hiking trails, picnicking, playground, concession, camping, tent and trailer sites (Mar-Nov; dump station, electrical hookups), cabins (Mar-Dec). Visitor center, eve programs. Standard fees. 5 mi NW on VA 3, then N on VA 347. Phone 804/493-8821.

Mount Vernon

(A-2) *See also Alexandria, Fairfax, Springfield; also see District of Columbia*

(16 mi S of Washington, D.C. on George Washington Memorial Pkwy)

What to See and Do

Grist Mill Historical State Park. This mill was reconstructed in 1930 on original foundation of a mill George Washington operated on Dogue Run. Visitor center, programs. (Memorial Day-Labor Day, daily) 3 mi W on VA 235. Phone 703/780-3383. ¢

Potomac Spirit. Offers round-trip, Potomac River cruises from Washington, D.C. to Mount Vernon. The five-hr excursion is sufficient for a complete tour of house, gardens, and tomb (late Mar-early June, one trip daily; early June-late Aug, two trips daily). Phone 202/554-7447.

Woodlawn Plantation. (1800-1805) In 1799 George Washington gave 2,000 acres of land as a wedding present to Eleanor Parke Custis, his foster daughter, who married his nephew, Major Lawrence Lewis. Dr.

George Washington's Mount Vernon

William Thornton, first architect of the US Capitol, then designed this mansion. The Lewises entertained such notables as Andrew Jackson, Henry Clay, and the Marquis de Lafayette. The house was restored in the early 1900s and later became the residence of a US senator; 19th-century period rms; many original furnishings. Formal gardens. (Mar-Dec, daily; closed Jan-Feb, Thanksgiving, Dec 25) A National Trust for Historic Preservation property. 3 mi W of George Washington Pkwy on US 1. Phone 703/780-4000. ¢¢¢ Also here is

Frank Lloyd Wright's Pope-Leighey House. (1940) Erected in Falls Church in 1940, the house was disassembled (due to the construction of a new highway) and rebuilt at the present site in 1964. Built of cypress, brick, and glass, the house is an example of Wright's "Usonian" structures, which he proposed as a prototype of affordable housing for Depression-era middle-income families; original Wright-designed furniture. (Mar-Dec, daily; closed Jan-Feb, Thanksgiving, Dec 25) A National Trust for Historic Preservation property. Combination ticket

for both houses avail. Phone 703/780-4000. ¢¢¢

Restaurant

★ ★ **MOUNT VERNON INN.** *On grounds of Mt Vernon (22121). 703/780-0011. www.mountvernon.org.* Hrs: 11 am-3:30 pm, 5-9 pm; Sun to 4 pm. Res accepted. Bar. Lunch $5.25-$8.50, dinner $12-$23.75. Child's menu. Specializes in mesquite-grilled seafood, game dishes. Own desserts. Waiters in Colonial costume. Hand-painted murals of Colonial scenes. Cr cds: A, DS, MC, V.
D̄

Natural Bridge

See also Lexington

Founded 1774 **Pop** 200 **Elev** 1,078 ft
Area code 540 **Zip** 24578
Information Natural Bridge of Virginia, US 11 and VA 130, PO Box 57; 540/291-2121 or 800/533-1410
Web www.naturalbridgeva.com

Native Americans worshiped at the stone bridge nature formed across a deep gorge; town and county were both named after it. The limestone arch, 215 feet high, 90 feet long, and 150 feet wide in some places, attracted the interest of Thomas Jefferson, who purchased the bridge and 157 surrounding acres from King George III for 20 shillings, about $2.49, in 1774. Fully appreciative of this natural wonder, Jefferson built a cabin for visitors and installed caretakers. His guest book reads like a colonial "Who's Who." Surveyed by George Washington and painted by many famous artists, the bridge easily accommodates US 11. The Glenwood Ranger District of the Washington and Jefferson National Forests has its office in Natural Bridge.

What to See and Do

Cave Mountain Lake Recreation Area. Swimming; picnicking, camping (fee). (May-Oct) 7 mi S via VA 130, right on VA 759, then right on Forest Service Rd 781 in George Washington and Jefferson national forests. Phone 540/291-2189. ¢¢

Natural Bridge. Self-guided tours (one hr). (Daily) Jct US 11 and VA 130; I-81, exit 175 or 180. Phone 540/291-2121. ¢¢ Ticket incl entrance to

    Caverns of Natural Bridge. More than 300 ft below ground on three levels; streams, hanging gardens of formations, flowstone cascade, totem pole, colossal dome, and more. One-mi guided tour (one hr). (Mar-Nov, daily) ¢¢¢

    Drama of Creation. Musical presentation, viewed from beneath Natural Bridge, incl light show cast under and across arch. (Nightly) Combination tickets can also incl

Natural Bridge Wax Museum. Wax figures depicting local history; self-guided factory tours. US 11 and VA 130. (Daily). ¢¢¢

Natural Bridge Zoo. State's largest and most complete zoo with over 400 reptiles, birds, and mammals. Petting area; safari shop; picnic grounds. (Mar-Nov, daily) I-81 between exits 175 and 180. Phone 540/291-2420. ¢¢

Motel/Motor Lodge

★ **WATTSTULL COURT.** *RR 1 Box 21, Buchanan (24066).* 540/254-1551. 26 rms. S, D $40-$48; each addl $3. Crib $4. Pet accepted. TV. Pool; wading pool. Restaurant 6 am-10 pm. Ck-out 11 am. Panoramic view of Shenandoah Valley. Cr cds: MC, V.
🐾 🏊 🖎 ♿

Hotel

★ ★ **NATURAL BRIDGE.** *US Hwy 11 (24578).* 540/291-2121; fax 540/291-1551; toll-free 800/533-1410. www. naturalbridgeva.com. 180 rms in hotel and inn. S, D $59-$129; under 18 free. Crib free. TV; cable. Indoor pool. Restaurant 7 am-9:30 pm. Bar 4-10 pm. Ck-out noon. Meeting rms. Business servs avail. Gift shop. Tennis. Miniature golf. Game rm. Cr cds: A, D, DS, MC, V.
🏌 🏊 🖎 ♿ SC

New Market

See also Basye, Harrisonburg, Luray

Settled 1761 **Pop** 1,637 **Elev** 1,060 ft **Area code** 540 **Zip** 22844

Information Shenandoah Valley Travel Association, PO Box 1040; 540/740-3132

Web www.svta.org

New Market, situated in the Shenandoah Valley, gained its niche in Virginia history on May 15, 1864 when, in desperation, Confederate General Breckinridge ordered the cadets from Lexington's Virginia Military Institute to join the battle against the forces of General Franz Sigel. The oldest was just 20, but they entered the fray fearlessly, taking prisoners and capturing a battery. Their heroism inspired the Confederate defeat of Sigel's seasoned troops.

What to See and Do

Bedrooms of America. Authentic furnishings from William and Mary through art deco periods. Antique dolls. Gift shop. (Daily; closed Dec

25) 9386 Congress St, I-81 exit 264. Phone 540/740-3512. ¢

Endless Caverns. Lighted display of unusual rock formations; stalagmites and stalactites, columns, shields, flowstone and limestone pendants, presented in natural color. Temperature 55°F summer and winter. Camping. Guided tours (75 min). (Daily; closed Dec 25) Via I-81, exit 257 or 264, then approx 3 mi on US 11 to entrance. ¢¢¢

New Market Battlefield State Historical Park. Site of Civil War Battle of New Market (May 15, 1864), in which 257 VMI cadets played a decisive role. Original Bushong farmhouse and outbuildings restored, period furnishings. Hall of Valor; exhibits; films. Scenic overlooks, walking tour. (Daily; closed Jan 1, Thanksgiving, Dec 24,25) 1 mi N of I-81 exit 264. Phone 540/740-3101. Also here is

New Market Battlefield Military Museum. Located on actual site of Battle of New Market, the museum houses a private collection of more than 2,000 military artifacts and genuine, personal artifacts of the American soldier from 1776 to the present. Incl uniforms, weapons, battlefield diaries, medals, mementos; film (30 min). Bookshop has more than 500 titles, some antique. Union and Confederate troop position markers are on museum grounds. (Mid-Mar-Nov, daily) George R. Collins Dr, ¼ mi N of I-81 exit 264. Phone 540/740-8065. ¢¢

Shenandoah Caverns. Elevator lowers visitors 60 ft to large subterranean rms, fascinating rock formations; snack bar, picnic areas. Interior a constant 54°F. (Daily; closed Dec 25) 4 mi N, off I-81 exit 269. Phone 540/477-3115. ¢¢¢¢

Motels/Motor Lodges

★ **BUDGET INN.** 2192 Old Valley Pike (22844). 540/740-3105; fax 540/740-3108; toll-free 800/296-6835. www.budgetinn.com. 14 rms, 5 with shower only. Mid-Apr-mid-Nov: S $24-$34; D $28-$44; each addl $3; under 12 free; higher rates special events; lower rates rest of yr. Crib $3. Pet accepted, some restrictions. TV; cable (premium). Playground. Complimentary coffee in lobby. Restaurant nearby. Ck-out 11 am. Business servs avail. Refrigerators. Picnic tables. Cr cds: A, C, D, DS, MC, V.

★ **QUALITY INN SHENANDOAH VALLEY.** 162 W Old Cross Rd (22844). 540/740-3141; fax 540/740-3250; toll-free 800/638-7949. www.qualityinn. com. 101 rms, 2 story. May-Oct: S $55-$70; D $70-$85; each addl $6; lower rates rest of yr. Crib free. TV; cable (premium); VCR avail. Pool. Sauna. Playground. Complimentary coffee in rms. Restaurant 6:30 am-9 pm. Ck-out noon. Coin lndry. Meeting rms. Business servs avail. In-rm modem link. Gift shops. Game rm. Miniature golf. Cr cds: A, C, D, DS, ER, MC, V.

Resort

★ **SHENVALEE GOLF RESORT.** 9660 Fairway Dr (22844). 540/740-3181; fax 540/740-8931. www.shenvalee.com. 42 rms, 1-2 story. Apr-Oct: S $55; D $62-$66; each addl $12; under 13 free; golf plan; lower rates rest of yr. Crib free. TV; cable. Pool; wading pool. Restaurant 6:15 am-9 pm; Sun to 8 pm. Bar 4:30 pm-midnight; wkends to 2 am. Ck-out 1 pm. Meeting rms. Business servs avail. Tennis. 27-hole golf privileges, greens fee $22-$25, putting green, driving range. Refrigerators. Balconies. Picnic tables. On 200 acres. Cr cds: A, C, D, DS, MC, V.

Newport News

(E-7) *See also Hampton, Norfolk, Portsmouth, Virginia Beach, Yorktown*

Settled 1619 **Pop** 180,150 **Elev** 25 ft **Area code** 757

Information Visitor Center, 13560 Jefferson Ave, 23603; 757/886-7777 or 888/4-WE-R-FUN

Web www.newport-news.org

One of the three cities (also see NOR-FOLK and PORTSMOUTH) that make up the Port of Hampton Roads, Newport News has the world's largest shipbuilding company, Newport News Shipbuilding. Fourteen miles long and 40 feet deep, Hampton Roads is one of the world's finest natural harbors, formed by the James, York, Elizabeth, and Nansemond rivers as they pass into Chesapeake Bay. The largest ships are accommodated at Newport News docks; huge tonnages of coal, ore, tobacco, and grain are shipped from the port annually. During the two World Wars it was a vitally important point of embarkation and supply. The area still has many important defense establishments.

Newport News is located on the historic Virginia Peninsula between Williamsburg and Virginia Beach. The peninsula contains Hampton, Yorktown, Jamestown, and Williamsburg. Some of the earliest landings in this country were here. The name of the town is said to derive from the good "news" of the arrival of Captain Christopher Newport, who brought supplies and additional colonists to the settlement at Jamestown.

What to See and Do

Fort Eustis. Headquarters of US Army Transportation Center. Self-guided auto tour avail; brochures at Public Affairs Office (Building 213). NW end of city on Mulberry Island, I-64 exit 250A. Phone 757/878-4920. **FREE** On grounds is

US Army Transportation Museum. Depicts development of Army transportation from 1776 to the present; "flying saucer," amphibious vehicles, trucks, helicopters. Gift shop. (Tues-Sun; closed hols) Phone 757/878-1115. **FREE**

Historic Hilton Village. Listed on the National Register of Historic Places, this village was built between 1918-1920 to provide wartime housing for workers at Newport News Shipbuilding. Architecturally significant neighborhood features 500 English cottage-style homes and antique and specialty shops. I-64 exit 263A, at Warwick Blvd and Main St. **FREE**

Mariners' Museum. Exhibits and displays represent international nautical history; ship models, figureheads, scrimshaw, paintings, decorative arts, and small craft. Age of Exploration Gallery chronicles advancements in shipbuilding, ocean navigation, and cartography that led to early transoceanic exploration. The Chesapeake Bay Gallery exhibits Native American artifacts, workboats, racing shells, multimedia exhibits, a working steam engine, and hundreds of artifacts and photos that tell the story of this body of water. The Crabtree Collection of Miniature Ships showcases 16 detailed miniatures that illustrate the evolution of the sailing ship. Small craft gallery showcases vessels from five continents. A short film, *Sea Power Beyond the Horizon,* shows the historic and modern importance of the sea. Historical interpreters; research library; museum shop. A 550-acre park on the James River features five-mi Noland Trail with 14 pedestrian bridges; picnic area. Guided tours. (Daily; closed Thanksgiving, Dec 25) Warwick Blvd and J. Clyde Morris Blvd; 2½ mi off I-64 exit 258A. Phone 757/596-2222. ¢¢

Newport News Park. Facilities of this 8,065-acre park incl freshwater fishing, canoes, paddleboats, boat rentals; history and nature trails, bicycle paths (rentals), archery, arboretum, discovery center, picnicking, Civil War earthworks, 188 campsites. (All yr) Some fees. Jct VA 105, 143, I-64 exit 250B. Phone 757/886-7912. ¢¢¢¢

Peninsula Fine Arts Center. Changing bimonthly exhibits ranging from national traveling exhibitions to regional artists; classes, workshops, and special events. Children's hands-on activity area; museum shop. (Daily; closed hols) 101 Museum Dr, I-64 exit 258A. Phone 757/596-8175. ¢¢

Virginia Living Museum. Exhibits on natural science; wildlife, all native to Virginia, living in natural habitats; indoor and outdoor aviaries; aquariums; wildflower gardens; planetarium with daily shows; observatory; children's hands-on Discovery Center. (Daily; closed hols) 524 J. Clyde Morris Blvd, I-64 exit 258A. Phone 757/595-1900.

Virginia War Museum. More than 60,000 artifacts, incl weapons, uniforms, vehicles, posters, insignias, and accoutrements relating to every major US military involvement from the Revolutionary War to the Vietnam War. Military history library and film collection. Civil War tours and educational programs avail. (Mon-Sat, also Sun afternoons; closed Jan 1, Thanksgiving, Dec 25). 9285 Warwick Blvd in Huntington Park, on US 60, I-64 exit 263A. Phone 757/247-8523. ¢¢

Motels/Motor Lodges

★ **COMFORT INN.** *12330 Jefferson Ave (23602). 757/249-0200; fax 757/249-4736; toll-free 800/368-2477. www.comfortinn.com.* 124 rms, 3 story. S $84; D $94; each addl $7; under 18 free. Crib free. Pet accepted. TV; cable (premium). Pool. Complimentary continental bkfst, coffee in rms. Restaurant adj 11 am-midnight. Ck-out noon. Coin lndry. Meeting rms. Business servs avail. In-rm modem link. Free airport transportation. Health club privileges. Some refrigerators. Cr cds: A, C, D, DS, ER, JCB, MC, V.

[D] [symbols: ⚑ ≈ ≈ 🔥 SC]

★ ★ **HAMPTON INN.** *12251 Jefferson Ave (23602). 757/249-0001; fax 757/249-3911. www.hamptoninn.com.* 120 rms, 4 story, 30 suites. Memorial Day-Labor Day: S, D $79-$89; suites $109-$139; under 18 free; higher rates special events; lower rates rest of yr. Crib free. TV; cable (premium). Complimentary continental bkfst. Coffee in rms. Restaurant opp open 24 hrs. Ck-out noon. Meeting rms. Business center. In-rm modem link. Bellhops. Sundries. Free airport transportation. Pool. Some fireplaces; refrigerator, microwave in suites. Picnic tables, grills. Cr cds: A, D, DS, MC, V.

[D] [symbols: ≈ ✈ ≈ 🔥 🏃]

Hotel

★ ★ ★ **OMNI NEWPORT NEWS HOTEL.** *1000 Omni Blvd (23606). 757/873-6664; fax 757/873-1732; toll-free 800/843-6664.* 183 rms, 9 story. Memorial Day-Labor Day: S, D $119; each addl $10; under 17 free; higher rates special events; lower rates rest of yr. Crib avail. TV; cable (premium), VCR avail. Coffee in rms.

Indoor pool; whirlpool, poolside serv. Restaurant 6:30 am-11 pm. Bar 11-2 am; piano bar Mon-Sat. Ck-out noon. Meeting rms. Business center. In-rm modem link. Gift shop. Exercise equipt; sauna. Cr cds: A, C, D, DS, JCB, MC, V.

[D] [symbols: ≈ 🏃 ≈ 🔥 SC 🏃]

Restaurants

★ ★ **AL FRESCO.** *11710 Jefferson Ave (23606). 757/873-0644.* Hrs: 11 am-2:30 pm, 5-10 pm; Mon to 9 pm; Sat from 5 pm. Closed Sun; hols. Res accepted. French, Vietnamese menu. Bar. A la carte entrees: lunch $5.25-$6.75, dinner $9.95-$18.95. Specialties: panache de mer, veal Oscar, scallops in oyster sauce. Mediterranean cafe atmosphere. Cr cds: DS, MC, V.

[D]

★ ★ **DAS WALDCAFE.** *12529 Warwick Blvd (23606). 757/930-1781.* Hrs: 11:30 am-2 pm, 5-10 pm; Sat from 4 pm; Sun 11:30 am-9 pm. Closed Mon; hols. Res accepted. German menu. Bar. Lunch, dinner $3.75-$13.50. Specialties: schnitzel, rouladen, hazelnut cake. Cr cds: A, D, MC, V.

★ ★ **HERMAN'S HARBOR HOUSE.** *663 Deep Creek Rd (23606). 757/930-1000.* Hrs: 11:30 am-2:30 pm, 5-10 pm; Sat from 5 pm; Sun brunch 11:30 am-3 pm. Closed Dec 25. Res accepted. Bar. Lunch $4.95-$9.95, dinner $8.95-$19.95. Specializes in local seafood, steak. Nautical decor. Cr cds: A, DS, MC, V.

[D] [SC] [symbol]

★ ★ **PORT ARTHUR.** *11137 Warwick Blvd (23601). 757/599-6474.* Hrs: 11:30 am-10 pm; Fri, Sat to 10:30 pm; Sun noon-10 pm; Sun buffet noon-3 pm, 5:30-9 pm. Closed Thanksgiving, Dec 25. Res accepted. Chinese, American menu. Bar. Lunch $3.95-$5.95, dinner $5.95-$14.95. Complete meals: dinner $17.50-$63. Wkend buffet: dinner $7.95. Child's menu. Specialties: Phoenix nest, shrimp kew, Peking duck. Family-owned. Cr cds: A, DS, MC, V.

Norfolk (F-8)

Founded 1682 **Pop** 243,403 **Elev** 12 ft
Area code 757
Information Norfolk Convention and
Visitors Bureau, 232 E Main St, 23510;
757/664-6620 or 800/368-3097
Web www.norfolkcvb.com

Suburbs Chesapeake, Hampton,
Newport News, Portsmouth, Virginia
Beach. (See individual alphabetical
listings.)

This city is part of the Port of
Hampton Roads. It is a bustling trade
center and has many historic, cultural, and resort areas nearby to
attract the tourist. Harbor tours
depart from Norfolk's downtown
waterfront.

In 1682 the General Assembly
bought from Nicholas Wise, a pioneer settler, 50 acres on the Elizabeth
River for "ten thousand pounds of
tobacco and caske." By 1736 the
town that developed was the largest
in Virginia. On January 1, 1776, Norfolk was shelled by the British and
later burned by the colonists to prevent a British takeover. The battle
between the *Merrimac* and the *Moni-
tor* in Hampton Roads in March 1862
was followed by the fall of the city to
Union forces in May of that year. In
1883 the first shipment of coal to the
port by the Norfolk and Western Railway (now Norfolk Southern) began a
new era of prosperity for the city.

Norfolk and Portsmouth are connected by bridge tunnels and a
pedestrian ferry. Norfolk houses the
largest naval facility in the world. It
is also headquarters for the United
States Navy's Atlantic Fleet and
NATO's Allied Command Atlantic.
Norfolk has shipbuilding and ship
repair companies, consumer and
industrial equipment manufacturers,
and food-processing plants. The city
ships coal, tobacco, grain, seafood,
and vegetables. It is also the region's
cultural center, home to the Virginia
Opera, Virginia Symphony, Virginia
Waterfront International Arts Festival, and Virginia Stage Company.

Old Dominion University (1930),
Virginia Wesleyan College (1967),
Norfolk State University (1935), and
Eastern Virginia Medical School
(1973) are located here. This area is
also the headquarters for year-round
resort activities. Within a 50-mile
radius are ocean, bay, river, and
marsh fishing and hunting; nearby
there are 25 miles of good beaches.
The 17.6-mile-long Chesapeake Bay
Bridge-Tunnel between Norfolk and
the Delmarva Peninsula opened in
1964; toll for passenger cars is $10,
including passengers.

Transportation

Car Rental Agencies. See IMPOR-
TANT TOLL-FREE NUMBERS.

Public Transportation. Buses (Tidewater Regional Transit), phone 757/640-
6300.

Rail Passenger Service. Amtrak
800/872-7245.

Airport Information

Norfolk International Airport. Information 757/857-3351; lost and
found 757/857-3344; weather
757/666-1212.

What to See and Do

Chrysler Museum of Art. Art treasures representing nearly every
important culture, civilization, and
historical period of the past 4,000
yrs. Photography gallery; fine collection of Tiffany decorative arts and
glass, incl the 8,000-piece Chrysler
Institute of Glass. (Wed-Sun; closed
hols) 245 W Olney Rd, at Mowbray
Arch. Phone 757/664-6200. ¢¢

**General Douglas MacArthur Memor-
ial.** Restored former city hall (1847)
where MacArthur is buried. Nine galleries contain memorabilia of his life
and military career. There are three
other buildings on MacArthur Sq: a
theater where a film biography is
shown, a gift shop, and the
library/archives. (Daily; closed Jan 1,
Thanksgiving, Dec 25) City Hall Ave
and Bank St. Phone 757/441-2965.
DONATION

Hermitage Foundation Museum.
Guided tours of fine arts museum in
Tudor-style mansion. Collections of
tapestries, Chinese bronzes and jade,
ancient glass. (Daily; closed Jan 1,
Thanksgiving, Dec 25) 7637 North
Shore Rd. Phone 757/423-2052. ¢¢

Hunter House Victorian Museum.
Built in 1894 and rich in architectural details, the house contains the Hunter family's collection of Victorian furnishings and decorative pieces, incl a Renaissance Revival bedchamber suite, a nursery with children's playthings, an inglenook, and stained-glass windows; lavish period reproduction floor and wall coverings, lighting fixtures, and drapery. Also exhibited is a collection of early-20th-century medical memorabilia. Tours begin every 30 min. (Apr-Dec, Wed-Sat, also Sun afternoons; closed Jan 1, Thanksgiving, Dec 25). 240 W Freemason St. Phone 757/623-9814. ¢¢

Moses Myers House. (1792) Excellent example of Georgian architecture; many pieces of original furniture, silver and china. (Apr-Dec, Tues-Sun; rest of yr, Tues-Sat; closed hols) 331 Bank St. Phone 757/333-6283. ¢¢

Nauticus, the National Maritime Center. Interprets aspects from marine biology and ecology to exploration, trade, and shipbuilding. Interactive computer exhibits allow visitors to navigate a simulated ocean voyage, design a model ship, pilot a virtual reality submarine, and view actual researchers at work in two working marine laboratories. Active US Navy ships and scientific research vessels periodically moor at Nauticus and open to visitors. Also 350-seat, 70mm wide-screen theater; shark petting tank. (May-Sept, daily; rest of yr, Tues-Sun; closed Jan 1, Thanksgiving, Dec 25). 1 Waterside Dr. Phone 757/664-1000. ¢¢¢¢ Also here is

Hampton Roads Naval Museum.
Interprets the extensive naval history of the Hampton Roads area; incl detailed ship models, period photographs, archaeological artifacts, and a superior collection of naval prints and artwork. (Daily; closed Jan 1, Thanksgiving, Dec 25) Phone 757/444-8971. **FREE**

Norfolk Botanical Garden. Azaleas, camellias, rhododendrons, roses (May-Oct), dogwoods, and hollies on 155 acres. Japanese, Colonial, perennial, and rose gardens; flowering arboretum; Hill of Nations; fragrance garden for the visually impaired; picnicking, restaurant, and gift shop; tropical pavilion. Flowering displays best from early Apr-Oct. Gardens (daily; closed special events). Information center (daily; closed Jan 1, Dec 25). Narrated boat ride (30 min) and tram tours (mid-Mar-Labor Day, daily; through Oct wkends, trams only). 6700 Azalea Garden Rd, adj Norfolk International Airport. Phone 757/441-5830. ¢¢¢

Norfolk Naval Base and Norfolk Naval Air Station. The largest naval installation in the world. Ship visitors should check in at the Naval Base Pass Office on Hampton Blvd, opp Gate 5. Naval base tours are also offered. Tour buses from Tour and Information Office, 9079 Hampton Blvd (Apr-Oct, daily). Hampton Blvd and I-564. Phone 757/444-7955. ¢¢

St. Paul's Episcopal Church. (1739) Only building to survive burning of Norfolk in 1776. (Tues-Fri, also by appt) 201 St. Paul's Blvd, at City Hall Ave. Phone 757/627-4353. **Donation**

Sightseeing tours.

American Rover. This 135-ft, three-masted topsail passenger schooner cruises the "smooth waters" of Hampton Roads historical harbor; spacious sun decks; below-deck lounges; concessions. Tour passes historic forts, merchant and US Navy ships. Some tours pass the naval base (inquire for tour schedule). (Apr-mid-Oct, two- and three-hr tours daily) Waterside Marina, Waterside Dr exit off I-264. Phone 757/627-SAIL.

Carrie B Harbor Tours. Replica of 19th-century riverboat takes narrated 90-min tour of naval shipyard and inner harbor (Apr-Oct, daily); narrated 2½ hr tour of naval base (Apr-Oct, daily); 2½ hr sunset cruise to Hampton Roads and naval base (June-Labor Day, daily). Departs from the Waterside. (Also see PORTSMOUTH) Phone 757/393-4735.

Spirit of Norfolk. Harbor cruise aboard 600-passenger cruise ship. Captain's narration highlights the harbor's famous landmarks, incl Waterside Festival Marketplace, Portsmouth Naval Hospital, Old Fort Norfolk, Blackbeard's hiding place, Norfolk Naval Base, and downtown area's dynamic skyline. Luncheon cruise (Tues-Sun); eve dinner cruise (Tues-Sun); moonlight party cruise (Fri-Sat, in season). Departs from the Waterside. Phone 757/625-1748.

Virginia Zoological Park. A combination zoo, park, and conservatory. Playground, tennis courts, basketball courts; picnic area, concession. (Daily; closed Jan 1, Dec 25). 3500 Granby St. ¢¢

Waterside Festival Marketplace. A waterfront pavilion creating a lively marketplace with more than 90 shops, restaurants. (Daily; closed Thanksgiving, Dec 25) Bordering the Waterside are the city's marina and dock areas, where harbor tour vessels take on passengers. 333 Waterside Dr. A brick promenade skirting the marina connects the Waterside to

> **Town Point Park.** Home to Norfolk Festevents, the park hosts more than 100 free outdoor concerts, parties, dances, movies, and festivals each yr. 120 W Main St. Phone 757/441-2345.

Willoughby-Baylor House. (1794) Restored town house with period furnishings; herb and flower garden adj. (By appt; inquire at Moses Myers House) 601 E Freemason St. Phone 757/664-6200. ¢¢

Special Events

Virginia Waterfront International Arts Festival. Eighteen days of classical and contemporary music, dance, visual arts and theater performances. Phone 757/664-6492. Late Apr-mid-May.

International Azalea Festival. Downtown and Norfolk Botanical Garden. To honor NATO. Parade, coronation ceremony, air show (held at Norfolk Naval Air Station), events, concerts, fair, ball, entertainment. Late Apr.

Harborfest. Town Point Park, downtown waterfront on Wayside Dr. Sailboat and speedboat races, tall ships, ship tours, waterskiing, military demonstrations, entertainment, children's activities, fireworks, seafood. First full wkend June. Phone 757/441-2149.

Virginia Symphony. Chrysler Hall and other select locations. Five performance series. Phone 757/892-6366. Sept-May.

Virginia Children's Festival. Town Point Park. More than 200 educational, creative, and interactive activities; entertainment. Early Oct. Phone 757/441-2149.

Virginia Opera. Harrison Opera House and other select locations. Statewide opera company; traditional and contemporary works. Features young American artists. Phone 757/623-1223. Oct-Apr.

Motels/Motor Lodges

★ ★ **BEST WESTERN CENTER INN.** *235 N Military Hwy (23502). 757/461-6600; fax 757/466-9093; toll-free 800/237-5517. www.bestwestern.com.* 152 rms, 2 story. Memorial Day-Labor Day: S $59-$69; D $69-$99; each addl $10; suites $149-$179; under 13 free; higher rates: hols (3-day min), Jazz Festival; lower rates rest of yr. Crib free. TV; cable (premium), VCR avail (movies). 2 pools, 1 indoor; whirlpool. Complimentary coffee in rms. Restaurant 6 am-2 pm, 5-10 pm; Sat, Sun from 7 am. Bar. Ck-out noon. Coin lndry. Meeting rms. Business servs avail. In-rm modem link. Free airport transportation. Exercise equipt; sauna. Many refrigerators; microwaves avail. Picnic tables. Near airport. Cr cds: A, C, D, DS, MC, V.

[D] [≈] [✕] [⊠] [⊛] [SC]

★ **COMFORT INN.** *8051 Hampton Blvd (23505). 757/451-0000; fax 757/451-8394; res 800/228-5150. www.comfortinn.com.* 120 rms, 2 story. S, D $59-$80; each addl $5; under 18 free. Crib free. TV; cable (premium). Indoor pool; whirlpool. Complimentary continental bkfst. Restaurant nearby. Ck-out 11 am. Coin lndry. Business servs avail. In-rm modem link. Refrigerators; some microwaves. Cr cds: A, C, D, DS, JCB, MC, V.

[D] [≈] [⊠] [⊛]

★ **ECONO LODGE.** *9601 4th View St (23503). 757/480-9611; fax 757/480-1307; res 800/553-2666. www.econolodge.com.* 71 units, 3 story, 22 kits. Mid-May-Labor Day: S $54.95/ D $64.95; each addl $5; kit. units $69.95; under 18 free; wkly rates; higher rates: some hols, special events; lower rates rest of yr. Pet accepted, some restrictions; $50 deposit. TV; cable (premium), VCR avail (movies). Complimentary continental bkfst. Restaurant nearby. Ck-out 11 am. Business servs avail. Coin lndry. Exercise equipt. Refrigerators.

Ocean; fishing pier. Beach adj. Cr cds: A, C, D, DS, JCB, MC, V.

D 🔌 🏋 🛒 🔥

★ ★ **HAMPTON INN.** *1450 N Military Hwy (23502). 757/466-7474; fax 757/466-0117; res 800/426-7866. www. hamptoninn.com.* 130 units, 2 story. Late May-early Sept: S $65-$69; D $75; under 18 free; lower rates rest of yr. Crib free. TV; cable (premium). Pool. Coffee in rms. Restaurant opp 7 am-11 pm. Ck-out noon. Business servs avail. In-rm modem link. Valet serv. Free airport transportation. Health club privileges. Cr cds: A, C, D, DS, MC, V.

D 🛒 🛫 🛒 🔥

★ **HOLIDAY SANDS MOTEL AND TOWER.** *1330 E Oceanview Ave (23503). 757/583-2621; fax 757/587-7540; toll-free 800/525-5156.* 95 units, 2-5 story, 74 kits. Memorial Day-Labor Day: S, D $50-$95; each addl $5; suites $85-$105; kit. units $70-$95; under 12 free; lower rates rest of yr. Crib free. Meeting rms. TV; cable (premium). Heated pool. Complimentary continental bkfst. Restaurant nearby. Ck-out 11 am. Business servs avail. Coin lndry. Free airport transportation. Exercise equipt. Refrigerators, microwaves. Private patios, balconies. On beach. Cr cds: A, C, D, DS, MC, V.

D 🐾 🛒 🏋 🛒 🔥 SC

★ **SUPER 8 MOTEL.** *7940 Shore Dr (23518). 757/588-7888; fax 757/588-7888; toll-free 800/800-8000. www. super8.com.* 74 units, 3 story, 10 kit. units. June-Labor Day: S, D $46.95-$66; suites, kit. units $72.88-$89.47; higher rates: July 4, Labor Day; lower rates rest of yr. Crib free. TV; cable (premium). Complimentary continental bkfst. Restaurant nearby. Ck-out 11 am. Business servs avail. Some refrigerators, microwaves. Cr cds: A, C, D, DS, MC, V.

D 🛒 🔥 SC

Hotels

★ ★ **DOUBLETREE CLUB HOTEL.** *880 N Military Hwy (23502). 757/461-9192; fax 757/461-8290; res 800/933-9600. www.doubletreehotel.com.* 208 rms, 14 story. S $64-$115; D $74-$123; each addl $10; suites $175; under 18 free; wkend rates. Crib free.

TV, cable (premium). Pool. Restaurant 6:30 am-10:30 pm. Bar 11-1 am. Ck-out noon. Meeting rms. Business center. Exercise equipt. Free airport transportation. Microwaves avail. Balconies. Shopping mall adj. Cr cds: A, C, D, DS, ER, JCB, MC, V.

D 🛒 🏋 🛒 🔥 SC 🛫

★ ★ ★ **HILTON.** *1500 N Military Hwy (23502). 757/466-8000; fax 757/466-8802; toll-free 800/445-8667. www. hilton.com.* 250 rms, 6 story. S $94-$139; D $104-$149; each addl $15; suites $170-$360; under 18 free; package plans. Crib free. TV; cable (premium). Pool; whirlpool, poolside serv. Coffee in rms. Restaurant 6:30 am-midnight. Bars 4 pm-1 am; entertainment. Ck-out 1 pm. Convention facilities. Business servs avail. In-rm modem link. Gift shop. Beauty shop. Free airport transportation. Lighted tennis. Exercise equipt; sauna. Mini-bars. Luxury level. Cr cds: A, C, D, DS, ER, JCB, MC, V.

D 🎿 🛒 🏋 🛫 🛒 🔥 SC

★ ★ **JAMES MADISON.** *345 Granby St (23510). 757/622-6682; fax 757/623-5949; toll-free 888/402-6682.* 124 units, 8 story. S, D $70-$150; each addl $10; under 16 free; wkend rates. Crib free. TV; cable (premium). Restaurant 6:30 am-2:30 pm, 4-10 pm. Bar from 4 pm. Ck-out noon. Meeting rms. Business servs avail. In-rm modem link. Health club privileges. Cr cds: A, D, DS, MC, V.

D 🛒 🔥

★ ★ ★ **MARRIOTT NORFOLK WATERSIDE .** *235 E Main St (23510). 757/627-4200; fax 757/628-6466. www.marriott.com.* 404 rms, 24 story. S, D $109-$165; suites $250-$600. Crib free. Pet accepted; $35. Garage parking $8; valet $10. TV; cable (premium). Indoor pool; whirlpool, poolside serv. Coffee in rms. Restaurant 6-11 am, 5:30-11 pm. Bar 11-1 am. Ck-out noon. Coin lndry. Convention facilities. Business center. In-rm modem link. Concierge. Gift shop. Exercise equipt; sauna. Game rm. Refrigerator, wet bar in suites. Luxury level. Cr cds: A, C, D, DS, ER, JCB, MC, V.

D 🔌 🛒 🏋 🛒 🔥 SC 🛫

★ ★ **RADISSON HOTEL NORFOLK.** *700 Monticello Ave (23510). 757/627-*

5555; fax 757/627-5921; res 800/333-3333. www.radisson.com. 332 rms, 12 story, 7 suites. Apr-Oct: S, D $139; suites $249; each addl $12; under 17 free; lower rates rest of yr. Crib avail. Pet accepted, some restrictions. Valet parking avail. Pool. TV; cable (premium). Complimentary coffee in rms, newspaper, toll-free calls. Restaurant 6:30 am-10 pm. Bar. Ck-out noon, ck-in 4 pm. Conference center, meeting rms, Business center. Bellhops. Concierge serv. Dry cleaning. Gift shop. Salon/barber avail. Exercise equipt. Golf, 18 holes. Tennis, 5 courts. Video games. Cr cds: A, C, D, DS, MC, V.

★ ★ ★ **SHERATON NORFOLK.** *777 Waterside Dr (23510). 757/622-6664; fax 757/625-8271; res 800/325-3535. www.sheraton.com.* 446 rms, 10 story. S, D $79-$149; each addl $15; suites $200-$600; under 18 free; wkend rates. Crib free. Pet accepted; $35. Valet parking $9.50. TV, cable (premium), VCR avail. Pool; poolside serv. Restaurant 6:30 am-10 pm; wkends to 11 pm. Rm serv to midnight. Bars 11-2 am; entertainment wkends. Ck-out noon. Convention facilities. Business center. In-rm modem link. Gift shop. Health club privileges. Dockage. Some refrigerators. Balconies. Atriumlike lobby. On harbor. Luxury level. Cr cds: A, C, D, DS, JCB, MC, V.

B&B/Small Inn

★ ★ ★ **PAGE HOUSE.** *323 Fairfax Ave (23507). 757/625-5033; fax 757/623-9451; toll-free 800/599-7659. www.pagehouseinn.com.* 7 rms, 1 with shower only, 3 story, 3 suites. S, D $110-$135; suites $140-$175. Children under 12 yrs only by res. TV; cable (premium), VCR avail. Complimentary full bkfst. Restaurant nearby. Ck-out 11 am, ck-in 4-6 pm. Business servs avail. In-rm modem link. Some in-rm whirlpools. Refrigerator in suites. Totally restored Georgian Revival residence (1898) in historic district. Totally nonsmoking. Cr cds: A, MC, V.

Restaurants

★ ★ **BAKER'S CRUST.** *330 W 21st St (23517). 757/625-3600. www.bakerscrust.com.* Specializes in smoked chicken, penne pasta, Jamaica roaster, steak crepe. Hrs: 8 am-10 pm; Fri, Sat to 11 pm. Wine, beer. Lunch $5.95; dinner $10.95-$20.95. Child's menu. Entertainment. Cr cds: A, DS, MC, V.

★ **THE BANQUE.** *1849 E Little Creek Rd (23518). 757/480-3600.* Hrs: 6 pm-2 am. Closed Mon; Thanksgiving, Dec 24-25. Res accepted. Bar. A la carte entrees: dinner $5.95-$14.95. Specializes in prime rib, shrimp. Entertainment. Western dcor. Cr cds: A, DS, MC, V.

★ ★ **FREEMASON ABBEY.** *209 W Freemason St (23510). 757/622-3966. www.cvent.net/restaurants/cvi/freemason/.* Hrs: 11:30 am-10 pm; Fri, Sat to 11 pm; Sun brunch 9:30 am-2 pm. Closed Jan 1, Thanksgiving, Dec 25. Bar. Lunch $3.95-$9.95, dinner $9.95-$17.95. Sun brunch $5.95-$8.95. Child's menu. Specializes in whole Maine lobster, prime rib. Renovated church (1873); many antiques. Cr cds: A, D, DS, MC, V.

★ ★ ★ **LA GALLERIA.** *120 College Pl (23510). 757/623-3939.* Hrs: 11:30 am-2:30 pm, 5:30-11:30 pm; Mon to 11 pm; Fri, Sat to midnight. Closed Sun; Thanksgiving, Dec 25. Res accepted. Italian menu. Bar 11:30 am-2:30 pm, 4:30 pm-2 am. Lunch $3.95-$7.95, dinner $11.95-$19.95. Child's meals. Specialty: salmon La Galleria. Own baking, pasta. Valet parking. Outdoor dining. Modern decor. Cr cds: A, D, MC, V.

★ ★ **THE MAX.** *1421 Colley Ave (23517). 757/625-0259.* Hrs: 11 am-10 pm; Fri, Sat to 2 am; Sun brunch 11 am-2:30 pm. Closed Thanksgiving, Dec 25. Bar. Lunch $2.95-$7.95, dinner $2.95-$16.95. Sun brunch $5-$6.95. Child's menu. Specializes in pasta, fresh vegetables, veal. Parking. Outdoor dining. Carnival and novelty items displayed. Cr cds: DS, MC, V.

★★ **MONASTERY.** *443 Granby St (23510). 757/625-8193.* Hrs: 11:30 am-2:30 pm, 5-10 pm; May-Labor Day from 5 pm. Closed Mon; Easter, Thanksgiving, Dec 25; also July-Aug. Res accepted; required Fri, Sat. Czech, Eastern European menu. Bar. Lunch $2.75-$8.50, dinner $4.75-$22. Specialties: roast duck, Wiener schnitzel, goulash. Antique mirrors, original works by local artists. Cr cds: A, C, D, DS, MC, V.
D

★★★ **SHIP'S CABIN.** *4110 E Ocean View Ave (23518). 757/362-4659. www.shipscabin.com.* Hrs: 5:30-9:30 pm; Fri, Sat to 10:30 pm; Sun 5-9 pm. Res accepted. Bar. Wine list. Dinner $12.95-$18.95. Specializes in grilled fish and meat. Own baking. Parking. Fireplaces. Outdoor dining. View of Chesapeake Bay. Cr cds: A, DS, MC, V.
D SC

★★ **TODD JURICH'S BISTRO.** *210 W York St (23510). 757/622-3210. www.toddjurichbistro.com.* Hrs: 11:30 am-2:30 pm, 5:30-10 pm; Fri to 11 pm; Sat 5:30-11 pm. Closed Sun; hols. Bar. Lunch $5-$10, dinner $11.95-$22.95. Specializes in regional cuisine. Own pastries, pasta. Cr cds: A, C, D, DS, MC, V.
D

★★ **UNCLE LOUIE'S.** *132 E Little Creek Rd (23505). 757/480-1225. www.unclelouies.com.* Hrs: 8 am-11 pm; Fri, Sat to midnight. Sun 8 am-10 pm. Closed Thanksgiving, Dec 25. Res accepted. Bar. Bkfst $3.50-$6.95, lunch, dinner $3.50-$16.95. Child's menu. Specializes in fresh seafood, prime meats, New York deli sandwiches. Entertainment Wed, Sat. Cr cds: A, D, DS, MC, V.
D

Unrated Dining Spot

DOUMAR'S. *1919 Monticello Ave (23517). 757/627-4163.* Hrs: 8 am-11 pm. Closed Sun; hols. A la carte entrees: bkfst, lunch, dinner 70¢-$2.30. Ice cream 90¢-$3.40. Specializes in sandwiches, ice cream, hand-rolled cones. Parking. 1950s-style drive-in with addl seating inside. Abe Doumar invented the ice cream cone in 1904; his original cone-making machine is on display here. Family-owned. Cr cds: A, MC, V.

Orange

See also Charlottesville, Culpeper

Founded 1749 **Pop** 4,123 **Elev** 521 ft **Area code** 540 **Zip** 22960

This is the seat of Orange County, named for William, Prince of Orange, in 1734. Located in the Piedmont (foothills) of the Blue Ridge Mountains, Orange was settled by Germans under the leadership of Alexander Spotswood between 1714 and 1719.

This is riding and hunting country, drawing its livelihood from farming, livestock, and light industry. There are many antebellum houses in the county.

What to See and Do

James Madison Museum. Exhibits commemorating Madison's life and his contributions to American history; also Orange County history and Hall of Agriculture that incl an 18th-century homestead. (Mar-Nov, daily; rest of yr, Mon-Fri) 129 Caroline St. Phone 540/672-1776. ¢¢

⭐ **Montpelier.** Residence of James Madison, fourth president of US. Madison was the third generation of his family to live on this extensive plantation. He inherited Montpelier and enlarged it twice. After his presidency he and Dolley Madison retired to the estate, which Mrs. Madison sold after the president's death to pay her son's gambling debts. In 1901 the estate was bought by William du Pont, who enlarged the house, added many outbuildings, incl a private railroad station, built greenhouses, and planted gardens. Today, under the stewardship of the National Trust for Historic Preservation, a long-term research and preservation project, "The Search for James Madison," has begun. Self-guided tours of arboretum, nature trails, and formal garden. (Daily; closed Jan 1, Thanksgiving, Dec 25; also first Sat Nov) 4 mi SW, on VA 20. Phone 540/672-0006. ¢¢¢

B&Bs/Small Inns

★ ★ ★ **HIDDEN INN.** *249 Caroline St (22960). 540/672-3625; fax 540/672-5029; toll-free 800/841-1253. www. hiddeninn.com.* 10 rms, 2 story, 4 bldgs. S $59-$89; D $79-$129; each addl $20; suites $139-$169. TV in living rm. Complimentary full bkfst; afternoon refreshments. Ck-out noon, ck-in 3 pm. Business servs avail. Health club privileges. Some in-rm whirlpools. Balconies. Each rm individually decorated; some with canopy bed, fireplace. Late 19th-century residence; on 7½ wooded acres. Totally nonsmoking. Cr cds: A, MC, V.

★ ★ **HOLLADAY HOUSE.** *155 W Main St (22960). 540/672-4893; fax 540/672-3028; toll-free 800/358-4422. www.symweb.com/holladay.* 6 rms, 3 story, 2 suites, 1 kit. unit. S, D $95-$135; each addl $25; suite $175-$195; kit. unit $130-$155; wkly rates. TV in some rms; cable. Complimentary full bkfst. Restaurant adj 7 am-6 pm. Ck-out 11 am, ck-in 4 pm. Business servs avail. Fireplace, whirlpool. Federal-style residence (ca 1830). Totally nonsmoking. Cr cds: A, DS, MC, V.

Pearisburg

See also Blacksburg, Radford

Pop 2,729 **Elev** 1,804 ft
Area code 540 **Zip** 24134

What to See and Do

Walnut Flats. Fishing in Dismal Creek; hunting (in season), hiking, primitive camping. Dismal Falls and Flat Top Mtn are here. 11 mi S on VA 100, then 10½ mi W on VA 42 to County 606, N 1 mi to County 201, 2½ mi. Phone 540/552-4641. **FREE** Approx ½ mi from Walnut Flats on County 201 is

White Pine Horse Camp. Primitive camping, horse trails. Phone 540/552-4641. **FREE**

White Rocks Recreation Area. Fishing in Big Stony Creek; hunting (in season), hiking, camping (fee). (Apr-Nov) 17 mi E via VA 613, 635 in George Washington and Jefferson national forests. Phone 540/552-4641.

Pentagon City

(See also Arlington County (Ronald Reagan Washington-National Airport Area))

Petersburg

(E-6) *See also Hopewell, Richmond*

Settled 1645 **Pop** 33,740 **Elev** 87 ft
Area code 804
Information Petersburg Visitors Center, 425 Cockade Alley, 23803; 804/733-2402 or 800/368-3595

This city, Lee's last stand before Appomattox (1864-1865), was settled in 1645 when the General Assembly authorized construction of Fort Henry at the falls of the Appomattox River. In 1784 three separate towns united to become the single city of Petersburg.

British troops under Generals Benedict Arnold and William Phillips occupied the town in 1781; on May 24 that same year Cornwallis started the journey to his surrender at Yorktown. Between the Revolutionary War and Civil War the town was a popular stopping place with a social life that, for a time, eclipsed that of Richmond.

Physically untouched during the early years of the Civil War (though the town sent 17 companies to the front), Petersburg in 1864 was the scene of Lee's final struggle against Grant. In April 1865, when Lee's supply routes were finally cut and he was forced to evacuate the city, the Confederacy collapsed. A week later Lee surrendered at Appomattox.

The shattered city made a new start after the war, showing amazing recuperative powers; in 1870, Petersburg had 20 more industries than there had been in 1850. Today, besides being a storehouse of Colonial and Civil War history, Petersburg is a thriving industrial city.

What to See and Do

Appomattox River Park. A 137-acre park with canal for canoeing or fishing; access to rapids; picnic area. (Mid-Apr-Oct, daily) Western part of town, on River Rd. Phone 804/733-2394.

Blandford Church (1735) and **Cemetery** (1702) Church, since 1901 a memorial to the Confederacy, has 15 Tiffany stained-glass windows. (Daily; closed hols) 321 S Crater Rd. ¢¢

Centre Hill Mansion. (1823) Federalist mansion visited by Presidents Tyler, Lincoln, and Taft. Chandeliers, finely detailed carvings; antiques, 1886 Knabe Art grand piano with hollywood inlaid on rosewood. (Daily; closed hols) Center Hill. ¢¢

Farmers Bank. (1817) Banking memorabilia incl original plates and press for printing Confederate currency. Tours depart from Visitor Center, Old Market Sq. (Apr-Oct, daily) 19 Bollingbrook St. ¢¢

Fort Lee. Army training center in WWI and WWII. 3 mi NE on VA 36. Here is

US Army Quartermaster Museum. Uniforms, flags, weapons, equestrian equipt from 200 yrs of military service. Civil War and Memorial rooms. (Tues-Sun; closed Jan 1, Thanksgiving, Dec 25) Phone 804/734-4203. **FREE**

Lee Memorial Park. Facilities of this 864-acre park incl lake (launch fee), fishing (fee; license required); game fields and courts (fee), picnic area. (Daily; lake facilities closed mid-Oct-mid-Apr) Southern part of town, off Johnson Rd. Phone 804/733-2394. Also here is

USSSA Softball Hall of Fame Museum. Honors outstanding persons in amateur softball. Numerous displays, exhibits, photographs; seven-min film. (Daily; closed hols) 3935 S Crater Rd, 1 mi off I-95. Phone 804/732-4099. ¢

Lee's Retreat. A 98-mi driving tour follows route of General Robert E. Lee's retreat from Petersburg to Appomattox. Roadside pull-overs, signs, and audio interpretation at important Civil War sites. For brochures, maps, and audio tapes, contact the Petersburg Visitors Center. Phone 800/6-RETREAT. **FREE**

Pamplin Park Civil War Site. Site of General Ulysses S. Grant's decisive victory over Confederate forces in 1865. This 422-acre park incl battle trails, reconstructed soldier huts, plantation home. Interpretive Center, and museum. Guided tours avail. (Daily; closed Jan 1, Thanksgiving, Dec 25) 6125 Boydton Plank Rd. Phone 804/861-2408. Also here is

National Museum of the Civil War Soldier. Exhibit on the Civil War's common soldier, one of the country's largest Civil War bookshops. Gift shop; restaurant.

Poplar Grove (Petersburg) National Cemetery. On self-guided tour of Petersburg National Battlefield (see). Of 6,315 graves, 4,110 are unidentified. S off I-85.

St. Paul's Episcopal Church. (1856) Lee worshiped here during the siege of Petersburg (1864-1865). Open on request (Mon-Thurs). 110 N Union between W Washington and Tabb sts. Phone 804/733-3415.

Siege Museum. Greek Revival building houses exhibits describing the ten-month Civil War siege of Petersburg. Film *The Echoes Still Remain*, with Joseph Cotten, is shown every hr on the hr. (Daily; closed hols) 15 W Bank St. Phone 804/733-2402. ¢¢

Trapezium House. (1817) Built by eccentric Irish bachelor Charles O'Hara in the form of a trapezium, with no right angles and no parallel sides. O'Hara is said to have believed the superstitions of his West Indian servant, who thought that ghosts and evil spirits inhabited right angles. Tours depart from Siege Museum, 15 W Bank St. (Apr-Oct, daily) Market and High sts. ¢¢

Motels/Motor Lodges

★ ★ **BEST WESTERN.** *12205 S Crater Rd (23805). 804/733-0600; fax 804/862-4549. www.bestwestern.com.* 138 rms, 1-2 story. S, D $45.95-$69.95;

each addl $5; under 18 free. Crib $5. Pet accepted; $5. TV; cable (premium). Pool; wading pool. Playground. Restaurant 5:30 am-10 pm. Bar noon-midnight. Ck-out 11 am. Coffee in rms. Coin lndry. Business servs avail. In-rm modem link. Sundries. Lighted tennis. Lawn games. Miniature golf. Some refrigerators. Picnic tables. Cr cds: A, D, DS, MC, V.

★ **DAYS INN.** *12208 S Crater Rd (23805). 804/733-4400; fax 804/861-9559; toll-free 877/512-4400. www.thedaysinn.com/petersburg.* 155 rms, 2 story. S, D $65-$70; each addl $5; kit. suites $75-$80. Crib free. Pet accepted; $5. TV; cable (premium). Coffee in rms. Pool; wading pool. Playground. Restaurant adj 5:30 am-10 pm. Ck-out 11 am. Coin lndry. Meeting rms. Business servs avail. In-rm modem link. Sundries. Putting green. Exercise equipt. Refrigerators, microwaves. Cr cds: A, C, D, DS, MC, V.

Restaurants

★ **ALEXANDER'S.** *101 W Bank St (23803). 804/733-7134.* Hrs: 9 am-9 pm; Mon, Tues to 3:30 pm. Closed Sun; Jan 1, Thanksgiving, Dec 25; also wk of July 4. Italian, Greek, American menu. Wine, beer. Bkfst $1.50-$4, lunch $4.50-$6.50, dinner $6.95-$11.99. Child's menu. Specialties: veal a la Greca, souvlaki, stuffed chicken breast. In old town storefront. Cr cds: MC, V.

Petersburg National Battlefield

See also Hopewell, Petersburg, Richmond

The campaign that spelled doom for the Confederacy occurred in a huge 40-mile semicircle around Richmond and Petersburg at the price of 70,000 Union and Confederate casualties.

After his unsuccessful attempt to take Richmond by frontal assault (at

Cold Harbor, June 3, 1864), General Grant withdrew and attacked Petersburg. After four days of fighting and failing to capture the city, Grant decided to lay siege. Petersburg was the rail center that funneled supplies to Lee and Richmond.

The siege lasted ten months, from June 15, 1864, to April 2, 1865, with the two armies in almost constant contact. When Petersburg finally fell, Lee's surrender was only a week away.

The park, more than 2,700 acres, preserves Union and Confederate fortifications, trenches, and gun pits. Another unit of the battlefield, Five Forks Unit, is located 23 miles to the west. Park (daily). Living history programs daily during summer. Access for the disabled includes several paved trails and ramps to the Visitor Center. For further information contact the Superintendent, 1539 Hickory Hill Rd, Petersburg 23803-4721; phone 804/732-3531. Golden Eagle, Golden Age, and Golden Access Passports honored (see MAKING THE MOST OF YOUR TRIP).

What to See and Do

Battery 5. Strongest original Confederate position, captured on opening day of battle. From here "the Dictator," a Union mortar, shelled Petersburg, 2½ mi away. A similar mortar is nearby.

Battery 8. Confederate artillery position captured and used by Union as Fort Friend.

Battery 9. Confederate position on original line. Site of reconstructed Union camp and living history programs.

City Point Unit. (See HOPEWELL)

Colquitt's Salient. Section of Confederate defense line.

The Crater. Hole remaining after Union troops tunneled beneath Confederate artillery position and exploded four tons of powder (July 30, 1864). The resulting breach in Confederate lines failed as a major breakthrough. Several special monuments in vicinity.

First Maine Monument. Memorial to Maine dead in greatest regimental loss in a single action of the war.

Five Forks Unit. (1,115 acres) This road junction, beyond Lee's extreme right flank; led to the only remaining

Confederate supply line, the South Side Railroad. The Battle of Five Forks (Apr 1, 1865) saw Union forces under General Philip H. Sheridan smash Confederates commanded by General George Pickett and gain access to the tracks beyond. On Apr 2 Grant ordered an all-out assault, crumbling Lee's right flank. Only a heroic stand by Confederate forces at Fort Gregg held off the Union advance while Lee evacuated Petersburg on the night of Apr 2. Visitor contact station (summer). Approx 6 mi SW via VA 613 (White Oak Rd), to jct Dinwiddie Courthouse Rd (VA 627) and Wheeler Pond Rd (VA 645). Phone 804/265-8244. **FREE**

Fort Haskell. One of the points where Union troops stopped a desperate attempt by Lee to break the siege.

Fort Stedman. Lee's "last grand offensive" concentrated here (Mar 25, 1865). The battle lasted four hrs; the Confederates failed to hold their breakthrough.

Gracie's Dam. Site of one of several Confederate dams intended to flood area between lines.

Harrison's Creek. First Grant (June 1864), then Lee (Mar 1865) had advances checked here.

Spring Garden. Heaviest Union artillery concentration during Battle of Crater was along this ridge.

Visitor Center. Information, exhibits; maps for self-guided tours. (Daily; closed Jan 1, Dec 25) Self-guided tour starts near center building. Off VA 36.

Portsmouth

(F-8) *See also Chesapeake, Hampton, Newport News, Norfolk, Virginia Beach*

Founded 1752 **Pop** 100,565 **Elev** 15 ft
Area code 757

Information Portsmouth Convention and Visitors Bureau, 505 Crawford St, Suite 2, 23704; 757/393-5327 or 800/767-8782

Web www.portsmouth.va.us

Connected to Norfolk by two bridge tunnels and a pedestrian ferry that cross the Elizabeth River, Portsmouth is part of the great Hampton Roads port, unrivaled for commercial shipping and shipbuilding activity. It is also the headquarters of the United States Coast Guard Atlantic Fleet.

In Gosport, long a part of Portsmouth, Andrew Sprowle, a Scot, built a marine yard in 1767 which became in turn a British naval repair station and, after the Revolutionary War, a federal navy yard. Now called the Norfolk Naval Shipyard, it is the largest naval shipyard in the world. The *Chesapeake,* sister of the *Constitution* and one of the US Navy's first warships, was built here. So was the *Merrimac,* which was seized by the Confederates, changed into an ironclad in 1861, and rechristened the CSS *Virginia.* The oldest drydock (1831) here is still in use.

What to See and Do

***Carrie B* Harbor Tours.** Replica of 19th-century riverboat makes narrated tour (90-min) of naval shipyard and inner harbor (Apr-Oct, daily); narrated tour (2½ hrs) of naval base and Hampton Roads (Apr-May and Sept-Oct, daily); sunset cruise (2½ hrs) to Hampton Roads and naval base (June-Labor Day, daily). Departs from Portside, 6 Crawford Pkwy. Phone 757/393-4735.

Hill House. Headquarters of the Portsmouth Historical Association. Built in early 1820s, this four-story English basement-style (with a raised basement) house contains original furnishings collected by generations of the Hill family. In near-original condition, the house has undergone only limited renovation through the yrs. Garden restored. (Apr-Dec, Wed, Sat and Sun) 221 North St. Phone 757/393-0241. ¢¢

Historic houses. Portsmouth has over 300 yrs of history represented by more than 20 examples of Colonial, Federal, and antebellum houses. Among them is the Nivison-Ball House (ca 1730-1750), 417 Middle St, where Andrew Jackson and General Lafayette were entertained. *These houses are private and may be viewed only from the exterior.* Obtain Olde Towne Portsmouth walking tour brochures with map and descriptions of churches, homes, and old buildings from the Visitor Center at High St Landing. Phone 757/393-5111.

Monumental United Methodist Church. (1772) Methodist. Oldest Methodist congregation in the South; history rm. Guided tour (Mon-Fri, by appt; closed hols). 450 Dinwiddie St, 1 blk N of High St. Phone 757/397-1297.

⭐ **The Portsmouth Museums.** Located in a four-blk radius, the museum complex has facilities housing artistic, educational, and historic exhibits. Museums (Memorial Day-Labor Day daily; closed Jan 1, Thanksgiving, Dec 25). Phone 757/393-8983. Incl

Children's Museum of Virginia. More than 60 interactive activities in 12 areas; planetarium. (Mid-June-Labor Day, Mon-Sat, also Sun afternoons) 221 High St. ¢¢

Court House Galleries. Changing exhibits. 420 High St. ¢

Lightship Museum. Built in 1915, commissioned in 1916 as *Lightship 101,* it served 48 yrs in Virginia, Delaware, and Massachusetts. Retired in 1964 and renamed *Portsmouth.* London Slip and Water St. ¢

Naval Shipyard Museum. Thousands of items of naval equipt, plus flags, uniforms, prints, maps, and models, incl models of the CSS *Virginia;* the US Ship-of-the-line *Delaware,* built in Portsmouth; and the first ship drydocked in the US. 2 High St, on Elizabeth River. ¢

Trinity Church. Episcopal. Oldest church building (1762) and parish in Portsmouth. Legend says the church bell cracked while ringing out news of Cornwallis' surrender; it was later recast. Confederate Memorial window. Commodore James Barron, many colonial patriots are buried here. Open on request (Mon-Fri); office behind church in parish hall. 500 Court St. Phone 757/393-0431.

Motel/Motor Lodge

★ ★ **HOLIDAY INN OLDE TOWNE.** 8 Crawford Pkwy (23704). 757/393-2573; fax 757/399-1248. 220 rms, 4 story. S $60-$89; D $60-$99; each addl $10; suites $130-$161; studio rms $75-$150; under 19 free; wkend rates; higher rates Harborfest. Crib free. Pet accepted. TV; cable (pre-

mium). Pool. Coffee in rms. Restaurant 6:30 am-10 pm. Bar noon-2 am. Ck-out noon. Coin lndry. Meeting rms. Business servs avail. In-rm modem link. Exercise equipt. Refrigerators avail. Dockage, marina adj. Cr cds: A, D, DS, MC, V.

D ⬛ ⬛ ⬛ ⬛ ⬛

Hotel

★ ★ ★ **RENAISSANCE PORTSMOUTH.** 425 Water St (23704). 757/673-3000. www.renaissancehotels. com. 244 rms, 16 story. S, D $225-$275; under 17 free. Crib avail. TV; cable (premium). Indoor pool; whirlpool. Restaurant 6:30 am-10 pm. Bar to midnight. Ck-out noon, ck-in 3 pm. Meeting rms. Business center. In-rm modem link. Concierge. Exercise equipt. Minibars; many refrigerators in suites. Cr cds: A, D, DS, MC, V.

⬛ ⬛ ⬛ ⬛ ⬛

Restaurants

★ ★ **CAFE EUROPA.** 319 High St (23704). 757/399-6652. Hrs: 11:30 am-2 pm, 5-9:30 pm; Fri, Sat to 10:30 pm. Closed Sun, Mon; hols; also mid-Aug-mid-Sept. Res accepted; required Fri, Sat. Continental menu. Bar. Lunch $4.50-$12, dinner $9.50-$15.95. Specialties: salmon Russian style, snail tureen, veal Tuscany. Intimate European atmosphere; Mucha prints. Cr cds: MC, V.

D

★ **CIRCLE SEAFOOD.** 3010 High St (23707). 757/397-8196. Hrs: 8 am-10 pm; Fri, Sat to 11 pm; Sun brunch noon-9 pm. Res accepted. Bar. Bkfst $2.50-$6.50, lunch $3.95-$14.95, dinner $7.95-$19.95. Sun brunch $10.95. Child's menu. Specializes in steak, seafood. Salad bar. Pianist Mon, Wed-Fri. Rotunda dining rm with extensive buffet. Cr cds: D, DS, MC, V.

D ⬛

★ ★ **SCALE O' DE WHALE.** 3515 Shipwright St (23703). 757/483-2772. Hrs: 11:30 am-2:30 pm, 5-9:30 pm; Fri, Sat to 10:30 pm. Closed hols. Res accepted. Serv bar. Lunch $4.50-$8.25, dinner $9.95-$17.95. Child's menu. Specializes in seafood, market price lobster, steak. Outdoor dining. At end of pier, dockage. Nautical decor; ship models, antiques, scrimshaw, kerosene lights. Cr cds: A, DS, MC, V.

Radford

(E-4) *See also Blacksburg, Salem*

Settled 1756 **Pop** 15,859 **Elev** 1,820 ft
Area code 540 **Zip** 24141
Information Chamber of Commerce, 1126 Norwood St; 540/639-2202
Web www.radfordchamber.com

What to See and Do

Claytor Lake State Park. Consists of 472 acres in wooded hills adjacent to 5,000-acre lake. Swimming, sand beach, bathhouse, fishing, boating (ramp, rentals, marina); hiking and bridle trails, picnicking, concession, tent and trailer sites (electrical hookups, Apr-Sept), cabins (Mar-early Dec). Visitor center, interpretive programs. Standard fees. Park office and visitor center in Howe House (1876-1879), built on land once settled by Dunkers (Dunkards), a religious sect that fled persecution in Germany in the 1720s. On VA 660, 6 mi SW, just S of I-81 exit 101. Phone 540/674-5492.

Radford University. (1910) 9,142 students. Flossie Martin Gallery in Powell Hall houses visual arts with an emphasis on regional and contemporary; changing exhibits. Corinna de la Burde Sculpture Court, adj to the gallery, is an open-air museum displaying large-scale sculpture; changing exhibits, and permanent installations. Archives in the McConnell Library contain pamphlets, campus information, local history, oral history of Appalachia, and rare books. Greenhouse (daily). Dedmon Center, a recreation-convocation complex, features air-supported roof, arena seating 5,600; swimming pool; indoor tennis and handball courts. (Daily) On US 11, I-81 exit 109. Phone 540/831-5324.

Special Event

The Long Way Home. Outdoor historical drama by Earl Hobson Smith depicts the true story of Mary Draper Ingles, survivor of the 1755 Draper's Meadow Massacre, and her heroic 850-mi flight to warn settlers of Native American attacks. Contact PO Box 711; phone 540/639-0679. Thurs-Sun, eves, Mid-June-Aug.

Motels/Motor Lodges

★ ★ **BEST WESTERN INN.** *1501 Tyler Ave (24141). 540/639-3000; fax 540/633-0251; toll-free 800/628-1955. www.bestwestern.com.* 72 rms, 2 story. S $60-$80; D $72-$90; each addl $5; under 18 free; higher rates univ events. Crib free. Pet accepted. TV; cable (premium). Indoor pool; wading pool, whirlpool. Ck-out noon. Business servs avail. Sundries. Exercise equipt; sauna. Bathrm phones; some refrigerators. Cr cds: A, D, DS, MC, V.

★ **COMFORT INN.** *4424 Cleburne Blvd, Dublin (24084). 540/674-1100; fax 540/674-2644; toll-free 800/638-7949. www.comfortinn.com.* 98 rms, 2 story. S $56-$72; D $61-$78; each addl $6; under 18 free; higher rates univ events. Crib free. TV; cable (premium). Pool. Complimentary continental bkfst, coffee in lobby. Restaurant adj 5-10 pm. Ck-out noon. Meeting rm. Business servs avail. Valet serv. Sundries. Some in-rm whirlpools; microwaves avail. Cr cds: A, C, D, DS, ER, JCB, MC, V.

★ **DOGWOOD LODGE.** *7073 Lee Hwy (24141). 540/639-9338.* 15 rms. S $28; D $33-$36; each addl $5; higher rates univ events. Crib $5. Pet accepted. TV; cable (premium). Restaurant nearby. Ck-out 11 am. Cr cds: DS, MC, V.

★ **EXECUTIVE MOTEL.** *7498 Lee Hwy (24143). 540/639-1664; fax 540/633-1737; toll-free 888/393-8483.* 27 rms, 13 with shower only, 2 story. Apr-Nov: S $32.50-$36.50; D $36.50-$46.50; under 12 free; higher rates special events; lower rates rest of yr. Crib free. Pet accepted, some restrictions; $4. TV; cable (premium), VCR. Complimentary coffee in lobby. Restaurant adj 6 am-11 pm. Ck-out 11 am. Health club privileges. Refrigerators; microwaves avail. Cr cds: A, C, D, DS, MC, V.

Reston

See also Dulles International Airport Area

Richmond

(E-6) *See also Ashland, Hopewell, Petersburg*

Settled 1607 **Pop** 197,790 **Elev** 150 ft
Area code 804
Information Convention and Visitors Bureau, 550 E Marshall St, 23219; 804/782-2777 or 800/370-9004
Web www.richmondva.org

There have been few dull moments in Richmond's history. Native Americans and settlers fought over the ground on which it now stands. In 1775 Patrick Henry made his "liberty or death" speech in St. John's Church, and in 1780 the city was named capital of the state. At that time Virginia extended all the way to the Mississippi. British soldiers plundered it brutally in the Revolutionary War. As the capital of the Confederacy from 1861-1865, it was constantly in danger. Finally in 1865 the city was evacuated and retreating Confederate soldiers burned the government warehouse; a portion of the rest of the city also went up in flames.

However, Richmond did survive. As Virginia's capital, it proudly exemplifies the modern South. It is a city industrially aggressive yet culturally aware, respectful of its own historical background yet receptive to new trends in architecture and modes of living. Richmond esteems both the oldest monuments and the newest skyscrapers.

Tobacco and tobacco products, paper and paper products, aluminum, chemicals, textiles, printing and publishing, and machinery contribute to the city's economy. Richmond is also an educational center; Virginia Commonwealth University, Virginia Union University, and the University of Richmond are based here.

What to See and Do

Agecroft Hall. Half-timbered Tudor manor built in the late 15th century near Manchester, England. Disassembled, brought here, and rebuilt during the late 1920s in a spacious setting of formal gardens and grassy terraces overlooking the James River. English furnishings from 16th and 17th centuries. Audiovisual presentation explains history of house. (Tues-Sun; closed hols) Cary St exit off I-195, turn onto N Thompson Ave, then right on Cary to Malvern, then left on Cantebury to 4305 Sulgrave Rd. Phone 804/353-4241. ¢¢

⭐ **Capitol Square.** Bounded by Broad, Governor, Bank, and 9th sts, Downtown. Phone 804/784-5736. On Capitol Sq are

Equestrian Statue of Washington. By Thomas Crawford; cast in Munich over an 18-yr period. Base features allegorical representations of six famous Revolutionary War figures from Virginia. 9th and Grace sts.

Governor's Mansion. (1813) This two-story Federal-style house was built after the capital was moved from Williamsburg. Oldest governor's mansion in the US still in use as a governor's residence. Tours (by appt). E of State Capitol. Phone 804/371-2642. **FREE**

State Capitol. (1785-1788) Modeled after La Maison Carrée, an ancient Roman temple at Nímes, France, the Capitol was designed by Thomas Jefferson. In this building, where America's oldest continuous English-speaking legislative bodies still meet, is the famous Houdon statue of Washington. The rotonda features the first interior dome in the US; here Aaron Burr was tried for treason, Virginia ratified the Articles of Secession, and

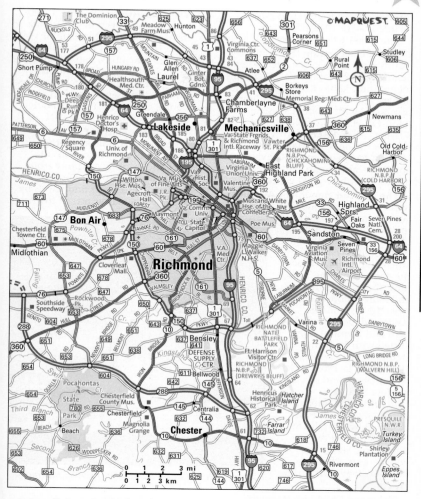

Robert E. Lee accepted command of the forces of Virginia; the Confederate Congress also met in the building. (Mon-Sat, also Sun afternoons; closed Jan 1, Thanksgiving, Dec 25) 9th and Grace sts, Capitol Sq. Phone 804/698-1788. Also on Capitol Sq are

Virginia State Library and Archives. Outstanding collection of books, maps, manuscripts. (Mon-Sat; closed hols) 800 E Broad St. Phone 804/692-3500. **FREE**

Church Hill Historic Area. Neighborhood of 19th-century houses, more than 70 of which predate Civil War. Some Church Hill houses are open Historic Garden Week (see SPECIAL

EVENTS). Bounded by Broad, 29th, Main, and 21st sts, E of Capitol Sq. In center of Church Hill is

St. John's Episcopal Church. (1741) Where Patrick Henry delivered his stirring "liberty or death" speech. Reenactment of Second Virginia Convention (late May-early Sept, Sun). Guided tours. (Daily; closed hols) 25th and Broad sts. Phone 804/648-5015. W of Church Hill is

Edgar Allan Poe Museum. Old Stone House portion is thought to be oldest structure in Richmond (1737). Three additional buildings house Poe mementos; James Carling illustrations of "The Raven"; scale model of Richmond of Poe's time. Guided tours. (Tues-Sun; closed hols). 1914 E Main St. Phone 804/648-5523. ¢¢

City Hall Observation Deck. Eighteenth-floor observation deck offers panoramic view of the city, incl capitol grounds, James River, and Revolutionary and Civil War-era buildings contrasted with modern skyscrapers. (Mon-Fri) 900 E Broad St. Phone 804/646-7000. **FREE** Across the street is the old **City Hall** (1886-1894), a restored Gothic Revival building featuring an elaborate central court with arcaded galleries.

⭐ **The Fan and Monument Avenue.** Named for the layout of streets that fan out from Monroe Park toward the western part of town. Historical neighborhood has restored antebellum and turn-of-the-century houses, museums, shops, restaurants, and famed Monument Ave. The fashionable boulevard, between Lombard and Belmont sts, is dotted with imposing statues of Generals Lee, Stuart, and Jackson, of Jefferson Davis, and of Commodore Matthew Fontaine Maury, inventor of the electric torpedo. Bounded by Franklin St and Monument Ave, Boulevard, Main, and Belvidere sts. Phone 804/643-3589. Within the area are

Richmond Children's Museum. Exhibits on arts, nature, and the world around us designed for children 2-12 yrs old; many hands-on exhibits. (July-Aug, daily; rest of yr, Tues-Sun; closed hols) 2626 W Broad St. Phone 804/474-2667 or 877/295-2667. ¢¢

Science Museum of Virginia. Hands-on museum. Major exhibits incl aerospace, computers, electricity, visual perception, physical phenomena, and astronomy, and Foucault pendulum. The Ethyl Universe Planetarium Space Theater features Omnimax films and planetarium shows (inquire for schedule). (Tues-Sun; closed Thanksgiving, Dec 25) 2500 W Broad St, N of Monument Ave. Phone 804/864-1400.

Virginia Historical Society. Comprehensive collection of Virginia history housed in Museum of Virginia History with permanent and changing exhibits, and Library of Virginia History with historical and genealogical research facilities. (Mon-Sat, museum also Sun afternoons; closed hols) 428 N Boulevard St. Phone 804/358-4901. ¢¢

Virginia Museum of Fine Arts. America's first state-supported museum of art. Collections of paintings, prints, sculpture from major world cultures; Russian Imperial Easter eggs and jewels by Faberge; decorative arts of the Art

Robert E. Lee Statue on Monument Avenue, Richmond

Nouveau and Art Deco movements; sculpture garden; changing exhibits. Cafeteria. (Tues-Sun; closed hols) Boulevard St and Grove Ave. Phone 804/340-1400. **FREE**

Federal Reserve Money Museum. Exhibits of currency, incl rare bills; gold and silver bars; money-related artifacts. (Open by appt only; closed hols) 701 E Byrd St, Downtown, on first floor of bank. Phone 804/697-8000. **FREE**

Hollywood Cemetery. (1847) James Monroe, John Tyler, Jefferson Davis, other notables, and 18,000 Confederate soldiers are buried here; audiovisual program (Mon-Fri). (Daily) 412 S Cherry St, at Albemarle St. Phone 804/648-8501. **FREE**

Jackson Ward. Historic downtown neighborhood that was home to many famous black Richmonders, incl Bill "Bojangles" Robinson. Area has numerous 19th-century, Greek Revival, and Victorian buildings with ornamental ironwork that rivals the wrought iron of New Orleans. Bounded by I-95, 7th, Broad, and Belvidere sts. Within the ward are

Bill "Bojangles" Robinson Statue. Memorial to the famous dancer who was born at 915 N 3rd St. Corner of Leigh and Adams sts.

Black History Museum and Cultural Center. Limited editions, prints, art, photographs; African memorabilia; Sam Gilliam collection. (Tues-Sun 10-5 pm). Clay St. Phone 804/780-9093. ¢¢

Maggie Walker National Historic Site. Commemorates life and career of Maggie L. Walker, daughter of former slaves, who overcame great hardships to become successful in banking and insurance; early advocate for women's rights and racial equality. Two-story, red brick house was home to her family 1904-1934. (Mon-Sat; closed Jan 1, Thanksgiving, Dec 25) 600 N 2nd St. Phone 804/771-2017. **FREE**

John Marshall House. (1790) Restored house of famous Supreme Court justice features original woodwork and paneling; family furnishings, and mementos. (Tues-Sun; closed hols) Combination ticket avail for Marshall House, Valentine Museum, Museum of the Confederacy, White House of the Confederacy. 818 E Marshall St. Phone 804/648-7998.

Kanawha Canal Locks. Impressive stone locks were part of nation's first canal system, planned by George Washington. Narrated audiovisual presentation explains workings of locks and canal. Picnic grounds. (Mon-Sat) 12th and Byrd sts, Downtown. Phone 780/010-7840 or 804/649-2800. **FREE**

RICHMOND'S HISTORICAL LEGACY

Richmond was the Civil War "Capital of the Confederacy," and this aspect of its past can easily be recalled on a two-hour, two-mile walking tour of the city center. The city also enjoys other, less-troubling claims to historical fame, which will be pointed out along the way. Begin this walk at the Virginia State Capitol, designed in 1785 by Thomas Jefferson, himself a state governor, in the style of a classical temple. Surrounded by Capitol Square's expanse of well-tended lawn, it displays such majesty that it still commands the eye despite the modern-day structures that surround it. Step inside the Rotunda to see the same life-size statue of George Washington, the only one executed of him from life. From Capitol Square, walk north (right) on 9th Street across Broad Street to the neighborhood once known as Court End, which now bustles with students and faculty of the Medical College of Virginia. At 818 East Marshall Street (intersecting 9th) stands the most important residence of Court End, the home of John Marshall, the distinguished chief justice of the US Supreme Court from 1801 to 1835. Built in 1790, the two-story brick house where he lived for 45 years is a museum dedicated to his memory. Though it's a seven-block detour, head west on Marshall Street to 2nd Street and turn north (right) two blocks to 110 East Leigh Street, the Maggie Walker National Historic Site. A museum, the modest two-story brick home on a quiet residential street honors a black woman of impressive ability. Despite physical handicaps, Walker became America's first female bank president, establishing the Penny Savings Bank in 1903 as a way of helping local blacks during the Jim Crow period. Double back via Marshall Street past the John Marshall House, to the Valentine Museum at 1015 East Clay Street. A small, innovative museum with a contemporary outlook, it focuses on the people and history of Richmond. Conclude the tour a block down the street at 12th and East Clay at the adjacent Museum of the Confederacy and the White House of the Confederacy. Not surprisingly, the museum emphasizes Southern leaders, featuring mementos of General Robert E. Lee. The White House, a neoclassical mansion built in 1818, recounts the home life during the Civil War of Confederate President Jefferson Davis and his wife Varina.

Meadow Farm Museum. (General Sheppard Crump Memorial Park) Living history farm museum depicting rural life in the 1860s. Orientation center, farmhouse, barn, outbuildings, crop demonstration fields, 1860s doctor's office. Also a 150-acre park with picnic shelters, playground. (Mar-Dec, Tues-Sun) 12 mi NW via I-95 N, I-295 W, Woodman Rd S exit, at Courtney and Mountain rds. Phone 804/501-5520. ¢

Monumental Church. (1812) Located on the Medical College of Virginia campus of Virginia Commonwealth University. Octagonal domed building designed by Robert Mills, architect of the Washington Monument. Commemorative structure was built on site where many prominent persons, incl the governor, perished in a theater fire in 1811. Interior closed. Behind the church is the distinctive Egyptian Building (1845). 1224 E Broad St, N of Capitol Sq.

Museum of the Confederacy. Contains the nation's largest collection of Confederate military and civilian artifacts, incl uniforms, equipt, flags, personal belongings of Jefferson Davis, Robert E. Lee, and J.E.B. Stuart, documents, manuscripts, and artwork. (Daily; closed Jan 1, Thanksgiving, Dec 25) 1201 E Clay St, N of Capitol Sq. Phone 804/649-1861. ¢¢

Parks. For general information contact the Department of Parks and Recreation. Phone 804/780-5733.

Bryan. A 279-acre park, 20 acres of which are an azalea garden with more than 55,000 plants (best viewed late Apr-mid-May). Picnic facilities, tennis courts. Bellevue Ave and Hermitage Rd. **FREE**

James River. Five sections. Fishing, pedestrian bridges with overlook of James River; whitewater canoe and inner-tube accesses; bird-watching, wildlife sanctuary, self-guided tours, bicycle and hiking trails, visitor center with display, information station, interpretive programs. W 22nd St and Riverside Dr. **FREE**

Lewis Ginter Botanical Garden. Victorian-era estate features the Grace Arents Garden and the Henry M. Flagler Perennial Garden; seasonal floral displays; emphasis on daffodils, daylilies, azaleas, and rhododendrons. (Daily) 1800 Lakeside Ave, in Lakeside. Phone 804/262-9887. ¢¢

Maymont. Dooley mansion, late Victorian in style, houses art collection and decorative arts exhibits (Tues-Sun; fee). Also here are formal Japanese and Italian gardens, an arboretum, a nature center with wildlife habitat for native species, an aviary, a children's farm, and a working carriage collection. (Daily) 1700 Hampton St at Pennsylvania Ave. Phone 804/358-7166. **FREE**

Pocahontas State Park. More than 7,000 acres; Swift Creek Lake. Swimming, pool, bathhouse, fishing, boating (launch, rentals, electric motors only); hiking trails, bicycle path (rentals), picnicking, concession, tent and trailer sites (seasonal), group cabins. Nature center; eve interpretive programs (summer). Standard fees. (Daily) S on US 10, then W on VA 655. Phone 804/796-4255.

William Byrd. Incl 287 acres of groves, artificial lakes, picnic areas. Tennis courts, softball fields, fitness course. Amphitheater (June-Aug). Virginia's WWI memorial, a 240-ft, pink brick carillon tower. Boulevard St and Idlewood Ave. Nearby is

St. John's Episcopal Church. (1741) Where Patrick Henry delivered his stirring "liberty or death" speech. Reenactment of Second Virginia Convention (late May-early Sep, Sun). Guided tours. (Daily; closed hols) 25th & Broad Sts. Phone 804/648-5015. ¢¢ W of Church Hill is

Shopping.

17th Street Market. Farmers market built on site of Native American trading village. Seasonal produce, flowers, holiday greens. (Daily) 17th St between E Main and E Market sts.

6th Street Marketplace. Restored area of shops, restaurants, entertainment. 6th St between Coliseum and Grace St, Downtown.

Carytown. Eight blks of shops, restaurants, theaters adj to historic Fan neighborhood. W Cary St, between Boulevard St and I-95.

Shockoe Slip. Restored area of historic buildings and gaslit cobblestone streets; shopping, restaurants, galleries. E Cary St between 12th and 14th sts, Downtown.

White House of the Confederacy

Sightseeing.

Historic Richmond Tours. Offers guided van tours with pickup at Visitor Center and major hotels (daily); res required. Also guided walking tours (Apr-Oct, daily; fee). Phone 804/649-0711. ¢¢¢¢

Paddlewheeler *Annabel Lee*. Triple-decked, 350-passenger, 19th-century-style riverboat cruises the James River. Narrated tour; entertainment. Lunch, brunch, dinner, and plantation cruises. (Apr-Dec, at least one cruise Tues-Sun) Departs from Intermediate Terminal. Phone 804/377-2020.

Plantation Tours. The Richmond-Petersburg-Williamsburg area has many fine old mansions and estates. Some are open most of the yr; others only during Historic Garden Week (see SPECIAL EVENTS). The Metro Richmond Visitors Center has maps, information folders, suggestions. (Daily) 1710 Robin Hood Rd. Phone 804/783-7450.

Valentine Museum. Traces history of Richmond. Exhibits focus on city life, decorative arts, costumes and textiles, industrial and social history; tour of restored 1812 Wickham House. Lunch served in walled garden (Apr-Oct). (Daily; closed hols). 1015 E Clay St, N of Capitol Sq. Phone 804/649-0711. ¢¢

Virginia Aviation Museum. Exhibits and artifacts on the history of aviation, with emphasis on Virginia pioneers. (Daily; closed Thanksgiving, Dec 25) 5701 Huntsman Rd in Sandston, at Richmond International Airport. Phone 804/236-3622. ¢¢

Virginia House. A Tudor building constructed of materials from Warwick Priory (built in England in 1125 and rebuilt in 1565 as a residence); moved here in 1925. West wing is modeled after Sulgrave Manor, at one time the home of Lawrence Washington. Furniture, tapestries, and paintings from 15th to 20th centuries. Formal gardens. Tours by appt only exc during Historic Garden Week (see SPECIAL EVENTS). (Fri-Sun, otherwise by appt; closed hols) 4301 Sulgrave Rd, ½ mi off VA 147 (Cary St), in Windsor Farms. Phone 804/353-4251. ¢¢

Virginia War Memorial. Honors Virginians who died in WWII, Korean, and Vietnam wars. Mementos of battles; eternal flame; more than 12,000 names engraved on glass and marble walls. (Daily) 621 S Belvidere St, downtown at N end of Robert E. Lee Bridge. **FREE**

White House of the Confederacy. Classical Revival house (1818) used by Jefferson Davis as his official residence during period when Richmond was capital of the Confederacy. Abraham Lincoln met with troops here during Union occupation of the city. Restored to pre-wartime appearance; original furnishings. (Daily; closed Jan 1, Thanksgiving, Dec 25) 12th and E Clay sts, N of Capitol Sq. Phone 804/649-1861. Combination ¢¢¢

Wilton. (1753) Georgian mansion built by William Randolph III. Fully paneled, authentic 18th-century furnishings. Headquarters of National Society of Colonial Dames in Virginia. (Tues-Sun; closed hols) Open during Historic Garden Week (see SPECIAL EVENTS). 215 S Wilton Rd off Cary St, 8 mi W. Phone 804/282-5936. ¢¢

Special Events

Historic Garden Week in Virginia. Many private houses and gardens of historic or artistic interest are opened for this event, which incl more than 200 houses and gardens throughout the state. Tours. Contact 12 E Franklin St, 23219; 804/644-7776. Mid-late Apr.

June Jubilee. Downtown. Performing and visual arts festival with ethnic foods, folk dances, music, crafts. First wkend in June.

Virginia State Fair. Animal and 4-H contests, music, horse show, carnival. Phone 804/228-3200. Late Sept-Oct 1.

Richmond Newpapers Marathon. Last Sun Oct.

Motels/Motor Lodges

★ **AMERISUITES.** 4100 Cox Rd, Glen Allen (23060). 804/747-9644; fax 804/346-9320; toll-free 800/833-1516. www.amerisuites.com. 126 suites, 6 story. S, D $90-$109; under 18 free. Crib free. TV; cable (premium). Pool. Complimentary continental bkfst. Restaurant nearby. Ck-out noon. Meeting rms. Business center. Coin lndry. Exercise equipt. Microwaves. Cr cds: A, C, D, DS, MC, V.
ⅅ 🏊 🐥 🛏 🐾 SC 🐥

★★ **COURTYARD BY MARRIOTT.** 6400 W Broad St (23230). 804/282-1881; fax 804/288-2934; res 800/321-2211. www.marriott.com. 145 rms, 3 story. S, D $119; suites $149; wkend rates. Crib free. TV; cable (premium). Pool; whirlpool. Coffee in rms. Complimentary full bkfst. Bar. Ck-out noon. Coin lndry. Business servs

avail. In-rm modem link. Valet serv. Sundries. Exercise equipt. Some refrigerators. Cr cds: A, C, D, DS, MC, V.
ⅅ 🏊 🐥 🛏 🐾

★ **FAIRFIELD INN.** 7300 W Broad St (23294). 804/672-8621; fax 804/755-7155; toll-free 800/228-2800. www.fairfieldinn.com. 124 rms, 2 story. S, D $61-$89; each addl $5; suite $129; under 18 free. Crib $10. TV; cable (premium). Complimentary continental bkfst. Restaurant adj 11-2 am. Ck-out noon. Business servs avail. In-rm modem link. Pool. Refrigerator, microwave in suite. Picnic tables. Cr cds: A, D, DS, MC, V.
ⅅ 🏊 🛏 🐾 SC

★★ **HAMPTON INN.** 10800 W Broad St, Glen Allen (23060). 804/747-7777; fax 804/747-7069. www.hamptoninn.com. 136 rms, 5 story. S, D $95-$109; each addl $7; under 18 free. Crib free. TV; cable (premium). Complimentary continental bkfst. Restaurant nearby. Ck-out noon. Meeting rms. Business servs avail. In-rm modem link. Bellhops. Exercise equipt. Pool. Picnic table. Cr cds: A, D, DS, MC, V.
ⅅ 🏊 🐥 🛏 🐾

★★ **HOLIDAY INN RICHMOND AIRPORT.** 5203 Williamsburg Rd (23150). 804/222-6450; fax 804/226-4305; toll-free 800/465-4329. www.richmondhotels.net/airport.htm. 230 rms, 3-6 story. S, D $84-$99; under 19 free. Pet accepted, some restrictions; $25. TV; cable (premium). Pool. Coffee in rms. Restaurant 6 am-2 pm, 4-11 pm. Bar. Ck-out noon. Meeting rms. Business servs avail. In-rm modem link. Bellhops. Free airport transportation. Exercise rm. Refrigerators, microwaves avail. Cr cds: A, C, D, DS, JCB, MC, V.
ⅅ 🐾 🏊 🛏 🐾 SC 🐥

★ **LA QUINTA INN.** 6910 Midlothian Tpke (23225). 804/745-7100; fax 804/276-6660; toll-free 800/531-5900. www.laquintainn.com. 130 rms, 3 story. S, D $58-$65; each addl $5; under 18 free. Crib free. Pet accepted, some restrictions. TV; cable (premium). Pool. Complimentary continental bkfst. Restaurant adj. Ck-out noon. Business servs avail. In-rm modem link. Cr cds: A, D, DS, MC, V.
ⅅ 🐾 🏊 🛏 🐾 SC

★ ★ **QUALITY INN WEST END.**
8008 W Broad St (23294). 804/346-0000; fax 804/346-4547. www.quality inn.com. 191 rms, 6 story. Apr-Oct: S, D $79-$149; each addl $10; under 18 free; lower rates rest of yr. Pet accepted, fee. Crib free. TV; cable (premium). Pool. Coffee in rms. Complimentary continental bkfst. Restaurant nearby. Ck-out 11 am. Exercise rm. Meeting rms. Business servs avail. In-rm modem link. Microwaves avail. Cr cds: A, C, D, DS, ER, JCB, MC, V.

[D] [☎] [≈] [≧] [🔥] [SC] [🚶]

★ **RED ROOF INN RICHMOND SOUTH.** *4350 Commerce Rd (23234). 804/271-7240; fax 804/271-7245; res 800/843-7663. www.redroof.com.* 108 rms, 2 story. S $35.99-$49.99; D $42.99-$65.99; under 18 free; higher rates race wkends. Pet accepted. TV; cable (premium). Complimentary coffee in lobby. Restaurant nearby. Ck-out noon. Business servs avail. Some refrigerators, microwaves. Cr cds: A, C, D, DS, MC, V.

[D] [☎] [≈] [🔥]

Hotels

★ ★ **BERKELEY HOTEL.** *1200 E Cary St (23219). 804/780-1300; fax 804/648-4728; toll-free 888/780-4422. www.berkeleyhotel.com.* 55 rms, 6 story. S $145-$180; D $155-$190; each addl $15; under 18 free; wkend rates. Crib free. TV; cable (premium), VCR avail. Pool privileges. Coffee in rms. Restaurant 7 am-2 pm, 6-10 pm; Fri, Sat to 11 pm; Sun to 9 pm. Bar 11:30 am-2 pm, 5:30 pm-midnight. Ck-out noon. Meeting rms. Business servs avail. In-rm modem link. Concierge. Valet parking $10. Health club privileges. Bathrm phones. Cr cds: A, C, D, DS, MC, V.

[≈] [D] [≧] [🔥] [SC]

★ ★ **CROWNE PLAZA.** *555 E Canal St (23219). 804/788-0900; fax 804/788-0791; res 800/227-6963. www.crowneplaza.com.* 299 rms, 16 story. Apr-June, Sept-Oct: S, D $179; each addl $10; suites $249-$895; under 18 free; wkend rates; lower rates rest of yr. Crib free. TV; cable (premium). Indoor pool; whirlpool. Coffee in rms. Restaurant 6 am-11 pm. Bar 4 pm-1:30 am. Ck-out noon.

Convention facilities. Business center. In-rm modem link. Concierge. Gift shop. Exercise rm. Cr cds: A, C, D, DS, MC, V.

[D] [≈] [🚶] [≧] [🔥] [🚶]

★ ★ ★ **HILTON RICHMOND AIRPORT.** *5501 Eubank Rd, Sandston (23150). 804/226-6400; fax 804/226-1269; toll-free 800/445-8667. www.hilton.com.* 160 rms, 5 story, 122 suites. S, D $79-$159; family, wkend rates. Crib free. TV; cable (premium). Pool; whirlpool. Coffee in rms. Restaurant 6:30 am-10 pm. Rm serv 24 hrs. Bar 11 am-midnight. Ck-out noon. Meeting rms. Business servs avail. In-rm modem link. Bellhops. Valet serv. Sundries. Free airport transportation. Exercise equipt. Some balconies. Cr cds: A, C, D, DS, JCB, MC, V.

[D] [≈] [🚶] [≧] [🔥] [SC]

★ ★ ★ ★ ★ **THE JEFFERSON.** *101 W Franklin St (23220). 804/788-8000; fax 804/225-0334; toll-free 800/424-8014. www.jefferson-hotel.com.* As a national historic landmark and a charter member of Historic Hotels of America, this property stands as a monument to this southern capital's grandiloquence. Completely renovated to its original 1890s splendor, the lobby boasts a 35-foot, Tiffany stained-glass skylight, a cascading staircase, and 70-foot ceilings. 260 rms, 9 story. Apr-mid-June and mid-Sept-early Dec: S $235-$285; D $255-$305; each addl $20; suites $335-$1,600; under 18 free; package plans; lower rates rest of yr. Crib free. Valet parking $12. TV; cable (premium), VCR avail. Pool. Restaurant 6:30 am-midnight (see also LEMAIRE). Rm serv 24 hrs. Bar 11-2 am. Ck-out noon. Meeting rms. Business center. In-rm modem link. Concierge serv. Exercise equipt. Refrigerators, minibars. Cr cds: A, C, D, DS, JCB, MC, V.

[D] [≈] [🚶] [≧] [🔥] [SC] [🚶]

★ ★ ★ **MARRIOTT RICHMOND.** *500 E Broad St (23219). 804/643-3400; fax 804/788-1230; res 800/228-9290. www.marriott.com.* 400 rms, 17 story. S, D $169; each addl $10; suites $200-$700; under 18 free; wkend rates. Crib free. TV; cable (premium). Indoor pool; whirlpool, poolside serv, lifeguard. Coffee in rms. Restaurant 6:30

am-10 pm. Bar 11-1 am. Ck-out noon. Coin lndry. Convention facilities. Business center. In-rm modem link. Concierge. Exercise equipt; sauna. Game rm. Some bathrm phones, refrigerators. Luxury level. Cr cds: A, C, D, DS, JCB, MC, V.

⬛🏊🏃🗻🐾🏃

★★★ **MARRIOTT RICHMOND WEST.** *4240 Dominion Blvd (23060). 804/965-9500; fax 804/965-5559. www.marriott.com.* 242 rms, 6 story. S, D $79-$250; under 17 free. Crib avail. TV; cable (premium). Indoor pool; whirlpool. Restaurant 6:30 am-10 pm. Bar to 11 pm. Ck-out 11 am, ck-in 3 pm. Meeting rms. Business center. In-rm modem link. Concierge. Exercise equipt. Refrigerators avail. Cr cds: A, DS, JCB, MC, V.

🏃⬛🏊🏃

★★★ **OMNI RICHMOND HOTEL.** *100 S 12th St (23219). 804/344-7000; fax 804/648-1029; res 800/843-6664. www.omnihotels.com.* 361 units, 19 story. Mid-Apr-mid-June, mid-Sept-mid-Nov: S $139; D $154; each addl $15; suites $209-$450; under 18 free; package plans; lower rates rest of yr. Crib free. TV; cable (premium). Indoor pool; poolside serv. Coffee in rms. Restaurant 6:30 am-11 pm. Bar noon-1 am. Ck-out noon. Convention facilities. Business center. In-rm modem link. Concierge. Shopping arcade. Health club privileges. Minibars. Luxury level. Cr cds: A, C, D, DS, MC, V.

⬛🏊🗻🐾🏃

★★★ **SHERATON.** *6624 W Broad St (23230). 804/285-2000; fax 804/288-3961; toll-free 800/228-9000. www.sheraton.com.* 372 rms, 3-8 story. S, D $154-$170; suites $200-$475; under 18 free; wkend rates. Crib free. TV; cable (premium), VCR avail. Indoor/outdoor pool; poolside serv. Playground. Coffee in rms. Restaurant 5-10 pm. Rm serv 6 am-midnight. Bar noon-2 am; entertainment. Ck-out noon. Meeting rms. Business center. In-rm modem link. Bellhops. Valet serv. Gift shop. Airport transportation. Lighted tennis. Exercise equipt. Some private patios. Luxury level. Cr cds: A, C, D, DS, JCB, MC, V.

⬛🎾🏊🏃🗻🐾SC🏃

B&Bs/Small Inns

★★ **EMMANUEL HUTZLER HOUSE.** *2036 Monument Ave (23220). 804/353-6900. www.bensonhouse.com.* 4 rms, 3 story. S $105-$140; D $115-$160. Children over 12 yrs only. TV; cable. Complimentary full bkfst, coffee in library. Restaurant nearby. Ck-out noon, ck-in 4 pm. Luggage handling. Health club privileges. Built 1914; antiques. Totally nonsmoking. Cr cds: A, D, DS, MC, V.

🗻🐾

★★ **LINDEN ROW INN.** *100 E Franklin St (23219). 804/783-7000; fax 804/648-7504; toll-free 800/348-7424. www.lindenrowinn.com.* 70 rms, 4 story, 7 suites. S, D $119-$179; each addl $10; suites $129-$209. TV; cable (premium). Complimentary continental bkfst. Coffee in rms. Dining rm (public by res) 11 am-2:30 pm, 5:30-10 pm. Ck-out 11 am, ck-in 3 pm. Business servs avail. In-rm modem link. Bellhops. Valet serv. Concierge. Health club privileges. In block of Greek Revival rowhouses (1847), around courtyard thought to be boyhood playground of Edgar Allan Poe; antique and period furnishings and decor. Cr cds: A, D, DS, MC, V.

🗻🐾

★ **THE PATRICK HENRY INN.** *2300 E Broad St (23223). 804/225-0477.* 3 rms. Apr-June, Oct-Nov: S $95-$135; D $115-$135; each addl $10; family, wkly, wkend rates; hol wkends (2-day min); higher rates special events; lower rates rest of yr. TV; cable. Complimentary continental bkfst, coffee in rms. Ck-out noon, ck-in 3 pm. Luggage handling. Street parking. Refrigerators. Greek Revival antebellum row house (ca 1855); garden patio, carriage house. Cr cds: A, MC, V.

🐾SC

All Suite

★★ **EMBASSY SUITES.** *2925 Emerywood Pkwy (23294). 804/672-8585; fax 804/672-3749; toll-free 800/362-2779. www.embassysuites.com.* 224 suites, 8 story. Suites $119-$185; each addl $20; under 18 free. Crib free. TV; cable (premium). Indoor pool;

whirlpool. Complimentary full bkfst. Restaurant 11 am-10 pm. Bar to 11 pm. Ck-out noon. Coin lndry. Meeting rms. Business center. In-rm modem link. Gift shop. Exercise equipt; sauna. Refrigerators, micro-waves; wet bar in suites. Cr cds: A, C, D, DS, JCB, MC, V.

Extended Stay

★★ **RESIDENCE INN BY MAR-RIOTT.** *2121 Dickens Rd (23230). 804/285-8200; fax 804/285-2530; res 800/331-3131. www.residenceinn.com.* 80 kit. suites, 2 story. S, D $119-$159; monthly, wkly, wkend rates. Crib free. Pet accepted, some restric-tions; $50. TV; cable (premium), VCR avail (movies). Pool. Complimentary continental bkfst. Ck-out noon. Coin lndry. Meeting rm. Business servs avail. In-rm modem link. Valet serv. Microwaves; many fireplaces. Private patios, balconies. Picnic tables, grills. Cr cds: A, C, D, DS, JCB, MC, V.

Restaurants

★★ **ACACIA.** *3325 W Cary St (23221). 804/354-6060. www.acacia restaurant.com.* Menu changes daily. Hrs: 11:30 am-9:30 pm. Closed Sun, Mon. Res accepted. Wine list. Lunch $5.95-$9.95; dinner $10.50-$24.95. Entertainment. In an old renovated church. Cr cds: A, D, DS, MC, V.

★★ **AMICI.** *3343 W Cary St (23221). 804/353-4700. amiciristorante.net.* Hrs: 11:30 am-2:30 pm, 5:30-10 pm; Fri, Sat to 11 pm; Sun from 5:30 pm. Closed hols. Res accepted. Northern Italian menu. Bar. A la carte entrees: lunch $7.95-$12.95, dinner $13.95-$23.95. Specializes in pasta, game, seafood. Own breads. Outdoor din-ing. Cr cds: A, D, DS, MC, V.

★ **CAFFE DI PAGLIACCI.** *214 N Lombardy St (23220). 804/353-3040. caffedipagliacci.com.* Hrs: 5-10 pm; Fri, Sat to 11 pm. Closed Sun; hols. Res accepted. Italian menu. Bar. Prices: $8.95-$19.95. Specializes in pasta, veal. Own desserts. Casual decor. Cr cds: A, C, D, DS, MC, V.

★★★ **DINING ROOM.** *1200 E Cary St (23219). 804/780-1300. berkleyhotel. com.* Hrs: 7 am-10 pm. Res accepted. Wine list. Bkfst, lunch $6.95-$12.95; dinner $24-32. Child's menu. Enter-tainment. European ambiance. Cr cds: A, C, D, DS, MC, V.

★★★ **THE FROG AND THE RED-NECK.** *1423 E Cary St (23219). 804/648-3764. www.frogandredneck.com.* Hrs: 5:30-10 pm; Sat 5-10:30 pm. Closed Sun; hols. Res accepted. Regional American menu. Bar. Wine list. Dinner $9.75-$26.25. Specialties: soft shell crab, jumbo lump crab cakes, buffalo. Contemporary decor, with a touch of Art Deco. Muraled walls. Totally nonsmoking. Cr cds: A, D, DS, MC, V.

★★ **HALF WAY HOUSE.** *10301 Jef-ferson Davis Hwy (23237). 804/275-1760.* Hrs: 11:30 am-2 pm, 5:30-9 pm; Sat, Sun from 5:30 pm. Res accepted. Bar. Lunch $8-$17, dinner $17-$32. Specialties: lobster Von Grinegan, filet mignon, Colonial chicken and beef pies. Parking. Antique-furnished manor house (1760) was stop on Petersburg stage-coach line until late 19th century; hosted Washington, Lafayette, Patrick Henry, Jefferson, among oth-ers. Used as a Union headquarters during 1864 siege of Richmond. Cr cds: A, D, DS, MC, V.

★★ **HELEN'S.** *2527 W Main St (23220). 804/358-4370.* Menu changes wkly. Hrs: 5:30-9:30 pm. Closed Mon, hols. Res accepted. Wine list. Dinner $18-$24. Entertainment. Cr cds: A, MC, V.

★★ **INDOCHINE.** *2923 W Cary St (23221). 804/353-5799.* Hrs: 5-9:30 pm. Closed Sun; Memorial Day, Dec 25. Res required Fri, Sat dinner. Viet-namese menu. Bar. Dinner $16.95-$20.95. Specialties: crispy softshell crab; scallops and shrimp in curry sauce; crispy salmon filet with spicy apple-cognac sauce. Own baking. French Colonial atmosphere; green-ery throughout. Totally nonsmoking. Cr cds: A, DS, MC, V.

★ ★ ★ **KABUTO JAPANESE HOUSE OF STEAK.** *8052 W Broad St (23294). 804/747-9573.* Hrs: 11:30 am-2 pm, 5-9:30 pm; Fri to 10 pm; Sat 4:30-10 pm; Sun 4-10 pm. Closed Thanksgiving, Dec 25. Res accepted. Japanese menu. Bar. Complete meals: lunch $7.50-$11.25, dinner $12.50-$24. Child's menu. Specializes in Teppanyaki cooking. Sushi bar. Parking. Japanese-style building. Cr cds: A, D, DS, MC, V.

[D] [⊒]

★ ★ **LA PETIT FRANCE.** *2108 Maywill St (23230). 804/353-8729.* Hrs: 11:30 am-2 pm, 5:30-10 pm; Sat 5:30-11 pm. Closed Sun, Mon; hols; also last 2 wks Aug. Res accepted. French menu. Serv bar. Wine list. A la carte entrees: lunch $8.95-$13.95, dinner $21.50-$29.95. Child's menu. Specializes in seafood, veal. Family-owned. Jacket (dinner). Cr cds: A, D, DS, MC, V.

[D] [⊒]

★ ★ ★ **LEMAIRE.** *101 W Franklin (23220). 804/788-8000. www.jefferson-hotel.com.* An elegant dining experience with the best of southern hospitality, this restaurant is located within the landmark hotel of Richmond, The Jefferson. Guests have a choice of several dining rooms, from the glass-enclosed conservatory to the mahogany-paneled library filled with antique, leather-bound volumes. Hrs: 6:30 am-2 pm, 5:30-10:30 pm. Closed Memorial Day. Res accepted. Bar. A la carte entrees: bkfst $2.25-$10.88, lunch $11-$18, dinner $30-$37. Buffet: bkfst, lunch $11.95-$15.95. Child's menu. Specializes in regional cuisine. Valet parking. Pianist. Seven small dining rms. Cr cds: A, D, DS, MC, V.

[D] [⊒]

★ **MILLIE'S.** *2603 E Main St (23223). 804/643-5512. www.milliesdiner.com.* Specializes in Thai spicy shrimp with asparagus, shiitakes, red cabbages, cilantro, and peanuts tossed with linguine; seared tuna with artichoke hearts; herbed buffalo salad. Hrs: 11 am-10:30 pm; Sat 10 am-10:30 pm; Sun 9 am-3 pm, 5:30-9:30 pm. Closed Mon. Wine list. Lunch $6-$11; dinner $19.95-$24.95. Entertainment. In front of old tobacco

warehouses, huge collection of old 45 singles with mini-jukeoxes in booths. Open kitchen. Cr cds: A, DS, MC, V.

[D] [⊒]

★ ★ ★ **THE ORIGINAL BOOK-BINDER'S.** *2306 E Cary St (23223). 804/643-6900.* Specializes steaks, seafood. Hrs: 4:30-10 pm; Sun to 9 pm. Closed hols. Res accepted. Bar. Wine list. Dinner complete meals: $16.95-$35. Child's menu. Valet parking. Family-owned. Cr cds: A, D, DS, MC, V.

★ **O'TOOLES.** *4800 Forest Hill Ave (23225). 804/233-1781.* Hrs: 11-2 am; Sun to midnight. Closed Dec 24, 25. Bar. Lunch $3.75-$8, dinner $4.25-$12.95. Child's menu. Specializes in seafood, steak, barbecued dishes. Pianist. Parking. Irish pub decor. Family-owned. Cr cds: A, MC, V.

[D] [⊒]

★ ★ **PEKING PAVILION.** *1302 E Cary St (23219). 804/649-8888.* Hrs: 11:30 am-2:15 pm, 5-9:30 pm; Fri to 10:30 pm; Sat 5-10:30 pm; Sun brunch 11:30 am-2 pm. Closed Thanksgiving. Res accepted. Chinese menu. Bar. Lunch $5.20-$8.55, dinner $6.75-$23.95. Sun brunch $9.95. Specialties: Peking duck, seafood delight, chicken imperial. Oriental antiques; teakwood sculpture. Cr cds: A, MC, V.

★ ★ ★ **RUTH'S CHRIS STEAK HOUSE.** *11500 Huguenot Rd (23113). 804/378-0600. www.sizzlingsteak.com.* Hrs: 5-10 pm; Fri, Sat to 11 pm; Sun to 9 pm. Closed hols. Res accepted. Bar. A la carte entrees: dinner $19.95-$32.95. Specializes in steak, lobster. Organist Tues-Sun. Parking. Outdoor dining. Cr cds: A, D, DS, MC, V.

[D] [⊒]

★ **SAM MILLER'S WAREHOUSE.** *1210 E Cary St (23219). 804/644-5465. www.sammillers.com.* Hrs: 11 am-11 pm; Sun 10 am-10 pm. Res accepted. Lunch $4.95-$12.50, dinner $14-$30. Sun brunch $6-$13.95. Child's menu. Specializes in fresh seafood, live Maine lobster, prime Western beef. Lobster tank. In historic district; display of antique mirrors. Cr cds: A, D, DS, MC, V.

[⊒]

★★ **SKILLIGALEE.** *5416 Glenside Dr (23228). 804/672-6200. www.skilligalee. com.* Hrs: 11:30 am-4 pm, 5-10 pm; Fri to 10:30 pm; Sat 5-10:30 pm; Sun 5-9 pm. Closed Thanksgiving, Dec 25. Bar. A la carte entrees: lunch $5.95-$11.95, dinner $15.95-$25.95. Child's menu. Specializes in fresh seafood, soups. Raw bar. Own salad dressing. Parking. Nautical decor with fireplace. Family-owned. Cr cds: A, DS, MC, V.

D ⊣

★ **STRAWBERRY STREET CAFE.** *421 Strawberry St (23220). 804/353-6860. www.strawberrystreetcafe.com.* Specializes in crab cakes, chicken pot pie, salad bar. Hrs: 11:30 am-10:30 pm; Fri to midnight; Sat 11 am-midnight; Sun 10 am-10:30 pm. Res accepted. Wine list. Lunch $5.50-$9.50; dinner $7.95-$16.95. Child's menu. Entertainment. Stained glass throughout restaurant. Cr cds: A, MC, V.

⊣

★ **TANGLEWOOD ORDINARY.** *2210 River Rd W, Maidens (23102). 804/556-3284. www.ordinary.com.* Hrs: 5-9 pm; Sun noon-8 pm. Closed Mon-Tues; hols. Res accepted; required Wed. Traditional Southern menu. Wine, beer. Complete meals: dinner $12. Specializes in chicken, roast beef, seasoned vegetables, ham. Casual dining in log cabin building. Collection of *The Saturday Evening Post* dating from 1913. Totally non-smoking.

★★ **TOBACCO COMPANY.** *1201 E Cary St (23219). 804/782-9431. www. thetobaccocompany.com.* Hrs: 11:30 am-2:30 pm, 5:30-10:30 pm; Sun 11 am-2:30 pm, 5:30-9:30 pm. Closed Jan 1, Dec 25. Res accepted. Bar 11:30-2 am. A la carte entrees: lunch $6.99-$11.95, dinner $17.95-$29.95. Sun brunch $4.95-$15.95. Specializes in prime rib, fresh fish. Own baking. Band Mon-Sat. In former tobacco warehouse (ca 1880); built around skylit atrium with antique cage elevator; many unusual antiques. Cr cds: A, D, MC, V.

D ⊣

★ **TRAK'S.** *9115 Quioccasin Rd (23229). 804/740-1700.* Hrs: 11 am-10 pm; Fri, Sat to 11 pm. Closed Sun; hols. Res accepted. Greek, Italian menu. Lunch $5-$7, dinner $8.95-$15.95. Child's menu. Specialties: Helen's a la Greek, Mediterranean lovers, Greek sampler. Parking. Greek artwork. Cr cds: A, D, DS, MC, V.

D ⊣

★★ **YEN CHING.** *6601 Midlothian Tpke (23225). 804/276-7430.* Hrs: 11:30 am-9:30 pm; Fri, Sat to 11 pm. Closed Thanksgiving. Res required. Chinese menu. Bar. Lunch, dinner $7.95-$22.95. Specializes in Hunan and Szechuan dishes. Parking. Chinese tapestries and art. Cr cds: A, MC, V.

D ⊣

Unrated Dining Spots

BYRAM'S LOBSTER HOUSE. *3215 W Broad St (23230). 804/355-9193. www.byrams.com.* Hrs: 11:30 am-10 pm; early-bird dinner Mon-Fri 3:30-6 pm. Closed Jan 1, Dec 25. Res accepted. Continental menu. Bar. Lunch $5.50-$13.95, dinner $8.95-$25.95. Specializes in seafood, beef. Parking. Local artwork, Greek reproductions. Family-owned. Cr cds: A, D, DS, MC, V.

SC ⊣

FAROUK'S HOUSE OF INDIA. *3033 W Cary St (23221). 804/355-0378.* Hrs: 11:30 am-3 pm, 5:30-10:30 pm. Res accepted. Indian menu. Lunch $6.95-$8.95, dinner $6.95-$12. Buffet: lunch $6.99. Specialties: curries, biryanies, tandoori. Cr cds: A, D, DS, MC, V.

D SC ⊣

Richmond National Battlefield Park

See also Ashland, Richmond

(Headquarters located at 3215 E Broad St, in Chimborazo Park)

A total of seven Union drives on Richmond, the symbol of secession, were made during the Civil War. Richmond National Battlefield Park,

770 acres in ten different units, preserves sites of the two efforts that came close to success—McClellan's Peninsula Campaign of 1862 and Grant's attack in 1864.

Of McClellan's campaign, the park includes sites of the Seven Days' Battles at Chickahominy Bluffs, Beaver Dam Creek, Gaines' Mill (Watt House), and Malvern Hill. Grant's campaign is represented by the battlefield at Cold Harbor, where on June 3, 1864, Grant hurled his army at fortified Confederate positions, resulting in 7,000 casualties in less than one hour. Confederate Fort Harrison, Parker's Battery, Drewry's Bluff (Fort Darling), and Union-built Fort Brady are also included. Park (daily).

What to See and Do

Main Visitor Center. Information, exhibits, film, slide program. (Daily; closed Jan 1, Thanksgiving, Dec 25) In Chimborazo City Park. 3215 E Broad St, on US 60 E in Richmond. Phone 804/226-1981. **FREE** From here start

> **Self-guided tour.** Auto drive (60 mi) with markers, maps, recorded messages providing background, detailed information for specific places. Visitors may select own route, incl all or part of the drive.

Other Visitor Centers. Cold Harbor, 16 mi NE on VA 156 (daily, unstaffed) and Fort Harrison, 10 mi SE on VA 5 and Battlefield Park Rd (June-Aug, daily). **FREE**

Roanoke

(E-4) *See also Salem*

Settled 1740 **Pop** 94,911 **Elev** 948 ft
Area code 540
Information Roanoke Valley Convention & Visitors Bureau, 114 Market St, 24011; 540/342-6025 or 800/635-5535
Web www.visitroanokeva.com

Roanoke was incorporated in 1882 when it became a junction of the Norfolk and Western Railway and the Shenandoah Valley Railroad. Before that, the town was called Big Lick

(salt marshes in the area attracted big game).

It is the cultural, industrial, commercial, convention, and medical center for western Virginia. Manufactured products include railroad cars, fabricated steel, fabrics, apparel, furniture, flour, wood products, electronic equipment, plastics, cosmetics, and locks.

Set in the Shenandoah Valley between the Blue Ridge and the Allegheny mountains, it is near the outdoor attractions of the huge Washington and Jefferson national forests (see HARRISONBURG) and the Blue Ridge Parkway (see).

What to See and Do

Blue Ridge Parkway. (see) Runs on crest of mountains both north and south of Roanoke. Narrow in parts; limited restaurants. Beautiful seasonal views from overlooks. 6 mi E on US 460 or 3 mi S on US 220.

Center in the Square. Restored 20th-century furniture warehouse housing five independent cultural organizations: three museums, incl Art Museum of Western Virginia, and two professional theater companies (see SPECIAL EVENT). (Tues-Sun; closed hols) 1 Market Sq, Downtown. Phone 540/342-5700. Also here are

> **History Museum of Western Virginia.** Permanent exhibits deal with Roanoke history from days of Native Americans to present. Archives, library (by appt). (Tues-Sun; closed hols) Phone 540/342-5770. ¢

> **Science Museum of Western Virginia & Hopkins Planetarium.** Museum contains hands-on exhibits in the natural and physical sciences: animals of land and ocean, computers, TV weather station. Workshops, programs, and classes for children and adults; special exhibits. Hopkins Planetarium shows films. (Tues-Sun; closed hols) Phone 540/342-5710. ¢¢¢

George Washington and Jefferson National Forests. (see HARRISONBURG)

Mill Mountain Zoological Park. Zoo sits atop Mill Mtn; offers picnic areas with magnificent views of city and valley. (Daily; closed Dec 25) Off US

220/I-581 and Blue Ridge Pkwy. Phone 540/343-3241. ¢¢¢

Virginia Museum of Transportation. Vehicles from the past and present. Large steam, diesel, and electric locomotive collection. Aviation exhibits; model of miniature traveling circus. Hands-on exhibits. (Mar-Dec, daily; rest of yr, Wed-Sun; closed hols) 303 Norfolk Ave, Downtown. Phone 540/342-5670. ¢¢¢

Virginia's Explore Park. This 1,300-acre living history museum and nature center features re-created frontier settlement that depicts life in western Virginia in 1671, 1740 and 1850. Six mi of hiking trails. Picnic areas. (May-Oct, Wed-Sun) Mi 115 on Blue Ridge Pkwy. Phone 800/842-9163. ¢¢¢

Special Events

Virginia State Championship Chili Cookoff. City Market. Teams compete to represent Virginia in World Cook-off. Samples, entertainment. Contact Roanoke Special Events Committee, 210 Reserve Ave SW, 24016. Phone 540/342-4716. First Sat May.

Festival in the Park. Art exhibits, crafts, sports, food, parade, entertainment. Two wkends beginning Fri before Memorial Day. Phone 757/625-1445.

Mill Mountain Theatre. Center in the Square. Musicals, comedies, dramas. Nightly Tues-Sun; Sat, Sun matinees. For res phone 540/342-5740. Regular season, Oct-Aug.

Motels/Motor Lodges

★ **BEST INN.** 501 Orange Ave (24016). 540/342-8961; fax 540/342-3813; toll-free 800/237-8466. 150 rms, 2 story. S, D $39.95-$89.95. Crib free. TV; cable (premium), VCR avail. Pool; wading pool. Complimentary bkfst buffet. Coffee in rms. Restaurant 7 am-9 pm. Bar from 5 pm. Ck-out noon. Business servs avail. In-rm modem link. Bellhops. Valet serv. Microwaves avail. Cr cds: A, C, D, DS, ER, JCB, MC, V.
D ⇌ ⇛ ⧖ SC

★ **CLARION HOTEL.** 2727 Ferndale Dr NW (24017). 540/362-4500; fax 540/362-4506; toll-free 800/228-5050.

www.clarionhotel.com. 154 rms, 5 story. S $89-$129; D $99-$129; each addl $10; under 18 free; wkend rates. Crib free. Pet accepted; $50 deposit. TV; cable (premium). Indoor/outdoor pool; whirlpool. Restaurant 6 am-10:30 pm. Complimentary coffee in rms. Bar 11:30 am-11 pm. Ck-out noon. Meeting rms. Business servs avail. In-rm modem link. Bellhops. Valet serv. Sundries. Free airport transportation. Lighted tennis. 18-hole golf privileges. Exercise equipt. Bathrm phones. Picnic tables, grills. Cr cds: A, C, D, DS, ER, JCB, MC, V.
D ⇌ ⧖ ⇛ ⊠ ✈ ⇛ ⧖ SC

★ **COLONY HOUSE MOTOR LODGE.** 3560 Franklin Rd SW (24014). 540/345-0411; res 800/552-7026. 69 rms, 2 story. S $46; D $58-$68; each addl $5; under 13 free. Crib avail. TV; cable. Complimentary continental bkfst. Restaurant adj 11 am-10 pm. Ck-out 11 am. Meetng rms. Business servs avail. Valet serv. Health club privileges. Pool. Bathrm phone, in-rm whirlpool, refrigerator in suites. Cr cds: A, C, D, DS, MC, V.
D ⇛ ⇛ ⧖ SC

★ **DAYS INN.** 8118 Plantation Rd (24019). 540/366-0341; fax 540/366-3935; toll-free 800/329-7466. www.daysinn.com. 123 rms, 2 story. S $45-$60; D $55-$65; each addl $6; suites $80; under 12 free. Crib avail. TV; cable (premium), VCR avail. Pool. Restaurant 6-10:30 am, 5-10 pm. Bar 4:30-11 pm. Ck-out noon. Meeting rms. Business servs avail. In-rm modem link. Valet serv. Free airport transportation. Cr cds: A, C, D, DS, JCB, MC, V.
D ⇛ ⇛ ⧖ SC

★★ **HAMPTON INN.** 3816 Franklin Rd SW (24014). 540/989-4000; fax 540/989-0250. www.hamptoninn.com. 59 rms, 2 story. May-Nov: S $58-$62; D $68-$72; family rates; higher rates special events. Crib free. TV; cable (premium), VCR avail. Complimentary continental bkfst. Restaurant adj 10:30 am-9 pm; wkends from 8 am. Ck-out 11 am. Coin lndry. Meeting rm. Business servs avail. In-rm modem link. Valet serv. Health club privileges. Some refrigerators, microwaves. Cr cds: A, C, D, DS, MC, V.
D ⇛ ⧖

★ ★ **HAMPTON INN AIRPORT.**
6621 Thirlane Rd (24019). 540/265-2600; fax 540/366-2091; res 800/426-7866. www.hamptoninn.com. 79 rms, 2 story. S $70-$72; D $76-$80; suites $103; under 18 free; higher rates: graduation, sporting events. Crib free. Valet parking $20. TV; cable (premium), VCR. Complimentary coffee in lobby. Restaurant nearby. Ck-out 11 am. Meeting rms. Business servs avail. Valet serv. Sundries. Coin lndry. Free airport transportation. Exercise equipt. Heated pool. Refrigerators, microwaves; some bathrm phones; in-rm whirlpool in suites. Cr cds: A, C, D, DS, MC, V.

D ⊷ 𝕏 ⊠ ⚲

★ ★ **HOLIDAY INN.** *4468 Starkey Rd (24014). 540/774-4400; fax 540/774-1195; toll-free 888/228-5040. www. holiday-inn.com.* 196 rms, 5 story. S, D $88-$102; suites $128-$153; under 18 free; wkend rates. Crib free. Pet accepted; $10. TV; cable (premium). Pool; poolside serv. Restaurant 6:30 am-10 pm. Bar 4 pm-2 am; entertainment. Ck-out noon. Meeting rms. Business servs avail. In-rm modem link. Bellhops. Valet serv. Concierge. Free airport, bus depot transportation. Golf privileges. Health club privileges. Some wet bars; microwaves avail. Luxury level. Cr cds: A, C, D, DS, MC, V.

D ⊷ 𝕏 ⊠ ⚲

★ ★ **HOLIDAY INN.** *6626 Thirlane Rd NW (24019). 540/366-8861; fax 540/366-1637; res 888/337-1385. www. holiday-inn.com/hotels/roaap.* 161 rms, 2 story. S, D $74-$85; under 18 free; wkend, special event rates. Crib free. TV; cable (premium), VCR avail. Pool; wading pool. Complimentary coffee in rms. Restaurant 6 am-10 pm. Bar. Ck-out noon. Coin lndry. Meeting rms. Business servs avail. In-rm modem link. Bellhops. Valet serv. Sundries. Airport, bus depot transportation. Tennis privileges. Golf privileges. Health club privileges. Some bathrm phones. Cr cds: A, C, D, DS, JCB, MC, V.

𝕏 D 𝕗 ⊷ ✈ ⊠ ⚲ SC

★ **RAMADA INN.** *1927 Franklin Rd SW (24014). 540/343-0121; fax 540/342-2048; res 800/272-6232. www. ramada.com.* 127 rms, 4 story. S $58; D $64; each addl $7; under 18 free; higher rates special events. Pet accepted. TV; cable. Pool. Complimentary full bkfst. Coffee in rms. Restaurant 11:30 am-2:30 pm, 4:30-9:30 pm. Bar 4:30 pm-2 am. Ck-out noon. Coin lndry. Meeting rms. Business servs avail. In-rm modem link. Health club privileges. Sundries. Near river. Cr cds: A, D, DS, MC, V.

D ⊷ ⊷ ⊠ ⚲

★ **SLEEP INN.** *4045 Electric Rd (24014). 540/772-1500; fax 540/772-1500; toll-free 800/628-1929.* 103 rms, shower only, 2 story. No elvtr. S $55.95-$60.95; D $60.95-$65; each addl $6; under 18 free. Crib free. TV; cable (premium), VCR. Complimentary continental bkfst. Restaurant nearby. Ck-out noon. Meeting rm. Business servs avail. In-rm modem link. Valet serv. Health club privileges. Microwaves avail. Cr cds: A, C, D, DS, ER, JCB, MC, V.

D ⊠ ⚲ SC

★ **TRAVELODGE.** *2619 Lee Hwy S, Troutville (24175). 540/992-6700; fax 540/992-3991; res 800/578-7878. www.travelodge.com/troutville109699.* 108 rms. S $45; D $52; each addl $6; kit. units $45; under 18 free; wkly rates. Crib free. Pet accepted; $6. TV; cable (premium). Pool. Playground. Complimentary continental bkfst. Coffee in rms. Restaurant nearby. Ck-out 11 am. Meeting rms. Business servs avail. Some refrigerators, microwaves. Cr cds: A, D, DS, MC, V.

D ⊷ ⊷ ⊠ ⚲ SC

Hotels

★ ★ ★ **HOTEL ROANOKE AND CONFERENCE CENTER.** *110 Shenandoah Ave (24016). 540/985-5900; fax 540/853-8290.* 332 rms, 7 story. S $119-$145; D $129-$155; each addl $10; suites $165-$450; under 18 free; wkend, hol rates; higher rates: graduation, football. Crib free. Valet parking $5. TV; cable (premium). Complimentary coffee in lobby. Restaurant 6:30 am-10 pm; Sat from 7 am; Sun 7 am-9 pm. Bar 11 am-midnight; Fri, Sat to 1 am; entertainment Fri, Sat. Ck-out noon. Convention facilities. Business center. In-rm modem link. Gift shop. Free airport, RR station transportation. Tennis privileges. Golf privileges, pro, putting green, driving range. Exercise equipt. Pool; whirlpool. Some refrigerators, fireplaces. Cr cds: A, C, D, DS, ER, JCB, MC, V.

🅳 🛏 🌊 🏋 🛎 🔥 SC 🐾 🏂

★ ★ ★ **PATRICK HENRY HOTEL.** *617 S Jefferson St (24011). 540/345-8811; fax 540/342-9908; toll-free 800/303-0988. patrickhenryroanoke.com.* 117 kit. units, 10 story. S $99; D $109; each addl $10; suites $125-$250; under 18 free; monthly rates. Crib avail. TV; cable (premium). Complimentary continental bkfst. Restaurant 11:30 am-11 pm. Bar 4 pm-2 am. Ck-out noon. Guest lndry. Meeting rms. Business servs avail. In-rm modem link. Barber, beauty shop. Free airport transportation. Health club privileges. Refrigerators; microwaves avail. Cr cds: A, C, D, DS, MC, V.

🅳 🌊 🔥

★ ★ **WYNDHAM ROANOKE AIR-PORT HOTEL.** *2801 Hershberger Rd NW (24017). 540/563-9300; fax 540/366-5846; res 800/996-3426. www.wyndham.com.* 320 rms, 8 story. S, studio rms $74-$134; D $84-$150; each addl $10; suites $210-$250; under 18 free; golf, wkend rates. Crib free. Pet accepted, some restrictions; $10. TV; cable (premium), VCR avail. 2 pools, 1 indoor; whirlpool, poolside serv. Restaurant 6:30 am-10 pm. Bars 11-1 am. Ck-out noon. Convention facilities. Business servs avail. Concierge. Gift shop. Free airport transportation. Lighted tennis. Exercise equipt; sauna. Some refrigerators. Private patios, balconies. Luxury level. Cr cds: A, C, D, DS, ER, JCB, MC, V.

🏂 🅳 🌊 🛏 🏋 ✈ 🌊 🔥

B&B/Small Inn

★ ★ **CLAIBORNE HOUSE.** *185 Claiborne Ave, Rocky Mt (24151). 540/483-4616.* 5 rms, 2 story. Some rm phones. S, D $75-$125. TV in some rms; cable (premium). Complimentary full bkfst. Complimentary coffee in rms. Ck-out 11 am, ck-in 3 pm. Business servs avail. Game rm. Built in 1895; Victorian-style decor. Totally nonsmoking. Cr cds: MC, V.

🌊 🔥

Restaurants

★ ★ **BILLY'S RITZ.** *102 Salem Ave SE (24011). 540/342-3937.* Hrs: 5-10:30 pm; Fri, Sat to midnight. Closed hols; Jan 1-16. Bar. Dinner $13-$25. Specializes in steak, pork chops, seafood. Outdoor dining. Three dining areas with eclectic decor. Cr cds: A, D, DS, MC, V.

🅳 🍽

★ ★ **CHARCOAL STEAK HOUSE.** *5225 Williamson Rd (24012). 540/366-3710. www.charcoalsteakhouse.com.* Hrs: 11 am-10 pm; Sat from 5 pm; Sun 5-9 pm; Sun brunch 10:30 am-2:30 pm. Closed Mon. Res accepted. Bar. Lunch $4.95-$11.50, dinner $9.95-$24. Child's menu. Specializes in prime rib, steak, seafood. Entertainment. Parking. Cr cds: A, D, DS, MC, V.

🅳 🍽

★ ★ **KABUKI JAPANESE STEAK HOUSE.** *3503 Franklin Rd SW (24014). 540/981-0222.* Hrs: 5-10:30 pm; Fri, Sat 4:30-11 pm. Closed hols; also Jan 2, Super Bowl Sun. Res accepted; required Fri, Sat. Japanese menu. Bar. Complete meals: dinner $10.45-$24.45. Child's menu. Specializes in Teppanyaki cooking. Parking. Japanese antique display. Cr cds: A, D, DS, MC, V.

🅳 🍽

★ ★ ★ **LIBRARY.** *3117 Franklin Rd (24014). 540/985-0811.* Hrs: 6 pm-midnight. Closed Sun; hols. Res accepted. French, American menu. Bar. Wine cellar. Dinner $12.95-$29.95. Specialties: roast rack of lamb, Dover sole, steak Diane. Own pastries. Parking. Antique books on display. Jacket. Cr cds: A, D, DS, MC, V.

🅳 🍽

★ **SUNNYBROOK INN.** *7342 Plantation Rd NW (24019). 540/366-4555. www.sunnybrookinn.com.* Hrs: 7 am-8 pm; Fri, Sat to 9 pm; Sun to 7 pm. Closed Dec 25. Res accepted. Wine, beer. Bkfst $3-$6, lunch $4-$8, dinner $6-$17. Buffet: (Fri, Sat) dinner $12.99-$17.99; (Sun) lunch, dinner $9. Child's menu. Specialties: oysters, country ham, fresh mountain trout. Salad bar. Parking. Outdoor dining.

In Colonial Revival farmhouse (1912). Cr cds: D, MC, V.

D ⊒

Salem

(E-4) *See also Roanoke*

Founded 1802 **Pop** 24,747 **Elev** 1,060 ft **Area code** 540 **Zip** 24153

Information Salem/Roanoke County Chamber of Commerce, 9 N College Ave, PO Box 832; 540/387-0267

Salem, part of the industrial complex of the Roanoke Valley, shares with Roanoke the beautiful setting between the Blue Ridge and Allegheny mountains. Historic markers throughout Salem indicate the city's colonial heritage.

What to See and Do

Dixie Caverns. Stalactites in lofty chambers; modern lighting system makes 45-min tour comfortable as well as interesting. Pottery shop and mineral shop (all yr). Camping facilities (fee). (Daily; closed Dec 25) Off I-81 at exit 132. Phone 540/380-2085. ¢¢¢

Roanoke College. (1842) 1,750 students. One of the few Southern colleges to remain open during Civil War. Many historic buildings, some antebellum. Olin Hall, fine arts building, has theater, art gallery, and sculptures. Excellent exhibit of paintings, photographs, and other items concerning Mary, Queen of Scots (by appt only; phone 540/375-2487). Tours. College Ave, off I-81. Phone 540/375-2282.

Motels/Motor Lodges

★ ★ **HOLIDAY INN.** *1671 Skyview Rd (24153).* 540/389-7061; fax 540/389-7060; toll-free 800/465-4329. *www. holiday-inn.com.* 102 rms, 3 story. S, D $52-$89; each addl $6; under 19 free. Crib free. TV; cable (premium). Pool; wading pool. Complimentary continental bkfst. Restaurant 6:30 am-2 pm, 5-10 pm. Ck-out noon. Meeting rms. Business servs avail. In-rm modem link. Bellhops. Valet serv.

Sundries. Cr cds: A, C, D, DS, ER, JCB, MC, V.

D ⊠ ⊠ ⊠ SC

★ ★ **HOLIDAY INN.** *1535 E Main St (24153).* 540/986-1000; fax 540/986-0355; toll-free 800/465-4329. *www. holiday-inn.com.* 70 rms, 3 story. S $55; D $60-$65; each addl $7; under 19 free. Crib free. TV; cable (premium), VCR avail (movies). Complimentary continental bkfst. Ck-out 11 am. Business servs avail. In-rm modem link. Sundries. Exercise equipt. Refrigerators, microwaves. Cr cds: A, D, DS, MC, V.

D 乂 ⊠ ⊠ SC

★ **QUALITY INN.** *179 Sheraton Dr (24153).* 540/562-1912; fax 540/562-0507; res 800/228-5151. *www.quality inn.com.* 120 rms, 2 story. S $51-$57; D $54-$61; each addl $6; under 18 free. Crib free. Pet accepted, some restrictions; $6. TV; cable (premium), VCR avail. Pool. Complimentary continental bkfst. Coffee in rms. Restaurant 5-9 pm. Bar 5 pm-11 pm. Ck-out 11 am. Meeting rms. Coin lndry. Business servs avail. Airport transportation. Putting green. Exercise equipt. Balconies. Cr cds: A, D, DS, JCB, MC, V.

D 🐾 ⊠ 乂 ⊠ ⊠

Restaurant

★ **SHANGHAI.** *1416 Colorado St (24153).* 540/389-4151. Hrs: 11:30 am-10 pm; Fri to 10:30 pm; Sat 5-10:30 pm; Sun from noon; Sun brunch to 2:30 pm. Closed Thanksgiving, Dec 25. Chinese menu. Bar. Lunch $2.95-$4.95, dinner $4.95-$8.95. Buffet: lunch $4.50, dinner $6.95. Sun brunch $4.50. Child's menu. Specialties: beef imperial, General Tso's chicken. Chinese decor with mural, vases. Cr cds: A, D, DS, MC, V.

D ⊒

Shenandoah National Park

See also Front Royal, Luray, New Market, Waynesboro

About 450 million years ago the Blue Ridge was at the bottom of a sea.

The picturesque Shenandoah Valley

Today it averages about 2,000 feet above sea level; some 300 square miles of the loveliest Blue Ridge area are included in Shenandoah National Park.

The park is 80 miles long and from 2 to 13 miles wide. Running its full length is the 105-mile Skyline Drive. Main entrances are the North Entrance (Front Royal), from I-66, US 340, US 522, and VA 55; Thornton Gap Entrance (31.5 miles south), from US 211; Swift Run Gap Entrance (65.7 miles south), from US 33; and the South Entrance (Rockfish Gap), from I-64, US 250, and the Blue Ridge Parkway (see). The Drive, twisting and turning along the crest of the Blue Ridge, is one of the finest scenic trips in the East. Approximately 70 overlooks give views of the Blue Ridge, the Piedmont, and, to the west, the Shenandoah Valley and the Alleghenies.

The Drive offers much, but the park offers more. Exploration on foot or horseback attracts thousands of visitors who return again and again. Most of the area is wooded, predominantly in white, red, and chestnut oak, with hickory, birch, maple, hemlock, tulip poplar, and nearly 100 other species scattered here and there. At the head of Whiteoak Canyon are hemlocks more than 300 years old. The park bursts with color and contrast in the fall, which makes this season particularly popular with visitors. The park is a sanctuary for deer, bear, fox, and bobcat, along with more than 200 varieties of birds.

Accommodations are available in the park, with lodges, motel-type units, and cabins at Big Meadows and Skyland and housekeeping cabins at Lewis Mountain. For reservations and rates (which vary), contact ARA-MARK Virginia Sky-Line Company, Inc, PO Box 727, Luray 22835-9051; phone 800/999-4714. Nearby communities provide a variety of accommodations. In the park there are restaurants at Panorama, Skyland, and Big Meadows; light lunches and groceries are available at Elkwallow, Big Meadows, Lewis Mountain, and Loft Mountain waysides.

The park is open all year; lodge and cabin accommodations, usually March-December; phone ahead for schedule. Skyline Drive is occasionally closed for short periods during November-March. As in all national parks, pets must be on a leash. The speed limit is 35 miles per hour. $10/car/week, annual permit $20; Golden Age, Golden Access, and Golden Eagle passports accepted (see MAKING THE MOST OF YOUR TRIP).

Park Headquarters is five miles east of Luray on US 211. Detailed information and pamphlets may be obtained by contacting Superintendent, Shenandoah National Park, 3655 US 211 E, Luray 22835; phone 540/999-3500.

What to See and Do

Camping. First-come, first-served tent and trailer sites (no hookups) at Mathews Arm, Lewis Mtn, and Loft Mtn. Big Meadows requires res (phone 800/365-CAMP). Fourteen-day limit. Campers must register and check out. (Spring-fall) Write Park Superintendent, 3655 US 211 E, Luray 22835, for information. ¢¢¢

Fishing. Trout. Regulations and directions at entrance stations, Dickey Ridge, Panorama, Big Meadows, and Loft Mtn. State or five-day nonresident license necessary.

Hiking. The 500 mi of trails incl 101 mi of Appalachian Trail. Along the trail, which winds 2,100 mi from Maine to Georgia, are numerous side trails to mountaintops, waterfalls, and secluded valleys. Trail crosses Skyline Dr at several points and can be entered at many overlooks. Overnight backcountry use requires a permit. No open fires are allowed. Regulations and permits may be obtained at any park entrance station, visitor center, or at Park Headquarters. Backcountry may be closed during periods of high fire danger. Visitor Centers and lodges post schedules of eve programs and ranger-led hikes. Self-guided walks ranging from ½ to two hrs are at Dickey Ridge (Mi 4.6), Skyland (Mi 1.7), Big Meadows (Mi 51.1), Lewis Mtn (Mi 57.5), and Loft Mtn (Mi 79.5).

Interpretive program. Guided walks, illustrated campfire talks. (Usually mid-June-mid-Oct; rest of yr, on a limited basis) Obtain schedule at Park Headquarters, entrance stations, visitor centers, and concessions.

Picnicking. Near Dickey Ridge Visitor Center, Elkwallow, Pinnacles, Big Meadows, Lewis Mtn, South River, Loft Mtn.

⭐ **Points of special interest on Skyline Drive.** (Mileposts are numbered north to south, starting at Front Royal. Periods of operation are estimated—phone ahead.)

Big Meadows. (3,500 ft) Accommodations, restaurant; store, gas; tent and trailer sites; picnic grounds; nature trail. (Usually Apr-Nov) Mi 51.1.

Byrd Visitor Center. Exhibits, information, book sales, orientation programs, maps. (Usually Apr-Nov, daily) Mi 51.

Dickey Ridge Visitor Center. Exhibits, programs, information, book sales; picnic grounds. (Usually Apr-Nov, daily) Mi 4.6.

Elkwallow. (2,445 ft) Picnic grounds; food, store. (May-Oct, daily) Mi 24.1.

Lewis Mountain. (3,390 ft) One-two bedrm cabins with heat; tent and trailer sites; picnic grounds, store. (Usually May-Oct) Mi 57.5.

Loft Mountain. (3,380 ft) Picnicking, camping (May-Oct); wayside facility; gas, store (May-Oct). Mi 79.5.

Loft Mountain Information Center. Exhibits, information; programs, nature trail. (Usually May-Nov) Mi 79.5.

Marys Rock Tunnel. (2,545 ft) Drive goes through 600 ft of rock (clearance 13 ft). Mi 32.4.

Panorama. (2,300 ft) Dining rm, gift shop. Trail to Marys Rock. Closed in winter. Mi 31.5, at jct US 211.

Pinnacles. (3,500 ft) Picnic grounds. Mi 36.7.

Skyland. (3,680 ft) Accommodations, restaurant, gift shop; guided trail rides; Stony Man Nature Trail. Mi 41.7.

South River. (2,940 ft) Picnic grounds, 2½-mi round trip trail to falls. Mi 62.8.

Riding. Many mi of horseback trails. Trail rides (ponies for children) for rent at Skyland.

Skyline Drive

(see Shenandoah National Park)

South Boston

(F-5) *See also Clarksville, Danville*

Pop 8,491 **Elev** 407 ft **Area code** 804
Zip 24592

What to See and Do

Staunton River State Park. Approx
1,300 acres of woods, meadows, and
lengthy shoreline on John H. Kerr
Reservoir (Buggs Island Lake). Swimming pool, wading pool, bathhouse,
fishing, boating (ramp); hiking and
nature trails, tennis courts, picnic
facilities, shelters, children's playground, concession, tent and trailer
sites, seven cabins (Mar-Dec). Standard fees. 8 mi NE on VA 304, then
11 mi SE on VA 344. Phone 804/572-
4623.

South Hill

See also Clarksville

Pop 4,403 **Elev** 440 ft **Area code** 804
Zip 23970

Motels/Motor Lodges

★★ **BEST WESTERN INN.** *I-85 and
US 58 (23970). 804/447-3123; fax
804/447-4237; res 800/528-1234.
www.bestwestern.com.* 151 rms, 2
story. S $52-$59; D $58-$65; each
addl $6; under 19 free. Crib free. Pet
accepted. TV; cable (premium).
Heated pool; wading pool. Complimentary continental bkfst. Coffee in
rms. Restaurant adj open 24 hrs. Bar
5 pm-1 am. Ck-out 11 am. Coin
lndry. Meeting rms. Free airport, bus
depot transportation. Exercise equipt.
Health club privileges. Game rm. Cr
cds: A, C, D, DS, MC, V.

★★ **HAMPTON INN.** *200 Thompson
Rd (23970). 804/447-4600; fax 804/
447-2553. www.hamptoninn.com.* 55
rms, 3 story, 6 suites. June-Sept: S, D
$65-$74; suites $125; under 18 free;

lower rates rest of yr. Crib free. TV;
cable (premium). Complimentary
continental bkfst, coffee in rms.
Restaurant nearby. Ck-out 11 am.
Meeting rms. Business servs avail. In-
rm modem link. Sundries. Coin
lndry. Exercise equipt. Pool. Some
refrigerators, microwaves. Cr cds: A,
C, D, DS, ER, JCB, MC, V.

★★ **HOLIDAY INN EXPRESS.** *101
Thompson St (23950). 804/955-2777;
fax 804/955-2700; res 800/465-4329.
www.holiday-inn.com.* 55 rms, 2 story.
Memorial Day-Labor Day: S, D $58-
$80; each addl $5; suites $85-$100;
under 18 free; lower rates rest of yr.
Crib free. TV; cable (premium). Complimentary continental bkfst. Restaurant nearby. Ck-out 11 am. Meeting
rm. Business servs avail. In-rm
modem link. Sundries. Exercise
equipt. Pool. Refrigerators. Cr cds: A,
C, D, DS, JCB, MC, V.

Springfield

(B-1) *See also Alexandria, Arlington
County (Ronald Reagan Washington-
National Airport Area), Fairfax, Mount
Vernon; also see District of Columbia*

Pop 30,417 **Elev** 300 ft **Area code** 703

Motels/Motor Lodges

★ **COMFORT INN.** *6560 Loisdale Ct
(22150). 703/922-9000; fax 703/971-
6944; toll-free 800/228-5150. www.
comfortinn.com.* 112 rms, 5 story. S,
D $89; under 18 free. Pet accepted.
TV; cable (premium). Complimen-
tary continental bkfst. Ck-out noon.
Meeting rms. Business servs avail.
In-rm modem link. Valet serv.
Health club privileges. Refrigerators,
microwaves avail. Cr cds: A, C, D,
DS, MC, V.

★ **DAYS INN.** *6721 Commerce St
(22150). 703/922-6100; fax 703/922-
0708; toll-free 800/329-7466. www.
daysinn.com.* 179 rms, 6 story. Apr-
Oct: S, D $62-$105; each addl $6,

under 18 free; wkly, monthly rates; lower rates rest of yr. Crib free. TV; cable (premium). Pool; lifeguard. Restaurant 6 am-1 pm, 5-8 pm; Sun to 1 pm. Ck-out noon. Meeting rms. Business servs avail. Valet serv. Health club privileges. Refrigerators avail. Cr cds: A, C, D, DS, ER, MC, V.
[D] [≈] [≈] [≈] [SC]

★ **DAYS INN POTOMAC MILLS.** 14619 Potomac Mills Rd, Woodbridge (22192). 703/494-4433; fax 703/385-2627; res 800/543-2392. www.daysinn. com. 176 rms, 9 story. S $68-$78; D $75-$85; each addl $7; suites $89; under 18 free. Crib free. Pet accepted, some restrictions. TV; cable. Pool; lifeguard. Complimentary continental bkfst. Restaurant adj 6 am-midnight. Ck-out noon. Coin lndry. Meeting rms. Business servs avail. In-rm modem link. Valet serv. Sundries. Exercise equipt. Some refrigerators, minibars. Cr cds: A, C, D, DS, MC, V.
[D] [≈] [≈] [✗] [≈] [≈] [SC]

★★ **HAMPTON INN.** 6550 Loisdale Ct (22150). 703/924-9444; fax 703/924-0324; toll-free 800/426-7866. www. hamptoninn.com. 153 rms, 7 story. Apr-June: S, D $89-$99; under 18 free; lower rates rest of yr. Crib free. Pet accepted. TV; cable (premium). Pool. Complimentary continental bkfst. Restaurant nearby. Ck-out noon. Valet serv. Health club privileges. Some refrigerators; microwaves. Cr cds: A, C, D, DS, MC, V.
[D] [≈] [≈] [≈] [≈] [SC]

Hotel

★★★ **HILTON.** 6550 Loisdale Rd (22150). 703/971-8900; fax 703/971-8527. www.hilton.com. 246 rms, 12 story. Mar-July: S $117; D $127; each addl $10; suites $270; under 18 free; wkend rates; lower rates rest of yr. Crib free. TV; cable (premium), VCR avail. Indoor pool; lifeguard. Complimentary coffee in rms. Restaurant 6:30 am-10 pm. Bar 2 pm-2:30 am; entertainment Thurs-Sat. Ck-out 1 pm. Meeting rms. Business servs avail. In-rm modem link. Concierge. Gift shop. Health club privileges. Some refrigerators. Cr cds: A, D, DS, MC, V.
[D] [≈] [≈] [≈]

Restaurant

★★ **MIKE'S AMERICAN GRILL.** 6210 Backlick Rd (22150). 703/644-7100. www.mikesamerican-gar.com. Hrs: 11:30 am-10:30 pm; Fri, Sat noon-midnight; Sun noon-10 pm. Closed Thanksgiving, Dec 25. Bar. Lunch, dinner $8.95-$17.95. Specializes in grilled meats, seafood, vegetarian cuisine. Warehouse decor. Cr cds: A, MC, V.
[D]

Staunton

(D-5) See also Harrisonburg, Waynesboro

Settled 1736 **Pop** 23,853 **Elev** 1,385 ft **Area code** 540 **Zip** 24401
Information Travel Information Center, 1250 Richmond Rd; 540/332-3972 or 800/332-5219

To historians, Staunton (STAN-ton) is known as the birthplace of Woodrow Wilson, and to students of government, as the place where the city manager plan was first conceived and adopted. Set in fertile Shenandoah Valley fields and orchards between the Blue Ridge and Allegheny mountain ranges, the area around Staunton produces poultry, livestock, and wool. Manufacturing firms in the city make air conditioners, razors, candy, and clothing.

A Ranger District office of the George Washington and Jefferson national forests is located here.

What to See and Do

Augusta Stone Church. (1747) Oldest Presbyterian church in continuous use in state. Once used as fort during Native American raids. Museum of early church artifacts (by appt). 7 mi N on US 11 in Fort Defiance. Phone 540/248-2634.

Frontier Culture Museum. Living history museum consists of working farms brought together from England, Germany, Northern Ireland, and an American farm. The European farms represent what America's early settlers left; the American farm, from the Valley of Virginia, reflects the blend of the various European influences. Visitors are able to see and take part in life as it was lived on these 17th-, 18th-, and 19th-century farmsteads. Costumed interpreters demonstrate daily life at all four sites. Visitor center. (Daily; closed first wk Jan, Thanksgiving, Dec 25) I-81 exit 222, US 250 W. 1290 Richmond Rd. Phone 540/332-7850. ¢¢¢

Gypsy Hill Park. Lake stocked with fish, swimming (late May-Labor Day, fee); lighted softball field with concession stand, outdoor basketball courts, tennis, 18-hole golf, picnicking, miniature train ride, playgrounds, fairgrounds. (Daily) Off Churchville and Thornrose aves. Phone 540/332-3945.

McCormick Memorial Wayside. Cyrus McCormick's first reaper is displayed here. Picnic grounds. (Daily) 16 mi SW via US 11, I-81; 1 mi E of I-81 on VA 606 near Steeles Tavern. Phone 540/377-2255. **FREE**

Trinity Episcopal Church. (1855) Founded as Augusta Parish Church (1746), original building on this site served as Revolutionary capitol of state for 16 days in 1781. Open on request (Mon-Fri). 120 W Beverley St. Phone 540/886-9132.

✪ Woodrow Wilson Birthplace and Presidential Museum. Restored Greek Revival manse with period furnishings and Wilson family mementos from 1850s; museum building on grounds houses sene-gallery presidential exhibit, "The Life and Times of Woodrow Wilson," and his 1919 Pierce-Arrow limousine. Victorian gardens. (Daily; closed Jan 1, Thanksgiving, Dec 25) 24 N Coalter St, near I-81, I-64, and US 11. Phone 540/885-0897. ¢¢¢

Special Event

Jazz in the Park. Gypsy Hill Park. Thurs nights. July-Aug.

Motels/Motor Lodges

★ ★ **BEST WESTERN INN.** 260 Rowe Rd (24401). 540/885-1112; toll-free 800/752-9471. www.bestwestern. com. 80 rms, 4 story. May-Oct: S $62-$75; D $72-$85; each addl $8; under 18 free; family rates; higher rates: graduation, fall foliage; lower rates rest of yr. Crib free. TV; cable. Com-

plimentary continental bkfst, coffee in rms. Restaurant adj 6:30 am-9 pm. Ck-out 11 am. Business servs avail. Valet serv. Sundries. Indoor pool. Some refrigerators. Cr cds: A, C, D, DS, JCB, MC, V.
D ⊠ ⊠ ⊠ SC

★ **BUDGET HOST.** 3554 Lee Jackson Hwy, Greenville (24401). 540/337-1231; fax 540/337-0821. 32 rms, 2 story. May-Nov: S $35-$45; D $45-$75; each addl $6; under 12 free; wkly rates; lower rates rest of yr. Crib free. Pet accepted, some restrictions; $6. TV; cable (premium). Pool; wading pool. Playground. Complimentary continental bkfst. Restaurant nearby. Ck-out 11 am. Refrigerators. Private patios, balconies. Picnic tables. Cr cds: A, D, DS, MC, V.
🐾 ⊠ ⊠ ⊠ SC

★ **COMFORT INN.** 1302 Richmond Ave (24401). 540/886-5000; fax 540/886-6643; res 800/228-5150. www.comfortinn.com. 98 rms, 5 story. May-Oct: S $67-$114; D $77-$114; each addl $10; under 18 free; higher rates special events; lower rates rest of yr. Crib avail. Pet accepted, some restrictions. TV; cable (premium). Pool. Complimentary continental bkfst, coffee in rms. Restaurant adj open 24 hrs. Ck-out 11 am. Business servs avail. Refrigerators, microwaves. Cr cds: A, D, DS, MC, V.
D 🐾 ⊠ ⊠ ⊠

★ ★ **HOLIDAY INN.** I-81; Hwy 275 (24401). 540/248-6020; fax 540/248-2902; toll-free 800/465-4329. www.holidayinnstaunton.com. 116 rms, 4 story. Mid-Mar-mid-Nov: S, D $79-$89; suites $95; under 17 free; golf plans; lower rates rest of yr. Crib free. TV; cable (premium). Indoor/outdoor pool; poolside serv. Restaurant 6 am-10 pm. Bar 4 pm-11 pm; entertainment. Ck-out noon. Meeting rms. Business servs avail. In-rm modem link. Valet serv. Sundries. Free airport transportation. Lighted tennis. 18-hole golf, greens fee $25, pro, putting green, driving range. Exercise equipt. Refrigerator, wet bar in suites. Some balconies. Cr cds: A, C, D, DS, ER, JCB, MC, V.
D 🏌 ⊠ 🏋 ⊠ ⊠ SC

★ **SHONEY'S MOTOR INN.** I-81 & Rte 250 (24402). 540/885-3117; fax

540/885-5620; toll-free 800/222-2222. 91 rms, 2 story. S $48; D $55; each addl $6; under 18 free. Crib free. TV; cable (premium). Indoor pool; whirlpool. Complimentary continental bkfst. Restaurant 6 am-11 pm; Fri, Sat to 1 am. Ck-out noon. Business servs avail. Valet serv. Sundries. Exercise equipt; sauna. Some in-rm whirlpools. Cr cds: A, C, D, DS, ER, MC, V.

B&Bs/Small Inns

★★ **BELLE GRAE INN.** 515 W Frederick St (24401). 540/886-5151; fax 540/886-6641. www.virginia.org/bellegrae. 14 rms, 2 story. Some rm phones. S, D $95-$150; each addl $25; suites $140-$170; higher rates wkends. Children over 12 yrs only. TV in most rms. Complimentary full bkfst; afternoon refreshments. Dining rm 7:30-9:30 am, 6-9 pm. Ck-out 11 am, ck-in 3 pm. Meeting rms. Business servs avail. Airport, RR station, bus depot transportation. Tennis privileges. Golf privileges. Fireplaces. Private patios, balconies. 1870s restored Victorian mansion. Each rm individually decorated; antiques. Cr cds: A, MC, V.

★★ **FREDERICK HOUSE.** 28 N New St (24401). 540/885-4220; fax 540/885-5180; toll-free 800/334-5575. www.frederickhouse.com. 19 units, 2 story, 9 suites. S, D $75-$170; each addl $25; suites $95-$170; wkly rates. Crib $10. TV; cable. Complimentary full bkfst. Ck-out 11 am, ck-in 3 pm. Tennis privileges. Golf privileges. Health club privileges. Private patios, balconies. Picnic tables. Encompasses 6 adj townhouses built 1810-1919. Antiques and period furnishings. Mary Baldwin College adj. Totally nonsmoking. Cr cds: A, D, DS, MC, V.

★★★ **SAMPSON EAGON INN.** 238 East Beverley St (24401). 540/886-8200; toll-free 800/597-9722. www.eagoninn.com. 5 rms, 1 with shower only, 2 story. S, D $94-$120; each addl $20; wkends (2-day min). Children over 12 yrs only. TV; cable, VCR (free movies). Complimentary full bkfst; afternoon refreshments. Ck-out 11 am, ck-in 4 pm. Business servs avail. Health club privileges.

Antiques. Restored antebellum home (1800) adj to Woodrow Wilson birthplace. Cr cds: A, MC, V.

★★ **THORNROSE HOUSE.** 531 Thornrose Ave (24401). 540/885-7026; fax 540/885-6458; res 800/861-4338. www.thornrosehouse.com. 5 rms, 2 story. No rm phones. S $60-$80; D $70-$90. Complimentary full bkfst. Ck-out 11 am, ck-in 3 pm. Georgian Revival house (1912); wrap-around veranda. Antiques; fourposter and brass beds. Opp park. Totally nonsmoking. Cr cds: A, MC, V.

Restaurants

★ **THE PULLMAN RESTAURANT.** 36 Middlebrook Ave (24401). 540/885-6612. www.thepullman.com. Seafood menu. Specializes in steak, seafood. Hrs: 11 am-10 pm; Fri, Sat to 11 pm; Sun to 9 pm. Closed hols. Res accepted. Wine list. Lunch, dinner $3.95-$16.95. Sun brunch $6.95-$15.95. Child's menu. Entertainment. Cr cds: A, D, DS, MC, V.

★ **ROWE'S.** 74 Rowe Rd (24401). 540/886-1833. www.mrsrowes.com. Hrs: 7 am-9 pm; Sun to 7 pm. Closed hols. Res accepted. Wine, beer. Bkfst $2-$5, lunch $3-$6, dinner $5-$13. Child's menu. Specializes in country ham, chicken, catfish. Country atmosphere. Family-owned since 1947. Cr cds: D, MC, V.

Strasburg

See also Front Royal, Winchester, Woodstock

Founded 1761 **Pop** 4,017 **Elev** 578 ft
Area code 540 **Zip** 22657

Information Chamber of Commerce, PO Box 42; 540/465-3187

Lying at the base of Massanutten Mountain and on the north fork of the Shenandoah River, Strasburg was founded in 1761 by German settlers. Prospering in the early 19th century as a center of trade and flour milling, the village later became identified with the manufacture of high quality pottery, earning the nickname "Pottown" after the Civil War. The town's location on the Manassas Gap Railroad and the Shenandoah Valley Turnpike gave Strasburg a pivotal role in Stonewall Jackson's Campaign of 1862. The first western Virginia town to be served by two railroads, Strasburg became prominent after 1890 as a railroad town, manufacturing center, and home of printing and publishing businesses.

Today Strasburg, located near the entrance to the Skyline Drive, offers historical and cultural museums. It attracts visitors with its antebellum and Victorian architecture and its burgeoning art community. The town calls itself the "antique capital of Virginia" because of its many antique shops.

What to See and Do

Belle Grove. (1794) The design of this limestone mansion reflects the influence of Thomas Jefferson. Used as Union headquarters during the Battle of Cedar Creek, Oct 19, 1864. Unusual interior woodwork; herb garden in rear. Guided tours. (Apr-Oct, daily) A National Trust for Historic Preservation property. (See SPECIAL EVENTS) 4 mi N on US 11. Phone 540/869-2028. ¢¢¢

Hupp's Hill Battlefield Park and Study Center. Former campsite for six different Civil War generals' troops, now a museum and hands-on interpretive center. Artifacts, documents, exhibits. Guided battlefield tours (by appt; fee). (Daily; closed hols) I-81 to exit 298, S ½ mi on US 11. Phone 540/465-5884. ¢¢

Strasburg Museum. Blacksmith, cooper, and potter shop collections; displays from colonial homes; relics from Civil War and railroad eras; Native American artifacts. Housed in Southern Railway Depot. (May-Oct, daily) E King St. Phone 540/465-3175. ¢

Special Events

Mayfest. Celebration of town's German heritage with parade, entertainment and arts, crafts, antiques, and foods fairs. Third wkend May.

Wayside Theatre. Professional performances. Wed-Sun. Res required. On US 11, I-81 exit 302. Phone 540/869-1776. Late May-mid-Oct and Dec.

Battle of Cedar Creek Reenactment. Belle Grove. Mid-Oct. Phone 830/278-2016.

B&Bs/Small Inns

★ ★ ★ **HOTEL STRASBURG.** *213 S Holliday St (22657). 540/465-9191; fax 540/465-4788; toll-free 800/348-8327. www.svta.org/thehotel.* 29 rms, 17 with shower only, 3 story. S, D $79; suites $112-$175; under 16 free; golf plan. Crib free. TV; cable. Complimentary continental bkfst (Mon-Fri). Restaurant (see also HOTEL STRASBURG). Bar. Ck-out 11 am, ck-in 2 pm. Meeting rm. Business servs avail. Health club privileges. Some in-rm whirlpools. Beach nearby; swimming privileges. Victorian building; antiques. Cr cds: A, C, D, DS, MC, V.
⊷ ⊠ 🐾 SC

★ ★ ★ **WAYSIDE INN.** *7783 Main St, Middletown (22645). 540/869-1797; fax 540/869-6038. www.waysideofva. com.* 22 rms, 3 story. S, D $95-$145; each addl $20; suites $145; under 12 free. Crib free. TV; cable. Restaurant (see also WILKINSON'S TAVERN). Bar 11 am-midnight. Ck-out 11 am, ck-in 2 pm. Meeting rms. Business servs avail. Boating, swimming nearby. Restored Colonial-era bldg; antiques. An inn since 1797. Cr cds: A, C, D, DS, MC, V.
D 🐾 SC

Restaurants

★ ★ ★ **HOTEL STRASBURG.** *213 S Holliday St (22657). 540/465-9191. www.svta.org/thehotel.* Hrs: 11:30 am-2:30 pm, 5-9 pm; Fri, Sat 8 am-2:30 pm, 5-10 pm; Sun 8 am-9 pm. Res accepted; required Sat. Continental menu. Bar from 11 am. Bkfst $4.95, lunch $5.25-$6.95, dinner $7.95-$18.95. Buffet: bkfst (Sat, Sun) $4.95, lunch (Mon-Fri) $5.95. Sun brunch $8.95. Child's menu. Specialties: tournados Jack Daniels, chicken

Shenandoah. Totally nonsmoking. Cr cds: A, D, DS, MC, V.

★★ **WILKINSON'S TAVERN.** *7783 E Main St (US 11), Middletown (22645). 540/869-1797.* Hrs: 7 am-3 pm, 5-9 pm; Fri, Sat to 10 pm; Sun 8 am-3:30 pm, 5-9 pm; Sun brunch 11:30 am-3:30 pm. Res accepted; required Sat. Bar 11 am-midnight. Bkfst $2.75-$6.95, lunch $4.95-$8.95, dinner $14.95-$21.95. Sun brunch $14.95. Child's menu. Specializes in fresh seafood, chicken, vegetarian dishes. In restored Colonial-era inn; many antiques. Cr cds: A, D, DS, MC, V.
SC

Suffolk

(see Portsmouth)

Surry

See also Colonial Parkway, Jamestown (Colonial National Historical Park), Newport News, Williamsburg

Pop 262 **Elev** 122 ft **Area code** 757 **Zip** 23883

What to See and Do

Chippokes Plantation State Park. Plantation continuously operated since 1619. Approx 1,600 acres. Swimming pool, fishing; hiking and bicycle paths, interpretive tour road, picnicking, concession. Visitor center, programs. Tours of mansion, carriage house, kitchen, and formal gardens (Memorial Day-Labor Day, Wed-Sun; Apr-Oct wkends). (See SPECIAL EVENT) Farm and Forestry Museum (Memorial Day-Labor Day, Wed-Sun; Apr-Oct, wkends). Standard fees. 6 mi E via VA 10, 634. Across James River from Jamestown. Phone 757/294-3625. ¢

Special Event

Pork, Peanut, and Pine Festival. Chippokes Plantation. Pork products, peanuts, crafts, pine decorations. Third wkend July.

Tangier Island

Settled 1666 **Pop** 604 **Elev** 3 ft
Area code 757 **Zip** 23440

Bought from Native Americans for two overcoats, Tangier was first settled by a mainland family named West. In 1686 John Crockett moved here with his four sons and four daughters. They were later joined by a few other families. Descendants of these families now populate the island. Life is simple and lacks most urban complexities. Most of the men are anglers, oystering and clamming in one season, crabbing in another.

This tranquil little island (approximately four miles long) is 12 miles out in Chesapeake Bay. The island offers good duck hunting, fishing, swimming, and relaxation. There is an airfield here, and there are excursion boats from Reedville and Onancock, Virginia, and Crisfield, Maryland. Accommodations include a boarding house, Chesapeake House, with seven rooms, family-style meals. Contact PO Box 194; phone 757/891-2331 for reservations.

Tappahannock

See also Lancaster, Montross, Richmond

Founded 1680 **Pop** 2,068 **Elev** 22 ft
Area code 804 **Zip** 22560
Information Chamber of Commerce, PO Box 481; 804/443-5241

Bartholemew Hoskins patented the first land here in 1645. Following his lead, others came and a small village soon sprang up, known at that time as Hobbes His Hole. Formally chartered in 1682 as New Plymouth, the town was to experience yet another name change. Built around the Rappahannock River, which means "running water," the town port became known as Tappahannock or "on the running water." Four hundred men gathered here in 1765 to protest the Stamp Act.

Today the area around Prince and Duke streets and Water Lane of Tappahannock has been declared a historic district. Highlights include the beautifully renovated Ritchie House, the Anderton House, once used for the prizing of tobacco into hogsheads, and Scot's Arms Tavern.

Motels/Motor Lodges

★ **DAYS INN.** *Rte 17 Tappahannock Blvd (22560). 804/443-9200; fax 804/443-2663; toll-free 800/329-7466. www.daysinn.com.* 60 rms, 2 story. S, D $44-$49; each addl $6; under 12 free. Crib free. TV; cable. Complimentary continental bkfst. Ck-out 11 am. Business servs avail. Cr cds: A, D, DS, MC, V.

D ⩬ 🐾 SC

★ **SUPER 8.** *US 17 and US 360 (22560). 804/443-3888; fax 804/443-3888; res 800/800-8000. www.super8. com.* 43 rms, 2 story. Apr-Sept: S $49.88; D $55.88; each addl $5; under 12 free; lower rates rest of yr. Pet accepted. TV; cable. Complimentary coffee in lobby. Restaurant opp 6 am-11 pm. Ck-out 11 am. Meeting rms. Business servs avail. Some refrigerators. Cr cds: A, D, DS, MC, V.

🦅 D ⩬ 🐾

Restaurant

★★ **LOWERY'S SEAFOOD RESTAURANT.** *US 17 & 360 (22560). 804/443-4314. www.lowerysrestaurant. com.* Hrs: 7:30 am-9 pm. Closed Dec 25. Bkfst $1.75-$6.75, lunch $3.25-$19, dinner $7-$19. Specializes in fresh local seafood. Own salad dressing. Antique cars on display. Cr cds: A, D, MC, V.

D ⩬

Triangle

See also Alexandria, Fredericksburg; also see District of Columbia

Pop 5,500 **Elev** 150 ft **Area code** 703 **Zip** 22172

Information Prince William County/Manassas Conference and Visitors Bureau, 8609 Sudley Rd, Suite 105, Manassas 20110; 703/396-7130

Web www.visitpwc.com

Quantico Marine Corps Base is three miles east of town.

What to See and Do

Marine Corps Air-Ground Museum. Chronological presentation of the Marine Corps Air-Ground Team's role in American history; artifacts on exhibit incl aircraft, engines, armor, tracked and wheeled vehicles, artillery, small arms, uniforms, dioramas, and photographs in pre-WWII aviation hangars. (Apr-late Nov, Tues-Sun) 2 mi E, in OCS area on Quantico Marine Corps Base. Phone 703/640-7965. **FREE**

Prince William Forest Park. Consists of 18,000 acres. Hiking, bicycling, picnicking, camping (14-day limit; no hookups; fee; group cabins by res only), trailer campground off VA 234 (fee; hookups, showers, lndry). Naturalist programs. (Daily) From I-95, ¼ mi W on VA 619. Phone 703/221-7181. ¢¢

Tyson's Corner

See also Arlington County (Ronald Reagan Washington-National Airport Area), Fairfax, Falls Church, McLean; also see District of Columbia

Pop 18,540 **Area code** 703

Information Fairfax County Convention and Visitors Bureau, 8300 Boone Blvd, Suite 450, Tysons Corner 22182; 703/790-3329 or 800/7-FAIRFAX

Web www.visitfairfax.org

This Virginia suburban area of Washington, D.C., is the location of one of the largest shopping centers in the nation.

Motel/Motor Lodge

★ **COMFORT INN.** *1587 Spring Hill Rd, Vienna (22182). 703/448-8020; fax 703/448-0343; res 800/228-5150. www.comfortinntysons.com.* 250 rms, 3 story. S, D $115.95-$125.95; each addl $5; suites $125.95-$145.95; under 18 free. Crib free. Pet accepted, some restrictions; $25 deposit. TV; cable (premium). Pool; lifeguard. Complimentary continental bkfst. Coffee in rms. Ck-out noon. Coin lndry. Meeting rms. Business servs avail. In-rm modem link. Valet serv. Free airport transportation. Health club privileges. Refrigerators, microwaves avail. Cr cds: A, C, D, DS, ER, JCB, MC, V.

D 🐾 ⇰ 🔀 🐾 SC

Hotels

★ ★ ★ **HILTON HOTEL.** *7920 Jones Branch Dr, McLean (22102). 703/847-5000; fax 703/761-5100; toll-free 800/932-3322. www.hilton.com.* 458 units, 9 story. S $150-$210; D $170-$230; each addl $20; suites $375-$1,750; package plans. Crib free. TV; cable (premium), VCR avail (free movies). Indoor pool; lifeguard. Complimentary coffee in rms. Restaurant 6:30 am-11 pm. Rm serv 6-2 am. Bar 11-2 am; entertainment. Ck-out noon. Convention facilities. Business center. In-rm modem link. Gift shop. Exercise equipt; sauna. Minibars; refrigerators avail. Atrium lobby; marble floors, fountain. Luxury level. Cr cds: A, C, D, DS, ER, JCB, MC, V.

D ⇰ 🏋 🔀 🐾 SC 🏃

★ ★ ★ **MARRIOTT TYSON'S COR-NER .** *8028 Leesburg Pike, Vienna (22182). 703/734-3200; fax 703/734-5763; toll-free 800/228-9290. www.marriott.com.* 390 units, 15 story. S, D $184-$199; suites $375; family rates; wkend packages. Crib free. TV; cable (premium). Indoor pool; whirlpool, poolside serv, lifeguard. Restaurant 6:30 am-11 pm. Bar 4:30 pm-1 am; Fri to 2 am; Sat 7 pm-2 am; closed Sun. Ck-out noon. Convention facilities. Business center. In-rm modem link. Gift shop. Coin lndry. Some covered parking. Exercise equipt; sauna. Refrigerators avail. Luxury level. Cr cds: A, C, D, DS, ER, JCB, MC, V.

D ⇰ 🏋 🔀 🐾 SC 🏃

★ ★ ★ ★ **THE RITZ-CARLTON, TYSON'S CORNER.** *1700 Tyson's Blvd, McLean (22102). 703/506-4300; fax 703/506-2694; toll-free 800/241-3333. www.ritzcarlton.com.* Near downtown Washington, this prop-

erty has 398 rooms and suites and is filled with the expected lavish touches of rich wood, exquisite fabrics, and fresh flowers. Listen to live entertainment in the lobby lounge after a strenuous day in the adjacent Tyson's Galleria, a premier shopping and dining center, or choose one of ten different therapeutic massages at the Eden Spa. 399 rms, 24 story. S, D $170-$260; suites $375-$2,400; under 18 free; monthly rates. Crib free. Valet parking $16. TV; cable (premium), VCR avail (movies $4). Indoor pool; whirlpool, lifeguard. Restaurant. Afternoon tea in lounge. Rm serv 24 hrs. Bar 11:30-1 am; entertainment. Ck-out noon. Convention facilities. Business center. In-rm modem link. Concierge serv. Gift shop. Beauty shop. Tennis privileges. 18-hole golf privileges, greens fee $75, pro, putting green, driving range. Exercise rm; sauna. Massage. Bathrm phones, minibars; microwaves avail. Luxury level. Cr cds: A, C, D, DS, JCB, MC, V.

D 🏋 🖐 ⇰ 🏋 🔀 🐾 🏃

★ ★ ★ **SHERATON PREMIER.** *8661 Leesburg Pike, Vienna (22182). 703/448-1234; fax 703/893-8193; res 800/325-3535. www.sheraton.com.* 437 rms, 24 story. S $185-$215; D $205-$235; each addl $20; suites $375-$2,000; under 17 free; wkly rates. Crib free. TV; cable (premium), VCR avail. 2 pools, 1 indoor; whirlpool, poolside serv, lifeguard. Complimentary coffee in rms. Restaurant 6:30 am-midnight. Rm serv 24 hrs. Bars 11-1 am. Ck-out noon. Convention facilities. Business center. In-rm modem link. Concierge. Gift shop. Beauty shop. Free airport transportation. Lighted tennis privileges. 18-hole golf privileges, pro, greens fee. Racquetball. Exercise equipt; sauna. Massage. Health club privileges. Bathrm phones; some refrigerators. Cr cds: A, C, D, DS, MC, V.

D ⇰ 🏋 🔀 🐾 🏃 🏋 🖐

All Suite

★ ★ **EMBASSY SUITES.** *8517 Leesburg Pike, Vienna (22182). 703/883-0707; fax 703/883-0694; toll-free 800/362-2779. www.embassysuites.com.* 232 suites, 8 story. S, D $169-$189; each addl $10; under 12 free; wkend rates. Crib free. TV; cable (premium). Indoor pool; whirlpool. Complimentary full bkfst, coffee in rms. Restaurant 11:30 am-11 pm. Bar. Ck-out noon. Business servs avail. In-rm modem link. Gift shop. Exercise equipt; sauna. Refrigerators, microwaves, wet bars. Cr cds: A, C, D, DS, JCB, MC, V.

Extended Stay

★★ **RESIDENCE INN BY MARRIOTT.** 8616 Westwood Ctr Dr, Vienna (22182). 703/893-0120; fax 703/790-8896; res 800/331-3131. www.residenceinn.com. 96 kit. suites, 2 story. Kit. suites $179-$229; each addl $10; under 18 free; wkend rates. Crib free. Pet accepted; $150 and $5/day. TV; cable (premium). Pool; whirlpool, lifeguard. Complimentary continental bkfst. Restaurant nearby. Ck-out noon. Coin lndry. Meeting rm. Business servs avail. In-rm modem link. Valet serv. Lighted tennis. Health club privileges. Many fireplaces. Picnic tables, grills. Cr cds: A, C, D, DS, JCB, MC, V.

Restaurants

★★ **AARATHI.** 409 Maple Ave E, Vienna (22180). 703/938-0100. Hrs: 11:30 am-2:30 pm, 5:30-10 pm; Fri, Sat to 10:30 pm. Closed July 4, Dec 25. Res accepted; required Fri, Sat dinner. Indian menu. Serv bar. Lunch $4.95-$8.50, dinner $4.95-$12.95. Lunch buffet $6.95. Specializes in tandoori, curry and vegetarian dishes. Cr cds: A, D, DS, MC, V.

★★ **BISTRO 123.** 246 E Maple Ave, Vienna (22180). 703/938-4379. www.bistro123vienna.com. Hrs: 11:30 am-2 pm, 5:30-10 pm; Fri to 10:30 pm; Sat 5:30-10:30 pm. Closed Sun. Res accepted. French menu. Bar. Lunch $3.50-$9.95, dinner from $11.95. Complete meals: dinner $34.95. Specialties: paté, lobster bisque, beef. Own desserts. Parking. Outdoor dining. Cr cds: A, MC, V.

★★ **BONAROTI.** 428 Maple Ave E, Vienna (22180). 703/281-7550. Hrs: 11:30 am-3 pm, 5-10:30 pm; Sat 5-11

pm. Closed Sun; hols. Res accepted. Italian menu. Bar. Lunch $8.95-$13.95, dinner $13.95-$22.95. Child's menu. Specializes in veal, pasta, seafood. Own pastries, pasta. Italian art. Totally nonsmoking. Cr cds: A, D, DS, MC, V.

★★ **CLYDE'S.** 8332 Leesburg Pike, Vienna (22182). 703/734-1901. www.clydes.com. Hrs: 11-2 am; Sun brunch 10 am-4 pm. Res accepted. Bar. A la carte entrees: lunch $4.95-$10.95, dinner $6.50-$15.50. Child's meals. Specializes in pasta, seafood, sandwiches. Parking. Original art collection. Cr cds: A, C, D, DS, MC, V.

★★ **HUNAN LION.** 2070 Chain Bridge Rd, Vienna (22182). 703/734-9828. www.hunanlion.com. Hrs: 11:30 am-10:30 pm; Fri, Sat to 11 pm. Closed Thanksgiving. Res accepted. Chinese menu. Bar. Lunch $6-$8, dinner $6-$10.50. Specialties: triple delicacy prawns, orange beef, General Tso's chicken. Parking. Cr cds: A, D, DS, MC, V.

★★★ **LA PROVENCE.** 144 W Maple Ave, Vienna (22180). 703/242-3777. Hrs: 11:30 am-2:30 pm, 5:30-10 pm. Closed Sun; most major hols. Res accepted; required Fri, Sat dinner. French Provençal menu. Serv bar. Wine list. Lunch $9.95-$12.95, dinner $15.95-$22.95. Specialties: bouillabaisse, duck confit. Own baking. Large flower murals. Totally nonsmoking. Cr cds: A, D, DS, MC, V.

★★★ **LE CANARD.** 132 Branch Rd, Vienna (22180). 703/281-0070. www.lecanardrestaurant.com. Hrs: 11:30 am-2:30 pm, 5:30-10:30 pm; Fri to 11 pm; Sat 5:30-11 pm; Sun from 5:30 pm. Res accepted; required Fri, Sat. French menu. Bar to 2 am. Wine list. Lunch $9.95-$11.25, dinner $15.95-$24.95. Specializes in fresh seafood, veal, beef. Own pastries. Piano bar. Cr cds: A, D, DS, MC, V.

★★★ **MAESTRO.** 1700 Tysons Blvd (22102). 703/506-4300. Hrs: 6:30 am-10 pm; Sat, Sun 1-4:30 pm; Sun brunch 11 am-2:30 pm. Res accepted. Wine list. Breakfast $9-$16, lunch $9-$24. A la carte entrees: dinner $18-

$40. Sun brunch $45. Child's meals. Specializes in seafood, lamb chops, prime aged beef. Harpist. Valet parking. Cr cds: A, D, DS, MC, V.
[D] [⊖]

★★ **MARCO POLO.** *245 Maple Ave W, Vienna (22180). 703/281-3922. www.marcopolorestaurant.com.* Hrs: 11:30 am-10:30 pm; Fri, Sat to 11 pm; early-bird dinner Thurs 5:30-7:30 pm. Closed Sun exc Mother's Day. Res accepted. Continental, Northern Italian menu. Serv bar. Lunch $6-$9, dinner $11-$18. Buffet: lunch (Tues-Fri) $8.25, dinner (Thurs) $14.50. Specializes in fresh seafood, fresh pasta, veal. Parking. Cr cds: A, DS, MC, V.
[D] [⊖]

★★★ **MORTON'S OF CHICAGO.** *8075 Leesburg Pike, Vienna (22182). 703/883-0800. www.mortons.com.* Hrs: 11:30 am-2:30 pm, 5:30-11 pm; Sat from 5:30 pm; Sun 5-10 pm. Closed hols. Res accepted; required Thurs-Sat. Bar. Wine list. A la carte entrees: lunch $8-$19.95, dinner $19.95-$29.95. Specializes in steak, seafood. Valet parking. Jacket. Cr cds: A, D, DS, MC, V.
[D] [⊖]

★★★ **NIZAM'S.** *523 Maple Ave W, Vienna (22180). 703/938-8948.* Hrs: 11 am-3 pm, 5-10 pm; Sat 5-11 pm; Sun 4-9 pm. Closed Mon; also Jan 1, Thanksgiving, Dec 25. Res accepted, required Fri, Sat. Turkish menu. Serv bar. Lunch $5.25-$10.50, dinner $11.95-$17.50. Specializes in beef, lamb, chicken. Turkish artwork. Totally nonsmoking. Cr cds: A, D, MC, V.
[D] [SC]

★★ **PANJSHIR II.** *224 W Maple Ave, Vienna (22180). 703/281-4183.* Hrs: 11:30 am-2 pm, 5-10 pm; Sun 5-9 pm. Closed Jan 1, July 4, Thanksgiving. Res accepted. Afghan menu. Bar. Lunch $5.95-$7.25, dinner $9.95-$13.25. Specializes in kebabs, saffron rice, vegetarian dishes. Parking. Cr cds: A, DS, MC, V.
[D] [⊖]

★★ **PHILLIPS SEAFOOD GRILL.** *8330 Boone Blvd, Vienna (22182). 703/442-0400. www.phillips.com.* Hrs: 11:30 am-9 pm; wkends to 10 pm. Closed Dec 25. Res accepted;

required Fri, Sat dinner. Bar. Lunch $5.95-$9.95, dinner $12.99-$25.99. Prix fixe: lunch, dinner $15.99-$21.99. Child's menu. Specialties: crab cakes, free-range chicken, raw bar. Parking. Outdoor dining. Hickory wood-burning grills. Family-owned. Cr cds: A, D, DS, MC, V.
[D] [⊖]

★★★ **PRIMI PIATTI.** *2013 I St NW, Vienna (22182). 202/223-3600. www. sidewalk.com.* Hrs: 11:30 am-2:30 pm, 5:30-10 pm; Fri to 10:30 pm; Sat 5:30-10:30 pm. Closed Sun; hols. Res accepted; required Fri, Sat. Italian menu. Bar. Lunch $9-$14.95, dinner $11-$23. Specializes in contemporary Italian cuisine. Valet parking. Outdoor dining. Cr cds: A, DS, MC, V.
[D]

★★★ **RITZ-CARLTON, THE RESTAURANT.** *1700 Tyson's Blvd (22102). 703/506-4300.* Specializes in seafood, lamb chops, prime aged beef. Hrs: 6:30 am-2 pm, 6-9 pm. Res accepted. Wine list. Bkfst a la carte entrees: $9-$16; lunch a la carte entrees: $9-$24; dinner a la carte entrees: $18-$40. Sun brunch $45. Child's menu. Entertainment: harpist. Valet parking. Cr cds: A, D, DS, MC, V.

★★ **TARA THAI.** *226 Maple Ave W, Vienna (22180). 703/255-2467. www. tarathai.com.* Hrs: 11:30 am-3 pm, 5-10 pm; Fri to 11 pm; Sat noon-3:30 pm, 5-11 pm; Sun noon-3:30 pm, 5-10 pm. Closed Dec 25. Res accepted; required Fri, Sat dinner. Thai menu. Bar. Lunch $3.95-$7.95, dinner $6.95-$12.95. Specializes in fresh seafood, grilled fish. Parking. Underwater ocean decor. Totally nonsmoking. Cr cds: A, D, DS, MC, V.
[D]

★★ **THAT'S AMORE.** *150 Branch Rd SE, Vienna (22180). 703/281-7777. www.thatsamore.com.* Hrs: 11:30 am-10:30 pm; Fri to midnight; Sat 4 pm-midnight; Sun 4-9:30 pm. Closed Labor Day, Thanksgiving, Dec 25. Italian menu. Bar. A la carte entrees: lunch $5.95-$9.95, dinner $15-$38. Specializes in pasta, seafood, chicken. Parking. Cr cds: A, D, DS, MC, V.
[D]

★ **WU'S GARDEN.** *418 Maple Ave E, Vienna (22180). 703/281-4410.* Hrs: 11:30 am-10 pm; Sat noon-11 pm.

Closed Thanksgiving. Res accepted. Chinese menu. Bar. Lunch $4-$7, dinner $7.95-$12. Specialties: Kung Pao chicken, crispy shrimp with walnuts. Parking. Oriental screens and artwork. Cr cds: A, D, DS, MC, V.
D

Virginia Beach

(F-8) *See also Chesapeake, Hampton, Newport News, Norfolk, Portsmouth*

Pop 425,257 **Elev** 12 ft **Area code** 757
Information Visitor Information Center, 2100 Parks Ave, 23451; 757/437-4882 or 800/446-8038
Web www.vbfun.com

For those who seek year-round recreation, Virginia Beach is the answer. A renovated resort area with a three-mile boardwalk and 28 miles of oceanfront and bay beaches offer visitors myriad activities: surfing, swimming, fishing, boating, waterskiing; in-line skating, bowling, tennis, golf, bicycling, and an amusement park and arcade games.

After a full day, there's nothing like dinner and a night out. Virginia Beach delivers with many fine restaurants serving fresh seafood, and nightclubs, concerts, and theaters catering to all musical tastes. With activities for all ages and hundreds of places to stay in all price ranges, Virginia Beach is one of the most popular resorts on the East Coast.

What to See and Do

Adam Thoroughgood House. (ca 1680) One of the oldest remaining brick houses in US; restored, furnished; restored gardens. (Apr-Dec, Tues-Sun; rest of yr, Tues-Sat; closed hols) 1636 Parish Rd. Phone 757/431-4000. ¢¢

Association for Research and Enlightenment. Headquarters for study and research of work of psychic Edgar Cayce. Visitor Center has bookstore, library, displays, ESP-testing machine, movie, and daily lecture. (Daily; closed Thanksgiving, Dec 25) 67th St and Atlantic Ave. Phone 757/428-3588. **FREE**

Contemporary Art Center of Virginia. This 32,000-square-ft facility is devoted to presentation of 20th-century art through exhibitions, education, performing arts, and special events. (Mon-Sat, Sun afternoons;

Virginia Beach

closed hols) 2200 Parks Ave. Phone 757/425-0000. ¢¢

First Landing/Seashore State Park.
More than 2,700 acres with lagoons, cypress trees, and sand dunes. Swimming at own risk, fishing, boating (ramp); hiking, bicycle, and self-guided nature trails; picnicking, tent and trailer sites (Mar-Nov; fee), 20 cabins (open all yr round). Visitor center, interpretive programs. Access for disabled to nature trail. (Daily) Standard fees. 5 mi N on US 60 at Cape Henry. Phone 757/412-2300. ¢¢

Fishing. In the Lynnhaven and Rudee Inlets for channel bass, speckled trout, spots, croakers, flounder, and whiting in season; in the Back Bay area, 18 mi S on VA 615, for largemouth black bass, pickerel, and perch. Pier fishing and surf casting from piers jutting into the Atlantic and piers in the Chesapeake Bay. Reef, deep-sea, and Gulf Stream fishing from charter boats, for sea bass, weakfish, flounder, cobia, bonito, tuna, marlin, false albacore, blue, and dolphin. Lake and stream fishing at Lake Smith, Lake Christine, and the inland waterways of the Chesapeake and Albemarle Canal. Crabbing for blue crabs in Lynnhaven waters, Linkhorn Bay, and Rudee Inlet. (No license or closed season for saltwater fishing.)

Francis Land House Historic Site and Gardens. Late 18th-century plantation home features period rms, special exhibits, gardens, and museum gift shop. (Tues-Sat, also Sun afternoons; closed hols) 3131 Virginia Beach Blvd, on the S side of the boulevard, between Rosemont Rd and Lynnhoven Pkwy. Phone 757/431-4000. ¢¢

Lynnhaven House. (ca 1725). This stately story-and-a-half masonry structure is a well-preserved example of 18th-century architecture and decorative arts. (May and Oct, wkends only; June-Sept, Tues-Sun) Phone 757/460-1688. ¢¢

Motor World Your Place to Race. Park incl go-carts, arcade. Also a 36-hole miniature Shipwreck Golf Course, batting cages, and large Children's Zone. (May-early Sept, daily) 700 S Birdneck Rd. Phone 757/422-6419.

Norwegian Lady Statue. A gift to Virginia Beach from the people of Moss, Norway. The statue commemorates the tragic wreck of the Norwegian bark *Dictator* off the shores of Virginia Beach in 1891. 25th St and Boardwalk.

Ocean Breeze Water Park. "Get wet, get wild" at this Caribbean paradise with slides, wave pool, rapids, and children's water amusements (mid-May-early Sept, daily). 849 General Booth Blvd. Phone 800/678-WILD. Combination ticket ¢¢¢¢

Old Cape Henry Lighthouse and Memorial Park. First US-government-built lighthouse (ca 1791). On Fort Story, an active army base. 6 mi N on US 60.

Old Coast Guard Station. Former Coast Guard Station (1903); visual exhibits of numerous shipwecks along the Virginia coastline tell of past bravery and disaster. "The War Years" exhibit relates United States Coast Guard efforts during WWI and WWII. Photographs, ship models, artifacts. Gift shop. (Memorial Day-Sept, daily; rest of yr, Tues-Sun; closed hols) 24th St and Atlantic Ave. Phone 757/422-1587. ¢¢

Virginia Marine Science Museum. Live animals, interactive exhibits, six-story screen, 300-seat **IMAX 3-D** theater. Exhibits incl ocean aquarium with sharks, large fish; sea turtle aquarium; seal and other habitats; aviary; salt marsh preserve; touch tank; river rm; garden. (Daily; closed Thanksgiving, Dec 25) 717 General Booth Blvd, 2 mi S of resort area. ¢¢

Special Events

Winter whale-watching boat trips. Phone 757/437-4882. Mon, Wed, Fri-Sun. Jan-Mar.

Virginia Saltwater Fishing Tournament. The Commonwealth of Virginia sponsors this annual program. No entry fee or registration requirements; open to everyone who fishes in tournament waters and complies with tournament rules. For information contact Virginia Saltwater Fishing Tournament, 968 S Oriole Dr, Suite 102, 23451; phone 757/491-5160. Mar-Dec.

Pungo Strawberry Festival. Sat and Sun of Memorial Day wkend.

Boardwalk Art Show. Works by more than 350 artists from US and abroad. Mid-June.

East Coast Surfing Championship.
Fourth wkend Aug. Phone 830/278-2016.

Neptune Festival. Last two wks Sept.

Motels/Motor Lodges

★ **COMFORT INN.** *2800 Pacific Ave (23451). 757/428-2203; fax 757/422-6043; res 800/228-5150. www.comfort inn.com.* 135 rms, 7 story. Memorial Day-Labor Day: S, D $109-$159; each addl $10; under 15 free; family rates; lower rates rest of yr. Crib free. TV; cable (premium). Indoor/outdoor pool; whirlpool. Complimentary continental bkfst. Restaurant opp 11 am-11 pm. Ck-out 11 am. Coin lndry. Meeting rms. Business servs avail. In-rm modem link. Bellhops. Valet serv. Exercise equipt. Game rm. Some refrigerators; microwaves avail. Cr cds: A, C, D, DS, ER, JCB, MC, V.
⬛ 🛄 🏊 🏃 📶 🐾

★ **COMFORT INN.** *2015 Atlantic Ave (23451). 757/425-8200; fax 757/425-6521; res 800/228-5160. www.comfort inn.com.* 83 kit. suites, 10 story. Mid-June-mid-Aug: S, D $165-$225; each addl $10; under 12 free; lower rates rest of yr. Crib free. TV; cable (premium). Indoor pool; whirlpool. Complimentary continental bkfst. Restaurant adj 6:30 am-10 pm. Ck-out 11 am. Business center. In-rm modem link. Bellhops. Exercise equipt. Refrigerators, microwaves. Private patios. On ocean. Cr cds: A, C, D, DS, MC, V.
⬛ 🛄 🏋 🏊 🏃 📶 🐾 🏃

★★ **COURTYARD BY MARRIOTT.** *5700 Greenwich Rd (23462). 757/490-2002; fax 757/490-0169; toll-free 800/321-2211. www.marriott.com.* 146 rms, 3 story. Memorial Day-Labor Day: S, D $75-$99; suites $110-$120; under 12 free; wkly, wkend rates; lower rates rest of yr. Crib free. TV; cable (premium). Pool; whirlpool. Coffee in rms. Bar. Ck-out noon. Business servs avail. In-rm modem link. Valet serv. Exercise equipt. Some refrigerators. Cr cds: A, C, D, DS, JCB, MC, V.
⬛ 🏊 🏃 📶 🐾 SC

★ **DAYS INN.** *3107 Atlantic Ave (23451). 757/428-7233; fax 757/491-1936; toll-free 800/292-3297. www.thedays.com/virginiabeach06421.* 121

units, 8 story. Late June-early Sept: S, D $135-$225; each addl $10; under 12 free; golf plans; lower rates rest of yr. Crib free. Pet accepted; $10. TV; cable (premium). Indoor pool; whirlpool. Restaurant 7-11 am, noon-2 pm, 6-10 pm. Bar from 5 pm. Ck-out 11 am. Coin lndry. Meeting rms. Business servs avail. In-rm modem link. Golf privileges. Some refrigerators; microwaves avail. Balconies. On ocean; beach. Cr cds: A, C, D, DS, MC, V.
⬛ 🐾 🏊 📶 🐾 SC 🐾

★ **ECONO LODGE.** *2109 Atlantic Ave (23451). 757/428-2403; fax 757/422-2530. www.econolodge.com.* 55 rms, 10 story. Memorial Day-Labor Day: S, D $120-$189; each addl $8; kit. units $149-$199; under 18 free; lower rates rest of yr. Crib free. TV; cable (premium). Indoor pool. Ck-out 11 am. Business servs avail. In-rm modem link. Free garage parking. Cr cds: A, C, D, DS, MC, V.
⬛ 🏊 📶 🐾

★★ **FAIRFIELD INN.** *4760 Euclid Rd (23462). 757/499-1935; res 800/228-2800. www.fairfieldinn.com.* 134 rms, 3 story. Mid-May-Labor Day: S, D $62-$95; under 18 free; lower rates rest of yr. Crib free. TV; cable (premium). Pool. Complimentary continental bkfst. Restaurants nearby. Ck-out noon. Business servs avail. In-rm modem link. Cr cds: A, C, D, DS, MC, V.
⬛ 🏊 📶 🐾

★★ **HAMPTON INN.** *5793 Greenwich Rd (23462). 757/490-9800; fax 757/490-3573; toll-free 800/426-7866. www.hamptoninn.com.* 122 rms, 4 story. June-Aug: S $64-$76; D $66-$76; under 18 free; higher rates special events; lower rates rest of yr. Crib free. TV; cable (premium). Pool. Complimentary continental bkfst. Coffee in rms. Restaurant adj 6:30 am-11 pm. Ck-out noon. Meeting rm. Business servs avail. In-rm modem link. Exercise equipt. Microwaves avail. Cr cds: A, C, D, DS, MC, V.
⬛ 🏊 🏃 📶 🐾 SC

★★ **HOLIDAY INN.** *5655 Greenwich Rd (23462). 757/499-4400; fax 757/473-0517; toll-free 800/567-3856. www.holiday-inn.com.* 328 rms, 6 story. S, D $99-$129; suites $289.

Crib free. TV; cable (premium). 2 pools, 1 indoor; whirlpool. Complimentary coffee in rms. Restaurant 6:30 am-10 pm. Bar 11 am-10 pm. Ck-noon. Convention facilities. Business servs avail. In-rm modem link. Bellhops. Concierge. Valet serv. Free airport transportation. Exercise equipt; sauna. Cr cds: A, D, MC, V.

D ⇔ ⊼ ≦ 🔥

★★ **HOLIDAY INN.** *3900 Atlantic Ave (23451). 757/428-1711; fax 757/ 425-5742; res 800/942-3224. www. holiday-inn.com.* 266 rms, 7 story, 55 kits. Mid-June-Labor Day: S, D $149-$189; suites $184-$249; each addl $10; under 19 free. Crib free. TV; cable (premium). Indoor/outdoor pool; poolside serv (summer). Free supervised children's activities (Memorial Day-Labor Day); ages 3-12. Complimentary coffee in rms. Restaurant 6:30 am-2 pm, 5-11 pm (in season), to 10 pm rest of yr. Bar 4-11 pm. Ck-out 11 am. Meeting rms. Business servs avail. Bellhops. Gift shop. Exercise equipt. Refrigerators. Balconies. On ocean. Cr cds: A, C, D, DS, ER, JCB, MC, V.

D ⇔ ⊼ ≦ 🔥 SC

★★ **HOLIDAY INN.** *2607 Atlantic Ave (23451). 757/491-6900; fax 757/ 491-2125. www.holiday-inn.com.* 143 rms, 10 story, 18 kit. suites. Mid-June-Labor Day: S, D $159-$199; each addl $10; kit. suites $199-$219; under 17 free; family rates; wkly rates; higher rates special events. Crib free. TV; cable (premium). Indoor pool; whirlpool. Complimentary coffee in rms. Restaurant 7 am-10 pm. Bar 5-10 pm. Ck-out 11 am. Meeting rms. Business servs avail. In-rm modem link. Bellhops. Valet serv. Coin lndry. Exercise equipt. Refrigerators; some in-rm whirlpools, microwaves. Balconies. On beach. Cr cds: A, DS, MC, V.

D ⇔ ⊼ ≦ 🔥

★★ **HOLIDAY INN.** *21st & Atlantic Ave (23451). 757/491-1500; fax 757/ 491-1945; toll-free 800/882-3224. www. holiday-inn.com.* 150 rms, 12 story. June-Sept: S, D $99-$199; each addl $10; under 18 free; lower rates rest of yr. TV; cable (premium). Indoor pool; whirlpool. Coffee in rms. Restaurant 6:30 am-10 pm. Bar 11 am-10 pm. Ck-out 11 am. Meeting rms. Business servs avail. In-rm modem link. Bell-

hops. Refrigerators; microwaves avail. Balconies. On ocean; swimming beach. Cr cds: A, DS, MC, V.

D ⇔ ≦ 🔥

★ **QUALITY INN.** *705 Atlantic Ave (23451). 757/428-8935; fax 757/425-2769; toll-free 800/445-8667. www. qualityinn.com.* 120 rms, 6 story. Memorial Day-Labor Day: S $165; D $175; each addl $10; under 18 free; lower rates rest of yr. Crib free. TV; cable (premium), VCR avail. Indoor/outdoor pool; whirlpool, poolside serv. Coffee in rms. Restaurant 7 am-midnight. Rm serv to 10 pm. Bar noon-1:30 am. Ck-out 11 am. Meeting rms. Business servs avail. In-rm modem link. Bellhops. Valet serv. Exercise equipt; sauna. Lawn games. On ocean; beach. Cr cds: A, C, D, DS, ER, MC, V.

⇔ ⊼ ≦ 🔥 SC

★★★ **RAMADA PLAZA.** *5700 Atlantic Ave (23451). 757/428-7025; fax 757/321-2468; res 800/298-2054. www.ramada.com.* 216 rms, 17 story. May-Sept: S, D $165-$210; suites $230-$280; each addl $10; under 18 free; lower rates rest of yr. TV; cable (premium), VCR avail. Indoor/outdoor pool; whirlpool, poolside serv, lifeguard in season. Supervised children's activities (mid-June-Labor Day); ages 5-11. Coffee in rms. Restaurant 7 am-10 pm. Bar 3 pm-1 am. Ck-out 11 am. Meeting rms. Business center. In-rm modem link. Concierge. Gift shop. Exercise equipt; sauna. Many refrigerators, microwaves. Balconies. On ocean; oceanfront deck, swimming beach. Most rms with ocean view. Luxury level. Video games. Cr cds: A, C, D, DS, MC, V.

D ⬥ ⬥ ⇔ ⊼ ≦ 🔥 ⊼

★★ **SEA GULL MOTEL.** *2613 Atlantic Ave (23451). 757/425-5711; fax 757/425-5710; toll-free 800/426-4855. www.vabeach.com/seagull.* 51 units, 4 story, 9 kit. units. Memorial Day-Labor Day: S, D $120-$138; each addl $10; kit. units $130-$155; family, wkly rates; lower rates rest of yr. Crib $5. TV; cable (premium). Indoor pool; whirlpool, poolside serv. Restaurant 7 am-10 pm, seasonal. Bar. Ck-out 11 am. Business servs avail. Refrigerators. On ocean, swimming beach. Cr cds: DS, MC, V.

⇔ ≦ 🔥 SC

Hotels

★ **CLARION HOTEL PEMBROKE.**
*4453 Bonney Rd (23462). 757/473-
1700; fax 757/552-5778; toll-free
800/847-5202. www.clarionhotel.com.*
149 rms, 8 story. Memorial Day-
Labor Day: S, D $89-$159; each addl
$10; suites, studio rms $109-$159;
under 12 free; lower rates rest of yr.
Crib free. TV; cable (premium).
Indoor pool; whirlpool, poolside
serv. Complimentary coffee in rms.
Restaurant 6:30-10:30 pm; Sat, Sun
7:30-11:30 pm. Bars 5-10 pm. Meeting rms. Business center. In-rm
modem link. Exercise equipt; sauna.
Some refrigerators, microwaves. Cr
cds: A, C, D, DS, ER, JCB, MC, V.

🄳 ⊵ 🕴 🔄 🐾 SC 🏃

★★ **DOUBLETREE HOTEL.** *1900
Pavilion Dr (23451). 757/422-8900;
fax 757/425-8460; toll-free 800/333-
3333. www.doubletree.com.* 292 rms,
12 story. Late May-early Sept: S, D
$159; each addl $10; suites $165-
$395; under 17 free; wkend rates;
lower rates rest of yr. Crib free. TV;
cable (premium). Indoor pool.
Restaurant 6:30 am-2 pm, 5-10 pm.
Bar from 4 pm; entertainment. Ck-
out 11 am. Convention facilities.
Business center. In-rm modem link.
Gift shop. Tennis. Exercise equipt;
sauna, steam rm. Some refrigerators.
Cr cds: A, C, D, DS, ER, JCB, MC, V.

🄳 🗝 ⊵ 🕴 🔄 🔥 SC 🏃

★★★ **FOUNDERS INN AND CON-
FERENCE CENTER.** *5641 Indian
River Rd (23464). 757/424-5511; fax
757/366-0613; toll-free 800/926-4466.
www.foundersinn.com.* 249 rms.
Memorial Day-Labor Day: S, D $89-
$159; each addl $15; suites $159-
$700; lower rates rest of yr; family,
wkly rates; golf plans. Crib free. TV;
cable (premium), VCR avail (movies).
2 pools, 1 indoor; lifeguard (summer). Playground. Supervised children's activities (Memorial Day-Labor
Day); ages 3-17. Restaurant 6 am-10
pm; dinner theatre. Rm serv to 11
pm. Ck-out noon. Meeting rms. Business center. In-rm modem link.
Concierge. Shopping arcade. Free
valet parking. Free airport, bus depot
transportation. Lighted tennis, pro.
Golf privileges, greens fee $29-59,
pro. Exercise rm; sauna. Indoor racquetball court. Lawn games. Bicycle

rentals. Bathrm phones, refrigerators.
Balconies. Picnic tables. Cr cds: A,
DS, MC, V.

🄳 🗝 ⊵ 🕴 🔄 🐾 🏃 🎿

★★★ **OCEAN SANDS RESORT.**
*2207 Atlantic Ave (23451). 757/428-
5141; fax 757/422-8436; toll-free 800/
874-8661. www.oceansandsresort.com.*
111 rms, 14 story. Late May-Labor
Day: S, D $130-$142; each addl $8;
under 12 free; higher rates Memorial
Day wkend; lower rates rest of yr.
Crib free. TV; cable (premium).
Heated pool; whirlpool. Restaurant 7
am-11 pm (seasonal). Bar 11-2 am.
Ck-out 11 am. Business servs avail.
In-rm modem link. Coin lndry. Airport transportation. Refrigerators;
some microwaves. Private patios; balconies. On beach. Cr cds: A, D, DS,
MC, V.

🄳 ⊵ 🕴 🔄 🔥

★★★ **SHERATON OCEANFRONT
HOTEL.** *Oceanfront at 36th St (23451).
757/425-9000. www.sheraton.com.* 204
rms, 15 story. S, D $175-$225; under
17 free. Crib avail. TV; cable (premium). Pool; whirlpool. Restaurant
6:30 am-10 pm. Bar to midnight. Ck-
out noon, ck-in 3 pm. Meeting rms.
Business center. In-rm modem link.
Concierge. Exercise equipt. Minibars;
many refrigerators in suites. Cr cds:
A, D, DS, MC, V.

⊵ 🕴 🔄 🐾 🏃

Resort

★★★ **VIRGINIA BEACH RESORT.**
*2800 Shore Dr (23451). 757/481-9000;
fax 757/496-7429; res 800/468-2722.
www.virginiabeachresort.com.* 295
suites, 8 story. Memorial Day-Labor
Day: S, D $165-$344; each addl $10;
under 18 free; lower rates rest of yr.
Crib free. TV; cable (premium).
Indoor/outdoor pool; whirlpool,
poolside serv. Supervised children's
activities (Memorial Day-Labor Day);
ages 4-14. Coffee in rms. Restaurant
6:30 am-11 pm. Bar. Ck-out 11 am.
Coin lndry. Convention facilities.
Business center. In-rm modem link.
Gift shop. Airport, bus depot transportation. Tennis privileges. Golf
privileges. Exercise equipt; sauna. Private beach. Bicycles. Refrigerators,

microwaves. Balconies. On bay. Cr
cds: A, C, D, DS, MC, V.

Restaurants

★ ★ **ALDO'S.** *1860 Laskin Rd (23454).
757/491-1111. www.gohamptonroad.
com.* Hrs: 11 am-11 pm; Fri, Sat to
12:30 am; Sun 4-11 pm. Closed
Thanksgiving, Dec 25. Res accepted.
Italian menu. Bar. A la carte entrees:
lunch, dinner $4.99-$27. Child's
menu. Specializes in seafood, pizza.
Entertainment Tues-Sat. Outdoor dining. Contemporary decor. Cr cds: A,
DS, MC, V.

★ ★ **BLUE PETE'S SEAFOOD AND
STEAK.** *1400 N Muddy Creek Rd
(23456). 757/426-2005.* Hrs: 6-10 pm.
Closed Sun. Bar. Dinner $7.50-
$29.95. Child's menu. Specializes in
fresh seafood, biscuits, Angus steak.
Own desserts. Parking. Outdoor dining. Located on creek in wooded
area. Cr cds: A, DS, MC, V.

★ ★ **COASTAL GRILL.** *1427 N Great
Neck Rd (23454). 757/496-3348.* Hrs:
5:30-11 pm; Sat 5 pm-midnight; Sun
5-9:30 pm. Closed hols. Bar. A la
carte entrees: dinner $3.95-$17.95.
Child's menu. Specializes in fresh
fish, chicken. Parking. Cr cds: A,
MC, V.

★ ★ **DUCK-IN RESTAURANT AND
GAZEBO.** *3324 Shore Dr (23451).
757/481-0201. www.duck-in.com.* Specializes in seafood, steaks, pasta,
chowders. Hrs: 11 am-10 pm; Fri, Sat
to 11 pm; Sun 9 am-10 pm. Wine
list. Lunch $5.99-$9.99; dinner
$8.99-$17.99. Child's menu. Entertainment. Cr cds: A, C, D, DS, MC, V.

★ ★ **IL GIARDINO.** *910 Atlantic Ave
(23451). 757/422-6464. www.
ilgiardino.com.* Hrs: 5-11:30 pm; Fri,
Sat to midnight. Closed Thanksgiving, Dec 25. Res accepted. Italian
menu. Bar. Dinner $9.95-$22.95.
Child's menu. Specializes in seafood,
veal. Entertainment in season. Valet
parking. Outdoor dining. Wood-
burning pizza oven. Cr cds: A, D, DS,
MC, V.

★ ★ **INLET.** *3319 Shore Dr (23451).
757/481-7300. www.theinletrestaurant.
com.* Hrs: 11-2 am; Nov-Mar 5-11
pm; Sun brunch 10 am-2 pm. Res
accepted. Bar. Lunch $3.95-$9.95,
dinner $9.95-$24.95. Sun brunch
$9.95. Child's menu. Specializes in
fresh seafood. Lobster tank. Raw bar.
Valet parking. Outdoor dining. On
Lynnhaven Inlet; 2-story saltwater
aquarium in dining area. Cr cds: A,
D, MC, V.

★ ★ ★ **LE CHAMBORD.** *324 N Great
Neck Rd (23454). 757/498-1234.* Hrs:
11:30 am-3 pm, dinner from 6 pm.
Closed Jan 1, Dec 25. Res accepted;
required wknd. French, continental
menu. Bar. Wine list. Lunch $5.95-
$8.95, dinner $5.95-$22.95. Special-
ties: rack of lamb, poached salmon,
veal tenderloin. Jazz pianist Fri-Sat.
Modern Mediterranean-style decor;
fireplaces in lounge area, dining rm.
Cr cds: A, D, DS, MC, V.

★ ★ **THE LIGHTHOUSE.** *1st St and
Atlantic Ave (23451). 757/428-7974.
www.thelighthouseva.com.* Hrs: noon-
9:30 pm; Sat, Sun from 10 am; Sun
brunch to 3 pm; early-bird dinner 5-
6:30 pm. Res accepted. Bar. Lunch
$4.95-$18.95, dinner $6.95-$25.95.
Sun brunch $17.95. Child's menu.
Specialties: she-crab soup, whole lobster, prime rib. Patio dining. View of
ocean or inlet. Family-owned. Cr cds:
A, D, DS, MC, V.

★ ★ **LUCKY STAR.** *1608 Pleasure
House Rd (23455). 757/363-8410.* Hrs:
5:30-10 pm. Closed Sun; some major
hols. Res accepted; required Fri, Sat.
Bar. A la carte entrees: dinner $5.50-
$22. Specialties: tuna Stremberg,
Chesapeake Bay crab cakes (in sea-
son), bayou banana split. Parking.
Local artwork. Totally nonsmoking.
Cr cds: A, MC, V.

★ ★ **LYNNHAVEN FISH HOUSE.**
*2350 Starfish Rd (23451). 757/481-
0003. www.lynnhavenfishhouse.com.*
Hrs: 11:30 am-10:30 pm. Closed
Thanksgiving, Dec 25. Bar. A la carte
entrees: lunch $5.95-$10.95, dinner
$13.95-$21.95. Child's menu. Specializes in seafood. Lobster tank.

Valet parking. On Lynnhaven fishing pier. Cr cds: A, D, DS, MC, V.
D

★ **PUNGO GRILL.** *1785 Princess Anne Rd (23456).* 757/426-6655. Hrs: 11 am-8 pm; Fri, Sat to 9:30 pm. Closed Mon; Thanksgiving, Dec 24, 25; also Jan-Feb. Res accepted. Regional American, continental menu. Bar. Lunch $4.50-$12.50, dinner $8.95-$18.95. Child's menu. Specializes in Cajun soups, homemade desserts. Parking. Outdoor dining. Dining rm on enclosed porch of 1919 Aladdin house. Cr cds: D, MC, V.
D

★★ **RUDEE'S.** *227 Mediterranean Ave (23451).* 757/425-1777. *www.rudees. com.* Hrs: 11 am-midnight. Closed Thanksgiving, Dec 25. Bar. Lunch, dinner $4.95-$28.95. Sun brunch $4.95-$9.95. Child's menu. Specializes in fresh seafood, shrimp, hand-cut steak. Raw bar. Valet parking. Outdoor dining. Nautical decor; casual atmosphere. On inlet; transient slips avail for boats. Cr cds: A, D, DS, MC, V.
D

★ **SAN ANTONIO SAM'S.** *604 Norfolk Ave (23451).* 757/491-0263. Hrs: 4-11 pm. Closed Dec 24, 25. Tex-Mex menu. Bar. Dinner $4.99-$14.99. Child's menu. Specializes in fajitas, ribs, chili. Parking. Casual dining rm in renovated 1898 ice house. Cr cds: A, DS, MC, V.
D

★★ **TANDOM'S PINE TREE INN.** *2932 Virginia Beach Blvd (23452).* 757/340-3661. *www.tandoms.com.* Hrs: 11:30 am-2:30 pm, 5-9 pm; Fri, Sat to 10 pm; Sun 10:30 am-9 pm; Sun brunch to 2:30 pm. Closed Memorial Day, Labor Day. Res accepted. Bar. Lunch $4.95-$9.95, dinner $9.95-$19.95. Sun brunch $7.95-$10.95. Child's menu. Specialties: prime rib, veal Oscar. Salad bar. Pianist. Parking. 1930s style. Cr cds: A, MC, V.
D SC

★ **WATERMAN'S.** *415 Atlantic Ave (23451).* 757/428-3644. *www. watermans.com.* Hrs: 11 am-10 pm; Fri, Sat to 11 pm. Closed Thanksgiving, Dec 24 eve, 25. Res accepted.

Bar to midnight. A la carte entrees: lunch $5.95-$14.95, dinner $5.95-$22.95. Child's menu. Specializes in seafood, beef. Outdoor dining. Two dining areas, with ocean view. Cr cds: A, D, DS, MC, V.
D SC

Unrated Dining Spot

CUISINE AND COMPANY. *3004 Pacific Ave (23451).* 757/428-6700. Hrs: 9 am-8 pm; summer 9 am-9 pm. Closed Jan 1, Thanksgiving, Dec 25. Continental menu. Wine, beer. A la carte entrees: lunch, dinner $1.25-$12. Specializes in pasta, salads, specialty desserts. Parking. Cr cds: A, D, MC, V.
D

Warm Springs

See also Clifton Forge, Covington, Hot Springs, Monterey

Pop 425 **Elev** 2,260 ft **Area code** 540 **Zip** 24484

Nestled at the foot of Little Mountain (3,100 feet), the spring wildflowers and groves of fall foliage make Warm Springs a very scenic spot for sightseeing, hiking, or water activities. Visitors also enjoy walking tours to view the many historic buildings.

B&B/Small Inn

★★★ **INN AT GRISTMILL SQUARE.** *Rte 645 (24484).* 540/839-2231; fax 540/839-5770. *www.vainns. com/grist.htm.* 17 units, 1 and 2 bedrm. S, D $80-$100; inn apt: S $120; D $140; each addl $10; under 12 free; MAP avail. Crib free. TV; cable. Pool. Sauna. Complimentary continental bkfst. Restaurant (see also WATERWHEEL). Bar 5-10 pm. Ck-out noon, ck-in 2 pm. Business servs avail. In-rm modem link. Airport transportation. Tennis. 18-hole golf privileges, pro. Downhill ski 5 mi. Refrigerators, some fireplaces. Private patios. Picnic tables. Consists of 5 restored 19th-century buildings. Cr cds: DS, MC, V.

Restaurant

★ ★ ★ **WATERWHEEL.** *Gristmill Sq (24484). 540/839-2231. www.vainns. com/grist.htm.* Hrs: 6-9 pm; Fri, Sat to 10 pm; Sun brunch 11 am-2 pm. Res accepted. Contemporary American menu. Bar. Wine list. Dinner $18-$24. Specializes in fresh local trout, veal, homegrown vegetables. Own baking. Parking. In gristmill dating from turn of the century. Totally nonsmoking. Cr cds: A, MC, V.

Warrenton

See also Culpeper, Fairfax, Front Royal, Manassas

Pop 6,670 **Elev** 560 ft **Area code** 540 **Zip** 20186
Information Warrenton-Fauquier County Visitor Center, 183A Keith St; 540/347-4414 or 800/820-1021
Web www.fauquierchamber.org

The seat of Fauquier County, Warrenton was named for General Joseph Warren, who fought at Bunker Hill in the Revolutionary War. The town is situated in the valley of the Piedmont near the foothills of the Blue Ridge Mountains and is known for its cattle and Thoroughbred horse farms. Many old buildings and houses provide for an interesting walking tour of the town.

Special Event

Flying Circus. Flying shows of the barnstorming era, from comedy acts to precision and stunt flying. Rides, picnic area. 7 mi S on US 15/29, then 7 mi SE on US 17 near Bealeton. Phone 540/439-8661. Sun. May-Oct.

Motels/Motor Lodges

★ **COMFORT INN.** *7379 Comfort Inn Dr (20187). 540/349-8900; fax 540/347-5759; res 800/228-5150. www.comfortinn.com.* 97 rms. May-Oct: S, D $59-$79; each addl $8; suites $99-$125; under 18 free; mid-wk rates; lower rates rest of yr. Crib free. Pet accepted, some restrictions; $10/day. TV; cable (premium). Pool. Compli-

mentary continental bkfst. Coffee in rms. Ck-out 11 am. Coin lndry. Meeting rm. Business servs avail. In-rm modem link. Exercise equipt. Health club privileges. Refrigerators; microwaves avail. Whirlpool in some suites. Cr cds: A, D, DS, MC, V.

★ ★ **HAMPTON INN.** *501 Blackwell Rd (20186). 540/349-4200; fax 540/349-0061; toll-free 800/426-7866. www.hampton-inn.com.* 101 rms, 2 story. S, D $64-$79; under 18 free. Crib free. Pet accepted. TV; cable (premium), VCR (movies). Pool. Complimentary continental bkfst. Ck-out noon. Meeting rms. Business servs avail. Coin lndry. Exercise equipt. Refrigerators, microwaves avail. Picnic tables, grill. Cr cds: A, C, D, DS, MC, V.

Restaurant

★ ★ **NAPOLEON'S.** *67 Waterloo St (20186). 540/347-1200. www.napoleons restaurant.com.* Hrs: 11 am-midnight; Fri, Sat to 1 am. Closed Dec 25. Res accepted. Continental menu. Bar. Lunch $5.75-$7.95, dinner $9.95-$16.50. Specializes in veal, fresh fish, hand-cut beef. Outdoor dining. Historic 1838 mansion owned by Confederate General Eppa Hunton. Attractive flower gardens. Cr cds: A, D, DS, MC, V.

Washington

(C-7) See also Warrenton

Founded 1796 **Pop** 183 **Elev** 690 ft **Area code** 540 **Zip** 22747

The oldest of more than 25 American towns to be named after the first president, this town was surveyed in 1749 by none other than George Washington himself. The streets remain laid out exactly as surveyed and still bear the names of families who owned the land on which the town was founded. It is romantically rumored that Gay Street was named by the 17-year-old Washington after the lovely Gay Fairfax.

The town, seat of Rappahannock County, is situated in the foothills of the Blue Ridge Mountains, which dominate the western horizon.

What to See and Do

Mount Vernon. (see)

B&Bs/Small Inns

★★ **BLEU ROCK INN.** *12567 Lee Hwy (22747). 540/987-3190; fax 540/987-3193. www.innsandouts.com/bleu_rock_inn.* 5 rms, 2 story. No rm phones. S, D $125-$195. Closed Mon, Tues; Jan 1, Dec 24, 25. Complimentary full bkfst. Restaurant (see also BLEU ROCK INN). Ck-out 11 am, ck-in 3 pm. Business servs avail. Balconies. Restored farmhouse (1899) on lake; rustic setting; vineyard. Cr cds: A, C, D, DS, MC, V.
🄳 ⚡ ⊠ 🔥

★★★★★ **THE INN AT LITTLE WASHINGTON.** *309 Main St (22747). 540/675-3800; fax 540/675-3100.* Opulent appointments and meticulously gracious service have made this the quintessential country inn. Since 1978, Patrick O'Connell and Reinhardt Lynch have created unique, memorable experiences for guests in a sumptuous, Victorian atmosphere. The pilgrimage to this rural corner of Virginia, 70 miles west of D.C., is worth it to experience truly excellent hospitality. 14 rms in 2 bldgs, 1 with shower only, 2 story. S, D $290-$495; each addl in suite $50; suites $440-$580; higher rates wkendt, hols, May, and Oct. Inn closed Tues (exc May and Oct); also Dec 24, 25. Complimentary continental bkfst. Restaurant (see also THE INN AT LITTLE WASHINGTON). Bar. Ck-out noon, ck-in 3 pm. Business servs avail. Gift shop. Airport transportation. Some balconies. Bicycles. Cr cds: MC, V.
🄳 ⊠ 🔥

★★★ **MIDDLETON INN.** *176 Main St (22747). 540/675-2020; fax 540/675-1050; toll-free 800/816-8157.* 4 rms, 2 with shower only, 2 story, 1 cottage. S, D $195-$375; 2-day min hol wkends, Oct; higher rates Oct. Children over 12 yrs only. TV; cable (premium), VCR avail (movies). Complimentary full bkfst; afternoon refreshments. Restaurant nearby. Ck-out 11 am, ck-in 3 pm. Luggage handling. Business servs avail. Lawn games. Federal-style house built 1850; rural setting. Totally nonsmoking. Cr cds: A, MC, V.
⚡ 🦶 ⊠ 🔥

★★ **SYCAMORE HILL HOUSE AND GARDENS.** *110 Menefee Mnt Ln (22747). 540/675-3046.* 3 rms, 1 with shower only, 2 story. No rm phones. S, D $115-$165; higher rates: wkends, hols, month of Oct (2-day min). Children over 12 yrs only. Complimentary full bkfst; afternoon refreshments. Ck-out 11 am, ck-in 2 pm. Business servs avail. Luggage handling. Lawn games. On top of hill, view of mountains. Gardens. Totally nonsmoking. Cr cds: MC, V.
🄳 ⊠ 🔥

Restaurants

★★★ **BLEU ROCK INN.** *12567 Lee Hwy (22747). 540/987-3190. www.bleurockinn.com.* Hrs: 5:30-9 pm; Sun brunch 11 am-2 pm. Closed Mon, Tues; Dec 25. Res accepted. French, American menu. Serv bar. A la carte entrees: dinner $17.95-$24.95. Sun brunch $7.25-$24.95. Specializes in fresh seafood. Outdoor dining. French country decor; fireplaces, antiques. Family-owned. Totally nonsmoking. Cr cds: A, D, DS, MC, V.

★★ **FOUR AND TWENTY BLACKBIRDS.** *650 Zachary Taylor Hwy, Flint Hill (22627). 540/675-1111.* Hrs: 5:30-9 pm; Sun brunch 10 am-2 pm. Closed Mon, Tues; July 4, Dec 25; also 1st 2 wks of Jan and Aug. Res accepted; required Fri, Sat. Serv bar. Dinner $16-$22. Sun brunch $8-$12. Specializes in vegetarian dishes, eclectic regional dishes. Own pasta, ice cream. Entertainment. Parking. Originally built in 1910 as carpenter's shop. Totally nonsmoking. Cr cds: MC, V.

★★★★★ **THE INN AT LITTLE WASHINGTON.** *309 Middle and Main sts (22747). 540/675-3800.* This ultimate Virginia country destination has consistently won the accolades of discriminating epicureans from across the country. Innkeepers Patrick O'Connell and Reinhardt Lynch have served classically prepared, contemporary cuisine in a beautiful, English-country decor since 1978. Specializes in local rabbit braised in pressed apple cider, pan-roasted native wild rockfish. Hrs: 6-9:30 pm; Sat 5:30-10 pm; Sun from 4 pm. Closed Tues (exc May and Oct); also Dec 24, 25. Res accepted; required Fri, Sat. Wine cellar. Dinner prix fixe: $88-$116. Valet parking. Cr cds: MC, V.

D

Waynesboro

(D-5) *See also Charlottesville*

Settled ca 1739 **Pop** 19,520
Elev 1,300 ft **Zip** 22980
Information Waynesboro Augusta County Chamber of Commerce, 301 W Main St; 540/949-8203

Waynesboro is at the southern end of the Skyline Drive and the northern end of the Blue Ridge Parkway.

What to See and Do

P. Buckley Moss Museum. Museum's exhibits and programs examine the symbolism and aesthetic ideas of one of America's most notable living artists. (Mon-Sat; closed Jan 1, Thanksgiving, Dec 25) 150 P. Buckley Moss Dr. Phone 540/949-6473. **FREE**

Shenandoah National Park. (see) 1 mi E to Skyline Dr.

Shenandoah Valley Art Center. Art galleries, studios. Working artists; performing arts. (Tues-Sun) 600 W Main St. Phone 540/949-7662. **DONATION**

Sherando Lake Recreation Area. Facilities incl 21-acre lake with sand beach and bathhouses, swimming, fishing; picnicking, camping (Apr-Oct, fee). Amphitheater, campfire programs. (Apr-Nov, daily) 16 mi SW on Blue Ridge Pkwy, in George Washington and Jefferson national forests. Phone 540/942-5965. ¢¢

Special Event

Fall Foliage Festival. First and second wkends Oct.

Motels/Motor Lodges

★ **COMFORT INN.** *640 W Broad St (22980). 540/942-1171; fax 540/942-4785; res 800/228-5150. www.comfort inn.com.* 75 rms. S $45-$59; D $52-$69; each addl $5; under 18 free. Crib free. Pet accepted, some restrictions. TV; cable (premium). Pool; wading pool. Coffee in rms. Ck-out noon. Business servs avail. Valet serv. Downhill ski 20 mi. Health club privileges. Microwaves avail. Cr cds: A, C, D, DS, ER, JCB, MC, V.

D ⊚ ⤢ ⤢ ⤢ ⤢ SC

★ **DAYS INN.** *2060 Rosser Ave (22980). 540/943-1101; fax 540/949-7586; res 800/329-7466. www.daysinn. com.* 98 rms, 2 story. May-Oct: S $45-$75; D $50-$85; each addl $5; higher rates fall foliage, graduation; lower rates rest of yr. Crib free. Pet accepted; $6. TV; cable (premium). Pool. Restaurant adj 6 am-midnight. Ck-out 11 am. Meeting rms. Business servs avail. Valet serv. Game rm. Lawn games. Microwaves avail. Picnic tables. Cr cds: A, C, D, DS, MC, V.

D ⊚ ⤢ ⤢ ⤢ ⤢ ⤢

★★ **INN AT AFTON.** *US 250 and I-64 (22980). 540/942-5201; fax 540/943-8746; res 800/860-8559. www.comet. net/nelsoncty.* 118 rms, 2-3 story. No elvtr. May-Oct: S $60-$76; D $63-$81; each addl $7; under 18 free; higher rates special events; lower rates rest of yr. Crib free. Pet accepted. TV. Heated pool. Restaurant 7 am-2 pm, 5-10 pm. Bar 5 pm-12:30 am; entertainment Fri, Sat. Ck-out noon. Meeting rms. Business servs avail. Valet serv. Downhill ski 18 mi. Cr cds: A, C, D, DS, JCB, MC, V.

D ⊚ ⤢ ⤢ ⤢ ⤢ SC

B&B/Small Inn

★★★ **IRIS INN.** *191 Chinquapin Dr (22980). 540/943-1991; fax 540/942-2093. www.irisinn.com.* 9 rms, 2 story. S $75-$90; D $80-$100; each addl $20; suites $130-$140; wkend rates (2-day min). TV. Complimentary full bkfst. Ck-out 11 am, ck-in 3 pm. Balconies. Wooded setting overlooking Shenandoah Valley. Totally nonsmoking. Cr cds: MC, V.

D ⤢ ⤢

Williamsburg

(E-7) See also Colonial Parkway, Jamestown (Colonial National Historical Park), Newport News, Surry, Yorktown

Settled 1633 **Pop** 11,998 **Elev** 86 ft
Area code 757

Information Chamber of Commerce, 201 Penniman Rd, PO Box 3620, 23187; 757/229-6511

Web www.williamsburgcc.com

After the Native American massacre of 1622, this Virginia colony built a palisade across the peninsula between the James and York rivers. The settlement that grew up around the palisade was called Middle Plantation and is now the site of Colonial Williamsburg.

Middle Plantation figured prominently in Bacon's Rebellion against Governor Berkeley. In 1693, it was chosen as the site of the College of William and Mary, and in 1699, the seat of Virginia government was moved here. The capitol was built to replace the Jamestown statehouse, which had burned the year before. Renamed in honor of William III of England, the new capital gradually became a town of about 200 houses and 1,500 residents. For 81 years, Williamsburg was the political, social, and cultural capital of Virginia.

The colony's first successful printing press was established here by William Parks, and in 1736 he published Virginia's first newspaper. The capitol was the scene of such stirring colonial events as Patrick Henry's Stamp Act speech (1765).

The First Continental Congress was called from here by the dissolved House of Burgesses in 1774. Two years later, the Second Continental Congress was boldly led by delegates from Virginia to declare independence; George Mason's Declaration of Rights, which became the basis for the first ten amendments to the Constitution, was adopted here.

Williamsburg's exciting days came to an end in 1780 when the capital was moved to Richmond for greater safety and convenience during the Revolutionary War. For a century and a half it continued as a quiet little college town, its tranquility interrupted briefly by the Civil War. In 1917, when a munitions factory was built near the town and cheap housing for the factory's 15,000 workers was hastily erected, Williamsburg seemed destined to live out its days in ugliness.

In 1926, however, John D. Rockefeller, Jr. and Dr. W.A.R. Goodwin, rector of Bruton Parish Church, who saw the town as a potential treasure-house of colonial history, shared the broad vision that inspired the restoration of Williamsburg. For more than 30 years Rockefeller devoted personal attention to the project and contributed funds to accomplish this nonprofit undertaking.

Today, after many years of archaeological and historical research, the project is near completion. The Historic Area, approximately a mile long and a half-mile wide, encompasses most of the 18th-century capital. Eighty-eight of the original buildings have been restored; 50 major buildings, houses, and shops and many smaller outbuildings have been reconstructed on their original sites; 45 of the more historically significant buildings contain more than 200 exhibition rooms, furnished either with original pieces or reproductions and open to the public on regular seasonal schedules.

Visitors stroll Duke of Gloucester Street and mingle with people in 18th-century attire. Craftsmen at about 20 different shops ply such trades as wigmaking and blacksmithing, using materials, tools, and techniques of pre-Revolutionary times.

Williamsburg is beautiful year-round. November through March is an excellent time to visit, when it is less crowded and the pace is more leisurely; some holiday weekends may be busy. The Historic Area is closed to private motor vehicles 8 am-10 pm.

What to See and Do

America's Railroads on Parade. More than 4,000 square ft of model train layouts. Hands-on exhibits, gift shop. (Daily; closed Jan 1, Thanksgiving, Dec 25) 1915 Pocahontas Tr, in Village Shops at Kingsmill. Phone 757/220-8725. ¢¢

Busch Gardens Williamsburg. European-style themed park on 360 acres features re-created 17th-century German, English, French, Italian, Scottish, and Canadian villages. Attractions incl more than 30 thrill rides, incl Drachen Fire roller coaster, one of the nation's largest; 3-D movie *Haunts of the Olde Country,* with in-theater special effects; live shows, antique carousel, celebrity concerts, miniature of Le Mans racetrack, rides for small children. Themed restaurants; shops. Transportation around the grounds by sky ride or steam train. A computer-operated monorail links the park with the Anheuser-Busch Hospitality Center; brewery tour. Park (mid-May-Labor Day, daily; late Mar-mid-May, wkends; after Labor Day-Oct, Mon, Tues, Fri-Sun). 3 mi E on US 60. Phone 757/253-3000. ¢¢¢¢¢

Carter's Grove. (Part of Colonial Williamsburg) This James River site incl the Winthrop Rockefeller Archaeology Museum, the partially reconstructed Wolstenholme Towne, and an early-18th-century slave quarter. Also a 1755 mansion, located on 80-ft bluff overlooking the James River, that has been restored to its 1930s splendor. A one-way country road begins here and winds through woods, meadows, and marshes back to Williamsburg, or visitors may return via US 60. (Mid-Mar-Dec, Tues-Sun) 7 mi SE. ¢¢¢¢

College of William and Mary. (1693) 7,000 students. America's second-oldest college (only Harvard is older). Initiated honor system, elective system of studies, schools of law, modern languages; second to have school of medicine (all in 1779). Phi Beta Kappa Society founded here (1776). W end of Duke of Gloucester St. Phone 757/221-4000. On campus are

Earl Gregg Swem Library. Houses College Museum. Large display honoring the college's 300th anniversary. (Mon-Fri; closed hols)

Muscarelle Museum of Art. Traveling displays and exhibitions from an extensive collection. (Wed-Sun; closed hols) Phone 757/221-2700. **FREE**

Wren Building. Oldest (1695-1699, restored 1928) academic building in America; designed by the great English architect Sir Christopher Wren. Tours (Daily). **FREE**

Colonial Williamsburg. (Please note that Colonial Williamsburg is only a part of the town of Williamsburg. Other attractions are listed for which there are separate admission fees.) Colonial Pkwy & VA 132.

⭐ **Colonial Williamsburg Visitor Center.** Ticket sales, sightseeing information; orientation film; lodging and dining assistance; bookstore; transportation. Center (daily). Colonial Pkwy and VA 132. Contact the Colonial Williamsburg Foundation, PO Box 1776, 23187. Phone 757/220-7645.

Ticket information. An admission ticket is necessary to enjoy the full scope of Colonial Williamsburg. Three types of general admission tickets are avail: The **Basic Ticket** provides admission on the Colonial Williamsburg transportation system and entrance to the exhibits in the Historic Area for one day. (This ticket does *not* provide admission to the Governor's Palace, the DeWitt Wallace Decorative Arts Gallery, Carter's Grove, or the Abby Aldrich Rockefeller Folk Art Center.) The **Patriot's Pass** (valid one yr) provides admission on the transporgation system and entrance to all historic buildings, colonial houses, craft shops, Governor's Palace, Carter's Grove, DeWitt Wallace Decorative Arts Gallery, Abby Aldrich Rockefeller Folk Art Center, and historical film. Ticket prices vary. Phone 800/246-2099. ¢¢¢¢

Disabled Visitor Information. Efforts are made to accommodate the disabled while still retaining the authenticity of colonial life. Many buildings have wheelchair access once inside, but it should be noted that most buildings are reached by steps. Visitor Center has a list detailing accessibility of each building; wheelchair ramps may be made avail at some buildings. In addition, there are wheel-chair rentals and parking. A hands-on tour of several historic trades may be arranged for the visually impaired and sign language tours are avail with advance notice. Phone 800/246-2099.

Exhibition buildings.

The Capitol. House of Burgesses met here (1704-1779); scene of Patrick Henry's speech against Stamp Act. E end of Duke of Gloucester St. N of capitol, across Nicholson St, is

Public Gaol. Where debtors, criminals, and pirates (incl Blackbeard's crew) were imprisoned. A few steps W and back to Duke of Gloucester St is

Raleigh Tavern. Frequent meeting place for Jefferson, Henry, and other Revolutionary patriots; a social center of the Virginia Colony. Opp is

Wetherburn's Tavern. One of the most popular inns of the period.

Governor's Palace and Gardens. Residence of Royal Governor, one of the most elegant mansions in colonial America; set in ten-acre restored gardens. N end of Palace Green. ¢¢¢¢

Brush-Everard House. Home of early mayor, with programs on slave life. SE is

Peyton Randolph House. (1716) Home of president of First Continental Congress. Rochambeau's headquarters prior to Yorktown campaign. SW is

James Geddy House. Once home of a prominent silversmith with working brass, bronze, silver, and pewter foundry. Across Palace Green at corner of Prince George St is

Wythe House. Home of George Wythe, America's first law professor, teacher of Jefferson, Clay, and Marshall. This was Washington's headquarters before siege of Yorktown, Rochambeau's after.

The Magazine. Arsenal and military storehouse of Virginia Colony; authentic arms exhibited. Duke of Gloucester St, 1 blk E of Palace Green.

Abby Aldrich Rockefeller Folk Art Center. Outstanding collection of American folk art. Items in this collection were created by artists not trained in studio techniques, but who faithfully recorded aspects of everyday life in paintings, sculpture, needlework, ceramics, toys, and other media. York St ½ blk SE of capitol.

Public Hospital. Reconstruction of first public institution in the English colonies devoted exclusively to treatment of mental illness.

DeWitt Wallace Decorative Arts Gallery. Modern museum adjoining Public Hospital, features exhibits, lectures, films, and related programs centering on British and American decorative arts of the 17th to early 19th centuries.

Bruton Parish Church. One of America's oldest Episcopal churches, in continuous use since 1715. Organ recitals (Mar-Dec, Tues and Sat). (Daily; no tours during services) Duke of Gloucester St, just W of Palace Green. Phone 757/229-2891.

Courthouse. County and city business was conducted here from 1770 until 1932. The interior has been carefully restored to its original appearance. Visitors often participate in scheduled reenactments of court sessions. Duke of Gloucester St, E of Palace Green.

Ride with Me to Williamsburg. Informative and entertaining 90-min audiocassette describes events from Williamsburg's colorful colonial, revolutionary, and Civil War past. The town's famous restoration is summarized by one of the architects who worked on the project. Contact RWM Associates, PO Box 1324, Bethesda, MD 20817. Phone 301/299-7817.

Tours and entertainment.

Carriage and wagon rides. A drive through Historic Area in carriage or wagon driven by costumed coachman. General admission ticket holders may make reservations on day of ride at Lumber House ticket office. (Daily, weather permitting) ¢¢

Children's Tours. Special programs, tours, and experiences exclusively for children and families are offered in the summer.

Evening entertainment. Colonial Williamsburg presents "rollicking 18th-century plays" throughout the yr; wide variety of cultural events, concerts, and historical reenactments (fees vary). Chowning's Tavern offers colonial "gambols" (games), music, entertainment, and light food and drink (eves).

Historic trades. Craftsmen in 18th-century costume pursue old trades of apothecary, printer, bookbinder, silversmith, wigmaker, shoemaker, blacksmith, harnessmaker, cabinet-maker, miller, milliner, gunsmith, wheelwright, basketmaker, cook, cooper, and carpenter.

Lanthorn Tour. A costumed interpreter conducts eve walking tour of selected shops that are illuminated by candlelight. (Mar-Dec, daily) Phone 800/246-2099. ¢¢

Play Booth Theater. Scenes from 18th-century plays in open-air theater. Open to all Colonial Williamsburg ticket holders. (Spring-fall, daily)

Shopping. Superior wares typical of the 18th century are offered in nine restored or reconstructed stores and shops; items incl silver, jewelery, herbs, candles, hats, and books. Two craft houses sell approved reproductions of the antiques on display in the houses and museums.

Special focus and orientation tours. Orientation tours (30 min) for first-time visitors; special tours (90 min), called history walks, incl African-American life, gardens, religion, and women of Williamsburg. Res are avail at any ticket sales location.

York River State Park. A 2,500-acre park along the York River and its related marshes. Incl the Taskinas Creek National Estuarine Research Reserve. Fishing, boating (launch), canoe trips; hiking and bridle trails, picnicking, interpretive center, programs, nature walks. (Daily) Standard fees. 8 mi NW via I-64, exit 231B, then 1 mi N on VA 607 to VA 606 E. Phone 757/566-3036.

Special Events

Colonial Weekends. Package wkends on 18th-century theme, features introductory lecture, guided tours, banquet at Colonial Williamsburg. Jan-early Mar. Phone 800/246-2099.

Antiques Forum. Colonial Williamsburg. Mid-Feb. Phone 800/447-8679.

Washington's Birthday Celebration. Colonial Williamsburg. President's Day wkend. Phone 830/278-2016.

18th-Century Comedy. Williamsburg Lodge Auditorium. Phone 800/HISTORY. Sat nights, Mar-Dec.

Learning Weekend. Colonial Williamsburg. Family-oriented wkend of discovery on a single topic. Mar. Phone 830/278-2016.

Military Drill. On Market Sq Green. Costumed wkly drill by Williamsburg Independent Company. Mid-Mar-Oct. Phone 757/229-6511.

Fife and Drum Corps. Colonial Williamsburg. Performances in the Historic Area. Sat, Apr-Oct. Phone 757/220-7453.

Garden Symposium. Colonial Williamsburg. Lectures and clinics. Last wk Apr. Phone 800/447-8679.

Prelude to Independence. Colonial Williamsburg. Mid-May. Phone 800/447-8679.

Publick Times. Colonial Williamsburg. Re-creation of colonial market days; contests, crafts, auctions, military encampment. Labor Day wkend. Phone 800/447-8679.

Traditional Christmas Activities. Colonial Williamsburg. Featuring grand illumination of city; fireworks. Dec. Phone 800/447-8679.

Living History Programs. At Colonial Williamsburg. Incl *An Assembly, Cross or Crown,* and *Cry Witch!* Varying schedule wkly. Spring, summer, and fall.

Motels/Motor Lodges

★ ★ ★ **COLONIAL HOUSES-HISTORIC LOD.** *302-B Francis St (23185).* 757/565-8440; fax 757/565-8444. 77 rms in 27 Colonial houses and taverns, 1-2 story. Apr-Dec: S, D $215-$225/rm; 2-8 persons $285-$960/house; lower rates rest of yr. Crib $20. TV, cable (premium). Pool privileges. Dining facilities. Ck-out 11 am, ck-in 4 pm. Business center. In-rm modem link. Some houses are more than 200 yrs old; furnished in the period. Cr cds: A, D, DS, MC, V.

D 🐾 🔧 🛟 🐾 🏃

★★ **COURTYARD BY MARRIOTT.**
*470 McLaws Cir (23185). 757/221-
0700; fax 757/221-0741; toll-free
800/446-9244. www.marriott.com.* 151
rms, 4 story. Memorial Day-Labor
Day: S, D $135-145; suites $175-
$195; lower rates rest of yr. Crib free.
TV; cable (premium). Indoor/outdoor
pool; whirlpool. Complimentary coffee in rms. Bar 5-10 pm. Ck-out
noon. Coin lndry. Meeting rms. Business servs avail. In-rm modem link.
Valet serv. Concierge. Sundries. Exercise equipt. Game rm. Refrigerator in
suites. Balconies. Cr cds: A, C, D, DS,
MC, V.

D ⌨ 🏋 🍽 🔥 SC

★ **GOVERNOR'S INN.** *506 N Henry
St (23185). 757/229-1000; fax 757/
229-7019; toll-free 800/447-8679.* 200
rms, 3 story. May-Aug: S, D $89; fam-
ily rates; lower rates rest of yr. Closed
Jan-mid-Mar. Crib $8. Pet accepted.
TV; cable (premium). Pool. Complimentary coffee. Restaurant nearby.
Business servs avail. Sundries. Gift
shop. Tennis privileges. Golf privileges. Game rm. Cr cds: A, D, DS,
MC, V.

D 🐾 🎿 🍽 🔥 SC 🎾

★★ **HAMPTON INN.** *201 Bypass Rd
(23185). 757/220-0880; fax 757/229-
7175. www.hamptoninn.com.* 122 rms,
4 story. Mid-June-early Sept: S, D
$89-$109; lower rates rest of yr,
higher rates: July 4, Labor Day. Crib
free. TV; cable (premium). Indoor
pool; whirlpool. Complimentary
continental bkfst. Coffee in rms. Ck-
out 11 am. Meeting rm. Business
servs avail. Sauna. Game rm. Cr cds:
A, D, DS, MC, V.

D 🍽 🔥 🔥

★★ **HOLIDAY INN.** *725 Bypass Rd
(23185). 757/220-1776; fax 757/220-
3124; toll-free 800/465-4329. www.
holiday-inn.com.* 202 rms, 2 story.
Mid-June-late Aug: S, D $89-$129;
each addl $6; suite $129-$150; under
18 free; lower rates rest of yr. Crib
free. TV; cable (premium). Pool; wading pool, poolside serv. Playground.
Supervised children's activities
(Memorial Day-Labor Day); ages 4-
12. Restaurant 7 am-2 pm, 5-10 pm.
Bar from 4 pm; Sat, Sun from 1 pm.
Ck-out 11 am. Coin lndry. Meeting
rms. Business servs avail. Bellhops.
Valet serv. Concierge (in season).

Sundries. Lighted tennis. Game rm.
Lawn games. Picnic tables. Cr cds: A,
C, D, DS, JCB, MC, V.

D 🎿 🍽 🔥 🔥 SC

★★ **HOLIDAY INN.** *814 Capitol
Landing Rd (23185). 757/229-0200;
fax 757/220-1642; toll-free 800/465-
4329. www.holidayinn.com.* 139 rms, 3
story. Apr-Oct: S, D $89-$109; each
addl $6; under 18 free; wkend rates;
golf plan; lower rates rest of yr. Crib
free. TV; cable (premium). Indoor
pool; whirlpool, poolside serv. Complimentary coffee in rms. Restaurant
7 am-10 pm. Bar 5-11 pm. Ck-out
noon. Coin lndry. Meeting rms. Business servs avail. Bellhops. Gift shop.
Exercise equipt; sauna. Game rm.
Refrigerators, microwaves avail. Cr
cds: A, D, DS, JCB, MC, V.

D 🍽 🏋 🍽 🔥 SC

★★ **HOLIDAY INN EXPRESS.** *119
Bypass Rd (23185). 757/253-1663; fax
757/220-9117; res 800/465-4329.* 131
rms, 2 story. Mid-June-Labor Day: S,
D $72-$94; each addl $6; under 19
free; lower rates rest of yr. Crib free.
TV; cable (premium). Pool. Complimentary continental bkfst. Ck-out 11
am. Meeting rms. Business servs
avail. In-rm modem link. Cr cds: A,
C, D, DS, MC, V.

D 🍽 🔥 🔥

★ **HOWARD JOHNSON HOTEL.**
*7135 Pocahontas Tr (23185). 757/229-
6900; fax 757/220-3211; toll-free 800/
841-9100. www.hojohst.com.* 100 rms,
4 story. Mid-June-Labor Day (2-day
min wkends): S, D $89-$140; suites
$120-$150; under 18 free; lower rates
rest of yr. Crib free. TV; cable (premium). Pool; wading pool, poolside
serv. Complimentary coffee in rms.
Restaurant adj 7 am-2 pm. Ck-out
noon. Coin lndry. Meeting rms.
Business servs avail. Valet serv. Sundries. Health club privileges. Game
rms. Cr cds: A, C, D, DS, JCB, MC, V.

D 🍽 🔥 🔥 SC

★ **QUALITY INN.** *901 Capitol Landing Rd (23185). 757/229-4444; fax
757/220-9314; toll-free 800/638-7949.
www.qualityinn.com.* 94 rms, 1-2
story. May-Oct: S, D $59-$89; suites
$89-$109; lower rates rest of yr. Crib
free. TV; cable (premium). Pool; wading pool. Restaurant 7 am-10 pm.
Ck-out 11 am. Coin lndry. Bellhops.

Putting green. Refrigerators, microwaves avail. On 7½ wooded acres with small fishing lake. Cr cds: A, C, D, DS, ER, JCB, MC, V.

D 🛁 ⛱ 🛏 🐾 SC

★ **QUARTERPATH INN.** *620 York St (23185). 757/220-0960; fax 757/220-1531; toll-free 800/446-9222. www.quarterpathinn.com.* 130 rms, 2 story. Apr-Oct: S, D $62-$75; each addl $6; under 18 free; package plans; lower rates rest of yr. Crib free. Pet accepted, some restrictions. TV, cable (premium). Pool. Restaurant adj 4-10 pm. Ck-out noon. Meeting rm. Business servs avail. Some in-rm whirlpools. Cr cds: A, C, DS, MC, V.

D 🐾 ⛱ 🛏 🐾 SC

★ ★ **RADISSON FORT MAGRUDER INN.** *6945 Pocahontas Tr (23185). 757/220-2250; fax 757/220-3215; toll-free 800/582-1010.* 303 rms, 4 story. Apr-Oct: S $79-$129; D $99-$148; each addl $10; suites $145-$250; under 18 free; lower rates rest of yr. Crib free. TV; cable (premium). 2 pools, 1 indoor; wading pool, whirlpool. Coffee in lobby. Restaurant 6:30 am-10 pm. Bar 11:30-1 am. Ck-out 11 am. Coin lndry. Convention facilities. Business center. Bellhops. Concierge. Gift shop. Lighted tennis. Golf privileges, greens fee $65-$115. Exercise equipt; sauna. Game rm. Bicycles. Refrigerators, some in-rm whirlpools. Balconies; many private patios. Cr cds: A, C, D, DS, MC, V.

D 🏊 ⛱ 🎿 🛏 🐾 SC 🎿 🏂

★ ★ ★ **WILLIAMSBURG WOODLANDS.** *102 Visitor Center Dr (23185). 757/229-1000; fax 757/565-8942; toll-free 800/447-8679.* 315 rms. Apr-Dec: S, D $91-$125; each addl $8; golf, tennis packages; lower rates rest of yr. Crib free. TV. 2 pools; wading pool, lifeguard. Playground. Supervised children's activities (mid-June-Aug); ages 5-12. Restaurant (see also THE CASCADES). Ck-out 11 am. Meeting rms. Business servs avail. Bellhops. Valet serv. Sundries. Barber, beauty shop. Tennis. Golf privileges, putting green. Health club privileges. Lawn games. Miniature golf. Picnic tables. Cr cds: A, D, DS, MC, V.

🏂 D 🏊 ⛱ 🛏 🐾 SC

Hotels

★ ★ ★ **MARRIOTT'S MANOR CLUB.** *101 St. Andrews Dr (23188). 757/258-1120; fax 757/258-5705; toll-free 800/845-5279. www.marriott.com.* 135 kit. suites, 3 story. Memorial Day-Labor Day: kit. suites $264/day, $1,418/wk; family rates; lower rates rest of yr. Crib free. TV; cable (premium), VCR (movies). 2 pools, 1 indoor; whirlpools. Complimentary coffee in rms. Restaurant 11:30 am-9:30 pm. Ck-out 10 am. Meeting rms. Business servs avail. In-rm modem link. Concierge. Sundries. Gift shop. Lighted tennis. 45-hole golf, greens fee $50-$100, pro, putting green, driving range. Exercise equipt. Massage. In-rm whirlpools, refrigerators, microwaves, fireplaces. Balconies. Grills. Cr cds: A, C, D, DS, MC, V.

🏂 D 🏊 ⛱ 🎿 🛏 🐾

★ ★ ★ **MARRIOTT WILLIAMS-BURG.** *50 Kingsmill Rd (23185). 757/220-2500; fax 757/221-0653; toll-free 800/288-2662. www.marriott.com.* 295 rms, 6 story. Apr-mid-Nov: S, D $129-$200; suites $225-$500; family rates; package plans; lower rates rest of yr. Crib free. TV; cable (premium). Indoor/outdoor pool; whirlpool, poolside serv. Coffee in rms. Restaurant 6:30 am-10:30 pm. Bar. Ck-out noon. Convention facilities. Business center. In-rm modem link. Bellhops. Concierge. Gift shop. Tennis. Exercise equipt; sauna. Game rm. Rec rm. Refrigerators avail. Private patios, balconies. Cr cds: A, C, D, DS, ER, JCB, MC, V.

D 🏊 ⛱ 🎿 🛏 🐾 SC 🎿

★ ★ ★ **WILLIAMSBURG HOSPITALITY HOUSE.** *415 Richmond Rd (23185). 757/229-4020; fax 757/229-9557; toll-free 800/522-2063. www.williamsburghosphouse.com.* 297 rms, 4 story. Mid-Mar-Dec: S, D $123-$153; each addl $10; suites $250-$500; under 18 free; wkend rates; golf plan; lower rates rest of yr. Crib free. TV; cable (premium). Heated pool; poolside serv. Restaurant 6:30 am-11 pm. Bar 11:30-1 am. Ck-out noon. Meeting rms. Business servs avail. In-rm modem link. Concierge. Gift shop. Indoor parking. Health club privileges. Cr cds: A, C, D, DS, MC, V.

D ⛱ 🛏 🐾 SC

★★ **WILLIAMSBURG LODGE.** *310 S England St (23185). 757/229-1000; fax 757/220-7799; toll-free 800/447-8679. www.history.org.* 315 rms, 3 story. Mar-Dec: S, D $175-$235; each addl $20; suites $225-$450; lower rates rest of yr. TV, VCR avail. 3 pools; wading pool, whirlpool, poolside serv. Supervised children's activities (Memorial Day-Labor Day); ages 4-12. Complimentary coffee in rms. Restaurant 7 am-10 pm. Bar. Ck-out noon. Meeting rms. Business servs avail. In-rm modem link. Gift shop. Beauty shop. Tennis, pro. 45-hole golf, greens fee $95-$110, pro, putting green. Exercise equipt; sauna. Lawn games. Bicycle rentals. Some fireplaces. Some private patios. Lounge, verandas. Gardens; at edge of Colonial Williamsburg historic district. Cr cds: A, D, DS, MC, V.

Resorts

★★★ **KINGSMILL RESORT.** *1010 Kingsmill Rd (23185). 757/253-1703; fax 757/253-3993; toll-free 800/832-5665. www.kingsmill.com.* Elegantly set along the James River and neighboring a residential area of about 5,000 retirees and families, this 400-room, Busch Properties (one of the Anheuser-Busch Companies) resort offers extensive conference and recreational facilities including a marina, tennis, conference and sports centers, a spa, and four restaurants. Complimentary shuttles are provided to nearby attractions including Busch Gardens and Colonial Williamsburg. 407 rms, 2 story. Mar-Nov: S, D $189-$269; 1-bdrm suites $269-$339; 2-bdrm suites $448-$598; 3-bdrm suites $637-$867; family rates; golf, tennis plans; lower rates rest of yr. Crib free. TV; cable (premium), VCR avail. Indoor/outdoor pools; whirlpool. Supervised children's activities (Memorial Day-Labor Day); ages 5-12. Dining rm 6 am-10 pm. Rm serv to midnight. Bar from 10 am. Ck-out 11 am, ck-in 4 pm. Meeting rms. Business center. In-rm modem link. Concierge serv. Shopping arcade. Beauty shop. Lighted tennis, pro. Three 18-hole golf courses, one par-3 golf course, pro, driving range, putting green. Paddle boats. Marina privileges. Rac-

quetball courts. Entertainment. Exercise rm; sauna. Massage. Spa. Some refrigerators, fireplaces. Microwave in suites. Picnic tables, grills. Cr cds: A, C, D, DS, JCB, MC, V.

★★★★ **WILLIAMSBURG INN.** *312 E Francis St (23187). 757/220-7978; fax 757/220-7096.* Elegantly decorated in an English Regency style, this newly renovated Inn features 62 rooms and suites in the main building. Guestrooms were enlarged to include elaborate baths, and the original, specially designed furniture has been refinished and reupholstered. The property is adjacent to the Colonial Williamsburg Historic Area and has 173 acres to explore filled with shops, museums, horse-drawn carriages, and all the expected resort recreations. 91 rms, 2 story. S, D $245-$345; suites $410-$750; package plans. Crib $12. TV; cable (premium), VCR avail. 3 pools, 1 indoor; wading pool, whirlpool, poolside serv, lifeguard. Supervised children's activities (July 4-Labor Day); ages 4-12. Restaurant 7 am-10 pm (see also REGENCY DINING ROOM). Afternoon tea 4 pm. Rm serv 24 hrs. Bar 11:30 am-11 pm; entertainment. Ck-out noon, ck-in 3 pm. Meeting rms. Business center. In-rm modem link. Airport transportation. Concierge. Tennis, pro. 9-hole and two 18-hole golf courses, greens fee $95, pro, putting green. Exercise equipt; sauna, steam rm. Massage. Lawn games. Bicycle rentals. Card rm. Some refrigerators. Balcony, fireplace in suites. Cr cds: A, C, D, DS, MC, V.

B&Bs/Small Inns

★★ **COLONIAL CAPITAL BED AND BREAKFAST.** *501 Richmond Rd (23185). 757/229-0233; fax 757/253-7667; toll-free 800/776-0570. www.ccbb.com.* 5 rms, 3 story. No elvtr. Mid-Mar-Dec: S $85-$110; D $105-$135; each addl $20; suite $150; package plans; lower rates rest of yr. Children over 8 yrs only. Complimentary full bkfst. Restaurant adj 6:30 am-10 pm. Ck-out 11 am, ck-in 2 pm. Built in 1926; antiques. Totally nonsmoking. Cr cds: A, DS, MC, V.

★★ **COLONIAL GARDENS INN.**
1109 Jamestown Rd (23185). 757/220-8087; fax 757/253-1495; res 800/886-9715. www.ontheline.com/cgbb. 4 rms, 2 share bath, 2 story, 2 suites. S, D $105-$115; each addl $25; suites $130; wkends, hols (2-3 day min). TV; cable (premium), VCR (movies). Complimentary full bkfst; afternoon refreshments. Complimentary coffee in rms. Restaurant nearby. Ck-out 11 am, ck-in 4-6 pm. In-rm modem link. Luggage handling. Built 1960; Southern design. Antiques. Totally nonsmoking. Cr cds: A, MC, V.
◪ 🐾 **SC**

★★★ **EDGEWOOD BED AND BREAKFAST.** *4800 John Tyler Memorial Hwy, Charles City (23030). 804/829-2962; fax 804/829-2962.* 8 rms, 3 with shower only, 3 story. S, D $120-$198. Children over 12 yrs only. TV; VCR. Pool. Complimentary full bkfst. Restaurant nearby. Ck-out 11:30 am, ck-in 3 pm. Microwaves avail. Once part of the Berkeley Plantation; has served as church, post office, and nursing home. Cr cds: A, MC, V.
◪ 🐾

★★ **LEGACY OF WILLIAMSBURG BED AND BREAKFAST.** *930 Jamestown Rd (23185). 757/220-0524; fax 757/220-2211; toll-free 800/962-4722. www.legacyofwilliamsburgbb.com.* 4 rms, 2 story, 3 suites. Mar-Dec: S, D $95; suites $140. Adults only. TV in sitting rm; cable, VCR (free movies). Complimentary full bkfst. Restaurant nearby. Ck-out 10:30 am, ck-in by 5 pm. Business servs avail. Rec rm. Billiards. Some balconies. Built in 18th-century style; period antiques, furnishings; library. Large rear deck overlooks small ravine. Totally nonsmoking. Cr cds: A, MC, V.
◪ 🐾

★★★ **LIBERTY ROSE BED AND BREAKFAST.** *1022 Jamestown Rd (23185). 757/253-1260; toll-free 800/545-1825. www.libertyrose.com.* 4 rms, 2 story. S, D $135-$205; each addl $50. Children over 12 yrs only. TV; VCR (free movies). Complimentary full bkfst; afternoon refreshments. Restaurant nearby. Ck-out 11 am, ck-in 3 pm. Picnic tables. Built 1920; many antiques. Wooded grounds. Totally nonsmoking. Cr cds: A, MC, V.
◪ 🐾

★★ **NORTH BEND PLANTATION BED AND BREAKFAST.** *12200 Weyanoke Rd, Charles City (23030). 804/829-5176. www.northbend plantation.com.* 4 rms, 2 story. S $105-$140; D $115-$140; each addl $40. TV. Pool. Complimentary full bkfst. Restaurant nearby. Ck-out 11 am, ck-in 3 pm. Fireplaces. Greek Revival house (1819); antiques. Cr cds: MC, V.
◪ 🐾

★★ **PINEY GROVE.** *16920 Southall Plantation Ln, Charles City (23030). 804/829-2480; fax 804/829-6888. www.pineygrove.com.* 4 rms, 2 story, 1 suite. No rm phones. S, D $125-$150; suite $160; hols (2-day min). TV avail in some rms; cable, VCR avail (movies) in common rm. Complimentary full bkfst. Ck-out noon, ck-in 4 pm. Luggage handling. Pool. Lawn games. Refrigerators. 2 historic farmhouses (ca 1800). Totally nonsmoking. Cr cds: A, MC, V.
◪ ◪

★ **WAR HILL INN BED AND BREAKFAST.** *4560 Longhill Rd (23188). 757/565-0248; fax 757/565-4550; toll-free 800/743-0248. www.ngetaway.com/va/warhill.* 5 rms, 2 suites. No rm phones. S, D $75-$165; each addl $15; suites $105-$135. Crib free. TV; cable. Playground. Complimentary full bkfst. Restaurant nearby. Ck-out 11 am, ck-in 4 pm. On working farm; built 1969 in Colonial style. Totally nonsmoking. Cr cds: MC, V.
🧸 ◪ 🐾

★★★ **WILLIAMSBURG SAMPLER BED AND BREAKFAST.** *922 Jamestown Rd (23185). 757/253-0398; fax 757/253-2669; toll-free 800/722-1169. www.williamsburgsampler.com.* 4 rms, 3 story. Rm phones avail. S, D $100-$150. TV; cable (premium). Complimentary full bkfst. Restaurant nearby. Ck-out 11 am, ck-in 1 pm. Business servs avail. Picnic tables. Plantation-style house; fireplaces, antiques, Colonial-style furnishings; gardens. Near William and Mary College; walking distance to historic area. Totally nonsmoking. Cr cds: MC, V.
◪ 🐾

Restaurants

★★ **ABERDEEN BARN.** *1601 Richmond Rd (23185). 757/229-6661.*

www.aberdeen-barn.com. Hrs: 5-9:30 pm; Fri, Sat to 10 pm. Closed Thanksgiving, Dec 25; also 1st 2 wks Jan. Res accepted. Bar. Dinner $12.95-$38.95. Child's menu. Specializes in roast prime rib, seafood, baby back ribs. Parking. Open-hearth grill. Barnlike atmosphere; farm implements. Cr cds: A, D, MC, V.
D **⅃**

★ ★ **BERRET'S.** 199 S Boundary St (23185). 757/253-1847. www.berrets. com. Hrs: 11:30 am-10 pm. Closed Jan 1, Dec 25; also Mon in Jan and Feb. Res accepted. Regional American menu. Bar. Lunch $3.95-$8, dinner $4.95-$24.50. Child's menu. Specialties: Virginia crab cakes, lobster and crabmeat combo, seafood and herbs baked in parchment. Raw bar. Parking. Outdoor dining. Casual dining rm; fireplace, nautical decor. Cr cds: A, D, MC, V.
D **SC**

★ **THE CASCADES.** 104 Visitors Center Dr (23185). 757/229-1000. Hrs: 7:30-10 am, 11:30 am-2 pm, 5:30-9 pm; Sun brunch 8 am-2 pm. Res accepted. Bar. Bkfst $5-$7, lunch $6-$9, dinner $7-$19. Buffet: bkfst $7.50, lunch $6.95. Sun brunch $12.95. Child's menu. Specializes in Chesapeake Bay seafood. Parking. Overlooks ravine with cascading brook; contemporary decor. Cr cds: A, D, DS, MC, V.
D **⅃**

★ ★ **COACH HOUSE TAVERN.** 12604 Harrison Landing Rd, Charles City (23030). 804/829-6003. Hrs: 11 am-4 pm; Fri-Sat 6-9 pm; Sun brunch 11 am-4 pm. Closed Dec 25. Res accepted; required Fri-Sat. Bar. Lunch $3.95-$14.95. Complete meals: dinner $14-$26. Sun brunch $3.95-$14.95. Child's menu. Specializes in seafood, game, desserts. Parking. In coach house of Berkeley Plantation; view of grounds and plantation house. Cr cds: A, DS, MC, V.
D **⅃**

★ ★ ★ **FORD'S COLONY.** 240 Ford's Colony Dr (23188). 757/258-4107. www.fordscolony.com. Hrs: 6-9:30 pm; Sun brunch 11:30 am-2:30 pm. Closed Mon; also early Jan. Res accepted. Regional American menu. Bar. Wine cellar. Dinner $16-$28. Sun

brunch $18.95. Child's menu. Specializes in fresh seafood, rack of lamb. Large floral centerpiece, original artwork, fine china and crystal. Jacket (dinner). Cr cds: A, MC, V.
D

★ **GAZEBO HOUSE OF PAN-CAKES.** 409 Bypass Rd (23185). 757/220-0883. Hrs: 6 am-2 pm. Res accepted. A la carte entrees: bkfst $3.75-$7.75, lunch $2.50-$8.50. Child's menu. Specializes in pancakes, omelettes. Casual decor. Cr cds: D, DS, MC, V.
D **SC**

★ ★ **GIUSEPPE'S.** 5601 Richmond Rd (23188). 757/565-1977. www.giuseppes. com. Hrs: 11:30 am-2 pm, 5-9 pm; Fri, Sat to 9:30 pm. Closed Sun; hols. Italian menu. Bar. Lunch, dinner $4.25-$15.95. Child's menu. Specialties: pasta primavera, chicken Provençal. Parking. Patio dining. Cr cds: A, D, DS, MC, V.
D

★ ★ **INDIAN FIELDS TAVERN.** 9220 John Tyler Memorial Hwy, Charles City (23030). 804/829-5004. Hrs: 11 am-3:30 pm, 5-9 pm; Fri, Sat to 10 pm. Sun brunch to 3:30 pm. Closed Dec 24, 25; also Mon in Jan. Res accepted. Bar. Lunch $5.95-$14.95, dinner $17.95-$27.95. Sun brunch $7-$16.95. Child's menu. Specialties: crab cakes Harrison, bourbon chocolate pecan pie, bread pudding. Parking. Screened porch dining area. Turn-of-the-century farmhouse on working farm. Cr cds: A, DS, MC, V.
D **⅃**

★ ★ **JEFFERSON INN.** 1453 Richmond Rd (23185). 757/229-2296. Hrs: 4-11 pm. Closed Thanksgiving, Dec 24, 25. Res accepted. Italian, continental menu. Dinner $8.95-$21.95. Child's menu. Specializes in steak, fresh seafood, Southern favorites. Family-owned. Cr cds: A, DS, MC, V.
D

★ ★ **KING'S ARMS TAVERN.** Duke of Gloucester St (23185). 757/220-7010. Hrs: 11:30 am-2:30 pm, 5-9:30 pm. Closed Tues (Sept, Nov-mid Dec); also mid-Feb-mid-Mar. Res required dinner. Bar. Lunch $7.25-$9.50, dinner $17.75-$25.95. Child's menu. Specialties: game pie, peanut soup,

Virginia ham. Garden bar serv. Own apple cider. Garden dining. Colonial balladeers. Restored 18th century tavern; Colonial decor. Cr cds: A, D, DS, MC, V.

★ ★ ★ **KITCHEN AT POWHATAN.** *3601 Ironbound Rd (23188). 757/220-0741.* Hrs: 5:30-10 pm. Closed Mon. Res accepted. Bar. Dinner $15-$28. Prix fixe: dinner $40. Specializes in game, seafood, regional cuisine. Parking. In 1737 structure on grounds of Powhatan Plantation. Cr cds: A, D, DS, MC, V.

★ ★ **KYOTO JAPANESE STEAK AND SEAFOOD HOUSE.** *1621 Richmond Rd (23185). 757/220-8888. www.kyoto2.com.* Hrs: noon-midnight; to 10 pm off-season. Res accepted. Chinese menu. Bar. Lunch $4.95-$6.95, dinner $6.95-$19.95. Child's menu. Specialties: steamed whole fish, General Tso's chicken, Peking duck. Parking. Outdoor dining. Large dining area decorated with Chinese screens and art objects. Gift shop. Fish pond. Karaoke. Cr cds: A, D, DS, MC, V.
D SC

★ ★ ★ **LA TRELLIS.** *403 Duke of Gloucester St (23185). 757/229-8610. www.dessertstodiefor.com.* Hrs: 11 am-9:30 pm; Sun brunch to 3 pm. Closed hols. Res accepted. Bar 11:30 am-10:30 pm. Lunch $5.50-$9.95, dinner $14.50-$24. Sun brunch $5.50-$14.95. Specializes in fresh seafood, pasta. Own ice cream. Entertainment wkends. Outdoor dining under trees. Cr cds: A, MC, V.
D

★ ★ **LE YACA.** *1915 Pocahontas Tr #C10 (23185). 757/220-3616.* Hrs: 11:30 am-2 pm, 6-9:30 pm; Mon from 6 pm. Closed Sun. Res accepted. Southern French menu. Bar. Wine cellar. Lunch $6.50-$13.50. Complete meals: dinner $22-$42. Specialties: open-spit leg of lamb, marquise au chocolat. Salad bar (lunch). Own pastries. Cr cds: A, DS, MC, V.
D

★ **OLD CHICKAHOMINY HOUSE.** *1211 Jamestown Rd (23185). 757/229-4689.* Hrs: 8:30-10:15 am, 11:30 am-2:15 pm. Closed Thanksgiving, Dec 25; also 2 wks mid-Jan. Wine, beer. Bkfst $.95-$7.75, lunch $2-$6.98.

Specialties: ham on hot biscuits, Brunswick stew, chicken and dumplings. Gift shop. 18th-century stagecoach stop atmosphere. Totally nonsmoking. Cr cds: MC, V.

★ ★ **PEKING.** *122 Waller Mill Rd (23185). 757/229-2288. www.peking-va.com.* Hrs: 11:30 am-10 pm; Fri, Sat to 11 pm; brunch 11:30 am-2:30 pm; dinner buffet 5:30-8:30 pm. Closed Thanksgiving. Res accepted; required wkends. Chinese menu. Bar. Lunch, dinner $6.95-$9.95. Buffet: lunch $4.95, dinner $6.95. Sun brunch $4.95. Specialties: General Tso's chicken, Emperor's shrimp, Peking chicken. Cr cds: A, D, DS, MC, V.
D

★ ★ **PRIME RIB HOUSE.** *1433 Richmond Rd (23185). 757/229-6823.* Hrs: 4:30-10 pm; Fri, Sat to 11 pm. Southwestern menu. Bar. A la carte entrees: dinner $9.95-$17.95. Child's menu. Specializes in prime rib, fresh seafood, Angus steak. Casual decor. Cr cds: A, D, DS, MC, V.
D

★ ★ ★ **REGENCY DINING ROOM.** *136 E Francis St (23185). 757/229-1000. www.history.org.* Hrs: 7-10 am, noon-2 pm, 6-9 pm; Sun brunch noon-2 pm. Res accepted. Continental menu. Bar. Wine list. Bkfst $9-$14, lunch $10-$17. A la carte entrees: dinner $27-$39. Sun brunch $27.50-$32. Specialties: snapper or veal with crabmeat, rack of lamb. Own baking. Parking. Jacket. Cr cds: A, D, DS, MC, V.
D

★ ★ **SEASONS CAFE.** *110 S Henry (23185). 757/259-0018.* Hrs: 11 am-10 pm; Fri, Sat to 11 pm. Sun brunch 11 am-3 pm. Closed Dec 25. Res accepted. Continental menu. Bar. Lunch $8-$13, dinner $9-$19. Sun brunch $13.95. Child's menu. Specializes in steak, prime rib, pasta. Salad bar. Outdoor dining. Located in former post office. Cr cds: A, D, DS, MC, V.
D

★ ★ **SHIELDS TAVERN.** *Duke of Gloucester St (23185). 757/220-7677. www.cwf.org.* Hrs: 11:30 am-3 pm, 5-9:30 pm; Sun brunch 10 am-2:30 pm. Closed Jan. Res accepted. Bar. Lunch $5.95-$12.95, dinner $14.95-$24. Sun brunch $6.25-$10.95.

Child's menu. Specialties: filet mignon, cream of crayfish soup. 18th-century costumed balladeers. Outdoor dining. Twelve dining rms in authentically restored Colonial building. Totally nonsmoking. Cr cds: A, D, DS, MC, V.

D

★ **THAT SEAFOOD PLACE.** *1647 Richmond Rd (23185). 757/220-3011.* Hrs: 11:30 am-2:30 pm, 4:30-9 pm; Fri, Sat 4:30-10 pm; Sun noon-9 pm; summer hrs vary. Closed Dec 25. Res accepted. Bar. Lunch $4.95-$6.95, dinner $8.25-$18.50. Child's menu. Specialties: shrimp sampler, sauteed shrimp and scallops. Salad bar. Parking. Outdoor dining. Nautical decor. Cr cds: A, MC, V.

D ⊒

★★ **WHALING COMPANY.** *494 McLaw Cir (23185). 757/229-0275. www.thewhalingcompany.com.* Hrs: 4:30-10 pm; early-bird dinner Sun-Fri 4:30-6 pm. Res accepted. Bar. Dinner $9.95-$18.95. Child's menu. Specializes in fresh fish, steaks. Own bread. Parking. Nautical decor. Cr cds: A, D, DS, MC, V.

D ⊒

★★ **YORKSHIRE STEAK AND SEAFOOD HOUSE.** *700 York St (23185). 757/229-9790. www.yorkshire-wmbg.com.* Hrs: 4-10 pm; summer to 10:30 pm. Closed Dec 25. Res accepted. Bar. Dinner $10.95-$22.95. Child's menu. Specialties: shish kebab, prime rib. Parking. In Colonial-style building. Totally nonsmoking. Cr cds: A.

D SC

Winchester

(C-6) *See also Front Royal*

Settled 1732 **Pop** 23,585 **Elev** 720 ft
Area code 540
Information Winchester-Frederick County Visitor Center, 1360 S Pleasant Valley Rd, 22601; 540/662-4135 or 800/662-1360

This is the oldest colonial city west of the Blue Ridge, a Civil War prize that changed hands 72 times (once, 13 times in a day). Sometimes called the "apple capital of the world," it is located at the northern approach to the Shenandoah Valley.

George Washington, a red-haired 16-year-old, blithely headed for Winchester and his first surveying job in 1748, and began a decade of apprenticeship for the awesome military and political responsibilities he would later assume as a national leader. During the French and Indian Wars, Colonel Washington made the city his defense headquarters while he built Fort Loudoun in Winchester. Washington was elected to his first political office as a representative from Frederick County to the House of Burgesses.

At the intersection of travel routes, both east-west and north-south, Winchester grew and prospered. By the time of the Civil War it was a major transportation and supply center, strategically located to control both Union approaches to Washington and Confederate supply lines through the Shenandoah Valley. More than 100 minor engagements and six battles took place in the vicinity. General Stonewall Jackson had his headquarters here during the winter of 1861-1862. From his headquarters in Winchester, Union General Philip Sheridan started his famous ride to rally his troops at Cedar Creek, 11 miles away, and turn a Confederate victory into a Union rout.

Approximately 3.5 million bushels of apples are harvested annually in Frederick County and are one of Winchester's economic mainstays today. The world's largest apple cold storage plant and one of the world's largest apple processing plants are here.

What to See and Do

Abram's Delight and Log Cabin. (1754) Oldest house in city, restored, furnished in 18th-century style; boxwood garden; log cabin, basement kitchen. (Apr-Oct, daily; rest of yr, by appt, weather permitting) Inquire about combination ticket. 1340 S Pleasant Valley Ave. Phone 540/662-6519. ¢¢

First Presbyterian Church of Winchester. (1788) Building has been used as a church, a stable by Union troops in Civil War, a public school, and an armory; restored in 1941. (Daily) 116 S Loudoun St. Phone 540/662-3824.

Handley Library and Archives. Completed in 1913, public library was designed in Beaux Arts style. Rotunda is crowned on the outside with a copper-covered dome and on the inside by a dome of stained glass. Interesting interior features incl wrought-iron staircases and glass floors. Historical archives are housed on lower level (nonresident fee). (Mon-Sat; closed hols) 100 W Piccadilly St. Phone 540/662-9041.

Stonewall Jackson's Headquarters. Jackson's headquarters Nov 1861-Mar 1862; now a museum housing Jackson memorabilia and other Confederate items of the war yrs. (Apr-Oct, daily; rest of yr, by appt, weather permitting) Inquire about combination ticket. 415 N Braddock St. Phone 540/667-3242. ¢¢

Washington's Office-Museum. Building used by George Washington in 1755-1756 during construction of Fort Loudoun. Housed in this museum are French and Indian, Revolutionary, and Civil War relics. (Apr-Oct, daily; rest of yr, by appt, weather permitting) Jct Cork and Braddock sts. Phone 540/662-4412. ¢

Special Events

Historic Garden Tour. Open house and gardens in historic Winchester. Phone 540/662-6550. Mid-Apr.

Shenandoah Apple Blossom Festival. Apple Blossom Queen, parades, arts and crafts, band contests, music, food, and attractions. Phone 540/662-3863. Late-Apr early May.

Apple Harvest Arts & Crafts. Jim Barnett Park. Pie contests, apple-butter making, music, arts and crafts. Third wkend Sept.

Motels/Motor Lodges

★ ★ **BEST WESTERN LEE-JACKSON.** 711 Millwood Ave (22601). 540/662-4154; fax 540/662-2618; toll-free 800/528-1234. www.bestwestern. com. 140 rms, 2 story. Apr-Oct: S $52; D $57; each addl $5; suites $65-$70; kit. units $35 (14-day min); under 13 free; lower rates rest of yr. Crib avail. Pet accepted. TV; cable (premium). Pool. Restaurant 6 am-10 pm. Bar 5-10:30 pm. Ck-out noon. Coin lndry. Meeting rms. Business servs avail. Valet serv. Free airport transportation. Health club privileges. Some refrigerators, microwaves. Picnic tables, grills. Cr cds: A, C, D, DS, MC, V.

⊡ 🐾 ⤳ ≊ 🐾 SC

★ **COMFORT INN.** 167 Town Run Ln, Stephens City (22655). 540/869-6500; fax 540/869-2558; toll-free 800/228-5150. www.comfortinn.com. 58 rms, 2 story. S $43-$70; D $49-$80; each addl $6; under 18 free. Crib free. TV; cable (premium), VCR avail (movies). Pool. Complimentary continental bkfst. Restaurant adj 11 am-9 pm. Ck-out noon. Business servs avail. In-rm modem link. Sundries. Refrigerators, microwaves avail. Cr cds: A, C, D, DS, ER, JCB, MC, V.

⊡ ⤳ ≊ 🐾 SC

★ **ECONO LODGE.** 1593 Martinsburg Pike (22603). 540/662-4700; fax 540/665-1762; res 800/553-2666. 50 rms, 2 story. S $46.95; D $50.95; each addl $5; under 19 free. Crib free. TV; cable (premium). Complimentary continental bkfst. Restaurant nearby. Ck-out 11 am. Business servs avail. In-rm modem link. Cr cds: A, C, D, DS, MC, V.

⊡ ≊ 🐾

★ ★ **HAMPTON INN.** 1655 Apple Blossom Dr (22601). 540/667-8011; fax 540/667-8033. www.hamptoninn. com. 103 rms, 4 story. S, D $60-$67; under 18 free. Crib free. TV; cable (premium). Pool. Complimentary continental bkfst. Restaurant nearby. Ck-out noon. Meeting rms. Business servs avail. In-rm modem link. Valet serv. Golf privileges. Health club privileges. Cr cds: A, C, D, DS, JCB, MC, V.

🎿 ⊡ ≊ ⤳ 🐾

★ ★ **HOLIDAY INN.** 1017 Millwood Pike (22602). 540/667-3300; fax 540/722-2730. www.holiday-inn.com. 175 rms, 2 story. S, D $49-$79; each addl $6; under 18 free. Crib free. TV; cable. Pool. Restaurant 6:30 am-10 pm. Bar 5:30 pm-midnight. Ck-out noon. Meeting rms. Business servs avail. In-rm modem link. Bellhops. Valet serv. Sundries. Tennis. Health club privileges. Some refrigerators, microwaves. Balconies. Cr cds: A, C, D, DS, MC, V.

⬛ 🛠 🏊 🏋 🦺

★ **SHONEY'S INN.** *1347 Berryville Ave (22601). 540/665-1700; fax 540/ 665-3037; res 800/222-2222.* 98 rms, 4 with shower only, 3 story. May-Oct: S $53; D $58-$61; each addl $5; under 18 free; lower rates rest of yr. Crib free. TV; cable (premium). Indoor pool; whirlpool. Restaurant 6 am-11 pm; Fri, Sat to 1 am. Ck-out noon. Meeting rm. Business servs avail. Sundries. Valet serv. Exercise equipt; sauna. Some in-rm whirlpools, refrigerators, microwaves. Cr cds: A, C, D, DS, MC, V.

⬛ 🏊 🏋 🦺

★ **TRAVELODGE.** *160 Front Royal Pike (22602). 540/665-0685; fax 540/ 665-0689; toll-free 800/578-7878. www. travelodge.com.* 149 rms, 3 story. S $46-$63; D $52-$69; each addl $5; suites $125; under 17 free. Crib free. Pet accepted; $5. TV; cable (premium), VCR avail (movies). Heated pool. Complimentary continental bkfst, coffee in rms. Restaurant nearby. Ck-out 11 am. Coin lndry. Business servs avail. In-rm modem link. Health club privileges. Refrigerators, microwaves avail. Cr cds: A, C, D, DS, ER, JCB, MC, V.

⬛ 🏊 🦺 SC

B&Bs/Small Inns

★★★ **ASHBY INN.** *692 Federal St, Paris (20130). 540/592-3900; fax 540/592-3781. www.ashbyinn.com.* 9 rms, 3 story. Rm phones avail. S, D $130-$200; each addl $20; suite $220. Children over 10 yrs only. TV in some rms. Complimentary full bkfst. Restaurant (see also ASHBY INN). Ck-out noon, ck-in 3 pm. Business servs avail. Tennis privileges. Golf privileges. Lawn games. Library/sitting rm. Converted residence (1829) and one-rm schoolhouse; stone fireplace; antique furnishings. Totally nonsmoking. Cr cds: MC, V.

🦺 🐾 🛠

★★★ **THE INN AT VAUCLUSE SPRING.** *231 Vaucluse Spring Ln, Stephens City (22655). 540/869-0200; fax 540/869-9546; res 800/869-0525.* 12 rms, 2 story, 2 suites, 2 cottages.

No rm phones. S, D $135-$200; each addl $25; suites $135; cottages $210-$250; wkends, hols (2-day min). Children over 10 yrs only. Complimentary full bkfst. Ck-out 11 am, ck-in 3-5 pm. Business center. Luggage handling. Gift shop. X-country ski on site. Pool. Many in-rm whirlpools, fireplaces. Built in 1785; Federal-style decor. On 100 acres. Cr cds: MC, V.

🏃 ⬛ 🏊 🦺

★★★ **L'AUBERGE PROVENÇAL FRENCH COUNTRY INN.** *Rte 340 S, Boyce (22663). 540/837-1375; fax 540/837-2004; toll-free 800/638-1702. www.laubergeprovencale.com.* 14 rms, 2 story. S $120-$175; D $145-$195; suite $250-$325; each addl $35. Children over 10 yrs only. Complimentary full bkfst. Restaurant (see also L'AUBERGE PROVENÇALE). Rm serv to 11 pm. Ck-out 11 am, ck-in 3 pm. Free airport transportation. Tennis privileges. 36-hole golf privileges. Whirlpool. Health club privileges. Balcony. Originally a sheep farm (1753) owned by Lord Fairfax. French country decor. Cr cds: A, C, D, MC, V.

🛠 🦺 SC

Restaurants

★★★ **ASHBY INN.** *692 Federal St (20130). 540/592-3900. www.ashbyinn. com.* Hrs: 6-9 pm; Sun noon-2:30 pm. Closed Mon, Tues; hols. Res required. Serv bar. Dinner $17-$25. Sun brunch $21. Specializes in lamb, fresh seafood, crab cakes. Menu changes daily. Outdoor dining. Virginia hunt country atmosphere; antiques. Plank flooring dates back to original inn (1829). Cr cds: MC, V.

⬛

★★★ **L'AUBERGE PROVENÇALE.** *13630 Lord Fairfax Hwy, Boyce (22620). 540/837-1375. www.laubergeprovencale. com.* Hrs: 6-10:30 pm; Sun 5-9 pm. Closed Mon, Tues; July 4, Dec 25. Res accepted; required Fri-Sun. French Provençal menu. Bar. Wine cellar. Prix fixe: dinner $65. Specializes in seasonal creations featuring homegrown organic vegetables, fruits and herbs. Outdoor dining. Country inn with extensive art collection. Totally nonsmoking. Cr cds: A, D, DS, MC, V.

Wise

See also Big Stone Gap, Breaks Interstate Park

Pop 3,255 **Elev** 2,454 ft
Area code 540 **Zip** 24293

What to See and Do

Recreation Areas. In George Washington and Jefferson National Forest (see HARRISONBURG). **High Knob,** 4 mi S on US 23 to Norton, then 3 mi S via VA 619, 1½ mi E on FS Road 238. Camping, swimming, picnicking. Parking fee. **Bark Camp,** [E]4 mi S on US 23 to Norton, then 6 mi E on US 58A to Tacoma, then 4 mi S off VA 706, 3 mi S on VA 822. Camping, boating, fishing, picnicking. Parking fee. **Cave Springs,** 7 mi W of Big Stone Gap on US 58A, then 1 mi N on VA 622, then 3 mi W on VA 621. Camping (fee). Swimming. Parking fee. **North Fork of Pound Lake,** US 23 to Pound, then W on VA 671. Camping (fee), picnicking, swimming, boat ramp, hiking. Clinch Ranger District office is in Wise. Phone 540/328-2931.

Woodstock

See also Basye, Front Royal, Luray, New Market

Founded 1761 **Pop** 3,952 **Elev** 780 ft
Area code 540 **Zip** 22664
Information Chamber of Commerce, 143 N Main St, PO Box 605; 540/459-2542
Web www.woodstockva.com/chamber

A German immigrant, Jacob Mller, received a land grant from Lord Fairfax and came here in 1752 with his wife and six children. A few years later he set aside 1,200 acres for a town, first called Müllerstadt, later Woodstock. In a small log church here, John Peter Gabriel Mühlenberg, in January 1776, preached his famous sermon based on Ecclesiastes

3:1-8: "There is a time to every purpose...a time to war and a time to peace," at the end of which he flung back his vestments to reveal the uniform of a Continental colonel and began to enroll his parishioners in the army that was to overthrow British rule.

The *Shenandoah Valley-Herald,* a weekly newspaper established in 1817, is still published here.

What to See and Do

Shenandoah County Court House. (1792) Oldest courthouse still in use west of the Blue Ridge Mtns; interior restored to original design. (Mon-Fri) Main St.

Shenandoah Vineyards. Valley's first winery. Premium wines; hand-picked and processed in the European style. Picnic area. Tours, free tastings available. (Daily; closed Jan 1, Thanksgiving, Dec 25) From I-81 exit 279 at Edinburg, W on VA 675, make first right on VA 686, go 1½ mi to winery. Phone 540/984-8699. **FREE**

Woodstock Tower. Panoramic view of seven horseshoe bends of the Shenandoah River. 4 mi E on Mill Rd, crest of Massanutten Mtn.

Special Events

Shenandoah Valley Music Festival. Symphony pops, classical, folk, jazz, country and big band concerts. Pavilion and lawn seating. Outdoor pavilion on grounds of historic Orkney Springs Hotel in Orkney Springs. Contact Festival, PO Box 12; phone 540/459-3396. Four wkends, mid-July-Labor Day wkend.

Shenandoah County Fair. One of the oldest county fairs in the state. Harness racing last four days. Late Aug-early Sept. Phone 540/459-3867.

Motels/Motor Lodges

★ **BUDGET HOST.** *1290 S Main St (22664). 540/459-4086; fax 540/459-4043; res 800/283-4678. www.budgethost.com.* 43 rms, 1-2 story. S $30; D $37-$40; each addl $5; under 6 free; wkly rates. Crib $5. Pet accepted, some restrictions. TV; cable. Pool. Restaurant 6:30 am-9 pm; Sun from 7 am. Ck-out 11 am. Coin lndry. Business servs avail. Downhill ski 20 mi. Picnic tables. Cr cds: A, DS, MC, V.

★ **RAMADA INN.** *1130 Motel Dr (22664). 540/459-5000; fax 540/459-8219; toll-free 800/272-6232. www. ramada.com.* 124 rms, 3 story. May-Oct: S $62; D $70; each addl $8; under 18 free; lower rates rest of yr. Crib free. TV; cable (premium). Heated pool. Restaurant 7 am-1:30 pm, 5-9 pm. Bar 5 pm-midnight. Ck-out noon. Meeting rms Business servs avail. Valet serv. Sundries. Some refrigerators. Cr cds: A, C, D, DS, JCB, MC, V.

B&B/Small Inn

★ ★ ★ **INN AT NARROW PAS-SAGE.** *Rte 11; 30 Chapman Landing Rd (22664). 540/459-8000; fax 540/459-8001; toll-free 800/459-8002. www.innatnarrowpassage.com.* 12 rms, 2 with bath, 2 story. Rm phones avail. S, D $95-$145; each addl $10. TV. Complimentary full bkfst. Ck-out 11 am, ck-in 2 pm. Meeting rms. Business servs avail. Lawn games. On river; canoeing. Historic inn (1740), used as headquarters by General Stonewall Jackson during Civil War. Totally nonsmoking. Cr cds: DS, MC, V.

Restaurant

★ ★ **SPRING HOUSE TAVERN.** *325 S Main St (US 11) (22664). 540/459-4755.* Hrs: 11 am-midnight; Sun noon-10 pm; Sun brunch 10 am-1:30 pm. Closed hols. Res accepted. Bar from 5 pm. Bkfst $4.25-$6, lunch $3.95-$6.25, dinner $9.95-$20.25. Sun brunch $6.50. Child's menu. Salad bar. 5 dining rms incl a log lounge. Early American antiques, artifacts. Cr cds: A, D, DS, MC, V.

Wytheville

(E-3) *See also Marion*

Founded 1792 **Pop** 7,804 **Elev** 2,284 ft **Area code** 540 **Zip** 24382
Information Wytheville-Wythe-Bland Chamber of Commerce, 150 E Monroe St, PO Box 563; 540/223-3365
Web chamber.wytheville.com

With lead mines and the only salt mine in the South nearby, Wytheville was a Union target during the Civil War. One story states a detachment of Union cavalry attempted to take the town in July, 1863, only to be thwarted by Molly Tynes, who rode 40 miles over the mountains from Rocky Dell to tell the countryside that the Yankees were coming. The alerted home guard turned them away. A transportation center today, Wytheville is a vacationland nestled between the Blue Ridge and Allegheny mountains. Rural Retreat Lake is nearby. Wythe Ranger District office for the George Washington and Jefferson national forests (see HARRISON-BURG) is located here.

What to See and Do

Big Walker Lookout. A 120-ft observation tower at 3,405-ft elevation; swinging bridge. Gift shop; snack bar. (Apr-late May, Thurs-Sun; Memorial Day-Oct, Tues-Sun) 12 mi N on US 52; on Big Walker Mtn Scenic Byway. Phone 276/228-4401. ¢¢

Shot Tower Historical Park. (1807) On bluff overlooking New River. One of three shot towers still standing in US; fortresslike stone shaft has 2½ ft thick walls rising 75 ft above ground and boring 75 ft below to a water tank. Molten lead was poured through sheet iron colanders from the tower top; during the 150-ft descent it became globular before hitting the water. Pellets were then sorted by rolling them down an incline; well-formed shot rolled into a receptacle; faulty ones zig-zagged off and were remelted. Visitor center, programs; hiking trails, picnicking. (Memorial Day-Labor Day, daily) Standard fees. At Jackson's Ferry, 6 mi E on I-81, then 7 mi S on US 52; or I-77 S, Poplar Camp exit. Phone 540/699-6778. ¢

Wytheville State Fish Hatchery. Approx 150,000 pounds of rainbow trout produced annually. Five-tank aquarium; displays. Self-guided tours. (Daily) 12 mi SE on US 52 to VA 629. Phone 276/637-3212. **FREE**

Special Event

Chautauqua Festival. Held over a nine-day period. Incl parade, educational events, performing arts, art shows, children's activities, music, food, entertainment. Third wk June.

Motels/Motor Lodges

★ ★ **BEST WESTERN.** 355 Nye Rd (24382). 540/228-7300; fax 540/228-4223. www.bestwestern.com. 100 rms, 2 story. Apr-Oct: S $45-$60; D $50-$66; each addl $6; under 18 free; higher rates special events; lower rates rest of yr. Crib free. Pet accepted. TV, cable (premium). Pool. Complimentary continental bkfst. Ck-out noon. Business servs avail. Valet serv. Microwaves avail. Cr cds: A, C, D, DS, MC, V.
D ⬜ ⬜ ⬜ ⬜ SC

★ **COMFORT INN.** 315 Holston Rd (24382). 540/228-4488; fax 540/228-4092; res 800/228-5150. 80 rms, 2 story. S $58; D $68; each addl $5; under 18 free. Crib free. TV; cable (premium). Pool. Complimentary continental bkfst. Restaurant nearby. Ck-out 11 am. Business servs avail. Cr cds: A, C, D, DS, JCB, MC, V.
D ⬜ ⬜ ⬜

★ **DAYS INN.** 150 Malin Dr (24382). 540/228-5500; fax 540/228-6301; toll-free 800/329-7466. www.daysinn.com. 118 rms, 1-3 story. Apr-Oct: S, D $48-$58; each addl $5; under 17 free; higher rates: hols, Bristol auto races; lower rates rest of yr. Crib free. TV; cable (premium). Complimentary coffee in lobby. Restaurant adj 6 am-midnight. Ck-out noon. Business servs avail. Microwaves avail. View of mountains. Cr cds: A, C, D, DS, MC, V.
D ⬜ ⬜ SC

★ **ECONO LODGE.** 1160 E Main St (24382). 540/228-5517; fax 540/228-5517; toll-free 800/228-5050. www.econolodge.com. 72 rms, 2 story. Apr-Oct: S $35.95-$55.95; D $38.99-$58.99; each addl $5; under 18 free; higher rates special events; lower rates rest of yr. Crib free. TV; cable. Complimentary coffee in lobby. Restaurant adj 11 am-9:30 pm. Ck-out 11 am. Business servs avail. Cr cds: A, C, D, DS, MC, V.
D ⬜ ⬜ SC

★ ★ **HOLIDAY INN.** 1800 E Main St (24382). 540/228-5483; fax 540/228-5417; toll-free 800/465-4329. www.holiday-inn.com. 199 rms, 1-4 story. Mar-Oct: S $49-$70; D $54-$70; each addl $5; suites $104-$150; under 18 free; wkly rates; higher rates auto races; lower rates rest of yr. Crib free. Pet accepted. TV; cable (premium). Pool; wading pool. Restaurant 6 am-2 pm, 5-9 pm. Bar. Ck-out 11 am. Meeting rms. Business servs avail. Cr cds: A, C, D, DS, JCB, MC, V.
D ⬜ ⬜ ⬜ ⬜ SC

★ **RAMADA INN.** 955 Peppers Ferry Rd (24382). 540/228-6000; fax 540/228-6009; toll-free 800/272-6232. www.ramada.com. 154 rms, 2 story. S $64-$85; D $69-$85; each addl $5; under 18 free. Crib free. Pet accepted. TV; cable (premium). Pool. Coffee in rms. Restaurant 6:30 am-9 pm. Bar 5-11 pm; Sun 6 pm-midnight. Ck-out noon. Coin lndry. Meeting rms. Business servs avail. Cr cds: A, C, D, DS, ER, JCB, MC, V.
D ⬜ ⬜ ⬜ SC

★ **SHENANDOAH INN.** 140 Lithia Rd (24382). 540/228-3188; fax 540/228-6458. 100 rms, 1-2 story. S $35-$45; D $43-$60; each addl $6; under 16 free; wkly, wkend, hol rates; higher rates some special events. Crib free. Pet accepted; $5. TV; cable. Complimentary coffee in lobby. Restaurant nearby. Ck-out 11 am. Balconies. Cr cds: A, C, D, DS, MC, V.
D ⬜ ⬜ ⬜ SC

Restaurant

★ **LOG HOUSE.** 520 E Main St (24382). 540/228-4139. Hrs: 11 am-10 pm. Closed Sun; Dec 25. Res accepted. Wine, beer. Lunch $2.99-$15.50, dinner $5.55-$16.95. Child's menu. Specialties: beef stew, stuffed chicken breast. Outdoor dining. Colonial motif; built 1776. Cr cds: A, D, MC, V.

Yorktown

See also Colonial Parkway, Gloucester, Jamestown (Colonial National Historical Park), Newport News, Williamsburg

Founded 1691 **Pop** 203 **Elev** 54 ft
Information Colonial National Historical Park, PO Box 210, 23690; 757/898-3400
Web www.nps.gov/colo

Free land offered in 1630 to those adventurous enough "to seate and inhabit" the 50-foot bluffs on the south side of the York River "formerly known by ye Indyan name of Chiskiacke" brought about the beginning of settlement. When the Assembly authorized a port, started in 1691, the town slowly expanded and in the following years became a busy shipping center, with prosperity reaching a peak about 1750. From then on the port declined along with the Tidewater Virginia tobacco trade.

Yorktown's moment in history came in 1781. British commander Cornwallis, after raiding up and down Virginia with minimal resistance from the Marquis de Lafayette, was sent here to establish a naval base in which supplies and reinforcements could be shipped to him. The Comte de Grasse's French fleet effectively blockaded the British, however, by controlling the mouth of the Chesapeake Bay. At the Battle of the Capes on September 5, 1781, a British fleet sent to investigate the French presence was defeated by the French. Cornwallis found himself bottled up in Yorktown by combined American and French forces under Washington, which arrived on September 28.

Shelling began October 9. The siege of Yorktown ended on October 17 with Cornwallis requesting terms of capitulation. On October 19, Cornwallis' troops marched out with flags and arms cased, their bands playing. Then they laid down their arms, bringing the last major battle of the Revolutionary War to a close.

Yorktown Battlefield, part of Colonial National Historical Park, surrounds the village. Though Yorktown itself is still an active community, many surviving and reconstructed colonial structures supply an 18th-century atmosphere.

What to See and Do

Grace Episcopal Church. (1697) Walls of local marl (a mixture of clay, sand, and limestone); damaged in 1781, gutted by fire in 1814. A 1649 communion service is still in use. (Daily) Church St. Phone 757/898-3261.

⭐ **Yorktown Battlefield.** Surrounds and incl part of town. Remains of 1781 British fortifications, modified and strengthened by Confederate forces in Civil War. Reconstructed American and French lines lie beyond. Roads lead to headquarters, encampment areas of Americans, French. Admission fee incl access to Visitor Center, battlefield tour, Moore House, and Nelson House. Golden Access, Age, and Eagle passports honored (see MAKING THE MOST OF YOUR TRIP). ¢¢ Stop first at

Visitor Center. Information; special exhibits, General Washington's field tents. (Daily; closed Dec 25) E side of town, at end of Colonial Pkwy. Phone 757/898-3400.

Self-guided battlefield tour. Markers, displays aid in visualizing siege. Highlights incl headquarters sites of Lafayette, von Steuben, Rochambeau, Washington; American Battery #2; Grand French Battery; a key point is Surrender Field where British forces laid down their arms.

Moore House. In this 18th-century house the "Articles of Capitulation" were drafted. These were signed by General Washington in the captured British Redoubt #10 on Oct 19. (Mid-June-mid-Aug, daily; spring and fall, wkends) Located along battlefield tour road. Phone 757/898-3400. W of here on VA 238 is

Yorktown National Civil War Cemetery. 2,183 interments (1,436 unknown).

Yorktown Victory Monument. Elaborately ornamented 95-ft granite column memorializes American-French alliance in Revolutionary War. E end of Main St. Then proceed to

Nelson House. Original restored mansion built by "Scotch Tom" Nelson in the early 1700s. Home of his grandson, Thomas Nelson, Jr., a signer of the Declaration of Independence. Impressive example of Georgian architecture. (Apr-Oct, daily) Nelson and Main sts.

Yorktown Victory Center. Museum of the Revolutionary War chronicles the struggle for independence from the beginnings of colonial unrest to the formation of the new nation. Exhibit galleries, living history Continental Army encampment, and late-18th-century farm. (Daily; closed Jan 1, Dec 25) Combination ticket with Jamestown Settlement (see JAMESTOWN COLONIAL NATIONAL HISTORICAL PARK) avail. ½ mi W on VA 238. Phone 757/253-4838. ¢¢¢¢

Special Event

Yorktown Day. Observance of America's Revolutionary War victory at Yorktown in 1781. Oct 19.

Motels/Motor Lodges

★ ★ **DUKE OF YORK MOTOR HOTEL.** *508 Water St (23690). 757/898-3232; fax 757/898-5922.* 57 rms, 2-3 story. Memorial Day-Labor Day: S, D $74; each addl $10; lower rates rest of yr. TV. Pool. Restaurant (hrs vary). Ck-out noon. Business servs avail. Some refrigerators. Balconies. Opp beach; overlooks river. Cr cds: A, C, D, DS, MC, V.
⊠ ⊠ ⊠

★ **YORKTOWN MOTOR LODGE.** *8829 George Washington Hwy (23692). 757/898-5451; fax 757/898-1766; toll-free 800/950-4003.* 42 rms, 1 story. Memorial Day-Labor Day: S $45-$55; D $55-$75; each addl $5; under 18 free; lower rates rest of yr. Crib $5. TV; cable (premium). Pool. Playground. Restaurant adj 7 am-9 pm. Ck-out 11 am. Business servs avail.

Refrigerators, microwaves. Cr cds: A, D, DS, MC, V.
⊠ ⊠ ⊠ SC

Restaurants

★ ★ **NICK'S SEAFOOD PAVILION.** *324 Water St (23690). 757/887-5269. www.switchboard.com.* Hrs: 11 am-10 pm. Closed Dec 25. Continental menu. Lunch, dinner $7-$35. Child's menu. Specializes in fresh local seafood, lobster, seafood kebab. Grecian atmosphere; art collection. Family-owned. Cr cds: A, D, DS, MC, V.
D

★ ★ **RIVER'S INN.** *8109 Yacht Haven Dr, Gloucester Point (23062). 804/642-9942.* Hrs: 11:30 am-3 pm; 5:30-9 pm; Fri, Sat to 10 pm. Closed Dec 25. Res accepted. Seafood menu. Bar. Lunch $5-$8, dinner $15-$21. Child's menu. Specialties: pan-fried crab cakes, Chesapeake blue plate, blue cheese salmon. Outdoor dining. View of marina and York River; nautical decor and artwork. Cr cds: A, MC, V.
D

WEST VIRGINIA

The wild, rugged topography that made settlement of this area difficult in the early days has today made West Virginia a paradise for outdoor enthusiasts. The state's ski industry has taken advantage of the highest total altitude of any state east of the Mississippi River by opening several Alpine and Nordic ski areas. Outfitters offer excellent whitewater rafting on the state's many turbulent rivers. Rock climbing, caving, and hiking are popular in the Monongahela National Forest, and West Virginia also boasts an impressive state park system, as well as extensive hunting and fishing areas.

The nickname "mountain state" gives only a hint of West Virginia's scenic beauty, which is unsurpassed in the East. West Virginia is also a land of proud traditions, with many festivals held throughout the year as tributes to the state's rich heritage. These events include celebrations honoring the state's sternwheel riverboat legacy, its spectacular autumn foliage, and even its strawberries, apples, and black walnuts.

Population: 1,807,000
Area: 24,282 square miles
Elevation: 240-4,863 feet
Peak: Spruce Knob (Pendleton County)
Entered Union: June 20, 1863 (35th state)
Capital: Charleston
Motto: Mountaineers are always free
Nickname: Mountain State
Flower: Rhododendron
Bird: Cardinal
Tree: Sugar Maple
Fair: Aug 2003, in Lewisburg
Time Zone: Eastern
Website: www.state.wv.us/tourism

The occupation of West Virginia began with the Mound Builders, a prehistoric Ohio Valley culture that left behind at least 300 conical earth mounds that challenge the imagination. Many have been worn away by erosion, but excavations in some have revealed elaborately adorned human skeletons and artifacts of amazing beauty and utility.

Pioneers who ventured into western Virginia in the 18th century found fine vistas and forests, curative springs, and beautiful rivers. George Washington and his family frequented the soothing mineral waters of Berkeley Springs (see), and White Sulphur Springs (see) later became a popular resort among the colonists. But much of this area was still considered "the wild West" in those days, and life here was not easy.

The Commonwealth of Virginia largely ignored its western citizens—only one governor was elected from the western counties before 1860. When the counties formed their own state during the Civil War, it was the result of many years of strained relations with the parent state. The move had been debated over the years and the war finally provided the opportunity the counties needed to break away from Virginia. Although many sentiments in the new state remained pro-South, West Virginia's interests were best served by staying with the Union.

The first land battle of the Civil War took place in the western counties (see PHILIPPI) soon after Fort Sumter was fired upon in April 1861. Through the rest of 1861 and into 1862, Union forces under Generals George McClellan and William S. Rosecrans chased the Confederates back toward rebel Virginia. Succeeding battles were fought farther and farther south until major Confederate resistance became impossible. For the rest of the war, Confederate Army activity in the state was limited to destructive lightning raids designed to wreck railroad lines and damage Union supply sources.

The war left West Virginia a new state, but like other war-ravaged areas, it had suffered heavy losses of life and property. The recovery took many years. West Virginians eventually rebuilt their state; new industry was developed, railroads were built, and resources like coal, oil, and natural gas brought relative prosperity.

West Virginia continues to be an important source of bituminous coal and a major producer of building stone, timber, glass, and chemicals. The state is also the home of such technological wonders as the National Radio Astronomy Observatory (see MARLINTON), where scientists study the universe via radio telescopes, and the New River Gorge Bridge (see GAULEY BRIDGE), the world's longest steel span bridge.

When to Go/Climate

West Virginia summers are hot and humid, although temperatures in elevated areas rarely top 90°F. Snowfall can range up to 10-15 feet in some areas.

AVERAGE HIGH/LOW TEMPERATURES (°F)

CHARLESTON

Jan 41/23	**May** 76/52	**Sept** 79/57
Feb 45/26	**June** 83/60	**Oct** 68/44
Mar 57/35	**July** 86/64	**Nov** 57/36
Apr 67/43	**Aug** 84/63	**Dec** 46/28

ELKINS

Jan 38/16	**May** 71/44	**Sept** 74/50
Feb 41/18	**June** 78/52	**Oct** 64/37
Mar 52/27	**July** 80/57	**Nov** 53/30
Apr 62/35	**Aug** 79/56	**Dec** 43/21

Parks and Recreation Finder

Directions to and information about the parks and recreation areas below are given under their respective town/city sections. Please refer to those sections for details.

NATIONAL PARK AND RECREATION AREAS

Key to abbreviations. I.H.S. = International Historic Site; I.P.M. = International Peace Memorial; N.B. = National Battlefield; N.B.P. = National Battlefield Park; N.B.C. = National Battlefield and Cemetery; N.C.A. = National Conservation Area; N.E.M. = National Expansion Memorial; N.F. = National Forest; N.G. = National Grassland; N.H.P. = National Historical Park; N.H.C. = National Heritage Corridor; N.H.S. = National Historic Site; N.L. = National Lakeshore; N.M. = National Monument; N.M.P. = National Military Park; N.Mem. = National Memorial; N.P. = National Park; N.Pres. = National Preserve; N.R.A. = National Recreational Area; N.R.R. = National Recreational River; N.Riv. = National River; N.S. = National Seashore; N.S.R. = National Scenic Riverway; N.S.T. = National Scenic Trail; N.Sc. = National Scientific Reserve; N.V.M. = National Volcanic Monument.

Place Name	Listed Under
Gauley River N.R.A.	SUMMERSVILLE
Harpers Ferry N.H.P.	HARPERS FERRY
Monongahela N.F.	ELKINS
New River Gorge N.Riv.	HINTON

STATE PARK AND RECREATION AREAS

Key to abbreviations. I.P. = Interstate Park; S.A.P. = State Archaeological Park; S.B. = State Beach; S.C.A. = State Conservation Area; S.C.P. = State Conservation Park; S.Cp. = State Campground; S.F. = State Forest; S.G. = State Garden; S.H.A. = State Historic Area; S.H.P. = State Historic Park; S.H.S. = State Historic Site; S.M.P. = State Marine Park; S.N.A. = State Natural Area; S.P. = State Park;

CALENDAR HIGHLIGHTS

MAY

Webster Springs Woodchopping Festival (Webster Springs). Southeastern World Woodchopping Championships; state championship turkey calling contest, draft horse pull, horse show, fireman's rodeo; arts and crafts, music, parades, concessions.

Vandalia Gathering (Charleston). A festival of traditional arts; craft demonstrations, clogging, gospel music, fiddling, banjo picking, special exhibits. Phone 304/558-0220.

JUNE

Mountain Heritage Arts and Crafts Festival (Harpers Ferry). More than 190 craftspeople and artisans demonstrate quilting, wool spinning, pottery throwing, vegetable dyeing, and other crafts; concerts. Also in September. Phone 304/725-2055 or 800/624-0577.

JULY

Jamboree in the Hills (Wheeling). A four-day country music festival featuring more than 30 hours of music; top country stars. Camping available. Phone 800/624-5456.

AUGUST

State Fair (Lewisburg). Fairgrounds. Exhibitors from a number of other states; horse shows, harness racing. Phone 304/645-1090.

SEPTEMBER

Sternwheel Regatta Festival (Charleston). Sternwheel and towboat races, parades, contests, hot air balloon race, fireworks; nationally known entertainers nightly; arts and crafts. Phone 304/348-6419.

Stonewall Jackson Heritage Arts and Crafts Jubilee (Weston). Jackson's Mill State 4-H Conference Center. Mountain crafts, music, dance, and food. Phone 304/269-1863.

OCTOBER

Mountain State Forest Festival (Elkins). Some events on campus of Davis & Elkins College. Queen Silvia is crowned; carnival, parades, entertainment, tilting at rings on horseback, sawing and woodchopping contests, marksmanship tests, State Championship Fiddle and Banjo Contest, juried craft fair and art exhibit. Phone 304/636-1824.

Bridge Day (Fayetteville). New River Gorge Bridge. Bridge is opened to pedestrians; parachutists test their skills by jumping off the bridge and floating to the bottom of the gorge. Contact Fayetteville Chamber of Commerce, phone 304/465-5617.

S.P.C. = State Public Campground; S.R. = State Reserve; S.R.A. = State Recreation Area; S.Res. = State Reservoir; S.Res.P. = State Resort Park; S.R.P. = State Rustic Park.

Place Name	Listed Under
Audra S.P.	BUCKHANNON
Babcock S.P.	BECKLEY
Beartown S.P.	HILLSBORO
Beech Fork S.P.	HUNTINGTON
Berkeley Springs S.P.	BERKELEY SPRINGS
Blackwater Falls S.P.	DAVIS
Blennerhassett Island S.H.P.	PARKERSBURG
Bluestone S.P.	HINTON

Cabwaylingo S.F.	WILLIAMSON
Cacapon Resort S.P.	BERKELEY SPRINGS
Calvin Price S.F.	HILLSBORO
Camp Creek S.P.	PRINCETON
Canaan Valley Resort S.P.	DAVIS
Carnifex Ferry Battlefield S.P.	SUMMERSVILLE
Cass Scenic Railroad S.P.	MARLINTON
Cathedral S.P.	AURORA
Cedar Creek S.P.	WESTON
Coopers Rock S.F.	MORGANTOWN
Droop Mountain Battlefield S.P.	HILLSBORO
Grave Creek Mound S.P.	WHEELING
Greenbrier S.F.	WHITE SULPHUR SPRINGS
Hawk's Nest S.P.	GAULEY BRIDGE
Holly River S.P.	WEBSTER SPRINGS
Kanawha S.F.	CHARLESTON
Kumbrabrow S.F.	WEBSTER SPRINGS
Lost River S.P.	MOOREFIELD
North Bend S.P.	PARKERSBURG
Panther S.F.	BLUEFIELD
Pinnacle Rock S.P.	BLUEFIELD
Pipestem S.Res.P.	HINTON
Point Pleasant Battlefield Monument S.P.	POINT PLEASANT
Prickett's Fort S.P.	FAIRMONT
Seneca S.F.	MARLINTON
Stonewall Jackson Lake S.P.	WESTON
Tomlinson Run S.P.	WEIRTON
Twin Falls Resort S.P.	BECKLEY
Tygart Lake S.P.	GRAFTON
Watoga S.P.	HILLSBORO
Watters Smith Memorial S.P.	CLARKSBURG

Water-related activities, hiking, riding, various other sports, picnicking, and visitor centers, as well as camping, are available in many of these areas. There is a small fee for swimming and game court use. Campgrounds with picnic facilities are available in 22 state parks and forests; all have drinking water and sanitary facilities; some have showers, coin laundries, utility hookups; two-week limit; $6-$14/night for six persons or less, $1 each additional person. Camping season runs from mid-April-October in all parks except Canaan Valley and Pipestem resorts, which are open year-round. Campground reservations may be made at Babcock, Beech Fork, Blackwater Falls, Bluestone, Canaan Valley Resort, Cedar Creek, Chief Logan, Holly River, North Bend, Pipestem Resort, Stonewall Jackson Lake, Tomlinson Run, Twin Falls Resort, Tygart Lake, and Watoga state parks and at Greenbrier and Kanawha state forests. There is a $5 handling fee; reservations must be made 7-14 days in advance. Camping at all other state parks is on a first-come, first-served basis. Pets on leash only. Many cabins and lodges are available for seasonal or year-round use; seven-day minimum second Monday in June-Labor Day. Most parks are open daily, 8 am-sunset. For information and reservations contact individual parks or phone 800/225-5982 (except AK and HI).

SKI AREAS
Place Name	**Listed Under**
Canaan Valley Resort S.P.	DAVIS
Elk River Touring Center	MARLINTON
Oglebay Resort Park	WHEELING

Snowshoe Mountain Resort	MARLINTON
Timberline Four Seasons Resort	DAVIS
White Grass Touring Center	DAVIS
WinterPlace Ski Resort	BECKLEY

FISHING AND HUNTING

In addition to a million acres of prime federal hunting and fishing land, West Virginia has 48 wildlife management areas. Nonresident statewide fishing license $30; three-day license $5. Nonresident (except KY, OH, PA) hunting, basic license, $100; archery deer, muzzleloader deer, and turkey stamps $25; six-day, small-game license $20. Nonresident migratory waterfowl stamp $5. A conservation stamp is required in addition to all regular hunting and fishing licenses (nonresident $5). Contact the Division of Natural Resources, Wildlife Resources Section, State Capitol Complex, Building 3, Charleston 25305, phone 304/558-2771.

Driving Information

Children under nine must be in an approved passenger restraint anywhere in vehicle; ages three-eight may use a regulation safety belt; children under three years must use an approved safety seat. Phone 304/746-2121.

INTERSTATE HIGHWAY SYSTEM

The following alphabetical listing of West Virginia towns in *Mobil Travel Guide* shows that these cities are within ten miles of the indicated interstate highways. A highway map, however, should be checked for the nearest exit.

Highway Number	Cities/Towns within ten miles
Interstate 64	Beckley, Charleston, Huntington, Lewisburg, Nitro, White Sulphur Springs.
Interstate 70	Wheeling.
Interstate 77	Charleston, Parkersburg, Princeton, Ripley; also see WV Tpke.
Interstate 79	Charleston, Clarksburg, Fairmont, Morgantown, Sutton.
Interstate 81	Martinsburg.

Additional Visitor Information

Travel materials, including information on accommodations, skiing, caving, rock climbing, whitewater rafting, and other activities, are available from the West Virginia Division of Tourism, State Capitol Complex, 2101 Washington St E, Charleston 25305, phone 800/225-5982. The Information & Education Section, Department of Natural Resources, State Capitol, Charleston 25305, publishes a monthly magazine, *Wonderful West Virginia*.

Information on hiking along the completed portion of the Allegheny Trail, including a hiking guide (fee), is available from the West Virginia Scenic Trails Association, 633 West Virginia Ave, Morgantown 26505. The trail runs north-south from the Pennsylvania state line near Coopers Rock State Forest to Peters Mountain, SE of Lindside, at the Virginia state line.

There are several welcome centers in West Virginia; visitors who stop by will find information and brochures most helpful in planning stops at points of interest. Locations are as follows: on I-64, westbound near White Sulphur Springs and eastbound near Huntington; on I-81, southbound by the West Virginia/Maryland border and northbound near the West Virginia/Virginia border; on I-79, southbound N of Morgantown; on I-77, southbound near Mineral Wells; on I-70, westbound near the West Virginia/Pennsylvania border. The West Virginia Information Center is located at Harpers Ferry. All centers are open (daily; closed January 1, Thanksgiving, December 25). Personnel at any of these locations will also assist visitors in making lodging reservations. In addition, information may be obtained at the Capitol Guides Desk in the rotunda of the State Capitol at Charleston (Memorial Day-Labor Day, Monday-Saturday, also Sunday afternoons).

SPRUCE KNOB/MONONGAHELA HIGH COUNTRY (APPROX 150 MI)

In the big cities of the Mid-Atlantic, it is sometimes hard to believe that there is a vast and rugged mountain wilderness just to the west. You can find plenty of this unspoiled nature in West Virginia, where soaring mountain ridges stretch into the distance and countless splashing streams beckon. This one-day, 150-mile loop out of the pretty college town of Elkins takes you through some of the Mid-Atlantic's most scenic mountain terrain. The route criss-crosses 100,000-acre Spruce Knob-Seneca Rocks National Recreation Area in the Monongahela National Forest. From Elkins, take US 250 south through the national forest to Thornwood. Mile after mile, the road climbs and dips alongside splashing streams. At Thornwood, head north on State Route 28 toward Riverton. Two miles south of Riverton, turn west (left) onto Forest Service Road 112 and follow the signs to Spruce Knob, about 15 miles. At an altitude of 4,861 feet, Spruce Knob is the state's loftiest mountain peak—although peak isn't really an apt description. The summit is a broad, oddly flat plateau scattered with piles of age-smoothed rocks. A thin forest of red spruce, stunted by the strong and nearly constant westerly winds, struggles for a foothold. This is one of the most remote and rugged areas of the Mid-Atlantic that can be reached in a passenger sedan. A rock-lined trail leads to the Observation Tower, a three-story stone structure that boosts sightseers above the trees for a majestic 360-degree panorama. Return to Route 28 and continue north to Seneca Rocks, a slender 900-foot-high forested ridge favored by rock climbers. You can watch them from the Discovery Center or take the easier 1½-mile trail to the summit. Pause for snacks or lunch at Harper's Old Country Store. To continue, head west on Route 55 to Harmon and pick up Route 32 north to Davis. The road passes alongside 6,000-acre Canaan Valley Resort State Park, where you can stop to hike, bicycle, or go for a swim in the outdoor pool. A year-round resort, the park operates a downhill skiing complex. In summer, the chairlift will carry you to the top for grand views. About 15 miles long and three miles wide, the valley is situated at an altitude of 3,200 feet, which all but guarantees moderate summer temperatures. Just to the north, the town of Davis has become a major center for mountain biking, mostly on abandoned U.S. Forest Service roads. Outfitters offer rentals and maps. On the edge of Davis, turn left into Blackwater Falls State Park, a rumpled expanse of woodland ridges and valleys cut by the impressively deep canyon of the Blackwater River. Motorists approach the park's 55-room lodge on a long, winding road that carries them deeper and deeper into the forest. Suddenly a clearing appears, revealing the lodge clinging to the precipitous edge of the canyon. The river races far below, the thunder of crashing whitewater clearly audible. Visitors can view the 65-foot plunge of Blackwater Falls from the canyon rim just upriver from the lodge or descend 214 steps to its base. In summer, the beach at little Pendleton Lake makes a refreshing rest stop. Continue north two miles to Thomas, an old mining town built in a double tier on a mountainside, and then return to Elkins on US 219 south.

CANYON COUNTRY–AROUND NEW RIVER GORGE (APPROX 300 MI)

The New River, a twisted strand of tumbling water, has cut a deep and narrow gorge for more than 50 miles through the rugged mountains of southeastern West Virginia. Rafting enthusiasts consider the New to be one of the best whitewater rivers in the nation. It's also very pretty to look at while standing on a cliff's edge high above. This two-day, 300-mile scenic drive out of Charleston, which circles the gorge, provides plenty of scenic viewing opportunities. At the same time, the tour offers a look at the state's coal-mining heritage. At the turn of the century King Coal ruled the gorge, and at one time two dozen coal-mining towns prospered on the banks of the New. Now, much of the gorge is protected as the New River Gorge National River. From Charleston, head east on US 60, following the old Midland Trail up the Kanawha River. In the first few miles, the highway winds past industrial plants, which are interesting to see in their ugly strangeness. The mountain scenery begins in about 30 miles at Gauley Bridge, where the New flows into the Kanawha. Here, as the New begins to display whitewater turbulence, the road climbs steeply and you spot the first of many waterfalls spilling from overhead. One of finest gorge views is just ahead at Hawk's Nest State Park, which has a 31-room lodge at cliff's edge. A steep hiking trail down to the river provides a chance to stretch your legs. About 25 minutes on, detour south on US 19 to Canyon Rim Visitor Center, which provides information about the park and the region. You also get a good look at the New River Gorge Bridge, one of the highest bridges in the country. Linking the north and south rims of the gorge, it has become famous for its once-a-year parachute jumps in October. Dozens of parachutists leap from its concrete safety barriers and float 876 feet to the river sandbar below. A stairway takes you partway down the cliff for more river and bridge views. Continue east on US 60 to State Route 41, where you again detour south (right) to Babcock State Park to see its old stone gristmill and to try its hiking trails. Back on US 60, head east to Route 20 south to Hinton, a picturesque riverfront town. A river-level road leads to views of Sandstone Falls on the New. You can stay in Hinton or continue south on Route 20 to Pipestem Resort State Park, a 4,000-acre preserve with a 113-room lodge and an 18-hole golf course. From Pipestem, double back on Route 20 to Route 3 west to US 19 north to Beckley. Here you can ride a coal car deep into the Beckley Exhibition Coal Mine. From Beckley, take Route 61 north to Glen Jean and then head east on Route 25 to Thurmond, a former riverside mining boom town. The still-active train tracks run down the main street next to the sidewalk. An Amtrak station doubles as a railroad museum. Return to Route 61 north to I-64/I-77 and back to Charleston.

Aurora

See also Davis, Grafton

Settled 1787 **Pop** 150 **Elev** 2,641 ft
Area code 304 **Zip** 26705

Located at the summit of Cheat
Mountain, Aurora offers visitors
clean air and high altitude.

What to See and Do

Cathedral State Park. Hiking trails
through 132 acres of deep, virgin
hemlock forest; x-country skiing, picnicking. Standard hrs. 1 mi E on US
50. Phone 304/735-3771.

Beckley

(D-3) *See also Gauley Bridge, Hinton*

Founded 1838 **Pop** 17,254 **Elev** 2,416
ft **Area code** 304
Information Southern West Virginia
Convention and Visitors Bureau, PO
Box 1799, 25802; 304/252-
2244 or 800/VISIT-WV
Web www.visitwv.org

The "smokeless coal capital of
the world" is a center for
more than 200 small mining
and farming towns. Beckley is
situated on a high plateau
surrounded by fertile valleys.
During the Civil War the village was held at various times
by both armies; Union troops
shelled it in 1863. Coal was
found here in 1774 but was
not mined until 1890. Smokeless coal became the standard
bunker fuel during World War
I, and the demand continued
for years thereafter. Beckley
now serves as a commercial,
medical, and tourist center.

What to See and Do

Babcock State Park. More
than 4,100 acres of rugged
mountain scenery with trout
stream and waterfalls, views
of New River Canyon, rhododendrons (May-July); restored

operating gristmill. Swimming pool,
lake and stream fishing, boating
(rowboat, paddleboat rentals); hiking
trails, horseback riding, game courts
(equipt rentals), x-country skiing,
camping (electrical hookups), 26 cabins (rentals, spring and fall). Nature
and recreation programs (summer).
Standard hrs, fees. (Mid-Apr-Oct) 13
mi NE via US 19 to WV 41, near Lan-
disburg. Phone 304/438-3003.

Beckley Exhibition Coal Mine. Riding
tours in coal cars through 1,500 ft of
underground passageways, constant
56°F temperature; museum, coal
company house, superintendent of
coal mines house, church, campground. (Apr-Oct, daily) 1½ mi SE
off I-77, exit 44 on Ewart Ave in New
River Park. Phone 304/256-1747.
¢¢¢

**Grandview Unit of New River Gorge
National River.** Nearly 900 wooded
acres at the northern end of the New
River Gorge National River area (see
HINTON); offers spectacular overlooks of New River Gorge and Horseshoe Bend; rhododendron gardens.
Hiking trails, game courts (some
fees), x-country skiing, picnicking,
playgrounds, concession. Outdoor
dramas (June-Labor Day, Tues-Sun). 5

Sunrise on the New River Gorge

mi SE on US 19, then 5 mi NE via Airport, Glen Hedrick and Grandview rds. Contact Superintendent, PO Box 246, Glen Jean 25846. Phone 304/763-3715.

Lake Stephens. A 303-acre lake with swimming, fishing, boating; trailer camping (hookups). W of town. Phone 304/934-5323.

Plum Orchard Lake Wildlife Management Area. More than 3,200 acres with rabbit, grouse, squirrel hunting. Also 202-acre lake with more than six mi of shoreline; boating; fishing for bass, channel catfish, crappie, and bluegill; picnicking, playground, camping. 11 mi N on I-77 to Pax exit, then E on Rural Rte 23. Phone 304/469-9905.

Skiing. WinterPlace Ski Resort. On southern West Virginia's highest peak. Two quad, three triple, two double chairlifts; two surface lifts; ski school, rentals; snowmaking; snowtubing; cafeteria, lounge; restaurants; entertainment; children's program; sporting goods shops. Night skiing. Twenty-seven runs; longest run 1¼ mi; vertical drop 603 ft. Snowboard park. (Dec-late Mar, daily) 17 mi S via I-77 exit 28 (Ghent/Flat Top), follow signs. Phone 304/787-3221 or 800/607-SNOW. ¢¢¢¢

Twin Falls Resort State Park. Approx 4,000 acres with restored pioneer house and farm. Swimming pool; hiking trails, 18-hole golf course, clubhouse, tennis, game courts, picnicking, playground, restaurant, lodge, camping, 14 cabins (equipt rentals). Recreation center, programs. Standard hrs, fees. (Daily) 25 mi SW via WV 16 and WV 54, then W on WV 97, near Maben. Phone 304/294-4000.

Whitewater rafting. Many outfitters offer guided trips on the New and Gauley rivers. For a list of outfitters, contact the Southern West Virginia Convention and Visitors Bureau, PO Box 1799, 25802. Phone 304/252-2244.

Youth Museum of Southern West Virginia. Hands-on exhibits, planetarium, log house. (May-Labor Day, daily; rest of yr, Tues-Sat) Ewart Ave, in New River Park. Phone 304/252-3730. ¢¢

Special Events

Theatre West Virginia. Cliffside Amphitheatre. Outdoor musical dramas. Grandview Park, W on I-64, exit 129B, follow signs. Mid-June-mid-Aug. Contact PO Box 1205, 25802; 304/256-6800 or 800/666-9142.

Appalachian Festival. Tamarack. Exhibitions and demonstrations of native crafts; entertainment, food. Aug. Phone 304/252-7328.

Motels/Motor Lodges

★ **COMFORT INN.** *1909 Harper Rd (25801).* 304/255-2161; fax 304/255-2161; res 888/259-8542. www.comfort inn.com. 130 rms, 3 story. S, D $69-$110; under 19 free. Crib free. Pet accepted. TV; cable (premium). Complimentary continental bkfst. Restaurant nearby. Ck-out noon. Coin lndry. Meeting rms. Business servs avail. In-rm modem link. Sundries. Downhill ski 15 mi. Exercise equipt. Refrigerators, microwaves. Cr cds: A, C, D, DS, JCB, MC, V.
D ⊗ ⊠ ⊠ ⊠ SC

★ ★ **HAMPTON INN.** *110 Harper Park Dr (25801).* 304/252-2121; fax 304/255-6238; toll-free 800/426-7866. www.hamptoninn.com. 108 rms, 5 story. S, D $68-$99; under 18 free; higher rates Bridge Day. Crib free. TV; cable (premium). Pool. Complimentary continental bkfst, coffee in rms. Restaurant adj. Ck-out noon. Meeting rms. Business servs avail. In-rm modem link. Valet serv. Exercise equipt. Downhill ski 15 mi. Some refrigerators. Cr cds: A, C, D, DS, MC, V.
D ⊠ ⊠ ⊠ ⊠ SC

★ ★ **HOLIDAY INN.** *1924 Harper Rd (25801).* 304/255-1511; fax 304/256-0526; res 800/233-1466. www.holiday-inn.com. 104 rms, 3 story. No elvtr. Apr-Oct: S, D $59-$119; under 19 free; package plans; lower rates rest of yr. Crib free. TV; cable (premium). Heated pool. Restaurant 6 am-2 pm, 5-10 pm. Bar 3 pm-3 am; Sun to 1 am. Coffee in rms. Ck-out 1 pm. Exercise equipt. Coin lndry. Business servs avail. In-rm modem link. Valet serv. Downhill ski 15 mi. Some in-rm

whirlpools, refrigerators, microwaves.
Cr cds: A, C, D, DS, MC, V.

Berkeley Springs

See also Martinsburg

Founded 1776 **Pop** 735 **Elev** 612 ft
Area code 304 **Zip** 25411
Information Berkeley Springs-Morgan
County Chamber of Commerce, 127
Fairfax St; 304/258-3738 or 800/447-8797
Web www.berkeleysprings.com

Popularized by George Washington,
who surveyed the area for Lord Fairfax in 1748, Berkeley Springs is the
oldest spa in the nation. Fairfax later
granted the land around the springs
to Virginia. The town is officially
named Bath, for the famous watering
place in England, but the post office
is Berkeley Springs. The waters,
which are piped throughout the
town, are fresh and slightly sweet,
without the medicinal flavor of most
mineral springs. Washington and his
family returned again and again. The
popularity of the resort reached its
peak after the Revolutionary War,
becoming something of a summer
capital for Washingtonians in the
1830s. But like all resort towns,
Berkeley Springs declined as newer,
more fashionable spas came into
vogue. The Civil War completely
destroyed the town's economy.
Today, the town is again visited for
its healthful waters, spas, and charming downtown.

What to See and Do

Berkeley Springs State Park. Famous
resort with health baths of all types
(fees); five warm springs. Main bathhouse (daily; closed hols). Roman
bathhouse with second-floor
museum (Memorial Day-mid-Oct,
daily). Swimming pool (Memorial
Day-Labor Day, daily; fee). Center of
town. Phone 304/258-2711. Overlooking park is

The Castle. (1886) English-Norman castle built by Colonel
Samuel Taylor Suit for his fiancee
has the flavor of England's famous
Berkeley Castle, where King
Edward II was murdered in 1327.
Battlement tower walls are
indented with the cross of St.
George. Furnished with 17th- and
18th-century antiques; contains
pine-paneled library, carved staircase, interesting collections. Gift
shop. Tours. (Daily) Phone
304/258-3274. ¢¢¢

Cacapon Resort State Park. More
than 6,100 acres with swimming,
sand beach, fishing, boating (rowboat and paddleboat rentals); hiking
and bridle trails, horseback riding,
18-hole golf course, tennis, game
courts, x-country skiing, picnicking,
playground, concession, restaurant,
lodge. No camping; 30 cabins.
Nature, recreation programs. Nature
center. Standard hrs, fees. 10 mi S off
US 522. Phone 304/258-1022.

**Sleepy Creek Wildlife Management
Area.** Approx 23,000 acres of rugged
forest offer wild turkey, deer, grouse,
and squirrel hunting; boating and
bass fishing on 205-acre lake; primitive camping (fee). Also 70 mi of hiking trails crossing two mountains,
several valleys. 15 mi SE, E of US
522. Phone 304/754-3855.

View from Prospect Peak. Potomac
River winds through what the
National Geographic Society has
called one of the nation's outstanding vistas. On WV 9, near town.

Special Event

Apple Butter Festival. Crafts demonstrations, music, contests. Columbus
Day wkend. Phone 800/447-8797.

Motel/Motor Lodge

★ **SUPER 8.** *118 Limestone Rd, Hancock (21750). 301/678-6101; fax
301/678-5376. www.super8.com.* 50
rms, 2 story. S, D $60-$85; under 18
free. Crib free. Pet accepted.TV; cable
(premium). In-rm modem link. Complimentary continental bkfst. Restaurant nearby. Ck-out noon. Some
refrigerators. Cr cds: A, C, D, DS,
MC, V.

GEORGE WASHINGTON'S SPA AND BERKELEY SPRINGS

Tucked in a narrow, rock-shadowed valley along the Cacapon River, the little mountain community of Berkeley Springs has transformed itself into "Spa Town USA." A total of five separate spas employ more than 40 massage therapists—three times the number of practicing lawyers, town officials claim. The clustering of so many spas in the town is relatively new, but Berkeley Springs has a long heritage as a spa destination. Well before white settlers arrived, Native Americans sought out the warm, 74.3-degree mineral springs. Still bubbling forth from the base of Warm Springs Ridge at 2,000 gallons per minute, the water was believed to have curative powers. George Washington, who first visited the springs in 1748 as a 16-year-old surveyor, returned nearly a dozen times in later years seeking health benefits. In 1776, he and prominent friends and family established the Town of Bath, intent on making it a popular spa, and the first bath houses were built. Because of this, Berkeley Springs claims to be "the country's first spa." You can explore the town's spa heritage in a 30-minute, half-mile stroll in Berkeley Springs State Park, which doubles as the community's town square. One of America's most curious public parklands, the seven-acre Berkeley Springs State Park operates year-round as a very affordable government-run spa. Begin a loop around the park at the large public swimming pool, fed by spring waters. Heading clockwise, take a peek inside the Main Bath House, where you can enjoy a private hot-tub soak and Swedish-style massage. Continue on to a stone-lined natural pool of flowing spring water, dubbed George Washington's Bath Tub in his honor. Move on to the Gentlemen's Spring House, where you are welcome to draw jugs of the famed drinking water for free. Conclude this plunge into historic bathing with a look into the Roman Bath House, where you can indulge in a private hot-tub soak without an accompanying massage.

Resorts

★ ★ **CACAPON STATE PARK.** *818 Cacapon Cr (25411). 304/258-1022; fax 304/258-5323; res 800/225-5982. www.cacaponresort.com.* 48 rms, 3 story, 31 kit. cabins. Apr-Oct: S, D $64-$70; each addl $6; kit. cabins, $282-$648/wk; lower rates rest of yr. Crib free in lodge, $5 in cabins. TV; cable (premium). Dining rm 7 am-9 pm; winter 8 am-7 pm. Ck-out noon, ck-in 3 pm. Meeting rms. In-rm modem link. Gift shop. Tennis. 18-hole golf, greens fee $25-$30, putting green, driving range. Game rm. Rec rm. Picnic tables. Near lake; boat rentals, sandy beach. Hiking trails. Naturalist program (Apr-Oct). State-operated. Cr cds: A, D, DS, MC, V.

D ♿ ⚕ 🎿 ⛷ 🛶 🔥

★ ★ **COOLFONT RESORT.** *3621 Cold Run Valley Rd (25411). 304/258-4500; fax 304/258-5499; toll-free 800/888-8768. www.coolfont.com.* 19 rms in main building, 2 story, 34 cottages. MAP, Oct: S $111-$201; D $174-$268; each addl $84-$94; cottages $112-$144; package plans; fitness plan; wkends, hols (3 day min);

lower rates rest of yr. Crib $10. Heated indoor pool; whirlpool. Playground. Supervised children's activities (June-Aug; wkends only rest of yr); ages 5-12. Complimentary coffee in rms. Dining rm 8 am-2 pm, 5:30-8:30 pm; Fri, Sat to 9:30 pm; Sun 8 am-3 pm, 5:30-8 pm. Snacks. Picnics. Bar; entertainment Sat. Ck-out 11 am, ck-in 4 pm. Gift shop. Coin lndry. Meeting rms. In-rm modem link. Tennis. Swimming beach; boats. X-country ski on site. Fishing. Sleighing. Hiking. Lawn games. Exercise rm; sauna. Massage. Microwaves avail. Some refrigerators, balconies. Picnic tables. Secluded woodland resort on 1,350 acres. Cr cds: A, D, DS, MC, V.

D ♿ ⚕ ⛷ ⛷ 🛶 🏃 🏊 🔥

B&Bs/Small Inns

★ ★ ★ **COUNTRY INN.** *207 S Washington St (25411). 304/258-2210; fax 304/258-3986; toll-free 800/822-6630. www.countryinnwv.com.* 70 rms, 13 share bath, 3 story. S, D $39-$115; each addl $15; suites $175; hol wkends 2-night min; some wkday rates. TV; cable (premium), VCR avail (movies). Dining rm 7-11 am, 11:30 am-2 pm, 5-9 pm; Fri, Sat to 10 pm. Private club 11 am-11 pm; entertainment Sat, Sun. Ck-out noon, ck-in 3 pm. Meeting rms. Business servs avail. Gift shop. Massage. Colonial design. Mineral baths and spa. Cr cds: A, C, D, DS, MC, V.

D ⌖ 🔥 SC

★ ★ ★ **HIGHLAWN INN.** *304 Market St (25411). 304/258-5700; toll-free 888/290-4163. www.highlawninn.com.* 12 rms in 4 buildings, 2-3 story. No rm phones. S, D $85-$195; whirlpool suite $195. Children over 14 only. TV; cable (premium), VCR (movies). Complimentary full bkfst; afternoon refreshments. Ck-out noon, ck-in 2 pm. Some whirlpools, fireplaces. Victorian mansion; built 1897. Antiques. Cr cds: MC, V.

D ⌖ 🔥

Bethany

See also Weirton, Wheeling

Pop 985 **Elev** 932 ft **Area code** 304 **Zip** 26032

What to See and Do

Bethany College. (1840) 800 students. Founded by Alexander Campbell, the leading influence in the 19th-century religious movement that gave rise to the Disciples of Christ, Churches of Christ, and Christian churches. Historic buildings on 300-acre campus incl Old Main, styled after the University of Glasgow in Scotland; Pendleton Heights, a 19th-century house used as the college president's residence; Old Bethany Meeting House (1852), Delta Tau Delta Founder's House (1854), and the

    Campbell Mansion. A 24-rm house where Campbell lived; antique furnishings. On property is hexagonal brick study, one-rm schoolhouse, and smokehouse. The Campbell family cemetery, "God's Acre," is across from the mansion. (Apr-Oct, Tues-Sun; rest of yr, by appt) Phone 304/829-7285. ¢¢

Bluefield

(E-3) See also Princeton

Founded 1889 **Pop** 11,451 **Elev** 2,611 ft **Area code** 304 **Zip** 24701
Information Convention and Visitors Bureau, 500 Bland St, PO Box 4099; 304/325-8438 or 800/221-3206
Web www.bluestonecvb.com

Named for the bluish chicory covering the nearby hills, Bluefield owes its existence to the Pocahontas Coal Field. The town came to life in the 1880s when the railroad came through to transport coal. This commercial and industrial center of southern West Virginia is known as nature's "air-conditioned city" because of its altitude—one-half mile above sea level. Bluefield has a sister city by the same name in Virginia, directly across the state line.

What to See and Do

Eastern Regional Coal Archives. Center highlights the history of West Virginia coal fields; exhibits, photographs, mining implements; films, research material. (Mon-Fri afternoons; closed hols) In Craft Memorial Library, 600 Commerce St. Phone 304/325-3943. **FREE**

Panther State Forest. More than 7,800 acres of rugged hills. Swimming pool (Memorial Day-Labor Day), fishing; hunting, hiking trails, picnicking, playground, concession, camping. Standard hrs, fees. 50 mi NW off US 52 near Panther. Phone 304/938-2252.

Pinnacle Rock State Park. Approx 250-acre park contains a 15-acre lake and interesting sandstone formations, which resemble a giant cockscomb. Hiking, picnicking. Standard hrs, fees. 7 mi NW on US 52. Phone 304/248-8565.

Motels/Motor Lodges

★ **ECONO LODGE.** *3400 Cumberland Rd (24701). 304/327-8171; fax 304/324-4259. www.econolodge.com.* 47 rms, 2 story. S, D $49-$54; each addl $5; under 18 free. Crib free. Pet accepted; $10. TV; cable (premium). Coffee in lobby. Complimentary continental bkfst. Restaurant nearby. In-rm modem link. Ck-out 11 am. Business servs avail. Some refrigerators. Cr cds: A, C, D, DS, MC, V.

★★ **HOLIDAY INN.** *3350 Big Laurel Hwy (24701). 304/325-6170; fax 304/323-2451; toll-free 800/465-4329. www.holiday-inn.com.* 120 rms, 2 story. S, D $73-$90; each addl $10; suites $120-$150; under 18 free. Crib free. Pet accepted. TV; cable (premium), VCR avail. Heated pool. Saunas. Restaurant 6 am-2 pm, 5 pm-10 pm. Rm serv. Ck-out noon. Meeting rms. In-rm modem link. Exercise equipt. Valet serv Mon-Fri. Cr cds: A, C, D, DS, ER, JCB, MC, V.

★ **RAMADA INN.** *3175 E Cumberland Rd (24701). 304/325-5421; fax 304/325-6045; res 800/333-3333. www.ramada.com.* 98 rms, 2 story. May-early Sept: S $63; D $90; each addl $5; under 18 free; wkend, wkly rates; ski plans; wkends; lower rates rest of yr. Crib free. Pet accepted. TV; cable (premium), VCR avail. Restaurant 6 am-10 pm. Rm serv 24 hrs. Bar 5 pm-1 am; entertainment Fri, Sat. Ck-out noon. Meeting rms. Business servs avail. In-rm modem link. Bellhops. Valet serv. Sundries. Exercise equipt; saunas. Heated indoor pool; wading pool, whirlpool, poolside serv. Game rm. Rec rm. Some refrigerators; microwaves avail. Cr cds: A, C, D, DS, MC, V.

Restaurant

★ **MAYFLOWER I.** *105 Hockman Pike (24605). 540/322-4578.* Hrs: 4-9:30 pm; Sat 2-9 pm; Sun 11:30 am-8 pm. Closed Mon; hols. Seafood menu. Dinner $6.30-$18. Child's menu. Specializes in seafood platters. Casual atmosphere with nautical decor. Cr cds: MC, V.

Buckhannon

(C-4) *See also Elkins, Philippi, Weston*

Settled 1770 **Pop** 5,725 **Elev** 1,433 ft **Area code** 304 **Zip** 26201
Information Buckhannon-Upshur Chamber of Commerce, 16 S Kanawha St, PO Box 442; 304/472-1722

What to See and Do

Audra State Park. Approx 360 acres offer swimming in a natural mountain stream surrounded by tall timber; bathhouse. Hiking trails, picnicking, playground, concession, tent and trailer camping. Standard hrs, fees. 8 mi N on US 119, then 6 mi E on WV 11. Phone 304/457-1162.

Holly River State Park. More than 8,100 acres and the second largest state park in the state. Camping, cabins, picnicking, hiking. Standard fees. 32 mi S of Buckhannon on WV 20. Phone 304/493-6353.

West Virginia State Wildlife Center. Fenced-in habitats of approx 50 species of birds and animals native to West Virginia, incl deer, elk, buffalo, timber wolf, mountain lion, and black bear. Loop walkway (1¼ mi). Trout pond; picnicking, concession. (May-Oct, daily; Apr and Nov, wkends and hols only; Dec-Mar, days vary) 12 mi S on WV 4, 20. Phone 304/924-6211. ¢

West Virginia Wesleyan College. (1890) 1,600 students. An 80-acre campus featuring Georgian architecture. Wesley Chapel, the largest place of worship in the state, contains a Casavant organ with 1,474 pipes. College Ave and Meade St. Phone 304/473-8000.

Special Event

West Virginia Strawberry Festival. Parades, dances, exhibits, air show, arts and crafts, other activities. Phone 304/472-9036. Usually wk before Memorial Day.

Motels/Motor Lodges

★ **CENTENNIAL MOTEL.** *22 N Locust St (26201).* 304/472-4100; fax 304/472-4100. 25 rms. S $36.95-$42.95; D $42.95-$48.95; each addl $6; under 12 free. Crib free. Pet accepted. TV; cable (premium). Complimentary coffee in lobby. Restaurant nearby. Ck-out noon. Cr cds: A, D, DS, MC, V.

★★ **BICENTENNIAL MOTEL.** *90 E Main St (26201).* 304/472-5000; fax 304/472-9159; res 800/762-5137. 50 rms, 2 story. S, D $59-$69; each addl $5; under 12 free. Crib free. Pet accepted; $10. TV; cable (premium). Pool. Playground. Restaurant 6 am-9 pm. Private club 4 pm-midnight. Ck-out noon. Meeting rms. Business servs avail. In-rm modem link. Sundries. Some refrigerators. Picnic tables, grills. Cr cds: A, D, DS, MC, V.

Charleston

(D-3) See also Nitro

Settled 1794 **Pop** 53,421 **Elev** 601 ft
Area code 304
Information Convention & Visitors Bureau, Charleston Civic Center, 200 Civic Center Dr, 25301; 304/344-5075 or 800/733-5469
Web www.charlestonwv.com

Charleston, the state capital, is the trading hub for the Great Kanawha Valley, where deposits of coal, oil, natural gas, and brine have greatly contributed to this region's national importance as a production center for chemicals and glass. Two institutions of higher learning, West Virginia State College and the University of Charleston, are located in the metropolitan area. Charleston is also the northern terminus of the spectacular West Virginia Turnpike.

Daniel Boone lived around Charleston until 1795. During his residence he was appointed a lieutenant colonel in the county militia in 1789 and was elected to the Virginia assembly the same year. The area became important as a center of salt production in 1824, when steam engines were used to operate brine pumps. After Charleston became the capital of West Virginia in 1885, following a dispute with Wheeling, the town came into its own. During World War I, an increased demand for plate and bottle glass, as well as for high explosives, made Charleston and the nearby town of Nitro (see) boom.

What to See and Do

Coonskin Park. Recreation area incl swimming, fishing for bass and cat-

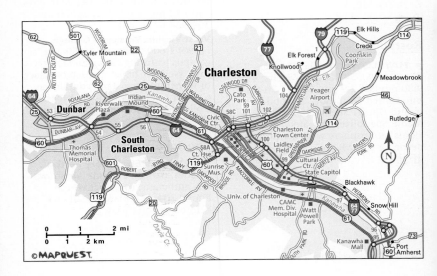

State Capitol, Charleston

fish, pedal boating; hiking trails, 18-hole golf, miniature golf, tennis. Picnicking, playground, concession. (Daily; closed Dec 25; some activities seasonal) Fees for activities. ¾ mi N off WV 114. Phone 304/341-8000.

Cultural Center. The Center houses the Division of Culture and History and Library Commission; archives library (Mon-Sat); state museum; special events, changing exhibits. (Daily; closed hols) Next to state capitol, on Greenbrier St. Phone 304/558-0220. **FREE** Also here is

> **Mountain Stage.** Live public radio show heard on stations nationwide; features jazz, folk, blues, and rock. Visitors may watch show; afternoon performances (Sun). Phone 304/342-5757. ¢¢

Elk River Scenic Drive. Beautiful drive along the Elk River from Charleston northeast to Sutton (approx 60 mi). Begins just north of town; take US 119 NE to Clendenin, then WV 4 NE to US 19 in Sutton.

Kanawha State Forest. Approx 9,300 acres with swimming pool, bathhouse (Memorial Day-Labor Day); hunting, hiking, interpretive trail for the disabled, horseback riding, x-country skiing, picnicking, playground, concession, camping. Standard hrs, fees. 7 mi S off US 119. Phone 304/558-3500.

State Capitol. (1932) One of America's most beautiful state capitols, the building was designed by Cass Gilbert in Italian Renaissance style. Within the gold-leaf dome, which rises 300 ft above the street, hangs a 10,080-piece, hand-cut imported chandelier weighing more than two tons. Guided tours avail. (Mon-Fri, Sat afternoons) On river at E Kanawha Blvd between Greenbrier St and California Ave. Phone 304/558-4839. **FREE** Across the grounds is the

> **Governor's Mansion.** (1925) Beautiful Georgian structure of red Harvard brick with white Corinthian columns. Tours (Thurs and Fri, also by appt). 1716 Kanawha Blvd E. Phone 304/558-3809. **FREE**

Sunrise Museum. On 16 acres of wooded grounds with gardens and trails, this art and science museum is housed in two historic mansions built by William MacCorkle, ninth governor of West Virginia. Guided tours by appt. (Wed-Sun; closed hols) 746 Myrtle Rd, across South Side Bridge. Phone 304/344-8035. ¢¢

Art Museum. American paintings, graphics, and sculpture from 19th through 20th centuries; rotating exhibits; films and lectures. Phone 800/344-8035. ¢¢

Science Museum. Exhibits in natural sciences and technology; planetarium, programs, lectures. Interactive exhibits, demonstrations. Phone 800/344-8035. ¢¢

West Virginia State College. (1891) 4,635 students. On campus are Davis Fine Arts Building with periodic exhibits (Mon-Sat; closed hols); Asian art collection in library (daily; closed hols); and East Hall (1895), formerly president's residence. Tours. 8 mi W via I-64 exit 50, in Institute. Phone 304/766-3000.

Whitewater rafting. Many outfitters offer guided rafting, canoeing, and fishing trips on the New and Gauley rivers. For a list of outfitters contact the West Virginia Division of Tourism, Research, and Development, 90 Mac Corkle Ave SW, South Charleston, WV 25303. Phone 800/225-5982.

Special Events

Vandalia Gathering. A festival of traditional arts; craft demonstrations, clogging, gospel music, fiddling, banjo picking, special exhibits. Memorial Day wkend. Phone 304/558-0220.

Sternwheel Regatta Festival. Sternwheeler and towboat races, parades, contests, hot-air balloon race, fireworks; nationally known entertainers nightly; arts and crafts. Late Aug-early Sept. Phone 304/348-6419.

Motels/Motor Lodges

★ ★ **DAYS INN.** *6400 SE MacCorkle Ave (25304). 304/925-1010; fax 304/925-1364; res 800/329-7466. www.daysinn.com.* 147 rms, 2-3 story. S, D $55-$95; each addl $5; under 12 free. Crib free. Pet accepted, some restrictions. TV; cable (premium). Complimentary continental bkfst, coffee in rms. Restaurant nearby. Ck-out 11 am. Meeting rms. Business servs avail. In-rm modem link. Sundries. Valet serv. Exercise equipt. Pool. Many refrigerators, microwaves. Cr cds: A, D, DS, MC, V.
🄳 🐾 ⊷ 🖍 ⊷ 🖎

★ ★ **HAMPTON INN.** *1 Virginia St W (25302). 304/343-9300; fax 304/342-9393. www.hamptoninn.com.* 110 rms, 5 story. S, D $81-$94; each addl $5; under 18 free; higher rates basketball tournament. Crib free. TV; cable (premium). Heated pool; whirlpool. Complimentary continental bkfst. Restaurant nearby. Ck-out noon. Meeting rm. Business servs avail. Exercise rm. Sundries. Free airport, RR station transportation. Cr cds: A, D, DS, MC, V.
🄳 ⊷ 🖍 ⊷ 🖎 SC

★ ★ **HAMPTON INN.** *1 Preferred Pl (25309). 304/746-4646; fax 304/746-4665. www.hamptoninn.com.* 104 rms, 6 story. S $78-$135; D $83-$135; each addl $5; under 18 free. Crib free. TV; cable (premium). Heated indoor pool; whirlpool. Complimentary continental bkfst. Coffee in rms. Restaurant adj 10-1 am. Ck-out noon. Meeting rms. Business center. In-rm modem link. Sundries. Coin lndry. Free airport transportation. Valet serv. Exercise equipt. Some in-rm whirlpools, refrigerators, microwaves. Cr cds: A, C, D, DS, JCB, MC, V.
🄳 ⊷ 🖍 ⊷ 🖎 SC 🖍

★ ★ **HOLIDAY INN.** *600 Kanawha Blvd E (25301). 304/344-4092; fax 304/345-4847; toll-free 800/465-4329. www.holiday-inn.com.* 256 rms, 12 story. S, D $69-$109; each addl $6; under 18 free; suites $169-$375; wkend rates; package plans. Crib $8. TV; cable (premium). Heated pool. Restaurant 6:30 am-2 pm; dining rm 5-10 pm. Bar 4 pm-2 am; closed Sun. Coffee in rms. Ck-out noon. Convention facilities. Business servs avail. In-rm modem link. Coin lndry. Valet serv. Barber, beauty shop. Gift shop. Garage $2/day. Free airport transportation. Exercise equipt. Some refrigerators, wet bars. Some rms with river view. Cr cds: A, C, D, DS, JCB, MC, V.
🄳 ⊷ 🖍 ⊷ 🖎 SC

★ ★ **HOLIDAY INN EXPRESS - CIVIC CENTER.** *100 Civic Center Dr (25301). 304/345-0600; fax 304/343-1322. www.charleston-holidayinn.com.* 196 rms, 6 story. S, D $81-$91; under 18 free; wkend rates. Crib free. Pet accepted, some restrictions; $15. TV; cable, VCR avail. Restaurant nearby 6 am-midnight. Complimentary continental bkfst. Coffee in rms. Ck-out noon. Coin lndry. Meeting rms. Business servs avail. In-rm moden link. Exercise equipt. Bellhops. Valet serv. Free airport transportation. Some refrigerators. Cr cds: A, C, D, DS, JCB, MC, V.

⬛ D ⬛ ⬛ SC

★ **KANAWHA CITY MOTOR LODGE.** *3103 MacCorkle Ave SE (25304). 304/344-2461; fax 304/345-1419.* 50 rms, 2 story. S $51-$60; D $56-$61; each addl $5; kit. units $62; under 18 free. Crib $5. TV; cable (premium). Complimentary coffee in lobby. Restaurant nearby. Ck-out 1 pm. Business servs avail. Charleston Memorial Hospital opp. Cr cds: A, C, D, DS, MC, V.

D ⬛ ⬛ SC

★ **RED ROOF INN.** *6305 MacCorkle Ave SE, Kanawha City (25304). 304/925-6953; fax 304/925-8111; toll-free 800/843-7663. www.redroof.com.* 108 rms, 2 story. Apr-Oct: S $39-$44; D $42-$70; each addl $5; under 18 free; higher rates special events; lower rates rest of yr. Crib free. Pet accepted. TV; cable (premium). Complimentary coffee in lobby. Restaurant adj 6 am-10:30 pm. Ck-out noon. Business servs avail. Cr cds: A, C, D, DS, MC, V.

D ⬛ ⬛ ⬛ SC

Hotel

★ ★ ★ **MARRIOTT TOWN CENTER CHARLESTON.** *200 Lee St E (25301). 304/345-6500; fax 304/353-3722; toll-free 800/228-9290. www.marriott.com.* 352 rms, 15 story. S, D $59-$129; suites $275-$295; wkend rates. Garage $4.50/day. Crib free. TV; cable (premium), VCR avail. Heated indoor pool; whirlpool, poolside serv. Coffee in rms. Restaurant 6:30 am-11 pm; Sun 7 am-10 pm; dining rm 5:30-11 pm. Rm serv. Bar 11-1 am. Coffee in rms. Ck-out noon. Coin lndry. Free airport transportation. Meeting rms. Business center. In-rm modem link. Gift shop. Bellhops. Valet serv. Exercise equipt; sauna. Some refrigerators. Luxury level. Many balconies. Cr cds: A, C, D, DS, MC, V.

D ⬛ ⬛ ⬛ ⬛ SC ⬛

Restaurants

★ ★ **BLOSSOM DELI.** *904 Quarrier St (25301). 304/345-2233.* Hrs: 8 am-9 pm; Mon to 3 pm; Fri to 10 pm; Sat 10 am-3 pm, 5-10 pm. Closed Sun; hols. Res accepted (dinner). Eclectic menu. Bkfst $1-$2, lunch $5.50-$17.25, dinner $8.25-$17.50. Specialties: create your own pasta, Mediterranean chicken, filet au poivre. Street parking. Decor of 1940s; soda fountain, dairy bar. Totally nonsmoking. Cr cds: A, D, DS, MC, V.

D

★ ★ **CHEF DAN'S.** *222 Leon Sullivan Way (25301). 304/344-2433.* Hrs: 11 am-9 pm; Fri to 10 pm; Sat 4-10 pm. Closed Sun, Mon; hols. Continental menu. Bar. Lunch, dinner $3.95-$17.95. Buffet: lunch $8.95. Child's menu. Specializes in pasta, pizza. Bistro decor. Cr cds: A, D, DS, MC, V.

D SC ⬛

★ ★ ★ **JOE FAZIO'S SPAGHETTI HOUSE.** *1008 Bullitt St (25301). 304/344-3071.* Hrs: 5-10 pm. Closed Mon; Jan 1, Easter, Dec 24, 25. Res accepted. Italian, American menu. Serv bar. Dinner $11-$21. Child's menu. Specializes in veal, chicken, steak. Parking. Family-owned. Cr cds: A, D, MC, V.

D SC

★ ★ ★ **LAURY'S.** *350 MacCorkle Ave SE (25314). 304/343-0055.* Hrs: 11 am-2 pm, 5-11 pm; Sat 5-10 pm. Closed Sun; hols. Res accepted. Continental menu. Bar. Lunch $4.95-$10.95, dinner $12.95-$49.95. Specialties: châteaubriand, veal, rack of lamb, lobster diablo. Entertainment Fri, Sat. Near Kanawha River. Renovated train depot. Cr cds: A, C, D, DS, MC, V.

D SC ⬛

Charles Town

See also Harpers Ferry, Martinsburg, Shepherdstown; also see Winchester, VA

Founded 1786 **Pop** 2,907 **Elev** 530 ft
Area code 304 **Zip** 25414

Information Jefferson County Chamber of Commerce, 201 Frontage Rd, PO Box 426; 304/725-2055

Web www.jeffersoncounty.com/chamber

Charles Town is serene, aristocratic, and full of tradition, with orderly, tree-shaded streets and 18th-century houses. It was named for George Washington's youngest brother, Charles, who laid out the town and named most of the streets after members of his family. Charles Washington's family lived here for many years. Charles Town is also famed as the place where John Brown was jailed, tried, and hanged in 1859 after his raid on Harpers Ferry.

What to See and Do

Charles Town Races and Gaming. Thoroughbred racing; clubhouse, video machines, dining rm. (Daily; closed hols) 1 mi E on US 340. Phone 304/725-7001. **FREE**

Jefferson County Courthouse. (1836) This red brick, Georgian Colonial structure was the scene of John Brown's trial, one of three treason trials held in the US before WWII. The courthouse was shelled during the Civil War but was later rebuilt; the original courtroom survived both the shelling and fires and is open to the public. In 1922, leaders of the miners' armed march on Logan City were tried here; one, Walter Allen, was convicted and sentenced to ten yrs. (Mon-Fri; closed hols) Corner of N George and E Washington sts. Phone 304/728-3240. **FREE**

Jefferson County Museum. Houses John Brown memorabilia, old guns, Civil War artifacts. (Apr-Nov, Mon-Sat) N Samuel and E Washington sts. Phone 304/725-8628. **Donation**

Site of John Brown Gallows. Marked by pyramid of three stones supposedly taken from Brown's cell in Charles Town jail. At execution, 1,500 troops were massed around the scaffold. Some were commanded by Major Thomas "Stonewall" Jackson; among them was John Wilkes Booth, Virginia militiaman. S Samuel and Hunter sts.

Tours of Charles Town. Historical walking tours; candlelit tours of Jefferson County Courthouse (eves);

carriage rides. All tours by appt. Phone 304/728-7713. **FREE**

Zion Episcopal Church. (1852) Buried in cemetery around church are about 75 members of Washington family, as well as many Revolutionary War and Confederate soldiers. (Interior, by appt) E Congress between S Mildred and S Church sts. Phone 304/725-5312.

Special Events

Founders Day-Washington Heritage. Exhibits, performances, tours. First wkend May. Phone 800/733-5469.

Jefferson County Fair. Livestock show, entertainment, amusement rides, exhibits. Late Aug. Phone 304/728-7415.

Motels/Motor Lodges

★ **TOWNE HOUSE MOTOR LODGE.** *549 E Washington St (25414).* 304/725-8441; fax 304/725-5484; toll-free 800/227-2339. 115 rms, 2 story. Mar-mid-Nov: S $30-$45; D $35-$45; each addl $5; lower rates rest of yr. Crib free. TV; cable (premium). Pool. Restaurant adj 7 am-8 pm; Fri, Sat to 9 pm. Ck-out 11 am. Business servs avail. Refrigerators. Cr cds: A, C, D, DS, MC, V.
🅳 ⛱ 🛰 🐾

★ **TURF MOTEL.** *608 E Washington St (25414).* 304/725-2081; fax 304/728-7605; toll-free 800/422-8873. 45 rms, 2 story, 6 kits. June-Labor Day: S, D $42-$60; each addl $2-$5; suites $80-$160; kit. units $65-$85; lower rates rest of yr. Crib free. Pet accepted; $50. TV; cable (premium). Pool. Restaurant 6:30 am-9 pm; Fri, Sat to 10 pm. Rm serv. Bar 10-2 am. Ck-out 11:30 am. Business servs avail. In-rm modem link. Free RR station transportation. Some balconies. Refrigerators, microwaves avail. Cr cds: A, C, D, DS, MC, V.
🅳 🐾 ⛱ 🛰 🐾 SC

Chesapeake and Ohio Canal National Historical Park

(See Maryland)

Clarksburg

(C-4) *See also Fairmont, Grafton, Weston*

Settled 1773 **Pop** 16,743 **Elev** 1,007 ft
Area code 304 **Zip** 26301
Information Greater Bridgeport Conference and Visitors Center, 164 W Main St, Bridgeport 26330; 304/842-7272 or 800/368-4324
Web www.bridgeport-clarksburg.com

In the heart of the West Virginia hills, Clarksburg is the trading center for an area of grading lands, coal mines, and oil and gas fields. The Criminal Justice Information Services Division of the FBI is located here. During the Civil War it was an important supply base for Union troops. The famous Civil War General "Stonewall" Jackson was born in Clarksburg in 1824. His statue stands before the courthouse.

What to See and Do

North Bend Rail Trail. Seventy-one mi of scenic countryside trails featuring 13 tunnels, numerous bridges, and several historic sites. Bike, hike, or horseback ride trail from nearby Wilsonburg to North Bend State Park (see PARKERSBURG). I-79, exit 119 to US 50. Phone 304/643-2500. **FREE**

Salem International University. (1888) 750 students. On campus is the Jennings Randolph Center (by appt; fee), which houses papers and memorabilia of the former senator. 12 mi W in Salem. Phone 304/782-5011. Also here is

    Fort New Salem. Collection of 20 log houses from throughout the state were relocated to campus;

pioneer history is re-created through crafts and folklore. Special events throughout the yr (fee); summer concerts (July, Sat eves). (Memorial Day wkend-Oct, Wed-Sun; Apr-mid-May, Mon-Fri) Phone 304/782-5245. ¢¢

Stealey-Goff-Vance House. (1807) House restored by Harrison County Historical Society as museum with period rms, antique furniture, tools, Native American artifacts. (May-Sept, Fri, limited hrs) 123 W Main St. Phone 304/842-3073. ¢

Watters Smith Memorial State Park. More than 500 acres on Duck Creek with visitor center/museum and 19th-century pioneer homestead. Swimming pool (seasonal); hiking, game courts, picnicking, playground, concession. Recreation building. Standard hrs, fees. 8 mi S on US 19, then SE on unnumbered road. Phone 304/745-3081.

Special Event

West Virginia Italian Heritage Festival. Italian arts, music, contests, entertainment. Labor Day wkend. Phone 304/622-7314.

Motels/Motor Lodges

★ ★ **HOLIDAY INN CLARKSBURG.** *100 Lodgeville Rd, Bridgeport (26330). 304/842-5411; fax 304/842-7258; res 800/465-4329. www.holiday-inn.com.* 159 rms, 2 story. S, D $79-$110; under 19 free. Crib free. Pet accepted. TV; cable (premuim). Pool. Restaurant 6 am-11 am, 5-10 pm; Sat, Sun 7 am-11 am, 5-10 pm. Private club 5 pm-10 pm; closed Sat, Sun. Coffee in rms. Ck-out noon. Meeting rms. Business servs avail. In-rm modem link. Valet serv. Sundries. Some refrigerators. Airport transportation. Cr cds: A, C, D, DS, JCB, MC, V.
🅳 ⬛ ⬛ ⬛ ⬛ ⬛

★ ★ **RAMADA LIMITED.** *250 Emily Dr (26301). 304/623-2600; fax 304/622-5240; res 800/272-6232. www.ramada.com.* 112 rms, 2 story. S, D $49.95-$54.95; each addl $5; under 18 free. Crib free. TV; cable (premium). Complimentary continental bkfst. Coffee in rms. Restaurant adj 11 am-10 pm. Ck-out noon. Meeting rms. Business servs avail. In-rm modem link. Sundries. Some Refrigerators. Cr cds: A, D, DS, MC, V.

★ **SLEEP INN.** *115 Tolley Dr, Bridgeport (26330). 304/842-1919; fax 304/842-9524; res 800/753-3746. www.sleepinn.com.* 73 rms, 2 story. S $59; D $69; under 18 free. Crib free. Pet accepted. TV; cable (premium), VCR avail. Complimentary continental bkfst. Restaurant nearby. Ck-out 11 am. Meeting rms. Business servs avail. Coin lndry. Valet serv. Microwaves, refrigerators avail. Cr cds: A, D, DS, JCB, MC, V.

Restaurants

★ ★ ★ **JIM REID'S.** *1422 Buckhannon Pike, Nutter Fort (26301). 304/623-4909.* Hrs: 11 am-2 pm, 5-10 pm; Sun noon-8 pm. Closed Mon; hols. Res accepted. Bar. Wine list. Complete meals: lunch $4.25-$6.50, dinner $11-$25. Child's menu. Specializes in fresh seafood, prime rib, steak. Family-owned. Cr cds: A, D, MC, V.

★ ★ **MINARD'S SPAGHETTI INN.** *813 E Pike St (26301). 304/623-1711.* Hrs: 11 am-10 pm; Fri, Sat to 11 pm. Closed hols. Res accepted. Italian menu. Wine, beer. Lunch $4.50-$6.75, dinner $7-$24. Child's menu. Specializes in steak, spaghetti. Italian decor. Cr cds: A, D, DS, MC, V.

Davis

See also Aurora, Elkins

Founded 1883 **Pop** 624 **Elev** 3,099 ft
Area code 304 **Zip** 26260
Information West Virginia Mountain Highlands, PO Box 1456, Elkins 26241; 304/636-8400

Davis, the highest town in the state, was founded by Henry Gassaway Davis, US senator from 1871-1883. Senator Davis established the first

night train in America (1848). He and his son-in-law, Senator Stephen B. Elkins, became wealthy from coal, lumber, and railroading.

What to See and Do

Blackwater Falls State Park. This 1,688-acre park incl a deep river gorge with 66-ft falls of dark, amber-colored water. Swimming in lake (fee), bath houses (Memorial Day-Labor Day), fishing, boating (rowboat, paddleboat rentals); nature trails, horseback riding; x-country ski trails, center (rentals, school); sledding, picnicking, playground, concession, lodge, cabins, tent and trailer campground. Nature, recreation programs and tours. Paved falls viewing area for the disabled. Standard hrs, fees. 2 mi W off WV 32. Phone 304/259-5216.

Canaan Valley Resort State Park. Approx 6,000 acres incl valley 3,200 ft above sea level, which is surrounded by spectacular mountain peaks. Swimming pool, bathhouse, fishing, boating; hiking trails, 18-hole golf course, tennis courts, skiing, ice rink, playground, lodge, cabins, camping (dump station). Nature, recreation programs. Standard hrs, fees. 9 mi S on WV 32. Phone 304/866-4121.

Ski areas.

Timberline Four Seasons Resort. Triple, two double chairlifts; patrol, school, SKIwee program, rentals; snowmaking; restaurant, bar; nursery; lodging, night skiing and special events. Thirty-five slopes and trails; longest run two mi, vertical drop 1,000 ft. (Dec-Apr, daily) X-country skiing. Chairlift rides (July-Oct, Sat and Sun, also Mon hols). 8 mi S off WV 32. Phone 304/866-4801. ¢¢¢¢

White Grass Touring Center. Thirty-six mi of x-country trails, some machine-groomed; patrol, school, rentals; snowfarming; restaurant; telemark slopes, guided tours. (Late Nov-Mar, daily) 9 mi S on WV 32 to Freeland Rd; ½ mi N of Canaan Valley Resort State Park. Phone 304/866-4114. ¢¢¢

Whitewater rafting. Many outfitters offer guided trips on the Cheat River. For a list of outfitters contact the West Virginia Division of Tourism,

Research, and Development, 90 Mac Corkle Ave SW, South Charleston, WV 25303 Phone 800/225-5982.

Special Event

Tucker County Alpine Winter Festival. Governor's Cup ski races. First wkend Mar. Phone 304/866-4121.

Motel/Motor Lodge

★★ **ALPINE LODGE.** *Williams Ave (26260).* 304/259-5245; fax 304/259-5168. 46 rms, 1-2 story. S, D $59-$80; each addl $2. Crib $5. TV; cable (premium). Indoor pool. Restaurant 6 am-9 pm. Ck-out 11 am. Coin lndry. Business servs avail. In-rm modem link. Sundries. Downhill ski 10 mi; x-country ski 2 mi. Refrigerators. Cr cds: A, C, D, DS, MC, V.

Resorts

★★ **BLACKWATER LODGE.** *County Rte 29 (26260).* 304/259-5216; fax 304/259-5881; res 800/225-5982. 54 rms in lodge, 1-2 story, 26 kit. cabins (1, 2 and 4 bedrm). S, D $68-$78; each addl $6; cabins for 2-8, $90-$150, $450-$900/wk; free in lodge. Heated indoor pool. whirlpool. TV in lodge; cable (premium). Playground. Supervised children's activites; ages 6-12. Dining rm 7 am-9 pm. Lodge: ck-out noon, ck-in 3 pm. Cabins: ck-out 10 am, ck-in 4 pm. Coin lndry. Meeting rms. Business servs avail. In-rm modem link. Tennis. Downhill ski 10 mi; x-country ski on site. Exercise equipt. Lawn games. Gift shop. Game rm. Picnic tables, grills. All state park facilities avail. Lake swimming. Cr cds: A, D, DS, MC, V.

★★★ **CANAAN VALLEY RESORT AND CONFERENCE CENTER.** *HC 70 Box 330 (26260).* 304/866-4121; fax 304/866-2172; toll-free 800/622-4121. www.canaanresort.com. 250 rms, 2 story. June-mid-Oct, late-Dec-mid-Mar: S, D $89-$99; each addl $7; suites $120; 2-4 bedrm cabins $690-$1,140/wk; family rates; package plans; lower lodge rates rest of yr. Deposit required. Crib $7; free in lodge. TV; cable (premium). 2 pools,

1 indoor; whirlpool, lifeguard (outside). Playground. Supervised child's activities (winter, summer); ages 6-12. Dining rm 7 am-11 pm, noon-2 pm, 5-9 pm. Snack bars; box lunches, picnics. Private club 4 pm-midnight. Coffee in rms. Ck-out 11 am, ck-in 4 pm. Grocery 2 mi. Coin lndry. Convention facilities. Business servs avail. In-rm modem link. Gift shop. Sports dir. Lighted tennis, pro. 18-hole golf, greens fee $24-$33, putting green, driving range, miniature golf. Downhill/x-country ski on site. Naturalist program. Bicycles. Lawn games. Entertainment, movies. Rec rm. Game rm. Exercise rm; sauna. Fishing privileges. Some refrigerators. Fireplace in cabins. Picnic tables. Camping sites avail. Cr cds: A, D, DS, MC, V.

Elkins

(C-4) *See also Buckhannon, Davis, Philippi*

Founded 1890 **Pop** 7,032 **Elev** 1,830 ft **Area code** 304 **Zip** 26241
Information West Virginia Mountain Highlands, PO Box 1456; 304/636-8400

Elkins was named for US Senator Stephen B. Elkins, an aggressive politician and powerful industrial magnate who was Secretary of War under Benjamin Harrison (1888-1892). This town is in a coal and timber region and is also a railroad terminus and trade center. Some of the finest scenery in the state can be seen in and around Elkins.

What to See and Do

Bowden National Fish Hatchery. Produces brook, brown, and rainbow trout for stocking in state and national forest streams; also striped bass for Chesapeake Bay restoration project. Hatchery (daily). Visitor center (Memorial Day-mid-Oct, daily). 10 mi E on Old US 33. Phone 304/637-0238. **FREE**

Spruce Knob/Seneca Rocks National Recreation Area

Monongahela National Forest. This 901,000-acre forest, in the heart of the Alleghenies, has some of the loftiest mountains in the East. Spruce Knob (4,862 ft) is the highest point in the state. Headwaters of the Ohio and Potomac rivers are here. The forest is a meeting ground of northern and southern plant life, with stands of red spruce and northern hardwoods joining with oak, hickory, and other southern hardwoods. There are also many interesting secondary and tertiary plants and wildflowers. Several recreation areas, incl five wilderness areas, Spruce Knob/Seneca Rocks National Recreation Area near Petersburg (see), and Blue Bend and Lake Sherwood recreation areas near White Sulphur Springs (see), are all located within the forest. Swimming, fishing, boating; hunting, hiking, rock climbing, caving, picnicking, camping (fee). Fees charged at the more developed recreation sites. Part of the Greenbrier River Trail (see MARLINTON) runs through the southern section of the forest. Forest headquarters in Elkins; Cranberry Mountain Visitor Center near Marlinton (see); and Seneca Rocks Visitor Center in Seneca Rocks (see PETERSBURG). Entrance is E of town on US 33. Contact Supervisor, US Department of Agriculture Building, 200 Sycamore St. Phone 304/636-1800.

The Old Mill. (1877) A gristmill powered by water turbines rather than a waterwheel. It was also used for planing wood and for producing white flour. Today it still uses water power to grind corn, wheat, rye, and buckwheat. Observation hive has live bees. West Virginia crafts shop incl rug weaving. (Memorial Day-Labor Day, Mon-Sat) 25 mi E via US 33 to WV 32 N, in Harman. Phone 304/227-4466. **DONATION**

Special Events

Augusta Festival. On campus of Davis & Elkins College, 100 Sycamore St. Celebration of traditional folk life and arts, featuring local and national performers, dances, juried craft fair, storytelling sessions, children's activities, and homemade foods. Mid-Aug. Phone 304/637-1209.

Mountain State Forest Festival. Some events on campus of Davis & Elkins College. Queen Silvia is crowned; carnival, parades, entertainment, tilting at rings on horseback, sawing and woodchopping contests, marksmanship tests, State Championship Fiddle and Banjo Contest; juried craft fair and art exhibit. Late Sept-early Oct. Phone 304/636-1824.

Motels/Motor Lodges

★ **ECONO LODGE INN.** *40 Cherry St; Rte 1 Box 15 (26241). 304/636-5311; fax 304/636-5311; toll-free 800/446-6900. www.econolodge.com.* 72 rms, 1-2 story. S $42-$47; D $47-$52; each addl $5; suites $54-$69; kit. units $56-$70; under 18 free; package plans; higher rates Forest Festival. Crib $5. Pet accepted; $5. TV; cable (premium). Indoor pool. Complimentary continental bkfst. Ck-out 11 am. Coin lndry. Meeting rms. Business servs avail. In-rm modem link. Some refrigerators. Cr cds: A, C, D, DS, MC, V.

D ⤳ ⊠ 🔥 SC

★ ★ **ELKINS MOTOR LODGE.** *Harrison Ave (26241). 304/636-1400; fax 304/636-6318; toll-free 877/636-1863.* 54 rms. 1-2 story. S, D $41-$50; each addl $3; suites $75. Crib $3. Pet accepted; $5. TV; cable (premium). Restaurant 5-10 pm; Sun to 8 pm. Private club 4:30 pm-1 am. Ck-out noon. Meeting rms. Business servs avail. In-rm modem link. Free airport transportation. Refrigerators, microwaves avail. Cr cds: A, D, DS, MC, V.

D ⊠ 🔥

★ **FOUR SEASONS MOTEL.** *1091 Harrison Ave (26241). 304/636-1990; fax 304/636-6475; toll-free 800/367-7130. www.elkinsfourseasons.com.* 14 rms, 1-2 story. $38-$48; each $3; under 12 free; wkly rates. Crib free. TV; cable (premium). Complimentary coffee in lobby. Restaurant nearby. Ck-out 11 am. Refrigerators. Cr cds: A, D, DS, MC, V.

⊠ 🔥 SC

★ **SUPER 8 MOTEL.** *350 Beverly Pike; Rte 219 S (26241). 304/636-6500; fax 304/636-6500; toll-free res 800/800-8000. www.super8.com.* 44 rms, 2 story. S, D $48-$60; each addl $6; under 12 free; higher rates: Forest Festival, graduation, ski wk. Crib free. Pet accepted. TV; cable (premium). Complimentary continental bkfst, coffee in lobby. Restaurant opp 7 am-10 pm. Ck-out 11 am. Business servs avail. In-rm modem link. Some refrigerators. Cr cds: A, C, D, DS, MC, V.

D ⊠ 🔥 SC

B&Bs/Small Inns

★ **THE POST HOUSE BED AND BREAKFAST.** *306 Robert E. Lee Ave (26241). 304/636-1792.* 5 rms, 2 share bath, 2 story. S $64; D $65; each addl $10. Closed Nov-June. TV; cable (premium). Complimentary continental bkfst. Restaurant nearby. Ck-out 11 am, ck-in 2 pm. Massage. Built in 1936. Totally non-smoking.

⊠ 🔥

SENECA ROCKS

Serious rock climbers rate West Virginia's massive Seneca Rocks as one of the top East Coast destinations for their sport. More than 375 major mapped climbing routes ascend the sheer, slender rocks that thrust 900 feet above the tumbling North Fork River. On any nice day you're apt to see a half-dozen or more climbers laboriously pulling themselves, hand over hand, slowly up the wall. It might take them hours to get to the top; you can enjoy the same view from the summit as they get, but without the effort. A 1½-mile foot trail–rated only moderately difficult–zig zags to the top. Heavily traveled and well-marked, it is a non-climber's introduction to West Virginia's panoramic vistas. A notable West Virginia landmark, the dramatic rock formation is worth a visit simply as a scenic attraction. From the edge of the river, which tumbles in a fury of white water, a thickly forested ridge forms an imposing pedestal for the rocks. From this base, the twin towers seem to leap into the sky. They form a rough, craggy wall with a knife's-edge point barely 15 feet wide. Begin your ascent near the foot of the rocks at Seneca Rocks Discovery Center, a beautiful structure of stone and glass. Inside, exhibits detail the natural history of the rocks; outside, the deck is positioned for great views of the climbers. The hiker's trail to the top begins just across the river from the Discovery Center. It climbs steadily through shady woods. Sturdy benches are placed along the way if you need to rest. At several especially steep points, stone steps seem to stretch endlessly above, but that's only your imagination. From the summit overlooks, the view of the river-traced valley below is a generous reward for your pains. Give yourself an hour to reach the top, 30 minutes to enjoy your lofty perch and another 30 minutes for the much easier descent. Afterward, cross the road (State Route 55) for refreshments in the village of Seneca Rocks at Harper's Old Country Store, which looks much as it must have on its opening day in 1902.

★★★ **THE WARFIELD HOUSE.**
318 Buffalo St (26241). 304/636-4555;
res 888/636-4555. www.warfieldhouse
bandb.com. 5 air-cooled rms, 2 story.
No rm phones. Apr-Nov: S, D $79-
$89; each addl $10; package plans.
Children over 12 yrs only. TV; cable
(premium) in common rm. Complimentary continental bkfst, coffee in
rms. Ck-out 11 am, ck-in 3-6 pm.
Business servs avail. Luggage handling. Street parking. Built in 1901;
Colonial Revival style. Totally nonsmoking. Cr cds: MC, V.
⊠ 🐾 SC

Restaurant

★★ **CHEAT RIVER INN.** *US 33E*
(26241). 304/636-6265. www.cheat
riverlodge.com. Hrs: 4-10 pm. Closed
Mon, major hols. Res accepted. Bar.
Dinner $14-$26. Specializes in
seafood, prime beef, and rainbow
trout. Child's menu. Outdoor dining.
Mounted fish on display. Cr cds: D,
DS, MC, V.
D ⊠

Fairmont

(B-4) *See also Clarksburg, Morgantown*

Settled 1793 **Pop** 19,097 **Elev** 883 ft
Zip 26554
Information Convention & Visitors
Bureau of Marion County, 110
Adams St, PO Box 58, 26555-0058;
304/368-1123 or 800/834-7365
Web www.marioncvb.com

Fairmont was a Union supply depot
plundered by Confederate cavalry in
April 1863. General William Ezra
Jones's division swept through town,
took 260 prisoners, destroyed the
$500,000 bridge across the Monon-
gahela River, and raided the governor's residence. After the war,
resources in the region were developed and coal became the mainstay.
Today Fairmont manufactures aluminum, mine machinery, and other
products.

What to See and Do

Fairmont State College. (1867) 7,000
students. On campus is a one-rm
schoolhouse with original desks,
books, and other artifacts related to
early era of education (Apr-Oct,
schedule varies). Locust Ave. Phone
304/367-4000.

Marion County Museum. Displays of
B & O china, five furnished rms covering 1776-1920s; doll, train, and toy
collection. (Mon-Sat; closed hols)
Adams St, adj to courthouse. Phone
304/367-5398. **FREE**

Prickett's Fort State Park. Approx
200 acres with reconstructed 18th-
century log fort, Colonial trade and
lifestyle demonstrations by costumed
interpreters, outdoor historical drama
(July, Wed-Sat). Boating (ramps); picnicking. Visitor center. Fort and
museum (mid-Apr-Oct, daily).
Museum (fee). I-79 exit 139, then 2
mi W. Phone 800/304-3633.

Special Event

Three Rivers Festival. Palatine Park.
Entertainment, parade, Civil War
reenactment, carnival, games. Third
wkend May. Phone 304/363-2625.

Motels/Motor Lodges

★★ **COMFORT INN AND SUITES.**
1185 Airport Rd (26554). 304/367-
1370; fax 304/367-1806; toll-free
800/228-5150. www.comfortinn.com.
82 rms, 2 story, 18 suites. S, D $59-
$79; suites $95; under 18 free; higher
rates special events. Crib free. TV;
cable (premium). Complimentary
continental bkfst, coffee in rms.
Restaurant nearby. Ck-out noon.
Meeting rms. Business servs. In-rm
modem link. Sundries. Exercise
equipt. Pool. Refrigerator, microwave
in suites. Cr cds: A, C, D, DS, JCB,
MC, V.
D ⊠ 🏋 ⊠ 🐾 SC

★★ **HOLIDAY INN.** *930 E Grafton*
(26554). 304/366-5500; fax 304/363-
3975; toll-free 800/465-4329. www.
holiday-inn.com. 106 rms, 2 story. S,
D $69-$99; under 18 free; higher
rates: WVU football games, graduation. Crib free. Pet accepted. TV;
cable (premium). Pool. Restaurant 6
am-2 pm, 5-10 pm. Coffee in rms.
Bar. Ck-out noon. Meeting rms. Busi-

ness servs avail. In-rm modem link. Bellhops. Valet serv. Sundries. Some refrigerators. Cr cds: A, C, D, DS, MC, V.

★ **RED ROOF INN.** *50 Middletown Rd (26554).* 304/366-6800; *fax 304/366-6812; toll-free 800/733-7663. www.redroof.com.* 108 rms, 2 story. S, D $39.95-65.99; each addl $3; under 18 free. Crib free. Pet accepted. TV. Complimentary coffee in lobby. Restaurant nearby. Ck-out noon. Business servs avail. Cr cds: A, C, D, DS, MC, V.

Restaurant

★ ★ **MURIALE'S.** *1742 Fairmont Ave, South Fairmont (26554).* 304/363-3190. Hrs: 11 am-9 pm; Fri, Sat to 10 pm. Closed Dec 25. Italian, American menu. Bar. Lunch $5-$8, dinner $8-$24. Child's menu. Specializes in lasagne, ravioli, steak. Family-owned. Cr cds: A, C, D, DS, MC, V.

Franklin

(F-7) *See also Petersburg, zz also see 3013*

Settled 1794 **Pop** 797 **Elev** 1,731 ft **Area code** 304 **Zip** 26807
Information West Virginia Mountain Highlands, PO Box 1456, Elkins 26241; 304/636-8400

What to See and Do

Seneca Caverns. Caves contain magnificent stalagmites and stalactites; were used as a refuge by the Seneca people. (Daily) Approx 15 mi NW on US 33 to Riverton, then 3 mi E. Phone 304/567-2691. ¢¢

Special Event

Treasure Mountain Festival. Square dancing, clogging; parade, gospel and mountain music, drama; rifle demonstration, cross-cut sawing contest; children's contests, games; trail rides craft exhibits, country food. Third wkend Sept. Phone 304/249-5422.

Gauley Bridge

See also Beckley, Charleston, Summersville

Pop 738 **Elev** 680 ft **Area code** 304 **Zip** 25085
Information Upper Kanawha Valley Chamber of Commerce, PO Box 831, Montgomery 25136; 304/442-5756

This town at the junction of the New and Gauley rivers was the key to the Kanawha Valley during the Civil War. In November 1861 Union General W. S. Rosecrans defeated Confederate General John B. Floyd, a victory that assured Union control of western Virginia. Stone piers of the old bridge, which was destroyed by retreating Confederates in 1861, can be seen near the present bridge.

What to See and Do

Contentment Museum Complex. (ca 1830) Former residence of Confederate Colonel George W. Imboden contains original woodwork, period furniture, toy collection. Adj Fayette County Historical Society Museum features displays of Native American relics, local artifacts, Civil War items; restored one-rm schoolhouse. (June-Aug, Mon-Sat; rest of yr, by appt) 7 mi E on US 60, 1 mi E of Hawk's Nest State Park. Phone 304/658-5695. ¢¢

Hawk's Nest State Park. Approx 280 acres on Gauley Mtn, with fine views of New River Gorge from rocks 585 ft above the river. A 600-ft aerial tramway carries passengers to canyon floor. Swimming pool, fishing; hiking trails, tennis, picnic area, playground, concession, restaurant, lodge. Log museum with early West Virginia artifacts (May-Nov, daily; free). Standard hrs, fees. 6 mi E on US 60. Phone 304/658-5212.

New River Gorge Bridge. A masterpiece of engineering, this four-lane, single arch steel-span bridge rises 876 ft above the New River Gorge National River (see HINTON), making it the second-highest bridge in the US, and at 3,030 ft, the longest bridge of its type in the world. Just north of the bridge on US 19 is the Canyon Rim Visitors Center (daily; closed Dec 25), providing two overlooks of the bridge and river, a 70-ft descending boardwalk, slide presentation, exhibits, and ranger-guided walks (May-Oct). 13 mi SE on US 60, then 6 mi SW on US 19, near Fayetteville. Phone 304/574-2115.

Whitewater rafting. Many outfitters offer guided trips on the New and Gauley rivers. For a list of outfitters contact the West Virginia Division of Tourism, Research, and Development, 90 Mac Corkle Ave SW, South Charleston 25303. Phone 800/225-5982.

Special Event

Bridge Day. New River Gorge Bridge. Bridge is opened to pedestrians; parachutists test their skills by jumping off the bridge and floating to the bottom of gorge. Third Sat Oct. Phone 304/442-5756.

Motel/Motor Lodge

★ ★ **HAWKS NEST STATE PARK LODGE.** *Rte 60, Ansted (25812). 304/658-5212; fax 304/658-4549; toll-free 800/225-5982.* 31 rms, 4 story. Late May-early Sept: S, D $70; each addl $6; suites $66-$82; under 13 free; lower rates rest of yr. Crib free. TV; cable (premium). Pool. Playground. Dining rm 7 am-9 pm; Dec-Feb to 8 pm. Ck-out noon. Meeting rm. Business servs avail. In-rm modem link. Some Refrigerators. Gift shop. Tennis. Golf privileges. Balconies. View of mountains. 1,100-ft vertical tramway to marina. Cr cds: A, D, DS, MC, V.

[D] [🎿] [🎣] [🏊] [📶] [🐾] [SC]

B&B/Small Inn

★ ★ **GLEN FERRIS INN.** *US 60, Glen Ferris (25090). 304/632-1111; fax 304/632-0113; toll-free 800/924-6093.* 16 rms. 3 story. S, D $60-$75; suite $100-$130. crib free. TV; cable (premium). Dining rm 6 am-9 pm; Sun from 7 am. Ck-out 11 am. Ck-in 4

pm. Meeting rm. Business servs avail. Renovated 1840's inn, originally Federal style in design; built by grandson of one of signers of Declaration of Indepedence. Overlooks Kanawha Falls. Totally nonsmoking. Cr cds: A, DS, MC, V.

[D] [🐾] [📶] [🐾]

Grafton

(B-4) *See also Clarksburg, Fairmont, Morgantown, Philippi*

Founded 1856 **Pop** 5,489 **Elev** 1,004 ft **Area code** 304 **Zip** 26354

Information Grafton-Taylor County Convention and Visitors Bureau, 214 W Main St, Rm 205; 304/265-3938

Mother's Day started in Grafton in 1908 when Anna Jarvis observed the anniversary of her mother's death during a religious service. The idea caught on nationally, and in 1914 President Woodrow Wilson issued a proclamation urging nationwide observance. The International Shrine to Motherhood in the original Mother's Day church is located at 11 East Main Street.

During the Civil War Grafton was an important railroad center; 4,000 Union troops camped here before the Battle of Philippi in 1861. General McClellan also had his headquarters in the town. The first land soldier killed in the war, T. Bailey Brown, fell at Grafton. He is buried in the Grafton National Cemetery.

What to See and Do

Tygart Lake State Park. This scenic 2,100-acre park contains one of the largest concrete dams east of the Mississippi (1,900 by 209 ft). Swimming, waterskiing, fishing, boating (ramp, rentals, marina); hiking, game courts, picnic area, playground, concession, lodge, tent and trailer camping, ten cabins. Nature and recreation programs, dam tours (summer; phone 304/265-1760). Standard hrs, fees. 2 mi S off US 119, 250. Phone 304/265-3383.

Special Event

Taylor County Fair. Fairgrounds, US 50. Horse racing, livestock shows, auctions, carnival, crafts. Last wk July. Phone 304/265-4155.

Motels/Motor Lodges

★ **CRISLIP MOTOR LODGE.** *300 Moritz Ave (26354). 304/265-2100; fax 304/265-2017.* 40 rms, 2 story. S, D $46-$50; each addl $5; Crib free. Pet accepted; $5/day. TV; cable (premium). Pool. Complimentary coffee in rms. Restaurant nearby. Ck-out 11 am. Business servs avail. In-rm modem link. Sundries. Cr cds: A, D, DS, MC, V.

★★ **TYGART LAKE STATE PARK LODGE.** *Rte 1 (26354). 304/265-6144; fax 304/265-6147; res 800/225-5982. www.tygartlake.com.* 20 rms, 1 story. May-Oct: S, D $65-$77; each addl $6; cabins $456-$510/wk; under 13 free; golf plans; lower rates Nov, Dec. Closed Jan-Apr. Crib $5.45/day. TV; cable (premium). Free supervised child's activities (Memorial Day-Labor Day). Restaurant 8 am-8 pm. Ck-out noon. Meeting rm. In-rm modem link. Rec rm. Gift shop. Playground. Lawn games. Picnic tables. Rms overlook lake. Cr cds: A, D, DS, MC, V.

Harpers Ferry

See also Charles Town, Martinsburg, Shepherdstown

Settled 1732 **Pop** 307 **Elev** 247 ft
Area code 304 **Zip** 25425

Information Jefferson County Chamber of Commerce, 201 Frontage Rd, PO Box 426, Charles Town 25414; 304/725-2055

Web www.jeffersoncounty.com/chamber

Scene of abolitionist John Brown's raid in 1859, Harpers Ferry is at the junction of the Shenandoah and Potomac rivers, where West Virginia, Virginia, and Maryland meet. A US armory and rifle factory made this an important town in early Virginia; John Brown had this in mind when he began his insurrection. He and 16 other men seized the armory and arsenal the night of October 16 and took refuge in the engine house of the armory when attacked by local militia. On the morning of the 18th the engine house was stormed, and Brown was captured by 90 marines from Washington under Brevet Colonel Robert E. Lee and Lt J.E.B. Stuart. Ten of Brown's men were killed, including two of his sons. He was hanged in nearby Charles Town

Harpers Ferry

(see) for treason, murder, and inciting slaves to rebellion.

When war broke out, Harpers Ferry was a strategic objective for the Confederacy, which considered it the key to Washington. "Stonewall" Jackson captured 12,693 Union prisoners here before the Battle of Antietam in 1862. The town changed hands many times in the war, during which many buildings were damaged. In 1944 Congress authorized a national monument here, setting aside 1,500 acres for that purpose. In 1963 the same area was designated a National Historical Park, now occupying more than 2,200 acres.

What to See and Do

⭐ **Harpers Ferry National Historical Park.** Here the old town has been restored to its 19th-century appearance; exhibits and interpretive presentations explore the park's relation to the water-power industry, the Civil War, John Brown, and Storer College, a school established for freed slaves after the war. A Visitor Center is located just off US 340. Visitors should park there; a bus will take them to Lower Town. Contact the Visitor Center, PO Box 65. Phone 304/535-6298. ¢¢ A walking tour of the park follows:

Information Center. Restored Federalist house built in 1859 by US government as residence for the master armorer of the US Armory. During the Civil War it was used as headquarters by various commanding officers. Also on this street is the site of the US Armory that John Brown attempted to seize; it was destroyed during the Civil War. S side of Shenandoah St near High St. Phone 304/535-6029. Farther down Shenandoah St and right under the trestle is

The Point. Three states, West Virginia, Virginia, and Maryland, and two rivers, the Shenandoah and Potomac, meet at the Blue Ridge Mtns. Back under the trestle is

John Brown's Fort. Where John Brown made his last stand; rebuilt and moved near original site. On Arsenal Sq. Across the street is

John Brown Museum. Contains an exhibit and film on John Brown and a ten-min slide presentation on the history of the park. Exiting

the museum to the right is High St, which has two Civil War museums and two black history museums. Up the stone steps from High St is

Harper House. Three-story stone house built between 1775-1782 by founder of town; both George Washington and Thomas Jefferson were entertained as overnight guests. Restored and furnished with period pieces. Behind this house is

Camp Hill. Four restored, private houses built 1832-1850. Continue up the hill to the

Ruins of St. John's Episcopal Church. Used as a guardhouse and hospital during the Civil War. Approx 100 yards farther is

Jefferson's Rock. From here Thomas Jefferson, in 1783, pronounced the view "one of the most stupendous scenes in nature." Farther along, above the cemetery, is

Lockwood House. (1848) Greek Revival house used as headquarters, barracks, and stable during Civil War; later used as classrm building by Storer College (1867), which was founded to educate freed men after the war.

Other buildings. Open to the public during the summer are the dry goods store, provost, office, and blacksmith shop.

John Brown Wax Museum. Sound and animation depict Brown's exploits, incl the raid on Harpers Ferry. High St. Phone 304/535-6342. ¢¢

Whitewater rafting. Many outfitters offer guided trips on the Shenandoah and Potomac rivers. For a list of outfitters contact the West Virginia Division of Tourism, Research, and Development, 90 Mac Corkle Ave SW, South Charleston 25303. Phone 800/225-5982.

Special Events

Mountain Heritage Arts and Crafts Festival. More than 190 craftspeople and artisans demonstrate quilting, wool spinning, pottery throwing, vegetable dyeing, and other crafts; concerts. Second full wkend June and last full wkend Sept. Phone 304/725-2055.

Election Day 1860. More than 100 people in 19th-century attire reenact the 1860 presidential election. Second Sat Oct. Phone 304/535-6298.

Old Tyme Christmas. Caroling, musical programs, children's programs, taffy pull, candlelight walk. First two wkends Dec. Phone 304/535-2627.

Motel/Motor Lodge

★ **COMFORT INN.** *Rte 340 & Union St (25425). 304/535-6391; fax 304/535-6395; toll-free 800/228-5150. www.comfortinn.com.* 50 rms, 2 story. Apr-Oct: S, D $69-$75; each addl $6; Special events (2-day min); under 18 free; lower rates rest of yr. Crib free. TV; cable (premium), VCR avail (movies). Complimentary continental bkfst. Coffee in rms. Restaurant nearby. Ck-out 11 am. Sundries. Business servs avail. In-rm modem link. Health club privileges. Refrigerators avail. Cr cds: A, C, D, DS, MC, V.
D ⊠ 🐾 SC

Hillsboro

(C-1) *See also Marlinton*

Settled 1765 **Pop** 243 **Elev** 2,303 ft **Area code** 304 **Zip** 24946
Information West Virginia Mountain Highlands, PO Box 1456, Elkins 26241; 304/636-8400

Civil War troops marched through Hillsboro and Confederates camped in town before the decisive Battle of Droop Mountain. Novelist Pearl S. Buck was born in her grandparents' house while her parents, missionaries on leave from China, were visiting.

What to See and Do

Beartown State Park. Approx 110 acres of dense forest with unique rock formations created by erosion; boardwalk with interpretive signs winds through park. Standard hrs. 1½ mi S off US 219. Phone 304/653-4254.

Droop Mountain Battlefield State Park. Encompasses approx 285 acres on site where on Nov 6, 1863, Union forces under General William W. Averell defeated Confederates under General John Echols, destroying the last major rebel resistance in the state. Park features graves, breastworks, and monuments. Hiking, picnic areas, playground. Museum. Battle reenactments (second wk Oct, every even yr). Standard hrs. 5 mi S on US 219. Phone 304/653-4254.

🌟 **Pearl S. Buck Birthplace Museum.** (Stulting House) Birthplace of Pulitzer and Nobel Prize-winning novelist, restored to its 1892 appearance; original and period furniture; memorabilia. Sydenstricker House, home of Buck's father and his ancestors, was moved 40 mi from its original site and restored here. Guided tours. (May-Oct, Mon-Sat, also Sun afternoons) ½ mi N on US 219. Phone 304/653-4430. ¢¢

Watoga State Park. More than 10,100 acres make this West Virginia's largest state park. Watoga, derived from the Cherokee term *watauga,* means "river of islands." It aptly describes the Greenbrier River, which forms several mi of the park's boundary. Swimming pool, bathhouses, fishing, boating on 11-acre Watoga Lake (rentals); hiking and bridle trails, horseback riding, tennis, game courts, x-country skiing, picnicking, playground, concession, restaurant (seasonal), tent and trailer camping, 33 cabins. Brooks Memorial Arboretum; nature, recreation programs (summer). Standard hrs, fees. 1 mi N on US 219, then SE. Phone 304/799-4087. Adj to the park is

Calvin Price State Forest. This vast, undeveloped forest has more than 9,400 acres for fishing; deer and small-game hunting, hiking, and primitive camping (fee). Phone 304/799-4087.

Hinton

See also Beckley

Founded 1873 **Pop** 2,880 **Elev** 1,382 ft **Area code** 304 **Zip** 25951

Information Summers County Chamber of Commerce, 200 Ballangee St; 304/466-5332

Hinton, a railroad town on the banks of the New River, is the seat of Summers County, where the Bluestone and Greenbrier rivers join the scenic and protected New River.

What to See and Do

Bluestone State Park. More than 2,100 acres on Bluestone Lake, which was created by the Bluestone Dam. Swimming pool (Memorial Day-Labor Day), wading pool, bathhouses, waterskiing, fishing, boating (ramps, marina nearby; canoe, rowboat, and motorboat rentals); hiking trails, game courts, picnicking, playground, tent and trailer camping (dump station), 25 cabins. Nature, recreation programs (summer). Gift shop. Standard hrs, fees. 5 mi S on WV 20. Phone 304/466-2805.

New River Gorge National River. One of the oldest rivers on the continent, the New River rushes northward through a deep canyon with spectacular scenery. The 52-mi section from Hinton to Fayetteville is popular among outdoor enthusiasts, especially whitewater rafters and hikers. The Hinton Visitor Center is located along the river at WV 3 Bypass (Memorial Day-Labor Day, daily); phone 304/466-0417. A yr-round visitor center is located on US 19 near the New River Gorge Bridge (see GAULEY BRIDGE). For further information and a list of whitewater outfitters contact Superintendent, PO Box 246, Glen Jean 25846. Phone 304/465-0508.

Pipestem Resort State Park. More than 4,000 acres with 3,600-ft aerial tramway to Bluestone River complex. Swimming, bathhouses, fishing, canoeing, paddleboating; hiking trails, horseback riding, nine- and 18-hole golf courses, miniature golf, tennis, archery, lighted game courts, x-country skiing, sledding, playground, two lodges, four restaurants, tent and trailer camping (dump station), 25 cabins. Visitor center; nature, recreation programs. Aerial tramway, arboretum, observation tower. Amphitheater; dances. Standard hrs, fees. 12 mi SW on WV 20. Phone 304/466-1800.

Resort

★ ★ ★ **MOUNTAIN CREEK LODGE.** *Pipestem State Park, Pipestem (25979). 304/466-1800; fax 304/466-5679; toll-free 800/922-5582.* 143 units in 2 bldgs, 7 story, 30 lodge rms, 26 kit. cottages. May-Sept: S $62; D $68; lodge rms (Nov-Mar only): S $46; D $52; each addl $6; under 13 free; suites $90-$165; 2-4 bedrm cottages $575-$754/wk; varied lower rates rest of yr. Crib $6. TV; cable (premium), VCR avail (movies $4). 2 pools, 1 indoor; wading pool, lifeguard, poolside servs. Playground. Restaurants (see also BLUESTONE DINING ROOM and MOUNTAIN CREEK). Bar (seasonal). Snack bars. Coin laundry. Ck-out noon, ck-in 4 pm; cottages ck-out 10 am, ck-in 4 pm. Meeting rms. Business servs avail. In-rm modem link. Grocery 3 mi. Lighted tennis. 18-hole golf. X-country ski on site; sleighing, tobogganing. Exercise equipt; sauna. Gift shop. Lawn games. Soc dir. Rec rm; entertainment in summer. Many balconies. Some refrigerators. Picnic tables. Mt Creek Lodge (open May-Oct) located at foot of Bluestone Canyon; accessible only by aerial tram. Resort state-owned, operated; all state park facilities avail to guests. Cr cds: A, DS, MC, V.

🅓 ♨ ➤ ⅋ ⻆ ⩟ ⩞ ⻣ SC

B&B/Small Inn

★ **PENCE SPRINGS HOTEL.** *Rte 3, Pence Springs (24962). 304/445-2606; fax 304/445-2204; toll-free 800/826-1829.* 15 units, 2 story, 1 cottage. Apr-Dec: S $59.50-$89.50; D $69.50-$99.50; cottage $350; under 3 free; wkly rates; lower rates rest of yr. Crib $10. Complimentary full bkfst. Dining rm 8-10 am, 5-9 pm; wknd hrs vary. Bar 5 pm-midnight. Ck-out 11 am, ck-in 4 pm. Meeting rms. Business servs avail. Lawn games. Picnic tables. On high plateau overlooking Greenbrier River valley. Cr cds: A, C, DS, MC, V.

🅓 ⅋ ⩞ ⻣ SC

Restaurants

★ ★ **BLUESTONE DINING ROOM.** *Pipestem Resort, Pipestem (25979). 304/466-1800.* Hrs: 7 am-2 pm, 5:30-9 pm. Wine, beer. Bkfst $3.95-$7.95, lunch $5.95-$7.95, dinner $9.95-$15.95. Buffet: bkfst $5.50, lunch $6.95, dinner $10-$20. Child's menu. Specializes in seafood, steak, country dishes. Outdoor dining. View of gorge and mts. Cr cds: D, MC, V.

D ➡

★ **KIRK'S.** *HC 76 Box 3 (25951). 304/466-4600.* Hrs: 6:30 am-9 pm. Closed Thanksgiving, Dec 25. Bkfst, lunch $3-$5, dinner $5-$12.25. Specialties: Kirk's hot dogs, fried chicken, stuffed baked potatoes. Own desserts. Outdoor dining. On New River near Bluestone Resort Park; patio overlooks river. Cr cds: A, MC, V.

D ➡

★ ★ **MOUNTAIN CREEK.** *Pipestem Resort, Pipestem (25979). 304/466-1800.* Hrs: 7 am-2 pm, 5:30-9 pm; Tues, Thurs 7-11 am, 5:30-9 pm; Sat to 10 pm. Closed Nov-May. Res accepted (dinner). French, American menu. Bar. Bkfst $2.25-$4.50, lunch $4.95, dinner $14.95-$27. Child's menu. Specialties: roasted pork filet, rack of lamb, prime rib of beef, seafood. Own pastries. Park in Pipestem Resort State Park. Dining rm at 1,000-ft-deep gorge; accessible by tram only. Totally nonsmoking. Cr cds: D, MC, V.

D ➡

★ ★ **OAK SUPPER CLUB.** *Just N of Pipestem State Park entrance, Pipestem (25979). 304/466-4800.* Hrs: 5:30-9 pm. Closed Thanksgiving, Dec 25; also Jan-Mar. Res accepted. Bar. Dinner $10.95-$24.95. Child's menu. Specializes in pork, duckling, fresh mountain trout. Named for 800 year-old white oak on grounds. Dining rm overlooks mountains. Family-owned. Cr cds: MC, V.

D

Huntington (D-2)

Founded 1871 **Pop** 51,475 **Elev** 564 ft
Area code 304
Information Cabell-Huntington Convention and Visitors Bureau, PO Box 347, 25708; 304/525-7333 or 800/635-6329
Web www.wvvisit.org

The millionaire president of the Chesapeake & Ohio Railroad, Collis P. Huntington, founded this city and named it for himself. Originally a rail and river terminus, commerce and industry have made it the second-largest city in the state. Thoroughly planned and meticulously laid out, Huntington is protected from the Ohio River by an 11-mile floodwall equipped with 17 pumping stations and 45 gates. Glass, railroad products, and metals are important city industries.

What to See and Do

Beech Fork State Park. Nearly 4,000 acres on 720-acre Beech Fork Lake. Fishing, boating (ramp, marina); hiking trails, physical fitness trail, tennis, game courts, picnicking, camping. Store. Visitor center; nature, recreation programs (summer). Meeting rms. Standard hrs, fees. Approx 15 mi SE via WV 10, then 7 mi W on Hughes Branch Rd, near Bowen. Phone 304/528-5794.

Camden Park. Amusement park with 27 rides, games, concession; boat and train rides, log flume, miniature golf, roller rink, picnicking. (Mid-Apr-Memorial Day, Sat, Sun; Memorial Day-Labor Day, Tues-Sun) Rides individually priced; also unlimited ride plan. US 60 E. Phone 304/429-4231. ¢¢¢

East Lynn Wildlife Management Area. Almost 23,000 acres used primarily by sportsmen; trails, primitive camping (fee). 15 mi SE via WV 152 and WV 37, near East Lynn. Phone 304/675-0871.

Heritage Village. Restored Victorian B & O Railroad yard surrounding brick courtyard. Restaurant in original passenger station (1887), restored Pullman car, shops in renovated freight and box cars, warehouses. (Mon-Sat) 11th St and Veterans Memorial Blvd. Phone 304/696-5954. **FREE**

Huntington Museum of Art. Museum with American and European paintings, prints, and sculpture; Herman P. Dean Firearms Collection; Georgian silver; Asian prayer rugs; pre-

Columbian art; Appalachian folk art; Ohio Valley historical and contemporary glass. Complex incl exhibition galleries, library, studio workshops, amphitheater, auditorium, sculpture garden, observatory, art gallery for young people, nature trails. (Tues-Sat, also Sun afternoons; closed hols) 2033 McCoy Rd; I-64 exit 8. Phone 304/529-2701. **FREE**

Industrial tours.

Blenko Glass Company, Inc. Famous glass factory; makers of Country Music Award, presidential gifts, and original supplier to Colonial Williamsburg. Visitor center (daily; closed hols) has stained glass from nine leading studios; observation gallery for viewing hand-blown glassmaking and blown stained glass. (Mon-Fri; closed hols; also first two wks July, Dec 25-Jan 1) Museum of Historical Glass; Garden of Glass beside three-acre lake. 16 mi E via US 60, in Milton; I-64 exit 28. Phone 304/743-9081. **FREE**

Motels/Motor Lodges

★ ★ **DAYS INN.** *5196 US Rte 60 E (25705). 304/733-4477; fax 304/733-4493; res 800/694-8999. www.daysinn.com.* 153 rms, 2 story. S, D $55-$85; each addl $5; under 16 free. Crib free. TV; cable (premium). Complimentary continental bkfst, coffee in rms. Restaurant nearby. Ck-out noon. Meeting rms. Business servs avail. In-rm modem link. Coin lndry. Sundries. Indoor pool. Many refrigerators, microwaves. Picnic tables, grills. Cr cds: A, C, D, DS, MC, V.
🅳 ⛱ 📶 🐾 SC

★ ★ **RADISSON HOTEL.** *1001 3rd Ave (25701). 304/525-1001; fax 304/525-1048; toll-free 800/333-3333. www.radisson.com.* 202 rms, 11 story. S, D $79-$119; each addl $10; suites $300-$400; under 18 free; wkend rates. Crib free. TV; cable (premium), VCR avail. Heated pool. Coffee in rms. Restaurant 6:30 am-11 pm; Fri, Sat to midnight. Rm serv. Bar 4 pm-midnight. Ck-out noon. Meeting rms. Business center. In-rm modem link. Shopping arcade. Valet parking. Airport, RR station, bus depot transportation. Exercise equipt; sauna.

Valet serv. On Ohio River. Cr cds: A, C, D, DS, ER, JCB, MC, V.
🅳 ⛱ 🏋 📶 🐾 SC 🏋

★ **RED ROOF INN.** *5190 US Rte 60E (25705). 304/733-3737; fax 304/733-3786; toll-free 800/733-7663. www.redroof.com.* 108 rms, 2 story. S, D $40-$70; each addl $5; under 18 free. Crib free. Pet accepted. TV; cable. Ck-out noon. Business servs avail. In-rm modem link. Refrigerators, microwaves avail. Cr cds: A, C, D, DS, MC, V.
🅳 🐾 📶 🐾 SC

★ ★ **STONE LODGE.** *5600 Rte 60 E (25705). 304/736-3451; fax 304/736-3451.* 120 rms, 3 story. S, D $49-$65; each addl $5; under 18 free. Crib free. TV; cable (premium). Pool. Restaurant 4-10 pm. Complimentary continental bkfst, coffee in rms. Ck-out noon. Meeting rms. Business servs avail. Sundries. Valet serv. Private patios, balconies. Refrigerators avail. Cr cds: A, C, D, DS, MC, V.
🅳 ⛱ 📶 🐾 SC

Restaurants

★ ★ **HERITAGE STATION.** *11th St and Veterans Memorial Blvd (25701). 304/523-6373.* Hrs: Apr-Sept: 11 am-10 pm, Fri, Sat to 10:30 pm; Oct-Mar: 11 am-9:30 pm; Fri, Sat 11 am-10 pm. Closed Sun; hols. Res accepted. Bar. Lunch, dinner $6-$28. Specializes in seafood, pasta, steak, burgers. Outdoor dining. Former railroad station built in 1887; memorabilia, antiques. Cr cds: A, C, D, DS, MC, V.
🅳 📶

★ ★ **REBELS & REDCOATS TAVERN.** *412 W 7th Ave (25701). 304/523-8829.* Hrs: 11 am-10 pm, 5:30-10 pm. Closed Sun, hols; also wk of July 4. Res accepted. Continental menu. Bar. Wine cellar. Lunch $6-$9, dinner $9-$42. Specialties: veal Oscar, châteaubriand bouquetiere, prime rib. Colonial decor; fireplace. Family-owned. Cr cds: A, DS, MC, V.
🅳 📶

Lewisburg

See also White Sulphur Springs

Founded 1782 **Pop** 3,624 **Elev** 2,099 ft **Area code** 304 **Zip** 24901
Information Greenbrier County Convention and Visitors Center, 105 Church St; 304/645-1000 or 800/833-2068
Web www.greenbrierwv.com

At the junction of two important Native American trails, the Seneca (now US 219) and the Kanawha (now US 60), Lewisburg was the site of colonial forts as well as a Civil War battle. The town's 236-acre historic district has more than 60 buildings from the 18th and 19th centuries in a variety of architectural styles.

What to See and Do

Lost World Caverns. Scenic trail over subterranean rock mountain; prehistoric ocean floor; stalagmites, stalactites; flow stone, ribbons, hex stones. Self-guided tours (daily; closed hols). 1 mi N on Fairview Rd. Phone 304/645-6677. ¢¢¢

North House Museum. Colonial and 19th-century objects and artifacts. (Mon-Sat) 301 W Washington. Phone 304/645-3398. ¢¢

Old Stone Presbyterian Church. (1796) Original log church (1783) was replaced by present native limestone structure. (Daily) 200 Church St. Phone 304/645-2676. **FREE**

Organ Cave. One of the longest caves in the US. Forty-five mi of mapped passageways. (Daily) 417 Masters Rd, Ronceverte 24970. Phone 304/645-7600.

Special Event

State Fair. Fairgrounds, 2 mi S on US 219. Exhibitors from a number of other states; horse shows, harness racing. Mid-Aug. Phone 304/645-1090.

Motels/Motor Lodges

★ ★ **BRIER INN.** *540 N Jefferson St (24901). 304/645-7722; fax 304/645-7865. www.brierinn.com.* 162 units, 2 story. Apr-Oct: S $54; D $59; each addl $5; suites $95-$100; kit. units $65-$70; under 12 free; higher rates state fair; lower rates rest of yr. Crib $5. Pet accepted, some restrictions; $10. TV; cable, VCR avail (movies). Pool. Restaurant 11 am-10 pm; Fri, Sat to 11 pm. Bar 10-2 am; entertainment Fri. Ck-out 11 am. Meeting rms. Business servs avail. In-rm modem link. Exercise rm. Cr cds: A, D, DS, MC, V.
D 🐾 ➳ 👗 ✈ 🖼 🔥

★ **ECONO LODGE FORT SAVANNAH MOTEL.** *204 N Jefferson St (24901). 304/645-3055; fax 304/645-3033; toll-free 800/283-4678.* 66 rms, 2 story. S $36-$50; D $42-$65; each addl $5; under 18 free. Crib free. Pet accepted; $10. TV; cable. Pool; whirlpool. Restaurant 6 am-10 pm. Ck-out noon. Business servs avail. Airport transportation. Balconies. Cr cds: A, C, D, DS, MC, V.
D 🐾 ➳ 🖼 🔥 SC

★ **DAYS INN.** *635 N Jefferson St (24901). 304/645-2345; fax 304/645-5501; toll-free 800/325-2525. www.daysinn.com.* 26 rms. S, D $50-$85; each addl $6; higher rates special events. Crib free. Pet accepted, some restrictions; $10. TV; cable (premium). Complimentary coffee in lobby. Restaurant nearby. Ck-out 11 am. Business servs avail. Airport transportation. Health club privileges. Cr cds: A, D, DS, MC, V.
🐾 🖼 🔥 SC

B&B/Small Inn

★ ★ ★ **GENERAL LEWIS INN.** *301 E Washington St (24901). 304/645-2600; fax 304/645-2601; toll-free 800/628-4454. www.generallewisinn.com.* 25 rms, 2 story. S $89-$94; D $94-$135; each addl $12; higher rates special events; package plans. Crib free. TV; cable. Dining rm 7 am-9 pm. Rm serv. Bar 11 am-9 pm. Ck-out 11 am. Health club privileges. Part of building dates from 1834. Antiques; gardens. Totally nonsmoking. Cr cds: A, DS, MC, V.
D 🖼 🔥

Marlinton

See also Hillsboro

Settled 1749 **Pop** 1,204 **Elev** 2,130 ft
Area code 304 **Zip** 24954
Information West Virginia Mountain
Highlands, PO Box 145, Elkins
26241; 304/636-8400

Marlinton is the seat of Pocahontas
County, an area known for its wide
variety of outdoor recreational
opportunities. A Ranger District
office of the Monongahela National
Forest (see ELKINS) is located in the
town.

What to See and Do

Cass Scenic Railroad State Park.
Steam train makes eight-mi round-
trip (90 min) up the mountain to
Whittaker (daily) and 22-mi round-
trip (4½ hr) to top of Bald Knob
(Tues-Sun); picnic stopover; dinner
trains (some Sat starting in June; call
for res). On 1,089-acre property are
two museums, a country store, and
14 renovated logging camp houses
now serving as tourist cottages. Picnicking, camping. Standard hrs, fees.
5 mi E on WV 39, then 19 mi N on
WV 28 to WV 66 in Cass. Phone
304/456-4300. ¢¢¢¢¢

**Cranberry Mountain Visitor Center-
Monongahela National Forest.**
Exhibits, videos, and publications on
conservation and forest manage-
ment. (Apr-Nov, daily) Approx 7 mi
NW of Mill Point via US 219 and
WV 39. Phone 304/653-4826. **FREE**
2 mi W is

> **Cranberry Glades.** A USDA Forest
> Service botanical area. Approx 750
> acres featuring open bog fringed by
> forest and alder thicket. Boardwalk
> with interpretive signs. Guided
> tours leave from visitor center
> (June-Labor Day, wkends). Glades
> (yr-round, weather permitting).
> Phone 304/653-4826. **FREE**

Greenbrier River Trail. Part of the
state park system, this 76-mi trail
runs along the Greenbrier River from
the town of Cass, on the north,
through Marlinton to North Cald-
well, on the south; passes through

small towns, over 35 bridges, and
through two tunnels. Originally the
trail was part of the Chesapeake &
Ohio Railroad. Activities incl back-
packing, bicycling, and x-country
skiing; trail also provides access for
fishing and canoeing. No developed
sites. Phone 304/799-4087.

**National Radio Astronomy Observa-
tory.** Study of universe by radio tele-
scopes. Slide show, exhibits, and
one-hr bus tour of site. (Mid-June-
Labor Day wkend, daily; Memorial
Day wkend-mid-June and after Labor
Day-Oct, Sat and Sun) 5 mi SE on
WV 39, then 21 mi N on WV 28, 92
in Green Bank. Phone 304/456-2209.
FREE

**Pocahontas County Historical
Museum.** Displays on history of the
county from its beginnings to present. Extensive photo collection.
(Early June-Labor Day, daily) On US
219 S, at WV 39. Phone 304/799-
4973. ¢

Seneca State Forest. Approx 12,000
acres with fishing and boating on
four-acre lake; hunting, hiking trails,
picnicking, playground, camping,
eight rustic cabins. Standard hrs,
fees. 5 mi E via WV 39, then 10 mi
NE on WV 28. Phone 304/799-6213.

Ski areas.

> **Elk River Touring Center.** Features
> 34 mi of x-country trails in the
> Monongahela National Forest;
> rentals; restaurant; lodging. Night
> skiing. Also guided mountain bike
> tours, cave tours in season. 16 mi
> N on US 219, follow signs, near
> Slatyfork. Phone 304/572-3771.
> ¢¢¢¢¢

> **Snowshoe Mountain Resort.** Four
> quad, seven triple chairlifts; two
> handle tows; patrol, school,
> rentals; snowmaking; restaurants,
> lodging, nursery, health club, four
> pools. Fifty-six slopes and trails;
> longest run 6,200 ft; vertical drop
> 1,500 ft. Night skiing. (Mid-Nov-
> mid-Apr, daily) Summer activities
> incl horseback riding, fishing, hik-
> ing. 26 mi N on US 219, near
> Slatyfork. ¢¢¢¢¢

Special Event

Pioneer Days. Craft exhibits and
demonstrations; horse-pulling contests, frog and turtle races; bluegrass
and mountain music shows; "4-by-4"

pulling; parade; antique car show. Early- mid-July. Phone 304/799-4315.

Martinsburg

(B-6) *See also Berkeley Springs, Charles Town, Harpers Ferry, Shepherdstown; also see Hagerstown, MD*

Settled 1732 **Pop** 14,972 **Elev** 457 ft
Area code 304 **Zip** 25401
Information Martinsburg-Berkeley County Chamber of Commerce, 198 Viking Way; 304/267-4841 or 800/332-9007
Web www.berkeleycounty.org

Martinsburg is located in the center of an apple- and peach-producing region in the state's eastern panhandle. Because of its strategic location at the entrance to the Shenandoah Valley, the town was the site of several battles during the Civil War. The famous Confederate spy Belle Boyd was a resident. Officially chartered in 1778, Martinsburg is recognized for the preservation of its many 18th- and 19th-century houses and mercantile and industrial buildings.

What to See and Do

General Adam Stephen House. (1789) Restored residence of Revolutionary War soldier and surgeon Adam Stephen, founder of Martinsburg. Period furnishings; restored smokehouse and log building. (May-Oct, Sat and Sun, limited hrs; also by appt) 309 E John St. Phone 304/267-4434. **FREE** Adj is

  Triple-Brick Building. Completed in three sections just after the Civil War, the structure was used to house railroad employees. A museum of local history is located on the top two floors. (May-Oct, Sat and Sun, limited hrs; also by appt) Phone 304/267-4434. **FREE**

Special Event

Mountain State Apple Harvest Festival. Parade, celebrity breakfast, contests, entertainment, Apple Queen coronation, square dancing, grand ball, arts and crafts show. Phone 304/263-2500. Third wkend Oct.

Motels/Motor Lodges

★ **COMFORT INN.** *1872 Edwin Miller Blvd (25401). 304/263-6200; fax 304/267-0995; toll-free 800/228-5150. www.comfortinn.com.* 109 rms, 5 story, 11 suites. Apr-Oct: S, D $49-$125; each addl $10; suites $98; under 18 free; wkend, hols rates; lower rates rest of yr. Crib free. TV; cable (premium). Pool. Complimentary continental bkfst. Restaurant adj 11 am-10 pm. Ck-out noon. Coin lndry. Meeting rms. Business servs avail. In-rm modem link. Sundries. Gift shop. Valet serv. Exercise equipt. Game rm. Some refrigerators, microwaves, minibars. Cr cds: A, C, D, DS, JCB, MC, V.
🄳 ⇋ 🏋 ⊠ 🔥 SC

★★ **COMFORT SUITES.** *Rte 9 E (25401). 304/263-8888; fax 304/263-1540; res 800/517-4000; toll-free 800/228-5050. www.comfortinn.com.* 76 rms, 3 story. May-Oct: S, D $68-$90; each addl $5; under 18 free; lower rates rest of yr. Crib free. TV; cable (premium), VCR avail. Pool. Complimentary continental bkfst. Restaurant nearby. Ck-out 11 am. Meeting rms. Business servs avail. In-rm modem link. Coin lndry. Golf privileges. Valet serv. Exercise equipt. Refrigerators, microwaves. Cr cds: A, C, D, DS, JCB, MC, V.
🄳 ⇋ 🏋 🏋 ⊠ 🔥 SC

★★ **HOLIDAY INN.** *301 Foxcroft Ave (25401). 304/267-5500; fax 304/264-9157; toll-free 800/465-4329. www.holiday-inn.com.* 120 rms, 5 story. Apr-Oct: S, D $59-$89; under 17 free; lower rates rest of yr. Crib free. Pet accepted, some restrictions. TV; cable (premium). 2 pools, 1 indoor; whirlpool, poolside servs. Restaurant 6:30 am-10 pm; Sun 7 am-9 pm. Rmserv. Bar 4 pm-1 am. Coffee in rms. Ck-out noon. Meeting rms. Business servs avail. In-rm modem link. Coin lndry. Valet serv. Lighted tennis, pro. Exercise rm; saunas. Lawn games. Some refrigerators. Cr cds: A, C, D, DS, JCB, MC, V.
🄳 ⚓ 🏌 ⇋ 🏋 ⊠ 🔥 SC

★ **KNIGHTS INN.** *1997 Edwin Miller Blvd (25401). 304/267-2211; fax*

304/267-9606; toll-free 800/843-5644. www.knightsinn.com. 59 rms, 1-2 story, 6 kits. Apr-Dec: S, D $46-$57; each addl $5; kits. $46.95-$55; under 17 free; lower rates rest of yr. Crib free. Pet accepted $5/day. TV; cable (premium), VCR avail. Complimentary coffee in lobby. Restaurant adj 6 am-11 pm. Ck-out 11 am. Business servs avail. In-rm modem link. Sundries. Refrigerators, microwaves. Cr cds: A, C, D, DS, JCB, MC, V.

★ **SUPER 8 MOTEL.** *2048 Edwin Miller Blvd (25401). 304/263-0801; fax 304/263-0801; toll-free 800/800-8000. www.super8.com.* 43 rms, 3 story. June-Sept: S, D $45-$55; each addl $6; under 16 free; wkly, wkend rates; higher rates special events; lower rates rest of yr. Crib free. Pet accepted. TV; cable (premium). Restaurant adj 6 am-11 pm. In-rm modem link. Ck-out 11 am. Meeting rms. Cr cds: A, C, D, DS, JCB, MC, V.

Resort

★ ★ ★ **WOODS RESORT & CONFERENCE CENTER.** *Mountain Lake Rd, Hedgesville (25427). 304/754-7977; fax 304/754-8146; toll-free 800/248-2222. www.thewoodsresort. com.* 60 rms in 3-building lodge, 14 kit. cabins. MAP: D $78.50-$98.50/ person; EP: S, D $89-$109; each addl $11; kit. cabins $138; under 5 free; wkends (2-night min). Crib free. TV; cable (premium), VCR avail. 4 pools, 1 indoor; wading pools, whirlpool, lifeguard. Supervised child's activities (June-Aug); ages 6-12. Complimentary coffee in lobby. Dining rm 7 am-3 pm, 5-9 pm; Fri 5-10 pm; Sat 3-10 pm; Sun 3-9 pm. Box lunches, picnics. Bar noon-midnight; entertainment Sat. Ck-out noon, ck-in 4 pm. Playground. Grocery 2½ mi. Coin lndry. Gift shop. Package store 12 mi. Meeting rms. Business servs avail. In-rm modem link. Indoor/outdoor lighted tennis. 36-hole golf privileges, greens fee $18-$50, pro. Horseback riding. Fishing. Exercise rm; sauna. Massage. Lawn games. Refrigerators, balconies. Some fireplaces. Whirlpools in lodge rms. Private patios. Cr cds: A, C, D, DS, MC, V.

Moorefield

See also Petersburg

Settled 1777 **Pop** 2,375 **Elev** 821 ft
Area code 304 **Zip** 26836
Information West Virginia Mountain Highlands, PO Box 1456, Elkins 26241; 304/636-8400

What to See and Do

Lost River State Park. More than 3,700 acres where Lee's White Sulphur Springs was once a famous resort; an original cabin still stands; museum. Swimming pool, wading pool (Memorial Day-Labor Day); hiking trails, horseback riding, tennis, game courts, picnicking, playground, restaurant, 24 cabins. Recreation building; nature programs (summer); scenic overlooks. Standard hrs, fees. 18 mi E on WV 55 to Baker, then 13 mi S on WV 259, near Mathias. Phone 304/897-5372.

Special Event

Hardy County Heritage Weekend. Tours of antebellum houses, medieval jousting, crafts, traditional events. Last full wkend Sept. Phone 304/538-6560.

Morgantown

(B-4) *See also Fairmont*

Settled 1776 **Pop** 26,809 **Elev** 892 ft
Area code 304 **Zip** 26505
Information Greater Morgantown Convention and Visitors Bureau, 709 Beechurst Ave; 304/292-5081 or 800/458-7373

Web www.mgtn.com

Morgantown is both an educational and industrial center. West Virginia University was founded here in 1867, the Morgantown Female Collegiate Institute in 1839. Known internationally for its glass, Morgantown is home to a number of glass plants which produce wares ranging from lamp parts to decorative paper weights and crystal tableware. The town is also home to a number of research laboratories maintained by the federal government.

What to See and Do

Coopers Rock State Forest. More than 12,700 acres. Trout fishing; hunting, hiking trails to historical sites; Henry Clay iron furnace (1834-1836). X-country ski trails, picnicking, playground, concession, tent and trailer camping. Standard hrs, fees. 10 mi E on I-68. Phone 304/594-1561. Adj is

Chestnut Ridge Regional Park. Swimming beach, fishing; tent and trailer camping (hookups, dump station), rustic cabins, lodge (fees), hiking, picnicking, x-country ski trails (Dec-Feb). Nature center. Park (daily). Phone 304/594-1773.

West Virginia University. (1867) 22,712 students. University has 15 colleges. Tours (Mon-Sat; for res phone 304/293-3489). The Visitors Center in the Communications Building on Patterson Dr has touch-screen monitors and video presentations about the university and upcoming special events (phone 304/293-6692 for 24-hr event information). Of special interest on the downtown campus are Stewart Hall and the university's original buildings, located on Woodburn Cir. In the Evansdale area of Morgantown are the Creative Arts Center, the 75-acre Core Arboretum, the 63,500-seat Coliseum, and the

Cook-Hayman Pharmacy Museum. Re-creates pharmacy of yesteryear with old patent medicines. (Mon-Fri; wkends by request; closed hols) Health Sciences Center North, rm 1136. Phone 304/293-5101. **Donation**

Personal Rapid Transit System (PRT). A pioneering transit system, the PRT is the world's first totally automated system. Operating without conductors or ticket takers, computer-directed cars travel between university campuses and downtown Morgantown. (Mon-Sat; may not operate hols and university breaks) Phone 304/293-5011. ¢

Whitewater rafting. Many outfitters offer guided trips on the Cheat and Tygart rivers. For a list of outfitters

contact the Greater Morgantown Convention and Visitors Bureau, 709 Beechurst Ave; Phone 800/458-7373.

Special Events

Mason-Dixon Festival. Morgantown Riverfront Park. River parade, boat races, arts and crafts, concessions. Mid-Sept. Phone 304/599-1104.

Mountaineer Balloon Festival. Morgantown Municipal Airport. Hot-air balloon races, carnival, music, food. Mid-Oct. Phone 304/296-8356.

Motels/Motor Lodges

★ **COMFORT INN.** *225 Comfort Inn Dr (26508). 304/296-9364; fax 304/296-0469; toll-free 800/228-5150. www.comfortinn.com.* 80 rms, 2 story. S, D $59-$139; each addl $5; suites $80-$115; kit. units $45-$95; under 18 free; higher rates: football wkends, graduation. Crib free. Pet accpeted. TV; cable (premium), VCR avail. Pool; whirlpool. Complimentary continental bkfst, coffee in rms. Restaurant adj 11 am-10 pm; Fri, Sat to 2 pm; Sun noon-9 pm. Ck-out noon. Meeting rm. Business servs avail. In-rm modem link. Sundries. Valet serv. Exercise equipt. Cr cds: A, C, D, DS, MC, V.
🅳 ➜ 🕇 ⊠ 🐾 SC

★ **ECONO LODGE.** *15 Commerce Dr, Westover (26507). 304/296-8774; fax 304/296-8774; toll-free 800/446-6900. www.econolodge.com.* 81 rms, 2 story. S, D $58; each addl $5; under 18 free. Crib free. TV; cable (premium). Restaurant nearby. Ck-out noon. Business servs avail. Valet serv. Cr cds: A, D, DS, MC, V.
🅳 ⊠ 🐾 SC

★ **ECONO LODGE.** *3506 Monongahela Blvd (26505). 304/599-8181; fax 304/599-8181; res 800/446-6900. www.econolodge.com.* 71 rms, 2 story. S, D $66; higher rates: football wkends, graduation. Crib $5. Pet accepted. TV; cable (premium). Complimentary continental bkfst. Restaurant adj 6 am-midnight. Ck-out 11 am. Business servs avail. In-rm modem link. Some refrigerators. Sundries. Cr cds: A, C, D, DS, MC, V.
🅳 ➜ ⊠ 🐾

★ ★ **HAMPTON INN.** *1053 Van Voorhis Rd (26505). 304/599-1200; fax 304/598-7331. www.hamptoninn.com.* 107 rms, 5 story. S, D $68-$104; suites $140 under 18 free; higher rates special events. Crib free. TV; cable (premium), VCR avail. Complimentary continental bkfst; coffee in rms. Restaurant adj. Ck-out noon. Meeting rm. Business servs avail. In-rm modem link. Valet serv. Cr cds: A, C, D, DS, JCB, MC, V.

🅳 ➶ 🐾

★ ★ **HOLIDAY INN.** *1400 Saratoga Ave (26505). 304/599-1680; fax 304/598-0989; toll-free 800/465-4329. www.holiday-inn.com.* 147 rms, 2-4 story. S, D $69-$85; under 18 free; higher rates: graduation, athletic events. Crib free. Pet accepted, $10. TV; cable (premium). Pool. Restaurant 6-11 am, 5-10 pm. Bar 4 pm-2 am. Coffee in rms. Ck-out noon. Meeting rms. Business servs avail. In-rm modem link. Valet serv. Cr cds: A, C, DS, MC, V.

🅳 ➶ ⇌ ➶ 🐾 SC

★ **RAMADA INN.** *US 119 N, I-68 & I-79 (26506). 304/296-3431; fax 304/296-8841; toll-free 800/834-9766. www.ramada.com.* 149 rms, 4 story. S, D $75-$185; each addl $5; suites, studio rms $100-$220; under 18 free; higher rates: special events, football games, Dec 31, Memorial Day wkend, graduation. Crib free. Pet accepted; $75. TV; cable (premium). Heated pool. Restaurant 6 am-10 pm. Bar 11 am-1 am, Sat to 2 am. Entertainment Wed, Fri, Sat. Complimentary continental bkfst, coffee in rms. Ck-out noon. Coin lndry. Meeting rms. Business servs avail. In-rm modem link. Sundries. Gift shop. Free airport transportation. Valet serv. Exercise equipt. Some refirgerators. Cr cds: A, C, D, DS, ER, JCB, MC, V.

🅳 ➶ ⇌ ☀ ➶ 🐾 SC

Hotel

★ ★ **HISTORIC CLARION HOTEL MORGAN.** *127 High St (26505). 304/292-8200; fax 888/241-7944; res 800/252-7466. www.clarionhotelmorgan.com.* 76 rms, 5 story. S, D $95-$130; under 12 free; monthly rates; higher rates: football season, graduation. Crib free. TV; cable (premium). Coffee in rms. Complimentary continental bkfst. Ck-out 11 am.

Meeting rms. Business servs avail. Exercise equipt. In-rm modem mlink. Valet serv. Refrigerators. Historic brick hotel (1925). Cr cds: A, C, D, DS, MC, V.

🅳 ☀ ⇌ 🐾

Resort

★ ★ ★ **LAKEVIEW RESORT.** *1 Lakeview Dr (26508). 304/594-1111; fax 304/594-9472; toll-free 800/624-8300. www.lakeviewresort.com.* 187 rms, 1-3 story. Apr-Nov: S, D $79-$199; each addl $10; suites $250-$450; under 18 free; summer, winter rates; golf plans; lower rates rest of yr. Crib free. TV; cable (premium). 4 pools, 2 indoor; whirlpool, poolside serv, lifeguard. Dining rms 6:30 am-10 pm. Bar 11-1 am; Sun from 1 pm; entertainment Mon-Sat. Coffee in rms. Ck-out 2 pm, ck-in 4 pm. Meeting rms. Business center. In-rm modem link. Valet serv. Gift shop. Free airport transportation. Playground. Supervised children's activites; ages 4-15. Indoor tennis. Two 18-hole golf courses, greens fee $39-$79, pro. Rec rm. Exercise rm; sauna. Massage. Some refrigerators. On 400 acres. Cr cds: A, C, D, DS, MC, V.

🅳 ☀ ☀ ⇌ ☀ ⇌ 🐾 SC ☀

B&B/Small Inn

★ **FIELDCREST MANOR BED AND BREAKFAST.** *1440 Stewartstown Rd (26505). 304/599-2686; fax 304/599-3796; res 866/599-2686. www.fieldcrestmanor.com.* 5 rms, 2 story. S $75; D $90; under 10 free; package plans; wkends, hols (2-day min). TV; cable (premium). Complimentary full bkfst. Ck-out 11 am, ck-in 3 pm. Business servs avail. In-rm modem link. Built in 1900; hillside location. Totally nonsmoking. Cr cds: A, MC, V.

⇌ 🐾

Restaurants

★ ★ **BACK BAY.** *1869 Mileground (26505). 304/296-3027. www.backbaywv.com.* Hrs: 11 am-9:30 pm; Fri to 10:30 pm; Sat 4-10:30 pm; Sun noon-9 pm. Closed hols. Bar. Lunch $3.95-$7.95, dinner $7.25-$21.95. Specializes in fresh seafood, prime rib, Cajun dishes. Nautical atmosphere. Cr cds: A, D, DS, MC, V.

🅳

★ **PUGLIONI'S.** *1137 Van Voorhis Rd (26505). 304/599-7521.* Hrs: 11 am-10 pm; Fri, Sat to 10 pm. Closed hols. Italian menu. Bar. Lunch $3.75-$8.95, dinner $7-$15. Child's menu. Specialties: pasta carbonara, pasta bellagio, chicken putanesca. Own pasta. Parking. Cr cds: A, D, DS, MC, V.
D

Nitro

(D-2) *See also Charleston*

Founded 1918 **Pop** 6,824 **Elev** 604 ft
Area code 304 **Zip** 25143
Information Putnam County Chamber of Commerce, 5664 WV Rte 34, PO Box 553, Teays 25569; 304/757-6510
Web www.putnamcounty.org

Nitro experienced explosive growth around a huge smokeless powder plant during World War I, when the town's population reached 35,000 overnight and some 3,400 buildings were erected. When the war ended the demand for smokeless powder fizzled and the town dried up; factory buildings were scrapped and whole houses were shipped down the river. Now a western suburb of Charleston, Nitro produces chemicals.

What to See and Do

Tri-State Greyhound Park. Indoor grandstand, clubhouse, concessions. (Mon-Sat eves; matinees Sat, Sun, and hols) Must be 18 to wager. E via I-64 exit 47A to Goff Mountain Rd, then to Greyhound Dr in Cross Lanes. Phone 304/776-1000.

Waves of Fun. Water park featuring three water slides, wave pool, swimming areas, bathhouse, tube rentals (fee), lockers, concessions; miniature golf. (Memorial Day-June, wkends; early June-Labor Day, daily) W via I-64 exit 39, then 3 mi S on WV 34, at Valley Park in Hurricane. Phone 304/562-0518. ¢¢¢

Motels/Motor Lodges

★ **ECONO LODGE.** *4115 1st Ave (25143). 304/755-8341; fax 304/755-2933; res 800/780-7234. www.econolodge.com.* 42 rms, 1-3 story. No elvtr. S, D $56-$66; under 12 free. Crib $6. Pet accepted; $10. TV; cable (premium). Restaurant adj open 24 hrs. Meeting rm. Ck-out 11 am. Business servs avail. Cr cds: A, C, D, DS, MC, V.
D ≥ ≥ 🔥 ➡

★ **COMFORT INN.** *102 Racer Dr, Cross Lanes (25313). 304/776-8070; fax 304/776-6460. www.comfortinn. com.* 112 rms, 2 story. S $62-$75; D $67-$79; each addl $5; under 18 free. Crib free. TV; cable (premium). Pool; whirlpool. Complimentary continental bkfst. Coffee in rms. Restaurant adj 7 am-midnight. Bar 4 pm-12 am; Fri, Sat to 2 am. Ck-out noon. Meeting rms. Business servs avail. Sundries. Exercise rm. Microwaves avail. Cr cds: A, C, D, DS, MC, V.
D ≥ 𝒳 ≥ 🔥 SC

★ ★ **SUPER 8.** *419 Hurricane Creek Rd, Hurricane (25526). 304/562-3346; fax 304/562-7408; res 800/800-8000. www.super8.com.* 146 rms, 2 story. Apr-Sept: S, D $40-$56; each addl $5; under 16 free; wkly rates; higher rates special events; lower rates rest of yr. Crib $5. Pet accepted, some restrictions; $10. TV; cable (premium). Pool. Complimentary continental bkfst. Restaurant adj 7 am-10 pm. Ck-out noon. Coin lndry. Business servs avail. In-rm modem link. Sundries. Game rm. Some refrigerators; microwaves avail. Picnic tables, grills. Cr cds: A, C, D, DS, MC, V.
D ➡ ≥ ≥ 🔥 SC

Restaurants

★ **DIEHL'S.** *152 Main Ave (25143). 304/755-9353.* Hrs: 10:30 am-9 pm; Sun 11 am-8 pm. Closed Mon. Lunch $3-$6, dinner $3.50-$7. Specializes in home-cooked meals. Casual decor. Cr cds: A, DS, MC, V.
D ≥

★ ★ ★ **WELLINGTON'S.** *1 Dairy Rd, Poca (25159). 304/755-8219. www. wellingtons.webatonce.com.* Hrs: 11 am-2 pm, 5-10 pm; Mon 5-10 pm; Sat 5-10 pm; early-bird dinner 5-6:30

pm. Closed Sun; hols. Res accepted. Continental menu. Bar. Lunch $5.95-$9.95, dinner $15-$24. Lunch buffet $5.75. Specialties: beef Wellington, shrimp and scallop tower, steak Diane. Piano Sat. Intimate atmosphere. Totally nonsmoking. Cr cds: A, C, D, DS, MC, V.

D

Parkersburg (B-3)

Settled 1785 **Pop** 33,099 **Elev** 616 ft
Area code 304 **Zip** 26101
Information Parkersburg/Wood Co Convention & Visitor's Bureau, 350 7th St; 304/428-1130 or 800/752-4982
Web www.parkersburgcvb.org

In 1770 George Washington came to this area to inspect lands awarded to him by Virginia for his military services. After the Revolutionary War, Blennerhassett Island, in the Ohio River west of Parkersburg, was the scene of the alleged Burr-Blennerhassett plot. Harman Blennerhassett, a wealthy Irishman, built a lavish mansion on this island. After killing Alexander Hamilton in a duel, Aaron Burr came to the island, allegedly with the idea of seizing the Southwest and setting up an empire; Blennerhassett may have agreed to join him. On December 10, 1806, the plot was uncovered. Both men were acquitted of treason but ruined financially in the process. The Blennerhassett mansion burned in 1811 but was later rebuilt.

Today Parkersburg is the center for many industries, including glass, chemicals, petrochemicals, and ferrous and other metals. Fishing is popular in the area, especially below the Belleville and Willow Island locks and dams on the Ohio River.

What to See and Do

Actors Guild Playhouse. Musical, comedic, and dramatic performances. (Fri-Sun) 8th and Market sts. Phone 304/485-1300. ¢¢

Blennerhassett Island Historical State Park. A 500-acre island accessible only by sternwheeler. There are self-guided walking tours of the island; horse-drawn wagon rides; tours of the Blennerhassett mansion. Bicycle rentals, picnicking, concession. (May-Labor Day, Tues-Sun, also hols; Sept-Oct, Thurs-Sun) Tickets avail for boat ride at Blennerhassett Museum. 2 mi S in Ohio River. Phone 304/420-4800. ¢¢

Blennerhassett Museum. Features archaeological and other exhibits relating to history of Blennerhassett Island and Parkersburg area; incl arti-

Blennerhassett Mansion, Blennerhassett Island Historical State Park

facts dating back 12,000 yrs. Theater with video presentation. (May-Oct, Tues-Sun; rest of yr, Sat and Sun; closed Jan 1, Thanksgiving, Dec 25) 2nd and Juliana sts. Phone 304/420-4840. ¢

City Park. A 55-acre wooded area with the Cooper Log Cabin Museum, which dates from 1804. Swimming pool, fishing, paddle boats; miniature golf, tennis, shelters and picnic facilities. Park Ave and 23rd St. Phone 304/424-8572.

Middleton Doll Company. Tour of vinyl and porcelain doll factory (20 min). Factory store (Mon-Sat; closed hols) 2 mi W via US 50, at 1301 Washington Blvd in Belpre, OH. Phone 740/423-1481. **FREE**

Mountwood Park. Wooded area with fishing, boating (no gasoline motors); hiking, mountain bike, nature trails, picnic area. 12 mi E via US 50 to Volcano Rd. Phone 304/679-3611. **FREE**

North Bend State Park. Approx 1,400 acres in the wide valley of the North Fork of the Hughes River; scenic overlooks of famous horseshoe bend. Swimming pool, bathhouse, fishing; miniature golf, tennis, game courts; hiking, bicycle, and bridle trail; 71-mi North Bend Rail Tr (see Clarksburg). Picnicking, playground, concession, restaurant, lodge, tent and trailer camping (dump station), eight cabins. Nature, recreation programs. Nature trail for disabled. Standard hrs, fees. 22 mi E on US 50, then 7 mi SE on WV 31, near Cairo. Phone 304/643-2931.

Parkersburg Art Center. Changing exhibits. (Tues-Sun; closed hols) 725 Market St. Phone 304/485-3859. ¢

Rubles Sternwheelers Riverboat Cruises. To Blennerhassett Island. (May-early Sept, Tues-Sun; early Sept-Oct, Thurs-Sun) Depart from Point Park, 2nd and Ann sts. Phone 740/423-7268. ¢¢¢

Special Events

Parkersburg Homecoming. Point Park, just off WV 68 at foot of 2nd St. Riverfront celebration features entertainment, parade, sternwheeler races, waterskiing show, miniature car races, fireworks. Third wkend Aug. Phone 304/422-3588.

West Virginia Honey Festival. 4-H Grounds. Honey-related exhibits, baking, food, arts and crafts. Mid-Sept. Phone 304/428-1130.

Motels/Motor Lodges

★★ **HOLIDAY INN.** *Rte 50 & I-77 (26104).* 304/485-6200; fax 304/485-6261. www.holiday-inn.com. 149 rms, 2 story. S, D $55-$97; wkend packages. Crib free. TV; cable (premium). Heated indoor pool; whirlpool. Restaurant 6 am-9 pm; Sat from 7 am; Sun 7 am-2 pm, 5-8 pm. Bar 11 am-midnight. Ck-out noon. Coin lndry. Meeting rms. Business servs avail. In-rm modem link. Bellhops. Game rm. Valet serv. Exercise equipt; sauna. Some refrigerators. Some balconies. Cr cds: A, D, DS, MC, V.

⬛ 🏊 🧍 ⬇ 🔥 SC

★★ **NORTH BEND STATE PARK LODGE.** *Rural Rte 1 Box 221, Cairo (26337).* 304/643-2931; fax 304/643-2970; toll-free 800/225-5982. www.northbendsp.com. 29 rms, 2 story, 8 cabins. Memorial Day wkend-Labor Day: S, D $51-$67; each addl $6; 2-3 bedrm cabins $528-$666/wk; under 12 free; lower rates rest of yr. Crib free. TV. Playground. Free supervised children's activities. Restaurant 7 am-8 pm. Rm serv. Ck-out noon (lodge), 10 am (cabins). Metting rms. Business servs avail. Sundries. Gift shop. Tennis. Picnic tables, grills. On river. View of mountains. State owned, operated. Cr cds: A, D, DS, MC, V.

⬛ 🎿 ⬇ 🔥 SC

★ **RED ROOF INN.** *3714 E 7th St (26104).* 304/485-1741; fax 304/485-1746; toll-free 800/733-7663. www.redroof.com. 106 rms, 2 story. S, D $40-$52; each addl $5; under 18 free. Crib free. Pet accepted. TV; cable (premium). Coin lndry. Exercise equipt. Ck-out noon. Meeting rms. Business servs avail. In-rm modem link. Valet serv. Cr cds: A, C, D, DS, MC, V.

⬛ 🐾 ⬇ 🔥 SC

Hotel

★★★ **HISTORIC BLENNERHAS-SETT.** *320 Market St (26101).* 304/422-3131; fax 304/485-0267;

toll-free 800/262-2536. www.
blennerhassett.com. 104 rms, 5 story.
S, D $95-$115; each addl $6; suites
$145-$165; under 18 free. Crib free.
Pet accepted; $10. TV; cable (pre-
mium), VCR avail. Coffee in rms.
Restaurant 6 am-10 pm. Rm serv. Bar
11-1 am. Ck-out noon. Meeting rms.
Business servs avail. In-rm modem
link. Gift shop. Valet parking. Free
airport transportation. Valet serv.
Restored Victorian hotel built in
1889. Cr cds: A, D, DS, MC, V.

B&B/Small Inn

★ ★ ★ **WILLIAMS' HOUSE BED
AND BREAKFAST.** 5406 Grand Central Ave, Vienna (26105). 304/295-
7212; fax 304/295-5550. 5 rms, 3
story. No elvtr. Some rm phones. S
$65; D $74; suite $89; wkend May-
Nov (2-night min); each addl $10.
Crib $10. TV; cable (premium), VCR
avail (movies). Complimentary full
bkfst. Ck-out 11:30 am, ck-in 3 pm.
Business servs avail. Airport transportation. Exercise equipt. Pool.
Lawn games. Microwaves avail. Valet
serv. Picnic tables, grills. Built in
1920; antiques. Totally nonsmoking.
Cr cds: MC, V.

Restaurants

★ **MOUNTAINEER FAMILY
RESTAURANT.** 4006 E 7th St (26101).
304/422-0101. Open 24 hrs. Closed
hols. Bkfst $1.95-$7.95, lunch $2.75-
$6.95, dinner $6-$13. Child's menu.
Specializes in steak, seafood, chicken.
Cr cds: MC, V.

★ ★ **POINT OF VIEW.** Blennerhassett
Heights Rd (26101). 304/863-3366.
www.pointofviewrestaurant.com. Hrs:
11:30 am-2 pm, 5-9:30 pm; Fri, Sat
5-10 pm. Closed Sun; Jan 1, Dec 25.
Bar. Lunch $4-$8, dinner $10-$30.
Child's menu. Specializes in prime
rib, fresh seafood, steak. Own baking. View of Blennerhassett Island.
Family-owned. Cr cds: A, D, DS,
MC, V.

Petersburg

(E-6) See also Franklin, Moorefield

Settled 1745 **Pop** 2,423 **Elev** 937 ft
Area code 304 **Zip** 26847

Information West Virginia Mountain
Highlands, 1200 Harrison Ave, Lower
Level, Suite A, Elkins 26241;
304/636-8400

A Ranger District office of the
Monongahela National Forest (see
ELKINS) is located in Petersburg.

What to See and Do

Monongahela National Forest. Recreation area is popular for canoeing,
hiking, and other outdoor sports.
Camping (fee). USDA Forest Service,
H659, PO Box 240. Phone 304/257-
4488. **FREE**

Smoke Hole Caverns. Caverns were
used centuries ago by the Seneca
both for shelter and the smoking of
meat. During the Civil War they
were used by troops on both sides for
storing ammunition. Later, they hid
"moonshiners," illegal distillers of
corn whiskey. It is claimed the caverns contain the longest ribbon stalactite and the second-highest cave
rm in the world. Guided tours. Large
gift shop with wildlife exhibits; concessions. Tours. (Daily; closed
Thanksgiving, Dec 25) 8 mi S on WV
28 and 55. Phone 304/257-4442. ¢¢¢

Motels/Motor Lodges

★ ★ **HERMITAGE MOTOR INN.**
203 Virginia Ave (26847). 304/257-
1711; fax 304/257-4330; toll-free
800/437-6482. 38 rms, 2 story. S
$47; D $55; each addl $6; under 12
free. Crib $5. TV; cable (premium).
Pool. Complimentary continental
bkfst. Restaurant 11 am-9 pm; Sat 4-
9 pm; Sun 11 am-3 pm. Ck-out
noon. Business servs avail. In-rm
modem link. Some reffrigerators.
Gift shop. shopping arcade. Craft
shop, bookstore in 1840s inn. Cr
cds: A, C, D, DS, MC, V.

★ **SMOKE HOLE HOTEL & LOG
CABINS.** WV 28 S; HC 59 Box 39,

Seneca Rocks (26884). 304/257-4442; fax 304/257-2745; toll-free 800/828-8478. www.smokehole.com. 10 rms, 3 suites, 35 cottages. S, D $49-$79; each addl $10; kit. cottages $94-$189; wkends (2-day min), hols (3-day min), family, wkly rates. TV; cable (premium). Pool. Playground. Ck-out 11 am. In-rm modem link. Gift shop. Lawn games. Refrigerators in cabins. Adj Smoke Hole Caverns. Cr cds: A, D, DS, MC, V.

Philippi

See also Buckhannon, Clarksburg, Grafton

Settled 1780 **Pop** 2,870 **Elev** 1,307 ft
Area code 304 **Zip** 26416
Information Barbour County Chamber of Commerce, PO Box 5000; 304/457-1958

The first land battle of the Civil War, a running rout of the Confederates known locally as the Philippi Races, was fought here on June 3, 1861. A historical marker on the campus of Alderson-Broaddus College marks the site. The Union attacked to protect the Baltimore & Ohio Railroad, whose main line between Washington and the West ran near the town.

What to See and Do

Barbour County Historical Society Museum. This B & O Railroad station (1911), used until 1956, is now restored as a museum; also local arts and crafts. (May-Oct, daily; rest of yr, by appt) 146 N Main St. Phone 304/457-4846.

Covered bridge. Spanning Tygart River since 1852; restored in recent years; believed to be the only two-lane bridge of its type still in daily use on a federal highway (US 250). Phone 304/645-7195.

Special Events

Blue & Gray Reunion. Commemorates the first land battle of the Civil War; reenactment, parade, crafts.

First wkend June. Phone 304/457-4265.

Barbour County Fair. Fairgrounds, 5 mi SE on US 250. Horse and antique car shows, quilt and livestock exhibits, carnival rides, nightly entertainment, parade, and more. Phone 304/457-3254. Wk before Labor Day. Phone 304/823-1328.

Motel/Motor Lodge

★ **PHILIPPI LODGING.** *Rte 4 Box 155 (26416). 304/457-5888; fax 304/457-5888.* 39 rms, 2 story. S, D $50-$80; each addl $6; under 12 free. Crib free. Pet accepted. TV; cable (premium). Complimentary coffee in lobby. Restaurant adj 6 am-9 pm. Ck-out 11 am. Business servs avail. In-rm modem link. Cr cds: A, C, D, DS, MC, V.

Point Pleasant

See also Ripley

Settled 1774 **Pop** 4,637 **Elev** 569 ft
Area code 304 **Zip** 25550
Information Mason County Area Chamber of Commerce, 305 Main St; 304/675-1050

On October 10, 1774, British-incited Shawnees under Chief Cornstalk fought a battle here against 1,100 frontiersmen. The colonists won and broke the Native American power in the Ohio Valley. Historians later argued that this, rather than the battle at Lexington, Massachusetts, was the first battle of the Revolutionary War. In 1908 the US Senate rewrote history by recognizing this claim.

What to See and Do

Krodel Park and Lake. A 44-acre park with a replica of Fort Randolph (ca 1775). Fishing (license required), paddle boats (fee); miniature golf (fee), playground, camping (Apr-Nov; fee). 1 mi SE via WV 62/2. Phone 304/675-1068. **FREE**

McClintic Wildlife Management Area.
Approx 2,800 acres with primitive
camping (fee). Also fishing and hunting (licenses required). 7 mi NE off
WV 62. Phone 304/675-0871.

**Point Pleasant Battle Monument
State Park.** An 84-ft granite shaft was
erected here in 1909, after the US
Senate agreed to a claim made by
historians that the first battle of the
Revolutionary War was fought here.
Park also contains a marker where
Joseph Celeron de Bienville buried a
leaden plate in 1749, claiming the
land for France, and the graves of
Chief Cornstalk and "Mad Anne"
Bailey, noted pioneer scout. 1 Main
St, in Tu-Endie-Wei Park (Native
American for "where two rivers
meet"). Phone 304/675-0869. **FREE**
Also here is

> **Mansion House.** (1796) Oldest log
> building in Kanawha Valley,
> restored as a museum. (May-Oct,
> daily) Phone 304/675-0869. **FREE**

West Virginia State Farm Museum.
Contains more than 30 farm buildings depicting early rural life, incl a
log church, one-rm schoolhouse,
kitchen, scale house, and four-unit
building. Barn contains mount of
one of the largest horses in the
world; also animals. (Apr-Nov, Tues-
Sun) 4 mi N via WV 62, adj to
county fairgrounds. Phone 304/675-
5737. **FREE**

Special Event

Mason County Fair. County Fairgrounds. Livestock show, arts and
crafts, contests, Nashville entertainers. Mid-Aug. Phone 304/675-5463.

Motel/Motor Lodge

★ ★ **LOWE HOTEL.** *401 Main St
(25550).* 304/675-2260. 30 rms, 3
story. S $44; D $48; suites $58-$54.
Crib free. TV; cable (premium); VCR
avail. Complimentary coffee in
lobby. Restaurant nearby. Ck-out
noon. Meeting rms. Business servs
avail. Some refrigerators. Cr cds: A,
C, D, DS, MC, V.

Princeton

(E-3) *See also Bluefield*

Settled 1826 **Pop** 6,347 **Elev** 2,446 ft
Area code 304 **Zip** 24740
Information Princeton-Mercer
County Chamber of Commerce, 910
Oakvale Rd; 304/487-1502
Web www.pmcc.com

Princeton is the southern terminus
of the spectacular 88-mile West Virginia Turnpike and a trade center for
an agricultural, industrial, and coal
mining area.

What to See and Do

Camp Creek State Park. Approx 500
acres. Fishing; hiking trails, game
courts, biking, horseback riding, picnicking, playgrounds, camping. Standard hrs, fees. 13 mi N on I-77, exit
20, then 2 mi NW, at Camp Creek.
Phone 304/425-9481.

Motels/Motor Lodges

★ **COMFORT INN.** *Ambrose Ln and
US 460 W (24740).* 304/487-6101; fax
304/425-7002; res 800/228-5150.
www.comfortinn.com. 51 rms, 2 story.
S, D $65-$85; each addl $6; under 18
free. Crib free. TV; cable (premium).
Complimentary continental bkfst.
Restaurant nearby. Ck-out noon.
Business servs avail. In-rm modem
link. Valet serv. Downhill ski 20 mi.
Whirlpool. Cr cds: A, C, D, DS, JCB,
MC, V.

★ **DAYS INN.** *347 Meadowfield Ln
(24740).* 304/425-8100; fax 304/487-
1734; res 800/329-7466. *www.days
inn.com.* 122 rms, 2 story. S $58-
$63; D $63-$78; kit. units $150;
under 16 free. Crib free. Pet
accepted; $6. TV; cable (premium).
Heated indoor pool; whirlpool.
Coin lndry. Complimentary continental bkfst, coffee in rms. Restaurant adj 6 am-10 pm. Ck-out 11 am.
Business servs avail. In-rm modem
link. Meeting rm. Sundries. Downhill ski 15 mi. Valet serv. Cr cds: A,
D, DS, ER, JCB, MC, V.

Restaurant

★ **JOHNSTON'S INN.** *805 Old Oak Vale Rd (US 460) (24740). 304/425-7591.* Hrs: 6:30 am-9:30 pm; Fri, Sat to 10:30 pm. Closed Thanksgiving, Dec 25. Res accepted. Bar from 11:30 am; Sun 3-10 pm. Bkfst $2-$5.50, lunch $5-$7, dinner $8-$16. Child's menu. Specializes in steak, seafood, desserts. Salad bar. Own salad dressings. Tiffany lamps, artwork, antiques. Family-owned. Cr cds: A, D, DS, MC, V.

D ⟶

Ripley

See also Point Pleasant

Settled 1768 **Pop** 3,263 **Elev** 616 ft
Area code 304 **Zip** 25271

What to See and Do

Washington's Lands Museum and Park. Housed in converted river lock building and restored Sayre Log House; exhibits trace the pioneer and river history of the area. Park, on the Ohio River, has picnicking and boat launching facilities. Museum (Memorial Day-Labor Day, Sat-Sun afternoons). 6 mi N via I-77 exit 146 to Ravenswood, then 2½ mi S on WV 68. Phone 304/372-5343. **DONATION**

Special Events

Mountain State Art & Craft Fair. Cedar Lakes Conference Center. Features traditional crafts, art, folk music, and foods. Early July. Phone 304/372-7860 or 304/372-7866.

West Virginia Black Walnut Festival. 25 mi E on US 33/119 in Spencer. Parade, carnival, band festival, car show, contests, livestock show, arts and crafts. Mid-Oct. Phone 304/927-1780.

Motels/Motor Lodges

★★ **BEST WESTERN MCCOYS INN AND CONFERENCE CENTER.** *701 Main St (25271). 304/372-9122; fax 304/372-4400; res 800/288-9122. www.bestwestern.com.* 140 rms, 2 story. S, D $59-$79; suites $150; under 12 free. Crib $3. TV; cable (premium). Pool. Complimentary continental bkfst, coffee in rms. Restaurant 11 am-10 pm; closed Sun. Ck-out 11 am. Coin lndry. Exercise equipt; steam rm. Massage. Valet serv. Meeting rms. Business servs avail. In-rm modem link. Sundries. Some in-rm whirlpools, refrigerators, fireplaces. Cr cds: A, C, D, DS, MC, V.

D ⟶ ⟶ ⟶ ⟶ SC

★★ **HOLIDAY INN EXPRESS.** *1 Hospitality Dr (25271). 304/372-5000; fax 304/372-5600; toll-free 800/465-4329. www.holiday-inn.com.* 65 rms, 2 story. S, D $55-$79; suites $99-$120; under 18 free; higher rates Mountain State Arts and Crafts Fair. Crib free. TV; cable (premium). Complimentary continental bkfst, coffee in rms. Restaurant adj 6:30 am-11 pm. Ck-out 11 am. Meeting rms. Business servs avail. In-rm modem link. Coin lndry. Exercise equipt. Cr cds: A, C, D, DS, MC, V.

D ⟶ ⟶

Shepherdstown

See also Charles Town, Harpers Ferry, Martinsburg; also see Frederick, Hagerstown, MD

Settled ca 1730 **Pop** 803 **Elev** 406 ft
Area code 304 **Zip** 25443

Information Jefferson County Chamber of Commerce, 201 Frontage Rd, PO Box 426, Charles Town 25414; 304/725-2055

Web www.jeffersoncounty.com/chamber

In 1787 Shepherdstown was the site of the first successful public launching of a steamboat. However, James Rumsey, inventor of the craft, died before he could exploit his success. Rival claims by John Fitch, and Robert Fulton's commercial success with the *Clermont* 20 years later, have clouded Rumsey's achievement.

The state's first newspaper was published here in 1790, and Shepherdstown almost became the national capital. (George Washington considered it as a possible site, according to letters in the Library of Congress.) Shepherdstown is also the location of one of the early grist-mills, which is believed to have been constructed around 1739 and finally ceased production in 1939. This is the oldest continuously settled town in the state.

What to See and Do

Historic Shepherdstown Museum. Artifacts dating to 1700s, incl many items concerning the founding of the town. Guided tours (by appt). (Apr-Oct, daily) In old Entler Hotel (1786), German and Princess sts. Phone 304/876-0910. **FREE** Also avail here are

Guided walking tours. Historic sites in Shepherdstown. Phone 304/876-0910. ¢¢

B&Bs/Small Inns

★ ★ ★ **BAVARIAN INN & LODGE.** *Rte 34 (25443). 304/876-2551; fax 304/876-9355. www.bavarianinnwv.com.* 73 rms, 2 in main bldg, 3-4 story, 4 chalets. S, D $105-$272; each addl $10; suites $210-$275; under 12 free; package plans; golf plan. Crib $10. TV; cable (premium), VCR avail. Pool; poolside serv. Complimentary coffee. Dining rm (see also BAVARIAN INN AND LODGE RESTAURANT). Bar 5 pm-midnight; Sun from 1 pm. Ck-out noon, ck-in 3 pm. Meeting rms. Business servs avail. In-rm modem link. Gift shop. Tennis. Golf privileges, putting green. Exercise equipt. Some in-rm whirlpools, fireplaces. Balconies. Totally non-smoking. Cr cds: A, C, D, DS, MC, V.

★ ★ ★ **THOMAS SHEPHERD INN.** *300 W German St (25443). 304/876-3715; fax 304/876-3313; res 888/889-8952. www.thomasshepherdinn.com.* 6 rms, 2 story. S, D $85-$101; wkends (2-day min); higher rates wkends. Children over 8 yrs only. TV, VCR in sitting rm (movies). Complimentary full bkfst. Ck-out 11 am, ck-in 2-6 pm. Business servs avail. In-rm modem link. Tennis privileges. Golf privileges. Fireplaces. Federal-style house (1868) on land originally owned by town founder

Thomas Shepherd. Totally nonsmoking. Cr cds: A, DS, MC, V.

Restaurants

★ ★ ★ **BAVARIAN INN AND LODGE.** *Rte 34 (25443). 304/876-2551. www.bavarianinnwv.com.* Hrs: 7:30-10:30 am, 11:30 am-2:30 pm, 5-10 pm; Sat from 4 pm; Sun noon-9 pm. Res accepted. German, continental menu. Bar 5 pm-midnight; Sun from 1 pm. Wine list. Bkfst $4.50-$9.75, lunch $5.50-$17.50, dinner $15-$30. Child's menu. Specializes in veal, game (in season), vegetarian dishes. Own baking. Parking. Entertainment. Fireplaces. Antiques. Overlooks Potomac River. Family-owned. Cr cds: A, D, DS, MC, V.

★ **OLD PHARMACY CAFE & SODA FOUNTAIN.** *138 E German St (25443). 304/876-2085.* Hrs: 11 am-9 pm; Fri, Sat to 10 pm. Entertainment Thurs-Sat evenings. Closed Jan 1, Thanksgiving, Dec 25. Res accepted. Bar. Wine, beer. Lunch $5.95-$8.95, dinner $15-$18. Child's menu. Specializes in gourmet sandwiches, vegetarian dishes, eclectic regional dishes. Street parking. In former pharmacy (1911); many original pieces incl a marble soda fountain. Cr cds: D, DS, MC, V.

★ ★ ★ **YELLOW BRICK BANK & LITTLE INN.** *201 German at Princess St (25443). 304/876-2208.* Hrs: 11:30 am-10 pm; Sun brunch 11 am-4 pm. Entertainment Fri, Sat. Closed Thanksgiving, Dec 25. Res accepted. Bar. A la carte entrees: lunch $5-$14, dinner $15-$25. Sun brunch $5-$14. Specializes in seafood, pasta, regional cuisine. Own baking. Street parking. Wood burning oven. In 1910 bank building in historic commercial district. Overnight stays avail. Cr cds: D, MC, V.

Summersville

See also Gauley Bridge

Founded 1824 **Pop** 3,294 **Elev** 1,894 ft **Area code** 304 **Zip** 26651
Information Chamber of Commerce, 411 Old Main Dr, PO Box 567; 304/872-1588

Twenty-year-old Nancy Hart led a surprise Confederate attack on Summersville in July 1861, captured a Union force, and burned the town. She was captured but her jail guard succumbed to her charms. The guard was then disarmed and killed by the young woman. She escaped to Lee's lines. After the war she returned to Summersville.

What to See and Do

Carnifex Ferry Battlefield State Park. Here on Sept 10, 1861, 7,000 Union troops under General William S. Rosecrans fought and defeated a lesser number of Confederates under General John B. Floyd. The 156-acre park incl Patteson House Museum (Memorial Day-wkend after Labor Day, Sat, Sun, hols), which displays Civil War relics. Hiking trails, picnicking, game courts, playgrounds, concession. Civil War reenactment (weekend after Labor Day). Park (May-early Sept, daily). 12 mi W on WV 39, then SE on WV 129, near Kesslers Cross Lanes. Phone 304/872-0825. **FREE**

Gauley River National Recreation Area. Designated a federally protected area in Oct 1988, the 25-mi stretch of the Gauley from the Summersville Dam west to just above the town of Swiss is famous for whitewater rafting. There are no developed sites. Large tracts of land along river are privately owned. For further information and a list of whitewater outfitters contact Superintendent, New River Gorge National River, PO Box 246, Glen Jean 25846. Phone 304/465-0508.

Summersville Lake. A 2,700-acre lake. Swimming, waterskiing, fishing, boating; hiking, picnicking. Battle

Run Campground is 3 mi W on WV 129 (fee). (May-Oct, daily) Fee for some activities. 5 mi S on US 19. Phone 304/872-3459.

Special Events

Nicholas County Fair. 3 mi N at Nicholas County Memorial Park. Midway; flower show; agricultural and crafts exhibits. July. Phone 304/872-1454.

Nicholas County Potato Festival. Citywide. Incl parades, entertainment, volleyball tournament, arts and crafts show, bed races. First full wk Sept. Phone 304/872-3722.

Motels/Motor Lodges

★ ★ **BEST WESTERN.** *1203 S Broad St (26651). 304/872-6900; fax 304/872-6908; res 800/214-9551. www.bestwestern.com.* 57 rms, 3 story. April-Oct: S, D $50-$83; each addl $5; under 12 free; lower rates rest of yr. Crib free. Pet accepted, some restrictions; $5. TV; cable (premium), VCR avail (movies). Complimentary continental bkfst. Coffee in rms. Restaurant 11 am-10 pm. Bar. Coin lndry. Ck-out 11 am. Business servs avail. In-rm modem link. Some refrigerators. Microwave avail. Cr cds: A, C, D, DS, MC, V.

★ **COMFORT INN.** *903 Industrial Dr N (26651). 304/872-6500; fax 304/872-3090; toll-free 800/872-1752. www.comfortinn.com.* 99 rms, 2 story. June-Oct: S, D $69-$90; each addl $5-$7; suites $90-$125; under 18 free; lower rates rest of yr. Crib free. Pet accepted, some restrictions; $5. TV; cable (premium), VCR avail (movies). Heated pool; wading pool. Complimentary continental bkfst. Restaurant nearby. Ck-out 11 am. Coin lndry. Meeting rms. In-rm modem link. Exercise equipt; sauna. Gift shop. Valet serv. Refrigerator in suites. Microwaves avail. Picnic tables. Cr cds: A, C, D, DS, MC, V.

★ **SLEEP INN.** *701 Professional Park Dr; (26651). 304/872-4500; fax 304/872-0288; res 800/872-1751. www.sleepinn.com.* 97 rms, 2 story. June-Oct: S, D $50-$66; each addl $5; under 18 free; higher rates special events; lower rates rest of yr. Crib free. Pet accepted, some restrictions; $5. TV; cable (premium), VCR avail (movies). Heated pool. Complimentary continental bkfst. Restaurant adj 11 am-10 pm. Ck-out 11 am. Coin lndry. Meeting rms. Business servs avail. In-rm modem link. Sundries. Lawn games. Refrigerators, microwaves avail. Cr cds: A, C, D, DS, MC, V.

Sutton

Settled 1826 **Pop** 1,011 **Elev** 840 ft
Area code 304 **Zip** 26601

What to See and Do

Sutton Lake. Dam is one mi E. Swimming in designated areas, boat launch (fee); camping (May-Dec; some electric hookups; fees) at Gerald R. Freeman Campground, 16 mi E on WV 15; and at Mill Creek-Bakers Run Area, 16 mi SE on WV 17. Phone 304/765-2816.

Motel/Motor Lodge

★ ★ **DAYS INN.** *2000 Sutton Ln (26601). 304/765-5055; fax 304/765-2067; res 800/329-7466. www. flatwoodsusa.com.* 200 units, 5 story. Mar-Nov: S $75; D $90; each addl $5; suites $135-$160; under 13 free; lower rates rest of yr. Crib free. TV; cable (premium). Heated indoor pool. Restaurant 5-10 pm; Sun 6-10 am. Bar 5 pm-midnight. Coffee in rms. Ck-out 11 am. Meeting rms. Business servs avail. In-rm modem link. Sundries. Gift shop. Exercise equipt; sauna. Many balconies. Some refrigerators. Cr cds: A, D, DS, MC, V.

Webster Springs

Settled 1860 **Pop** 990 **Elev** 1,509 ft
Area code 304 **Zip** 26288
Information Mayor's Office, 146 McGraw Ave; 304/847-5411

Once a resort famed for its medicinal "lick," or spring, the town is now a trading center and meeting place for sportsmen.

What to See and Do

Holly River State Park. More than 8,000 acres of heavy forest with excellent trout fishing in Laurel Fork. Swimming pool, bathhouse; hiking trails to waterfalls and Potato Knob, tennis, game courts, picnicking, playground, restaurant (seasonal), camping (dump station), nine cabins. Nature, recreation programs (summer). Standard hrs, fees. 20 mi N on WV 20 to Hacker Valley, then 1 mi E. Phone 304/493-6353.

Kumbrabow State Forest. More than 9,400 acres of wild, rugged country with trout fishing; deer, turkey, and grouse hunting; hiking trails, x-country skiing, picnicking, playground, tent and trailer camping, five rustic cabins. Standard hrs, fees. 25 mi NE on WV 15, then 5 mi N, near Monterville. Phone 304/335-2219.

Special Events

Webster Springs Woodchopping Festival. Southeastern World Woodchopping Championships; state championship turkey calling contest, draft horse pull, horse show, fireman's rodeo; arts and crafts, music, parades, concessions. Memorial Day wkend. Phone 304/847-7666.

Webster County Fair. 11 mi S on WV 20 to 4-H Camp Caesar. Rides, agricultural exhibits, entertainers, horse show. Labor Day wk. Phone 304/226-3888.

Weirton

(A-4) *See also Wheeling, zz also see 2565*

Founded 1910 **Pop** 20,411 **Elev** 760 ft
Area code 304 **Zip** 26062
Information Chamber of Commerce, 3200 Maine St; 304/748-7212

Weirton has been a steel producing town since its founding in 1910 by Ernest T. Weir, who also founded the Weirton Steel Company. In 1984 Weirton Steel became the largest employee-owned steel company in the world. Modern plants produce tin plate and hot-rolled, cold-rolled, and galvanized steels for containers, automobiles, appliances, and other products.

What to See and Do

Mountaineer Racetrack & Resort. Thoroughbred racing on one-mi track; three restaurants. (Mon, Thurs-Sun) 12 mi N on WV 2. Phone 304/387-2400.

Tomlinson Run State Park. Approx 1,400 acres. Swimming pool, bathhouse, fishing, boating on 27-acre lake (rowboat and paddleboat rentals); hiking trails, miniature golf, tennis, picnicking, playground, tent and trailer camping (dump station). Nature, recreation programs (summer). Standard hrs, fees. 15 mi N off WV 8. Phone 304/564-3651.

Weirton Steel Corp and Half Moon Industrial Park. Tours of Alpo and others. Contact Chamber of Commerce for details. Phone 304/748-7212.

Weston

See also Buckhannon, Clarksburg

Settled 1784 **Pop** 4,317 **Elev** 1,009 ft
Area code 304 **Zip** 26452

Information Lewis County Convention and Visitors Bureau, 345 Center St, PO Box 379; 304/269-7328

Surveyed originally by "Stonewall" Jackson's grandfather, Weston today is a center for coal, oil, and gas production, as well as the manufacture of glass products. The Weston State Hospital, completed in 1880 and said to be the largest hand-cut stone building in the nation, is located in town.

What to See and Do

Cedar Creek State Park. More than 2,400 acres. Swimming pool, bathhouse, fishing, boating (rentals); hiking trails, miniature golf, tennis, game courts, picnicking, playground, concession, tent and trailer camping (dump station). Park office in restored log cabin. Standard hrs, fees. 31 mi SW off US 33/119, near Glenville. Phone 304/462-8517.

Jackson's Mill State 4-H Conference Center. First camp of its kind in US; 43 buildings, gardens, swimming pool, amphitheater, interfaith chapel. Picnicking. 4 mi N off US 19. Phone 304/269-5100. Also here is

   Jackson's Mill Historic Area. Incl Blaker's Mill, an operating water-powered gristmill; blacksmith shop; McWharten cabin (ca 1700s); Mary Conrad's cabin (ca 1800s); and Jackson's Mill Museum, where "Stonewall" Jackson lived and worked as a boy. Museum represents grist and saw milling agriculture and home arts of the area as practiced 100 yrs ago. (Memorial Day-Labor Day, Tues-Sun; May and after Labor Day-mid-Oct, wkends only) Phone 304/269-5100. ¢¢

Stonewall Jackson Lake and Dam. Approx 2,500-acre lake with over 82 mi of shoreline created by impounding the waters of the West Fork River. Swimming, scuba diving, waterskiing, fishing, boating (ramps, rentals, marinas); picnicking, camping. Visitor center. Just S off I-79 exit 96, follow signs to dam. Phone 304/269-4588.

Stonewall Jackson Lake State Park. Approx 3,000 acres. Fishing, boating (launch, marina); nature and fitness trails, picnicking, playground, camping (hookups). Visitor center. Standard hrs, fees. 11 mi S on US 19. Phone 304/269-0523.

Special Events

Horse show. Trefz Farm, 3 mi E on US 33. Saddle, walking, harness, pony, western, and Arabian riding.Usually July. Phone 304/269-3257.

Stonewall Jackson Heritage Arts & Crafts Jubilee. Jackson's Mill State 4-H Conference Center. Mountain crafts, music, dance, and food. Labor Day wkend. Phone 304/269-1863.

Motel/Motor Lodge

★ **COMFORT INN.** *Rte 33 E & I-79 (26452). 304/269-7000; fax 304/269-7011; toll-free 800/228-5150. www. comfortinn.com.* 62 rms, 2 story. S, D $49-$89; under 18 free. Crib free. Pet accepted; $10. TV; cable (premium). Heated pool. Restaurant 6 am-9 pm. Bar 5-9 pm. Complimentary continental bkfst, coffee in rms. Ck-out noon. In-rm modem link. Balconies. Cr cds: A, C, D, DS, MC, V.

Wheeling (B-4)

Settled 1769 **Pop** 31,419 **Elev** 678 ft **Area code** 304 **Zip** 26003

Information Convention & Visitors Bureau, 1401 Main St; 304/233-7709 or 800/828-3079

Web www.wheelingcvb.com

Wheeling stands on the site of Fort Henry, built in 1774 by Colonel Ebenezer Zane and his two brothers, who named the fort for Virginia's Governor Patrick Henry. In 1782 the fort was the scene of the final battle of the Revolutionary War, a battle in which the valiant young pioneer Betty Zane was a heroine. The fort had withstood several Native American and British sieges during the war. However, during the last siege (after the war was officially ended), the defenders of the fort ran out of powder. Betty Zane, sister of the colonel, volunteered to run through the gun-

fire to the outlying Zane cabin for more. With the powder gathered in her apron, she made the 150-yard trek back to the fort and saved the garrison. Zane Grey, a descendant of the Zanes, wrote a novel about Betty and her exploit.

Today Wheeling is home to many industries, including producers of steel, iron, tin, chemical products, pottery, glass, paper, tobacco, plastics, and coal.

What to See and Do

The Artisan Center. Restored 1860s Victorian warehouse houses River City Ale Works, West Virginia's largest brew pub. "Made in Wheelingî crafts and exhibits; artisan demonstrations. (Daily) Heritage Sq, 1400 Main St. Phone 304/233-4555. **FREE**

Grave Creek Mound State Park. Features nation's largest prehistoric Adena burial mound—79 ft high, 900 ft around, 50 ft across the top. Some excavating was done in 1838; exhibits in Delf Norona Museum and Cultural Center (daily; fee). 9 mi S via WV 2, on Jefferson Ave in Moundsville. Phone 304/843-1410.

Jamboree, USA. Live country music shows presented by WWVA Radio since 1933. (Sat) Capitol Music Hall, 1015 Main St. Phone 304/234-0050. ¢¢¢¢

Kruger Street Toy & Train Museum. Collection of antique toys, games, and playthings. (Daily; Jan-Apr) 144 Kruger St. Phone 304/242-8133. ¢¢

Oglebay Resort Park. A 1,650-acre municipal park. Indoor and outdoor swimming pools, fishing, paddle boating on three-acre Schenk Lake; three 18-hole golf courses, miniature golf, tennis courts, picnicking, restaurant, snack shop, cabins, lodge. Train ride; 65-acre Good Children's Zoo with animals in natural habitat. Benedum Natural Science Theater; garden center; arboretum with 4 mi of walking paths; greenhouses; observatory. Fee for most activities. 3 mi NE of I-70, on WV 88. Phone 304/243-4000. Also in park is

   Mansion Museum. Period rms, exhibits trace history from 1835-present. (Daily) Phone 304/242-7272. ¢¢

Jamboree

Site of Fort Henry. Bronze plaque marks location of fort that Betty Zane saved. Main St, near 11th St. Phone 304/233-7709.

West Virginia Independence Hall-Custom House. (1859) Site of meeting at which Virginia's secession from the Union was declared unlawful and the independent state of West Virginia was created. The building, used as a post office, custom office, and federal court until 1912, has been restored. It now houses exhibits and events relating to the state's cultural heritage incl an interpretive film and rms with period furniture. (Mar-Dec, daily; rest of yr, Mon-Sat; closed state hols) 16th and Market sts. Phone 304/238-1300. ¢¢

Wheeling Park. Approx 400 acres. Swimming pool, water slide, boating on Good Lake; golf, miniature golf, indoor/outdoor tennis, ice-skating (rentals), picnicking, playground, refreshment area with video screen and lighted dance floor. Aviary. Fees for activities. (Daily; some facilities seasonal) 5 mi E on US 40. Phone 304/242-3770.

Special Events

Jamboree in the Hills. 15 mi W off I-70 exit 208 or 213, in St. Clairsville, OH. A four-day country music festival featuring more than 30 hrs of music; top country stars. Camping avail.Third wkend July. Phone 800/624-5456.

Oglebayfest. Oglebay Resort Park. Country fair, artists' market, fireworks, parade, ethnic foods, contests, square and round dancing, entertainment. First wkend Oct. Phone 304/243-4000.

City of Lights. Oglebay Resort Park. A 350-acre lighting display featuring lighted buildings, holiday themes with more than 500,000 lights, incl 28-ft candy canes and giant swans on Schenk Lake. Winter Fantasy in Good Zoo. Nov-Jan. Phone 304/243-4000.

Motels/Motor Lodges

★ ★ **BEST WESTERN INN.** *949 Main St (26003). 304/233-8500; fax 304/233-8500; toll-free 800/780-7234. www.bestwestern.com.* 80 rms, 4 story. S, D $56-$88; each addl $8; suites $136; under 12 free; higher rates wkends, special events. Crib free. Pet accepted $10. TV; cable (premium). Complimentary continental bkfst, coffee in rms. Restaurant 11 am-10 pm; Sat, Sun from 7 am. Bar 11-2 am. Ck-out 11 am. Meeting rms. Business servs avail. In-rm modem link. Exercise equipt; sauna. Valet serv. Cr cds: A, C, D, DS, MC, V.

[D] [🏊] [🏃] [≋] [👐] [SC]

★ **DAYS INN.** *I-70 and Dallas Pike Exit 11, Triadelphia (26059).* *304/547-0610; fax 304/547-9029; res 800/329-7466. www.daysinn.com.* 106 rms, 2 story. S, D $54-$70; each addl $6; under 18 free. Crib free. Pet accepted. TV; cable (premium), VCR avail. Pool. Complimentary continental bkfst. Bar 5 pm-1 am, closed Sun. Ck-out noon. Meeting rm. Business servs avail. In-rm modem link. Some in-rm whirlpools. Cr cds: A, C, D, DS, MC, V.

[D] [🏃] [≋] [≋] [👐]

★★ **HAMPTON INN.** *795 National Rd (26003).* *304/233-0440; fax 304/233-2198; toll-free 800/426-7866. www.hamptoninn.com.* 104 rms, 5 story. S, D, suites $79-$94; under 18 free; wkends (2-day min). Crib free. TV; cable (premium), VCR avail. Complimentary continental bkfst. Restaurant adj 6:30 am-11 pm. Coffee in rms. Ck-out noon. Meeting rms. Business servs avail. In-rm modem link. Valet serv. Exercise equipt. Refrigerator, wet bar in suites. Cr cds: A, C, D, DS, MC, V.

[D] [🏃] [≋] [👐] [SC]

Resort

★★★ **OGLEBAY CONFERENCE CENTER.** *Oglebay Park (26003).* *304/243-4000; fax 304/243-4070; toll-free 800/624-6988. www.oglebay-resort.com.* 212 rms in 2-story lodge, chalets; 49 kit. cottages (2-6 bedrm). S, D $99-$200; suites $190-$490; kit. cottages $625-$1,350/wk; golf plans. Valet parking avail. Crib free. Pet accepted. TV; cable (premium), VCR avail (movies). 2 pools, 1 indoor; wading pool, whirlpool, poolside serv, lifeguard. Playground. Supervised children's activities (June-Aug); ages 6-14. Dining rm 6:30-10:30 am, noon-2 pm, 5-9 pm. Box lunches, snack bar. Lounge noon-midnight. Coffee in rms. Ck-out 11 am, ck-in 3 pm. Grocery ½ mi. Package store 2 mi. Gift shop. Game rm. Meeting rms. Business center. In-rm modem link. Coin lndry. Valet serv. Airport, bus depot transportation. Lighted tennis courts, pro. Four 18-hole golf courses, greens fee, par-3 golf, pro, driving range, miniature golf. Down-

hill ski ½ mi. Stocked lake. Paddleboats. Lawn games. Children's zoo. Stables. Fishing. Exercise equipt. Massage. Some refrigerators, fireplaces, private patios, balconies. Picnic tables, grills. Mansion museum, garden center. Rustic setting in Oglebay Park. Cr cds: A, C, D, DS, MC, V.

[D] [🐎] [🎿] [🎱] [🐟] [≋] [🏊] [🏃] [≋] [👐] [🏃]

Restaurants

★★★ **ERNIE'S ESQUIRE.** *1055 E Bethlehem Blvd (26003).* *304/242-2800.* Hrs: 11 am-midnight; Fri to 1 am; Sat to 2 am; Sun to 10:30 pm; Sun brunch noon-2 pm. Closed Dec 25. Res accepted. Continental menu. Bar. Wine list. Lunch $3.75-$8.95, dinner $11-$29. Sun brunch $8.95. Child's menu. Specializes in fresh seafood, beef. Own baking. Entertainment Fri, Sat. Valet parking. 6 rms, each with different decor. Family-owned. Cr cds: A, D, DS, MC, V.

[D] [≋]

White Sulphur Springs

See also Lewisburg; also see Covington, VA

Settled 1750 **Pop** 2,315 **Elev** 1,923 ft **Area code** 304 **Zip** 24986

Information Chamber of Commerce, PO Box 11, 24986; 304/536-2500

Web www.wssswv.com

In the 18th century White Sulphur Springs became a fashionable destination for rich and famous colonists, who came for the "curative" powers of the mineral waters. It has, for the most part, remained a popular resort ever since. A number of US presidents summered in the town in the days before air conditioning made Washington habitable in hot weather. The John Tylers spent their honeymoon at the famous "Old White" Hotel. In 1913 the Old White Hotel gave way to the present Greenbrier Hotel, where President Wilson honeymooned with the second Mrs. Wilson. During World War II the hotel served as an internment camp for German and Japanese diplomats and, later, as a hospital.

The first golf course in America was laid out near the town in 1884, but the first game was delayed when golf clubs, imported from Scotland, were held for three weeks by customs men who were suspicious of a game played with "such elongated black-jacks or implements of murder."

What to See and Do

Fishing, swimming, boating, camping, hiking. In Monongahela National Forest (see ELKINS): Blue Bend Recreation Area, 6 mi N on WV 92, then 4 mi W on WV 16/21; Lake Sherwood Recreation Area, 23 mi N via WV 92, then 11 mi NE on WV 14. Phone 304/536-2144.

Greenbrier State Forest. More than 5,100 acres. Swimming pool (Memorial Day-Labor Day), bass fishing in Greenbrier River; hunting, hiking trails, picnicking, playground, tent and trailer camping, 12 cabins. Nature, recreation programs (summer). Standard hrs, fees. 3 mi W on US 60, then 1½ mi S on Harts Run Rd. Phone 304/536-1944.

Memorial Park. Swimming pool (Memorial Day-Labor Day; fee); tennis courts, ball fields, track, horseshoe pits, playground. (Daily) Greenbrier Ave.

National Fish Hatchery. Rainbow trout in raceways and ponds. Visitor center has display pool, aquariums, and exhibits. (Memorial Day-Labor Day, daily) 400 E Main St, on US 60. Phone 304/536-1361. **FREE**

Special Event

Dandelion Festival. Entertainment, exhibits; arts and crafts. Memorial Day wkend. Phone 304/536-2323.

Motel/Motor Lodge

★ **OLD WHITE MOTEL.** *865 E Main St (24986). 304/536-2441; fax 304/536-1836; toll-free 800/867-2441. www.oldwhitemotel.com.* 26 rms; 6 rms with shower only. S $37; D $55; each addl $3; under 12 free; higher rates special events. Crib free. Pet accepted, some restrictions. TV; cable (premium). Pool. Coffee in lobby.

Restaurant adj 7:30 am-9 pm. Ck-out noon. Cr cds: A, C, D, DS, MC, V.

Resort

★ ★ ★ ★ **THE GREENBRIER.** *300 W Main St (US 60) (24986). 304/536-1110; fax 304/536-7854; toll-free 800/453-4858. www.greenbrier.com.* This century-old resort offers recreations ranging from award-winning golf and tennis for the traditionalist to whitewater rafting and four-wheeling for the adventurer to luxurious spa treatments and fitness activities for the self-indulgent. Accommodations range from rooms and suites to three-bedroom cottages, and dining and entertainment covers intimate and elegant to clubby and casual. It's virtually impossible to tire of the choices. 596 rms in hotel, 6 story, 103 guest house rms. MAP, Apr-Oct: S, D, guest rms $210-$292; each addl $125; cottages $339-$399; suites $361-$399; wkend, family rates; tennis, golf plans; lower rates rest of yr. Serv charge of $21/person/day. Crib free. TV; cable, VCR avail. 2 pools, 1 indoor; whirlpool, wading pool, poolside serv, lifeguard. Playground. Supervised child's activities. Dining rms 7:30 am-9:30 pm (see also THE GREENBRIER MAIN DINING ROOM and THE TAVERN ROOM). Box lunches, snack bar. Rm serv 24 hrs. Bars 11-2 am. Ck-out noon, ck-in 3 pm. Convention facilities. Business center. In-rm modem link. Extensive shopping arcade. Airport, RR station, bus depot transportation. Sports dir. 5 indoor, 15 outdoor tennis courts, pro. Lighted, heated platform tennis. Three 18-hole golf courses, greens fee $135, pro, 2 putting greens, driving range. Canoeing; rafting (seasonal). Ice-skating (seasonal). Horse-drawn sleighing and carriage rides. Stables, English saddles. Fitness trail. Bicycling. Lawn games. Trap and skeet shooting. Hunt club and game preserve. British regulation croquet court. Soc dir; movies, dancing, entertainment. Bowling; indoor games. Extensive exercise rm; sauna, steam rm. Spa. Some refrigerators; microwaves avail; fireplace in cottages. Private patios, balconies. Cr cds: A, D, DS, MC, V.

Restaurants

★ ★ ★ **THE GREENBRIER MAIN DINING ROOM.** *300 W Main St (24986). 304/536-1110. www. greenbrier.com.* Hrs: 7:30-10 am, 6:30-9 pm. Res required. Continental menu. Private club 5 pm-1 am. Wine cellar. Prix fixe: bkfst $20-$25, dinner $80-$90. Serv charge 17.5 percent; addl serv charge for alcoholic beverages. Child's menu. Specializes in veal, fresh seafood, vegetarian dishes. Own baking. Chamber music at dinner. Valet parking. Jacket (dinner). Cr cds: A, D, MC, V.

ⅅ

★ ★ ★ ★ **THE TAVERN ROOM.** *300 W Main St (24986). 304/536-1110. www.greenbrier.com.* Open from April through late October, this intimate restaurant is just one of the many gastronomic indulgences available at The Greenbrier resort. New American dishes, including the favorite five-onion soup and several great rotisserie selections, are presented with warm, attentive service. The adjacent wine bar is the perfect spot for live piano and a glass or bottle from the extensive cellar. Specializes in fresh seafood, veal, beef. Hrs: 7-9:30 pm. Closed Dec-Apr. Res required. Bar. Wine cellar. Dinner prix fixe: $100-$105. 17.5 percent serv charge. Child's menu. Entertainment: pianist. Valet parking. Jacket. Cr cds: A, D, MC, V.

ⅅ

Williamson

Founded 1892 **Pop** 3,414 **Elev** 665 ft
Area code 304 **Zip** 25661
Information Tug Valley Chamber of Commerce, 45 E 2nd Ave, PO Box 376; 304/235-5240
Web www.tugvalleychamberof commerce.com

The center of the "billion-dollar coal field," Williamson is truly a coal town; the walls of the local Chamber of Commerce building, at the west corner of Courthouse Square, are made of coal. The surrounding Tug River Valley was the scene of the bitter Hatfield-McCoy mountaineer family feud.

What to See and Do

Cabwaylingo State Forest. Approx 8,100 acres. Swimming pool (Memorial Day-Labor Day), fishing; hunting, hiking trails, game courts, picnicking, playground, concession, tent and trailer camping (dump station), 13 cabins. Standard hrs, fees. 38 mi N off US 52, WV 152 near Wilsondale. Phone 304/385-4255.

Matewan. This tiny hamlet was the site of the famous feud between the West Virginia Hatfields and the Kentucky McCoys. On Election Day, Aug 7, 1882, three McCoy sons stabbed and shot Ellison Hatfield. Devil Anse Hatfield avenged his brother by executing the three McCoys. Soon Kentucky bounty hunters made raids into West Virginia to capture the Hatfields, who retaliated in 1888 by attacking a McCoy homestead. By 1890 the killings had ended but the feud continued to be sensationalized. In 1920, Matewan was the scene of a shootout between union organizers and coal company operators that left ten dead, incl the mayor. 12 mi SW via WV 49. Phone 304/426-4239.

Special Event

King Coal Festival. Entertainment, exhibits; theatrical presentation; country music, square dancing. Mid-Sept. Phone 304/235-5560.

ATTRACTION LIST

Attraction names are listed in alphabetical order followed by a symbol identifying their classification and then city. The symbols for classification are: [S] for Special Events and [W] for What to See and Do

17th Street Market [W] *Richmond, VA*

18th-Century Comedy [S] *Williamsburg, VA*

6th Street Marketplace [W] *Richmond, VA*

Abby Aldrich Rockefeller Folk Art Center [W] *Williamsburg, VA*

Abe's Buggy Rides [W] *Lancaster, PA*

Abington Art Center [W] *Jenkintown, PA*

Abram's Delight and Log Cabin [W] *Winchester, VA*

Academy Art Museum [W] *Easton, MD*

Academy of Music [W] *Philadelphia, PA*

Academy of Natural Sciences Museum [W] *Philadelphia, PA*

ACC Crafts Fair [S] *Baltimore, MD*

Actors Guild Playhouse [W] *Parkersburg, WV*

Adam Thoroughgood House [W] *Virginia Beach, VA*

African American Civil War Memorial [W] *Washington, DC*

African-American Museum Philadelphia [W] *Philadelphia, PA*

African Art Museum of Maryland [W] *Columbia, MD*

Agecroft Hall [W] *Richmond, VA*

"Ag Hill," The College of Agriculture [W] *State College, PA*

Agricultural Expo and Fair [S] *Cumberland, MD*

Air Power Park and Aviation History Center [W] *Hampton, VA*

Albemarle County Courthouse [W] *Charlottesville, VA*

Alcoa Building [W] *Pittsburgh, PA*

Alexandria Black History Resource Center [W] *Alexandria, VA*

Algonkian [W] *Fairfax, VA*

A. Lincoln's Place [W] *Gettysburg, PA*

Allegheny College [W] *Meadville, PA*

Allegheny County Courthouse [W] *Pittsburgh, PA*

Allegheny National Forest [W] *Warren, PA*

Allegheny Observatory [W] *Pittsburgh, PA*

Allegheny Portage Railroad National Site [W] *Altoona, PA*

Allegheny Portage Railroad National Historic Site [W] *Ebensburg, PA*

Alpine Mountain Ski Area [W] *Stroudsburg, PA*

Alsatia Mummers Halloween Parade Festival [S] *Hagerstown, MD*

American Music Theater Festival [S] *Philadelphia, PA*

American Red Cross [W] *Washington, DC*

American Rover [W] *Norfolk, VA*

American Swedish Historical Museum [W] *Philadelphia, PA*

America's Railroads on Parade [W] *Williamsburg, VA*

Amish Country Tours [W] *Lancaster, PA*

Amish Farm and House [W] *Lancaster, PA*

Amish Village [W] *Bird-in-Hand, PA*

Amstel House Museum [W] *New Castle, DE*

Amtrak Station [W] *Wilmington, DE*

Anacostia Museum, Smithsonian Institution [W] *Washington, DC*

Anderson House Museum [W] *Washington, DC*

Andy Warhol Museum [W] *Pittsburgh, PA*

Angle, The [W] *Gettysburg National Military Park, PA*

Annapolis by Candlelight [S] *Annapolis, MD*

Anne Spencer House [W] *Lynchburg, VA*

Annual Event [W] *Washington Crossing Historic Park (Bucks County), PA*

Anthracite Heritage Museum [W] *Scranton, PA*

Antietam National Battlefield [W] *Hagerstown, MD*

Antique Aircraft Fly-In [S] *Cambridge, MD*

Antique Automobile Club [S] *Hershey, PA*

Antique Car Show [S] *Fairfax, VA*

Antique Row [W] *Philadelphia, PA*

Antiques Forum [S] *Williamsburg, VA*

Apothecary Museum [W] *Bethlehem, PA*

Appalachian Festival [S] *Beckley, WV*

Apple Blossom Festival [S] *Gettysburg, PA*

Apple Butter Festival [S] *Berkeley Springs, WV*

Applefest [S] *Franklin (Venango County), PA*

Apple Harvest Arts & Crafts [S] *Winchester, VA*

Apple Harvest Festival [S] *Gettysburg, PA*

Appomattox Courthouse Building [W] *Appomattox Court House National Historical Park, VA*

Appomattox Court House National Historical Park [W] *Lynchburg, VA*

Appomattox Court House National Historical Park [W] *Lynchburg, VA*

Appomattox River Park [W] *Petersburg, VA*

Arch Street Meetinghouse [W] *Philadelphia, PA*

Area of Embarkation [W] *Washington Crossing Historic Park (Bucks County), PA*

Arlington County Fair [S] *Arlington County (Ronald Reagan Washington-National Airport Area), VA*

Arlington House, the Robert E. Lee Memorial [W] *Arlington County (Ronald Reagan Washington-National Airport Area), VA*

Arlington National Cemetery [W] *Arlington County (Ronald Reagan Washington-National Airport Area), VA*

Army 10-miler [S] *Arlington County (Ronald Reagan Washington-National Airport Area), VA*

Army-Navy Football Game [S] *Philadelphia, PA*

Art Barn [W] *Washington, DC*

Art Festival and Octoberfest [S] *Carlisle, PA*

Arthur M. Sackler Gallery [W] *Washington, DC*

Artisan Center, The [W] *Wheeling, WV*

Art Museum [W] *Charleston, WV*

Art Museum of the Americas, OAS [W] *Washington, DC*

Arts and Industries Building [W] *Washington, DC*

Artscape [S] *Baltimore, MD*

Asa Packer Mansion [W] *Jim Thorpe, PA*

Ash-Lawn Highland [W] *Charlottesville, VA*

Assateague Island [W] *Chincoteague, VA*

Assateague Island National Seashore [W] *Ocean City, MD*

Assateague State Park [W] *Ocean City, MD*

Association for Research and Enlightenment [W] *Virginia Beach, VA*

Athenaeum, The [W] *Alexandria, VA*

Athenaeum of Philadelphia [W] *Philadelphia, PA*

At Sea [W] *Washington, DC*

Atwater Kent Museum [W] *Philadelphia, PA*

Audra State Park [W] *Buckhannon, WV*

Augusta Festival [S] *Elkins, WV*

Augusta Stone Church [W] *Staunton, VA*

August Court Days [S] *Leesburg, VA*

Auto Tape Tour [W] *Valley Forge National Historical Park, PA*

Auto tours [W] *Wellsboro, PA*

Autumn Glory Festival [S] *Oakland (Garrett County), MD*

Autumn Leaf Festival [S] *Clarion, PA*

Babcock State Park [W] *Beckley, WV*

Babe Ruth Birthplace/Baseball Center [W] *Baltimore, MD*

Bach Festival [S] *Bethlehem, PA*

Backbone Mountain [W] *Oakland (Garrett County), MD*

Baker Mansion Museum [W] *Altoona, PA*

Balch Institute for Ethnic Studies [W] *Philadelphia, PA*

Bald Eagle [W] *Lock Haven, PA*

Baldwin-Reynolds House Museum [W] *Meadville, PA*

Ball's Bluff Battlefield [W] *Leesburg, VA*

Baltimore Center for the Performing Arts—Morris Mechanic Theater [W] *Baltimore, MD*

Baltimore Maritime Museum [W] *Baltimore, MD*

Baltimore Museum of Art [W] *Baltimore, MD*

Baltimore Museum of Industry [W] *Baltimore, MD*

Baltimore Orioles (MLB) [W] *Baltimore, MD*

Baltimore Patriot. [W] *Baltimore, MD*

Baltimore Ravens (NFL) [W] *Baltimore, MD*

Baltimore Streetcar Museum [W] *Baltimore, MD*

Baltimore Zoo [W] *Baltimore, MD*
Band concerts [S] *New Castle, DE*
B & O Railroad Museum [W] *Baltimore, MD*
Bandstand concerts [S] *Rehoboth Beach, DE*
Banning Park [W] *Wilmington, DE*
Barbara Fritchie House and Museum [W] *Frederick, MD*
Barbour County Fair [S] *Philippi, WV*
Barbour County Historical Society Museum [W] *Philippi, WV*
Bark Peeler's Convention [S] *Galeton, PA*
Barns-Brinton House [W] *Kennett Square, PA*
Barns of Wolf Trap [S] *Fairfax, VA*
Barter Theatre [S] *Abingdon, VA*
Basilica of the National Shrine of the Assumption [W] *Baltimore, MD*
Basilica of the National Shrine of the Immaculate Conception [W] *Washington, DC*
Battery 5 [W] *Petersburg National Battlefield, VA*
Battery 8 [W] *Petersburg National Battlefield, VA*
Battery 9 [W] *Petersburg National Battlefield, VA*
Battlefield Museum [W] *Manassas (Bull Run) National Battlefield Park, VA*
Battle Monument [W] *Baltimore, MD*
Battle of Cedar Creek Reenactment [S] *Strasburg, VA*
Bavarian Summer Fest [S] *Denver/Adamstown, PA*
Beall-Dawson House [W] *Rockville, MD*
Bear Creek Ski Area [W] *Allentown, PA*
Beartown State Park [W] *Hillsboro, WV*
Beckley Exhibition Coal Mine [W] *Beckley, WV*
Bedford County Courthouse [W] *Bedford, PA*
Bedrooms of America [W] *New Market, VA*
Beech Fork State Park [W] *Huntington, WV*
Bel Air Mansion [W] *Bowie, MD*
Bel Air Stable [W] *Bowie, MD*
Belle Boyd Cottage [W] *Front Royal, VA*
Belle Grove [W] *Strasburg, VA*
Bellevue State Park [W] *Wilmington, DE*
Belmont (The Gari Melchers Estate and Memorial Gallery) [W] *Fredericksburg, VA*
Bendigo State Park [W] *Kane, PA*

Benedum Center for the Performing Arts [W] *Pittsburgh, PA*
Berkeley Springs State Park [W] *Berkeley Springs, WV*
Berks County Heritage Center [W] *Reading, PA*
Bethany College [W] *Bethany, WV*
Beth Sholom Synagogue [W] *Jenkintown, PA*
Betsy Ross House [W] *Philadelphia, PA*
Beyond the Garden Gates Tour [S] *Frederick, MD*
Bicentennial Tower [W] *Erie, PA*
Big Boulder [W] *White Haven, PA*
Big Meadows [W] *Shenandoah National Park, VA*
Big Walker Lookout [W] *Wytheville, VA*
Bill "Bojangles" Robinson Statue [W] *Richmond, VA*
Bird-in-Hand Farmers' Market [W] *Bird-in-Hand, PA*
Bishop White House [W] *Philadelphia, PA*
Black History Museum and Cultural Center [W] *Richmond, VA*
Black History Recreation Trail [W] *Washington, DC*
Black Moshannon State Park [W] *Bellefonte, PA*
Blackwater Creek Natural Area [W] *Lynchburg, VA*
Blackwater Falls State Park [W] *Davis, WV*
Blackwater National Wildlife Refuge [W] *Cambridge, MD*
Blair County Arts Festival [S] *Altoona, PA*
Blair House [W] *Washington, DC*
Blandford Church [W] *Petersburg, VA*
Blenko Glass Company, Inc [W] *Huntington, WV*
Blennerhassett Island Historical State Park [W] *Parkersburg, WV*
Blennerhassett Museum [W] *Parkersburg, WV*
Blessing of the Fleet and Historical Pageant [S] *Leonardtown, MD*
Block House of Fort Pitt [W] *Pittsburgh, PA*
Bloomsburg Fair [S] *Bloomsburg, PA*
Bloomsburg Theatre Ensemble [S] *Bloomsburg, PA*
Bloomsburg University of Pennsylvania [W] *Bloomsburg, PA*
Blue & Gray Reunion [S] *Philippi, WV*
Bluebird Gap Farm [W] *Hampton, VA*
Blue Knob [W] *Bedford, PA*
Blue Mountain [W] *Allentown, PA*
Blue Ridge Farm Museum [W] *Martinsville, VA*

Blue Ridge Folklife Festival [S] *Martinsville, VA*

Blue Ridge Parkway [W] *Roanoke, VA*

Blue Ridge Parkway [W] *Roanoke, VA*

Blue Rocks [W] *Hamburg, PA*

Bluestone State Park [W] *Hinton, WV*

B'nai B'rith Klutznick Museum [W] *Washington, DC*

Boardwalk Arts Festival [S] *Bethany Beach, DE*

Boardwalk Art Show [S] *Virginia Beach, VA*

Boat House Row [W] *Philadelphia, PA*

Boat trips [W] *Annapolis, MD*

Bob Hoffman Weightlifting Hall of Fame [W] *York, PA*

Bombay Hook National Wildlife Refuge [W] *Smyrna, DE*

Bonham House [W] *York, PA*

Book and the Cook, The [S] *Philadelphia, PA*

Bourse, The [W] *Philadelphia, PA*

Bowden National Fish Hatchery [W] *Elkins, WV*

Bowhunter's Festival [S] *Galeton, PA*

Bowman's Hill [W] *Washington Crossing Historic Park (Bucks County), PA*

Boyce Park Ski Area [W] *Pittsburgh, PA*

Boyertown Museum of Historic Vehicles [W] *Pottstown, PA*

Braddock's Grave [W] *Uniontown, PA*

Bradford Landmark Society [W] *Bradford, PA*

Brandywine Battlefield [W] *Kennett Square, PA*

Brandywine Creek State Park [W] *Wilmington, DE*

Brandywine River Museum [W] *Kennett Square, PA*

Brandywine Springs Park [W] *Wilmington, DE*

Brandywine Zoo and Park [W] *Wilmington, DE*

Brethren's House [W] *Bethlehem, PA*

Brick Hotel Gallery and Manney Collection of Belter Furniture [W] *Odessa, DE*

Bridge Day [S] *Gauley Bridge, WV*

Brinton 1704 House [W] *West Chester, PA*

Bristol Caverns [W] *Bristol, VA*

Bristol Motor Speedway [S] *Bristol, VA*

Brookmere Farm Vineyards [W] *Lewistown, PA*

Brookside Gardens [W] *Silver Spring, MD*

Brunswick Museum [W] *Frederick, MD*

Brunswick Tours [W] *Lancaster, PA*

Brush-Everard House [W] *Williamsburg, VA*

Bruton Parish Church [W] *Williamsburg, VA*

Bryan [W] *Richmond, VA*

Bryce Resort [W] *Basye, VA*

Bryn Athyn Cathedral [W] *Willow Grove, PA*

Bube's Brewery [W] *Lancaster, PA*

Buckaloons Recreation Area [W] *Warren, PA*

Buckroe Beach [W] *Hampton, VA*

Bucks County River Country [W] *New Hope, PA*

Bucktail Natural Area [W] *Lock Haven, PA*

Bufano Sculpture Garden [W] *Baltimore, MD*

Bull Run [W] *Fairfax, VA*

Bull Run School House [W] *Lock Haven, PA*

Bureau of Engraving and Printing [W] *Washington, DC*

Burial Ground of Congregation Mikveh Israel [W] *Philadelphia, PA*

Burke Lake [W] *Fairfax, VA*

Burton-Ingram House [W] *Lewes, DE*

Busch Gardens Williamsburg [W] *Williamsburg, VA*

Bushkill Falls [W] *Bushkill, PA*

Bushy Run Battlefield [W] *Greensburg, PA*

Bus Tour [W] *Valley Forge National Historical Park, PA*

Byrd Visitor Center [W] *Shenandoah National Park, VA*

Cabin John Regional Park [W] *Bethesda, MD*

Cabwaylingo State Forest [W] *Williamson, WV*

Cacapon Resort State Park [W] *Berkeley Springs, WV*

Caleb Pusey Home, Landingford Plantation [W] *Chester, PA*

Caledonia State Park [W] *Chambersburg, PA*

Calvert Marine Museum [W] *Leonardtown, MD*

Calvin Price State Forest [W] *Hillsboro, WV*

Camden Park [W] *Huntington, WV*

Camelback Ski Area [W] *Tannersville, PA*

Campbell Mansion [W] *Bethany, WV*

Camp Creek State Park [W] *Princeton, WV*

Camp Hill [W] *Harpers Ferry, WV*

Camping [W] *Blue Ridge Parkway, VA*

Camping [W] *Shenandoah National Park, VA*

Canaan Valley Resort State Park [W] *Davis, WV*

Canal Museum [W] *Easton, PA*

C & O Historical Society Archives [W] *Clifton Forge, VA*

Candy Americana Museum [W] *Lancaster, PA*

Cannon Ball House & Marine Museum [W] *Lewes, DE*

Canoe Creek State Park [W] *Altoona, PA*

Canoeing [W] *Stroudsburg, PA*

Canoeing, rafting, kayaking, and tubing. Kittatinny Canoes [W] *Milford, PA*

Cape Henlopen State Park [W] *Lewes, DE*

Capital Children's Museum [W] *Washington, DC*

Capitol, The [W] *Harrisburg, PA*

Capitol, The [W] *Washington, DC*

Capitol, The [W] *Williamsburg, VA*

Capitol Hill buildings [W] *Harrisburg, PA*

Capitol Square [W] *Richmond, VA*

Capitol Theatre [W] *Chambersburg, PA*

Car and Carriage Museum [W] *Luray, VA*

Carlisle Barracks [W] *Carlisle, PA*

Carlyle House [W] *Alexandria, VA*

Carnegie Mellon University [W] *Pittsburgh, PA*

Carnegie Museums of Pittsburgh, The [W] *Pittsburgh, PA*

Carnegie Science Center, The [W] *Pittsburgh, PA*

Carnifex Ferry Battlefield State Park [W] *Summersville, WV*

Carousel World [W] *New Hope, PA*

Carpenters' Hall [W] *Philadelphia, PA*

Carpenter Shop [W] *Bradford, PA*

Carriage and wagon rides [W] *Williamsburg, VA*

Carrie B Harbor Tours [W] *Norfolk, VA*

Carrie B Harbor Tours [W] *Portsmouth, VA*

Carter Barron Amphitheater [W] *Washington, DC*

Carter Reception Center [W] *Irvington, VA*

Carter's Grove [W] *Williamsburg, VA*

Carytown [W] *Richmond, VA*

Cascades Trail [W] *Blue Ridge Parkway, VA*

Casemate Museum [W] *Hampton, VA*

Casselman Bridge and State Park [W] *Grantsville, MD*

Cass Scenic Railroad State Park [W] *Marlinton, WV*

Cathedral of Learning [W] *Pittsburgh, PA*

Cathedral State Park [W] *Aurora, WV*

Catholic University of America [W] *Washington, DC*

Catlin House [W] *Scranton, PA*

Catoctin Colorfest [S] *Thurmont, MD*

Catoctin Mountain National Park [W] *Thurmont, MD*

Cave Mountain Lake Recreation Area [W] *Natural Bridge, VA*

Caverns [W] *Harrisonburg, VA*

Caverns of Natural Bridge [W] *Natural Bridge, VA*

Cedar Creek State Park [W] *Weston, WV*

Cedar Crest College [W] *Allentown, PA*

Cedarville State Forest [W] *Waldorf, MD*

Center in the Square [W] *Roanoke, VA*

Centipede Tours [W] *Philadelphia, PA*

Central Counties Concerned Sportsmen Annual Show [S] *Clearfield (Clearfield County), PA*

Central Market House [W] *York, PA*

Central Moravian Church [W] *Bethlehem, PA*

Central Pennsylvania Festival of the Arts [S] *State College, PA*

Centre County Grange Fair [S] *State College, PA*

Centre County Library and Historical Museum [W] *Bellefonte, PA*

Centre Hill Mansion [W] *Petersburg, VA*

Chaddsford Winery [W] *Kennett Square, PA*

ChambersFest [S] *Chambersburg, PA*

Chancellorsville Visitor Center [W] *Fredericksburg and Spotsylvania National Military Park, VA*

Chapel of the Centurion [W] *Hampton, VA*

Chapman State Park [W] *Warren, PA*

Charles Carroll, Barrister House [W] *Annapolis, MD*

Charles Center [W] *Baltimore, MD*

Charles Town Races and Gaming [W] *Charles Town, WV*

Chatham [W] *Danville, VA*

Chatham Manor [W] *Fredericksburg and Spotsylvania National Military Park, VA*

Chautauqua Festival [S] *Wytheville, VA*

Cherry Blossom Festival [S] *Washington, DC*

Cherry Festival [S] *North East, PA*

Chesapeake and Ohio Canal Boat Rides [W] *Washington, DC*

Chesapeake Appreciation Days [S] *Annapolis, MD*

Chesapeake Bay Bridge [W] *Annapolis, MD*

Chesapeake Bay Maritime Museum [W] *St. Michael's, MD*

Chesapeake Jubilee [S] *Chesapeake, VA*

Chestnut Ridge Regional Park [W] *Morgantown, WV*

Children's Museum of Virginia [W] *Portsmouth, VA*

Children's Tours [W] *Williamsburg, VA*

Chilhowie Apple Festival [S] *Marion, VA*

Chinatown [W] *Washington, DC*

Chincoteague Power Boat Regatta [S] *Chincoteague, VA*

Chinn House Ruins [W] *Manassas (Bull Run) National Battlefield Park, VA*

Chippokes Plantation State Park [W] *Surry, VA*

Chocolate Lovers' Weekend [S] *Hershey, PA*

Choo-Choo Barn, Traintown, USA [W] *Lancaster, PA*

Christ Church [W] *Alexandria, VA*

Christ Church [W] *Philadelphia, PA*

Christ Church Burial Ground [W] *Philadelphia, PA*

Christian Heurich Mansion [W] *Washington, DC*

Christmas [S] *Bethlehem, PA*

Christmas at Oatlands [S] *Leesburg, VA*

Christmas Candlelight Tour [S] *Fredericksburg, VA*

Christmas in Annapolis [S] *Annapolis, MD*

Christmas in Hershey [S] *Hershey, PA*

Christmas Open House [S] *Harmony, PA*

Chrysler Museum of Art [W] *Norfolk, VA*

Church Hill Historic Area [W] *Richmond, VA*

Church Home and Hospital [W] *Baltimore, MD*

City Court House [W] *Baltimore, MD*

City Hall [W] *Baltimore, MD*

City Hall [W] *Philadelphia, PA*

City Hall Observation Deck [W] *Richmond, VA*

City of Baltimore Conservatory [W] *Baltimore, MD*

City of Lights [S] *Wheeling, WV*

City Park [W] *Parkersburg, WV*

City Point Unit [W] *Petersburg National Battlefield, VA*

City Point Unit of Petersburg National Battlefield [W] *Hopewell, VA*

Civil War Heritage Days [S] *Gettysburg, PA*

Civil War Library and Museum [W] *Philadelphia, PA*

Civil War Reenactment [S] *Bedford, PA*

Clara Barton National Historic Site [W] *Bethesda, MD*

Clara Barton National Historic Site [W] *Washington, DC*

Clarion County Historical Society [W] *Clarion, PA*

Claude Moore Colonial Farm [W] *McLean, VA*

Claws 'N Paws Wild Animal Park [W] *Hawley, PA*

Clayton, the Henry Clay Frick Home [W] *Pittsburgh, PA*

Claytor Lake State Park [W] *Radford, VA*

Clear Creek State Park [W] *Brookville, PA*

Clearfield County Fair [S] *Clearfield (Clearfield County), PA*

Cliffview Trading Post [W] *Galax, VA*

Cliveden [W] *Philadelphia, PA*

Clover Hill Tavern and outbuildings [W] *Appomattox Court House National Historical Park, VA*

Coast Day [S] *Lewes, DE*

Cockpit in Court Summer Theatre [W] *Baltimore, MD*

Cockpit in Court Summer Theatre [S] *Baltimore, MD*

Codorus State Park [W] *Hanover, PA*

Coleman Memorial Park [W] *Lebanon, PA*

College of William and Mary [W] *Williamsburg, VA*

College Park Aviation Museum [W] *College Park, MD*

Colonel Crawford Park [W] *Meadville, PA*

Colonial farm [W] *George Washington Birthplace National Monument, VA*

Colonial Mansions [W] *Philadelphia, PA*

Colonial Pennsylvania Plantation [W] *Media, PA*

Colonial Weekends [S] *Williamsburg, VA*

Colonial Williamsburg Visitor Center [W] *Williamsburg, VA*

Colonial Williamsburg [W] *Williamsburg, VA*

Colquitt's Salient [W] *Petersburg National Battlefield, VA*

Columbia County Historical Society [W] *Bloomsburg, PA*

Columbia Festival of Arts [S] *Columbia, MD*

Columbus Chapel—Boal Mansion Museum [W] *State College, PA*

Colvin Run Mill Historic Site [W] *McLean, VA*

Compass Inn Museum [W] *Ligonier, PA*

Concentration Valley [W] *Washington Crossing Historic Park (Bucks County), PA*

Concerts [S] *Washington, DC*

Concord Point Lighthouse [W] *Havre de Grace, MD*

Conemaugh Gap [W] *Johnstown, PA*

Cone Park Trail [W] *Blue Ridge Parkway, VA*

Conewago Chapel [W] *Hanover, PA*

Confederate Cemetery [W] *Appomattox Court House National Historical Park, VA*

Confederate Cemetery [W] *Fredericksburg, VA*

Confederate Fort [W] *Jamestown (Colonial National Historical Park), VA*

Congress [W] *Washington, DC*

Congress Hall [W] *Philadelphia, PA*

Conneaut Cellars Winery [W] *Conneaut Lake, PA*

Conrad Weiser Homestead [W] *Reading, PA*

Constitution Gardens [W] *Washington, DC*

Contemporary Art Center of Virginia [W] *Virginia Beach, VA*

Contentment Museum Complex [W] *Gauley Bridge, WV*

Cook Forest State Park [W] *Clarion, PA*

Cook-Hayman Pharmacy Museum [W] *Morgantown, WV*

Coonskin Park [W] *Charleston, WV*

Cooper Cabin [W] *Butler, PA*

Coopers Rock State Forest [W] *Morgantown, WV*

Corbit-Sharp House [W] *Odessa, DE*

Corcoran Gallery of Art [W] *Washington, DC*

CoreStates US Pro Cycling Championship [S] *Philadelphia, PA*

Cornwall Iron Furnace [W] *Cornwall, PA*

Coryell's Ferry [W] *New Hope, PA*

County Courthouse [W] *Gloucester, VA*

County jail [W] *Appomattox Court House National Historical Park, VA*

County parks [W] *Fairfax, VA*

County parks. Blue Spruce [W] *Indiana, PA*

County parks. South Park [W] *Pittsburgh, PA*

Courthouse [W] *Williamsburg, VA*

Court House Galleries [W] *Portsmouth, VA*

Covered bridge [W] *Philippi, WV*

Covered Bridge & Arts Festival [S] *Bloomsburg, PA*

Covered bridges [W] *Doylestown (Bucks County), PA*

Cowanesque Lake [W] *Mansfield, PA*

Crab Festival [S] *St. Mary's City, MD*

Craft demonstrations and sales [W] *Blue Ridge Parkway, VA*

Craggy Gardens Trail [W] *Blue Ridge Parkway, VA*

Craggy Gardens Visitor Center [W] *Blue Ridge Parkway, VA*

Cranberry Glades [W] *Marlinton, WV*

Cranberry Mountain Visitor Center-Monongahela National Forest [W] *Marlinton, WV*

Crater, The [W] *Petersburg National Battlefield, VA*

Crawford County Fair [S] *Meadville, PA*

Crayola Factory, The [W] *Easton, PA*

Crook Farm [W] *Bradford, PA*

Crook Farm Country Fair [S] *Bradford, PA*

Crossing, The [W] *Washington Crossing Historic Park (Bucks County), PA*

Crystal Cave Park [W] *Kutztown, PA*

Crystal Grottoes Caverns [W] *Boonsboro (Garrett County), MD*

Culp's Hill [W] *Gettysburg National Military Park, PA*

Cultural Center [W] *Charleston, WV*

Cumberland County Historical Society and Hamilton Library Association [W] *Carlisle, PA*

Cumberland Knob Contact Station [W] *Blue Ridge Parkway, VA*

Cunningham Falls State Park [W] *Thurmont, MD*

Cyclorama Center [W] *Gettysburg National Military Park, PA*

Cylburn Arboretum [W] *Baltimore, MD*

Dale House [W] *Jamestown (Colonial National Historical Park), VA*

Dandelion Festival [S] *White Sulphur Springs, WV*

Daniel Boone Homestead [W] *Reading, PA*

Daniel Weaver Company, The [W] *Lebanon, PA*

Dankfest [S] *Harmony, PA*

Dans Mountain State Park [W] *Cumberland, MD*

Danville Harvest Jubilee [S] *Danville, VA*

Danville Museum of Fine Arts and History [W] *Danville, VA*

Danville Science Center [W] *Danville, VA*

DAR Headquarters [W] *Washington, DC*

Das Awkscht Fescht [S] *Allentown, PA*

Dauphin County Courthouse [W] *Harrisburg, PA*

David Bradford House [W] *Washington, PA*

David Wilmot's Burial Place [W] *Towanda, PA*

D.C. United (MLS) [W] *Washington, DC*

DeBence Antique Music World [W] *Franklin (Venango County), PA*

Decatur House Museum [W] *Washington, DC*

Declaration House [W] *Philadelphia, PA*

Decoy Festival [S] *Havre de Grace, MD*

Decoy Museum [W] *Havre de Grace, MD*

Deep Creek Lake State Park [W] *Oakland (Garrett County), MD*

Delaware Agricultural Museum and Village [W] *Dover, DE*

Delaware Archeology Museum [W] *Dover, DE*

Delaware Art Museum [W] *Wilmington, DE*

Delaware History Museum [W] *Wilmington, DE*

Delaware Museum of Natural History [W] *Wilmington, DE*

Delaware Public Archives [W] *Dover, DE*

Delaware Seashore State Park [W] *Rehoboth Beach, DE*

Delaware State Fair [S] *Dover, DE*

Delaware State Museums [W] *Dover, DE*

Delaware State Visitor Center [W] *Dover, DE*

Delaware Water Gap [W] *Bushkill, PA*

Delaware Water Gap [W] *Shawnee on Delaware, PA*

Delaware Water Gap [W] *Stroudsburg, PA*

Delgrossos Park [W] *Altoona, PA*

Department of Commerce Building [W] *Washington, DC*

Department of Energy [W] *Washington, DC*

Department of Justice Building [W] *Washington, DC*

Department of State Building [W] *Washington, DC*

Department of the Interior [W] *Washington, DC*

Department of the Treasury [W] *Washington, DC*

Deshler-Morris House [W] *Philadelphia, PA*

Devil's Den [W] *Gettysburg National Military Park, PA*

Devon Horse Show [S] *Philadelphia, PA*

DeWitt Wallace Decorative Arts Gallery [W] *Williamsburg, VA*

Dickey Ridge Visitor Center [W] *Shenandoah National Park, VA*

Dickinson College [W] *Carlisle, PA*

Dingmans Falls and Silver Thread Falls [W] *Milford, PA*

Disabled Visitor Information [W] *Williamsburg, VA*

DiscoverSea Shipwreck Museum [W] *Fenwick Island, DE*

Dixie Caverns [W] *Salem, VA*

Doctor's Office [W] *Lewes, DE*

Dogan House [W] *Manassas (Bull Run) National Battlefield Park, VA*

Dogwood Festival [S] *Charlottesville, VA*

Dominion Wine Cellars [W] *Culpeper, VA*

Doncaster Demonstration Forest [W] *La Plata, MD*

Donegal Mills Plantation & Inn [W] *Wrightsville (York County), PA*

Doorways to Old Virginia [W] *Alexandria, VA*

Dorney Park and Wildwater Kingdom [W] *Allentown, PA*

Douthat State Park [W] *Clifton Forge, VA*

Dover Downs [S] *Dover, DE*

Dover Heritage Trail [W] *Dover, DE*

Drake Well Museum [W] *Titusville, PA*

Drama of Creation [W] *Natural Bridge, VA*

Droop Mountain Battlefield State Park [W] *Hillsboro, WV*

Dr. Samuel A. Mudd House Museum [W] *Waldorf, MD*

Drum Corps International-Eastern Regional Championship [S] *Allentown, PA*

Drumfest [S] *Cumberland, MD*

Dumbarton Oaks [W] *Washington, DC*

Dupont-Kalorama Museum Walk [W] *Washington, DC*

Duquesne Incline [W] *Pittsburgh, PA*

Duryea Day Antique & Classic Auto Show [S] *Pottstown, PA*

Dutch Wonderland [W] *Lancaster, PA*

Earl Gregg Swem Library [W]
    Williamsburg, VA
Earth and Mineral Sciences Museum
    [W] *State College, PA*
East Broad Top Railroad [W] *Orbiso-*
    nia, PA
East Cemetery Hill [W] *Gettysburg*
    National Military Park, PA
East Coast Surfing Championship [S]
    Virginia Beach, VA
Easter Decoy & Art Festival [S] *Chin-*
    coteague, VA
Easter Egg Roll [S] *Washington, DC*
Eastern Market [W] *Washington, DC*
Eastern Mennonite University [W]
    Harrisonburg, VA
Eastern Regional Coal Archives [W]
    Bluefield, WV
Eastern Shore Chamber Music Festi-
    val [S] *Easton, MD*
Eastern Sports & Outdoor Show [S]
    Harrisburg, PA
East Lynn Wildlife Management Area
    [W] *Huntington, WV*
Eckley Miners' Village [W] *Hazleton,*
    PA
Edgar Allan Poe Grave [W] *Baltimore,*
    MD
Edgar Allan Poe House [W] *Baltimore,*
    MD
Edgar Allan Poe Museum [W] *Rich-*
    mond, VA
Edgar Allan Poe National Historic
    Site [W] *Philadelphia, PA*
Eisenhower National Historic Site
    [W] *Gettysburg, PA*
Eisenhower National Historic Site
    [W] *Gettysburg National Military*
    Park, PA
Eldred World War II Museum [W]
    Port Allegany, PA
Election Day 1860 [S] *Harpers Ferry,*
    WV
Elfreth's Alley [W] *Philadelphia, PA*
Elfreth's Alley Fete Days [S] *Philadel-*
    phia, PA
Elizabeth Myers Mitchell Art Gallery
    [W] *Annapolis, MD*
Elk Mountain Ski Center [W] *Carbon-*
    dale, PA
Elk Neck State Forest [W] *Elkton, MD*
Elk Neck State Park [W] *Elkton, MD*
Elk River Scenic Drive [W] *Charleston,*
    WV
Elk River Touring Center [W] *Marlin-*
    ton, WV
Elk Run Trail [W] *Blue Ridge Parkway,*
    VA
Elkwallow [W] *Shenandoah National*
    Park, VA

Ellicott City B & O Railroad Station
    Museum [W] *Ellicott City, MD*
Elmwood Park Zoo [W] *Norristown,*
    PA
Emancipation Oak [W] *Hampton, VA*
Emancipation Statue [W] *Washington,*
    DC
Embassy Row [W] *Washington, DC*
Endless Caverns [W] *New Market, VA*
Enoch Pratt Free Library [W] *Balti-*
    more, MD
Ephrata Cloister [W] *Ephrata, PA*
Equestrian Statue of Washington [W]
    Richmond, VA
Erie Art Museum [W] *Erie, PA*
Erie National Wildlife Refuge [W]
    Meadville, PA
Erie Zoo [W] *Erie, PA*
Eternal Light Peace Memorial, The
    [W] *Gettysburg National Military*
    Park, PA
Evangelical Reformed Church [W]
    Frederick, MD
Evans Farm [W] *McLean, VA*
Evening entertainment [W] *Williams-*
    burg, VA
Evening Parade [S] *Washington, DC*
Evergreen House [W] *Baltimore, MD*
Everhart Museum [W] *Scranton, PA*
Exhibition buildings [W] *Williams-*
    burg, VA
Explorers Hall [W] *Washington, DC*
Fairmont State College [W] *Fairmont,*
    WV
Fairmount Park [W] *Philadelphia, PA*
Fairmount Park Historical Christmas
    Tours [S] *Philadelphia, PA*
Fairy Stone State Park [W] *Mar-*
    tinsville, VA
Fall Festival [S] *Frederick, MD*
Fall Foliage Festival [S] *Jim Thorpe, PA*
Fall Foliage Festival [S] *Waynesboro,*
    VA
Fall Foliage Festival Days [S] *Bedford,*
    PA
Fall Harvest Festival and Craft Show
    [S] *Havre de Grace, MD*
Fallingwater [W] *Pittsburgh, PA*
Fallingwater (Kaufmann Conserva-
    tion on Bear Run) [W] *Con-*
    nellsville, PA
Falls Church, The [W] *Falls Church,*
    VA
Fallsington Day [S] *Bristol (Bucks*
    County), PA
Family burial ground [W] *George*
    Washington Birthplace National
    Monument, VA
Fan, The [W] *Richmond, VA*
Farmers' and Threshermen's Jubilee
    [S] *Somerset, PA*

Farmers Bank [W] *Petersburg, VA*

Farmer's Market and Auction [W] *Waldorf, MD*

Fashion Centre at Pentagon City [W] *Arlington County (Ronald Reagan Washington-National Airport Area), VA*

FBI Headquarters [W] *Washington, DC*

Federal Hill [W] *Baltimore, MD*

Federal Reserve Building [W] *Washington, DC*

Federal Reserve Money Museum [W] *Richmond, VA*

Federal Trade Commission Building [W] *Washington, DC*

Federal Triangle [W] *Washington, DC*

Fell's Point [W] *Baltimore, MD*

Fenwick Island Lighthouse [W] *Fenwick Island, DE*

Fenwick Island State Park [W] *Fenwick Island, DE*

Festival in the Park [S] *Danville, VA*

Festival in the Park [S] *Roanoke, VA*

Festival of American Folklife [S] *Washington, DC*

Festival of Leaves [S] *Front Royal, VA*

Fife and Drum Corps [S] *Williamsburg, VA*

Finance Building [W] *Harrisburg, PA*

Firefighters Historical Museum [W] *Erie, PA*

Fireman's Hall Museum [W] *Philadelphia, PA*

Fire Museum of Maryland [W] *Towson, MD*

Fire Museum of York County [W] *York, PA*

First Assembly Day [S] *Jamestown (Colonial National Historical Park), VA*

First Bank of the United States, The [W] *Philadelphia, PA*

First Landing/Seashore State Park [W] *Virginia Beach, VA*

First landing site [W] *Jamestown (Colonial National Historical Park), VA*

First Maine Monument [W] *Petersburg National Battlefield, VA*

First Presbyterian Church of Winchester [W] *Winchester, VA*

First Unitarian Church [W] *Baltimore, MD*

Fishing [W] *Blue Ridge Parkway, VA*

Fishing [W] *Harrisonburg, VA*

Fishing [W] *Shenandoah National Park, VA*

Fishing [W] *Virginia Beach, VA*

Fishing contests and tournaments [S] *Ocean City, MD*

Fishing, swimming, boating, camping, hiking [W] *White Sulphur Springs, WV*

Five Forks Unit [W] *Petersburg National Battlefield, VA*

Flaming Foliage Festival [S] *Lock Haven, PA*

Flat Rock Trail [W] *Blue Ridge Parkway, VA*

Flowerdew Hundred [W] *Hopewell, VA*

Flying Circus [S] *Warrenton, VA*

Folger Shakespeare Library [W] *Washington, DC*

Folk Art Center [W] *Blue Ridge Parkway, VA*

Folk Craft Center & Museum [W] *Bird-in-Hand, PA*

Folk Festival [S] *Kutztown, PA*

Folk Festival [S] *Pittsburgh, PA*

Fondo del Sol [W] *Washington, DC*

Fonthill Museum [W] *Doylestown (Bucks County), PA*

Footbridge, The [W] *St. Michael's, MD*

Ford's Theatre [W] *Washington, DC*

Fort Augusta [W] *Lewisburg, PA*

Fort Bedford Park and Museum [W] *Bedford, PA*

Fort Christina Monument [W] *Wilmington, DE*

Fort Cumberland Trail [W] *Cumberland, MD*

Fort Delaware State Park [W] *Odessa, DE*

Fort Delaware State Park [W] *Wilmington, DE*

Fort Dupont Park [W] *Washington, DC*

Fort Dupont Sports Complex [W] *Washington, DC*

Fort Dupont Summer Theatre [S] *Washington, DC*

Fort Early [W] *Lynchburg, VA*

Fort Eustis [W] *Newport News, VA*

Fort Frederick State Park [W] *Hagerstown, MD*

Fort Haskell [W] *Petersburg National Battlefield, VA*

Fort Hunter Mansion [W] *Harrisburg, PA*

Fort Hunter Park [W] *Harrisburg, PA*

Fort Lee [W] *Petersburg, VA*

Fort Ligonier [W] *Ligonier, PA*

Fort Ligonier Days [S] *Ligonier, PA*

Fort McHenry National Monument and Historic Shrine [W] *Baltimore, MD*

Fort Mifflin [W] *Philadelphia, PA*

Fort Monroe [W] *Hampton, VA*

Fort Necessity National Battlefield [W] *Uniontown, PA*

Fort New Salem [W] *Clarksburg, WV*

Fort Pitt Museum [W] *Pittsburgh, PA*
Fort Roberdeau [W] *Altoona, PA*
Fort Stedman [W] *Petersburg National Battlefield, VA*
Fort Stevens Park [W] *Washington, DC*
Fort Ward Museum and Historic Site [W] *Alexandria, VA*
Fort Washington National Park [W] *Washington, DC*
Fort Washington State Park [W] *Ft Washington, PA*
Fort Zeller [W] *Lebanon, PA*
Forum Building [W] *Harrisburg, PA*
Founder's Day [S] *Charlottesville, VA*
Founders Day-Washington Heritage [S] *Charles Town, WV*
Founders Hall [W] *Hershey, PA*
Fountain of Faith [W] *Falls Church, VA*
Fountain Square Holiday Celebration [S] *Dulles Intl Airport Area, VA*
Fountain Square Ice Rink [S] *Dulles Intl Airport Area, VA*
Franciscan Monastery [W] *Washington, DC*
Francis Land House Historic Site and Gardens [W] *Virginia Beach, VA*
Frank Buchman House [W] *Allentown, PA*
Franklin and Marshall College [W] *Lancaster, PA*
Franklin County Fair [S] *Chambersburg, PA*
Franklin Court [W] *Philadelphia, PA*
Franklin Delano Roosevelt Memorial [W] *Washington, DC*
Franklin Institute Science Museum [W] *Philadelphia, PA*
Franklin Mint Museum [W] *Media, PA*
Franklin Silver Cornet Band Concerts [S] *Franklin (Venango County), PA*
Frank Lloyd Wright's Pope-Leighey House [W] *Mount Vernon, VA*
Frederick Douglass National Historic Site, "Cedar Hill" [W] *Washington, DC*
Fredericksburg Area Museum (Town Hall) [W] *Fredericksburg, VA*
Fredericksburg Masonic Lodge #4, AF and AM [W] *Fredericksburg, VA*
Fredericksburg National Cemetery [W] *Fredericksburg and Spotsylvania National Military Park, VA*
Fredericksburg Visitor Center [W] *Fredericksburg and Spotsylvania National Military Park, VA*

Freedom Park [W] *Arlington County (Ronald Reagan Washington-National Airport Area), VA*
Free Library [W] *Philadelphia, PA*
Freer Gallery [W] *Washington, DC*
French Azilum [W] *Towanda, PA*
French Creek State Park [W] *Pottstown, PA*
Frick Art and Historical Center, The [W] *Pittsburgh, PA*
Frick Art Musuem, The [W] *Pittsburgh, PA*
Frick Park [W] *Pittsburgh, PA*
Friendship Hill National Historic Site [W] *Uniontown, PA*
Friends Meeting House [W] *York, PA*
Frontier Culture Museum [W] *Staunton, VA*
Fulton Opera House [W] *Lancaster, PA*
Furnace Town [W] *Salisbury, MD*
Gadsby's Tavern Museum [W] *Alexandria, VA*
Gallery, The [W] *Philadelphia, PA*
Gambrill State Park [W] *Frederick, MD*
Garden Symposium [S] *Williamsburg, VA*
Garden Week [S] *Charlottesville, VA*
Garden Week in Historic Lexington [S] *Lexington, VA*
Garrett County Fair [S] *Oakland (Garrett County), MD*
Garrett State Forest [W] *Oakland (Garrett County), MD*
Gateway Center [W] *Pittsburgh, PA*
Gathland State Park [W] *Boonsboro (Garrett County), MD*
Gauley River National Recreation Area [W] *Summersville, WV*
Gazela of Philadelphia [W] *Philadelphia, PA*
General Adam Stephen House [W] *Martinsburg, WV*
General Douglas MacArthur Memorial [W] *Norfolk, VA*
General Gates' House [W] *York, PA*
General Lee's Headquarters [W] *Gettysburg, PA*
General Services Administration Building [W] *Washington, DC*
George C. Marshall Museum [W] *Lexington, VA*
George Mason University [W] *Fairfax, VA*
George Read II House [W] *New Castle, DE*
George Rogers Clark Memorial [W] *Charlottesville, VA*
George Taylor House and Park [W] *Allentown, PA*
Georgetown [W] *Washington, DC*

Georgetown Garden Tour [S] *Washington, DC*

Georgetown House Tour [S] *Washington, DC*

Georgetown University [W] *Washington, DC*

George Washington and Jefferson National Forests [W] *Harrisonburg, VA*

George Washington and Jefferson National Forests [W] *Marion, VA*

George Washington and Jefferson National Forests [W] *Roanoke, VA*

George Washington Birthday Celebrations [S] *Alexandria, VA*

George Washington Birthplace National Monument [W] *Fredericksburg, VA*

George Washington Masonic National Memorial [W] *Alexandria, VA*

George Washington's Ferry Farm [W] *Fredericksburg, VA*

George Washington's Headquarters [W] *Cumberland, MD*

George Washington University [W] *Washington, DC*

Germania Old Home Day [S] *Galeton, PA*

Germantown [W] *Philadelphia, PA*

Gettysburg Battle Theatre [W] *Gettysburg, PA*

Gettysburg College [W] *Gettysburg, PA*

Gettysburg National Cemetery, The [W] *Gettysburg National Military Park, PA*

Gettysburg Scenic Rail Tours [W] *Gettysburg, PA*

Ghosts of Gettysburg Candlelight Walking Tours [W] *Gettysburg, PA*

Ghost Tours [W] *New Hope, PA*

Gifford Pinchot State Park [W] *York, PA*

Glasshouse [W] *Jamestown (Colonial National Historical Park), VA*

Glencairn Museum [W] *Willow Grove, PA*

Gloria Dei Church National Historic Site ("Old Swedes") [W] *Philadelphia, PA*

God's Acre [W] *Bethlehem, PA*

Goodwill Industries Embassy Tour [S] *Washington, DC*

Gordon-Roberts House [W] *Cumberland, MD*

Goshen Pass [W] *Lexington, VA*

Gouldsboro State Park [W] *Mount Pocono, PA*

Goundie House [W] *Bethlehem, PA*

Government House [W] *Annapolis, MD*

Government Printing Office [W] *Washington, DC*

Governor's Mansion [W] *Charleston, WV*

Governor's Mansion [W] *Richmond, VA*

Governor's Palace and Gardens [W] *Williamsburg, VA*

Grace Episcopal Church [W] *Yorktown, VA*

Gracie's Dam [W] *Petersburg National Battlefield, VA*

Graeme Park [W] *Willow Grove, PA*

Grand Caverns Regional Park [W] *Harrisonburg, VA*

Grand Opera House [W] *Wilmington, DE*

Grandview Cemetery [W] *Johnstown, PA*

Grandview Unit of New River Gorge National River [W] *Beckley, WV*

Grave Creek Mound State Park [W] *Wheeling, WV*

Grave of Captain John Green [W] *Bristol (Bucks County), PA*

Grave of "Molly Pitcher" [W] *Carlisle, PA*

Gravity Coach [W] *Hawley, PA*

Gray Line bus tours [W] *Philadelphia, PA*

Gray Line bus tours [W] *Washington, DC*

Grayson Highlands State Park [W] *Abingdon, VA*

Great Allentown Fair [S] *Allentown, PA*

Great Delaware Kite Festival [S] *Lewes, DE*

Great Falls of the Potomac [W] *Washington, DC*

Great Frederick Fair [S] *Frederick, MD*

"The Great Square" [W] *Easton, PA*

Green, The [W] *New Castle, DE*

Greenbelt Park [W] *College Park, MD*

Greenbrier River Trail [W] *Marlinton, WV*

Greenbrier State Forest [W] *White Sulphur Springs, WV*

Greenbrier State Park [W] *Hagerstown, MD*

Green Ridge State Forest [W] *Cumberland, MD*

Greenstone Trail [W] *Blue Ridge Parkway, VA*

Greenwood Furnace State Park [W] *Lewistown, PA*

Greer House [W] *New Castle, PA*

Grey Towers [W] *Milford, PA*

Gridley's Grave [W] *Erie, PA*

Grist Mill Historical State Park [W] *Mount Vernon, VA*

Guided Bus and Walking Tours [W] *Pittsburgh, PA*

Guided walking tours [W] *Shepherdstown, WV*

Gunpowder Falls State Park [W] *Baltimore, MD*

Gunston Hall [W] *Alexandria, VA*

Gypsy Hill Park [W] *Staunton, VA*

Hagerstown Railroad Heritage Days [S] *Hagerstown, MD*

Hagerstown Roundhouse Museum [W] *Hagerstown, MD*

Hagley Museum [W] *Wilmington, DE*

Haines Mill Museum [W] *Allentown, PA*

Halfway Park Days [S] *Hagerstown, MD*

Hall of Presidents and First Ladies [W] *Gettysburg, PA*

Hammond-Harwood House [W] *Annapolis, MD*

Hampton Bay Days [S] *Hampton, VA*

Hampton Carousel [W] *Hampton, VA*

Hampton Cup Regatta [S] *Hampton, VA*

Hampton Jazz Festival [S] *Hampton, VA*

Hampton National Historic Site [W] *Towson, MD*

Hampton Roads Naval Museum [W] *Norfolk, VA*

Hampton University [W] *Hampton, VA*

Handley Library and Archives [W] *Winchester, VA*

Hans Herr House [W] *Lancaster, PA*

Harbor cruises [W] *Baltimore, MD*

Harbor Expo [S] *Baltimore, MD*

Harborfest [S] *Norfolk, VA*

Harborplace [W] *Baltimore, MD*

Hardy County Heritage Weekend [S] *Moorefield, WV*

Harley-Davidson, Inc [W] *York, PA*

Harmony Museum [W] *Harmony, PA*

Harness racing [S] *Ocean City, MD*

Harness racing [W] *Washington, DC*

Harper House [W] *Harpers Ferry, WV*

Harpers Ferry National Historical Park [W] *Harpers Ferry, WV*

Harrington Raceway [S] *Dover, DE*

Harrison's Creek [W] *Petersburg National Battlefield, VA*

Harriton House [W] *King of Prussia, PA*

Hartslog Day [S] *Huntingdon, PA*

Hartwood [W] *Pittsburgh, PA*

Harvest Days [S] *Lancaster, PA*

Harvest Moon Festival [S] *Wilmington, DE*

Haverford College [W] *Philadelphia, PA*

Hawk Mountain Sanctuary [W] *Hamburg, PA*

Hawk's Nest State Park [W] *Gauley Bridge, WV*

Head House Open Air Craft Market [S] *Philadelphia, PA*

Hebrew Tabernacle Reproduction [W] *Lancaster, PA*

Heinz Chapel [W] *Pittsburgh, PA*

Heisey Museum, The [W] *Lock Haven, PA*

Henry Clay Frick Fine Arts Building [W] *Pittsburgh, PA*

Heritage Center Museum of Lancaster County [W] *Lancaster, PA*

Heritage Day [S] *Bowie, MD*

Heritage Village [W] *Huntington, WV*

Heritage Wine Cellars [W] *North East, PA*

Hermitage Foundation Museum [W] *Norfolk, VA*

Herrington Manor State Park [W] *Oakland (Garrett County), MD*

Hershey Gardens [W] *Hershey, PA*

Hershey Museum [W] *Hershey, PA*

Hersheypark [W] *Hershey, PA*

Hersheypark Arena [W] *Hershey, PA*

Hersheypark Balloonfest [S] *Hershey, PA*

Hersheypark Stadium/Star Pavilion [W] *Hershey, PA*

Hershey's Chocolate World [W] *Hershey, PA*

Hiawatha [W] *Williamsport, PA*

Hibernia County Park [W] *Downingtown, PA*

Hibernia Mansion Christmas Tours [S] *Downingtown, PA*

Hickory Run State Park [W] *White Haven, PA*

Hidden Valley Ski Area [W] *Somerset, PA*

High Country Arts & Craft Fair [S] *Clearfield (Clearfield County), PA*

Highland County Maple Festival [S] *Monterey, VA*

Highlands, The [W] *Ft Washington, PA*

Hiking [W] *Shenandoah National Park, VA*

Hill House [W] *Portsmouth, VA*

Hills Creek State Park [W] *Mansfield, PA*

Hill-to-Hill Bridge [W] *Bethlehem, PA*

Hiram R. Burton House [W] *Lewes, DE*

Hirshhorn Museum and Sculpture Garden [W] *Washington, DC*

Historical Society of Berks County [W] *Reading, PA*

Historical Society of Frederick County Museum [W] *Frederick, MD*

Historical Society of Pennsylvania [W] *Philadelphia, PA*

Historical Society of Talbot County [W] *Easton, MD*

Historical Society of York County [W] *York, PA*

Historic Annapolis Foundation [W] *Annapolis, MD*

Historic Annapolis Foundation Welcome Center and Museum Store [W] *Annapolis, MD*

Historic Bartram's Garden [W] *Philadelphia, PA*

Historic Bethlehem Inc's 18th-Century Industrial Quarter [W] *Bethlehem, PA*

Historic Christ Church [W] *Irvington, VA*

Historic District [W] *Bloomsburg, PA*

Historic Fallsington [W] *Bristol (Bucks County), PA*

Historic Garden Tour [S] *Winchester, VA*

Historic Garden Week [S] *Fredericksburg, VA*

Historic Garden Week in Virginia [S] *Richmond, VA*

Historic Hanna's Town [W] *Greensburg, PA*

Historic Hilton Village [W] *Newport News, VA*

Historic houses [W] *Portsmouth, VA*

Historic Houses of Odessa [W] *Odessa, DE*

Historic Lancaster Walking Tour [W] *Lancaster, PA*

Historic Michie Tavern [W] *Charlottesville, VA*

Historic Richmond Tours [W] *Richmond, VA*

Historic Rock Ford [W] *Lancaster, PA*

Historic Schaefferstown [W] *Cornwall, PA*

Historic Schaefferstown Events [S] *Cornwall, PA*

Historic Shepherdstown Museum [W] *Shepherdstown, WV*

Historic St. Mary's City [W] *St. Mary's City, MD*

Historic trades [W] *Williamsburg, VA*

Historic Yellow Springs [W] *Downingtown, PA*

History Museum of Western Virginia [W] *Roanoke, VA*

Hoge-Osmer House [W] *Franklin (Venango County), PA*

Holiday in Lexington [S] *Lexington, VA*

Holley Ross Pottery [W] *Canadensis, PA*

Holliday Lake State Park [W] *Appomattox Court House National Historical Park, VA*

Holly River State Park [W] *Buckhannon, WV*

Holly River State Park [W] *Webster Springs, WV*

Hollywood Cemetery [W] *Richmond, VA*

Holocaust Memorial [W] *Baltimore, MD*

Holts Landing State Park [W] *Bethany Beach, DE*

Holy Trinity (Old Swedes) Church and Hendrickson House [W] *Wilmington, DE*

Home of General Henry "Light Horse Harry" Lee [W] *Alexandria, VA*

Homes and Gardens Tour [S] *Leesburg, VA*

Homestead, The [W] *Hot Springs, VA*

Hometown Holidays [S] *Rockville, MD*

Homewood House Museum [W] *Baltimore, MD*

Hooray for Hopewell Festival [S] *Hopewell, VA*

Hope Lodge [W] *Ft Washington, PA*

Hopewell Furnace National Historic Site [W] *Pottstown, PA*

Hopewell Furnace National Historic Site [W] *Pottstown, PA*

Horseback Riding [W] *Blue Ridge Parkway, VA*

Horse-drawn carriage tours [W] *Frederick, MD*

Horse racing [S] *Philadelphia, PA*

Horse racing. Delaware Park [S] *Wilmington, DE*

Horseshoe Curve Visitors Center [W] *Altoona, PA*

Horse show [S] *Weston, WV*

House Office Buildings [W] *Washington, DC*

House tours [S] *Alexandria, VA*

Howard County Center of African-American Culture [W] *Columbia, MD*

Howard County Fair [S] *Ellicott City, MD*

Howard University [W] *Washington, DC*

Hoyt Institute of Fine Arts [W] *New Castle, PA*

Hugh Mercer Apothecary Shop [W] *Fredericksburg, VA*

Hugh Moore Park [W] *Easton, PA*

Humpback Bridge [W] *Covington, VA*

Humpback Rocks Visitor Center [W] *Blue Ridge Parkway, VA*

Hungry Mother Arts and Crafts Festival [S] *Marion, VA*

Hungry Mother State Park [W] *Marion, VA*

Hunter House Victorian Museum [W] *Norfolk, VA*

Huntington Museum of Art [W] *Huntington, WV*

Huntsdale Fish Hatchery [W] *Carlisle, PA*

Hupp's Hill Battlefield Park and Study Center [W] *Strasburg, VA*

Hyner View [W] *Lock Haven, PA*

Idlewild Park [W] *Ligonier, PA*

Inclined Plane Railway [W] *Johnstown, PA*

Inclines [W] *Pittsburgh, PA*

Independence Hall [W] *Philadelphia, PA*

Independence National Historical Park [W] *Philadelphia, PA*

Independence Seaport Museum [W] *Philadelphia, PA*

Independence Square [W] *Philadelphia, PA*

Indian Caverns [W] *Huntingdon, PA*

Indian Echo Caverns [W] *Harrisburg, PA*

Industrial tours [W] *Huntington, WV*

Information Center [W] *Harpers Ferry, WV*

International Azalea Festival [S] *Norfolk, VA*

Interpretive program [W] *Shenandoah National Park, VA*

Interpretive programs [W] *Blue Ridge Parkway, VA*

Iron Gate Gorge [W] *Clifton Forge, VA*

Islamic Center [W] *Washington, DC*

Italian Lake [W] *Harrisburg, PA*

Italian Market [W] *Philadelphia, PA*

Iwo Jima Statue [W] *Arlington County (Ronald Reagan Washington-National Airport Area), VA*

Iwo Jima Statue [W] *Washington, DC*

Jack Frost [W] *White Haven, PA*

Jackson's Mill Historic Area [W] *Weston, WV*

Jackson's Mill State 4-H Conference Center [W] *Weston, WV*

Jackson Ward [W] *Richmond, VA*

Jamboree in the Hills [S] *Wheeling, WV*

Jamboree, USA [W] *Wheeling, WV*

James A. Michener Art Museum [W] *Doylestown (Bucks County), PA*

James Buchanan's Wheatland [W] *Lancaster, PA*

James Fort site [W] *Jamestown (Colonial National Historical Park), VA*

James Geddy House [W] *Williamsburg, VA*

James L. Kelso Bible Lands Museum [W] *Pittsburgh, PA*

James Madison Museum [W] *Orange, VA*

James Madison University [W] *Harrisonburg, VA*

James Monroe Museum [W] *Fredericksburg, VA*

James River [W] *Richmond, VA*

James River Wayside [W] *Blue Ridge Parkway, VA*

Jamestown Settlement [W] *Jamestown (Colonial National Historical Park), VA*

Jamestown Weekend [S] *Jamestown (Colonial National Historical Park), VA*

Janes Island State Park [W] *Crisfield, MD*

Japanese Exhibition House [W] *Philadelphia, PA*

Jazz in the Park [S] *Staunton, VA*

Jefferson County Courthouse [W] *Charles Town, WV*

Jefferson County Fair [S] *Charles Town, WV*

Jefferson County Museum [W] *Charles Town, WV*

Jefferson's Poplar Forest [W] *Lynchburg, VA*

Jefferson's Rock [W] *Harpers Ferry, WV*

Jeff Matthews Memorial Museum [W] *Galax, VA*

Jennings Environmental Education Center [W] *Butler, PA*

Jeweler's Row [W] *Philadelphia, PA*

Jewish Historical Society of Maryland [W] *Baltimore, MD*

Jimmy Stewart Museum [W] *Indiana, PA*

Jim Thorpe Memorial [W] *Jim Thorpe, PA*

Jim Thorpe River Adventures, Inc [W] *Jim Thorpe, PA*

John Brown Museum [W] *Harpers Ferry, WV*

John Brown's Fort [W] *Harpers Ferry, WV*

John Brown Wax Museum [W] *Harpers Ferry, WV*

John Chads House [W] *Kennett Square, PA*

John Dickinson Plantation [W] *Dover, DE*

John F. Kennedy Center for the Performing Arts [W] *Washington, DC*

John Fox, Jr., House & Museum [W] *Big Stone Gap, VA*

John Harris Mansion [W] *Harrisburg, PA*

John Heinz National Wildlife Refuge at Tinicum [W] *Philadelphia, PA*

John Marshall House [W] *Richmond, VA*

Johns Hopkins Medical Institutions [W] *Baltimore, MD*

Johns Hopkins University [W] *Baltimore, MD*

Johnson Victrola Museum [W] *Dover, DE*

Johnstown Flood Museum [W] *Johnstown, PA*

Johnstown Flood National Memorial [W] *Johnstown, PA*

John Wilkes Booth Escape Route [W] *Waldorf, MD*

John Wilkes Booth Escape Route Tour [S] *Waldorf, MD*

Jonathan Hager Frontier Craft Day [S] *Hagerstown, MD*

Jonathan Hager House and Museum [W] *Hagerstown, MD*

Joseph Meyerhoff Symphony Hall [W] *Baltimore, MD*

Joseph Priestley House [W] *Danville, PA*

Joseph R. Grundy Observatory [W] *Lancaster, PA*

Judiciary Square [W] *Washington, DC*

July 4 Celebration [S] *Washington, DC*

Jumonville Glen [W] *Uniontown, PA*

June Jubilee [S] *Richmond, VA*

June Tolliver House [W] *Big Stone Gap, VA*

Kanawha Canal Locks [W] *Richmond, VA*

Kanawha State Forest [W] *Charleston, WV*

Kemerer Museum of Decorative Arts [W] *Bethlehem, PA*

Kenilworth Aquatic Gardens [W] *Washington, DC*

Kenmore [W] *Fredericksburg, VA*

Kennywood Park [W] *Pittsburgh, PA*

Kettle Creek [W] *Lock Haven, PA*

Keystone Country Festival [S] *Altoona, PA*

Killens Pond State Park [W] *Dover, DE*

King Coal Festival [S] *Williamson, WV*

King Street [W] *Alexandria, VA*

Kinzua Bridge State Park [W] *Kane, PA*

Kinzua Dam and Allegheny Reservoir [W] *Warren, PA*

Kipona [S] *Harrisburg, PA*

Kooser [W] *Somerset, PA*

Korean War Memorial [W] *Washington, DC*

Koziar's Christmas Village [W] *Reading, PA*

Krodel Park and Lake [W] *Point Pleasant, WV*

Kruger Street Toy & Train Museum [W] *Wheeling, WV*

Kumbrabow State Forest [W] *Webster Springs, WV*

Labor Department [W] *Washington, DC*

Lackawanna Coal Mine Tour [W] *Scranton, PA*

Lackawanna County Stadium [W] *Scranton, PA*

Lacrosse Hall of Fame Museum [W] *Baltimore, MD*

Ladew Topiary Gardens [W] *Cockeysville, MD*

Lafayette College [W] *Easton, PA*

Lafayette House [W] *Alexandria, VA*

Lafayette Square [W] *Washington, DC*

Lake Fairfax [W] *Fairfax, VA*

Lakemont Park [W] *Altoona, PA*

Lake Moomaw [W] *Covington, VA*

Lake Shenandoah [W] *Harrisonburg, VA*

Lake Stephens [W] *Beckley, WV*

Lake Wallenpaupack [W] *Hawley, PA*

Lancaster County Courthouse Historic District [W] *Lancaster, VA*

Landis Valley Museum [W] *Lancaster, PA*

Land Lighthouse [W] *Erie, PA*

Land of Little Horses [W] *Gettysburg, PA*

Lanthorn Tour [W] *Williamsburg, VA*

Laurel Blossom Festival [S] *Jim Thorpe, PA*

Laurel Caverns [W] *Uniontown, PA*

Laurel Highlands River Tours [W] *Uniontown, PA*

Laurel Hill [W] *Somerset, PA*

Laurel Tour [S] *Clearfield (Clearfield County), PA*

Learning Weekend [S] *Williamsburg, VA*

Lee Chapel [W] *Lexington, VA*

Lee-Fendall House [W] *Alexandria, VA*

Lee Memorial Park [W] *Petersburg, VA*

Lee's Retreat [W] *Petersburg, VA*

Lehigh County Museum [W] *Allentown, PA*

Leitersburg Peach Festival [S] *Hagerstown, MD*

LeMoyne House [W] *Washington, PA*

Leonard Calvert Monument [W] *St. Mary's City, MD*

L.E. Smith Glass Co [W] *New Stanton, PA*

Lewes-Cape May, NJ, Ferry [W] *Lewes, DE*

Lewes Garden Tour [S] *Lewes, DE*

Lewes Historical Society Complex [W] *Lewes, DE*

Lewis and Clark Monument [W] *Charlottesville, VA*

Lewis Ginter Botanical Garden [W] *Richmond, VA*

Lewis Mountain [W] *Shenandoah National Park, VA*

Lexington Carriage Company [W] *Lexington, VA*

Lexington Market [W] *Baltimore, MD*

Liberty Bell Pavilion [W] *Philadelphia, PA*

Liberty Bell Shrine [W] *Allentown, PA*

Library Hall [W] *Philadelphia, PA*

Library of Congress [W] *Washington, DC*

Library of Pittsburgh [W] *Pittsburgh, PA*

Lightship Museum [W] *Portsmouth, VA*

Ligonier Highland Games and Gathering of the Clans of Scotland [S] *Ligonier, PA*

Ligonier Ice Fest [S] *Ligonier, PA*

Lime Kiln Arts Theater [S] *Lexington, VA*

Lincoln Caverns [W] *Huntingdon, PA*

Lincoln Highway Heritage Corridor [W] *Greensburg, PA*

Lincoln Homestead [W] *Harrisonburg, VA*

Lincoln Memorial [W] *Washington, DC*

Lincoln Museum [W] *Washington, DC*

Lincoln Room Museum [W] *Gettysburg, PA*

Lincoln Train Museum, The [W] *Gettysburg, PA*

Linden Hall [W] *Connellsville, PA*

Linn Cove Information Center [W] *Blue Ridge Parkway, VA*

Linville Falls Trail [W] *Blue Ridge Parkway, VA*

Little League Baseball Museum [W] *Williamsport, PA*

Little League Baseball International Headquarters [W] *Williamsport, PA*

Little League World Series [S] *Williamsport, PA*

Little Pine State Park [W] *Williamsport, PA*

Little Round Top [W] *Gettysburg National Military Park, PA*

Live Bethlehem Christmas Pageant [S] *Bethlehem, PA*

Living History Programs [S] *Williamsburg, VA*

Living Treasures Animal Park [W] *New Castle, PA*

Lock Ridge Furnace Museum [W] *Allentown, PA*

Lockwood House [W] *Harpers Ferry, WV*

Loft Mountain [W] *Shenandoah National Park, VA*

Loft Mountain Information Center [W] *Shenandoah National Park, VA*

London Town [W] *Annapolis, MD*

The Long Way Home [S] *Radford, VA*

Longwood Gardens [W] *Kennett Square, PA*

Lost River Caverns [W] *Bethlehem, PA*

Lost River State Park [W] *Moorefield, WV*

Lost World Caverns [W] *Lewisburg, WV*

Lotus Blossom Festival [S] *Frederick, MD*

Loudoun Hunt Pony Club Horse Trials [S] *Leesburg, VA*

Loudoun Museum [W] *Leesburg, VA*

Lovely Lane Museum [W] *Baltimore, MD*

Luckenbach Mill [W] *Bethlehem, PA*

Lums Pond State Park [W] *Odessa, DE*

Luray Caverns [W] *Luray, VA*

Luray Singing Tower [W] *Luray, VA*

Luray Zoo [W] *Luray, VA*

Lutheran Theological Seminary [W] *Gettysburg, PA*

Lyceum, The [W] *Alexandria, VA*

Lycoming County Fair [S] *Williamsport, VA*

Lynnhaven House [W] *Virginia Beach, VA*

Mabry Mill [W] *Blue Ridge Parkway, VA*

Mabry Mill Trail [W] *Blue Ridge Parkway, VA*

Magazine, The [W] *Williamsburg, VA*

Maggie Walker National Historic Site [W] *Richmond, VA*

Magna Entertainment Corporation [W] *Washington, PA*

Magoffin House Museum [W] *Mercer, PA*

Maier Museum of Art [W] *Lynchburg, VA*

Main Visitor Center [W] *Richmond National Battlefield Park, VA*

Manassas Museum, The [W] *Manassas, VA*

Mann Center for the Performing Arts [S] *Philadelphia, PA*

Mansion House [W] *Point Pleasant, WV*

Mansion Museum [W] *Wheeling, WV*

Maple Festival [S] *Somerset, PA*

Maple Syrup Demonstration [S] *Thurmont, MD*

Margaret Brent Memorial [W] *St. Mary's City, MD*

Marietta House Museum [W] *Bowie, MD*

Marine Barracks [W] *Washington, DC*

Marine Corps Air-Ground Museum [W] *Triangle, VA*

Marine Corps Museum [W] *Washington, DC*

Marine Mammal Pavilion [W] *Baltimore, MD*

Mariners' Museum [W] *Newport News, VA*

Marion County Museum [W] *Fairmont, WV*

Market Square Fair [S] *Fredericksburg, VA*

Martin Luther King Memorial Library [W] *Washington, DC*

Mary Ball Washington Museum and Library Complex [W] *Lancaster, VA*

Maryland Days [S] *St. Mary's City, MD*

Maryland Historical Society Library of Maryland [W] *Baltimore, MD*

Maryland House and Garden Pilgrimage [S] *Baltimore, MD*

Maryland Indian Cultural Center [W] *Waldorf, MD*

Maryland Institute, College of Art [W] *Baltimore, MD*

Maryland Preakness Celebration [S] *Baltimore, MD*

Maryland Renaissance Festival [S] *Annapolis, MD*

Maryland Science Center & Davis Planetarium [W] *Baltimore, MD*

Maryland Seafood Festival [S] *Annapolis, MD*

Maryland Sheep and Wool Festival [S] *Ellicott City, MD*

Mary McLeod Bethune Memorial [W] *Washington, DC*

Mary Merritt Doll Museum [W] *Pottstown, PA*

Marys Rock Tunnel [W] *Shenandoah National Park, VA*

Mary Washington College [W] *Fredericksburg, VA*

Mary Washington House [W] *Fredericksburg, VA*

Mary Washington Monument [W] *Fredericksburg, VA*

Mason County Fair [S] *Point Pleasant, WV*

Mason-Dixon Festival [S] *Morgantown, WV*

Mason-Dixon Line Marker [W] *Salisbury, MD*

Masonic Cemetery [W] *Fredericksburg, VA*

Massanutten One-room School [W] *Luray, VA*

Matewan [W] *Williamson, WV*

Mayfair Festival of the Arts [S] *Allentown, PA*

Mayfest [S] *Strasburg, VA*

Mayfest Street Festival [S] *Luray, VA*

Maymont [W] *Richmond, VA*

Mazza Vineyards [W] *North East, PA*

McClintic Wildlife Management Area [W] *Point Pleasant, WV*

McConkey Ferry Inn [W] *Washington Crossing Historic Park (Bucks County), PA*

McConnell's Mill State Park [W] *New Castle, PA*

McCormick Memorial Wayside [W] *Staunton, VA*

McDowell Hall [W] *Annapolis, MD*

McHenry Highland Festival [S] *Oakland (Garrett County), MD*

MCI Center [W] *Washington, DC*

McLean House and outbuildings [W] *Appomattox Court House National Historical Park, VA*

Meadowcroft Museum of Rural Life [W] *Washington, PA*

Meadow Farm Museum [W] *Richmond, VA*

Meadowlark Botanical Gardens [W] *Fairfax, VA*

Meek's Store and Meek's Storehouse [W] *Appomattox Court House National Historical Park, VA*

Mellon Arena [W] *Pittsburgh, PA*

Memorial Amphitheatre [W] *Arlington County (Ronald Reagan Washington-National Airport Area), VA*

Memorial Building [W] *Washington Crossing Historic Park (Bucks County), PA*

Memorial Church [W] *Jamestown (Colonial National Historical Park), VA*

Memorial Day Celebration [S] *State College, PA*

Memorial Day Ceremony [S] *Washington, DC*

Memorial Day Service [S] *Arlington County (Ronald Reagan Wash-*

ington-National Airport Area), VA

Memorial Flagstaff [W] *Washington Crossing Historic Park (Bucks County), PA*

Memorial House [W] *George Washington Birthplace National Monument, VA*

Memorial Park [W] *White Sulphur Springs, WV*

Memorials to State Units [W] *Gettysburg National Military Park, PA*

Memorytown, USA [W] *Mount Pocono, PA*

Mennonite Heritage Center [W] *Quakertown (Bucks County), PA*

Mennonite Information Center [W] *Lancaster, PA*

Mercer Mile [W] *Doylestown (Bucks County), PA*

Mercer Museum of the Bucks County Historical Society [W] *Doylestown (Bucks County), PA*

Merchant's Exchange, The [W] *Philadelphia, PA*

Merchants Hope Church [W] *Hopewell, VA*

Meridian International Center [W] *Washington, DC*

Merli-Sarnoski Park [W] *Carbondale, PA*

Merritt's Museum of Childhood [W] *Pottstown, PA*

Mid-Atlantic Air Museum [W] *Reading, PA*

Mid-Atlantic Maritime Festival [S] *St. Michael's, MD*

Middlecreek Wildlife Management Area [W] *Lebanon, PA*

Middleton Doll Company [W] *Parkersburg, WV*

Military Drill [S] *Williamsburg, VA*

Mill Bridge Village [W] *Lancaster, PA*

Miller Hall Planetarium and Sawhill Art Gallery [W] *Harrisonburg, VA*

Miller House [W] *Hagerstown, MD*

Mill Grove [W] *King of Prussia, PA*

Mill Mountain Theatre [S] *Roanoke, VA*

Mill Mountain Zoological Park [W] *Roanoke, VA*

Minnie V [W] *Baltimore, MD*

Misery Bay [W] *Erie, PA*

Miss Hampton II Harbor Cruises [W] *Hampton, VA*

Monocacy National Battlefield [W] *Frederick, MD*

Monongahela Incline [W] *Pittsburgh, PA*

Monongahela National Forest [W] *Elkins, WV*

Monongahela National Forest [W] *Petersburg, WV*

Montage Ski Area [W] *Scranton, PA*

Montgomery County Agricultural Fair [S] *Gaithersburg, MD*

Monticello [W] *Charlottesville, VA*

Monticello Visitors Center [W] *Charlottesville, VA*

Montpelier [W] *Orange, VA*

Montpelier Mansion [W] *Laurel, MD*

Monumental Church [W] *Richmond, VA*

Monumental United Methodist Church [W] *Portsmouth, VA*

Monuments [W] *Charlottesville, VA*

Moore House [W] *Yorktown, VA*

Moraine State Park [W] *Butler, PA*

Moravian College Alumni Association Antiques Show [S] *Bethlehem, PA*

Moravian Museum (Gemein Haus) [W] *Bethlehem, PA*

Moravian Pottery and Tile Works [W] *Doylestown (Bucks County), PA*

Morgan Log House [W] *Kulpsville, PA*

Morgan State University [W] *Baltimore, MD*

Morris Arboretum of the University of Pennsylvania [W] *Philadelphia, PA*

Morton Homestead [W] *Chester, PA*

Morven Park [W] *Leesburg, VA*

Moses Myers House [W] *Norfolk, VA*

Mother Seton House [W] *Baltimore, MD*

Motor World Your Place to Race [W] *Virginia Beach, VA*

Mountain Craft Days [S] *Somerset, PA*

Mountaineer Balloon Festival [S] *Morgantown, WV*

Mountaineer Racetrack & Resort [W] *Weirton, WV*

Mountain Farm Trail [W] *Blue Ridge Parkway, VA*

Mountain Heritage Arts and Crafts Festival [S] *Harpers Ferry, WV*

Mountain Lake [W] *Blacksburg, VA*

Mountain Playhouse [S] *Ligonier, PA*

Mountain Stage [W] *Charleston, WV*

Mountain State Apple Harvest Festival [S] *Martinsburg, WV*

Mountain State Art & Craft Fair [S] *Ripley, WV*

Mountain State Forest Festival [S] *Elkins, WV*

Mountain Streams & Trails Outfitters [W] *Uniontown, PA*

Mount Airy Lodge Ski Area [W] *Mount Pocono, PA*

Mount Clare Museum House [W] *Baltimore, MD*

Mt Davis [W] *Somerset, PA*

Mount Hope Estate & Winery [W] *Manheim, PA*

Mount Nittany Vineyard & Winery [W] *State College, PA*

Mount Olivet Cemetery [W] *Frederick, MD*

Mount Rogers National Recreation Area [W] *Marion, VA*

Mount St. Mary's College and Seminary [W] *Emmitsburg, MD*

Mount Tone Ski Resort [W] *Carbondale, PA*

M̦tter Museum [W] *Philadelphia, PA*

Mount Vernon [W] *Alexandria, VA*

Mount Vernon [W] *Washington, DC*

Mount Vernon [W] *Washington, VA*

Mount Vernon Place United Methodist Church [W] *Baltimore, MD*

Mountwood Park [W] *Parkersburg, WV*

MPT (Maryland Public Television) [W] *Baltimore, MD*

Muddy Run LLC [W] *Lancaster, PA*

Muhlenberg College [W] *Allentown, PA*

Mummer's Museum [W] *Philadelphia, PA*

Mummer's Parade [S] *Philadelphia, PA*

Muscarelle Museum of Art [W] *Williamsburg, VA*

Museum [W] *Fredericksburg and Spotsylvania National Military Park, VA*

Museum [W] *Hampton, VA*

Museum and Library of the Historical Society of Cocalico Valley [W] *Ephrata, PA*

Museum of American Art of the Pennsylvania Academy of the Fine Arts [W] *Philadelphia, PA*

Museum of Anthracite Mining [W] *Ashland, PA*

Museum of Art [W] *Pittsburgh, PA*

Museum of Natural History [W] *Pittsburgh, PA*

Museum of North Carolina Minerals [W] *Blue Ridge Parkway, VA*

Museum of Photographic History [W] *Pittsburgh, PA*

Museum of Small Town Life [W] *Dover, DE*

Museum of the Confederacy [W] *Richmond, VA*

Museum Shop (Pemberton House) [W] *Philadelphia, PA*

Musical programs [S] *Washington, DC*

Music at Gretna [S] *Lancaster, PA*

Music Hall [W] *Pittsburgh, PA*

Musikfest [S] *Bethlehem, PA*

MV *Lady Baltimore* [W] *Baltimore, MD*

Narrated cruises [W] *Baltimore, MD*

Narrows, The [W] *Cumberland, MD*

NASA/Goddard Visitor Center [W] *College Park, MD*

NASA Visitor Center [W] *Chincoteague, VA*

Nassawango Iron Furnace [W] *Salisbury, MD*

National Academy of Sciences [W] *Washington, DC*

National Air and Space Museum [W] *Washington, DC*

National Aquarium [W] *Baltimore, MD*

National Aquarium [W] *Washington, DC*

National Archives [W] *Washington, DC*

National Aviary [W] *Pittsburgh, PA*

National Building Museum [W] *Washington, DC*

National Capital Trolley Museum [W] *Silver Spring, MD*

National Civil War Wax Museum [W] *Gettysburg, PA*

National Colonial Farm [W] *Washington, DC*

National Fish Hatchery [W] *White Sulphur Springs, WV*

National Gallery of Art [W] *Washington, DC*

National Hard Crab Derby & Fair [S] *Crisfield, MD*

Nationality Days [S] *Ambridge, PA*

National Library of Medicine [W] *Bethesda, MD*

National Memorial Arch [W] *Valley Forge National Historical Park, PA*

National Museum of African Art [W] *Washington, DC*

National Museum of American Jewish History [W] *Philadelphia, PA*

National Museum of American History [W] *Washington, DC*

National Museum of American Art [W] *Washington, DC*

National Museum of Health and Medicine [W] *Washington, DC*

National Museum of Natural History [W] *Washington, DC*

National Museum of the Civil War Soldier [W] *Petersburg, VA*

National Museum of Women in the Arts [W] *Washington, DC*

National Outdoor Show [S] *Cambridge, MD*

National Presbyterian Church and Center [W] *Washington, DC*

National Radio Astronomy Observatory [W] *Marlinton, WV*

National Shrine Grotto of Lourdes [W] *Emmitsburg, MD*

National Shrine of the Sacred Heart [W] *Hazleton, PA*

National Toy Train Museum [W] *Lancaster, PA*

National Wax Museum of Lancaster County [W] *Lancaster, PA*

National Wildlife Visitor Center [W] *Laurel, MD*

National Zoological Park [W] *Washington, DC*

Native American Heritage Festival and Powwow [S] *Clarksville, VA*

Natural Bridge [W] *Natural Bridge, VA*

Natural Bridge Wax Museum [W] *Natural Bridge, VA*

Natural Bridge Zoo [W] *Natural Bridge, VA*

Natural Chimneys Jousting Tournament [S] *Harrisonburg, VA*

Natural Chimneys Regional Park [W] *Harrisonburg, VA*

Natural Tunnel State Park [W] *Big Stone Gap, VA*

Nature Center [W] *Washington, DC*

Nauticus, the National Maritime Center [W] *Norfolk, VA*

Naval Shipyard Museum [W] *Portsmouth, VA*

Navy Museum [W] *Washington, DC*

Navy Yard [W] *Washington, DC*

Nay Aug Park [W] *Scranton, PA*

Neas House Museum [W] *Hanover, PA*

Nelson House [W] *Yorktown, VA*

Nemours Mansion and Gardens [W] *Wilmington, DE*

Neptune Festival [S] *Virginia Beach, VA*

New Castle Court House Museum [W] *New Castle, DE*

New Germany State Park [W] *Grantsville, MD*

New Hall Military Museum [W] *Philadelphia, PA*

New Hope & Ivyland Railroad [W] *New Hope, PA*

New Hope Arts and Crafts Festival [S] *New Hope, PA*

Newlin Mill Park [W] *Media, PA*

New Market Battlefield Military Museum [W] *New Market, VA*

New Market Battlefield State Historical Park [W] *New Market, VA*

New Market Days [S] *Frederick, MD*

Newport News Park [W] *Newport News, VA*

New River Gorge Bridge [W] *Gauley Bridge, WV*

New River Gorge National River [W] *Hinton, WV*

Newseum, The [W] *Arlington County (Ronald Reagan Washington National Airport Area), VA*

"New Towne" [W] *Jamestown (Colonial National Historical Park), VA*

New Year's Eve Extravaganza [S] *Baltimore, MD*

New York Avenue Presbyterian Church [W] *Washington, DC*

Nicholas County Fair [S] *Summersville, WV*

Nicholas County Potato Festival [S] *Summersville, WV*

Norfolk Botanical Garden [W] *Norfolk, VA*

Norfolk Naval Base and Norfolk Naval Air Station [W] *Norfolk, VA*

Northampton County Historical Society [W] *Easton, PA*

North Bend Rail Trail [W] *Clarksburg, WV*

North Bend State Park [W] *Parkersburg, WV*

Northern Virginia Fine Arts Festival [S] *Dulles Intl Airport Area, VA*

North House Museum [W] *Lewisburg, WV*

North Museum of Natural History and Science [W] *Lancaster, PA*

North Office Building [W] *Harrisburg, PA*

Northwest River Park [W] *Chesapeake, VA*

Northwest Trading Post [W] *Blue Ridge Parkway, VA*

Norwegian Lady Statue [W] *Virginia Beach, VA*

Oatlands [W] *Leesburg, VA*

Occoneechee State Park [W] *Clarksville, VA*

Ocean Breeze Water Park [W] *Virginia Beach, VA*

Octagon , The [W] *Washington, DC*

Oglebayfest [S] *Wheeling, WV*

Oglebay Resort Park [W] *Wheeling, WV*

Ohiopyle State Park [W] *Uniontown, PA*

Oktoberfest [S] *Dulles Intl Airport Area, VA*

Old Barn [W] *Bradford, PA*

Old Bedford Village [W] *Bedford, PA*

Old Cape Henry Lighthouse and Memorial Park [W] *Virginia Beach, VA*

Old Chapel [W] *Bethlehem, PA*

Old Church Tower [W] *Jamestown (Colonial National Historical Park), VA*

Old City Hall [W] *Philadelphia, PA*

Old Coast Guard Station [W] *Virginia Beach, VA*

Old Court House Museum [W] *Lynchburg, VA*

Old Dover Days [S] *Dover, DE*

Old Dutch House [W] *New Castle, DE*

Old Economy Village [W] *Ambridge, PA*

Old Executive Office Building [W] *Washington, DC*

Old Fashioned Sunday [S] *Lancaster, PA*

Old Fiddler's Convention [S] *Galax, VA*

Old Fiddlers' Picnic [S] *Downingtown, PA*

Old Jail, The [W] *Chambersburg, PA*

Old Jail Museum [W] *Jim Thorpe, PA*

Old Jail Museum [W] *Leonardtown, MD*

Old Library Museum [W] *New Castle, DE*

Old Main [W] *State College, PA*

Old Mill, The [W] *Elkins, WV*

Old One-Room Schoolhouse #8 [W] *Bradford, PA*

Old Otterbein United Methodist Church [W] *Baltimore, MD*

Old Pine St Presbyterian Church [W] *Philadelphia, PA*

Old Presbyterian Meeting House [W] *Alexandria, VA*

Old Salem Church [W] *Fredericksburg and Spotsylvania National Military Park, VA*

Old Senate Chamber [W] *Washington, DC*

Old Slave Block [W] *Fredericksburg, VA*

Old State House, The [W] *Dover, DE*

Old St George's United Methodist Church [W] *Philadelphia, PA*

Old St. Mary's Church [W] *Philadelphia, PA*

Old Stone House [W] *Washington, DC*

Old Stone Presbyterian Church [W] *Lewisburg, WV*

Old Town Mall [W] *Baltimore, MD*

Old Trinity Church, Dorchester Parish [W] *Cambridge, MD*

Old Tyme Christmas [S] *Harpers Ferry, WV*

Ole Bull State Park [W] *Galeton, PA*

Opera Company of Philadelphia, The [W] *Philadelphia, PA*

Organ Cave [W] *Lewisburg, WV*

Organization of American States (OAS) [W] *Washington, DC*

Other buildings [W] *Harpers Ferry, WV*

Other Visitor Centers [W] *Richmond National Battlefield Park, VA*

Otterbein "Homesteading." [W] *Baltimore, MD*

Outlet Shopping [W] *Reading, PA*

Oxon Hill Farm [W] *Washington, DC*

Oyster and Maritime Museum of Chincoteague [W] *Chincoteague, VA*

Oyster Festival [S] *Chincoteague, VA*

Packet Boat *Marshall* [W] *Lynchburg, VA*

Packwood House Museum [W] *Lewisburg, PA*

Paddlewheeler *Annabel Lee* [W] *Richmond, VA*

Pageant of Peace [S] *Washington, DC*

Page County Heritage Festival [S] *Luray, VA*

Pamplin Park Civil War Site [W] *Petersburg, VA*

Panorama [W] *Shenandoah National Park, VA*

Panther State Forest [W] *Bluefield, WV*

Paramount's Kings Dominion [W] *Ashland, VA*

Parker Dam [W] *Clearfield (Clearfield County), PA*

Parkersburg Art Center [W] *Parkersburg, WV*

Parkersburg Homecoming [S] *Parkersburg, WV*

Parks [W] *Richmond, VA*

Parkway Craft Center [W] *Blue Ridge Parkway, VA*

Parry Barn [W] *New Hope, PA*

Parry Mansion Museum [W] *New Hope, PA*

Patapsco Valley State Park [W] *Ellicott City, MD*

Patrick Henry Home "Scotchtown" [W] *Ashland, VA*

Patrick Henry National Memorial (Red Hill) [W] *Brookneal, VA*

Patriot. , The [W] *St. Michael's, MD*

Patterson Park [W] *Baltimore, MD*

Pavilion at the Old Post Office [W] *Washington, DC*

P. Buckley Moss Museum [W] *Waynesboro, VA*

Peabody Institute of the Johns Hopkins University [W] *Baltimore, MD*

Peaks of Otter Visitor Center [W] *Blue Ridge Parkway, VA*

Pearl S. Buck Birthplace Museum [W] *Hillsboro, WV*

Pearl S. Buck House [W] *Doylestown (Bucks County), PA*

PECO Energy Company [W] *Aberdeen, MD*
PECO Energy Jazz Festival [S] *Philadelphia, PA*
Peddler's Village [W] *New Hope, PA*
Peninsula Fine Arts Center [W] *Newport News, VA*
Penn Memorial Landing Stone [W] *Chester, PA*
Penn National Race Course [W] *Harrisburg, PA*
Pennsbury Manor [W] *Bristol (Bucks County), PA*
Penn's Cave [W] *State College, PA*
Penn-Shore Vineyards and Winery [W] *North East, PA*
Penn's Landing [W] *Philadelphia, PA*
Penn's Woods West-Folk & Arts Festival [S] *Mercer, PA*
Pennsylvania Ballet [W] *Philadelphia, PA*
Pennsylvania Hospital [W] *Philadelphia, PA*
Pennsylvania Lumber Museum [W] *Galeton, PA*
Pennsylvania Military Museum [W] *State College, PA*
Pennsylvania National Horse Show [S] *Harrisburg, PA*
Pennsylvania Renaissance Faire [S] *Manheim, PA*
Pennsylvania State Farm Show [S] *Harrisburg, PA*
Pennsylvania State Laurel Festival [S] *Wellsboro, PA*
Pennsylvania State University [W] *State College, PA*
Pennsylvania Trolley Museum [W] *Washington, PA*
Pentagon, The [W] *Arlington County (Ronald Reagan Washington-National Airport Area), VA*
Pentimenti Gallery [W] *Philadelphia, PA*
People's Place, The [W] *Bird-in-Hand, PA*
Performing arts [W] *Philadelphia, PA*
Personal Rapid Transit System (PRT) [W] *Morgantown, WV*
Pest House Medical Museum [W] *Lynchburg, VA*
Petersen House [W] *Washington, DC*
Peter Wentz Farmstead [W] *Norristown, PA*
Peyton Randolph House [W] *Williamsburg, VA*
Philadelphia 76ers (NBA) [W] *Philadelphia, PA*
Philadelphia Carriage Company [W] *Philadelphia, PA*

Philadelphia Eagles (NFL) [W] *Philadelphia, PA*
Philadelphia Flower Show [S] *Philadelphia, PA*
Philadelphia Flyers (NHL) [W] *Philadelphia, PA*
Philadelphia History Museum—The Atwater Kent [W] *Philadelphia, PA*
Philadelphia Museum of Art [W] *Philadelphia, PA*
Philadelphia Open House [S] *Philadelphia, PA*
Philadelphia Orchestra [W] *Philadelphia, PA*
Philadelphia Phillies (MLB) [W] *Philadelphia, PA*
Philadelphia Savings Fund Society Building [W] *Philadelphia, PA*
Philadelphia Theatre Company [W] *Philadelphia, PA*
Philadelphia Zoo [W] *Philadelphia, PA*
Phillips Collection [W] *Washington, DC*
Philosophical Hall [W] *Philadelphia, PA*
Philpott Lake [W] *Martinsville, VA*
Phipps Conservatory [W] *Pittsburgh, PA*
Phipps Conservatory Flower Shows [S] *Pittsburgh, PA*
Physick House [W] *Philadelphia, PA*
Picnic area [W] *George Washington Birthplace National Monument, VA*
Picnicking [W] *Shenandoah National Park, VA*
Pier 6 Concert Pavilion [W] *Baltimore, MD*
Pimlico Race Course [S] *Baltimore, MD*
Pine Grove Furnace State Park [W] *Carlisle, PA*
Pinnacle Rock State Park [W] *Bluefield, WV*
Pinnacles [W] *Shenandoah National Park, VA*
Pioneer Cemetery [W] *Franklin (Venango County), PA*
Pioneer Days [S] *Marlinton, WV*
Pioneer Tunnel Coal Mine and Steam Lokie Ride [W] *Ashland, PA*
Pipestem Resort State Park [W] *Hinton, WV*
Pittsburgh Children's Museum [W] *Pittsburgh, PA*
Pittsburgh Irish Festival [S] *Pittsburgh, PA*
Pittsburgh Penguins (NHL) [W] *Pittsburgh, PA*

Pittsburgh Pirates (MLB) [W] *Pittsburgh, PA*

Pittsburgh Public Theater [S] *Pittsburgh, PA*

Pittsburgh/Shop 'N Save Three Rivers Regatta [S] *Pittsburgh, PA*

Pittsburgh Steelers (NFL) [W] *Pittsburgh, PA*

Pittsburgh Symphony Orchestra [S] *Pittsburgh, PA*

Pittsburgh Zoo, The [W] *Pittsburgh, PA*

Planetarium [W] *Reading, PA*

Plank House [W] *Lewes, DE*

Plantation Tours [W] *Richmond, VA*

Play Booth Theater [W] *Williamsburg, VA*

Please Touch Museum for Children [W] *Philadelphia, PA*

Plum Orchard Lake Wildlife Management Area [W] *Beckley, WV*

Pocahontas County Historical Museum [W] *Marlinton, WV*

Pocahontas State Park [W] *Richmond, VA*

Pocono Indian Museum [W] *Bushkill, PA*

Pocono Knob [W] *Mount Pocono, PA*

Pocono Whitewater Adventures [W] *Jim Thorpe, PA*

Pohick Bay Regional Park [W] *Alexandria, VA*

Pohick Episcopal Church [W] *Alexandria, VA*

Point, The [W] *Harpers Ferry, WV*

Point Lookout State Park [W] *St. Mary's City, MD*

Point of Honor [W] *Lynchburg, VA*

Point Pleasant Battle Monument State Park [W] *Point Pleasant, WV*

Points of special interest on Skyline Drive [W] *Shenandoah National Park, VA*

Point State Park [W] *Pittsburgh, PA*

Point-to-Point Steeplechase [S] *Cockeysville, MD*

Pony Penning [S] *Chincoteague, VA*

Poplar Grove (Petersburg) National Cemetery [W] *Petersburg, VA*

Poplar Hill Mansion [W] *Salisbury, MD*

Pork, Peanut, and Pine Festival [S] *Surry, VA*

Portage Station Museum [W] *Ebensburg, PA*

Portsmouth Museums, The [W] *Portsmouth, VA*

Port Tobacco [W] *La Plata, MD*

Potomac Park (East and West) [W] *Washington, DC*

Potomac Spirit [W] *Mount Vernon, VA*

Potomac State Forest [W] *Oakland (Garrett County), MD*

Pottsgrove Manor [W] *Pottstown, PA*

Powel House [W] *Philadelphia, PA*

PP & L Montour Preserve [W] *Danville, PA*

PPG Place [W] *Pittsburgh, PA*

PPL [W] *Hawley, PA*

Prelude to Independence [S] *Williamsburg, VA*

Presbyterian Church [W] *Fredericksburg, VA*

President Kennedy's Gravesite [W] *Washington, DC*

Presque Isle State Park [W] *Erie, PA*

Prestwould [W] *Clarksville, VA*

Prickett's Fort State Park [W] *Fairmont, WV*

Prince Gallitzin State Park [W] *Altoona, PA*

Prince George County Heritage Fair [S] *Hopewell, VA*

Princess Anne [W] *Salisbury, MD*

Prince William County Fair [S] *Manassas, VA*

Prince William Forest Park [W] *Triangle, VA*

Professional sports [W] *Baltimore, MD*

Professional sports [W] *Philadelphia, PA*

Professional sports [W] *Pittsburgh, PA*

Professional sports [W] *Washington, DC*

Promised Land State Park [W] *Hawley, PA*

Public Gaol [W] *Williamsburg, VA*

Public Hospital [W] *Williamsburg, VA*

Publick Times [S] *Williamsburg, VA*

Public Works Museum & Streetscape [W] *Baltimore, MD*

Pungo Strawberry Festival [S] *Virginia Beach, VA*

Pymatuning Spillway [W] *Conneaut Lake, PA*

Pymatuning State Park [W] *Conneaut Lake, PA*

Quiet Valley Living Historical Farm [W] *Stroudsburg, PA*

Quilt Show [S] *Fairfax, VA*

Quilt Show [S] *Fredericksburg, VA*

Rabbit's Ferry House [W] *Lewes, DE*

Raccoon Creek State Park [W] *Ambridge, PA*

Radford University [W] *Radford, VA*

Railfest [S] *Altoona, PA*

Railroader's Memorial Museum [W] *Altoona, PA*

Railroad Museum of Pennsylvania [W] *Lancaster, PA*

Raleigh Tavern [W] *Williamsburg, VA*

Randolph-Macon College [W] *Ashland, VA*

Randolph-Macon Women's College [W] *Lynchburg, VA*
Raystown Lake [W] *Huntingdon, PA*
Reading Public Museum and Art Gallery [W] *Reading, PA*
Recreation [W] *Galax, VA*
Recreation area [W] *Aberdeen, MD*
Recreation Areas [W] *Wise, VA*
Red Arrow Tour [W] *Wellsboro, PA*
Red Cross Waterfront Festival [S] *Alexandria, VA*
Reeds Gap State Park [W] *Lewistown, PA*
Refuge Waterfowl Museum [W] *Chincoteague, VA*
Regional parks [W] *Fairfax, VA*
Renwick Gallery [W] *Washington, DC*
Replica of the *Stourbridge Lion* [W] *Honesdale, PA*
Reservoir Park [W] *Harrisburg, PA*
Reston Town Center [W] *Dulles Intl Airport Area, VA*
Restored buildings [W] *Lewes, DE*
Richland Balsam Trail [W] *Blue Ridge Parkway, VA*
Richmond Children's Museum [W] *Richmond, VA*
Richmond National Battlefield Park [W] *Richmond, VA*
Richmond Newpapers Marathon [S] *Richmond, VA*
Ride with Me to Williamsburg [W] *Williamsburg, VA*
Riding [W] *Shenandoah National Park, VA*
Ridley Creek State Park [W] *Media, PA*
Ringing Rocks Park [W] *Pottstown, PA*
Rising Sun Tavern [W] *Fredericksburg, VA*
Riverfront Park [W] *Harrisburg, PA*
Riverside Park [W] *Lynchburg, VA*
River tours [W] *Uniontown, PA*
Riverview Park [W] *Pittsburgh, PA*
River Walk Art Festival [S] *York, PA*
Roadside America [W] *Shartlesville, PA*
Roanoke College [W] *Salem, VA*
Robert E. Lee Monument [W] *Charlottesville, VA*
Robert Fulton Birthplace [W] *Lancaster, PA*
Robin Hood Dell East [W] *Philadelphia, PA*
Robin Hood Dell East [S] *Philadelphia, PA*
Robinson House Museum [W] *Wellsboro, PA*
Rock Creek Park [W] *Washington, DC*
Rockhill Trolley Museum [W] *Orbisonia, PA*
Rockingham County Fair [S] *Harrisonburg, VA*

Rockville Bridge [W] *Harrisburg, PA*
Rockwood Museum [W] *Wilmington, DE*
Rocky Gap Music Festival [S] *Cumberland, MD*
Rocky Gap State Park [W] *Cumberland, MD*
Rocky Grove Fair [S] *Franklin (Venango County), PA*
Rocky Knob Information Station [W] *Blue Ridge Parkway, VA*
Rocky Knob Trail [W] *Blue Ridge Parkway, VA*
Rocky Mount Historic Site [W] *Bristol, VA*
Rodef Shalom Biblical Botanical Garden [W] *Pittsburgh, PA*
Rodin Museum [W] *Philadelphia, PA*
Roger Brooke Taney Home [W] *Frederick, MD*
Rose Festival [S] *Manheim, PA*
Rose Hill Manor Children's Museum [W] *Frederick, MD*
Roswell Historic Ruins [W] *Gloucester, VA*
Rubles Sternwheelers Riverboat Cruises [W] *Parkersburg, WV*
Ruins of St. John's Episcopal Church [W] *Harpers Ferry, WV*
Sailing tours [W] *Annapolis, MD*
Sailor's Creek Battlefield Historic State Park [W] *Farmville, VA*
St. Clements Island-Potomac River Museum [W] *Leonardtown, MD*
St. George's Episcopal Church and Churchyard [W] *Fredericksburg, VA*
St. James House [W] *Fredericksburg, VA*
St. John's Church [W] *Hampton, VA*
St. John's Church Georgetown Parish [W] *Washington, DC*
St. John's College [W] *Annapolis, MD*
St. John's Episcopal Church [W] *Richmond, VA*
St. Mark's Church [W] *Jim Thorpe, PA*
St. Mary's County Fair [S] *Leonardtown, MD*
St. Mary's County Oyster Festival [S] *Leonardtown, MD*
St. Mary's Square [W] *St. Michael's, MD*
St. Mary's Square Museum [W] *St. Michael's, MD*
St. Mary's Whitechapel Church [W] *Lancaster, VA*
St. Paul's Episcopal Church [W] *Norfolk, VA*
St. Paul's Episcopal Church [W] *Petersburg, VA*

St. Peter's Church [W] *Philadelphia, PA*

St. Vincent Archabbey and College [W] *Ligonier, PA*

Salem International University [W] *Clarksburg, WV*

Salisbury Zoological Park [W] *Salisbury, MD*

Sandcastle Water Park [W] *Pittsburgh, PA*

Sandy Point State Park [W] *Annapolis, MD*

Savage River State Forest [W] *Grantsville, MD*

Saylor Park Cement Industry Museum [W] *Allentown, PA*

S. B. Elliott [W] *Clearfield (Clearfield County), PA*

Scarecrow Festival [S] *New Hope, PA*

Schenley Park [W] *Pittsburgh, PA*

Schifferstadt [W] *Frederick, MD*

Schriver House [W] *Gettysburg, PA*

Schuylkill Center for Environmental Education [W] *Philadelphia, PA*

Science Museum [W] *Charleston, WV*

Science Museum of Virginia [W] *Richmond, VA*

Science Museum of Western Virginia [W] *Roanoke, VA*

Scottish Christmas Walk [S] *Alexandria, VA*

Scottish Rite Cathedral [W] *New Castle, PA*

Scranton Iron Furnaces [W] *Scranton, PA*

Sea Witch Halloween and Fiddlers' Festival [S] *Rehoboth Beach, DE*

Self-guided battlefield tour [W] *Yorktown, VA*

Self-guided tour [W] *Richmond National Battlefield Park, VA*

Self-guided trails [W] *Blue Ridge Parkway, VA*

Seltzer's Lebanon Bologna Company [W] *Hershey, PA*

Seminary Ridge [W] *Gettysburg National Military Park, PA*

Senate Office Buildings [W] *Washington, DC*

Senator John Heinz Regional History Center, The [W] *Pittsburgh, PA*

Seneca Caverns [W] *Franklin, WV*

Seneca Creek State Park [W] *Gaithersburg, MD*

Seneca State Forest [W] *Marlinton, WV*

Separation Day [S] *New Castle, DE*

Sesame Place [W] *Bristol (Bucks County), PA*

Sesame Place [W] *Philadelphia, PA*

Seton Shrine Center [W] *Emmitsburg, MD*

Settlers Landing Monument [W] *Hampton, VA*

Sewall-Belmont House [W] *Washington, DC*

Shad Festival [S] *Bethlehem, PA*

Shawnee [W] *Bedford, PA*

Shawnee Mountain Ski Area [W] *Shawnee on Delaware, PA*

Shawnee Place Play & Water Park [W] *Shawnee on Delaware, PA*

Sheep Dog Trials [S] *Leesburg, VA*

Sheep Shearing [S] *Lancaster, PA*

Shempp Toy Train Collection [W] *Williamsport, PA*

Shenandoah Apple Blossom Festival [S] *Winchester, VA*

Shenandoah Caverns [W] *Harrisonburg, VA*

Shenandoah Caverns [W] *New Market, VA*

Shenandoah County Court House [W] *Woodstock, VA*

Shenandoah County Fair [S] *Woodstock, VA*

Shenandoah National Park [W] *Charlottesville, VA*

Shenandoah National Park [W] *Harrisonburg, VA*

Shenandoah National Park [W] *Luray, VA*

Shenandoah National Park [W] *Waynesboro, VA*

Shenandoah River [W] *Harrisonburg, VA*

Shenandoah Valley Art Center [W] *Waynesboro, VA*

Shenandoah Valley Folk Art and Heritage Center [W] *Harrisonburg, VA*

Shenandoah Valley Music Festival [S] *Woodstock, VA*

Shenandoah Vineyards [W] *Woodstock, VA*

Shenango Lake [W] *Sharon, PA*

Sherando Lake Recreation Area [W] *Waynesboro, VA*

Sherwood Gardens [W] *Baltimore, MD*

Shockoe Slip [W] *Richmond, VA*

Shopping [W] *Philadelphia, PA*

Shopping [W] *Richmond, VA*

Shopping [W] *Williamsburg, VA*

Shops at National Place [W] *Washington, DC*

Shops at the Bellevue [W] *Philadelphia, PA*

Shot Tower Historical Park [W] *Wytheville, VA*

Showcase of Nations Ethnic Festivals [S] *Baltimore, MD*

Siege Museum [W] *Petersburg, VA*

Sightseeing [W] *Richmond, VA*

Sightseeing boat tours [W] *Alexandria, VA*

Sightseeing tours [W] *Lancaster, PA*

Sightseeing tours [W] *Norfolk, VA*

Sightseeing tours [W] *Philadelphia, PA*

Sightseeing tours [W] *Pittsburgh, PA*

Sightseeing tours [W] *Washington, DC*

Sightseeing tours. Captain Barry's Back Bay Cruises & Expeditions [W] *Chincoteague, VA*

Sightseeing USA/Lenzner Coach USA [W] *Pittsburgh, PA*

Silver Lake [W] *Harrisonburg, VA*

Site of Fort Henry [W] *Wheeling, WV*

Site of John Brown Gallows [W] *Charles Town, WV*

Six Flags America [W] *Washington, DC*

Sizerville State Park [W] *Port Allegany, PA*

Ski areas [W] *Allentown, PA*

Ski areas [W] *Carbondale, PA*

Ski areas [W] *Davis, WV*

Ski areas [W] *Marlinton, WV*

Ski areas [W] *White Haven, PA*

Skiing. Blue Knob Ski Area [W] *Bedford, PA*

Skiing. Mountain View Ski Area [W] *Edinboro, PA*

Skiing. Seven Springs Mountain Resort Ski Area [W] *Donegal, PA*

Skiing. Ski Denton/Denton Hill [W] *Galeton, PA*

Skiing. Ski Liberty [W] *Gettysburg, PA*

Skiing. Spring Mountain Ski Area [W] *Limerick, PA*

Skiing. Tanglwood [W] *Hawley, PA*

Skiing. Wintergreen Resort [W] *Charlottesville, VA*

Skiing. WinterPlace Ski Resort [W] *Beckley, WV*

Ski Roundtop [W] *York, PA*

Ski Sawmill Family Resort [W] *Wellsboro, PA*

Skyland [W] *Shenandoah National Park, VA*

Skyline Caverns [W] *Front Royal, VA*

Sky Meadows State Park [W] *Front Royal, VA*

Sleepy Creek Wildlife Management Area [W] *Berkeley Springs, WV*

Slifer House Museum [W] *Lewisburg, PA*

Small Ships Review, The [S] *Sharon, PA*

Smallwood State Park [W] *La Plata, MD*

Smithfield Plantation [W] *Blacksburg, VA*

Smithsonian Institution [W] *Washington, DC*

Smoke Hole Caverns [W] *Petersburg, WV*

Smyrna Museum [W] *Smyrna, DE*

Snowshoe Mountain Resort [W] *Marlinton, WV*

Society Hill Area [W] *Philadelphia, PA*

Soldier Life Program [W] *Valley Forge National Historical Park, PA*

Soldiers and Sailors Memorial Hall and Military History Museum [W] *Pittsburgh, PA*

Soldiers Delight Natural Environment Area [W] *Towson, MD*

Soldiers' National Museum [W] *Gettysburg, PA*

Somerfest [S] *Somerset, PA*

Somerset Historical Center [W] *Somerset, PA*

Sotterley Plantation [W] *Leonardtown, MD*

South Office Building [W] *Harrisburg, PA*

South River [W] *Shenandoah National Park, VA*

South River Meeting House [W] *Lynchburg, VA*

South St [W] *Philadelphia, PA*

Southwest Virginia Museum [W] *Big Stone Gap, VA*

Special focus and orientation tours [W] *Williamsburg, VA*

Spirit of Norfolk [W] *Norfolk, VA*

Spring Fling [S] *Clarion, PA*

Spring Garden [W] *Petersburg National Battlefield, VA*

Springhouse [W] *Bethlehem, PA*

Springs Folk Festival [S] *Grantsville, MD*

Springs Folk Festival [S] *Somerset, PA*

Springs Museum [W] *Grantsville, MD*

Spruce Forest Artisan Village [W] *Grantsville, MD*

Spruce Forest Summerfest and Quilt Show [S] *Grantsville, MD*

Stabler-Leadbeater Apothecary Museum [W] *Alexandria, VA*

Stacking of Arms [W] *Appomattox Court House National Historical Park, VA*

Star-Spangled Banner Flag House and 1812 Museum [W] *Baltimore, MD*

State Capitol [W] *Charleston, WV*

State Capitol [W] *Richmond, VA*

State Fair [S] *Lewisburg, WV*

State Fair [S] *Towson, MD*

State House [W] *Annapolis, MD*

State Museum of Pennsylvania, The [W] *Harrisburg, PA*

State parks [W] *Bedford, PA*
State parks [W] *Clearfield (Clearfield County), PA*
State parks [W] *Lock Haven, PA*
State parks [W] *Somerset, PA*
Station Square [W] *Pittsburgh, PA*
Staunton River State Park [W] *South Boston, VA*
Stealey-Goff-Vance House [W] *Clarksburg, WV*
Steamtown National Historic Site [W] *Scranton, PA*
Stenton House [W] *Philadelphia, PA*
Stephen Foster Memorial [W] *Pittsburgh, PA*
Steppingstone Museum [W] *Havre de Grace, MD*
Sternwheel Regatta Festival [S] *Charleston, WV*
Stirling Street [W] *Baltimore, MD*
Stock car races [S] *Martinsville, VA*
Stoevers Dam Recreational Area [W] *Lebanon, PA*
Stone Bridge [W] *Manassas (Bull Run) National Battlefield Park, VA*
Stone House [W] *Manassas (Bull Run) National Battlefield Park, VA*
Stone Row [W] *Jim Thorpe, PA*
Stonewall Jackson Heritage Arts & Crafts Jubilee [S] *Weston, WV*
Stonewall Jackson House [W] *Lexington, VA*
Stonewall Jackson Lake and Dam [W] *Weston, WV*
Stonewall Jackson Lake State Park [W] *Weston, WV*
Stonewall Jackson Memorial Cemetery [W] *Lexington, VA*
Stonewall Jackson on Little Sorrel [W] *Charlottesville, VA*
Stonewall Jackson's Headquarters [W] *Winchester, VA*
Stonewall Jackson Shrine [W] *Fredericksburg and Spotsylvania National Military Park, VA*
Story Book Forest [W] *Ligonier, PA*
Stoudt's Black Angus [W] *Denver/Adamstown, PA*
Stourbridge Rail Excursions [W] *Honesdale, PA*
Stoy Museum of the Lebanon County Historical Society [W] *Lebanon, PA*
Strasburg Museum [W] *Strasburg, VA*
Strasburg Railroad [W] *Lancaster, PA*
Stratford Hall Plantation [W] *Montross, VA*
Street Fair [S] *Ephrata, PA*
Street Rod Roundup [S] *Cumberland, MD*
Stroud Mansion [W] *Stroudsburg, PA*

Sturgis Pretzel House [W] *Lancaster, PA*
Sully [W] *Fairfax, VA*
Summer [W] *Basye, VA*
Summer Concerts [S] *Dulles Intl Airport Area, VA*
Summerfair [S] *Carlisle, PA*
Summersville Lake [W] *Summersville, WV*
Sunrise Museum [W] *Charleston, WV*
Supreme Court of the United States [W] *Washington, DC*
Surf Fishing Tournaments [S] *Fenwick Island, DE*
Surratt House and Tavern [W] *Waldorf, MD*
Susquehanna State Park [W] *Havre de Grace, MD*
Sutton Lake [W] *Sutton, WV*
Swallow Falls State Park [W] *Oakland (Garrett County), MD*
Swarthmore College [W] *Chester, PA*
Swigart Auto Museum [W] *Huntingdon, PA*
Swiss Pines [W] *King of Prussia, PA*
Symphony of Lights [S] *Columbia, MD*
Tangier Island Cruises [W] *Crisfield, MD*
Tannery [W] *Bethlehem, PA*
Taste of D.C. [S] *Washington, DC*
Taste of the Town [S] *Dulles Intl Airport Area, VA*
Taylor County Fair [S] *Grafton, WV*
Teddy Bear's Picnic [S] *New Hope, PA*
Temple University [W] *Philadelphia, PA*
Tercentenary Monument [W] *Jamestown (Colonial National Historical Park), VA*
Textile Museum [W] *Washington, DC*
Thaddeus Kosciuszko National Memorial [W] *Philadelphia, PA*
Thanksgiving Day Parade [S] *Philadelphia, PA*
Theaters [W] *Baltimore, MD*
Theaters [W] *Washington, DC*
Theatre West Virginia [S] *Beckley, WV*
Theodore Roosevelt Memorial [W] *Washington, DC*
Third Haven Friends Meeting House [W] *Easton, MD*
Thomas Jefferson Memorial [W] *Washington, DC*
Thomas L. Kane Memorial Chapel [W] *Kane, PA*
Thomas T Thaber Museum of the Lycoming County Historical Society [W] *Williamsport, PA*
Thompson Country Store [W] *Lewes, DE*
Thoroughbred racing [S] *Laurel, MD*

Three Centuries Tours of Annapolis [W] *Annapolis, MD*

Three Rivers Arts Festival [S] *Pittsburgh, PA*

Three Rivers Festival [S] *Fairmont, WV*

Ticket information [W] *Williamsburg, VA*

Timberline Four Seasons Resort [W] *Davis, WV*

Tioga-Hammond Lakes [W] *Mansfield, PA*

Tioga Point Museum [W] *Towanda, PA*

Tionesta Reservoir [W] *Clarion, PA*

Tobacco auctions [W] *Danville, VA*

Tobyhanna State Park [W] *Mount Pocono, PA*

Todd House [W] *Philadelphia, PA*

Toll Gate House [W] *Cumberland, MD*

Tomb of the Unknowns [W] *Arlington County (Ronald Reagan Washington-National Airport Area), VA*

Tomlinson Run State Park [W] *Weirton, WV*

Top of the World [W] *Baltimore, MD*

Torpedo Factory Arts Center [W] *Alexandria, VA*

Totem Pole Playhouse [S] *Chambersburg, PA*

Tour-Ed Mine and Museum [W] *Pittsburgh, PA*

Tourmobile Sightseeing [W] *Washington, DC*

Tours [W] *Valley Forge National Historical Park, PA*

Tours and entertainment [W] *Williamsburg, VA*

Tours of Charles Town [W] *Charles Town, WV*

Town Point Park [W] *Norfolk, VA*

Towson State University [W] *Towson, MD*

Traditional Christmas Activities [S] *Williamsburg, VA*

Trail of the Lonesome Pine [S] *Big Stone Gap, VA*

Trail of the Trees [W] *Blue Ridge Parkway, VA*

Trails [W] *Jamestown (Colonial National Historical Park), VA*

Trapezium House [W] *Petersburg, VA*

Trap Pond State Park [W] *Dover, DE*

Treasure Mountain Festival [S] *Franklin, WV*

Trexler-Lehigh County Game Preserve [W] *Allentown, PA*

Trexler Memorial Park [W] *Allentown, PA*

Trinity Chapel [W] *Frederick, MD*

Trinity Church [W] *Portsmouth, VA*

Trinity Episcopal Church [W] *Staunton, VA*

Triple-Brick Building [W] *Martinsburg, WV*

Triple W Riding Stable [W] *Honesdale, PA*

Tri-State Greyhound Park [W] *Nitro, WV*

Trout Gallery, The [W] *Carlisle, PA*

Trout Hall [W] *Allentown, PA*

Troxell-Steckel House and Farm Museum [W] *Allentown, PA*

Tuckahoe State Park [W] *Easton, MD*

Tuckahoe Steam and Gas Show and Reunion [S] *Easton, MD*

Tucker County Alpine Winter Festival [S] *Davis, WV*

Tudor Place [W] *Washington, DC*

Twin Brook Winery [W] *Lancaster, PA*

Twin covered bridges [W] *Bloomsburg, PA*

Twin Falls Resort State Park [W] *Beckley, WV*

Twin Lakes [W] *Kane, PA*

Twin Lakes State Park [W] *Keysville, VA*

Two Mellon Bank Center [W] *Pittsburgh, PA*

Tygart Lake State Park [W] *Grafton, WV*

Tyler Arboretum [W] *Media, PA*

Tyler's Cruises [W] *Crisfield, MD*

Unfinished Railroad [W] *Manassas (Bull Run) National Battlefield Park, VA*

Union Station [W] *Washington, DC*

United States Naval Academy [W] *Annapolis, MD*

University of Delaware Mineral Collection [W] *Newark, DE*

University of Delaware [W] *Newark, DE*

University of Maryland at Baltimore [W] *Baltimore, MD*

University of Maryland [W] *College Park, MD*

University of Pennsylvania Museum of Archaeology and Anthropology [W] *Philadelphia, PA*

University of Pennsylvania [W] *Philadelphia, PA*

University of Pittsburgh [W] *Pittsburgh, PA*

University of Virginia [W] *Charlottesville, VA*

US Army Ordnance Museum [W] *Aberdeen, MD*

US Army Quartermaster Museum [W] *Petersburg, VA*

US Army Transportation Museum [W] *Newport News, VA*

US Botanic Gardens [W] *Washington, DC*

US Holocaust Memorial Museum [W] *Washington, DC*

US Mint [W] *Philadelphia, PA*

US National Arboretum [W] *Washington, DC*

US Navy Memorial [W] *Washington, DC*

US Powerboat Show [S] *Annapolis, MD*

US Sailboat Show [S] *Annapolis, MD*

USS *Olympia.* [W] *Philadelphia, PA*

USSSA Softball Hall of Fame Museum [W] *Petersburg, VA*

USX Tower [W] *Pittsburgh, PA*

Utz Quality Foods, Inc [W] *Hanover, PA*

Vagabond Players [W] *Baltimore, MD*

Valentine Museum [W] *Richmond, VA*

Valley Forge National Historical Park [W] *Downingtown, PA*

Valley Forge National Historical Park [W] *King of Prussia, PA*

Valley Forge National Historical Park [W] *Norristown, PA*

Valley Railroad Museum [W] *Towanda, PA*

Vandalia Gathering [S] *Charleston, WV*

Venango County Court House [W] *Franklin (Venango County), PA*

Victorian Christmas Week [S] *Lancaster, PA*

Victorian Ice Cream Festival [S] *Wilmington, DE*

Victorian Sunday [S] *Williamsport, PA*

Vietnam Veterans Memorial [W] *Washington, DC*

View from Prospect Peak [W] *Berkeley Springs, WV*

Vineyard and Winery Tours [W] *Leesburg, VA*

Virginia Air and Space Center and Hampton Roads History Center [W] *Hampton, VA*

Virginia Aviation Museum [W] *Richmond, VA*

Virginia Children's Festival [S] *Norfolk, VA*

Virginia Highlands Festival [S] *Abingdon, VA*

Virginia Historical Society [W] *Richmond, VA*

Virginia Horse Center [W] *Lexington, VA*

Virginia House [W] *Richmond, VA*

Virginia Institute of Marine Science, College of William and Mary [W] *Gloucester, VA*

Virginia Lake Festival [S] *Clarksville, VA*

Virginia Living Museum [W] *Newport News, VA*

Virginia Marine Science Museum [W] *Virginia Beach, VA*

Virginia Military Institute [W] *Lexington, VA*

Virginia Museum of Fine Arts [W] *Richmond, VA*

Virginia Museum of Natural History [W] *Martinsville, VA*

Virginia Museum of Transportation [W] *Roanoke, VA*

Virginia Mushroom and Wine Festival [S] *Front Royal, VA*

Virginia Opera [S] *Norfolk, VA*

Virginia Quilt Museum [W] *Harrisonburg, VA*

Virginia Saltwater Fishing Tournament [S] *Virginia Beach, VA*

Virginia Scottish Games [S] *Alexandria, VA*

Virginia's Explore Park [W] *Roanoke, VA*

Virginia State Championship Chili Cookoff [S] *Roanoke, VA*

Virginia State Fair [S] *Richmond, VA*

Virginia State Library and Archives [W] *Richmond, VA*

Virginia Symphony [S] *Norfolk, VA*

Virginia War Memorial [W] *Richmond, VA*

Virginia War Museum [W] *Newport News, VA*

Virginia Waterfront International Arts Festival [S] *Norfolk, VA*

Virginia Zoological Park [W] *Norfolk, VA*

Visitor Center [W] *Fredericksburg, VA*

Visitor Center [W] *George Washington Birthplace National Monument, VA*

Visitor Center [W] *Jamestown (Colonial National Historical Park), VA*

Visitor Center [W] *Manassas (Bull Run) National Battlefield Park, VA*

Visitor Center [W] *Petersburg National Battlefield, VA*

Visitor Center [W] *Uniontown, PA*

Visitor Center [W] *Valley Forge National Historical Park, PA*

Visitor Center [W] *Yorktown, VA*

Visitor Center-Electric Map-Gettysburg Museum of the Civil War [W] *Gettysburg National Military Park, PA*

Visitor Centers [W] *Blue Ridge Parkway, VA*

Voice of America [W] *Washington, DC*

Wagner Free Institute of Science [W] *Philadelphia, PA*

Waldameer Park & Water World [W] *Erie, PA*

Walking or driving tour of Fredericksburg [W] *Fredericksburg, VA*

Walking tour [W] *Charlottesville, VA*

Walking tour of historic sites [W] *Alexandria, VA*

Walking tours [W] *Annapolis, MD*

Walnut Flats [W] *Pearisburg, VA*

Walnut Street Theatre [W] *Philadelphia, PA*

Walters Art Museum [W] *Baltimore, MD*

Wanamaker, Kempton & Southern, Inc [W] *Hamburg, PA*

Ward Museum of Wildfowl Art [W] *Salisbury, MD*

Warren County Fair [S] *Front Royal, VA*

Warren County Garden Tour [S] *Front Royal, VA*

Warren Rifles Confederate Museum [W] *Front Royal, VA*

Warrington Friends Meeting House [W] *York, PA*

Washington and Lee University [W] *Lexington, VA*

Washington Capitals (NHL) [W] *Washington, DC*

Washington County Museum of Fine Arts [W] *Hagerstown, MD*

Washington Crossing [W] *Washington Crossing Historic Park (Bucks County), PA*

Washington Crossing Historical Park [W] *New Hope, PA*

Washington Dolls' House & Toy Museum [W] *Washington, DC*

Washington Harbour [W] *Washington, DC*

Washington Headquarters [W] *Valley Forge National Historical Park, PA*

Washington Memorial Chapel [W] *Valley Forge National Historical Park, PA*

Washington Monument [W] *Baltimore, MD*

Washington Monument [W] *Washington, DC*

Washington Monument State Park [W] *Boonsboro (Garrett County), MD*

Washington Mystics (WNBA) [W] *Washington, DC*

Washington National Cathedral [W] *Washington, DC*

Washington National Cathedral Open House [S] *Washington, DC*

Washington Redskins (NFL) [W] *Washington, DC*

Washington's Birthday Celebration [S] *Williamsburg, VA*

Washington's Lands Museum and Park [W] *Ripley, WV*

Washington's Office-Museum [W] *Winchester, VA*

Washington Square [W] *Philadelphia, PA*

Washington Wizards (NBA) [W] *Washington, DC*

Watch and Clock Museum, The [W] *Lancaster, PA*

Waterford [W] *Leesburg, VA*

Waterfowl Festival [S] *Easton, MD*

Waterfowl Week [S] *Chincoteague, VA*

Waterrock Knob Information Center [W] *Blue Ridge Parkway, VA*

Waterside Festival Marketplace [W] *Norfolk, VA*

Waterworks [W] *Bethlehem, PA*

Watoga State Park [W] *Hillsboro, WV*

Watson-Curtze Mansion [W] *Erie, PA*

Watters Smith Memorial State Park [W] *Clarksburg, WV*

Waves of Fun [W] *Nitro, WV*

Wayne County Fair [S] *Honesdale, PA*

Wayne County Historical Society Museum [W] *Honesdale, PA*

Wayne Memorial Blockhouse [W] *Erie, PA*

Wayside Theatre [S] *Strasburg, VA*

Weavertown One-Room Schoolhouse [W] *Bird-in-Hand, PA*

Webster County Fair [S] *Webster Springs, WV*

Webster Springs Woodchopping Festival [S] *Webster Springs, WV*

Weirton Steel Corp and Half Moon Industrial Park [W] *Weirton, WV*

Wendell August Forge, Inc [W] *Mercer, PA*

Western Maryland Scenic Railroad [W] *Cumberland, MD*

Western Maryland Station Center [W] *Cumberland, MD*

Western Pennsylvania Laurel Festival [S] *Brookville, PA*

West Front [W] *Washington, DC*

Westmoreland County Courthouse [W] *Greensburg, PA*

Westmoreland Museum of American Art [W] *Greensburg, PA*

Westmoreland State Park [W] *Montross, VA*

West Virginia Black Walnut Festival [S] *Ripley, WV*

West Virginia Honey Festival [S] *Parkersburg, WV*

West Virginia Independence Hall-Custom House [W] *Wheeling, WV*

West Virginia Italian Heritage Festival [S] *Clarksburg, WV*

West Virginia State College [W] *Charleston, WV*

West Virginia State Farm Museum [W] *Point Pleasant, WV*

West Virginia State Wildlife Center [W] *Buckhannon, WV*

West Virginia Strawberry Festival [S] *Buckhannon, WV*

West Virginia University [W] *Morgantown, WV*

West Virginia Wesleyan College [W] *Buckhannon, WV*

Wetherburn's Tavern [W] *Williamsburg, VA*

Wheatfield and Peach Orchard, The [W] *Gettysburg National Military Park, PA*

Wheeling Park [W] *Wheeling, WV*

Whipple Dam State Park [W] *State College, PA*

White Arrow Tour [W] *Wellsboro, PA*

White Clay Creek State Park [W] *Newark, DE*

White Grass Touring Center [W] *Davis, WV*

White House, The [W] *Washington, DC*

White House of the Confederacy [W] *Richmond, VA*

White Pine Horse Camp [W] *Pearisburg, VA*

White Rocks Recreation Area [W] *Pearisburg, VA*

White's Mill [W] *Abingdon, VA*

Whitetop Ramp Festival [S] *Marion, VA*

White Water Adventurers [W] *Uniontown, PA*

Whitewater rafting [W] *Beckley, WV*

Whitewater rafting [W] *Charleston, WV*

Whitewater rafting [W] *Davis, WV*

Whitewater rafting [W] *Gauley Bridge, WV*

Whitewater rafting [W] *Harpers Ferry, WV*

Whitewater rafting [W] *Jim Thorpe, PA*

Whitewater rafting [W] *Morgantown, WV*

Whitworth Guns on Oak Hill [W] *Gettysburg National Military Park, PA*

Widener University [W] *Chester, PA*

Wilderness Voyagers [W] *Uniontown, PA*

Wildflower Preserve [W] *Washington Crossing Historic Park (Bucks County), PA*

Wildlife Learning Center [W] *Conneaut Lake, PA*

William Byrd [W] *Richmond, VA*

William Paca Garden [W] *Annapolis, MD*

William Paca House [W] *Annapolis, MD*

Williamsport C & O Canal Days [S] *Hagerstown, MD*

Willingtown Square [W] *Wilmington, DE*

Willoughby-Baylor House [W] *Norfolk, VA*

Wilmington & Western Railroad [W] *Wilmington, DE*

Wilmington Garden Day [S] *Wilmington, DE*

Wilson-Warner House [W] *Odessa, DE*

Wilton [W] *Richmond, VA*

Wine Country Harvest Festival [S] *North East, PA*

Wine Festival [S] *Leesburg, VA*

Wine in the Woods [S] *Columbia, MD*

Winery tours [W] *North East, PA*

Winter [W] *Basye, VA*

Winterfest [S] *Oakland (Garrett County), MD*

Winterthur Museum, Garden, and Library [W] *Wilmington, DE*

Winterthur Point-to-Point Races [S] *Wilmington, DE*

Winter whale-watching boat trips [S] *Virginia Beach, VA*

Wolf Trap Farm Park for the Performing Arts [S] *Fairfax, VA*

Wolf Trap Farm Park for the Performing Arts [S] *Washington, DC*

Woodlawn Plantation [W] *Mount Vernon, VA*

Woodrow Wilson Birthplace and Presidential Museum [W] *Staunton, VA*

Woodrow Wilson House [W] *Washington, DC*

Woodsmen's Carnival [S] *Galeton, PA*

Woodson Law Office [W] *Appomattox Court House National Historical Park, VA*

Woodstock Tower [W] *Woodstock, VA*

Wopsononock Mountain [W] *Altoona, PA*

"Wreck of the Old 97" Marker [W] *Danville, VA*

Wren Building [W] *Williamsburg, VA*

Wye Oak State Park [W] *Chesapeake Bay Bridge Area, MD*

Wythe House [W] *Williamsburg, VA*
Wytheville State Fish Hatchery [W]
    Wytheville, VA
Yellow Arrow Tour [W] *Wellsboro, PA*
Yellow Creek State Park [W] *Indiana,
    PA*
Yellow House [W] *Washington, DC*
York County Colonial Court House
    [W] *York, PA*
York River State Park [W] *Williams-
    burg, VA*
Yorktown Battlefield [W] *Yorktown,
    VA*
Yorktown Day [S] *Yorktown, VA*
Yorktown National Civil War Ceme-
    tery [W] *Yorktown, VA*
Yorktown Victory Center [W] *York-
    town, VA*
Yorktown Victory Monument [W]
    Yorktown, VA
Youth Museum of Southern West Vir-
    ginia [W] *Beckley, WV*
Zion Episcopal Church [W] *Charles
    Town, WV*
Zion Lutheran Church [W] *Manheim,
    PA*
ZooAmerica [W] *Hershey, PA*
Zwaanendael Museum [W] *Lewes, DE*

LODGING LIST

Establishment names are listed in alphabetical order followed by a symbol identifying their classification and then city and state. The symbols for classification are: [AS] for All Suites, [BB] for B&Bs/Small Inns, [CAS] for Casinos, [CC] for Cottage Colonies, [CON] for Villas/Condos, [CONF] for Conference Centers, [EX] for Extended Stays, [HOT] for Hotels, [MOT] for Motels/Motor Lodges, [RAN] for Guest Ranches, and [RST] for Resorts

1740 HOUSE [BB] *New Hope, PA*
1880'S MADISON HOUSE [BB] *Lynchburg, VA*
200 SOUTH STREET INN [BB] *Charlottesville, VA*
A-1 ECONOMY INN [MOT] *Somerset, PA*
AARON BURR HOUSE [BB] *New Hope, PA*
ABBEY GREEN MOTOR LODGE [MOT] *West Chester, PA*
ABERCROMBIE BADGER BED AND BREAKFAST [BB] *Baltimore, MD*
ADAM'S MARK HOTEL [HOT] *Philadelphia, PA*
ADAMS OCEANFRONT VILLAS [MOT] *Rehoboth Beach, DE*
ADDEY'S INN OF HERSHEY [MOT] *Hershey, PA*
ADMIRAL [MOT] *Rehoboth Beach, DE*
ADMIRAL FELL INN [BB] *Baltimore, MD*
AIRPORT PLAZA HOTEL [MOT] *Pittsburgh Intl Airport Area, PA*
ALDEN HOUSE BED AND BREAKFAST [BB] *Lancaster, PA*
ALEXANDER WITHROW INN [BB] *Lexington, VA*
ALLENBERRY RESORT INN [RST] *Carlisle, PA*
ALLENWOOD MOTEL [MOT] *Allentown, PA*
ALPINE MOTEL [MOT] *Abingdon, VA*
AMERICAN INN OF BETHESDA [MOT] *Bethesda, MD*
AMERISUITES [MOT] *Richmond, VA*
ANGLER'S MOTEL [MOT] *Lewes, DE*
ANTRIM 1844 [BB] *Emmitsburg, MD*
APPALACHIAN TRAIL INN [MOT] *Carlisle, PA*
APPLEBUTTER INN [BB] *Butler, PA*
APPLETREE BED AND BREAKFAST [BB] *Pittsburgh, PA*
ASHBY INN [BB] *Winchester, VA*

ATHERTON HOTEL [HOT] *State College, PA*
ATLANTIC BUDGET INN [MOT] *Fenwick Island, DE*
ATLANTIC BUDGET INN, THE [MOT] *Rehoboth Beach, DE*
ATLANTIC VIEW MOTEL [MOT] *Rehoboth Beach, DE*
AUSTRALIAN WALKABOUT INN BED AND BREAKFAST [BB] *Lancaster, PA*
AUTOPORT MOTEL & RESTAURANT [MOT] *State College, PA*
BAILIWICK INN [BB] *Fairfax, VA*
BALADERRY INN [BB] *Gettysburg, PA*
BARLEY SHEAF FARM BED & BREAKFAST [BB] *New Hope, PA*
BATTLEFIELD BED AND BREAKFAST INN [BB] *Gettysburg, PA*
BAVARIAN INN & LODGE [BB] *Shepherdstown, WV*
BAYBERRY INN BED AND BREAKFAST [BB] *Somerset, PA*
BAYMONT INN [MOT] *Harrisburg, PA*
BAY RESORT MOTEL [MOT] *Rehoboth Beach, DE*
BEACH VIEW MOTEL [MOT] *Rehoboth Beach, DE*
BEACON [MOT] *Lewes, DE*
BEAVER VALLEY MOTEL [MOT] *Beaver Falls, PA*
BEECHMONT BED AND BREAKFAST INN [BB] *Hanover, PA*
BEL AIRE HOTEL COMPLEX [MOT] *Erie, PA*
BELLE GRAE INN [BB] *Staunton, VA*
BERKELEY HOTEL [HOT] *Richmond, VA*
BERLIN ATLANTIC [BB] *Ocean City, MD*
BEST INN [MOT] *Gettysburg, PA*
BEST INN [MOT] *Roanoke, VA*
BEST WESTERN [MOT] *Alexandria, VA*
BEST WESTERN [MOT] *Annapolis, MD*
BEST WESTERN [MOT] *Ashland, VA*

BEST WESTERN [MOT] *Basye, VA*
BEST WESTERN [MOT] *Bedford, PA*
BEST WESTERN [MOT] *Blacksburg, VA*
BEST WESTERN [MOT] *Carlisle, PA*
BEST WESTERN [MOT] *Charlottesville, VA*
BEST WESTERN [MOT] *Downingtown, PA*
BEST WESTERN [MOT] *Fredericksburg, VA*
BEST WESTERN [MOT] *La Plata, MD*
BEST WESTERN [MOT] *Lynchburg, VA*
BEST WESTERN [MOT] *Manassas, VA*
BEST WESTERN [MOT] *Newark, DE*
BEST WESTERN [MOT] *Nitro, WV*
BEST WESTERN [MOT] *Petersburg, VA*
BEST WESTERN [MOT] *Summersville, WV*
BEST WESTERN [MOT] *West Chester, PA*
BEST WESTERN [MOT] *Wytheville, VA*
BEST WESTERN ALPINE LODGE [MOT] *Davis, WV*
BEST WESTERN BRADDOCK MOTOR INN [MOT] *Cumberland, MD*
BEST WESTERN BRANDYWINE VALLEY INN [MOT] *Wilmington, DE*
BEST WESTERN BWI AIRPORT [MOT] *Baltimore/Washington International Airport Area, MD*
BEST WESTERN CAVALIER INN [MOT] *Charlottesville, VA*
BEST WESTERN CENTER CITY HOTEL [MOT] *Philadelphia, PA*
BEST WESTERN CENTER INN [MOT] *Norfolk, VA*
BEST WESTERN COUNTRY OVEN [MOT] *Harrisburg, PA*
BEST WESTERN CUPBOARD INN [MOT] *Lewisburg, PA*
BEST WESTERN EAST MOUNTAIN INN [MOT] *Wilkes-Barre, PA*
BEST WESTERN EDEN RESORT INN AND CONFERENCE CENTER [MOT] *Lancaster, PA*
BEST WESTERN FLAGSHIP OCEANFRONT [MOT] *Ocean City, MD*
BEST WESTERN GENETTI HOTEL AND CONFERENCE CENTER [MOT] *Wilkes-Barre, PA*
BEST WESTERN GENETTI MOTOR LODGE [MOT] *Hazleton, PA*
BEST WESTERN GOLDEN LEAF [MOT] *Rehoboth Beach, DE*
BEST WESTERN GRAND VICTORIA INN [MOT] *Towanda, PA*
BEST WESTERN HOTEL [MOT] *Philadelphia, PA*

BEST WESTERN HOTEL AND CONFERENCE CENTER [MOT] *Baltimore, MD*
BEST WESTERN INN [MOT] *Emporia, VA*
BEST WESTERN INN [MOT] *Gettysburg, PA*
BEST WESTERN INN [MOT] *Hershey, PA*
BEST WESTERN INN [MOT] *Indiana, PA*
BEST WESTERN INN [MOT] *King of Prussia, PA*
BEST WESTERN INN [MOT] *Lexington, VA*
BEST WESTERN INN [MOT] *Luray, VA*
BEST WESTERN INN [MOT] *Manassas, VA*
BEST WESTERN INN [MOT] *Marion, VA*
BEST WESTERN INN [MOT] *Martinsville, VA*
BEST WESTERN INN [MOT] *Milford, PA*
BEST WESTERN INN [MOT] *Radford, VA*
BEST WESTERN INN [MOT] *Reading, PA*
BEST WESTERN INN [MOT] *South Hill, VA*
BEST WESTERN INN [MOT] *Staunton, VA*
BEST WESTERN INN [MOT] *Wheeling, WV*
BEST WESTERN INN [MOT] *York, PA*
BEST WESTERN INN & CONFERENCE CENTER [MOT] *Du Bois, PA*
BEST WESTERN KEY BRIDGE [MOT] *Arlington County (Ronald Reagan Washington-National Airport Area), VA*
BEST WESTERN LEE-JACKSON [MOT] *Winchester, VA*
BEST WESTERN MCCOY'S INN AND CONFERENCE CENTER [MOT] *Ripley, WV*
BEST WESTERN MOUNTAIN VIEW [MOT] *Covington, VA*
BEST WESTERN MOUNT VERNON [MOT] *Alexandria, VA*
BEST WESTERN PARKWAY CENTER [MOT] *Pittsburgh, PA*
BEST WESTERN PLAZA MOTOR LODGE [MOT] *Breezewood, PA*
BEST WESTERN POCONO INN [MOT] *Stroudsburg, PA*
BEST WESTERN ST. MICHAEL'S MOTOR INN [MOT] *St. Michael's, MD*

BETHANY ARMS [MOT] *Bethany Beach, DE*

BIG MEADOWS LODGE [MOT] *Luray, VA*

BIRCHWOOD [MOT] *Chincoteague, VA*

BIRD-IN-HAND FAMILY INN [MOT] *Bird-in-Hand, PA*

BISHOP'S HOUSE [BB] *Easton, MD*

BLACK HORSE LODGE & SUITES [MOT] *Denver/Adamstown, PA*

BLACK WALNUT BED & BREAKFAST COUNTRY INN [BB] *Milford, PA*

BLACK WALNUT POINT INN [BB] *St. Michael's, MD*

BLACKWATER LODGE [RST] *Davis, WV*

BLEU ROCK INN [BB] *Washington, VA*

BOARDWALK PLAZA HOTEL [HOT] *Rehoboth Beach, DE*

BOAR'S HEAD INN [RST] *Charlottesville, VA*

BOULEVARD BED AND BREAKFAST, THE [BB] *Wilmington, DE*

BRAFFERTON INN [BB] *Gettysburg, PA*

BRANDYWINE RIVER HOTEL [BB] *Kennett Square, PA*

BRANDYWINE SUITES HOTEL [HOT] *Wilmington, DE*

BRANDYWINE VALLEY COUNTRY ESTATE [HOT] *Newark, DE*

BREAKS INTERSTATE [MOT] *Breaks Interstate Park, VA*

BRIER INN [MOT] *Lewisburg, WV*

BRIGHTON SUITES HOTELS [MOT] *Rehoboth Beach, DE*

BROOKSHIRE INNER HARBOR SUITE HOTEL [HOT] *Baltimore, MD*

BRUNSWICK HOTEL [HOT] *Lancaster, PA*

BUDGET HOST [MOT] *Bristol, VA*

BUDGET HOST [MOT] *Staunton, VA*

BUDGET HOST [MOT] *Woodstock, VA*

BUDGET HOST FORT SAVANNAH MOTEL [MOT] *Lewisburg, WV*

BUDGET HOST INN [MOT] *Somerset, PA*

BUDGET HOST INN [MOT] *York, PA*

BUDGET HOST PATRIOT INN [MOT] *Bloomsburg, PA*

BUDGET INN [MOT] *Dover, DE*

BUDGET INN [MOT] *New Market, VA*

BUDGET MOTEL [MOT] *Stroudsburg, PA*

CABINS AT BROOKSIDE [MOT] *Luray, VA*

CACAPON STATE PARK [RST] *Berkeley Springs, WV*

CAESARS PARADISE STREAM [RST] *Mount Pocono, PA*

CAESARS POCONO PALACE RESORT [RST] *Stroudsburg, PA*

CAESAR'S POCONO RESORTS [RST] *Tannersville, PA*

CANAAN VALLEY RESORT AND CONFERENCE CENTER [RST] *Davis, WV*

CANYON MOTEL [MOT] *Wellsboro, PA*

CAPITOL HILL SUITES [HOT] *Washington, DC*

CARMEL COVE BED AND BREAKFAST [BB] *Oakland (Garrett County), MD*

CARNEGIE HOUSE [BB] *State College, PA*

CASTLE IN THE SAND HOTEL [MOT] *Ocean City, MD*

CATOCTIN INN [BB] *Frederick, MD*

CAYMAN SUITES [MOT] *Ocean City, MD*

CEDAR GABLES SEASIDE INN [BB] *Chincoteague, VA*

CELIE'S WATERFRONT BED AND BREAKFAST [BB] *Baltimore, MD*

CENTENNIAL MOTEL [MOT] *Buckhannon, WV*

CENTER CITY HOTEL [HOT] *Washington, DC*

CENTRE BRIDGE INN [BB] *New Hope, PA*

CHANNEL BASS INN [BB] *Chincoteague, VA*

CHANNEL INN HOTEL [MOT] *Washington, DC*

CHESAPEAKE BAY LIGHTHOUSE BED AND BREAKFAST [BB] *Annapolis, MD*

CHESAPEAKE LANDING [BB] *Rehoboth Beach, DE*

CHESAPEAKE WOOD DUCK INN [BB] *St. Michael's, MD*

CHESTER HOUSE [BB] *Front Royal, VA*

CHRISTLEN MOTEL [MOT] *Baltimore, MD*

CHURCHILL, THE [HOT] *Washington, DC*

CLAIBORNE HOUSE [BB] *Roanoke, VA*

CLARION FONTAINEBLEAU [HOT] *Ocean City, MD*

CLARION HOTEL [MOT] *Roanoke, VA*

CLARION HOTEL PEABODY COURT [HOT] *Baltimore, MD*

CLARION HOTEL PEMBROKE [HOT] *Virginia Beach, VA*

CLARION INN [MOT] *Hagerstown, MD*

CLARION INN [MOT] *Lewistown, PA*
CLARION INN [MOT] *Scranton, PA*
CLARION INN AND CONVENTION
    CENTER [MOT] *Carlisle, PA*
CLIFF PARK INN [BB] *Milford, PA*
CLIFTON COUNTRY INN, THE [BB]
    Charlottesville, VA
CLUB HOTEL BY DOUBLETREE
    [HOT] *Philadelphia, PA*
COCONUT MALORIE HOTEL
    RESORT [HOT] *Ocean City, MD*
COLLEGE MOTEL [MOT] *Gettysburg,
    PA*
COLONIAL CAPITAL BED AND
    BREAKFAST [BB] *Williamsburg,
    VA*
COLONIAL GARDENS INN [BB]
    Williamsburg, VA
COLONIAL HOUSES-HISTORIC LOD
    [MOT] *Williamsburg, VA*
COLONIAL MOTEL [MOT]
    Gettysburg, PA
COLONY HOUSE MOTOR LODGE
    [MOT] *Roanoke, VA*
COMFORT INN [MOT] *Abingdon, VA*
COMFORT INN [MOT] *Alexandria, VA*
COMFORT INN [MOT] *Annapolis, MD*
COMFORT INN [MOT] *Ashland, VA*
COMFORT INN [MOT] *Beckley, WV*
COMFORT INN [MOT] *Bethlehem, PA*
COMFORT INN [MOT] *Blacksburg, VA*
COMFORT INN [MOT] *Bristol, VA*
COMFORT INN [MOT] *Chesapeake
    Bay Bridge Area, MD*
COMFORT INN [MOT] *Chincoteague,
    VA*
COMFORT INN [MOT] *Covington, VA*
COMFORT INN [MOT] *Culpeper, VA*
COMFORT INN [MOT] *Dover, DE*
COMFORT INN [MOT] *Doylestown
    (Bucks County), PA*
COMFORT INN [MOT] *Easton, MD*
COMFORT INN [MOT] *Emporia, VA*
COMFORT INN [MOT] *Erie, PA*
COMFORT INN [MOT] *Fairfax, VA*
COMFORT INN [MOT] *Farmville, VA*
COMFORT INN [MOT] *Fredericksburg,
    VA*
COMFORT INN [MOT] *Gettysburg, PA*
COMFORT INN [MOT] *Greensburg, PA*
COMFORT INN [MOT] *Harpers Ferry,
    WV*
COMFORT INN [MOT] *Harrisonburg,
    VA*
COMFORT INN [MOT] *Johnstown, PA*
COMFORT INN [MOT] *King of
    Prussia, PA*
COMFORT INN [MOT] *Lynchburg, VA*
COMFORT INN [MOT] *Mansfield, PA*

COMFORT INN [MOT] *Martinsburg,
    WV*
COMFORT INN [MOT] *Morgantown,
    WV*
COMFORT INN [MOT] *New Castle, PA*
COMFORT INN [MOT] *Newark, DE*
COMFORT INN [MOT] *Newport News,
    VA*
COMFORT INN [MOT] *Nitro, WV*
COMFORT INN [MOT] *Norfolk, VA*
COMFORT INN [MOT] *Ocean City,
    MD*
COMFORT INN [MOT] *Philadelphia,
    PA*
COMFORT INN [MOT] *Philadelphia,
    PA*
COMFORT INN [MOT] *Pikesville, MD*
COMFORT INN [MOT] *Pottstown, PA*
COMFORT INN [MOT] *Princeton, WV*
COMFORT INN [MOT] *Radford, VA*
COMFORT INN [MOT] *Reading, PA*
COMFORT INN [MOT] *Salisbury, MD*
COMFORT INN [MOT] *Springfield, VA*
COMFORT INN [MOT] *Staunton, VA*
COMFORT INN [MOT] *Summersville,
    WV*
COMFORT INN [MOT] *Tyson's Corner,
    VA*
COMFORT INN [MOT] *Virginia Beach,
    VA*
COMFORT INN [MOT] *Virginia Beach,
    VA*
COMFORT INN [MOT] *Warrenton, VA*
COMFORT INN [MOT] *Waynesboro,
    VA*
COMFORT INN [MOT] *Westminster,
    MD*
COMFORT INN [MOT] *Weston, WV*
COMFORT INN [MOT] *White Haven,
    PA*
COMFORT INN [MOT] *Winchester, VA*
COMFORT INN [MOT] *Wytheville, VA*
COMFORT INN AND SUITES [MOT]
    Fairmont, WV
COMFORT INN AT SHADY GROVE
    [MOT] *Gaithersburg, MD*
COMFORT INN BALLSTON [MOT]
    *Arlington County (Ronald Reagan
    Washington-National Airport
    Area), VA*
COMFORT INN DULLES AIRPORT
    [MOT] *Dulles Intl Airport Area,
    VA*
COMFORT INN EAST [MOT]
    Harrisburg, PA
COMFORT INN VIRGINIA HORSE
    CENTER [MOT] *Lexington, VA*
COMFORT SUITES [MOT] *Allentown,
    PA*

COMFORT SUITES [MOT]
Chesapeake, VA
COMFORT SUITES [MOT] *Chesapeake Bay Bridge Area, MD*
COMFORT SUITES [MOT] *Laurel, MD*
COMFORT SUITES [MOT]
Martinsburg, WV
CONLEY INN [MOT] *Beaver Falls, PA*
CONLEY RESORT INN [MOT] *Butler, PA*
COOLFONT RESORT [RST] *Berkeley Springs, WV*
COUNTRY INN [BB] *Berkeley Springs, WV*
COUNTRY INN & SUITES [MOT]
Pittsburgh, PA
COUNTRY LIVING INN [MOT]
Lancaster, PA
COURTYARD BY MARRIOTT [MOT]
Alexandria, VA
COURTYARD BY MARRIOTT [MOT]
Annapolis, MD
COURTYARD BY MARRIOTT [MOT]
Arlington County (Ronald Reagan Washington-National Airport Area), VA
COURTYARD BY MARRIOTT [MOT]
Arlington County (Ronald Reagan Washington-National Airport Area), VA
COURTYARD BY MARRIOTT [MOT]
Baltimore/Washington International Airport Area, MD
COURTYARD BY MARRIOTT [MOT]
Charlottesville, VA
COURTYARD BY MARRIOTT [MOT]
Cockeysville, MD
COURTYARD BY MARRIOTT [MOT]
College Park, MD
COURTYARD BY MARRIOTT [MOT]
Dulles Intl Airport Area, VA
COURTYARD BY MARRIOTT [MOT]
Dulles Intl Airport Area, VA
COURTYARD BY MARRIOTT [MOT]
Fairfax, VA
COURTYARD BY MARRIOTT [MOT]
Gaithersburg, MD
COURTYARD BY MARRIOTT [MOT]
Hampton, VA
COURTYARD BY MARRIOTT [MOT]
Manassas, VA
COURTYARD BY MARRIOTT [MOT]
Richmond, VA
COURTYARD BY MARRIOTT [MOT]
Rockville, MD
COURTYARD BY MARRIOTT [MOT]
Silver Spring, MD
COURTYARD BY MARRIOTT [MOT]
Virginia Beach, VA

COURTYARD BY MARRIOTT [HOT]
Washington, DC
COURTYARD BY MARRIOTT [MOT]
Williamsburg, VA
COURTYARD BY MARRIOTT [MOT]
Willow Grove, PA
COURTYARD BY MARRIOTT [MOT]
Wilmington, DE
COURTYARD BY MARRIOTT VALLEY FORGE [MOT] *King of Prussia, PA*
COZY COUNTRY INN THURMONT [MOT] *Thurmont, MD*
CRESCENT LODGE [BB] *Canadensis, PA*
CRISLIP MOTOR LODGE [MOT]
Grafton, WV
CROSS CREEK RESORT [RST]
Titusville, PA
CROSS KEYS MOTOR INN RESTAURANT [MOT]
Gettysburg, PA
CROWNE PLAZA [MOT] *Harrisburg, PA*
CROWNE PLAZA [HOT] *Philadelphia, PA*
CROWNE PLAZA [HOT] *Pittsburgh Intl Airport Area, PA*
CROWNE PLAZA [HOT] *Richmond, VA*
CROWNE PLAZA WASHINGTON-NATIONAL AIRPORT [HOT]
Arlington County (Ronald Reagan Washington-National Airport Area), VA
DARLEY MANOR INN BED AND BREAKFAST [BB] *Wilmington, DE*
DAYS INN [MOT] *Aberdeen, MD*
DAYS INN [MOT] *Allentown, PA*
DAYS INN [MOT] *Arlington County (Ronald Reagan Washington-National Airport Area), VA*
DAYS INN [MOT]
Baltimore/Washington International Airport Area, MD
DAYS INN [MOT] *Blacksburg, VA*
DAYS INN [MOT] *Brookville, PA*
DAYS INN [MOT] *Butler, PA*
DAYS INN [MOT] *Carlisle, PA*
DAYS INN [MOT] *Chambersburg, PA*
DAYS INN [MOT] *Charleston, WV*
DAYS INN [MOT] *Charlottesville, VA*
DAYS INN [MOT] *Chesapeake, VA*
DAYS INN [MOT] *Clarion, PA*
DAYS INN [MOT] *Clearfield (Clearfield County), PA*
DAYS INN [MOT] *Donegal, PA*

DAYS INN [MOT] *Dulles Intl Airport Area, VA*
DAYS INN [MOT] *Easton, MD*
DAYS INN [MOT] *Emporia, VA*
DAYS INN [MOT] *Farmville, VA*
DAYS INN [MOT] *Frederick, MD*
DAYS INN [MOT] *Gettysburg, PA*
DAYS INN [MOT] *Hagerstown, MD*
DAYS INN [MOT] *Harrisburg, PA*
DAYS INN [MOT] *Harrisonburg, VA*
DAYS INN [MOT] *Hershey, PA*
DAYS INN [MOT] *Huntingdon, PA*
DAYS INN [MOT] *Huntington, WV*
DAYS INN [MOT] *Leesburg, VA*
DAYS INN [MOT] *Lewisburg, PA*
DAYS INN [MOT] *Lewisburg, WV*
DAYS INN [MOT] *Lexington, VA*
DAYS INN [MOT] *Lynchburg, VA*
DAYS INN [MOT] *Manassas, VA*
DAYS INN [MOT] *Meadville, PA*
DAYS INN [MOT] *New Stanton, PA*
DAYS INN [MOT] *Petersburg, VA*
DAYS INN [MOT] *Princeton, WV*
DAYS INN [MOT] *Roanoke, VA*
DAYS INN [MOT] *Scranton, PA*
DAYS INN [MOT] *Springfield, VA*
DAYS INN [MOT] *State College, PA*
DAYS INN [MOT] *Sutton, WV*
DAYS INN [MOT] *Tappahannock, VA*
DAYS INN [MOT] *Towson, MD*
DAYS INN [MOT] *Virginia Beach, VA*
DAYS INN [MOT] *Waldorf, MD*
DAYS INN [MOT] *Waynesboro, VA*
DAYS INN [MOT] *Wheeling, WV*
DAYS INN [MOT] *Wytheville, VA*
DAYS INN & SUITES [MOT] *Cumberland, MD*
DAYS INN INNER HARBOR HOTEL [MOT] *Baltimore, MD*
DAYS INN POTOMAC MILLS [MOT] *Springfield, VA*
DE SOTO HOLIDAY HOUSE [MOT] *Bradford, PA*
DINNER BELL INN [MOT] *Rehoboth Beach, DE*
DOE RUN LODGE RESORT AND CONFERENCE CENTER [RST] *Blue Ridge Parkway, VA*
DOGWOOD LODGE [MOT] *Radford, VA*
DOLLAR INN [MOT] *Somerset, PA*
DOUBLETREE [HOT] *Charlottesville, VA*
DOUBLETREE [HOT] *Rockville, MD*
DOUBLETREE CLUB HOTEL [HOT] *Norfolk, VA*
DOUBLETREE GUEST SUITES [HOT] *Philadelphia, PA*

DOUBLETREE HOTEL [HOT] *Arlington County (Ronald Reagan Washington-National Airport Area), VA*
DOUBLETREE HOTEL [HOT] *Philadelphia, PA*
DOUBLETREE HOTEL [HOT] *Virginia Beach, VA*
DOUBLETREE HOTEL [HOT] *Wilmington, DE*
DOUBLETREE INN AT THE COLONNADE [HOT] *Baltimore, MD*
DRIFTWOOD MOTOR LODGE [MOT] *Chincoteague, VA*
DUKE OF YORK MOTOR HOTEL [MOT] *Yorktown, VA*
DULING-KURTZ HOUSE & COUNTRY INN [BB] *West Chester, PA*
DUTCH INN [MOT] *Martinsville, VA*
ECONO LODGE [MOT] *Bedford, PA*
ECONO LODGE [MOT] *Berkeley Springs, WV*
ECONO LODGE [MOT] *Bluefield, WV*
ECONO LODGE [MOT] *Erie, PA*
ECONO LODGE [MOT] *Morgantown, WV*
ECONO LODGE [MOT] *Morgantown, WV*
ECONO LODGE [MOT] *Norfolk, VA*
ECONO LODGE [MOT] *Rehoboth Beach, DE*
ECONO LODGE [MOT] *Virginia Beach, VA*
ECONO LODGE [MOT] *Washington, PA*
ECONO LODGE [MOT] *Williamsport, PA*
ECONO LODGE [MOT] *Winchester, VA*
ECONO LODGE [MOT] *Wytheville, VA*
ECONO LODGE INN [MOT] *Elkins, WV*
ECONO LODGE INN [MOT] *Lynchburg, VA*
ECONO LODGE INN OUTLET VILLAGE [MOT] *Reading, PA*
EDGEWOOD BED AND BREAKFAST [BB] *Williamsburg, VA*
EDGEWOOD MANOR INC [BB] *Martinsburg, WV*
ELKINS MOTOR LODGE [MOT] *Elkins, WV*
ELKTON LODGE [MOT] *Elkton, MD*
EMBASSY SQUARE SUMMERFIELD SUITES BY WYNDHAM [HOT] *Washington, DC*

EMBASSY SUITES [AS] *Arlington County (Ronald Reagan Washington-National Airport Area), VA*

EMBASSY SUITES [HOT] *Baltimore/Washington International Airport Area, MD*

EMBASSY SUITES [AS] *Richmond, VA*

EMBASSY SUITES [AS] *Tyson's Corner, VA*

EMBASSY SUITES [AS] *Washington, DC*

EMBASSY SUITES UPTOWN [AS] *Washington, DC*

EMMANUEL HUTZLER HOUSE [BB] *Richmond, VA*

EMPIRE MOTOR LODGE ABINGDON [MOT] *Abingdon, VA*

ENGLISH INN OF CHARLOTTESVILLE [MOT] *Charlottesville, VA*

EVERMAY ON THE DELAWARE [BB] *New Hope, PA*

EXECUTIVE CLUB SUITES [MOT] *Alexandria, VA*

EXECUTIVE CLUB SUITES [MOT] *Arlington County (Ronald Reagan Washington-National Airport Area), VA*

EXECUTIVE MOTEL [MOT] *Ocean City, MD*

EXECUTIVE MOTEL [MOT] *Radford, VA*

FAIRFIELD INN [MOT] *Baltimore/Washington International Airport Area, MD*

FAIRFIELD INN [MOT] *Chesapeake, VA*

FAIRFIELD INN [MOT] *Frederick, MD*

FAIRFIELD INN [MOT] *Richmond, VA*

FAIRFIELD INN [MOT] *Virginia Beach, VA*

FAIRVILLE INN [BB] *Kennett Square, PA*

FALLS PORT INN & RESTAURANT [BB] *Hawley, PA*

FARNSWORTH HOUSE INN [BB] *Gettysburg, PA*

FIELDCREST MANOR BED AND BREAKFAST [BB] *Morgantown, WV*

FOREST HILLS MOTEL [MOT] *Bowie, MD*

FOUNDERS INN AND CONFERENCE CENTER [HOT] *Virginia Beach, VA*

FOUNTAIN HALL BED AND BREAKFAST [BB] *Culpeper, VA*

FOUR POINTS BY SHERATON [MOT] *Blacksburg, VA*

FOUR POINTS BY SHERATON [MOT] *Greensburg, PA*

FOUR POINTS BY SHERATON [MOT] *Hagerstown, MD*

FOUR POINTS BY SHERATON [MOT] *Harrisonburg, VA*

FOUR POINTS BY SHERATON HOTEL [HOT] *Pittsburgh, PA*

FOUR POINTS BY SHERATON [MOT] *Stroudsburg, PA*

FOUR SEASONS HOTEL PHILADELPHIA [HOT] *Philadelphia, PA*

FOUR SEASONS HOTEL WASHINGTON D. C. [HOT] *Washington, DC*

FOUR SEASONS MOTEL [MOT] *Elkins, WV*

FOX AND HOUND BED AND BREAKFAST [BB] *New Hope, PA*

FOX HILL INN [BB] *Marion, VA*

FREDERICK HOUSE [BB] *Staunton, VA*

FREDERICKSBURG COLONIAL INN [BB] *Fredericksburg, VA*

FRENCH MANOR [BB] *Mount Pocono, PA*

GARDEN AND THE SEA INN, THE [BB] *Chincoteague, VA*

GARDEN SPOT MOTEL [MOT] *Lancaster, PA*

GASLIGHT INN [BB] *Gettysburg, PA*

GATEWAY RESORT HOTEL [MOT] *Ocean City, MD*

GENERAL LEWIS INN [BB] *Lewisburg, WV*

GENERAL SUTTER INN [BB] *Lancaster, PA*

GENETTI HOTEL & SUITES [HOT] *Williamsport, PA*

GEORGETOWN INN [HOT] *Washington, DC*

GETTYSTOWN INN BED & BREAKFAST [BB] *Gettysburg, PA*

GIBSON'S LODGINGS [BB] *Annapolis, MD*

GLASBERN INN, THE [BB] *Allentown, PA*

GLASS HOUSE INN [MOT] *Erie, PA*

GLENDORN - A LODGE IN THE COUNTRY [BB] *Bradford, PA*

GLEN FERRIS INN [BB] *Gauley Bridge, WV*

GOLDEN PHEASANT INN [BB] *New Hope, PA*

GOLDEN PLOUGH INN [BB] *New Hope, PA*

GOVERNOR CALVERT HOUSE [BB] *Annapolis, MD*
GOVERNORS HOUSE HOTEL [HOT] *Washington, DC*
GOVERNOR'S INN [MOT] *Williamsburg, VA*
GRAMERCY BED AND BREAKFAST [BB] *Pikesville, MD*
GRAND HYATT WASHINGTON [HOT] *Washington, DC*
GRAVES' MOUNTAIN LODGE [RAN] *Culpeper, VA*
GREENBRIER, THE [RST] *White Sulphur Springs, WV*
GRESHAM'S LAKE VIEW MOTEL [MOT] *Hawley, PA*
HALEY FARM BED AND BREAKFAST [BB] *Oakland (Garrett County), MD*
HAMILTON CROWNE PLAZA, THE [HOT] *Washington, DC*
HAMPTON INN [MOT] *Alexandria, VA*
HAMPTON INN [MOT] *Allentown, PA*
HAMPTON INN [MOT] *Baltimore, MD*
HAMPTON INN [MOT] *Baltimore/Washington International Airport Area, MD*
HAMPTON INN [MOT] *Baltimore/Washington International Airport Area, MD*
HAMPTON INN [MOT] *Beckley, WV*
HAMPTON INN [MOT] *Blacksburg, VA*
HAMPTON INN [MOT] *Chambersburg, PA*
HAMPTON INN [MOT] *Charleston, WV*
HAMPTON INN [MOT] *Charleston, WV*
HAMPTON INN [MOT] *Charlottesville, VA*
HAMPTON INN [MOT] *Chesapeake, VA*
HAMPTON INN [MOT] *Du Bois, PA*
HAMPTON INN [MOT] *Emporia, VA*
HAMPTON INN [MOT] *Erie, PA*
HAMPTON INN [MOT] *Fairfax, VA*
HAMPTON INN [MOT] *Frederick, MD*
HAMPTON INN [MOT] *Gaithersburg, MD*
HAMPTON INN [MOT] *Hampton, VA*
HAMPTON INN [MOT] *Harrisburg, PA*
HAMPTON INN [MOT] *Harrisburg, PA*
HAMPTON INN [MOT] *Harrisonburg, VA*
HAMPTON INN [MOT] *Lynchburg, VA*
HAMPTON INN [MOT] *Morgantown, WV*
HAMPTON INN [MOT] *Newport News, VA*

HAMPTON INN [MOT] *Norfolk, VA*
HAMPTON INN [MOT] *Pittsburgh, PA*
HAMPTON INN [MOT] *Pittsburgh, PA*
HAMPTON INN [MOT] *Pittsburgh Intl Airport Area, PA*
HAMPTON INN [MOT] *Richmond, VA*
HAMPTON INN [MOT] *Roanoke, VA*
HAMPTON INN [MOT] *Scranton, PA*
HAMPTON INN [MOT] *South Hill, VA*
HAMPTON INN [MOT] *Springfield, VA*
HAMPTON INN [MOT] *State College, PA*
HAMPTON INN [MOT] *Virginia Beach, VA*
HAMPTON INN [MOT] *Warrenton, VA*
HAMPTON INN [MOT] *Wheeling, WV*
HAMPTON INN [MOT] *Wilkes-Barre, PA*
HAMPTON INN [MOT] *Williamsburg, VA*
HAMPTON INN [MOT] *Willow Grove, PA*
HAMPTON INN [MOT] *Winchester, VA*
HAMPTON INN [MOT] *York, PA*
HAMPTON INN AIRPORT [MOT] *Roanoke, VA*
HARBOR COURT [HOT] *Baltimore, MD*
HARBOR VIEW [MOT] *Rehoboth Beach, DE*
HARBOURTOWNE GOLF RESORT AND CONFERENCE CENTER [RST] *St. Michael's, MD*
HARRY PACKER MANSION [BB] *Jim Thorpe, PA*
HAWKS NEST STATE PARK LODGE [MOT] *Gauley Bridge, WV*
HAWTHORN SUITES [MOT] *Pittsburgh, PA*
HAY ADAMS HOTEL [HOT] *Washington, DC*
HENLEY PARK HOTEL [HOT] *Washington, DC*
HENLOPEN HOTEL [MOT] *Rehoboth Beach, DE*
HENRY CLAY INN [BB] *Ashland, VA*
HERMITAGE MOTOR INN [MOT] *Petersburg, WV*
HERR TAVERN AND PUBLICK HOUSE, THE [BB] *Gettysburg, PA*
HERSHEY FARM MOTOR INN [MOT] *Lancaster, PA*
HERSHEY LODGE & CONVENTION CENTER [HOT] *Hershey, PA*
HIDDEN INN [BB] *Orange, VA*
HIDDEN VALLEY RESORT CONFERENCE CENTER [RST] *Somerset, PA*

HIGHLAND INN [BB] *Monterey, VA*
HIGHLAWN INN [BB] *Berkeley Springs, WV*
HILLBROOK INN [BB] *Charles Town, WV*
HILTON [HOT] *King of Prussia, PA*
HILTON [HOT] *Lynchburg, VA*
HILTON [HOT] *Norfolk, VA*
HILTON [HOT] *Pikesville, MD*
HILTON [HOT] *Springfield, VA*
HILTON AIRPORT [HOT] *Philadelphia, PA*
HILTON ALEXANDRIA MARK CENTER [HOT] *Alexandria, VA*
HILTON AND TOWERS [HOT] *Arlington County (Ronald Reagan Washington-National Airport Area), VA*
HILTON AND TOWERS [HOT] *Washington, DC*
HILTON CAPITOL [HOT] *Washington, DC*
HILTON GARDEN INN [HOT] *Lancaster, PA*
HILTON HOTEL [HOT] *Allentown, PA*
HILTON HOTEL [HOT] *Columbia, MD*
HILTON HOTEL [HOT] *Gaithersburg, MD*
HILTON HOTEL [HOT] *Harrisburg, PA*
HILTON HOTEL [HOT] *Pittsburgh, PA*
HILTON HOTEL [HOT] *Tyson's Corner, VA*
HILTON HOTEL AND TOWERS [HOT] *Baltimore, MD*
HILTON RICHMOND AIRPORT [HOT] *Richmond, VA*
HILTON WASHINGTON EMBASSY ROW [HOT] *Washington, DC*
HISTORIC BLENNERHASSETT [HOT] *Parkersburg, WV*
HISTORIC CLARION HOTEL MORGAN [HOT] *Morgantown, WV*
HISTORIC STRASBURG INN [BB] *Lancaster, PA*
HOLIDAY INN [MOT] *Alexandria, VA*
HOLIDAY INN [MOT] *Alexandria, VA*
HOLIDAY INN [MOT] *Arlington County (Ronald Reagan Washington-National Airport Area), VA*
HOLIDAY INN [MOT] *Baltimore, MD*
HOLIDAY INN [MOT] *Beaver Falls, PA*
HOLIDAY INN [MOT] *Beckley, WV*
HOLIDAY INN [MOT] *Bethesda, MD*
HOLIDAY INN [MOT] *Bethlehem, PA*
HOLIDAY INN [MOT] *Bluefield, WV*
HOLIDAY INN [MOT] *Carlisle, PA*
HOLIDAY INN [MOT] *Charleston, WV*

HOLIDAY INN [MOT] *Charlottesville, VA*
HOLIDAY INN [MOT] *Chesapeake, VA*
HOLIDAY INN [MOT] *Clarion, PA*
HOLIDAY INN [MOT] *College Park, MD*
HOLIDAY INN [MOT] *Culpeper, VA*
HOLIDAY INN [MOT] *Cumberland, MD*
HOLIDAY INN [MOT] *Denver/Adamstown, PA*
HOLIDAY INN [MOT] *Du Bois, PA*
HOLIDAY INN [MOT] *Dulles Intl Airport Area, VA*
HOLIDAY INN [MOT] *Erie, PA*
HOLIDAY INN [MOT] *Fairfax, VA*
HOLIDAY INN [MOT] *Fairmont, WV*
HOLIDAY INN [MOT] *Fredericksburg, VA*
HOLIDAY INN [MOT] *Gaithersburg, MD*
HOLIDAY INN [MOT] *Hampton, VA*
HOLIDAY INN [MOT] *Harrisburg, PA*
HOLIDAY INN [MOT] *Harrisburg, PA*
HOLIDAY INN [MOT] *Harrisburg, PA*
HOLIDAY INN [MOT] *Hershey, PA*
HOLIDAY INN [MOT] *Indiana, PA*
HOLIDAY INN [HOT] *Johnstown, PA*
HOLIDAY INN [MOT] *King of Prussia, PA*
HOLIDAY INN [MOT] *Lancaster, PA*
HOLIDAY INN [MOT] *Laurel, MD*
HOLIDAY INN [MOT] *Leesburg, VA*
HOLIDAY INN [MOT] *Lynchburg, VA*
HOLIDAY INN [MOT] *Manassas, VA*
HOLIDAY INN [MOT] *Martinsburg, WV*
HOLIDAY INN [MOT] *McLean, VA*
HOLIDAY INN [MOT] *Morgantown, WV*
HOLIDAY INN [MOT] *Newark, DE*
HOLIDAY INN [MOT] *Oil City, PA*
HOLIDAY INN [MOT] *Parkersburg, WV*
HOLIDAY INN [HOT] *Philadelphia, PA*
HOLIDAY INN [MOT] *Pittsburgh, PA*
HOLIDAY INN [MOT] *Pittsburgh, PA*
HOLIDAY INN [MOT] *Pittsburgh, PA*
HOLIDAY INN [MOT] *Pittsburgh, PA*
HOLIDAY INN [MOT] *Pittsburgh, PA*
HOLIDAY INN [MOT] *Pittsburgh, PA*
HOLIDAY INN [MOT] *Reading, PA*
HOLIDAY INN [MOT] *Roanoke, VA*
HOLIDAY INN [MOT] *Roanoke, VA*
HOLIDAY INN [MOT] *Salem, VA*
HOLIDAY INN [MOT] *Salem, VA*
HOLIDAY INN [MOT] *Scranton, PA*
HOLIDAY INN [MOT] *Staunton, VA*
HOLIDAY INN [MOT] *Uniontown, PA*

HOLIDAY INN [MOT] *Virginia Beach, VA*
HOLIDAY INN [MOT] *Virginia Beach, VA*
HOLIDAY INN [MOT] *Virginia Beach, VA*
HOLIDAY INN [MOT] *Virginia Beach, VA*
HOLIDAY INN [MOT] *Waldorf, MD*
HOLIDAY INN [MOT] *West Chester, PA*
HOLIDAY INN [MOT] *West Middlesex, PA*
HOLIDAY INN [MOT] *Wilkes-Barre, PA*
HOLIDAY INN [MOT] *Williamsburg, VA*
HOLIDAY INN [MOT] *Williamsburg, VA*
HOLIDAY INN [MOT] *Williamsport, PA*
HOLIDAY INN [MOT] *Winchester, VA*
HOLIDAY INN [MOT] *Wytheville, VA*
HOLIDAY INN [MOT] *York, PA*
HOLIDAY INN [MOT] *York, PA*
HOLIDAY INN AND SUITES [MOT] *Alexandria, VA*
HOLIDAY INN CAPITOL [HOT] *Washington, DC*
HOLIDAY INN CAPITOL HILL [HOT] *Washington, DC*
HOLIDAY INN CENTRAL [HOT] *Washington, DC*
HOLIDAY INN CHESAPEAKE HOUSE [MOT] *Aberdeen, MD*
HOLIDAY INN CLARKSBURG [MOT] *Clarksburg, WV*
HOLIDAY INN EXPRESS [MOT] *Brookville, PA*
HOLIDAY INN EXPRESS [MOT] *Danville, VA*
HOLIDAY INN EXPRESS [MOT] *Dulles Intl Airport Area, VA*
HOLIDAY INN EXPRESS [MOT] *Easton, MD*
HOLIDAY INN EXPRESS [MOT] *Gettysburg, PA*
HOLIDAY INN EXPRESS [MOT] *Hopewell, VA*
HOLIDAY INN EXPRESS [MOT] *Lexington, VA*
HOLIDAY INN EXPRESS [MOT] *Philadelphia, PA*
HOLIDAY INN EXPRESS [MOT] *Pottstown, PA*
HOLIDAY INN EXPRESS [MOT] *Ripley, WV*
HOLIDAY INN EXPRESS [MOT] *South Hill, VA*
HOLIDAY INN EXPRESS [MOT] *Williamsburg, VA*
HOLIDAY INN EXPRESS - CIVIC CENTER [MOT] *Charleston, WV*
HOLIDAY INN GEORGETOWN [HOT] *Washington, DC*
HOLIDAY INN INNER HARBOR [HOT] *Baltimore, MD*
HOLIDAY INN MEADOWLANDS [MOT] *Washington, PA*
HOLIDAY INN NORTH [MOT] *Fredericksburg, VA*
HOLIDAY INN NORTH [MOT] *Wilmington, DE*
HOLIDAY INN OCEANFRONT [MOT] *Ocean City, MD*
HOLIDAY INN OLDE TOWNE [MOT] *Portsmouth, VA*
HOLIDAY INN RICHMOND AIRPORT [MOT] *Richmond, VA*
HOLIDAY INN SELECT [MOT] *Baltimore, MD*
HOLIDAY INN SELECT [MOT] *Lynchburg, VA*
HOLIDAY INN SELECT [HOT] *Wilmington, DE*
HOLIDAY SANDS MOTEL AND TOWER [MOT] *Norfolk, VA*
HOLLADAY HOUSE [BB] *Orange, VA*
HOLLILEIF BED & BREAKFAST [BB] *New Hope, PA*
HOMESTEAD , THE [RST] *Hot Springs, VA*
HOMESTEAD MOTOR LODGE [MOT] *Gettysburg, PA*
HOMEWOOD SUITES [MOT] *King of Prussia, PA*
HOMEWOOD SUITES HOTEL [MOT] *Alexandria, VA*
HOPKINS INN [BB] *Baltimore, MD*
HOTEL DUPONT, THE [HOT] *Wilmington, DE*
HOTEL DU VILLAGE [BB] *New Hope, PA*
HOTEL GEORGE [HOT] *Washington, DC*
HOTEL HARRINGTON [HOT] *Washington, DC*
HOTEL HERSHEY, THE [RST] *Hershey, PA*
HOTEL LOMBARDY [HOT] *Washington, DC*
HOTEL MONTICELLO [HOT] *Washington, DC*
HOTEL ROANOKE AND CONFERENCE CENTER [HOT] *Roanoke, VA*
HOTEL ROUGE [MOT] *Washington, DC*

HOTEL STRASBURG [BB] *Strasburg, VA*

HOTEL WASHINGTON [HOT] *Washington, DC*

HOWARD JOHNSON [MOT] *Danville, VA*

HOWARD JOHNSON [MOT] *Harrisonburg, VA*

HOWARD JOHNSON [MOT] *Lynchburg, VA*

HOWARD JOHNSON [MOT] *Salisbury, MD*

HOWARD JOHNSON EXPRESS INN [MOT] *Waldorf, MD*

HOWARD JOHNSON HOTEL [MOT] *Williamsburg, VA*

HOWARD JOHNSON HOTEL AND SUITES [MOT] *Newark, DE*

HOWARD JOHNSON INN [MOT] *Lancaster, PA*

HOWARD JOHNSON INN [MOT] *Lexington, VA*

HOWARD JOHNSON INN [MOT] *Mercer, PA*

HOWARD JOHNSON INN [MOT] *New Stanton, PA*

HOWARD JOHNSON MOTOR LODGE [MOT] *Bradford, PA*

HOWARD JOHNSON MOTOR LODGE [MOT] *Harrisburg, PA*

HOWARD JOHNSON OCEANFRONT [MOT] *Ocean City, MD*

HUMMINGBIRD INN [BB] *Lexington, VA*

HUNTINGDON MOTOR INN [MOT] *Huntingdon, PA*

HUNTINGFIELD MANOR [BB] *Chesapeake Bay Bridge Area, MD*

HYATT [HOT] *Arlington County (Ronald Reagan Washington-National Airport Area), VA*

HYATT [HOT] *Dulles Intl Airport Area, VA*

HYATT FAIR LAKES [HOT] *Fairfax, VA*

HYATT REGENCY [HOT] *Arlington County (Ronald Reagan Washington-National Airport Area), VA*

HYATT REGENCY [HOT] *Baltimore, MD*

HYATT REGENCY [HOT] *Bethesda, MD*

HYATT REGENCY [HOT] *Dulles Intl Airport Area, VA*

HYATT REGENCY [HOT] *Washington, DC*

HYATT REGENCY PHILADELPHIA AT PENN'S LANDING [HOT] *Philadelphia, PA*

HYATT REGENCY PITTSBURGH IN'L AIRPORT [HOT] *Pittsburgh Intl Airport Area, PA*

IMPERIAL HOTEL [BB] *Chesapeake Bay Bridge Area, MD*

INN AT AFTON [MOT] *Waynesboro, VA*

INN AT BUCKEYSTOWN [BB] *Frederick, MD*

INN AT BUCKHORN [MOT] *Bloomsburg, PA*

INN AT CANAL SQUARE [BB] *Lewes, DE*

INN AT FORDHOOK FARM, THE [BB] *Doylestown (Bucks County), PA*

INN AT GEORGIAN PLACE [BB] *Somerset, PA*

INN AT GOVERNMENT HOUSE [BB] *Baltimore, MD*

INN AT GRISTMILL SQUARE [BB] *Warm Springs, VA*

INN AT HENDERSON'S WHARF [BB] *Baltimore, MD*

INN AT LEVELFIELD [BB] *Lancaster, VA*

INN AT LITTLE WASHINGTON, THE [BB] *Washington, VA*

INN AT MITCHELL HOUSE [BB] *Chesapeake Bay Bridge Area, MD*

INN AT MONTCHANIN VILLAGE [BB] *Wilmington, DE*

INN AT MONTICELLO [BB] *Charlottesville, VA*

INN AT NARROW PASSAGE [BB] *Woodstock, VA*

INN AT NICHOLS VILLAGE [MOT] *Scranton, PA*

INN AT OAKMONT [BB] *Pittsburgh, PA*

INN AT OLDE NEW BERLIN [BB] *Shamokin Dam, PA*

INN AT PERRY CABIN, THE [RST] *St. Michael's, MD*

INN AT PHILLIPS MILL [BB] *New Hope, PA*

INN AT READING [MOT] *Reading, PA*

INN AT THE CANAL [BB] *Elkton, MD*

INN AT TURKEY HILL [BB] *Bloomsburg, PA*

INN AT UNION RUN [BB] *Lexington, VA*

INN AT VAUCLUSE SPRING, THE [BB] *Winchester, VA*

INN AT WALNUT BOTTOM [BB] *Cumberland, MD*

INNE AT WATSON'S CHOICE [BB] *Uniontown, PA*

INNKEEPER [MOT] *Hopewell, VA*

INNKEEPER MOTOR LODGE [MOT] *Danville, VA*

INN OF SHAMOKIN DAM [MOT] *Shamokin Dam, PA*

INNS AT DONECKERS, THE [BB] *Ephrata, PA*

INNS OF ADAMSTOWN [BB] *Denver/Adamstown, PA*

INN TO THE WOODS [BB] *New Hope, PA*

IRIS INN [BB] *Waynesboro, VA*

ISLAND MOTOR INN [MOT] *Chincoteague, VA*

JAMES GETTYS HOTEL [AS] *Gettysburg, PA*

JAMES MADISON [HOT] *Norfolk, VA*

JEFFERSON, THE [HOT] *Richmond, VA*

JEFFERSON, THE [HOT] *Washington, DC*

JORDAN HOLLOW FARM INN [BB] *Luray, VA*

JOSEPH AMBLER INN [BB] *Willow Grove, PA*

JW MARRIOTT HOTEL [HOT] *Washington, DC*

KALORAMA GUEST HOUSE [BB] *Washington, DC*

KALORAMA GUEST HOUSE [BB] *Washington, DC*

KALTENBACH'S BED AND BREAKFAST [BB] *Wellsboro, PA*

KANAWHA CITY MOTOR LODGE [MOT] *Charleston, WV*

KELLER INN [MOT] *Lancaster, PA*

KENMORE INN [BB] *Fredericksburg, VA*

KENT MANOR INN [BB] *Chesapeake Bay Bridge Area, MD*

KESWICK HALL AT MONTICELLO [RST] *Charlottesville, VA*

KING'S COTTAGE BED & BREAKFAST [BB] *Lancaster, PA*

KINGSMILL RESORT [RST] *Williamsburg, VA*

KNIGHTS INN [MOT] *Greensburg, PA*

KNIGHTS INN [MOT] *Martinsburg, WV*

KNIGHTS INN [MOT] *Somerset, PA*

KORMANSUITES [HOT] *Philadelphia, PA*

LAKE MOTEL [MOT] *Clarksville, VA*

LAKE SIDE MOTOR COURT [MOT] *Oakland (Garrett County), MD*

LAKEVIEW RESORT [RST] *Morgantown, WV*

LANSDOWNE CONFERENCE RESORT [RST] *Leesburg, VA*

LANTERN LODGE MOTOR INN [MOT] *Lebanon, PA*

LA QUINTA INN [MOT] *Bristol, VA*

LA QUINTA INN [MOT] *Pittsburgh Intl Airport Area, PA*

LA QUINTA INN [MOT] *Richmond, VA*

LA RESERVE CENTER CITY BED & BREAKFAST [BB] *Philadelphia, PA*

LATHAM HOTEL [HOT] *Philadelphia, PA*

LATHAM HOTEL GEORGETOWN, THE [HOT] *Washington, DC*

L'AUBERGE PROVENCAL FRENCH COUNTRY INN [BB] *Winchester, VA*

LAZYJACK INN [BB] *St. Michael's, MD*

LEESBURG COLONIAL INN [BB] *Leesburg, VA*

LEGACY OF WILLIAMSBURG BED AND BREAKFAST [BB] *Williamsburg, VA*

LIBERTY ROSE BED AND BREAKFAST [BB] *Williamsburg, VA*

LIGHTHOUSE CLUB HOTEL, THE [HOT] *Ocean City, MD*

LIGHTHOUSE INN [MOT] *Chincoteague, VA*

LINCOLN SUITES [AS] *Washington, DC*

LINDEN ROW INN [BB] *Richmond, VA*

LITTLE RIVER INN [BB] *Leesburg, VA*

LODGE AT CHALK HILL [MOT] *Uniontown, PA*

LOEWS ANNAPOLIS HOTEL [HOT] *Annapolis, MD*

LOEWS L'ENFANT PLAZA HOTEL [HOT] *Washington, DC*

LOEWS PHILADELPHIA HOTEL [HOT] *Philadelphia, PA*

LOGAN INN [BB] *New Hope, PA*

LONGDALE INN [BB] *Clifton Forge, VA*

LOWE HOTEL [MOT] *Point Pleasant, WV*

LURAY CAVERNS MOTEL [MOT] *Luray, VA*

LYNCHBURG MANSION BED AND BREAKFAST [BB] *Lynchburg, VA*

MADISON HOTEL, THE [HOT] *Washington, DC*

MAGEE'S MAIN STREET INN [BB] *Bloomsburg, PA*

MAIN STREET INN [MOT] *Buckhannon, WV*

MANSION INN [BB] *New Hope, PA*

MAPLE HALL COUNTRY INN [BB] *Lexington, VA*

MARINER MOTEL [MOT] *Chincoteague, VA*

MARRIOTT ANNAPOLIS WATERFRONT [HOT] *Annapolis, MD*

MARRIOTT AT METRO CENTER
[HOT] *Washington, DC*
MARRIOTT BETHESDA [HOT]
Bethesda, MD
MARRIOTT BWI AIRPORT [HOT]
*Baltimore/Washington
International Airport Area, MD*
MARRIOTT CONFERENCE CENTER
WESTFIELDS [RST] *Dulles Intl
Airport Area, VA*
MARRIOTT CRYSTAL CITY [HOT]
*Arlington County (Ronald Reagan
Washington-National Airport
Area), VA*
MARRIOTT CRYSTAL GATEWAY
[HOT] *Arlington County (Ronald
Reagan Washington-National
Airport Area), VA*
MARRIOTT FAIRVIEW PARK [HOT]
Falls Church, VA
MARRIOTT GREENBELT [HOT]
College Park, MD
MARRIOTT HARRISBURG [HOT]
Harrisburg, PA
MARRIOTT INNER HARBOR
BALTIMORE [HOT] *Baltimore,
MD*
MARRIOTT KEY BRIDGE [HOT]
*Arlington County (Ronald Reagan
Washington-National Airport
Area), VA*
MARRIOTT NORFOLK WATERSIDE
[HOT] *Norfolk, VA*
MARRIOTT PHILADELPHIA [HOT]
Philadelphia, PA
MARRIOTT PHILADELPHIA AIRPORT
[HOT] *Philadelphia, PA*
MARRIOTT PHILADELPHIA WEST
[HOT] *Philadelphia, PA*
MARRIOTT PITTSBURGH AIRPORT
[HOT] *Pittsburgh Intl Airport
Area, PA*
MARRIOTT PITTSBURGH CITY
CENTER [HOT] *Pittsburgh, PA*
MARRIOTT RICHMOND [HOT]
Richmond, VA
MARRIOTT RICHMOND WEST
[HOT] *Richmond, VA*
MARRIOTT'S HUNT VALLEY INN
[HOT] *Cockeysville, MD*
MARRIOTT'S MANOR CLUB [HOT]
Williamsburg, VA
MARRIOTT SUITES BETHESDA [AS]
Bethesda, MD
MARRIOTT SUITES WASHINGTON
DULLES [HOT] *Dulles Intl
Airport Area, VA*

MARRIOTT TOWN CENTER
CHARLESTON [HOT]
Charleston, WV
MARRIOTT TYSONS CORNER [HOT]
Tyson's Corner, VA
MARRIOTT WARDMAN PARK HOTEL
[HOT] *Washington, DC*
MARRIOTT WASHINGTON [HOT]
Washington, DC
MARRIOTT WASHINGTON CENTER
GAITHERSBURG [HOT]
Gaithersburg, MD
MARRIOTT WASHINGTON DULLES
AIRPORT [HOT] *Dulles Intl
Airport Area, VA*
MARRIOTT WATERFRONT HOTEL
BALTIMORE [HOT] *Baltimore,
MD*
MARRIOTT WILLIAMSBURG [HOT]
Williamsburg, VA
MARTHA WASHINGTON INN, THE
[BB] *Abingdon, VA*
MARYLAND INN [BB] *Annapolis, MD*
MAYNEVIEW BED AND BREAKFAST
[BB] *Luray, VA*
MCINTOSH INN [MOT] *King of
Prussia, PA*
MCINTOSH INN [MOT] *Newark, DE*
MCKEE'S MOTEL [MOT] *Butler, PA*
MELODY MOTOR LODGE [MOT]
Connellsville, PA
MELROSE HOTEL [HOT] *Washington,
DC*
MEMORYTOWN [MOT] *Mount
Pocono, PA*
MENDENHALL HOTEL [MOT]
Kennett Square, PA
MERCERSBURG INN [BB]
Chambersburg, PA
MERRY SHERWOOD PLANTATION
[BB] *Ocean City, MD*
MIDDLETON INN [BB] *Washington,
VA*
MIDTOWN MOTEL [MOT] *Port
Allegany, PA*
MILTON HALL BED AND BREAKFAST
INN [BB] *Covington, VA*
MILTON MOTEL [MOT] *Hershey, PA*
MIMSLYN INN [MOT] *Luray, VA*
MISS MOLLY'S INN [BB]
Chincoteague, VA
MORRISON-CLARK INN [BB]
Washington, DC
MORRISON HOUSE [HOT]
Alexandria, VA
MOTEL 6 [MOT] *Erie, PA*
MOTEL 6 [MOT] *Washington, PA*
MOUNTAIN CREEK LODGE [RST]
Hinton, WV

MOUNTAIN LAUREL RESORT AND
SPA [RST] *White Haven, PA*
MOUNTAIN VIEW INN [MOT]
Greensburg, PA
MR. MOLE BED AND BREAKFAST
[BB] *Baltimore, MD*
MYER MOTEL [MOT] *Milford, PA*
NASSAU MOTEL [MOT] *Ocean City,
MD*
NATURAL BRIDGE [HOT] *Natural
Bridge, VA*
NEMACOLIN WOODLANDS RESORT
[RST] *Uniontown, PA*
NEWMYER HOUSE [BB] *Connellsville,
PA*
NITTANY LION INN [BB] *State
College, PA*
NORMANDY INN [HOT] *Washington,
DC*
NORRIS HOUSE INN [BB] *Leesburg,
VA*
NORTH BEND PLANTATION BED
AND BREAKFAST [BB]
Williamsburg, VA
NORTH BEND STATE PARK LODGE
[MOT] *Parkersburg, WV*
OAKS VICTORIAN INN [BB]
Blacksburg, VA
OCEAN SANDS RESORT [HOT]
Virginia Beach, VA
OCEANUS MOTEL [MOT] *Rehoboth
Beach, DE*
O'FLAHERTY'S DINGELDEIN HOUSE
[BB] *Lancaster, PA*
OGLEBAY CONFERENCE CENTER
[RST] *Wheeling, WV*
OLD WHITE MOTEL [MOT] *White
Sulphur Springs, WV*
OMNI CHARLOTTESVILLE HOTEL
[HOT] *Charlottesville, VA*
OMNI HOTEL AT INDEPENDENCE
PARK [HOT] *Philadelphia, PA*
OMNI NEWPORT NEWS HOTEL
[HOT] *Newport News, VA*
OMNI RICHMOND HOTEL [HOT]
Richmond, VA
OMNI SHOREHAM HOTEL [HOT]
Washington, DC
OMNI WILLIAM PENN HOTEL [HOT]
Pittsburgh, PA
ONE WASHINGTON CIRCLE HOTEL
[HOT] *Washington, DC*
OSCEOLA MILL COUNTRY INN, THE
[BB] *Blue Ridge Parkway, VA*
PAGE HOUSE [BB] *Norfolk, VA*
PARK HYATT PHILADELPHIA AT THE
BELLEVUE [HOT] *Philadelphia,
PA*
PARK HYATT WASHINGTON [HOT]
Washington, DC

PARSONAGE INN [BB] *St. Michael's,
MD*
PATRICK HENRY HOTEL [HOT]
Roanoke, VA
PATRICK HENRY INN, THE [BB]
Richmond, VA
PEAKS OF OTTER LODGE [MOT] *Blue
Ridge Parkway, VA*
PENCE SPRINGS HOTEL [BB] *Hinton,
WV*
PENN NATIONAL INN AND GOLF
CLUB [BB] *Chambersburg, PA*
PENN'S VIEW HOTEL [HOT]
Philadelphia, PA
PENN WELLS HOTEL & LODGE
[HOT] *Wellsboro, PA*
PENN WELLS LODGE [MOT]
Wellsboro, PA
PHILIPPI LODGING [MOT] *Philippi,
WV*
PHILLIPS BEACH PLAZA HOTEL
[MOT] *Ocean City, MD*
PHOENIX PARK HOTEL [HOT]
Washington, DC
PINEAPPLE HILL BED AND
BREAKFAST [BB] *New Hope, PA*
PINE BARN INN [BB] *Danville, PA*
PINE HILL FARM BED AND
BREAKFAST [BB] *Milford, PA*
PINEHURST INN BED AND
BREAKFAST [BB] *Hershey, PA*
PINE KNOB INN [BB] *Canadensis, PA*
PINES MOTEL [MOT] *Crisfield, MD*
PINE TREE FARM BED AND
BREAKFAST [BB] *Doylestown
(Bucks County), PA*
PINEY GROVE [BB] *Williamsburg, VA*
PLAZA HOTEL [MOT] *Hagerstown,
MD*
POCONO MANOR INN AND GOLF
CLUB [RST] *Mount Pocono, PA*
POCONO RAMADA INN [MOT]
White Haven, PA
PONDA - ROWLAND BED AND
BREAKFAST [BB] *Wilkes-Barre,
PA*
POST HOUSE BED AND BREAKFAST,
THE [BB] *Elkins, WV*
PRINCE GEORGE INN [BB] *Annapolis,
MD*
PRINCESS ROYALE OCEANFRONT
HOTEL [HOT] *Ocean City, MD*
PRIORY INN [BB] *Pittsburgh, PA*
PROSPECT HILL PLANTATION INN
[BB] *Charlottesville, VA*
PUMP HOUSE INN [BB] *Canadensis,
PA*

QUALITY HOTEL [MOT] *Arlington County (Ronald Reagan Washington-National Airport Area), VA*

QUALITY INN [MOT] *Ashland, VA*

QUALITY INN [MOT] *Bedford, PA*

QUALITY INN [MOT] *Carlisle, PA*

QUALITY INN [MOT] *Danville, PA*

QUALITY INN [MOT] *Erie, PA*

QUALITY INN [MOT] *Falls Church, VA*

QUALITY INN [MOT] *Front Royal, VA*

QUALITY INN [MOT] *Gettysburg, PA*

QUALITY INN [MOT] *Lebanon, PA*

QUALITY INN [MOT] *Ocean City, MD*

QUALITY INN [MOT] *Ocean City, MD*

QUALITY INN [MOT] *Pocomoke City, MD*

QUALITY INN [MOT] *Salem, VA*

QUALITY INN [MOT] *Virginia Beach, VA*

QUALITY INN [MOT] *Williamsburg, VA*

QUALITY INN [MOT] *Williamsport, PA*

QUALITY INN [MOT] *York, PA*

QUALITY INN AND SUITES [MOT] *Aberdeen, MD*

QUALITY INN AND SUITES [MOT] *Chambersburg, PA*

QUALITY INN BREEZE MANOR [MOT] *Breezewood, PA*

QUALITY INN IWO JIMA [MOT] *Arlington County (Ronald Reagan Washington-National Airport Area), VA*

QUALITY INN MOTOR LODGE [MOT] *Gettysburg, PA*

QUALITY INN ON THE LAKE [MOT] *Clarksville, VA*

QUALITY INN SHENANDOAH VALLEY [MOT] *New Market, VA*

QUALITY INN WEST END [MOT] *Richmond, VA*

QUALITY SUITES [MOT] *Rockville, MD*

QUARTERPATH INN [MOT] *Williamsburg, VA*

QUO VADIS BED & BREAKFAST [BB] *Franklin (Venango County), PA*

RADISSON [MOT] *Alexandria, VA*

RADISSON [HOT] *Annapolis, MD*

RADISSON [MOT] *Hampton, VA*

RADISSON [HOT] *Williamsport, PA*

RADISSON BARCELO [HOT] *Washington, DC*

RADISSON CROSS KEYS [HOT] *Baltimore, MD*

RADISSON FORT MAGRUDER INN [MOT] *Williamsburg, VA*

RADISSON HOTEL [MOT] *Huntington, WV*

RADISSON HOTEL [HOT] *Philadelphia, PA*

RADISSON HOTEL [HOT] *Scranton, PA*

RADISSON HOTEL GREEN TREE [HOT] *Pittsburgh, PA*

RADISSON HOTEL NORFOLK [HOT] *Norfolk, VA*

RADISSON HOTEL SHARON [HOT] *West Middlesex, PA*

RADISSON PENN HARRIS HOTEL [HOT] *Harrisburg, PA*

RADISSON VALLEY FORGE HOTEL [HOT] *King of Prussia, PA*

RADNOR HOTEL [HOT] *Philadelphia, PA*

RAMADA [MOT] *Blacksburg, VA*

RAMADA [MOT] *Pittsburgh, PA*

RAMADA INN [MOT] *Altoona, PA*

RAMADA INN [MOT] *Bluefield, WV*

RAMADA INN [MOT] *Breezewood, PA*

RAMADA INN [MOT] *Bristol, VA*

RAMADA INN [MOT] *Charlottesville, VA*

RAMADA INN [MOT] *Du Bois, PA*

RAMADA INN [MOT] *Edinboro, PA*

RAMADA INN [MOT] *Erie, PA*

RAMADA INN [MOT] *Fredericksburg, VA*

RAMADA INN [MOT] *Hazleton, PA*

RAMADA INN [MOT] *Lancaster, PA*

RAMADA INN [MOT] *Lancaster, PA*

RAMADA INN [MOT] *Lexington, VA*

RAMADA INN [MOT] *Ligonier, PA*

RAMADA INN [MOT] *Luray, VA*

RAMADA INN [MOT] *Morgantown, WV*

RAMADA INN [MOT] *New Castle, DE*

RAMADA INN [MOT] *Pikesville, MD*

RAMADA INN [MOT] *Roanoke, VA*

RAMADA INN [MOT] *Somerset, PA*

RAMADA INN [MOT] *State College, PA*

RAMADA INN [MOT] *Woodstock, VA*

RAMADA INN [MOT] *Wytheville, VA*

RAMADA INN AT THE OUTLETS [MOT] *Reading, PA*

RAMADA INN CONFERENCE CENTER [MOT] *Salisbury, MD*

RAMADA LIMITED [MOT] *Clarksburg, WV*

RAMADA LIMITED OCEANFRONT [MOT] *Ocean City, MD*

RAMADA PLAZA [MOT] *Virginia Beach, VA*

RAMADA PLAZA SUITES AND
    CONFERENCE CENTER [MOT]
    Pittsburgh, PA
RED CARPET [MOT] *Charlottesville,
    VA*
RED CARPET INN [MOT] *Bristol, VA*
RED CARPET INN [MOT] *Gettysburg,
    PA*
RED ROOF INN [MOT] *Alexandria, VA*
RED ROOF INN [MOT] *Charleston,
    WV*
RED ROOF INN [MOT] *Fairmont, WV*
RED ROOF INN [MOT] *Harrisburg, PA*
RED ROOF INN [MOT] *Huntington,
    WV*
RED ROOF INN [MOT] *Manassas, VA*
RED ROOF INN [MOT] *Parkersburg,
    WV*
RED ROOF INN [MOT] *Pittsburgh, PA*
RED ROOF INN [MOT] *Pittsburgh Intl
    Airport Area, PA*
RED ROOF INN [MOT] *Washington,
    PA*
RED ROOF INN RICHMOND SOUTH
    [MOT] *Richmond, VA*
REFUGE INN [MOT] *Chincoteague, VA*
RENAISSANCE HARBORPLACE
    HOTEL [HOT] *Baltimore, MD*
RENAISSANCE MAYFLOWER HOTEL
    [HOT] *Washington, DC*
RENAISSANCE PHILADELPHIA
    AIRPORT [HOT] *Philadelphia,
    PA*
RENAISSANCE PITTSBURGH HOTEL
    [HOT] *Pittsburgh, PA*
RENAISSANCE PORTSMOUTH [HOT]
    Portsmouth, VA
RENAISSANCE WASHINGTON DC
    HOTEL [HOT] *Washington, DC*
RESIDENCE INN BY MARRIOTT [EX]
    *Arlington County (Ronald Reagan
    Washington-National Airport
    Area), VA*
RESIDENCE INN BY MARRIOTT [EX]
    Bethesda, MD
RESIDENCE INN BY MARRIOTT [EX]
    Dulles Intl Airport Area, VA
RESIDENCE INN BY MARRIOTT [EX]
    Richmond, VA
RESIDENCE INN BY MARRIOTT [EX]
    Tyson's Corner, VA
RICHARD JOHNSTON INN [BB]
    Fredericksburg, VA
RITTENHOUSE HOTEL, THE [HOT]
    Philadelphia, PA
RITZ-CARLTON, PENTAGON CITY,
    THE [HOT] *Arlington County
    (Ronald Reagan Washington-
    National Airport Area), VA*

RITZ-CARLTON, PHILADELPHIA,
    THE [HOT] *Philadelphia, PA*
RITZ-CARLTON, TYSON'S CORNER,
    THE [HOT] *Tyson's Corner, VA*
RITZ-CARLTON, WASHINGTON
    D.C., THE [HOT] *Washington,
    DC*
RIVER HOUSE INN [BB] *Pocomoke
    City, MD*
RIVER INN [HOT] *Washington, DC*
RIVERSIDE INN [BB] *Edinboro, PA*
ROBERT JOHNSON HOUSE [BB]
    Annapolis, MD
ROBERT MORRIS INN [BB] *Easton,
    MD*
ROCKVALE VILLAGE INN [MOT]
    Lancaster, PA
RODEWAY INN [MOT] *New Castle,
    DE*
RODEWAY INN [MOT] *Philadelphia,
    PA*
RODEWAY INN [MOT] *State College,
    PA*
RODEWAY INN & SUITES [MOT]
    Hershey, PA
ROEBLING INN ON THE DELAWARE
    [BB] *Hawley, PA*
ROSALOE MOTEL [MOT] *Hot Springs,
    VA*
SAFARI MOTEL [MOT] *Ocean City,
    MD*
SAHARA MOTEL [MOT] *Ocean City,
    MD*
ST. JAMES SUITES [AS] *Washington,
    DC*
ST. MICHAEL'S HARBOUR INN AND
    MARINA [HOT] *St. Michael's,
    MD*
ST. REGIS WASHINGTON, THE [HOT]
    Washington, DC
SAMPSON EAGON INN [BB]
    Staunton, VA
SANDCASTLE [MOT] *Rehoboth Beach,
    DE*
SCARLETT HOUSE BED AND
    BREAKFAST [BB] *Kennett
    Square, PA*
SEA ESTA MOTEL III [MOT] *Rehoboth
    Beach, DE*
SEA GULL MOTEL [MOT] *Virginia
    Beach, VA*
SEA SHELL [MOT] *Chincoteague, VA*
SETTLERS INN AT BINGHAM PARK
    [BB] *Hawley, PA*
SEVEN SPRINGS MOUNTAIN
    RESORT [RST] *Donegal, PA*
SHADOWBROOK RESORT [RST]
    Scranton, PA
SHANNON INN [MOT] *Stroudsburg,
    PA*

SHAWNEE INN [RST] *Shawnee on Delaware, PA*

SHELDON'S MOTEL [MOT] *Keysville, VA*

SHENANDOAH INN [MOT] *Wytheville, VA*

SHENVALEE GOLF RESORT [RST] *New Market, VA*

SHERATON [HOT] *Richmond, VA*

SHERATON BALTIMORE NORTH HOTEL [HOT] *Towson, MD*

SHERATON BARCELO [HOT] *Annapolis, MD*

SHERATON BUCKS COUNTY HOTEL [HOT] *Norristown, PA*

SHERATON COLLEGE PARK [HOT] *College Park, MD*

SHERATON CRYSTAL CITY HOTEL [HOT] *Arlington County (Ronald Reagan Washington-National Airport Area), VA*

SHERATON GREAT VALLEY HOTEL [HOT] *Downingtown, PA*

SHERATON HOTEL [HOT] *Columbia, MD*

SHERATON HOTEL [HOT] *Pittsburgh, PA*

SHERATON INN [HOT] *Allentown, PA*

SHERATON INN [HOT] *Dover, DE*

SHERATON INN [HOT] *Fredericksburg, VA*

SHERATON INN [HOT] *Harrisburg, PA*

SHERATON INN [HOT] *Reading, PA*

SHERATON INNER HARBOR HOTEL [HOT] *Baltimore, MD*

SHERATON INTERNATIONAL ON BWI AIRPORT [HOT] *Baltimore/Washington International Airport Area, MD*

SHERATON NORFOLK [HOT] *Norfolk, VA*

SHERATON OCEANFRONT HOTEL [HOT] *Virginia Beach, VA*

SHERATON PHILADELPHIA AIRPORT HOTEL [HOT] *Philadelphia, PA*

SHERATON PREMIER [HOT] *Tyson's Corner, VA*

SHERATON RESTON [HOT] *Dulles Intl Airport Area, VA*

SHERATON RITTENHOUSE SQUARE [HOT] *Philadelphia, PA*

SHERATON SOCIETY HILL HOTEL [HOT] *Philadelphia, PA*

SHERATON SUITES [AS] *Alexandria, VA*

SHERATON SUITES [HOT] *Wilmington, DE*

SHERATON UNIVERSITY CITY HOTEL [HOT] *Philadelphia, PA*

SHERWOOD MOTEL [MOT] *Wellsboro, PA*

SHONEY'S INN [MOT] *Winchester, VA*

SHONEY'S MOTOR INN [MOT] *Staunton, VA*

SIGN OF THE SORREL HORSE [BB] *Doylestown (Bucks County), PA*

SILVER THATCH INN [BB] *Charlottesville, VA*

SIMMONS MOTEL [MOT] *Hershey, PA*

SKYLAND LODGE [MOT] *Luray, VA*

SKYTOP LODGE [RST] *Canadensis, PA*

SLEEP INN [MOT] *Clarksburg, WV*

SLEEP INN [MOT] *Johnstown, PA*

SLEEP INN [MOT] *Roanoke, VA*

SLEEP INN [MOT] *Summersville, WV*

SMITHTON BED & BREAKFAST COUNTRY INN [BB] *Ephrata, PA*

SMOKE HOLE HOTEL & LOG CABINS [MOT] *Petersburg, WV*

SOFITEL [HOT] *Philadelphia, PA*

SPINNERS MOTOR INN [MOT] *Hershey, PA*

SPINNING WHEEL BED AND BREAKFAST [BB] *Chincoteague, VA*

STEELES TAVERN MANOR [BB] *Lexington, VA*

STERLING INN [BB] *Mount Pocono, PA*

STEVENS MOTEL [MOT] *State College, PA*

STONE LODGE [MOT] *Huntington, WV*

STONE MANOR [BB] *Frederick, MD*

STRATFORD INN [MOT] *Danville, VA*

SUMMIT INN RESORT [RST] *Uniontown, PA*

SUNRISE MOTOR INN [MOT] *Chincoteague, VA*

SUPER 8 [MOT] *Allentown, PA*

SUPER 8 [MOT] *Bristol, VA*

SUPER 8 [MOT] *Clarion, PA*

SUPER 8 [MOT] *Erie, PA*

SUPER 8 [MOT] *Nitro, WV*

SUPER 8 [MOT] *Tappahannock, VA*

SUPER 8 MOTEL [MOT] *Carlisle, PA*

SUPER 8 MOTEL [MOT] *Chesapeake, VA*

SUPER 8 MOTEL [MOT] *Cumberland, MD*

SUPER 8 MOTEL [MOT] *Elkins, WV*

SUPER 8 MOTEL [MOT] *Manassas, VA*

SUPER 8 MOTEL [MOT] *Martinsburg, WV*

SUPER 8 MOTEL [MOT] *Mount Pocono, PA*

SUPER 8 MOTEL [MOT] *Norfolk, VA*

SUPER 8 NORTH [MOT]
  Fredericksburg, VA
SUTTON MOTEL [MOT] *Elkton, MD*
SWATARA CREEK INN [BB] *Lebanon, PA*
SWISS WOODS BED & BREAKFAST [BB] *Lancaster, PA*
SYCAMORE HILL HOUSE AND GARDENS [BB] *Washington, VA*
TAFT BRIDGE INN [BB] *Washington, DC*
TARA COUNTRY INN [BB] *Sharon, PA*
TATTERSALL INN [BB] *New Hope, PA*
TEN-ELEVEN CLINTON [BB] *Philadelphia, PA*
THOMAS BOND HOUSE [BB] *Philadelphia, PA*
THOMAS SHEPHERD INN [BB] *Shepherdstown, WV*
THORNROSE HOUSE [BB] *Staunton, VA*
TIDES, THE [RST] *Irvington, VA*
TIDES [MOT] *Ocean City, MD*
TIDEWATER INN AND CONFERENCE CENTER [HOT] *Easton, MD*
TOFTREES RESORT [RST] *State College, PA*
TOPAZ HOTEL [HOT] *Washington, DC*
TOWANDA MOTEL & RESTAURANT [MOT] *Towanda, PA*
TOWNE HOUSE INN [BB] *Du Bois, PA*
TOWNE HOUSE MOTOR LODGE [MOT] *Charles Town, WV*
TRAVELERS MOTEL [MOT] *Alexandria, VA*
TRAVELODGE [MOT] *Chambersburg, PA*
TRAVELODGE [MOT] *Elkins, WV*
TRAVELODGE [MOT] *Lexington, VA*
TRAVELODGE [MOT] *Roanoke, VA*
TRAVELODGE [MOT] *Winchester, VA*
TREMONT HOTEL [HOT] *Baltimore, MD*
TURF MOTEL [MOT] *Charles Town, WV*
TURF VALLEY HOTEL AND COUNTRY CLUB [HOT] *Ellicott City, MD*
TURNING POINT INN [BB] *Frederick, MD*
TWIN TURRETS INN [BB] *Pottstown, PA*
TYGART LAKE STATE PARK LODGE [MOT] *Grafton, WV*
UPTOWNER [MOT] *Huntington, WV*
VANDIVER INN [BB] *Havre de Grace, MD*
VENICE INN [MOT] *Hagerstown, MD*

VICTORIAN INN BED AND BREAKFAST [BB] *Lock Haven, PA*
VILLAGE INN [BB] *Bird-in-Hand, PA*
VILLAGE INN [MOT] *Harrisonburg, VA*
VINE COTTAGE INN [BB] *Hot Springs, VA*
VIRGINIA BEACH RESORT [RST] *Virginia Beach, VA*
WADE'S POINT INN [BB] *St. Michael's, MD*
WARFIELD HOUSE, THE [BB] *Elkins, WV*
WAR HILL INN BED AND BREAKFAST [BB] *Williamsburg, VA*
WARWICK HOTEL [HOT] *Philadelphia, PA*
WASHINGTON COURT HOTEL ON CAPITOL HILL [HOT] *Washington, DC*
WASHINGTON MONARCH HOTEL [HOT] *Washington, DC*
WASHINGTON SUITES [HOT] *Alexandria, VA*
WASHINGTON SUITES HOTEL [HOT] *Washington, DC*
WATERGATE, THE [HOT] *Washington, DC*
WATERLOO COUNTRY INN [BB] *Salisbury, MD*
WATERSIDE MOTOR INN [MOT] *Chincoteague, VA*
WATSON HOUSE [BB] *Chincoteague, VA*
WATTSTULL COURT [MOT] *Natural Bridge, VA*
WAYNE HOTEL [HOT] *King of Prussia, PA*
WAYSIDE INN [BB] *Strasburg, VA*
WEDGWOOD INN [BB] *New Hope, PA*
WELLESLEY INN [MOT] *Chesapeake, VA*
WESTFIELD MOTOR INN [MOT] *Lancaster, PA*
WESTIN CONVENTION CENTER HOTEL [HOT] *Pittsburgh, PA*
WESTIN EMBASSY ROW [HOT] *Washington, DC*
WESTIN GRAND [HOT] *Washington, DC*
WESTIN PHILADELPHIA, THE [HOT] *Philadelphia, PA*
WHISPERING PINES MOTEL [MOT] *Irvington, VA*
WHITEHALL INN [BB] *New Hope, PA*
WHITE ROSE MOTEL [MOT] *Hershey, PA*

WHITE SWAN TAVERN [BB]
   Chesapeake Bay Bridge Area, MD
WIDOW KIP'S COUNTRY INN [BB]
   Basye, VA
WILLARD INTER-CONTINENTAL
   WASHINGTON [HOT]
   Washington, DC
WILLIAM PAGE INN [BB] *Annapolis,*
   MD
WILLIAM PENN INN [BB] *Norristown,*
   PA
WILLIAMSBURG HOSPITALITY
   HOUSE [HOT] *Williamsburg,*
   VA
WILLIAMSBURG INN [RST]
   Williamsburg, VA
WILLIAMSBURG LODGE [HOT]
   Williamsburg, VA
WILLIAMSBURG SAMPLER BED AND
   BREAKFAST [BB] *Williamsburg,*
   VA
WILLIAMSBURG WOODLANDS
   [MOT] *Williamsburg, VA*
WILLIAMS' HOUSE BED AND
   BREAKFAST [BB] *Parkersburg,*
   WV
WILL O' THE WISP [MOT] *Oakland*
   (Garrett County), MD
WILLOW VALLEY RESORT [RST]
   Lancaster, PA
WILSON-LEE HOUSE BED AND
   BREAKFAST [BB] *Cape Charles,*
   VA
WINDSOR INN [BB] *Washington, DC*

WINDSOR PARK HOTEL [MOT]
   Washington, DC
WINTERGREEN RESORT [RST]
   Charlottesville, VA
WOODFIN SUITES HOTEL [MOT]
   Rockville, MD
WOODLANDS INN AND RESORT,
   THE [RST] *Wilkes-Barre, PA*
WOODRUFF HOUSE BED AND
   BREAKFAST [BB] *Luray, VA*
WOODS RESORT & CONFERENCE
   CENTER [RST] *Martinsburg, WV*
WYDNOR HALL INN [BB] *Bethlehem,*
   PA
WYNDHAM [HOT] *King of Prussia, PA*
WYNDHAM CITY CENTER [HOT]
   Washington, DC
WYNDHAM FRANKLIN PLAZA
   HOTEL [HOT] *Philadelphia, PA*
WYNDHAM GARDEN HOTEL [HOT]
   Harrisburg, PA
WYNDHAM INNER HARBOR HOTEL
   [HOT] *Baltimore, MD*
WYNDHAM ROANOKE AIRPORT
   HOTEL [HOT] *Roanoke, VA*
WYNDHAM WILMINGTON [HOT]
   Wilmington, DE
YORKTOWNE HOTEL [HOT] *York, PA*
YORKTOWN MOTOR LODGE [MOT]
   Yorktown, VA
ZWAANENDAEL INN [HOT] *Lewes,*
   DE

RESTAURANT LIST

Establishment names are listed in alphabetical order followed by a symbol identifying their classification and then city and state. The symbols for classification are: [RES] for Restaurants and [URD] for Unrated Dining Spots.

110 RESTAURANT AND BAR [RES] *King of Prussia, PA*
1789 [RES] *Washington, DC*
1902 LANDMARK TAVERN [RES] *Pittsburgh, PA*
208 TALBOT [RES] *St. Michael's, MD*
701 RESTAURANT [RES] *Washington, DC*
A AND J [RES] *Rockville, MD*
AARATHI [RES] *Tyson's Corner, VA*
ABERDEEN BARN [RES] *Charlottesville, VA*
ABERDEEN BARN [RES] *Williamsburg, VA*
ACACIA [RES] *Richmond, VA*
ACCOMAC INN [RES] *York, PA*
ADDIE'S [RES] *Rockville, MD*
ADITI [RES] *Washington, DC*
AFTERWORDS [URD] *Washington, DC*
AIR TRANSPORT COMMAND [RES] *New Castle, DE*
ALAMO [RES] *College Park, MD*
ALDO'S [RES] *Virginia Beach, VA*
ALEXANDER'S [RES] *Petersburg, VA*
ALFRED'S VICTORIAN RESTAURANT [RES] *Harrisburg, PA*
AL FRESCO [RES] *Newport News, VA*
ALLEGRO [RES] *Altoona, PA*
ALOHA [RES] *St. Mary's City, MD*
ALPENHOF BAVARIAN [RES] *Reading, PA*
ALPINE [RES] *Arlington County (Ronald Reagan Washington-National Airport Area), VA*
AMICI [RES] *Richmond, VA*
AMISH BARN [RES] *Bird-in-Hand, PA*
ANDALUCIA [RES] *Rockville, MD*
ANDALUCIA DE BETHESDA [RES] *Bethesda, MD*
ANGELINA'S [RES] *Baltimore, MD*
ANNA MARIA'S [RES] *Washington, DC*
ANTIQUE AIRPLANE [RES] *Reading, PA*
ANTRIM 1844 [RES] *Emmitsburg, MD*
APPENNINO [RES] *Allentown, PA*
AQUARELLE [RES] *Washington, DC*
ARLINGTON DINER [RES] *Stroudsburg, PA*

ARMAND'S CHICAGO PIZZERIA [URD] *Washington, DC*
ARROYO GRILLE [RES] *Philadelphia, PA*
ARSENAL AT NEW CASTLE [RES] *New Castle, DE*
ARTHUR'S [RES] *Downingtown, PA*
ARTIE'S [RES] *Fairfax, VA*
ASHBY INN [RES] *Winchester, VA*
ASHBY'S OYSTER HOUSE [RES] *Lewes, DE*
ASHLEY ROOM [RES] *St. Michael's, MD*
ATHENS STEAK HOUSE [RES] *Bristol, VA*
ATLANTIC [RES] *Baltimore, MD*
AU PETIT PARIS [RES] *Cumberland, MD*
AUSTIN GRILL [RES] *Bethesda, MD*
AUSTIN GRILL [RES] *Washington, DC*
AZALEA [RES] *Philadelphia, PA*
BACCHUS [RES] *Washington, DC*
BACCHUS BETHESDA [RES] *Bethesda, MD*
BACK BAY [RES] *Morgantown, WV*
BACK BURNER [RES] *Wilmington, DE*
BAILIWICK INN [RES] *Fairfax, VA*
BAKER'S CRUST [RES] *Norfolk, VA*
BANGKOK STEAKHOUSE [RES] *Falls Church, VA*
BANQUE, THE [RES] *Norfolk, VA*
BARON'S INNE [RES] *King of Prussia, PA*
BAVARIAN INN AND LODGE [RES] *Shepherdstown, WV*
BAY HUNDRED RESTAURANT [RES] *St. Michael's, MD*
BAY LEAF [RES] *Allentown, PA*
BAYOU [RES] *Havre de Grace, MD*
BEAVER HOUSE [RES] *Stroudsburg, PA*
BEDUCI [RES] *Washington, DC*
BENIHANA [RES] *Pittsburgh, PA*
BERLENGAS [RES] *Philadelphia, PA*
BERRET'S [RES] *Williamsburg, VA*
BERTHA'S [RES] *Baltimore, MD*
BERTINE'S NORTH CARIBBEAN [RES] *Charlottesville, VA*
BETHESDA CRAB HOUSE [RES] *Bethesda, MD*
BILBO BAGGINS [RES] *Alexandria, VA*

BILLY MARTIN'S TAVERN [RES]
    Washington, DC
BILLY'S RITZ [RES] *Roanoke, VA*
BISTRO 123 [RES] *Tyson's Corner, VA*
BISTRO 1717 [RES] *Wilmington, DE*
BISTRO BIS [RES] *Washington, DC*
BISTRO BISTRO [RES] *Arlington
    County (Ronald Reagan
    Washington-National Airport
    Area), VA*
BISTRO FRANCAIS [RES] *Washington,
    DC*
BISTRO ST. MICHAELS [RES] *St.
    Michael's, MD*
BISTROT LEPIC [RES] *Washington, DC*
BLACK HORSE [RES]
    Denver/Adamstown, PA
BLACK OLIVE [RES] *Baltimore, MD*
BLACK TRUMPET [RES] *Wilmington,
    DE*
BLACK WALNUT [RES] *Doylestown
    (Bucks County), PA*
BLAIR MANSION INN [RES] *Silver
    Spring, MD*
BLEU ROCK INN [RES] *Washington,
    VA*
BLOSSOM DELI [RES] *Charleston, WV*
BLUE ANGEL [RES] *Philadelphia, PA*
BLUE COAT INN [RES] *Dover, DE*
BLUE MOON [RES] *Rehoboth Beach,
    DE*
BLUE MOUNTAIN FAMILY
    RESTAURANT [RES]
    Shartlesville, PA
BLUE OCEAN [RES] *Fairfax, VA*
BLUE PETE'S SEAFOOD AND STEAK
    [RES] *Virginia Beach, VA*
BLUE POINT GRILL [RES] *Alexandria,
    VA*
BLUESTONE DINING ROOM [RES]
    Hinton, WV
BOCCACCIO [RES] *Baltimore, MD*
BOILING SPRINGS TAVERN [RES]
    Carlisle, PA
BOMBAY BISTRO [RES] *Fairfax, VA*
BOMBAY BISTRO [RES] *Rockville, MD*
BOMBAY CLUB [RES] *Washington, DC*
BOMBAY DINING [RES] *Bethesda, MD*
BOMBAY PALACE [RES] *Washington,
    DC*
BONAROTI [RES] *Tyson's Corner, VA*
BONFIRE [RES] *Ocean City, MD*
BOOKBINDER'S 15TH STREET
    SEAFOOD HOUSE [RES]
    Philadelphia, PA
BOURBON STREET [RES] *New Hope,
    PA*
BRANDYWINE ROOM [RES]
    Wilmington, DE

BRASSERIE PERRIER [RES]
    Philadelphia, PA
BREAD LINE, THE [URD] *Washington,
    DC*
BRIDGE, THE [RES] *St. Michael's, MD*
BRIDGET FOY'S SOUTH STREET
    GRILL [RES] *Philadelphia, PA*
BROOKSIDE [RES] *Luray, VA*
BROWNIE'S IN THE BURG [RES]
    Stroudsburg, PA
BROWN PELICAN [RES] *Frederick, MD*
BUA [RES] *Washington, DC*
BUDDAKAN [RES] *Philadelphia, PA*
BUON GIORNO [RES] *Bethesda, MD*
BURMA [RES] *Washington, DC*
BUSARA [RES] *Washington, DC*
BUTTERY, THE [RES] *Lewes, DE*
BYRAM'S LOBSTER HOUSE [URD]
    Richmond, VA
CAB FRYE'S TAVERN [RES] *Pottstown,
    PA*
CAFE [RES] *Bethlehem, PA*
CAFE ALLEGRO [RES] *Pittsburgh, PA*
CAFE ATLANTICO [RES] *Washington,
    DC*
CAFE AT THE FRICK [RES] *Pittsburgh,
    PA*
CAFE BETHESDA [RES] *Bethesda, MD*
CAFE BRETTON [RES] *Annapolis, MD*
CAFE DALAT [RES] *Arlington County
    (Ronald Reagan Washington-
    National Airport Area), VA*
CAFE EUROPA [RES] *Portsmouth, VA*
CAFE HON [RES] *Baltimore, MD*
CAFE LUIGI [RES] *Bethlehem, PA*
CAFE MILANO [RES] *Washington, DC*
CAFE MOZART [RES] *Washington, DC*
CAFE NORMANDIE [RES] *Annapolis,
    MD*
CAFE OGGI [RES] *McLean, VA*
CAFE TAJ [RES] *McLean, VA*
CAFE TROIA [RES] *Towson, MD*
CAFFE DI PAGLIACCI [RES]
    Richmond, VA
CALIFORNIA CAFE [RES] *Carlisle, PA*
CALVERT GRILLE [RES] *Alexandria,
    VA*
CALVERT HOUSE INN [RES] *College
    Park, MD*
CANDLELIGHT INN [RES] *Bethlehem,
    PA*
C & O [RES] *Charlottesville, VA*
CAPITAL GRILLE, THE [RES]
    Washington, DC
CARBONE'S [RES] *Greensburg, PA*
CARLTON [RES] *Pittsburgh, PA*
CARLYLE GRAND CAFE [RES]
    *Arlington County (Ronald Reagan
    Washington-National Airport
    Area), VA*

CARMASSI'S TUSCANY GRILL [RES] *Pittsburgh, PA*
CARMELLO'S [RES] *Charlottesville, VA*
CARMELLO'S AND LITTLE PORTUGAL [RES] *Manassas, VA*
CARROL'S CREEK [RES] *Annapolis, MD*
CASABLANCA [RES] *Willow Grove, PA*
CASBAH [RES] *Pittsburgh, PA*
CASCADES, THE [RES] *Williamsburg, VA*
CASHION'S EAT PLACE [RES] *Washington, DC*
CATACOMBS AT BUBE'S BREWERY [RES] *Lancaster, PA*
CATALAN WEST [RES] *Washington, DC*
CATHERINE'S AT SPINNER'S [RES] *Hershey, PA*
CENTRE BRIDGE INN [RES] *New Hope, PA*
CESCO TRATTORIA [RES] *Bethesda, MD*
C.F. FOLKS [URD] *Washington, DC*
CHADAGAN'S [RES] *Mercer, PA*
CHARCOAL STEAK HOUSE [RES] *Roanoke, VA*
CHARLESTON [RES] *Baltimore, MD*
CHART HOUSE [RES] *Alexandria, VA*
CHEAT RIVER INN [RES] *Elkins, WV*
CHEESE CELLAR CAFE & BAR [RES] *Pittsburgh, PA*
CHEF DAN'S [RES] *Charleston, WV*
CHEF'S SECRET [RES] *College Park, MD*
CHESAPEAKE LANDING SEAFOOD [RES] *St. Michael's, MD*
CHEZ ANDRE [RES] *Alexandria, VA*
CHEZ GERARD AUTHENTIC FRENCH RESTAURANT [RES] *Uniontown, PA*
CHEZ LA MER [RES] *Rehoboth Beach, DE*
CHIAPPARELLI'S OF LITTLE ITALY [RES] *Baltimore, MD*
CHINA PALACE [RES] *Pittsburgh, PA*
CHRIS' STEAK HOUSE [RES] *Gaithersburg, MD*
CHRISTOPHER MARKS [RES] *Washington, DC*
CHURCH BREW WORKS, THE [RES] *Pittsburgh, PA*
CIRCA [RES] *Philadelphia, PA*
CIRCLE SEAFOOD [RES] *Portsmouth, VA*
CIRCULAR DINING ROOM [RES] *Hershey, PA*
CITRONELLE [RES] *Washington, DC*
CITY LIGHTS [RES] *Baltimore, MD*
CITY TAVERN [RES] *Philadelphia, PA*

CLIFFSIDE [RES] *Pittsburgh, PA*
CLYDE'S [RES] *Columbia, MD*
CLYDE'S [RES] *Dulles Intl Airport Area, VA*
CLYDE'S [RES] *Tyson's Corner, VA*
CLYDE'S [RES] *Washington, DC*
COACH HOUSE TAVERN [RES] *Williamsburg, VA*
COAL BARON [RES] *Uniontown, PA*
COASTAL GRILL [RES] *Virginia Beach, VA*
COCK N' BULL [RES] *New Hope, PA*
COCO LOCO [RES] *Washington, DC*
COLUMBUS INN [RES] *Wilmington, DE*
COMMON PLEA [RES] *Pittsburgh, PA*
CONNAUGHT PLACE [RES] *Fairfax, VA*
COOPER'S SEAFOOD HOUSE [RES] *Scranton, PA*
COPELAND'S OF NEW ORLEANS [RES] *Alexandria, VA*
COPELAND'S OF NEW ORLEANS [RES] *Rockville, MD*
COPPER KETTLE [RES] *Chambersburg, PA*
COPPI'S VIGORELLI [RES] *Washington, DC*
CORINTHIAN [RES] *Annapolis, MD*
COTTONWOOD CAFE [RES] *Bethesda, MD*
COUNTRY CAFE [RES] *Hot Springs, VA*
COUNTRY COTTAGE [RES] *Somerset, PA*
COUNTRY CUPBOARD [RES] *Lewisburg, PA*
COUNTRY ROAD INN [RES] *Summersville, WV*
COVENTRY FORGE INN [RES] *Pottstown, PA*
COWBOY CAFE [RES] *Arlington County (Ronald Reagan Washington-National Airport Area), VA*
COYOTE CROSSING [RES] *Philadelphia, PA*
COZY [RES] *Thurmont, MD*
CRAB SHANTY [RES] *Ellicott City, MD*
CRAZY SWEDE [RES] *Havre de Grace, MD*
CRISFIELD [RES] *Silver Spring, MD*
CROWN STERLING [RES] *Lynchburg, VA*
CUISINE AND COMPANY [URD] *Virginia Beach, VA*
CUTTALOSSA INN [RES] *New Hope, PA*
CUVEE NOTREDAME [RES] *Philadelphia, PA*
DA DOMENICO [RES] *McLean, VA*

DALESIO'S OF LITTLE ITALY [RES] *Baltimore, MD*
D & S BRASSERIE [RES] *Lancaster, PA*
DANSBURY DEPOT [URD] *Stroudsburg, PA*
DANTE [RES] *McLean, VA*
DARK HORSE [RES] *Philadelphia, PA*
DAS WALDCAFE [RES] *Newport News, VA*
DAVE AND ANDY'S ICE CREAM PARLOR [URD] *Pittsburgh, PA*
DC COAST [RES] *Washington, DC*
DELRAY VIETNAMESE GARDEN [RES] *Bethesda, MD*
DEUX CHEMINEES [RES] *Philadelphia, PA*
DIEHL'S [RES] *Nitro, WV*
D'IGNAZIO'S TOWNE HOUSE [RES] *Media, PA*
DILWORTHTOWN INN DINING ROOM, THE [URD] *West Chester, PA*
DIMITRI'S [RES] *Hershey, PA*
DIMITRI'S [RES] *Philadelphia, PA*
D'IMPERIO'S [RES] *Pittsburgh, PA*
DINARDO'S [RES] *Philadelphia, PA*
DINING ROOM, THE [RES] *Abingdon, VA*
DINING ROOM [RES] *Richmond, VA*
DISTRICT CHOPHOUSE [RES] *Washington, DC*
DOBBIN HOUSE [RES] *Gettysburg, PA*
DONECKERS [RES] *Ephrata, PA*
DON'S SEAFOOD [RES] *Chincoteague, VA*
DOUMAR'S [URD] *Norfolk, VA*
DUANGRAT'S [RES] *Falls Church, VA*
DUCK-IN RESTAURANT AND GAZEBO [RES] *Virginia Beach, VA*
DUE [RES] *Pikesville, MD*
DULING-KURTZ HOUSE [RES] *West Chester, PA*
EASTERN CHINESE [RES] *Bethlehem, PA*
EASTVILLE MANOR [RES] *Cape Charles, VA*
EAST WIND [RES] *Alexandria, VA*
ECCO CAFE [RES] *Alexandria, VA*
ED'S STEAK HOUSE [RES] *Bedford, PA*
EHRHARDT'S LAKESIDE [RES] *Hawley, PA*
ELYSIUM [RES] *Alexandria, VA*
EMBERS [RES] *Ocean City, MD*
ERNIE'S CORK & BOTTLE [RES] *Wheeling, WV*
ERNIE'S ESQUIRE [RES] *Wheeling, WV*

ESPOSITO'S/PIZZA 'N PASTA, THE [URD] *Fairfax, VA*
EVANS SEAFOOD [URD] *St. Mary's City, MD*
EVERMAY [RES] *New Hope, PA*
FACCIA LUNA [RES] *Alexandria, VA*
FACCIA LUNA [RES] *Arlington County (Ronald Reagan Washington-National Airport Area), VA*
FAGER'S ISLAND [RES] *Ocean City, MD*
FAIRFAX ROOM [RES] *Washington, DC*
FAMOUS 4TH STREET DELICATESSEN [URD] *Philadelphia, PA*
FARMHOUSE, THE [RES] *Allentown, PA*
FARNSWORTH HOUSE [RES] *Gettysburg, PA*
FAROUK'S HOUSE OF INDIA [URD] *Richmond, VA*
FEDERAL GRILL [RES] *Allentown, PA*
FELICIA'S [RES] *Philadelphia, PA*
FILOMENA [RES] *Washington, DC*
FIREPLACE [RES] *Scranton, PA*
FISHERMAN'S INN AND CRAB DECK [RES] *Chesapeake Bay Bridge Area, MD*
FISH MARKET [RES] *Alexandria, VA*
FLAMING PIT [RES] *Gaithersburg, MD*
FOONG LIN [RES] *Bethesda, MD*
FORD'S COLONY [RES] *Williamsburg, VA*
FORK [RES] *Philadelphia, PA*
FORTUNE [RES] *Dulles Intl Airport Area, VA*
FOUNDERS, THE [RES] *Philadelphia, PA*
FOUNTAIN RESTAURANT [RES] *Philadelphia, PA*
FOUR AND TWENTY BLACKBIRDS [RES] *Washington, VA*
FRAN O'BRIEN'S STADIUM STEAK HOUSE [RES] *Washington, DC*
FRASCATI [RES] *Bethesda, MD*
FRATELLI [RES] *Washington, DC*
FRED'S [RES] *Annapolis, MD*
FREEMASON ABBEY [RES] *Norfolk, VA*
FROG AND THE REDNECK, THE [RES] *Richmond, VA*
FULLMOON SALOON [RES] *Rehoboth Beach, DE*
GABRIEL [RES] *Washington, DC*
GABRIEL'S [RES] *Frederick, MD*
GADSBY'S TAVERN [RES] *Alexandria, VA*
GALILEO [RES] *Washington, DC*
GAMBLE MILL TAVERN [RES] *Bellefonte, PA*

GARDEN AND THE SEA INN, THE
[RES] *Chincoteague, VA*
GARRETT'S [RES] *Washington, DC*
GAZEBO HOUSE OF PANCAKES [RES]
Williamsburg, VA
GENO'S [URD] *Philadelphia, PA*
GEORGETOWN INN [RES] *Pittsburgh,
PA*
GEORGIA BROWN'S [RES]
Washington, DC
GERANIO [RES] *Alexandria, VA*
GERARD'S PLACE [RES] *Washington,
DC*
GERMANO'S TRATTORIA [RES]
Baltimore, MD
GILLIGAN'S [RES] *Lewes, DE*
GINGERBREAD MAN [RES]
Gettysburg, PA
GIUSEPPE'S [RES] *Williamsburg, VA*
GOLDEN BULL GRAND CAFE [RES]
Gaithersburg, MD
GOLDEN PHEASANT INN [RES] *New
Hope, PA*
GOODFELLAS [RES] *Charlottesville,
VA*
GRACIE'S 21ST CENTURY CAFE [RES]
Pottstown, PA
GRAND CONCOURSE [RES]
Pittsburgh, PA
GREENBRIER MAIN DINING ROOM,
THE [RES] *White Sulphur
Springs, WV*
GREEN HILLS INN [RES] *Reading, PA*
GREEN ROOM [RES] *Wilmington, DE*
GREEN TREE [RES] *Leesburg, VA*
GRIFFIN'S [RES] *Annapolis, MD*
GRILL FROM IPANEMA [RES]
Washington, DC
GROFF'S FARM RESTAURANT [RES]
Lancaster, PA
GUAPO'S [RES] *Washington, DC*
GUARDS [RES] *Washington, DC*
GYPSY ROSE [RES] *Limerick, PA*
HAAD THAI [RES] *Washington, DC*
HAAG'S HOTEL [RES] *Shartlesville, PA*
HAANDI [RES] *Bethesda, MD*
HAANDI [RES] *Falls Church, VA*
HALF WAY HOUSE [RES] *Richmond,
VA*
HAMPTON'S [RES] *Baltimore, MD*
HANNA'S MARINA DECK [RES] *Ocean
City, MD*
HARBOUR LIGHTS [RES] *St. Michael's,
MD*
HARD TIMES CAFE [URD] *Alexandria,
VA*
HARD TIMES CAFE [URD] *Rockville,
MD*
HARDWARE STORE [RES]
Charlottesville, VA

HARPOON HANNA'S [RES] *Fenwick
Island, DE*
HARRIS CRAB HOUSE [RES]
Chesapeake Bay Bridge Area, MD
HARRISON'S HARBOR WATCH [RES]
Ocean City, MD
HARRY BROWNE'S [RES] *Annapolis,
MD*
HARRY'S SAVOY GRILL [RES]
Wilmington, DE
HAYDN ZUG'S [RES] *Lancaster, PA*
HEART-IN-HAND [RES] *Fairfax, VA*
HELEN'S [RES] *Donegal, PA*
HELEN'S [RES] *Richmond, VA*
HENNINGER'S TAVERN [RES]
Baltimore, MD
HERITAGE STATION [RES]
Huntington, WV
HERMAN'S HARBOR HOUSE [RES]
Newport News, VA
HERMITAGE INN [RES] *Fairfax, VA*
HERO'S AMERICAN [RES] *Manassas,
VA*
HERR TAVERN & PUBLICK HOUSE,
THE [RES] *Gettysburg, PA*
HIGH COUNTRY [RES] *Blue Ridge
Parkway, VA*
HOBBIT [RES] *Ocean City, MD*
HOGATE'S [RES] *Washington, DC*
HOTEL STRASBURG [RES] *Strasburg,
VA*
HOT ROD CAFE MONTICELLO [RES]
Sharon, PA
HOUSE OF CHANG PEKING II [RES]
Altoona, PA
HUNAN CHINATOWN [RES]
Washington, DC
HUNAN LION [RES] *Tyson's Corner,
VA*
HUNTER'S TAVERN [RES] *Easton, MD*
HYEHOLDE [RES] *Pittsburgh Intl
Airport Area, PA*
IKAROS [RES] *Baltimore, MD*
IL BORGO [RES] *McLean, VA*
IL CIGNO [RES] *Dulles Intl Airport
Area, VA*
IL FORNO PIZZERIA [RES]
Gaithersburg, MD
IL GIARDINO [RES] *Virginia Beach, VA*
IL PIZZICO [RES] *Rockville, MD*
IL PORTO [RES] *Alexandria, VA*
INDIA GARDEN [RES] *Pittsburgh, PA*
INDIAN FIELDS TAVERN [RES]
Williamsburg, VA
INDIA PALACE [RES] *Wilmington, DE*
INDOCHINE [RES] *Richmond, VA*
INLET [RES] *Virginia Beach, VA*
INN AT LITTLE WASHINGTON, THE
[RES] *Washington, VA*
INN AT PHILLIPS MILL [RES] *New
Hope, PA*

INN OF THE FALCON [RES]
Bethlehem, PA
IRONHORSE [RES] Ashland, VA
ITALIAN BISTRO [RES] Philadelphia,
PA
IVY INN [RES] Charlottesville, VA
JAKE'S RESTAURANT [RES]
Philadelphia, PA
JALEO [RES] Washington, DC
JEAN-MICHEL [RES] Bethesda, MD
JEANNE'S [RES] Lynchburg, VA
JEANNIER'S [RES] Baltimore, MD
JEAN PIERRE'S [RES] New Hope, PA
JEFFERSON, THE [RES] Washington,
DC
JEFFERSON HOUSE, THE [RES]
Norristown, PA
JEFFERSON INN [RES] Williamsburg,
VA
JENNY'S [RES] New Hope, PA
J G COOK'S RIVERVIEW INN [RES]
Wilmington, DE
J GILBERT'S STEAKHOUSE [RES]
McLean, VA
JIMMY TSANG'S [RES] Pittsburgh, PA
JIM REID'S [RES] Clarksburg, WV
JOE FAZIO'S SPAGHETTI HOUSE
[RES] Charleston, WV
JOHANSSON'S [RES] Westminster, MD
JOHN STEVEN, LTD. [RES] Baltimore,
MD
JOHNSTON'S INN [RES] Princeton,
WV
JOSEPH AMBLER INN [RES] Willow
Grove, PA
JOSEPH POON [RES] Philadelphia, PA
JOY AMERICA CAFE [RES] Baltimore,
MD
J. PAUL'S [RES] Washington, DC
J. R.'S GOODTIMES [RES] McLean, VA
JUNCTION 808 [RES] Hagerstown, MD
J.W.'S STEAKHOUSE [RES] Arlington
County (Ronald Reagan
Washington-National Airport
Area), VA
KABUKI JAPANESE STEAK HOUSE
[RES] Roanoke, VA
KABUL CARAVAN [RES] Arlington
County (Ronald Reagan
Washington-National Airport
Area), VA
KABUTO JAPANESE HOUSE OF
STEAK [URD] Richmond, VA
KANSAS CITY PRIME [RES]
Philadelphia, PA
KAWASAKI [RES] Baltimore, MD
KAYA [RES] Pittsburgh, PA
KAZAN [RES] McLean, VA

KENNEDY-SUPPLEE MANSION [RES]
Valley Forge National Historical
Park, PA
KENNETT SQUARE INN [RES] Kennett
Square, PA
KID SHELLEENS [RES] Wilmington,
DE
KIMBERTON INN [RES] Valley Forge
National Historical Park, PA
KING'S ARMS TAVERN [RES]
Williamsburg, VA
KING'S CONTRIVANCE [RES]
Columbia, MD
KINKEAD'S [RES] Washington, DC
KIRK'S [RES] Hinton, WV
KITCHEN AT POWHATAN [RES]
Williamsburg, VA
KLONDIKE KATE'S [RES] Newark, DE
KNAVE OF HEARTS [RES]
Philadelphia, PA
KNIGHT HOUSE [RES] Doylestown
(Bucks County), PA
KOBALT [RES] Washington, DC
KRAZY KAT'S [RES] Wilmington, DE
KRUPIN'S [RES] Washington, DC
KYOTO [RES] Chesapeake, VA
KYOTO JAPANESE STEAK AND
SEAFOOD HOUSE [RES]
Williamsburg, VA
LA BERGERIE [RES] Alexandria, VA
LA CHAUMIERE [RES] Washington,
DC
LA COLLINE [RES] Washington, DC
LA COTE D'OR CAFE [RES] Arlington
County (Ronald Reagan
Washington-National Airport
Area), VA
LA FAMIGLIA [RES] Philadelphia, PA
LAFAYETTE [RES] Washington, DC
LA FERME [RES] Bethesda, MD
LA FOURCHETTE [RES] Washington,
DC
LA GALLERIA [RES] Norfolk, VA
LA LA LAND [RES] Rehoboth Beach,
DE
LA MICHE [RES] Bethesda, MD
LAMP POST [RES] Rehoboth Beach, DE
LANDINI BROTHERS [RES]
Alexandria, VA
LANDMARK CRAB HOUSE [RES]
Chincoteague, VA
LANDMARK STEAKHOUSE [RES]
Lynchburg, VA
LA PETITE AUBERGE [RES]
Fredericksburg, VA
LA PETIT FRANCE [RES] Richmond,
VA
LA PIAZZA CAFE [RES] Quakertown
(Bucks County), PA

LA PROVENCE [RES] *Tyson's Corner, VA*
LA SCALA [RES] *Baltimore, MD*
LA TRELLIS [RES] *Williamsburg, VA*
L'AUBERGE CHEZ FRANCOIS [RES] *McLean, VA*
L'AUBERGE PROVENCAL [RES] *Winchester, VA*
LAUREL BRIGADE INN [RES] *Leesburg, VA*
LAURIOL PLAZA [RES] *Washington, DC*
LAURY'S [RES] *Charleston, WV*
LAVANDOU [RES] *Washington, DC*
L'AVVENTURA [RES] *Charlottesville, VA*
LEBANESE TAVERNA [RES] *Washington, DC*
LE BAR LYONNAIS [RES] *Philadelphia, PA*
LE BEC-FIN [RES] *Philadelphia, PA*
LE CANARD [RES] *Tyson's Corner, VA*
LE CHAMBORD [RES] *Virginia Beach, VA*
LEE'S [RES] *Stroudsburg, PA*
LEESBURG COLONIAL INN [RES] *Leesburg, VA*
LEGAL SEAFOODS [RES] *Washington, DC*
LE GAULOIS [RES] *Alexandria, VA*
LEMAIRE [RES] *Richmond, VA*
LE MONT [RES] *Pittsburgh, PA*
LE POMMIER [RES] *Pittsburgh, PA*
LE REFUGE [RES] *Alexandria, VA*
LES HALLES [RES] *Washington, DC*
LE VIEUX LOGIS [RES] *Bethesda, MD*
LEWNES' STEAKHOUSE [RES] *Annapolis, MD*
LE YACA [RES] *Williamsburg, VA*
LIBERATORE'S [RES] *Towson, MD*
LIBRARY [RES] *Roanoke, VA*
LIGHTHOUSE [RES] *Lewes, DE*
LIGHTHOUSE, THE [RES] *Virginia Beach, VA*
LINWOOD'S CAFE [RES] *Pikesville, MD*
LITTLE ITALY [RES] *Cape Charles, VA*
LITTLE VIET GARDEN [RES] *Arlington County (Ronald Reagan Washington-National Airport Area), VA*
LOCKS POINTE [RES] *Chesapeake, VA*
LOG CABIN [RES] *Lancaster, PA*
LOG HOUSE [RES] *Wytheville, VA*
LONDON GRILLE [RES] *Pittsburgh, PA*
LOS SARAPES [RES] *Doylestown (Bucks County), PA*
LOTUS INN [RES] *King of Prussia, PA*
LOWERY'S SEAFOOD RESTAURANT [RES] *Tappahannock, VA*

LUCKY STAR [RES] *Virginia Beach, VA*
LUIGINO [RES] *Washington, DC*
LYNNHAVEN FISH HOUSE [RES] *Virginia Beach, VA*
LYNNHAVEN INN [RES] *New Castle, DE*
MAESTRO [RES] *Tyson's Corner, VA*
MAHARAJA [RES] *Charlottesville, VA*
MAIN DINING ROOM [RES] *Charlottesville, VA*
MAINLAND INN [RES] *Kulpsville, PA*
MAIN STREET DEPOT [RES] *Bethlehem, PA*
MAKOTO RESTAURANT [RES] *Washington, DC*
MANADA HILL INN [RES] *Harrisburg, PA*
MANAYUNK BREWING CO [RES] *Philadelphia, PA*
MANDARIN TANG [RES] *Easton, PA*
MANGO MIKE'S [RES] *Alexandria, VA*
MARCO POLO [RES] *Tyson's Corner, VA*
MARKER RESTAURANT & LOUNGE [RES] *Philadelphia, PA*
MARKET INN [RES] *Washington, DC*
MARKET STREET BAR AND GRILL [RES] *Dulles Intl Airport Area, VA*
MATUBA [RES] *Arlington County (Ronald Reagan Washington-National Airport Area), VA*
MATUBA [RES] *Bethesda, MD*
MAX, THE [RES] *Norfolk, VA*
MAX & ERMA'S [RES] *Pittsburgh, PA*
MAX'S ALLEGHENY TAVERN [RES] *Pittsburgh, PA*
MAYFLOWER I [RES] *Bluefield, WV*
MCCORMICK AND SCHMICK'S [RES] *Washington, DC*
MEETING PLACE [RES] *Brookville, PA*
MELITTA'S GASTHAUS [RES] *Petersburg, VA*
MELROSE [RES] *Washington, DC*
MENDENHALL INN [RES] *Kennett Square, PA*
MENDOCINO GRILL AND WINE BAR [RES] *Washington, DC*
MERCERSBURG INN [RES] *Chambersburg, PA*
MESKEREM [RES] *Washington, DC*
MICHAEL'S [RES] *Philadelphia, PA*
MIDDLETON TAVERN [RES] *Annapolis, MD*
MIKE'S AMERICAN GRILL [RES] *Springfield, VA*
MILLIE'S [RES] *Richmond, VA*
MILTON INN, THE [RES] *Cockeysville, MD*
MINARD'S SPAGHETTI INN [RES] *Clarksburg, WV*

MINSI TRAIL INN [RES] *Bethlehem, PA*
MONASTERY [RES] *Norfolk, VA*
MONOCLE [RES] *Washington, DC*
MONROE'S [RES] *Alexandria, VA*
MONTE CARLO LIVING ROOM [RES]
   Philadelphia, PA
MONTEREY BAY FISH GROTTO [RES]
   Pittsburgh, PA
MONTGOMERY'S GRILLE [RES]
   Bethesda, MD
MOONSTRUCK [RES] *Philadelphia, PA*
MORRISON-CLARK [RES] *Washington,
   DC*
MORTON'S OF CHICAGO [RES]
   Tyson's Corner, VA
MORTON'S OF CHICAGO [RES]
   Washington, DC
MOUNTAIN CREEK [RES] *Hinton, WV*
MOUNTAINEER FAMILY
   RESTAURANT [RES]
   Parkersburg, WV
MOUNT VERNON INN [RES] *Mount
   Vernon, VA*
MT. WASHINGTON TAVERN [RES]
   Baltimore, MD
MRS. K'S TOLL HOUSE [RES] *Silver
   Spring, MD*
MR. SMITH'S [RES] *Washington, DC*
MR. YUNG'S [RES] *Washington, DC*
MURIALE'S [RES] *Fairmont, WV*
MURPHY'S OF D.C. [RES]
   Washington, DC
NAIS CUISINE [RES] *Philadelphia, PA*
NAM'S [RES] *Bethesda, MD*
NAPOLEON'S [RES] *Warrenton, VA*
NARROWS [RES] *Chesapeake Bay
   Bridge Area, MD*
NATHAN'S [RES] *Washington, DC*
NEW HEIGHTS [RES] *Washington, DC*
NEW SMITHVILLE COUNTRY INN
   [RES] *Kutztown, PA*
NICK'S SEAFOOD PAVILION [RES]
   Yorktown, VA
NINO BARSOTTI'S [RES] *Donegal, PA*
NIZAM'S [RES] *Tyson's Corner, VA*
NORMANDIE FARM [RES] *Rockville,
   MD*
NORTHWOODS [RES] *Annapolis, MD*
OAKHURST TEA ROOM [RES]
   Somerset, PA
OAK SUPPER CLUB [RES] *Hinton, WV*
OBELISK [RES] *Washington, DC*
OBRYCKI'S CRAB HOUSE [RES]
   Baltimore, MD
OCCIDENTAL GRILL [RES]
   Washington, DC
OCEAN CLUB [RES] *Ocean City, MD*
ODETTE'S [RES] *New Hope, PA*
O'DONNELL'S [RES] *Bethesda, MD*

OLD ANGLER'S INN [RES] *Rockville,
   MD*
OLD CHICKAHOMINY HOUSE [RES]
   Williamsburg, VA
OLD EBBITT GRILL [RES] *Washington,
   DC*
OLDE GREENFIELD INN [RES]
   Lancaster, PA
OLDE MUDD TAVERN [RES]
   Fredericksburg, VA
OLD EUROPE [RES] *Washington, DC*
OLD MILL ROOM [RES]
   Charlottesville, VA
OLD PHARMACY CAFE [RES]
   Shepherdstown, WV
OLD SOUTH MOUNTAIN INN [RES]
   Boonsboro (Garrett County), MD
OLD WHARF INN [RES] *Chesapeake
   Bay Bridge Area, MD*
O'LEARY'S SEAFOOD [RES] *Annapolis,
   MD*
OPUS 251 [RES] *Philadelphia, PA*
OREGON GRILLE, THE [RES]
   Cockeysville, MD
ORIGINAL BOOKBINDER'S, THE
   [RES] *Richmond, VA*
ORIGINAL PANCAKE HOUSE [RES]
   Bethesda, MD
O'TOOLES [RES] *Richmond, VA*
OTTO'S BRAUHAUS [RES] *Willow
   Grove, PA*
OVAL ROOM [RES] *Washington, DC*
OVERTURES [RES] *Philadelphia, PA*
PALACE OF ASIA [RES] *Ft Washington,
   PA*
PALM, THE [RES] *Philadelphia, PA*
PALM [RES] *Washington, DC*
PALM COURT [RES] *Dulles Intl Airport
   Area, VA*
PALOMA [RES] *Philadelphia, PA*
PANINO [RES] *Manassas, VA*
PANJSHIR [RES] *Falls Church, VA*
PANJSHIR II [RES] *Tyson's Corner, VA*
PAOLO'S [RES] *Washington, DC*
PARKHURST [RES] *Luray, VA*
PASION! [RES] *Philadelphia, PA*
PASTA PIATTO [RES] *Pittsburgh, PA*
PEACOCK ON THE PARKWAY [RES]
   Philadelphia, PA
PEAKS OF OTTER [RES] *Blue Ridge
   Parkway, VA*
PEARLY BAKER'S ALE HOUSE [RES]
   Easton, PA
PEERCE'S PLANTATION [RES]
   Towson, MD
PEKING [RES] *Williamsburg, VA*
PEKING CHEERS [RES] *Gaithersburg,
   MD*
PEKING GOURMET INN [RES] *Falls
   Church, VA*

PEKING PAVILION [RES] *Richmond, VA*
PEKING SUPREME [RES] *Gaithersburg, MD*
PENN ALPS [RES] *Grantsville, MD*
PENN BREWERY [RES] *Pittsburgh, PA*
PESCE [RES] *Washington, DC*
PHILADELPHIA FISH [RES] *Philadelphia, PA*
PHILIPPI INN [RES] *Philippi, WV*
PHILLIPS CRAB HOUSE [RES] *Ocean City, MD*
PHILLIPS' FLAGSHIP [URD] *Washington, DC*
PHILLIPS SEAFOOD GRILL [RES] *Tyson's Corner, VA*
PHILLIPS SEAFOOD HOUSE [RES] *Ocean City, MD*
PICCOLO MONDO [RES] *Pittsburgh, PA*
PICCOLO MONDO [RES] *Wilmington, DE*
PIERPOINT [RES] *Baltimore, MD*
PILIN THAI [RES] *Falls Church, VA*
PINE BARN INN [RES] *Danville, PA*
PINE GRILL [RES] *Somerset, PA*
PIZZERIA PARADISO [RES] *Washington, DC*
P. J. SKIDOO'S [RES] *Fairfax, VA*
PLAIN AND FANCY FARM [RES] *Bird-in-Hand, PA*
PLOUGH & THE STARS [RES] *Philadelphia, PA*
POD [RES] *Philadelphia, PA*
POINT OF VIEW [RES] *Parkersburg, WV*
POINT VIEW INN [RES] *Oakland (Garrett County), MD*
POLI [RES] *Pittsburgh, PA*
POLO GRILL [RES] *Baltimore, MD*
PORT ARTHUR [RES] *Newport News, VA*
POSITANO [RES] *Wilmington, DE*
POWERHOUSE [RES] *White Haven, PA*
PRIMANTI BROTHERS [RES] *Pittsburgh, PA*
PRIME RIB [RES] *Baltimore, MD*
PRIME RIB [RES] *Washington, DC*
PRIME RIB HOUSE [RES] *Williamsburg, VA*
PRIMI PIATTI [RES] *Tyson's Corner, VA*
PRIMI PIATTI [RES] *Washington, DC*
PRINCE MICHEL [RES] *Culpeper, VA*
PUFFERBELLY [RES] *Erie, PA*
PUGLIONI'S [RES] *Morgantown, WV*
PULCINELLA [RES] *McLean, VA*
PULLMAN RESTAURANT, THE [RES] *Staunton, VA*
PUMP HOUSE INN [RES] *Canadensis, PA*

PUNGO GRILL [RES] *Virginia Beach, VA*
QUAKER STEAK & LUBE [RES] *Sharon, PA*
QUEEN BEE [RES] *Arlington County (Ronald Reagan Washington-National Airport Area), VA*
RAKU [RES] *Bethesda, MD*
RAKU [RES] *Washington, DC*
RANGOON BURMESE RESTAURANT [RES] *Philadelphia, PA*
REBELS & REDCOATS TAVERN [RES] *Huntington, WV*
RED HORSE STEAK HOUSE [RES] *Hagerstown, MD*
RED HOT AND BLUE [RES] *Arlington County (Ronald Reagan Washington-National Airport Area), VA*
RED HOT & BLUE [RES] *Rockville, MD*
RED SAGE [RES] *Washington, DC*
RED TOMATO CAFE [RES] *Bethesda, MD*
REDWOOD [RES] *Lexington, VA*
REGENCY DINING ROOM [RES] *Williamsburg, VA*
RENATO [RES] *Fredericksburg, VA*
RESTAURANT 821 [RES] *Wilmington, DE*
RESTAURANT NORA [RES] *Washington, DC*
RESTAURANT SCHOOL, THE [URD] *Philadelphia, PA*
RICCIUTI'S [RES] *Rockville, MD*
RICHARDSON'S [RES] *Hagerstown, MD*
RICO'S [RES] *Pittsburgh, PA*
RISTORANTE PANORAMA [RES] *Philadelphia, PA*
RITZ-CARLTON, THE GRILL [RES] *Arlington County (Ronald Reagan Washington-National Airport Area), VA*
RITZ-CARLTON, THE RESTAURANT [RES] *Tyson's Corner, VA*
RIVER'S INN [RES] *Yorktown, VA*
ROCCO CAPRICCIO [RES] *Baltimore, MD*
ROCK BOTTOM BREWERY [RES] *Bethesda, MD*
ROCOCO [RES] *Philadelphia, PA*
ROCOCO'S [RES] *Charlottesville, VA*
ROLLER'S [URD] *Philadelphia, PA*
ROOF TERRACE [RES] *Washington, DC*
ROTHWELL'S GRILLE [RES] *Towson, MD*
ROUGE 2003 [RES] *Philadelphia, PA*
ROWE'S [RES] *Staunton, VA*
ROY'S PLACE [RES] *Gaithersburg, MD*
R. T.'S [RES] *Alexandria, VA*

R. T.'S SEAFOOD KITCHEN [RES]
Arlington County (Ronald Reagan
Washington-National Airport
Area), VA
RUBY LOUNGE [RES] Baltimore, MD
RUDEE'S [RES] Virginia Beach, VA
RUDY'S 2900 [RES] Westminster, MD
RUSSIA HOUSE [RES] Dulles Intl
Airport Area, VA
RUSTY RUDDER [RES] Rehoboth
Beach, DE
RUTH'S CHRIS STEAK HOUSE [RES]
Baltimore, MD
RUTH'S CHRIS STEAKHOUSE [RES]
Bethesda, MD
RUTH'S CHRIS STEAK HOUSE [RES]
Richmond, VA
SABER ROOM [RES] Wilkes-Barre, PA
SACHIKO'S PORTERHOUSE [RES]
Lynchburg, VA
SAIGON GOURMET [RES]
Washington, DC
SAIGONNAIS [RES] Washington, DC
ST. MICHAEL'S CRAB HOUSE [RES]
St. Michael's, MD
SALOON, THE [RES] Philadelphia, PA
SAM AND HARRY'S [RES] Washington,
DC
SAM MILLER'S WAREHOUSE [RES]
Richmond, VA
SAMMY AND NICK'S [RES] Hampton,
VA
SAM SNEAD'S TAVERN [RES] Hot
Springs, VA
SAN ANTONIO SAM'S [RES] Virginia
Beach, VA
SAN CARLO'S [RES] York, PA
SANTA FE CAFE [RES] College Park,
MD
SANTA FE EAST [RES] Alexandria, VA
SASSAFRAS [URD] Philadelphia, PA
SCALE O' DE WHALE [RES]
Portsmouth, VA
SCHAEFER'S CANAL HOUSE [RES]
Elkton, MD
SCHNITZELHOUSE [RES]
Charlottesville, VA
SCOTLAND YARD [RES] Alexandria,
VA
SEA CATCH [RES] Washington, DC
SEASONS [RES] Washington, DC
SEASONS CAFE [RES] Williamsburg,
VA
SEAWELL'S ORDINARY [RES]
Gloucester, VA
SECRET GARDEN BEEWON [RES]
Falls Church, VA
SEQUOIA [RES] Washington, DC
SERBIAN CROWN [RES] McLean, VA

SERRANO [RES] Philadelphia, PA
SETTLERS INN, THE [RES] Hawley, PA
SEVEN SEAS [RES] Rockville, MD
SEVEN STARS INN [RES] Valley Forge
National Historical Park, PA
SEVENTH STREET GRILLE [RES]
Pittsburgh, PA
SHANGHAI [RES] Salem, VA
SHIELDS TAVERN [RES] Williamsburg,
VA
SHIP'S CABIN [RES] Norfolk, VA
SIAM ASIAN BISTRO [RES] Dulles Intl
Airport Area, VA
SIDESTREETS [RES] Ellicott City, MD
SIGN OF THE SORREL HORSE [RES]
Doylestown (Bucks County), PA
SILK PURSE & SOW'S EAR [RES]
Wilmington, DE
SILVER DINER [RES] Arlington County
(Ronald Reagan Washington-
National Airport Area), VA
SILVER DINER [RES] Rockville, MD
SIR WALTER RALEIGH [RES]
Gaithersburg, MD
SIR WALTER RALEIGH INN [RES]
Falls Church, VA
SKILLIGALEE [RES] Richmond, VA
SMOKEY PIG [RES] Ashland, VA
SOBA LOUNGE [RES] Pittsburgh, PA
SONOMA [RES] Philadelphia, PA
SOTTO SOPRA [RES] Baltimore, MD
SOUTH AUSTIN GRILL [RES]
Alexandria, VA
SOUTH STREET DINER [RES]
Philadelphia, PA
SPIKE AND CHARLIE'S [RES]
Baltimore, MD
SPOTTED HOG [RES] New Hope, PA
SPRING HOUSE TAVERN [RES]
Woodstock, VA
STAZI MILANO [RES] Jenkintown, PA
STEAMERS SEAFOOD [RES]
Chincoteague, VA
STEELHEAD GRILL [RES] Pittsburgh,
PA
STEPHEN'S [RES] Philadelphia, PA
STONEBAR INN [RES] Stroudsburg, PA
STRAWBERRY STREET CAFE [RES]
Richmond, VA
STRIPED BASS [RES] Philadelphia, PA
SUNNYBROOK INN [RES] Roanoke,
VA
SUN PORCH [RES] Uniontown, PA
SURF N' TURF [RES] Johnstown, PA
SUSANNA FOO [RES] Philadelphia, PA
SUSHI-KO [RES] Washington, DC
SUSHI TWO [RES] Pittsburgh, PA
SWANN CAFE [RES] Philadelphia, PA
SWANN LOUNGE [URD] Philadelphia,
PA

SWEETWATER TAVERN [RES] *Dulles Intl Airport Area, VA*
SYDNEY'S SIDE STREET [RES] *Rehoboth Beach, DE*
TABERNA DEL ALABARDERO [RES] *Washington, DC*
TABOO [RES] *Chesapeake, VA*
TACHIBANA [RES] *McLean, VA*
TAMBELLINI [RES] *Pittsburgh, PA*
TANDOM'S PINE TREE INN [RES] *Virginia Beach, VA*
TANGERINE [URD] *Philadelphia, PA*
TANGLEWOOD ORDINARY [RES] *Richmond, VA*
TAQUET [RES] *King of Prussia, PA*
TARA THAI [RES] *Bethesda, MD*
TARA THAI [RES] *Tyson's Corner, VA*
TASTE OF SAIGON [RES] *Rockville, MD*
TAURASO'S [RES] *Frederick, MD*
TAVERN, THE [RES] *Abingdon, VA*
TAVERN [RES] *State College, PA*
TAVERN, THE [RES] *West Middlesex, PA*
TAVERNA CRETEKOU [RES] *Alexandria, VA*
TAVERN BY THE LAKE [RES] *Mount Pocono, PA*
TAVERN ROOM, THE [RES] *White Sulphur Springs, WV*
TAVOLA TOSCANA [RES] *Wilmington, DE*
T. C. TROTTER'S [RES] *Lynchburg, VA*
TEATRO GOLDONI [RES] *Washington, DC*
TEL-AVIV CAFE [RES] *Bethesda, MD*
TEMPO [RES] *Alexandria, VA*
TERRACE [RES] *Kennett Square, PA*
TERRACE ROOM [URD] *Pittsburgh, PA*
TERSIGUEL'S [RES] *Ellicott City, MD*
TESSARO'S [RES] *Pittsburgh, PA*
THAI HUT [RES] *Alexandria, VA*
THAI KINGDOM [RES] *Washington, DC*
THAI PLACE [RES] *Pittsburgh, PA*
THAT'S AMORE [RES] *Rockville, MD*
THAT'S AMORE [RES] *Towson, MD*
THAT'S AMORE [RES] *Tyson's Corner, VA*
THAT SEAFOOD PLACE [RES] *Williamsburg, VA*
THOMAS ENGLAND HOUSE [RES] *Smyrna, DE*
THYME SQUARE [RES] *Bethesda, MD*
TIJUANA TAXI [RES] *Rehoboth Beach, DE*
TIN ANGEL [RES] *Pittsburgh, PA*
TIO PEPE [RES] *Baltimore, MD*

TIVOLI [RES] *Arlington County (Ronald Reagan Washington-National Airport Area), VA*
TOBACCO COMPANY [RES] *Richmond, VA*
TODD JURICH'S BISTRO [RES] *Norfolk, VA*
TOKYO TEAHOUSE [RES] *Mount Pocono, PA*
TOM & TERRY'S [RES] *Fenwick Island, DE*
TOMBS [RES] *Washington, DC*
TOM SARRIS' ORLEANS HOUSE [RES] *Arlington County (Ronald Reagan Washington-National Airport Area), VA*
TOM'S KITCHEN [RES] *Hazleton, PA*
TONY AND JOE'S SEAFOOD PLACE [RES] *Washington, DC*
TONY CHENG'S MONGOLIAN BARBECUE [RES] *Washington, DC*
TORTILLA FACTORY [RES] *Dulles Intl Airport Area, VA*
TOSCANA CUCINA RUSTICA [RES] *Philadelphia, PA*
TOWN AND COUNTRY GRILLE [RES] *King of Prussia, PA*
TRAGARA [RES] *Bethesda, MD*
TRAK'S [RES] *Richmond, VA*
TREATY OF PARIS [RES] *Annapolis, MD*
TWO QUAIL [RES] *Washington, DC*
UMBRIA [RES] *Philadelphia, PA*
UNCLE LOUIE'S [RES] *Norfolk, VA*
UNION CANAL HOUSE [RES] *Hershey, PA*
UNION STREET PUBLIC HOUSE [RES] *Alexandria, VA*
UPPER DECK [RES] *Pocomoke City, MD*
VEGA GRILL [RES] *Philadelphia, PA*
VELLEGGIA'S [RES] *Baltimore, MD*
VERMONT FLATBREAD CO [RES] *Pittsburgh, PA*
VETRI [RES] *Philadelphia, PA*
VICINO [RES] *Silver Spring, MD*
VICKERS [RES] *Downingtown, PA*
VICTORIAN MANOR [RES] *State College, PA*
VIDALIA [RES] *Washington, DC*
VILLA D'ESTE [RES] *Alexandria, VA*
VILLAGE BISTRO [RES] *Arlington County (Ronald Reagan Washington-National Airport Area), VA*
VILLAGE INN [RES] *Dover, DE*
VILLA STRAFFORD [RES] *King of Prussia, PA*
VINCENTE'S [RES] *Wilmington, DE*
VINEYARD [RES] *Bristol, VA*

WARNER'S GERMAN RESTAURANT [RES] *Cumberland, MD*

WASHINGTON HOUSE [RES] *Lancaster, PA*

WASHINGTON HOUSE [RES] *Quakertown (Bucks County), PA*

WATERMAN'S [RES] *Virginia Beach, VA*

WATERMAN'S CRAB HOUSE [RES] *Chesapeake Bay Bridge Area, MD*

WATERWHEEL [RES] *Warm Springs, VA*

WATERWORKS CAFE [RES] *Wilmington, DE*

WAYNE'S BAR-B-QUE [RES] *Baltimore, MD*

WAYSIDE INN [RES] *Smyrna, DE*

WELLINGTON'S [RES] *Nitro, WV*

WHALING COMPANY [RES] *Williamsburg, VA*

WHARF [RES] *Alexandria, VA*

WHITE DOG CAFE [RES] *Philadelphia, PA*

WILD ONION [RES] *King of Prussia, PA*

WILKINSON'S TAVERN [RES] *Strasburg, VA*

WILLARD ROOM [RES] *Washington, DC*

WILLIAM PENN INN [RES] *Norristown, PA*

WILLSON-WALKER HOUSE [RES] *Lexington, VA*

WINFIELD'S [RES] *Dulles Intl Airport Area, VA*

WOODEN ANGEL [RES] *Beaver Falls, PA*

WOO LAE OAK [RES] *Arlington County (Ronald Reagan Washington-National Airport Area), VA*

WU'S GARDEN [RES] *Tyson's Corner, VA*

YELLOW BRICK BANK & LITTLE INN [RES] *Shepherdstown, WV*

YEN CHING [RES] *Richmond, VA*

YE OLDE CONCORDVILLE INN [RES] *West Chester, PA*

YORK INN [RES] *Cockeysville, MD*

YORKSHIRE STEAK AND SEAFOOD HOUSE [RES] *Williamsburg, VA*

ZED'S ETHIOPIAN CUISINE [RES] *Washington, DC*

ZOCALO [RES] *Philadelphia, PA*

CITY INDEX

Aberdeen, MD, 85
Abingdon, VA, 355
Alexandria, VA, 256
Allentown, PA, 171
Altoona, PA, 174
Ambridge, PA, 175
Annapolis, MD, 85
Appomattox Court House National
    Historical Park, VA, 364
Arlington County (Ronald Reagan
    Washington-National Airport
    Area), VA, 365
Ashland, PA, 176
Ashland, VA, 372
Aurora, WV, 528
Baltimore, MD, 92
Baltimore/Washington International
    Airport Area, MD, 108
Basye, VA, 374
Beaver Falls, PA, 176
Beckley, WV, 528
Bedford, PA, 177
Bellefonte, PA, 178
Berkeley Springs, WV, 530
Bethany, WV, 532
Bethany Beach, DE, 7
Bethesda, MD, 110
Bethlehem, PA, 178
Big Stone Gap, VA, 374
Bird-in-Hand, PA, 181
Blacksburg, VA, 375
Bloomsburg, PA, 182
Bluefield, WV, 532
Blue Ridge Parkway, VA, 376
Booker T. Washington National Mon-
    ument, VA, 378
Boonsboro (Garrett County), MD,
    115
Bowie, MD, 115
Bradford, PA, 184
Breaks Interstate Park, VA, 379
Breezewood, PA, 184
Bristol, VA, 379
Bristol (Bucks County), PA, 185
Brookneal, VA, 381
Brookville, PA, 186
Buckhannon, WV, 533
Bucks County, PA, 186
Bushkill, PA, 187
Butler, PA, 187
Cambridge, MD, 116
Canadensis, PA, 188
Cape Charles, VA, 381
Cape Henry Memorial, VA, 382

Carbondale, PA, 189
Carlisle, PA, 190
Chambersburg, PA, 192
Charleston, WV, 534
Charles Town, WV, 537
Charlottesville, VA, 382
Chesapeake, VA, 388
Chesapeake and Ohio Canal
    National Historical Park, MD,
    116
Chesapeake and Ohio Canal
    National Historical Park, VA,
    390
Chesapeake and Ohio Canal
    National Historical Park, WV,
    539
Chesapeake Bay Bridge Area, MD,
    117
Chester, PA, 194
Chincoteague, VA, 390
Clarion, PA, 195
Clarksburg, WV, 539
Clarksville, VA, 394
Clearfield (Clearfield County), PA,
    196
Clifton Forge, VA, 394
Cockeysville, MD, 119
College Park, MD, 120
Colonial National Historical Park,
    VA, 395
Colonial Parkway, VA, 395
Columbia, MD, 122
Conneaut Lake, PA, 196
Connellsville, PA, 197
Coraopolis, PA, 198
Cornwall, PA, 198
Covington, VA, 396
Crisfield, MD, 123
Culpeper, VA, 396
Cumberland, MD, 123
Danville, PA, 198
Danville, VA, 397
Davis, WV, 540
Delaware Water Gap, PA, 199
Denver/Adamstown, PA, 200
Donegal, PA, 201
Dover, DE, 7
Downingtown, PA, 201
Doylestown (Bucks County), PA, 203
Du Bois, PA, 204
Dulles Intl Airport Area, VA, 399
Easton, MD, 125
Easton, PA, 205
Ebensburg, PA, 206

Edinboro, PA, 206
Elkins, WV, 541
Elkton, MD, 127
Ellicott City, MD, 128
Emmitsburg, MD, 129
Emporia, VA, 403
Ephrata, PA, 207
Erie, PA, 208
Fairfax, VA, 403
Fairmont, WV, 544
Falls Church, VA, 406
Farmville, VA, 408
Fenwick Island, DE, 10
Fort Delaware State Park, DE, 11
Franklin, WV, 545
Franklin (Venango County), PA, 211
Frederick, MD, 130
Fredericksburg, VA, 408
Fredericksburg and Spotsylvania
    National Military Park, VA,
    414
Front Royal, VA, 414
Ft Washington, PA, 211
Gaithersburg, MD, 133
Galax, VA, 416
Galeton, PA, 212
Gauley Bridge, WV, 545
George Washington Birthplace
    National Monument, VA, 416
Gettysburg, PA, 213
Gettysburg National Military Park,
    PA, 218
Gibsonia, PA, 219
Gloucester, VA, 417
Grafton, WV, 546
Grantsville, MD, 135
Great Dismal Swamp National
    Wildlife Refuge, VA, 417
Greensburg, PA, 219
Hagerstown, MD, 136
Hamburg, PA, 220
Hampton, VA, 418
Hanover, PA, 221
Harmony, PA, 222
Harpers Ferry, WV, 547
Harrisburg, PA, 222
Harrisonburg, VA, 420
Havre de Grace, MD, 138
Hawley, PA, 226
Hazleton, PA, 228
Hershey, PA, 228
Hillsboro, WV, 549
Hinton, WV, 549
Honesdale, PA, 232
Hopewell, VA, 422
Hopewell Furnace National Historic
    Site, PA, 232
Hot Springs, VA, 423
Huntingdon, PA, 233
Huntington, WV, 551
Indiana, PA, 233
Irvington, VA, 424

Jamestown (Colonial National His-
    torical Park), VA, 425
Jenkintown, PA, 234
Jim Thorpe, PA, 235
Johnstown, PA, 235
Kane, PA, 237
Kempton, PA, 237
Kennett Square, PA, 237
Keysville, VA, 427
King of Prussia, PA, 239
Kulpsville, PA, 242
Kutztown, PA, 242
Lancaster, PA, 242
Lancaster, VA, 428
La Plata, MD, 139
Laurel, MD, 139
Lebanon, PA, 249
Leesburg, VA, 428
Leonardtown, MD, 140
Lewes, DE, 11
Lewisburg, PA, 250
Lewisburg, WV, 553
Lewistown, PA, 251
Lexington, VA, 431
Ligonier, PA, 252
Limerick, PA, 252
Lock Haven, PA, 253
Luray, VA, 434
Lynchburg, VA, 436
Manassas, VA, 439
Manassas (Bull Run) National Battle-
    field Park, VA, 441
Manheim, PA, 254
Mansfield, PA, 254
Marion, VA, 442
Marlinton, WV, 554
Martinsburg, WV, 555
Martinsville, VA, 443
McLean, VA, 444
Meadville, PA, 255
Media, PA, 255
Mercer, PA, 256
Milford, PA, 257
Monroeville, PA, 258
Monterey, VA, 446
Montross, VA, 446
Moorefield, WV, 556
Morgantown, WV, 556
Mount Pocono, PA, 258
Mount Vernon, VA, 446
Natural Bridge, VA, 447
Newark, DE, 14
New Castle, DE, 15
New Castle, PA, 260
New Hope, PA, 260
New Market, VA, 448
Newport News, VA, 449
New Stanton, PA, 265
Nitro, WV, 559
Norfolk, VA, 452
Norristown, PA, 266
North East, PA, 267

Oakland (Garrett County), MD, 141
Ocean City, MD, 142
Odessa, DE, 17
Oil City, PA, 267
Orange, VA, 457
Orbisonia, PA, 267
Parkersburg, WV, 560
Pearisburg, VA, 458
Pennsylvania Dutch Area, PA, 268
Pentagon City, VA, 458
Petersburg, VA, 458
Petersburg, WV, 562
Petersburg National Battlefield, VA, 460
Philadelphia, PA, 268
Philippi, WV, 563
Pikesville, MD, 147
Pittsburgh, PA, 294
Pittsburgh Intl Airport Area, PA, 309
Pocomoke City, MD, 148
Point Pleasant, WV, 563
Port Allegany, PA, 311
Portsmouth, VA, 461
Pottstown, PA, 311
Princeton, WV, 564
Quakertown (Bucks County), PA, 313
Radford, VA, 463
Reading, PA, 314
Rehoboth Beach, DE, 17
Reston, VA, 464
Richmond, VA, 464
Richmond National Battlefield Park, VA, 475
Ripley, WV, 565
Roanoke, VA, 476
Rockville, MD, 149
St. Mary's City, MD, 151
St. Michael's, MD, 153
Salem, VA, 480
Salisbury, MD, 156
Scranton, PA, 316
Shamokin Dam, PA, 318
Sharon, PA, 319
Shartlesville, PA, 319
Shawnee on Delaware, PA, 320
Shenandoah National Park, VA, 480
Shepherdstown, WV, 565
Silver Spring, MD, 157
Skyline Drive, VA, 482
Smyrna, DE, 21
Somerset, PA, 320
South Boston, VA, 483
South Hill, VA, 483
Springfield, VA, 483

State College, PA, 323
Staunton, VA, 484
Strasburg, VA, 486
Stroudsburg, PA, 325
Suffolk, VA, 488
Summersville, WV, 567
Surry, VA, 488
Sutton, WV, 568
Tangier Island, VA, 488
Tannersville, PA, 327
Tappahannock, VA, 488
Thurmont, MD, 158
Titusville, PA, 328
Towanda, PA, 328
Towson, MD, 159
Triangle, VA, 489
Tyson's Corner, VA, 489
Uniontown, PA, 329
Valley Forge National Historical Park, PA, 332
Virginia Beach, VA, 493
Waldorf, MD, 161
Warm Springs, VA, 499
Warren, PA, 333
Warrenton, VA, 500
Washington, DC, 31
Washington, PA, 334
Washington, VA, 500
Washington Crossing Historic Park (Bucks County), PA, 335
Waynesboro, VA, 502
Webster Springs, WV, 568
Weirton, WV, 569
Wellsboro, PA, 335
West Chester, PA, 337
West Middlesex, PA, 338
Westminster, MD, 162
Weston, WV, 569
Wheeling, WV, 570
White Haven, PA, 339
White Sulphur Springs, WV, 572
Wilkes-Barre, PA, 340
Williamsburg, VA, 503
Williamson, WV, 574
Williamsport, PA, 341
Willow Grove, PA, 343
Wilmington, DE, 22
Winchester, VA, 513
Wise, VA, 516
Woodstock, VA, 516
Wrightsville (York County), PA, 344
Wytheville, VA, 517
York, PA, 344
Yorktown, VA, 519

Notes

Notes

Mobil Travel Guides

Please check the guides you would like to order:

☐ 0-7627-2619-9
California
$18.95

☐ 0-7627-2618-0
Florida
$18.95

☐ 0-7627-2612-1
Great Lakes
Illinois, Indiana, Michigan,
Ohio, Wisconsin
$18.95

☐ 0-7627-2610-5
Great Plains
Iowa, Kansas, Minnesota,
Missouri, Nebraska, North
Dakota, Oklahoma, South
Dakota
$18.95

☐ 0-7627-2613-X
Mid-Atlantic
Delaware, Maryland,
Pennsylvania, Virginia,
Washington D.C., West
Virginia
$18.95

☐ 0-7627-2614-8
**New England and Eastern
Canada**
Connecticut, Maine, Massachu-
setts, New Hampshire, Rhode
Island, Vermont, Canada
$18.95

☐ 0-7627-2616-4
New York/New Jersey
$18.95

☐ 0-7627-2611-3
Northwest
Idaho, Montana, Oregon, Wash-
ington, Wyoming, Canada
$18.95

☐ 0-7627-2615-6
Southeast
Alabama, Arkansas, Georgia, Ken-
tucky, Louisiana, Mississippi,
North Carolina, South Carolina,
Tennessee
$18.95

☐ 0-7627-2617-2
Southwest
Arizona, Colorado, Nevada, New
Mexico, Texas, Utah
$18.95

Please ship the books above to:

Name: _____

Address: _____

City: _____ State: _____ Zip: _____

Total Cost of Book(s) $_____	☐ Please charge my credit card.
Shipping & Handling $_____ (Please add $3.00 for first book $1.50 for each additional book)	☐ Discover ☐ Visa ☐ MasterCard ☐ American Express
Add 8.75% sales tax $_____	Card #_____
Total Amount $_____	Expiration _____
☐ My Check is enclosed.	Signature _____

Please mail this form to: **Mobil Travel Guides**
1460 Renaissance Drive, Suite 401
Park Ridge, IL 60068

Mobil
Travel Guide®

Northwest
Idaho
Montana
Oregon
Washington
Wyoming
Alberta
British Columbia
Manitoba

Great Plains
Iowa
Kansas
Minnesota
Missouri
Nebraska
North Dakota
Oklahoma
South Dakota

Great Lakes
Illinois
Indiana
Michigan
Ohio
Wisconsin

**New England
Eastern Canada**
Connecticut
Maine
Massachusetts
New Hampshire
Rhode Island
Vermont
New Brunswick
Nova Scotia
Ontario
Prince Edward
  Island
Quebec

California

**New York
New Jersey**

Southwest
Arizona
Colorado
Nevada
New Mexico
Texas
Utah

Southeast
Alabama
Arkansas
Georgia
Kentucky
Louisiana
Mississippi
North Carolina
South Carolina
Tennessee

Florida

Mid-Atlantic
Delaware
Maryland
Pennsylvania
Virginia
Washington, D.C.
West Virginia

Add your opinion!

Help make the Guides even more useful. Tell us about your experiences with the hotels and restaurants listed in the Guides (or ones that should be added).

Find us on the Internet at www.mobiltravelguide.com/feedback

Or copy the form below and mail to Mobil Travel Guides, 1460 Renaissance Drive, Suite 401, Park Ridge, IL 60068. All information will be kept confidential.

Your name _____   Were children with you on trip? ☐ Yes ☐ No

Street _____   Number of people in your party _____

City/State/Zip _____   Your occupation _____

Establishment name_____   ☐ Hotel ☐ Resort ☐ Restaurant
☐ Motel ☐ Inn ☐ Other

Street_____   City_____   State _____

Do you agree with our description? ☐ Yes ☐ No   If not, give reason_____

Please give us your opinion of the following:

Decor	Cleanliness	Service	Food
☐ Excellent	☐ Spotless	☐ Excellent	☐ Excellent
☐ Good	☐ Clean	☐ Good	☐ Good
☐ Fair	☐ Unclean	☐ Fair	☐ Fair
☐ Poor	☐ Dirty	☐ Poor	☐ Poor

2003 Guide rating _____ ★
Check your suggested rating
☐ ★
☐ ★★
☐ ★★★
☐ ★★★★
☐ ★★★★★
☐ ✓unusually good value

Date of visit _____   First visit? ☐ Yes ☐ No

Comments _____

Establishment name_____   ☐ Hotel ☐ Resort ☐ Restaurant
☐ Motel ☐ Inn ☐ Other

Street_____   City_____   State _____

Do you agree with our description? ☐ Yes ☐ No   If not, give reason_____

Please give us your opinion of the following:

Decor	Cleanliness	Service	Food
☐ Excellent	☐ Spotless	☐ Excellent	☐ Excellent
☐ Good	☐ Clean	☐ Good	☐ Good
☐ Fair	☐ Unclean	☐ Fair	☐ Fair
☐ Poor	☐ Dirty	☐ Poor	☐ Poor

2003 Guide rating _____ ★
Check your suggested rating
☐ ★
☐ ★★
☐ ★★★
☐ ★★★★
☐ ★★★★★
☐ ✓unusually good value

Date of visit _____   First visit? ☐ Yes ☐ No

Comments _____

Notes

Notes